			House		Senate	
Winner's Electoral College Vote %	Winner's Popular Vote %	Congress	Majority Party	Minority Party	Majority Party	Minority Party
**	No popular vote	1st	38 Admin †	26 Opp	17 Admin	9 Opp
		2nd	37 Fed ††	33 Dem-R	16 Fed	13 Dem-R
**	No popular vote	3rd	57 Dem-R	48 Fed	17 Fed	13 Dem-R
		4th	54 Fed	52 Dem-R	19 Fed	13 Dem-R
**	No popular vote	5th	58 Fed	48 Dem-R	20 Fed	12 Dem-R
		6th	64 Fed	42 Dem-R	19 Fed	13 Dem-R
HR**	No popular vote	7th	69 Dem-R	36 Fed	18 Dem-R	13 Fed
		8th	402 Dem-R	39 Fed	25 Dem-R	9 Fed
92.0	No popular vote	9th	116 Dem-R	25 Fed	27 Dem-R	7 Fed
		10th	118 Dem-R	24 Fed	28 Dem-R	6 Fed
69.7	No popular vote	11th	94 Dem-R	48 Fed	28 Dem-R	6 Fed
		12th	108 Dem-R	36 Fed	30 Dem-R	6 Fed
59.0	No popular vote	13th	112 Dem-R	68 Fed	27 Dem-R	9 Fed
		14th	117 Dem-R	65 Fed	25 Dem-R	11 Fed
84.3	No popular vote	15th	141 Dem-R	42 Fed	34 Dem-R	10 Fed
		16th	156 Dem-R	27 Fed	35 Dem-R	7 Fed
99.5	No popular vote	17th	158 Dem-R	25 Fed	44 Dem-R	4 Fed
		18th	187 Dem-R	26 Fed	44 Dem-R	4 Fed
HR	39.1 †††	19th	105 Admin	97 Dem-J	26 Admin	20 Dem-J
		20th	119 Dem-J	94 Admin	28 Dem-J	20 Admin
68.2	56.0	21st	139 Dem	74 Nat R	26 Dem	22 Nat R
		22nd	141 Dem	58 Nat R	25 Dem	21 Nat R
76.6	54.5	23rd	147 Dem	53 AntiMas	20 Dem	20 Nat R
		24th	145 Dem	98 Whig	27 Dem	25 Whig
57.8	50.9	25th	108 Dem	107 Whig	30 Dem	18 Whig
		26th	124 Dem	118 Whig	28 Dem	22 Whig
79.6	52.9					
–	52.9	27th	133 Whig	102 Dem	28 Whig	22 Dem
		28th	142 Dem	79 Whig	28 Whig	25 Dem
61.8	49.6	29th	143 Dem	77 Whig	31 Dem	25 Whig
		30th	115 Whig	108 Dem	36 Dem	21 Whig
56.2	47.3	31st	112 Dem	109 Whig	35 Dem	25 Whig
–	–	32nd	140 Dem	88 Whig	35 Dem	24 Whig
85.8	50.9	33rd	159 Dem	71 Whig	38 Dem	22 Whig
		34th	108 Rep	83 Dem	40 Dem	15 Rep
58.8	45.6	35th	118 Dem	92 Rep	36 Dem	20 Rep
		36th	114 Rep	92 Dem	36 Dem	26 Rep
59.4	39.8	37th	105 Rep	43 Dem	31 Rep	10 Dem
		38th	102 Rep	75 Dem	36 Rep	9 Dem
91.0	55.2					
–	–	39th	149 Union	42 Dem	42 Union	10 Dem
		40th	143 Rep	49 Dem	42 Rep	11 Dem
72.8	52.7	41st	149 Rep	63 Dem	56 Rep	11 Dem
		42nd	134 Rep	104 Dem	52 Rep	17 Dem
81.9	55.6	43rd	194 Rep	92 Dem	49 Rep	19 Dem
		44th	169 Rep	109 Dem	45 Rep	29 Dem
50.1	47.9 †††	45th	153 Dem	140 Rep	39 Rep	36 Dem
		46th	149 Dem	130 Rep	42 Dem	33 Rep
58.0	48.3	47th	147 Rep	135 Dem	37 Rep	37 Dem
–	–	48th	197 Dem	118 Rep	38 Rep	36 Dem
54.6	48.5	49th	183 Dem	140 Rep	43 Rep	34 Dem
		50th	169 Dem	152 Rep	39 Rep	37 Dem

Source for election data: Svend Peterson, *A Statistical History of American Presidential Elections*. New York: Frederick Ungar Publishing, 1963. Updates: Richard Scammon, *America Votes* 19. Washington, D.C.: Congressional Quarterly, 1991; *Congressional Quarterly Weekly Report*, Nov. 7, 1992, p. 3552.

Abbreviations:

Admin = Administration supporters
AntiMas = Anti-Masonic
Dem = Democratic
Dem-R = Democratic-Republican
Fed = Federalist

Dem-J = Jacksonian Democrats
Nat R = National Republican
Opp = Opponents of administrat
Rep = Republican
Union = Unionist

Understanding American Government

The Essentials

Susan Welch

The Pennsylvania State University

John Gruhl

University of Nebraska ~ Lincoln

John Comer

University of Nebraska ~ Lincoln

Susan M. Rigdon

University of Illinois at Urbana ~ Champaign

 WADSWORTH
CENGAGE Learning

Australia • Brazil • Canada • Mexico • Singapore • Spain • United Kingdom • United States

WADSWORTH
CENGAGE Learning

Understanding American Government, The Essentials
Susan Welch, John Gruhl, John Comer, Susan M. Rigdon

Publisher: Clark Baxter

Executive Editor: Carolyn Merrill

Associate Development Editor: Rebecca Green

Editorial Assistant: Katherine Hayes

Technology Project Manager: Gene Ioffe

Marketing Manager: Trent Whatcott

Marketing Assistant: Aimee Lewis

Marketing Communications Manager: Heather Baxley

Project Manager: Joshua Allen

Creative Director: Rob Hugel

Art Director: Maria Epes

Print Buyer: Rebecca Cross

Permissions Editor: Roberta Broyer

Production Service: The Book Company, Gary Kliewer

Text Designer: Carolyn Deacy

Photo Researcher: Katharine S. Cebik

Copy Editor: Pam Rockwell

Cover Designer: Carolyn Deacy

Cover Image: ©Wally McNamee/CORBIS

Compositor/Production Service: Graphic World

Printer: Transcontinental/Beauceville

For product information and technology assistance, contact us at
Cengage Learning Academic Resource Center, 1-800-423-0563
For permission to use material from this text or product,
submit all requests online at **www.cengage.com/permissions**
Further permissions questions can be emailed to
permissionrequest@cengage.com

Library of Congress Control Number: 2007942787

ISBN-13: 978-0-495-50117-6

ISBN-10: 0-495-50-117-4

Wadsworth Cengage Learning
10 Davis Drive
Belmont, CA 94002-3098
USA

Cengage Learning products are represented in Canada by Nelson Education, Ltd.

For your course and learning solutions, visit **academic.cengage.com**

Purchase any of our products at your local college store or at our preferred online store **www.ichapters.com**

Printed in Canada
1 2 3 4 5 6 7 11 10 09 08 07

BRIEF CONTENTS

CONTENTS

Links between People and Government

CHAPTER 7

Elections 166

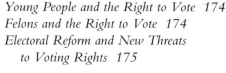

CHAPTER 11
The Judiciary 318

PART FOUR

Civil Liberties and Rights

CHAPTER 12
Civil Liberties 344

As we were writing this book, we joked that we should title it *What Introductory Students Should Know About American Government, Without Any Extraneous Details or Unnecessary Filler, But With Enough Examples and Anecdotes to Make It Interesting.* In a nutshell, this is the approach we've taken.

Understanding American Government: The Essentials isn't a brief book, a bare-bones book that addresses only the "nuts and bolts" of American government. But neither is it a long book that touches on tangential points that are unnecessary for introductory students. Rather, it's a medium-length book that can work by itself for a quarter-long or semester-long course. Yet it's short enough that it can be used with a topical book or a reader as well.

We're excited by this book. The length seems just right—long enough to explain what needs to be explained and to include interesting tidbits in the process but short enough to be readable. The chapters are streamlined, so they move along. They're written in a language that's accessible to introductory students. We think this book will be a very effective teaching tool.

The Organization and Contents of the *Essentials* Edition

This *Essentials* edition is a shortened and considerably rewritten version of our previous *Understanding American Government*. To achieve this shorter book, we have consolidated coverage of the Constitution and federalism and of elections and money and politics. We have also grouped our discussion of policy into domestic and foreign policies. We have dropped sections that seemed less "essential" than the rest of the book and edited and shortened throughout to make the book even more concise and readable.

We start each chapter with a short vignette that illustrates, often in a rather humorous way, some important point in the chapter. At the end of each chapter, we

have added 20 multiple-choice questions, providing an opportunity for students to test their comprehension of the chapter.

We're sympathetic to the argument that educated people should know important concepts, events, and persons that have shaped our society and government, and we're conscious of our responsibility to advance students' cultural literacy. Thus, we've identified Key Terms and also Key Names in each chapter, and we've provided longer lists of these terms and names than other texts do. These lists, of course, don't include every term, event, or name that has influenced American government, but they do include every one that is given space in our chapters.

The marked erosion of presidential popularity, the continuing war on Iraq, the political and policy impact of the "war on terror," and the race for the 2008 presidential election provide new issues of interest for analysts of American government and they are covered in this edition. The 2006 elections are discussed in several chapters, and enough time has passed that we have been able to describe several of the consequences of that election. The changing role of the electronic media in elections is another topic of interest that is more fully covered here.

Continuing Features

Past users of our larger edition will recognize several continuing emphases. We want the students reading this book to understand how the everyday practice of politics, including the dwindling of a perceived electoral presidential mandate and the difficulties of congressional leadership on foreign policy, is rooted in the larger principles of government and political culture. We want to convey to students, whether they are taking this course as an elective or a requirement, why it is important for every American to understand how our government functions. We hope they find that it is also an interesting and often exciting subject that has relevance to almost every aspect of their lives. We believe an introductory course succeeds if most students develop an understanding of the major concepts of our form of government, an interest in learning more about politics, and an ability to analyze political issues and evaluate the news they hear about them.

Students should come out of an introductory course with a firm grounding in the essential "nuts and bolts" of American government, but it is also crucial that they understand the political environment in which government functions. We offer the essentials of American government, but we also want the student to understand why (and sometimes how) these important features have evolved, their impact on government and individuals, and why they are controversial (if they are) and worth learning about. For example, we prefer that students leave the course remembering why government tries to regulate corporations, how it does so, and the political factors that lead to stronger or weaker regulations rather than memorizing specific regulatory acts. The latter will change or soon be forgotten, but understanding the "whys" will help the student understand the issues long after the course is over.

A particular emphasis throughout the book is on the *impact* of government: how individual features of government affect its responsiveness to different groups (in Lasswell's terms, "Who gets what and why?"). We realize that nothing in American politics is simple; rarely does one feature of government produce, by itself, a clear outcome. Nevertheless, we think that students will be more willing to learn about government if they see some relationships between how government operates and the impact it has on them as American citizens. For example, students who do not understand why learning about voter registration laws is important may "see the light" when they understand the link between such laws and low voter turnout.

We hope a greater understanding of and appreciation for American government may encourage those not already engaged in civic and political activities to become more active citizens. Though students did vote at a higher rate in 2004 than they have in decades, a 2006 survey by the National Constitution Center found that more teenagers could identify the Three Stooges (59%) than could name the three branches of government, six times as many knew the hometown of Bart Simpson than knew where Abraham Lincoln came from, and not even 2% could correctly identify James Madison.

The organization of the book is straightforward. After material on democracy, the Constitution, and federalism, the book covers linkages, then institutions. Civil liberties and rights are treated after the chapter on the judiciary, and chapters on domestic and foreign policy conclude the book.

But the book is flexible enough that instructors can modify the order of the chapters. Some instructors will prefer to cover institutions before process. Others may prefer to discuss civil liberties and rights when discussing the Constitution.

Our book features include a civil rights chapter that integrates a thorough treatment of constitutional issues concerning minorities and women, a discussion of the civil rights and women's rights movements, and contemporary research on the political status of these groups. We include in this chapter the special legal problems of Hispanics and American Indians.

Substantive policy chapters reinforce the emphasis on the impact of government action. The domestic policy chapter reviews fiscal policy, focusing on taxes and tax reform, before moving to a consideration of various kinds of income support programs, including agricultural subsidies, that have an impact on the distribution of income in our society. The chapter closes with a discussion of health care issues. The chapter on foreign policy places current foreign policy issues in the context of the history of our foreign policy aims, especially since World War II, and features new issues arising from the post–9/11 world.

We are pleased to be able to write this new version of our text and, at the same time, continue to improve the text further in ways suggested by our students and readers. We have been extremely pleased by the reaction of instructors and students to the eleven editions of our larger book. We were especially gratified to have won three times the American Government Textbook Award from the Women's Caucus for Political Science of the American Political Science Association.

Special Features

Beginning with the first edition, our text has provided features especially designed to involve students in the controversies—and excitement—of American politics.

American Diversity

In many chapters, "American Diversity" boxes illustrate the impact of the social diversity of the American population on political life. These boxes help students understand how a variety of backgrounds and attitudes shape views of politics and positions on issues.

Boxes

In each chapter, boxes highlighting interesting aspects of American politics draw the students into the material. Many illustrate how government and politics really work in a particular situation—how a corporation lobbies for government benefits, how a seemingly powerless group is able to organize for political action, how interest groups solicit money by mail, and how political polls are done. Others highlight features of government that may be of particular interest to students—how ethnicity shapes voting behavior and how teen pregnancies and abortions affect the abortion debate.

Other Features

Several other features also help students organize their study.

Key Terms

Key terms are boldfaced within the text and listed at the end of each chapter and in the glossary.

Key Names

Key individuals covered in the chapter are boldfaced and listed at chapter's end as an aid for reviewing.

Test Yourself

A set of 20 multiple-choice questions follows each chapter.

Supplements for Instructors

 Power Lecture Disk with JoinIn for *Understanding American Government: The Essentials*

- **Interactive PowerPoint Lectures** This one-stop lecture and class preparation tool makes it easy for you to assemble, edit, and present custom lectures for your course, using Microsoft® PowerPoint®. The interactive PowerPoint lectures bring together text-specific outlines; audio and video clips from historic to current events; animated learning modules illustrating key concepts; and tables, statistical charts, graphs, and photos from the book, as well as outside sources. In addition, you can add your own materials—culminating in a powerful, personalized, media-enhanced presentation.

- **Test Bank in Microsoft Word and Exam-View® Computerized Testing** with a large array of well-crafted multiple-choice and essay questions, along with their answers and page references.

- **Instructor's Manual** with learning objectives, chapter outlines, discussion questions, suggestions for stimulating class activities and projects, tips on integrating media into your class, including step-by-step instructions on how to create your own podcasts, suggested readings and Web resources, and a section specially designed to help teaching assistants and adjunct instructors.

- **JoinIn** JoinIn on TurningPoint for *Understanding American Government: The Essentials* Book-specific clicker questions test and track student comprehension of key concepts. Political Polling questions simulate voting, engage the classroom, foster dialogue on group behaviors and values, and add personal relevance; results can be compared to national data, leading to lively discussions. Visual Literacy questions tied to images from your book add useful pedagogical tools and high-interest feedback during your lecture. Save the data from your students' responses all semester—track their progress and show them how political science works by incorporating this exciting new tool into your classroom. *Contact your Cengage representative for more information about JoinIn and our exclusive infrared or radio-frequency hardware solutions.*

- **Resource Integration Guide** outlines the rich collection of resources available to instructors and students within the chapter-by-chapter framework of the book, suggesting how and when each supplement can be used to optimize learning.

CENGAGENOW—at http://academic.cengage.com/cengagenow/

Adopting instructors will be given password-protected access to course management tools so that they can assign and supervise their students' use of CengageNOW if they wish to do so.

WebTutor™

Rich with content for your American government course, this Web-based teaching and learning tool includes course management, study/mastery, and communication tools. Use WebTutor to provide virtual office hours, post your syllabus, and track student progress with WebTutor's quizzing material. For students, WebTutor offers real-time access to interactive online tutorials and simulations, practice quizzes, and Web links—all correlated to *Understanding American Government: The Essentials.* Available in WebCT and Blackboard.

Political Theatre DVD

Video and audio clips drawn from key political events from the last seventy-five years: presidential speeches, campaign ads, debates, news reports, national convention coverage, demonstrations, speeches by civil rights leaders, and more.

JoinIn for Political Theatre

For even more interaction, combine **Political Theatre** with the innovative teaching tool of a classroom response system through JoinIn™. Poll your students with questions we've created for you or create your own. Built within the Microsoft® PowerPoint® software, it's easy to integrate into your current lectures, in conjunction with the "clicker" hardware of your choice.

ABC News Videos for American Government

A collection of three- to six-minute video clips on relevant political issues. They serve as great lecture or discussion launchers. On VHS or DVD.

Video Case Studies for American Government

Free to adopters, this award-winning video contains twelve case studies on the debate on recent policy issues, such as affirmative action. Each case ends with questions designed to spark classroom discussion.

 Turnitin®

This proven online plagiarism-prevention software promotes fairness in the classroom by helping students learn to cite sources correctly and allowing instructors to check for originality before reading and grading papers. Turnitin® quickly checks student papers against billions of pages of Internet content, millions of published works, and millions of student papers and within seconds generates a comprehensive originality report. A booklet, *How to Avoid Plagiarism Using Turnitin,* is also available; ask your Cengage representative for details.

Building Democracy: Readings in American Government

This extraordinary collection provides access to over 500 historical documents and scholarly readings to create the ideal supplement for any American Government course. Cengage Custom Solutions' intuitive **TextChoice** website at **www.textchoice.com/democracy/** allows you to quickly browse the collection, preview selections, arrange your table of contents, and create a custom cover that will include your own course information. Or if you prefer, your local representative will be happy to guide you through the process.

Consider for Students, available packaged with the book

CengageNOW

CengageNOW, updated and enhanced for 2008, will generate a personalized study plan for each student and direct them to the appropriate premium resources, including an integrated online e-book, new interactive Simulations, Election Updates, Participation exercises, Video Case Studies, MicroCase exercises, Internet activities, web links, and Timelines. Visit **http://academic.cengage.com/cengagenow/** to access sign-in for those who purchased a book with ThomsonNOW or the chance to purchase access.

Companion Website for *Understanding American Government: The Essentials*—at www.academic.cengage.com/

Students will find free and open access to Learning Objectives, Quizzes, Chapter Glossaries, Flash Cards, Crossword Puzzles, and Internet activities.

The Handbook of Selected Court Cases

Includes more than thirty Supreme Court cases.

The Handbook of Selected Legislation and Other Documents

Features excerpts from twelve laws passed by the U.S. Congress that have had a significant impact on American politics.

Election 2006: An American Government Supplement

By John A. Clark and Brian Schaffner, this election booklet uses real examples that address both the 2006 congressional and gubernatorial races, making the concepts covered come alive for students.

American Government: Using MicroCase ExplorIt, Ninth Edition

By Barbara Norrander, this Windows-compatible package includes access to MicroCase datasets and a workbook. Students make their own decisions about the issues as they analyze and interpret current NES and GSS data.

Acknowledgments

We would like to thank the many people who have aided and sustained us during the lengthy course of this project.

We first want to thank Michael Steinman, our original coauthor and the original primary author of Chapters 1, 9, and 10, who helped plan the original edition of the book and continued his coauthorship for several editions. The shape of the book still reflects his insights and efforts. Then, we thank Margery Ambrosius and Jan Vermeer for their intellectual contributions to this book through their coauthorship in previous editions. Our current and former University of Nebraska and Penn State colleagues have been most tolerant and helpful. We thank them all. In particular, we appreciate the assistance of Philip Dyer, David Forsythe, John Hibbing, Robert Miewald, John Peters, David Rapkin, and Beth Thiess-Morse, who provided us with data,

bibliographic information, and other insights that we have used here. Susan Welch's Penn State colleagues Ron Filippelli and Ray Lombra have been a source of encouragement, support, and many interesting political insights.

We are also grateful to the many other readers of our manuscript and earlier editions of the book, as listed here. Without their assistance the book would have been less accurate, less complete, and less lively. And thanks, too, to those instructors who have used the book and relayed their comments and suggestions to us. Our students at the University of Nebraska have also provided invaluable reactions to previous editions.

Our editors at Cengage Learning also deserve our thanks. Clark Baxter was a continual source of encouragement and optimism from the beginning of the first edition through the beginning of the ninth edition. Carolyn Merrill, our current editor, urged us to write this *Essentials* version, and we are grateful that she did. Special thanks go to our crack production team of Dusty Friedman, our production editor; Kate Cebik, our photo researcher; and Pam Rockwell, our copyeditor. They were always willing to do a little more.

Reviewers of the New Edition

Melinda K. Blade, Academy of Our Lady of Peace; Bert C. Buzan, California State University–Fullerton; Stefanie Chambers, Trinity College; David V. Edwards, University of Texas at Austin; Robert Glen Findley, Odessa College; Bernard-Thompson Ikegwuoha, Green River Community College; Terri Johnson, University of Wisconsin–Green Bay; Michael K. Moore, University of Texas at Arlington; Catherine C. Reese, Arkansas State University; K. L. Scott, University of Central Florida; Richard S. Unruh, Fresno Pacific University; Alex H. Xiao, Sacramento City College.

Reviewers of Previous Editions

Alan Abramowitz, *State University of New York at Stony Brook;* Larry Adams, *Baruch College–City University of New York;* Danny M. Adkison, *Oklahoma State University;* James Alt, *Harvard University;* Margery Marzahn Ambrosius, *Kansas State University;* Kevin Bailey, *North Harris Community College;* Bethany Barratt, *Roosevelt University;* Kennette M. Benedict, *Northwestern University;* James Benze, *Washington and Jefferson College;* Timothy Bledsoe, *Wayne State University;* Jon Bond, *Texas A&M University;* Paul R. Brace, *New York University;* Joseph V. Brogan, *La Salle University;* James R. Brown Jr., *Central*

Washington University; Kent M. Brudney, *Cuesta Community College*; Chalmers Brumbaugh, *Elon College*; Alan D. Buckley, *Santa Monica College*; Richard G. Buckner Jr., *Santa Fe Community College*; Ronald Busch, *Cleveland State University*; Carl D. Cavalli, *Memphis State University*; Richard A. Champagne, *University of Wisconsin, Madison*; Mark A. Cichock, *University of Texas at Arlington*; Michael Connelly, *Southwestern Oklahoma State University*; Gary Copeland, *University of Oklahoma*; George H. Cox Jr., *Georgia Southern College*; Paige Cubbison, *Miami-Dade University*; Landon Curry, *Southwest Texas State University*; Jack DeSario, *Case Western Reserve University*; Robert E. DiClerico, *West Virginia University*; Ernest A. Dover Jr., *Midwestern State University*; Georgia Duerst-Lahti, *Beloit College*; Ann H. Elder, *Illinois State University*; Ghassan E. El-Eid, *Butler University*; C. Lawrence Evans, *College of William and Mary*; Rhodell J. Fields, *St. Petersburg College*; Murray Fischel, *Kent State University*; Bobbe Fitzhugh, *Eastern Wyoming College*; Jeff Fox, *Catawba College*; Stephen I. Frank, *St. Cloud State University*; Marianne Fraser, *University of Utah*; Jarvis Gamble, *Owens Community College*; Sonia R. Garcia, *St. Mary's University*; David Garrison, *Collin County Community College*; Phillip L. Gianos, *California State University–Fullerton*; Doris A. Graber, *University of Illinois–Chicago*; Michael Graham, *San Francisco State University*; Ruth M. Grubel, *University of Wisconsin–Whitewater*; Stefan D. Haag, *Austin Community College*; Larry M. Hall, *Belmont University*; Edward Hapham, *University of Texas–Dallas*; Peter O. Haslund, *Santa Barbara City College*; Richard P. Heil, *Fort Hays State University*; Peggy Heilig, *University of Illinois at Urbana*; Craig Hendricks, *Long Beach City College*; Marjorie Hershey, *Indiana University*; Kay Hofer, *Southwest Texas State University*; Samuel B. Hoff, *Delaware State College*; Robert D. Holsworth, *Virginia Commonwealth University*; Jesse C. Horton, *San Antonio College*; Gerald Houseman, *Indiana University*; Timothy Howard, *North Harris College*; Peter G. Howse, *American River College*; David W. Hunt, *Triton College*; Pamela Imperato, *University of North Dakota*; Jerald Johnson, *University of Vermont*; Loch Johnson, *University of Georgia*; Evan M. Jones, *St. Cloud State University*; Joseph F. Jozwiak Jr., *Texas A&M University–Kingsville*; Matt Kerbel, *Villanova University*; Marshall R. King, *Maryville College*; Orma Lindford, *Kansas State University*; Peter J. Longo, *University of Nebraska–Kearney*; Roger C. Lowery, *University of North Carolina–Wilmington*; H. R. Mahood, *Memphis State University*; Kenneth M. Mash, *East Stroudsburg University*; Alan C. Melchior, *Florida International University*; A. Nick Minton, *University of Massachusetts–Lowell*; Matthew Moen, *University of Maine*; Michael K. Moore, *University of Texas at Arlington*; Michael Nelson, *Vanderbilt University*; Bruce Nesmith, *Coe College*; Walter Noelke, *Angelo State University*; Thomas Payette, *Henry Ford Community College*; Theodore B. Pedeliski, *University of North Dakota*; Jerry Perkins, *Texas Tech University*; Toni Phillips, *University of Arkansas*; C. Herman Pritchett, *University of California–Santa Barbara*; Charles Prysby, *University of North Carolina–Greensboro*; Sandra L. Quinn-Musgrove, *Our Lady of the Lake University*; Donald R. Ranish, *Antelope Valley Community College*; Linda Richter, *Kansas State University*; Jerry Sandvick, *North Hennepin Community College*; James Richard Sauder, *University of New Mexico*; Eleanor A. Schwab, *South Dakota State University*; Earl Sheridan, *University of North Carolina–Wilmington*; Edward Sidlow, *Northwestern University*; Cynthia Slaughter, *Angelo State University*; John Squibb, *Lincolnland Community College*; Glen Sussman, *Old Dominion University*; M. H. Tajalli-Tehrani, *Southwest Texas State University*; Kristine A. Thompson, *Moorehead State University*; R. Mark Tiller, *Austin Community College*; Gordon J. Tolle, *South Dakota State University*; Susan Tolleson-Rinehart, *Texas Tech University*; Bernadyne Weatherford, *Rowan College of New Jersey*; Richard Unruh, *Fresno Pacific College*; Jay Van Bruggen, *Clarion University of Pennsylvania*; David Van Heemst, *Olivet Nazarene University*; Kenny Whitby, *University of South Carolina*; Donald C. Williams, *Western New England College*; James Matthew Wilson, *Southern Methodist University*; John H. Wilson Jr., *Itawamba Community College*; Clifford J. Wirth, *University of New Hampshire*; Ann Wynia, *North Hennepin Community College*; Mary D. Young, *Southwestern Michigan College*.

SUSAN WELCH received her A.B. and Ph.D. degrees from the University of Illinois at Urbana–Champaign. She is currently Dean of the College of the Liberal Arts and Professor of Political Science at The Pennsylvania State University. Her teaching and research areas include legislatures, state and urban politics, and women and minorities in politics. She has edited the *American Politics Quarterly*.

JOHN GRUHL, a Professor of Political Science, received his A.B. from DePauw University in Greencastle, Indiana, and his Ph.D. from the University of California at Santa Barbara. Since joining the University of Nebraska faculty in 1976, he has taught and researched in the areas of judicial process, criminal justice, and civil rights and liberties. He has won University of Nebraska campuswide and systemwide distinguished teaching awards and has become a charter member of the university's Academy of Distinguished Teachers.

JOHN COMER is a Professor of Political Science at the University of Nebraska. He received his A.B. in political science from Miami University of Ohio in 1965 and his Ph.D. from Ohio State University in 1971. His teaching and research focus on interest groups, public opinion, voting behavior, and political parties.

SUSAN RIGDON received A.B. and Ph.D. degrees in political science from the University of Illinois in 1966 and 1971. She has taught American government at several institutions in the United States and China and has other teaching and research interests in comparative government, poverty and development, and culture and politics. She is a Research Associate in Anthropology at the University of Illinois at Urbana–Champaign.

Wayne Joseph grew up as a black American in Louisiana. He had typical black experiences—being called "nigger" by white kids and being harassed by police officers. His race influenced his choice of a high school and the various girls he dated and the first woman he married. He cultivated an interest in African American literature. He wrote about Black History Month. All along, he assumed his ancestry was approximately 70 percent African.

As a high school principal in suburban Los Angeles, he saw a TV program about a company that offers DNA testing to determine one's ancestry. He was curious, so he ordered the kit. He swabbed the insides of his cheeks, as instructed, and then returned the swabs. Several weeks later, he received the results. According to his DNA, his ancestry is actually 57 percent European, 39 percent Native American, 4 percent Asian—and 0 percent African. He was shocked. He asked his mother if he had been adopted. (He hadn't been.) His sister and his kids, named Martin and Kenya, who assumed their ancestry was African, also were stunned. Eventually, Joseph concluded, "Now I'm a metaphor for America."[1]

Americans take pride in their form of government but express ambivalence toward the political process. We cherish the Declaration of Independence and the Constitution and love the symbols of democracy. We visit Washington, D.C. to marvel at the Washington Monument, the Jefferson and Lincoln memorials, the Capitol, and the White House. We show these symbols of our democracy to our children, hoping they will learn to revere them too.

But at the same time that we point with pride to the documents and symbols of American democracy, we often seem unwilling to accept the realities of democratic practice or to spend the time it takes to familiarize ourselves with the candidates and issues.[2] We assume that political conflict entails mere self-interest, and we tag interest groups and political parties as "special interests." We refer to debates over issues as "partisan bickering" or "ideological posturing." We don't like the partisan labels of "Democrat" and "Republican" or the ideological labels of "liberal" and "conservative." We want nonpartisan, nonideological solutions to society's problems. But when our officials do come to agreement, we call their compromises "selling out." In other words, we love the concept of democracy but hate the rough-and-tumble, the give-and-take, and the conflict of democracy in action.[3]

An era without "politics as usual"—without conflict and debate and without partisanship and ideology—isn't going to happen. People who expect such an era are demonstrating their ignorance or naivete (or childishness, in the view of one observer[4]). Different people have different values and different goals as well as different means to reach them. "Things get disagreeable because people disagree."[5] This is why we have politics.

Politics is the means by which individuals' and groups' interests compete to shape government's impact on society's problems.[6] This text examines politics as it affects competition for and performance in government office and efforts to influence policy made by government officials.

In their attempts to shape policy, individuals and groups compete, and government's role is to mediate among them, resolving conflicts and formulating policies that represent a collective view. Thus, politics is essential to governing. More than two thousand years ago, the Greek philosopher **Aristotle** wrote that politics is the most noble endeavor in which people can engage, because it helps individuals know themselves and forces individuals to relate to others. Through political participation, individuals pursue their own needs and interests, but they must consider the needs and interests of fellow citizens. In other words, through politics we learn to balance our own desires against the good of the community as a whole.

Today, Americans are less inclined to share Aristotle's conception of politics than they are the cynical view of novelist Gore Vidal: "Who collects what money from whom in order to spend on what is all there is to politics."[7] Yet the ideals of our founders and the beliefs of our citizens today are about far more than who collects what to spend where.

This chapter begins the discussion by profiling the American people and identifying the political values we share. It also briefly describes how democracy, when practiced by people who are racially, ethnically, religiously, and economically diverse and scattered across a vast and varied landscape, is destined to be characterized as much by competition and conflict as by cooperation and community.

A Demographic Profile

When the nineteenth-century poet Walt Whitman wrote, "Here is not merely a nation but a teeming Nation of nations," he said a lot about our country and its politics.[8] It is a cliché, yet true, that the United States is a land of immigrants, peopled by individuals from all over the world. Americans are a conglomeration of races, ethnicities, cultural traditions, and religions—what one historian calls "a collision of histories"[9]—as well as the usual mixture of socioeconomic classes.

Our diversity was foreshadowed by the word *America*. The continent was named by a German mapmaker working in a French college, who intended to honor an Italian explorer (Amerigo Vespucci) sailing under the Portuguese flag.[10]

Immigration and Ethnic Diversity

Long before the Europeans arrived, the population of North America was characterized by cultural diversity. The first inhabitants probably crossed a land bridge from Asia thousands of years ago, and others may have sailed to South America and migrated north. Although often characterized by the single term *Indians* or *Native Americans,* the first immigrants were competitive and at times at war with each other, and their differences were

Immigrants crowd a New York City neighborhood in 1890.

substantial enough to doom eighteenth-century efforts to form pan-Indian alliances against European colonization.[11] Today, the U.S. Census Bureau recognizes 562 different tribes, many fewer than three hundred years ago but still suggestive of the array of diverse cultures that predated European settlement.

The umbrella term *European* itself is somewhat deceptive in that European settlers emigrated from countries that not only differed linguistically, religiously, and politically but also had often been at war with one another. Migrants carried these conflicts with them to America.

Because the colonies were ruled from England, and its language and culture were dominant, we tend to think of early Americans as Anglos and Protestants. But the earliest European settlers of the southwestern and southeastern territories were more likely to be Roman Catholics from Spain and France. The current states of Arizona, New Mexico, California, and Texas were populated by Mexican Catholics of mixed Spanish and Indian

descent. Over time, Germany, distinctly non-Anglo and evenly split between Catholics and Protestants, provided more immigrants to America than England did.

The immigrants often self-segregated into territories—Puritans in Massachusetts, Quakers in Pennsylvania and Rhode Island, and Catholics in Maryland—which later became states. Their different beliefs and traditions contributed to the rise of distinctive local cultures and state governments.

Like Europeans, Africans, too, came from a huge continent that encompassed many languages, cultures, and religions. Although the European slave trade was concentrated in the African coastal areas, the men and women forcibly removed to the Americas did not share a common tradition. But their experience united most in a common condition as noncitizens lacking all political and economic rights.

After the Revolution and the formation of the United States, the new government began to articulate an immigration policy, removing it from the hands of state governments but provoking disagreements over the standards for admission ever since. In 1807, Congress prohibited the "importation" of people for slavery. (This prohibition took effect in 1808, the soonest it could under the Constitution.)

The ethnic and racial composition of the American population broadened in the mid- to late-nineteenth century as new waves of settlers came from southern and eastern Europe, China, and Japan, as well as from Ireland and Germany. They included large numbers of Roman, Eastern, and Russian Orthodox Catholics; Jews; and some Buddhists. An 1882 law prohibited further immigration from China, and a 1907 agreement with Japan restricted new Japanese entries to the Hawaiian Islands. But immigration continued at high levels into the twentieth century, peaking in the 1890s through the 1910s.

This surge led to efforts to slow the pace of immigration. Between the 1920s and 1960s, immigration was open mainly to those from the European countries represented in the American population at the time of the 1910 census, thereby favoring the British, German, and other northern Europeans and penalizing the southern and eastern Europeans.

The civil rights movement led to the end of the nationality restrictions in place since the 1920s. In 1965, the old quota system that favored northern European applicants was scrapped, and the door was opened to people of every nationality and thus of every race and religion.

People in some political categories have been given preferential treatment. During the Cold War, virtually everyone fleeing a communist country, including Cubans, Russians, Eastern Europeans, Vietnamese, Cambodians, and Laotians, were allowed in. Following the Tiananmen Square massacre in Beijing in 1989, thousands of Chinese students were granted permanent residency.

People with immediate family members who are U.S. citizens are given preferential treatment. Therefore, when permanent residents become citizens—and one-third of all Americans who are foreign-born *are* naturalized citizens—their immediate family members living outside the United States automatically qualify for their own residency visas.[12] People with specific job skills, such as science, engineering, or computer training, are also given preferential treatment under the law. In practice, however, only a fraction of them are given a visa. For 2008, the U.S. Citizenship and Immigrations Services reached its limit for these applications in a single day. (And even then, it accepted less than half of the applicants.)[13] These two categories—applicants who are immediate family members and those who have specific job skills—tend to conflict because legal immigration is so restricted. The more who are accepted in one category, the fewer who can be accepted in the other. The current law favors the first category, but most reform proposals, driven by the corporate need for more high-tech workers, would increase the second category at the expense of the first one.

In 2004, immigrants were admitted from 188 countries. More new arrivals were born in Mexico than in any other country, followed by persons born in India and China.[14] This ensures that current trends in the ethnic diversification of the American population will continue and explains why Hispanics, who accounted for less than 7 percent of the population in the 1990 census, are now nearly 15 percent of the population and America's largest ethnic minority.

Rivaling the surge in legal immigration in the 1990s and 2000s are the millions of illegal immigrants in the 2000s, most of whom entered the country by crossing the Mexican border. The number of undocumented people, estimated between ten and twelve million, is increasing annually at almost the same rate as the legal immigrants.

Combining legal and illegal immigrants, the United States has the most foreign-born residents since the U.S. Census Bureau started keeping such statistics in 1850. Foreign-born residents make up nearly 15 percent of the American population.[15] (See Figure 1.)

Immigration and Political Cleavage

Antiforeign, or nativist, sentiments have been common throughout our history. Some native-born Americans have feared economic competition from newcomers or have perceived those who speak a language other than English and who follow traditions and religions different from theirs as a cultural threat. These sentiments usually have been greatest when immigration levels have been highest, which is why strong nativist sentiments influenced the politics of the mid-1800s, the late 1800s and early 1900s, the 1920s, and the 1990s, and why they are again a force in the early 2000s.

The wave of immigration produced by Ireland's potato famine in the 1840s created a fever of anti-Irish and anti-Catholic sentiment, which found expression in the Know-Nothing Party. The wave in the late 1800s and

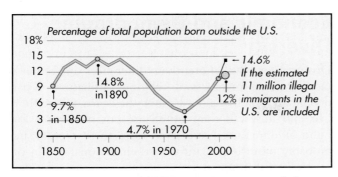

FIGURE 1 • Immigrants as a Percentage of the American Population *The number of immigrants relative to our population peaked in the 1890s and 1910s, but the percentage today is nearly that level if illegal immigrants are included.*
SOURCE: Time, Inc., 10/30/2006, p. 45. Reprinted by permission.

early 1900s prompted a reaction against big-city political machines, which were supported by immigrant voters, and sparked the creation of the Progressive movement (discussed in Chapter 6). This wave also prompted concerted efforts to establish the American flag as a national symbol for the diverse immigrants.[16] Public schools started flying the flag in 1890; the Pledge of Allegiance was adopted in 1892; people started saluting the flag in 1898; Flag Day was created in 1916; and a federal law prohibiting mutilation of the flag was passed in 1917.[17]

Patriotic fervor during World War I sparked hostility toward German Americans, and the Russian Revolution led to the Red Scare of the 1920s and the deportation of many Russian and Eastern European immigrants. During World War II, Japanese Americans were targeted as potential collaborators with Japan. Their property was confiscated, and they were imprisoned in camps under military guard.

Today, there is much concern about immigration, both legal and illegal, but especially illegal. This immigration has led to increased human smuggling, drug trafficking, and other crime. It has provoked citizen anger over our uncontrolled borders and the governmental expenses for immigrants' health care, and employers' frustration over their inability to get legal status for undocumented workers. Aside from these problems, many Americans simply fear increasing immigration, whether legal or illegal, as a threat to American culture. For some, this means a threat to the dominance of Anglo Americans in our society.

This fear led to the defeat of immigration reform in 2007. The Bush administration and the Democratic leaders of Congress had agreed to compromise legisla-

tion that would have tightened border control while establishing a guest worker program and creating a legal path toward citizenship for current illegal aliens. However, vocal conservatives, rallied by radio and television commentators, pressured Congress to reject the legislation.

Although each generation of immigrants has faced resentment from preceding generations, each has contributed to the building of America. Early European immigrants settled the eastern seaboard and pushed west to open the frontier. Africans' slave labor helped create the South's economy. Germans and Scandinavians developed the Midwest into an agricultural heartland, and free blacks and Irish, Italian, Polish, and Russian newcomers provided labor for America's industrial revolution and turned many cities into huge metropolises. Chinese immigrants helped build the transcontinental railroad linking East and West, and Japanese and Hispanics helped make California our top food producer. More recently, young Chinese and Indian immigrants have figured prominently in high-tech industries, and older Indian immigrants have dominated the motel business in the United States. All immigrant groups have gone on from their initial roles to play a fuller part in American life. Today's immigrant groups almost certainly will follow this pattern.

Immigration and Religious Diversity

The eighteenth-century French philosopher Voltaire, a leader of the Enlightenment, once wrote that a nation with one church will have oppression; with two, civil war; with a hundred, freedom.[18] We know that many of our earliest settlers—French Huguenots, German Anabaptists, British Methodists, Catholics, and Quakers—came here to escape religious intolerance in Europe. Once here, however, many found it necessary to establish separate communities to ensure freedom for their form of religious practice. Maryland, New Jersey, and Pennsylvania were conceived and established as "plantations of religion" for protection of specific religious groups.[19] Rhode Island was founded by the religious dissident Roger Williams, who, after being expelled from Massachusetts's Puritan society, bought land from the Narragansett Indians and founded a new colony for other religious outcasts.

With independence, the United States disassociated itself not just from the government of England but from its state religion, the Church of England (the Anglican church), which was, and is today, headed by the British monarch. Some at the Constitutional Convention wanted to name the Episcopalian church, which was the newly independent Anglican church in the United States, as our state church, but most knew that such a provision would never be accepted in a country with such religious diversity. Yet six of the thirteen original states did establish an official religion, and some levied a religious tax, leaving it to individual taxpayers to designate which church would receive their tax payments.[20]

Despite the diversity in religious practice, instruction and textbooks in public schools drew much of their content from the Protestant Bible. School officials maintained that their instruction was "nonsectarian," but their reluctance to remove blatantly anti-Catholic material led to the creation of Catholic church-run schools, which remain today an alternative to public schools. Occasionally, religious differences led to violence, as in Philadelphia's Bible riots of 1843, when Protestants burned down a Catholic school and thirteen people were killed.[21] The Know-Nothing Party, which was an outgrowth of nativist societies (and which was so secretive that when its members were asked questions about the party or its candidates, they would reply that they didn't know—hence the party's common name), won popularity during this period by spreading fear of a Catholic takeover. Catholic-Protestant conflict lasted well into the twentieth century and sometimes trumped ethnicity. In places, Protestants of various national origins joined forces against Catholics of various national origins, passing "puritan Sunday" laws that prohibited Catholic church dances, singing parties, and serving alcohol on the Sabbath.[22] Being all white and all Christian did not spare communities from exclusionary and repressive assimilationist tactics or violence against those of a different ancestry or religion. Claims that our political unity is being undermined by ethnic and religious diversity are not new.

America's religious profile is changing along with its ethnic makeup. Although a large majority (83 percent) still identify as Christians, Americans now claim affiliation with an estimated 1600 different religions and denominations, including three million Jews, one to three million Muslims, one million Buddhists, and three-quarters of a million Hindus.[23] To some observers, these figures represent the potential for social fragmentation; but a proliferation of religious affiliations may both bolster liberty and serve as its measure.

Economic and Demographic Diversity

Diversity involves more than differences in people's race, national origin, and religious affiliation. What people do for a living, how much they earn, where they live, and how old they are all are potential bases for political differences, and over time these factors are probably more important than their national origin or religious affiliation.

Economic diversity especially is important. Some prefer to think of America as a country without social classes (or without any classes except a middle class), but we do have a range of social classes, from the lower class to the middle class to the upper class, and with multiple levels in each one.

Many like to think of America as a land of opportunity, but opportunity knocks harder and louder for those who are better off. Most of those who are born poor stay poor. Although our society is not as class conscious as many others, our personal economic situations play an important part in shaping our views toward politics and our roles in the political process. Most people who are poor, for example, do not vote, but those who do vote tend to vote Democratic. Most people who are well-off do vote, and they are more likely to vote Republican than Democratic.

Regional and residential differences also are important. The sharpest split historically has been between the North and the South, as a result of the division over the right of southern states to secede from the Union in order to maintain a regional economic system rooted in slavery and the Civil War that resulted from this division. Other regional differences exist as well. People on the East Coast and West Coast tend to have different views than those in the middle of the country. Residential differences shape politics too. City dwellers have different views than rural residents, and suburbanites may have different views than either.

Age differences also can affect political orientation. The needs and interests of older citizens are substantially different from those of young adults. Older citizens vote at higher rates, and their interest groups are among the most powerful in the country. This fact has made economic security and health care for senior citizens high-priority policy issues, even while the number of children living in poverty is increasing.

Diversity and Identity Politics

It has become increasingly common for people to assume a hyphenated identity—that is, to identify themselves by both their family heritage and their citizenship. Today the hyphen has been dropped, but many of us cling to a two-part (or more) identity as an African, Arab, Chinese, Cuban, Irish, Italian, Japanese, Mexican, Polish, or—fill in the blank—American. Tiger Woods describes himself as a "Cablinasian"—Caucasian, black, American Indian, and Asian.

This tendency distinguishes contemporary Americans from earlier generations of immigrants, whose children didn't want to be seen as greenhorns (newcomers) still attached to the old countries. And those whose families had lived here for generations rarely called themselves British, Dutch, German, or Swedish Americans. If asked about their heritage, they may well have responded as Theodore Roosevelt, the descendant of Dutch immigrants, did when he declared himself an "American-American."[24]

Today's emphasis upon hyphenated identities may be the result of the civil rights movement, as more people began to take pride in their family's ancestry, and government affirmative action programs, which treat individuals as members of groups eligible to receive preferences in getting jobs or government contracts or in gaining admission to selective colleges. Although these developments in the 1960s and 1970s involved African Americans primarily, parallel equal rights movements and affirmative action programs involved other racial minorities and women as well. The emphasis upon hyphenated identities may also be the result of the current wave of immigration from Latin America and Asia. These immigrants often cite their national origins.

For whatever reasons, an individual's race, ethnicity, or gender has taken on added political importance. The use of such factors to influence the division of public resources has given rise to **identity politics.** This is the practice of organizing on the basis of one's racial identity, ethnic identity, gender, or sexual orientation to compete for public resources and to influence public policy.[25]

American Indians reflect the tug of identity politics in recent decades. Their once dwindling—apparently dwindling—population is now burgeoning. Their numbers began increasing with the Indian rights movement in the 1960s, as more people with Indian ancestry felt new pride and reclaimed their heritage. The environmental movement in the 1970s prompted others to view earlier Indians as good stewards of the land and wildlife. The enactment of affirmative action programs and the growth of the gambling industry on reservation land undoubtedly attracted still others. As a result, each census from 1970 through 2000 has found more Americans identifying themselves as Indians. This includes persons who have full Indian ancestry and those who have only partial or distant (or imagined) Indian ancestry, who did not choose to identify themselves as Indians in earlier decades. According to the Census, then, the population of Indians has doubled since 1960.[26] (However, according to birth and death records, the population has not grown nearly so much.[27])

Despite their common usage, some categories employed in identity politics are simplistic. *African* is a category that includes African Americans whose ancestors have been in the country since the seventeenth century and also first-generation immigrants who came after laws restricting immigration from Africa were lifted in the 1960s. Since that change, more Africans have come to the United States than were brought here against their will during all the years of slavery.[28]

Hispanic, which refers to people with a Spanish-speaking background, is a catch-all term for Mexicans, Puerto Ricans, Cubans, and others with national origins in Central and South America and the Caribbean. It also includes those whose origin is Spain or Portugal. Most don't consider themselves part of a common

The new National Museum of the American Indian on the Washington Mall reflects identity politics. Native Americans lobbied for the museum, consulted on its design, and here participated in opening ceremonies.

AP Images/Pablo Martinez Monsivais

group,[29] and most don't call themselves "Hispanics." Traditionalists often use *Hispanic,* whereas activists usually say *Latino.* Those who derive from Spain or Portugal tend to favor *Hispanic.* They believe that *Latino* excludes those not from Latin America. Those who derive from south of the border increasingly favor *Latino.*[30] (Because of their lack of agreement, our text uses the terms *Hispanic* and *Latino* interchangeably.) Instead of a collective identity, they identify with others of their national origin.[31]

Different groups live in different parts of the United States. Mexican Americans are heavily concentrated in the Southwest, although they're spreading throughout the country, including the Midwest and the South. Puerto Ricans tend to live in New York, Boston, Chicago, and other cities in the North. Cuban Americans are heavily concentrated in South Florida.

Moreover, Hispanics don't share a common race. Some are brown-skinned, others are black-skinned, and still others are white-skinned. Many are an amalgam of European, African, and American Indian ancestry that makes it impossible to classify them by race. Thus, they're considered an ethnic group and a statistical category rather than a distinct race. In short, the term *Hispanic* encompasses many diverse groups of people.

Paradoxically, identity politics has intensified during a period in which racial and ethnic boundaries are blurring (see the box "Racial Identity and the Census in an Age of DNA Testing"). DNA testing has shown how problematic the concept of race is when used as a census category in the United States.

Intermarriage has complicated the concept of race. So much racial and ethnic mixing has occurred that by the 1990 census one hundred million Americans could name no specific ancestry, or they reported multiple ancestries.[32] And intermarriage is increasing. Although 93 percent of whites and 87 percent of blacks still marry within-group, a third of all Hispanic and Asian marriages are mixed.[33] Among third-generation Hispanics and Asians, over half of their marriages are mixed.[34] In this context, it's worth noting that 23 percent of all births in the United States in 2005 were to foreign-born women, who are overwhelmingly Hispanic and Asian. Should this pattern continue, by 2050 the majority of Americans would be of mixed race.[35] However, this pattern may not continue. The number of Hispanics and Asians has become so large that Hispanic and Asian immigrants are beginning to marry Hispanic and Asian natives rather than Anglos.[36]

Political Culture

In recent years, the concept of *diversity* has become a civic virtue. Yet our national motto is *E Pluribus Unum* ("Out of Many, One") referring to the union of many states. In some minds, it also refers to the molding of one people from many origins and traditions. But given our diversity, do we have enough commonality to form a political culture? A **political culture** is a shared body of values and beliefs that shapes perceptions and attitudes toward politics and government and in turn influences political behavior.

The Importance of Political Culture

For their vitality and stability, governments rely on the support of citizens—their identification with the country and its method of governing and their adoption of the values and behavior necessary to sustain the system. Without this support, governments would be ineffective and perhaps unable to gain obedience except through coercion.

In a democracy, sharing a political culture does not mean that citizens must agree on specific issues or even on the government's role in dealing with the country's problems. Democracy embraces conflict and competition just as it requires cooperation and a sense of community. The essence of political culture is agreement not on specific issues but on fundamental principles and on rights and obligations of citizenship and the rules for participating in the political process. These shared values reduce the strains produced by our differences and allow us to compete, even intensely, on some issues while cooperating on others.

Learning Political Culture

Whether the newly created United States of America came about by the "design of Providence," a "lucky accident," or the Founders' skill in shaping a workable constitution, it faced a problem common to all political systems—how to create a national identity among the citizenry.[37] The Founders spoke of a united country—a people with a common ancestry, a shared language, the same religion, and the same political principles. From what you have read earlier in this chapter, you know this view was in some part wishful thinking. Moreover, Americans were divided into states, and they were more

RACIAL IDENTITY AND THE CENSUS IN AN AGE OF DNA TESTING

Nineteenth-century laws that segregated blacks and whites prompted people to think about which persons were black and which ones were white. For precision, the **United States Census** developed multiracial categories for those of mixed black and white heritage, terming them *mulatto* and even categorizing them further as *quadroon* or *octoroon* for those with one-fourth or one-eighth African American ancestry.

Now the commercial availability of **DNA testing** has brought a new twist to racial and ethnic self-identification by providing a scientific basis for one's ancestry. The results have surprised many Americans. Historian Henry Louis Gates led nine prominent African Americans through a search for their ancestors, including DNA tests.[1] Gates, an African American scholar, was amazed to learn that 50 percent of his genetic heritage was European, including an Ashkenazi (Jewish) woman. Others, too, were surprised that their ancestors included Asians, American Indians, and, of course, whites. Pennsylvania State University students in a race and ethnicity class, in which DNA testing is available, often discover mixed-race ancestry they knew nothing about.

The mixed-race ancestry revealed by DNA testing has implications for the United States Census, which is taken every ten years. The census establishes the size and geographical distribution of the population. Its primary purpose is to determine the states' number of seats in the House of Representatives. But the census is also used in the enforcement of federal laws and policies, such as the Voting Rights Law and various affirmative action policies, and implementation of federal programs, such as grants to cities and states based on

Wayne Joseph, who was featured in the chapter's opening vignette, was astounded when DNA testing revealed his ancestry.

Courtesy of Wayne Joseph

their size and composition. As a member of the House committee that oversees the Census Bureau bluntly put it, "The numbers drive the dollars."[2] What appears to be a straightforward statistical procedure, then, often becomes a contentious political issue.

Since the first census in 1790, Americans have been counted by race. Through the 1950 census, race was established by the census taker's observation. In the 1980 census, race was determined by self-identification. In the 1990 census, each person was given four categories to choose from—white, black, American Indian (or Native Alaskan), and Asian (or Pacific Islander)—but was allowed to claim Hispanic ethnic heritage in addition to his or her racial ancestry.

As a result of immigration and interracial marriage, many Americans complained that they couldn't choose a single category—they were multiracial. For example, former general and secretary of state Colin Powell, who is considered African American, was born to immigrants from Jamaica, but his

maternal grandmother was a Scot and his family was issued a Scottish family crest.[3] Although the 2000 census didn't include a multiracial category, it did allow each person to check multiple boxes. (This census also offered five categories, separating Native Hawaiians and Pacific Islanders from Asians.)

Yet only 2.4 percent of Americans checked multiple boxes, and thereby identified themselves as multiracial, way below the actual percentage of Americans who are multiracial. Many Hispanics are mixed race, and by some estimates three-fourths of African Americans are mixed race.[4]

Even if more people had checked multiple boxes, it would tell us only how many were willing to identify themselves as multiracial. It wouldn't tell us which ancestry predominates, let alone which ancestries actually exist in their genes. The refinement of the census seems simplistic compared with the sophistication of DNA testing.

The increasing fragmentation of the racial categories, as revealed in the census and especially through DNA testing, poses a general question: How should race be identified? What proportion of genetic inheritance is necessary to categorize a person as a member of a race? And is one's genetic inheritance as important as one's culture and life experiences? DNA testing may force us to rethink the way we identify and classify people by race in an increasingly multiracial society.

[1]*African American Lives* (PBS video, 2006).
[2]Representative Thomas C. Sawyer (D-Ohio), quoted in Lawrence Wright, "One Drop of Blood," *New Yorker,* July 25, 1994, 47.
[3]The Scotsman Website (thescottsman. scotsman.com/index.cfm?id 535722004).
[4]"Politics of Identity Resurface with Census," *Champaign-Urbana News-Gazette,* March 25, 2001, B8.

attached to their state than to the country. It was not until after the Civil War, when a spirit of nationalism swept the country, that Americans' attachment to the Union was solidified. (Then writers began referring to the United States with the singular *is* rather than the plural *are*.[38])

Most Founders believed that an educated citizenry was essential to the survival of the new republic, and advocates of public education such as Daniel Webster and Thomas Jefferson argued that only educated citizens would be able to understand public issues, elect virtuous leaders, and "sustain the delicate balance between liberty and order in the new political system."[39] As the public school system emerged, increasing emphasis was placed on the "training of citizens in patriotism, political knowledge, and public affairs."[40] Although schools were then (as they are now) under local control, there was some common content in civic education throughout the country. The public schools became a primary agent in fostering our political culture.

The mass media emerged as another important agent (discussed in Chapters 3 and 4). Newspapers, magazines, radio, and then television all provided infor-mation about the workings of the government and the rules of the game. At the same time, they persuaded Americans, either explicitly or implicitly, to support the government and accept the rules. Television especially provided shared experiences to its viewers.

Today, one of the most controversial issues in the debate over what is required to sustain a political culture is whether all citizens should speak a common language. The Founders took it for granted that English would be the national language, and **Noah Webster's** 1783 textbook promoting "a new national language to be spelled and pronounced differently from British English" was one of the first attempts to create an American national identity.[41] Webster, a Connecticut school teacher, wanted British textbooks banned from the classroom, saying that the wiping out of old-world maxims had to begin in infancy: "Let the first word he lisps be Washington."[42] In 1828, Webster published the *Dictionary of American English*—a dictionary "suited to the needs of the American people"—because, he argued, Americans could never accept the British definitions of senate, congress, assembly, and courts.[43] Another objective was to standardize the multitude of dialects, some mutually unintelligible, spoken by

Assimilation can take awhile. These children of Asian immigrants—from Taiwan, India, the Philippines, Bangladesh, and Korea—have grown up in America but feel, one said, "like the hyphen" in Asian-American—that is, between Asian and American.

Americans of the time.[44] Today, the United States has fewer spoken dialects than any other large country in the world, a considerable accomplishment given the diversity of our collective heritage and strong regional cultures.

Webster's belief that a single language was essential to developing a common political culture has been reinforced by generations of Americans, as each immigrant group has learned the English language (and contributed its own words in the process). The wave of immigration in recent years, especially from Spanish-speaking countries, has led to fears that new immigrants aren't learning the language. Twenty-seven states have passed laws establishing English as the official language, and the federal government requires minimal competency in English as part of the civics test for U.S. citizenship. Actually, however, the new immigrants are learning the language, as Chapter 13 details, but there are so many newcomers that people keep hearing the foreign languages of the recent arrivals.

The Core Values

Some people think that Americans are too diverse to share a common set of political values, and, in fact, some people argue that every country in the world is composed of "competing political cultures, not a single political culture."[45] Although our "nation of nations" is crosscut with cultural, political, and economic cleavages, most Americans do share some basic values.

The words many Americans use to characterize their society and government often come from the second paragraph of the Declaration of Independence: "We hold these Truths to be self-evident, that all Men are created equal, that they are endowed by the Creator with certain unalienable Rights, that among these are Life, Liberty, and the Pursuit of Happiness." These words suggest the basic beliefs on which the American system was founded—universal truths that can be known, equality before the law, belief in a higher power that transcends human law, and rights that are entitlements at birth and therefore can be neither granted nor taken away by government. The fundamental concept is liberty, especially the freedom to pursue one's livelihood and other personal goals that lead to a "happy" life.

Here we look briefly at the core values of American democracy. Chapter 2 explains how they are expressed in the Constitution.

Individual Liberty

Our belief in **individual liberty** stems from the motives of our ancestors who immigrated to America. Some, who were religious minorities in their countries, came to avoid religious persecution. Others came for economic opportunity. Of these, some immigrants were dirt-poor, and they saw America as an opportunity to become rich. Other immigrants were already well-to-do, but they saw America as an opportunity for greater wealth. Both those who came for religious reasons and those who came for economic reasons were suspicious of authority and hierarchy and distrustful of government. They were "runaways from authority."[46] In America, they sought to escape the heavy hand of government, either in imposing restrictions on their religion or taxes on their wealth. Thus, they conceptualized freedom as *freedom from* government—freedom to be left alone—and they passed these views down to later generations.[47]

Our belief in individual liberty also derives from the Judeo-Christian belief that every individual has equal worth before God and from the writings of English philosophers that every individual has natural rights from God. The views of seventeenth-century philosopher **John Locke** permeate the Declaration of Independence and the Constitution. Locke articulated the concept of **natural rights,** which are inherent, so they exist as soon as people are born; unalienable, so they cannot be taken away by rulers; and self-evident, so they can be known to all.[48]

Influenced by these ideas, early Americans emphasized individual liberty over other goals of government, and later Americans have reinforced this emphasis. Thus, liberty is clearly reflected in both the Bill of Rights adopted by the Founders and in court rulings articulated by later generations of judges. Liberty is also reflected in the way we talk. Most Americans speak of "the government"—that is, a government in opposition to the people—rather than "our government."[49]

These values have molded popular expectations. Immigrants still come to America to be their own boss. Living in a society with a clear commitment to individual liberty can be exciting and liberating. The flip side of the coin is that people also are at liberty to fail and face the consequences. And people who are limited by prejudice or poverty are given less help by government in overcoming these problems than people are given in other countries, which put more emphasis on the community as a whole rather than on the individual.[50]

Of course, the emphasis on individual liberty isn't absolute. Some restrictions are imposed on individual rights for the good of the community. For example, local zoning laws may restrict the liberty of one person to build a gas station in a residential neighborhood out of consideration for the neighborhood's residents. But our emphasis on individual liberty means that for better or worse—actually, for better *and* worse—there are fewer restrictions than in other countries where different values prevail.

A lively debate in recent decades has been sparked by those who believe that individual liberty has been overemphasized at the expense of community interests. Advocates of this position believe that our fixation on individual rights has led to a declining sense of community and, in everyday behavior, a general lack of civility among Americans. They advocate revitalizing the concept of citizenship, including the responsibility to participate in public life and "the qualities of character that self-government requires."[51] They call their program *communitarianism* and claim that it is actually closer to the Founders' conception of freedom than is the modern celebration of the unencumbered individual.

Political Equality

The Judeo-Christian belief that all people are equal in the eyes of God led logically to other concepts of equality, such as **political equality.** The ancient Greek emphasis on the opportunity and responsibility of all citizens to participate in ruling their city-states also contributed to our notion of political equality. Thus, the Declaration of Independence proclaims that "all Men are created equal." This does not mean that all people are born with equal ability. It means that all citizens are born with equal standing before the government and are entitled to equal rights.

In the early years of our country, however, as in the ancient Greek city-states, full rights of citizenship were conferred only on those thought to have the intellectual and moral judgment to act in the public interest. In both Greece and the United States, such thinking denied political rights to slaves, who were believed incapable of independent judgment, and to women, whose knowledge was seen as limited to the private or domestic sphere. This left a deep tension between the religious view that sees each individual as equal before God and the historical concept of differential political rights. Over time, this conflict was resolved in favor of the inherent worth and the political equality of each individual. The closing of this gap was noted by President Lyndon Johnson when he signed the Civil Rights Act of 1964 into law: "those who are equal before God shall now also be equal in the polling places, in the classrooms, in the factories. . . ."[52]

Long before the Civil Rights Act, however, most Americans considered themselves relatively equal socially and politically, if not economically. **Alexis de Tocqueville,** a perceptive Frenchman who traveled through the United States in the 1830s, observed that Americans felt more equal to one another than Europeans did. He attributed this feeling to the absence of a hereditary monarchy and aristocracy in this country. Americans did not look up to royalty and aristocrats as their "betters" the way Europeans did.[53]

Popular Sovereignty

The belief in political equality led to **popular sovereignty,** or rule by the people. If individuals are equal, no one person or small group has the right to rule others. Instead, the people collectively rule themselves. President **Abraham Lincoln** expressed this concept in the Gettysburg Address when he spoke of "government of the people, by the people, for the people."

Popular sovereignty, then, led to our form of government, a **democracy.** The word *democracy,* derived from the Greek language, means "authority of the people." If political authority resides in the people, then the people have the right to govern themselves. This, of course, entails a government by the many rather than by the few (aristocracy or oligarchy or theocracy) or by just one (monarchy or dictatorship).

Majority Rule

The belief in political equality also led to the practice of **majority rule.** If people are equal, officials should be chosen and policies should be adopted according to the greater number. Otherwise, some people—the minority—would have more authority than the others.

Majority rule helps provide the support necessary for a government. Those in the minority go along because they accept this principle and they expect to be in the majority on other issues or at other times. (It helps if everyone wins some of the time and no one loses all of the time.[54]) They also go along because they expect those in the majority to respect their rights. Thus, majority rule entails minority rights.

Minority Rights

The Founders were concerned about the rights of political and religious minorities. As a result of the expansion of individual rights in the twentieth century, Americans today are concerned about the rights of racial, ethnic, and sexual minorities as well.

Although **minority rights** are necessary to preserve majority rule in the long run, the two concepts clash with each other on a daily basis. It's useful to view them as opposite ends of a continuum. If one concept is overemphasized, the other is underemphasized. For a democratic government, it's a delicate balance—really, a constant struggle—to find an appropriate accommodation between the two concepts. Because the majority has more power, it tends to flex its muscles at the expense of the minority. The most egregious example has been the enslavement, segregation, and discrimination directed at African Americans, but other examples occur every day in our society.

Economic Rights

The American Revolution was triggered by the colonists' perception that the British Parliament was imposing unfair taxation and economic policies that benefited England rather than the colonies. To an extent, the colonists fought the Revolution to be left alone to pursue their livelihoods and to retain their wealth, or at least to ensure that they would not have to give up their wealth without their consent.

Economic freedom, specifically the **right to own property,** is an adjunct to our concepts of individual liberty and natural rights. Locke considered this right an important natural right. According to Locke, when people work the land, clearing it and planting it, they mix their labor with it. This work makes the land their property. Although Americans had gotten the land through theft from the Indians or through luck from their ancestors (who had gotten it for little or nothing by a royal grant in colonial times), in this view the important thing is what they do with the land. Farmers start with dirt and grasses and trees, and they create productive land. Some inevitably accumulate more property and create more wealth than others. Thus, the right to property leads to significant inequality of wealth. Yet Locke thought it would lead to greater productivity for society.[55]

Just as tension exists between individual liberty and the good of all and between majority rule and minority rights, tension also exists between the political equality the Declaration avows and the property rights the Constitution protects. (The latter will be discussed in Chapter 2.) In reality, people who amass more wealth than others also exert more power over government.

The ancient Greeks, as well as some Founders such as Thomas Jefferson, feared that democracy could not tolerate extremes of wealth and poverty. They thought that a wealthy minority, out of smugness, and an impoverished minority, out of desperation, would seek their own improvement and disregard the public interest. Most Founders worried less about this. They thought they could create a government that would protect individual diversity, including economic disparity, and still survive.

But the pursuit of political equality in a real world of great economic inequities has led government to a greater role in regulating economic activity than the Founders ever anticipated. When we discuss antitrust laws and unfair business practices and when we discuss welfare, health care, and Social Security policies, we're implicitly debating whether government should reduce inequalities of wealth.

We can see that democratic principles sometimes contradict each other. Americans have struggled for more than two centuries to reconcile their political practice with their democratic aims and to perfect a governmental system that was revolutionary for its time. We will see these contradictions many times in this book as we explore how government actually works.

Conclusion: Is Government Responsive?

This book is organized around the theme of government responsiveness. How responsive are government officials and policies to popular demands? The conclusion of each chapter will try to answer this question as it applies to whichever aspect of American government is covered in that chapter. (This will be more evident in the remaining chapters than in this introductory chapter.)

To work, democracy requires citizens to participate in politics—some to run for office, others to help in campaigns, and most to vote in elections. Democracy also encourages citizens to speak their mind and to petition the government as means of influencing other citizens and elected officials.

Americans love the idea that the average person has a say in government. Voting is the basic way, and the easiest way, to do so, yet barely half of eligible Americans vote in presidential elections, far fewer in congres-

Americans, such as this man in St. Petersburg, Florida, are very patriotic, but many don't participate in our democracy.

sional elections held in between presidential elections, and fewer still in local elections. Only a tiny minority, the political activists, take full advantage of the opportunities to participate. One-fifth of all Americans do nothing political; they don't even discuss politics.[56]

Even after 9/11, when Americans were expressing a more favorable view of government, there was no increase in political participation. There was flag waving and a proliferation of flag magnets on cars, and there was vocal support for our troops abroad, but these actions don't make the country a democracy.

Many Americans practice "couch-potato politics," refusing to accept the responsibilities of national citizenship.[57] In fact, a majority of Americans think it is possible to be patriotic without getting involved in political or civic life.[58]

Why do these Americans like their government on paper but dislike participating in it? Are they too busy to be bothered? Or has government failed? Are its laws and policies not what the people want? Have the people been turned off because the media emphasize negative aspects of government? Have the people been alienated because some individuals and groups wield disproportionate

power? Have average citizens been shut out of the process? Or is the problem the fault of the citizens and not of government at all? When asked, "What's wrong with government?" Americans typically cite elected officials, political parties, special interests, or the media. Rarely do they blame the voters or the public in general.

Dropping out of the political process because we think it is futile or controlled by others is like cutting off our nose to spite our face. Throughout this book, we'll see that government *is* responsive—but to people and groups who participate in politics. The old adage "the squeaky wheel gets the grease" applies to government as well as to other things in society.

Americans often say, "It's all politics." *Of course it is!* Diverse people and groups have different views about what the government should do. In a democracy, they're free to express their views and to influence their officials and institutions to adopt them. So debates about issues and conflicts over elections are political. They reflect the competition inherent in a democracy.

Ignoring politics and the institutions that represent the people to their government, such as political parties and interest groups, would not eliminate politics. Neither would muzzling political parties and interest groups. Rather, these actions would eliminate the most effective ways yet developed for the public, especially average people, to influence government decisions.

In the coming chapters, we'll examine the major institutions and processes of our republic, describing their evolution since the Founding and explaining their operation today.

Key Terms

politics   2
identity politics   7
political culture   8
United States Census   9
DNA testing   9
individual liberty   11

natural rights   11
political equality   12
popular sovereignty   12
democracy   12
majority rule   12
minority rights   13
right to own property   13

Key Names

Aristotle   2
Noah Webster   10

John Locke   11
Alexis de Tocqueville   12
Abraham Lincoln   12

1. We have politics because
   a. we have politicians.
   b. political parties create conflict.
   c. we have disagreeable people.
   d. too many people don't want what's best for society.
   e. people often have different values and goals.

2. Aristotle thought all but which of the following?
   a. Politics is a noble endeavor.
   b. Politics helps individuals know themselves.
   c. Politics prevents society from coming together.
   d. Politics helps individuals relate to others.
   e. Politics forces individuals to consider the interests of fellow citizens.

3. There has been cultural diversity in North America since the
   a. time of the Native Americans.
   b. time the first European settlers arrived.
   c. time the first African slaves arrived.
   d. late-nineteenth-century immigrants came.
   e. late-twentieth-century immigrants came.

4. Today the number of illegal immigrants to the United States each year is estimated to be _____ the number of legal immigrants.
   a. more than
   b. much more than
   c. about the same as
   d. less than
   e. much less than

5. As a result of current legal and illegal immigration to the United States, we have
   a. the highest percentage of foreign-born residents in our history.
   b. a lower number of foreign-born residents than we had in the late 1800s and early 1900s.
   c. about the same percentage and number of foreign-born residents that we had at the time of the Civil War.
   d. a higher percentage of foreign-born residents than we had in the late 1800s and early 1900s.
   e. the highest number of foreign-born residents in our history.

6. Which statement isn't true? Nativist sentiments
   a. fortunately haven't surfaced since the early 1900s.
   b. occur when Americans fear economic competition from newcomers.
   c. are greatest when immigration levels are highest.
   d. occur when newcomers are perceived as a cultural threat.
   e. are a political force today.

7. Our religious diversity has led to
   a. religious conflict through history.
   b. religious uniformity today.
   c. religious freedom.
   d. religious oppression.
   e. both a. and c.

8. The United States has
   a. no social classes.
   b. just a middle class.
   c. a huge middle class and tiny upper and lower classes.
   d. a full range of social classes.
   e. multiple classes, but it doesn't matter because those who want to move up have ample opportunity to do so.

9. The most significant regional split in the United States is between the
   a. East and West.   b. North and South.
   c. the coasts and the heartland.
   d. the mountains and the flatlands.
   e. the industrial regions and the agricultural regions.

10. The term *identity politics* refers to the
    a. tendency of newcomers to muscle their way into the system.
    b. rejection of hyphenated labels we see today.
    c. attachment that European Americans have to their ancestral country.
    d. the importance of ethnic or racial ancestry in politics today.
    e. desire of people to be considered full-fledged Americans.

11. The term *Hispanic* refers to
    a. brown-skinned people in the Southwest.
    b. a cohesive group of people.
    c. residents with a Spanish-speaking background.
    d. a distinct race of people.
    e. recent immigrants from Latin America.

12. DNA testing will
    a. finally enable us to classify people in one racial category or another.
    b. force the Census Bureau to eliminate its category of "mulatto."
    c. make the current racial categories seem simplistic.
    d. help the Census Bureau perfect its system of classification.
    e. simplify the administration of government programs based on race.

13. Noah Webster was a significant figure because he
    a. attempted to create and standardize American English.
    b. was an early president.
    c. was an important member of Congress.
    d. was a chief justice of the Supreme Court.
    e. established the first factory in America.

14. Americans' emphasis on individual liberty came from
    a. early settlers who were runaways from authority.
    b. those who came to America to practice their religion as they saw fit.
    c. those who came to America to make money.
    d. those who came to America because they desired a society that emphasized the community.
    e. all but d.

15. To a significant extent, our concept of natural rights came from _____ and was articulated by _____.
    a. the ancient Greeks; Aristotle
    b. the Judeo-Christian tradition; John Locke
    c. the backlash against European religious persecution; Noah Webster
    d. the Judeo-Christian tradition; Charles de Montesquieu.
    e. England's Anglican Church; John Locke

16. Our core value of equality emphasizes equal
    a. ability.   b. virtue.
    c. respect.   d. rights.
    e. talents.

17. President Abraham Lincoln's statement in the Gettysburg Address about "government of the people, by the people, for the people" refers to the concept of
    a. individual liberty.   b. political equality.
    c. popular sovereignty.   d. direct democracy.
    e. minority rights.

18. A major conflict among our core values is between majority rights and
    a. popular sovereignty.   b. minority rights.
    c. democracy.   d. individual liberty.
    e. political equality.

19. The core value that has been the most important in our political culture is
    a. individual liberty.   b. political equality.
    c. popular sovereignty.   d. majority rule.
    e. minority rights.

20. Our government is responsive to
    a. nobody really.
    b. those who are uninterested in politics.
    c. those who are patriotic.
    d. those who practice "couch-potato politics."
    e. those who participate in politics.

Even if this couple marries in a state that allows same-sex couples to marry, their marriage won't be recognized by other states or by the federal government.

Chuck Nacke/Woodfin Camp & Associates

When the Hawaii Supreme Court ruled in 1993 that homosexual couples might be allowed to marry in that state, social conservatives in other states worried that their states would have to recognize the marriages if these couples ever moved from Hawaii, because the Constitution's **full faith and credit clause** requires each state to recognize the contracts made in other states. Conservatives also worried that homosexuals would travel to Hawaii just to get married and then return to their states as married couples.[1] So conservatives pushed Congress to pass the Defense of Marriage Act, which allows states to disregard same-sex marriages performed in other states. The act also withholds federal recognition of same-sex marriages and denies federal benefits, such as Social Security, to same-sex couples. As a result, even couples in states that later allowed same-sex marriages, such as Massachusetts, are not considered married according to the federal government. Thus, Congress took over a traditional state responsibility—deciding who is married. Conservatives' abhorrence of same-sex marriages trumped their preference for states' rights. This is just one example of the continuously shifting balance of power between the federal and state governments.

Early settlers came to America for different reasons. Some came to escape religious persecution, others to establish their own religious orthodoxy. Some came to avoid debtors' prison, others to get rich. Some came to flee the closed society of the Old World, others to make money for their families or employers in that world. Some came as free persons, others as indentured servants or slaves. Few came to practice self-government. Yet the desire for self-government was evident from the beginning.[2] The settlers who arrived in Jamestown in 1607 established the first representative assembly in America. The Pilgrims, who reached Plymouth in 1620, drew up the Mayflower Compact in which they vowed to "solemnly & mutually in the presence of God, and one of another, covenant and combine our selves together into a civill body politick." They pledged to establish laws for "the generall good of the colonie" and in return promised "all due submission and obedience."[3]

During the next century and a half, the colonies adopted constitutions and elected representative assemblies. Of course, the colonies lived under British rule; they had to accept the appointment of royal governors and the presence of British troops. But a vast ocean separated the two continents. At such distance, Britain could not wield the control it might at closer reach. It had to grant the colonies a measure of autonomy, which they used to practice the beginnings of self-government.

These early efforts toward self-government led to conflict with the mother government. In 1774, the colonies established the Continental Congress to coordinate their actions. Within months, the conflict reached flash point, and the Congress urged the colonies to form their own governments. In 1776, the Congress adopted the Declaration of Independence.

After six years of war, the Americans accepted the British surrender. At the time it seemed they had met their biggest test. Yet they would find fomenting a revolution easier than fashioning a government, and drafting a declaration of independence easier than crafting a constitution.

The Articles of Confederation

Even before the war ended, the Continental Congress passed a constitution, and in 1781 the states ratified it. This first constitution, the **Articles of Confederation,** formed a "league of friendship" among the states. As a confederation, it allowed each state to retain its "sovereignty" and "independence." That is, it made the states supreme over the federal government. Under the Articles, however, Americans would face problems with both their national and state governments.

[handwritten: congressional powers were strictly limited]

National Government Problems

The Articles of Confederation established a Congress, but they limited the powers that Congress could exercise, and they provided no executive or judicial branch. The Articles reflected the colonial experience under the British government. The leaders feared a powerful central government with a powerful executive like a king. They thought such a government would be too strong and too distant to guarantee individual liberty. Furthermore, the Articles reflected a lack of national identity among the people. Most did not yet view themselves as Americans. As Edmund Randolph remarked, "I am not really an American, I am a Virginian."[4] Consequently, the leaders established a very decentralized government that left most authority to the states.

The Articles satisfied many people. Most Americans worked small farms, and although many of them sank into debt during the depression that followed the war, they felt they could get the state governments to help them. They realized they could not influence a distant central government as readily.

But the Articles frustrated bankers, merchants, manufacturers, and others in the upper classes. They envisioned a great commercial empire replacing the agricultural society that existed in the late eighteenth century. More than local trade, they wanted national and even international trade. For this they needed uniform laws, stable money, sound credit, and enforceable debt collection. They needed a strong central government that could protect them against debtors and against state governments sympathetic to debtors. The Articles provided neither the foreign security nor the domestic climate necessary to nourish these requisites of a commercial empire.

After the war, the army disbanded, leaving the country vulnerable to hostile forces surrounding it. Britain maintained outposts with troops in the Northwest Territory (the Midwest today), in violation of the peace treaty, and an army in Canada. Spain, which had occupied Florida and California for a long time and had claimed the Mississippi River valley as a result of a treaty before the war, posed a threat. Barbary pirates from North Africa seized American ships and sailors. (See box "The Black Flag on the High Seas.")

[handwritten: A lack of unity lack recognize of a government]

[handwritten: No National Law. that was easily identified]

Congress could not raise an army, because it could not draft individuals directly, or finance an army, because it could not tax individuals directly. Instead, it had to ask the states for soldiers and money. The states, however, were not always sympathetic to the problems of the distant government. And although Congress could make treaties with foreign countries, the states made (and broke) treaties independently of Congress. Without the ability to establish a credible army or negotiate a binding treaty, the government could not get the British troops to leave American soil or the Spanish government to permit navigation on the Mississippi River.[5]

In addition to an inability to confront foreign threats, the Articles demonstrated an inability to cope with domestic crises. The country bore a heavy war debt that brought the government close to bankruptcy. Since Congress could not tax individuals directly, it could not shore up the shaky government. The states competed with each other for commercial advantage. As independent governments, they imposed tariffs on goods from other states. The tariffs slowed the growth of businesses.

In short, the government under the Articles of Confederation seemed too decentralized to ensure either peace or prosperity. The Articles, one leader concluded, gave Congress the privilege of asking for everything while reserving to each state the prerogative of granting nothing.[6] A similar situation exists today in the United Nations, which must rely on the goodwill of member countries to furnish troops for its peace-keeping forces and dues for its operating expenses.[7]

State Government Problems

Other conflicts arose closer to home. State constitutions adopted during the American Revolution made the state legislatures more representative than the colonial legislatures had been. Most state legislatures also began to hold elections every year. The result was heightened interest among candidates and turnover among legislators. In the eyes of national leaders, there was much pandering to voters and horse trading by politicians as various factions vied for control. The process seemed up for grabs. According to the Vermont Council of Censors, laws were "altered—realtered—made better—made worse; and kept in such a fluctuating position that persons in civil commission scarce know what is law."[8] In short, state governments were experiencing more democracy than any other governments in the world at the time. National leaders, stunned by the changes in

THE BLACK FLAG ON THE HIGH SEAS

Americans faced attacks from pirates as well as threats from foreign powers. As many as a hundred merchant ships sailed from American ports to Mediterranean cities each year, bringing salted fish, flour, sugar, and lumber and returning with figs, lemons, oranges, olive oil, and opium. Barbary pirates from North Africa—Tripoli (now Libya), Tunis (Tunisia), Algeria, and Morocco—preyed upon ships in the Mediterranean Sea, seizing sailors, holding them for ransom or pressing them into slavery, and extorting money from shippers and governments.[1] Historians estimate that a million Europeans and Americans were kidnapped or enslaved by these pirates in the seventeenth and eighteenth centuries.

Although American ships were protected by the British navy (and by the British government's willingness to pay tribute) during colonial times, they were not shielded after independence. The weakness of the government under the Articles of Confederation left the ships' crews to fend for themselves. The marauding pirates were not only a nasty rebuke to American merchants' desire for international trade but also to our citizens' belief in free trade on the seas, without acts of violence or demands for payments.

The conflict was mostly over riches—the Barbary states used piracy to finance their governments—but it also reflected religious conflict. The Barbary states were Muslim, and although their societies would not be called fundamentalist or Islamist today—in fact, they treated their Jewish residents better than most European societies did at the time—their leaders told American officials that the Koran gave them the right to enslave infidels.[2]

The piracy would not cease until the new government under the Constitution created a strong navy and fought the Barbary Wars (1801–1805)—the first deployment of the American military overseas.[3]

[1] Other pirates patrolled the Caribbean, with some operating out of New Orleans.

[2] Previously, European states had held Muslim slaves.

[3] This led to the line in the Marines Corps anthem "to the shores of Tripoli."

SOURCES: Christopher Hitchens, "Black Flag," *New York Times Book Review*, August 21, 2005, 7–8; Max Boot, *The Savage Wars of Peace* (New York: Basic Books, 2002), 3–29.

FOUNDING MOTHERS

Charles Francis Adams, a grandson of President John Adams and Abigail Adams, declared in 1840, "The heroism of the females of the Revolution has gone from memory with the generation that witnessed it, and nothing, absolutely nothing remains upon the ear of the young of the present day."[1] That statement remains true today; in the volumes written about the revolutionary and Constitution-making era, much is said of the "Founding Fathers" but little about the "Founding Mothers." Although no women were delegates to the Constitutional Convention, in various ways besides birthing and rearing the children and maintaining the homes women contributed significantly to the founding of the country. Many contributed directly to the political ferment of the time. Their political role during the revolutionary and Constitution-making era was probably greater than it would be again for a century.

Before the Revolutionary War, women were active in encouraging opposition to British rule. Groups of women, some formed as the "Daughters of Liberty," organized resistance to British taxes by leading boycotts of British goods such as cloth and tea; they made their own cloth, hosting spinning bees, and their own drinks from native herbs and flowers.

A few women were political pamphleteers, helping increase public sentiment for independence. One of those pamphlet writers, Mercy Otis Warren, from Boston, was thought to be the first person to urge the Massachusetts delegates to the Continental Congress to vote for separation from Britain.[2] She also wrote poems advocating independence and plays satirizing British officials and sympathizers among the colonists (although the plays could only be read, not staged, because Puritan Boston forbade theater). Throughout the period before and after the Revolution, Warren shared her political ideas in personal correspondence with leading statesmen of the time, such as John Adams and Thomas Jefferson. Later, she wrote a three-volume history of the American Revolution.

When the Declaration of Independence was drafted, the printer—a publisher in Maryland named Mary Katherine Goddard—printed her own name at the bottom of the Declaration in support of the signers who were in hiding from the British.

Because the Continental Army lacked money to pay, feed, and clothe the troops, women raised funds, canvassing door to door, and also made clothes for the soldiers. One group of women in Philadelphia made 2200 shirts.

During the Revolutionary War, many women followed their husbands into battle. As part of the American army, most filled traditional women's roles as cooks, seamstresses, and nurses, but there are reports of women swabbing cannons with water to cool them and firing cannons when their husbands were wounded. After Margaret Corbin's husband was killed, she manned his artillery piece and was wounded three times. Later she received pay as a disabled soldier, including the ration for rum or whiskey.

the few years since the Revolution, considered this development an "excess of democracy."

These leaders, most of whom were wealthy and many of whom were creditors, pointed to the laws passed in some states that relieved debtors of some of their obligations. The farmers in debt pressed the legislatures for relief that would slow or shrink the payments owed to their creditors, and some legislatures granted such relief.

These laws worried the leaders, and **Shays's Rebellion** in western Massachusetts in 1786 and 1787 frightened them. Boston merchants who had loaned Massachusetts money during the war insisted on being repaid in full so they could trade with foreign merchants. The state levied steep taxes that many farmers could not pay during the hard times. The law authorized foreclosure—sale of the farmers' property to recover unpaid taxes—and jail for the debtors. The law essentially transferred wealth from the farmers to the merchants. The state government wasn't as sympathetic to debtors as some other states were. The farmers protested the legislature's refusal to grant any relief from the law. Bands of farmers blocked entrances to courthouses where judges were scheduled to hear cases calling for foreclosure and jail. Led by Daniel Shays, some marched to the Springfield arsenal to seize weapons. Although they were defeated by the militia, their sympathizers were victorious in the next election.

Farmer protested about taxes & wealth going to merchants & debtors going to jail.

This English political cartoon satirizes a gathering of leading women of North Carolina who drew up a resolution to boycott taxed English goods.

battle. One wrapped tight bandages around her breasts and served three years and survived two wounds. Fellow soldiers thought she was a young man slow to grow a beard.[3] Still other women fought to defend their homes using hatchets, farm implements, and pots of boiling lye in addition to muskets.

Women also served as spies. When British soldiers commandeered one house for their quarters, the mother asked if she and her children could remain. One night she overheard the officers plotting a surprise attack on Washington's camp, and she sneaked out of town to warn the camp. A sixteen-year-old girl rode forty miles to warn a militia of another pending attack.[4]

Women were so prominent in the war that British general Lord Cornwallis said, "We may destroy all the men in America, and we shall still have all we can do to defeat the women."[5]

Following independence, a few women continued an active political role. Mercy Otis Warren campaigned

against the proposed Constitution because she felt it was not democratic enough. Abigail Adams called for new laws, unlike English laws which gave all power to husbands, that would provide some equality between husbands and wives. She also called for formal education for girls.

Yet independence did not bring an improvement in the political rights of women. It would be another century before the rights of women would become a full-fledged part of our national political agenda.

[1] Quoted in Linda Grant De Pauw and Conover Hunt, *Remember the Ladies* (New York: Viking, 1976), 9.

[2] Alice Felt Tyler, *Freedom's Ferment* (New York: Harper & Row), 1962.

[3] Cokie Roberts, *Founding Mothers* (New York: HarperCollins, 2004), 79–82.

[4] Mrs. Betsey Loring also made a heroic contribution to the cause by keeping a British general so "lustily occupied" in Philadelphia that he failed to move his troops to Valley Forge, where he could have destroyed the Continental Army. Alas, her motive was not patriotism; she sought a position in the British army for her husband. Roberts, *Founding Mothers,* xviii.

[5] Ibid., xix.

Both the revolt and the legislature's change in policy scared the wealthy. To them it raised the specter of mob rule. Nathaniel Gorham, the president of the Continental Congress and a prominent merchant, wrote Prince Henry of Prussia, announcing "the failure of our free institutions" and asking whether the prince would agree to become king of America (the prince declined).[9] Just months after the uprising, Congress approved a convention for "the sole and express purpose of revising the Articles of Confederation."

To a significant extent, then, the debate at the time reflected a conflict between two competing visions of the future American political economy—agricultural or commercial.[10] Most leaders espoused the latter, and the

combination of national problems and state problems prompted them to push for a new government.[11]

The Constitution

The Constitutional Convention

The Setting

The **Constitutional Convention** convened in Philadelphia, then the country's largest city, in 1787. State legislatures sent fifty-five delegates. They met at the Pennsylvania State House—now Independence Hall—in the same room where many of them had signed the

Handout annotation: Heuristics → the art to shape of the world so you can win.
↑ rules & ways you make decisions

Declaration of Independence eleven years earlier. Delegates came from every state except Rhode Island, whose farmers and debtors feared that the convention would weaken states' powers to relieve debtors of their debts.

All of the delegates were men (see the box "Founding Mothers"). They were distinguished by their education, experience, and enlightenment. **Benjamin Franklin,** of Pennsylvania, was the best-known American in the world. He had been a printer, scientist, and diplomat. At eighty-one, he was the oldest delegate. **George Washington,** of Virginia, was the most respected American in the country. As the commander of the revolutionary army, he was a national hero. He was chosen to preside over the convention. The presence of men like Franklin and Washington gave the convention legitimacy.

The delegates quickly determined that the Articles of Confederation were beyond repair. Rather than revise them, as instructed by Congress, the delegates decided to draft a new constitution.[12]

The Predicament

Annotation: Fear of anarchy & tyranny. ← sense of coats

The delegates came to the convention because they thought their government was too weak, yet the Americans had fought the Revolution because they chafed under a government that was too strong. "The nation lived in a nearly constant alternation of fears that it would cease being a nation altogether or become too much of one."[13] People feared both anarchy and tyranny.

This predicament was made clear by the diversity of opinions among the leaders. At one extreme was Patrick Henry, of Virginia, who had been a firebrand of the Revolution. He feared that the government would become too strong, perhaps even become a monarchy, in reaction to the problems with the Articles. He said he "smelt a rat" and did not attend the convention. At the other extreme was Alexander Hamilton, of New York, who had been an aide to General Washington during the war and had seen the government's inability to supply and pay its own troops. Ever since, he had called for a stronger national government and had suggested even a monarchy. He did attend the convention but, finding little agreement with his proposals, participated infrequently.

In between was **James Madison,** of Virginia. Small and frail, timid and self-conscious as a speaker, he was nonetheless an intelligent and savvy politician. He had operated behind the scenes to organize the convention and to secure Washington's attendance. (He announced

that Washington would attend without asking Washington first. Washington, who was in retirement, had not planned to attend but reluctantly agreed to do so because of the expectation that he would.[14]) Madison, who had studied other countries' governments, had secretly drafted a plan for a new government, one that was a total departure from the government under the Articles and one that would set the agenda for the convention. During the convention, Madison was "up to his ears in politics, advising, persuading, softening the harsh word, playing down this difficulty and exaggerating that, engaging in debate, harsh controversy, polemics, and sly maneuver."[15] In the end, his views more than anyone else's would prevail, and he would be known as the Father of the Constitution.[16]

Consensus

Despite disagreements, the delegates did see eye to eye on the most fundamental issues. They agreed that the government should be a **republic**—a form of government that derives its power from the people and whose officials are accountable to the people. The term more specifically refers to an indirect democracy in which the people vote for at least some of the officials who represent them.[17]

They also agreed that the national government should be stronger than under the Articles and that it should have three separate branches—legislative, executive, and judicial—to exercise the three functions of government—making, administering, and judging the laws. They thought that both the legislative and executive branches should be strong.

Conflict

Although there was considerable agreement over the fundamental principles and elemental structure of the new government, the delegates quarreled about the specific provisions concerning representation, slavery, and trade.

Representation Sharp conflict was expressed between delegates from large states and those from small states over representation. Large states sought a strong government that they could control; small states feared a strong government that could control them.

When the convention began, the Virginia Plan, drafted by Madison, was introduced. According to this plan, the legislature would be divided into two houses, with representation based on population in each. But delegates from the small states calculated that the three largest states would have a majority of the representatives and could dominate the legislature.

These delegates countered with the New Jersey Plan. According to this plan, the legislature would consist of one house, with representation by states, which would have one vote each. This was exactly the same as the structure of Congress under the Articles, also designed to prevent the largest states from dominating the legislature.

James Wilson, of Pennsylvania, asked for whom they were forming a government—"for men, or for the imaginary beings called states?"[18] But delegates from the small states would not budge. Some threatened to leave the government and align themselves with a European country instead.[19]

The convention deadlocked, and some delegates left for home. George Washington wrote that he almost despaired of the likelihood of reaching any agreement. To ease tensions, Benjamin Franklin suggested that the delegates begin each day with a prayer, but they could not agree on this either; Alexander Hamilton insisted they did not need "foreign aid."

Faced with the possibility that the convention would disband without a constitution, the delegates, after weeks of frustrating debate, compromised. Delegates from Connecticut and other states proposed a plan in which the legislature, Congress, would have two houses. In one, the **House of Representatives,** representation would be based on population, and members would be elected by voters. In the other, the **Senate,** representation would be by states, and members would be selected by state legislatures. Presumably, the large states would dominate the former, the small states the latter (see the box "The Undemocratic Senate"). The delegates narrowly approved this **Great Compromise,** or Connecticut Compromise.[20] The compromise has been called "great" because it not only resolved this critical issue but paved the way for resolution of other issues.

This decision began a pattern that continues to this day. When officials face implacable differences, they try to compromise, but the process is not easy. It is an apt choice of words to say that officials "hammer out" a compromise; it is not a coincidence that we use *hammer* rather than a softer metaphor.

Slavery In addition to conflict between large states and small states over representation, conflict emerged between northern states and southern states over slavery, trade, and taxation.

With representation in one house based on population, the delegates had to decide how to apportion the seats. They agreed that Indians would not count as part of the population but differed about slaves. Delegates from the South, where slaves made up one-third of the population, wanted slaves to count fully in order to boost the number of southern representatives. Although slaves had not been counted at all under the Articles or under any state constitution, southerners argued that their use of slaves produced wealth that benefited the entire nation. Delegates from the North, where most states had outlawed slavery or at least the slave trade after the Revolution, did not want slaves to count at all. Gouverneur Morris, of Pennsylvania, said the southerners' position

> comes to this: that the inhabitant of Georgia and South Carolina who goes to the coast of Africa, and in defiance of the most sacred laws of humanity tears away his fellow creatures from their dearest connections and damns them to the most cruel bondages, shall have more votes in a government instituted for the protection of the rights of mankind than the citizen of Pennsylvania or New Jersey who views with a laudable horror so nefarious a practice.[21]

Others pointed out that slaves were not considered persons when it came to rights such as voting. Nevertheless, southerners asserted that they would not support the constitution if slaves were not counted at least partially. In the **Three-fifths Compromise,** the delegates agreed that three-fifths of the slaves would be counted in apportioning the seats.

This compromise expanded the political power of the people who were oppressing the slaves. The votes of southern whites became worth more than those of northerners in electing members to the House of Representatives and also in electing presidents (because the number of presidential electors for each state was based on the number of members in Congress from the state). By 1860, nine of the fifteen presidents, including all five who served two terms, were slave owners.[22] Ultimately, twelve presidents were slave owners.

Southerners pushed through two other provisions addressing slavery. One forbade Congress from banning the importation of slaves before 1808; another required free states to return escaped slaves to their owners in slave states. In these provisions, southerners won most of what they wanted; even the provision permitting Congress to ban the importation of slaves in 1808 was little limitation because by then planters would have enough slaves to fulfill their needs by natural population increases. In return, northerners, who represented ship-

After slavery was abolished and the right to vote was extended to racial minorities and women, the equal representation of states in the Senate is perhaps the most undemocratic aspect left in the Constitution.[1]

Because each state gets two senators regardless of its population, small or sparsely populated rural states enjoy disproportionate representation relative to their size. California, the most populous state, and Wyoming, the least populous state, have equal representation, although California has seventy times more people. Therefore, voters in California have one-seventieth as much representation, or power, in the Senate as voters in Wyoming have.

The equal representation of states in the Senate is not the result of some grand theory of government. As explained in the text, it was a major concession to the small states to maintain their allegiance to the country and to obtain their support for the Constitution. At that time, people identified more closely with their state than with the nation as a whole. Today, our mass society, mass media, and transportation networks weaken these ties and strengthen our sense of national identity.

Do the people in small states have special needs to protect that would justify their greater representation? The Constitution, including the Bill of Rights and later amendments, guarantees fundamental rights. Federal laws and court decisions preserve various rights. Federalism, which splits power between the national government and the state governments, provides states with more authority than they would have in nonfederal systems. Do the people in small states have additional needs to protect beyond these? If so, what are they? And are these needs greater than the needs of other people who do not get extra representation, such as the people who are short or fat or disabled, or the people who have been the victims of widespread discrimination, such as African Americans or Native Americans, just to name a few groups?

What if a similar rationale were applied to African Americans? If the 12 percent of Americans who are black had as many senators representing them as the 12 percent of Americans who live in our smallest states have representing them, the Senate would include forty-four black senators. Would this seem fair?

Yet even if most Americans decide that the equal representation in the Senate is unfair and undemocratic, it is unlikely they could change it. The Constitution stipulates, "No state, without its consent, shall be deprived of its equal suffrage in the Senate."[2] Furthermore, Article 5, which addresses amendments, limits amendments in two categories. The provision regarding the importation of slaves could not be amended until 1808, and the provision regarding the representation in the Senate cannot be amended ever.

Some constitutional scholars suggest that an amendment repealing this provision could be adopted first and an amendment altering the representation itself could be adopted next. Other scholars think the courts would not tolerate this obvious sabotage of the Founders' intentions.[3] Regardless, it is a moot point, because amendment of the Constitution requires ratification by three-fourths of the states. Just thir-

pers, got authority for Congress to regulate commerce by a simple majority rather than a two-thirds majority. Thus northerners conceded these two provisions reinforcing slavery in order to benefit shippers.[23]

Yet the framers were embarrassed by the hypocrisy of claiming to have been enslaved by the British while allowing enslavement of African Americans. Their embarrassment is reflected in their language. The three provisions reinforcing slavery never mention "slavery" or "slaves"; one gingerly refers to "free persons" and "other persons."

Slavery was the most divisive issue at the convention. As Madison noted, "The real difference of interests lay, not between the large and small, but between the northern and southern states. The institution of slavery and its consequences formed the line of discrimination."[24] The unwillingness to tackle the slavery issue more directly has been called the "Greatest Compromise" by one political scientist.[25] But an attempt to abolish slavery would have caused the five southern states to refuse to ratify the Constitution.

Trade and Taxation

Slavery also underlay a compromise on trade and taxation. With a manufacturing economy, northerners sought protection for their businesses. In particular, they wanted a tax on manufactured products imported from Britain. Without a tax, British goods would be cheaper than

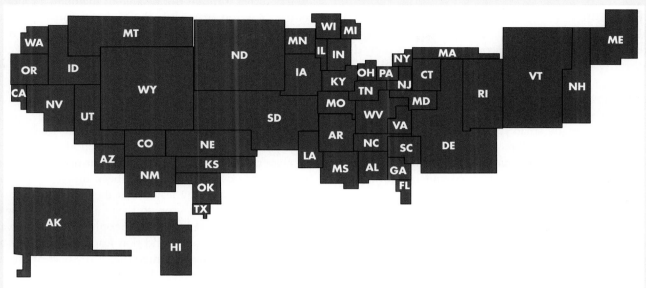

The size of each state in this map reflects the relative power of its citizens in the Senate.

FIGURE 1

SOURCE: Michael Lind, "75 Stars," *Mother Jones* (January-February 1998), p. 130. Reprinted with permission.

teen states can block an amendment favored by the rest of the country. The thirteen smallest states, with only 5 percent of the nation's population, thus can thwart the wishes of the thirty-seven largest states, with 95 percent of the nation's people.

[1] Most information in this box is from Robert A. Dahl, *How Democratic Is the American Constitution?* (New Haven, Conn.: Yale University Press, 2001).

[2] This provision is reinforced by Article 4, which stipulates that "no . . . state shall be formed by the junction of two or more states, or parts of states, without the consent of . . . the states concerned." Thus, small states cannot be forced to combine as a way to reduce their representation.

[3] J. W. Peltason, *Corwin and Peltason's Understanding the Constitution,* 9th ed. (New York: Holt, Rinehart and Winston, 1982), 113. For a creative alternative, see Michael Lind, "75 Stars," *Mother Jones* (January-February 1998), 44–49.

northern products; but with a tax, northern products would be more competitive—and prices for northern and southern consumers would be higher. With an agricultural economy, southerners sought free trade for their plantations. They wanted a guarantee that no tax would be levied on agricultural commodities exported to Britain. Such a tax would make their commodities less competitive abroad and, they worried, amount to an indirect tax on slavery—the labor responsible for the crops. The delegates resolved these issues by allowing Congress to tax imported goods but not exported ones.

After seventeen weeks of debate, thirty-nine of the original fifty-five delegates signed the Constitution on September 17, 1787. Some delegates had left when they saw the direction the convention was taking, and three others refused to sign, feeling that the Constitution gave too much authority to the national government. Most of the rest were not entirely happy with the result (even Madison, who was most responsible for the content of the document, was despondent that his plan for a national legislature was compromised by having one house with representation by states), but they thought it was the best they could do.

Features of the Constitution

Years later, however, a British prime minister said the American Constitution was "the most wonderful work ever struck off at a given time by the brain and purpose of man."[26] To see why it was unique, we'll examine its major features.

A Republic

The Founders distinguished between a democracy and a republic. For them, a *democracy* meant a **direct democracy,** which permits citizens to vote on most issues, and a *republic* meant an **indirect democracy,** which allows citizens to vote for their representatives, who make governmental policies.

Although many small towns in New England used (and some still use) a direct democracy, the Founders opposed a direct democracy for the whole country. Some city-states of ancient Greece and medieval Europe had a direct democracy but could not sustain it. A large country, the Founders thought, would have even less ability to do so because people could not be brought together in one place to debate and vote. Moreover, the Founders believed that people could not withstand the passions of the moment, so they would be swayed by a demagogue to take unwise action. Eventually, democracy would collapse into tyranny.

The Founders favored a republic because they believed that the government should be based on the consent of the people and that the people should have some voice in choosing their officials. So the Founders provided that the people would elect representatives to the House. They also provided that the state legislators, themselves elected by the people, would select their state's senators as well as their state's electors for the Electoral College, which chooses the president. In this way, the people would have a voice but one partially filtered through their presumably wiser representatives.

The Founders' views reflect their ambivalence about the people. Rationally, they believed in popular sovereignty, but emotionally, they feared it. New England clergyman Jeremy Belknap voiced their ambivalence when he declared, "Let it stand as a principle that government originates from the people; but let the people be taught . . . that they are not able to govern themselves."[27]

The Founders would have been aghast at the proliferation of such experiments in direct democracy as initiatives, referenda, and recall elections in many states. The **initiative** process allows citizens and interest groups to collect signatures on petitions and place a proposal on the ballot. If enough voters favor the proposal, it becomes law.[28] The **referendum** process allows the legislature to place a proposal on the ballot. **Recall elections** enable voters to remove officials from office before their terms expire.

The Founders considered a democracy radical and a republic only slightly less radical. Because they believed that the country could not maintain a democracy, they worried that it might not be able to maintain a republic either. It is said that when the Constitutional Convention ended, Benjamin Franklin was approached by a woman who asked, "Well, Doctor, what have we got, a republic or a monarchy?" Franklin responded, "A republic, Madam, if you can keep it."

Fragmentation of Power

Other countries assumed that a government must have a concentration of power to be strong enough to govern. However, when the Founders made our national government more powerful than it had been under the Articles of Confederation, they feared that they also had made it more capable of oppression, so they fragmented its power.

The Founders believed that people are selfish, always coveting more property, and that leaders always lust after more power. They assumed that this aspect of human nature is unchangeable. Madison speculated, "If men were angels, no government would be necessary." "Alas," he added, "men are not angels." Therefore, "in framing a government which is to be administered by men over men, the great difficulty lies in this: you must first enable the government to control the governed; and in the next place oblige it to control itself."[29] The Founders decided that the way to oblige the government to control itself was to structure it so as to prevent any one leader, group of leaders, or factions of people from exercising power over more than a small part of it. Thus the Founders fragmented government's power. This is reflected in three concepts they built into the structure of government—federalism, separation of powers, and checks and balances. (The Founders' views are conveyed in the *Federalist Papers,* especially in Nos. 10 and 51, which are included in the Appendix of this text.)

Federalism The first division of power was between the national government and the state governments. This division of power is called **federalism.**[30] The U.S. government under the Articles of Confederation had been **confederal** (as the Confederacy of southern states during the Civil War would also be); that is, the state governments wielded most authority. The national government exercised only the powers given it by the state governments. At the other extreme, most foreign governments had been **unitary;** the central government wielded all authority.[31]

The Founders, who had had unhappy experiences with a confederal system (their own government under

Anti-Federalists → feared the power of a distant government & a constitution without a bill of rights.

pg 38

the Articles) and a unitary system (the English government during colonial times), wanted to avoid both types. Instead, they sought a strong national government but reasonably strong state governments as well. They invented a federal system as a compromise between the confederal and unitary systems.

They saw federalism as a way to provide sufficient power for the government to function while checking excessive power that could lead to tyranny. They worried about the **"mischiefs of factions"**—groups seeking something for themselves without regard for the rights of others or the well-being of all.[32] According to Madison, factions could be controlled through federalism.[33] A faction might dominate one state but would be less able to dominate many states. (Nevertheless, we should note that federalism is not necessary for a democratic government. Some unitary governments, such as those of Britain and Sweden, are among the most democratic in the world today.)

The Constitution delegates some powers to the national government and reserves other powers for the state governments. Authority over foreign affairs—to make treaties, repel attacks, and declare war—is given to the national government. Authority to print and coin money and to regulate interstate commerce was also given to the national government, and authority to tax was given to both levels. These provisions ensured a stronger national government in foreign and domestic matters than under the Articles.[34] In addition, the Constitution's **supremacy clause** declares that the Constitution is the supreme law of the land and that any laws and treaties made "in pursuance thereof" also are the supreme law of the land whenever they conflict with state laws or actions. But authority over many other matters, including broad authority to provide for the welfare of the people, was given to the state governments. The **Tenth Amendment,** which reflects the general understanding of the time, stipulates that the powers not delegated to the national government are reserved for the states. So this guarantee ensured reasonably strong state governments as well.[35]

Yet the Constitution's language is so general and so succinct that it is very ambiguous. This made the document acceptable to both advocates of a strong national government and supporters of strong state governments, but it also made the document flexible so it could be interpreted as later generations desired or critical challenges required. The language could support either **nation-centered federalism,** which underscores the power of the nation in the arrangement, or **state-centered federalism,** which emphasizes the power of the states.

Finally, we should note that the term *federalism* is often misunderstood because people refer to our national government as the *federal government*. So the word that actually describes the division of power between the national and state governments is also used in this context to refer to just the national government.

Separation of powers The second division of power was within the national government. The power to make, administer, and judge the laws was split into three branches—legislative, executive, and judicial (see Figure 2). In the legislative branch, the power was split further

written By Madison & Hamilton. → Propaganda → state legislature to ratified the constitution

Branch:	Legislative Congress		Executive Presidency	Judicial Federal Courts
	House	Senate	President	Judges
Officials chosen by:	People	People, (originally, state legislatures)	Electoral College, whose members are chosen by the people (originally, by state legislatures)	President, with advice and consent of Senate
For term of:	2 years	6 years	4 years	Life
To represent primarily:	Common people	Wealthy people	All people	Constitution
	Large states	Small states		

FIGURE 2 • **Separation of Powers** *Separation of powers, as envisioned by the Founders, means not only that government functions are to be performed by different branches but also that officials of these branches are to be chosen by different people, for different terms, and to represent different constituencies.*

into two houses. This **separation of powers** contrasts with the parliamentary systems in most developed democracies, in which the legislature is supreme. In parliamentary systems, both executive and judicial officials are drawn from the legislature and are responsible to it. There is no separation of powers.

To reinforce the separation of powers, officials of the three branches were chosen by different means. Representatives were elected by the people (at that time mostly white men who owned property), senators were selected by the state legislatures, and the president was selected by the Electoral College, whose members were selected by the states. Only federal judges were chosen by officials in the other branches. They were nominated by the president and confirmed by the Senate. Once appointed, however, they were allowed to serve for "good behavior"—essentially for life—so they had much independence. (Since the Constitution was written, the Seventeenth Amendment has provided for election of senators by the people, and the state legislatures have provided for election of members of the Electoral College by the people.)

Officials of the branches were also chosen at different times. Representatives were given a two-year term, senators a six-year term (with one-third of them up for reelection every two years), and the president a four-year term. These staggered terms would make it less likely that temporary passions in society would bring about a massive switch of officials or policies.

The Senate was designed to act as a conservative brake on the House, due to senators' selection by state legislatures and their longer terms. Upon his return, Thomas Jefferson, who was in France during the Constitutional Convention, met with George Washington over breakfast. Jefferson protested the establishment of a legislature with two houses. Washington supposedly asked, "Why did you pour that coffee into your saucer?" "To cool it," Jefferson replied. Similarly, Washington explained, "We pour legislation into the senatorial saucer to cool it."[36]

Separation of powers creates the opportunity for **divided government.** Rather than one political party controlling both elected branches, one party might win the presidency while the other party wins a majority of seats in one or both houses of Congress. Divided government has been common throughout the nation's history. Since the emergence of the Democratic and Republican party system (1856), it has occurred as a result of two of every five elections.[37] Since World War II, it has been the dominant mode of government.[38] In this way, American voters have added another element to Madison's concept of separation of powers.

Checks and balances To guarantee separation of powers, the Founders built in overlapping powers called **checks and balances** (see Figure 3). Madison suggested that "the great security against a gradual concentration of the several powers in the same department consists in giving those who administer each department the necessary constitutional means and personal motives to resist encroachments by the others. . . . *Ambition must be made to counteract ambition.*"[39] To that end, each branch was given some authority over the others. If one branch abuses its power, the others can use their checks to thwart it.

Thus rather than a simple system of separation of powers, ours is a complex, even contradictory, system of both separation of powers and checks and balances. The principle of separation of powers gives each branch its own sphere of authority, but the system of checks and balances allows each branch to intrude into the other branches' spheres. For example, because of separation of powers, Congress makes the laws; but due to checks and balances, the president can veto them and the courts can rule them unconstitutional. In these ways, all three branches are involved in legislating. One political scientist calls ours "a government of separated institutions competing for shared powers."[40]

With federalism, separation of powers, and checks and balances, the Founders expected conflict. They invited the parts of government to struggle against each other to limit any part's ability to dominate the rest. The Founders hoped for "balanced government." The national and state governments would represent different interests, as would the branches within the national government. The House would represent the "common" people and the large states; the Senate, the wealthy people and the small states; the president, all the people; and the Supreme Court, the Constitution. Although each part would struggle for more power, it could not accumulate enough to dominate the others. Eventually, it would have to compromise and accept policies that would be in the interest of all of the parts and their constituencies.

Motives of the Founders

To understand the Constitution better, it is useful to consider the motives of the Founders. Were they selfless patriots, sharing their wisdom and experience? Or were they selfish property owners, protecting their interests?

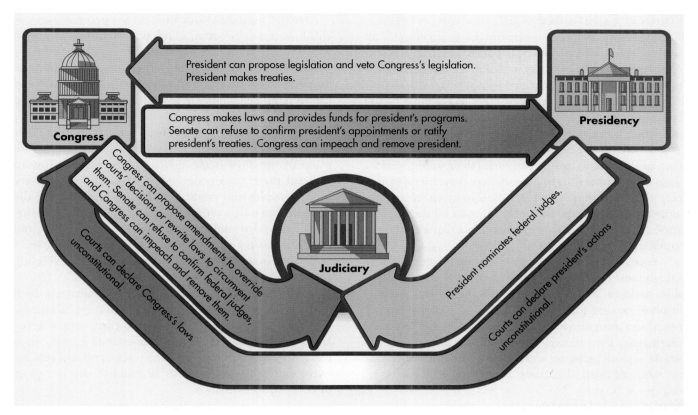

FIGURE 3 • **Checks and Balances** *Most of the major checks and balances among the three branches are explicit in the Constitution, although some are not. For example, the courts' power to declare congressional laws or presidential actions unconstitutional—their power of "judicial review"—is not mentioned.*

Let's consider the philosophical ideas, political experience, and economic interests that influenced the Founders.

Philosophical Ideas

The Founders were well-educated intellectuals who incorporated philosophical ideas into the Constitution. At a time when the average person did not dream of going to college, a majority of the Founders graduated from college. As learned men, they shared a common library of writers and philosophers.

The Founders reflected the ideals of the Enlightenment, a pattern of thought emphasizing the use of reason, rather than tradition or religion, to solve problems. They studied past governments to determine why the governments had failed in the hope that they could apply these lessons to the present. From all accounts, they engaged in a level of debate that was rare in politics, citing philosophers ranging from the ancient Greeks to the modern British and French.

The writings of **John Locke,** as explained in Chapter 1, underlay many of the ideas of the Found-

ers. In addition to his views on natural rights and property rights, the Founders endorsed Locke's views about the relationship between the people and their government. Locke maintained that the people come together to form a government through a **social contract**—an implied agreement between the people and their government—that establishes a **limited government,** strong enough to protect their rights but not so strong as to threaten these rights. This government should not act without the consent of the governed.[41]

The views of **Charles de Montesquieu,** an eighteenth-century French philosopher, also influenced the debate at the convention and the provisions of the Constitution. Although others had suggested separation of powers before, Montesquieu refined the concept and added that of checks and balances. The Founders cited him more than any other thinker.[42] (Presumably, they cited him more than Locke because by this time Locke's views had so permeated American society that the Founders considered them just "common sense."[43])

Political Experience

Although the Founders were intellectuals, they were also experienced and practical politicians who had "to operate with great delicacy and skill in a political cosmos full of enemies."[44]

The Founders brought extensive experience to the convention. Eight had signed the Declaration of Independence, and thirty-nine had served in Congress. Seven had been governors, and many had held other state offices. Some had helped write their state constitutions. The framers drew on this experience. For example, although they cited Montesquieu in discussing separation of powers, they also referred to the experience of colonial and state governments that already had some separation of powers.[45]

As practical politicians, "no matter what their private dreams might be, they had to take home an acceptable package and defend it—and their own political futures—against predictable attack."[46] So, they compromised the difficult issues and ducked the stickiest ones. Ultimately, they pieced together a document that allowed each delegate to return home and announce that his state had won something.

Economic Interests

At the same time, the Founders represented an elite that sought to protect its property from the masses. The delegates to the convention included prosperous planters, manufacturers, shippers, and lawyers. About one-third were slave owners. Most came from families of prominence and married into other families of prominence. Not all were wealthy, but most were at least well-to-do. Only one, a delegate from Georgia, was a yeoman farmer like most men in the country. In short, "this was a convention of the well-bred, the well-fed, the well-read, and the well-wed."[47]

The Founders championed the right to property. The promise of land and even riches had enticed many immigrants to come to America.[48] A desire for freedom from arbitrary taxes and trade restrictions had spurred some colonists to fight in the Revolution.[49] And the inability of the government under the Articles of Confederation to provide a healthy economy had prompted the Founders to convene the Constitutional Convention. They apparently agreed with Madison that "the first object of government" is to protect property.[50] They worried that a democratic government, responding to popular pressures, might appropriate their property or impose high taxes to help less wealthy people. They wanted a government that could resist such populism.

Yet the Founders' emphasis on property was not as elitist as it might seem. Land was plentiful, and with westward expansion, more would be available. Already most men were middle-class farmers who owned some property. Even those who owned no property could foresee the day when they would, so most wanted to protect property.

The Founders diverged from the farmers in their vision to create a national commercial economy in place of the small-scale agricultural economy. Toward this end, the Founders desired to protect other property, such as wealth and credit, in addition to land.[51] So the delegates included provisions to protect commerce, including imports and exports, contracts, and debts, and provisions to regulate currency, bankruptcy, and taxes.[52] (See the box "Constitutional Provisions Protecting Property.")

Political scientists and historians have debated which of these three influences on the Founders—philosophical, political, or economic—was most important. Actually, the influences are difficult to separate because they reinforce each other; the framers' ideas, political experience, and economic interests all point to the same sort of constitution.[53]

Ratification of the Constitution

Ratification was uncertain. Many people opposed the Constitution, and a lively campaign against it appeared in newspapers, pamphlets, and mass meetings.

Knowing opponents would charge the framers with setting up a national government to dominate the state governments; those who supported the Constitution ingeniously adopted the name **Federalists** to empha-

stopping the majority → from holding power. Sep. of powers, limits on Gov power, Check & Balances.

size a real division of power between the national and state governments. They dubbed their opponents **Anti-Federalists** to imply that their opponents did not want a division of power between the governments.

The Anti-Federalists faulted the Constitution for lacking a bill of rights. The framers had not included one because most states already had one in their constitutions. The framers also thought that fragmenting power would prevent any branch from becoming strong enough to deny individual rights. Yet critics demanded provisions protecting various rights, and the Federalists promised to propose amendments guaranteeing these rights as soon as the government began.

The Anti-Federalists also criticized the Constitution for other reasons. Localists at heart, they were wary of entrusting power to officials far away. They worried that the central government would accumulate too much power and the presidency would become a monarchy or Congress an aristocracy. One delegate to the Massachusetts convention blasted the Federalists:

> These lawyers, and men of learning and moneyed men, that talk so finely, and gloss over matters so smoothly, to make us poor illiterate people swallow down the pill, expect to get into Congress themselves; they expect to . . . get all the power and all the money into their own hands, and then they will swallow up all us little folks . . . just as the whale swallowed up Jonah![54]

But the Anti-Federalists had no alternative plan. They were divided, with some wanting to amend the Articles of Confederation and others wanting to reject both the Articles and the Constitution in favor of some yet undetermined form of government. Their lack of unity on an alternative was instrumental in their inability to win support.[55]

Within six months, nine states ratified the new Constitution, and the new government, with George Washington as president, began in 1788. Within one year, the four remaining states approved the Constitution.

Although this process might seem unremarkable today, this marked the first time that a nation had proposed a new government and then asked the people to approve or reject it. And the process occurred with little violence or coercion. As a constitutional historian observed, "The losers were not jailed, hanged, or politically disabled. They did not boycott, take up arms, or go into exile. They continued, as before, to be full and free citizens, but now living in a new republic."[56]

CONSTITUTIONAL PROVISIONS PROTECTING PROPERTY

Numerous constitutional provisions, some obvious and others not, were designed to protect property:

Provision	Effect
"The Times, Places and Manner of holding Elections for Senators and Representatives, shall be prescribed in each State by the Legislature thereof."	Allows states to set property qualifications to vote.
"The Congress shall have Power . . . To coin Money."	Centralizes currency.
"No State shall . . . emit bills of credit."	Prevents states from printing paper money.
"Congress shall have Power . . . To establish uniform Laws on the subject of Bankruptcies."	Prevents states from relieving debtors of the obligation to pay.
"The Congress shall have Power . . . To regulate Commerce . . . among the several States."	Centralizes commerce regulation and thereby establishes a national economy.
"No State shall . . . pass any . . . Law impairing the Obligation of Contracts."	Prevents states from relieving debtors of the obligation to pay and thereby establishes stable business arrangements.
"The United States shall guarantee to every State [protection] against domestic Violence."	Protects states from debtor uprisings.
"The Congress shall have Power . . . To provide for calling forth the Militia to execute the Laws of the Union, suppress insurrections."	Protects creditors from debtor uprisings.

refer to pg 51

Faction → A group whether its a majority or minority united by a common passion adverse by a common

Changing the Constitution

The framers expected their document to last; Madison wrote, "We have framed a constitution that will probably be still around when there are 196 million people."[57]

Check & Balances → way to ensure each branch of government have equal balance of powers & Checks on other branches
pg 31

Bicameralism → House & Senate. —two/state. *population*

Authorities empty barrels of beer after the Eighteenth Amendment, which prohibited alcohol, was adopted in 1919. The Twenty-first Amendment repealed the Eighteenth in 1933.

Library of Congress

Yet, because the framers realized it would need some changes, they drafted a Constitution that can be changed either formally by amendment or informally by judicial interpretation or political practice. In doing so, they left a legacy for later governments. "The example of changing a Constitution, by assembling the wise men of the state, instead of assembling armies," Jefferson noted, "will be worth as much to the world as the former examples we had given them."[58]

By Constitutional Amendment

That the Articles of Confederation could be amended only by a unanimous vote of the states posed an almost insurmountable barrier to any change at all. The framers of the Constitution made sure that this experience would not repeat itself. Yet they did not make amendment easy; the procedures, though not requiring unanimity, do require widespread agreement. More than nine thousand amendments have been proposed in Congress, but only twenty-seven (including the ten in the Bill of Rights) have been adopted.[59]

Procedures The procedures for amendment entail action by both the national government and the state governments. Amendments can be proposed either by a two-thirds vote of both houses of Congress or by a national convention called by Congress at the request of two-thirds of the state legislatures. Congress then specifies which way amendments must be ratified—either by three-fourths of the state legislatures or by ratifying conventions in three-fourths of the states. Among these avenues, the usual route has been proposal by Congress and ratification by state legislatures.

Amendments In the first Congress under the Constitution, the Federalists fulfilled their promise to support a bill of rights. Madison drafted twelve amendments, Congress proposed them, and the states ratified ten of them in 1791. This Bill of Rights includes freedom of conviction and expression and numerous rights for criminal defendants. (These will be covered fully in Chapter 12.)

Among the other seventeen amendments to the Constitution, the strongest theme is the expansion of citizenship rights:[60]

- Abolition of slavery (Thirteenth, 1865)
- Equal protection, due process of law (Fourteenth, 1868)
- Right of black men to vote (Fifteenth, 1870)
- Direct election of senators (Seventeenth, 1913)
- Right of women to vote (Nineteenth, 1920)
- Right of District of Columbia residents to vote in presidential elections (Twenty-third, 1960)
- Abolition of poll tax in federal elections (Twenty-fourth, 1964)
- Right of persons eighteen and older to vote (Twenty-sixth, 1971)

In recent decades, two amendments proposed by Congress were not ratified by the states. One would have provided equal rights for women (discussed in Chapter 13), and the other would have given congressional representation to the District of Columbia as though it were a state.

Although the Constitution expressly provides for change by amendment, its ambiguity about some subjects and silence about others virtually guarantees change by interpretation and practice as well.

By Judicial Interpretation

If there is disagreement about what the Constitution means, who is to interpret it? Although the Constitution does not say, the judicial branch has taken on this role. To decide disputes before them, the courts must determine what the relevant provisions of the Constitution mean. By saying that the provisions mean one thing rather than another, the courts can, in effect, change the Constitution. Woodrow Wilson called the Supreme Court "a constitutional convention in continuous session." The Court has interpreted the Constitution in ways that bring about the same results as new amendments. (Chapters 11, 12, and 13 provide many examples.)

By Political Practice

Political practice has accounted for some very important changes. These include the rise of political parties and the demise of the Electoral College as an independent body. They also include the development of the cabinet to advise the president and the development of the committee system to operate the two houses of Congress. (Chapters 6, 7, and 8 explain these changes.)

The Founders would be surprised to learn that only seventeen amendments, aside from the Bill of Rights, have been adopted in over two hundred years. In part this is due to their wisdom, but in part it is due to changes in judicial interpretation and political practice, which have combined to create a "living Constitution."

Evolution of the Constitution and Federalism

The Constitution and the practice of federalism have evolved since the Founding. This section will bring them up-to-date.

Early Conflicts

The country faced secessionist threats almost immediately after its creation—by southern states when the Federalists (under John Adams) were in power and then by New England states when the Jeffersonians (under Thomas Jefferson) were in power. These threats were averted, but frequent conflicts between the nation and the states arose.

Supreme Court Rulings

The Supreme Court became the principal arbiter of the Constitution and soon faced questions about national supremacy. **John Marshall,** chief justice of the United States from 1801 to 1835, was a Federalist, a firm believer in a strong national government, and the decisions of his Court supported this view.

The Marshall Court established the legal bases for the supremacy of national authority over the states. Among the Marshall Court's most important rulings was **McCulloch v. Maryland** in 1819.[61] The case grew out of a dispute over the establishment of a national bank. The bank was unpopular because it competed with smaller banks operating under state laws and because some of its branches engaged in reckless and even fraudulent practices. When the government of Maryland levied a tax on the currency issued by the branch in Baltimore, the bank's constitutionality was called into question and a case was brought before the Court. The claim was that Congress, by establishing a national bank, infringed on the states' authority.

Marshall's ruling upheld the establishment of the bank and struck down the tax by the state. "[T]he power to tax involves the power to destroy," Marshall wrote, and the states shouldn't have the power to destroy the bank, because the bank was "necessary and proper" to carry out Congress's powers to collect taxes, borrow money, regulate commerce, and raise an army. Marshall maintained that if the goal of the legislation is legitimate, "all means which are appropriate, which are plainly adapted to that end, which are not prohibited, but consistent with the letter and spirit of the Constitution, are constitutional."

Thus, Marshall interpreted "necessary" quite loosely. The bank was not essential, but it was useful. This interpretation of the **necessary and proper clause** allowed Congress, and thus the national government, to wield much more authority than the Constitution appeared to grant. This interpretation recognized the existence of **implied powers**—ones implicit in the explicit powers specifically cited—for the national government. It meant that Congress can legislate in almost any area it wishes. Thus, the Marshall Court embraced nation-centered federalism. By laying the foundation for a strong national government for our rapidly expanding nation, *McCulloch* would become one of the two most important rulings of the Marshall Court and indeed of the Supreme Court ever. (The other was *Marbury* v. *Madison,* which will be covered in Chapter 11.)

Conflicts between the nation and the states continued, and debates over slavery exacerbated them. These conflicts led to southern states' efforts to secede from the Union and to the Civil War.

The Civil War and Reconstruction

The Civil War, from 1861 through 1865, and Reconstruction, from the end of the war through 1876, constituted a "second American Revolution."[62] After the bloodletting and scorched earth, more than six hundred thousand soldiers lay in graves—one of every seven men between the ages of fifteen and thirty—and parts of the South lay in waste. The North's victory preserved the Union, but it did far more than this. It also altered the Constitution—in the minds of the people and in formal amendments to the document.

Although the North's leader, President **Abraham Lincoln,** a Republican, held views that would be considered racist today (he believed that black people were inherently inferior and that they should emigrate from the United States),[63] he despised slavery because it deprived persons of their unalienable rights to life, liberty, and the pursuit of happiness promised by the Declaration of Independence. But efforts to abolish slavery were constrained by the political climate, and Lincoln was a practical politician. Before the war, he was willing to allow slavery in the southern states as long as the Union was preserved. But one year into the war, he found this goal too limited.[64] Abolitionist sentiment was spreading in the North, providing Lincoln the opportunity to lead efforts to abolish slavery as well as preserve the Union. In the process, he helped reinvent America.

The Emancipation Proclamation

The **Emancipation Proclamation** offered the promise of redefining the Constitution. President Lincoln announced the proclamation in September 1862 and ordered it to take effect in January 1863. The document proclaimed that the slaves "shall be . . . forever free" in the Confederate states where the Union army was not in control. Its language limited its sweep, for it exempted those parts of the Confederate states where the Union army was in control and also the slave states that remained loyal to the Union (Delaware, Kentucky, Maryland, and Missouri). And despite its language, it could not be enforced in the parts of the Confederate states where the Union army was not in control. Thus, as a legal document, the proclamation was problematic. However, as a symbolic measure, it was successful. The proclamation made clear that the war was not anymore just to preserve the Union, but to abolish slavery as well. It captured people's imagination, and when slaves heard about it, many left their plantations and some joined the Union army. The desertion sowed confusion in the South and denied a reliable labor force to the region.

The Gettysburg Address

President Lincoln's **Gettysburg Address** set the tone for new interpretations of the Constitution.[65] The battle at Gettysburg, Pennsylvania, in 1863, was a Union victory and the turning point in the Civil War. Lincoln was invited to deliver "a few appropriate remarks" during the dedication of the battlefield where many had fallen. Lincoln was not the main speaker, and his speech was not long. The main speaker took two hours, recounting the battle and reciting the names of the generals and even some of their soldiers; Lincoln took two minutes to give a 268-word speech. (He spoke so briefly that the photographer, with his clumsy equipment and its slow exposure, failed to get a single photograph.) Lincoln used the occasion to advance his ideal of equality.

He began: "Four score and seven [eighty-seven] years ago our fathers brought forth on this continent a new nation, conceived in liberty and dedicated to the proposition that all men are created equal." Here

This view of the remains of Richmond, Virginia, conveys the destruction of the Civil War.

Library of Congress

Lincoln referred not to the Constitution of 1787 but to the Declaration of Independence of 1776. For Lincoln, the Constitution had abandoned the principle of equality that the Declaration had promised. He sought to resurrect this principle. Lincoln did not mention slavery or the Emancipation Proclamation, which were divisive. A shrewd politician, he wanted people to focus on the Declaration, which was revered.

Lincoln concluded by addressing "the great task remaining before us . . . that we here highly resolve that these dead shall not have died in vain, that this nation, under God, shall have a new birth of freedom, and that government of the people, by the people, for the people shall not perish from the earth." This phrase, which Lincoln made famous, was borrowed from a speaker at an antislavery convention.[66] It depicted a government elected by all the people, to serve all the people.[67] Lincoln's conclusion reinforced his introduction—both emphasized equality.

Although his speech was brief, Lincoln used the word *nation* five times, including the phrase "a new nation." His purpose was not to encourage support for the Union, but to urge people to think of the nation as a whole, its identity now forged in a bloody war of brother against brother, rather than as simply a collection of individual states with their own interests.[68]

Thus the president essentially added the Declaration's promise of equality to the Constitution, and he substituted his vision of a unified nation for the Founders' precarious arrangement of a balance of power between the nation and the states. According to one historian, "He performed one of the most daring acts of open-air sleight-of-hand ever witnessed by the unsuspecting. . . .The crowd departed with a new thing in its ideological luggage, that new constitution Lincoln had substituted for the one they brought with them."[69]

The Gettysburg Address was heard by an audience of perhaps fifteen thousand, but its language was spread through word of mouth and newspapers and eventually by politicians and teachers. It was read and repeated, and sometimes memorized, by generations of schoolchildren. Although some critics at the time perceived what Lincoln was attempting—the *Chicago Times* quoted the Constitution to the president and charged him with betraying the document he swore to uphold—most citizens came to accept Lincoln's addition. His speech, which has been called "the best political address" in the country's history, thus became "the secular prayer of the postbellum American Republic."[70] (The speech is reprinted in the Appendix.)

The Reconstruction Amendments

If the Gettysburg Address became the preamble of the new constitution, the **Reconstruction Amendments** became its body. These three amendments, adopted from 1865 through 1870, began to implement the promise of equality and the vision of a unified nation rather than a collection of individual states.

The Thirteenth Amendment abolished slavery, essentially constitutionalizing the Emancipation Proclamation.

The Fourteenth Amendment declared that all persons born or naturalized in the United States are citizens, overturning the Supreme Court's ruling before the Civil War that blacks, whether slave or free, could not be citizens.[71] The Fourteenth Amendment also included the equal protection clause, which requires states to treat persons equally, and the due process clause, which requires states to treat persons fairly. The equal protection clause would become the primary legal means to end discrimination, and the due process clause would become the primary legal means to give persons the full benefit of the Bill of Rights.[72] This amendment, one legal scholar observes, was "a revolutionary change. The states were no longer the autonomous sovereigns that they thought they were when they claimed the right of secession. They were now, in fact, servants of their people. [They] existed to guarantee due process and equal justice for all."[73]

The Fifteenth Amendment extended the right to vote to blacks. Because women could not vote at the time, the amendment essentially provided the right to vote to black men.

As important as the substantive content of these amendments was a procedural provision authorizing Congress to enforce them. ("Congress shall have power to enforce this article by appropriate legislation.") That is, the amendments gave Congress broad power, beyond that granted in the original Constitution, to pass new laws to implement the amendments. Consequently, the federal government would come to oversee and even intervene in the policies of state and local governments to make sure that these governments did not disregard the guarantees of the amendments. These amendments thus marked the start of a trend of federalizing the Constitution by increasing the power of Congress.[74] Five later amendments also would include this provision.

During Reconstruction, the Union army occupied the South and enforced the amendments and congressional laws implementing them. But southern whites resisted, and eventually northern whites grew weary of the struggle. At the same time, there was a desire for healing between the two regions and lingering feelings for continuity with the past. In 1876, the two national political parties, the Democrats and the Republicans, struck a deal to withdraw the Union army and to allow the southern states to govern themselves again. The entrenched attitudes of southern whites prompted them to establish segregation and discrimination in place of slavery, thus preventing blacks from enjoying their new rights. As a result, the new constitution stressing equality and powers of the national government to enforce equality, as envisioned by Lincoln, would not really come into being until the 1950s and 1960s, when the civil rights movement, Supreme Court rulings, presidential initiatives, and congressional acts would converge to give effect to the ideal of racial equality. In the meantime, the new constitution would lay, in our collective consciousness, as an unfulfilled promise, occasionally emerging to foster greater equality.[75]

During the industrialization and urbanization that followed the Civil War, the national government continued to extend its reach and expand its power, but more significant changes would occur during the Great Depression.

In the 1920s, the economy and stock market were booming. Herbert Hoover capitalized on the country's prosperity in the 1928 election.

The Great Depression and the New Deal

The Great Depression began when the stock market crashed in 1929. Wealthy people lost their investments, and business activity declined. Ordinary people lost their jobs, with a quarter of them becoming unemployed. Many people lost their savings when the banks collapsed. Unlike today, there was no systematic program of relief—no unemployment compensation, no food stamps, no welfare. Cities and states, which had provided aid to the poor, were overwhelmed; they didn't have the funds or organizations to cope with the increasing needs. Private charities didn't have enough resources to assume the burden. So, millions of Americans were hungry and homeless, and many of them were hopeless. Their suffering and dislocation threatened the political stability of the country.

President Herbert Hoover, expecting the economy to right itself, resisted aggressive action and as a result lost his bid for reelection to **Franklin Roosevelt,** a Democrat, in 1932. President Roosevelt immediately initiated an ambitious program, heralded as "a new deal for the American people," to stimulate the economy and help the people who were suffering. Within his first hundred days, Congress had passed numerous proposals to regulate the activities of business and labor and establish a national welfare system. FDR's program and his administration came to be known as the **New Deal.**

This era also altered the Constitution—not by formal amendments, but through judicial rulings and political practice. In the process, it changed the minds of the people.[76] As a result, we replaced our small, limited government, as envisioned by the Founders, with a big, activist government.

Judicial Rulings

In the late nineteenth and early twentieth centuries, a laissez-faire economic philosophy was popular in this country and was reflected in governmental policies. According to this philosophy, government should not interfere in the economy (*laissez-faire* means "leave it alone" in French). Although government could *aid* businesses, it should not *regulate* them.[77] People who believed this philosophy thought it would create a robust and efficient economy. Indeed, industrialization produced an array of new products for consumers and an increase in personal wealth for owners, but it also led to negative consequences for employees, who were forced to labor in harsh, even dangerous, conditions for long hours and little pay.

During the Depression, many people who lost their job lost their ability to put food on the table. Breadlines and soup kitchens were common. Here the unemployed wait for coffee and doughnuts at one of fifty-two relief kitchens in New York City in 1934.

For decades, when Congress and state legislatures passed laws regulating child labor, maximum hours of work, and minimum wages for work, the Supreme Court usually followed the traditional philosophy and declared the laws unconstitutional. After Roosevelt took office and Congress passed the laws implementing his recovery program, the Court's majority often declared these laws unconstitutional as well. The impasse reached a climax in 1935 and 1936 when the Court invalidated twelve laws—the core of FDR's program. The Court's resistance made clear that the New Deal reforms were not simply fine-tuning governmental policy toward the economy, but were overhauling the long-standing policy.[78] In response to the Court's resistance, members of Congress introduced thirty-nine constitutional amendments to reverse the Court's rulings.

After Roosevelt was resoundingly reelected in 1936, intense pressure from the president, Congress, and the public prompted two justices who had voted against government regulation of business to switch sides and vote for such regulation in 1937. The switch allowed the government to extend its reach far beyond what was thought permissible just a few years before.

These transformative rulings created a "constitutional revolution."[79] They took the place of formal amendments to the Constitution, which were no lon-ger necessary once the Court acquiesced to the policies of the president and Congress. As a result, government could regulate businesses when the public believed that regulation would be beneficial.

Political Practice

Before the Depression, Washington, D.C., had been "a sleepy southern town," in the eyes of reporters.[80] When Roosevelt took office, he was uncertain exactly what to do, but he was willing to experiment. Roosevelt's personality and ambitious ideas attracted hundreds of thousands of people to the Capital, some simply relieved to find a job, but others excited to work for the government. These reformers brought new ideas, even radical ideas for the time, that would receive consideration in the depths of the Depression. As federal efforts to provide relief and regulation spread throughout the country, many other people got jobs in federal offices outside Washington.

Within six years of Roosevelt's taking office, the number of federal workers in the District of Columbia had more than doubled,[81] the number of federal workers in the country had almost doubled, and the size of the federal budget had almost doubled.[82] In the process, the scope of the federal government had expanded considerably. In short, the country got big government and activist government in less than a decade. These changes were so dramatic that one political scientist has said they created a "second American republic."[83]

Roosevelt's exuberance and experimentation had given people hope. As the country gradually pulled out of the Depression (though the country would not fully recover until the economic activity generated by World War II provided the final boost), people gave Roosevelt credit, electing him to an unprecedented four terms and returning Democrats to Congress to support him.[84]

Ever since, Americans, albeit to different degrees, have expected the government to tackle society's problems. While sometimes mouthing the language of the Founders—for example, Thomas Jefferson's assertion, "That government is best which governs least"—they have generally accepted the reality of the government that was expanded during the Depression.[85]

The changes during the Depression would lay the foundation for the government of the 1960s, which would promote the equality advanced during the Civil War. Without a powerful government pushing for change, the entrenched attitudes supporting segregation and discrimination would not have been overcome.

A Combination of Constitutions

As a result of President Lincoln and the Radical Republicans in the 1860s and 1870s and President Roosevelt and the New Deal Democrats in the 1930s and 1940s, our government is very different from the one the Founders bequeathed us.[86] Later generations of Americans made the eighteenth-century Constitution work in the nineteenth century, and then they made it work in the twentieth century—by remaking that Constitution. Changes in the nineteenth century added the concept of equality and elevated the national government over the state governments. Changes in the twentieth century transformed a relatively small, limited government into a very large, activist government.

The original Constitution and the remade Constitution reflect competing visions. Should we emphasize liberty or equality? Should we demand that individuals solve their own problems or ask government to help them? Americans have not reconciled these visions. Sometimes we cling to the Founders' Constitution; other times we embrace the post–Civil War and post-Depression Constitution. In political debates, politicians, commentators, or citizens take positions without articulating, perhaps without even realizing, that these positions hark back to the Founders' Constitution, whereas opponents espouse views that rely on the post–Civil War and post-Depression Constitution. Although, of course, we have only one Constitution on paper, we have two constitutions coexisting, sometimes uneasily, in our minds and in government policies.[87] As a consequence of our history, then, we actually have a combination of constitutions.

Conclusion: Does the Constitution Make the Government Responsive?

The Constitution established a government that has survived for over two centuries. Although the United States is considered a relatively young country, it has one of the oldest constitutions in the world. As a result, the United States has the oldest democracy, oldest republic, and oldest federal system in the world.[88]

In the Constitution, the Founders set forth a mechanism to govern a vast territory and to provide for majority rule while allowing minority rights. This government has enabled more people to live in liberty and in prosperity than the people of any nation before or since.[89] Americans have been grateful, venerating the Founders and embracing the Constitution as a secular Bible. Citizens consult it for guidance and cite it for support at the same time they debate the meaning of its provisions.

Despite its status as a political icon, however, the Constitution has been copied by few countries.[90] Although provisions of the Bill of Rights, such as freedom of speech, and of the Fourteenth Amendment, such as the equal protection clause, have been adopted by other countries,[91] the structure of our government has been less popular. Among the twenty-two democratic countries that have remained stable since 1950,[92] only five others have a federal system with significant power at the state level, only three others have a bicameral legislature with significant power in both houses, and only four others have one house with equal representation for the states regardless of their population. No others have a presidential system, and only two others have a judicial system that exercises judicial review of national legislation.[93] Our Constitution and governmental structure are seen more as a reflection of historical factors and political compromises than as a desirable form of government.

The Founders did leave important problems unresolved for succeeding generations. Most notable was slavery and the treatment of African Americans. Also troublesome was the uncertain relationship between the nation and the states. As we have seen, later Americans would have to tackle these problems, and in the process they, too, would contribute to the Constitution. Succeeding generations remade the Constitution most noticeably in the wake of the Civil War and the Great Depression, and they remade it more than many Americans realize.

The relationship between the nation and the states, even after the Civil War, remains unclear. Students picture federalism as a layer cake, with one distinct layer of authority for the states topped by another distinct layer of authority for the national government. In practice, our federalism resembles a marble cake, with two distinct colors—not layers—swirled throughout. In **marble-cake federalism,** the levels of government are distinct, but their powers are not. The two levels interact and share authority, and it becomes difficult to delineate precisely what things each level does. Marble-cake federalism has been the pattern since the New Deal expanded the role of the national government and blurred the distinction between the two levels.

Federalism does enable the states to serve as **experimental laboratories**—"laboratories of democracy" in the words of Supreme Court Justice Louis Brandeis—in which innovative states can pioneer public policies that, if successful, can be copied by other states or the national government. No-fault automobile insurance, "lemon laws" permitting the buyers of new but defective cars to return them, and "no-call laws" allowing phone customers to block telemarketing calls all began in a state. Now physician-assisted suicide is being tried in Oregon. As experimental laboratories, the states can be more responsive to their citizens. At the same time, however, federalism makes it more difficult to impose national solutions even when national problems are crying for action. Reluctant states can stymie such action.

Debates over federalism, usually couched in terms of "states' rights," continue, but as one member of Congress observed about his colleagues, they "don't really believe in states' rights; they believe in deciding the issue at whatever level of government they think will do it their way. They want to be Thomas Jefferson on Monday, Wednesday, and Friday and Alexander Hamilton on Tuesday and Thursday and Saturday."[94] This inconsistency means that we decide the locus of power—the level of government—for each specific issue according to the politics at that particular time (as the chapter's opening vignette suggests).

Despite the major changes brought about by the Civil War and the Great Depression, and all the changes brought about by other events at other times, the basic structure of government and the underlying fragmentation of power in the Constitution remain. The combination of federalism, separation of powers, and checks and balances, along with the unique method for choosing the president, make our government perhaps "the most intricate ever devised."[95] It is also perhaps "the most opaque . . . , confusing, and difficult to understand."[96]

The structure of government and fragmentation of power make it difficult for citizens to hold their leaders accountable. If you disapprove of some policy, whom do you hold accountable in the next election—the president, the Senate, the House of Representatives, the unelected judges, or the state governments? Usually there is divided responsibility, resulting in less accountability.

Of course, the Founders sought a government that would be responsive to the people only to a limited extent. The Constitution created a republic, which granted the people the right to elect some representatives who would make their laws. In this way, the people had more say in government than the people in other countries at the time. Yet the Constitution was expected to filter the public's passions and purify their selfish desires. Thus the original Constitution allowed citizens to vote only for members of the House of Representatives—not for members of the Senate or the president. Furthermore, it fragmented power, so a single group could not control the entire government. Amendments to the Constitution that have expanded opportunities for citizens to participate in government have done little to modify the structure of government or its fragmentation of power.

This configuration has prevented many abuses of power, although it has not always worked. During the Vietnam War and the Iraq War, for example, one branch—the presidency—exercised vast power whereas the others acquiesced.

This configuration has also provided the opportunity for one branch to pick up the slack when the others became sluggish. The overlapping of powers ensured by checks and balances allows every branch to act on virtually every issue it wants to. In the 1950s, President Eisenhower and Congress were reluctant to push for civil rights, but the Supreme Court did so by declaring segregation unconstitutional.

But the system's very advantage has become its primary disadvantage. In their efforts to fragment power so that no branch could accumulate too much, the Founders divided power to the point where the branches sometimes cannot wield enough. In their efforts to build a government that requires a national majority to act, they built one that allows a small minority to block action.

This problem has become increasingly acute as society has become increasingly complex. Like a mechanical device that operates only when all of its parts function in harmony, the system moves only when there is consensus or compromise. Consensus is rare in a large, heterogeneous society; compromise is common, but it requires more time as well as the realization by competing interests that they cannot achieve much without engaging in it.

At best, the system moves inefficiently and incrementally; at worst, it moves hardly at all. The Constitution has established a government that is slow to respond to change. "By intent," one political scientist noted, "the U.S. government works within a set of limits designed to prevent it from working too well."[97] Therefore, the system tends to preserve the status quo and to respond to the groups that benefit from the status quo.

Although the changes made in the wake of the Depression brought us big, activist government, they did not negate all of our historical aversion to such government. We still have a more limited government than other advanced industrialized countries. Contrary to what many Americans believe, our taxes are lower and governmental policies in numerous areas, such as health care, welfare, and transportation, are less ambitious.[98] This, of course, limits our ability to address our problems.

Yet some political scientists believe the American people actually prefer a system that is hard to move. Because the people are suspicious of government, they may be reluctant to let one party dominate it and use it to advance that party's policies. In surveys, many people—a quarter to a third of those polled—say they think it is good for one party to control the presidency and the other to control Congress.[99] In presidential and congressional elections, more than a quarter of the voters split their ticket between the two parties.[100] As a result, from 1969 through 2000, opposing parties controlled the executive branch and both houses of the legislative branch for all but six years. The Republicans captured the presidency and both branches of Congress from 2001 to 2006 (except for one year, when a Republican senator defected, giving the Democrats a temporary majority). However, the voters again divided control in the congressional elections of 2006, electing Democratic majorities to both houses of Congress.

Such divided government reinforces the fragmentation of power in a way that makes it difficult, if not impossible, for citizens to pin responsibility on particular officials and parties for the decisions and policies of government. "If no individual or institution possesses the authority to act without the consent of everybody else in the room, then nobody is ever at fault if anything goes wrong. Congress can blame the president, the president can blame the Congress or the Supreme Court, the Supreme Court can blame the Mexicans or the weather in Ohio."[101] If citizens cannot determine who is responsible for what, they cannot hold those individuals accountable and make them responsive.

Key Terms

Key Names

1. The Constitution's full faith and credit clause
   a. requires each state to recognize the contracts made in other states.
   b. requires the states to pay bills they owe to other states.
   c. underscores the power of the states.
   d. requires the states to pay bills they owe to the federal government.
   e. requires any state to accept a homosexual marriage conducted in another state.

2. The Articles of Confederation reflected Americans'
   a. desire for a strong central government.
   b. desire for a federal form of government.
   c. identity as American citizens.
   d. fear of a strong central government.
   e. fear of strong state governments.

3. The United States under the Articles of Confederation had a _____ form of government.
   a. federal
   b. state-centered federal
   c. confederal
   d. nation-centered federal
   e. unitary

4. Before the Constitution was drafted, many average Americans wanted _____, but the elites wanted _____.
   a. a strong central government; strong state governments
   b. an economy based on trade; an economy based on agriculture
   c. an agricultural economy; a commercial empire
   d. an economy based on national trade; an economy based on local trade
   e. a government that would enforce debtors' obligations; a government that might reduce debtors' obligations

5. Delegates to the Constitutional Convention generally agreed that
   a. slavery should continue.
   b. the government should be a republic.
   c. taxes on imported and exported goods should be allowed.
   d. the large states should have more representation than the small states.
   e. slaves should count in calculating representation.

6. The Founders' preference for indirect democracy reflected their views that the
   a. people should have some say in government.
   b. people can't be trusted.
   c. officials should obtain the consent of the governed before enacting any laws.
   d. officials should exercise their own independent judgment when enacting the laws.
   e. both a. and b.

7. The Founders devised a federal system as a compromise between
   a. unitary and confederal systems.
   b. a democracy and a republic.
   c. parliamentary government and presidential government.
   d. separation of powers and checks and balances.
   e. nation-centered federalism and state-centered federalism.

8. The ruling in *McCulloch* v. *Maryland* is important for all but which of the following reasons?
   a. It laid the foundation for a strong national government.
   b. It interpreted the necessary and proper clause broadly.
   c. It limited Congress's power to tax.
   d. It recognized implied powers of Congress.
   e. It allowed the national government to tackle more problems.

9. Choosing the officials of different branches by different means and for different terms reinforces the concept of
   a. federalism.
   b. separation of powers.
   c. checks and balances.
   d. a. and b.
   e. b. and c.

10. The term *divided government* refers to
    a. federalism.
    b. separation of powers.
    c. checks and balances.
    d. fragmentation of power in general.
    e. one party controlling the presidency and the other party controlling one or both houses of Congress.

11. The principle of separation of powers is diluted by the
    a. fragmentation of power in our government.
    b. federal arrangement of state and national authority.
    c. Bill of Rights.
    d. system of checks and balances.
    e. concept of popular sovereignty.

12. Representation in the Senate gives disproportionate power to
    a. large states.
    b. medium-sized states.
    c. small states.
    d. different states at different times; there's no pattern.
    e. no states, because they all get equal representation.

13. The Founders were
    a. idealists who sought the best government possible.
    b. practical politicians who were willing to compromise.
    c. well-to-do individuals who wanted to protect their property.
    d. all of the above.
    e. just b. and c.

14. The Founders drew from _____ for the idea of limited government and from _____ for the idea of separation of powers.
    a. Charles de Montesquieu; John Locke
    b. John Locke; Thomas Jefferson
    c. George Washington; John Adams
    d. Alexander Hamilton; Charles de Montesquieu
    e. John Locke; Charles de Montesquieu

15. Which of the Founders was most responsible for the Constitution?
    a. George Washington
    b. Benjamin Franklin
    c. Thomas Jefferson
    d. James Madison
    e. Alexander Hamilton

16. The effect of the Civil War was to
    a. expand the authority of the national government.
    b. simply preserve the Union.
    c. return the Constitution to the Founders' understanding.
    d. restore the status quo that had existed before the war.
    e. enlarge the powers of the state governments.

17. The Gettysburg Address was significant primarily because President Lincoln
    a. honored Union soldiers for their bravery.
    b. analyzed the outcome of the battle.
    c. condemned southern politicians for starting the war.
    d. emphasized his original goal of preserving the Union.
    e. tried to add the notion of equality to the Constitution.

18. The Reconstruction Amendments
    a. abolished slavery.
    b. extended the right to vote to blacks.
    c. began to implement the promise of equality from the Union's victory in the Civil War.
    d. shifted power from the states to the federal government.
    e. did all of the above.

19. Which of the following statements about the impact of the Great Depression and the New Deal isn't true?
    a. They had no effect on our interpretation of the Constitution.
    b. They caused the size of the bureaucracy and the size of the budget to nearly double.
    c. Judicial rulings allowed more government regulation of business.
    d. They transformed small, limited government into big, activist government.
    e. They prompted the public to alter its traditional views about big government.

20. The success of our Constitution is reflected in all but which of the following?
    a. The number of years it has survived
    b. The way it allows government to act quickly
    c. The way it allows one branch of government to act if other branches aren't acting
    d. The way it fosters compromise
    e. The way it enables one part of government to check abuses of power by another part

Key: 1-a; 2-d; 3-c; 4-c; 5-b; 6-e; 7-a; 8-c; 9-b; 10-e; 11-d; 12-c; 13-d; 14-e; 15-d; 16-a; 17-e; 18-e; 19-a; 20-b.

The environmental group Greenpeace tries to influence public opinion with attention-grabbing costumes and stunts.

ho Seung-Hui, a 23-year-old senior English major at Virginia Tech, was viewed by classmates and teachers as a disturbed young man who wrote obscene and violent stories in his English classes, took photos of women's legs with a camera concealed under his desk, and had, on occasion, stalked women on campus.[1] His abnormal and hostile behavior was a subject of many discussions among faculty in the English department, and his behavior had been reported on occasion to the campus police and mental health departments. When he indicated he might commit suicide, he was referred off campus for psychiatric evaluation, but no treatment was ever provided.

Despite his violent images and disturbed behavior, Mr. Cho was able to purchase a 22-caliber semiautomatic weapon on the web from a licensed dealer in Wisconsin. He bought a second semiautomatic weapon, a Glock pistol, in Roanoke, Virginia, 40 miles from the Virginia Tech campus, and 10-round magazines from dealers on e-Bay. He also purchased hollow point bullets, those that cause severe flesh wounds by expanding and mushrooming once inside the body, and practiced shooting at a Roanoke firing range.

On April 16, 2007, Mr. Cho entered a campus building, fired 170 shots and killed 30 faculty and students, after earlier killing two others in a dorm room. Afterwards, many speculated how such a disturbed individual with records of both mental instability and contact with the police (though no formal arrest or convictions) might have freely and legally obtained semiautomatic weapons.

The answer is that America, unique among Western nations, has only limited gun regulation. Though the sale of semiautomatic weapons was outlawed in 1994 legislation, that legislation expired in 2004, and no new legislation has been passed. Despite the fact that for decades public opinion has shown majority support for stricter regulation, most states and the federal government have not enacted effective legislation for semiautomatic weapons.[2] Many states do not regulate handguns either, though federal law does require background checks for gun purchasers.

Opponents of gun regulation are well organized through the National Rifle Association, which is very vocal, provides substantial support to candidates running for election, and can be a powerful force against candidates who support stricter gun control. Supporters of gun regulation are less intense and less well organized. Even periodic mass murders, like that of Mr. Cho and before him the Columbine school shooting, cause only a minimal spurt in calls for stricter legislation.

Public opinion is often contradictory. The public is hostile toward political leaders for failing to respond to the public's needs, yet, at the same time, complains that leaders simply follow the latest polls. Many are angry with the government. They do not trust it; they think it is too big and spends too much money. Yet they like the services it provides, and very few are willing to cut spending to eliminate services or programs that benefit them.

This chapter explores public opinion to better understand these contradictions. It describes how public opinion is formed and measured, assesses how informed and knowledgeable the public is with respect to public affairs, discusses the role of ideology in American politics, treats some divisions within the population over issues, and concludes with an assessment of the extent to which government is responsive to public opinion.

Nature of Public Opinion

Public opinion can be defined as the collection of individual opinions toward issues or objects of general interest—that is, those that concern a significant number of people. Opinion can be positive or negative about something. The distinction between positive or negative, yes or no, for or against an issue is called the direction of public opinion. On any given issue or personality, some people are positive, others negative.

Intensity reflects the strength of public opinion. The public may have rather weak feelings about an issue or feel quite strongly about it. Intense opinions often drive behavior. Many people now oppose the invasion of Iraq, for example, but only the most intense people protest it in the streets. Public opinion is not very intense on most issues. A small minority may feel intensely about any issue, but a majority rarely does.

Opinions also vary in stability. Some constantly change, whereas others rarely do. Stable opinions are often intense and grounded in a great deal of information—though not necessarily accurate. Feelings of attachment to American political parties tend to be stable, while opinions toward candidates and public officials, particularly high-profile ones like the president, fluctuate in response to changing events and circumstances. President George W. Bush began his presidency with 60 percent of the public approving the job he was doing. This rose to 90 percent shortly

OPINIONS ON SAME-SEX MARRIAGE

All issues have a moral element, but those that are primarily moral have the greatest potential to divide. Slavery was a moral issue that almost destroyed the nation. In the first decades of the twentieth century, prohibition—banning the sale of alcoholic beverages—was a divisive moral issue.

Abortion emerged as a moral issue in the 1970s and remains so today. Although Americans are highly supportive of abortion when the health and safety of the mother is a concern, they are quite divided when the issue is ending an unwanted pregnancy.

In the 1990s, the rights of gays and lesbians became a politically visible moral issue. During the past decade, Americans have been increasingly willing to extend rights to gays and lesbians. A majority of Americans have endorsed equal rights with respect to job opportunities, but it has only been in the last few years that a majority accepts that homosexual relations between consenting adults should be legal. The right of gays and lesbians to serve in the military has been another contested topic. The "don't ask, don't tell" policy has led to the expulsion of hundreds of members of the armed forces, even though 80 percent of the public now believe that gays and lesbians should serve. Support for allowing homosexual couples to form civil unions and enjoy some of the same rights as married couples has also increased. In 1996, about one-third favored such unions; eight years later nearly two-thirds did.

Increasing acceptance of gays and lesbians is driven to a large extent by their greater visibility. Seven out of ten Americans report knowing someone who is gay or lesbian. With increased interaction and acquaintance comes tolerance. However, public support for same-sex marriages is considerably lower. Only 37 percent of the public favors same-sex marriages. Many Americans associate marriage with their religious traditions, and many of those traditions do not approve of homosexuality.

The trend toward greater tolerance is likely to continue because younger generations are much more accepting than are older generations. Although nearly two-thirds of those over sixty-five oppose same-sex marriages, less than one-third of those between eighteen and thirty-four do. Thus, as the older generations pass from the scene, public opinion is likely to continue to become more accepting.

after 9/11 and has dropped steadily to only 30 percent in mid-2007 (see Figure 1).

Formation of Public Opinion

People learn and develop opinions about government and politics through the process of **political socialization.** As with learning in other spheres, individuals learn about politics by being exposed to new information supplied or filtered through parents, peers, schools, the media, political leaders, and the community. These **agents of political socialization** introduce each new generation to the rights and responsibilities of citizenship (see Chapter 1) as well as shape opinions and positions toward officeholders and political issues. Individuals, particularly adults, also learn about politics and develop opinions through personal experiences.

Political learning begins at an early age and continues throughout life. In young children, learning is influenced by reasoning capacity and expectations.[3] Preschoolers are unable to distinguish political from nonpolitical objects. Some are unable to separate political figures from cartoon characters, and some confuse religion with politics. A significant number of five- and six-year-olds report that the president takes his orders from God.[4] By first grade, these confusions are resolved, and children begin to see government as distinct and unique.[5]

However, the inability to understand abstract concepts or complex institutions means the conception of government is limited. Most identify government with the president.[6] Children at a very early age recognize him. In a recent year, 97 percent of a group of fourth graders were able to identify the president by name,[7] a proportion that has stayed constant for several decades.[8] Many, no doubt, see him on TV and understand that he is the leader of the nation. Experiences with parents and other adults provide children with a basis for understanding their relationship with authority figures with whom they have no contact.[9] Feelings children have toward parents are generalized to the president. Studies in the 1950s found children describ-

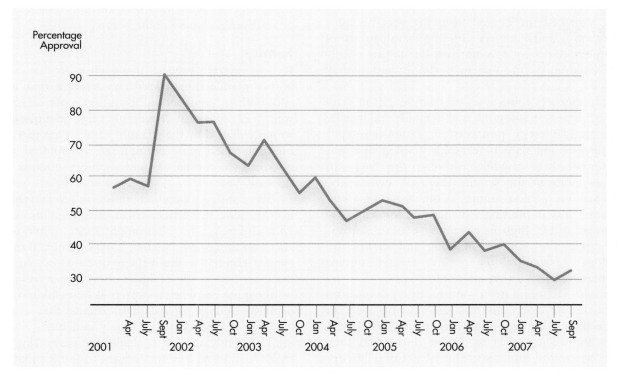

FIGURE 1 • **George W. Bush's Approval Ratings Peaked after 9/11, Then Declined**
SOURCE: Gallup Poll Tuesday Briefing, April 13, 2004. Update http://poll.gallup.com/content/default.aspx?ci=1723. Data are nationwide polls with sample sizes of 1000–1200 and a margin of error of 3 percent.

ing the president as good and helpful;[10] many saw him as more powerful than he really is.[11] A more recent study notes children are considerably less likely to evaluate the president as good, and this extends from fourth to eighth grade.[12] Children today may have a greater capacity to draw a distinction between the institutional presidency and the individual who occupies the office.

Older children are introduced to political ideas and political institutions in school and through the media. Their concept of government broadens to include Congress, the act of voting, and ideas such as freedom and democracy. The positive view of government reflected in feelings toward the president gives way to more complex and realistic images. The process can be accelerated by political events and the reaction of others to them. Children were much less positive toward the president and government in the 1970s than in the 1960s. The Watergate scandal in 1973 lowered both adults' and children's evaluations of the president.[13] The Clinton sexual scandals and the impeachment proceedings of 1998, however, had no impact on adult evaluations of the president and government, and presumably none on children. The approval ratings of the president reached record levels, and confidence in the executive branch remained unchanged from the year before.[14] Even when scandal lowers children's evaluations of government, the effect may not last. The negative feelings of children during Watergate diminished as they aged.[15]

In adolescence, political understanding expands still further. Children discuss politics with family and friends. By the middle teens, positions on issues develop.[16] Some fifteen- and sixteen-year-olds develop opinions that resemble those of adults. Although they begin to recognize faults in the system, they still believe the United States is the best country in the world. They rate the country low in limiting violence and fostering political morality but high in providing educational opportunities, a good standard of living, and science and technology.[17] For most, the positive feelings toward government learned earlier are reinforced.

In adulthood, opinions toward specific personalities and policies develop, and political activity becomes more serious. Although most Americans revere the country and do not want to change the system, they tend to be cynical and distrustful of political leaders. Some of this negative feeling grows out of Americans' dislike of conflict and partisanship in politics.[18] Some is caused by media coverage, which not only highlights conflict but often exaggerates it. At the same time, the media are committed to and supportive of the American system.[19] Americans may get angry with their government, but, except for the Civil War, it has never boiled over to the point of mass violence directed toward political institutions or leaders.

Critical comments about government and political leaders sharply declined after 9/11, but that cessation was short-lived. Most Americans felt gratitude toward the brave souls—many of whom lost their lives—who courageously marched to aid those under attack. Yet, except for those who were called to serve in the armed forces or who were able to volunteer to help in the World Trade Center cleanup, Americans were not asked to translate these positive feelings into action. Though commentators on 9/11 and immediately afterward predicted that nothing would ever be the same, for most Americans life did return to normal quickly and with it, skepticism toward government.

Agents of Political Socialization

It is the agents of political socialization—principally the family and schools—that are responsible for ensuring that each new generation of Americans resembles those generations that have come before.

Family

Recent research suggests that each of us may be born with a predilection toward conservatism or liberalism and with a predilection for other political traits as well.[20] Despite that, children's party identification is strongly shaped by their family. Families are particularly important in shaping the opinions of children because of strong emotional ties and exclusive control during the early years.[21]

The family influences opinions in several ways aside from genetic ties. Parents share their opinions directly with children, who often adopt those opinions. They say or do things that children imitate. Children overhear parents' comments about the political parties and adopt them as their own. Children also transfer feelings toward parents to political objects. When children harbor negative feelings toward their parents, they are more likely to be negative toward the president.[22]

The family also partly shapes the personality of the child. A child who is encouraged to speak up at home is likely to do so in public. Children also inherit their social and economic position from their parents, which influences not only how they view themselves but also how they view the world and how the world views them. A child from a wealthy family begins with advantages and opportunities that a child from a poor family can only dream about.

Children are more likely to reflect their parents' views when these views are clearly communicated and important. Parents often, if unintentionally, convey how they feel about political parties during election campaigns and children pick it up. Other opinions are less likely to be communicated to children. Seventy percent of high school seniors were able to correctly identify the party of their parents, but no more than 36 percent could identify their parents' opinion on other issues.[23]

However, even where parental influence is strong, it is not immutable. As young adults leave their parents' circle, agreement between their opinions, including party allegiance, and those of their parents, declines. New agents and experiences come into play.[24] Even among younger children, parental influence may not be as strong as in the past. Parents no longer have exclusive control during a child's preschool years, and the number of households with both parents working or with a single parent who works means less contact with parents. Others can be expected to fill this void. Today, schools often deal with problems the family dealt with in the past. While parental influence may be declining, whether or not one is raised in the traditional two-parent family or one with a single parent has little or no impact on important political opinions and political behavior.[25]

School

A child of our acquaintance who came to the United States at the age of five could not speak English and did not know the name of his new country. After a few months of kindergarten, he knew that George Washington and Abraham Lincoln were good presidents, he was able to recount stories of the Pilgrims, he could draw the flag, and he felt strongly that the United States was the best country in the world. This child illustrates the importance of the school in political socialization and how values and symbols of government are explicitly taught in American schools, as they are in schools in every nation.[26]

Although we do not understand exactly which aspects of formal schooling influence political opinions, there is little doubt that education and years of formal schooling—the skills it provides and experiences it represents—make a difference. People who have more education are more interested in and knowledgeable about politics.[27] They are also more likely to participate

© Robin Nelson/Black Star

This boy, at a white supremacist rally, likely was socialized in these views by his parents.

in politics and to be politically tolerant.[28] Yet education does not seem to lead to a greater appreciation of the real workings of democracy, that is, a form of government where there are disagreements typically resolved through bargaining and compromise.[29] Education does not prepare citizens for how democracy works in practice, or how to recognize that disagreement is fundamental to democratic processes, or how to build positive feelings toward these processes.

How do the schools influence the political opinions of children? Schools promote patriotic rituals. They often begin each day with the Pledge of Allegiance and include patriotic songs and programs in many activities. In the lower grades, children celebrate national holidays such as Presidents' Day and Thanksgiving and learn the history and symbols associated with them. Involvement in such activities fosters love and respect of country.

In the upper grades, mock elections, conventions, and student government introduce students to the operation of government. School clubs operate with democratic procedures and reinforce the concepts of voting and majority rule. The state of Illinois let the state's elementary school children vote to select the official state animal, fish, and tree, conveying the message that voting is the way issues are decided.

Textbooks often foster commitment to government and the status quo. Those used in elementary grades emphasize compliance with authority and the need to be a "good" citizen. Even textbooks in advanced grades present idealized versions of the way government works and exaggerate the role of citizens in holding public officials accountable and in shaping public policy. Textbooks are less likely, however, to emphasize the need for citizens to uphold democratic values such as participating in politics and tolerating others' views. Nor do they help students understand that conflicts and differences of opinion are inevitable in a large and diverse society and that the role of politics is to address and resolve these disagreements.

The number of civics courses taken in high school improves students' knowledge of government and politics and fosters beliefs that government pays attention to people and that elections are important in holding government responsible. Courses during the senior year are particularly important. Seniors are ready to make the transition to adulthood and thus government and politics may be more meaningful.[30]

Reading habits and language skills are also important to democratic citizenship. Those who spend time reading are more likely to reflect attributes of democratic citizenship—including knowledge of public affairs, interest in politics, and tolerance—than those who do not.[31] Proficiency with language is important, too, as language is the mechanism for communicating and assessing information and evaluating new ideas and arguments.[32]

Teachers as role models also contribute in significant ways. Perceptions that school administrators and teachers are fair are linked with expressions of trust toward other people.[33]

In sum, the major impact of schooling from kindergarten through high school seems to be that it creates "good" citizens—citizens who accept political authority and the institutions of government and who also limit their political activities to the conventional and routine, such as voting in elections. In this way, elementary and secondary education serves government and

the status quo in ways that the dominant interests in society prefer. Schools are not particularly effective at fostering political participation and commitment to democratic values. Nor do they provide students with the skills to critically assess social, political, and economic structures that are at the root of problems and strategies for dealing with injustice and effecting political change.[34] In this regard, the failure of schools is often attributed to the "hidden curriculum."[35] Schools are not democratic institutions where students are encouraged to participate in a meaningful way. Indeed, most schools foster a climate averse to controversy. Such an environment is unlikely to produce active and engaged citizens.

The impact of college often broadens students' perspectives and leads to greater understanding of the world around them. They become more open and tolerant. They become less rigid and bound by tradition. Most students go to college to get a better job, make more money, prepare for a specific career, broaden their knowledge of the world, or learn about things that interest them. Some attend because their parents insist or because everyone else is going. Few go to college seeking to become more tolerant, but this is often the result. College students are more open and tolerant than the population as a whole, and the longer they are in college, the more open and tolerant they become—seniors more so than freshmen, and graduate students more so than undergraduates.[36]

Some recent commentators argue that college professors indoctrinate students and even suggest that state legislatures should investigate such "indoctrination."[37] In fact, a survey showed that 64 percent of the social science faculty in the nation's colleges identify themselves as liberal, and only 20 percent regard themselves as conservative. However, faculty in other fields are less liberal. For example, only 30 percent of the business faculty identify themselves as liberal.

The idea that professors are indoctrinating students seems unlikely, however. For example, at the height of the Vietnam War (1968–1971), students were more likely to identify themselves as liberal than students before or after the war, and after the war, fewer declared themselves liberal.[38] During the same period, the outlook of college faculty changed very little. Thus students are not simply a reflection of their college teachers. At large universities, where the largest percentage of students attend, the environment is sufficiently diverse to reinforce many points of view. Moreover, it is college that provides students with the self-confidence and independence that enable them to resist indoctrination.[39] Today, more college freshmen are moderates than liberals.[40]

On issues, college freshmen look much like the population as a whole, liberal on some issues but conservative on others. They are liberal in wanting the government to do more to control the sale of handguns, provide national health care to cover everyone's medical costs, and guarantee homosexuals the right to marry and in believing that racial discrimination remains a problem. They are conservative in attitudes about crime: majorities wish to retain the death penalty and believe that the courts show too much concern for the rights of criminals. Small majorities are pro-choice, favor affirmative action, and support taxing the rich more (see Table 1). During the past few years, freshmen have become slightly more liberal in their opinions as well as in their self-identification.[41]

The most distinctive characteristic of college freshmen in recent years has been their low interest in politics,[42] although since 2001, there has been a slight increase. But the 22 percent who report frequently talking about politics is far less than the high of 60 percent in 1968, during the Vietnam era.[43]

Peers

In many instances, peers simply reinforce the opinions of the family or school. When there is a conflict between peer and parental socialization, peers sometimes win but only on issues of special relevance to youth. Peers have the most influence when the peer group is attractive to the individual and when the individual spends time with the group. With growing numbers of single-parent families and working parents, parental influence may be diminishing and friends and associates may be taking on greater importance than adults.

Mass Media

The primary effect of the media on children is to increase their level of information about politics. The primary effect on adults is to influence what they think about—that is, the issues, events, and personalities they pay attention to.[44] The media also influence opinions about issues and individuals; in recent years, the media have reflected a high degree of cynicism and negativism toward political leaders. Research

Table 1	Opinions of College Freshmen in 2005	
The federal government should do more to control the sale of handguns.		79%
A national health care plan is needed to cover everyone's medical costs.		74%
There is too much concern in the courts for the rights of criminals.		58%
Same-sex couples should have the right to legal marital status.		58%
Wealthy people should pay a larger share of taxes than they do now.		58%
Abortion should be legal.		55%
Marijuana should be legalized.		38%
Federal military spending should be increased.		34%
The death penalty should be abolished.		33%
It is important to have laws prohibiting homosexual relationships.		27%
Racial discrimination is no longer a major problem in America.		21%

The percentages are those agreeing strongly or somewhat with the statement.

SOURCE: "Attitudes and Characteristics of Freshmen," *Chronicle of Higher Education*, February 3, 2006. On the web at http://chronicle.com/premium/stats/freshmen/2006/data.htm #political.79%

Televised images of American soldiers' abuse of Iraqi prisoners jailed at the Abu Ghraib prison outside Baghdad influenced public opinion in the Middle East as well as in the United States.

shows that changes in public opinion tend to follow sentiments expressed by television news commentators.[45] The impact of the media is explored in more detail in Chapter 4.

Adult Socialization

Not all political socialization occurs in the preadult years. Opinions develop and change throughout life as one experiences new and different things. Marriage, divorce, unemployment, a new job, or a move to a new location can affect political opinions.[46]

Economic, political, and social events have the potential to change the way Americans think about politics. Many hard hit by the Great Depression were drawn to politics seeking help. Most, voting for the first time, cast their ballot for the Democrats in 1932 and continued to vote Democratic throughout their lifetimes. World War II and the attack on Pearl Harbor shaped the opinions of a generation of Americans. The Vietnam War moved many college students to the streets in protest, whereas others moved to Canada to avoid the draft. In contrast, the short-term impact of the terrorist attacks on the Pentagon and the World Trade Center pushed the public closer to government, although the impact soon dissipated (see the box "The Short-Term Impact of 9/11 on Public Opinion").[47]

Impact of Political Socialization

Each new generation of Americans is socialized to a large extent by the one preceding it. In many ways, each new generation will look and act much like the one that came before. In this sense, political socialization represents a stabilizing and conserving influence. Typically, it leads to support for and compliance with government and the social order. Although many disagree with particular government policies, few question the basic structure of government.

THE SHORT-TERM IMPACT OF 9/11 ON PUBLIC OPINION

Although the Great Depression had a long-lasting impact on American public opinion, and the Japanese attack on Pearl Harbor changed Americans' views of their role in the world conflict taking place, the influence on public opinion of the traumatic attacks of 9/11 was intense but short-lived. Before the terrorist attacks, many Americans took government for granted and considered it unimportant and irrelevant to their lives. The booming economy and surging stock market during the 1990s led to complacency. Moreover, cynicism about government was fueled by a steady stream of negative commentary about the government emanating from the media and politicians who found it useful for their careers.

But the smoke and devastation of 9/11 had an immediate impact on Americans' attitudes. From the ashes of the World Trade Center and Pentagon sprang a feeling of patriotism, national unity, and a willingness to help others and see the nation through a difficult crisis. Suddenly government was a positive force. More than 80 percent, compared with just 50 percent the year before, had a favorable view of the national government, and trust in government nearly doubled following the attacks.[1] The public standing of the president and Congress similarly surged, as government seemed necessary again. As someone remarked, "the only persons going up the stairs of the World Trade Center while everyone else was going down were government officials. The events brought home the fact that the government does important work."[2]

Perhaps these positive changes after 9/11 would have been longer lasting if the nation had been called upon to sacrifice as it had in World War II. Instead, the president and Republicans in Congress used 9/11 to push a partisan agenda, tax cuts for the rich, a war in Iraq, and a great increase in presidential power. The president did not urge the nation to use less energy to check growing U.S. dependence on foreign oil, which in turn increases our vulnerability to instability in the Middle East. Nor did he call on the nation to support higher taxes to pay for the war in Iraq and Afghanistan. The president's advice to Americans was "Live your lives, hug your children."[3] "Go shopping" (to stimulate the economy) was the call. Asking Americans to act as if nothing had happened, the president got his wish and may have also squelched the willingness of large numbers of Americans to offer a helping hand when the nation needed it.

[1] Alexander Stille, "Suddenly, Americans Trust Uncle Sam," New York Times, November 3, 2001, online article.
[2] "Public Opinion Six Months Later," Pew Research Center for the People and the Press, news release, March 7, 2002.
[3] Benjamin Wallace-Wells, "Mourning Has Broken," Washington Monthly, October 2003, 16–18.

Measuring Public Opinion

Pollsters measure public opinion by asking individuals to answer questions in a survey or poll. Of course, there are other techniques used to measure opinion, and before scientific polls these techniques were all that were available. Elected officials consider the opinions of people who talk to them or write or e-mail them; journalists gauge public opinion by talking selectively to individuals; letters written to newspaper editors or newspaper editorials are a measure of public opinion. Protests and demonstrations also reflect public opinion. All of these techniques provide an incomplete picture, however. Letters or messages to public officials and newspapers are more likely to come from people with extreme opinions[48] or from those with writing skills—that is, people with more education. Editorial opinion is even less likely to provide an accurate picture of public opinion because most newspaper publishers tend to be conservative, and this view is often reflected in their editorials. In most presidential elections in the twentieth century, newspapers favored the Republican candidate by about three to one.[49] The exception to this was that more newspapers endorsed John Kerry than George W. Bush in 2004 by a small margin.[50]

Today, pollsters initiate the expression of public opinion by conducting a poll. Rather than focus on what the public is concerned about, polls concentrate on what pollsters and their sponsors are most interested in. For this reason, many issues of public importance never become subjects of a poll. In spite of this, polling remains the only accurate way to assess what the nation as a whole thinks about political issues and public officials. While not perfect, polls are the best measure of public opinion.

Early Polling Efforts

The first attempts to measure popular sentiments on a large scale were the **straw polls** (or unscientific polls) developed by newspapers in the nineteenth century.[51] In 1824, the *Harrisburg Pennsylvanian,* in perhaps the first poll assessing preferences for candidates, sent reporters to check on support for the four presidential contenders that year. The paper reported that Andrew Jackson was the popular choice over John Quincy Adams, Henry Clay, and William H. Crawford. Jackson did receive the most popular votes, but John Quincy Adams was elected president after the contest was decided by the House of Representatives. Toward the end of the nineteenth century, the *New York Herald* regularly tried to forecast election outcomes in local, state, and national races. During presidential election years, the paper collected estimates from reporters and political leaders across the country and predicted the Electoral College vote by state.

Straw polls are still employed today. Some newspapers have interviewers ask adults at shopping malls and other locations about their voting preferences. Several television networks run Internet polls about serious and trivial issues. CNN asks viewers of its early evening news show to register their opinions on different issues and reports the results before the broadcast ends. Major events often trigger media polls. After each presidential debate, national media invite people to cast a vote via the web on who won. Preferences are electronically recorded and tabulated. Straw polls are unscientific because there is no way to ensure that the sample of individuals giving opinions is representative of the larger population. If these polls are unrepresentative, they are unlikely to reflect public opinion accurately.

The famed *Literary Digest* poll is a good example of an unrepresentative poll. The magazine conducted polls of presidential preferences between 1916 and 1936. As many as eighteen million ballots were mailed out to persons drawn from telephone directories and automobile registration lists. Although the purpose was less to measure public opinion than to boost subscriptions, the *Literary Digest* did predict the winners in 1924, 1928, and 1932. In 1936, however, the magazine predicted Alfred Landon would win, but Franklin D. Roosevelt won by a landslide. The erroneous prediction ended the magazine's polling, and in 1938 the *Literary Digest* went out of business.

Why did the *Literary Digest* miss in 1936? The sample was biased. Working class and poor people, the people most likely to vote for Roosevelt, the Democrat, did not own telephones and automobiles in the depths of the Great Depression.[52] Since the sample was drawn from telephone directories and auto registrations, these potential Roosevelt voters were significantly underrepresented.

Emergence of Scientific Polling

Scientific polling began after World War I, inspired by the new field of business known as marketing research. After the war, demand for consumer goods rose, and American businesses, no longer engaged in the production of war materials, turned to satisfying consumer demand. Businesses used marketing research to identify what consumers wanted and, perhaps more important, how products should be packaged so consumers would buy them. The American Tobacco Company changed from a green to a white package during World War II because it found that a white package was more attractive to women smokers.[53]

The application of mathematical principles of probability was also important to the development of scientific polling. To determine the frequency of defects in manufactured products, inspectors made estimates on the basis of a few randomly selected items, called a **sample.** It was a simple matter to extend the practice to individuals and draw conclusions regarding a large population based on findings from a smaller, randomly selected sample.

In the early 1930s, **George Gallup** and several others, using probability-based sampling techniques, began polling opinions on a wide scale. In 1936, Gallup predicted that the *Literary Digest* would be wrong and that Roosevelt would be reelected with 55.7 percent of the vote. Gallup's accurate prediction of the outcome lent credibility to probability-based polls, even though he underestimated Roosevelt's actual vote. In time, Gallup Polls would become a feature of American politics and probability-based polls the standard for those wanting accuracy in knowing what the public thinks.

Increasingly, government used polls. In 1940, Roosevelt became the first president to use polls on a regular basis, employing a social scientist to measure trends in public opinion toward the war in Europe.

Use of Polls

Many major American universities have a unit that performs survey research, and there are hundreds of commercial marketing research firms, private pollsters, and newspaper polls. For politicians, polls almost have become what the Oracle of Delphi was to the ancient Greeks and Merlin was to King Arthur—a divine source of wisdom. During a budget debate between President Clinton and congressional Republicans, Republicans used polls that told them promising to "put the government on a diet" would be popular in the upcoming 1996 election. Polls led Clinton to counter by accusing the Republicans of trying to cut Medicare. When the media wanted to make sense of the debate, they conducted more polls.[54]

Use by Politicians

Beginning in the 1960s, presidents increasingly turned to polls to assess the public's thinking on issues.[55] President Clinton took the use of polls to a new high. He spent more on polling than all previous administrations combined and tested every significant policy idea and the language to promote it.[56] Weekly polls shaped his centrist message, leading to his reelection in 1996. If polls showed a position to be popular, Clinton was likely to adopt it as his own. He embraced welfare reform, a Republican idea opposed by Democrats in Congress and liberals in his administration, partly because it was popular.[57] A White House poll in 1997 suggested that Americans preferred using the budget surplus to bolster Social Security rather than administer a Republican-preferred tax cut. In his State of the Union address, he called on Congress to "save Social Security first." Clinton even used polls to select a vacation spot.[58] Rather than vacation on Martha's Vineyard and play golf, Clinton went hiking in the Rockies instead, having been told by a consultant that golf was a Republican sport and that the voters he needed to win were campers.

Of course, Clinton did not always adopt positions because they were popular. He bucked public opinion and many leaders of his own party in his support for NAFTA (the North American Free Trade Agreement) and was again out of step with public opinion in his support for a multibillion-dollar bailout when the Mexican peso collapsed. He also defied public opinion

Harry Truman exults in incorrect headlines, based on faulty polls and early returns, the morning after he won the 1948 election.

in sending troops to Bosnia. To his surprise, his standing in the polls rose.[59]

George W. Bush expressed disdain for the polling done by the Clinton White House. In fact, however, the Bush administration does poll on national security and everything else.[60] As a result of its polling, the Bush administration has mastered the use of **crafted talk,** which enables politicians to move from the center and cater to the views of their more extreme base—all while appearing to remain in the middle.[61] Thus, whereas Clinton relied on polls to identify policies with broad public support, Bush relies on them to package—some might say camouflage—policies favored by his conservative base so these policies appear more attractive to mainstream voters.[62]

For example, Bush proposed partial privatization of Social Security. But his pollsters learned that the word *privatization* scared the public by implying that the government would no longer guarantee a lifetime income, as Social Security does. Instead, the president opted to use such terms as *retirement security, personal accounts, choice,* and *opportunity*—without changing the substance of his proposal.

The president also proposed the elimination of the inheritance tax, which was triggered when wealthy people died and left their estates to their heirs. Traditionally this tax was called the "estate tax" because it was imposed on the people with large estates. But the president and congressional Republicans called it the "death tax" to convey the notion that it was imposed on people when they die—that is, on everyone. In fact, it was imposed on just the wealthiest 1–2 percent. Yet the phrase *death tax* was a rhetorical success, persuading a majority of middle-class Americans to favor its elimination, even though it would never affect them.

Poll findings encouraged the administration to describe President Bush's energy plan as "balanced" and "comprehensive" and one that relies on "modern" methods to prevent environmental damage. The findings also prompted officials to call his proposal to give parents vouchers that would enable them to send their children to private schools "school choice" or "opportunity scholarships" rather than "school vouchers" or "aid to private schools."

Crafted talk often comes from the use of **focus groups,** which are small groups of average men and women brought together to share their reactions to candidates or policies or to the language used to refer to them. A focus group is not a scientific poll, and the participants might not be a cross-section of the population, but the process allows political consultants to explore participants' feelings in depth. The consultants search for the language, whether positive toward their side or negative toward the other side, that produces the desired effect on the participants. This language then can be used on the general public; it can be incorporated into speeches or commercials. The same process is employed by market researchers to sell corporations' products.

Many private pollsters work for one party or candidate. Although they undoubtedly wish to collect accurate data for their clients, their goal is to present their client in the most favorable light.[63] They may sometimes manipulate the wording of questions to benefit their client. The results, when publicized, give the impression that the public thinks something that, in fact, it does not.

Push polls are an egregious example of misuse. Here is how push polls work. A pollster for Jones asks whether the person called supports John Jones, Mary Smith, or is undecided in the upcoming congressional election. If the answer is Smith or undecided, the voter is asked a hypothetical question that leaves a negative impression. "If you were told that Smith drives a high-powered sports car at dangerous speeds through residential neighborhoods, would it make a difference in your vote?" The voter is then asked her preference again. Naturally, the level of support for Smith falls a great deal. The goal is to see whether certain "information" can "push" voters away from a candidate or a neutral opinion and toward the candidate favored by those doing the poll.[64] Learning the weaknesses of the opposition has always been a part of politics, but push polls seek to manipulate opinion, and they often distort the facts, including candidates' records.

An even more vicious tactic is to pump thousands of calls into a district or state under the guise of conducting a poll but with the intent of spreading false information about a candidate. Senator John McCain (R-Ariz.) accused the George W. Bush campaign of spreading false information in the guise of a poll in the 2000 South Carolina primary when both were seeking the Republican presidential nomination. Rumors were spread that McCain had become mentally unstable as a result of his imprisonment by the North Vietnamese in the Vietnam War and had fathered an illegitimate black child (in fact, he and his wife had adopted a child). This phony poll halted McCain's momentum, which had been surging until this primary. Both the push poll and

This gimmick may have attracted customers, but it was not a scientific way to measure opinion about President Clinton's impeachment.

the phony poll are violations of polling ethics and corruptions of the political process.

Use by Media

Along with polling by candidates, polls by news organizations have also increased. The number of network-sponsored **tracking polls,** in which a small number of people are polled on successive evenings throughout a campaign in order to assess changes in the level of voter support, began to be used in 1988 and exploded in 2000. Virtually every news organization of any size has since then featured daily tracking polls during election campaigns.[65] Tracking polls monitor the movement of candidates during the campaign, who is gaining and who is falling behind. This horse race aspect of the campaign makes a good story and attracts viewers. Pollsters and media are starting this intensive coverage earlier and earlier.

The ease of conducting polls explains, in part, their increasing use. Pollsters can conduct a poll at a moment's notice and have results within hours. This ease often leads to abuse. On clearly defined issues where the public has thought about something carefully and holds strong views, such as the vote in an election taking place

in a few days, a well-designed poll can provide an accurate picture of the public's views. However, polls taken well in advance of the election are flawed simply because voters have not made up their minds. Early polls tend to measure how well the public knows various candidates rather than specific opinions about them. Poll results reflecting support for candidates seeking office for the first time, or in primary elections, often jump up and down simply because voters do not know much about the candidates.

Even when issues are well defined and opinions are fairly stable, it is increasingly difficult to obtain a sample that provides a representative picture of public opinion. Many respondents refuse to be interviewed[66]—some because they don't want to be bothered, others because they fear they'll be asked to buy something or contribute money. Response rates for telephone surveys have also decreased because of extensive cell phone use and call-screening technologies that allow potential respondents to avoid calls altogether.[67] Nonrespondents, those who refuse to be polled or cannot be reached, are an increasing proportion of those called and can be as high as 80 percent. Pollsters are concerned that these nonresponse rates reflect the views of stay-at-homes who are too bored, too infirm, or too lonely to hang up rather than the views of Americans as a whole.[68] However, those who participate in these national polls differ little from those who do not, at least on issues that matter to pollsters.[69]

Other problems make it difficult for pollsters to get an accurate reading of public opinion. For example, there is the tendency of some respondents to express an opinion when they don't have one. No one wants to appear uninformed. Some respondents volunteer an answer even though they know little or nothing about a subject. The problem is getting worse as pollsters increasingly probe topics on which the public has no opinion and on which there is little reason to believe it should. For example, pollsters asked citizens whether the levies in New Orleans were strong enough to hold back the surge of a major hurricane and whether the U.S. military has enough troops on the ground in Iraq to win the war.

Polls taken within a few days of the elections asking about vote choice, on the other hand, tend to be quite accurate. All eight of the election eve polls in the 1996 presidential election predicted the winner, and the average error was tiny.[70] In 2000, the Democratic and Republican candidates each received 48 percent of the vote, with Gore a half million votes ahead. The election proved too close to call, but all election eve polls predicted the candidates' totals within each poll's margin of error. The polls taken the day before the 2004 election also were quite accurate, despite the closeness of the election. The average of fourteen major newspaper and network commercial polls had Kerry at 47.4 percent and Bush at 48.9 percent. The actual vote was 48 percent to 51 percent.[71]

Election day **exit polls** are ubiquitous and controversial features of media coverage. Before election day, the networks identify key precincts around the nation. On election day, as voters leave these precincts, pollsters ask them how they voted. Their responses, coupled with early returns and an analysis of how these precincts voted in past elections, are used to project the winner in the current election. When enough precincts in a state have been analyzed, the networks "call" the state for the winner. Since the 1960s, television networks have used exit polls to project the winners before all of the votes have been counted. To reduce costs, the networks jointly contract with one polling service, so they all receive the same data, and usually they all project the same winner about the same time. Because of fierce competition among the networks, however, each tries to beat the others, even if only by minutes.

Usually the exit polls have been accurate, but not always. At 7:50 P.M. on election night in 2000, the networks declared Democratic candidate Al Gore the winner in Florida. Because the election was very close and Florida had many electoral votes, it was already clear that whoever won this state probably would win the election. About 9:30 P.M., the polling service that conducted the exit polls notified the networks to pull back. Florida was "too close to call." At 2:15 A.M. the next morning, the networks declared Republican candidate George W. Bush the winner in Florida, and thus the next president of the United States, with 271 electoral votes, just 1 more than needed. They flashed their prepared graphics with a beaming Bush. But as more ballots were counted, Bush's lead in Florida eroded. About 3:30 A.M., the networks again pulled back. Florida again was "too close to call." Despite Dan Rather's assertion that if CBS called a state, "you can put it in the bank," the networks botched their calls two times in one night.

What happened? The election in Florida, as nationally, was extremely close and the polling sample was too small. (The networks, which had been taken over by huge corporations such as General Electric, slashed costs so much that the polling service couldn't sample enough precincts.[72]) Those who were polled were not sufficiently representative of all who voted.[73] (Absentee ballots cast before the election, which tend to be Republican votes, were not included.) And a significant number of voters in one large county who intended to vote for Gore marked their ballots, which were designed in a confusing fashion, in a way that nullified their votes. Of course, they did not realize this, and they told pollsters they voted for Gore. So they were counted as Gore voters in the exit polls but not in the actual tally.

The wrong calls were not merely an embarrassment to the networks. Because the networks initially called Florida for Gore ten minutes before polling places in the state's western panhandle closed, it is possible that a few Republicans on their way to vote might have turned around and gone home. Because the networks later called Florida for Bush, proclaiming him the "forty-third president," it is likely that many people around the country considered Bush the legitimate winner even when the networks eventually decided that the election was too close to call after all. Then in the postelection contest, when the two sides struggled for public support, Gore was put in the position of appearing to take Bush's victory, and his presidency, away from him.

Although the networks vowed to fix the polls, more problems popped up during the 2004 election. Exit polls showed John Kerry beating George Bush by a substantial margin. An aide took the president aside to tell him that he was going to lose. Of course, he did not. It is difficult to know just what happened. The pollsters may have oversampled Kerry voters or undersampled Bush voters by accident, but there is no evidence that Bush voters are more reluctant to be polled. An alternative explanation is that the actual votes may have been tampered with. Postelection investigations showed some fraud, though not enough to change any state's election results. However, the peculiar, and difficult to explain, finding is that the difference in the Democratic vote between the exit polls and the final tally was greatest in swing states, in areas with electronic voting machines, and in states with Republican governors.[74]

Even accurate and reliable polls can affect politics in a negative way. Poor standing in the polls may discourage otherwise viable candidates from entering a race, leaving the field to others who have less chance of winning or who lack the skills necessary to govern effectively. In 2000, several potential Republican candidates passed up the presidential race when early polls suggested that George W. Bush was the odds-on favorite to win the Republican nomination. And, in an unprecedented move, in 2002 Senator Robert Torricelli (D-N.J.) withdrew from his reelection race just thirty-six days before the election when polls showed that he could not win (he had been censured by the Senate for unethical conduct).

Additionally, polls can have a negative effect on political campaigns. Prior to polling, the purpose of campaigns was to reveal the candidates' views on the issues and their solutions to the pressing problems of the day. Instead, polls find out what the voters want, and the candidates then adopt positions and develop images to suit the voters. Too often, they follow the voters rather than lead them. They consider this strategy safer than trying to educate the public about complex problems or new solutions. Former senator Daniel Patrick Moynihan (D-N.Y.) decried politicians' addiction to poll results. "We've lost our sense of ideas that we stand by, principles that are important to us," he said.[75]

Poll results can also influence fund-raising, and without money, potential candidates cannot get traction in an election. Donors, especially large donors, want to give their money to candidates who have a good chance of winning, and with small poll numbers, potential candidates find it hard to raise the money that could give their candidacy visibility and raise those numbers. Governor Tom Vilseck (D-Iowa) entered the race for the 2008 presidential election and withdrew just two months later, never getting more than a couple of percentage points in the polls and being unable to raise funds.

It is possible that the sheer number of polls may lead everyone to take them less seriously. Still, it is unlikely that ambitious politicians bent on winning will abandon something that may help them win.

In spite of problems and abuses, polls still provide a valuable service to the nation. If direct democracy, like the New England town meeting, is the ideal, the use of public opinion polls is about as close as the modern state is likely to get to it. Polls help interpret the meaning of elections. When voters cast their ballots for one candidate over another, all anyone knows for sure is that a majority preferred one candidate. Polls can help reveal what elections mean in terms of policy preferences and thus help make the government more responsive to voters. Republicans claimed their victory in the 1994 congressional elections was an indication that voters supported the party's Contract with America, a series of policies the party vowed to enact if it won a majority in the House. Polls showed that most Americans had never heard of it. Although the hostility of average Americans toward polls may mean that pollsters will have to work harder to get an accurate picture of public opinion, they remain the best reflection of what Americans think about politics and politicians.

Knowledge and Information

Asking citizens their opinions on matters of public policy, candidates for public office, and the operation and institutions of government presumes they possess sufficient knowledge and information to form opinions and that expressions of opinion reflect real preferences. But Americans are often vague on the details of their government and who represents them.

Only one-fourth can name their two senators,[76] and only one-third can name their U.S. representative.[77] More than one-third don't know the party of their representative,[78] and 40 percent don't know which party controls Congress.[79] Prior to the 2004 election, 14 percent incorrectly identified the Democrats as controlling the House of Representatives and 30 percent confessed that they didn't know which party was the majority. Knowledge about the Senate was no higher.[80]

Many Americans are unable to identify prominent political personalities. Fourteen percent were unable to identify Vice President Dick Cheney, prior to his and George W. Bush's re-election in 2004 was less well recognized during his term than was Cheney during his. Ronald Reagan's vice president, George H.W. Bush.[81] Only a small percentage of Americans can identify a single piece of legislation passed by Congress.[82] In fact, more people can identify television personalities than major political figures.[83] In spite of increases in education, levels of knowledge regarding politics have not changed much since the 1940s.[84]

Although Americans revere the Constitution and see it as a blueprint for democracy, many do not know what is in it. One-third think it establishes English as the country's official language, and one-sixth think it establishes America as a Christian nation. One-fourth can't name a single First Amendment right (freedom to assemble and petition government, freedom to practice any religion, freedom of speech, and freedom for the press), and only 6 percent can name all four.[85]

Misperception regarding government policies is widespread, which means that many members of the public are asking to be manipulated by candidates for office. Although polls showed Americans in favor of reducing the size of the federal government, most have no idea whether the size of government is growing or shrinking.[86] Most Americans feel that the country spends too much on foreign aid and think we should cut its amount, but one-half estimate foreign aid to be about fifteen times greater than it is. Asked what an appropriate spending level would be, the average answer is eight times more than the country spends.[87] In one poll, nearly half of the public had an opinion on a nonexistent Public Affairs Act. Fearing to admit that they had never heard of it, these people gave an opinion anyway, just as they would for real policies they had never heard of.[88]

Despite these levels of ignorance, some argue that average citizens know what they need to know to make sound political judgments.[89] Most citizens take an active interest in politics and pay attention when they have a personal stake. Eighty percent know that Congress passed a law requiring employers to provide family leave following the birth of a child or in an emergency. When times are bad, voters do tune in to government more. With the war in Iraq and a shaky economy, six in ten Americans reported giving the 2004 presidential election a lot of thought as early as February, much earlier than in 2000. Over half reported more enthusiasm for voting, up 15 percent from 2000.[90] Greater interest and concern translated into higher turnout.

The average American may not know details of government, but most have strong opinions they rely on, opinions about whether things are going well or not.[91] Is a candidate running an effective campaign? If not, can one expect him or her to run the country? Can a candidate hold his or her own in debates? All are cues reflecting whether or not a candidate can handle the job.

At the same time, lack of knowledge is an impediment to holding government accountable and responsible to the people. Those who are less politically knowledgeable find it difficult to sort through the claims and counterclaims of politicians. Some support candidates and policies that work against their self-interest. By their lack of information, they are asking to be manipulated, and they are.[92]

Politicians often contribute to citizen ignorance and misperception. They often avoid discussing issues, especially controversial ones, or worse, mislead by trumpeting suspect or false information. Eight out of ten Americans continued to believe Iraq had weapons of mass destruction despite none being found.[93] Nearly one-half responded that Saddam Hussein was directly involved in carrying out the 9/11 attacks with no evidence supporting such a link.[94] The Bush administration had encouraged these views, orchestrating officials' comments to assert explicitly that Iraq had weapons of mass destruction and to suggest implicitly that Iraq was linked to al-Qaeda. Even when no weapons of mass destruction were found during the war and when no significant link to al-Qaeda was found by the 9/11

DOUBTING THE HOLOCAUST?

A major problem for pollsters is designing questions that accurately measure opinions. Do you agree that it's not the case that a few words don't make a lot of difference in a poll question? You do, don't you? Questions with a double negative are difficult to understand. Results from such questions are unreliable. Poorly worded questions can confuse respondents and cause pollsters to draw the wrong conclusions.

The point was illustrated in a poll to discover the proportion of Americans who doubt that the Holocaust happened. The survey asked the following question: "As you know, the term Holocaust usually refers to the killing of millions of Jews in Nazi death camps during World War II. Does it seem possible or does it seem impossible to you that the Nazi extermination of the Jews never happened?" The results: 22 percent said it was possible that the Holocaust never happened; another 12 percent were not sure. The conclusion: About one-third of the country either doubted that the Holocaust occurred or were uncertain.

Since no reputable historian denies that the Holocaust happened, this "finding" was shocking. Commentators reflected on how the public could be so ill-informed regarding a major event, not just of the twentieth century, but of recorded history.

But the wording of the question was the culprit. Another version asked, "Does it seem possible to you that the Nazi extermination of Jews never happened, or do you feel certain that it happened?" This time only 1 percent said it was possible that the Holocaust never happened. Eight percent were unsure, and 90 percent were certain that it happened.

Why the difference? A study of thirteen polls, with estimates of Holocaust doubters ranging from 1 to 46 percent, found that high estimates resulted from confusing language.

SOURCE: Richard Morin, "From Confusing Questions, Confusing Answers," *Washington Post National Weekly Edition*, July 18, 1994, 37.

Commission, the administration was reluctant to correct the record.[95]

It is hard work to stay informed. It takes time and energy. With work and family, average men and women have little time for politics. But failure to stay informed means that politicians can often ignore what the public wants.

Ideology

Average Americans hold opinions on a variety of different issues. These opinions may be consistent with each other and reflect a broader framework or worldview, what scholars call an **ideology,** or they may be inconsistent and unrelated. One might, for example, express support for government assistance to farmers hit by hard times but oppose it for out-of-work steelworkers whose jobs have been outsourced to foreign countries.

Most Americans lack an ideological worldview; that is, they do not have a consistent and coherent set of opinions on political issues. Nor are they consistent in evaluations of candidates for public office or political parties. Yet the major contemporary ideologies, liberalism and conservatism, are useful in thinking about public opinion and understanding the institutions of American politics and political and social conflicts in society. Liberalism is sometimes identified by the label *left* or *left wing* and conservatism by the label *right* or *right wing*. These terms date from the French National Assembly of the early nineteenth century when liberal parties occupied the left side of the chamber and conservative parties occupied the right.

Modern liberalism, used in the American political context, embodies the notion that government can be a positive and constructive force in society, responsible for assisting individuals, businesses, and communities in dealing with social and economic problems. Franklin Roosevelt and the Democrats' New Deal policies of the 1930s were enacted to relieve the economic hardships of the Great Depression and limit the harsh consequences of an unrestrained free market economy through government regulation and control. Central to liberalism is the belief that government has a responsibility to make life better for average men and women. This can mean support for government regulations as well as for taxes to pay for government programs. And it has meant support for civil rights legislation to promote equality for racial minorities and women.

At the same time, contemporary **liberals** combine their support for government action to bring about social and economic equality with a belief that government should stay out of the way in other issues such as abortion and contraception, the so-called **social issues.** Keeping government out of the bedroom is sometimes a rallying cry for liberals. Liberals also tend to be opposed to other government invasions of privacy, such as monitoring phone calls, reading material, and Internet activity.

Modern conservatism generally encompasses the notion that individuals and communities are better off without government assistance and regulation in economic areas. Central to conservatism is the belief that the free market should be allowed to function unencumbered by government rules and regulations, and individuals, rather than the government, are responsible for their own economic well-being. Short of harming others, individuals should be allowed to do as they please in their economic lives. Consistent with this view, government is necessarily small, and where there is a need for government, it is best if it is at the state or local rather than the more distant federal level. While conservatism subscribes to a diminished role for government, throughout the nation's history it has been associated with the promotion of commercial and business interests that has led at times to large subsidies and other government benefits for businesses, corporations, and favored occupational groups such as farmers.

However, many modern **conservatives** would like government to impose a standard of behavior—for example, restrict or outlaw abortion and contraception and thus prod people to be more responsible about sex. Unlike the economy and race where conservatives oppose government action to bring about a particular outcome, for social issues such as abortion, contraceptive rights, and same-sex marriage many conservatives favor big government regulation of behavior. President Bush proposed laws that would spend federal money to teach sexual abstinence to teenagers and outlaw same-sex marriages and late-term abortions. Some conservatives also favor government action to monitor communication, restrict political activity, and abolish some rights of defendants in a time of war. So, for example, the Bush administration and, in some cases, the Republican congressional majority after 9/11 put in place policies to monitor certain telephone communications, obtain information on individual's book purchases and library checkouts, and to

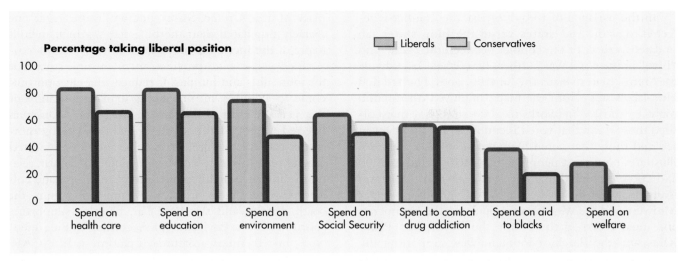

Percentage taking liberal position

Liberals   Conservatives

Spend on health care · Spend on education · Spend on environment · Spend on Social Security · Spend to combat drug addiction · Spend on aid to blacks · Spend on welfare

FIGURE 2 • **Liberals and Conservatives Differ on Spending for Safety Net and Environmental Issues** *The proportions are those who want to increase spending on each area.* SOURCE: General Social Survey, 2002 (N's = 602 to 1,301).

restrict the rights of those accused of sympathy toward terrorists organizations.

However, not all conservatives agree on these big government activities. Many traditional "small government" conservatives are appalled at these invasions of privacy, whether political or sexual, and many oppose what they label George W. Bush's big government conservatism. One commentator dubbed him the "nanny-in-chief" of the "nanny state."[96]

These broad descriptions capture the core ideas of liberalism and conservatism, but individual politicians, political parties, and most Americans reflect them imperfectly. Though liberalism and conservatism are not political parties, in contemporary America one finds more liberals in the Democratic Party and more conservatives in the Republican. There is, however, broad consensus on some issues, that government has a role to play in making people's lives better. But the extent of that role is the subject of vigorous debate.

Americans tend to be conservative on some matters and liberal on others. A little more than a third identify themselves as conservative, and a little more than a fourth identify themselves as liberal. However, more—about 40 percent—identify themselves as **moderate** or middle of the road, neither liberal nor conservative.[97] Because moderates are the swing group, not only in voting but also in building support for policies, public officials will sometimes move to the middle or even to the opposite ideological group in constructing propos-

als in order to garner majority support. President Bill Clinton endorsed a major overhaul of the nation's welfare program, limiting government assistance to families in need, typically considered a conservative position. President George W. Bush, while governing mostly from the right, confounded some conservatives by proposing an expansion of the Medicare program to include a drug benefit for seniors, usually considered a liberal position. Both Presidents Clinton and Bush adopted positions from the opposite side of the ideological spectrum in an effort to attract political support from political moderates (Figure 2).

Public Opinion in Red States and Blue States

Liberalism and conservatism not only find expression in partisan differences but also reflect geographical differences. Ideological divisions have strong historical roots stemming from differences between northerners and southerners going back to the time of America's founding. The Civil War (1861–1865) was a stark manifestation of these divisions. After the Civil War and continuing to this day, the more conservative agrarians in the Midwest have often found themselves in alliance with the southern agrarians against the more liberal urbanites in the East.

In the parlance of today's media, the conflict is referred to as the **red states** versus the **blue states** (an updated version of the conflict between the "gray" and "blue" in the Civil War). Others have labeled the divide the "retro" states versus the "metro" ones. The red and blue labels stem from the maps employed on election night by the TV networks in 2000 and 2004 that colored those states that voted Republican for president in red and those that voted Democratic in blue. Figure 3 illustrates how most people in each state voted in 2000 and 2004. Presented this way, it appears that the nation is divided, with majorities in New England, the upper Midwest, and the West Coast supporting the Democrats and most voters in the South, the Border and Plains states, and the Rocky Mountain West supporting the Republicans. The red states comprise most of the land-mass of the United States but are more rural and sparsely populated than the blue states, which include many of the metropolitan centers.

Red versus blue provides an interesting story line for journalists and pundits. It reduces the election outcome to a simple and intriguing explanation and one that is easily grasped by average Americans. Conservative red America has been described as religious, moralistic, patriotic, white, masculine, and less educated. Liberal blue America has been depicted as secular, relativistic, internationalist, multicultural, feminine, and college educated. Reds are seen as supporting guns, the death penalty, and the Iraq War, blues as supporting abortion and the environment. According to the stereotypes, in red America Saturday's pastime is NASCAR; Sunday's is church. In blue America, Saturday is for the

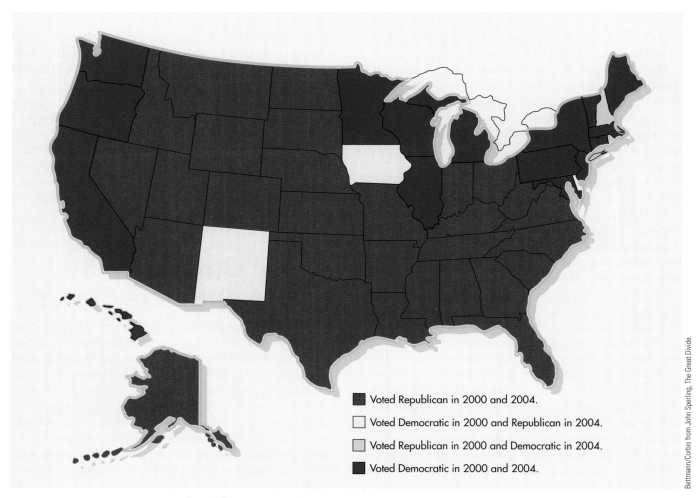

Voted Republican in 2000 and 2004.

Voted Democratic in 2000 and Republican in 2004.

Voted Republican in 2000 and Democratic in 2004.

Voted Democratic in 2000 and 2004.

FIGURE 3 • **Party Strength Displays Geographic Patterns**

farmer's market, and Sunday is for reading the *New York Times*.[98]

There are differences between red states and blue states. Religion is one difference. The red states encompass the **Bible belt**, a broad area of the country where most people identify with a religion and evangelical Protestants are common. This area comprises most of the South and parts of Kansas and Missouri. In contrast, the West Coast and parts of the Southwest are much more secular. Forty-four percent of those living in red states identify themselves as born-again Christians; only 26 percent in blue states do. Many fewer people in the blue states identify with any religious organization. A much smaller margin separates church attendance patterns, because only a minority of red staters and blue staters attend church weekly, though somewhat more red staters do.[99] These religious differences are significant, because in recent national elections, born-again Christians and regular church attenders have been more likely to vote Republican than those with weaker religious faith. After the 2004 election, a map circulated on the Internet, identifying the states that supported Kerry as one country—the "United States of Canada," as though they had seceded and joined Canada—and the states that supported Bush as another country—"Jesusland."

Other differences also reflect more conservative values in the red states. For example, in red states, women are less active in politics, less likely to hold political office, have lower incomes, and are less likely to be managers and professionals than in the blue states. Red states impose more restrictions on abortion and incorporate more abstinence education in sex education classes (see Table 2).

Red states are more hostile to labor unions, so they have adopted laws that enable many companies to avoid unionizing their workforce. Wal-Mart, which began in Arkansas and then spread through the South, does everything in its power to keep its workers from forming or joining unions. In contrast, blue states are more hospitable to labor unions. Cities such as New York, Chicago, and San Francisco are union bastions.[100]

For the 2004 election, the stereotypes were on full display. During the spring primaries, a conservative interest group ran a commercial opposing the candidacy of Howard Dean, Vermont's governor, who was running for the Democratic nomination for president. In the commercial, average people advised Dean to "take his tax-hiking, government-expanding, latte-drinking, sushi-eating, Volvo-driving, *New York Times*-reading, body-piercing, Hollywood-loving, left-wing freak show

Table 2	State Laws Affecting Reproductive and Homosexual Rights

An analysis of twenty-five categories of state laws affecting reproductive and homosexual rights, ranging from laws restricting contraception and abortion to laws recognizing same-sex partnerships, found sharp differences among the states. The states with the most restrictive laws were all red states, and the states with the most permissive laws were almost all blue states. (New Mexico was the exception, although it voted Democratic in 2000 and nearly did so again in 2004.)

Most Restrictive States	Most Permissive States
Ohio and South Dakota (tied for most restrictive)	New York and New Mexico (tied for most permissive)
Indiana	
North Dakota	New Jersey
Oklahoma	Washington
Mississippi	California
Kentucky	Vermont
Utah	Massachusetts
Nebraska	New Hampshire
Missouri	Connecticut
	Hawaii

SOURCE: Analysis conducted by the National Gay and Lesbian Task Force and two pro-choice groups—Ipas and the SisterSong Women of Color Reproductive Health Collective. David Crary, "In Gay, Reproductive Rights Rankings, S. Dakota, Ohio Last," *Lincoln Journal Star*, June 1, 2006, 4A.

back to Vermont, where it belongs." During the fall campaign, John Kerry, the Democratic nominee from "Taxachusetts," was derided for his ability to speak French.

Based on such differences, in the aftermath of the 2004 election, one commentator declared that "the red states get redder, the blue states get bluer, and the political map of the United States takes on the coloration of the Civil War."[101] One adviser to President Bush commented, "You've got 80 percent to 90 percent of the country that look at each other like they are on separate planets."[102] Conservatives sneer at blue staters for being chardonnay-sipping elitists out of touch with average people, while liberals deride red staters for being beer-guzzling, gun-toting rednecks. However, these stereotypes are exaggerated and lack historical context.

In each category there is a mix of values and opinions, as Senator Barack Obama (D-Ill.) so eloquently stated at the Democratic National Convention. "We worship an awesome God in the blue states, and we don't like federal agents poking around our libraries in the red states. We coach Little League in the blue states and have gay friends in the red states. There are patriots who opposed the war in Iraq and patriots who supported it. We are one people, all of us pledging allegiance to the Stars and Stripes, all of us defending the United States of America." Indeed, polling data confirm a mix of opinions and reveal surprisingly little difference between red and blue. Citizens in red states are only slightly more conservative than those in blue states. And as Figure 4 shows, majorities in red states are usually on the same side of various issues as majorities in blue states.

And although many in the media, based on exit polls, pointed to "moral values" as the reason for George W. Bush's victory in 2004, further analysis revealed that moral values were no more likely to be mentioned as a reason for voting Republican than in either of the two previous elections. When voters identified their main concerns in the election, they were much more likely to mention war and terrorism than moral values. Among those who did cite moral values, one-fourth to one-third voted for Kerry. The relative absence of clear-cut divisions appears even in personal contexts. When unmarried Americans were asked whether they would be "open to marrying someone who held significantly different political views" from their own, 57 percent said they would.[103]

Like other simple story lines about politics, the characterizations of the states contain some truth but are exaggerated. They apply to a minority of the populations in the red and blue states. They apply most clearly to political activists and political junkies—the people who are the most involved and most interested in politics.

These partisans in both parties are sharply divided, and increasingly so.[104] The characterizations apply more and more to elected officials, who themselves are increasingly polarized.[105] Most are nominated in primaries, and primaries are dominated by the more extreme members of their parties. Only 15 percent of the public votes in primary elections, and these are the most partisan voters. Republican candidates have to appease conservatives in their party, whereas Democratic candidates have to appease liberals in their party. Moreover, with little competition in most congressional districts, the more extreme and polarized views are not effectively challenged. And the campaign finance system may contribute to the polarized atmosphere by rewarding those candidates whose allegiance to a single issue or cause is most fierce.

The media also contribute to the sense that the nation is divided. The media tend to frame issues as debates and elections as contests between two sharply opposing sides. With the proliferation of cable TV channels, talk radio shows, and Internet blogs, the public can tune to those voices, and only those

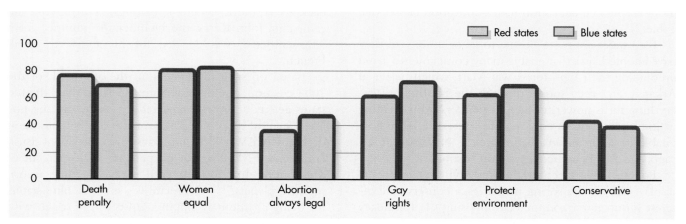

FIGURE 4 • **Red- and Blue-State Voters Have Similar Opinions on Many Controversial Issues** *These are proportions of voters who (1) favor the death penalty; (2) believe in an equal women's role; (3) believe abortion should be legal under all conditions; (4) oppose discrimination against gays and lesbians; (5) believe we should do whatever it takes to protect the environment; and (6) see themselves as conservative.*
SOURCE: 2002 Pew National Survey reported in Fiorina, 2005.
The American Prospect, Feb. 2005. © Tom Tomorrow.

voices, with which they agree. This prompts the media to enlist the voices who are extreme in their positions and hostile to the opposition. In contrast, in the early decades of television, there were only three national networks, which sought high ratings by not targeting their newscasts toward any one segment of the audience.

With political activists and public officials generally representing the more extreme views in their party, and the media usually emphasizing those views and characterizing opposing views as un-American, it is not surprising that our political debate has become more polarized despite the fact that the average Americans are not extreme in either direction.

Public Opinion Toward Race

Public opinion has influenced, as well as responded to, the progress of the African American struggle for equality. Polls extending as far back as the 1940s show white America increasingly opposed to segregation and discrimination, at least in principle.[106] In fact, the change might be characterized as revolutionary. Whereas only one-third of whites accepted the idea of black and white children going to the same schools in 1942, in the 1980s more than 90 percent approved. Today nearly

everyone approves. Over 80 percent respond that they have no objection to sending their children to schools where more than half of the students are black. Nearly two-thirds say they would not object to schools where most of the students are black. The percentage of people believing that whites have a right to keep African Americans out of their neighborhoods has been cut in half since 1963.[107] Thirty-eight percent of whites were against laws forbidding interracial marriage in 1963; 85 percent were opposed in 1996.[108] Most Americans say they would vote for a black candidate for president.

Public opinion can change because individuals change or because older individuals with one set of opinions are replaced by a new generation with a different set of opinions. Changes in whites' racial opinions through the 1960s occurred for both reasons. Older whites with more stereotyped views of blacks were replaced by a younger generation who were more tolerant. At the same time, the civil rights movement prompted many Americans to reconsider their views on race.

Since the 1970s, most changes occurred because of the replacement of older, more prejudiced whites with younger, less prejudiced ones. Differences in socialization between those born in the 1920s and 1930s and those born in the 1950s and 1960s have led to much greater support for racial integration. More change can be expected in the future as today's teens age and replace older Americans. For example, a majority of white

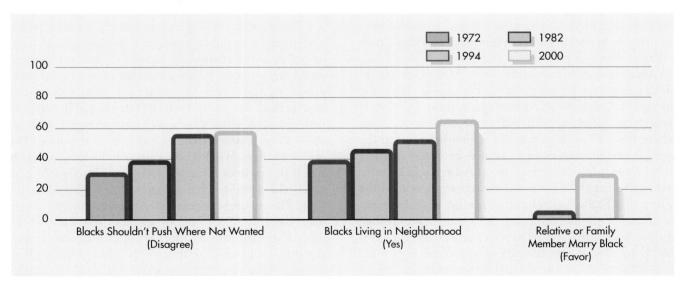

FIGURE 5 • Whites Have Grown More Accepting of Blacks
SOURCE: General Social Survey, Selected Years (N's range from 1,130 in 1990 to 2,070 in 2000). Data from whites only. By permission of Mike Luckovich and Creators Syndicate, Inc. ©Tribune Media Services, Inc. All Rights Reserved. Reprinted with permission.

adults believe the reason that blacks lag behind whites in jobs, education, and income is because they fail to take advantage of opportunities available to all, whereas a large plurality of white teens believe discrimination by whites is responsible.[109]

While white Americans accept integration, they have been much slower to accept government initiatives to achieve it. For example, although racially segregated schools often are in poor central-city areas and offer inferior education, busing to achieve racial balance in schools has never had much appeal to whites. Only about one-third would support it.

Why is there a discrepancy between the increasing majorities of whites who support integration and the majorities who believe that government should not make special efforts to help minorities? In some cases, unwillingness on the part of whites to endorse government initiatives to end segregation reflects racist sentiments.[110] Although only 10 percent of white Americans respond that differences in jobs, housing, and income between whites and blacks are the result of biological differences,[111] 43 percent cling to the racist belief that it is lack of motivation and will power on the part of blacks.[112] Thus anywhere from 10 to 40 percent of white Americans harbor racist beliefs in spite of their willingness to accept blacks, live in integrated neighborhoods, and have their children attend integrated schools.

However, some whites oppose government help for blacks on principle. They object to being told what to do by government or feel government assistance for blacks is discrimination against whites. For some, government help violates their sense that individuals have a responsibility to provide for themselves.

Another reason that some white Americans are reluctant to accept government intervention is that many do not see the need. African Americans and white Americans live in very different perceptual worlds. Anywhere from 40 to 60 percent of whites believe that the average African American is as well or better off than the average white American in schooling, job, income, and health care.[113] This is a direct contradiction to the reality that blacks lag behind whites on virtually every social and economic indicator. But misperceptions such as these lead many whites to reject any government effort to equalize the social and economic standing of the races. Whites who more accurately recognize the plight of black Americans are more likely to accept the government's role in providing equal education for black

and white children and ensuring that blacks are treated equally by courts and police.[114]

Blacks, not unexpectedly, see things differently. A majority view themselves trailing whites in education, income, jobs, and health care, and of course this is the reality.[115] Moreover, 44 percent believe that they personally have been denied a job or promotion because of race.[116]

Like whites, African Americans have become somewhat less supportive of government initiatives. In 1964, 92 percent thought the federal government should ensure blacks fair treatment in jobs; by 1996, only 64 percent did. Support for government assistance in school integration has also declined. Some blacks fear that government initiatives will only antagonize whites. Others fear that black children will suffer if they are in a climate where they are an unwanted minority. Still others believe government is ineffective in bringing about an end to discrimination.

Conclusion: Is Government Responsive to Public Opinion?

In a democracy, government should be responsive to the wishes of the people. Those wishes, collectively, comprise public opinion. But is government responsive?

The most direct way to assess whether public policy is responsive to public opinion is to compare changes in policy with changes in opinion. One study compared responses to policy questions in several hundred public opinion surveys conducted over a forty-five year period. On more than 300 items, public opinion had changed. And when opinions changed, policies also changed more than two-thirds of the time. The policy changes matched the opinion changes especially when the opinion changes were large and stable (and when the opinion changes moved in a liberal direction). The researchers concluded that the policy changes may have caused the opinion changes about half of the time. However, the opinion changes probably caused the policy changes, or they both affected each other, the rest of the time. On important issues, when changes in public opinion were clear-cut, policy usually became consistent with opinion.[117]

Yet policy isn't as consistent with opinion now as it used to be. Twenty years ago congressional laws reflected public opinion polls about 60 percent of the time; more recently the figure is 40 percent.[118] This change may reflect the growing polarization among public officials and political activists. This change may also reflect the gerrymandering of legislative districts, which provides most members of the House of Representatives with a safe seat—either safely Republican and conservative or safely Democratic and liberal. Representatives from those districts don't have to cater to centrist opinion in their district as much as they did in the past.[119]

Public officials also pay attention to the intensity of public opinion. Elected officials may support a minority opinion that is intensely held. President Bush continues to push tax cuts, whereas a majority of Americans prefer their tax dollars be used to reduce the deficit or fund social programs.[120] The president is responding to his core constituency that strongly favors tax cuts. A minority with intense feelings is more likely to make financial contributions, provide campaign help, and ultimately vote for a candidate who does what they want or against a candidate who does the opposite than is a majority with weaker feelings.

There are other reasons why public policy may not reflect public opinion. Interest groups, political parties, and public officials' own preferences influence policy, and they may not agree with public opinion. Before the 2006 election, for example, Republicans held solid majorities in both the House and Senate. After newly elected and reelected members were seated in January 2007, the Democrats controlled both houses. Polls showed that large majorities of the public voted for the Democrats because they thought we should not be in Iraq. Though public opinion was heavily in favor in 2003 when we invaded Iraq, by 2006 majorities blamed the Republicans for getting us into the war and then mismanaging it. Newly elected Democrats pledged to reflect their constituents' attitudes and get us out of the war, which was rapidly becoming a quagmire.

Yet, just a few weeks after the new Democratic congress was sworn in in January 2007, the president decided to send more troops to Iraq, to escalate the war—in the administration parlance, to have a "surge" of troops. Though Democrats protested, there was little they could do, short of cutting off all funding. This illustrates that though government can be responsive to public opinion, responsiveness is not always in the short term and sometimes happens only after months and years.

Some observers worry that political activists and interest groups manipulate public opinion through the increasingly intrusive media, which distort the issues and blind the public to its own self-interest. Even when public opinion accurately reflects the public's real attitudes, this opinion is not sacred. Public officials do not have to follow public opinion. The course of action favored by a majority may not be the best course. The Founders didn't want public opinion necessarily to become public policy. They established a federal system with separation of powers and checks and balances to ensure that the majority, in the heat of the moment, cannot work its will easily.

In our system, therefore, we should not expect public policy always and instantaneously to match public opinion. However, the fact that governmental policy usually reflects majority opinion, especially when that opinion is large and stable, does indicate that the government generally is responsive.

Key Terms

Key Names

1. Which is true?
   a. The majority of Americans support the regulation of gun sales and, accordingly, federal policy outlaws gun ownership.
   b. The majority of Americans support the regulation of gun sales and, accordingly, federal policy significantly limits the sale of both handguns and semiautomatic weapons.
   c. The majority of Americans support the regulation of gun sales and sales of some guns are regulated.
   d. The majority of Americans oppose gun regulation and, accordingly, federal policy does not regulate the sale of any type of gun.
   e. The majority of Americans oppose regulation and, accordingly, only the sale of ammunition is regulated.

2. A flag-waving protest against the Iraq war is an example of
   a. an intense public opinion.
   b. political socialization.
   c. insurrection.
   d. government instability.
   e. responsiveness to public opinion.

3. Agents of political socialization include
   a. your college or university.
   b. your mom.
   c. your high school friends.
   d. the cable network you watch.
   e. all of the above.

4. Which of the following is *not* a common way for schools to affect political attitudes?
   a. Patriotic rituals such as the Pledge of Allegiance and teaching patriotic songs
   b. Civics textbooks
   c. Student government and mock elections
   d. Stimulating students to speak out on controversial issues
   e. Teaching reading and improving language facility

5. Which of the following is true of high schools' contributions to students' learning about politics?
   a. Tends to support the political status quo
   b. Tends to promote radical change in our political system
   c. Tends to promote democratic values
   d. Tends to foster attitudes challenging the status quo
   e. Tends to present a realistic picture of the way government really works

6. Which of the following is *not* true about college education and political socialization?
   a. Over time, students' political ideologies change more than those of professors.
   b. Students were more liberal during the Vietnam War than before or after.
   c. Most college freshmen are very conservative.
   d. Most college freshmen report low levels of political interest.
   e. Students leave college more tolerant than when they entered.

7. We are likely to get the most accurate views of public opinion by using
   a. straw polls.
   b. push polls.
   c. crafted talk.
   d. probability-based polls.
   e. multiple focus groups.

8. An example of a push poll is
   a. a survey done by providing a phone number for TV viewers to call in to express an opinion on a presidential debate.
   b. a group of randomly selected voters being asked about a candidate's views on gun control.
   c. a mechanism to reduce refusal rates by potential respondents to a survey by pushing them to answer.
   d. a phone bank of callers who provide new, mostly accurate, information about a candidate while pushing voters to vote in the upcoming election.
   e. a telephone poll that asks respondents how they would feel about a candidate about whom the pollsters provide selective, usually negative, information.

9. Tracking polls can be misleading because
   a. new candidates often are unknown.
   b. samples are likely biased toward those who will talk to interviewers.
   c. some respondents will offer an opinion when they have no information.
   d. new technology, such as cell phones and answering machines, bias the samples.
   e. all of the above.

10. In the 2000 election, the outcome in Florida differed from the exit poll results for all of the following reasons *except*
    a. voters who voted absentee were not included in the exit polls.
    b. voters in one large county were confused by the ballot, intending to vote for Gore but in fact voting for a third-party candidate.
    c. exit polls were designed to favor Republicans.
    d. the election was very close and polls cannot reliably predict very close races.
    e. exit poll samples were too small to provide a reliable sample.

11. Polling during campaigns can
    a. disadvantage candidates without a lot of name recognition.
    b. favor those who start from an underdog position.
    c. minimize the need for campaign funding.
    d. allow more of a focus on the substantive issues of the campaign.
    e. provide the party in the White House with an advantage.

12. Which is true about public knowledge of politics?
    a. Most citizens can name both of their U.S. Senators but don't know who Dick Cheney is.
    b. Most citizens know who Dick Cheney is and can identify several pieces of important legislation.
    c. Most citizens know who Dick Cheney is and can name at least one First Amendment right.
    d. Most Americans can name all four freedoms in the First Amendment.
    e. Most Americans cannot identify Dick Cheney but do know that Congress passed a Family Leave Act.

13. Red states
    a. are most likely to be found in the South and Plains states.
    b. are most likely to be found in the Northeast and West coast.
    c. have citizens who are more liberal than in the blue states.
    d. are less religious than citizens in the blue states.
    e. tend to vote Democratic in presidential elections and Republican in congressional ones.

14. Which is true of public opinion on the issue of gay and lesbian rights?
    a. Americans are becoming more supportive of gay and lesbian rights.
    b. Americans are more likely to favor gay marriage than other types of gay and lesbian rights.
    c. The "don't ask, don't tell" policy has led to only a handful of dismissals from the military service.
    d. The older generation is more supportive of gay and lesbian rights than younger people.
    e. Most Americans oppose the rights of gays and lesbians to serve in the military.

15. Which is true of ideology in America?
    a. Most conservatives favor government intervention to promote economic equality and to regulate personal morality.
    b. Most liberals favor government intervention to promote economic equality and to regulate personal morality.
    c. Conservatives are divided over whether government should regulate personal morality.
    d. Most liberals favor government intervention to promote personal morality but not economic equality.
    e. Generally speaking, regulating personal morality and economic equality are not political issues.

16. Which is true about racial attitudes?
    a. White support for integration in the schools and neighborhoods has decreased over the past thirty years.
    b. Whites are more likely than they were in the 1960s to favor government action to reduce black and white inequality.
    c. Most whites understand that blacks do not have equal employment and housing opportunities.
    d. Support for government action to remedy racial discrimination has increased among blacks during the past thirty years.
    e. Most whites favor school and housing integration.

17. President Bush decided to send more troops to Iraq after the 2006 election. This is an example of
    a. elected officials responding to majority public opinion.
    b. congressional war powers.
    c. a public opinion mandate.
    d. response to National Guard commanders.
    e. the fact that responsiveness is not always short term.

18. The Founders
    a. wanted government to be directly and immediately responsive to public opinion.
    b. built in checks and balances to temper the responsiveness of the government to public opinion.
    c. favored a monarchy with the king standing between public opinion and government action.
    d. believed in unfettered democracy.
    e. were impatient when public policy was not responsive to public opinion.

19. After 9/11,
    a. positive opinions toward government increased.
    b. negative opinions toward government increased.
    c. public officials called on the public to make significant economic sacrifices to fight terror.
    d. interest in government decreased.
    e. presidential popularity fell.

20. Sometimes majority public opinion is not consistent with public policy because
    a. policy makers disagree with public opinion.
    b. the minority has very intense views.
    c. powerful interest groups may support the minority opinion.
    d. sometimes there is a lag between changing opinion and changing policy.
    e. all of the above.

Key: 1-c; 2-a; 3-e; 4-d; 5-a; 6-c; 7-d; 8-e; 9-e; 10-c; 11-a; 12-c; 13-a; 14-a; 15-a; 16-c; 17-e; 18-b; 19-a; 20-e

Jessica Lynch.

You may have heard the story of Jessica Lynch early during the Iraq war. Just nineteen years old, from a small town—a hollow nestled in the mountains of West Virginia—Jessica Lynch was an army private who served as a supply clerk. She was in a convoy that got separated from its unit, after taking multiple wrong turns, and got lost in the desert, when it was ambushed by Iraqis. In the skirmish, she was shot and stabbed, but she was a fearless fighter, killing several attackers. She was ready to die rather than surrender. Yet she and some others were captured. Although she was taken to an Iraqi hospital, the Iraqi doctors refused to treat her and an Iraqi soldier sodomized her. Fortunately, U.S. Special Forces conducted a daring night raid on the hospital in the face of hostile fire—a video taken through night lenses showed the raid in a dramatic iridescent green—and rescued her. Or so the media reported.

Jessica became the media star of the war—a combination of a female Rambo and "the Mona Lisa of Operation Iraqi Freedom."[1] In the ambush, eleven soldiers were killed, and five others were wounded, including a Native American woman. But Jessica, with her blond hair and blue eyes, became the media darling. She was featured not only in the daily newspapers and newscasts but on the cover of a magazine and as the subject of a song. She was offered university scholarships, cars, and money to tell her story to the media. NBC proposed a movie; CBS offered, in addition to a movie, a documentary, a book, and an opportunity to co-host an MTV special.

But most of what was reported by the media wasn't true.[2] Her convoy was ambushed, and in the melee her vehicle rammed into an army truck and turned over. This collision caused her injuries. She was not shot, nor stabbed. She had not fired her rifle, because it had jammed. When she was captured and taken to the hospital, the Iraqi doctors treated her, and they contacted the U.S. military to pick her up. The Iraqi soldiers had left the hospital two days before the American soldiers arrived. There was no hostile fire, and Jessica was handed over as promised. Thus, the real story was much less dramatic than the media version.

So how did the phony story get reported? A high administration official gave reporters inaccurate information from U.S. intelligence,[3] and the media ran with it, exaggerating the information for dramatic effect. The story became so thrilling that when the administration learned the truth, it was slow to correct the story. Then, when a military officer contradicted the reports, the media themselves were slow to correct the story.[4] The administration and the media both had reasons to perpetuate this fairy tale. The push to Baghdad had bogged down, and the military and White House welcomed a positive story. The media always seek a dramatic story featuring human interest and strong emotions to attract an audience of readers, listeners, or viewers.

Meanwhile, Jessica, recovering from serious injuries, was unable to remember much about the incident. But she did criticize the military for using her to generate popular support for the war.

A *medium* transmits something. The mass media—which include newspapers, magazines, books, radio, television, movies, records, and the Internet—transmit communications to masses of people.

Although the media don't constitute a branch of government or even an organization established to influence government, such as a political party or an interest group, they have an impact on government. In addition to providing entertainment, the media provide information about government and politics. This chapter focuses on the news media—the part of the media that delivers the news about government and politics.

The Media State

The media have developed and flourished to an extent the Founders could not have envisioned. As one political scientist noted, the media have become "pervasive . . . and atmospheric, an element of the air we breathe."[5] Without exaggeration, another observer concluded, "Ancient Sparta was a military state. John Calvin's Geneva was a religious state. Mid–nineteenth-century England was Europe's first industrial state, and the contemporary United States is the world's first media state."[6]

Americans spend more time being exposed to the media than doing anything else. In a year, according to one calculation, the average full-time worker puts in 1824 hours on the job, 2737 hours in bed, and 3256 hours exposed to the media (almost 9 hours a day).[7] Ninety-eight percent of American homes have a radio, and the same percentage have a television. For years, more homes had a television than had a toilet.[8] Almost 20 percent of children younger than two have a television in their bedroom; more than 40 percent of children between four and six do; and almost 70 percent of older children do. A third of children younger than six live in homes where the television is left on all or most of the time.[9] The average child (from eight years old on) or

adult watches television three hours a day.[10] By the time the average child graduates from high school, he or she has spent more time in front of the tube than in class.[11] By the time the average American dies, he or she has spent one-and-a-half years just watching television commercials.[12]

With the evolution in digital technology, such as the Internet, companies are working "to weave media and electronic communication into nearly every waking moment of our lives."[13] Already, kids and young adults expose themselves to multiple media simultaneously. One study found that eight- to eighteen-year-olds on average pack in eight-and-a-half hours of media in six-and-a-half hours of time. Up to a third of them say they pay attention to more than one medium "most of the time," usually music or television while using the computer.[14]

As Internet use has shot up, it has cut into family time more than anything else. Although the average Internet user spends 30 minutes less time watching television than before, he or she spends 70 minutes less time interacting with family members than before.[15]

The rest of this section will examine three continuing trends in journalism: the shifting dominance of various media, the increasing concentration of the media, and the increasing atomization of the media.

Dominance of the Media

For many years newspapers were the dominant medium. There were no "mass media" until the advent of broadcasting. Radio, which became popular in the 1920s, and television, which became popular in the 1950s, reached people who could not or would not read. Television especially became so central and influential in American life that one scholar speculated that the second half of the twentieth century will go down in history as "the age of television."[16]

As television grew in popularity, newspapers waned. People did not need their headlines anymore, and many people did not want their in-depth coverage either. Newspapers have struggled for readers and advertisers, and many have folded. Since 1960, more than 300 daily papers have disappeared.[17] Since 1970, the percentage of regular readers has declined (from 78 percent of adults to 42 percent).[18] The percentage of young adult regular readers has declined the most. (In 1966, 58 percent of first-year college students said "keeping up-to-date with political affairs" was an "essential" or "very important" goal. In 1998, only 26 percent held this view.)[19] Even after 9/11, which prompted a surge of interest in foreign affairs, readership continued to decline.[20]

For several decades the evening newscasts of the major networks—ABC, CBS, and NBC—replaced newspapers as the dominant medium for coverage of politics. However, the audience for the evening newscasts has declined with the rise of cable television, talk radio, and the Internet. (Since the mid-1990s, the percentage of regular viewers of the networks' evening newscasts has dropped from 60 percent to 34 percent.[21]) These other media allow people to get the news at different times and in various formats.

These trends will likely continue. Newspapers will lose more readers while television will lose its dominance and the Internet will gain new users.[22]

Today, different media appeal to different groups. Seniors read newspapers and watch the major networks' evening newscasts, whereas young adults are more likely to surf the Web. The cable networks attract the least educated, and news magazines, political magazines, and the Internet attract the most educated (see Table 1 and Figure 1). Conservatives tend to watch Fox television and listen to talk radio, whereas liberals tend to watch the Public Broadcasting System (PBS) and listen to National Public Radio (NPR).[23] Conservatives and liberals both scan the Web but favor different sites.

Concentration of the Media

Journalism is a big business, and it has become a bigger business in recent decades. First, small media organizations owned by local families or local companies were taken over by chains (owning multiple newspapers, radio stations, *or* television stations) or conglomerates (owning multiple newspapers, radio stations, *and* television stations). Then large media organizations were taken over by chains or conglomerates. Finally, chains and conglomerates were bought out by larger chains and conglomerates.

Seven huge companies—Time Warner, Viacom, News Corporation, Sony, General Electric, Bertelsmann, and Disney—form the top tier of media conglomerates. Time Warner, the largest, has over eighty thousand employees and $30 billion in annual revenues. It boasts 50 percent of the online business, 20 percent of the cable television business, 18 percent of the movie business, and 16 percent of the record business in the country. It also has 160 magazines, five publishing houses, and "Looney Tunes" cartoons.[24] Twenty other companies, which are major players in one or two types of the media, form a second tier of media conglomerates.[25] Their goal is to control the information and entertainment markets of the future. Media conglomerates want to offer all media—television stations, radio stations, newspapers, magazines, books, movies, records, and computer services—in various formats at all times of the day. Each conglomerate seeks to become the sole source of all your news and entertainment.

An early expectation for the Internet—that it would provide unlimited diversity and offer an alternative to established media—is already being dashed as powerful conglomerates are racing to swallow their competitors and influence the government to adopt policies that will lock in their advantage.[26]

This trend toward concentration of the media is certain to continue. It will provide much more convenience, at somewhat more cost, for consumers, but it

Table 1	Number of Years after Introduction to Attract Fifty Million Users

Medium	Years
Radio	38
Television	13
Internet	4

SOURCE: "Ticker," *Brill's Content,* March 1999, 128.

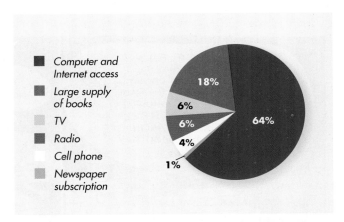

FIGURE 1 • **If you were stranded on a deserted island . . .** *and could take only one of the following with you, which would you take?* SOURCE: Asked of 1000 households with Internet access. IPSOS Insight U.S. Express Omnibus, August 2004, cited in "Primary Sources," *Atlantic Monthly,* January-February, 2005, 54.

will pose problems for a democracy that relies on the media to inform its citizens.

This trend already makes some problems apparent. The news comes from fewer sources than it used to. Although there are tens of thousands of media entities in the United States, the numbers are misleading. Chains and conglomerates own the television stations with most of the viewers, the radio stations with most of the listeners, and the newspapers and magazines with most of the readers.[27] One media analyst, referring to these chains and conglomerates, observed, "Two dozen profit-driven companies, owned and managed by billionaires operating in barely competitive markets, account for nearly the entirety of the U.S. media culture."[28] Just ten companies publish the newspapers that reach 51 percent of the readers.[29] Six companies broadcast to 42 percent of the radio audience, and five companies broadcast to 75 percent of the television audience.[30] Six companies have more than 80 percent of the cable television market. Four companies sell almost 90 percent of all music recordings, and six companies earn more than 90 percent of all film revenues.[31] One company controls over 70 percent of live music concerts in the country.[32]

Moreover, just one wire service—the Associated Press (AP)—supplies the international and national news for most newspapers. Only four television networks—ABC, CBS, NBC, and CNN—furnish the news for most television stations.

With fewer sources of news, there is a narrower range of views—less of a marketplace of ideas—than is healthy for a democracy. Instead, a small number of powerful people provide information and opinion—essentially, define reality—for the rest of the people.

These chains and conglomerates have begun to exercise their power through political activism and censorship. During the Iraq War, Clear Channel Communications, the largest radio chain with over twelve hundred stations nationwide, organized pro-war rallies in seven major cities.[33] Cumulus Media, the second largest radio chain, halted airplay of Dixie Chicks songs on its country stations after a member of the band criticized President Bush.[34] (Then NBC and the CW network refused to run commercials for a documentary about the group because the commercials included statements about the president.[35]) Comcast, the largest cable company, and CNN, owned by Time Warner, rejected peace groups' attempts to buy time for antiwar ads.[36] Sinclair Broadcast Group, the largest television chain with sixty-two stations, forbade its ABC affiliates from airing *Nightline* the night Ted Koppel read the names of military personnel killed in Iraq. The company said the show would "undermine" the war effort.[37] Two weeks before the presidential election, the company ordered its stations to broadcast a film in prime time accusing John Kerry of betraying American prisoners when he returned from Vietnam and testified against the war.[38] (The company modified this directive after intense criticism prompted some advertisers to pull their commercials, some viewers to threaten a boycott, some shareholders to vow a revolt, and its stock to plummet.) These instances, although relatively minor in themselves, are ominous signs for the future. It would be naive not to expect more attempts by media chains and conglomerates to flex their muscles.

In addition, the chains and conglomerates have exercised self-censorship when news coverage has threatened corporate interests. ABC killed a story that Disney, its owner, followed employment practices that allowed the hiring of convicted pedophiles at its parks.[39] NBC broadcast a report about defective bolts used in airplanes and bridges built by GE, its owner, and by other companies, but the references to GE were removed. When the president of NBC News complained about the removal and corporate interference in their newscasts, the boss of GE poked a finger in his chest and shouted, "You work for GE!"[40]

Another problem resulting from concentration of the media is financial pressure to reduce the quality of news coverage. News organizations are expected to

... IN THE INTEREST OF FULL DISCLOSURE, WE REMIND VIEWERS THAT THE COMPANY WHICH OWNS THIS NEWS OPERATION ALSO OWNS YOUR NEWSPAPER, THE RADIO STATION YOU LISTEN TO, ALL YOUR MAGAZINES, MOST OF THE COMPANIES WE REPORT ON, AS WELL AS SEVERAL BRANCHES OF GOVERNMENT AND SOME KEY ELECTED OFFICIALS ...

YOU HAVE TO ADMIRE THEIR CANDOR.

caglecartoons.com

match other divisions in their corporations and generate sizable profits each year. Corporate officers feel the heat from Wall Street analysts and major stockholders, who are more concerned with the value of the stock than the quality of the journalism. As a result, costs are cut—some reporters are let go, while others are shifted from time-consuming in-depth or investigative reporting to more superficial stories.[41] A reporter for a mid-size newspaper in Illinois admitted, "If a story needs a real investment of time and money, we don't do it anymore." He lamented, "Who the hell cares about corruption in city government, anyway?"[42]

Another problem resulting from concentration of the media is a decline of local news. When a train derailed in Minot, North Dakota, and released over 200,000 gallons of ammonia, authorities tried to notify residents to avoid the area and to stay indoors. But when police called the six local commercial radio stations, nobody answered. The stations were all owned and programmed by Clear Channel, based in San Antonio, Texas.[43] By the next day, three hundred people had been hospitalized, and pets and livestock had been killed.[44]

Atomization of the Media

Despite the increasing concentration of the media, a contrary trend—an atomization of the media—has also developed in recent decades. Whereas concentration has led to a national media, atomization has fragmented the influence of the national media. The major newspapers and broadcast networks have lost their dominance, and other media, some not even considered news organizations, have played a significant role in politics.

This trend is partly the result of technological changes, particularly the development of cable television and the Internet. Cable television, with a multiplicity of channels, can offer more specialization in programming. It can provide **narrowcasting** to appeal to small segments of the audience in contrast to major networks' **broadcasting** to appeal to the overall audience. For example, C-SPAN covers Congress on three channels and, unlike the networks, lingers on members' speeches and committees' hearings. Other national cable networks cater to blacks and Hispanics.[45] A cable system in Los Angeles and New York caters to Jews. A cable channel in California broadcasts in Chinese, one in Hawaii broadcasts in Japanese, and one in Connecticut and Massachusetts broadcasts in Portuguese. Stations in New York also provide programs in Greek, Hindi, Korean, and Russian.

Cable television can also offer twenty-four-hour news, as CNN, Fox, and MSNBC do.

The Internet features additional news sites. Major newspapers post their articles on websites before the papers themselves are delivered. Online "magazines" also address politics. During the congressional impeachment of President Clinton, one online magazine—*Salon*—revealed that the Republican representative spearheading the effort (Henry Hyde of Illinois) had had an adulterous relationship. Self-styled "journalists" even post their "news" as well. Matt Drudge offers political gossip on his own website, the Drudge Report, which originated in his one-bedroom apartment.[46]

The trend toward atomization of the media is also partly the result of the populist backlash against government officials and established journalists, perceived as "Washington insiders," that characterized American politics in the 1980s and 1990s. This is reflected in the popularity of radio talk shows. Many stations have such programs, and many people tune in.[47] Their numbers make talk radio a force in politics. Its middle-class audience acts as a national jury on governmental controversies. The populist backlash also is reflected in the increasing attention paid to fringe media by the public. In the 1992 presidential campaign, the *Star,* a supermarket tabloid, published allegations by Gennifer Flowers, a former nightclub singer, that she had had a twelve-year affair with Bill Clinton while he was governor of Arkansas. The major media hesitated to repeat the *Star's* story—they had nothing but scorn for the tabloids, which, they insisted, did not practice true journalism—but within days most gave in, under the pretense of debating the propriety of reporting personal matters. Flowers then appeared on *A Current Affair,* a syndicated television show, rated Clinton as a lover on a scale from 1 to 10, and sang "Stand by Your Man." Thus Flowers did not need to take her story to the major media; she got the tabloid media to tell it and pay her for it ($150,000 from the *Star* and $25,000 from *A Current Affair*).[48]

During the impeachment of President Clinton, Larry Flynt, the publisher of *Hustler* magazine, was offended by what he considered to be the hypocrisy of the president's adversaries. He offered to pay for information about any affairs that Republican leaders had. Ultimately, he published an article about an affair involving the Speaker of the House designate, Robert Livingston (R-La.). Although the article appeared only in his magazine, the revelation received publicity in other media and caused Livingston to resign.

Because the public pays attention to the fringe media more than it used to, politicians have begun to use these media. Instead of announcing their candidacy at a press conference, as politicians traditionally did, some have announced their candidacy on television talk shows. During the campaign, they have appeared on other television shows. Clinton played the saxophone on the *Arsenio Hall Show,* and Bush kissed the host on the *Oprah Winfrey Show.* Candidates swapped jokes with Jay Leno and David Letterman—and prayed they would not end up looking silly. All this blurs the line between politics and entertainment. When Senator Bill Bradley (Dem-N.J.), campaigning for the Democratic nomination for president, appeared at a Houston radio station that was ranked number one among men in the area, he expected to discuss his new book. Instead, the disc jockeys had two women disrobe from the waist up to report his reaction.[49]

Politicians have to be good sports, because people who pay little attention to political news do pay attention to these shows. Almost a third of adults said they get political information from late-night comedy shows; over a third of those under thirty said these shows are their *primary* source of political news.[50] So it may not be a joke when Letterman proclaims, "The road to the White House goes through me!" (But Letterman himself may be out of date, as young viewers pay more attention to Jon Stewart and Stephen Colbert than to Leno and Letterman.)

Because of the expanding role of fringe media, mainstream journalists envision a shrinking role for themselves. They no longer monopolize the market of political information; they no longer control the gates through which such information must pass.

This trend toward atomization of the media has significant implications beyond its impact on the established media and their professional journalists. Although this trend makes the news more accessible to more people, it also makes the news less factual, less reliable, and less analytical.

The proliferation of news outlets and the availability of newscasts around the clock create intense competition for news stories. The media have more space or time to fill than information to fill it. So they feel pressure to find new stories or identify new angles of old stories. In addition, they use talk shows that blend news, opinion, gossip, rumor, and speculation, because these shows are cheap to produce and, if the hosts and guests are provocative, entertaining for viewers. The media can fill their time and attract an audience. But the result is a commingling of facts and nonfacts. Then these facts and nonfacts are repeated by other organizations seeking to make sure that they are not left behind. In the rush to broadcast and publish, the media put less emphasis on assessing the accuracy of the content they disseminate than they used to. The "great new sin," a veteran reporter observed, is not being inaccurate but being boring.[51]

Interest groups exploit the competition among the media and aggravate the problem. In the 2004 presidential campaign, the "Swift Boat Veterans for Truth" ran a TV commercial charging that John Kerry had not deserved his medals from the Vietnam War. The "facts" alleged in the commercial apparently were false, and the commercial originally was run in only a few cities, but it had a whopping impact on the election. Its metamorphosis from a local ad to dominant news story illustrates how news often is disseminated today. The ad and the charges against John Kerry were first publicized by conservative bloggers who made no attempt to discern the truth of the charges by seeking official records or interviewing people who were actually there. Talk radio, dominated by conservatives, picked up the story. Radio commentators, whose staple is opinions about opinions, had no interest in discerning the truth of the charges either. Then Fox News, the generally Republican television network, publicized the ad, prompting MSNBC and CNN to do so too. Meanwhile, Bush contributors donated more money so the ad could be run nationally and frequently. Eventually, the mainstream media felt obligated to address it as well. Thus, the dishonest commercial became the major story of the campaign for a month and a major factor in the outcome of the election.[52] (However, if Kerry had responded more effectively, he might have defused its impact.)

The fringe media also aggravate the problem. Their goal is entertainment and their audience is politically unsophisticated, so these media are less careful about the accuracy of the information they disseminate. Some pay for stories, possibly encouraging people to lie for the money; many sensationalize stories, possibly distorting the truth. Although the mainstream media are also commercial enterprises subject to the pressures of the marketplace, they have a tradition to uphold. Reporters at major newspapers and broadcast networks often speak of their responsibility to follow journalistic standards, whereas members of the fringe media some-

"I just feel fortunate to live in a world with so much disinformation at my fingertips."

to calm me down. She held onto me, allowing me to place my leg on her shoulder as it was hanging free. . . . I thought that my face had been blown off, so I made the remark that I wouldn't be pretty again LOL. Of course the medics all rushed with reassurance which was quite amusing as I know what I look like now and I don't even want to think about what I looked like then.[57]

Similar to talk radio, blogs can act like "a lens, focusing attention on an issue until it catches fire."[58] Senate Majority Leader Trent Lott (R–Miss.), at a one-hundredth birthday party for Senator Strom Thurmond (R–S. C.) in 2002, made a remark seeming to praise Thurmond's past advocacy of racial segregation. Although the mainstream media ignored the remark, the blogs kept it alive until other media addressed it. Two weeks later, Lott resigned his leadership position.

Yet blogs can also perpetuate falsehoods. Blogs are free of the constraints of the mainstream media, such as objectivity and accountability. Bloggers have no editors or fact checkers—the layers of "review, revision, and correction" that the major media have.[59] So some blogs are pure hoakum—for example, that the U.S. government, rather than al Qaeda, destroyed the World Trade Center; that a cruise missile, rather than a hijacked jet, hit the Pentagon; and that United Flight 93 was shot down by an Air Force fighter, rather than forced down by its own passengers. And an increasing number of bloggers are partisan operatives who have been trained to engage in "guerrilla Internet activism" while presenting themselves as average people.[60] Their fealty to the truth may be far less than their passion for the cause. One falsely claimed that Barack Obama was educated at an Islamist madrassah (an Islamic school that teaches fundamentalist religious doctrine) as a child in Indonesia.

Meanwhile, the public is lost in this factual free-for-all. Most citizens are not well versed in the issues or very knowledgeable about the politicians. Without the help of professional journalists, many are not able to separate the blarney from the gospel truth when candidates and officials speak.

In sum, two opposite trends—concentration of the media and atomization of the media—are occurring. The key question is how much control the media con-

times reflect the views of radio talk show host Don Imus, who asserted, "The news isn't sacred to me. It's entertainment . . . designed to revel in the agony of others."[53] (Imus was fired in 2007 after making a racial slur about Rutgers University women basketball players, but his attitude about the news lives on in other hosts.)

The Internet aggravates the problem even more. Any person with a computer and a phone line can create an independent web log—a **blog**—to convey his or her information or views worldwide. Blogs are an alternative to mainstream journalism, serving as "the voice of the little guy" in a world of media giants.[54] Unlike "the sober, neutral drudges of the establishment press, the bloggers are class clowns and crusaders, satirists and scolds."[55] Some attract thousands or even hundreds of thousands of visitors per day. The most popular political blog—Daily Kos—has 600,000 readers each day, which is more than all but a handful of newspapers.[56]

About two hundred American soldiers in Iraq keep blogs, describing *their* war. "Sergeant Lizzie" described the result of a roadside bomb under her Humvee:

I started to scream bloody murder, and one of the other females on the convoy came over, grabbed my hand and started

glomerates will exercise and how much news and how many views will emerge through other outlets. Financial pressures are bearing down, and powerful corporations are trying to dominate the media business. In the future, the huge conglomerates likely will dominate more than they do now, while independent voices from the Internet will break through on issues that have a human interest angle.

Relationship between the Media and Politicians

"Politicians live—and sometimes die—by the press. The press lives by politicians," according to a former presidential aide. "This relationship is at the center of our national life."[61]

Although this relationship was not always so close—President Herbert Hoover once refused to tell a reporter whether he enjoyed a baseball game he attended[62]—politicians and journalists now realize that they need each other. Politicians need journalists to reach the public and to receive feedback from the public. They scan the major newspapers in the morning and the network newscasts in the evening. President Lyndon Johnson watched three network newscasts on three televisions simultaneously. (Presidents Ronald Reagan, who read mostly the comics, and George W. Bush, who reads mostly the sports section, are exceptions to the rule.)[63] In turn, journalists need politicians to cover government. They seek a steady stream of fresh information to fill their news columns and newscasts.

The close relationship between the media and politicians is both a **symbiotic relationship,** meaning they use each other for their mutual advantage, and an **adversarial relationship,** meaning they fight each other.

Symbiotic Relationship

President Johnson told individual reporters, "You help me, and I'll help make you a big man in your profession." He gave exclusive interviews and, in return, expected favorable coverage.

Reporters get information from politicians in various ways. Some reporters are assigned to monitor beats. Washington beats include the White House, Congress,

the Supreme Court, the State Department, the Defense Department, and some other departments and agencies. Other reporters are assigned to cover specialized subjects, such as economics, energy issues, and environmental problems, which are addressed by multiple departments or agencies.

The government has press secretaries and public information officers who provide reporters with ideas and information for stories. The number of these officials is significant; one year the Defense Department employed almost fifteen hundred people just to handle press relations.[64] The Bush White House employs over fifty.[65] The Department of Homeland Security has an entertainment liaison office to provide information to help moviemakers and, at the same time, get moviemakers to portray the department positively.[66]

The government supplies reporters with a variety of news sources, including copies of speeches, summa-

Henry Groskinsky, New York City

Because President Richard Nixon moved awkwardly—his gestures were out of sync with his words—he was not effective on television. He reminded some people of a marionette; one man made this doll for the president.

ries of committee meetings, news releases, and news briefings about current events. Officials also grant interviews, hold press conferences, and stage "media events." The vast majority of reporters rely on these sources rather than engage in more difficult and time-consuming investigative reporting.

Interviews

Interviews show the symbiotic nature of the relationship between reporters and politicians. During the early months of the Reagan presidency, *Washington Post* writer William Greider had a series of eighteen off-the-record meetings with budget director David Stockman. Greider recounted:

> *Stockman and I were participating in a fairly routine transaction of Washington, a form of submerged communication which takes place regularly between selected members of the press and the highest officials of government. Our mutual motivation, despite our different interests, was crassly self-serving. It did not need to be spelled out between us. I would use him and he would use me. . . . I had established a valuable peephole on the inner policy debates of the new administration. And the young budget director had established a valuable connection with an important newspaper. I would get a jump on the unfolding strategies and decisions. He would be able to prod and influence the focus of our coverage, to communicate his views and positions under the cover of our "off the record" arrangement, to make known harsh assessments that a public official would not dare to voice in the more formal setting of a press conference, speech, or "on the record" interview.[67]*

Leaks

Interviews can result in **leaks**—disclosures of information that officials want to keep secret. Others in the administration, the bureaucracy, or Congress use leaks for various reasons.

Officials in the administration might leak information about a potential policy—float a trial balloon—and then gauge the reaction to it without committing themselves in case it is shot down. As a result of bureaucratic infighting, officials might leak to prod the president or high-ranking official into taking some action[68] or to prevent the president or high-ranking official from taking some action. When President George W. Bush decided to appoint a Clinton administration attorney to be an antiterrorism adviser, Vice President Cheney's office leaked information to discredit the attorney and block the appointment.[69] (The attempt failed.)

Officials might leak to force public debates on matters that would otherwise be addressed behind closed doors. After Congress investigated the intelligence failures leading up to the terrorist attacks on September 11, 2001, someone leaked the information that the National Security Agency—the ultrasecret agency that engages in electronic surveillance around the world—had intercepted al-Qaeda messages on September 10 saying "Tomorrow is zero day" and "The match begins tomorrow" but had not translated the messages from Arabic until September 12.

Officials might leak to shift blame for mistakes or problems. When the Iraqi insurgency cast doubt upon our presumed victory in the Iraq War, officials apparently from the State Department leaked information suggesting that the Pentagon had rushed the country into war. Then officials apparently from the Pentagon leaked information claiming that the CIA had exaggerated the intelligence about Iraq's nuclear weapons program. Then officials apparently from the CIA leaked information indicating that the administration had distorted the intelligence about Iraq's weapons of mass destruction. Each group tried to absolve itself of the blame as the war turned sour.

Officials might leak to hurt an adversary. Diplomat Joseph Wilson was sent to Niger, which exports uranium, to investigate the possibility that Iraq had sought a type of uranium used in nuclear weapons. Wilson found no evidence to support the claim. Yet President Bush included the claim as a fact in his next State of the Union address, and others in the administration repeated it to persuade the public to support a war against Iraq. Breaking his silence, Wilson wrote an article in the *New York Times* maintaining that the administration had "twisted" the intelligence to "exaggerate" the threat. In retaliation, officials in the White House leaked the identity of Wilson's wife, Valerie Plame, who had worked for the CIA as an undercover spy.[70] Unmasking Plame effectively ended her career as a spy and jeopardized the operations she had established and contacts she had made in foreign countries.[71]

Officials might leak embarrassing information to help an ally or protect themselves. By leaking this information at a particular time or in a particular way, they can minimize the damage it would otherwise cause. So, officials leak embarrassing information during holidays or weekends, when the news receives less attention. They leak to small- or medium-size newspapers rather than to the *New York Times* or the *Washing-*

After diplomat Joseph Wilson (right) challenged an administration claim that Iraq had sought uranium for nuclear weapons, administration officials leaked the identity of his wife, Valerie Plame (left), who had been a CIA undercover agent.

Presidents as far back as George Washington have been enraged by leaks. Reagan said he was "up to my keister" in leaks, and Nixon established a "plumbers" unit to wiretap aides and plug leaks once they learned who was responsible. George W. Bush, embarrassed about leaks revealing that the CIA operates secret prisons in foreign countries and the National Security Agency (NSA) wiretaps American citizens who make phone calls to foreign countries, launched the most extensive crackdown since Nixon. FBI investigations and CIA polygraph tests targeted government employees considered possible sources for the reports, and the Justice Department warned media organizations of prosecution, under a 1917 statute, for revealing secret information.[76]

Leaks may serve the public by disclosing information that otherwise would not be available, but leaks would serve the public better if reporters explained the leakers' motives so the public could understand the bureaucratic or ideological conflict driving the story. Yet reporters are wary of antagonizing the leakers—their sources—for fear of not getting a story next time.

Leaks often enable reporters to break stories before their competitors can report them. Competition for these **scoops** is intense. During the 2004 presidential campaign, CBS showed a letter regarding George W. Bush's National Guard service. In its zeal for a scoop, CBS aired the story before verifying the authenticity of the letter.[77] It turned out that the letter had been forged and the network had been snookered, which proved highly embarrassing to CBS and costly to Dan Rather, who lost his anchor position.

ton Post because these influential papers dislike giving prominent play to stories broken by less prestigious papers.[72] After President George H.W. Bush nominated Clarence Thomas to the Supreme Court, an official in the Bush administration leaked the fact that Thomas had experimented with marijuana in college. The official's purpose was to inoculate Thomas from the greater controversy that could have occurred if the press had discovered and revealed this fact closer to the confirmation vote.[73]

Despite the common belief that leaks are from low-level employees of the opposite party, most are from high-ranking officials of the president's party. "The ship of state," one experienced reporter noted, "is the only kind of ship that leaks mainly from the top."[74] During the Vietnam War, President Johnson himself ordered an aide to leak the charge that steel companies were "profiteering" from the war. After an executive complained, Johnson assured him that "if I find out some damn fool aide did it, I'll fire the sonuvabitch!"[75] During the Iraq War, President Bush authorized an aide to leak classified information to counter mounting criticism about the administration's use of intelligence before the war.

Press Conferences

Press conferences also show the symbiotic nature of the relationship between reporters and politicians. Theodore Roosevelt, who was the first president to cultivate close ties to correspondents, started the **presidential press conference** by talking to reporters while getting shaved.[78] Franklin Roosevelt, who was detested by newspaper publishers, realized that the press conference could help him reach the public. He held fre-

"What do you want to know, boys?" President Franklin Roosevelt (front) holds a casual press conference in 1935.

quent informal sessions around his desk and provided a steady stream of news, which editors felt obligated to publish. This news publicized his policies at the same time that editors were ranting against them. John Kennedy saw that the press conference could help him reach the public more directly if he allowed the networks to televise it live.[79] Then editors could not filter his remarks.

As a result, presidents and their aides transformed the conference into a carefully orchestrated media show. Now an administration schedules a conference when it wants to convey a message. Aides identify potential questions, and the president rehearses appropriate answers. (Former press secretaries brag that they predicted at least 90 percent of the questions asked—and often the reporters who asked them.[80]) During the conference, the president calls on the reporters he wants. Although he cannot ignore those from the major news organizations, he can call on

others who he expects will lob soft questions. The George W. Bush administration even gave press credentials to a Republican operative posing as a real reporter so he would ask the questions the president wanted to answer.[81]

Beaming the conference to the nation results in less news than having a casual exchange around the president's desk, which used to reveal his thinking about policies and decisions. Appearing in millions of homes, the president cannot be as open and cannot allow himself to make a gaffe in front of the huge audience.

The transformation of the conference frustrates reporters and prompts them to act as prosecutors. As one press secretary observed, they play a game of "I gotcha."[82] Still, reporters value the conference. Editors consider the president's remarks news, so the conference helps reporters do their job. It also gives them a chance to bask in the limelight.

Media Events

"Media events" also show the symbiotic nature of the relationship between reporters and politicians. Staged for television, these events usually pair a photo opportunity with a speech to convey a strong impression of a politician's position on an issue.

The **photo opportunity** (often simply called a *photo op*) frames the politician against a backdrop that symbolizes the points the politician is trying to make. Photo ops for economic issues might use factories—bustling to represent success or abandoned to represent failure. The strategy is the same as that for advertisements of merchandise: Combine the product (the politician) with the symbols in the hope that the potential buyers (the voters) will link the two.[83] In the 1996 presidential campaign, Bob Dole, who was having trouble attracting young voters, arranged for a photo op at the Rock and Roll Hall of Fame rather than at, say, the Lawrence Welk Museum.

In the run-up to the 2004 presidential election, employees of the Homeland Security Department were told to provide one homeland security photo op a month as a way to link President Bush with 9/11 and the war on terrorism.[84]

Photo ops can be misleading. To persuade people that President Bush's tax cuts, which were designed primarily to benefit wealthy taxpayers, would help working Americans, the Speaker of the House, Dennis Hastert (R–Ill.), asked well-heeled lobbyists who favored the tax cuts to dress as construction workers and appear in photo ops featuring "a sea of hard hats" and signs proclaiming, "Tax Relief for Everyone." The lobbyists were urged to participate: "WE DO NEED BODIES—they must be DRESSED DOWN, appear to be REAL WORKER types, etc."[85] After Saddam Hussein's regime was overthrown during the Iraq War, his statue was pulled down by a crowd of joyous Iraqis in a spontaneous celebration. Or so it appeared. The incident convinced many Americans that the Iraqis were grateful for our presence. In reality, the incident was staged as a photo op by the American military. The statue, which was attached to a cable, was pulled down by a tank, and the Iraqis, who were transported to the square for the cameras, numbered only 30 to 40. A video that was taken from a distance revealed a more accurate version than the close-up that was shown on television screens.[86]

The speech at a media event is not a classical oration or even a cogent address with a beginning, middle, and

© Brooks Kraft/Corbis

After the initial phase of the Iraq War in May 2003, President Bush used the opportunity for a dramatic photo op designed for his reelection campaign. Landing a navy jet on an aircraft carrier off the California coast, he swaggered across the deck, sporting a flight suit and backslapping the sailors. Standing under a banner that proclaimed "Mission Accomplished," he (prematurely) announced the end of major combat in Iraq.

end. It is an informal talk that emphasizes a few key words or phrases or sentences—almost slogans, because television editors allot time only for a short **sound bite.** And the amount of time is less and less. In 1968, the average sound bite of a presidential contender on the evening news was about forty-two seconds, but in 1988 it was under ten seconds, and since then has dropped to less than eight seconds.[87]

Speechwriters plan accordingly. "A lot of writers figure out how they are going to get the part they want onto television," a former presidential aide explained. "They think of a news lead and write around it. And if the television lights don't go on as the speaker is approaching that news lead, he skips a few paragraphs and waits until they are lit to read the key part."[88] This approach does not produce coherent speeches, but the people watching on television won't know, and the few watching in person don't matter because they are just props.

Perhaps more than any other source of news, media events illustrate the reliance of politicians on television and of television on politicians. The head of CBS News said, "I'd like just once to have the courage to go on the air and say that such and such a candidate went to six cities today to stage six media events, none of which had anything to do with governing America."[89] Yet television fosters these events, and despite occasional swipes by correspondents, networks continue to show them.

Adversarial Relationship

Although the relationship between the media and politicians is symbiotic in some ways, it is adversarial in others. Since George Washington's administration, when conflicts developed between Federalists and Jeffersonians, the media have attacked politicians and politicians have attacked the media. During John Adams's administration, Federalists passed the Sedition Act of 1798, which prohibited much criticism of the government. Federalist officials used the act to imprison Jeffersonian editors. Later, President Andrew Jackson proposed a law to allow the government to shut down "incendiary" newspapers. Even now, a former press secretary commented, "there are very few politicians who do not cherish privately the notion that there should be some regulation of the news."[90]

The adversarial relationship stems from a fundamental difference in perspectives. Politicians use the media to persuade the public to accept their policies, so they want the media to act as conduits, conveying their messages, exactly as they deliver them, to the public. But journalists see themselves not as conduits for the politicians but as servants of the people in a democracy. They examine and question officials and policies so the public can learn more about them. According to one correspondent, "My job is not to say here's the church social with the apple pie, isn't it beautiful?"[91]

In contemporary society, information is power. To the extent that the administration controls the flow of information, it can achieve its policy goals. To the extent that the media disseminate contradictory information, they can ensure that these policy goals will be subject to public debate.

Inevitably, politicians fall short of their goals, and many blame the media for their failures. They confuse the message and the messenger, like Russian Tsar Peter the Great, who, when notified in 1700 that his army had lost a battle, promptly ordered the messenger strangled. When President Kennedy became upset by the *New York Times*'s coverage of Vietnam, he asked the paper to transfer its correspondent from Vietnam. (The *Times* refused.) When President Nixon became angry at major newspapers and networks, he had Vice President Spiro Agnew lash out at them. He also ordered the Department of Justice to investigate some for possible antitrust violations and the Internal Revenue Service to audit some for possible income tax violations. When aides to President George W. Bush read a *Washington Post* article questioning the truthfulness of the president's statements, they suggested that the reporter be removed from the White House beat. (The *Post* refused.[92])

However, it would be incorrect to think that the relationship between the media and politicians is usually adversarial. Normally, it is symbiotic. Although journalists like to think of themselves as adversaries who stand up to politicians, most of them rely on politicians most of the time.[93]

Yet the relationship has become more adversarial since the Vietnam War and the Watergate scandal fueled cynicism about government's performance and officials' honesty.[94] Many reporters, according to the editor of the *Des Moines Register*, "began to feel that no journalism is worth doing unless it unseats the mighty."[95] New reporters especially began to feel this way. Senator Alan Simpson (R–Wyo.) asked the daughter of old friends what she planned to do after graduating from journalism school. "I'm going to be one of the hunters," she replied. When he asked, "What are you going to hunt?" she answered, "People like you!"[96]

In response, politicians, fearing that they will say something that will be used against them, have restricted reporters' access. In turn, reporters, worrying that they will not get the information they need to do their job, have complained that politicians are not accessible. During the George W. Bush presidency, one lamented, "The idea of a truly open press conference, an unscripted political debate, a leisurely and open . . . conversation between political leaders, or even a one-on-one interview between a member of the press and an undefended politician had become almost quaint in conception."[97] (See the box "He Wasn't a Straight Shooter.")

At the same time, politicians have become more sophisticated in their efforts to **spin** the media—to portray themselves and their programs in the most favorable

When Vice President Cheney accidentally shot a fellow hunter on a Texas ranch, neither he nor his staff nor the White House reported it to the press. The next day, the ranch's owner reported it to the local newspaper. Despite the media's demands for statements or interviews, the vice president refused to respond for four more days. The White House tried to shift the spotlight from the vice president, claiming the accident was the victim's fault. Finally, Cheney agreed to an interview with Republican-friendly Fox news.[1]

Comedians had a field day using the vice president as a punch line. Jay Leno on *The Tonight Show with Jay Leno,* NBC: "I'm surprised Dick Cheney loves to hunt so much. The five times the government tried to give him a gun, he got a deferment." Jimmy Kimmel on *Jimmy Kimmel Live,* ABC: "Kind of a sad study out today that single women over the age of 35 are more likely to be shot by the vice president than find a husband."

Why all the jokes? Why such media clamor? This incident resembles previous incidents in which the media seemed to make a mountain out of a molehill. Vice President Dan Quayle, appearing in a grade-school class for a photo op, misspelled the word "potato." President Jimmy Carter, fishing in Georgia, shooed away a swamp rabbit approaching his boat and gnashing its teeth. This led to stories about the "killer rabbit." Although these incidents themselves were truly minor, they reflected shortcomings already perceived by reporters and people. The Quayle incident reflected doubts about the "Veep's" smarts, and the Carter incident reflected conclusions about the administration's haplessness.[2] These spontaneous and comprehensible incidents brought "all the abstractions together into one concrete image."[3]

Although Vice President Cheney's reluctance to report and acknowledge the shooting may have been due simply to his personal anguish, the merciless jokes reflected the journalists' beliefs that the vice president, and administration foreign policies for which he has been a driving force, are secretive, arrogant, and even incompetent. So the incident—a poor decision, which led to an unfortunate result, which was not acknowledged until the outcry became too great—stands in for aspects of the war on terrorism and the war in Iraq. And it represents the journalists' feelings that the vice president, though a good shot, hasn't been a straight shooter.

[1]Vice President Cheney's standard contract for public appearances stipulates that the temperature be set at 68 degrees; an array of diet sodas be available; and any televisions be pre-tuned to Fox News. *Wait, Wait, Don't Tell Me,* NPR, March 25, 2006.
[2]Mark Z. Barabak, "Political Blunders Crumble Careers," *Lincoln Journal Star,* February 20, 2006, A7.
[3]Psychologist Anthony Pratkanis, quoted in ibid.

light, regardless of the facts, and to shade the truth. Politicians' spin prompts reporters to become more cynical. "They don't explicitly argue or analyze what they dislike in a political program but instead sound sneering and supercilious about the whole idea of politics."[98] Reporters' cynicism then prompts politicians to escalate their efforts to spin the media, which prompts reporters to escalate their comments that politicians are insincere or dishonest. And so the cycle continues.

After Vice President Al Gore announced his candidacy for president in 2000 from his family's farm in Carthage, Tennessee, ABC correspondent Diane Sawyer conducted an interview reflecting these dynamics. She began, "Are you really a country boy?" He replied, "I grew up in two places. I grew up in Washington, D.C. [as the son of a senator from Tennessee], and I grew up here. My summers were here. Christmas was here." Sawyer taunted Gore, "You mucked pigpens?" Gore answered, "I cleaned out the pigpens . . . and raised cattle and planted and plowed and harvested and took in hay." Sawyer, not satisfied, challenged Gore in an attempt to show that he was a hypocrite: "I have a test for you. Ready for a pop quiz? . . . How many plants of tobacco can you have per acre? . . . What is brucellosis? . . . What are cattle prices roughly now? . . . When a fence separates two farms, how can you tell which farm owns the fence?" By announcing from his family's farm, Gore was trying to convey his rural roots; by interviewing him in this manner, Sawyer was trying to question his sincerity.[99]

The increasingly adversarial relationship is also due to other factors mentioned earlier in the chapter. There are so many media, with so much space to fill, that they have a voracious appetite for news and a strong incentive to compete against each other for something "new." As a result, they often magnify trivial things. And because the fringe media now play a more prominent role, and because their stories eventually appear in the mainstream media, all media pay more attention to politicians' personal shortcomings with sex, drugs, and alcohol and raise more questions about politicians' "character" than they ever used to.[100] In 1977, one of every two hundred stories on network newscasts was about a purported scandal; in 1997 (*before* the Monica Lewinsky affair was revealed), one of every seven stories was.[101]

After 9/11, reporters were sensitive to, and even intimidated by, the public's fear and anger from the terrorist attacks and its vocal support for the Iraq War. Consequently, reporters relaxed their stance. But they became more adversarial again when the American victory evaporated during the Iraqi insurgency.

Yet the apparent toughness usually is "a toughness of demeanor" rather than a toughness of substantive journalism.[102] Reporters exhibit tough attitudes rather than conduct thorough investigations and careful analyses. In fact, few engage in investigative journalism.[103] Before hurricane Katrina, reporters failed to notice that the Federal Emergency Management Administration (FEMA) was headed by political hacks rather than by people experienced in disaster response. Nor did reporters question why a study found that employees' morale at FEMA was lower than that at any other federal agency.[104] Before the coal mine accidents in 2006, reporters failed to examine the impact of significant changes in mine safety regulations and enforcement by the Bush administration.[105]

Relationship between the Media and Recent Administrations

Franklin Roosevelt created the model that most contemporary presidents use to communicate with the public. Newspaper publishers, who were conservative businessmen, had no use for Roosevelt and his policies. In fact, a correspondent recalled, "The publishers didn't just disagree with the New Deal. They hated it. The reporters, who liked it, had to write as though they hated it too."[106] Recognizing that he would not receive favorable coverage, Roosevelt realized that he would have to reach the public another way. He used press conferences to provide a steady stream of news about his policies. He also used radio talks, which he called **fireside chats,** to advocate his policies and reassure his listeners in the throes of the Depression. He had a fine voice and a superb ability to speak informally—he talked about his family, even his dog. He drew such an audience that he was offered as much airtime as he wanted (though he was shrewd enough to realize that too much would result in overexposure). This tactic enabled him to avoid the filters of reporters and editors and to take his case directly to the people.[107]

In addition, Roosevelt was the first president to seek systematic feedback from the people. He used public opinion polls to gauge people's views toward his policies. Thus for him, communication was a two-way process—to the people and from the people.

Reagan Administration

Ronald Reagan refined the model. As a young man, Reagan idolized Roosevelt, even developing an imitation with an appropriate accent and a cigarette holder.[108] As president, Reagan duplicated Roosevelt's success in using the media. Although Reagan's command of the facts about his proposals and government programs was uncertain, his ability to convey his broad themes was uncanny. Reporters dubbed him the "Great Communicator."

As Roosevelt used radio, Reagan used television. By the time he reached the White House, after a career as an actor in movies and television, Reagan had mastered the art of speaking and performing in front of live audiences and on camera.[109] Tall, handsome, and poised, he knew exactly how to use an inflection, a gesture, or a tilt of his head to keep all eyes and ears focused on him. His speeches and even his casual comments were highly effective.

His aides knew how to make his appearances especially impressive. The administration knew that the media would cover the president extensively to fill their news columns and newscasts. An aide explained the strategy: "The media, while they won't admit it, are not in the news business; they're in entertainment. We tried to create the most entertaining, visually attractive scene to fill that box [the TV screen], so that the networks would have to use it."[110]

Aides sent advance agents days or weeks ahead of the president to prepare the "stage" for media events—the specific location, backdrops, lighting, and sound equipment. A trip to Korea was designed to show "the commander in chief on the front line against communism." An advance man went to the demilitarized zone separating North and South Korea and negotiated with the

News photo of President Reagan in Korea, staged to reflect "American strength and resolve."

Army and Secret Service for the most photogenic setting. He demanded that the president be allowed to use the most exposed bunker, which meant that the army had to erect telephone poles and string thirty thousand yards of camouflage netting to hide Reagan from North Korean sharpshooters. The advance man also demanded that the Army build camera platforms on a hill that remained exposed but offered the most dramatic angle to film Reagan surrounded by sandbags. Although the Secret Service wanted sandbags up to Reagan's neck, the advance man insisted that they be no more than four inches above his navel so viewers would get a clear picture of the president wearing his flak jacket and demonstrating "American strength and resolve."[111]

The Reagan administration also developed the technique of highlighting a single theme with a single message for every day and every week to emphasize whatever proposal the president was pushing at the time. The administration then arranged the president's appearances and offered the media information that would reinforce the message. Aides strictly controlled the president. They determined "the line of the day" and instructed him on what to say. They also instructed him not to answer reporters' questions about other matters. They didn't want other remarks to overshadow the message of the day. The strategy was to set the agenda rather than letting the media set it.[112]

By alternately using and avoiding the media, President Reagan's administration managed the news more than any previous administration.

Clinton Administration

In his use of the media, **Bill Clinton** emulated Roosevelt and Reagan. Like Roosevelt, he tried to leapfrog journalists to reach citizens directly.[113] Like Reagan, he tried to focus on one issue at a time to shape public opinion on that issue.

Clinton was knowledgeable about policies, perhaps the most knowledgeable president ever, and he was articulate when speaking. Unlike Roosevelt and Reagan, however, Clinton was not enthralling. He lacked discipline, talking too long and giving too many details for most listeners. He strayed from his message of the day or the week, blurring his focus. Consequently, many people said they didn't know what he wanted to do. Yet Clinton was empathetic, conveying the feeling that he cared for others, so many people said they thought he understood the problems of people like them.

Clinton was especially effective one-on-one with reporters because of his knowledge and his charm. One network correspondent who was not a supporter said, "He is the most charming man I have ever met."[114]

But Clinton inspired visceral hatred from some opponents even before he set foot in the White House. Perhaps it was because he represented the excesses of the baby boom generation, having engaged in sexual affairs and drug use, or because his independent-minded wife, Hillary, reflected the nontraditional gender roles of that generation. Or perhaps it was because his election cast doubt on conservatives' expectations that Republicans had a lock on the White House and would continue the "Reagan revolution." For whichever reason, some conservative commentators, interest groups, and congressional investigators made a concerted effort from the outset of his administration to undermine his presidency. They magnified minor miscues into major scandals and fed accusations and rumors, some completely unfounded, to reporters.[115] News organizations allowed themselves to be manipulated by Clinton's opponents because, due to the atomization of the media, they were competing with other organizations. They aired charges before verifying them because other organizations, including fringe media, had done so or would do so if given a chance. Also, as one reporter later acknowledged, "There's no denying that we give more coverage to stories when someone is shouting."[116] So Clinton faced a hostile press from the start.[117]

As investigations into the Whitewater land deal, revelations about the president's personal life, and concerns about his party's fundraising prompted ethical questions, they dominated the news and hindered his efforts to convey his messages and accomplish his goals. The Clintons became bitter toward the media, and reporters became cynical toward the administration. They thought Clinton did not tell the truth or at least did not leave an accurate impression; they considered him "a master of lawyerly evasion."[118] So they looked for falsity or hypocrisy behind his actions and statements.

George W. Bush Administration

The **George W. Bush** administration has emulated the Reagan administration in trying to manage the news by alternately using and avoiding the media.

Aides establish a message for every day and e-mail talking points to administration officials, instructing them to address these ideas. The president voices the message at his appearances, and backdrops bearing the message printed as a slogan reinforce it. Administration officials who are contacted by the press repeat it. All are expected to "stay on message."

Otherwise, access to the president and White House officials is strictly limited. The president is made available for speeches to friendly audiences or for a few questions from a few reporters at the White House. Press conferences are rarely scheduled. Bush has held far fewer conferences than other modern presidents.[119] Interviews are occasionally granted, but questions must be submitted in advance. Reporters who displease the administration are punished by losing their access.[120] When veteran reporter Helen Thomas of the Associated Press displeased the president, he refused to answer her questions at press conferences for three years.[121] As a result of this process, according to President Reagan's communications aide, "this is the most disciplined White House in history."[122]

When the president attended a meeting in Ireland, an Irish reporter who had submitted questions in advance was dissatisfied when the president answered in generalities. She interrupted him and pressed him for more specific answers. Her behavior was so unusual that it became a news story. Unlike most American reporters, she did not worry about future access to the White House.

The administration's communications strategy also entails a very active and well-financed public relations machine. The administration contracts with public relations firms and advertising agencies to produce pseudo news reports, purporting to be actual news stories, which portray the administration as vigilant and compassionate.[123] These are distributed to television stations around the country, which integrate them into their newscasts. To viewers, they appear to be news rather than propaganda. In a two-and-a-half-year period, seven cabinet departments spent $1.6 billion on 343 public relations contracts for news releases and other services.[124] The administration even paid some real reporters to say positive things about the administration's policies.

President Bush is not comfortable in front of television cameras. Initially, he shunned the role of "communicator in chief." When aides scheduled public appearances, he bristled.[125] When he gave formal speeches or made informal remarks, he often looked awkward and sounded inarticulate. Reporters observed that he was "perhaps the least confident public performer of the modern presidency."[126] An aide to the previous president commented, "In the Clinton administration, we worried the president would open his zipper, and in the Bush administration, they worry the president will open his mouth."[127] As governor of Texas, Bush had worked behind the scenes and evidently expected to do the same as president.

The terrorist attacks thrust Bush into the public role he had avoided. Although he failed to return to the White House on September 11 to reassure Americans from the Oval Office,[128] later he visited the site of the World Trade Center and galvanized public support when he picked up a bullhorn and talked to the workers. Gradually, he grew into his new role, appearing more comfortable on the national stage. Converting "grief to anger to action,"[129] he rallied the public behind the war on terrorism and the war in Afghanistan.

Bush's strength is to speak to moral clarity. The terrorist attacks allowed Bush to talk in these terms. But September 11 was "one of history's rare unnuanced days," a presidential adviser admitted.[130] On other issues, where there is less moral clarity, such as the clash between Israelis and Palestinians, Bush is less effective. His black-and-white view of the world and his "poverty of language"[131] make it difficult for him to convey any nuances in his comments. (He told one senator, "I don't do nuance."[132]) On these issues, he can seem simpleminded, and he has sent confusing and contradictory messages to the public and to foreign countries affected by our policies.

Bush's speechwriters are quite good at expressing his ideals and very effective in communicating with his supporters. They incorporate religious language to appeal to evangelical Christians.[133] In addition to references to *evil* and *evildoers,* there are terms, such as *work of mercy* and *wonder-working power,* that are recognized by the devout. When the president announced the invasion of Afghanistan, his speech included allusions to Revelation, Isaiah, Job, Matthew, and Jeremiah.[134] The president, however, did spur a backlash in the United States and abroad when he called the war on terrorism a *crusade,* thus linking it to the Crusades by European Christians against Eastern Muslims in the Middle Ages.

Although his formal speeches are good, Bush tends to stumble when he speaks without a script. At times he forgets his train of thought, makes up words, and leaves listeners bewildered.[135] But his lack of polish didn't seem to hurt him in the polls, at least until his policies became unpopular. He talks like many men, in his tone and simple words—even the belligerence in his voice— and thus relates well to many voters. Sounding like a frontier sheriff in the Wild West, he declared that Osama bin Laden was "wanted, dead or alive." When Iraqi insurgents began to use roadside bombs against American soldiers, Bush threatened, "Bring 'em on." While some people were appalled by such comments, others liked the swagger in his delivery and the confidence in his gestures, at least until his policies led the country into a quagmire in Iraq. Then the swagger and confidence began to ring hollow. One observer calls Bush "a master of the American vernacular, that form of expression which eschews slickness and makes a virtue of the speaker's limitations."[136]

Relationship between the Media and Congress

Members of Congress also use the media but have less impact. They hire their own full-time press secretaries, who churn out press releases, distribute television tapes, and arrange interviews with reporters.[137] The Senate and House of Representatives provide recording studios for members and allow television cameras into committee rooms and C-SPAN into the chambers. Yet members still have trouble attracting the media's eye. One president can be the subject of the media's focus, but 535 members of Congress cannot. Only a handful of powerful (or, occasionally, colorful) members receive coverage from the national media. Other members get attention from their home-state or district media, but those from large urban areas with numerous representatives get little publicity or scrutiny even there.[138]

Congressional committees also use the media to influence public opinion. During the Whitewater hearings, President Clinton talked with a Republican senator on the investigating committee. "They were impugning Hillary," he recalled, "and I asked this guy, 'Do you really think my wife and I did anything wrong in this Whitewater thing?' He just started laughing. He said, 'Of course you didn't do anything wrong. That's not the point. The point of this is to make people think you did something wrong.' "[139]

Relationship between the Media and the Supreme Court

Unlike presidents and members of Congress, justices of the Supreme Court shun the media. They rarely talk to reporters, and they also forbid their law clerks from talking to the press. They try to convey the impression that they are not engaged in politics and therefore should not answer reporters' questions or concern themselves with public opinion.

As a result, the media do not cover the Supreme Court nearly as much as the presidency or Congress. Few newspapers have a full-time Court reporter; no newsmagazines or television networks do. In one recent year, only twenty-seven reporters had Court press credentials, whereas an estimated seventeen hundred reporters had White House press credentials.[140]

When the media do cover the Supreme Court, they focus on the Court's rulings.[141] They seldom investigate or peer behind the Court's curtains. They often ignore even relevant concerns, such as questions about the justices' health. Most reporters on this beat, called "Washington's most deferential press corps,"[142] reject the role of watchdog. Consequently, the justices are shielded from both the legitimate investigation and the excessive scrutiny that officials in the other branches are subjected to.

Bias of the Media

Every night, Walter Cronkite, former anchor for *CBS Evening News,* signed off by saying, "And that's the way it is," implying that the network held a huge mirror to the world and returned a perfect reflection to its viewers, without selection or distortion. But the media do not hold a mirror. They hold a searchlight that seeks and illuminates some things instead of others.[143]

From all the events that occur in the world every day, the media can report only a handful as the news of the day. Even the fat *New York Times,* whose motto is "All the News That's Fit to Print," cannot include all the news. The media must decide what events are newsworthy. They must decide where to report these—on the front page or at the top of the newscast, or in a less prominent position. Then they must decide how to report them. When the Wright brothers invited reporters to Kitty Hawk, North Carolina, to observe the first airplane flight in 1903, none considered it newsworthy enough to cover. After the historic flight, only seven American newspapers reported the flight, and only two reported it on their front page.[144]

In making these decisions, it would be natural for journalists' attitudes to affect their coverage. As one acknowledged, a reporter writes "from what he hears and sees and how he filters it through the lens of his own experience. No reporter is a robot."[145]

Political Bias

Historically, the press has been politically biased. The first papers, which were established by political parties, parroted the party line. Even the independent papers that succeeded them advocated one side or the other. The attitudes of publishers, editors, and reporters seeped—sometimes flooded—into their prose.

But the papers gradually abandoned their ardor for editorializing and adopted the **practice of objectivity** to attract and retain as many readers as possible. This means that in news stories (not in editorials or columns) they try to present the facts rather than their opinions. When the facts are in dispute, they try to present the positions of both sides. They are reluctant to evaluate these positions. Even when one side makes a false or misleading assertion, they are hesitant to notify their readers. Instead, they rely upon the other side to do so. They hope that their readers can discern which is accurate.

Although most mainstream media today follow the practice of objectivity, the public still thinks the press is biased. Many people think the press is "out to get" the groups they identify with. Executives believe the press is out to get businesses, and laborers believe it is out to get unions. Conservatives believe the press is biased against conservatives, and liberals believe it is biased against liberals. Republicans believe the press is biased against Republicans, and Democrats believe it is biased against Democrats.[146]

Indeed, the public is more critical today, when most media at least attempt to be objective, than in the past, when the media did not even pretend to be. Back then, citizens could subscribe to whichever local paper reflected their own biases. Now, as local newspapers and television stations have given way to national newspapers and networks, and as independently owned newspapers and television stations have given way to large chains and conglomerates, people have less opportunity to follow only those media that reflect their views. People with strong views are disappointed with this more balanced coverage. So partisans on both sides criticize the same media for being biased—though in opposite directions.

To assess the presence and the direction of **political bias,** it is necessary to examine the differences in coverage by the advocacy media and the mainstream media; the differences in coverage of elections and issues; and the differences in coverage of domestic policies and international policies.

Bias in the Advocacy Media

Some media do not try to be neutral. Advocacy media intentionally tilt one way or the other and seek an audience of people who share their views. Advocacy media can be found at both ends of the political spectrum, though far more are conservative than liberal.

Because conservatives perceived a liberal bias in the mainstream media, they established their own media in the 1980s and 1990s. This vocal complex includes newspapers, such as the *Wall Street Journal* (editorial page), the *Washington Times,* and the *New York Post,* various magazines, numerous radio and television talk shows and Internet websites, plus a network of columnists, commentators, and think tanks. These journalists, seeing themselves as part of an ideological movement, as members of the same team, are unabashedly conservative.

Their role in talk radio has been especially powerful. The rise of talk radio began in the 1980s when the daytime television audience was mostly female and the daytime radio audience was mostly male, and a gender gap emerged in political preferences, with men becoming more conservative and women remaining more liberal. At the same time, a backlash grew against feminism and affirmative action among middle-class and lower-middle-class whites. Many stations decided to capture these listeners by airing their views.[147]

Today, more than thirteen hundred talk stations fill the airwaves, and more than a fifth of American adults consider talk radio their primary source for news.[148] The vast majority of talk shows are hosted by conservative commentators,[149] such as Rush Limbaugh, Sean Hannity, Bill O'Reilly, G. Gordon Liddy,[150] Oliver North, and numerous others. The Republican National Committee, in fact, has a Radio Services Department that provides talking points to these hosts every day so that they will reinforce the message from the Bush White House.[151] According to one analysis, 91 percent of the talk on the 257 news/talk stations owned by the top five conglomerates was conservative; only 9 percent was liberal.[152]

The conservative advocacy media also include the Fox News Channel. Fox is the first major network to *narrowcast*—intentionally appeal to a narrow segment of the entire audience—rather than broadcast.[153] Owned by a conservative media mogul and operated by a former Republican consultant, Fox appeals to conservatives disenchanted with the mainstream media.[154] It presents a skewed lineup of commentators and guests, featuring prominent conservatives with strong personalities paired with relatively unknown liberals with relatively weak personalities. Fox also follows the talking points from the Republican National Committee. After years of critical coverage of President Clinton, Fox offered fawning coverage of President Bush (criticizing him only after the failures in the Iraq War became obvious).

Throughout its programming, the network blurs the distinction between news and commentary. For instance, when reporting on a proposal by President Bush to cut taxes, the network ran a line along the bottom of the screen urging, "Cut 'em already."[155] When reporting on Swiss protesters against the Iraq War, an anchor referred to the demonstrators as "hundreds of knuckleheads." Another referred to France, which opposed the war, as a member of the "axis of weasels." The network then ran that phrase along the bottom of the screen when reporting about France. Fox aired relentlessly upbeat coverage of the Iraq War. Its correspondents were urged to downplay American casualties. (A memo from a senior executive instructed: "Do not fall into the easy trap of mourning the loss of U.S. lives.") They were also told to refer to Marine snipers as "sharpshooters," because the word *snipers* has a negative connotation. And all along, the network questioned the patriotism of liberals and critics of the war.[156] When apparent progress in the war deteriorated, Fox scaled back its coverage rather than report the shortcomings and failures.[157] Not until numerous conservatives began to criticize the war did Fox air critical views. Fox launched a crusade against the supposed "War on Christmas" in 2005, criticizing businesses and individuals who wished folks "Happy Holidays" instead of "Merry Christmas." It broadcast fifty-eight segments in one five-day period.[158]

A former Fox correspondent said it was common to hear producers remind them, "We have to feed the core"—that is, their conservative viewers.[159] Yet the network retains a veneer of neutrality. It claims to be "fair and balanced" and "spin free." The marketing strategy is to attract viewers by offering them conservative commentary but also the reassurance that this commentary is truth rather than opinion.[160]

The conservative media also include Christian radio networks, television organizations, and more than thirteen hundred radio and television stations.[161] These media address political issues as well as spiritual matters.

Although liberals have as many magazines and Internet websites, the only advocacy media they dominate are documentary films.[162] For example, Michael Moore's films, such as *Fahrenheit 9/11,* also offer a combination of facts, opinions, and speculation, though from the left rather than the right.

Bias in the Mainstream Media

Although the advocacy media are far more slanted, allegations of bias are leveled against the mainstream media far more often. Conservative groups and commentators, especially, claim that these media are biased toward liberal candidates and policies.[163]

Journalists for the mainstream media are not very representative of the public. They are disproportionately college-educated white males from the upper middle class. They are disproportionately urban and secular, rather than rural and religious, and they are disproportionately Democrats or independents leaning to the Democrats, rather than Republicans or independents leaning to the Republicans. Likewise, they are disproportionately liberals rather than conservatives.[164]

Journalists who work for the most influential organizations—large newspapers, wire services, newsmagazines, and radio and television networks—are more likely to be Democrats and liberals than those who work for less prominent organizations—small newspapers and radio and television stations.[165] Journalists in the most influential organizations are more likely than the public to support the liberal position on issues. At the same time, they support capitalism and do not think that our institutions "need overhaul."[166] Thus, they are not extremely liberal.

Focusing on journalists' backgrounds and attitudes assumes that these color journalists' coverage. But several factors mitigate the effect of these traits. Most journalists chose their profession not because of a commitment to an ideology, but because of the opportunity to rub elbows with powerful people and be close to exciting events. "Each day brings new stories, new dramas in which journalists participate vicariously."[167] As a result, most journalists "care more about the politics of an issue than about the issue itself,"[168] so they are less likely to express their views about the issue. In addition, mainstream organizations pressure journalists to muffle their views because of a conviction that it is professional to do so and also a desire to avoid the headaches that could arise otherwise—debates among their staffers, complaints from their audience, perhaps even complaints from the White House or Congress.[169] Some organizations fear public perceptions of reporters' bias so much that they restrict reporters' private lives, forbidding any political activity, even outside the office and on their own time.[170]

For these reasons, mainstream media do not exhibit nearly as much political bias toward candidates or policies as would be expected from journalists' backgrounds and attitudes.

To measure bias, researchers use a technique called content analysis. They scrutinize newspaper and television stories to determine whether there was an unequal amount of coverage, unequal use of favorable or unfavorable statements, or unequal use of a positive or negative tone. They consider insinuating verbs ("he conceded" rather than "he said") and pejorative adjectives ("her weak response" rather than "her response"), and for television stories, they evaluate the announcers' nonverbal communication—voice inflection, eye movement, and body language.

Bias in Elections

Researchers have examined media coverage of presidential campaigns the most and have found relatively little bias. The media typically gave the two major candidates equal attention, and they usually avoided any favorable or unfavorable statements in their news stories. They typically provided diverse views in editorials and columns, with some commentary slanting one way and other commentary slanting the opposite way. The authors of a study examining forty-six newspapers concluded that American newspapers are "fairly neutral."[171]

Other studies have reached similar conclusions about various media.[172] An analysis of the data from fifty-nine studies found no significant bias in newspapers, a little (pro-Republican) bias in newsmagazines, and a little (pro-Democratic) bias on television networks.[173]

Overall, there is less bias than the public believes or the candidates feel. When candidates complain, they are usually objecting to bad news or are trying to manipulate the media. The strategy is to put reporters on the defensive so that they will go easier on the candidate or harder on the opponent in the future, just as sports coaches "work the refs" over officiating calls.

Yet the way in which the media cover campaigns can have different implications for different candidates. The media report the facts that one candidate is leading while the other is trailing, that one campaign is surging while the other is slipping. "We all respond like Pavlov's dogs to polls," an experienced correspondent explained.[174] This coverage has positive implications for those who are leading or surging—swaying undecided voters, galvanizing campaign workers, and attracting financial contributions—and negative implications for those who are trailing or slipping. Such coverage does not benefit one party over the other party in election after election, but it can benefit one party's candidate over the other party's candidate in a particular election.[175] People who support the losers consider such reporting biased. Journalists, however, consider it simply a reflection of reality.

Another habitual practice has different implications for different candidates. The press pays more attention to minor things that are easy to report—and easy to ridicule—than to substantive issues that are difficult to explain.[176] Hence the voluminous coverage about President Clinton's sexual affairs. Although reporters are willing to criticize or even ridicule candidates about minor matters, they are usually reluctant to challenge them on substantive issues. Doing so would require more knowledge about substantive policies or more nerve to draw conclusions about these policies than most reporters have.

Likewise, when covering presidential debates, the press pays more attention to style and tactics than to substantive issues—more attention to how something was said than to what was said.[177] Reporters act more like theater critics than helpful guides to confused voters. These practices do not reflect bias by reporters as much as they reflect superficiality in reporting.

There are two exceptions to the generalization that overt political bias in elections is minimal. First, the media usually give short shrift to third-party candidates.[178] Ralph Nader, who first ran for president in 2000, was well known and held views partly shared by numerous voters, but he received scant coverage. When he held enthusiastic rallies on college campuses and in large coliseums, the national media virtually ignored them. Only when the election between Gore and Bush tightened and it appeared that Nader might be a spoiler did the national media pay attention. Then they focused on his potential as a spoiler rather than on his views that had attracted the crowds.[179]

Second, newspapers traditionally print editorials and columns that express opinions. In editorials before elections, papers endorse candidates. Most owners are Republican, and many influence the editorials. Since the first survey in 1932, more papers have endorsed the Republican presidential candidate, except in the elections of 1964, 1992, and 2004, when Kerry edged Bush in endorsements—212 to 199.[180]

Bias against All Candidates and Officials

Some critics charge that a general bias exists against all candidates and officials—a negative undercurrent in reporting about government, regardless of who or what is covered. President Nixon's first vice president, Spiro Agnew, called journalists "nattering nabobs of negativism." Critics believe that this bias increased after the Vietnam War and the Watergate scandal made reporters more cynical.

There is considerable validity to this charge. Analyses of newspapers, magazines, and television networks show that the overwhelming majority of stories about government and politicians are neutral.[181] However, the rest are more often negative than positive.[182]

Emphasizing the negative distorts what candidates say. In the 1996 presidential campaign, 85 percent of the candidates' comments made a positive case for the candidates, but 85 percent of the media's coverage dwelled on the negative attacks by the candidates.[183] Emphasizing the negative also distorts what officials do. The *Washington Post* reported that Senator Robert Byrd (D-W. Va.) got the National Park Service to fund a project for his state, including the renovation of a train station—for his "personal pork barrel." "Why did the National Park Service spend $2.5 million turning a railroad station into a visitor center for a town with a population of eight?" The compelling reason—Senator Robert C. Byrd, "who glides past on Amtrak's Cardinal Limited from time to time, heading to and from his home in Sophia, a few miles south." But Byrd did not ride that train, and that train did not go to that town. Moreover, the Interior Department recommended the project; it was not "slipped" into other legislation "unwanted," as the article claimed. When the reporter was questioned, he replied with disgust, "Look, everyone knows that this is the way the world works in Washington. What's the big deal?" Indeed, this is the way things work in Washington sometimes, but apparently not this time. This article, which prompted editorials in newspapers across the country, reinforced readers' cynicism.[184]

Emphasizing the negative conveys the impression that the individuals involved are unworthy of the office they seek or the one they hold. It ultimately conveys the impression that the political process itself is contemptible.[185]

Bias toward Issues

The relative lack of bias in the coverage of elections (except for the negative tone against all candidates) does not necessarily mean there is no bias in the coverage of issues. Because elections are highly visible and candidates are very sensitive about the coverage, the media take more care to be neutral for elections than for issues.

Domestic issues Empirical studies of the coverage of several domestic issues, including abortion, school busing, and nuclear power, indicate a tilt toward the liberal positions.[186] Anecdotal reports of the coverage of other domestic issues, such as gay rights, gun control, capital punishment, the environment, and homelessness, also suggest some bias toward the left.[187]

At the same time, the media exaggerate crimes, drugs, and other urban pathologies that stereotype African Americans and, to a lesser extent, Hispanics.[188] In this respect, they don't reflect a bias toward the left.

Popular television programs, movies, and records often promote social ideas or trends characterized as liberal, such as diversity, multiculturalism, acceptance of racial minorities, acceptance of casual sex, and disparagement of traditional religion. Conservative Christians, especially, feel that their beliefs are under daily attack by the "liberal media." (However, television programs and movies also glorify violence and guns—and since 9/11, torture of suspected terrorists[189]—which don't reflect liberal values. Moreover, television programs and movies rarely have their female characters choose an abortion when they face an unwanted pregnancy.[190]) These programs might have as much or even more effect on individuals' views than the news does. But this chapter focuses on the news media, not the entertainment media, which are beyond the scope of this text.

Although debates about bias revolve around liberalism and conservatism, perhaps the question actually should be reframed: Does the coverage of domestic issues reflect class bias? An examination of the debate over the North American Free Trade Agreement (NAFTA), drafted to ease trade between American and Canadian and Mexican companies, showed more emphasis on the benefits of free trade than on the loss of jobs from the treaty. Thus, the media reflected the views of businesses more than those of workers.[191]

Analysts now suggest that for domestic issues, the most significant bias is not liberal or conservative but upper-middle class over working class.[192] This bias usually favors the liberal positions on social issues and the conservative, or business, positions on economic issues.[193] This bias closely reflects the college education and social class of most journalists. Most journalists are "unlikely to have any idea what it means to go without health insurance, to be unable to locate affordable housing, to have their children in underfunded and dilapidated schools, to have relatives in prison or on the front lines of the military, [or] to face the threat of severe poverty."[194]

Foreign issues The bias in the coverage of foreign issues is quite different from that of domestic issues. The mainstream media toe the government line (at least until it becomes obvious that the administration's policy isn't working). This is often the conservative position.[195]

During the Cold War, this meant harsh attacks on not only the Soviet Union but also leftist Latin American regimes.[196] During the Persian Gulf War, this meant jingoistic coverage and unquestioning acceptance of administration claims.[197] Even during the Vietnam War, which is often cited as an example of harsh criticism of governmental policies, the media in fact offered blindly positive coverage for many years and then relatively restrained criticism near the end of the war.[198]

This bias, reflecting governmental policy, was apparent after the 2001 terrorist attacks. The media not only quoted the president and other officials extensively, as would be expected, but they also adopted the mindset and language of administration officials. An analysis of the editorials of twenty metropolitan newspapers showed that they echoed the president's rhetoric, magnifying our feelings of fear and portraying a conflict between values decreed by God and evil perpetrated by

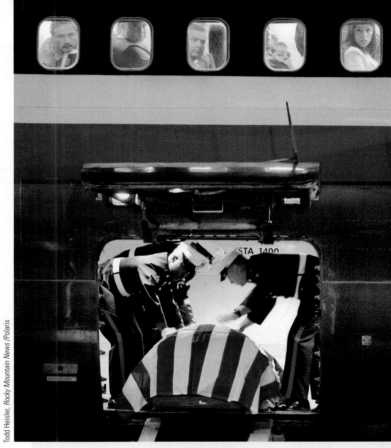

Todd Heisler, Rocky Mountain News /Polaris

The Bush administration has tried to prevent journalists from photographing coffins returning from the Iraq War, usually flying the coffins to military bases in the middle of the night. But a journalist observed this coffin coming home to Reno, Nevada.

the terrorists and their supporters. Like the president, the newspapers emphasized urgent action over debate and national unity over dissent.[199] The television networks also followed the administration, featuring patriotic logos and melodramatic music.

Some media went further. Two newspapers fired columnists who criticized the president's delayed return to the Capitol on September 11, and cable systems yanked *Politically Incorrect*, whose host Bill Maher questioned the president's use of the word *cowardly* to refer to the terrorists.[200] CNN's head warned the staff, "If you get on the wrong side of public opinion, you are going to get into trouble."[201] The patriotic fervor diminished media coverage and therefore public awareness of important matters, such as Arab opinion, the conflict between the Israelis and the Palestinians, and the disagreements among the countries fighting terrorism.[202]

A majority of Americans have had serious misperceptions about important questions relating to the Iraq War, according to a study based on a series of seven polls spanning nine months. Respondents were asked whether world public opinion favored the United States's going to war, whether there was clear evidence that Saddam Hussein was working with al-Qaeda, and whether weapons of mass destruction were found during the war. (Responses to the second and third questions are shown in Figure 2.) Respondents were asked what their primary source of news is and how often they watch, listen to, or read this source.

Respondents' misperceptions varied according to the media they followed. Those who watched Fox had the most misperceptions, whereas those who watched public television or listened to public radio had the fewest.[1] The misperceptions were not due to people's paying little attention to the news. Just the opposite: those who watched Fox more often had more misperceptions than those who watched it less often.

The results not only suggest biased or superficial coverage by some media

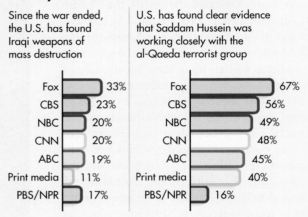

Primary news source for those who believe:

Since the war ended, the U.S. has found Iraqi weapons of mass destruction		U.S. has found clear evidence that Saddam Hussein was working closely with the al-Qaeda terrorist group	
Fox	33%	Fox	67%
CBS	23%	CBS	56%
NBC	20%	NBC	49%
CNN	20%	CNN	48%
ABC	19%	ABC	45%
Print media	11%	Print media	40%
PBS/NPR	17%	PBS/NPR	16%

FIGURE 2 • Misperceptions and their origins

SOURCE: Program on International Policy at the University of Maryland and Knowledge Networks. Poll of 3334 adults, conducted January–September 2003, with a margin of error of 1.7 percent (www.knowledgenetworks.com/ganp). © Rob Rogers reprinted by permission of United Features Syndicate.

more than others but the results also have policy implications. Respondents' misperceptions were related to their support for the war. Those with the most misperceptions expressed the most support for the war.

Remarkably, in 2006 50 percent of Americans still believed that Iraq had weapons of mass destruction leading up to the war.[2]

[1]Researchers tried to control for the possibility that people presort themselves according to ideology by comparing the same demographic groups for each source and also by comparing similar political groups—for example, they compared people who planned to vote for Bush in 2004 and watched Fox with people who planned to vote for Bush but followed other media.

[2]Charles J. Hanley, "Half of Americans Still Believe WMD Claims, Polls Show," *Lincoln Journal Star*, August 9, 2006, 1A.

This bias was also evident in coverage of the Iraq War. In the run-up to the war, the sources cited in television news were overwhelmingly prowar—according to one study, 71 percent were prowar, whereas only 3 percent were antiwar[203]—and the pundits appearing on television talk shows were heavily prowar as well. Although there were snippets of doubt and clips of protests on television newscasts, there was no substantive debate.[204]

The media conveyed, without examination, officials' assertions that there was a link between Saddam Hussein and 9/11. They also conveyed, without examination, officials' assertions that Iraq possessed weapons of mass

destruction—biological, chemical, and nuclear weapons. For many people, these became primary justifications for the war. (See the box "What You Watch Affects What You Believe"). Yet no evidence of either claim has been found (at least as of fall, 2007).

During the war, the networks used special music, graphics, and promotions to dramatize American patriotism and evoke viewers' emotions. Fox and MSNBC used the administration's moniker for the war, "Operation Iraqi Freedom," and most networks used the administration's term *coalition forces,* thus endorsing the administration's claim that there was a broad coalition. (In fact, the war was fought by troops from the United States, with some troops from Great Britain, fewer troops from South Korea, Italy, and Poland, and token representation from other countries.) CNN, with audiences around the globe, used two news teams to cover the war. One team, beamed to the United States, was overtly prowar; the other team, beamed to the rest of the world, was more neutral.[205] And, for good measure, MSNBC removed Phil Donohue from his afternoon show out of fear that his liberal sensibilities would offend conservative viewers during wartime.[206]

Throughout the war, the American media, compared with European and Middle Eastern media, sanitized the combat. They were slow to report negative news[207] and reluctant to depict the blood and gore—the reality of war—in both words and pictures of both Americans and Iraqis.[208] For example, the media reported that U.S. bombers were "softening up" Iraqi defenses. The Air Force commander was amused by the phrase. "We're not softening them up," he said. "We're killing them."[209] When the behavior by American soldiers at Baghdad's Abu Ghraib prison was disclosed, the worst abuses weren't covered by many news organzations.[210] The media sanitized the coverage because "the dirty little secret of much war 'news' is that much of the audience wants to entrance itself into emotional surrender, and news officials want to elicit precisely that surrender."[211] The media did not offer grimmer reports and starker photographs until the insurgency and the lack of real security in Iraq became apparent.

For some time, the media were cowed by the power of the administration as well as by the demands of the public. Officials insinuated that any criticism, even questioning, by reporters was unpatriotic. Officials also issued veiled threats to reporters. The White House press secretary remarked, "People had better watch what they say."[212] Another official ominously warned a reporter that his name was on "a list," presumably of disloyal journalists who would be watched and, perhaps, dealt with.[213] The administration also threatened to deny access to reporters who displeased officials. This would mean no interviews, no tips or leaks, no invitations to special events, and no seats on the plane for presidential trips. Because access is all important, this would make it difficult for reporters to do their jobs. The result was a chilling effect on reporters, editors, and executives.[214] So most media, including supposedly "liberal newspapers" such as the *New York Times* and the *Washington Post,* were little more than stenographers, writing down and passing on administration statements without serious ques-

tioning. In the run-up to the war, the *Post* had 140 front-page articles making the administration's case for the war and only a handful questioning the administration's claims.[215] Later, the *Post* acknowledged that its reporting before the war and early in the war was "strikingly one-sided at times."[216] (Ironically, Comedy Central's humor in "fake news" shows left a more accurate impression than the networks' newscasts did.)[217]

As the aftermath of the invasion revealed serious flaws in U.S. policy, many media became more critical. The *Times* apologized for its lack of scrutiny and skepticism of administration claims.[218] Its apology prompted a letter to the editor that could have been sent to most American news organizations:

> *I've followed all the stories and the "spin" to create a case for war from the beginning. . . . As a university student, I sat through it and asked questions as cabinet members made their case for war. In the sixteen months leading up to my activation to fight in Iraq as a tank platoon commander, I felt that this spin was an effort to find a magic button of support with the citizenry. . . .*
>
> *So off I went, to lead my men on this quest. We fought and died holding up the soldiers' end of the democratic bargain. I lived with many of the young men fighting and dying who had such blind faith in our system of government. They felt it was just right to do what we were doing, even though many of them could not explain or justify why.*
>
> *So on this Memorial Day weekend, as I sit and think about what I've done, the people who have been hurt, the future of this ongoing tragedy, I come to this conclusion: Shame on you.*[219]

The mainstream media reflect the government line on foreign policy because they rely on government officials as their sources for most news.[220] They fear losing access to these officials. This means that their stories will bear officials' imprint. It also means that their stories will revolve around debates among officials—what "he said" versus what "she said." When there is little dissent within the government, as in the run-up to the Iraq War, there is little coverage of opposing views by the media, even if there are alternative views in our society.[221] Journalists seem flummoxed when they can't frame an issue as a debate between opposing groups of officials.

Perceptions of Bias

We have seen that in the mainstream media there is minimal bias in favor of particular candidates or parties in elections, and there is some liberal bias in the coverage of social issues, some conservative bias in the coverage of economic issues, and often conservative bias in the coverage of foreign policy. Overall, however, there is far less political bias than many people believe. In particular, there is far less liberal bias than many conservatives believe.[222] Why do so many people perceive so much bias?

As noted earlier, there is some negative bias against all candidates and officials. People sense this bias against the candidates or officials on their side but don't see it against the candidates or officials on the other side. In addition, people hear aides to the candidates or officials complain about the media without realizing that the aides are simply "working the refs" rather than sincerely lodging a complaint.[223] Also, people hear the steady drumbeat from interest groups and talk shows that the media are biased against their side. Eventually, they come to believe it. They don't realize that the leaders of interest groups and hosts of talk shows are just trying to get people riled up so they will join the group, make a contribution, subscribe to a magazine, or listen to the show. One influential conservative downplayed liberal bias in an interview but at the same time was claiming liberal bias in subscription pitches for his magazine.[224] Karl Rove, President Bush's top aide, has also dismissed the idea of liberal bias in the media.[225]

Yet many conservatives among the public assume the existence of liberal bias. Studies show that strong partisans with strong views perceive more bias than average people.[226] When strong partisans on opposite sides evaluate the same stories in the same media, both groups see bias against their side, even when the stories are balanced.[227] Certain that their side is correct, they consider coverage that is actually balanced as slanted because it gives their opponents more credence than their opponents deserve. And although these partisans say that biased coverage will not affect them, they fear it will affect others who are less aware or astute.[228] When strong partisans evaluate coverage that is clearly biased toward their side, they see no bias or less bias than average people.[229] They consider this coverage fair, because in their eyes it reports the "truth."

Even if people's perceptions are inaccurate reflections of media coverage, their perceptions determine which newscasts they will watch. As a result of conservatives' criticism over the years, some mainstream media have become cowed. CNN has ordered producers to include more conservatives than liberals in their stories.[230] During the 2004 presidential campaign, CBS twice postponed a documentary on the faulty intelligence about Iraq's purported weapons of mass destruction. The network said that it would show the documentary after the election, when the network could not be accused of trying to affect the election's outcome.[231]

Commercial Bias

Although the public dwells on charges of political bias, **commercial bias** is far more pervasive and important in understanding media coverage of politics. As Ted Koppel, former anchor of ABC's *Nightline,* notes, "The accusation that [the] news has a political agenda misses the point. Right now, the main agenda is to give the people what they want. It is not partisanship but profitability that shapes what you see."[232]

Reasons for Commercial Bias

Traditionally, the mainstream media believed they had a "public trust" to meet journalistic standards and provide important news. Newspapers made less money than other businesses, and television news divisions consistently lost money. When *60 Minutes* first aired, the head of CBS told the creator of the show, "Make us proud."[233] The show became a hit, and in its first decade it made so much profit—more than the Chrysler Corporation did during the same years[234]—that the executives started telling the producers, "Make us money!"[235] At the same time, television newscasts became more popular and even profitable. This transformation of the news from an economic backwater to a profit stream has had a huge impact on the mainstream media.

As private businesses, American media, except for public broadcasting, are run for a profit. The larger their audience, the more they can charge for their advertising. An increase or decrease of 1 percent in the ratings of a television news program in New York City, for example, can mean a difference of $5 million in advertising for the year.[236] NBC's news division generated 40 to 50 percent of NBC's overall profit in recent years, with its entertainment and sports divisions dividing the rest.[237] Local stations' news programs also provide 40 to 50 percent of the stations' overall profit.[238]

With chains and conglomerates taking over most media, the pressure to make a sizable profit has escalated. In the 1970s, big-city newspapers expected to make a 7 or 8 percent profit; today, chains and conglomerates expect these papers to make a 20 to 30 percent profit.[239] Corporate executives worry that financial analysts will consider them a poor investment and mutual fund managers will refuse to buy or keep their stock if their earnings fall below those available "from investments anywhere else in the financial universe, from a shirt factory in Thailand to the latest Internet start-up."[240]

The pressure to make a profit and the need to attract an audience shape the media's presentation of the news and lead to commercial bias. Sometimes this means that the media deliberately print or broadcast what their advertisers want. CBS bowed to demands by Procter & Gamble that it drop episodes of *Family Law* dealing with gun ownership, capital punishment, interfaith marriage, and abortion.[241] Sometimes the media censor themselves. In 2004, VH1 and MTV pulled clips of, and refused to run ads for, the documentary *Super Size Me*, which shows what happened to a guy who ate every meal at McDonald's for a month. They feared losing advertising from fast-food restaurants.[242]

Usually, though, commercial bias means that the media print or broadcast what the public wants, which is to say what the public finds entertaining. (See box "Color and the Clicker.") This creates a "conflict between being an honest reporter and being a member of show business,"

AMERICAN DIVERSITY

COLOR AND THE CLICKER

Television news features African Americans in "lights-and-sirens" stories about crimes and drugs and in other stories about urban pathologies, such as single parenthood, that reinforce negative stereotypes.[1] However, television news shuns African Americans in other contexts—not just in the newscasts that focus on government officials but also in the newsmagazines, such as *Dateline, 20/20, 60 Minutes,* and *48 Hours,* that air human dramas.[2] A network staff member lamented, "Can't we do a story about day-care centers and have a black day-care owner. . . ? Why can't they be regular, normal people doing regular, normal things that aren't just associated with their ethnic backgrounds? It makes me sick."[3]

A producer working on a story about a mental disability was searching for a family who had a child with that disability. "I found a great, great upper-middle-class family in Miami, but they were black. I was told . . . : 'Find another family.'" Many network staff members have had similar experiences.

"It's a subtle thing," said one. "A story involving blacks takes longer to get approved. And if it is approved, chances are that it will sit on the shelf a long time before it gets on the air. No one ever says anything. The message gets through."

Sometimes it's not so subtle. Staffers were told by executives that a particular story was "not a good story for us" or that it would "not have broad appeal in the Midwest and in the South." Instead, they were told to feature "families with lots of blond-haired, blue-eyed children."[4]

One reporter observed, "They whisper it, like cancer: 'Is she white?'"

"'Yeah, she's white.'"

"'Are you sure?'"

"'Well, it says they are from Slovakian descent; I'm assuming.'"

"'Well, go out and check.'"

A producer on an evening newscast, working on a health series, found a story about a doctor who encouraged women to get mammograms. The doctor hauled her equipment to beauty parlors where she could test the women conveniently. But when the executive producer saw the piece, he exclaimed, "You didn't tell me that the doctor was black . . . that the people were black!" And he spiked the story.

This pattern is pervasive. A senior executive at a major network confessed, "It's our dirty little secret."

The reason? Research shows the demographic makeup of the audience for every program, and minute-by-minute ratings reveal which stories attract and keep an audience. Many middle-class whites don't want to watch stories about either lower-class people or racial minorities. When such stories come on, these viewers click to another channel. The networks, under pressure to boast the most viewers to generate the most profits for their corporate owners, cater to the tastes of middle-class whites—the largest segment of the audience.

What appears to be racial bias by the networks is actually commercial bias, just as we have seen that what appears to be political bias by the media is usually commercial bias. But the commercial bias here has racial implications, just as the commercial bias elsewhere has political implications. As a result, television news, which could forge understanding between the races by showing sympathetic people of all colors facing common challenges, makes little effort to do so. Instead, it accepts the subtle racism of those white viewers who won't watch the same story if it portrays black folks rather than white folks.

[1] Jeff Cohen, "Racial Tension," *Brill's Content,* October 1999, 54.

[2] The record of *60 Minutes* is not as bad as the others, perhaps because *60 Minutes* is the only one without prime-time competition. Robert Schmidt, "Airing Race," *Brill's Content,* October 2000, 145.

[3] Av Westin, "The Color of Rating," *Brill's Content,* April 2001, 84. Quotations are from this article, unless otherwise noted.

[4] Schmidt, "Airing Race," 114–115.

a network correspondent confessed, "and that conflict is with me every day."[243] When Dan Rather was asked why CBS devoted time to the demolition of O. J. Simpson's house two years after his trial, Rather answered, "Fear. . . . The fear that if we don't do it, somebody else will, and when they do it, they will get a few more readers, a few more listeners, a few more viewers than we do. The result is the 'Hollywoodization of the news.'"[244]

The dilemma is most marked for television. Many people who watch news on television are not interested in politics; a majority, in fact, say that newscasts devote too much time to politics.[245] Some watch newscasts because they were watching another program before the news, others because they were planning to watch another program after the news. Networks feel pressure "to hook them and keep them."[246] Therefore, networks try to make the everyday world of news seem as exciting as the make-believe world depicted in their entertainment programs. One network instructed its staff, "Every news story should, without any sacrifice of probity or responsibility, display the attributes of fiction, of drama. It should have structure and conflict, problem and denouement, rising action and falling action, a beginning, a middle, and an end."[247] As one executive says, television news is "**infotainment.**"[248]

Consequences of Commercial Bias

The media's commercial bias has important consequences. One is to sensationalize the news. The anthrax infections that occurred after the terrorist attacks in 2001 deserved our full attention, but the media would not let up. Even after the initial flurry of reports, they ran one overwrought piece after another. *Time* magazine featured families who bought gas masks. The *Washington Post* wrote that America is "on the verge" of "public hysteria."[249] In fact, few people panicked. In polls, large majorities expressed concern but not fear. Yet the media realized that generating fear would force people to pay attention to the news.

The media's tendencies to sensationalize the news are evident in their coverage of Jessica Lynch, as described in the chapter's opening vignette.

Another consequence of commercial bias is to feature human interest over serious news. In 2005, the three main television networks devoted a total of eighty-four minutes to Michael Jackson's trial for child molesting but only eighteen minutes to the massive genocide in Darfur, Sudan.[250] In 2006, *Time* magazine paid a reported $4 million for photos of Brad Pitt and Angelina Jolie's baby but let go two top-notch investigative reporters because the magazine couldn't afford them any longer.[251]

The media's tendencies to sensationalize the news and to feature human interest over serious news lead to greater emphasis on scandal, sex, and crime. During President Clinton's terms, the media provided saturation coverage of the Whitewater scandal[252] and various other scandals, although a succession of special prosecutors could find nothing more damning than that the president lied about having sexual relations with a White House intern named Monica Lewinsky.[253]

The media plunged into the affair with abandon.[254] The *Los Angeles Times* assigned twenty-six reporters to examine Lewinsky's life, interviewing babysitters and kindergarten classmates.[255] The networks even interviewed one person who had eaten lunch with her three years earlier. The public was offered breathless reports about phone sex, the president's cigar as a sex toy, and the intern's dress with a semen stain. There was tittering about the "distinguishing characteristics" of the president's genitals—and

The media frenzy over anthrax prompted some families, like this one in Chicago, to buy gas masks.

© Time Life Pictures/Getty Images

speculation about how this would be proved or disproved in court.

Although the national media cover crime extensively, the local media cover it even more fully. Local television news is, in Ralph Nader's words, "something that jerks your head up every ten seconds, whether that is shootings, robberies, sports showdowns, or dramatic weather forecasts."[256] Media consultants advise local stations how to attract the largest audience and make the most money for their chain or conglomerate.[257] The saying "If it bleeds, it leads" expresses, tongue in cheek, many stations' programming philosophy. Thus, crime coverage fills one-third of local newscasts.[258] A week before the presidential election, local stations in Columbus, Ohio, devoted more than twice as much time to various crimes than to the election, although the outcome in the state, and in the nation, was in doubt.[259] One station, however, did find time for an undercover investigation of a topless car wash.

A jaded reporter put it bluntly: "It doesn't matter what kind of swill you set in front of the public. As long as it's got enough sex and violence in it, they'll slurp it up."[260] (Even so, American stations do not go as far as the Bulgarian program *The Naked Truth,* which had women disrobe as they read the news.)

Another consequence of commercial bias is to highlight conflict. Stories about conflict provide drama. Reporters, one admits, are "fight promoters" rather than consensus builders.[261] So reporters frame issues as struggles between opposite camps. After the murderous rampage at Columbine High School in Littleton, Colorado, the media posed the question, Was the incident caused by the availability of guns in our society *or* by the glorification of violence in the media? In this moronic debate, the media prodded people to choose sides, as though the cause had to be one *or* the other rather than a combination of the two or something else entirely.

Sometimes this practice is taken to the extreme. Some stories about Holocaust survivors include bizarre statements by Holocaust deniers claiming that the Nazis didn't have a plan to exterminate European Jews or that Hitler wasn't aware of the effort or that the Germans didn't kill many Jews. The stories present these absurd statements as though they constitute an opposing opinion entitled to a public hearing.[262] With their fixation on controversy, the media allow themselves to be manipulated by ignorant or unscrupulous people. In the process, they promote confusion among people who don't know any better.

By highlighting conflict and framing issues as though they have two—and only two—sides, the media polarize the public, which makes it harder for people to accept compromises as solutions to problems and harder for politicians to forge compromises. In fact, the media belittle compromises. They portray politicians on one side as losing or "giving in" when they should have been fighting to win. Thus, the media reinforce some citizens' naive belief that politicians need not and should not compromise. As one reporter admits, "the middle ground, the sensible center, is dismissed as too squishy, too dull, too likely to send the audience channel surfing."[263]

Another consequence of commercial bias is to use a **game orientation** in reporting about competing candidates, officials, or parties.[264] The assumption is that politics is a game and politicians, whether candidates campaigning for election or officials performing in office, are the players. The corollary to the assumption is that the players are self-centered and self-interested. They are seeking victory for themselves and defeat for their opponents, and they are relatively unconcerned about the consequences of their proposals or of government's policies. With this orientation, reporters spotlight politicians' strategies and tactics, and they slight the substance and impact of politicians' proposals and policies.

The game orientation appeals to journalists because it generates human interest. It offers new story lines as new information comes to light, much like a board game where "chance" cards inject unexpected scenarios and alter the players' moves and the game's outcomes. This orientation also appeals to journalists because it is easy and relatively free from charges of partisan or ideological bias. (Stories emphasize which contestants are winning, not which ones should win or what consequences might result.) If journalists seriously examined policies and proposals instead of using the game orientation, they would be less able to offer human interest and would be more vulnerable to charges of bias.

The game orientation attracts an audience, but it breeds more cynicism. It creates the impression that politics is just a game, not an essential activity for a democratic society; that politicians are just the players, not our representatives; that politicians act just in their self-interest, not in the public interest; and that politicians' goal is just to beat others, not to make good public policy.

For elections, the game orientation results in what is called **horse race coverage,** with "front-runners,"

"HURRAH FOR OLD TIPPECANOE."

HARD CIDER AND LOG CABIN ALMANAC 18 FOR 41

HARRISON AND TYLER.

NEW YORK:
TURNER & FISHER, 52 CHATHAM STREET,
AND No. 11 NORTH SIXTH STREET, PHILADELPHIA.
Of whom may be had all the Principal Almanacs now Published.

© The Granger Collection, New York/The Granger Collection

Long before television cameras, candidates shaped their image. In 1840, William Henry Harrison campaigned as the log cabin and hard cider candidate, even though his father was a wealthy planter, a Virginia governor, and a signer of the Declaration of Independence. To underscore his purported origins, Harrison gave Indian war whoops at rallies.

taken by commercial organizations but they also conduct polls themselves.[268] Nowadays, coverage of polls takes more space than coverage of candidates' speeches, and it usually appears as the lead or next-to-lead story.[269]

Even after elections, the game orientation continues. When Clinton proposed a plan to overhaul the welfare system, all major newspapers focused on the political implications for his reelection; few even explained the plan, let alone its substantive implications.[270]

Commercial bias in the media leads to additional consequences for television specifically. One is to emphasize events, or those parts of events, that have visual interest. The networks have people whose job is to evaluate all film for visual appeal. Producers seek the events that promise the most action, camera operators shoot the parts of the events with the most action, and editors select the portions of the film with the most action.[271] Television thus focuses on disasters and protests far more than their occurrence justifies, and it displays the interesting surface rather than the underlying substance of these events—for example, the protest rather than the cause of the anger.

Another consequence of commercial bias for television is to cover the news very briefly. A half-hour newscast has only nineteen minutes without commercials. In that time, the networks broadcast only a third as many words as the *New York Times* prints on its front page alone. Although cable television has ample time, it follows this format, too, endlessly repeating the same stories without adding new information.[272]

Television stories are short—about one minute each—because the networks think viewers' attention spans are short. Indeed, a survey found that a majority of eighteen- to thirty-four-year-olds with remote controls typically watch more than one show at once.[273] Thus, networks do not allow leaders or experts to explain their thoughts about particular events or policies. Instead, networks take sound bites to illustrate what was said. Although correspondents try to explain the events or policies, they have little time to do so.

A network correspondent was asked what went through his mind when he signed off each night. "Good night, dear viewer," he said. "I only hope you read the *New York Times* in the morning."[274]

When the chairman of the board of one network, in conversation with a former Reagan aide, asked what the networks could do to provide more responsible reporting, the aide answered, "Easy, . . . just eliminate ratings for news. You claim that news is not the same as

"dark horses," and "also-rans." Although the race was a staple of journalism even in the nineteenth century,[265] the proportion of election coverage focusing on the race has increased in recent decades.[266]

Today, horse race coverage dominates election reporting. As much as two-thirds of the reporting by newspapers, television networks, and websites features the horse race, and much of the remaining reporting features the candidates' strategies. Far less reporting examines the candidates' positions or proposals.[267]

The quintessential feature of horse race coverage—reporting of candidates' poll standings—has increased greatly. Not only do the media report the results of polls

entertainment. So why do you need ratings?" The chairman sighed, "Well, that's our big money-maker, the news."[275] A former network executive concluded, "Because television can make so much money doing its worst, it often can't afford to do its best."[276]

Overall, commercial bias in the media results in no coverage or superficial coverage of many important stories. This, more than any political bias, makes it difficult for citizens, particularly those who rely on television, to become well informed. During the year before the September 11 terrorist attacks, al-Qaeda was mentioned only once on the networks' evening newscasts.[277] However, seven months before the airplane hijackings, a report predicting a "catastrophic attack" was issued by a government commission. A statement warning that Osama bin Laden's network was the "most immediate and serious threat" facing the country was made by the CIA director at a Senate hearing. Their dire predictions generated little interest among the media. Since the terrorist attacks, the media have paid more attention to foreign affairs, yet they continue to reflect the trends that typified news coverage before 9/11.

Conclusion: Are the Media Responsive?

To make a profit, the media have to be responsive to the people. They present the news they think the people want. Because they believe the majority desire entertainment, or at least diversion, rather than education, they structure the news toward this goal.[278] For the majority who want entertainment, national and local television and radio provide it. For the minority who want education, the better newspapers and magazines provide it. Public radio, with its morning and evening newscasts, and public television, with its nightly newscast, also provide quality coverage. In addition, Internet websites provide news on demand. The media offer something for everyone.

When officials or citizens get upset with the media, they pointedly ask, "Who elected you?" Journalists reply that the people—their readers or listeners or viewers—"elected" them by paying attention to their news columns or newscasts.

To say that the media are responsive, however, is not to say that they perform well. Giving the people what they want most is not necessarily serving the country best. "This business of giving people what they want is a dope pusher's argument," says a former president of NBC

News. "News is something people don't know they're interested in until they hear about it. The job of a journalist is to take what's important and make it interesting."[279]

Instead, the media personalize and dramatize the news. The result is to simplify the news. Superficial coverage of complex events leaves the public unable to understand these events and ultimately unable to force the government to be responsive.

Even though the media give the people what they want, the people criticize the media. People rank the press the lowest in public esteem of all professional groups except lawyers.[280] People also express less support for freedom of the press. Even before the 2001 terrorist attacks, which spurred public desire for national unity, a majority said the press has too much freedom. In fact, a majority said the media should not be allowed to endorse or criticize political candidates, and a third said the media should not be allowed to publish a story without government approval.[281]

Almost two-thirds tell pollsters that the media "don't get the facts straight."[282] Actually, the media usually do get the facts straight, but the nature of their reporting leads to this charge. The practice of objectivity—repeating what he said versus what she said without evaluating the truth of either—passes along false and misleading statements and confuses people rather than enlightens them.[283]

At the same time, the media's practices alienate the people from their government. The negative bias against all candidates and officials undermines them directly, and the game orientation undermines them subtly. The emphasis on conflict, though intriguing the public, polarizes and alienates the public.

The result of these practices may be to foster **media malaise** among the public.[284] This is a feeling of cynicism and distrust, perhaps even despair, toward government and officials. Indeed, according to a survey, the public is even more cynical than journalists themselves. Seventy-seven percent of the public gave government officials a low rating for honesty and ethics, whereas only 40 percent of the journalists did.[285] Most of the public believed that politicians could "never" be trusted to do the right thing. Yet the journalists saw the American political process as "a flawed but basically decent means of reconciling different points of view and solving collective problems."[286] They apparently report in a more cynical fashion than they actually feel because of the conventions of contemporary journalism. But the public, though deploring these practices, evidently sees them as reflections of reality. Thus, cynical coverage by the press leads to even more cynical attitudes in the citizenry.[287]

The cynical attitudes have important implications for politics. They likely reduce satisfaction with candidates and officials and reduce turnout in elections. At the same time, they probably increase votes for "outsiders" who present themselves as "nonpoliticians."

In short, one writer observes, "the press, which in the long run cannot survive if people lose interest in politics, is acting as if its purpose was to guarantee that people are repelled by public life."[288]

The media's problems are compounded by a declining interest in politics and a decreasing number of people who read newspapers or watch newscasts (greater than the increasing number of people who search the Web for news). Although the public is better educated now than in the 1960s, it is less likely to follow the news and less able to answer questions about the government.[289] People under thirty-five especially reflect these trends. To retain their shrinking audience, many newspapers and newscasts have revamped their formats to replace hard news with soft features. If this process continues, it will have disturbing implications. Citizens who are not aware of the news or who do not understand it cannot fulfill their role in a democracy.

The problem is circular, as one political scientist points out:

Because most members of the public know and care relatively little about government, they neither seek nor understand high-quality political reporting and analysis. With limited demand for first-rate journalism, most news organizations cannot afford to supply it, and because they do not supply it, most Americans have no practical source of the information necessary to become politically sophisticated.[290]

Individual journalists are aware of the shortcomings of contemporary journalism but pessimistic about their ability to improve the coverage. Because of commercial pressures, they are experiencing low morale in newsrooms across the country.[291]

Nevertheless, we should not lose sight of the fact that the American media, despite their shortcomings, provide very fast and relatively accurate reports of events. They also probe wrongdoing in society. Thus, they serve as a check on government in many situations. As a former government official noted, "Think how much chicanery dies on the drawing board when someone says, 'We'd better not do that; what if the press finds out?'"[292]

Key Terms

narrowcasting   79
broadcasting   79
blog   81
symbiotic relationship   82
adversarial relationship   82
leaks   83
scoops   84
presidential press conference   84
photo opportunity   86

sound bite   86
spin   87
fireside chats   89
practice of objectivity   93
political bias   93
commercial bias   100
infotainment   102
game orientation   103
horse race coverage   103
media malaise   105

Key Names

Franklin Roosevelt   89
Ronald Reagan   89
Bill Clinton   90
George W. Bush   91

1. Which of the following has not been a trend in media use in recent decades?
   a. Newspapers have been losing readers.
   b. Major television networks' newscasts have been losing viewers.
   c. People have been seeking more neutral news.
   d. Cable television networks' news shows have been gaining viewers.
   e. Internet news sources have been gaining users.

2. The increasing concentration of the media in recent decades has meant which of the following?
   a. more financial resources for journalists to use
   b. higher-quality news coverage
   c. a race to control the supply of information and entertainment in the future
   d. more investigative reporting
   e. a greater variety of news sources for people to get news from

3. What consequences result from the increasing atomization of the media in recent decades?
   a. Articles in the fringe media have been taken seriously.
   b. News stories are edited less carefully than before.
   c. The mainstream media are given less respect than they used to get.
   d. More false information is presented as "news."
   e. All of the above.

4. The symbiotic relationship between the media and politicians is reflected in all but which of the following?
   a. spin
   b. photo ops
   c. press conferences
   d. interviews
   e. news releases

5. Most leaks of information come from
   a. reporters who have carefully investigated the subject.
   b. high-ranking officials who have political motives.
   c. bureaucrats who dislike the politicians.
   d. low-level officials who are disgruntled.
   e. members of the opposite party who want to embarrass the administration.

6. Which of the following statements about the relationship between the media and politicians is not correct?
   a. The relationship is more symbiotic than adversarial.
   b. There has been an increase in reporting on politicians' shortcomings concerning sex, drugs, and alcohol.
   c. The relationship became more adversarial after the Vietnam War and the Watergate scandal than it was before.
   d. There is extensive investigative reporting of government policies.
   e. Sometimes the government and the media compete because they're the two main sources of information in society.

7. The radio let President Franklin Roosevelt speak directly to the people, which enabled him to avoid
   a. the media malaise that would occur otherwise.
   b. the commercial bias of newspapers.
   c. relying on newspapers owned by his opposition.
   d. the political bias of television.
   e. questions from unfriendly reporters.

8. The Reagan administration's media strategy included all but which of the following?
   a. making the president visible to the public
   b. featuring a theme for the day or week
   c. making the president's appearances photogenic
   d. telling the president what to talk about
   e. making the president accessible to reporters

9. The most aggressive efforts to control the media and manage the news have come from the _____ administration.
   a. Carter
   b. Reagan
   c. George H. W. Bush
   d. Clinton
   e. George W. Bush

10. The practice of objectivity means all but which of the following?
    a. Reporters convey the facts rather than their opinions about the subject.
    b. Reporters present both sides of the dispute.
    c. Reporters quote the adversaries in the controversy.
    d. Reporters indicate if someone is lying or misleading people.
    e. Reporters convey the opinions of both sides of the controversy.

11. Coverage of election campaigns by the mainstream media reflects
    a. significant bias in favor of Democrats.
    b. significant bias in favor of Republicans.
    c. some bias in favor of both sides.
    d. relatively little political bias.
    e. no political bias at all.

12. There is some liberal bias in coverage of _____ and some conservative bias in coverage of _____ by the mainstream media.
    a. economic issues; social issues
    c. foreign policy issues; economic issues
    c. social issues; economic issues
    d. economic issues; foreign policy issues
    e. foreign policy issues; social issues

13. Media coverage of domestic social and economic issues combined might best be explained as reflecting a pattern of bias for _____ over _____ .
    a. the upper class; other classes
    b. liberals; conservatives
    c. the middle class; either the upper class or the lower class
    d. Republicans; Democrats
    e. the upper middle class; the working class

14. Commercial bias is based primarily on the media's need to
    a. make a profit.
    b. satisfy their advertisers.
    c. avoid political bias.
    d. satisfy Hollywood moguls.
    e. educate citizens in a democracy.

15. Except for stories about crimes and drugs, network news shows are reluctant to air stories featuring black people because
    a. of the networks' racial bias.
    b. of the networks' political bias.
    c. advertisers tell the networks that African Americans don't have enough "buying power."
    d. the networks worry that such stories will lead to media malaise.
    e. the networks know that many white viewers will change the channel.

16. The word *infotainment* reflects the media's
    a. political bias.
    b. commercial bias.
    c. emphasis upon informing our citizens.
    d. symbiotic relationship with politicians.
    e. adversary relationship with politicians.

17. Media coverage of the Jessica Lynch incident probably reflects media bias for
    a. a good story.
    b. the military.
    c. the Bush administration.
    d. the Iraq War.
    e. conservative foreign policies in general.

18. Covering news events as though they were athletic contests shows the media's
    a. adversarial relationship with politicians.
    b. symbiotic relationship with politicians.
    c. strict adherence to objectivity.
    d. commercial bias.
    e. political bias.

19. Coverage of the _____ usually dominates the mainstream media's election reporting.
    a. candidates' views
    b. "horse race"
    c. candidates' strategies
    d. government's policies
    e. candidates' criticisms of each other

20. The overall result of contemporary journalistic conventions is to foster _____ among the public.
    a. the illusion of objectivity
    b. a hunger for spin
    c. media malaise
    d. a disdain for commercial bias
    e. real respect for government and officials

Key: 1-c; 2-c; 3-e; 4-a; 5-b; 6-d; 7-c; 8-e; 9-e; 10-d; 11-d; 12-c; 13-e; 14-a; 15-e; 16-b; 17-a; 18-d; 19-b; 20-c.

A father and his son march in opposition to a congressional bill that would crack down on illegal immigrants.

Janette Fennell and her husband walked out the front door of their San Francisco house, and as they approached their Lexus in the driveway, they were confronted by carjackers and forced into the trunk. Their nine-month-old baby was left in his car seat on the driveway as the carjackers sped away. The carjackers stopped an hour and forty-five minutes later, abandoning the car in a wooded area forty miles from the city and leaving the Fennells in the trunk. By then it was hard to breathe, but, Janette said, "I started ripping apart everything I could get my hands on. . . . I kept ripping and uncovered what appeared to be a cable and a latch. I pulled it. The trunk opened." After almost two hours of "sheer terror," they were safe, and when they returned to the city their baby was still lying in his car seat in the driveway.

But Janette was furious that the trunk release latch was so hard to find. Researching the latches of other cars, she found that many cars didn't even have an internal release latch. She also found that almost 1200 people had been locked in their trunk, either by criminals or by accident, since 1970, and at least 260 had died of suffocation or heat stroke. The government didn't require an internal release latch. So the homemaker became a crusader. She formed an interest group—Trunk Releases Urgently Needed Coalition. TRUNC testified at government hearings and pestered the automakers until Ford agreed to install a glow handle and General Motors patented an automatic release that senses body movement and temperature, now standard equipment on their cars.[1]

In the United States, everything from fruits to nuts is organized. From apple growers to filbert producers, nearly every interest has an organization to represent it. These organizations touch nearly every aspect of our lives; members of the American College of Obstetrics and Gynecology bring us into the world, and members of the National Funeral Directors Association usher us out.

Organizations that try to achieve their goals with government assistance are **interest groups.** Fruit and nut growers want to get government subsidies and protection from imported products; doctors and funeral directors want to limit government regulation and oversight.

The effort of an interest group to influence government decisions is called **lobbying.** Lobbying may involve direct contact between a **lobbyist**—or consultant or lawyer, as they prefer to be called—and a government official, or it may involve indirect action, such as attempts to sway public opinion, which in turn influences government officials.

People organize and lobby to promote their interests and enhance their influence. "The modern government," one lobbyist observed, "is huge, pervasive, intrusive into everybody's life. If you just let things take their course and don't get involved in the game, you get trampled on."[2] The Founders feared the harmful effects of interest groups, which they called "factions." The Founders, however, didn't attempt to limit the opportunity for people to organize and speak out. When the Bill of Rights was adopted, the First Amendment protected the right to speak, assemble, and petition the government. Instead, James Madison sought to cure the **"mischiefs of faction"** by fragmenting government power through federalism, separation of powers, and checks and balances. These elements of the Constitution make it difficult for one or a few groups to control the government and override the interests of the people as a whole.

However, Americans today complain about interest groups, usually calling them "special interests." They think that everyone is represented in Washington except the people. Some analysts agree that that the constitutional checks don't prevent "special interests" from manipulating government for their own good, contrary to the interests of society as a whole.[3]

Do interest groups undermine the interests of the people? Or, by providing a means for the people to participate in the process, do they make government more responsive to the people? These difficult questions are explored in this chapter.

From a victim to an advocate: Jannette Fennell demonstrates a trunk release lever after TRUNC pressured automakers to install new levers.

Formation of Interest Groups

America is a nation of joiners. As early as the 1830s, the Frenchman **Alexis de Tocqueville,** who traveled throughout the country, saw the tendency of Americans to form and join groups: "In no country in the world has the principle of association been more successfully used or applied to a greater multitude of objects than in America."[4] Even now, Americans are more likely than citizens of other countries to belong to groups.[5]

Why Interest Groups Form

Groups organize in the United States for multiple reasons. The freedom to speak, assemble, and petition government, guaranteed in the **First Amendment,** facilitates group formation. Without such freedom, only groups favored by government or those with members willing to risk punishment for speaking out against government would exist. Groups also organize here because federalism creates two levels of government—the national government, and the state and local governments—that have significant authority. Groups try to influence both levels. Groups also organize here because the United States, compared with most countries, is racially, ethnically, and religiously diverse. This diversity gives rise to varying interests and conflicting views on public issues and consequently to groups that represent them.[6]

In addition to these reasons, which distinguish the United States from other countries, groups organize here and elsewhere because of social changes, economic pressures, and technological developments. As these disturb the status quo, groups organize to cope with the disturbances or to benefit from them. These historical factors come in waves, so the formation of interest groups occurs in waves.[7]

Social changes and economic pressures often lead to these surges. In the decades before the Civil War, debates over slavery led to the formation of abolitionist groups and, in response, proslavery groups. In the decades after the Civil War, rapid industrialization led to the formation of trade unions and business associations. The greatest surge in group formation occurred between 1900 and 1920. Stimulated by the shocks of industrialization, urbanization, and immigration, the United States Chamber of Commerce, American Farm Bureau Federation, National Association for the Advancement of Colored People (NAACP), and countless others were formed.[8]

Another great surge occurred in the 1960s and 1970s. The civil rights and antiwar movements created new groups, and their success spurred other groups representing racial minorities, women, consumers, the poor, the elderly, and the environment. Then the number of business groups surged in reaction to the success of consumer and environmental groups pushing government to regulate businesses.[9] In these two decades, the number of groups increased by 60 percent, and the number sending representatives to Washington doubled.[10]

Technological changes also accelerate group formation. In the 1960s and 1970s, computer-generated direct mail made it easier to recruit members and raise money. In the 1990s, the spread of personal computers and the growth of the Internet facilitated communication between people with an endless variety of narrow interests. The Internet is particularly useful for those wishing to organize citizen groups on a low budget.[11] It is also useful for groups outside the mainstream who wish to operate anonymously.

The chapter's opening vignette illustrates these factors. A social change—the crime of carjacking—created the problem, and another social change—consumer groups' willingness to challenge powerful automobile manufacturers—created the precedents that prompted Janette Fennell to form TRUNC. Technological developments—the computer and the Internet—enabled her to recruit members, raise money, publicize the group, and pressure the companies; and another technological development—the new internal release latches—enabled TRUNC to demand that the companies adopt them.

Through history there's a pattern of action and reaction. When government addresses a problem, people who are adversely affected organize to oppose the policy.[12] In 1890, Yosemite National Park was established to preserve a spectacular stretch of the Sierra Nevada mountains in California. Two years later, cattle ranchers, who wanted the land for grazing, proposed that the park be reduced by half. This prompted preservationists to form the **Sierra Club** to block the ranchers' proposal, which the new environmental organization did. The Sierra Club would become a major environmental organization.

Why People Join

Interest groups encounter resistance when they try to attract new members. Some people lack a sense of **political efficacy**—the belief that they can make a difference. Instead, they feel, "I'm just one person. What can I do?" Many people who possess a sense of political efficacy nevertheless are reluctant to join because they are unwilling to bear the costs—pay the dues or make the effort—of joining. And they assume that they will not have to bear the costs because others will do so instead. So they let others do the work. Yet they still expect to share the benefits if the group reaches its goal.[13] For example, if the group prods the government to reduce the water pollution in a local river or lake, everyone who uses the river or lake—not just the members of the group—will share the benefits of cleaner water. This is called the **free-rider problem.**[14] Why should people join if they don't have to?

To overcome this natural human resistance, groups offer a variety of benefits—psychological, social, and economic—to attract members. Groups, of course, offer the satisfaction that comes from doing good—helping promote a cause. So they emphasize the worthiness of their cause and often exaggerate the harm that will befall the country if their cause doesn't prevail. Groups also offer a sense of belonging with fellow citizens who share similar interests. So they host meetings, dinners, and other social activities to create a feeling of solidarity among members. The National Rifle Association (**NRA**), which

Preservationists formed the Sierra Club to protect the new Yosemite National Park, which cattle ranchers wanted to reduce by half.

lobbies against gun control, provides safety and training classes for new shooters and shooting competitions for children and women as well as for men. The NRA tries to enlist the whole family in its efforts. Groups also offer economic benefits. The American Association of Retired Persons **(AARP)** provides discounted drugs; discounted health, home, and auto insurance; a motor club; a travel service; investment counseling; and several magazines. These services lure millions of members and generate millions of dollars for the organization.

Some people join groups because they are coerced. Lawyers must join their state's bar association in a majority of states, and workers must join their industry's labor union in a majority of states.

Which People Join

Although America is a nation of joiners, many Americans don't take advantage of the opportunity to join interest groups. Some are more inclined to do so than others. Those with more education and higher incomes are much more likely to belong. They have greater interest in the news and government policies. They can afford membership dues, and they have the free time or flexible schedules that allow them to take part and the intellectual ability and social skills that enhance their participation. They also appear more attractive to many groups and therefore are more apt to be recruited.

Men are somewhat more likely to join than women, and whites are somewhat more likely to join than blacks.[15] The elderly and middle-aged participate at higher rates than the young.

Have People Stopped Joining?

A widely publicized book, *Bowling Alone,* documents the decline in group membership in recent decades.[16] A variety of organizations, from labor unions to churches, PTAs, and bowling leagues, have experienced a decline as Americans have become busier at work and at home.

More families are headed by a single parent or by two parents who work outside the home. Women's lives, especially, have changed over the past generation, with most women now in the paid workforce while still carrying the largest share of household and child-raising duties. Women used to be the backbone of many local educational, religious, civic, and political groups, but working women now have far less time and energy to devote to volunteer activities. The entrance of women into the workforce also means that most men do more around the house and with their children than their fathers did. This too decreases the time and energy available for organized groups.

At the same time, technology, from television to computers, has enabled us to create little islands of our own at our home; we don't need to join others for entertainment or even for interaction, which we can get online. Figuratively speaking, we still bowl, but we bowl alone.

This trend has unfortunate consequences. Fewer Americans are taking advantage of the opportunities to join the organizations that will represent them to officials. Even the decline in nonpolitical groups has repercussions for democracy. In these groups, as in political groups, members develop close personal relationships that foster discussion of public issues and trust among the citizens, which are important to a vibrant democracy. Involvement in groups teaches people how to run meetings, discuss issues, agree to disagree, and learn to cooperate to get things done. When groups elect their officers, the process reinforces the workings of representative democracy and the ideals of good citizenship, such as discussing, voting, and following established rules and procedures.[17]

Although formal membership in interest groups has decreased, membership in issue advocacy groups is increasing.[18] These groups, which are professionally managed, solicit "members" who "join" by donating money—writing an occasional check to support the organization's activities.[19] These **checkbook members** contribute to the cause but don't interact with other members. Membership in issue advocacy groups is increasing because people today have more money but less time to offer. These groups can succeed politically, but their members do lose the benefits of social interaction. The members especially lose the experiences of hearing divergent viewpoints and fashioning workable compromises.

Types of Interest Groups

Interest groups come in all sizes and configurations. Some have large memberships, such as the American Federation of Labor–Congress of Industrial Organizations (AFL-CIO), a labor union with 9 million members. Others have small memberships, such as the Mushroom Growers Association with only fourteen members. Some have no members at all. Corporations, which act as interest groups when they lobby government,[20] have managers and stockholders but no members in the usual sense.

Some interest groups are formally organized, with elected or appointed leaders, dues-paying members, regular meetings, and established bylaws. Others are loose-knit, with no leaders and few rules.

Political action committees (**PACs**), which are the part of an interest group that donates money to election campaigns, and "527 organizations," which are interest groups that sponsor political advertisements (explained further in Chapter 7), are specialized interest groups in modern American politics. Most large interest groups and corporations have a PAC, and an increasing number of groups have formed as a 527 organization. These entities, which are authorized by federal law, raise money through direct mail and the Internet. They have leaders, who articulate the group's views and decide how to spend the group's funds, and checkbook members, who decide whether the group's views merit their contributions.

Thus, interest groups can be distinguished according to their membership and their organizational structure. They can also be distinguished by their goals, as explained below.

Private Interest Groups

Private interest groups seek economic benefits for their members or clients. Examples include business, labor, and agriculture groups.

Business

Business organizations are the most numerous and among the most powerful interest groups in Washington (see Figure 1). Much of politics is essentially the interaction—some would say the confrontation—between business and government.[21] Business seeks to maximize profit, whereas government, at least sometimes, works to protect workers and consumers from the unfettered effects of profit-seeking businesses through regulation of employees' wages and working conditions, products' safety, and monopolistic practices.

Today, however, there is less confrontation between business and government than during other eras. The Republican Party has long favored business, and since the 1990s the Democratic Party, anxious to compete for campaign contributions, has often favored business too.[22] In a capitalist economy, there are powerful incentives and pressures for politicians of all political persuasions to accede to, rather than antagonize, business, which is so important to the nation's economic success.[23] If the economy falters, the politicians get blamed. So business usually does well, regardless of which party occupies the White House or dominates Congress.

The lobbying by the pharmaceutical industry illustrates the clout of the country's businesses. There may be no lobby in Washington as powerful as the pharmaceutical lobby. Well financed by drug companies, the industry spends over $100 million a year in lobbying and campaign contributions to obtain favorable legislation. The industry heavily supports Republican candidates and officeholders.[24]

The industry employs three thousand lobbyists, a third of whom are former federal officials who served as members or staffers in Congress or as bureaucrats in government agencies involved in health care.[25] In the K Street corridor, home to Washington's most prominent lobbying and law firms, there are 134 firms on the drug

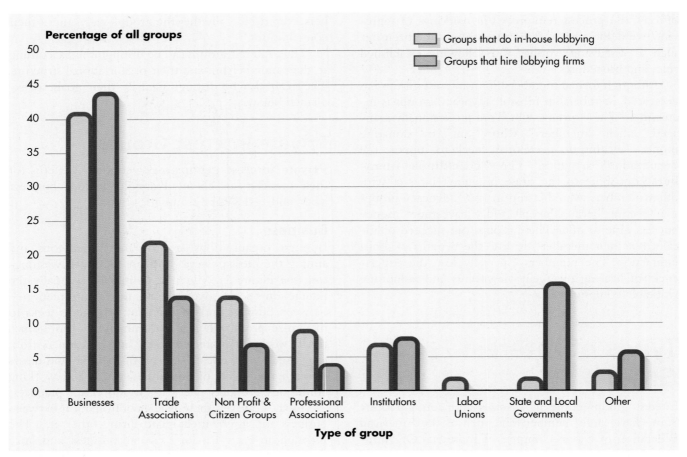

Percentage of all groups

Legend:
- Groups that do in-house lobbying
- Groups that hire lobbying firms

Type of group: Businesses, Trade Associations, Non Profit & Citizen Groups, Professional Associations, Institutions, Labor Unions, State and Local Governments, Other

FIGURE 1 • **Contemporary Interest Groups** *Business interests dominate the modern interest group system. This graph categorizes 2810 groups that maintain an office in Washington, D.C., and 6601 groups that lobby there.*

Data are based on filing reports with the government. Those identified as hiring lobbying firms represent only those with no in-house lobbyists.
SOURCE: Frank R. Baumgartner and Beth L. Leech, "Interest Niches and Policy Bandwagons: Patterns of Interest Group Involvement in National Politics," *Journal of Politics* 63 (November 2001): 1191–1213.

industry's payroll. One company alone, Bristol–Myers Squibb, retains fifteen firms with fifty-seven lobbyists.

The pharmaceutical industry has been especially powerful during the George W. Bush presidency. A big victory came with passage of the Medicare prescription drug bill, which subsidizes prescription drugs for senior citizens.[26] The pharmaceutical industry and health maintenance organizations spent an estimated $14 million to lobby for the bill. The bill not only guarantees huge sales for the companies but it includes some restrictions that enhance their profits. The bill forbids the government from negotiating for lower prices for the drugs, and it forbids the reimporting of drugs manufactured in the United States but sold abroad for less than they do here. The program is expected to ensure billions of dollars in profits for the industry. (See the box "Inter-

est Groups Respond to 9/11" for more coverage of business efforts to lobby the government.)

Given their political clout, it is no surprise that the drug companies are the most profitable of the largest corporations in America, with about $200 billion in annual profits from "take-home" prescriptions (that is, not counting drugs administered in hospitals, doctors' offices, or nursing homes.)[27]

Labor

Labor unions seek agreements with businesses and policies by government that protect workers' jobs, wages, and benefits and ensure the safety of workplaces. They channel money to election candidates, chiefly Democrats, though far less than businesses funnel to Republicans. In place of businesses' dollars, labor unions use their numbers—their members—to distribute campaign literature, man phone banks, and canvass door-to-door to get out the vote for their candidates.

The fight for the right to unionize was a bitter struggle in the late 1800s and early 1900s. Before federal legislation gave workers the right to organize, companies often brought in strikebreakers—men and women willing to work without a contract and, of course, without an inclination to join a union. And striking workers were often attacked by police or thugs hired by owners. Many large companies had a more potent arsenal than local police forces did. During this labor strife, hundreds or thousands of workers were killed. But some brutal incidents shocked the nation and led to the legislation that guaranteed the right to organize.

However, as unions boosted workers' standard of living in the 1950s and 1960s, unions came to be seen as less important. And as manufacturing jobs, which had been the backbone of union strength, dwindled in the 1970s, union membership declined. From 35 percent of the workforce in 1955, their membership dropped to 20 percent in 1983 and to only 13 percent today (see Figure 2).[28] With the decline in membership came a decline in political clout.[29]

Due to the strong antiunion sentiment in the South and Southwest, 84 percent of union members reside in just twelve states.[30] Their concentration, while enabling them to influence their state governments, limits their ability to influence the national government. Members of Congress lend a sympathetic ear to their own constituents or to the outside groups that offer large campaign contributions.

Although unions have gained new members by organizing teachers and government workers, they have not had the political power to overcome the antiunion efforts of businesses in parts of the country. In just five years during the 1990s, 125,000 employees lost their jobs for supporting a union.[31] Although such acts are illegal, they are rarely prosecuted and even then barely penalized.

Unions have charged Wal-Mart with preventing its workers from organizing for collective bargaining. When meat cutters at one Wal-Mart in Texas organized, executives shut down the meat counters in the Wal-Marts throughout Texas and five neighboring states. When employees at one Wal-Mart in Canada organized, executives closed the entire store.[32] As the largest private employer in the United States, Wal-Mart sets the standard for big-box retailers. They, too, try to prevent

IN MEMORY OF

IDA BRAYMAN

17 YEARS OLD

who was shot & killed by an Employer Feb. 5th 1913 during the great struggle of the Garment Workers of Rochester.

Copyrigted 1913 by U. G. W. Local 14 Rochester N. Y.

This postcard commemorates the death of a seventeen-year-old woman murdered while striking for recognition of her union, an eight-hour day, and extra pay for overtime and holidays.

unions in order to keep employees' wages and benefits low and to compete with Wal-Mart.[33] Unions have established two interest groups—Wake Up Wal-Mart and Wal-Mart Watch—to publicize company policies and to propose state and local laws that make it more difficult for the company to open new stores.[34]

Unions have also been hurt by global competition and government's unwillingness to protect American workers threatened by this competition. Fearful of losing their job or putting their employer at a disadvantage in a competitive market, workers are reluctant to strike. Without the threat of a strike, there is little reason to heed workers' demands.

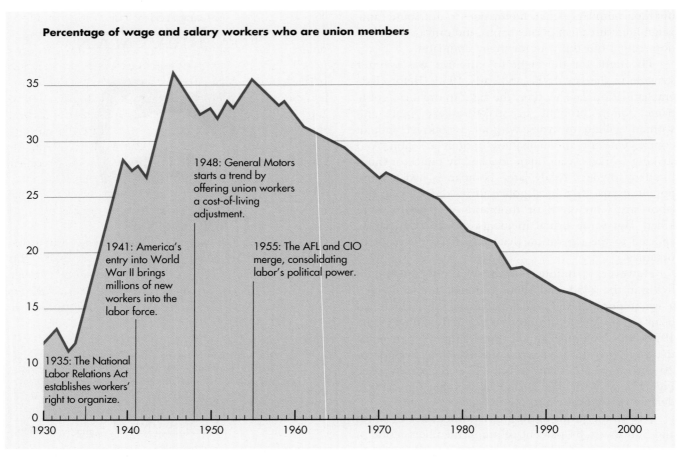

Percentage of wage and salary workers who are union members

1935: The National Labor Relations Act establishes workers' right to organize.

1941: America's entry into World War II brings millions of new workers into the labor force.

1948: General Motors starts a trend by offering union workers a cost-of-living adjustment.

1955: The AFL and CIO merge, consolidating labor's political power.

FIGURE 2 • **Union Membership in the United States**
SOURCE: U.S. Census Bureau, *Statistical Abstract of the United States,* online at www.census.gov/prod/www/statistical-abstract-02.html.

The decline of unions has led to lowered wages, directly because strong unions gain higher wages for their workers, and indirectly because higher wages for their workers pressure nonunion employers to pay high wages to nonunion workers as well. The decline in unions has also blunted the liberal thrust of American politics because unions lobby not only for workers' rights but for other progressive policies, such as government-funded health care.

In an effort to expand membership in recent years, unions have reached out to low-wage service workers, such as hotel maids and nursing home employees, and to some non-blue-collar workers, such as computer specialists in Silicon Valley[35] (and even to graduate teaching assistants at some major universities—other low-wage service workers!).[36] Nonetheless, labor still lags far behind business in ability to influence government.

Agriculture

Agricultural organizations are important in agricultural policy making. Large groups address general farm policy, and hundreds of commodity organizations promote their particular product and operate like business trade associations. So, cattle, milk, tobacco, cotton, and wool producers all have lobbies. Large agribusiness firms such as Cargill and Archer-Daniels-Midland also have their own lobbies in Washington.

Today, American agriculture is dominated by agribusiness and large corporate farms, so the agriculture groups are dominated by these interests. The small farmer plays a minor role, although politicians invoke the small farmer and the family farm—they call for policies that will "save" the family farmer—when they push for subsidies that will go to large corporate enterprises. Government spends more than $20 billion subsidizing crop production, or in some situations nonproduction, and most of this money goes to the largest and wealthiest—usually the corporate—farms.[37]

Public Interest Groups

Public interest groups lobby for political and social causes rather than financial gain for their members. Amnesty International lobbies for the rights of political prisoners around the world even though its members aren't prisoners. The National Taxpayers Union lobbies for reduced taxes; although its members would benefit from reduced taxes, so would everyone else who pays taxes.

Nearly all groups think of themselves as pursuing the "public" interest, even the private groups who are seeking financial gain for their members. But the term *public interest groups* refers only to those working for a cause rather than for personal or corporate interests.

The term doesn't mean that the groups are necessarily working in the public interest according to some objective measure or according to public opinion polls. People, of course, disagree whether specific groups are actually working in the public interest. For the abortion issue, both pro-choice and pro-life groups are public interest groups, even though the members of one side don't believe for a minute that the members of the other are working in the public interest.

Public interest groups increased dramatically during the 1960s and 1970s.[38] The various groups founded by Ralph Nader and committed to the safety of consumer products reflect this trend. Now there are twenty-five hundred public interest groups with 40 million members.[39]

Multiple-Issue Groups

Public interest groups are classified as multiple- or single-issue groups. Multiple-issue groups address a range of issues.

Racial and ethnic groups Organizations promoting the interests of racial and ethnic minorities are multiple-issue groups because they address various concerns of these people. Chapter 13 discusses these organizations and their role in the civil rights movement.

Women's groups Groups advocating women's equality range from large, mass-based organizations interested in numerous issues to smaller groups focused on fewer issues. The National Organization for Women (**NOW**) is the largest and most prominent, with 250,000 mem-

bers and chapters in each state.[40] It researches and lobbies at the national, state, and local levels in a number of policy areas, including reproductive freedom and economic rights. NOW's success has spurred the creation of conservative groups such as the Independent Women's Forum, which opposes government programs to achieve gender equality.[41] A few groups have organized specifically to elect women to office. The most successful is EMILY's List—*EMILY* stands for Early Money Is Like Yeast (it makes the "dough" rise), which recruits, trains, and funds pro-choice Democratic women to run for public office. The National Federation of Republican Women helps Republican women get elected.

Gay and lesbian groups Organizations promoting the interests of gays and lesbians fight for equal rights and more recently for same-sex marriage. The Lambda Defense Fund also represents gay and lesbian students who have been discriminated against or harassed in

AP/Wide World Photos

Mary Bonauto, a lawyer with Gay and Lesbian Advocates and Defenders, brought the lawsuit that led to the legalization of civil unions in Vermont and then another that resulted in the legalization of same sex marriage in Massachusetts.

We like to think that in a time of national crisis, we all pull together. But the efforts of interest groups to secure benefits from government don't stop because of a national tragedy. Rather, the groups refocus their appeals to take advantage of the situation.

In the wake of September 11, 2001, scores of lobbyists pleading for special interests repackaged their demands in patriotic wrapping. As television commentator Bill Moyers observed, "It didn't take long for wartime opportunists—the mercenaries of Washington, the lobbyists, lawyers, and political fundraisers—to crawl out of their offices on K Street to grab what they can for their clients."[1]

It began with the nation's airline industry. By September 22, the government had given the airlines a sweet deal to compensate for the drop in air travel: $5 billion in cash, plus $10 billion in loan guarantees. The airlines also won protection from lawsuits arising from the attacks, which would have cost them billions more. The bailout was so large that it exceeded the combined value of the major airlines: United, American, Delta, Northwest, US Airways, America West, and Continental.[2] In the blink of an eye and with virtually no debate, Congress approved the measure for an industry in which several carriers were near bankruptcy before 9/11 (and less than three years later, two carriers would be bankrupt again). And, of course, the American taxpayers received no ownership in the airlines for their huge investment.

One small carrier, Midway Airlines, which had declared bankruptcy in August, 2001, nonetheless got an $11 million bailout.[3]

The airlines' success prompted the manufacturers of small airplanes; the operators of small airports, flight schools, and skydiving companies; and even Alaska bush pilots whose business wasn't affected by the attacks to seek their own government handout.

Others followed the airlines' strategy. Steel companies, arguing that their product is essential to national security, lobbied for subsidies as well as restrictions on imports of less costly foreign steel. Although one or two steel mills could provide all the steel needed for defense,[4] the president approved restrictions on imports at a big cost to U.S. taxpayers. (The restrictions eventually had to be lifted after the World Trade Organization declared that they violated free-trade agreements.)

The Agricultural Act of 2001, which authorized $167 billion in farm subsidies, was retitled the Farm Security Act of 2001. A capital gains tax cut was marketed as a national security initiative by the National Taxpayers Union.

Ethanol producers asked for more subsidies to reduce the nation's dependence on foreign oil. Manufacturers of traffic signs proposed more spending on highway safety, arguing that traffic-routing devices would help motorists flee cities faster and safer during future terrorist attacks. The American Bus Association, representing a thousand private companies providing intercity bus service, lobbied for $400 million to improve bus security and safety and to retain bus drivers who had come to fear potential attacks.

---

school, and it educates teachers, administrators, and legislators about the challenges encountered by these students. The box "The Origin of Gay and Lesbian Rights Groups" and Chapter 12 discuss these organizations.

Religious groups Many religious denominations have organizations to represent their interests in Washington. Protestant groups lie on both sides and in the middle of the political spectrum and address a wide range of matters. Catholic groups are active in the antiabortion and antinuclear movements, and they have become outspoken in the immigration debate. Jewish groups lobby for liberal causes and emphasize Israel's security. Muslim groups lobby for Palestinian rights and favorable policies toward the countries with Islamic populations. They also advocate for fair treatment of American Muslims.[42]

Evangelical Protestant denominations—**the Christian right** (sometimes called the "religious right" to encompass conservative Jewish groups as well)—are the most potent religious force in American politics.[43] They are actively involved in the hot-button issues of abortion and homosexuality and in the related social issues of divorce, birth control, and women's rights. They oppose the teaching of evolution and the restrictions on religious symbols and practices in public schools and buildings. In general, they want government's laws and policies to be based on Christian principles and to be acknowledged as such. They push their agenda through religious schools; religious media, including newspapers,

Not to be outdone, bison producers also bellied up to the trough because, as they put it, fear of terrorism drove patrons from the fancy restaurants that serve bison steaks and burgers.

And the American Shore and Beach Preservation Association sought additional funds to maintain public beaches because "America needs to make a major commitment to its energy and water infrastructure, both for security and economic reasons."[5]

None of these groups was asking for anything different from what it had sought before 9/11. But 9/11 offered an opportunity to make a stronger argument for their requests. One lobbyist expressed what many others were thinking: "What happened was a tragedy certainly, but there are opportunities. We're in business. This is not a charity."[6] A member of Congress captured the view of lobbyists and lawmakers: "It's an open grab bag, so let's grab."[7]

"Pardon me, but could you tell us where the public trough is?"

[1] Bill Hogan, "Star-Spangled Lobbyists," *Mother Jones,* March-April 2002, 59–63.
[2] Alan Guebert, "Lugar's Proposal Calls Groups' Bluff," *Lincoln Journal-Star,* October 21, 2001.

[3] Sally B. Donnelly, "Largesse for a Defunct Airline," *Time,* December 17, 2001, 14.
[4] Hogan, "Star-Spangled Lobbyists."
[5] Ibid.

[6] David E. Rosenbaum, "Since Sept. 11 Lobbyists Use New Pitches for Old Pleas," *New York Times,* December 31, 2001, B1.
[7] Hogan, "Star-Spangled Lobbyists."

magazines, radio and television; and thousands of politically mobilized churches.[44]

The Christian Coalition, one prominent group, was formed in the 1980s by a television evangelist, Pat Robertson, who sought the Republican presidential nomination in 1988.[45] The Christian Coalition is heavily involved in politics and closely linked to the Republican Party. In the early 1990s, Coalition members were a majority in many Republican state and local party organizations.[46]

Robertson and fellow television preacher Jerry Falwell, who led the Moral Majority, issued provocative statements to rally conservative Christians. Falwell proclaimed that AIDS reflected "the wrath of a just God against homosexuals"[47] and that the 9/11 attacks re-

flected God's judgment of "the pagans, and the abortionists, and the feminists, and the gays and lesbians."[48] The two leaders urged the resignation or impeachment of President Clinton after his affair with Monica Lewinsky was revealed.[49] Their groups helped deliver the Republican presidential nomination to George W. Bush in 2000 by mobilizing their followers in opposition to his rival, Senator John McCain (R–Ariz.). And they helped deliver the presidential election to Bush in 2000 and 2004.

However, the sway of organized conservative Christian groups may have peaked.[50] With the election of Bush, the Christian right gained visibility and power in the highest reaches of government. Their leaders, seeing conservative Republicans in control of all three branches

THE ORIGIN OF GAY AND LESBIAN RIGHTS GROUPS

In the 1950s, homosexuals usually kept their sexual orientation private. When their orientation did come to public attention, homosexuals were characterized as deviates and subjected to humiliation. They were often fired (as they still can be in many places)

Consequently, gays and lesbians, especially those who hung out together, were extremely vulnerable to blackmail and to police harassment. Following a raid on a gay bar in 1954, a Miami newspaper headlined its story, "Perverts Seized in Bar Raid." A decade later, New York's liquor authority declared that a meeting of three or more homosexuals in a bar was reason enough for the bar to lose its license.[1] Although New York City boasted more liberal views than the rest of the country, police entrapment of homosexuals—plainclothes officers patronized the bars and waited for a proposition—was common through the 1960s. Discrimination in city hiring was abolished only in 1967 and in the fire and police departments well after that.

The first national group organized to speak for homosexuals was the Mattachine Society, founded in 1950 to raise political consciousness among gays and to fight the persecution of gays that came with the anti-Communist blacklisting in that decade.[2] But the Mattachine Society had branches in only a few cities, and these declined when it was discovered that some of the leaders were Communists.

Homosexuals continued to be ostracized by society until the modern gay rights movement began. In 1969, a police raid at a seedy bar—the Stonewall—in Greenwich Village, New York, sparked the movement. Rumored to be owned by the Mafia, the bar operated without a liquor license and served as a dope hangout. A private club, the Stonewall was a popular meeting place for a diverse group of gay men, "including drag queens, hippies, street people, and uptown boys slumming."[3] That summer the city's police were cracking down on illegal bars, especially those frequented by gay men, Latinos, and blacks. Several gay bars had already been raided without incident before the Stonewall, but each raid heightened the anger and desperation in the gay community.

A small police unit entered the Stonewall at 3 A.M. The employees were arrested for selling liquor without a license, and the customers were asked to leave. When a police van arrived to take away the arrested employees, the crowd grew hostile and began to throw things—first coins, then cans and bottles, and then larger items. The police took refuge in the club, but the increasingly angry crowd pressed to break in, and the police drew their weapons. Soon lighter fluid and a match were thrown inside the building and a fire started, although any casualties were averted when police reinforcements arrived. The crowd, feeling empowered by its attempt to fight back, moved down the street shouting "gay power" and celebrating newfound strength and solidarity.

After the unrest ended, gays' sense of injustice and their pride from the protests were transformed into an organization, the Gay Liberation Front. Its founders were determined to use radical means to fight the discrimination against homosexuals. Not long after, moderate gays and lesbians broke from the Gay Liberation Front to form the Gay Activist Alliance. Later, other groups evolved that used mainstream politics and legal challenges to support the cause of equality for gays and lesbians. By the early 1970s, gay pride parades, usually held in late June to commemorate the anniversary of the Stonewall raid, were common in major cities, and gay rights organizations were actively working across the land.

Changes in the status of homosexuals soon followed. In 1973, the American Psychiatric Association removed homosexuality from its list of mental disorders. In the 1980s, the AIDS tragedy focused media attention on the gay community and brought public awareness to the discrimination issue. Entertainers and celebrities who acknowledged their homosexuality, and in some instances suffered from AIDS, raised public consciousness even more. As more homosexuals "came out of the closet," they received more support from straight people.

[1] Robert Amsel, "Back to Our Future? A Walk on the Wild Side of Stonewall," www.gayastrology.com/stonewall.shtml (excerpted from *Advocate*, September 19, 1987).

[2] The source for much of this discussion is Eric Marcus, *Making History: The Struggle for Gay and Lesbian Equal Rights, 1945–1990* (New York: HarperCollins, 1992); see also Jeffrey Schmalz, "Gay Politics Goes Mainstream," *New York Times Magazine*, October 11, 1992, 18ff.

[3] Amsel, "Back to Our Future?"

of the federal government, flexed their muscles. But the harder they pushed, the greater the backlash from moderate Americans.

The resistance was especially evident after the strident attempts to use Terri Schiavo's case as a rallying cry. Schiavo, who was 41 years old, had been in a persistent vegetative state for fifteen years. She could not eat, so she was kept alive by a feeding tube inserted into her abdomen. Her husband petitioned to remove the tube, but her parents resisted. After nineteen Florida courts heard the case, and all three levels of federal courts, including the U.S. Supreme Court, refused to intervene, the result was a court order to disconnect the tube. Conservative Christian groups, seeing a connection to their pro-life movement, made the case a cause celebre, pressuring Florida officials and then Congress to intervene and overturn the court rulings. Congress urged federal courts to hear the case, and President Bush interrupted a break at his ranch to return to the capital to sign the bill. The courts, however, rejected the plea. So did 70 percent of the public.[51] In their efforts to appeal to their base, the conservative Christian groups alienated moderate Americans.

Some evangelicals have become disillusioned because political activity has produced so little. Although they've defeated gay marriage at the ballot box in many states, they've not succeeded in eliminating abortion, reinstating school prayers, or reshaping school curricula to teach creationism or intelligent design along with evolution. Now some feel used by the Republican party—useful as loyal foot soldiers when it's time to march to the polls, but ignored when the GOP's bigwigs set the party's agenda and priorities.[52]

Yet at least part of the evangelical movement is broadening its focus to address environmental issues such as global warming. Although some leaders want to keep the focus on social issues, which brought the movement to prominence, other leaders see the environment as a practical way to expand their base as well as the right thing to do for poor people who are the ones most likely to suffer from global warming.

Moderate and liberal religious groups have also been calling for more attention to the plight of the poor.[53] These groups put greater weight on the Christian doctrine of helping the less fortunate than on the social issues that have mobilized conservative groups.[54]

Environmental groups Earth Day 1970 marked the beginning of the environmental movement in the United States. Spurred by an oil spill in California, a "teach-in" on college campuses became a day of environmental awareness for millions of Americans nationwide. A minority movement in the 1970s, the environmental lobby today is large and active, and its values are supported by most Americans.[55]

Some environmental groups, such as the Sierra Club, National Audubon Society, and Natural Resources Defense Council, have permanent offices in Washington with skilled professionals.[56] Other groups, such as Greenpeace, Earth First!, and the Sea Shepherds, which seek a green cultural revolution, shun conventional lobbying in favor of direct confrontation.

Like other movements, the environmental movement has divisions. Some environmentalists don't want to compromise with business, but others are willing to take small steps in the hope that these will lead to long strides down the road.

Environmental groups have been on the defensive during the administration of George W. Bush. Conservative Republicans often oppose environmental regulations, arguing that businesses should be allowed to regulate themselves. In response to the demands of its business allies, the administration has rolled back some environmental regulations adopted by the Clinton administration.[57]

Single-Issue Groups

Public interest groups include single-issue groups as well as multiple-issue groups. **Single-issue groups** are distinguished by their intense concern for a single issue. Their zeal makes these groups reluctant to compromise.

The NRA is an example. Its members are passionate in their opposition to gun control. They live in every congressional district, and they can be mobilized to contact their members of Congress. Although a majority of Americans have supported gun control for many years, the NRA has prevented Congress from passing most gun control proposals. And it has prevented the Treasury Department's Bureau of Alcohol, Tobacco, and Firearms from strictly enforcing the gun control laws that are on the books.[58]

The NRA campaigned for the election of George W. Bush, with a high-ranking official boasting that a Bush win would mean direct access to the Oval Office.[59] Indeed, the Bush administration has been a close ally. Reversing 60 years of government policy, the administration has adopted the position that the Second Amendment protects a right for individuals to keep and bear arms rather than the right of government to arm a militia to maintain domestic security.[60]

In 2004, congressional allies of the NRA blocked the renewal of the ban on assault weapons and semiautomatic rifles.

The NRA has been so successful that some politicians, especially in "red" states, who are inclined to support gun control measures, have concluded that the risks to their election or reelection are so great and the probabilities of passing gun control measures are so small that it's prudent to go along with the NRA and instead save their tough stands for some other issues. It was an indication of the NRA's success that following the Virginia Tech shootings in 2007 there were few calls for new gun control laws in Congress.

Yet the NRA may be shifting its focus. In recent years, the organization has become increasingly worried about the shrinking wildlife habitat available for hunting and fishing, as continued development near big cities has transformed fields and streams and as the Bush administration's energy policies have opened more federal land for oil and gas drilling. Rank-and-file members now consider the dwindling habitat a greater threat to their hunting and fishing than gun control legislation, and they have pressured their leaders to address this concern and qualify NRA support for the administration.[61]

The **pro-life** and **pro-choice groups** in the abortion debate are other examples of single-interest groups. Pro-life groups, such as the National Right to Life Committee, want a constitutional amendment banning all abortions. Because this is unlikely, they have pushed for federal and state laws restricting the availability of abortions, such as laws requiring waiting periods and parental notification or consent for minors. In some states they have pushed for extra-stringent building codes or staffing requirements for clinics. The goal is to make abortions more difficult for the woman, the doctor, and the clinic.[62] Like the Christian right, from which it draws members, the pro-life movement is closely allied with the Republican party. In 2004, it got the Republican Congress to forbid the late-term abortions ("intact dilation and extraction") called "partial birth abortions" by the movement and the media.

Pro-choice groups, such as the National Abortion Rights Action League (NARAL) and Planned Parenthood, want to maintain a woman's right to choose. (Often identified with abortion rights, Planned Parenthood also advocates for access to birth control, sex education in schools, and quality reproductive health care for women.) These groups are closely allied with the Democratic party.

"If you still want to belong to an organization dedicated to killing Americans, there's always the tobacco lobby."

Single-issue groups have increased in recent decades, alarming some observers and many politicians. When groups form around highly emotional issues and refuse to compromise, politicians can't deal with them as they deal with other groups, so the issues continue to boil,[63] consuming the time and energy of politicians at the expense of issues that many consider more important. On the other hand, single-issue groups have always been part of politics,[64] and they may represent interests that aren't represented by multiple-issue groups. Fears about single-issue groups may result from the groups' heavy media coverage, their exaggerated claims of influence, and, for some, their confrontational tactics.

Strategies of Interest Groups

Interest groups use several strategies to influence public policy. These include initiating favorable action, blocking unfavorable action, and influencing key appointments.

Initiating Action

Interest groups initiate governmental action that will help them. They lobby Congress to pass new laws, and because the president is involved and influential in this process, they lobby the administration to push these bills. After the terrorist attacks and the anthrax scare, there was concern that terrorists might use smallpox in future attacks. The government decided to stockpile smallpox vaccine. The pharmaceutical industry lobbied for a law that would grant the drug companies immunity in case the vaccine, which can have serious side effects, caused illness or death.[65] As the bill was working its way through Congress, one drug company, Eli Lilly, got the bill's sponsors to sneak in a provision that would grant immunity for another drug made by the company that was unrelated to the smallpox vaccine or to potential terrorist attacks. This provision was removed from the bill only when it was noticed by a few senators at the last minute.

Groups lobby the administration to adopt new policies for those subjects in which the president is authorized to adopt new policies without Congress passing new laws. When it was uncertain whether the United States would use economic sanctions or military attacks against Iraq in 1991, defense contractors lobbied for a war because they could sell more weapons to the government and they could see how their weapons performed on the battlefield. The National Wooden Pallet and Container Association, which represents companies that make the pallets used to transport supplies, and the Composite Can and Tube Institute, which represents companies that make cardboard containers and the tubes around which toilet paper and paper towels are wrapped, also lobbied for a war, because the government would buy more pallets and cardboard containers, toilet paper, and paper towels.

Groups also lobby the administration to increase or decrease the enforcement of federal laws that affect them. As the head of the executive branch, the president is responsible for executing the laws. But executing the laws isn't automatic. Sometimes the laws are ambiguous, so they can be interpreted one way or another. Sometimes an agency lacks enough trained personnel to enforce all the laws it's responsible for, so it has to choose which ones to enforce.

Groups lobby the bureaucracy to adopt new rules. Congress passes relatively general laws, and it delegates authority to the bureaucratic agencies that have expertise in the subject matter to adopt specific rules to implement the laws. These rules can be as important to the individuals or companies affected by them as the laws themselves are, so groups lobby the agencies to adopt favorable rules. When the Federal Aviation Administration (FAA), which regulates air travel, banned firearms from airplanes in the 1960s, the NRA persuaded it to allow knives. (This policy was still in effect on 9/11.)

Thus, bureaucrats, like members of Congress, are targets of lobbying. Enron CEO Ken Lay telephoned Curtis Hébert, appointed by President George W. Bush to head the Federal Energy Commission (FEC), to tell him that Enron would support him in his new job if he changed his views on electricity deregulation.[66]

Businesses, acting as interest groups, also lobby the bureaucracy to obtain **government contracts**—government orders to buy goods or services. Businesses are anxious to sell everything government wants to buy. These contracts cover things big and small. Halliburton got lucrative no-bid contracts to supply the troops in Iraq (so lucrative that the company was charging the government $100 for each 15-pound bag of laundry its workers put in washing machines and $45 for each case of soda),[67] while other companies got contracts to provide private soldiers for security details in Iraq. And companies that make playing cards vie for government contracts for the decks distributed as souvenirs to people who ride on "Air Force One"—the president's plane. These special cards are embossed with the presidential seal.

Blocking Action

Interest groups try to block governmental action that will harm them, so they do just the reverse of what groups do to initiate governmental action. They lobby Congress not to pass proposed bills and the administration not to push these bills. They lobby the administration not to adopt new policies under consideration. They also lobby the administration not to increase or decrease the enforcement of federal laws that affect them. They lobby the bureaucracy not to adopt new rules under consideration. After 9/11, the FAA finally banned knives from airplanes, but airlines lobbied against the change, asking how first-class passengers could eat their steak without a knife. If these efforts fail, groups might file a lawsuit either to delay the harmful action or to scuttle it altogether if the courts declare it illegal or unconstitutional.

Of these two strategies—initiating action and blocking action—interest groups resort to the latter more often. In our system of separation of powers, checks and balances, and federalism, power is fragmented and government is decentralized. Initiating action may require a group to clear each level—federal and state—and at the federal level, it requires a group to clear each part of each branch—for the legislative branch, the House and the Senate and multiple committees in each; for the executive branch, the White House, with the president's many advisers, and the bureaucracy, with its numerous agencies; and for the judicial branch, the several levels of courts. Groups wanting to change law or policy have to persuade officials at every step to go along. Groups wanting to keep the law or policy, however, only have to persuade officials—erect a barrier—at one point, any point, in the process. Our system, which was designed to prevent individuals or groups from taking control of the government, favors the status quo.

Either way, the process can be ongoing. Environmental groups persuaded the Clinton administration to impose more stringent efficiency standards for air conditioners to conserve energy. Then the manufacturers of air conditioners, more concerned about the short run, got the Bush administration to scale back these standards to save money in manufacturing costs. (More stringent standards require more expensive technology.) Then a federal court ruled that the Bush administration violated a law when it scaled back the standards.

Influencing Appointments

To shape government policy and accomplish their goals indirectly, interest groups also try to influence important appointments. The president nominates and the Senate confirms appointees to high positions in the executive branch and judges to the federal courts. Having a friend or ally in a key position can help secure a group's goals.

The auto industry opposed several nominees by President Clinton to head the National Highway Traffic Safety Administration, fearing that they were more concerned with safety and consumers than they were with the auto manufacturers. The pharmaceutical industry vetoed Dr. Alastair Wood, a drug safety expert who was under consideration by President George W. Bush to chair the Food and Drug Administration (FDA). Drug company CEOs complained that Wood was "too aggressive on drug safety issues."[68]

Increasingly, interest groups have tried to influence presidential appointments of federal judges, as will be covered in Chapter 11.

In following any of these strategies, like-minded groups may join together as **coalitions.** For example, amusement parks, lawn and garden centers, Kingsford charcoal, and 7-Eleven stores joined the Daylight Saving Time Coalition to lobby Congress to extend daylight saving time. All wanted additional evening daylight hours for the users of their services and products: amusement parks so customers can stay longer, lawn and garden centers so people can work in their yards later, Kingsford for

Jim West/Alamy

The First Amendment protects interest group speech, even repulsive speech such as this message from a church in Topeka, Kansas, whose members believe that God is punishing Americans for tolerating homosexual behavior.

barbecuers, and 7-Eleven for folks who prefer to drive or stop for a snack during daylight. Extending the daylight hours has boosted sales and profits for all.

Tactics of Interest Groups

To implement their strategies, interest groups employ a variety of tactics. Some try to influence policy makers directly, whereas others try to mold public opinion and influence policy makers indirectly.

Direct Lobbying Techniques

Direct lobbying usually entails contacts between lobbyists and officials. Thirty-two thousand lobbyists are registered in Washington.[69] Some are salaried employees of the groups they represent; others are contract lobbyists, "hired guns" who represent any individual or group willing to pay for the service. Contract lobbyists include numerous lawyers affiliated with the city's most prestigious law firms.

For direct lobbying, **gaining access** to the officials is essential. As busy people, the officials are protected by their receptionists and aides whose job is to shield the officials from those who would take up their time.

Former officials—members of Congress, aides to the president, experts in the bureaucracy—are recruited as lobbyists by firms because of their contacts and knowledge of the officials and policies they dealt with. An official with the Securities and Exchange Commission (SEC), which regulates the stock market, recognized "Washington's revolving-door tradition whereby high-ranking federal officials move into high-paying private industry jobs." With his contacts and knowledge, he expected "to springboard to at least a $300,000 salary" with a lobbying firm when he left the SEC.[70] Representative Billy Tauzin (R-La.), who steered the Bush administration's Medicare drug bill through the House, was rewarded by the pharmaceutical industry with a job as the head of the pharmaceutical lobby—for a salary of 2 million dollars a year.[71]

Former members of Congress are especially sought as lobbyists because they have an advantage in addition to their contacts and knowledge. They're allowed access to the private dining rooms and the floors of the House and the Senate, where no one else is allowed. They can button-hole current members just before a vote. When they first came to Washington, most of these officials planned to return home after their service, but the longer they lived in the capital, and experienced the highly charged atmosphere of the most political city in the country, the harder it got to return home. So they decided to remain as lobbyists. Since 1998, more than 250 members of Congress and 275 aides to the president have registered as lobbyists.[72] When Bob Dole (R-Kan.) resigned from the Senate to run for president in 1996, he said he'd have no place to go but back to his hometown of Russell, Kansas, if he lost the election. Instead, he joined a lobbying firm as a "rainmaker"—a prominent person who can attract clients who will bring millions of dollars to the firm.[73]

Usually both Democrats and Republicans are recruited, so firms have access to officials in both parties. This practice also ensures that firms maintain access when control of government shifts from one party to the other.

When the Republicans controlled Congress in the 1990s, however, they pressured the firms to employ only Republicans as lobbyists. And then they pressured the lobbyists to make campaign contributions only to Republican officeholders and candidates. The goal was to deprive the Democratic party of the funds necessary to remain competitive. The plan was dubbed the "K Street strategy" after the K Street corridor, home to lobbyists representing the nation's largest business corporations and trade associations.

House Republican leader Tom DeLay (R-Tex.) compiled a list of the four hundred largest contributors to the parties. Their lobbyists were summoned to his office, one by one, and shown their name in either the "friendly" (Republican) or "unfriendly" (Democratic) column, depending upon which party's candidates they had contributed to. DeLay told them, "If you want to play in our revolution, you have to live by our rules." Friendly lobbyists were invited to help write legislation affecting their clients. So, chemical industry lobbyists helped decide hazardous waste regulations, and oil company lobbyists helped determine energy policies. Defense contractors helped write weapons contracts.[74]

An old adage says, "Power corrupts and absolute power corrupts absolutely."[75] The Republicans' control of government and their aggressive efforts to ensure their control in the future led to increasing corruption. Eventually, this corruption became a factor in the Democratic victories in the 2006 elections. As a result of new Democratic majorities in Congress, the lobbying firms scurried to hire more Democratic lobbyists.[76]

Contacting Officials

The prototypical lobbying technique is to pay a visit or make a call to an official. Lobbyists don't need to contact every legislator. Rather, they contact key legislators—party leaders and the members who sit on the committees with jurisdiction over the subject of the lobbyists' concern—and the professional staffers serving those committees.[77]

Successful lobbying is based on friendship. As a former chair of one House committee observed, "The most effective lobbyists here are the ones you don't think of as lobbyists." Referring to one prominent Washington lobbyist, he said, "I don't think of him as a lobbyist. He's almost a constituent, or a friend." Barbara Boxer, then a representative (and now a senator; D-Cal.), referring to the same gentleman, described him as "a lovely, wonderful guy. In the whole time I've known him, he's never asked me to vote for anything." She joked that he's almost "a member of the family."[78]

Providing Expertise

When lobbyists contact officials, they might provide expertise that officials lack. Lobbyists make sure that they fully understand their client's business and the entire industry in which it operates and also the proposed policy or law under consideration. Consequently, lobbyists are an invaluable source of information for members of Congress and aides in the White House, who usually are generalists rather than experts. They rely on lobbyists to educate them. When Congress considered standards for high-definition TV in the 1990s, a representative of the Information Technology Association of America referred to "pixels." A member of Congress spoke up, "I'm trying to stay with you here, but one of the first times I ever took a ride on an airplane was when I came to Washington to take this seat, and I remember looking out the window and thought part of the wing was falling off when we landed because the flaps came up."[79] Lobbyists often draft legislation. A legislator may ask a lobbyist known to be an expert in an area to draft a bill, or a lobbyist may draft a bill and ask a legislator thought to be sympathetic to the cause to introduce the bill in Congress.

Giving Money

Lobbyists also give money, in the form of campaign contributions, to candidates for office and to officials running for reelection. They give to those they agree with and also those who are incumbents or favorites in elections. The money greases the skids—it ensures access. A longtime financial backer of Ronald Reagan said that having a dialogue with a politician is fine, "but with a little money they hear you better."[80] A Democrat commented in a similar vein, "Who do members of Congress see? They'll certainly see the one who gives the money. It's hard to say no to someone who gives you $5000."[81]

Despite its liberal reputation, the entertainment industry donated more money to Republican candidates (59 percent) than to Democratic candidates (41 percent) in the 2006 congressional elections. Hollywood studios even donated to conservative Republicans who sat on committees with jurisdiction over issues, such as intellectual property rights, important to the industry.[82] With the Republicans in the majority at the time, Hollywood moguls followed their business interests rather than their ideological views.

To give money, groups, including businesses and unions, set up PACs, which channel contributions to parties and candidates. This discussion presumes that the groups freely decide whether to contribute their money. However, once the parties and candidates got used to receiving contributions, and as they faced escalating costs for television advertising, they began to pressure the groups to make contributions. Republican leader Tom Delay told lobbyists they had "to pay to play"—that is, to contribute if they wanted to influence congressional bills or obtain government contracts.

Thus, leverage is exercised in both directions. The groups give money to the parties and candidates as a way to influence current and future officials, and the parties and candidates demand money from the groups as a way to finance their campaigns. With only some exaggeration, one might say that the groups are practicing a legalized form of bribery and the parties and candidates are practicing a legalized form of extortion.

Litigating in Court

Although interest groups do not lobby judges the way they do legislators and bureaucrats, some do use litigation to persuade courts to rule for their side in disputes over policies and laws. The groups might file a lawsuit, represent a defendant facing criminal prosecution, or submit a brief—written arguments—in favor of one side in the case.

Although most groups don't use litigation, some use it as their primary tactic, particularly those that lack influence with the legislative and executive branches. Litigation has been a successful strategy for civil rights organizations. Throughout the first half of the twentieth century, when Congress and presidents were unsympathetic to the rights of black Americans, the National Association for the Advancement of Colored People (NAACP) fought segregation in the courts. Litigation has been the usual strategy of civil liberties groups, especially the American Civil Liberties Union (ACLU). (These groups' efforts will be covered in Chapters 12 and 13.)

Environmental groups use litigation to challenge governmental policies toward environmental issues. On the local level, environmental groups file lawsuits to challenge new developments that threaten environmental damage. They hope to block the projects or, at least, to delay the projects, so the costs will increase and the developers will have an incentive to negotiate changes with the groups. Then for future projects, the developers might be willing to make concessions before the groups file a suit.

Indirect Lobbying Techniques: Going Public

Traditionally, lobbyists employed the direct lobbying techniques just addressed. But, increasingly, they have used the indirect lobbying techniques known as **going public**.[83] These techniques include mobilizing their supporters and molding public opinion. The goal is to get citizens to contact officials or to get them to vote in elections. In these ways, groups lobby indirectly.

Mobilizing Supporters

Groups mobilize their activists and other supporters—**the grass roots**—through direct mail, e-mail, websites, and faxes. To overcome people's inertia, groups often exaggerate their opponents' views or strength or the dire consequences that could result. They proclaim a monstrous adversary or predict a catastrophic defeat if their supporters don't heed the call. Their communications are "about scaring the hell out of people."[84]

The NRA is especially effective. It can generate thousands of letters, e-mails, or calls to members of Congress within days. The calls from irate members led one senator to remark, "I'd rather be a deer in hunting season than run afoul of the NRA crowd."[85] At rallies in 2000, NRA president Charlton Heston called the presidential election "the most important since the Civil War." If Gore won, he asserted, his Supreme Court will "hammer your gun rights into oblivion." Members turned out in droves, with the result that at least West Virginia, a traditional Democratic state, gave its electoral votes to Bush. Moral Majority leader Jerry Falwell activated his "gospel grapevine" to flood the White House and Congress with messages opposed to President Clinton's plan to allow homosexuals in the military. Warning of a radical homosexual rights agenda, Falwell urged viewers of his *Old Time Gospel Hour* to register their opinions.

Of course, the messages don't always succeed, especially if they don't reflect a broad base. Senator Tom Harkin (D-Iowa) received hundreds of letters opposing his antitobacco position, though from only one part of his state. The mystery was solved when he learned that all the letters came from employees of a Kraft food plant, owned by tobacco company RJ Reynolds.[86]

The messages should appear spontaneous and sincere. Groups often provide sample letters to aid their members, but these aren't as convincing as those written in a member's own words. Postcards with preprinted messages aren't very convincing either. With the Internet, groups are using online petitions. Although these aren't as effective as individual communications, a huge number of names may have an impact. MoveOn.org, a left-leaning website with an e-mail list of 1.8 million, can with the click of a mouse send hundreds of thousands of messages hurtling toward Washington.[87] MoveOn also tries to mold public opinion by soliciting money to air television commercials.

Molding Public Opinion

Groups try to mold public opinion through commercials on television and radio and ads in newspapers and magazines. Groups also stage media events, including photo ops, to attract media coverage.

Television programming can also mold public opinion. Lifetime, the television network targeted at women, has acted like an interest group in raising issues relevant to women through its issue-oriented programming. A movie featuring Academy Award-winning actress Mira Sorvino dealt with sex trafficking. Others have focused on stalking, spouse abuse, and DNA testing in rape cases. A documentary, *Terror in the Home,* prompted a 7000 percent increase in calls to the National Domestic Violence Hotline. A movie, *Video Voyeur: The Susan Wilson Story,* depicting spying by a creepy high-tech neighbor, led to the Video Voyeurism Protection Act of 2004.[88]

Framing the debate—causing people to view the debate one way rather than another—can be crucial in winning public support. Business groups that propose "tort reform," which would limit the money that courts can award to individuals injured in auto accidents, air disasters, unsuccessful surgeries, and other mishaps, focus on notorious cases in which the victims have gotten outrageous awards for minor injuries, such as the grandmother who spilled McDonald's coffee onto her lap and was awarded $2.9 million for her serious burns. (But the award was reduced to $840,000 by the judge and then reduced to some lower amount through negotiations between the two litigants to avoid an appeal.) These groups frame the debate as an overdue reform or, in malpractice cases, as a crucial reform if we want doctors to remain in the medical profession.[89] Lawyer groups that oppose "tort reform" instead focus on the poor victims seriously injured and left penniless by the careless behavior of large corporations or wealthy doctors.[90] These groups frame the debate as a denial of victims' rights to sue and receive compensation for their injuries and to hold corporations or doctors accountable—essentially, as the little guy versus the big bully.

Students sit-in at a segragated lunch counter in Jackson, Mississippi, during the civil rights era.

Occasionally, groups fabricate information. Although there's a cardinal rule that lobbyists should not mislead officials—they would never be trusted again—there's no comparable rule for not misleading the public. ExxonMobil, which opposes government efforts to reduce global warming, has tried to discredit the science of global warming. According to one calculation, the corporation gave $16 million to 43 groups between 1998 and 2005 to mislead the public into believing that the science is inconclusive and the scientists are in disagreement.[91] The corporation assumed it's not necessary to convince people that there's no global warming; it's only necessary to confuse them into thinking that the issue isn't resolved, so the difficult steps to counter it don't have to be taken yet.[92]

As elections approach, groups also rate members of Congress based on their votes or positions. The League of Conservation Voters identifies the "Dirty Dozen" among the congressional incumbents running for re-election. In 2006, the League also identified the "Oil Slick Seven" who favored the oil companies' interests the most.

Engaging in Protest If groups are excluded from the political process or if they simply lack the money necessary to organize throughout the country, they can turn to protest. When the House of Representatives passed a draconian bill that would urge more deportations of illegal aliens, deny social services for them, and subject anyone who helps them to five years in prison, legal immigrants worried because many Latino families have both legal and illegal immigrants. The bill would have split families, deporting some members and subjecting others to prison for helping them. Latino organizations, anxious to show the American people how valuable the immigrants are, announced a "Day Without Immigrants" in 2006. They urged workers to leave construction sites and restaurants undermanned, hotel rooms uncleaned, and crops unattended, and to march in the streets. They asked students to leave classrooms and join them. The marchers generated awareness of the issue, which usually is the first step in a long struggle.

The civil rights movement is the best example of a successful protest in twentieth-century America. By demonstrating against legalized segregation, black and some white protestors called attention to the discrepancy between the American values of democracy and equality and the inferior status of blacks in the South. The protestors also called attention to the contrast between their peaceful behavior and the police and vigilante brutality unleashed against them. In their marches, sit-ins, and other demonstrations, the protestors practiced **civil disobedience**—intentionally but peacefully violating laws and getting arrested, so they could challenge the laws in court. (See the box "Organizing Protest: the Montgomery Bus Boycott.")

Some environmental groups, such as Greenpeace, also practice civil disobedience. The organization got its start in 1971 when environmental and peace activists sent two boats to Amchitka Island (near Alaska) to protest a U.S. underground nuclear weapon test. In other protests, members placed themselves in the path of a harpoon to protect endangered whales and parachuted over coal-powered plants to protest acid rain. Their goal was to generate eye-catching publicity and energize the public.

Sometimes protest leads to hostility against, rather than sympathy for, the protesters. Antiwar demonstrations by college students in the 1960s and 1970s angered not only government officials, who targeted the leaders for harassment, but also ordinary citizens, including many who opposed the war itself. They were more antiprotest than antiwar.

Protest demands skill from the leaders and sacrifices from the followers. Continued participation, essential to real success, robs the activists of a normal life. They can face jail, physical harm, or even death, and they need discipline to refrain from violence, even when they are targeted for violence.

Once protest groups get a hearing—that is, once they find someone in government who is willing to listen—they often shift to an inside strategy, working with those in power rather than against them. They discard the demonstrations for more conventional lobbying techniques.

Success of Interest Groups

Politics is not a game of chance in which luck determines the winners and losers. Some groups are more successful than others because of their resources and goals.

Resources

Money usually is essential for success. Groups with more money can establish and operate an organization, hire experienced administrators and lobbyists, and make campaign donations. They can also try to mold public opinion through television commercials or other channels. This resource gives business groups a tremendous advantage in our political system.

Size—the number of members—can augment their money or might substitute for great wealth, especially if their members can be mobilized. AARP has 35 million members, senior citizens who focus on Social Security and health care and who vote in high numbers. They pay dues, so AARP has a big bankroll, but its power comes chiefly from its size.

The number of members relative to the number of potential members in a group can also be important. The American Medical Association (AMA) enrolled 70 percent or more of the nation's doctors for years, and it enjoyed a lot of clout. As its percentage of American doctors declined, its influence declined as well.

Cohesion and intensity might substitute for money and size. Public interest groups and especially single-issue groups, such as the pro-choice and pro-life groups, are most likely to have cohesive and intense members who can be mobilized to contact officials, write letters to the editor, persuade their friends, and vote.

The groups that marshal the greatest resources are most likely to win. In fact, they may overcome the majority view, as reflected in public opinion polls. Supporters of gun control have long had public opinion on their side, but their main group, the National Council to Control Handguns, has less money, fewer members, and less cohesion and intensity among its members than the NRA boasts. As a result, the NRA has triumphed over public opinion for decades.

Goals

Groups that promote change, especially sweeping change, usually are less successful than groups that work to preserve the status quo. In our system of separation of powers, checks and balances, and federalism, groups that promote change must persuade numerous officials in multiple institutions; groups that work to preserve the status quo may have to persuade only one key official, or perhaps several important officials, in just a single institution. Thus it is harder to produce government action than to prevent such action.

When President Clinton proposed his major health care reform, medical, dental, hospital, and insurance associations and companies voiced their opposition. The proposal became the most heavily lobbied initiative in history.[93] Given its scope, it was not a surprise that the proposal was defeated. Although health care costs continue to spiral out of control, significant reform may require a crisis, or at least the perception of a crisis, to overcome the resistance of the groups affected by it.

On the other hand, President Clinton's welfare reform, which was a major revision of an entrenched policy, was adopted. It set work requirements for the recipients, who are the poorest and least politically active Americans. They don't have strong interest groups representing them, so they were unable to block the new requirements.

Groups that seek narrow benefits for themselves, rather than broad policy changes for society, usually are more successful. If the provisions are complex, the media are less likely to call attention to them and the public is less likely to be aware of them. Virtually everyone is aware of hot-button issues such as abortion and capital punishment, but relatively few people are aware of technical provisions that regulate or tax businesses. The accountancy profession opposed regulations that would

ORGANIZING A BOYCOTT

The 1955 Montgomery, Alabama, bus boycott was the first successful civil rights protest, and it brought its twenty-six-year-old leader, Dr. **Martin Luther King, Jr.,** to national prominence.

Montgomery, like most southern cities, required blacks to sit in the back of public buses, reserving the seats in the front for whites. Between the two was a "no-man's-land" where blacks could sit if there were no whites. If whites boarded the bus and needed the seats, however, blacks had to move to the back.

One afternoon, **Rosa Parks,** a seamstress at a department store and a leader in the local NAACP, got on the bus to go home. The bus was crowded, and when a white man boarded, the driver called on the four blacks in the "no-man's-land" to move to the back. Three moved, but Parks, tired from a long day and tired of the racial injustice, refused. Under a law that gave him the authority to enforce segregation, the driver arrested her.

That evening, a group of women professors at the black college in Montgomery, led by Jo Ann Robinson, drafted a letter calling on their brothers and sisters to stay off the buses on Monday. Although fearful for their jobs and concerned that the state would cut the funding to the college if it became known that they had used state facilities to produce the letter, they worked through the night and made thirty-five thousand copies of their letter to distribute to the city's black residents.

The following day, black leaders agreed to the boycott, and on Sunday, black ministers encouraged their members to support the boycott. On Monday, 90 percent of black workers walked, shared rides in private cars, or took black-owned taxis. The boycott inspired confidence and pride in the black community. Hundreds of blacks jammed the courthouse, as nervous police looked on, to make sure that Rosa Parks was safely released after being convicted.

At a mass rally later that evening, Martin Luther King, Jr., cried out, "There comes a time when people get tired of being trampled over by the iron feet of oppression." Noting that the right to protest is the glory of American democracy, King appealed to the strong religious faith of the crowd:

"If we are wrong, God Almighty is wrong. . . . If we are wrong, Jesus of Nazareth was merely a utopian dreamer. . . . If we are wrong, justice is a lie." These words established King as a charismatic leader of the civil rights movement.

Due to its initial success, the boycott was extended. Each successive day was a trial for the residents and their leaders. Thousands had to find a way to get to work, and the leaders struggled to keep a massive carpool going. But each night's rally boosted morale for the next day's boycott. The rallies became prayer services, as the black community prayed for strength to keep on walking, for courage to remain nonviolent, and for divine guidance for their oppressors.

The city bus line was losing money. City leaders urged more whites to ride the buses to make up lost revenue, but few did. Black leaders, recognizing that the boycott could not continue forever, agreed to end it if the rules for "no-man's-land" were relaxed. In response, city leaders concluded that they were on the verge of breaking the boycott, and they rejected the offer. Police officers be-

---

make corporations' financial status more transparent in the 1990s. Few people, except for the executives in the corporations and auditing firms, were aware of the financial implications until Enron collapsed with the complicity of auditing firm Arthur Anderson.

Whole industries and individual corporations have gotten Congress to insert favorable provisions in tax laws. The tax code is riddled with exemptions for industries and corporations.[94] Some beneficiaries aren't identified by their name. A provision exempts Phillips Petroleum, identified in a law as a "corporation incorporated on June 13, 1917, which has its principal place of busi-

ness in Bartlesville, Oklahoma."[95] A representative from a district that has three national bakeries quietly inserted a provision into a tax bill that simply deleted "bakery drivers" from the list of occupations treated as employees.[96] The drivers, although hired by the bakeries, would be considered self-employed rather than bakery employees. This meant that the bakeries wouldn't have to pay Social Security, Medicare, or unemployment taxes on their drivers. (Instead, their drivers would have to pay extra Social Security and Medicare taxes themselves.) This ripoff was removed only when a congressional staffer noticed it and publicized it.

gan to harass carpoolers and issue bogus tickets for trumped-up violations.

City leaders issued an ultimatum—settle or face arrest. A white grand jury indicted more than one hundred boycott leaders for the alleged crime of organizing the protest. In the spirit of nonviolence, the leaders, including King, surrendered.

The decision to arrest the leaders proved to be the turning point of the boycott. The white editor of the local paper said it was "the dumbest act that has ever been done in Montgomery." With the mass arrests, the boycott finally received national attention. Reporters from all over the world streamed into Montgomery to cover the story. The boycott became a national event, and its leader, Martin Luther King, Jr., became a national figure.

A year later, the U.S. Supreme Court declared Alabama's local and state laws mandating segregation on buses unconstitutional. Only after the city complied with the Court's order did the boycott end.

When Rosa Parks died at the age of ninety-two in 2005, she was lauded as one of the key figures in the civil

Rosa Parks is fingerprinted in Montgomery, Alabama, after her arrest for refusing to give up her seat on the bus to a white man. Her refusal triggered a boycott of city buses that became the first successful civil disobedience in the civil rights movement and made Parks a hero to black and white Americans alike.

rights movement. Fifty thousand people filed through the U.S. Capitol Rotunda, where she lay in state, the first woman and second African American to be honored in this way. Thousands attended her funeral, and thousands more lined the streets to witness her casket pulled by a horse-drawn carriage to the cemetery.

SOURCES: Taylor Branch, *Parting the Waters: America in the King Years* (New York: Simon & Schuster, 1988), chs. 4 and 5; Juan Williams, *Eyes on the Prize* (New York: Viking, 1987).

Conclusion: Do Interest Groups Make Government More Responsive?

In an indirect democracy, as in the United States, citizens elect representatives to make decisions—pass laws and adopt policies—for them. The elections focus on a handful of issues or on the personalities of candidates; they aren't referendums on the gamut of matters pending at the time. The elections occur only periodically, and many citizens don't vote when the elections do roll around. So, the elections don't reflect people's views on many issues. To supplement the ballot box in our political system, interest groups play an important role. They offer citizens the opportunity to join, and they monitor the government and, when necessary, make their views known to our officials.

By joining and paying dues or making contributions, citizens essentially hire private representatives—

their groups' leaders—to act on their behalf much as citizens elect public officials to do so. Most citizens can't monitor the actions of the president, 535 members of Congress organized into almost two hundred committees and subcommittees, and more than one hundred bureaucratic agencies. And most citizens can't communicate their views to these officials, committees, and agencies. But interest groups can.

The theory that groups represent us and compete for the attention of and influence over government is called **pluralism.** There are many groups, plural groups, which spring up around every conceivable issue. Thousands of groups represent millions of Americans. According to the theory, the groups compete as businesses compete with other businesses to sell their products and services. In this way, the people are represented and appropriate policies—the survivors of spirited competition in the political marketplace—are adopted. Accordingly, our government is responsive to the people, even though many of them don't vote.

In fact, although many people do join groups—more people than in other countries—some people don't join groups, so these people aren't represented by groups, or at least by many groups or strong groups. The people who have the least education and the least income are the least likely to join groups. Therefore groups don't represent, or don't adequately represent, the poor, the working class (except for those in unions), and the politically disinterested. Instead, they disproportionately represent the well-to-do and their businesses. A political scientist's observation from 1960 remains valid today: "The flaw in the pluralist heaven is that the angelic chorus sings with an upper class accent."[97]

The middle class can wield power, through its sheer numbers, when it is very aware of and interested in an issue. And sometimes middle-class concerns do benefit working-class people as well. The middle-class members of AARP protect the interests of the elderly in general.

But the rapid proliferation and expanded power of interest groups in recent decades has led to what some political scientists call **hyperpluralism.** According to this view, the system now features so many groups with so many supporters and resources that it is difficult to find common ground to forge solutions to problems. The groups pull the government in too many directions, and they wield a de facto veto of proposals they dislike. The result is gridlock. The Clinton White House tried to work with eleven hundred interest groups on health care reform but still couldn't find an acceptable compromise.[98] And modern technology heightens the impact. A witness to congressional hearings on tax reform noticed that lobbyists used cell phones to start an avalanche of protests by phone and fax the instant anyone even *mentioned* something the groups opposed.[99]

In this climate, the groups make government responsive to their members, but their efforts prevent government from solving critical problems, even when a majority of the people want government to address these problems. So, ironically, as the groups are making government responsive to their members, they are rendering it unresponsive to the rest of society.

Of course, there are exceptions. Consider the successes of **Ralph Nader,** the son of Lebanese immigrants and a crusader for average Americans against the giants of corporate America. Nader spearheaded an array of interest groups, including Public Citizen, that attracted young professionals (dubbed "Nader's Raiders") and fought for safer products and a healthier environment. More than any other person, Nader is responsible for seat belts, air bags, padded dashboards, steering columns that won't impale drivers, and fuel tanks that won't explode upon collision. Because of Nader, drinking water, baby food, and dental X-rays are all safer. Infant pajamas are less likely to catch fire. To a significant extent, Nader is also responsible for the creation of important bureaucratic agencies—the Environmental Protection Agency (EPA); the Consumer Product Safety Commission (CPSC), which tries to ensure safe products; and the Occupational Safety and Health Administration (OSHA), which tries to ensure safe workplaces. Nader deserves credit for the Freedom of Information Act, which exposes government actions and ensures greater accountability.[100] His work is a testament to how much one person, working through interest groups, can do, even when that person is up against powerful opponents.

Key Terms

Key Names

1. What did the Frenchman Alexis de Tocqueville observe when he traveled through the United States in the 1830s?
   a. lingering feelings for mother England
   b. Americans' tendency to join groups
   c. idolization of the president
   d. Americans' reluctance to join groups
   e. a desire to return to a monarchy

2. Which of the following is not a reason why Americans are more likely to form and join interest groups than people in other countries?
   a. the First Amendment
   b. strong political parties
   c. federalism
   d. our racial and ethnic diversity
   e. our religious diversity

3. Through history, interest groups have most often formed when
   a. the president has been unpopular.
   b. political parties have been at their strongest.
   c. Congress has been unproductive.
   d. the presidency has been at its strongest.
   e. major social, economic, or technological changes have been occurring.

4. The surge in the formation and activity of interest groups in the 1960s and 1970s reflected all but which of the following?
   a. renewed interest in labor unions
   b. the civil rights movement
   c. the women's movement
   d. the environmental movement
   e. consumers' concerns about unsafe products

5. If someone doesn't join interest groups because she doesn't think she could make any difference, political scientists would say that she lacks
   a. a conscience.
   b. an understanding of politics.
   c. a sense of political efficacy.
   d. an awareness that others are joining interest groups.
   e. a willingness to fulfill her responsibilities in a democracy.

6. Interest groups face the _____ because potential members realize that they will share in the benefits of the groups' efforts without bearing any of the groups' costs or work.
   a. political efficacy problem
   b. membership dilemma
   c. free-rider problem
   d. work-cost dilemma
   e. iron law of oligarchy

7. Which of the following would you predict to be the most likely to join interest groups?
   a. Hispanic immigrants
   b. welfare recipients
   c. shopkeepers
   d. business executives
   e. recent college graduates

8. Interest groups establish PACs to
   a. recruit more members.
   b. channel their contributions to candidates in elections.
   c. mobilize their members.
   d. lobby the bureaucracy.
   e. handle any lawsuits they're involved in.

9. Which of the following is considered a private interest group?
   a. AARP   b. AFL-CIO
   c. Christian Coalition   d. NRA
   e. Planned Parenthood

10. Which generally are the most numerous and powerful interest groups?
    a. business groups
    b. environmental groups
    c. agriculture groups
    d. labor unions
    e. pro-life and pro-choice groups

11. Labor union membership has declined since its peak in the mid-twentieth century because of all but which of the following?
    a. their success in boosting members' wages
    b. business efforts to resist the formation of unions
    c. the decline of manufacturing jobs in the United States
    d. antiunion sentiment in the South and Southwest
    e. the failure of unions to try to organize big sectors of the workforce such as government employees

12. Public interest groups are those which
    a. lobby to increase the number and size of government agencies.
    b. pursue the real public interest.
    c. lobby for benefits that would go primarily to their members.
    d. follow public opinion about what government should do.
    e. lobby for causes rather than financial gain.

13. Single-issue groups are troublesome for politicians because they _____ than other groups.
    a. are more knowledgeable about their issue
    b. are less willing to compromise
    c. have more members
    d. have more money
    e. have more professional staffers

14. Which is likely to be more successful?
    a. a group trying to get Congress to pass a new law
    b. a group trying to get the administration to adopt a new policy
    c. a group trying to get Congress to add an amendment to an existing law
    d. a group trying to get the administration to expand enforcement of an existing law
    e. a group trying to defeat efforts by another group to repeal an existing law

15. Businesses that want to sell their products or services to government seek
    a. a new law authorizing them to do so.
    b. bureaucratic rules.
    c. a new policy authorizing them to do so.
    d. government contracts.
    e. executive agreements.

16. Groups that contribute money to politicians' campaigns want, at a minimum, _____ for their money.
    a. honest government
    b. access to the politicians
    c. efficient government
    d. favorable votes by the politicians
    e. good public policies

17. Which groups use litigation as a frequent tactic?
    a. groups that reflect majority opinion
    b. groups that have a lot of money
    c. groups that have a national profile
    d. groups that have a lot of members
    e. groups that lack influence with the legislative and executive branches.

18. Groups use the tactic of going public to
    a. mobilize their supporters.
    b. gain access to decision makers.
    c. persuade officials in bureaucratic agencies.
    d. influence the public.
    e. a and d.

19. Single-issue groups usually have _____, which helps them succeed.
    a. intense members
    b. public support
    c. a good cause
    d. a lot of money
    e. a lot of members

20. Interest groups don't represent, or adequately represent, all but which of the following?
    a. the poor
    b. the elderly
    c. most of the working class
    d. those with the least education
    e. those with the lowest incomes

Christian evangelicals have become a potent force within the Republican Party.

Democrats and Republicans differ about politics, of course, but do they differ about other things? Do they differ in cultural preferences, such as their tastes in reading and music? Democratic and Republican party operatives were asked questions about a variety of nonpolitical matters.[1] Their answers do reveal differences between the two parties' workers, even for things that have no overt political content.

When asked what was the most recent book they read, members of both parties cited the bestseller *The DaVinci Code,* but after this book Republicans were much more likely to cite religious books and self-help books than Democrats were.

When asked for their favorite magazine, members of both parties said they liked *Sports Illustrated,* but otherwise they diverged. Republicans favored a variety of sports and outdoors magazines, such as *Golf Digest* and *Field and Stream,* whereas Democrats favored literary magazines, especially the *New Yorker.*[2] Democrats were more likely to mention music magazines, such as *Rolling Stone* and *Spin,* than Republicans were.

Musical tastes also show similarities and differences. The operatives of both parties like rock music, but after that the Republicans are more likely to prefer country and the Democrats are more likely to prefer rap, R & B, blues, or reggae. There are further differences within these categories. The Democrats are drawn to less conventional music, citing artists classified by the music industry as alternative rock, alternative metal, alternative rap, and alternative country, whereas the Republicans cited more traditional singers and groups.

Overall, Republican operatives, reflecting the greater homogeneity within their party, differed among themselves less than Democratic operatives did.

Thus there are differences in cultural preferences as well as in political predilections, at least among the operatives of the two parties. In their attempts to appeal to the voters, then, Republican officials who invite an R & B group to entertain at their convention may be just as insincere as Democratic candidates who profess an interest in NASCAR.

James Madison, the "Father of the Constitution," warned against the "mischief of factions," which today would include interest groups and political parties. George Washington, the "Father of the Country," cautioned against the "baneful" effects of parties and called them the people's worst enemies. Years later, however, a respected political scientist, E. E. Schattschneider, claimed that "political parties created democracy and that democracy was impossible without them."[3]

The public reflects these contradictory views. Americans, especially young adults, are cynical about parties and believe we would be better off without them. People complain that politics is too **partisan**—that candidates and officials make decisions based on their party affiliation, rather than according to our country's needs. People say they're tired of "partisan bickering," as though the parties are arguing over nothing, like little children. Many believe that the parties create conflict where none really exists. Despite these views, however,

most people identify with one of the parties, and many people vote solely according to the party affiliations of the competing candidates.

This chapter examines American political parties to see why they persist—indeed, why they are important—despite the criticism they face. We'll start with an overview of American political parties.

Characteristics of American Parties

Political parties consist of three interrelated components: (1) the citizens who consider themselves members of the party, (2) the officeholders who are elected or appointed in the name of the party, and (3) the activists who run the party organization at the national, state, and local levels (see Figure 1).[4]

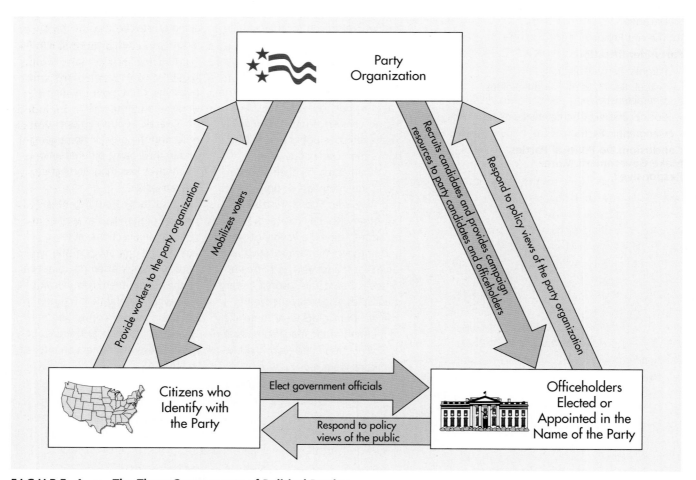

FIGURE 1 • **The Three Components of Political Parties**

The American party system is unusual among Western democracies, which can be seen when we examine its distinguishing features.

Two Major Parties

The American party system is a **two-party system.** Only two parties—the **Democratic Party** and the **Republican Party**—have a realistic chance to win the presidency or most seats in Congress. (Occasionally an independent wins a seat; today a socialist—Senator Bernie Sanders (Vt.)—holds a seat.)

Two-party systems are very rare. In Western Europe, **multiparty systems** are the rule. Italy has nine national parties and several regional parties; Germany has five national parties. Great Britain, although predominantly a two-party system, has several significant minor parties. Multiparty systems are also found in Canada, which has three parties, and Israel, which has more than twenty.

Why two parties in the United States? The most common explanation is that American elections, with our **single-member districts** and **winner-take-all provision,** favor two parties.[5] These features mean that only one individual—the one who receives the most votes—is elected from a district. Although these features seem natural, even inevitable, to Americans, they contrast with **proportional representation** (PR), which is employed in more democracies. PR systems use large multimember districts. In most PR systems, voters cast their ballot for a party slate, and each party receives the number of seats in the district according to its percentage of votes in the district.[6] (There's no winner-take-all provision.) Consequently, representation in the national legislature is roughly proportional to the popular vote each party receives nationwide.

In single-member-district, winner-take-all elections, only the major parties have a good shot at winning a legislative seat. Minor parties are less likely to emerge and, if they do, more likely to merge with a major party. In PR elections, even a modest showing—15 percent or less—may win a legislative seat, enabling a small party to have a voice and a base to attract more supporters in the next election. This prospect encourages minor parties.

Minor Parties

Although the American party system disfavors minor parties, also called "third parties," such parties do exist. Most, such as the Prohibition Party (since the 1860s),

which opposes the sale of alcoholic beverages, and the Communist Party USA (since the 1920s), which proposes the adoption of communism, receive little notice and few votes. But some, such as the Progressive Party in the late 1800s and early 1900s, have had a major impact on American politics.

Some minor parties are essentially an individual's organization. In 1968, Alabama's segregationist governor, George Wallace, split from the Democratic Party to run for president as the candidate of the American Independent Party. In 1992, Texas businessman Ross Perot decided to run for president. His willingness to use his personal fortune to fund an expensive campaign made him a visible alternative to the major-party candidates. He polled 19 percent of the votes, an extraordinary number for a minor party, but his total didn't influence the outcome, as he siphoned votes from both major-party candidates. However, his campaign did push the issue of the budget deficit to the top of the national agenda.

Consumer advocate **Ralph Nader** ran in 2000 and 2004. In 2000, he was the nominee of the Green Party, an offshoot of the antinuclear and environmental movements. He claimed that the major parties were simply pawns of corporate America, and he called for more checks on big business. In 2000, he received just 3 percent of the votes nationwide, but this tally included 97,000 voters in Florida. Because most Nader voters preferred Al Gore over George W. Bush, many of their votes would have gone to Gore if Nader hadn't been on the ballot. In the tight election, with Bush's 537-vote margin, Nader's votes were enough to deny Gore a victory in the state and, consequently, in the Electoral College.[7] (Of course, in an election this close, other factors affected the outcome as well.)

In 2004, Bush donors helped finance Nader's campaign in an attempt to pull votes from Democratic candidate John Kerrey,[8] but this time Nader received less than 1 percent of the votes and didn't affect the outcome in any state.

Despite Nader's impact as a spoiler, third parties must overcome substantial barriers to get established. Most Americans feel long-standing loyalty to one of the major parties. They also realize that minor-party candidates can't win, so most don't want to "waste their vote" or, worse, help their least liked candidate, as Nader's Florida voters helped Bush. Because voters realize that minor-party candidates can't win, such candidates can't raise the money or attract the media attention they need.[9] Although many Americans—over half in various polls—tell pollsters that they want alternatives to the two major parties, few voters ever cast a vote for a minor-party candidate.

Historically, minor parties do well only when the country faces social or economic challenges that the major parties have avoided. Then, once the minor parties make an impact, the major parties co-opt their ideas, and the minor parties, no longer needed, fade into oblivion. After Perot made the budget deficit a national issue, the incoming Clinton administration made the deficit its chief economic priority, and Perot's insistent demands diminished.

Moderate Parties

The American party system features relatively moderate parties. In a two-party system, both parties are "big tents" with diverse members. To win, they have to attract many voters. Unlike in a multiparty system, where parties can gain legislative seats without winning a majority in any district, American parties can't focus their campaigns on just one segment of the electorate. If they want to win, they must appeal to most of the electorate; they must choose pragmatism over ideological purity. Most voters cluster toward the middle, rather than at the extremes (see Figure 2), so the parties pitch their campaigns toward the middle, at least in national elections.

The Democrats position themselves in the center-left, and the Republicans position themselves in the center-right. For the presidency, the parties either nominate moderate candidates; or ideological candidates, once nominated, moderate their positions or at least obscure them. Bill Clinton became a "new Democrat," embracing some Republican ideas, such as free trade and welfare reform. George W. Bush called himself a "compassionate conservative," convincing many voters that he was actually a moderate (but couldn't say so without alienating conservative voters). Once in office, Clinton stayed in the middle, but

Bush turned back to the right to satisfy his conservative base. Bush's strategy worked while public fears of terrorist attacks were fresh—people were willing to go along then—but failed as the fears subsided.

Although the parties aim for the center, both have members and supporting interest groups—left of center in the Democratic Party and right of center in the Republican Party—tugging them toward the extreme. In recent decades, this tendency has been stronger in the Republican Party, as conservatives have wrested control of the party from moderates. Republican officeholders have been more conservative than Republican voters in many places. In the 1990s, Republican members of Congress shut down the government over a budget dispute and then impeached President Clinton over his sexual affair. For both matters, public opinion ran contrary to Republican efforts, and the president survived impeachment and won reelection. In the 2000s, after gaining the upper hand as a result of the 2000 election and the 9/11 attacks, Republicans again tried to implement a conservative agenda too extreme for public opinion, and Democratic majorities were elected to Congress in 2006.

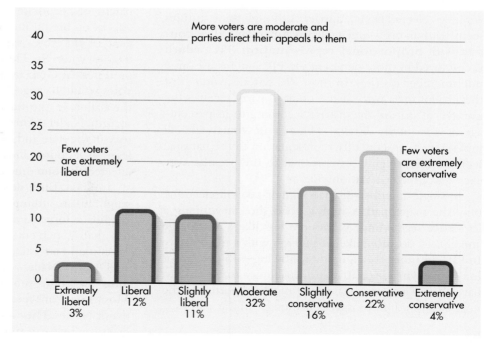

FIGURE 2 • **Where the Voters Are** *The labels indicate how the voters characterize themselves today. In recent years, more have characterized themselves as conservative than as liberal, but most have characterized themselves as moderate. Thus, the parties usually aim their campaigns at the middle.*
SOURCE: Data from General Social Survey, 2004.

Fragmented Parties

The American party system also features fragmented parties. The national, state, and local parties are relatively independent, rather than tightly knit in a hierarchical organization. Each level has its own power base and resources, so it can act according to its own interests. This result reflects our federalism, which fragments governmental power between the national and the state and local levels.

This fragmentation challenges the party's leaders who want to present a consistent message to voters and the party's officeholders who want to get their fellow officeholders to follow the party's positions. Although presidents usually get support from their party's officeholders,[10] the fragmentation allows the officeholders to go their own way. To get reelected, they only need the votes of their constituents—not the approval of the president or other leaders. When President Clinton proposed an increase in gas taxes to reduce the deficits, Sen. Herbert Kohl (D-Wisc.) told him the increase could be no more than 4.3 cents per gallon. Clinton had to accept Kohl's figure because the bill's outcome was in doubt and the senator's vote was important. When President Bush proposed immigration reform, conservative Republicans rebelled and refused to pass a bill that could attain bipartisan support.

Party Organization

Party organization reflects the fragmentation of the parties. Party organization isn't hierarchical, with the national party organization on the top and the local party organizations at the bottom. The national party organization doesn't dictate policies to or impose penalties on the lower-level organizations. Instead, party organization is layered, with each layer linked to, but independent of, the others.

National Party Organizations The **national party chair** heads the national party organization, called the **national committee.** The national party chair is appointed by the president or, for the opposition party, by its national committee. The national party chair raises money and speaks out on behalf of the party. The national committees rarely meet, although they do choose the site of their party's convention and determine the formula for calculating each state's number of delegates.

Both parties also have House and Senate campaign committees, which raise money, recruit candidates, and vet strategy for upcoming campaigns.[11] Representative Rahm Emanuel (D-Ill.) headed the Democratic Congressional Campaign Committee in 2006. A former ballet prodigy, he was charged with producing a House Democratic majority for the first time in twelve years. Hyperactive and ruthless—he was nicknamed "Rahmbo"—Emanuel recruited centrist candidates for conservative districts, such as retired NFL quarterback Heath Shuler of North Carolina. Shuler resisted Emmanuel's pleas to run, insisting that he wanted to spend time with his family. Emmanuel persisted, calling him five times a day. "He calls one morning: 'Heath, I'm taking my kids to school,' then

Representative Rahm Emanuel and Senator Charles Schumer headed the Democratic Congressional and Senatorial Campaign Committees for the 2006 elections. They recruited some traditional, masculine men to run in the more conservative districts and states. The winners included quarterback Heath Shuler (N. Car.) and sheriff Brad Ellsworth (Ind.) (above, top) in the House, and farmer John Tester (Mont.) (above, bottom) and former Marine Jim Webb (Va.) in the Senate.

AP Images/Darron Cummings

AP Images/Reed Saxton

he just hangs up," Shuler said. "At 11:30, he calls and says, 'I'm leaving my office to eat lunch with my kids.' Then, 'Heath, it's 3:30, and I'm walking into school.'"[12] Shuler relented—and won his election—and Emanuel delivered a majority for the Democrats.

State and Local Party Organizations State and local party organizations have chairs and committees to direct party activities at these levels. In some communities, the parties are so weak that there is little organization. In these communities, any citizens who want to become active in their party need only show up and pitch in at party meetings.

Now we'll turn to history to see how the parties arose and developed and to see what roles they've played in our political system.

The Rise of American Parties

The Founders dreaded the prospect of political parties, fearing that rival parties competing for their own interests rather than working for the common good would undermine the new nation and its fledgling government.[13] Instead they hoped, unrealistically, to govern by consensus.

Because of the Founders' misgivings, the Constitution doesn't mention political parties. Nevertheless, the Constitution created a government in which parties, or something like them, were inevitable. With popular election as the mechanism for selecting political leaders, an agency for organizing and mobilizing the supporters of competing candidates became a necessity.

Birth of Parties

With George Washington's unanimous election to the presidency in 1788, it appeared that the nation could be governed by consensus. But differences of opinion soon arose. **Alexander Hamilton,** Washington's secretary of the treasury, supported a strong national government. He and his supporters in Congress, who called themselves **Federalists,** were opposed by **Thomas Jefferson,** Washington's secretary of state, who feared a strong central government. The conflict led Jefferson to challenge John Adams for the presidency in 1796. Jefferson lost but then began to recruit political operatives in each state to mobilize support on his behalf. **Jeffersonians** estab-

lished newspapers to get out their message. In short, Jefferson created the first American political party. Backed by his new party, Jefferson ran for the presidency in 1800 and won.

Before Jefferson left office, most members of Congress—more than 90 percent—were either Jeffersonians (later called Jeffersonian Republicans) or Federalists and consistently voted in support of their party's positions.[14]

Development of Mass Parties

Andrew Jackson introduced the idea of a political party with a large following among rank-and-file voters. Running for president in 1828, Jackson reached out to the masses. His appeals drew five times more voters to the polls than in 1824. Jackson's opponents deplored his approach, calling him a "barbarian" and his campaign "the howl of raving democracy."[15]

Like Jefferson, Jackson saw the strength of American democracy in the common person. His administration fostered participation in government by the average American. Property ownership as a qualification for voting was lifted in the states that still had this requirement, and the franchise was extended to all white men. Members of the Electoral College were elected by the people rather than selected by state legislatures. Party conventions, with representatives from every state and locality, were established to nominate presidential candidates.[16] These reforms encouraged participation. Historians, assessing this era's emphasis on the common person, would refer to the spirit of **Jacksonian democracy.**

Reflecting the increased participation in election campaigns as well as the population growth in the country, the electorate continued to expand, doubling again by 1840.[17]

Golden Age of Mass Parties

Parties reached their high point after the Civil War. Party leaders controlled the nominations for public offices. Party organizations mobilized the voters during election campaigns. Voting rates also peaked during this half century.

Political Machines

Local parties created **political machines,** which were powerful organizations that could deliver the votes. These organizations, also known as "urban machines" because they were especially prevalent in big cities, flourished during this period, with some lasting until the middle of the twentieth century.

The machines were hierarchical organizations, unlike today's parties. A city was divided into small neighborhoods called precincts, and the precincts were grouped into larger neighborhoods called wards. Party operatives were designated as "precinct captains" and "ward heelers." Their job was to know their constituents, tend to their needs, and then get their votes for the party's candidates in the next election. The head of the machine was a boss, who often served as mayor, and who directed the organization and ran city government to maintain control for the party. (See the box "A Day in the Life of a Machine Politician.")

The machines relied on the votes of the poor and working class, many of whom had recently immigrated from Europe. Although most accounts of machine politics are negative, dwelling on corruption, the machines provided valuable services for their constituents.

Providing Welfare The machines served as an informal welfare system for poor people during an era before the government created any formal welfare system—Temporary Assistance, Food Stamps, Social Security, Medicare, or Medicaid. Party organizations would provide food, clothing, or housing to people who needed help.

Party workers were an early "Welcome Wagon" for fresh immigrants, meeting them on the dock as they came off the ship and helping them settle into their new community in this strange country.

Longtime Rep. Tip O'Neill (D-Mass.) told the story of Boston mayor James Curley, a leader of the city's Democratic organization in the early twentieth century. As winter approached, Curley called Filene's, a local department store, and told the owner he needed five thousand sweaters. When the owner balked, Curley reminded him that it was time to reassess Filene's property for tax purposes—a none-too-subtle threat that its taxes would go up if the sweaters weren't delivered. Of course, the sweaters were delivered and distributed to poor people in the city.[18]

Party machines weren't motivated by a spirit of altruism. Rather, they were motivated by self-interest. They did favors to get favors—votes—in return. As New York City's boss George Washington Plunkitt said, "If a family is burned out, I don't ask whether they are Republicans or Democrats. . . . I just get quarters for them, buy clothes for them if their clothes were burned up and fix them up

'til they get things runnin' again. It's philanthropy, but it's politics too—mighty good politics. Who can tell me how many votes one of these fires brings me?"[19]

Providing Jobs The machines also served as an informal employment agency. The machines controlled government jobs and operated a **patronage system.**[20] During this era, virtually all government jobs, from the mayor's top aide to street sweepers, went to political appointees. When one party captured control of city government, city workers who supported the other party would be fired and new workers who supported the winning party would be hired in their place. "To the victor belong the spoils," the saying went. So the patronage system also came to be known as the **spoils system.**

The practice began with the presidency of Andrew Jackson, whose supporters were on the western frontier rather than in the eastern cities. He wanted to open government jobs to common people rather than reserve them for the elites. In adopting this practice, the machines provided jobs to some middle-class people as well as to many poor people and new immigrants. By 1900, New York City's machine controlled 60,000 city jobs. In the 1960s and 1970s, Chicago's mayor Richard Daley, one of the last of the big-city bosses, controlled 35,000 city jobs and, indirectly through public contracts, 10,000 private ones.[21]

When the parties provided welfare and jobs, the recipients were not only grateful but indebted, so they supported the parties. Job holders were fearful of losing their jobs, so they formed an army of party workers during the campaign, going door to door and taking residents to the polls.

Turnout was sky-high during the era of machine politics. In the 1896 presidential election, party workers led 90 percent of eligible voters (outside the South) to the polls, an astonishing number when many voters lived in isolated rural areas and used horses and buggies for transportation.[22]

Engaging in Corruption Although the machines provided undeniable benefits, they also engaged in undeniable corruption (as the story about the sweaters illustrates). Bribes and kickbacks were common. Payoffs were necessary for businesses to obtain government contracts. The corruption eventually produced a backlash against the machines, and the public pressured their legislators to enact various reforms that led to the machines' gradual demise.

George Washington Plunkitt was a ward leader in the infamous Tammany Hall machine, the Democratic Party organization that governed New York City for seven decades in the late nineteenth and early twentieth centuries. Although Plunkitt was on the city payroll, he did not have a free ride. The demands of his job were exhausting. Providing social services to his constituents, he had opportunities to build support for the party.

Entries from Plunkitt's diary illustrate the typical tasks he faced each day.

- 2:00 A.M. Aroused from sleep by a bartender who asked me to go to the police station and bail out a saloon keeper who had been arrested for violating the excise law. Furnished bail and returned to bed at three o'clock.
- 6:00 A.M. Awakened by fire engines. Hastened to the scene of the fire . . . found several tenants who had been burned out, took them to a hotel, supplied them with clothes, fed them, and arranged temporary quarters for them.
- 8:30 A.M. Went to the police court to secure the discharge of six "drunks," my constituents, by a timely word to the judge. Paid the fines of two.
- 9:00 A.M. Appeared in the municipal district court to direct one of my district captains to act as counsel for a widow about to be dispossessed. . . . Paid the rent of a poor family and gave them a dollar for food.
- 11:00 A.M. At home again. "Fixed" the troubles of four men waiting

George Washington Plunkitt holds forth in his unofficial office, a boot-black stand at the New York County Court House.

for me: one discharged by the Metropolitan Railway for neglect of duty; another wanted a job on the road; the third on the subway; and the fourth was looking for work with a gas company.

- 3:00 P.M. Attended the funeral of an Italian. Hurried back for the funeral of a Hebrew constituent. Went conspicuously to the front both in the Catholic church and the synagogue.
- 7:00 P.M. Went to district headquarters to preside over a meeting of election district captains, submitted lists of all the voters in their districts and told who were in need, who were in trouble, who might be won over [to Tammany] and how.
- 8:00 P.M. Went to a church fair. Took chances on everything, bought ice cream for the young

girls and the children, kissed the little ones, flattered their mothers, and took the fathers out for something down at the corner.

- 9:00 P.M. At the clubhouse again. Spent $10 for a church excursion. Bought tickets for a baseball game. Listened to the complaints of a dozen pushcart peddlers who said they were being persecuted by the police. Promised to go to police headquarters in the morning and see about it.
- 10:30 P.M. Attended a Hebrew wedding reception and dance. Had previously sent a handsome wedding present to the bride.
- 12:00 A.M. In bed.

SOURCE: Alistair Cooke, *Alistair Cooke's America* (New York: Knopf, 1973), 290–291; adapted from William L. Riordon, *Plunkitt of Tammany Hall* (New York Dutton, 1963), 91–93.

Functions of Parties

When political parties were at the height of their power, they performed important functions for our society. When we speak of institutions performing "functions," we mean that institutions do things which society finds useful. These things become their functions. The parties' primary function, then as now, was to get their candidates elected, but to accomplish this goal they performed other functions—political and social functions—that society found useful.

The parties recruited candidates from among party operatives who had moved up the ladder from low-level jobs to more responsible jobs in the party. (The boss of New York City's machine began by delivering coal to poor people in the winter to keep them from freezing.) Once the workers had proven themselves, party leaders would consider them for elective office. The parties, of course, didn't want to be embarrassed, so the leaders chose carefully. They nominated a slate of candidates, up to mayor on the local level, governor on the state level, and president on the national level. Aspiring candidates who weren't nominated by their party couldn't run on their own. The parties controlled access to the ballot, and, regardless, everyone needed party support to win.

After the parties nominated their candidates, they ran their campaigns, mapping strategy and planning tactics. They supplied the funds and the workers. In the 1896 election, Republican workers brought 750,000 persons from all over the United States to the Ohio home of their candidate, William McKinley, who would greet the visitors from his front porch.[23]

We've already seen that the parties provided welfare and jobs to many people. The parties also provided political information to the people through party newspapers. Of course, these newspapers presented only one side, but they did inform party supporters about government and politics.[24] After gaining people's allegiance through these activities, the parties were in position to mobilize their people on election day.

If a party was successful, especially if it was successful over consecutive elections, it could control government. Elected officials—the party's members—would implement the party's policies. In this way, the party would make government responsive to most people, or at least to its supporters.

Thus, the value of political parties in a democracy was to give average people political power. As individuals, ordinary people were powerless. But as members of a large party, these people were powerful. Collectively, they could wield the power that only corporations or wealthy individuals could exercise on their own.

Now we see that the parties at that time benefited society and, in the process, strengthened themselves. The parties became strong because they performed political and social functions that made them indispensable to the people. But what would happen if the parties couldn't perform these functions anymore? We'll return to this question shortly.

The Decline of Parties

Political parties no longer are at the height of their power. Although many Americans think that the parties are too powerful today, the parties are far less powerful than they were in the second half of the nineteenth century or the first half of the twentieth century.

The Progressive Reforms

The parties began to decline as a result of the **Progressive movement,** which morphed into a third party—the Progressive Party—in the early 1900s. Middle-class people concerned about the corruption of big-city machines fueled the movement, which sought to wrest control from the machines and from the immigrants and poor people they served. The movement championed numerous reforms that reduced the corruption but also seriously weakened the power of the parties.

Election reforms included voter registration, the secret ballot, and primary elections. **Voter registration,** which required voters to register their name and address before an election, made it difficult for people who didn't live in a district to vote in the district and for parties to stuff ballot boxes with fraudulent votes. (Parties could no longer urge their workers to "vote early and vote often.") The **secret ballot** prevented party workers at the polls from knowing how their constituents actually voted. These reforms reduced the incidence of corruption, but primary elections undermined party control of nominations, which was more devastating. **Primary elections** allowed the party's voters to choose the party's nominees for the general elections. This meant that the party's leaders couldn't screen their workers and reward the most effective and most loyal with a nomination. Instead, the party's voters would choose whoever seemed the most appealing.

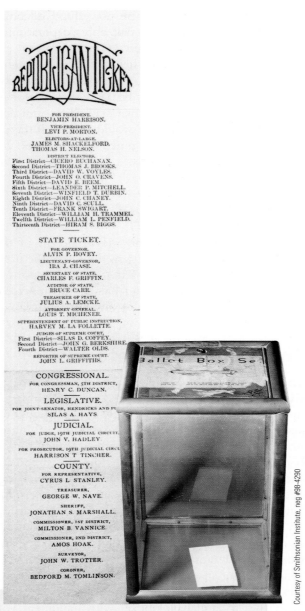

Until the 1890s, there was no pretense of secrecy in voting. Each party's ballot was a different color. Voters chose their party's ballot, like this Republican ballot for the 1888 election in Indiana, and placed it in a clear glass-sided ballot box.

Another reform was the introduction of **merit systems** for hiring government employees according to competence rather than party affiliation. Once merit systems were established, they were expanded, with more and more jobs falling under their purview. Eventually, the merit systems at the federal, state, and local levels replaced the patronage systems for all but a small number of jobs—the top aides to the president, governor, and mayor.

Although the Progressives never captured the presidency, their party became the most influential third party in American history, and their ideas were enacted into law throughout the country. As a result, political parties were weakened.

Functions of Parties, Revisited

Political parties don't perform the same functions, or to the same degree, that they did when they were in their heyday.

Diminution of Party Functions

Welfare and Jobs During the Depression, the federal government began to establish welfare programs—basic welfare, now known as Temporary Assistance, and Social Security. In later decades, it added Food Stamps, Medicare, and Medicaid. Poor people can get help for their basic needs and medical care. Elderly people of all classes get Social Security and Medicare. If workers are laid off, they can get unemployment compensation. Because people receive welfare from the government, they don't need the parties to provide it. As we've seen, the federal, state, and local governments established merit systems for government jobs in place of the parties' patronage systems, though some jobs—high-level positions—are still filled through political appointments.

Government welfare programs and merit systems severed the links between the parties and welfare recipients and between the parties and government employees. Because the parties no longer provided welfare and jobs, they no longer gained the allegiance of the beneficiaries. For the most part, these changes were advantageous—the government's welfare programs are systematic, rather than hit-or-miss efforts, and the merit systems ensure capable employees rather than partisan hacks. (We saw the result of political appointments when hurricane Katrina hit the Gulf Coast. The Bush administration had installed political operatives, rather than experienced managers, at the top of the Federal Emergency Management Administration (FEMA). Their incompetence was as obvious as it was disastrous.) Nonetheless, these changes weakened the parties.

Information The parties also lost their monopoly over political information. As independent newspapers replaced party papers, and as radio and television attracted a mass audience, people got their political information from many news organizations. People made up their own mind about how to vote rather than relied on their party.

Nominations and Campaigns The parties don't even perform their core political functions of nominating candidates and running campaigns as they used to.

Party voters in primary elections choose the nominees. The parties still hold their conventions, but the conventions merely ratify the choices of the voters and rally public support for the ticket.

Although the candidates receive money and advice from their party organization, they assemble their own campaign teams from the private sector because modern media elections require extensive expertise. A short list of the campaign specialists necessary for a high-profile office includes public opinion pollsters, computer programmers, and statisticians to assess voters' attitudes; radio and television producers, directors, writers, actors,

and a gamut of other specialists to make commercials; speech and drama coaches to help the candidates speak, gesture, and move effectively; radio and television time buyers and newspaper space buyers to place the ads in the most useful media at the most useful times; and direct-mail advertisers. These operations are very costly, so the candidates need to supplement campaign funds from the party with additional money from wealthy individuals and interest groups. If the candidates are elected, they will feel beholden to their donors, who may have different priorities than their party.

Americans decry the power of interest groups today, but these groups fund candidates' campaigns. As the parties have lost power, interest groups have gained it. Picture the parties and interest groups as the two ends of a teeter-totter—as the parties have gone down, interest groups have gone up.

For these reasons, elected officials are more independent of their party, and less obligated to follow its platform, than they used to be. Therefore, the parties aren't able to control the government as they used to.

Erosion of Popular Support

Because parties don't play all the roles they used to, people don't feel the same attachment they used to. The term **dealignment** refers to the diminished attachment to parties.[25] Many people aren't aligned with any party.

Increase in Independents One sign of dealignment is an increase in the proportion of the public calling themselves **independents.** This proportion has risen from less than 15 percent in 1960 to more than 40 percent in 2000.[26] The tendency for younger Americans in particular to consider themselves independent means that the electorate may become even more independent as older Americans die.

Increase in Split Tickets Another indication of dealignment is an increase in **split-ticket voting,** which is voting for a member of one party for one office and a member of another party for a different office—for example, voting for the Republican presidential candidate but a Democratic House candidate. Voters who split their ticket are motivated by something other than partisanship, such as the personalities of the candidates or the issues in the campaign. Ticket splitting is much more common than in the 1950s (see Figure 3).[27]

Disinterest in Parties Another sign of dealignment is disinterest in parties. The number of Americans who say

The David J. and Janice L. Frent Collection

Party officials no longer determine their nominee for president; party voters in primary elections do. In 1976, Democratic officials were reluctant to endorse Jimmy Carter, who was relatively inexperienced, but Democratic voters in the primaries liked his decency. Carter received enough support from them that the party had to nominate him. Although he won the general election (thus vindicating the voters in the primaries), he was unable to govern effectively (thus vindicating party officials). Consequently, in 1980 he lost his reelection bid.

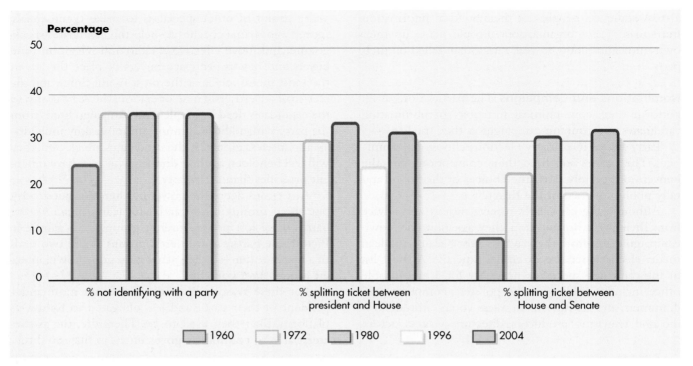

Percentage

Legend: 1960, 1972, 1980, 1996, 2004

Categories: % not identifying with a party, % splitting ticket between president and House, % splitting ticket between House and Senate

FIGURE 3 • **Erosion of Support for Parties**
SOURCE: National Election Studies, Center for Political Studies, University of Michigan, 1960–2004 (www.umich.edu/nes).

there is nothing they like or dislike about either the Democratic or Republican Party has increased.[28] Parties are simply not reaching many voters.[29]

With the decline in attachment comes a decline in participation, as Chapter 7 will address.

The Resilience of American Parties

The parties recognized their decline in the 1980s and have tried to revitalize themselves ever since. They have raised more money and bolstered their organizations, adding professional staffers and linking with political consultants. Although the parties remain weaker today than a century ago, they still play important roles in American politics.

Information

Parties increasingly provide information to their supporters through direct mail, on radio and television, and now on the Internet. During congressional and presi-

dential campaigns, party members might receive weekly or even more frequent messages from the national, state, and local party organizations and congressional campaign committees.

Nominations and Campaigns

Parties increasingly recruit candidates, encouraging individuals to run and providing them with an official or unofficial party endorsement and political advice and financial support. They host workshops on topics such as talking to reporters. Sometimes they offer the services of media consultants.

Governing

The parties' resilience is especially apparent in governing. The parties dominate Congress. The majority in each house chooses the leaders of that chamber (while the minority chooses its leaders). The majority sets the agenda, deciding which issues will be debated and which ones will be brought to a vote. The majority also controls each committee and subcommittee, where the work gets done.

Members of Congress usually vote with other members of their party, and members in the president's party usually follow the president's lead. Partisan voting in Congress has increased dramatically since the 1970s.[30] During the Bush presidency, House Republicans have voted together about 90 percent of the time, while the Democrats have voted together more than 85 percent of the time (on issues in which the parties opposed each other). (See Figure 4).

Before the 1980s, the Democratic Party included many southern moderates and conservatives, and the Republican Party included some northern moderates and liberals. Since then, southern conservatives have gravitated to the Republican Party, and northern liberals have gravitated to the Democratic Party (as we'll explain in the next section). Now both parties are more ideologically uniform.[31]

Partisan voting in recent years also reflects the conservative Republicans elected in the mid-1990s and the conservative president, George W. Bush, elected in 2000 and 2004. These conservative Republicans, determined to capitalize on their control of the White House and Congress (until 2006) and on the public unity following the 9/11 attacks, pushed a very conservative agenda. They pressured the remaining moderate Republicans to go along. The conservative media and interest groups did as well, calling the moderate Republicans "RINOs"— Republicans in name only.[32] Facing intense heat, the moderates wilted, hoping at least to show voters that the party could govern.[33] In response, the Democrats, who traditionally have been less unified than the Republicans, became more unified to withstand the Republicans' aggressive tactics. These dynamics led to more partisan voting by both parties' members.

Party-line voting is likely to remain high as long as each party has a distinct vision. However, a president committed to building bridges across partisan lines and a minority party willing to work with such a president would lead to less party-line voting.

Most Americans deplore the partisan wrangling now occurring, but clear partisan divisions do help voters recognize the differences between the parties and also help them hold elected officials accountable for their policies. Thus these divisions increase the likelihood of popular control of the government.

For example, consider the abortion issue. The Republican Party's position is pro-life, and the Democratic Party's position is pro-choice (though, of course, each party has pro-life and pro-choice members). Voting for a Republican candidate typically means supporting the pro-life position. If Republicans should build a solid and lasting majority, they would attempt to enact pro-life policies, as they did in the so-called partial birth abortion law (addressed in Chapter 12) and as Republican presidents did in appointing pro-life judges and authoring pro-life executive orders. The Democrats would do the reverse. This clear distinction between the parties enables the voters to choose the party and the position they favor. Of course, the voters' choice is complicated by the fact that the parties don't offer such clear distinctions on most other issues and also by the fact that many voters agree with one party on one issue and the other party on other issues.

Indeed, despite the increase in partisan voting, our system rarely resembles what political scientists call **responsible party government.** If the parties took clear positions on major issues, if elected officials tried to enact these positions into public policies, and if the voters recognized the parties' positions and the officials' actions, we would have responsible party government, as some European democracies do. In Great Britain, members of Parliament are tethered to their party. They are expected to vote with their party. If they defect too often, they can be prevented from running for reelection. Our system, with separation of powers, means that one party may control the presidency while the other controls one or both houses of Congress. This diffuses rather than pinpoints responsibility, and it makes responsible party government unlikely.

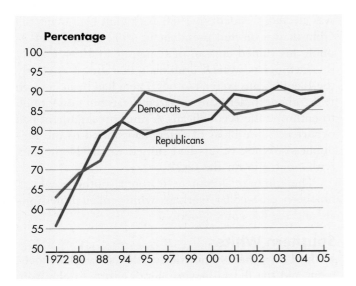

FIGURE 4 • **Party Unity in Congressional Voting**
SOURCE: *CQ Weekly,* January 3, 2004, 48.

Most Americans, who hold individualistic rather than communitarian values, would abhor the lock-step discipline of responsible party government. Yet our free-wheeling system, in which our elected representatives may disregard their party's positions, means that the voters don't know how their representatives voted on most matters, so the voters can't hold their representatives accountable for bad policies.

Realignments of American Parties

Although we have two competitive parties, at any given time, the two parties aren't evenly matched. Usually one is dominant, winning the presidency and Congress in election after election. Eventually, some major event, such as a war or a depression, destabilizes voters' party allegiance and triggers a massive movement of voters from one party to the other party, which then becomes the dominant party. This process in which one party loses many supporters to the other party is called a **realignment.**

These upheavals—revolutions without bloodshed—have occurred about every 32 to 36 years. Since the party system was established, there have been three major realignments—during the Civil War in the 1860s, the depression in the 1890s,[34] and the Great Depression in the 1930s.[35] There have also been minor realignments in which blocs of voters have switched sides. (See Figure 5.)

Major Realignment in the 1930s

The realignment of the 1930s set the stage for the politics of recent decades. The Republicans had dominated since the realignment of the 1890s. When the Great Depression rocked the country, those hit the hardest—poor people; working people; recent immigrants; and black Americans, who had favored Abraham Lincoln's party since the Civil War—turned to the Democrats, electing **Franklin Roosevelt** as president and Democratic majorities to Congress. The 1932 election started a major realignment, from Republicans to Democrats, and marked a new era. FDR would be elected an unprecedented four times, and Democrats would be swept into Congress. Many Republicans and new voters coming of age would become Democratic supporters.

Roosevelt's **New Deal coalition,** composed of city dwellers, blue-collar workers, Catholic and Jewish immigrants, blacks, and southerners, was a potent political force, but it included an uneasy alliance—conservative, rural, white southerners committed to racial segregation and liberal, urban, black and white northerners. After FDR's death, the coalition began to fray. With the civil rights movement, which alienated the South in 1964, and the Vietnam War, which split the party in 1968, the coalition continued to tear. Even though the Democrats would dominate Congress through the early 1990s, they would win the presidency only three times after Lyndon Johnson's victory in 1964.[36]

Remember the historical pattern—a new realignment every 32 to 36 years. If the pattern continued, there should have been another realignment during the 1960s. Republican Richard Nixon was elected president in 1968 and 1972, the latter in a landslide, but his Watergate scandal tarnished the Republicans' reputation and may have delayed or diminished the anticipated realignment, as the Democrats enjoyed large majorities in Congress and elected Jimmy Carter as president in 1976.

Minor Realignment in Recent Decades

But a conservative backlash arose by the decade's end, and Republican Ronald Reagan was elected president in 1980 (over Carter) and 1984, the latter in another landslide. Then his vice president, George H.W. Bush, was elected president in 1988. Although Democrat Bill Clinton was elected president in 1992 and 1996, Republicans gained control of Congress in 1994. Clearly, the Democrats weren't dominant, but almost as clearly, the Republicans weren't either. There had been enough realignment to dethrone the Democrats but not enough to enthrone the Republicans. A minor realignment had occurred. Some blocs of voters had shifted to the Republicans, while others had shifted to the Democrats, with a net gain for the GOP.

The minor realignment featured southern whites, northern blue-collar workers, white-collar professionals, and regular churchgoers.

Southern Whites

In the 1960s, the combination of the civil rights movement and the federal government's efforts to eliminate racial segregation caused many southern whites to leave their long-time home in the Democratic Party. Their

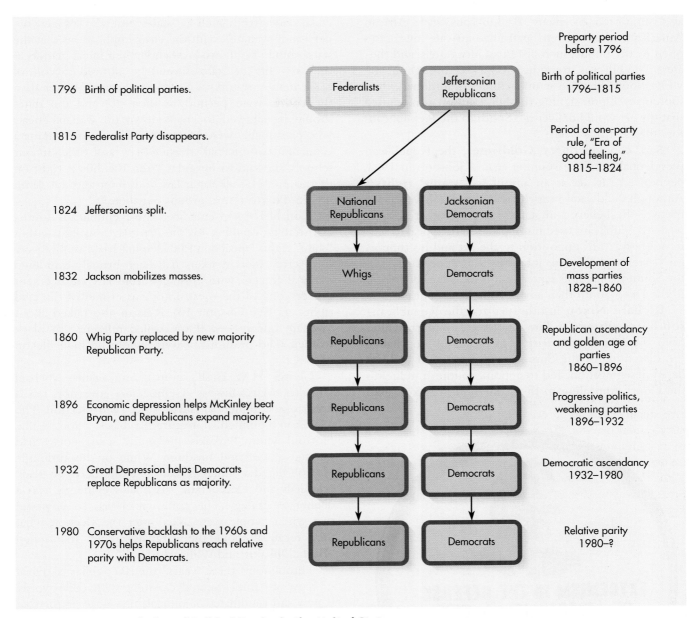

1796 Birth of political parties.

1815 Federalist Party disappears.

1824 Jeffersonians split.

1832 Jackson mobilizes masses.

1860 Whig Party replaced by new majority Republican Party.

1896 Economic depression helps McKinley beat Bryan, and Republicans expand majority.

1932 Great Depression helps Democrats replace Republicans as majority.

1980 Conservative backlash to the 1960s and 1970s helps Republicans reach relative parity with Democrats.

Preparty period before 1796

Birth of political parties 1796–1815

Period of one-party rule, "Era of good feeling," 1815–1824

Development of mass parties 1828–1860

Republican ascendancy and golden age of parties 1860–1896

Progressive politics, weakening parties 1896–1932

Democratic ascendancy 1932–1980

Relative parity 1980–?

Federalists — Jeffersonian Republicans — National Republicans — Jacksonian Democrats — Whigs — Democrats — Republicans — Democrats — Republicans — Democrats — Republicans — Democrats — Republicans — Democrats

FIGURE 5 • **Evolution of Political Parties in the United States**

move to the Republican Party was the most monumental switch in this minor realignment.

Before the 1960s, southern whites had been restive. President Harry Truman ordered the desegregation of the military after World War II, and the Democratic platform proposed civil rights legislation, prompting Strom Thurmond, Democratic governor of South Carolina, to form a breakaway party—the States' Rights Party, commonly called the Dixiecrats. Thurmond ran for president against Truman and carried four southern states. Although the Dixiecrats returned to the fold, southern discomfort with the party grew in the 1950s when northern Democrats again proposed civil rights legislation.

The exodus of southern conservatives gained momentum when the Democratic president **Lyndon Johnson** pushed and the Democratic Congress passed the landmark Civil Rights Act of 1964. This legislation, also supported by many Republicans, gave African Americans the right to patronize private businesses open to the public, such as restaurants, hotels, and theaters. The bill was strenuously opposed throughout the white South because it undermined traditional white supremacy. Upon signing the bill, Johnson commented that the act would deliver the South to the Republicans for "the next fifty years."[37]

Sure enough, **Barry Goldwater,** the Republican presidential nominee running against Johnson in 1964, denounced the act as an affront to **"states' rights."** Although Goldwater himself seemed not to have a racial motive—he believed in states' rights in other areas as well—Republicans used his opposition to appeal to segregationists.[38] His opposition to the act and his support for "states' rights" were interpreted as code for letting the South maintain its segregation. Goldwater did better in the Deep South than any previous Republican.

Richard Nixon institutionalized the Republicans' **southern strategy** to lure disaffected southern whites from the Democratic Party. He promised "to change the direction" of the Supreme Court, which had ordered desegregation, and to appoint southern judges to the Court. Appealing to the white voters, Nixon used

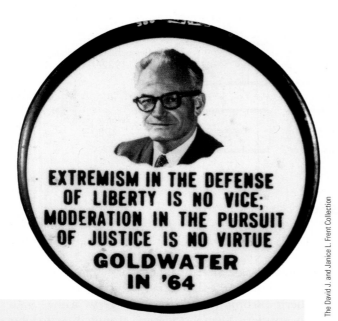

The David J. and Janice L. Frent Collection

Arizona Senator Barry Goldwater captured the Republican nomination for president in 1964. His acceptance speech, quoted on this campaign pin, reflected the new dominance of conservatives over moderates in the party.

racial code words such as "states' rights," "law and order," and "welfare," with the clear implications that the states should be allowed to handle their racial matters as they saw fit; the states should be allowed to control black demonstrators, rioters, and criminals better than the courts were permitting them to; and the states should be allowed to crack down on welfare cheats who presumably were African Americans. After taping a campaign commercial stressing "law and order in our schools," he said to his aides, "Yep, this hits it right on the nose. . . . It's all about law and order and the damn Negro–Puerto Rican groups out there."[39]

Ronald Reagan enhanced the Republicans' southern strategy, opening his presidential campaign with a "states' rights" speech in Philadelphia, Mississippi, where three civil rights workers had been brutally murdered by local citizens with assistance from law enforcement officers, one of the most notorious crimes of the civil rights era (see Chapter 13). Reagan also talked about "welfare queens"—a thinly veiled reference to black women who presumably were living the high life on welfare.

George H.W. Bush, campaigning against Michael Dukakis, Massachusetts' Democratic governor, ran a notorious commercial during the 1988 election. The television commercial featured a black felon, Willie Horton, whom Dukakis, under the state's policy, had granted a weekend furlough. While on his furlough, Horton raped a white woman. The link between black criminals and Democratic candidates evidently was a deliberate strategy. The commercial was so powerful that when people were asked after the election what they recalled about the campaign, they mentioned "Bush, Dukakis, and Willie Horton."[40]

Throughout these years, the Republicans' racial strategy was implemented carefully, with code words. Rarely did candidates or officials use racial epithets or praise segregation, as politicians of both parties did in previous generations. Whenever challenged about their racial strategy, they claimed that they hadn't made any racist statements.

But when Strom Thurmond, the Democrat who formed the Dixiecrats and later joined fellow southerners who switched to the Republicans, celebrated his hundredth birthday in 2002, Trent Lott, a Mississippi Republican and Senate majority leader, disregarded these norms. He declared that his state was proud to have voted for Strom Thurmond's ticket. "And if the rest of the country had followed our lead," he continued, "we wouldn't have had all these problems over the years either." Lott later apologized, but the public condemnation, including a rebuke by President Bush, forced him to resign his leadership position.

This realignment certainly doesn't mean that all or even most white southern Republican voters are racist. It does, however, mean that since 1964 the Republicans have strategically used a conservative and sometimes implicitly racist approach to race-related issues to build their dominance in the region, just as the Democrats did for generations before them.

Although racial attitudes were the early driving force in this realignment, southern whites' conservative views on other issues, ranging from foreign policies to gun control to religious matters, made the Republican Party a congenial home as well.

The southern strategy has proven highly successful for the Republican Party. The South went from a solidly Democratic region to a reliably Republican one. Since 1968, the Republicans have carried the South in all presidential elections, except when Georgian Jimmy Carter was the Democratic candidate in 1976. Even then, a majority of southern whites voted for the Republican, Gerald Ford. Since 1994, the Republicans have garnered a majority of southern whites' votes for their congressional and state and local candidates also. Meanwhile, southern blacks are the backbone of the southern Democratic Party.[41]

The shift of conservative southern whites to the Republican Party not only makes the South more Republican but it also makes the Republican Party more conservative and the party system more ideological. The southern Republican members of Congress, in general, are more conservative than the southern Democratic members they replaced, and they are more conservative than many northern Republican members. They push their party further to the right. At the same time, their departure from the Democratic Party makes that party more liberal. Thus the parties are more ideological and more polarized than before the shift.

Northern Blue-Collar Workers

Blue-collar ethnics who traced their origins to the waves of European immigrants, especially those from Catholic countries such as Ireland and Italy, were at the heart of Roosevelt's New Deal coalition.[42] But when southern whites left the Democratic Party, some northern blue-collar workers did too.[43]

With the New Deal's success and the 1950s' and 1960s' booming economy, blue-collar workers enjoyed the economic security that allowed them to consider

Strom Thurmond broke with the Democratic party to run for president in 1948 on the Dixiecrat segregation ticket. Later he became a Republican. In 2002, Senate leader and fellow Republican Trent Lott (center) congratulates him on his 100th birthday.

other issues. As the Democratic Party turned from bread-and-butter issues to civil rights, the Vietnam War, and women's equality—issues that motivated the upper middle class more than the lower middle class—some blue-collar workers abandoned the party. Although liberal on economic issues, they were conservative on social issues and on foreign policies. Many were attracted to the Republicans' emphasis on traditional values.

Reagan captured most of these voters, but when the economy reversed course for these workers, they turned back to the Democrats, supporting Clinton in 1992 and 1996. But then Bush captured most of them again. So the realignment of northern blue-collar workers wasn't as pronounced as that of southern whites, but it contributed to the minor realignment during these years.

White-Collar Professionals

Since the Depression, the more affluent, better-educated, white-collar workers voted Republican. But as blue-collar workers drifted from the Democratic

The Republican Party has tried to pull blue-collar workers away from their traditional home in the Democratic Party. As president, Ronald Reagan was especially effective in luring these voters.

© Andy Levin/Photo Researchers, Inc.

Catholics and Jews tended to be Democrats, and Protestants tended to be Republicans. As social issues gained attention over economic issues, this religious cleavage has diminished and a new cleavage has emerged—between those who are very religious and those who are not. Church attendance is more correlated with party affiliation than either income or education is. Weekly churchgoers congregate in the Republican Party, and nonreligious people connect with the Democratic Party.[46] This movement has benefited the Republican Party because there are more weekly churchgoers than nonreligious people, but the latter group is growing faster. (Among people 18 to 25 years old, 20 percent report no religious affiliation, up from 11 percent in the late 1980s.)[47]

The Supreme Court's abortion ruling in 1973 was the catalyst to the shift, prompting conservative Christians, who had deplored the sexual revolution and the secular drift of modern American society, to become politically active. They formed pro-life groups that coalesced into the Christian right. Eventually, the Christian right became one of the strongest forces in the Republican Party, along with big business. Former senator John Danforth (R-Mo.), himself a minister, observed that his party had been transformed "into the political arm of conservative Christians."[48]

The Net Result

In this minor realignment, the net result is a big gain for the GOP, because the southern whites, northern blue-collar workers, and regular churchgoers who left the Democratic Party far outnumber the white-collar professionals who left the Republican Party. This minor realignment has brought the Republicans to rough parity with the Democrats. A major realignment, which would have put the Republicans on top, didn't occur—because of dealignment or some other factor?

And a major realignment is not likely to occur now. In the early 2000s, with back-to-back elections of President Bush and congressional Republicans and with the patriotic fervor following the terrorist attacks, the Republicans had an opportunity to solidify and expand their gains. Karl Rove, the president's top adviser, strove mightily to engineer a permanent realignment. But the Republicans overreached, passing legislation that benefited their constituency of wealthy individuals and big businesses, including tax cuts for the wealthy and deregulation for the businesses, especially in energy, environment, and consumer matters. The

Party, white-collar professionals, including teachers, lawyers, doctors, and scientists, gravitated to it. (Most business executives remained in the Republican Party.)

White-collar professionals had more liberal attitudes toward foreign policies than blue-collar workers had. (Student demonstrators, many of whom would become professionals, infuriated the "hard hats" during the Vietnam War.) The professionals weren't as threatened by the civil rights, women's rights, or environmental movements as the laborers were. Indeed, many professionals embraced these movements. The professionals tended to support abortion rights—an unwanted pregnancy would interfere with their careers—and to have a "live-and-let-live" mindset, rather than a traditional-values mindset, toward homosexuality.[44] In recent elections, the Democrats have fared well in the affluent communities populated by white-collar professionals.[45]

Regular Churchgoers

Catholic and Jewish immigrants were also in Roosevelt's New Deal coalition. Since the Depression,

Republicans have allied themselves with conservative Christians, especially church-going Protestant evangelicals. George W. Bush uses their language.

Republicans also made prominent appeals to their constituency of religious conservatives, with heated rhetoric about gay marriage and abortion. Most damaging, they pursued an aggressive foreign policy, using the "war on terrorism" to launch a preemptive attack on Iraq. As the war dragged on and as the deficits—from tax cuts, war spending, and antiterrorism spending—soared, the Republicans provided the Democrats with an opening, which the Democrats took in 2006, regaining control of both houses of Congress (though by small margins).

As President Bush continued to lose popularity during his second term, the Republican Party also lost popularity. The GOP's image in the public's mind is lower than it has been at any time since 1992 (when the Gallup Poll began measuring public opinion on these questions).[49] The rough parity with the Democratic Party that it had achieved is in jeopardy, though it is too soon to know whether this Republican plunge is a long-term trend.

In the future, there may be new realignments, although they may occur more frequently than every 32 to 36 years, especially if the trend toward dealignment continues.[50] Today's voters are less attached to their parties, so it will take less to make them switch allegiance. Eventually, if the trend toward dealignment grows, we could reach the point where tomorrow's voters aren't attached to parties enough to align or realign themselves. Instead, they could form fluid coalitions that could change in every election.

Party Identification

Party identification is the psychological link that individuals feel toward a party. Unlike European parties, which have official members who pay dues and sign pledges accepting party principles, American parties don't offer formal membership. You're a Democrat or a Republican if you identify with that party.

A majority of Americans identify with a party. In 2006, 34 percent identified as Democrats, 30 percent as Republicans, and the rest as independents or supporters of another party.[51] For a glimpse of partisan differences from one generation to the next, see Figure 6.

We like to think that we're rational individuals exercising free will when we adopt a party, but that isn't the case for most people. Party identification typically is determined by our parents' party affiliation; our sexual, racial, ethnic, and religious characteristics; our socioeconomic characteristics; and our geographic factors.

The previous section of the chapter has indicated the party identification of some groups while explaining realignments, but we'll recapitulate those groups and address other groups here, so you'll have a complete picture of party identification today.

Parents' Party Affiliation

Party identification usually develops through the process of political socialization, explained in Chapter 3. Parents pass down their political views, including their party affiliation, to their children. If both parents identify with the same party, their children probably will as well. If one parent identifies with one party and the other parent identifies with the other party, their children get mixed signals and may be independent. If both parents are apolitical, their children also may reject both parties.

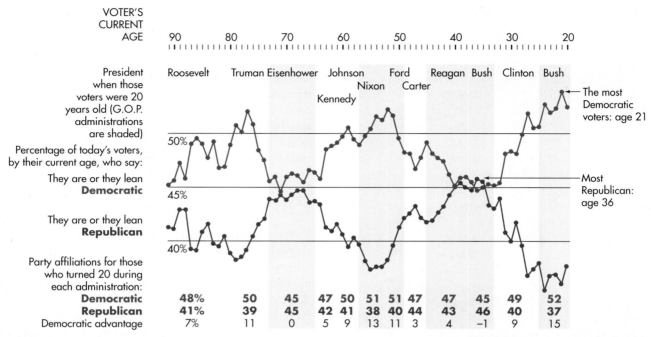

FIGURE 6 • **Party Affiliation by Generation** *Some new voters are affected by the political atmosphere that prevails when they come of age, and most continue to vote for the same party as they grow older. Those who came of age during the Depression, World War II, the Vietnam War, or the Watergate scandal were very likely to become Democrats. Those who came of age during the Eisenhower or Reagan years were less likely to do so. Those casting their first votes in recent years have been the most Democratic, and least Republican, voters of any generation.*

Your parents' party affiliation is the most important determinant of your party affiliation, but various characteristics and factors also come into play.

Sexual, Racial, Ethnic, and Religious Characteristics

The two genders and some racial groups, ethnic groups, and religious groups favor a particular party, so if you belong to one of these groups, it's likely that you'll favor the same party.

For generations, men and women voted similarly. Since women got the vote, most wives followed their husband's lead. In the 1980s, however, a **gender gap** emerged. During this conservative era, more men moved to the right than women did. Men liked Reagan's muscular foreign policy and his probusiness views. Since then women have preferred the Democrats' social policies, which use government to cushion life's hardships and to regulate business's impact on its employees and on the environment. Women also have disliked war and military spending more

than men have.[52] (The gap isn't due to abortion views. Men and women tend to favor, or disfavor, abortion equally.) The gap is most noticeable for working women and unmarried women. Men and stay-at-home moms are more likely to be Republicans, whereas other women are more likely to be Democrats.[53]

Homosexuals are presumed to be Democrats. They are difficult to poll because many feel vulnerable and reluctant to acknowledge their sexual orientation even in a confidential survey. But attacks from conservatives who espouse "traditional values"—against antidiscrimination laws, on the grounds that they amount to "preferential treatment," and against same-sex marriage, on the grounds that it undermines heterosexual marriage—undoubtedly have driven most gays and lesbians into the Democratic camp.

Racial minorities tend to favor the Democrats. African Americans cast a higher percentage of their votes for the Democratic candidates than any other group does. They have never left the New Deal coalition, and the Democratic Party has championed civil rights. Latinos aren't a monolithic group; they vary according to the countries they or their ancestors came from. Cuban Americans in South Florida are staunch Republicans, but other Latinos favor the Democrats, though to a lesser extent than African Americans do. Asians aren't a monolithic group either. They were thought to prefer the Republicans, but in recent elections they have turned to the Democrats.

Although some Latinos and Asians have lived in the United States for generations—Latinos in the Southwest predated Anglos in the East—many are immigrants or from families of recent immigrants. As relative newcomers, their party identification isn't as fixed as other Americans' identification is. Both parties are vying for their loyalty, especially for Latinos' allegiance, because their population is the fastest growing in the United States. The Republicans fear that they won't remain competitive if they can't convert more Latinos. The Bush administration has made a concerted effort to woo them. The president has given his weekly radio address in Spanish, has appointed an Hispanic as White House Counsel and then Attorney General, and has proposed immigration reform that would allow long-time illegal immigrants to work toward citizenship rather than be deported. His proposal has run counter to the views of his party's conservative base.

Most Jews are committed Democrats, but many Catholics are wavering after the minor realignment in recent decades. Now Catholics lean toward the Republicans. Regular churchgoers, whether Protestant or others, are very strong Republicans, and the nonreligious are almost as strong Democrats.

Socioeconomic Characteristics

Individuals' education, occupation, and income, which determine their social class, also influence their party identification. Although the parties used to split clearly along class lines—the upper classes were Republicans, and the lower classes were Democrats—that economic pattern has been blurred by the salience of social issues in recent decades. The upper class itself still prefers the Republicans, and the lower class strongly prefers the Democrats. But educational and occupational characteristics have created exceptions to the historical pattern.

Individuals with graduate degrees (beyond undergraduate school) have gravitated to the Democrats. They are part of the minor realignment that has occurred in recent decades. In addition, white-collar workers in the public sector—government and education—are mostly Democrats. On the other hand, white-collar workers in the private sector are disproportionately Republicans. Business executives appreciate Republican policies that maximize business opportunities and minimize government regulations.

Geographic Factors

Individuals' region of the country and type of community—urban, suburban, exurban, or rural—also influence their party identification.

The Great Plains and the Rocky Mountain West traditionally have been Republican bastions. The South, in the minor realignment of recent decades, has become another Republican region. The Northeast and the West Coast are mostly Democratic regions.

Big cities are strong Democratic locales, and small towns and rural areas are strong Republican locales. Suburbs lie in between. Some, which resemble the suburban stereotype as a posh home for big business executives, provide many Republican votes, though they have experienced Democratic inroads, and others, which lie near the city itself, provide many Democratic votes. Exurbs, which are the rapidly growing cities just beyond the suburbs, are heavily Republican.

For the last three categories addressed above—sexual, racial, ethnic, and religious characteristics; socioeconomic characteristics; and geographic factors—individuals grow up surrounded by people who share the same characteristics, or most of the same characteristics, and who live in the same region and in the same big city, suburb, or small town. These people reinforce the party affiliation that individuals get from their parents.

This party affiliation usually remains constant through life, but it can change if individuals change their social status—for example, getting a college degree, perhaps a graduate degree, pursuing a professional career, and making a higher income—and moving to a different place than their parents. Through these experiences, individuals will be exposed to different people and different ideas from the ones they were taught when growing up. Individuals' party affiliation can also change in response to major events. The Great Depression was a catalyst for some people; the civil rights movement and the Vietnam War were for others.

In the next chapter, we'll see that party identification is one factor—an important factor, but only one factor—that determines how people vote.

A STRICT FATHER OR A NURTURING PARENT?

Do we choose our political party based on our conception of an ideal family? Cognitive linguist George Lakoff thinks so. His research, which examines psychological dimensions of party identification, concludes that the major parties mirror competing conceptions of the ideal family. Republicans, especially conservatives, gravitate toward a "strict father family," and Democrats, especially liberals, gravitate toward a "nurturing parent family." Yet neither group realizes that their political affiliation may derive from their family beliefs.

Strict Father Family

Conservatives view the world as a dangerous place, brimming with evil and enticing with temptations. Children must be taught the difference between good and evil, and right and wrong. They must be disciplined, so they will learn to be strong and to make good choices. If they make bad choices, they must face the consequences. So par-

ents need to use punishment, perhaps even physical punishment, to teach children to obey.

The father is the protector of and provider for the family. He is also the moral authority, so he must exercise the upper hand over sexuality and reproduction.

To succeed in life, people need to compete with others. If children become self-disciplined, they can compete with others. If they succeed, their success will indicate that they are disciplined and moral. If they don't succeed, their lack of success will signal a lack of discipline and morality.

Applied to politics, the strict father becomes the government, whose job is to establish national security to protect the citizens and economic policies to promote prosperity. These are the most important things government does, so the military and the economy both should be robust.

Some citizens will be like mature and self-reliant children, and others will be like immature and dependent

children prone to whining. Government should allow the former the freedom to fulfill their self-interest. Government shouldn't coddle the latter; it shouldn't give these people things they don't deserve. Therefore government regulations that limit economic success should be reduced as much as possible, because they interfere with the opportunities of the self-reliant citizens, but government punishments for improper or immoral behavior should be increased as much as necessary, because they teach badly needed discipline to the dependent citizens.

In international politics, the strict father family model implies that the United States should act as the strict father to the international family. The United States' size and power and overall success indicate that Americans are more disciplined and moral than foreigners and deserve to dominate. According to this view, the country should never relinquish its military and economic superiority.

Conclusion: Do Political Parties Make Government More Responsive?

Although the Founders initially opposed the idea of political parties, some eventually turned to parties when they realized that there was no consensus to govern the country. Then, as now, there were sharp differences among the people. The leaders recognized that their ideas could prevail if they aligned with others to elect

their candidates. Parties arose, and continue, primarily as vehicles to organize people for elections.

The party label next to the candidate's name provides a cue for the voters who have little knowledge of the candidates or issues. These voters simply vote for their party. Even the voters who pay attention might be confused, because the campaigns might not illuminate the differences between the candidates or their stands on complex issues. These voters, too, can use the party label as a cue. Because the parties and their candidates have a history of taking positions and casting votes on issues, knowing a candidate's party provides a general understanding of the candidate's positions.

Nurturing Parent Family

The stereotypical nurturing parent would be a mother, but the concept of a nurturing parent family is based less on traditional notions than the strict father family, so a nurturing parent family could be headed by a mother or a father, or by both combined.

Liberals view the world as a place that can be and should be nurturing. Parents should nurture children and train them to be empathetic toward others. "In place of strict rules, there is a general 'ethics of care,' that says, 'Help, don't harm.'" When children do harm others, punishment should be restitution—paying back—rather than retribution.

The community should be emphasized as much as or more than the self. Therefore cooperation is valued more than competition. Those who need help should be given help. Yet, within a nurturing community, parents should grant children freedom to explore and grow as their individual personalities determine.

Interactions between parents and children should be based on mutual respect, and communications should be honest and two-way, taking each other's views into account. Thus although the parents are authority figures, they aren't as authoritarian as in the strict father family.

Applied to politics, the nurturing parent becomes the government, whose job is to protect the citizens, of course, but also to care for them, especially those who can't care for themselves. Government should strive for fairness between people and the well-being of all.

Government should also permit freedom for citizens to express their thoughts and opinions and pursue their interests and inclinations, as long as they don't harm others.

In international relations, the United States should be a good citizen in the world community, treating other countries with respect and emphasizing cooperation rather than confrontation.

You can apply these conceptions of families to a range of issues—for example, tax cuts, labor relations, immigration proposals, and the panoply of sexual matters, from sex education to birth control to abortion to homosexuality. Thus according to the strict father model, "Girls who get pregnant through illicit sex must face the consequences of their actions and bear the child."

Although everyone combines these two models, many people view the world mostly one way rather than the other. Lakoff estimates that 35 to 38 percent of the voters adhere to a strict father worldview and 35 to 39 percent adhere to a nurturing parent worldview. The rest blend the two models more equally, often using them in different spheres of their life, perhaps one at home and another at work. Lakoff thinks that a party can be successful if it can activate its model, through the words and the images used by its candidates, in the minds of the swing voters who blend the two models.

SOURCE: George Lakoff, "Framing the Dems," *American Prospect*, September, 2003, 32–35.

When parties attract individuals from divergent backgrounds and interests, they aid our society by mediating its conflicts, thereby contributing to political and social stability.

Although parties primarily organize people for elections, they also play important roles in governing. They formulate policy options and ultimately decide which ones to support and which ones to oppose.

In these ways, the parties help average Americans influence government officials and policies. By attracting and aggregating ordinary people, the parties give them political power. Otherwise, only wealthy people or celebrities would have the money or prominence to wield any clout. Thus the major contribution of parties to democracy is to make government more responsive to citizens.

The parties also provide a counterweight to interest groups. Although interest groups represent people, and large groups represent many people, they represent a narrower range of people—those with a particular interest—than parties. Each of the parties—the two "big tents"—tries to attract a majority of the people. When the parties succeed, they can check the influence of special interests.

There is no doubt that parties are weaker than they were a century ago. However, they have tried to halt their decline and have, in fact, experienced a resurgence in recent decades. All three components of parties—members, officeholders, and party organizations—have been reinvigorated. The number of people claiming partisan allegiance has grown slightly, while the number claiming independence and the number casting split tickets have shrunk slightly. Partisan voting in Congress has increased markedly. Party organizations have strengthened themselves considerably.

These changes have come at a time when conservatives, in response to the liberalism and secularism of the 1960s and 1970s, and the influence of these trends ever since, have launched aggressive attempts to redirect government policy. In doing so, the conservatives have made the Republican Party more cohesive and forced the Democratic Party to become more cohesive to defend its values. Once these cultural struggles subside, will the two parties be able to maintain the vigor they display today?

Of course, even today we don't have responsible party government. American parties don't perform in practice as they might in theory.

American citizens, especially young adults, are cynical toward parties. Yet the parties still serve important functions. Without parties, voters would face a bewildering array of candidates. They would be at the mercy of campaign consultants, big donors, special interests, and the media. Without parties, conflicts over how to use the nation's limited resources—what politics is about—would still exist, but narrower interests would have a freer hand, and average men and women would have less say.

The dean of American political scientists recently concluded that "we can be pretty sure that a country wholly without competitive parties is a country without democracy."[54] Although the existence of competitive parties is no guarantee that average men and women will prevail, they would most assuredly fail without parties.

Key Terms

partisan   140
two-party system   140
Democratic Party   140
Republican Party   140
multiparty systems   140
single-member districts   140
winner-take-all provision   140
proportional representation   140
national party chair   143
national committee   143
Federalists   144
Jeffersonians   144
Jacksonian democracy   144
political machines   144
patronage system   145

spoils system   145
Progressive movement   147
voter registration   147
secret ballot   147
primary elections   147
merit systems   148
dealignment   149
independents   149
split-ticket voting   149
responsible party government   151
realignment   152
New Deal coalition   152
"states' rights"   154
southern strategy   154
party identification   157
gender gap   157

Key Names

Ralph Nader   140
Alexander Hamilton   144
Thomas Jefferson   144
Andrew Jackson   144

Franklin Roosevelt   152
Lyndon Johnson   153
Barry Goldwater   154
Richard Nixon   154

1. Political parties consist of
   a. citizens who identify with a party.
   b. citizens who formally belong to a party.
   c. officeholders elected in the name of the party.
   d. party organizations.
   e. all of the above except b.

2. The American party system and electoral system are unusual in comparison with Western democracies for all but which of the following characteristics?
   a. a two-party system
   b. relatively small districts
   c. single-member districts
   d. districts with the winner-take-all provision
   e. proportional representation

3. The Founders _____ political parties.
   a. opposed the idea of
   b. were leery about them but recognized the inevitability of
   c. were neutral toward
   d. included a provision in the Constitution regarding
   e. welcomed the development of

4. Political machines were
   a. the epitome of mass parties.
   b. informal welfare organizations and job agencies.
   c. welcome wagons for new immigrants.
   d. corrupt.
   e. all of the above.

5. The patronage system
   a. provided government jobs to party supporters.
   b. replaced the spoils system.
   c. was used for relatively few jobs.
   d. depressed electoral turnout.
   e. provided jobs according to merit.

6. Through history, parties' primary function has been to
   a. nominate candidates.
   b. run campaigns.
   c. get their candidates elected.
   d. provide jobs.
   e. provide welfare.

7. The real value of parties in a democracy is to
   a. limit the power of the presidency.
   b. extend the power of interest groups.
   c. give some power to average people.
   d. check the power of Congress.
   e. boost the power of elites in society.

8. Since the last half of the 1800s and first half of the 1900s, parties have
   a. remained as powerful as they were then.
   b. gained some power.
   c. gained much power.
   d. lost some power.
   e. performed the same functions as they did then.

9. The Progressive movement resulted in all but which of the following?
   a. reduced corruption
   b. strengthened parties
   c. voter registration
   d. secret ballot
   e. primary elections

10. Which is not an indication of dealignment among voters?
    a. the decrease in party-line voting
    b. the movement of southern whites to the Republican Party
    c. the increase in independents
    d. the decline in interest in parties
    e. the increase in split-ticket voting

11. If we had _____, we would come closer to attaining responsible party government.
    a. less corruption
    b. more independent officeholders
    c. more merit systems
    d. more party discipline
    e. fewer political machines

12. The New Deal coalition included all but which of the following?
    a. Wall Street bankers
    b. city dwellers
    c. blue-collar workers
    d. Catholic and Jewish immigrants
    e. African Americans

13. In recent decades, we've experienced
    a. a major realignment favoring the Republicans.
    b. a major realignment favoring the Democrats.
    c. a minor realignment favoring the Republicans.
    d. a minor realignment favoring the Democrats.
    e. no significant realignment at all.

14. The most significant realignment in recent decades has occurred among
    a. Catholics.
    b. southern whites.
    c. white-collar professionals.
    d. northern blue-collar workers.
    e. Jews.

15. In recent decades, Republicans extensively used all but which tactic to lure southern whites?
    a. a southern strategy
    b. promises to change the direction of the Supreme Court
    c. racial code words and phrases
    d. overt racist remarks
    e. appeals to "states' rights"

16. The shift of southern whites to the Republican Party makes all but which of the following?
    a. the party system less polarized
    b. the South more Republican
    c. the Republicans more conservative
    d. the Democrats more liberal
    e. both parties more ideological

17. The religious cleavage between _____ is especially pronounced in American politics now.
    a. mainline Protestants and evangelical Protestants
    b. Protestants and Catholics
    c. Christians and Jews
    d. Judeo-Christian religions and other religions
    e. regular churchgoers and the nonreligious

18. The most important determinant of a person's party identification is the person's
    a. parents.
    b. gender.
    c. religion.
    d. job.
    e. wealth.

19. The Republican Party tends to reflect the _____, and the Democratic Party tends to reflect the _____.
    a. nurturing father family; nurturing mother family
    b. strict father family; nurturing parent family
    c. permissive parent; authoritarian parent
    d. nurturing parent family; strict father family
    e. strict father family; strict mother family

20. Political scientists consider political parties to be
    a. the reason why we have so much conflict in government.
    b. irrelevant as long as we have vigorous interest groups.
    c. essential for democracy.
    d. less important than interest groups.
    e. interesting to study but not very important for government.

Key: 1-e; 2-e; 3-a; 4-e; 5-a; 6-c; 7-c; 8-d; 9-b; 10-b; 11-d; 12-a; 13-c; 14-b; 15-d; 16-a; 17-e; 18-a; 19-b; 20-c.

Is presidential candidate Barack Obama ready for prime time?
Is America ready for a black president?

Does your mode of transportation influence your voting behavior? A 2004 survey of adults found that those who drove cars were more likely to vote Republican than those who biked, rode subways or buses, or walked. Moreover, drivers of SUVs, Chevys, Fords, and pickup trucks were even more Republican. And those who enjoyed NASCAR races were also reliably Republican.[1]

On the other hand, nondrivers were more Democratic. And those who drove Toyotas, Volvos, Suburus and other fuel-efficient cars were also likely to vote Democratic. In fact, five out of six owners of Volvos voted for **John Kerry**, the Democratic candidate in 2004.

So indeed it does suggest that transportation preferences affect voting. However, this relationship is more likely to be due to the link between transportation and other preferences that influence voting. Those who bike, ride buses or the subways are mostly urban, and ur-

ban voters tend to be Democratic. Those who drive pickup trucks are usually from rural areas or small towns where voters are Republican. Fords and Chevys are also popular in small towns. NASCAR supporters are disproportionately Southern or rural, too.

Cars also reflect lifestyle choices. Those who choose Volvos, Toyotas, and other fuel-efficient cars are more likely to be concerned about the environment, as are Democrats. Volvo owners especially are most interested in safety, and they are likely to be highly educated and urban residents where Volvos are available. Those who drive SUVs may be less likely to worry about global warming, a position that, at least until recently, was held more by Republicans than Democrats.

Thus, while cars, bikes, and driving do not have much to do with politics directly, they reflect the different choices, values, and conditions of life of those who own them.

Americans have fought and died in wars to preserve the rights of citizens to choose their leaders through democratic elections. Some have even died here at home trying to exercise these rights. Despite this, most Americans take these important rights for granted; about half do not bother to vote even in presidential elections, and fewer still participate in other ways.

Moreover, the process by which we choose our leaders, especially the president, has been sharply criticized in recent years. Critics charge that election campaigns are meaningless and offer little information to the voters, that candidates pander to the most ill-informed and mean-spirited citizens, and that public relations and campaign spending, not positions on issues or strength of character, determine the winners. Then in 2000, and again in 2004, it also became apparent that some voters' votes were not counted even when they went to the polls, largely due to defects in the election process itself.

In this chapter, we analyze why voting is important to a democracy and why, despite its importance, so few do it. Then we examine political campaigns and elections to see how they affect the kinds of leaders and policies we have. We will see that the lack of participation by many reinforces the government's responsiveness to those who do participate, especially those who are well organized.

The American Electorate

During the more than two centuries since the Constitution was written, two important developments have altered the right to vote, termed **suffrage.** First, suffrage gradually was extended to include almost all citizens aged eighteen or over. This expansion occurred largely through federal action: constitutional amendments, congressional acts, and Supreme Court decisions. Second, recently, serious issues of lack of access to the ballot have arisen. These limitations are largely being imposed by several states under the guise of ensuring that only eligible voters vote.

Early Limits on Voting Rights

Although the Declaration of Independence states that "all men are created equal," at the time of the Constitution and shortly thereafter the central political right of voting was denied to most Americans. States decided who would be granted suffrage. In some, only an estimated 10 percent of the white males could vote, whereas in others 80 percent could.[2]

Controversial property qualifications for voting existed in many states. Some argued that only those with an economic stake in society should have a say in political life. But critics of the property requirement repeated a story of Tom Paine's:

> *You require that a man shall have $60 worth of property, or he shall not vote. Very well . . . here is a man who today owns a jackass, and the jackass is worth $60.*
>
> *Today the man is a voter and he goes to the polls and deposits his vote. Tomorrow the jackass dies. The next day the man comes to vote without his jackass and he cannot vote at all. Now tell me, which was the voter, the man or the jackass?*[3]

Because the Constitution gave states the power to regulate suffrage, the elimination of property requirements was a gradual process. By the 1820s, most were gone, although some lingered to midcentury.

In some states, religious tests also were applied. A voter had to be a member of the "established" church or could not be a member of certain religions (such as Roman Catholicism or Judaism). However, religious tests disappeared even more quickly than property qualifications.

By the time of the Civil War, state action had expanded the rights of white men. However, neither slaves, Indians, nor free southern blacks could vote, although northern blacks could in a few states.[4] Women's voting rights were confined to local elections in a few states.[5]

Blacks and the Right to Vote

The Civil War began the long, slow, and often violent process of expanding the rights of blacks to full citizenship. Between 1865 and 1870, three amendments were passed to give political rights to former slaves and other blacks. One, the Fifteenth Amendment, prohibited the denial of voting rights on the basis of race and thus gave the right to vote to black men.

For a short time following the ratification of this amendment, a northern military presence in the South and close monitoring of southern politics enabled blacks to vote and hold office in the South, where 90 percent of all blacks lived. During this **Reconstruction** period, two southern blacks were elected to the Senate

RADICAL MEMBERS

OF THE FIRST LEGISLATURE AFTER THE WAR

SOUTH CAROLINA

Dusenberry	Mayes	Demars	Rivers	Miteford	Smith	Swails
McKinlay	Jillson	Brodie	Duncan	White	Pettengell	Perrin
Dickson	Lomax	Hayes	BOOZER	Barton	Hyde	James
Wilder	Jackson	Cain	Smythe	Boston	Lee	Johnston
Hoyt	Thomas	Maxwell	Wright	Shrewsbury	Simends	Wimbush
Randolph	Webb	Martin	MOSES	Mickey	Chesnut	Hayes
Harris	Bozeman	Cook	Sancho	Henderson	Mc Daniel	Farr
	Tomlinson	Miller	Sanders	Howell	Williams	Meade
	Wright *		Nuckles	Hayne	Gardner	Thompson
				Mobley		Rainey
				Hudson		
				Nash		
				Carmand		

* Afterwards associate Justice of the Supreme Court of the State

Library of Congress

Blacks comprised a majority of the population in South Carolina in 1866 and elected a black majority to the state legislature. The black legislators worked for civil rights, black male suffrage, and state constitutional reform. Radical was the name given to Republicans at that time.

and fourteen were elected to the House of Representatives between 1869 and 1876. One state, South Carolina, even had a black majority in its legislature. In most places, however, blacks did not dominate politics or even receive a proportional share of offices; whites saw blacks' political activities as a threat to their own dominance. White southerners began to prevent blacks from voting through intimidation that ranged from mob violence and lynchings to economic sanctions against blacks who attempted to vote.

Northerners tolerated these methods, both violent and nonviolent. The northern public and political leaders had lost interest in the fate of blacks or had simply grown tired of the struggle. In 1876, a compromise ended Reconstruction. In the wake of the disputed 1876 presidential election, southern Democrats agreed to support Republican Rutherford B. Hayes for president in return for an end to the northern military presence in the South and a hands-off policy toward activities there. By the end of the nineteenth century, blacks were effectively disfranchised in all of the South. The last southern black member of Congress served to 1901. Another would not be elected until 1972.

Southern constitutions and laws legitimized the loss of black voting rights. **Literacy tests** were often required, supposedly to make sure voters could read and write and thus evaluate political information. Most blacks, who had been denied education, were illiterate. Many whites also were illiterate, but fewer were barred from voting. Local election registrars exercised nearly complete discretion in deciding who had to take the test and how to administer and evaluate it. Educated blacks often were asked for legal interpretations of obscure constitutional provisions, which few could provide.

Some laws had exemptions that whites were allowed to take advantage of. An "understanding clause" exempted those who could not read and write but who could explain sections of the federal or state constitution to the satisfaction of the examiner, and a "good moral character clause" exempted those with such character. Again, local election registrars exercised discretion in deciding who understood the Constitution and who had good character. Finally, the **grandfather clause** exempted those whose grandfathers had the right to vote before 1867—that is, before blacks could legally vote in the South.

The **poll tax** also deprived blacks of voting rights. The tax, though only a couple of dollars, was often a sizable portion of working people's monthly income. In some states, individuals had to pay not only for the present election, but also for every past election in which they were eligible to vote but did not.

In the **white primary,** blacks were barred from voting in primary elections, where party nominees were chosen. Because the Democrats always won the general elections, the real contests were in the Democratic primaries. The states justified excluding blacks on the grounds that political parties were private rather than government organizations and thus could discriminate just as private clubs or individuals could.

Less formal means were also used to exclude blacks from voting. Registrars often closed their offices when blacks tried to register, or whites threatened blacks with the loss of jobs or housing if they tried to vote. Polling places were sometimes located far from black neighborhoods or were moved at the last minute without notify-

BLACKS AND HISPANICS IN OFFICE

Before the Voting Rights Act (VRA) in 1965, few African Americans held major public office. Only a handful were members of Congress, and few were state legislators, mayors of major cities, or other important political officers. Following the VRA, southern blacks began to have the political clout to elect members of their own race to office for the first time, and northern blacks began to increase their influence, winning races in districts where blacks were not always majorities. Progress, slow to be sure, has occurred; in 1970, there were only 179 blacks holding state and national legislative seats; by 2001, the number had more than tripled, to 633. Only two African Americans have won a governor's seat in modern times, Virginia's Douglas Wilder and, in 2006, Massachusetts' Deval Pat-

rick. In 2004, with blacks as both major party candidates in Illinois, Barack Obama (D-Ill.) won to become the only current African American member of the U.S. Senate and only the third to hold a Senate seat in the modern era.

Richard Hatcher, who became mayor of Gary, Indiana, in 1968, was the first African American mayor of a major U.S. city. By 2004, 530 African Americans served as black mayors in northern and southern cities, more than forty of them in cities of fifty thousand and more and many in communities where blacks are far less than half the population. Nationally, the number of black officeholders has increased from an estimated 1200 in 1969 to more than 9000 in 2001. Although this is far from proportional representation, it is a dramatic increase.

Hispanics, too, have improved their representation in political office. From a total of little more than 3000 Hispanic public officials in 1985, their numbers by 2004 had grown to more than 4600, including more than 200 state-elected legislators and executives.

In sum, though progress is slow, African Americans and Hispanics, like other ethnic groups, are achieving political power through elections. As a sign of their increased numbers and influence, both Hispanic and black elected officials are forming their own organizations to share ideas and plans.

SOURCE: *Statistical Abstract of the United States 2003* (Washington, D.C.: Government Printing Office, 2001), tabs. 408 and 417; website of the National Council of Black Mayors, Inc, www.blackmayors.org.

---

ing potential voters. If these means failed, whites threatened or practiced violence. In one election in Mobile, Alabama, whites wheeled a cannon to a polling place and aimed it at about one thousand blacks lined up to vote.

The treatment of blacks by the southern establishment was summarized on the floor of the Senate by South Carolina Senator Benjamin ("Pitchfork Ben") Tillman, who served from 1895 to 1918. As he put it, "We took the government away. We stuffed ballot boxes. We shot them. We are not ashamed of it."[6]

Over time, the Supreme Court and Congress outlawed the "legal" barriers to black voting in the South. The Court invalidated the grandfather clause in 1915 and the white primary in 1944. Through the Twenty-fourth Amendment, Congress abolished the poll tax for federal elections in 1964, and the Court invalidated the tax for state elections in 1966.[7] But threats of physical violence and economic reprisals still kept most southern blacks from voting. Although many blacks in the urban areas of the rim South (such as Florida, North

Carolina, Tennessee, and Texas) could and did vote, those in the rural South and most in the Deep South could not; in 1960, black voter registration ranged from 5 to 40 percent in southern states.[8] (See the box titled "Blacks and Hispanics in Office.")

The Voting Rights Act and Redistricting

Despite our shameful history of depriving African Americans the right to vote, today black voting rates approach those of whites. In the Deep South, much of this dramatic change was brought about by the 1965 passage of the **Voting Rights Act (VRA),** which made it illegal to interfere with anyone's right to vote. The act abolished the use of literacy tests, and, most important, it sent federal voter registrars into counties where less than 50 percent of the voting-age population (black and white) was registered. The premise of this requirement was that if so few had registered, there

Blacks line up to vote in Peachtree, Alabama, after enactment of the Voting Rights Act of 1965.

must be serious barriers to registration. Registrars were sent to all of Alabama, Mississippi, South Carolina, and Louisiana, substantial parts of North Carolina, and scattered counties in six other states.[9] Any changes in election procedures had to be approved by the Department of Justice or the U.S. District Court for the District of Columbia. States or counties had to show a clean record of not discriminating for ten years before they could escape this supervision. Those who sought to deter blacks from voting through intimidation now had to face the force of the federal government.

Though black registration had been increasing in the rim South due to voter registration and education projects, the impact of the VRA in the Deep South was dramatic.[10] Within a year after federal registrars were sent, hundreds of thousands of southern blacks were registered, radically changing the nature of southern politics. In the most extreme case, Mississippi registration of blacks zoomed from 7 to 41 percent. In Alabama, the black electorate doubled in four years. Due to these increases, not only have dozens of blacks been elected, but white politicians must now court black voters to get elected. Even the late George Wallace, the segregationist Alabama governor who had opposed the civil rights movement in the 1960s, eagerly sought black votes in the 1970s and 1980s.

The VRA was renewed and expanded in 1970, 1975, 1982, and again in 2006, despite some grumbling by white Republican conservatives about the continu-ing federal scrutiny of voting rights in the South. It now covers more states and other minorities, such as Hispanics, Asians, Native Americans, and Inuits (called Eskimos in the past), and thus serves as a basic protection for minority voting rights. For example, states must provide bilingual ballots in counties in which 5 percent or more of the population does not speak English.

The VRA dramatically changed the face of the electorate in the South and then later in other parts of the nation. Given the success of the VRA and faced with an expanded black electorate, some white officials in areas of large black populations used new means to diminish the political clout of African Americans. Their technique was **gerrymandering.** Through devices that political scientists call **"cracking, stacking, and packing,"** districts were drawn to minimize black representation, depending on the size and configuration of the black and white populations. *Cracking* divides significant, concentrated black populations into two or more districts so that none will have a black majority; *stacking* combines a large black population with an even greater white population; and *packing* puts a huge black population into one district rather than two, where blacks might otherwise approach a majority in each.

Initially, the Supreme Court was reluctant to find these practices illegal without specific proof that their intent was to discriminate against black voters.[11] But in 1982, congressional revision of the VRA required states with large minority populations to draw boundaries in

Even before women were given the right to vote nationally, they held political office. Women officeholders in colonial America were rare but not unknown. In 1715, for example, the Pennsylvania Assembly appointed a woman as tax collector.[1]

Elizabeth Cady Stanton, probably the first woman candidate for Congress, received twenty-four votes when she ran in 1866.[2] It was not until 1916 that the first woman member of Congress, **Jeannette Rankin** (R-Mont.), was actually elected. In 1872, Victoria Claflin Woodhull ran for president on the Equal Rights Party ticket teamed with abolitionist Frederick Douglass for vice president.

More than one-hundred thousand women now hold elective office, but many of these offices are minor. Inroads by women into major national offices have been slow. **Geraldine Ferraro**'s 1984 vice presidential candidacy was historic, but not victorious. In recent years, women have only gradually increased their membership in Congress. But in the 1992 elections, women candidates won striking increases in national legislative offices. Women have continued to gain seats and, after 2006, num-

AP Images/Christopher Morris/VII

For her or against her? Senator Hillary Clinton evokes strong feelings both ways. Here she attends the unveiling of the Smithsonian's official portrait of her as first lady.

ways to increase the probabilities that minorities will win seats. The focus of the voting rights legislation then turned from protecting the right of suffrage to trying to ensure that voting rights result in the election of African American and other minority officeholders. With this new statute as an indication of congressional intent, the Court then did strike down districting in North Carolina as inappropriately diluting black voting power.[12]

After the 1990 census, eleven new **majority-minority districts** were created for blacks and six for Hispanics. Partly as a result of this redistricting, blacks and Hispanics dramatically increased their congressional representation. Blacks were elected to Congress for the first time since Reconstruction in Alabama, Florida, North Carolina, South Carolina, and Virginia. Hispanics were elected for the first time ever in Illinois and New Jersey.[13] However, after this post–1990 redistricting, which used extensive gerrymandering to create the majority-minority districts, some white voters challenged their legality. In a series of cases, the Supreme Court then ruled that racial gerrymandering, the drawing of district lines specifically to concentrate racial minorities to try to ensure the election of minority representatives, is as constitutionally suspect as the drawing of district lines to diffuse minority electoral strength.[14] Despite the consequent redrawing of several majority-minority districts after the 1994 election, the African American incumbents were still able to win reelection in 1996 and after.

bered at least 16 percent of the House and 16 percent of the Senate. More than two-thirds of the women in each house are Democrats.[3] Nancy Pelosi (D-Cal.), as the first woman (and Italian American) Speaker of the House, is now third in the line of presidential succession.

Real progress has also been made in state and local governments. Women hold 12 percent of the governorships (Democrats) and 28 percent of the lieutenant governorships. In 1969, only 4 percent of the state legislators were women; today, 23 percent are. However, the rates of increase have slowed in recent years, with only a 2 percent growth in the past decade.[4] The proportion ranges widely, from not quite 9 percent in South Carolina to one-third or more in Maryland, Delaware, Arizona, Nevada, Vermont, and Washington. Women are also making inroads in local political offices.[5]

Does it make a difference in terms of policy to have women officeholders rather than men? Behavioral studies of women members of Congress and other legislative bodies indicate that they are, on the whole, more liberal than men.[6] Women tend to give issues relating to women, children, and the family higher priority than do male legislators.[7] Women are also less likely to be involved in corrupt activities.

As more and more women are getting graduate and professional education and working outside the home, and as the public increases its support for women in politics, the trend toward more women in public office will continue.

Of course, in 2007, many eyes are on Hillary Clinton (D-N.Y.), who is making a strong run for the presidency, leading her fellow Democratic candidates in polls through mid-2007. Polls show that she has both high positive evaluations and high negatives.[8] Most think she is a strong leader, but many do not trust her. At the same time, 96 percent of Americans say they would vote for a qualified woman for president.

[1]Joseph J. Kelley, *Pennsylvania: The Colonial Years* (Garden City, N.Y.: Doubleday, 1980), 143.

[2]Elisabeth Griffin, *In Her Own Right* (New York: Oxford University Press, 1983).

[3]Data are from Center for the American Woman and Politics, National Information Bank on Women in Public Office, Rutgers University, www.rci.rutgers.edu/cawp/pdf/elective.pdf.

[4]Kira Sanbonmatsu, *Democrats, Republicans, and the Politics of Women's Place* (Ann Arbor: University of Michigan Press, 2002).

[5]Data are from the Center for American Women and Politics, Rutgers University, 2006, www.cawp.rutgers.edu/Facts.html#leg.

[6]Susan Welch, "Are Women More Liberal Than Men in the U.S. Congress?" *Legislative Studies Quarterly* 10 (1985), 125–134.

[7]Sue Thomas and Susan Welch, "The Impact of Gender on Activities and Priorities of State Legislators," *Western Political Quarterly* 44 (1991), 445–456.

[8]"Sen. Clinton for President?" A Washington Post-ABC News Poll, reported in the July 17–23, 2006 *Washington Post National Weekly Review*, p. 13. The poll was based on telephone interviews with 1103 randomly chosen people; half were asked each question.

Creating majority–minority districts has affected the partisan composition of some southern states. Black voters were redistricted from solid Democratic districts to create new majority black districts. This left their old districts with Republican majorities and helped Republicans get their first victories in eighteen congressional districts in the 1994 elections.

Women and the Right to Vote

When property ownership defined the right to vote, women property owners could vote in some places. When property requirements were removed, suffrage came to be seen as a male right only. Women's right to vote was reintroduced in the 1820s in Tennessee school board elections.[15] From that time on, women had the vote in some places, usually only at the local level or for particular kinds of elections.

The national movement for women's suffrage did not gain momentum until after the Civil War. Before and during that war, many women helped lead the campaign to abolish slavery and establish full political rights for blacks. When black men got the right to vote after the Civil War, some women saw the paradox in their working to enfranchise these men when they themselves lacked the right to vote. Led by Susan B. Anthony, Elizabeth Cady Stanton, and others, they lobbied Congress and the state legislatures for voting rights for women.

The first suffrage bill was introduced in Congress in 1868 and each year thereafter until 1893. Most members were strong in their condemnation of women as potential voters. One senator claimed that if women could hold political views different from their husbands, it would make "every home a hell on earth."[16]

When Wyoming applied to join the Union in 1889, it had already granted women the right to vote. Congress initially tried to bar Wyoming from the Union for that reason, but then relented when the Wyoming territorial legislature declared, "We will remain out of the Union one hundred years rather than come in without the women." Still, by 1910, women had complete suffrage rights in only four western states.

Powerful interests opposed suffrage for women. Liquor interests feared that women voters would press for prohibition because many women had been active in the temperance (antiliquor) movement. Other businesses feared that suffrage would lead to reforms to improve working conditions for women and children. Southern whites feared that it would lead to voting by black women and then by black men. Political bosses feared that women would favor political reform. The Catholic Church opposed it as contrary to the proper role of women. According to some people, suffrage was a revolt against nature. Pregnant women might lose their babies, nursing mothers their milk, and women might grow beards or be raped at the polls (then frequently located in saloons or barber shops).[17] Others argued less hysterically that women should be protected from the unsavory practices of politics and should confine themselves to their traditional duties.

About 1910, however, the women's suffrage movement was reenergized, in part by ideas and tactics borrowed from the British women's suffrage movement. A new generation of leaders, including Alice Paul and Carrie Chapman Catt, began to lobby more vigorously, reach out to the working class, and engage in protest marches and picketing, all new features of American politics. In 1917, the National Women's Party organized around-the-clock picketing of the White House; their arrest and subsequent torture through beatings and forced feedings embarrassed the administration and won the movement some support. These incidents, plus contributions by women to the war effort during World War I, led to the adoption of the Nineteenth Amendment guaranteeing women the right to vote in 1920. Although only 37 percent of eligible women voted in the 1920 presidential election, as the habit of voting spread, women's voting rates equaled those of men. (See the box "Women in Office.")

Young People and the Right to Vote

Federal constitutional and legislative changes extended the franchise to young adults. Before 1971, almost all states required a voting age of nineteen or more. The service of eighteen-year-olds in the Vietnam War brought protests that if these men were old enough to die for their country, they were old enough to vote. Yielding to these arguments and to the general recognition that young people were better educated than in the past, Congress adopted and the states ratified the Twenty-sixth Amendment giving eighteen-year-olds the right to vote. As we will see, however, young people are a lot less likely to vote than other groups.

Felons and the Right to Vote

The restriction of felons' voting rights is an exception to the general liberalization of the right to vote. (Felons are those convicted of serious crimes.) Most states bar convicted felons from voting while in prison or on probation, but four states, including Florida and three other southern states with large black populations,[18] bar felons from voting forever. In some states, these laws stem from Reconstruction-era policies targeted to reduce the voting power of blacks. Since 2004, three states have reinstituted voting rights to felons after they serve their time.

Nationally, more than five million people are prevented from voting by felony convictions, including one in seven black men (in Alabama, one in three black men are barred).[19] Nationally, 40 percent of those barred from voting are black.[20] Analyses of the impacts of these laws suggest they have had a significant effect in putting conservative Republicans in office in states with large black populations.[21]

Some might argue that we should not worry about the voting rights of felons. Loss of voting rights might be seen as part of their punishment. However, most felons barred from voting have served their time and returned to society. Many times they were convicted as young people and have been law-abiding citizens for years or even decades since. Moreover, this particular punishment does not really seem to fit the crime.

In sum, only convicted felons, the mentally incapable, noncitizens, and those not meeting minimal residence requirements are legally barred from voting now. Voting has become an essential right of citizenship, except for felons, rather than a privilege just for those qualified by birth or property.

Electoral Reform and New Threats to Voting Rights

In recent elections, new threats to voting rights, especially voting rights of African Americans, have occurred. The most widely publicized problems were in the 2000 and 2004 elections. Months after the 2000 Presidential election that saw **Al Gore** win the popular vote but **George W. Bush** win the electoral vote and the Presidency, half of the electorate thought that the outcome was unfair or downright crooked. (See the section titled "The 2000 Election: A Perfect Storm.") Many African Americans, who believed they were systematically disfranchised by the way the election was run in Florida, were especially outraged. One of ten votes in largely African American precincts in Florida were thrown out as invalid, compared with one of thirty-seven in white precincts, significantly reducing the Democratic vote and changing the outcome of the presidential election.[22]

Voter Reform Legislation

The 2000 election revealed a number of problems with our electoral system. (The problems had existed for a long time, but in a close election they become more crucial.) Many areas had voting equipment that not only was old but also did not work well, resulting in many votes not being counted. Many states also had unclear laws governing procedures for recounts and challenges to voter eligibility.

To deal with some of these issues, Congress passed electoral reform legislation in 2002. This new legislation offered states funding to buy new, modern voting equipment; mandated statewide registration lists; and required states to train poll workers, post a list of voters' rights in each polling place, keep up-to-date computerized lists of voters, and allow voters whose names do not appear on the precinct lists to cast a provisional ballot, which can be accepted or challenged later.

This legislation did bring about some positive changes. Though most of the money to purchase the machines was not provided by the federal government, many areas did buy new electronic machines that work like ATMs, responding to touches on the screen.[23] And many states enacted new standards for counts and recounts. However, these changes brought new problems. Most technical experts, and many others, are fearful that some of the new electronic machines are open to fraud. One information-security expert argues that one particular system was "so deficient in security it could be compromised by a bright teenager intent on hacking an election."[24] The reason is that in most of the new machines there is no paper backup. Your vote for X could be counted as a vote for Y and you would never know it. To deal with this potential for fraud, California has required precincts to offer voters a choice of a paper ballot or an electronic one, and a proposed law to require paper backup for all these machines is on the ballot in California and being considered by other states.[25]

The requirement to have computerized, up-to-date lists of voters has also had unintended negative effects. States are purging registration lists, ostensibly to keep them up-to-date but sometimes to reduce the number of voters of the party not in control of the state's election machinery (in most states, elections are controlled by the office of the Secretary of State or some similar statewide office whose head is elected). Though states have a legitimate interest in making sure that voter lists reflect current voters and their addresses, sometimes purging reflects less high-minded motives. This tactic is used to disfranchise lower-income and minority voters or to reduce the other party's voters.[26] Sometimes private companies are hired to purge voter lists and are paid according to how many they purge. Florida, in trying to update its voter lists, purged twenty-two thousand black voters (largely Democratic) from the voter registration lists, but only sixty-one Hispanics (who, in Florida, are more likely than blacks to be Republicans). Florida officials claimed this partisan purge was accidental, though others disagreed.[27]

Voter Turnout

Paradoxically, as the *right* to vote has expanded, the proportion of eligible citizens *actually* voting has contracted.

Political Activism in the Nineteenth Century

In 1896, an estimated 750,000 people—5 percent of all voters—took train excursions to visit presidential candidate William McKinley at his Ohio home during the campaign.[28] This amazing figure is but one indication of the high level of intense political interest and activity in the late nineteenth century.

In those days, politics was an active, not a spectator, sport. People voted at high rates, as much as 80 percent in the 1840 presidential election,[29] and they were very partisan. They thought Independents were corrupt and ready to sell their votes to the highest bidder. In colonial America, voters usually voted by voice. By the mid-nineteenth century, most states used paper ballots. Elaborate and well-organized parties printed and distributed the ballots. Voters, after being coached by party leaders, simply dropped their party's ballot into the box. **Split-ticket voting**—that is, voting for candidates from different parties for different offices—and secrecy in making one's choice were impossible.[30]

Progressive Reforms

The **Progressive reforms** of the late nineteenth and early twentieth centuries brought radical changes to election politics. Progressive reformers, largely professional and upper middle class, sought to eliminate corruption from politics and voting. But they also meant to eliminate the influence of the lower classes, many of them recent immigrants. These two goals went hand in hand because the lower classes were seen as the cause of corruption in politics.

The Progressive movement was responsible for several reforms: primary elections, voter registration laws, secret ballots, nonpartisan ballots (without party labels), and the denial of voting rights for aliens, which removed a major constituency of the urban party machines. The movement also introduced the merit system for public employment to reduce favoritism and payoffs in hiring.

The reforms, adopted by some states at the end of the nineteenth century and by others much later, were largely effective in cleaning up politics. But the reformers also achieved, to a very large extent, their goal of eliminating the lower classes from politics. Taking away most of the reason for the existence of the political parties—choosing candidates and printing and distributing ballots—caused the party organization to decline, which, in turn, produced a decline in political interest and activity on the part of the electorate. Without strong parties to mobilize voters, only the most interested and motivated participated. The new restrictions on voting meant that voters had to invest more time, energy, and thought in voting. They had to think about the election months in advance and travel to city hall to register. As a consequence, politics began to be a spectator activity. Voter turnout declined sharply after the turn of the century.

Turnout figures from the nineteenth century are not entirely reliable and not exactly comparable with today's figures. In the days before voter registration, many aliens could vote, and some people voted twice. In some instances, more people voted in a state election than lived there! Nevertheless, it is generally agreed that turnout was very high in the nineteenth century and that it has diminished substantially; it dropped from more than 77 percent from 1840 to 1896 to 54 percent in the 1920 to 1932 era, when the Progressive reforms were largely in place. During the New Deal era, when the Democratic Party mobilized new groups of voters, turnout rose again, but it has never achieved the same levels as in the nineteenth century.

Election campaigns in the nineteenth century featured more hoopla, which generated tremendous turnout. This illustration shows the 1840 Whig gimmick—party members rolled a huge ball from town to town—that prompted the phrase "keep the ball rolling."

Courtesy of the Smithsonian Institute

Recent Turnout

Between 1964 and 2000, turnout in presidential elections slowly declined, from 62 percent to 52 percent, but that proportion increased significantly in 2004 to 58 percent.[31] The turnout for off-year congressional elections is even lower. It has not exceeded 45 percent since World War II, and in 2002 it was 42 percent.[32] Youth voting is abysmal in off-year elections; in 2002, for example, though 61 percent of the over-sixty-five age group turned out, only 15 percent of eighteen- to twenty-year-olds did. Turnout in primary elections is far lower still, sometimes as low as 10 percent.

Although nations count their turnouts differently, it is clear that Americans vote in much lower proportions than citizens of other Western democracies. Only Switzerland, which has allowed women to vote just since 1971, approximates our low-turnout levels. Within the United States, turnout varies greatly among the states. In the 2004 presidential election, for example, 77 percent of Minnesota's citizens voted, but only 46 percent of Hawaii's did.[33] Turnout tends to be lower in the South and higher in the northern Plains and Mountain states.[34]

Not only are voting rates low but even fewer participate actively in political campaigns. For example, in a recent year, about one-quarter of the population said that they worked for a party or candidate. About an equal proportion claimed that they contributed money to a party or a candidate. Smaller proportions attended political meetings or actually belonged to a political club. Unlike voting, rates of participation in campaigns have not declined over the past twenty years. This suggests that people are about as political as they always have been, but that something about elections themselves has decreased voter turnout. Indeed, more people give money to candidates and parties than they used to, probably because, unlike twenty years ago, candidates and parties now use mass mailings and the Internet to solicit funds from supporters.[35] Hundreds of thousands of potential donors can be reached in a very short time.

The differences in turnouts among states suggest that not only are there certain kinds of people who are unwilling to vote but there are also certain kinds of laws and political traditions that depress voter turnout.

Who Does Not Vote?

Voting is related to education, income, and occupation—that is, to socioeconomic class. Those who are more educated, have more money, and have higher-status jobs vote more often. If you are a college graduate, the chances are about 70 percent that you will vote; if you have less than a high school education, the chances are less than half that.[36] Differences between higher- and lower-income people are also quite large and growing. Although voting among all groups of Americans has declined in the past forty years, the proportion of college-educated persons who participated fell by less than 10 percent, while that of high school–educated persons dropped by nearly 20 percent. Education apparently is linked to voting because those with more years of education are more interested in, and knowledgeable about, politics.

Differences between voting rates of those in the middle and upper classes are much wider in the United States than elsewhere, and wider today than in nineteenth-century America.[37] Something unique about the contemporary American political system inhibits voting participation of all citizens, but particularly those whose income and educational levels are below the average.

Just as there is a strong class basis to voting, there is also a strong class basis for participation in campaign activities.[38] Those with more education and income are more likely to participate. Those with some college education actually increased their participation over the past twenty years, whereas those with less than a high school education decreased theirs. Thus, the class bias in participation, as in voting alone, has increased.[39]

Voting is also much more common among older people than younger people. Young people are volunteering in their communities in record numbers,[40] so why the low voting rates? Young people's initial tendency to vote is positively influenced by their parents' education and political engagement and by their own high school experiences and that of going on to college. Later in life, getting married, establishing a stable residence, and becoming active in the community are important to continuing their voting habits.[41] Thus, low turnouts may reflect many who grew up in homes where there was a low interest in government and the news; they did not learn that politics are important.[42] Then, too, like many of their elders, some young people cannot discern significant differences between the two major political parties, or they believe that candidates do not address issues of primary concern to young people. Low voter turnout is also a product of the high degree of mobility of young adults; they change their residences frequently and do not have time or do not take time to figure out how and where to register. Many young people are preoccupied with major life changes—leaving home, going to college, beginning their first full-time job, getting married, and starting a family.

In other kinds of political participation, even taking education into account, men usually participate slightly more than women, whites somewhat more than blacks, older people more than younger people, and southerners more than northerners. But these differences change over time. Young people participated more than their elders, and blacks more than whites, during the late 1960s and early 1970s.[43] The civil rights and anti–Vietnam War movements drew many young and black people into political activity.

Why Turnout Is Low

There are a number of other possible reasons more Americans, especially low-income and young Americans, do not vote.

Satisfaction among Nonvoters

One reason sometimes given for low rates of voter turnout is that nonvoters are satisfied; failing to vote is a passive form of consent to what government is doing.[44] This argument falls flat on two counts. First, voter turnout has decreased in an era when public trust in government has decreased, not increased. Second, if staying at home on Election Day were an indication of satisfaction, one would expect turnout to be lower among the well off, not among the working class and the poor.

Voters Are "Turned Off" by Political Campaigns

About one-third of a nonvoting group in the 1990 election, when asked why they did not vote, gave reasons suggesting they were disgusted with politics.[45] In explaining low turnout, analysts often point to the hateful advertising, attacks on other candidates, candidates who do not tell the truth about their positions, incessant polling, and lack of thoughtful media coverage.[46]

These analyses surely contain some grains of truth, but how many? After all, people who are most likely to pay attention to the media, watch the ads, hear about the polls, and follow the campaigns are the most likely to vote, not the least. It is possible that the increasingly media-oriented campaigns have decreased overall turnout during the past generation (and we will have more to say about these campaigns later in the chapter). In fact, turnout is inversely related to media spending; the more the candidates spend, the lower the turnout. But negative advertising does not affect turnout much, if at all,[47] and negative advertising and other media attention cannot explain the class bias in nonvoting.

In addition to the *quality* of the campaigns, some people think turnout has declined because our elections are so frequent, campaigns last so long, and so many offices are contested that the public becomes bored, confused, or cynical.[48] At the presidential level, the sheer quantity of coverage, much of it focused repetitively on "who's winning," may simply bore people. At the local level, voters elect so many officeholders, all the way down to weed and mosquito control commissioners, that many have no idea for whom or what they are voting. This proliferation of elective offices, thought by some to promote democracy and popular control, may promote only voter confusion and alienation. The problem is compounded because elections for different offices are held at different times. For example, most states have decided to hold elections for governor in non-presidential election years. This decision probably reduces presidential election turnout by 7 percent and may reduce by one-third the number of those who vote for governor in those states.[49] Primary elections also affect turnout. One estimate is that holding primary campaigns diminishes the general election turnout by 5 percent.[50]

By contrast, in Britain the time between calling an election (by the current government) and the actual election is only a month. On May 9, 2001, Prime Minister Tony Blair called the election, and on June 7, 2001, it was held. All campaigning was done during that time. There were no primaries. Moreover, as in most other parliamentary democracies, British citizens vote only for their representative in Parliament and (at one other time) for their local representative. Voters are not faced with choices for a myriad of offices they barely recognize.

Lack of Social Rootedness

Turnout is low partially because of what one analyst has called lack of "social rootedness."[51] Middle age, marriage, and residential stability lead to rootedness in one's community. Americans move around, marry late, and get divorced more than those in other nations. Mobility alone may reduce voting by as much as 9 percent. However, American turnout is still low, even taking into account these factors.

Americans living abroad, whether in the armed forces or for private reasons, have special barriers to registering and voting. In a bizarre development, in 2004, the Pentagon discouraged citizens living abroad from voting by shutting down a state-of-the-art website designed to make it easy for those citizens to register and obtain ballots.[52]

Barriers to Registration

Many people do not vote because they have not registered to vote. Most other democracies have nonpersonal systems of voter registration. That is, the state or parties are responsible for registering voters. Voter registrars go door-to-door to register voters, or voters are registered automatically when they pay taxes or receive public services. Usually, these registrar offices are nonpartisan and consider it their duty to register voters. Consequently, almost everyone is registered to vote.

The United States is unique in putting the responsibility for registering on the individual citizen. Moreover, registration is handled at the state level, usually by agencies controlled by one party or another. These conditions are a major impediment to voting. Only about 70 percent of U.S. citizens are registered.[53] Difficult registration procedures have a special impact on low-income Americans, who were 17 percent less likely to vote in states with difficult registration procedures than in other states.[54]

Given that states are laboratories—some things are tried in one state, other approaches tried in another—we know that some registration procedures encourage people to register and vote and others do not. One estimate is that voter turnout would be 9 percent higher if all states' procedures were similar to those of states that try to facilitate voter registration.[55] Procedures that work to increase voter registration include registration periods lasting up to Election Day (most states require registration at least twenty-five days before the election),[56] registration offices located in neighborhoods rather than just one central county office, registration by mail, registration offices open at convenient hours, and a policy of not purging voters from the registration lists who fail to vote.

In other jurisdictions, voter registrars do not provide these options, and some actually try to hinder groups working to increase registration. Some states do not allow volunteers to register voters outside the registration office.[57] Florida passed a law imposing fines of $250 for every voter registration form filed more than ten days after it is collected, even if a hurricane passes through in the meantime, and a fine of $5000 for every form that is not submitted. The Florida League of Voters, which has conducted nonpartisan voter registration drives for nearly seventy years, is suing to block the new rules, saying that its entire budget could be put at risk if a natural disaster or car accident or another such event delayed submission of forms.[58]

To increase registration, a national law—the **motor voter law**—allows people to register at public offices, such as the Department of Motor Vehicles and welfare offices.[59] The law led to the greatest expansion of voter registration in American history; five million new voters registered,[60] but it has not increased actual turnout.[61]

Failures of Parties to Mobilize Voters

Traditionally, political parties mobilized voters to turn out. In the 1980s and 1990s, however, the parties spent more time raising funds than mobilizing voters.[62] The failure of parties to mobilize voters is another reason for low voter turnout, especially among the working class and poor. Because of their low income, a majority of nonvoters are Democrats. If mobilized, they would probably vote for Democrats, but not to the degree many Republicans fear. In many elections, the preferences of nonvoters have simply reflected the preferences of voters.[63]

In 2004, both parties returned to their traditional mobilization function, a development that was likely responsible for the upswing in voting. Both put much emphasis on registering voters and getting them to the polls. Both parties used increasingly sophisticated technology to link information about each party supporter with neighborhood information. Each party communicated with its core supporters via e-mail and frequently urged them to register and vote.

Both parties have developed sophisticated databases recording individuals' residential location, gender, education, race, homeowner status, and many other variables. They gather data not just from public sources such as voter registration rolls and driver's license registrations, but also from consumer data from stores ranging from book vendors to auto dealerships. So, for example, we know that Republicans are more likely to drink bourbon and Democrats gin, Democrats buy Volvos and Republicans Fords and Chevys.[64] The Republicans have an even larger and more sophisticated database than the Democrats and are more likely to be able to cross-reference political and personal information.

In the past, Republicans have been most fearful of general get-out-the-vote efforts, because the Republicans have no interest in mobilizing lower- and lower-middle class voters. But now, with sophisticated databases, each party can target its own potential electorate.[65] However, Republicans are still more likely to oppose legislation making it easier for members of the general electorate to vote. States with the highest turnout tend to have active and liberal Democratic parties, giving voters a choice and thus a motive to vote.

Lack of Strong Labor Unions

Working-class citizens are much less likely to vote than white-collar and professional workers. Yet, among working people, union members are much more likely to vote than are others. This reflects the mobilization efforts of the unions. If union membership were larger, these mobilization efforts would likely expand the working-class electorate. Most other democracies have much stronger labor unions than the United States and

State Barriers to Voting

Some states work to facilitate voting turnout of those already registered while others do not. For example, some states do not provide sample ballots or publicize where voters should go to vote, while other states mail sample ballots and information about where to vote to registered voters. Some states have limiting polling hours, while others open the polls very early and keep them open until 9 P.M. or later so that voters can vote before or after work. About half the states, including most of those west of the Mississippi, allow voters to vote with absentee ballots, even if they are not planning to be absent from their homes on Election Day. Absentee balloting makes voting something that can be done at the voter's convenience. One observer remarked, "The concept of Election Day is history. Now it's just the final day to vote."[66] Though this is clearly an overstatement, almost all Oregon voters vote before Election Day, perhaps a harbinger of the future for other states.[67] To reach these early voters, parties must begin television advertising and flyer mailing much earlier. Providing information, extended polling hours, or absentee ballots has a positive impact on voting rates, particularly for those who have less education or who are younger.[68]

Other states make it harder to vote. The states with the highest barriers to voting tend to be states with the largest minority populations. Some estimates are that one out of four Ohio voters in 2004 experienced problems on voting day, including having to go to more than one polling place, having to wait more than twenty minutes to vote, or leaving the polls before voting. Nearly half of Ohio's African American population experienced one of those problems.[69] African Americans were also more likely to be asked for identification and to feel intimidated at the polls.

Many states are considering requiring identification at the polls, a change that could result in fewer low-income people voting.

Partisan Efforts to Discourage Voting

In the 2004 election, there were many instances of partisan attempts to deter registration and voting. Most of the examples that have come to light have been Republican efforts to deter Democrats, although undoubtedly there are reverse examples. In Nevada, the Republican National Committee employed a private company to register voters; it discarded those filled out by Democrats. In Wisconsin, Republicans tried to challenge thousands of registrants in heavily Democratic Milwaukee, and in one county in Ohio, some voters received an advisory on fake Board of Elections letterhead warning them that if they registered through the Kerry campaign or the NAACP they couldn't vote.[70]

Voting as a Rational Calculation of Costs and Benefits

Nonvoting may also be the result of a rational calculation of the costs and benefits of voting. When 35 percent of Americans think voting on *American Idol* is more important than voting for the president, obviously many voters do not think that the stakes in elections are great.[71] Economist Anthony Downs argues that people vote when they believe the perceived benefits of voting are greater than the costs.[72] If a voter sees a difference between the parties or candidates and favors one party's position over the other, that voter has a reason to vote and can expect some benefit from doing so. For that reason, people who are highly partisan vote more than those less attached to a party, and people with a strong sense of political efficacy, the belief they can influence government, vote more than others.

Voters who see no difference between the candidates or parties, however, may believe that voting is not worth the effort it takes and that it is more rational to abstain. In fact, 40 percent of nonvoters in 1990 gave only the excuse that they were "too busy," suggesting a large degree of apathy.[73] Others think that their vote does not matter. Perhaps misled by the continual public opinion polling and the widely publicized results, some may believe they don't need to vote.

Nevertheless, many people will vote even if they think there is no difference between the candidates because they have a sense of civic duty, a belief that their responsibilities as citizens include voting. In fact, more voters give this as an explanation for voting than any other reason, including the opportunity to influence policy.[74]

Downs assumes that the costs of voting are minimal, but, in reality, for many people the time, expense of time off from work or transportation costs, and possible embarrassment of trying to register are greater than the perceived benefits of voting. This is especially true for lower-income people who perceive that neither party is attentive to their interests. Moreover, they are especially vulnerable to a climate where voters are being challenged at the polls over their right to vote. That is why it is crucial that either the state or the parties provide services to help voters gain information about voting and even (in the case of parties) provide assistance in getting to the polls. The frequency, length, and media orientation of campaigns may lower the perceived benefits of voting for people of all incomes by trivializing the election and emphasizing the negative.

Voter turnout in the United States may not increase substantially until one of the political parties works to mobilize the traditional nonvoters through policies that appeal to them. For example, Roosevelt's New Deal mobilized thousands of new voters. If voters believe they have a reason to vote, then their calculation of the benefits of voting increases relative to the costs.

Presidential Nominating Campaigns

Many Americans believe in the Horatio Alger myth, which states that with hard work anyone can achieve great success. This myth has its parallel in politics, where it is sometimes said that any child can grow up to be president. In fact, only a few run for that office, and even fewer are elected. Most people have little chance of being president: they are unknown to the public; they do not have the financial resources or contacts to raise the money needed for a national campaign; they are the wrong race or gender; they have jobs they could not leave to run a serious campaign; and their friends would probably ridicule them for even thinking of such a thing.[75]

Who Runs for President and Why?

Most candidates for president are senators or governors.[76] In recent decades, governors (George W. Bush, **Bill Clinton**, **Ronald Reagan**, and Jimmy Carter) have been more successful than senators (George McGovern, Robert Dole, and John Kerry). Vice presidents also frequently run, but until George H. W. Bush's victory in 1988, they were not successful in the twentieth century.

Why do candidates run? An obvious reason is to gain the power and prestige of the Presidency. But they may have other goals as well, such as to gain support for a particular policy or set of ideas. Ronald Reagan, for example, clearly wanted to be president in part to spread his conservative ideology. Sometimes candidates

run for the presidency to be considered for the vice presidency, probably viewing it as an eventual stepping-stone to the Presidency. But only occasionally—most recently John Kerry picking **John Edwards**—do presidential candidates choose one of their defeated opponents to run as a vice presidential candidate.

How a Candidate Wins the Nomination

The nominating process is crucial in deciding who eventually gets elected. Boss Tweed once said, "I don't care who does the electing, so long as I get to do the nominating."[77] American presidential candidates are nominated through a process that includes the general public, the financial supporters of each party, and other party leaders.

Over time, voters and fundraisers have gained more power at the expense of party leaders. Presidential candidates try to win a majority of delegates at their party's national nominating convention in the summer preceding the November election. Delegates to those conventions are elected in state caucuses, conventions, and primaries. Candidates must campaign to win the support of those who attend caucuses and conventions and of primary voters.

Normally, candidates formally announce their candidacies in the year preceding the presidential election year. Their aim is to persist and survive the long primary and caucus season that begins in January of election year and continues until only one candidate is left. Candidates use a number of methods to maximize their chances of survival. They carefully choose the primaries they will enter and to which they will devote their resources. Candidates must enter enough primaries so they are seen as national, not regional, candidates, but they cannot possibly devote time and resources to every primary or caucus. Especially important are the early events—the Iowa caucus and the New Hampshire primary—and the larger state primaries.

Candidates try hard to raise substantial amounts of money early. A large war chest can mark a candidate as unbeatable. George W. Bush started strong in the 2000 primaries because he had raised millions more than all his opponents combined.

Candidates also try to find the position, slogan, or idea that will appeal to the most voters. In 1984, Ronald Reagan presented himself as the candidate embodying traditional America. As one of his staff aides

CAN AN AFRICAN AMERICAN BE ELECTED PRESIDENT?

Will the American presidency continue to be held only by white, non-Jewish males? Can an African American or a woman ever be elected? In the campaign leading to 2008, we will give these questions another test as the Democratic field includes a popular woman and a popular African American candidate.

Over the years, there has been some loosening of the informal restrictions that have limited the circle of potential candidates. In 1960, only 71 percent of all voters said they would vote for a Catholic for president and some doubted whether a Catholic could ever be elected.[1] Only one had ever run as a major party candidate, Alfred Smith, who was soundly defeated by Herbert Hoover in 1928. But in 1960, **John F. Kennedy** was elected, and that barrier was broken. In 2004, John Kerry's Catholicism did not seem to be an issue except for very

conservative members of his own church, who disdained his position on abortion and gay rights. The candidacy of Joseph Lieberman, an orthodox Jew, for vice president on the 2000 Democratic ticket was widely applauded.

Ronald Reagan broke the informal barrier about not electing divorced men to the presidency; in 2007, the frontrunner for the Republican ticket, Rudolph Guiliani, has been divorced twice.

But not being white has been a bigger barrier than religious diversity or marital status. Among campaigns during the past twenty years, race was probably most important in the 1988 campaign. It surfaced when the Republicans succeeded in tying Democratic candidate Michael Dukakis to Willie Horton, an African American convict who raped a woman while on furlough from prison. It also came up when **Jesse Jackson**'s prominence in the Democratic Party was highlighted and

made to seem somehow illegitimate and frightening. A campaign letter from the California Republican Party asked, "Why is it so urgent you decide now? Here are two [reasons]." Below the letter were two photos, one of Bush and Reagan, the other of Jackson and Dukakis. "If [Dukakis] is elected to the White House," it continued, "Jesse Jackson is sure to be swept into power on his coattails."[2]

This is not to say that all of those who voted against Jackson in the primaries or against the Democrats in the general election were racists. Jackson had no experience holding office and is identified with the most liberal wing of the Democratic Party.

In the 1990s, many voters, both Democratic and Republican, unsuccessfully tried to persuade Colin Powell to run for president. As a former chair of the Joint Chiefs of Staff, he did not have partisan experience but did have credibility as a potential candidate with

---

wrote in a campaign memo, "Paint RR as the personification of all that is right with, or heroized by, America."[78] George W. Bush capitalized on the sentiment that Bill Clinton's standard of personal morality was low, portraying himself as someone who would bring morality back to the White House.

To compete successfully, candidates also need considerable media coverage. They must convince reporters that they are serious candidates with a real chance of winning. Journalists and candidates establish expectations for how well each candidate should do based on poll results, the quality of a candidate's campaign organization, the amount of money and time spent in the campaign, and the political complexion of the state. If a candidate performs below expectations, this may be seen by the press as a weakness. Even if a candidate wins, the victory may be interpreted as a loss if it's by a

narrower margin than anticipated. On the other hand, a strong showing when expectations are low can mean a boost to a candidate's campaign. Consequently, candidates try to lower media expectations. Bill Clinton finished second in the New Hampshire primary in 1992, but because the top vote getter (Paul E. Tsongas) was from neighboring Massachusetts, Clinton's second place finish was considered a victory. Coming far from behind, he pronounced himself "the comeback kid," a designation that became the story of the primary.

In sum, the primary season is a game among the media, the candidates, and the voters, with the candidates trying to raise voter enthusiasm and lower media expectations simultaneously. One commentator has called the political reporters, consultants, and pollsters "the expectorate," the group who decides whether the candidate has done well enough.[79]

individuals across the political spectrum. More recently, Barack Obama, the sole African American U.S. Senator (D-Ill.), threw his hat into the ring, running as a candidate who can bring Americans together around common American values.

As the figure shows, only 6 to 7 percent of the public say they would not vote for a black or a woman who was their party's nominee, and a slightly lower proportion say they would not vote for a Jew. Although 6 to 7 percent is enough to make a difference in a close race, many more people today say they would vote for a black, Jew, or woman than said they would vote for a Catholic in 1960. John Kennedy's victory suggests that 6 or 7 percent is not an insurmountable barrier.

[1]Barry Sussman, "A Black or Woman Does Better Today Than a Catholic in '60," *Washington Post National Weekly Edition*, November 21, 1983, 42.

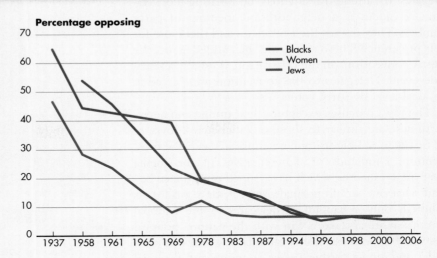

Percentage opposing

Legend: Blacks, Women, Jews

The question asked was, "If your party nominated a generally well-qualified man for president and he happened to be a black [Jew], would you vote for him?" or "If your party nominated a woman for president, would you vote for her if she were qualified for the job?" No questions were asked about African Americans until 1958. The 1961 data for blacks are from 1963. The 1994 and 1996 data are from the NORC's General Social Surveys. No data are available after 1996 for blacks and after 2000 for Jews.

[2]"Though This Be Meanness, Yet There Is a Method in It," *Washington Post National Weekly Edition*, October 10, 1988, 26.

SOURCE: www.cbsnews.com/htdocs/pdf/020306woman.pdf; Gallup Poll data from www.atheists.org/flash.line/atheism9.htm.

The common wisdom about presidential primaries is that the key ingredient is "momentum." That is, a candidate needs to win early, or at least do better than expected, to gain momentum, and then keep winning to maintain momentum. The "expectorate" needs to pronounce him a winner. In 1976, Jimmy Carter, then an unknown governor from Georgia, won the Iowa caucuses, which attracted tremendous media attention and, in turn, led to further primary wins and eventually the nomination. John Kerry, by winning Iowa and then New Hampshire in the 2004 Democratic primaries, gained so much momentum that he knocked the other candidates out of the race very quickly, in what was originally billed as a tightly contested race.

Candidates must avoid making a big mistake or, worse yet, being caught covering up a mistake or untruth. Gary Hart's 1988 candidacy collapsed when the media discovered that his marriage did not prevent him from having an affair with other women. He compounded the damage by lying. This incident raised questions about his character and honesty. In contrast, during the primary campaign, Clinton admitted his marriage was not perfect but did not flaunt ongoing affairs. (The Monica Lewinsky scandal occurred after he was in the White House and was already a popular president.)

Incumbent presidents seeking renomination do not have the same problems as their challengers. Incumbents usually have token or no opposition in the primaries. No incumbent who sought renomination was denied it in the twentieth century.

In addition to these general strategies, candidates must deal specifically with the particular demands of caucuses, conventions, and primaries.

Presidential Caucuses and Conventions

Some states employ caucuses and conventions to select delegates to attend presidential nominating conventions. A caucus is a neighborhood meeting of party members. They discuss the candidates and then vote for their preference. These results are then added across the state. A convention, on the other hand, is usually a statewide event. Delegates to the convention are elected at the local level by party voters.

The Iowa caucuses, except for their timing and newsworthiness, are similar to those in other states. Iowa, as the first state to hold its caucuses, normally gets the most attention. Thousands of representatives of the media cover these caucuses, which have gained importance beyond what one would normally expect for a small state. Although only a handful of delegates to the national convention are at stake, a win with the nation's political pros watching can establish a candidate as a serious contender and attract further media attention and financial donations necessary to continue the campaign.

Presidential Primaries

Delegates to presidential nominating conventions are also selected in direct primaries, sometimes called **presidential preference primaries.** In these elections, governed by state laws and national party rules, voters indicate a preference for a presidential candidate, or they vote for the delegates committed to a candidate, or both. (In states where voters merely indicate their preference, the delegates are actually selected in conventions, and the primaries are called "beauty contests" because they are meaningless in terms of winning delegates, though they can be important in showing popular support.) Like other primaries, presidential primaries can be open (to all voters) or closed (to nonmembers).

Through the 1960s, presidential preference primaries usually played an insignificant role in presidential nominations because only a handful of states employed primaries to select delegates. Thus Vice President **Hubert Humphrey** gained the Democratic Party's nomination in 1968 without winning a single primary. A majority of the delegates to the Democratic convention were selected through party caucuses and state conventions, where party leaders supportive of Humphrey had considerable influence. Humphrey's nomination severely divided the Democratic Party. Many constituencies within the party, particularly those opposed

Soliciting votes by giving speeches and making appearances was once considered beneath the dignity of the presidential office. William Jennings Bryan was the first presidential candidate to break with this tradition. In 1896, he traveled more than eighteen thousand miles and made more than six hundred speeches in an effort to win voters. One observer noted that he was "begging for the presidency as a tramp might beg for a pie." Although Bryan lost the election to William McKinley, his approach to campaigning became the standard. This photo illustrates how the term stump speech, used to refer to candidates' boilerplate campaign speeches, may have developed.

to the Vietnam War, charged that the nomination was controlled by party elites out of touch with rank-and-file Democrats.

Delegate Selection Reform

In response, the Democratic Party changed delegate selection procedures to make delegates more representative of Democratic voters. One change established quotas for blacks, women, and young people to reflect the groups' percentages in each state's population. These reforms significantly increased minority and female convention representation and, quite unexpectedly, made the primary the preferred method of nomination. Criteria of openness and representativeness could be more easily satisfied through primary selection. In recent years, more than 70 percent of the Democratic delegates have been chosen in primaries. The Democrats have replaced quotas for minorities with guidelines urging minority involvement in party affairs. However, the quota remains that half the delegates must be women.

The Republican Party has not felt as much pressure to reform its delegate selection procedures. Republicans have tried to eliminate discrimination and increase participation in the selection process.

Reforming the Nomination Process

Each election year political observers discuss changing the presidential nomination process. They correctly complain that primaries weaken political parties by removing the decision from party officials and that primaries have very low, unrepresentative turnouts. The primary electorate is often in the 25 to 35 percent range, sometimes even lower. Primary voters include the citizens who are most interested in politics. These citizens tend to hold more extreme views than other people. Thus Democratic primaries have a disproportionate number of liberals, and Republican primaries have a disproportionate number of conservatives. These primary voters pull the Democratic candidates further to the left and the Republican candidates further to the right than the candidates might choose to position themselves or than the electorate as a whole might want the candidates to position themselves.

Moreover, until 2008, the system gave disproportionate influence to two small states, Iowa and New Hampshire, that come first in the process. Voters in most other states did not get to see most candidates; they had already been weeded out by the time the April, May, and June primaries occurred. There are two advantages of giving disproportionate influence to small states that select their delegates early. Only in these first small states do candidates come in contact with voters on a very personal basis. In large states, the primaries are strictly media events. One estimate was that candidates in contested races might spend as much as one thousand days, collectively, in Iowa, far beyond what they could do in later primaries. In the 1996 campaign, one of every five New Hampshire voters had met a presidential candidate. In large states, most voters go through their entire lives without ever meeting a presidential candidate.[80]

Having small states at the beginning of the primary season also allows candidates to test their popularity without spending millions of dollars. Those who are successful could then attract funds for the larger, more expensive races. This system gives little-known candidates a better chance than most alternative arrangements would give.

However, this system meant that voters in our largest states had little say in the choice of their parties' nominees. Thus legislators in the larger states moved to get their states into the early action. In 2008, therefore, the system was quite different. The New Hampshire primary remained first, but a week later 22 states, including many large states, held primaries. This new lineup puts a much bigger premium on having money and gaining support early, since only media buys will allow candidates to be visible in so many large states simultaneously.

Rearranging the schedule does not address the central problem of primaries, removing power from political parties. Many people are glad that we no longer have the "smoke-filled rooms" where party bosses chose the nominees. Nevertheless the primary system has weakened political parties, and the small primary electorate is unrepresentative of the general public. Indeed, these voters might be less representative of the public than the party bosses who met in smoke-filled rooms. Certainly they know less about the nominees than the party bosses did. But the days when party leaders could anoint the nominees are probably gone forever.

The National Conventions

Once selected, delegates attend their party's national nominating convention in the summer before the November election. Changes in party rules have reduced the convention's role from an arena where powerful party leaders came together and determined the party's nominee to a body that ratifies a choice based on the outcome of the primaries and caucuses. That is, the conventions now routinely nominate whichever candidate wins the most primaries.

In the "old" days, often many ballots were necessary before a winner emerged. In 1924, it took the Democrats 103 ballots to nominate John W. Davis. Now nominees are selected on the first ballot. Sometimes commentators predict a close nomination race, which would force the decision to be made at the convention, but this hasn't happened since the primaries have been used extensively. Instead, the national party conventions served other purposes: to endorse the nominee and his choice for vice president, to construct a party platform,

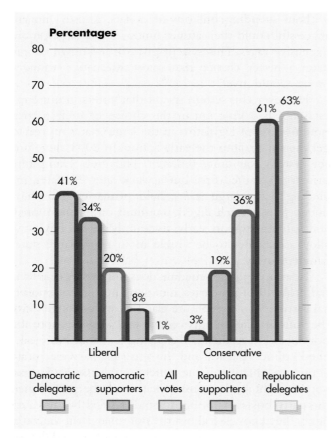

Percentages

- 41% Democratic delegates (Liberal)
- 34% Democratic supporters (Liberal)
- 20% All votes (Liberal)
- 8% Republican supporters (Liberal)
- 1% Republican delegates (Liberal)
- 3% Democratic delegates (Conservative)
- 19% Republican supporters (Conservative)
- 36% All votes (Conservative)
- 61% Republican supporters (Conservative)
- 63% Republican delegates (Conservative)

FIGURE 1 • National Convention Delegates Are More Ideologically Extreme Than Rank-and-File Members

SOURCE: Data are from delegate and public surveys reported in the *New York Times*, August 29, 2004, 13.

to whip up enthusiasm for the ticket among party loyalists, and to present the party favorably to the national viewing audience. Thus even without choosing the nominee, the national conventions give meaning to the notion of a national party.

After the reforms of 1972, convention delegates have become a more diverse group, especially on the Democratic side. In 2004, 50 percent of the Democratic and 43 percent of the Republican delegates were women; 18 percent of the Democratic and 6 percent of the Republican delegates were black. (Only 2 percent of Republican voters are black and 28 percent of Democratic voters are.) Similarly, Democratic delegates are much more likely to be Latino and very slightly more likely to be Asian than are Republican delegates.[81] Compared to the population, delegates to national party conventions are well educated and well off finan-

cially. Delegates also tend to be more ideologically extreme than each party's rank and file. Democratic delegates are more liberal and Republican delegates more conservative than their party's supporters and the public in general.

The Activities of the Convention

National party conventions are full of color and portray at least a semblance of excitement. They are a montage of balloons, placards, and demonstrations. Candidates and their lieutenants scurry in search of uncommitted delegates. Behind-the-scenes negotiators try to work out differences among factions of the party. Journalists are everywhere covering everything from the trivial to the momentous. The keynote address reviews the party's glorious past, speaks to a promising future, and levels attacks, usually relatively gentle, at the opposition. Each candidate is placed in nomination by a party notable who reviews the candidate's background and experience. The roll call of the states ratifies the party's choice, and on the last night delegates cheer the acceptance speeches of the presidential and vice presidential nominees. Those who contested the nomination often join the nominees on the platform at the end in a display of party unity.

During the convention, each party endorses a platform, a statement of what it plans to do dressed up in flowery language about how it is the only possible choice for patriotic Americans. Although platforms are filled with platitudes, they do have some substance. Most of the platforms contain pledges of proposed future actions, and most of those pledges are fulfilled.[82] Platforms do provide observant voters with information about what the party will do if elected.

Finally, the conventions close with the acceptance speeches of the presidential and vice presidential nominees, which are the highlights for most viewers.

Overall, the function of the conventions might best be summarized by the comment, "Conventions are now like bar mitzvahs. They are rites of passage. But rites of passage are very important in society. The guy is changing from a politician and a candidate to one of the two people who are going to be president for sure; it gives them a certain majesty."[83]

The Media and the Convention

With the beginning of radio coverage in 1924 and television coverage in 1940, the conventions have become media events. In 2004, there were six times as many media representatives as delegates at the conventions.[84]

You're ON TV

...before the greatest audience ever...
MORE THAN 70,000,000 VOTERS!

These Tips Tell How Your Behavior Can Win Democratic Votes From Our TV Audience...

Get into your place well *ahead* of time. The Hall can't look good across the nation with its bare seats showing, latecomers drifting in.

Stay in your place till *after* you're told we're off the air. Impatient delegates scuttling out of a littered Hall don't make a good picture.

Pay no attention to the cameras — then they'll pay more attention to *you*. You'll really get wiped out but fast if you insist on playing lens-mugger, hand-waver, TVbitionist.

Don't keep poking signs, banners, balloons up where they intercept cameras, personalities, speakers, candidates, all-Party displays.

Show your enthusiasm and enjoy it. But don't interrupt speakers incessantly, don't be a point-killer. Save your punching power for the real final round.

Remember — there's nothing phony about having good TV manners. It's just good sense. It's good for you, good for the Party.

We're Playing To The World's Greatest Audience—SHOW WHAT A GREAT PARTY WE ARE!

In the 1950s, at the dawn of the television age, Democratic Party leaders instruct their delegates how to behave on camera.

Courtesy of the Smithsonian Institute

The parties try to put on a show they hope will attract voters to their candidates, controlling who speaks and when. Polls usually show the party's candidate doing better during and after the party's convention, called the "convention bounce," though the effect does not last long.

When there are deep divisions in the party, it may be impossible to prevent them from surfacing at the convention during prime time. This has not happened for many years, since the classic 1968 Democratic Convention. It was filled with conflict—conflict inside the convention between the supporters of Hubert Humphrey and opponents of the Johnson policies on the Vietnam War and conflict outside the convention on the streets of Chicago between antiwar demonstrators and the Chicago police. Television covered both events, associating the division in the convention with the turmoil outside, and dimmed Humphrey's chances of winning the election.

Because subsequent conventions have been predictable, with few controversial issues, the major networks are no longer showing them "gavel to gavel," leaving that coverage to public television or specialty cable networks such as CNN and C-SPAN. The major networks showed only a few prime-time events of each 2004 national convention: the keynote speech; an occasional speech by a party luminary, such as President Clinton at the Democratic convention and Arnold Schwarzenegger, governor of California, at the Republican one; the vice presidential acceptance speech; and the presidential acceptance speech. This limited coverage is the logical outcome of the successful attempt of party leaders to control the conventions. If there's no controversy, there's no media attention.

Selecting a Vice Presidential Nominee

Selection of a vice presidential candidate normally is done by the party's presidential nominee and then merely ratified at the convention, although in 1956, Democratic presidential nominee Adlai Stevenson broke with tradition and left the decision to the convention.

Presidential candidates usually select a vice presidential nominee who can balance the ticket. What exactly does "balance" mean? A careful analysis of vice presidential choices of both parties since 1940 revealed that presidential candidates tend to balance the ticket in terms of age—choosing a running mate from a different age cohort, as John Kerry did with John Edwards.[85] Those with little Washington experience usually balance the ticket by choosing a Washington insider as a running mate (as, in 1992, outsider Clinton did by choosing Gore and as, in 2000, outsider George W. Bush did by choosing **Dick Cheney**). Although common wisdom also suggests that presidential candidates balance the ticket in terms of region (e.g., John F. Kennedy from Massachusetts chose Texan **Lyndon Johnson** in 1960) or ideology (e.g., the more liberal Michael Dukakis chose the more conservative Lloyd Bentsen in 1988), this happens only occasionally.[86] In 2004, both presidential candidates had running mates whose ideologies were similar to their own.

Gender traditionally has not been part of a ticket-balancing effort, but since Walter Mondale's historic choice of Geraldine Ferraro in 1984, women are sometimes among those given consideration.

The most important factor, however, is choosing a vice presidential running mate from a large state—the larger, the better.[87] Presidential candidates believe that choosing a vice presidential candidate from a large state will help win that state in the November election. In

When Bill Clinton selected Al Gore as his running mate in 1992, he chose someone who was from the same generation and region and who had the same ideology (moderate liberal). Although Gore, unlike Clinton, was a Washington insider, observers were surprised that there wasn't more effort to balance the ticket. Yet the two couples (including Hillary Clinton and Tipper Gore) developed a chemistry that energized their campaign.

fact, this is not true; the added advantage of a vice presidential candidate in his or her home state is less than 1 percent, and the bigger the state, the less the advantage.[88] About one-third of the vice presidential candidates since 1960, including John Edwards, did not even carry their home state.[89] Both Bush and Kerry ignored the large-state potential in choosing their running mates. Dick Cheney even joked about his home state's miniscule contribution to the Electoral College totals (Wyoming has just 3 votes of the 535 total).

Do vice presidential choices affect the election outcome? In most cases, no, although Kennedy's selection of Johnson probably enabled him to carry the state of Texas in the tight 1960 race.

Third-Party and Independent Nominees

Independent and third-party candidates are part of every presidential campaign. Most of the candidates are invisible to all except the most avid political devotee. It's not easy for independents to get on the ballot; state laws control access to the ballot, and state lawmakers are Republicans or Democrats. But in recent elections, strong independents have emerged with some frequency, including Ross Perot in 1992 and 1996, and Ralph Nader in 2000. The Nader candidacy probably cost Gore the election by taking some liberal votes in closely fought states.

The General Election Campaign

We take it for granted that the election campaign is what determines who wins, and it does have a modest effect.[90] But consider this: only twice since 1952 has the candidate who was ahead in the polls in July, before the national conventions, lost the election. Those years were 1988 when Dukakis led and 2000 when Al Gore led (and since Gore won the popular vote, perhaps his case is only a partial exception to the rule).[91] This suggests that although campaigns can make a difference, a lot of other factors determine who is elected.

Campaign Organization

Staffing the campaign organization is crucial, not only hiring talented people but also to getting those with considerable national campaign experience and a variety of perspectives. The candidate's own personal organization is only one part of the overall campaign organization. The national party organization and state parties also have some responsibilities, including the very important functions of registering potential party voters and getting them to the polls, as well as trying to make sure that the presidential candidate's local appearances will help the party's congressional and state candidates. Party organizations are also crucial in raising funds after the conventions, when direct fundraising by candidates is no longer legal if the candidate accepts public funding.

Campaign Strategies

In developing a strategy, candidates seek to do three things: mobilize those who are already loyal to them and their party, persuade independent voters that they are the best candidate, and try to convert the opposition. Most candidates emphasize mobilizing their own voters. Democrats have to work harder at this than Republicans because Democratic voters often do not vote and are more likely to vote for the other party than are Republicans.

Both parties must try to persuade independent voters, who are numerous and who are swing voters; their votes determine the outcome. In 1964, when Johnson trounced Republican Goldwater, 80 percent of Republicans voted for Goldwater. In 2006, a large majority of independents turned against the Republicans they had supported in 2004, and this switch led to the Democrats retaking the House and Senate.

The crucial strategic question is where to allocate resources of time and money: where to campaign, where to buy media time and how much to buy, and where to spend money helping local organizations.

Allocating Resources among States

Candidates must always remember that they have to win a majority of the Electoral College vote (see "The Electoral College" section later in this chapter). The most populous states, with the largest number of elec-

toral votes, are vital. Prime targets are those large states that could go to either party, such as, in 2004, Ohio, Pennsylvania, and of course Florida.

In recent years, candidates have been increasingly sophisticated about where to use their limited resources. Thus in the 2004 presidential campaign, there was little advertising or activity in several of the largest states—California, Illinois, New York, and Texas—because the first three were considered sure Kerry states and the last a sure Bush state. Instead, the campaign focused mostly on the so-called **battleground states,** or **swing states,** where the results were in doubt: not just the large states of Ohio, Pennsylvania, and Florida, but medium-sized states such as Wisconsin and Iowa and even smaller states such as New Mexico with its five electoral votes and New Hampshire with its four. As one indicator of attention, President Bush visited Pennsylvania eighteen times during the campaign, and Senator Kerry visited it twenty-two times. Ohio was John Kerry's most frequent stop (with twenty-six visits), and it was second for George W. Bush (with seventeen visits). Relatives of the candidates, entertainers, and party luminaries who campaigned for the candidates also focused on these swing states.

In focusing on swing states, candidates are attempting to expand their existing bases of support. Most of the Rocky Mountain states have been solidly Republican in their presidential loyalties. Republicans must build on this base and their strength in the South by carrying some of the large eastern or midwestern industrial states to win.

Democrats have a strategic problem given the near solid Rocky Mountain and Southern Republican bloc. Between the end of Reconstruction (in 1877) and 1948, the South was solidly Democratic. Since 1976, the Democrats have consistently lost the South, as we discussed in Chapter 6. Some strategists have urged the Democrats to win back the South by choosing more conservative candidates. Others have argued for a strategy to win without the South, aiming for the industrial states of the East and Midwest along with California and a few other states of the West. This was Clinton's winning strategy, although he did win three southern states in each election. (This strategy was also used successfully by the Republicans between the 1870s and the 1920s, when they were able to capture the White House regularly without ever winning a southern state.)

Creating Images

Largely through the media, candidates try to create a favorable image and portray the opponent in an unfa-

In 2004, George W. Bush campaigned on his role as commander in chief and was often photographed with the military.

© Brooks Kraft/Corbis

tion to domestic issues, the campaign was fought largely on the issue of who would be the stronger leader in a dangerous world. And the results indicated that those voters concerned about this issue voted strongly for Bush. By 2006, though, the unpopular war turned this key issue to a plus for Democrats.

Issue appeals are usually general, and often candidates do not offer a clear-cut choice even on the most important controversies of the time. For example, the 1968 presidential election offered voters little choice on Vietnam policy, because the positions of candidates Nixon and Humphrey appeared very similar.[92] Voters who wanted to end the war by withdrawing or others who wanted to escalate the war had no real choice between the candidates. In 2004, the situation was similar, with neither candidate offering an option to withdraw from Iraq, though Kerry appeared more willing to declare Iraq a failed venture.

Ideally, the major campaign themes and strategies have been put into place by the end of the summer, but these themes and strategies are revised and updated on a daily, sometimes hourly, basis as the campaign progresses. Decisions are made not only by the candidate and the campaign manager but also by a staff of key advisers that includes media experts and pollsters. Sophisticated polling techniques are used to produce daily reports on shifts in public opinion across the nation and in particular regions. Campaign trips are modified or scratched as the candidate's organization sees new opportunities. And media events can be planned to complement the paid advertising the candidate runs.

Campaign Communication

Candidates use multiple ways of communicating with their supporters and with the millions of swing voters who might vote either way. Campaign advertising, appearances on television, candidate debates, mass mailings, and many forms of electronic communication are all part of campaign communication. They inform, they help set the campaign agenda, and they help persuade voters.[93]

Media Advertising

Paid advertisements allow candidates to focus on points most favorable to their cause or to portray their opponents in the most negative light. In 2004, the presidential candidates and associated groups spent more than $1 billion on advertising in an attempt to sway public opinion.[94] Most advertising is done through television, although radio and the Internet also reach significant

vorable way. In 2000, George W. Bush used his warm personality to establish a positive image despite the concerns many voters had about his abilities. Voters were comfortable with Gore's abilities but had reservations about his personality. Moreover, after eight years of Clinton's evasions and lies about personal issues, Gore's exaggerations may have seemed too much like those of Clinton. In 2004, Bush tried to define himself as a resolute war leader and define Kerry as a "flip-flopper" with no principled positions. Kerry, in turn, painted Bush as an arrogant person unwilling to listen to criticisms or admit failures.

Issues can also be the basis for an appeal to voters. Democrats traditionally have used the "pocketbook" issues, arguing that economic times are better with Democratic presidents. In 2004, though, the Iraq War and the war on terrorism were the predominant issues of the campaign. Although Kerry sought to turn atten-

audiences.[95] Television ads were first used in the 1952 campaign. One, linking the Democratic Truman administration to the unpopular Korean War, showed two soldiers in combat talking about the futility of war. Then one of the soldiers is hit and dies. The other one exposes himself to the enemy and is also killed. The announcer's voice says, "Vote Republican."[96] Today's ads are shorter and less melodramatic but still appeal to emotions. The 1984 Reagan commercials hearkened back to an idyllic past before the turmoil of the 1960s and 1970s and proclaimed American greatness again. Their cheerful tag line was "It's morning in America."[97] (Many historic ads are available for viewing online at www.movingimage.us.)

There is both an art and a science to campaign ads. Most political ads are quite short, thirty or sixty seconds in length. Campaigns are sophisticated in placing ads. Selection of television shows and media markets is important. For example, in 2004, President Bush ran many of his ads on crime shows such as *Law and Order* and *NYPD Blue* because he thought there would be an audience of conservative men sympathetic to Republican appeals watching those shows. The Kerry campaign ran more ads on shows catering to women, such as *Judge Judy* and *Oprah,* and to younger and older men, such as the *Late Show with David Letterman*.[98] Kerry also advertised more on shows with African American stars. Both campaigns spent a lot to advertise on morning news shows and popular daytime shows such as *Dr. Phil*.[99] Both campaigns focused on the battleground states and wasted little of their advertising budget on states already thought to be sure for one candidate.[100] But within the battleground states, the Bush campaign focused more on the rural and exurban (outer suburban) areas than did the Kerry campaign.

Campaigns also have to decide what combination to run of positive ads, touting their own programs; negative ads, attacking their opponents; and response ads, responding to opponents' charges. Negative ads were more prominent in the 2004 election than in the recent past. The Bush campaign ran far more negative ads than the Kerry campaign.[101] This high level of negativity is unusual for an incumbent but probably reflected his low approval ratings. Strong front-runners tend to stay positive.[102] The 2004 election was so close that both sides made liberal use of negative ads. However, many ads were run not by the candidates themselves, but by independent advocacy groups.

Negative ads do provide some helpful information about issues, supplementing media news coverage, which focuses heavily on personalities, conflicts, and the "horse race" aspect of campaigns.[103] Many, though not all, negative ads contain a grain of truth. Kerry did vote for numerous tax increases, but not as many as the Republicans charged. Hundreds of thousands of jobs were lost during the Bush administration, but not as many as the Democrats claimed.

However, some negative ads are simply false. Among the most discussed negative ads in 2004 were those of the "Swift Boat Veterans for Truth." The group attacked Kerry's war record. (Kerry, as a young naval lieutenant, commanded a "swift boat" in the Vietnam War and won medals for heroism as well as for his wounds.) The Swift Boat Veterans did not serve with Kerry, and several were angry with him for opposing the war after returning from Vietnam. The Kerry campaign was slow to respond to these August ads and lost ground in the polls during this period despite the fact that independent reexaminations of the record found nothing to substantiate the Swift Boat Veterans' ad claims.

Sen. John Kerry (D-Mass.) needed hockey pads for the rough and tumble campaign of 2004.

Negative ads tend to reinforce viewers' previous beliefs. So, if you believed that Kerry wouldn't be a strong leader, or that Democrats wouldn't stand up to foreign threats, you would be more likely to believe the Swift Boat ads that questioned Kerry's Vietnam service and implicitly draw these damning conclusions. Campaign advisers think that negative ads are very effective, even though most people say they do not like them.[104] One adviser said, "People won't pay any attention [to positive ads]. Better to knock your opponent's head off."[105] Polls do show that negative ads can have a dramatic short-term effect on a candidate's standing. The Swift Boat commercials suggest that negative ads can have a long-term effect as well.

Some observers speculate that negative ads increase voter cynicism and thus depress turnout, but there is little evidence of this effect. However, there is evidence that Republicans and independents find negative ads more believable than Democrats do, perhaps because Republicans and independents are more cynical about politics and government to begin with.

Technology allows the opposition candidate's ads to be evaluated continuously and new ads prepared immediately to counter attacks that might be having an impact. After the Swift Boat fiasco, Kerry began responding to other negative ads. One day in October, the Kerry campaign learned that President Bush had just charged that Kerry would "weaken America and make the world more dangerous." Within three hours, the Kerry campaign had made an ad accusing Bush of "desperately attacking" Kerry. By late afternoon, the script and video were sent to reporters.[106] The Bush campaign had a similar instant-response operation.

Other checks do exist on negative campaigns.[107] One check is the press, which could point out errors of fact. In recent campaigns, the press has tried to do this. In 2004, fact-checkers were more active, and many papers ran critiques of the truthfulness of ads (and the statements in debates). In the process, however, the press often simply gave more attention to the negative messages.[108] Another check is the voters, who might become outraged. But although the voters complain, campaign research shows that negative ads often influence the voters, perhaps even the same ones who complain.

Historians tell us that negative campaigning is as American as apple pie. When Thomas Jefferson faced John Adams in 1796, a Federalist editorial prophesized that if Jefferson were elected, "[m]urder, robbery, rape, adultery and incest will be openly taught and practiced."[109] When Andrew Jackson ran for president in 1832, his mother was called a prostitute, his father a mulatto (someone of mixed races, black and white), his wife a profligate woman, and himself a bigamist.[110] A British observer of American elections in 1888 described them as a "tempest of invective and calumny . . . imagine all the accusations brought against all the candidates for the 670 seats in the English Parliament concentrated on one man, and read . . . daily for three months."[111]

Television Appearances and Media Events

Campaigns are expensive because they rely so heavily on the media to get the candidate's message to the voters. As one observer argued, "Today's presidential campaign is essentially a mass-media campaign. It is not that the mass media entirely determine what happens. . . . [b]ut it is no exaggeration to say that, for the large majority of voters, the campaign has little reality apart from the media version."[112]

Increasingly, candidates are getting free publicity by appearing on various television shows. In earlier elections, candidates appeared only on "serious" shows, such as the Sunday morning talk shows where candidates would be interviewed by one or more members of the press. Now it is increasingly common for candidates to appear in more informal, sometimes humorous, settings such as late night talk shows or comedy shows. The candidates hope to use these settings to show voters that they are approachable and down to earth. It also gives candidates a chance to poke fun at their own foibles and thus possibly defuse opponents' attacks.

National television appearances might be the only sight that voters in a majority of states ever get of the candidates. Given the increasing sophistication of the campaigns, most television and radio ads never appear in states that are solid for one candidate or another. Although voters in battleground states might consider it a blessing to not face an onslaught of campaign ads, voters in other states may feel less connected to the campaign.

Candidates spend most of their time going from media market to media market, hoping to get both national and local coverage.[113] Vice presidential candidates often appear in the smaller media markets, while the presidential contenders hit the major metro areas. They stage media events with photo opportunities in front of enthusiastic crowds and patriotic or other positive symbols.

Televised Debates

Candidates also use televised debates as part of their media campaigns. In 1960, Kennedy challenged Nixon to debate during their presidential campaigns. Nixon did not want to debate because as vice president he was already known and ahead in the polls. He remembered his first election to the House of Representatives when he challenged the incumbent to debate and, on the basis of his performance, won the election. Afterward he said the incumbent was a "damn fool" to debate. Nevertheless Nixon did agree to debate, and when the two contenders squared off, presidential debates were televised to millions of homes across the country for the first time.

Nixon dutifully answered reporters' questions and rebutted Kennedy's assertions. But Kennedy came to project an image. He sought to demonstrate his vigor, to compensate for his youth and inexperience. He also sought to contrast his attractive appearance and personality with Nixon's. So he quickly answered reporters' specific questions and then directly addressed viewers about his general goals. Kennedy's strategy worked. He appealed to people and convinced them that his youth and inexperience would not pose problems. While Kennedy remained calm, Nixon became nervous, smiling at inappropriate moments, with his eyes darting back and forth and beads of sweat rolling down his face, which had a five-o'clock shadow that projected a somewhat sinister look.

According to public opinion polls, people who saw the debates thought that Kennedy performed better in three of the four. (The only debate in which they thought Nixon performed better was the one in which the candidates were not in the same studio side-by-side. They were in separate cities, and with this arrangement Nixon was less nervous.) Yet people who heard the debates on radio did not think Kennedy performed as well. They were not influenced by the visual contrast between the candidates or the Kennedy strategy of looking directly into the camera. Clearly, television made the difference.

No more presidential debates were held for sixteen years. The candidates who were ahead did not want to risk their lead. But in 1976, President Ford decided to debate Carter, and in 1980, President Carter decided to debate Reagan. Both incumbents were in trouble, and they thought they needed to debate to win. Although President Reagan was far ahead in 1984, he decided to debate Mondale because he did not want to seem afraid. By agreeing to debate, he solidified the precedent begun anew in 1976.

In 2000, the media's low expectations for Bush's performance, coupled with his congenial, personal style, helped him hold his own or even win the debates in the view of many, even though the debates revealed his limited grasp of issues and misstatements of facts. Gore's mannerisms seemed stiff and overbearing. And the press, which is far more inclined to evaluate the debates as theater performances than as policy discussions, addressed Gore's body language more than Bush's grasp of issues and misstatements of facts.

Because candidates have different strengths, each campaign wants a debate format that builds on its candidate's strengths. The "debate about debates" has become as predictable a part of campaigns as the debates themselves. Representatives of candidates debate the number of debates, the formats, the topics to be covered, the size of the audience, even the size and shape of the podia. (In 1976, President Ford, who was tall, wanted a high podium so Jimmy Carter would appear even shorter than he was.) The 2004 debates were governed by a thirty-two-page set of rules agreed to by the candidates' representatives.

In 2004, those negotiating for Bush argued that the first debate should be about foreign policy, ostensibly

*Families all across the country gathered in front of their TVs to watch the first televised presidential debates in 1960, featuring Senator John F. Kennedy and Vice President **Richard Nixon**.*

Bush's strength. He thought he could easily show Kerry to have an uncertain grasp and a vacillating policy. Instead, Kerry looked assured and confident and attacked Bush's foreign policy mistakes throughout the debate. When cameras focused on Bush listening to Kerry, he looked surly and angry at being attacked. And when Bush responded, he wasn't able to offer a coherent defense of his policies. Consequently, although Kerry had been trailing in the polls before the debate, his performance in this debate narrowed the gap.

Bush was not used to direct criticism of his policies. Within the White House, criticism was not welcomed, and on the campaign trail, Bush usually spoke only to handpicked Republican supporters, whose tough questions tended to be about whether he liked broccoli or what he felt about his legacy.[114] Thus he did not have much recent experience facing criticism nor with presenting a serious counterargument to it. The ridicule and dismissiveness that he used in his campaign stump speeches did not work well when faced with a real-life opponent making real-life arguments on stage. The president prepared more for the second and third debates and looked more confident and pleasant. However, most people thought that Kerry bested Bush in those debates, too, but only by a small margin.[115]

A newer feature of debates is that in recent primary campaigns, various groups have sponsored debates among primary candidates. The results of these debates tend to be minimal, especially when as in the 2008 race, there are a lot of candidates. A debate among seven or ten candidates allows for even less direct exchange than a debate between two candidates. However, these debates are a way for the people who are paying attention to the election to learn more about the candidates.

E-Campaigning

Increasingly, candidates are relying on electronic communication to keep supporters informed about the campaign and the issues, to raise money, and to solicit volunteer activity. This includes websites, e-mail, blogs, podcasts, text messaging, and the use of the social networking sites like MySpace.

All the leading candidates for the presidency in 2008 had active websites. Those of the Democrats were more popular than those of the Republicans as measured by hits in early 2007. All candidates use e-mail to communicate with hundreds of thousands of people, making them feel like insiders and encouraging their continued support and allegiance. These e-mail messages supplement the use of direct postal mailings, which are more

expensive and less responsive to breaking events. An e-mail can be prepared and sent in a few hours; a direct mailing takes days or longer. In the 2004 election, the Kerry campaign had more than two million supporters on its e-mail lists, and the Republicans reportedly had as many as six million.

Podcasts to download are an even newer feature of e-campaigning, and the parties are also examining Internet social networks such as Friendster and Facebook to try to access groups of potential supporters.[116] In the 2006 elections, YouTube became a way for millions of Internet users to play and replay candidate mistakes. Senator George Allen's (R-Va.) comment calling an Indian American "macacca" was captured on camera and replayed to another 100,000 people. This no doubt contributed to his narrow defeat for reelection to the Senate. Several Democrats also tried to strategically use YouTube, MySpace, and Facebook as a positive asset to their 2008 campaigns.

YouTube gained national attention when one of the primary debates for each party was sponsored by YouTube, and members of the public asked the candidates questions via YouTube video. At first the Republicans did not want to have a debate in this format, but later agreed. YouTube allowed some voters to have a kind of personal contact with the candidates.

Blogs also have become a campaign tool. Candidates and their supporters can air their views and attack opponents through blogs, some of which are read by millions. Daily Kos, whose contributors are mostly liberals and Democrats, had nearly five million hits in one month in 2005.[117] Each blog site reaches a specialized group of people. Although talk radio is dominated by conservative Republicans, the most popular political blogs are those on the liberal side. Some observers argue that the web fits the style of Democrats well, with their propensity toward debate and disagreement, whereas the talk radio show, with its "on-message" tendencies, fits the Republican style.

Campaign Funding

Success in raising money is one of the keys to a successful political campaign. Former Speaker of the House of Representatives Tip O'Neill (D-Mass.) once said, "There are four parts to any campaign. The candidate, the issues . . . , the campaign organization, and the money. Without money you can forget the other three."[118]

We have conflicting attitudes about money in politics, however. On the one hand, without money, candidates or people with new political ideas could never become known in our massive and complex society. Television spreads names and ideas almost instantaneously, so having money to buy television time means that your ideas will be heard. In that sense, money contributes to open political debate. On the other hand, money can be a corrupting influence on politics. At the least, it can buy access to decision makers. At the worst, it can buy decisions. Money allows some points of view to be trumpeted while others are forced to whisper. Some candidates or groups can afford to spend hundreds of thousands of dollars for each prime-time minute of national television or for prestigious Washington law firms to lobby; others can afford only web pages and letters. Money increases the inequities in political life.

Americans have struggled with these contradictions about money and politics. Periodically, after a series of outrages relating to the impact of money on legislation, regulation, or elections, we pass laws seeking to reduce the impact of money in political life; but then, everyone finds ways around all the rules and a new cycle of outrage and legislation starts again.

A significant period of reform occurred in the early 1970s. Prompted by the increasing use of television in campaigns and the rising cost of buying television time, Congress passed a law regulating spending on advertising in 1971. The law limited the amount that candidates could donate to their own campaigns and required candidates to disclose the names and addresses of donors of more than $100. In the course of the Watergate investigations, it became clear that corporations were not abiding by these restrictions. Several corporations secretly funded President Nixon's reelection campaign. For example, Nixon's Justice Department negotiated a settlement favorable to the ITT Corporation in a pending legal dispute soon after an ITT subsidiary gave the Republican National Committee $400,000.[119] Altogether, twenty-one individuals and fourteen corporations were indicted for illegal campaign contributions, mostly but not entirely to the Nixon reelection campaign.

In response to these scandals, Congress again attempted to regulate campaign financing. New legislation was passed in 1974. The objectives of the 1974 law were to limit campaign spending, to make the campaign finance system more open by disclosing the names of donors, and to force candidates to be less reliant on a few big donors. The act also established the bipartisan **Federal Election Commission** (FEC) to

CLINTON'S YOUTUBE CAMPAIGN

Hillary Clinton's campaign gained considerable attention in mid 2007 when she used the web to ask her supporters to vote on a campaign song. She released a video on YouTube, "I Need Your Advice." In this short clip, she stated that whatever the choice of her supporters, "I make you this solemn and sacred promise: I won't sing it in public," then the video switched to the earlier unscripted YouTube video of her singing the national anthem way off key (she was unaware this was being taped). This latter YouTube video had gotten considerable press. A week later, she recorded another humorous video, again posted on YouTube, which included videos both of distinctly amateur efforts at creating songs for her contest and several people saying what a stupid idea this song contest was, followed by her comment thanking everyone for their help.

Then, in announcing the results of that election, she released a video vignette spoofing the last scene in the last *Sopranos* episode. In addition to creating good publicity for her campaign, these efforts were clearly designed to demonstrate both that she had a sense of humor and was in touch with popular culture. And, because of the novelty of the approach, the national press and other Internet sites talked about and linked to the video, thus garnering publicity beyond the initial YouTube users. Because she is typically portrayed as humorless, this little YouTube campaign could make an impact, even early in the campaign.

See: www.youtube.com/watch?v=3FV7XU-TLMU&NR=1; www.youtube.com/watch?v=LClOHUFUC5g&NR=1; www.hillaryclinton.com/blog/view/?id=8262.

enforce the law. However, within a decade, candidates and parties discovered ways to get around this law, and calls for further reform were finally answered by Congress when, in 2002, it passed what is called the McCain-Feingold Act. The chief aim of his act was to eliminate **soft money donations** (funds given to parties and other groups ostensibly for use other than campaigning). However loopholes were quickly found in this law, too.

Current regulations focus on disclosure, public funding, contribution limits, and spending limits in political campaigns.

Disclosure

Federal law requires candidates to disclose the source of their contributions. The **Federal Election Commission** provides public reports on who has given money to whom. Through this part of the law, journalists and the public can see what private interests are contributing and who the beneficiaries of their contributions are. In fact, you can look on the web and see who in your community has given to what candidates, campaign committees, or **PACS** (www.fecinfo.com/cgi-win/x_stateguide.exe?DoFn=&sYR=2006, see below). This is one aspect of the legislation that has been effective and relatively uncontroversial. Financers of independent groups must also be disclosed.

Public Funding

Since 1974, presidential candidates are eligible for public funding for the primary and general elections. The amount increases each year to take account of inflation. The funds come from a voluntary checkoff of $3 that individuals can make on their tax returns. If a candidate accepts public funding, he or she must adhere to certain spending limits. Candidates who do not accept public funding can spend as much as they can raise.

Once candidates receive their parties' nominations, public funding pays them each about $75 million for the general election campaign (also adjusted each election for inflation), and they can accept several million more from their party's national committee. At this point, fundraising is supposed to be officially over for the candidates. But this prohibition does not limit other groups from raising and spending money to sway public opinion and thereby help their favored candidate.

The public financing system is dying. In 2004, George W. Bush, John Kerry, and Howard Dean decided not to accept public money, so they had no spending limits at all at the primary stage.[120] Hillary Rodham Clinton announced in early 2007 that she would not accept public funding for either the primary or general election in 2008. [121] And then her chief opponents, John Edwards and Barack Obama, also rejected public funding. The reason that candidates reject public funding is that they can raise more money from private donors. Thus an arms race is renewed. As one of the commissioners of the Federal Election Committee remarked, "The 2008 race will be the longest and most expensive presidential election in American history. Top-tier candidates are going to have to raise $100 million by the end of 2007 to be a serious candidate."[122]

Contribution Limits

Federal law also regulates the amount that individuals and groups can give to candidates and campaigns. Individuals can now give $2000 per candidate per election. The law also regulates donations to national party committees, to state or local committees, and overall donations. Because of the legal restrictions of direct donations to candidates and campaigns, and because of new technology, some candidates have put a lot of effort into raising money through the Internet from people who are not fat cats. Howard Dean, the Democratic front-runner in the early 2004 primary season, first realized the potential of the Internet to link his supporters with the campaign and with each other. Tens of thousands of his supporters were in constant contact with the campaign through e-mail and were regularly solicited for funds. Seeing the success that Dean was having through the Internet, Kerry's staff advised him to mention his web address in his Iowa victory speech. This mention resulted in an instantaneous tenfold increase in hits on Kerry's website. After he won the **Super Tuesday** primaries, he took in $2.6 million in a single day.[123] Enough funds were raised by both Dean and Kerry in the primary season to allow both to reject public funding for their campaigns.

Although these small donations somewhat balance giving by the large donors, the fat cats had other places to play. The limits on direct contributions were negated in other ways through four huge, and largely related, loopholes: **independent spending,** PACs, soft money, 527 groups.

Spending Limits

Attempts to limit campaign spending have been ineffective. The Supreme Court knocked huge holes in campaign funding legislation when it struck down spending limits except in publicly funded presidential elections.[124] Because spending often goes to buy advertising, the Court argued that spending restrictions violated individuals' First Amendment right of free speech. Spending in a campaign enables candidates to get their message out. Giving money is a form of expression protected by the Constitution. Consequently, spending limits apply only in presidential races when candidates accept public funds.

Federal law classifies nonparty and candidate spending in different ways. We will discuss independent spending, political action committees (PACS), soft money, and 527 group spending.

Independent Spending Spending by nonparty groups is unregulated. In 1985, the Supreme Court ruled that groups, including PACs (discussed later) could spend unlimited amounts working on behalf of issues or candidates, publicly funded or not, as long as they do not give funds directly to parties or candidates.[125]

The Court assumed that this spending would be meaningfully independent. However, "independent" spending is often done by organized groups with indirect links to the candidate. Thus interest groups, through their PACs, can spend as much as they want as long as they are not actually campaigning for a candidate. Instead, they engage in "issues advocacy," usually targeted to promoting a particular candidate or party.[126] Thus anyone not officially part of a campaign or national party can spend as much as he or she wants. However, to be independent, a group cannot be officially linked to a candidate or party nor can it endorse a candidate or party.

Two examples illustrate how tenuous these definitions are. The Media Fund, run by a former Clinton White House adviser, ran television ads throughout the primary campaign. One featured a shot of a factory with the voice pointing out that "it's true that George W. Bush has created more jobs. Unfortunately, ..." The camera then reveals that the factory is in China, and the voice announces that most of the new jobs were in places like China.[127] The ad did not endorse Kerry but clearly worked in his interest. On the other side, the "Swift Boat Veterans for Truth" was financed largely by Bush supporters and advised by an attorney who was an official in the Bush campaign (and who resigned when this tie was revealed). Technically, however, the group was "independent" of the Bush campaign.

Political Action Committees Although federal legislation has limited group contributions to candidates, it does not limit individuals' contributions to groups. As a result, Political Action Committees (PACs) are a prominent feature of the campaign funding scene.

PACs are funded from dues and "voluntary" contributions from members in the case of labor unions and "voluntary" contributions from employees in the case of businesses. PACs are one way that individuals can channel more money to their favorite candidates. Individuals could give a limited amount directly to candidates and then give more money to each of several PACs, which in turn gives it to candidates.[128] About four hundred of the 4000 or so PACs give more than $100,000 in total. These wealthy PACs represent corporate interests, trade interests (groups of professionals or industries, such as the National Pork Producers Council), or issue coalitions.

Although PACs differ in the targets of their donations, they show a distinct preference for Republicans in the presidential races and for incumbents—Republicans or Democrats—in congressional races (see Figure 2). PACs usually want to give to the candidate they believe will win, normally the incumbents, so that they will have access to a policy maker. PACs also give money to members in districts where the PACs have a substantial interest, such as a large number of union members for a union PAC or a large factory for a corporate PAC.[129] PACs also target contributions to members of key congressional committees. For example, PACs organized by defense contractors give disproportionately to members who serve on the Armed Services Committees, which have a big role in deciding what weapons to purchase.[130]

Women's PACs, including EMILY's List, one of the biggest-spending PACs, are unusual in focusing most of their money on nonincumbents. Their goal is to get more women elected, which often means supporting nonincumbents with strong chances of winning.

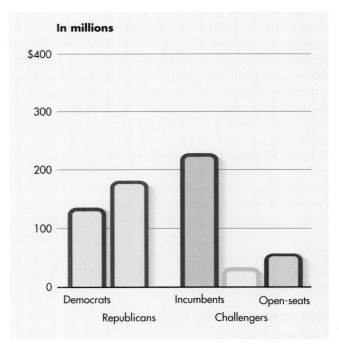

In millions

FIGURE 2 • **Recipients of Political Action Committee Donations in 2003–2004 Election Cycle** *PACs give overwhelmingly to incumbents. The donations charted here were to House and Senate candidates. Open seats are those races without an incumbent.*

SOURCE: U.S. Census Bureau, *Statistical Abstract of the United States,* 2006. (Washington, D.C.: Government Printing Office, 2006), table 414.

Soft Money Some campaign donations are so-called "soft money." Soft money is supposed to be used for such "party-building" activities as national party conventions, voter registration drives, direct mailings, polling, issue ads, and advertisements for nonfederal party candidates. Donors who wanted to give more than their legal federal maximum could give soft money to national party committees. Soft money was exempted from limitations of federal legislation because, in theory, it was not to be used for campaigns. In reality, most soft money is spent by independent groups for national television advertisements for the parties' candidates. [131]

527 Groups Big donors can give unlimited funds to so-called **527 groups,** named after the provision in the tax code authorizing them. These 527 groups also can spend independently. In the 2004 campaign, the most visible were MoveOn.org Voter Fund on the Democratic side and the Swift Boat Veterans for Truth group on the Republican side. These tax-exempt groups, and many others on both sides of the partisan divide, collected unregulated money from supporters of the candidates and then used that money to fund television advertisements. Neither fundraising nor expenditures of groups such as MoveOn.org or Swift Boat are limited by any federal laws so long as the groups are independent of the campaigns and do not endorse candidates. The organizers of 527 groups were often important party activists and donors. Thus the groups are technically independent, but in reality are closely linked to the candidates.

Overall, then, federal laws regulating campaign finance have been successful in requiring disclosure; somewhat successful in regulating donations to formal candidates, parties, and PACs; but remarkably unsuccessful in limiting the flow of money into the campaign process through soft money and 527 groups. Fat cats can, in fact, give as much as they want to work on behalf of their candidates, just not directly to the candidate or the party.

The Impact of our Campaign Finance System

There are many potential effects of our campaign finance system. In general, the perception that big money buys influence and access, if not actual votes, has a corrosive impact on public trust in government. Indeed, much of the public believes that most individuals in government are out to feather their own nests and that many are crooks. Some of the reasons for this low trust

have nothing to do with money. But public trust was certainly affected by the Watergate scandal in the 1970s, and it is likely that continuous revelations about big-money lobbying activity since then reinforce public cynicism and distrust.

American elections are funded, for the most part, by private money. It is therefore not surprising that candidates turn to people who have money to help with that funding. It is also not surprising that the current system alienates voters. Even if we believe that no votes are actually bought, the appearance of conflicts of interest that permeates the existing system and clearly disturbs the public should give pause to those interested in the health of our political system.

Walter Lippmann, a respected journalist, once said that American attitudes about corruption alternate between "fits and starts of unsuspecting complacency and violent suspicion."[132] We think nothing is wrong, and then we think everything is wrong. So it is with our views of campaign money. For several years after major post-Watergate campaign finance reforms in 1974, we thought things were going along pretty well. More recently, many people have become convinced that the nation is in terrible jeopardy because of the influence of money. This fear is compounded because money has helped bring about regulatory lapses, which in turn have been partly responsible for failures to check the dishonesty of many corporations, which in turn has led to eroding confidence in corporate America. So beyond leading Americans to grow cynical about government, the campaign finance system has indirectly helped lead to a loss of confidence in business, too.

Although a new campaign finance law was passed in 2002, it has had little impact. Elected officials appear to be more afraid of being without campaign donations than they are that the campaign finance system will further erode confidence in the whole political system. Ideologically, Democrats are more sympathetic to limiting the influence of big money, but practically, Democratic incumbents are heavily dependent on their PAC "fixes." Thus, neither party has much incentive to support campaign finance reform, despite the fact that the public is repelled by the existing system.

The Electoral College

All planning for the campaign has to take into account the peculiar American institution of the **Electoral College.** In the United States, we do not have a direct election of the president. Although Al Gore had over five hundred thousand more votes than George W. Bush in 2000, he lost the election. The Electoral College is another feature of the American constitutional system that limits democracy.[133]

The Way the System Works

What counts is the popular vote in each state, because that vote determines which candidate will receive the state's electoral votes. Each state has as many electors as its total representation in Congress (House plus Senate) (see Figure 3.4 in Chapter 3). The smallest states (and the District of Columbia) have three, whereas the largest state—California—has fifty-five. Voters choose electors of the Electoral College when they vote for president. Technically, they vote for the electors pledged to the candidate and whose names are on file with the state government. The outcome is not official until these electors gather in each state capital in December after the presidential election to cast their votes for president and vice president.

With the exception of Maine and Nebraska, which divide some of their Electoral College votes according to who wins in each congressional district, all of each state's electoral votes go to the candidate winning the most votes in that state. If one candidate wins a majority (270) of the electors voting across the United States, then the election is decided. If the electoral vote is tied, or if no candidate wins a majority, then the election is decided in the House of Representatives, where each state has one vote and a majority is necessary to win. This has not happened since 1824, when John Quincy Adams was chosen. If voting in the Electoral College for the vice president does not yield a majority, the Senate chooses the vice president, with each senator having one vote. If it should get to that stage, the largest and smallest states would have equal weight, a very undemocratic procedure.

Strategic Implications

The campaign strategies that candidates use are shaped by the Electoral College system. In general, candidates have incentives to spend more time in the large states where the majority of the electoral votes are. However, in recent campaigns, a disproportionate amount of time is spent on the so-called swing states, states that are not safe for one candidate or the other. That is why states such as New York and California had few political ads and visits by the campaigns. Their votes were considered to be safe for John Kerry, so neither Bush nor Kerry paid attention to the state. Without an

Electoral College system, both Bush and Kerry would have spent much more time in those states given their huge populations.

But the small states that tend to favor the existing system did not receive much attention either. The safe Republican states in the prairies, the South, and the Great Plains were ignored, too, by Bush as well as Kerry.

Rationale and Outcomes of the Electoral College

The Founders neither wanted nor envisioned a popular election of the president; selection of the president was placed in the hands of state elites, the electors. The Founders also agreed to enshrine the influence of small states (at that time, disproportionately Southern, slaveholding states) in the fundamental framework of the Constitution, and the Electoral College was one of the ways of doing that.[134]

The Founders assumed that the Electoral College would have considerable power, with each elector exercising independent judgment and choosing from among a large number of candidates. They did not foresee the development of political parties or the development of a political climate where the popular vote is considered the source of legitimacy for a candidate. In practice, as state parties developed, the electors became part of the party process, pledged to party candidates. Therefore electors usually rubber-stamp the choice of voters in each state rather than exercise their own judgment.

A discrepancy between the Electoral College and the popular vote outcome occurred three times in the nineteenth century (1824, 1876, and 1888). However, after more than a century of presidential elections whose outcome was known once the popular vote was tallied, and since the principle of "one person, one vote" has become enshrined in law and political culture, the American public has become used to thinking of elections as an expression of the will of the people.

When the 2000 election yielded an Electoral College winner who had not won the popular vote, there were immediate calls for the elimination or reform of the Electoral College system. However, these calls went nowhere, and the Electoral College remains.

Possible Reforms

The Electoral College was designed both to temper the influence of voters by establishing an intermediate body of electors who actually choose the president and to make sure that the South had a disproportionate influence on the choice of the president.[135] It is a distinctly undemocratic mechanism that institutionalizes in the presidential election process part of the excess weight given to smaller states in the United States Senate (because the number of electors for each state is based on the number of senators and representatives in each state).

Over the years, several proposed reforms have been considered. One reform would be to abolish the Electoral College altogether and leave the choice of president to the popular vote because direct election is a more understandable system. Direct election is not as simple as it seems, however, because when the election is close and there are third-party candidates who get more than a token vote, no candidate receives a majority of the votes. Some run-off system might be necessary.

Even though one might think support for a popular election would be overwhelming given the democratic values of our society, it is not. The Electoral College is based on states, so it encourages campaigns designed to win "states." In this sense, it reinforces the federal system. People in small states support it because their electoral votes are a larger proportion of the Electoral College than their actual votes are a proportion of all votes.

On the other hand, many political and legal experts believe the Electoral College system gives greater weight to a vote cast in a large state; a one-vote margin in Pennsylvania, for example, yields twenty-one votes for the winning candidate compared to only three votes in North Dakota. Thus it is more important to get that extra vote in Pennsylvania. Therefore, candidates focus their campaigns in, and appeals to, the large states with tight races.

In 2007, California Republicans introduced an item for public referendum that would divide California's electoral vote by winners of the most popular votes in each congressional district. This would immediately give Republicans about twenty additional electoral votes, changing the national electoral equilibrium, though it would reduce California's overall clout in the election. Such a change would presumably drive Democrats in minority Democratic states to propose the same thing, though it is hard for the minority party in a state to drive such a change in the absence of provisions for a referendum (a direct popular vote on legislation).

An even more undemocratic feature of the Electoral College is that not all states require their electors to cast their votes for the candidates who won the state vote. The **faithless elector** is one who casts his or her vote for a personal choice, even someone who was not on the ballot. Even though the intent of the Founders was to allow electors to cast their votes any way they desired, modern reformers have proposed that, in our more democratic era, electors should be bound by the wishes of the voters in their states. It is true that no faithless elector has ever made a difference in the outcome of an election, but in the 2000 election, as few as three faithless electors could have made a difference.

Another target of reform is the requirement that if the electoral vote is tied, the presidential choice is to be thrown to the House of Representatives. There is no expectation that each state's House delegation would vote for the presidential candidate that its state's voters chose; rather, states would reflect the majority party in their House delegation. Moreover, each state would have an equal vote. Alaska would carry the same clout as California. This is a very undemocratic feature of the process, and would probably cause a crisis if actually used to elect a candidate with a minority of the popular vote.

Voting Behavior

Voting behavior is shaped by party identification, candidate evaluations, and positions on the issues. We have discussed party identification in Chaper 5. Here we will examine candidate evaluations and issue positions and how the three factors work together.

Candidate Evaluations

Candidates' personalities and styles have had more impact since television has become voters' major source of information about elections. Reagan's popularity in 1984 is an example of the influence of a candidate and his personality. The perceived competence and integrity of candidates are other facets of candidate evaluation. Voters are less likely to support candidates who do not seem capable of handling the job, regardless of their issue positions. Jimmy Carter suffered in 1980 because of negative evaluations of his competence and leadership among voters.

Clinton's popularity puzzled some observers. Many voters did not like his evasions and his adulterous behavior, but they voted for him anyway. During the impeachment debates, many journalists expressed amazement that Clinton's popularity remained high. The public, more than journalists, seemed to be able to

"This year I'm not getting involved in any complicated issues. I'm just voting my straight ethnic prejudices."

separate his public and private roles. The public continued to support him because they felt he was doing a good job as president, not because they admired him personally.

Personality was important in the 2004 campaign. John Kerry seemed unable to connect with people and uncomfortable on the campaign trail. At times, he appeared to be going through the motions, playing a role. In answering questions, he often provided lengthy and detailed responses. George Bush, on the other hand, seemed more at ease, comfortable working the crowd. His responses were often truncated and general. However, both candidates' performances in the first debate belied these characterizations. Kerry appeared calm and at ease, his answers crisp and concise. Bush seemed impatient and snarly. Regardless, the image of Kerry as an effete, somewhat snobbish, Boston patrician who was out of touch with average Americans dogged him throughout the campaign.

Issues

Issues are a third factor influencing the vote. Although Americans are probably more likely to vote on issues now than they were in the 1950s, issues influence only some of the voters some of the time. In 2000 and 2004, voters saw themselves as much closer to the Democratic candidates than to Bush.[136]

To cast an **issue vote,** voters quite obviously must have a position on an issue. In recent elections, more than 80 percent of the public had a position on issues such as government spending, military spending, and women's rights.[137] An issue vote also requires the candidates to differ with respect to their issue positions and for the voters to recognize this difference. A substantial minority of voters are able to detect some differences among the issue positions of presidential candidates.[138] Lastly, voters must cast their vote for the candidate that reflects their position on the issue or at least the candidate that is closest to their issue position.

In every election since 1972, more than 70 percent of those who met these conditions cast issue votes.[139] Issues with the highest proportion of issue voting were those that typically divided Republicans and Democrats, such as government spending, military spending, and government aid to the unemployed and minorities. However, because many in the electorate were unable to define both their own and the candidates' positions on each issue, the proportion of the total electorate that can be said to cast an "issue vote" is usually less than 40 percent, and for some issues it is much less.[140] Abortion is another issue on which voters cast issue-related votes. In 1996, for example, about 60 percent of the voters cast issue-related votes on abortion. Of those voters (who had a position and also knew the candidates' position), 15 percent of those who opposed abortion under any conditions voted for Clinton, a supporter of abortion rights, compared with 81 percent of those who believed that abortion should be a matter of personal choice.[141]

Issue voting may be mostly an evaluation of the current incumbents. If voters like the way incumbents, or the incumbent's party, have handled the job in general or in certain areas—the economy or foreign policy, for example—they will vote accordingly, even without much knowledge about the specifics of the issues.

Voting on the basis of past performance is called **retrospective voting.** There is good evidence that many people do this, especially according to economic conditions.[142] Voters support incumbents if national income is growing in the months preceding the election. Since World War II, the incumbent party has won a presidential election only once when the growth rate was less than 3 percent (Eisenhower in 1956) and lost only twice when it was more than 3 percent (Ford in

1976 and Gore in 2000).[143] For example, in 2004, ninety-six percent of voters who strongly approved of Bush's handling of the economy voted for him; only 3 percent voted for John Kerry. Only 13 percent of those who strongly disapproved his handling voted for him, while 84 percent voted for Kerry.

Parties, Candidates, and Issues

All three factors—parties, candidates, and issues—clearly matter. Party loyalties are especially important because they help shape our views about issues and candidates. However, if issues and candidates did not matter, the Democrats would have won every presidential election between 1932 and 2000. Republican victories suggest that they often have had more attractive candidates (as in 1952, 1956, 1980, and 1984) or issue positions (in 1972 and in some respects in 1980). However, the Democrats' partisan advantage shrank throughout the 1980s. Although there are still more registered Democrats than Republicans in the United States, the margin is slight, and the number of independents is large enough to tilt the outcome.

Party loyalty, candidate evaluations, and issues are important factors in congressional elections just as in presidential ones. Voting in congressional elections is discussed in Chapter 7.

The 2000 Election:
A Perfect Storm

The election of 2000 demonstrates the antidemocratic nature of the Electoral College. It was won by George W. Bush, who got fewer votes than his rival, Al Gore. In another antidemocratic twist, the election was decided by the United States Supreme Court, when, by a 5–4 vote, it stopped the recount of votes going on at the order of the Florida Supreme Court. The division in the Electoral College was very close, and the decision rested on the outcome in Florida, where election mismanagement, partisan politics, and unavoidable human error came together to create chaos in a closely divided race.

Election Day exit polls of Florida voters showed Gore winning by a small margin. But after first declaring Gore the winner, the television networks declared Bush the winner, and then in the early morning hours decided it was too close to call. The election hung in the balance. Bush had a tiny lead of several hundred ballots.

Confusion reigned in the days afterward. The press and election observers reported several problems, some of them serious. Thousands of Gore votes were lost because of the strange "butterfly" ballot configuration in Palm Beach County, a heavily Democratic liberal county. The odd format, designed by the supervisor of elections in the county, made it difficult for some voters to determine which punch hole corresponded to which presidential candidate. (It was labeled the "butterfly ballot" because candidate names appeared on both sides of a row of vertical punch holes rather than only on one side, which is the standard, less-confusing format.) Even though the problem was recognized early on Election Day by some distraught voters leaving the polling places, there was no way that local election officials felt they could fix the problem then.

More than three thousand voters punched the hole registering a vote for Patrick Buchanan, listed to the right of Gore's name on the ballot. This is particularly ironic because the areas of Palm Beach County casting the most votes for Buchanan were those inhabited by mostly elderly Jewish voters, the least likely group to support Buchanan, who is thought to be anti-Semitic. As one elderly Jewish woman exclaimed after mistakenly voting for Buchanan, "I would rather have had a colonoscopy than vote for that son-of-a-bitch Buchanan."[144]

Nearly three thousand voted for Gore and the socialist candidate whose punch hole was underneath Gore, apparently thinking they voted for Joseph Lieberman, Gore's vice presidential running mate, whose name was under Gore's. (Bush lost about 1600 votes from those who voted for him and Buchanan.) While some spoiled ballots are normal in every election, this erratic pattern in one county was a result of the badly designed ballot. But there was nothing the Gore campaign could do. The ballot was designed by a Democratic supervisor of elections who made the candidates' names larger so elderly voters could read them easier. But the larger typeface actually made the format harder to understand. Nevertheless, a sample ballot had been printed in the local newspapers before the election, as is required in many states. Clearly there was no intention to deceive any voters.

There was also a problem with overseas ballots. Americans overseas have the right to vote. They must ask for a ballot before the election and mail it by the day of the election, but the ballot need not be received by local officials until ten days after the election. (This time allows for mail delays.) There are strict rules about how these ballots are to be certified to avoid vote fraud: for example, the ballots have to have legible overseas postmarks showing the ballot was cast on or before Election Day, a witness was present (a Florida requirement), and the voters had to have registered in advance. But hundreds of these ballots came in lacking postmarks (or having U.S. postmarks) or lacking a witness and from voters who were not registered. Many military personnel whose home state was Florida must have decided to vote after the election when the outcome appeared uncertain, and some may have been persuaded to do so by partisan groups. Under law, these ballots shouldn't have been counted, but the Bush campaign, assuming the ballots were mostly Republican, claimed that it would be unpatriotic not to count them. The Gore campaign was put in the untenable position of choosing either to accept the illegal Republican ballots or to appear to deny our overseas military personnel their right to vote.

After the election, Gore pursued a conservative strategy to deal with these problems that likely cost him the election. Nothing could be done about the butterfly ballot problem save a re-vote, and nothing in Florida law allowed that. To deal with tens of thousands of incompletely punched cards throughout the state, Gore asked for a recount in only four strongly Democratic counties. (Later, after the Bush campaign sued to stop the recount, Gore did challenge Bush to have a recount in every county, but he did not file suit to accomplish it.[145]) Finally, when the Florida Supreme Court mandated a recount in every county, so much time had elapsed that the U.S. Supreme Court threw up its hands and gave the election to Bush.

Gore's biggest mistake was to refrain from challenging the overseas votes, even the hundreds that were patently illegal under Florida laws. Indeed, 680 were flawed, including nearly 200 with U.S. postmarks, indicating that they had been mailed from within the country rather than from overseas; 344 were late, illegible, or missing postmarks; and even 38 reflected double voting by 19 voters.[146] Clearly the local election judges would have thrown these out had Democratic Party representatives challenged them. But they did not out of a timid concern about not wanting to appear against voting rights of overseas armed forces personnel, even fraudulent ones. As a consequence of the illegal military ballots alone, Gore lost Florida by 537 votes when his Election Day margin, that is, the margin given him by people who voted on Election Day rather than by mail ballot, was a 202-vote victory.[147]

The Bush postelection campaign was more skillful and more aggressive. Republican representatives urged election officials in Democratic-majority counties to follow the law in handling overseas ballots, so illegal ballots would not be counted; in Republican counties, they urged election officials to disregard the law, so illegal ballots would be counted.[148] (There is nothing illegal or even immoral about Republican supporters doing this, but the election officials should not have caved, and the Democratic representatives should have argued that the laws be followed.) At one point the Bush campaign even organized a demonstration to intimidate election officials in Miami-Dade County to stop conducting the recount they were in the middle of. Demonstrators barged into the building, yelling and pounding on doors. Photos from that event showed that many of the "demonstrators" were staffers in conservative congressional Republican offices who had been sent to Florida to do this, though at the time the election officials recounting the ballot did not know that. The demonstration succeeded in getting the officials to halt the recount.

In addition, the Bush campaign had strong political allies in Florida. Not only was Bush's brother the governor, but the secretary of state, who oversees the election system, was cochair of Bush's Florida campaign. Making little effort to appear nonpartisan, at every opportunity she ruled in favor of the Bush campaign and forced the Gore campaign to go to court to obtain recounts and redress. Time also worked in favor of the Bush campaign, because it held a narrow lead throughout the post-Election Day period and because it knew that the deadline for certifying Florida's electors would put pressure on the courts to stop the recount. Thus the Bush campaign used delaying tactics to slow and stop the recounts.

The outcome of this election will long be argued. It is likely that a bare majority of Florida voters, in fact, favored Gore.[149] Systematic analyses have proven that the Buchanan vote was inflated by at least 2500 votes intended for Gore in Palm Beach County.[150] As one commentator noted, "No election analyst will say with a straight face that the butterfly design didn't cost Al Gore the presidency."[151]

Of course, the overseas ballots contributed, too, by an unknown amount. That is, we know how many ballots were illegal, but we don't know for sure their distribution between Bush and Gore. Nearly two-thirds of the 2400 overseas ballots counted after November 7 were for Bush. Presumably the illegal overseas ballots also broke for Bush. Two independent scholars argue that the probability is about 99 percent that Gore would have won if the invalid overseas ballots were handled properly and a statewide recount was allowed under any reasonable standard for counting chads.[152]

The confusion surrounding the 2000 election outcome highlights an important aspect of our electoral process: state law and local policies determine the mechanics of presidential elections. The election brought into stark relief the problems that shoddy election procedures can create. Former president and Nobel Peace Prize winner Jimmy Carter, who, through his Carter Center, now works for peace and social justice around the world, is often invited to monitor elections in Asia and Africa and to attest to their fairness. He remarked, "I was really taken aback and embarrassed by what happened in Florida. If we were invited to go into a foreign country to monitor the election, and they had similar standards and procedures, we would refuse to participate at all."[153]

Voting Patterns in the 2004 Election

As we discussed in Chapter 4, popular parlance often refers to the solid Republican states as "red" states and the solid Democratic states as "blue" states because TV networks use red and blue to depict them on election night maps. Figure 4 (in Chapter 3; p. 66) illustrates the red states and blue states as well as the results of the 2004 election.

Although the press tends to discuss the red states and blue states as if they were fixed in concrete, of course they are not. There are a core of states that, in recent years, have voted solidly Republican and a core that have voted consistently Democratic, but many states change their majorities from one election to another. However, only one state (New Hampshire) voted Republican in 2000 but Democratic in 2004, and two states (New Mexico and Iowa) voted Democratic in 2000 but Republican in 2004.

Analysts of voting in the 2004 election discovered that the crude distinction between red and blue states disguises more telling voting patterns. Most red states are in the poorer half of the states as measured by per capita income. For example, twenty-six of the twenty-eight states with the lowest per capita income voted for Bush. Given that overall the poorer you are the more likely you are to vote Democratic and given that Bush's economic policies have favored the wealthy over the poor, this seems like a paradox.

In fact, in the poorer states, such as Oklahoma and Mississippi, the wealthy are very heavily Republican, voting Republican 80 percent of the time. In these red states, there is significant class voting. In the blue states, such as Maryland, New York, Connecticut, and California, the rich and the poor, on average, vote similarly. In blue states, rich people are only slightly more likely than poor people to be Republican. Rich people in the blue states are much more likely to be Democrats than they are in the poorer, red states.[154] "Class warfare," as evidenced through the ballot box, is much more prevalent in the red, Republican-voting states.

These patterns are new in American politics. But the 2004 election was also about continuity. Incumbent presidents usually win reelection; that happened fifteen out of the twenty times incumbents ran in the past century. Incumbents, such as Bush, whose party has just captured the White House almost always win; Jimmy Carter was the one exception. Although much was made in the media of Republican success due to "values issues" such as gay marriage, more systematic analyses suggest that these were not very important. Bush's margin compared to that in 2000 was slightly higher across the states, with the exception that in the states most directly affected by the World Trade Center attack (New York, New Jersey, and Connecticut) he gained more, nearly 6 percent.[155]

The Permanent Campaign

The **permanent campaign** is a term coined by political scientists to describe the current state of American electoral politics.[156] During each election cycle, the time between the completion of one election and the beginning of the next gets shorter and shorter. No longer does the election campaign start in the election year; now it is nearly a four-year process, as candidates hire consultants and fundraisers, assemble field operations, and commission polls.

Several factors are responsible for this change, some political and some technological. The political process has changed a great deal during the past twenty years. Primaries have become the chief means by which candidates get nominated, and parties have shrunk in importance in the nominating process. The necessity to win primaries in different regions of the nation means that potential candidates must start early to become known to key political figures, and ultimately to the voting public, in these states. In the "old days," candidates had to woo only party leaders, a process that, though not easy, was much less public and much less expensive than campaigning for primary victories.

Technology has also contributed to the permanent campaign. Certainly, in comparison to the turn of the twentieth century, transportation and communications technology have revolutionized campaigns. Then travel was by rail, ship, or horse, and candidates could not simply dart about the country spending the morning in New York City and the afternoon in Seattle. Telephone communication was primitive, and there were no radios or televisions. The idea of potential candidates spending four years publicly campaigning for office under these conditions would have been ludicrous.

But even in comparison with only thirty years ago, the media and information technology have revolutionized campaigning and thus have contributed to the permanent campaign. Modern computer and telephone technology enable the media and private organizations to take the pulse of the public through opinion polls almost continually. As polls have become more common, they have become a source of fascination to the media (and as pollsters have discovered that the media's appetite for polls is nearly insatiable, polls have proliferated). Whereas in the 1950s polls were rarely done and poll results were rarely discussed in media coverage of elections, by the 1980s hundreds of stories about each election campaign focused on poll results. Indeed, much of the media coverage of the campaign focuses on exactly that. In 2004, many news outlets carried daily polls during the last couple of months of the campaign. Thus candidates must pay attention to how well they do in the polls, which means they must begin campaigning early to earn name recognition from the public.

And, more generally, the fact that campaigns have become media events means that candidates must begin early to establish themselves as worthy of media attention. Until candidates have organizations, fundraisers, and pollsters, the media do not take them seriously. Nor would it be very rational to do otherwise, because a modern campaign cannot succeed without these things.

All of these factors—the decline of the party organizations and the increased importance of primaries, the growth of polling, and the overwhelming role the media now play in campaigns—have contributed to the perpetual motion that modern elections have become. These trends seem irreversible. Only the rolling back of the primary system would seem to make much difference, and that change is highly unlikely.

Conclusion: Do Elections Make Government Responsive?

Although election campaigns are far less successful in mobilizing voters and ensuring a high turnout today than they were a century ago, in a democracy we expect elections to allow us to control government. Through them we can "throw the rascals out" and bring in new faces with better ideas, or so we think. But other than to change the party that controls government, do elections make a difference?

In the popular press, we hear a lot about "mandates." A president with a **mandate** is one who is clearly directed by the voters to take some particular course of action—reduce taxes or begin arms control talks, for example. George W. Bush won a majority in 2004. Did he have a mandate? If so, what for? The largest proportion of the public, 41 percent, was concerned about national security issues, mainly the war in Iraq and terrorism.[157] Most of those people voted for Bush, but about one-third of Kerry voters thought this was the most important issue, too. So does that mean the president has a mandate to stay in Iraq until we "win," however we define a win, or is there a mandate to withdraw once elections are held? Or just to do what he thinks best?

And how about on domestic issues? More than 25 percent of voters reported that economic issues were the most important to them, and another 11 percent said domestic issues, such as health care and Social Security, were. Most voters concerned about domestic and economic issues favored Kerry, though some of Bush's supporters also thought this was most important. So Bush did not have a mandate on these issues, but as president would, of course, have to deal with them. Only about 10 percent said "cultural" issues were most important to them, and two-thirds of those voted for Bush.[158]

Did Bush have a mandate? Like most things in politics, the answer is not simple. Sometimes elections have an effect on policy, but often their effects are not clear-cut. In close elections, few would argue that there is a mandate. In 2000, voters favored the Democratic policy positions and did so in a time of peace and prosperity. A plurality gave their votes to Gore. Yet Bush became president and acted as though his narrow Electoral College victory was a mandate in support of his foreign policies and conservative domestic policies.

It is primarily political parties that translate the mix of various issues into government action because voters' issue positions influence their party loyalties and their candidate evaluations. Over time, a rough agreement usually develops between public attitudes and policies.[159] A vote for the candidate of one's own party is usually a reflection of agreement on at least some important issues. Once in office, the party in government helps sort out the issues for which there is a broad public mandate from those for which there is not.

Elections that appear to be mandates can become "mandates for disaster." More than one observer has pointed out that every twentieth-century president who won the election by 60 percent or more of the popular vote soon encountered serious political trouble. After his landslide in 1920, Warren Harding had his Teapot Dome scandal involving government corruption. Emboldened by his 1936 triumph, Franklin D. Roosevelt tried to pack the Supreme Court and was rebuffed on that issue. Lyndon Johnson won by a landslide in 1964 and was soon mired in Vietnam. Richard Nixon smashed George McGovern in 1972 but then had to resign because of Watergate. Ronald Reagan's resounding victory in 1984 (a shade less than 60 percent) was followed by the blunders of the Iran-Contra affair. Of these presidents, only Roosevelt was able to recover fully from his political misfortune. Reagan regained his personal popularity but seemed to have little influence on policy after Iran-Contra. One recent observer has argued that these disasters come because "the euphoria induced by overwhelming support at the polls evidently loosens the president's grip on reality."[160]

Elections can point out new directions for government and allow citizens to make it responsive to their needs, but the fact that many individuals do not vote means that the new directions may not reflect either the needs or wishes of the public. If election turnout falls too far, the legitimacy of elections may be threatened. People may come to believe that election results do not reflect the wishes of the majority. For this reason, the increase in turnout in 2004 should hearten all of us. If elections promote government responsiveness to those who participate in them, higher turnouts help increase responsiveness.

On the other hand, if we believe in democracy, we should be concerned about the decline in competitiveness of congressional elections. Essentially, in most states, state legislative majorities have had the capacity to determine election outcomes, including their own seats, for a decade. While the power to redistrict has always been in state legislative hands, the power and precision of new technology makes this power even greater. This is a significant challenge to responsiveness.

Key Terms

Key Names

TEST YOURSELF

1. Which is true of suffrage in 1789 when the Constitution was implemented?
   a. Almost all Americans could vote.
   b. Only a minority of Americans could vote.
   c. Almost all white people could vote.
   d. A majority of whites but only a minority of blacks could vote.
   e. Strict federal rules regulated voting rights.

2. The vignette concerning the relationship between driving and partisanship suggests
   a. partisanship is related to a variety of social and economic factors.
   b. partisanship is probably largely genetic.
   c. partisanship is probably unchangeable.
   d. partisanship has developed only with the development of the automobile.
   e. views on the environment are the most important factor shaping partisanship.

3. Religious tests for voting
   a. were never a part of American history.
   b. until 1925 barred Jews and Muslims from voting.
   c. were applied in all states in the late eighteenth century.
   d. persisted in some states until the middle of the twentieth century.
   e. largely died out by the 1820s.

4. The voting rights of black Americans
   a. were extended to all males beginning in the 1840s.
   b. were extended to all black people after the Civil War.
   c. were largely extinguished in the South during Reconstruction.
   d. were undermined by literacy tests and the grandfather clause.
   e. were promoted by literacy tests and the grandfather clause.

5. The Voting Rights Act
   a. was implemented during the Reconstruction period.
   b. targeted states with high black voting rates.
   c. did not apply to Northern states.
   d. had little impact on voting or registration.
   e. targeted areas with small black voter registration.

6. "Cracking, stacking, and packing" refers to
   a. ways of keeping partisan opponents from voting.
   b. ways to divide districts to minimize black electoral clout.
   c. ways to disenfranchise convicted felons.
   d. names for majority-minority congressional districts.
   e. the means that Democrats used to gain congressional seats in the South in the 1990s.

7. Which is *not* true about women's suffrage?
   a. Women voted in some states in the Revolutionary era.
   b. Reconstruction-era amendments to the Constitution gave women the right to vote.
   c. Women suffrage supporters were sometimes beaten and tortured.
   d. In the nineteenth century, women's suffrage was opposed by powerful religious interests.
   e. In the nineteenth century, women's suffrage was opposed by Southern whites.

8. Which is *not* true about women officeholders?
   a. The first woman was elected to Congress in 1916.
   b. A woman was not chosen to be Speaker of the House of Representatives until 2007.
   c. Congress has a larger proportion of women members than do state legislatures.
   d. Women still hold less than 20 percent of seats in Congress.
   e. A large proportion of women members of Congress are Democrats.

9. Which is true about the voting patterns of young people?
    a. They vote at about the same rate as older people.
    b. They vote at higher rates than older people.
    c. They are less likely to vote than older people.
    d. Their rates of voting declined in 2004 despite many attempts on college campuses to get them to turn out.
    e. They are much more Republican than older people.

10. Which is *not* a reason that explains failure of registered voters to vote?
    a. Nonvoters are more satisfied with the way things are going than voters.
    b. Potential voters may be turned off by the length and nature of political campaigns.
    c. Some states make it difficult for voters to vote.
    d. Parties no longer do a very good job of mobilizing voters.
    e. Labor unions are weaker than in decades past.

11. Which is true of presidential primaries?
    a. They have always been the chief mode of nominating presidential candidates.
    b. Turnout is typically about as high as in general elections.
    c. Candidates work to raise media expectations about their successes.
    d. Early primaries have had the least impact on the nomination process.
    e. Many large states have moved their primaries to earlier in the primary season.

12. Which is true of presidential nominating conventions?
    a. In recent years, it has taken several ballots to choose a presidential nominee in the Democratic convention.
    b. In recent years, it has taken several ballots to choose a presidential nominee in the Republican convention.
    c. Most television stations televise the conventions "gavel to gavel."
    d. The convention generally holds an open election for the vice presidential nominee.
    e. Conventions are important political rituals in modern society.

13. Which is true of campaign ads?
    a. Candidates place most ads in television shows that appeal to their potential supporters.
    b. Candidates place most ads on television shows that appeal to opposition voters.
    c. Negative ads were less widely used in 2004 than in the prior two elections.
    d. Negative ads have very little substantive content.
    e. Campaign ads must be truthful.

14. Televised presidential debates
    a. started when Jimmy Carter ran against Ronald Reagan.
    b. sway large proportions of voters.
    c. helped John Kennedy in his race with Richard Nixon.
    d. generally determine the outcome of an election.
    e. have occurred in every election since the Kennedy-Nixon race.

15. Which is true about campaign finance regulation?
    a. Public funding of presidential campaigns has eliminated most fundraising for presidential candidates.
    b. Disclosure provisions of the law have been largely successful in achieving the goals of allowing the public to know who is providing money to candidates.
    c. The Courts, holding that First Amendment rights do not apply to campaign advertising, have upheld most restrictions on campaign advertising.
    d. The McCain-Feingold law has closed most loopholes in campaign finance regulation.
    e. Individuals may give as much as they want to individual candidates, as long as they disclose their gifts.

16. Which is *not true* of the Electoral College system?
    a. It was originally an attempt to take the choice of the president out of the hands of popular majorities.
    b. It can lead to a candidate being elected who receives fewer popular votes than the opponent.
    c. It always reflects the majority will.
    d. It is an undemocratic part of our Constitution.
    e. It reinforces the federal system in certain ways.

17. Which is true of the 2000 election?
    a. George W. Bush received fewer votes than Al Gore.
    b. George W. Bush won in a landslide election.
    c. The butterfly ballot cost Al Gore thousands of votes in Pennsylvania.
    d. The Democrats challenged most overseas military ballots in Florida.
    e. The Supreme Court upheld most of Gore's challenges to Florida's actions.

18. Voters in red states
    a. are more likely to vote Democratic.
    b. are more likely to be liberal.
    c. are more likely to be poor.
    d. have few partisan differences between the rich and poor voters.
    e. changed their voting patterns between 2000 and 2004.

19. The permanent campaign reflects
    a. the advent of the primary system.
    b. technological changes.
    c. the rise of polling.
    d. none of the above.
    e. all of the above.

20. Which is necessary for issue voting to occur?
    a. Voters must have issue preferences.
    b. Candidates must have issue preferences.
    c. Voters must be able to tell the difference between issue positions of the candidates.
    d. Voters must vote on their issue preferences.
    e. All of the above.

21. Evaluations of political candidates
    a. are the most important factor predicting presidential votes.
    b. are unimportant in predicting presidential votes.
    c. are one of three key factors in predicting presidential votes.
    d. were not important in the Reagan elections.
    e. were not important in the election of 2004.

22. Which is true of election mandates?
    a. Winners of presidential elections generally have clear mandates on foreign policy.
    b. Winners of presidential elections generally have clear mandates on domestic policy.
    c. Recent presidents with strong mandates have often overreached and encountered political problems.
    d. The results of the 2004 election clearly indicated a mandate for President Bush to stay in Iraq until we won.
    e. The results of the 2000 election clearly provided a mandate for President Bush's conservative domestic policies.

23. Young people
    a. vote at higher rates than older people.
    b. sometimes believe that politics is for older people.
    c. are sometimes ignored by candidates.
    d. increased their 2004 turnout more than other groups.
    e. are not able to be mobilized by traditional grassroots efforts.

24. Which is true of public opinion toward potential presidential candidates?
    a. The public has become more supportive of non-white male candidates.
    b. More than half of the public would not support an African American for president.
    c. About a quarter of the public say they would not vote for a women for president.
    d. When John F. Kennedy was elected, nearly one-half of the public said they wouldn't vote for a Catholic.
    e. All are true.

25. It is likely true that Hillary Clinton's YouTube announcements discussed in text were
    a. designed to show that she is tough on crime.
    b. designed to appeal to the baby boomer generation.
    c. designed to show a sense of humor.
    d. designed to confront her major challengers on key issues of the campaign.
    e. designed to improve music education in America.

Key: 1-b; 2-a; 3-e; 4-d; 5-e; 6-b; 7-b; 8-c; 9-c; 10-a; 11-e; 12-c; 13-a; 14-c; 15-b; 16-c; 17-a; 18-c; 19-e; 20-e; 21-c; 22-c; 23-d; 24-a; 25-c

After the Democrats won a majority of seats in Congress in 2006, Representative Nancy Pelosi (D-Calif.) became the first woman ever elected Speaker of the House.

ouse members Emanuel Cleaver (D-Mo.) and Shelly Moore Capito (R-W.Va.) are trying to lead a crusade to bring more civility to the House of Representatives. Tired of highly partisan rhetoric, vitriolic exchanges, and personal insults, they decided to launch their movement with a "Civility Hour" on the floor of the House, where taxation policy could be discussed in a civil manner.[1] In the past years, representatives have been increasingly showing their contempt for fellow members. Rep. Marion Berry (D-Ark.) once dubbed another member a "Howdy Doody-looking nimrod" on the House floor,[2] while Jean Schmidt (R-Ohio) taunted John Murtha (D-Pa.) that "only cowards cut and run, marines never do." Murtha, who, as a World War II and Korean Marine veteran won a Bronze Star and two Purple Hearts, had called for a withdrawal from Iraq. This taunt led Martin Meehan (D-Mass.) to yell "you guys are pathetic!"[3] Vice President Dick Cheney and John McCain (R-Ariz.) both yelled, on other recent occa-

sions on the Senate floor, "F---you!"—Cheney to Patrick Leahy (D-Vt.) and McCain to fellow Republican John Cornyn (Tex.).

Though the civility hour sounded like a modest start to decreasing such toxicity, in the end the hour was cancelled when a debate on tort reform turned into a very uncivil discussion, with the Republicans charging the Democrats with not caring about national security and the Democrats returning the disparaging remarks.

But Cleaver and Capito are not deterred, deciding to form a Civility Task Force. Even those efforts have not gone far; the membership remains at two. As Cleaver lamented, "We haven't had to hire any new receptionists to handle all the phone calls and applications to join. But I'm confident that people will see the merit in this."[4]

Perhaps Cleaver and Capito's efforts will pick up steam. But if not, remarked Alcee Hastings (D-Fl.), "There's a rankle and a divisiveness here, and it's called democracy."[5]

Most Americans think the person who represents them in Congress does a very good job. They return them to office at impressively high rates. But most Americans do not think Congress as a whole does a very good job. Its approval ratings are often well below 50 percent; in mid-2007, they were hovering around 25 percent. How do we explain this contradiction?

In this chapter, we look at the current composition of Congress and ask how representative a body it is. We describe how Congress is organized and how it carries out its constitutional responsibilities, then look at how individual members carry out their duties in Washington and their districts and what makes them so popular back home that they usually get reelected. We look at the process by which members are elected. Finally, we look at Congress's relationship to the other branches of government and to the public.

Members and Constituencies

Members

The Founders clearly intended Congress to be the dominant branch of government. They laid out its role and powers in Article I, and their discussion takes up almost half the document. Despite its impressive formal powers, observers have always been skeptical of it.

Alexis de Tocqueville, for example, was not impressed with the status of members of Congress, noting that they were "almost all obscure individuals, village lawyers, men in trades, or even persons belonging to the lower class." His view was shared by another European visitor, Charles Dickens, who was shocked in 1842 to find Congress full of tobacco spitters who committed "cowardly attacks upon opponents" and seemed to be guilty of "aiding and abetting every bad inclination in the popular mind."[6] However one views their behavior, members of Congress were not then, and are not now, a cross section of the American public. But they are a more diverse group than the membership of Congresses of the eighteenth and nineteenth centuries ever were or thought they should be.

Who Can Serve?

The Constitution places few formal restrictions on membership in Congress. One must be twenty-five-years old to serve in the House and thirty in the Senate.

One must have been a citizen for at least seven years to be elected to the House and nine years to be elected to the Senate. Members must reside in the states from which they were elected, but House members need not reside in their own districts. As a practical matter, however, it is highly unlikely that voters will elect a person to represent their district who is not from the district or who does not maintain a residence there. Local identity is not as significant a factor in Senate races; national figures such as Robert Kennedy and Hillary Rodham Clinton, who established in-state residency within weeks or months of the election, both ran successful campaigns in New York.

Length of Service

Every member of the House stands for election every two years, and senators serve six-year terms, with one-third of the membership standing for election every two years. The Constitution placed no cap on how many times an individual can be elected to the House or Senate. In the early years, leaving one's home to serve in Congress was considered a great sacrifice. Washington was a muddy swamp, with debris-filled streets, farm animals running loose, and hot and humid weather with no relief in the pre-air-conditioning days. National transportation was so poor almost no one got home during a session. As late as the early 1900s, the median length of service for a representative was only five years.[7]

But as Washington became a power center and a much more livable and accessible city, members served longer. And as seats went uncontested in the one-party South, more legislators became career politicians, spending thirty and even forty years in Congress. These long-serving members began to dominate committee work and to control the legislative agenda.

Term Limits

During the height of public anger with government in the 1990s, there was a nationwide move to limit the number of terms that state and national legislators could serve. Although Congress narrowly defeated term-limit legislation, in twenty-three of twenty-four states that allow ballot initiatives, voters adopted term limits for their members of Congress and state legislators.

However, in 1995, in a 5–4 vote, the Supreme Court held term limits for members of Congress unconstitutional. By adding to the qualifications spelled out in the Constitution (age and citizenship), the Court ruled that states were in effect "amending" the Constitution.[8] By definition, then, such laws would be unconstitutional because the Constitution can be amended only through the processes of adoption and ratification it specifies, not by state or congressional laws.[9]

Constituencies

The district a member of Congress represents is called a **constituency.** The term is used to refer to both the area within the electoral boundaries and its residents. There are two senators from each state, so each senator's constituency is the entire state and all its residents. Most states have multiple House districts, though seven states (Alaska, Delaware, Montana, North Dakota, South Dakota, Vermont, and Wyoming) have populations so small that they are allotted only a single seat in the House of Representatives, so the entire state is the district. Except for those seven states, every House district must have (in accordance with the one-person, one-vote rule) roughly the same number of residents, so the number of districts in each state depends on its total population.

In states with large urban populations, several districts may exist within a single city. The logistics of campaigning are thus very different for a representative from New York City, whose district may be as small as 12 square miles, and one from Montana, who must cover the entire state (147,042 square miles).

Reapportionment

Initially, the House of Representatives had fifty-nine members, but as the nation grew and more states joined the Union, the size of the House increased too. Since 1910, it has had 435 members, except in the 1950s, when seats were temporarily added for Alaska and Hawaii. Every ten years, in a process called **reapportionment,** the 435 seats are allocated among the states based on the latest census. Since the first Congress, the number of constituents each House member represents has grown from 30,000 to roughly 700,000 currently.

Within a constant 435-seat House, states with fast-growing populations gain seats, whereas those with slow-growing or declining populations lose seats. Since World War II, population movement in the United States has been toward the South, West, and Southwest and away from the Midwest and Northeast. This has been reflected in the allocation of House seats. For example, from 1950 through 2000, California gained twenty-three seats and New York lost fourteen. In recent years, states such as Illinois, Wisconsin, Pennsylvania, and Ohio have lost House seats to states in the

In its early years, Washington, D.C., was described as "a miserable little swamp." When this photo was taken in 1882, it still retained the look and feel of a small town.

National Archives. Reprinted with permission.

South and West such as Arizona, California, Colorado, Florida, Georgia, Nevada, and Texas as well as California. The census counts all residents, irrespective of legal residency or citizenship, and several of the seat-gaining states are home to millions of undocumented residents. California, for example, the state with more illegal immigrants than any other, would have shown population loss since the last census if not for immigration.

Redistricting

States that gain or lose seats and states whose population shifts within the state (rural to urban or urban to suburban, for example) must redraw their district boundaries, a process called **redistricting.** This is always a hot political issue because the precise boundaries of a district determine the election prospects of candidates and parties. In fact, because in most states the state legislature controls the redistricting process, districts are normally drawn to benefit the party in control of the state legislature. A district whose boundaries are devised to maximize the political advantage of a party or a racial group is known as a **gerrymander** (see also Chapter 7). Majority parties in state legislatures persist in securing political advantage by drawing bizarrely shaped districts but still complying with the Supreme Court ruling that all congressional districts be approximately equal in population.

Before 1960, states often did not redistrict their state legislative and congressional boundaries to reflect population changes among the districts for fear that doing so would endanger incumbents and threaten rural areas whose populations were declining. Some legislative districts in urban areas had nineteen times as many residents as rural districts. When some state legislatures refused to reapportion themselves, the Supreme Court, in *Baker* v. *Carr* (1962), issued the first in a series of rulings forcing states to reapportion their legislative districts.[10] Two years later, the Court required congressional districts to be approximately equal in population, thus mandating the principle of "one person, one vote."[11] Although the decisions provoked strong opposition and a constitutional amendment was proposed to overturn them, over time the principle of one person, one vote has come to be widely accepted.

The redistricting process has been very important to underrepresented minorities, as we saw in Chapter 7).[12] However, redistricting has led to less representation in other ways. Software now available can measure voting patterns down to the block level. This allows legislators, using voter registration records that record party preferences, to draw district lines to create "safe" (noncompetitive) legislative districts for either the Republican or Democratic candidate. This is a serious problem for democratic accountability. Fair and competitive elections are the primary way the public exercises authority over government. In the run-up to the 2006 election, for example, some estimates were that only thirty congressional districts were truly competitive.

Tenure

Given that congressional seats have become ever more safe, congressional tenures have become ever longer.[13] In noncompetitive districts, members are almost certain to be reelected. Even after the 2006 election with many incumbents defeated, there were only 60 new members in the 110th Congress (2007–2009), compared to more than 100 a decade earlier.[14].

Congress as a Representative Body

What Does *Representative* Mean?

To take the measure of how representative Congress is, we first have to establish what *representation* means. During the Revolutionary War, John Adams said that the legislature to be created under the new government "should be an exact portrait, in miniature, of the people at large, as it should think, feel, reason, and act like them."[15] Benjamin Franklin said simply that Congress should be a mirror of the people. But should Congress look like a demographic cross section of the public or should its decisions reflect constituent issue positions? Or both? And should elected representatives use their delegated authority to act as their conscience dictated even when their action is not supported by a majority of their constituents?

A Congress that reflects the demographic mix of the country is one where descriptive representation is high. This kind of representation is not rooted in what legislators *do* but rather on their personal characteristics—what they *are,* or *are like.*[16] The rise of identity politics has increased demands for a Congress that better reflects the country's demographic profile, and so today it is more likely than ever that a predominantly Hispanic, white, or African American congressional district will be represented by a member of the corresponding ethnicity or race. But Congress is still far from representative in this sense (see the box "Congress Is Not a Cross Section of America").

For the first century of the Republic, the possibility of having citizen-legislators who were a cross section of the general public was just a

WHY ARE MY CONSTITUENTS SO ANGRY WITH ME?

HOW CAN THEY SAY I DON'T REPRESENT THEM?

I CAN BE SELFISH AND LAZY...

I LOOK OUT FOR MY OWN BEST INTEREST!

I'M SOMETIMES PREJUDICED AND SWEAR A LITTLE...

I NEVER HAVE ENOUGH MONEY... I EVEN BOUNCE A FEW CHECKS!

I HATE MAKING TOUGH DECISIONS

LOVE BEING THE CENTER OF ATTRACTION

I'VE BEEN KNOWN TO LIE CHEAT AND DRINK TOO MUCH!

HOW CAN THEY BE ANGRY?

HOW CAN THEY SAY I DON'T REPRESENT THEM??

I THINK I REPRESENT MOST OF THEM VERY WELL!!

Reprinted with permission

romantic notion. Only certain landed, business, or professional white men could even think about running for Congress. The first black men were not elected until the Reconstruction period after the Civil War, and the first woman was not elected until 1916. Today, although adults in all economic categories can meet the minimum requirements needed to stand for office, the demands of the nomination and selection process, especially campaign costs, limit the number of people who are able to run.

"Acting for" Representation

If Congress still has a way to go to *look* like the American public, does it act like them? Part of why we want Congress to look like America is that there is a relationship between a person's sex, race, ethnicity, income, and religious views and that person's position on issues.

But is there such a relationship? Do women, for example, really represent their constituents differently from their male colleagues? There is no guarantee that any one woman (or African American or Mexican American) will represent women (or blacks or Hispanics) collectively better than, say, a white man, or that a millionaire will not look out for the interests of blue-collar workers. And there is evidence that our overly broad categories do not capture similarities of interests. For example, first- and second-generation immigrants are not especially supportive of those recently arrived or of illegal immigrants, nor do Japanese American, Christian senators from Hawaii necessarily have the same perspective on the world as newly arrived immigrants from China and India or as Muslim Indonesians or

Pakistanis. Does Sen. Ken Salazar (D-Col.), a man whose family emigrated from Spain and helped found Santa Fe in the 1500s (before the *Mayflower* arrived), really share the same experiences as those who organize as Hispanic Americans?

There is reason to believe, however, that as women, blacks, Hispanics, and Asians increase their presence in Congress, so will the likelihood that the issues of greatest concern to them will be heard. It is hard to imagine that a Congress made up of blue-collar females would pass the same legislation as one made up of wealthy males. We cannot test that speculation, but we know that as the proportion of women in Congress has risen, so have the number of bills of special importance to women.[17]

One simple measure of "acting for" representation is party identification. Although only 62 percent of the public identifies with the two major parties, Republicans and Democrats hold 99.7 percent of the seats. (See Figure 1.)

Another measure of "acting for" representation is a legislator's voting record. By casting hundreds of votes each year, members try to represent the interests of their constituencies, bring benefits to the district, and in the process win support for reelection. Members must consider what benefits their districts as a whole as well as the needs of subgroups within the district, such as party voters, socioeconomic groups, and personal supporters.[18] Overall, if districts are filled with farmers, the members must represent farmers, whether or not they know anything about farming. Representatives of dis-

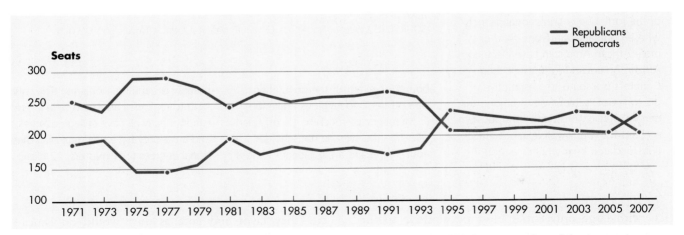

FIGURE 1 • **Makeup of the House of Representatives, by Party, 1971–2007** *Representation of the two major parties in the House has been much more equal since 1995 than in earlier decades, but other parties have been shut out.*
NOTE: Figures are for the first day of each Congress and do not include Independents or vacant seats.
SOURCE: *Congressional Quarterly Weekly Review, April 3, 2004, 790.*

CONGRESS IS NOT A CROSS SECTION OF AMERICA

Congress is not now, and never has been, a cross section of the American population (see Table). The citizens who serve in Congress are still disproportionately white and male: white non-Hispanic males, who make up about one-third of the total population, held about 70 percent of the seats in the House of Representatives and 81 percent of the seats in the Senate in 2006.

Women, who make up 51 percent of the nation's population, are the most underrepresented demographic group. They are just 17 percent of the House membership and 16 percent of the Senate's. Three states (Iowa, Delaware, and Vermont) have never elected a woman to Congress.[1] Most states do send at least one female representative, however, and California's delegation has twenty women, including both of its senators (California's representation accounts for almost one-quarter of all women in Congress).

Hispanic, Asian, and African Americans are below parity with their numbers in the population. But thirty-seven of the forty-one congressional districts whose populations are one-third or more African American have elected an African American to represent them.[2] Congress is also not representative of the range of religious views among the general public. Christianity and Judaism account for virtually all religious affiliations declared by members, although

	Table 1	Members of the 110th Congress: Not a Cross Section of the Public (2007–2009)*	
	Population (%)	House** (%)	Senate (%)
Women	51	17	16
African American	12.3	9.2	1
Hispanic	14	5.3	3
Asian Pacific	4	0.9	2
American Indian	0.7	0.2	0
Lawyer	0.3	37	57
Blue collar	25	2	3
Millionaires	0.7	27	40
Foreign born	13	2***	0***
Median age	35	56	60
Protestant	51†	56	56
Catholic	25†	29.6	24
Jewish	2.6†	6	13
Mormon	1.3†	2.5	5
Muslim	1–2†	0.2	0

*Does not include undecided House races as of November 15, 2006.

**Does not include nonvoting members from Puerto Rico, Guam, Samoa, the Virgin Islands, or the District of Columbia.

***Does not include those born abroad of American parents, such as John McCain.

†The U.S. Census does not collect data on religion so figures for the general population are estimates. Congressional affiliations are by self-declaration and will not add up to 100 percent because ten members specified other denominations and six gave no affiliation.

SOURCE: *CQ Weekly,* November 13, 2006; *National Journal,* November 10, 2006.

about 15 percent of the population claim other or no religious affiliation.

Members are much better off financially than the average householder: about 30 percent are millionaires and a number are multimillionaires.[3] They also tend to rank well above average in education; nearly all have college degrees, and a majority have graduate or professional degrees (141 masters, 224 law,

tricts with large universities must be sensitive to the reactions of students and professors even if they personally think academics have pointed heads.

For members to act as their constituents would if they were making policy themselves—to pursue policies they favor and vote as they would on issues—requires that members keep in close touch with the home district. And in fact most members do spend about half of each year in their districts. On the whole, the member's issue positions are usually not far from

20 in medicine, and 19 doctorates, including three political scientists). Although blue-collar workers constitute nearly one-quarter of the working population, only a dozen congressional members claim blue-collar backgrounds.[4]

The most common occupational background of congressional members has been the law. But this pattern is beginning to change as legislative careers have become more demanding. Today it is difficult for an attorney to maintain a law practice and also serve as a legislator. Ethics laws requiring financial disclosure and information about client relations have also discouraged practicing attorneys from running for congressional office. Although a majority of Senators were trained as lawyers, there are now more House members with backgrounds in business and public service than in the practice of law. But in this era of high technology, such fields as engineering and science still are barely represented in Congress. Increasingly, Congress is drawing its members from professional politicians; in 2006, 72 percent of House members and eighty-eight senators had held prior elective office. Fifty-two senators had served in the House before running for the Senate.[5]

Another dent in the citizen-legislator ideal has been the presence of "dynasty" families (the Adamses, Harrisons,

The Sanchez sisters—Loretta (left) and Linda—serve in the House of Representatives as Democrats representing two districts in Southern California.

Lodges, Kennedys, and Bushes). In the 108th, there were three pairs of siblings and twenty-six members whose parents had also served in Congress.[6]

Members of the Senate are even less a cross section of the American population than the House, but the Senate was established to represent the interests of the states, not to be a mirror of the people. Because representation in the Senate is based on a one-state, two-vote standard—not one-person, one-vote—the interests of low-population states are overrepresented and those of the larger, more urban, and more ethnically and racially diverse states are underrepresented.

[1]A list of all women who have served in the House can be found at www.loc/gov/thomas; those who have served in the Senate can be found at www.senate.gov/artandhistory/ history/common/briefing/women_senators.htm.

[2]Gregory L Giroux, "A Touch of Gray on Capitol Hill," *CQ Weekly,* January 31, 2005, 243.

[3]These are estimates drawn from members' financial disclosure statements, which do not provide exact figures on income. Members need only report income and assets within a broad dollar range. A few members do, however, release their tax statements.

[4]"A Touch of Gray," 241.

[5]Ibid., 242.

[6]*CQ's Politics in America 2004: The 108th Congress* (Washington, D.C.: CQ Press, 2003), 1133. Eleven of the twenty-six whose mother or father served in Congress directly succeeded their parent.

those of his or her party or the majority of the constituency *that votes.* But members are more likely to share the issue position of constituents when the issue is important to constituents and when their opinions are strongly held. Since constituents are often unin-

formed, divided, or apathetic, and most votes in Congress are on bills the electorate knows little about, members can vote their personal issue preferences, with their party, or with those constituents or donors who most forcibly make their positions known.

The first members of Congress made $6 a day, which paid for boardinghouse accommodations, firewood, candles, their meals, and a mileage allowance for travel to and from the capital.[1] Today, members receive a handsome salary indexed to inflation, a generous benefits package including full medical and dental care, and money for office, staff, mailing, and travel.

Personal Benefits

Salary

Congress has indexed its salaries to inflation so that members no longer have to vote each session on salary increases. Thus salaries have increased from $90,000 in 1989 to $165,200 in 2006. (Salaries of congressional leaders are somewhat higher.) Members are now among the top 5 percent of American wage earners.[2]

Health Care

For a modest monthly premium, members can opt for a first-class private health care plan or care at one of two military hospitals. Taxpayers spend millions more each year to keep a doctor and staff on site at the Capitol's Wellness Center, which also houses a pool and gymnasium.

Pensions

Members of Congress are required to pay Social Security taxes, but they also have 401(k) plans and a generous federal pension program. They can begin collecting as early as age fifty if they have served at least twenty years. Pensions cannot be higher than 80 percent of a member's final salary, and in general, those with decades of service receive about 75 percent of their salaries. If Congress voted to convert its pension system to the same kind of cash-balance plan many members have advocated for American workers, the value of their pensions would drop by as much as 60 percent.[3]

Benefits That Help Reelection Chances

Office and Clerical Support

Representatives are authorized to hire up to eighteen staff members, and they receive an allowance for office space and furniture in their home district. Senators' staff budgets vary with the population of their states. The average size of a Senator's personal staff is thirty-four full-time workers. Those who serve as committee chairs or in leadership positions have additional staff and larger expense allowances.

Travel and Mailing Allowances

Members receive an allowance for travel to and from their districts, adjusted according to their distance from Washington. They also receive mailing allowances called the franking privilege (discussed on page 224).

Studio Access

Television and radio recording studios are provided for preparing ads and sound bites for the news.

Other Perks

Members of Congress enjoy many other perquisites, including subsidized travel abroad; subsidized meals in the Senate and House dining rooms; free parking on Capitol Hill, on Washington streets, and at airports; free car washes; and a child care center.

A Final Benefit

Taxpayers fund life insurance policies and a death benefit equal to a year's salary for each member of Congress. And if a legislator so desires, the sergeant-at-arms will arrange for an undertaker to plan the member's final journey.

[1]Per diem and travel allowances for the first members were verified in 2002 when Senate custodial staff found an eighteenth-century ledger with payment accounts.
[2]Salaries of government officials can be found at www.usgovinfo.about.com. The website of the Center for Public Integrity (www.publicintegrity.org) is also excellent for tracking congressional pay and benefits.
[3]Now with Bill Moyers, Public Broadcasting System, July 2, 2004. www.pbs.org/now.

Constituents are becoming more active in communicating with their legislators, flooding them with faxes, e-mails, poll results, and mailgrams, often at the encouragement of radio or television talk shows or interest groups mobilizing their memberships. These communicative individuals, however, are often not representative of the majority in a member's constituency and tend to hold their positions with greater intensity than the average voter. As we saw in Chapter 3, Congress is more likely to respond to those with intensely held views. And Congress itself has become more extreme in its views than the public in general. Republican members have become more conservative and Democrats more liberal. Even though 42 percent of Americans still identify as "moderates," by 2004 only 8 percent of House members and 9 percent of the Senate were centrists.[19]

Electing Members of Congress

Elections determine who gets to represent the rest of us. Because reelection is an important objective for almost all members of Congress and *the* most important objective for many, members work at being reelected throughout their terms.[20] Most are successful, though senators are not as secure as members of the House.

Campaigns

In the nineteenth century, political parties organized congressional and presidential campaigns, and the candidates had relatively little to do. Today, however, congressional as well as presidential campaigns are candidate centered.

Congressional candidates usually hire the staff, raise the money, and organize their own campaigns. They may recruit campaign workers from local political parties; interest groups they belong to; unions, church, civic, or other voluntary organizations; or they may simply turn to friends and acquaintances.[21]

Political parties do have a significant role, however. National and local parties also recruit potential candidates. Presidents make personal appeals to fellow party members who they think can run strong races, and national campaign committees also recruit aggressively. Said one Democratic congressional campaign chair, "I'm not looking for liberals or conservatives. That's not my bag. I'm looking for winners."[22] Parties redouble their efforts when, as in recent elections, control of Congress is at stake. Besides, if candidates are not closely linked to parties, then, once elected, they are not as indebted to their party nor as obligated to reflect party views. Recognizing this, national parties have increasingly provided services to congressional candidates—helping them manage their campaigns, develop issues, advertise, raise money, and conduct opinion polls. National party organizations give substantial sums of money to congressional candidates.

In 2006, the Democrats worked especially hard to recruit candidates who would be seen as tough on national security. Thus they made a special effort to recruit those who had served in the military, such as Jim Webb (D-Va.), who upset incumbent Republican George Allen in Virginia, or who had moderate records, such as Bob Casey (D-Pa.), who defeated conservative Republican Rick Santorum in Pennsylvania.

Congressional Media Campaigns

To wage a serious campaign, the challenger or a contender for an open seat must wage a media campaign. Candidates hire media consultants and specialists in polling, advertising, and fundraising. The old-style politician who might have been effective in small groups but who cannot appear poised and articulate on television has given way to someone who can project an attractive television image. Candidates are elected on the basis of their media skills, which may not be the same skills as those needed to be a good lawmaker.

Campaign Money

An old adage says, "Half the money spent on campaigns is wasted. The trouble is, we don't know which half." This bromide helps explain why congressional campaigns are expensive. There is a kind of "campaign arms race" as each candidate tries to do what the other candidate does and a little more, escalating costs year by year.

Members of Congress are aggressive in soliciting for donations. They fear defeat in the next election and think that raising a lot of money can protect them. Senators, for example, must raise more than $20,000 each week during all six years of their term to fund an average-cost winning reelection campaign. A senator from a populous, high-cost state needs to raise substantially more. Hillary Clinton (D-N.Y.) and Rick Santorum (R-Pa.) spent more than $20 million in their 2006 reelection races (Santorum lost). Even popular small-state senators raise millions.

Until the 1960s, most fundraising by members of Congress was done in their home districts because members did not want their constituents to think they were influenced by Washington lobbyists. That has changed dramatically. Today, members of Congress are heavily supported by political action committees (PACs) and the majority of PAC funds are raised in Washington.[23] Well-known lobbyists get hundreds of invitations to congressional fundraisers every year.[24]

Incumbents: Unsafe at Any Margin?

Most members are reelected even if they have not done that much for their home districts.[25] Indeed, one Republican member remarked, "Let's face it, you have to be a bozo to lose this job."[26] Still, incumbents believe the best way to ensure victory is to be so good at serving the home district, so successful in getting money for their districts, and so well known to the voters that no serious rival will want to run. Incumbents hope poten-

Democrat Jim Webb, with his wife, celebrates his election to the Senate from Virginia. During his campaign, Webb criticized the Iraq War and wore the combat boots of his son, a Marine serving in the war. Webb was one of six Democratic challengers who unseated Republican incumbents in the 2006 elections, giving the Democrats a majority in the Senate.

AP/Wide World Photos

tial rivals will bide their time and wait for a better year or run for some other office.[27]

Given the advantages of office that incumbents have in name recognition and in favors they can do their constituents (for more on these advantages, see Box, *Pay and Perks of Office,* page 218), you may wonder why they worry about losing. But worry they do. One political scientist proclaimed that members feel "unsafe at any margin."[28] No matter how big their last victory, they worry that their next campaign will bring defeat. And despite the high reelection rate of incumbents, a few do lose. This fear prompts members

to spend even more of their energies preparing for the next campaign.

For the most part, this fear is misplaced. Turnover in Congress comes primarily from those who decide not to run. Even in the anti-incumbent election of 2006, less than 10 percent of House incumbents lost (all of them Republicans). In 2004, a more typical recent election, only 2 percent lost and only about three dozen of the 435 seats were even competitive.

The advantages of incumbency are becoming larger. State legislative majorities in 2001 drew most House districts in ways to make sure their fellow partisans had the safest seats possible. Mostly, they protected incumbents of their own party, but in doing so created safe seats for the other party, too. The only states to have many competitive seats were where district drawing was taken out of the hands of the legislature and placed in nonpartisan hands; Iowa is the best example. This gerrymandering has significant consequences for our democracy because it is primarily through elections that we hold public officials accountable.

House members really do have to offend their constituencies to lose. Senators are somewhat more vulnerable. Most senators are also reelected, but the probabilities of defeat are higher than for the House. In the late 1970s and early 1980s, it was not uncommon for a third of the senators running to be defeated. Those proportions have decreased, but in 2006 around 20 percent of senators running lost. Even so, the electoral benefit of incumbency still exists for the great majority of candidates who choose to run for reelection.[29]

Challengers

Another reason for the uneasiness of incumbents is that as their media and public relations sophistication has grown, so has that of their challengers. Still, without the advantages of incumbents' free mailing privileges and other opportunities to become well known to constituents, challengers have a difficult time. The best advice to someone who wants to be a member of Congress is to find an open seat.

To beat an incumbent, challengers need money. The more they spend, the more likely they are to win. In recent House campaigns, a challenger needed to spend at least $1 million to have even a one in four chance of winning—and the cost continues to rise.[30] Spending is important for challengers because they must make themselves known in a positive way, and they must suggest that something is wrong with the incumbent. Usu-

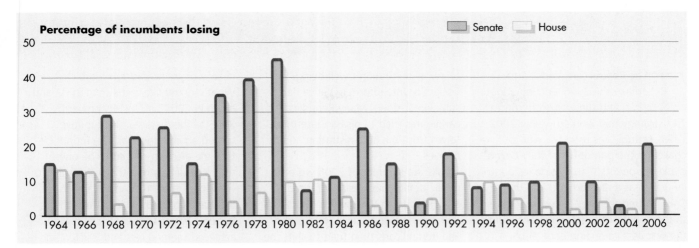

Percentage of incumbents losing

Senate ☐ House

FIGURE 2 • **House Incumbents Have Had Secure Jobs in Recent Years** *In the 1980s and 1990s, more House incumbents lost in the reapportionment years (1982 and 1992); in the 1970s, most lost in 1974, the Watergate year. In the 1960s, reapportionment occurred both before the 1964 and 1966 election. Senate results do not reflect this cycle because, of course, there is no redistricting of the Senate constituencies. Each senator represents the whole state.*
SOURCE: *Statistical Abstract of the United States 2004.*

ally, challengers will charge incumbents with ignoring the district, being absent from committee hearings or floor votes, being too liberal or too conservative, or voting incorrectly on a key issue. Sometimes, of course, the incumbent has been involved in a scandal, which offers a ready target for the challenger.[31]

Sometimes challengers will try unusual tactics to make themselves known. In the 2006 election, a Republican candidate rode an elephant, accompanied by a mariachi band, alongside the Rio Grande River to illustrate lax border control. The stunt resulted in interviews by several TV and radio commentators.

Senate challengers have a better chance than House challengers (see Figure 1). One reason is that Senate seats are bigger prizes and so attract stronger candidates. Then, too, in a statewide constituency there is a larger pool of challengers to draw on. Because they are often former governors or members of the House with a statewide reputation, Senate challengers are better known than House challengers.[32] One analysis of this showed that about 80 percent of voters recognized the name of the person running against their incumbent senator; less than 60 percent recognized the challenger to their House incumbent.[33]

Another reason Senate challengers have greater success is that most incumbents have not had personal contact with as high a proportion of voters as a representative due to the much greater number of people they represent. Also there is a wider range of views and

demands to satisfy in their larger and more heterogeneous constituencies.[34] Senators from the largest states have about a six- or seven-point electoral disadvantage compared with senators from the smallest states. Senators from the smallest states do about as well in retaining their seats as House members from their states.[35]

Voting for Congress

In Chapter 7, we reviewed the impact of parties, issues, and candidates on voting choices. The same factors influence voting choices in congressional races.

Party loyalty, candidate evaluations, and issues are important factors in congressional elections just as in presidential ones.[36] Party loyalty is even more important for congressional than for presidential elections because congressional elections are less visible, so more people base their vote on party identification. Incumbency is also much more important than in presidential races. The result is that increasingly, since about 1960, voters have split their tickets in voting for presidential and congressional candidates. Recently, Bill Clinton had to deal with a Republican majority in both houses during his second term, while George W. Bush had to work with a Democratic majority in each house after the 2006 midterm elections.

Normally, the party of a winning presidential candidate gains seats during a presidential election year and loses a number of seats in the midterm election. This

The Republicans decided to make the 2006 election about Iraq and the war on terrorism. This strategy had worked well in 2002 when Republicans used the war to challenge the patriotism of their Democratic opponents. The president's popularity was at a record high, and the "rally 'round the flag" effect worked to the benefit of the Republicans. And the war as a campaign issue also worked well for the Republicans in 2004, when voters decided that George Bush would be a stronger leader than his opponent, John Kerry.

But by 2006, the president's popularity had declined. The administration's poor response to the devastation of hurricane Katrina in New Orleans and the Mississippi Gulf Coast eroded his reputation as a strong leader and protector of the nation's well-being. His Social Security reform initiative had sunk like a stone. Many Republican candidates tried to disassociate themselves from the administration and its policies.

As the summer of 2006 wore on, public opinion increasingly turned against the Iraq War, which offered little hope of a quick or victorious end. The Republicans then tried to shift the focus to the war on terrorism, an issue in which the Republicans continued to have popular support. But the Democrats would not let them off the hook on Iraq, and Democratic candidates all over the country made Iraq an issue.

Republican candidates from the president on down grew increasingly insistent that a vote for the Democrats was a vote for the terrorists, but this charge grew increasingly ineffective. What worked like a charm in 2002 and again in 2004 had lost its power by 2006 as the majority of the public turned against the war. The month before the election proved to be one of the most deadly months in the war, with more than 100 Americans and thousands of Iraqis killed. The administration's promises that victory could be achieved seemed less and less realistic.

At the same time, the Republicans' messages were knocked off track by a series of scandals affecting Republican members of Congress. Two members of the House resigned because of crimes relating to financial corruption. Another member of the House resigned after the media revealed that he had been writing sexually suggestive text messages to teenaged boys who

maintains a sort of equilibrium in party control of Congress.[37] In 2006, voters delivered a rebuke to the Republicans, who lost 29 House seats and six Senate seats. This contrasted with the midterm elections of 1998 and 2002, when the president's party actually gained a few seats in the House and, in 2002, the Senate too.

To some extent, midterm election results are a referendum on how well citizens think the president is doing. In 1998, Clinton was given credit for the economic good times the country was experiencing, and in 2002, voters rewarded the Republicans for Bush's strong anti-terrorist stance. But by 2006, a majority of voters decided that the Iraq War was not going well nor was the war on terror and that the president and his party were not doing a competent job of leading the country.

The Advantages of Incumbency

Because reelection is an important objective for almost all members of Congress and the most important objective for many, much of the work members do throughout their term is targeted at getting reelected.

Incumbents are able to use the many advantages of incumbency to keep themselves in office.

Before they even take the oath of office, newly elected representatives are given an introduction to the advantages of incumbency. At meetings arranged by the Democratic and Republican leadership and by the House Administrative Committee, new members learn about free mailing privileges, computers and software to help them target letters to specialized groups of constituents, facilities to make videotapes and audiotapes to send to hometown media, and other "perks" designed to keep members in touch with their constituencies and, not coincidentally, to help win reelection (see the box "Pay and Perks of Office" on page 218).

Incumbents win because they are better known than nonincumbents. Voters have seen their representatives and senators on television or received mail from them, and they can give a general rating of their performance.[38] Although most voters can correctly identify their representatives and senators as liberal or conservative, only a small minority know how these legislators voted on any issue.[39] Therefore incumbents have the

were congressional pages. Media coverage of this story broadened to focus on the alleged cover-up of these messages by some members of the House Republican leadership. This story dominated the media in late September and early October, a time when many voters start to pay serious attention to the campaign.

In November, the Democrats captured majorities in both the House and Senate. Although the 31-vote shift to the Democrats in the House was not large by historical off-year standards, given that most districts were not considered to be in play at all, it was a substantial victory.

What determined the election?[1] About 40 percent of the public considered corruption and scandals extremely important to their vote, about the same proportion who thought the economy was important, who thought the war in Iraq was important, and who thought terrorism was important. Most of those who believed corruption, the war in Iraq, or the economy were important voted Democratic. A small majority of those who thought terrorism was important voted Republican. Republicans also won a majority of voters who believed that immigration and values issues such as abortion and same-sex marriage were important.

Exit polls indicated that the Democrats picked up support compared to 2004 in every demographic group: men, women, blacks, whites, Asians, and Latinos, small-town residents and denizens of large cities, the religious and the nonreligious, and people of all education, age, and income groups. Republicans won 81 percent of those who approved of the war in Iraq, and Democrats won 80 percent of those who disapproved of it. Unfortunately for the Republicans, substantially more disapproved of the war than approved of it. Those who approved of the president heavily voted Republican, and those who opposed him voted for the Democrats.

A telling statistic is that only one Republican candidate for Congress used the president's photo in his or her TV ads, whereas dozens of Democrats did as they tried to tie their opponents to an unpopular president. The congressional elections thus became a referendum on the president.

[1]"How Voters Feel," *USA Today,* November 8, 2006, 2A.

---

advantage of name recognition without the disadvantage of having voters know how they actually cast their votes on most pieces of legislation.

Incumbents' high level of public recognition is not so surprising given that members of Congress spend much of their time and energy looking for and using opportunities to make themselves known to their constituents. Members spend half or more of their days in their district, making an average of thirty-five trips home a year—at taxpayers' expense.[40] Congress is recessed during major holidays, part of the summer, and prior to elections—the House and Senate often do not meet at all in August, a month designated as a "District Work Period."

Casework

Arguably the main advantage of incumbency is the opportunity that being in office gives representatives to perform services and do favors for their constituents. Members send constituents calendars, U.S. flags that have flown over the Capitol, and publications of the federal government. This is one of the best ways members of Congress have to make themselves known in their districts and to create a kind of patron–client relationship. You will not read about this in the Constitution, where the duties of Congress are defined. But in practice, electoral politics has meant that members must spend a great deal of their time serving the specific interests of their districts, which are not necessarily synonymous with the interests of the nation as a whole. Members take this aspect of their representational responsibilities very seriously because it is their own constituents who will reelect them—or not.

Collectively, the House and Senate receive close to 200 million e-mail messages each year, and more than 18 million pieces of regular mail.[41] The work of answering questions and doing personal favors for constituents who write or call for help is called **constituency service** or **casework.** More than 30 percent of senators' staffs and almost half of all representatives' staffs are located in their home state or district offices to better serve constituents.[42]

Congressional staff function as red-tape cutters for everyone from elderly citizens having difficulties with Social Security to small-town mayors trying to get federal grants for new sewer systems. They provide information to students working on term papers, people looking for federal jobs, citizens puzzled about which federal agency to ask for assistance, or residents trying to get information about a relative in the military. Typically, responsibility for mediating with federal agencies is divided among the casework staffers by issue area, allowing them to specialize and resolve constituents' problems—passports, immigration, Social Security payments, and the like—more efficiently.

Of course, not all casework is directed toward winning reelection. Some members say they enjoy their casework more than their policy roles, perhaps because the results of casework are more immediate and tangible. Individually, they may have limited power in trying to get important legislation passed, but in dealing with a constituent's problems, their power is much greater because of their clout with bureaucrats. A phone call or letter to a federal agency will bring attention to the constituent's problem. And casework does allow members to build nonpartisan and seemingly nonpolitical ties with their constituents.

Mailing Privileges

For the 110th Congress, taxpayers will provide more than a half billion dollars for office and franking expenses (mailing costs).[43] The franking privilege is a great asset of incumbency because it allows members to write their constituents without paying for postage out of pocket or using campaign funds. (The frank is a facsimile of the member's signature, and it works like metered mail, with the frank appearing where the stamp would be.) It is not free; Congress pays the postal bill at the end of each year. The value of the frank has been estimated as equivalent to $350,000 in campaign contributions.

The frank helps each member increase name recognition (and newly elected members can begin using the frank immediately, even before they are sworn in). The frank cannot be used to send personal correspondence to constituents or to ask them for their vote or a campaign contribution, but members can send out newsletters that inform constituents of their work for the district or to survey constituents' issue positions. Much of the time, however, the frank is used to send constituents material they have requested, such as government forms or publications, and this too increases a member's name recognition.

Media Advantage

In addition to regular mailings, members use increasingly sophisticated production equipment and technology to make television and radio shows to send home. Constituents may see or hear stories about their representatives on local television and radio news programs produced in congressional studios by the representatives' own staff and paid for out of campaign or party funds. Members like to tape themselves at committee meetings asking questions or being referred to as "Mr. (or Madam) Chairman" (many members chair at least a subcommittee). The tape then is edited to a thirty-second sound bite and sent to local television stations. Often stations run these productions as news features without telling their viewers that they are essentially self-promotion pieces prepared by the members. Congressional staffers also write press releases about accomplishments of their bosses and fax them to local newspapers, which often print them as written.

Fundraising

Media access enhances another advantage of incumbency—the opportunity to raise funds from the hundreds of political action committees (PACs) that populate Washington. Eager to gain access to members of Congress, PACs make fundraising much easier for incumbents than challengers, as we pointed out in Chapter 7.

Committee assignments are also extremely important in fundraising. If a member wins a seat on one of the powerful "juice" committees—one that considers legislation important to big-money interests or that appropriates money—the chances of attracting large campaign donations are greatly increased.

Pork-Barrel Funding

Incumbents can gain the attention of or curry favor with constituents by obtaining funds for special projects, new programs, buildings, or other public works that bring jobs, benefits, and business to their districts or states. Such benefits are widely known as **pork-barrel projects.** A pork feature of virtually every annual budget is money for yet another bomber, fighter plane, weapon, or military construction project the Pentagon has not requested. Universities are also perennial winners in the pork sweepstakes, receiving several billion dollars for campus projects.

Because members consider pork-barrel projects crucial to their reelection chances, there is little support in Congress for eliminating projects most know to be unwise or wasteful. David Stockman, director of the Office of Management and Budget during the Reagan administration, observed, "There's no such thing as a fiscal conservative when it comes to his district."[44] Liberals and conservatives, Democrats and Republicans, protect these kinds of projects.

How Congress Is Organized

An institution with 535 voting members that must make thousands of policy decisions every year without benefit of a unified leadership is an institution not likely to work quickly or efficiently. Like all organizations, legislatures need some structure to be able to accomplish their purposes. Congress does have both a leadership system and a committee structure, but each is organized along party lines. Alongside this partisan organization exist many other groups—caucuses, coalitions, work and study groups, and task forces—whose membership cuts across party lines or reflects the division of interests within **party caucuses.** Some of this micro-organizing is a means of bypassing the committee system that dominates Congress's legislative and oversight functions.

The Evolution of Congressional Organization

The Constitution calls for the members of the House of Representatives to select a **Speaker of the House** to act as its presiding officer and for the vice president of the United States to serve as president (or presiding officer) of the Senate. But the Constitution does not say anything about the powers of these officials, nor does it require any further internal organization.

The first House, meeting in New York in 1789, had slow and cumbersome procedures. For its first several sessions, Congress's legislative work was accomplished by appointing ad hoc committees. By the Third Congress, there were about 350 committees, and the system had become unwieldy. Soon permanent committees were created, each with continuing responsibilities in one area, such as taxes or trade.[45]

As parties developed, the selection of the Speaker became a partisan matter, and the Speaker became as much a party leader as a legislative manager. The seventh Speaker, Henry Clay (Whig-Ky.), who served ten

Senator Ted Stevens (R-Alaska), called "Uncle Ted" by his constituents because of his ability to obtain federal money for the state, secured $1.5 million to replace this bus stop outside the Anchorage Museum of History and Art.

of the years between 1811 and 1825, transformed the speakership from a ceremonial office to one of real leadership. To maintain party loyalty and discipline, he used his powers to appoint committee members and chairs. Under Clay's leadership, the House was the dominant branch, but its influence declined when it, like the rest of government, could not cope with the divisiveness of the slavery issue. By 1856, it took 133 ballots to elect a Speaker. Many physical fights broke out on the House floor; duels were held outside.[46] A famous remark at the time was that "the only people in Congress who are not carrying a revolver are those carrying two revolvers."[47]

The Senate, a smaller body than the House, was less tangled in procedures, less rule-bound, and more effective in its operation. Its influence rose as visitors packed the Senate gallery to hear the great debates over slavery waged by Daniel Webster (Mass.), John C. Calhoun (S.C.), and Clay (who had moved from the House). During this era, senators were elected by state legislatures, not directly by the people. Thus they had strong

It may seem paradoxical that as the budget deficit grows, Congress spends more and more on small projects targeted to local constituencies. But the fact that members of Congress are elected by local constituencies builds a bias for local over national needs into the budget process. This preference is especially apparent in the work of the appropriations and authorization committees. Nothing gives senators and representatives more opportunity to prove to their states and districts that they are serving local needs than getting money earmarked for use at home.

An **earmark** is a specific amount of money designated—or set aside—at the request of a member of Congress, for a favored project, usually in his or her district. In 2006, Congress approved 13,012 earmarks at a cost of $67 billion.[1]

Many of these earmarks, or set asides as they are also called, qualify as what are popularly known as pork-barrel projects (see section on pork-barrel spending). The projects may benefit a special interest, create jobs, or help the local economy in some other way, but they are not in any sense priorities, at least not outside the district. And the special interests they benefit may be big campaign contributors.

The most successful earmarkers—not surprisingly—are the most senior and most powerful members of appropriations and authorization committees, but all members have the opportunity to include earmarks in the budgets of agencies they oversee. There is little systematic oversight of agency budgets, and once an earmark makes it into a budget bill that may be hundreds of pages long, there is little chance it will be seen by members. There is even less chance if the earmark is included in the committee report rather than as a line in the budget bill. Virtually no one outside the subcommittees may ever see these reports. This is one reason why earmarks are so hard to monitor or to remove from a budget. Another reason it is difficult to end the practice is because virtually everyone in Congress does it; earmarking is a beloved bipartisan tradition. Though the problem is worsening, it has continued in peacetime and wartime, when the budget is balanced and when it is in deep deficit. The practice is so common and such a necessary legislative skill that a Washington, D.C., firm offers a training seminar in how to get an earmark.[2]

Ted Stevens (R-Alaska), the former chair of the powerful Senate Appropriations committee, is a perennial earmark champion. In 2006, he got $325 million worth of earmarks for his state, drawing national attention for $223 million in a highway appropriation bill to construct a bridge to an island in Alaska with fifty residents promptly nicknamed, "The Bridge to Nowhere."

Citizens Against Government Waste (CAGW), which publishes an annual "Pig Book" and gives an "oinker of the month" award, estimated that about $29 billion of earmarked money was spent on close to ten thousand pork barrel projects in the 2006 election year.[3] Congress approved $13.5 million for the International Fund for Ireland and its World Toilet Summit; $1 million for water-free urinal conservation in Michigan; $235,000 for the National Wild Turkey Federation in South Carolina; $550,000 for the Museum of Glass in Tacoma, Washington;

---

local party ties. But the Senate, too, became ineffective as the nation moved toward civil war. Senators carried arms to protect themselves as debates over slavery turned to violence.

After the Civil War, with the Presidency weakened by the impeachment of Andrew Johnson, strong party leadership reemerged in the House, and a period of congressional government began. Speaker **Thomas Reed** (R–Me.), nicknamed "The Czar" by his colleagues, assumed the authority to name members and chairs of committees and to chair the **Rules Committee,** which decided which bills were to come to the floor for debate. A major consequence of the Speaker's extensive powers was increased party discipline. Members who voted against their party might be punished by a loss of committee assignments or chairmanships.

At the same time, both the House and the Senate became more professional. After the Civil War, the strengthening of parties and the growth of the one-party South, where Democrats controlled virtually all elective offices, made reelection easier, thus offering the possibility of a congressional career.

This desire for permanent careers in the House produced an interest in reform. Members wanted a chance at choice committee seats and did not want to be con-

and $150,000 for a boxing club in the home state of Senate majority leader Harry Reid. This is why CAGW's spending alert system (which mimics Homeland Security's color-coded graph) registers "low" only when Congress is in recess.

It is important to note, though, that the public are enablers of this behavior. Although we talk as if we want an ethical, high-minded Congress whose members are always responsive first to the national interest, when fragmented into individual constituents, the public often behaves quite differently. The average voter does expect his or her representative to deliver for the district. As one earmark critic says, "It is not about the size of your project. It's about the size of your politician."[4] And though many campaign donors undoubtedly do give to help reelect someone they believe in, it would surprise no one if big donors were giving to buy influence and access.

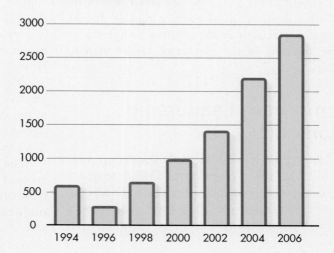

Number of earmarks

FIGURE 3 • Earmarks Have Increased Dramatically
In recent years, the number of earmarks have increased dramatically. Shown here are the earmarks in defense bills.
SOURCE: Congressional Research Service.

[1]Editorial, "The Speaker's Hard Lesson in Reform," *New York Times,* June 25, 2006, wk 11.
[2]David Baumann, "Tempest in a Barrel," *National Journal,* February 11, 2006, 58.

[3]Citizens Against Government Waste, "Pig Book," www.cagw.org/site/PageServer?pagename=reports_pigbook2006.

[4] Keith Ashdown of Taxpayers for Common Sense, quoted in Bill Marsh, "Pork Under Glass? Small Museums and their Patrons on Capitol Hill," *New York Times,* April 30, 2006, wk 4.

trolled by the Speaker. Resistance against the dictatorial practices of Reed and his successor, **Joseph Cannon** (R-Ill.), grew. Cannon, more conservative than many of his fellow Republicans, used his powers to block legislation he disliked, to punish those who opposed him, and even to refuse to recognize members who wished to speak. In 1910, there was a revolt against "**Cannonism,**" which had become a synonym for the arbitrary wielding of the Speaker's powers. The membership voted to remove the Speaker from the Rules Committee and to strip him of his authority to appoint committees and their chairs. The revolt weakened party influence because the Speaker could not punish members by removing them from committees. The committees became more independent too.

The Senate also was undergoing a major reform. The election of senators by state legislatures had made many senators pawns of special interests—the big monopolistic corporations (called trusts) and railroads. In a day when millionaires were not as common as now, the Senate was referred to as the "Millionaires' Club." Reformists pressured to establish the direct popular election of senators. After years of resistance to a constitutional amendment providing for its direct election, the Senate finally, under the threat of a call for a constitutional convention, which many members of Congress feared might lead to other changes in the Constitution, passed a direct-election amendment in 1912 which was ratified by the states a year later.[48]

These reforms of the early twentieth century dispersed power in both the House and the Senate and weakened leadership. House members no longer feared the kind of retribution levied by Speaker Cannon on members who deviated from party positions. In the Senate, popular elections made senators responsive to the diverse interests of the electorate rather than to party leaders.

Contemporary Leadership Positions

The Speaker of the House is the only leadership position specified in the Constitution. Other positions came into being with political parties. The Founders did not anticipate parties nor were there party organizations in Congress when it first met.

House Leadership Positions

The leaders of each party are selected by their respective members sitting in caucus—meeting as a group to conduct party business. Party caucus refers both to party meetings and to the party members collectively. The House Republican Caucus, for example, consists of all Republicans serving in the House, and the Democratic Caucus consists of all Democratic members (independents can caucus with either party, currently they caucus with the Democrats). As specified in the Constitution, the full House must elect the Speaker of the House, but it is a straight party-line vote, so the real selection is made in the majority party's caucus. Once elected, the Speaker becomes second in line to succeed to the Presidency, after the vice president. The Speaker's institutional task is to act as presiding officer and to see that legislation moves through the House.

The House party leadership positions, which have evolved through practice, include a majority leader, a minority leader, and majority and minority whips. The **majority leader** is second in command to the Speaker and is officially in charge of the party's legislative agenda (since the Speaker is technically an officer of the House, not of his party). The majority leader, working with the Speaker, also schedules votes on bills. The **minority leader** is, as the name suggests, the leader of the minority party.

Whips originated in the British House of Commons, where they were named after the "whipper-in," the rider who keeps the hounds together in a fox hunt. This aptly describes the whips' role in Congress. Party whips try to maintain contact with party members, determine which way they are leaning on votes, and attempt to gain their support. Assisting the majority and minority whips are a number of deputy and assistant whips who keep tabs on their assigned state delegations.

Because the Speaker is now more a party than an institutional leader, he or she is expected to use the speakership

Library of Congress

Vitriolic exchanges are not a new phenomenon in Congress. Shown here is a fight in the House of Representatives in 1798. After Rep. Matthew Lyon (Vt.) spit on Rep. Roger Griswold (Conn.) and the House refused to expel Lyon, Griswold attacked Lyon with a cane. Lyon defended himself with fire tongs as other members of Congress looked on—with some amusement, it seems.

to maximize partisan advantage in committee and staff appointments and to secure the passage of measures preferred by the party. For this reason, the person selected usually has been someone who has served in the House a long time, who is a skilled parliamentarian and an ideological moderate who can negotiate compromises and put together legislative majorities. By tradition, the Speaker does not cast a vote on most bills before the House, participating only on "symbolic or party-defining issues."[49]

Trying to win partisan support is often difficult, and the Speaker no longer has the powers of Joe Cannon, but the Speaker does have some rewards and punishments to dispense for loyalty and disloyalty. Speakers have a say in who gets to sit on which committees, which committees will be given jurisdiction over complex bills, what bills will come to the House floor for a vote and under what rules they will be considered, and how their party's congressional campaign funds are allocated. The Speaker also decides who will be recognized to speak on the floor of the House and whether motions are relevant. He or she has the authority to appoint members to conference and select committees and to control some material benefits, such as the assignment of extra office space. Speakers also have the power to name the chair of the Rules Committee and all of their party's members on the committee. Despite these formal powers, the Speaker must be persuasive to be effective.

In modern times, the only Speaker to attempt the level of control achieved by such strong predecessors as Reed and Cannon was **Newt Gingrich** (R–Ga.). Before his election in 1995, Gingrich had been the intellectual and tactical leader of conservative House Republicans. But Gingrich met with rebellion in his own party and had to fight back a challenge to his leadership in his third year. Gingrich's demands for party discipline in support of a national legislative program (the so-called Contract with America) undercut the power of committee chairs and also left many members with too little flexibility to respond to their constituencies, which risked their chances for reelection. This is one reason that an ideological moderate with a conciliatory manner is often sought for the Speaker's position.

Dennis Hastert (R–Ill.), Gingrich's successor in 1999, came to the leadership more in the mold of a traditional Speaker, even though he had been elected whip as the protégé of Majority Leader Tom ("the Hammer") Delay (R–Tex.), who almost made Gingrich look like a softie. Hastert had a friendly, low-key de-meanor and was seen as a mediator and persuader in contrast to the agenda-driven disciplinarians Gingrich and Delay. While at first he acted in a low-key manner, after the Republicans won the White House and regained control of the Senate in the 2000 elections, Hastert became a much more forceful leader, playing velvet-covered mallet to Delay's hammer in what some saw as a good cop–bad cop ploy.[50]

By the end of Bush's first term, Hastert and Delay were the White House's go-to team; they used House rules to dominate the legislative process—even more than Gingrich had—and twisted the arms of colleagues who were slow to support bills the president wanted enacted. Rather than being a strong leader in his own right, Hastert acted as a facilitator for the president's agenda and, in the eyes of his critics, as an "enabler" for Delay's strong-arm tactics.[51]

This worked well for Hastert until 2006 when Bush's poll ratings fell to historic lows. Whereas Delay was forced from office on ethics issues, Hastert was able to retain the speakership in part because he was, by contrast, such a low-key figure still little known to the public. A colleague called this "the political advantage of being boring."[52] In June 2006, Hastert became the longest-serving Republican Speaker, but his leadership was criticized over charges of his mismanagement of allegations of sexual harassment of House pages. When **Nancy Pelosi** (D–Ca.) became Speaker, she promised to be a leader of the House, not of her party, and to reduce partisanship in the legislative process.

Senate Leadership

The Senate has no leader comparable to the Speaker of the House. The vice president of the United States is formally the presiding officer and can attend and preside any time he chooses; part of his expense allowance is designated for Senate work. In reality, the vice president attends infrequently. He has relatively little power except that he is allowed to cast the tie-breaking vote in those rare instances when the Senate is evenly split. Therefore whenever a head count predicts a deadlocked vote on an important bill, the vice president shows up to preside. Consistent with the Bush administration's hands-on legislative strategy, Dick Cheney has been an active presence on Capitol Hill during his tenure as vice president, making regular trips to his office just off the Senate floor and holding weekly lunches with Republican Senators.

The Senate has an elected president pro tempore, by tradition the senior member of the majority party. It is an honorific post with few duties except to preside over the Senate in the absence of the vice president. In practice, during the conduct of routine day-to-day business, presiding duties are divided among junior senators. This releases the senior member from boring work while giving the Senate's newest members a chance to learn the rules and procedures.

As in the House, both parties also elect assistant floor leaders and whips to help maintain party discipline. These are important, if not essential, positions for working one's way into the top leadership in both the House and the Senate.

The position of Senate majority leader was not created until 1911 and has often been held by individuals of no particular distinction in their parties. The office has none of the speakership's potential for control of chamber proceedings. A congressional watcher once said the majority leader "is often more a coat-check attendant than a maitre d' or chef."[53] The instances of powerful majority leaders are few, the most notable being **Lyndon Johnson** (D-Tex.). He assumed office at a time when the Democrats had a slim hold on the Senate, giving him an opportunity to exercise his extraordinary powers of personal persuasion to keep party members in line on key votes. Johnson's reputation was

made through a combination of personality and mastery of the legislative process. There is nothing inherent in the office to give a majority leader the power Johnson had, and no one has had it since.

The Senate majority leader is a spokesperson for his party's legislative agenda and is supposed to help line up members' votes on key issues. But procedurally, the Senate is a free-for-all compared to the House, with "every man and woman for him- or herself."[54] Unlike the Speaker, the majority leader cannot control the terms under which a bill is considered on the floor nor can the majority leader stop a filibuster—a procedural maneuver that allows a minority to block a bill from coming to the floor by monopolizing the session with nonstop speeches. This means that a majority leader needs to do much more than keep his own party in line to keep legislation moving through the Senate. He can influence the general atmosphere of deliberation in the Senate by adopting an approach to working with the minority party that is either conciliatory or partisan. But whether he chooses the more traditional conciliatory and clubby approach of the former leader **Robert Dole** (R-Kan.), or the more aggressively partisan approach of Trent Lott (R-Miss.), the majority leader must be less strident than a Speaker like Gingrich and

As Senate majority leader, Lyndon Johnson (left), shown here with Sen. Theodore Green (D-R.I.), "used physical persuasion in addition to intellectual and moral appeals. He was hard on other people's coat lapels." If the man he was trying to persuade was shorter than Johnson, "he was inclined to move up close and lean over the subject of his persuasive efforts." If the man was taller, Johnson "would come at him from below, somewhat like a badger." Quotes are from Eugene McCarthy, Up 'til Now (New York: Harcourt, 1987).

less of an enforcer than Hastert, because those styles would never be accepted in the more egalitarian atmosphere of the Senate.

The Senate minority leader's job is similar to that of the majority leader in that its effectiveness depends on a limited package of incentives and procedural ploys to enforce party discipline. Historically, the Senate's majority and minority leaders have worked closely together to conduct Senate business, but this can break down if one is running for the Presidency or has other ambitions.

Both the majority and minority leaders must also articulate their parties' issue positions and try to win support for bills supported by their parties. In fulfilling this duty they may undercut their political viability at home if their constituents are more conservative or liberal than the leadership of the national parties. The current majority leader, **Harry Reid** (D-Nev.), a Democrat from a Republican state, is more conservative (an opponent of abortion rights, for example) than the Senate party caucus. By speaking out for a more liberal Democratic membership, he could endanger his own reelection. If a Senate leader also has presidential aspirations, as Bob Dole and more recently Bill Frist (R-Tenn.) did, the balancing act is even more difficult because he must carve out issue positions that distinguish him from other senators in his party who are also seeking the nomination. Robert Dole found it so difficult to carry out all of those roles simultaneously that he resigned from the Senate during his run for the Presidency.

Committees

Much of the work of Congress is done in committees. Observers of American politics take this for granted, yet the power of legislative committees is rare among Western democracies. In Britain, for example, committees cannot offer amendments that change the substance of a bill. In our Congress, the substance of a bill can be changed in committee even after its passage in both chambers.

The division of labor provided by committees and subcommittees enables Congress to consider a vast number of bills each year. If every member had to review every measure in detail, it would be impossible to deal with the current workload. Instead, most bills are killed in committee, leaving many fewer for each member to evaluate before a floor vote. Committees also help members develop specializations. Members who remain on the same committee for some time gain expertise and are less dependent on professional staff and executive agencies for background information.

Standing Committees

Today there are twenty **standing committees** in the House and sixteen in the Senate. Each deals with a different subject matter, such as finance or education or agriculture. Each has a number of subcommittees, totaling ninety-nine in the House and seventy-three in the Senate during the 109th Congress.[55] The number of committees and subcommittees fluctuates, declining during years of reform and cost-cutting and increasing during years of government growth. During the Bush administration, as government grew, with a new cabinet department and two new intelligence agencies, so did the number of congressional committees.

Nearly all legislation introduced in Congress is referred to a standing committee and then to a subcommittee. Subcommittees may hold public hearings to give interested parties a chance to speak for or against a bill. They also hold **markup** sessions to provide an opportunity for the committee to rewrite the bill. Following markup, the bill is sent to the full committee, which may also hold hearings. If approved there, it goes to the full House or Senate.

Party ratios—the number of Democrats relative to Republicans on each committee—are determined by the majority party in the House and negotiated by the leadership of both parties in the Senate. The ratios are generally set in rough proportion to party membership in the particular chamber, but the majority party gives itself a disproportionate number of seats on several key committees to ensure control.

Committee Membership

New members and members seeking committee changes express their preferences to their party's selection committee. The party tries to accommodate members' requests for assignments that will be most beneficial to their constituencies, but there is some self-selection by seniority. Historically, junior members did not ask for the most prestigious posts, but this tradition has broken down as freshmen have become bolder in their requests and even receive instruction in how to get the assignments they want. And if there are freshmen members whose reelection races are likely to be tough or who the party leadership believes have the potential to be future leaders, those members will likely be given helpful committee assignments. For example,

Barack Obama, thought to be a future Democratic star, was given a position on the influential Foreign Relations Committee in his freshman year, just as Hillary Clinton was given her first choices when she was a freshman.

The committees dealing with appropriations, taxes, and finance are always sought after because having a say in the allocation of money and how the tax burden falls on individuals and businesses gives members power and enhances their ability to help their home districts. These are sometime called "juice committees" because of the advantage they give members in squeezing interested parties for campaign contributions. Most members also want committee assignments that let them tell constituents they are working on problems of the district. Members from rural districts, for example, seek seats on committees that deal with agricultural and trade issues.

Media coverage is another criterion important in deciding committee preference. The work of some committees is more likely to be covered by television. Committees scrambled to hold attention-getting hearings on the new Department of Homeland Security and corporate fraud in 2002 and on 9/11 failures and the reorganization of intelligence agencies in 2004. Getting on the right committee is important to those who want to become nationally known. When a journalist once asked Senator Joseph Biden (D-Del.) why he was so newsworthy, Biden replied, "It's the committees, of course." Biden has served on the three committees with the greatest media exposure, and this prominence has made him a credible potential candidate for the Presidency in every Democratic primary season for the past twenty-five years.

The practice of filling each committee with representatives whose districts have an especially strong economic interest in its work encourages committees to be rather parochial in their outlook. It also leads to costly and wasteful legislation; if committee members' constituents benefit from programs under their jurisdiction, the members have no incentive to eliminate them or pare them back. This is one of the biggest weaknesses in the committee system.[56]

Committees are also often filled with members who have financial interests in the businesses they make policies for. Most members who sit on the banking committees own bank stock, many on agriculture committees own agribusiness stock, and those on the armed services committees hold stock in defense industries.[57] Senator Frist (R-Tenn.), an ex-surgeon who held stock in a huge hospital management company founded by his family (one that had paid multi-million dollar fines for overbilling), made it a legislative priority to help rewrite health care and medical malpractice laws. Billy Tauzin (R-La.), who, as chair of the Ways and Means Committee, shepherded Bush's Medicare drug benefit bill through Congress, immediately left Congress to take a million-dollar-a-year job as a lobbyist for pharmaceutical companies who will benefit from the legislation. And seven members of the House Appropriations Committee, Republicans and Democrats, have PACs that are headed by present or former lobbyists for businesses with issues before the committee.[58]

Committee Chairs

The chair is usually the most influential member of a committee. Chairs have the authority to call meetings, set agendas, and control committee staff and funds. In addition, chairs have strong substantive knowledge of the matters that come before their committees, and this, too, is a source of influence.

Historically, the member of the majority party with the longest service on a committee became its chair by the so-called **seniority rule.** The rule was adopted to protect committee members from powerful Speakers of the House, who often used their authority to award committee chairs to friends and allies. But it allowed members who were senile, alcoholic, or personally disliked by every member of the committee to become chairs if they were the most senior. It also led to chairs who were dictatorial and out of step with the rest of their party. In response to those complaints, in the early 1970s both parties agreed that the seniority rule no longer had to be followed. Since then, the Committee on Committees in the Republican caucus and the Steering and Policy Committee in the Democratic caucus have recommended chairs in addition to assigning committee seats. All members of each party caucus vote on these recommendations by secret ballot, although in some cases the result is a foregone conclusion. In the House, the Speaker has power to name members to the Rules Committee and to appoint or recommend the chairs of the most powerful committees.

Some members prefer the Speaker appointment system because they believe it can prevent potentially damaging intraparty fights over who will chair important committees, just as the seniority principle did. At the same time, it reduces the likelihood of producing the kind of autocratic chairs who were common under the seniority rule.

The end of the automatic seniority rule also brought a change in the behavior of senior members. Before 1975, committee chairs were less supportive of their party than other party members in roll-call votes.[59] They could go their own way with impunity because their powerful positions were guaranteed. Since 1975, committee chairs have had to be party loyalists if they want to keep their jobs. When Arlen Specter (R-Pa.), a supporter of abortion rights, made public statements after the 2004 elections that the Bush administration should send the Senate Supreme Court nominees who were moderates if it wanted to ensure confirmation, the White House made it clear that if Specter wanted to serve as chair of the Judiciary Committee, he would have to support any and all of the president's nominees to the federal courts

The same pattern holds true of those who are second, third, and fourth in seniority on each committee. They are now much less likely to deviate from their party's position. In that sense, the reforms have strengthened party influence in Congress, especially in the House, where it has led to a greater concentration of power, away from committees and to the leadership. During the Bush administration, however, the White House rather than the party leadership established policy for the Republican caucus. Thus the power of both House and Senate chairs diminished when Republicans controlled Congress.

Subcommittees

Each standing committee is divided into subcommittees with jurisdiction over part of the committee's area of responsibility. The House International Relations Committee, for example, has seven subcommittees—one each for the geographic areas of Africa, East Asia and the Pacific, the Western Hemisphere, the Middle East and South Asia, and Europe, one for oversight, and a newly created subcommittee on terrorism and proliferation issues.

In the days of the seniority rule, standing committee chairs chose the subcommittee chairs and controlled subcommittees' jurisdiction, budget, and staff. Since 1974, each House subcommittee operates semi-independently of the parent committee. Similar changes took place in the Senate. These reforms, sometimes called the "subcommittee bill of rights," allowed more members, especially newer members, to share in important decisions. In this way, they made Congress more democratic. But by diffusing power, they also made it less efficient because the very number of subcommittees contributed to government gridlock. Complex legislation might be sent to several subcommittees, each with its own interests and jurisdiction.

Under the Republican majority in the House, standing committee chairs reasserted control over their subcommittees. In 1999, new rules were adopted to streamline the legislative process and reduce the number of subcommittees.[60] These reforms have not ended the problem of overlapping jurisdictions. When President George W. Bush proposed establishing the cabinet-level Department of Homeland Security, for example, twelve House committees were involved in marking up the bill. And in general there is a tendency toward committee creep, with periods of committee reduction followed by periods of growth

Select, Special, Joint, and Conference Committees There are a few other types of congressional committees. *Select* or *special committees* are typically organized on a temporary basis to investigate a specific problem or to hold hearings and issue a report on special problems that arise, such as intelligence agency failures prior to 9/11 or government response to hurricane Katrina. These committees are disbanded when their work is completed. The exceptions are the House and the Senate Select Committees on Intelligence and the Senate Select Committee on Ethics, which are, in effect, permanent committees.

The four joint committees include members from both houses, with the chair alternating between a House and a Senate member. Conference committees, appointed whenever the Senate and the House pass different versions of the same bill, also have joint membership. Members from the committees that managed the bill in their respective chambers work out a single version for the full membership to vote on. Conference committees are dissolved after the compromise version is agreed on. Their work is discussed in greater detail in the section on lawmaking.

Task Forces

The traffic jams and turf wars surrounding much committee work have led members of Congress with strong interests in particular areas to look for ways to bypass the committee structure. Task forces and ad hoc committees have existed in the House for decades, used by Democratic and Republican leaders alike, to study major issues and draft legislation, usually to get around foot-dragging committees.[61]

Task forces can act more expeditiously than regular committees, but on the other hand, task forces bypass mechanisms for accountability to the public and to most rank-and-file members. Bills are written without formal hearings or the opportunity to point out any potential pitfalls and problems of the legislation. Rank-and-file members often face having to vote on a huge package of legislation about which they know only that they know little. In 2004, the House was embarrassed when it passed an appropriation bill that few had read. Someone had stuck in a provision allowing members of Congress to gain access to the personal income tax returns of private citizens. When it was reported in the press, a staff member confessed to adding it, and red-faced members removed it.

Staff and Support Agencies

Congress encompasses not only elected representatives but also a staff of more than twenty thousand, not including individuals employed in support positions such as security and maintenance. The cost of funding Congress in 2007 will be more than $4 billion.[62] But Congress cannot serve its proper role as a check on the executive branch if it does not have its own information base.

To this end, staff in support agencies carry out various research functions. The Government Accountability Office (GAO) checks on the efficiency and effectiveness of executive agencies, the Congressional Research Service (CRS) conducts studies of public issues and does specific research at the request of members, the Office of Technology Assessment provides long-range analyses of the effects of new and existing technology, and the Congressional Budget Office provides the expertise and support for Congress's budgeting job.

To research difficult problems, members can call on the seven hundred full-time congressional research staffers in the Library of Congress. These researchers have issue specializations and contacts with experts in the academic world, in all the federal agencies, and with the interest groups that lobby on behalf of these issues. No member of Congress would have the time to develop this kind of expertise, yet without it, competent legislation could not be written, and Congress would not have the background it needs to challenge facts and figures presented in communications from the executive branch.

What Congress Does

The importance of Congress is reflected in the major, explicit constitutional powers the Founders gave it: to lay and collect taxes, coin money, declare war and raise and support a military, and regulate commerce with foreign governments and among the states. Essentially, most of the named powers the Constitution gives to the national government were given to Congress. These and other powers specifically mentioned in the Constitution are called the **enumerated powers** of Congress. Congress also has **implied powers;** that is, it is permitted to make all the laws "necessary and proper" to carry out its enumerated powers. Although the Founders did not necessarily foresee it, this tremendous grant of power covers almost every conceivable area of human activity.

Lawmaking

In each congressional session in the past decade, between three thousand and seven thousand bills and resolutions have been introduced. Less than 10 percent of these measures pass, and most die in committee. Of those passed, many are noncontroversial, including the so-called "sense of the chamber" measures, such as resolutions congratulating the winners of the Super Bowl and taking note of the death of singer Ray Charles, or very specific bills, such as for the naming of a federal courthouse. In a sign of the times, even these conventionally nonpolitical resolutions became victims of partisanship in the 109th Congress when Majority Leader Frist refused to allow a vote on a congratulatory resolution offered by New Jersey's two Democratic senators. The resolution, noting the thirtieth anniversary of the Born to Run album, was a tip of the hat to their constituent, Bruce Springsteen. But Frist, who had sponsored his own resolutions honoring events in rock-and-roll and county music history, blocked the measure honoring Springsteen, for no apparent reason other than that Springsteen had campaigned for the Democratic presidential nominee in 2004.[63]

A number of the bills passed each year are private; they resolve an issue an individual or private party has with the government, such as citizenship status or a monetary claim. Our concern is with public bills, those that become laws affecting the general public.

Turning a bill into a law is like running an obstacle course. Opponents of a bill have an advantage because it is easier to defeat a bill than to pass one. Because of the need to win a majority at each stage, the end result is almost always a compromise. That does not mean a compromise of all interests, but only of those that manage to play a role in shaping a particular bill. The formal steps by which a bill becomes a law are important but do not reveal the bargaining and trade-offs at every step in the process.

Submission and Referral

Bills may be introduced in either the House or the Senate, except for tax measures (which according to the Constitution must be initiated in the House) and appropriations bills (which by tradition are introduced in the House). This reflects the Founders' belief that the chamber directly elected by the people should control the purse strings.

Although the president initiates about half of all legislation passed, only members of Congress can introduce bills. Interest groups, constituents, or the president must find a congressional sponsor for a proposed bill.[64] After a bill's introduction, it is referred to a standing committee by the Speaker of the House or the presiding officer in the Senate. The content of the bill largely determines where it will go, although the Speaker has some discretion, particularly over complex bills that cover more than one subject area. Many such bills are referred to more than one committee simultaneously.

Committee Action

Once the bill reaches a committee, it is assigned to the subcommittee that covers the appropriate subject area. One of the main functions of committees is to screen bills with little chance of passage. (If a committee kills a bill, there are procedures that members can use to try to get the bill to the floor, but these are used infrequently.) Bills receiving subcommittee approval go to full committee; hearings may be held at both levels.

Hearings on bills and the markup of bills are, unless otherwise specified, open to the public, although few people know about them or would have the time or opportunity to sit in. Consequently, lobbyists fill most of the hearing rooms. For critical meetings, lobbyists will hire messengers to stand in line for them, sometimes all night, and then pack the hearing room. Members who receive financial or other support from groups affected by the legislation often face intense and direct pressure to vote a particular way in committee. Sometimes lobbyists mob members as they leave the hearing room.

Scheduling and Rules

Once a House committee approves a bill, it is placed on one of four "calendars," depending on the subject matter of the bill. The Senate has just two calendars: one for private and public bills and another for treaties and nominations. Bills from each calendar are generally considered in the order in which they are reported from committee. In the House, the Rules Committee sets the terms of the debate over the bill by issuing a rule on it. The rule either limits or does not limit debate and determines whether amendments will be permitted. A rule forbidding amendments means that members have to vote yes or no on the bill; there is no chance to change it. If the committee refuses to issue a rule, the bill dies.

In earlier years, the Rules Committee was controlled by a coalition of conservative Democrats and Republicans who used their power to block liberal legislative proposals, including, for decades, meaningful civil rights proposals. Under recent Republican control the committee was dominated by the Speaker and the majority leadership. The powers inherent in the speakership allow the majority leadership to use or bend rules to force measures to the floor, where only a simple majority is necessary for passage. House members have few tactical options against a Speaker who uses his full powers to set the rules. And Hastert was willing to use the rules, not only by holding open vote counts until the leadership could round up enough votes to win passage but by preventing amendments and other changes in the leadership-agreed-upon wording of bills. In 2003, 76 percent of all House bills were heard under restricted rules, compared with 15 percent in 1977.[65] And after Bush's reelection in 2004, Hastert announced he would let no bill come to a vote unless it had the support of a majority of House Republicans even though it might have bipartisan majority support. The practice of advancing bills only when a majority of Republican members favor them means that the leadership never had to negotiate their passage with the Democrats. This, of course, outraged the Democrats.

Because the Senate is a smaller body, it can operate with fewer rules and formal procedures. It does not have a rules committee. A lot of work is accomplished through the use of privately negotiated unanimous consent agreements, which allow the Senate to dispense with standard rules and define terms for the debating and amendment of a specific bill. As the Senate's workload has increased and its sense of collegiality has decreased, it has become more difficult to get opponents to accept a unanimous consent agreement. A few senators can and do delay or kill important bills.

In a closely divided Senate, where no party can have de facto control without a majority of sixty, the arm-twisting tactics that the House leadership can use to enforce party discipline cannot work for the Senate leadership. The rules do not allow for it, and senators are more high-profile figures than representatives, many with their own political aspirations; they cannot easily be dictated to, even by their own leadership.

Debate and Vote

Debate on a bill is controlled by the bill managers, usually senior members of the committee that sent the bill to the full chamber. The opposition, too, has its managers, who schedule opposition speeches. "Debates" are not a series of fiery speeches of point and counterpoint. They are often boring recitations delivered to sparse audiences, some of whom are reading, conversing, or walking around. In the House after the time allotted for debate is over, usually no more than a day, the bill is reported for final action. And if a bill is brought to the floor under a rule allowing no amendments, even a day's debate can lead to no more than an up-or-down vote on the bill as presented.

In the Senate there is no way other than by a unanimous consent agreement to limit debate and no restrictions on adding amendments. Opponents can add all sorts of irrelevant amendments to pending legislation. One senator held up an antibusing bill for eight months with 604 amendments. The other major mechanism for delay in the Senate is the **filibuster.** This is a continuous speech made by one or more members to prevent the Senate from taking action on a bill. Before 1917, only unanimous consent could prevent an individual from talking. Today a **cloture** vote of three-fifths of the members closes or ends debate on an issue thirty hours after cloture is invoked. Then the measure must be brought to a vote. The filibuster developed in the 1820s when the Senate was divided between slave and free states. Unlimited debate maintained the deadlock.[66] For over a century, the filibuster was used primarily to defeat civil rights legislation. It took a cloture vote to end seventy-three days of debate and get the 1964 Civil Rights Act to the floor for a vote.

Both liberals and conservatives use filibusters (as they do nongermane amendments). During Bill Clinton's first year in office, Republicans used the filibuster quite frequently to block proposals from the Democratic Senate majority. After Republicans took control of the Senate in 1995, Democrats returned the favor. As the senate Republican caucus has become increasingly conservative, those who are moderates and active in the Centrist Coalition have frequently broken ranks with the leadership, especially on budgetary measures and judicial nominations. Along with Democrats they have used their powers to filibuster and to place holds on nominations and certain other items of business to freeze the agenda.

Filibusters prevent domination and precipitous action by the majority. But by requiring sixty votes to end debate, they impede the majority's right to legislate and they contribute to gridlock.[67] Their use by Democrats to block Bush nominees to the federal courts drew such anger from the Republican leadership that in 2005 Majority Leader Frist, calling it "minority tyranny," threatened to abolish the filibuster by getting a simple majority to support it as a rules change, a threat Sen. Trent Lott dubbed "the nuclear option." A bipartisan group of Republicans and Democrats opposed this option, but in exchange for the Republicans' joining the alliance, Democrats agreed to reserve their use of the filibuster against Bush's court nominees for exceptional cases. The agreement did not apply to other uses of the filibuster.

When members finally cast their votes on major public bills, they are usually voting on the general aim of the bill without knowing its exact provisions. Rarely does any member read a bill in full. The texts of laws like the No Child Left Behind Act, the first PATRIOT Act, NAFTA, and the prescription drug benefit for seniors run from eight hundred to more than one thousand pages. The very complex USA PATRIOT Act, which had serious implications for civil liberties, was rushed through Congress in just a few weeks with virtually no member having read it. When a measure passes, it is sent to the other chamber for action.

Conference Committee

The Constitution requires that the House and Senate pass an identical bill before it can become law, and since this rarely happens, the two versions must be reconciled. Sometimes the chamber that passed the bill last will simply send it to the other chamber for minor modifications. But if the differences between the two versions are not minor, a **conference committee** is set up to try to resolve them. The presiding officers of each chamber, in consultation with the chairs of the standing committees that considered the bill, choose the members of the committee. Both parties are represented, but there is neither a set number of conferees nor a rule requiring an equal number of seats for each chamber. If the leaders of both parties are strongly committed to passing a version of a bill, they may negotiate the compromise themselves and essentially impose it on the committee. They may even negotiate the final version with the president to avoid a veto. These negotiations can also be planned by the White House with the intent to limit the wiggle room party leaders have to negotiate compromises.

Conference committees, or the individuals in control of them, have tremendous latitude in how they resolve the differences between the House and Senate versions of a bill. One aide to the Clinton White House described these committees as "no-man's-land" because there are no formal rules governing how they operate.[68] Sometimes a bill is substantially rewritten, and occasionally a bill is killed. As President Reagan once said, "an apple and an orange could go into a conference committee and come out a pear."[69] The power of conference committees to alter bills after their passage is why they are sometimes called the "Third House" of Congress.[70]

Once the conference committee reaches an agreement, the bill goes back to each chamber, where its approval requires a majority vote. It cannot be amended at that point so is presented to the membership on a take-it-or-leave-it basis. In the Senate, however, any individual member can challenge a provision added in conference that was not related to the original bill. In practice, both House and Senate accept most conference reports because members of both parties in each chamber have participated in working out the compromise version. However, in the years of unified government—in Clinton's first years and during most of the second Bush administration—minority parties often felt so blocked out of the negotiations that determined the final wording of a bill that they refused to sign on to conference committee reports.

Clearly, conference committees can be very influential in determining the final provisions in major legislation, yet the work they do happens almost completely out of public view. Knowing how to win a seat on a conference committee—that is, to participate in rewriting an important piece of legislation—is an essential skill for any legislator who wants to wield influence.

As should be clear from this overview of the complex legislation process, to be a successful member of Congress—to get bills passed or to keep them from being passed, to influence other members, or to rise to a position of leadership—a legislator must know how to use the inner workings of the legislative process. The conference committee is an important part of that process, as is the tactical use of a full range of parliamentary rules and procedures within the congressional system.

Presidential Action and Congressional Response

The president may sign a bill, in which case it becomes law. The president may veto it, in which case it returns to Congress with the president's objections. The president also may do nothing, and the bill will become law after ten days unless Congress adjourns during that period.

Most presidents have not used the veto lightly, but when they do, Congress does not usually override them. A two-thirds vote in each house is required to override a presidential veto. Congress voted to override only nine of former President Reagan's seventy-eight vetoes, only one of President George H. W. Bush's forty-six, and only two of Clinton's thirty-four. George W. Bush did not exercise his veto power until his sixth year in office and as of late 2007 has vetoed two bills.

Lawmaking by Committee

The division of labor provided by committees and subcommittees enables Congress to consider a vast number of bills each year. If every member had to review every measure in detail, it would be impossible to deal with the current workload. Instead, most bills are killed in committee, leaving many fewer for each member to evaluate before a floor vote. Committees also help members develop specializations. Members who remain on the same committee for some time gain expertise and are less dependent on professional staff and executive agencies for information.

But committee government also has disadvantages. By splitting off into subcommittees and developing expertise in a few areas, a House member runs the danger of being more responsive to narrow interests and constituencies and less responsive to national objectives when making national policy. Over time, members of congressional subcommittees develop close relationships with lobbyists for the interest groups and staff in executive branch agencies affected by their work. Over the years, these three groups—legislators, lobbyists, and bureaucrats, sometimes called an "iron triangle"—get to know each other, often come to like and respect one another, and seek to accommodate each other's interests. The lobbyists likely provide money to help fund the legislators' campaigns. These personal relationships can result in favorable treatment of special-interest groups.

The division of authority and the specialization of individual members have often made it difficult for

Congress to get things done. Most members of the majority party in the Senate and about half of those in the House chair committees or subcommittees. With their own bases of power, they have the potential to act independently from party leaders. This can make it difficult for the opposition party in Congress to mount a coherent alternative to the president and opens the possibility for members of the president's own party to block his initiatives.

Many of the reforms of the Gingrich era were aimed at stemming the flow of power to committees and their chairs and channeling it back to the leadership in hopes of ending gridlock and enforcing party government. The second Bush administration took this a step further by setting the legislative agenda in the White House and insisting that the congressional leadership enforce it. This attempt to shut down the bipartisan negotiating and compromise common to the legislative process led to Democrats being frozen out of committees and negotiations where traditionally the minority party played a role. This in turn led to another kind of gridlock when Democrats and dissenting (usually centrist) Republicans, frustrated by being marginalized, resorted to obstructionist tactics (filibusters, holds on nominations, denial of unanimous consent agreements) as their only means to affect the process. The process also corrupted the independence of Congress as a separate branch of government. With the Republican congressional leadership doing the bidding of the White House, the independent powers of Congress eroded as their desire to hold the executive branch accountable dwindled.

Oversight

As part of the checks-and-balances principle, it is Congress's responsibility to make sure that the bureaucracy is administering federal programs as Congress intended. This monitoring function is called **oversight** and has become more important as Congress continues to delegate authority to the executive branch. For a variety of reasons, Congress is not especially well equipped, motivated, or organized to carry out its oversight function. Nevertheless, it does have several tools for this purpose.

One tool is the Government Accountability Office, created in 1921 and known as the General Accounting Office until 2004. The GAO functions as Congress's watchdog in oversight and is primarily concerned with making sure that money is used properly.

Another method of oversight, albeit not a very effective one, is committee hearings. Members can quiz representatives from agencies on the operation of their agencies, but often the hearings go into great detail about some particular problem of minor importance and neglect broader policy questions. Scheduling conflicts and the pressure of other business often mean that a member's attention is not focused on committee hearings. Nevertheless, officials in agencies view hearings as a possible source of embarrassment for their agency and spend a great deal of time preparing for them. This is especially true when Congress decides, often for political reasons, to seek maximum media coverage for hearings.

This attempt at publicity points to one of the problems with the use of these proceedings to carry out the oversight function: hearings are often held after oversight has failed. This was painfully clear after the corporate collapses of 2002—of Enron, Global Crossing, and WorldCom, for example—when four Senate and three House committees held hearings in succession, all vying for media time. But if Congress had exercised oversight and had not weakened the regulatory clout of the Securities and Exchange Commission, these scandals might not have occurred, and some of the enormous costs to employees and investors might have been prevented. Prominent members of oversight committees, such as Joseph Lieberman (D-Conn.) and Christopher Dodd (D-Conn.), who represent a state where some of the failed businesses were headquartered and who had received large campaign contributions from them, actively worked to prevent new regulations from being adopted. Occurring after the failures, the hearings were more aftersight than oversight but served as a way for Congress both to consider remedial measures and to make it seem like it was doing something about the problem.

The incentive of committee members to place constituent protection and the interests of big campaign donors above rule enforcement is one weakness of oversight. But the fragmentation of oversight responsibility is also a problem. There were at least seven Senate committees and six House committees with some oversight responsibility for the accounting and financial practices that led to so many industry bankruptcies in 2002. And many more committees were responsible for oversight of the defense and intelligence agencies whose failures were so widely publicized after 9/11.

Congress can also exercise its oversight function through informal means.[71] One way of doing this is to request reports on topics of interest to members or committees. In a given year, the executive branch might prepare five thousand reports for Congress.[72] Moreover, the chair and staff of the committee or subcommittee relevant to the agency's mission are consulted regularly by the agency. But one can question whether any serious oversight is exercised informally. There are few electoral or other incentives for members to become involved in the drudgery of wading through thousands of pages of reports or for doing a really thorough job in any area of oversight, at least until a crisis arises or public confidence in the economy or government institutions is threatened.

The primary means for congressional oversight is its control over the federal budget. Congress can cut or add to agencies' budgets and thereby punish or reward them for their performance. Members with authority over an agency's budget can use that power to get benefits for their constituents, and by going along with the members' wishes, agencies may stand a better chance of having their budget requests approved. There is an incentive in this relationship for congressional committees to exercise oversight, but increasingly Congress has failed to do so. It has allowed authorizing legislation for agencies as important as the Consumer Product Safety Commission, the U.S. Commission on Civil Rights, the Corporation for Public Broadcasting, and the Federal Election and Trade Commissions, among others, to expire. The agencies continue to function because Congress waives budget rules to provide annual funding for them without oversight by authorization committees.[73]

If Congress has received low marks for gridlock in legislating, it has been absent without leave in carrying out much of its oversight function. Many members of Congress have made the charge themselves, especially with respect to oversight of intelligence operations and defense policy and appropriations. In the wake of 9/11, the Bush administration encouraged Congress to neglect oversight in these areas by arguing that the president needed a free hand to wage the war on terrorism.

Former Senator Rick Santorum (R–Pa.) explained the weakening of oversight in the Republican-controlled Congress as a party preference: "Republicans don't enjoy oversight—not nearly as much as Democrats—and so . . . we don't do as much."[74] However, that is untrue. Representative Howard Waxman (D-Ca.) pointed to House Republicans' willingness to take "more than 140 hours of testimony to investigate whether the Clinton White House misused its holiday card database but less than five hours of testimony regarding how the Bush administration treated Iraqi detainees."[75] In fact, during the years when Republicans had majorities in Congress, the decade between 1997 and 2006, of the 1015 subpoenas issued by congressional committees to provide testimony or documents for congressional hearings, 1000 were for investigations of actions taken by the Clinton administration and 15 for investigations of the Bush administration.[76] In other words, members of Congress would rather exercise oversight on presidents from the opposing party.

Many congressional experts concur that since Bush became president Congress's oversight work has withered. Time and again the White House has refused to let officials testify at committee hearings, denied access to records and reports, and stonewalled on turning over subpoenaed materials. One Congress watcher called it "the battered Congress syndrome," because "the more the White House or executive branch officials defy Congress or slap Congress around, the more Congress submits. When executive officials testify, they frequently make clear that they have no intention of giving Congress what it wants."[77]

This was clear when Congress tried to exercise its oversight function prior to the war by asking the CIA for a National Intelligence Estimate of the threat Iraq presented. Few members saw anything more than an executive summary of the report, and access to it was in a secure room under guard. Even then, only members of committees with oversight responsibility for intelligence and defense issues were briefed on the contents of agency assessments of Iraq's weapons of mass destruction capabilities and possible links to the al-Qaeda terrorist network. When these briefings were later found to be based on information provided by a handful of unreliable Iraqi expatriates and forged documents, many Senators in both parties were livid. So were many CIA officers who knew that House and Senate intelligence committees had never seen the much more accurate assessments contained in the uncensored reports sent to the White House.[78]

When the Democrats became the majority of both the House and Senate in 2007, they immediately began to investigate a range of behaviors of the bureaucracy and the Bush administration, from the treatment of prisoners in Guantanamo to the firing of U.S. attorneys by the Attorney General. At each point, the administration resisted congressional attempts to obtain information. In mid-2007, the Congress issued subpoenas for information relating to the apparent firing of the attorneys for political purposes.

Budget Making

The topic of budget making may be dull, but without money government cannot function. Real priorities are reflected not in rhetoric but in the budget. An increasingly large part of the job of Congress is to pass a budget. The Constitution gave budget powers to Congress, but in the 1920s, Congress delegated its authority to prepare the annual budget to the president (through the Office of Management and Budget, or OMB).

Congress is aided in budget review by the Congressional Budget Office (CBO), which provides expertise to Congress on matters related to both the budget and the economy. Before the establishment of the CBO, members of Congress felt they were junior partners in budget making because they had to depend on information provided by the president, his budget advisers, and the OMB. Because the CBO is responsible to both parties in Congress, it provides a less politically biased set of forecasts about the budget than the administration or the leadership of either party would.

Characteristics of Budgeting

Historically, congressional budgeting has had two basic characteristics. First, the process is usually incremental; that is, budgets for the next year are usually slightly more than budgets for the current year. Normally, Congress does not radically reallocate money from one year to the next; members assume that agencies should get about what they received the previous year. This simplifies the work of all concerned. Agencies do not have to defend, or members scrutinize, all aspects of the budget. Second, Congress tends to spend more in election years and in times of unemployment.

There are exceptions to these general rules, such as times of war or domestic crisis. The first budget submitted after 9/11, for example, requested a huge increase in defense spending. Thereafter the increases were far larger than the annual budgets show because most of the money for the wars in Afghanistan and Iraq was requested in "supplementals," special appropriations bills that authorize spending not included in the fiscal year budget.

Authorizations and Appropriations

Each year, Congress passes a budget resolution that sets a dollar amount of spending for the fiscal year, but money is not appropriated in a single piece of legislation. Since the 1970s, the budget has been divided and reviewed as separate bills, each of which focuses on a different area of expenditure, such as defense. All budget legislation goes through a process similar to but more complicated than other bills. To grasp the complexity, it is necessary to understand the distinction between budget authorizations and budget appropriations. **Authorizations** are acts that enable agencies and departments to operate, either by creating them or by authorizing their continuance. They also establish the guidelines under which the agencies operate. Although authorization bills might specify funding levels, they do not actually provide the funding. **Appropriations** are acts that give federal agencies the authority to spend the money allocated to them. Both authorization and appropriations bills must pass each house, and differences must be resolved in conference.

Typically, authorizations precede appropriations, although this is not always the case. Budgetary procedures are not defined in the Constitution but are determined by House and Senate rules, which can be, and often have been, changed. The standing committees that oversee the work of the agency or program being funded usually work out the authorizations. The House Interior and Insular Affairs Committee and the Senate Energy and National Resources Committee, for example, review the authorization of the Park Service in the Department of the Interior; the agricultural committees write authorizations for the Department of Agriculture. Close ties often exist between the agency being reviewed and the authorizing committee, which can cause proposed funding levels to be set without consideration of the overall demand on federal revenues. But the real power to limit spending rests with the House and Senate appropriations committees.

Each of the two appropriations committees has subcommittees corresponding to the functional areas into which budget allocations are divided (lumped together somewhat differently in the House and the Senate). The chair of the two appropriations committees and the ranking minority member (and the ranking majority member in the Senate as well) can sit as members of any or all of the subcommittees, adding to their power. The Appropriations Committee assigns a spending limit for each area, and the relevant subcommittee then decides how to apportion it among the agencies in its jurisdiction. The power of those who chair appropriations subcommittees is suggested by their nickname, "The Cardinals." In reviewing an agency's proposed budget, the subcommittee is not bound to fund it at the level requested in the president's budget proposal or the authorization bill. Nor do a subcommittee's funding proposals have to be accepted by the whole committee.

Although appropriations subcommittees may develop close ties with the agencies they review, the committee as a whole does not, and it may not be as generous as its subcommittees. In the bills it sends to the floor for a vote, the Appropriations Committee can increase or cut the previous year's funding levels, or it can eliminate an agency altogether.

The House and Senate also have subcommittee-free budget committees, whose membership in the House overlaps with that of Appropriations and Ways and Means and must include representatives from the leadership of both parties. The budget committees work with the CBO on big-picture issues such as economic forecasting and fiscal planning, including deficit management and controlling overall spending. The House Budget Committee prepares a budget proposal that sets out spending goals in the context of projected federal revenues. Budget committees are not as powerful as Appropriations and neither the House nor Senate committee can enforce the spending limits they recommend.

During the budgetary process, committees hold hearings, but these have become a sideshow to the main event. The real decisions are made in private negotiations, and budgets are produced after months of direct negotiations among congressional leaders, their staff, administration aides, individual members, and the president. The rest of Congress is often left with a take-it-or-leave-it budget package laid out in separate bills for each functional area (roughly eleven) or in several omnibus appropriations bills.

Problems with the Budget Process

Almost everyone is critical of congressional budget making. One reason is that members simply cannot agree on spending for any fiscal year; it is not unusual for the new fiscal year to begin before Congress has passed all the necessary appropriations bills. Then, under time pressure, they will lump spending into several omnibus bills in order to keep government operating. These cumbersome bills are difficult to decipher and make oversight by scrutiny of agency budgets very difficult.

Another problem is that Congress does not honor its own budget resolutions, which establish the amount of total spending for each fiscal year. Congress has frequently outspent the dollar limit that it set.[79] As emergencies or unforeseen needs arise, Congress passes supplemental spending bills such as for Iraq and Afghanistan or to deal with a natural disaster like Katrina.

Congress also now consistently violates the pay-as-you-go (paygo) rule that requires all new spending to be offset by a revenue source. The paygo rule, established at the end of the first Bush administration and observed throughout Clinton's presidency, was one of several key factors that made it possible to balance the budget in 2000. When George W. Bush took office, the budget was in surplus, and both he and the Congress abandoned paygo. By the end of Bush's first term, all of the supplemental spending on war and emergencies, in addition to much of the budgeted spending, came from borrowing—from the Social Security Trust Fund, private citizens, and increasingly from foreign governments.

Many members are troubled by the fact that for decades Congress has been slowly ceding budget-setting power to the executive branch. White House staff typically get involved in negotiating final dollar amounts with congressional leaders, but the Bush administration superseded the conventional congressional bargaining process here too, often working out final versions of appropriations bills with the Republican leadership before conference committees ever met.

Members on the Job

This section examines how members of Congress go about the day-to-day business of legislating, budget making, oversight, and constituency service, as well as carrying out party caucus- and campaign-related activities.

Negotiating the Informal System

To be successful, representatives and senators must not only serve their constituents and get reelected but must also know how to work with their colleagues and how to maneuver within the intricate system of parliamentary rules, customs, and traditions that govern the House and Senate.

Informal Norms

First among the many lessons every new member must learn are the customary ways of interacting with colleagues both on and off the floor of Congress.[80] These **informal norms** help keep the institution running smoothly by attempting to minimize friction and allowing competition to occur within an atmosphere of civility. As in other American institutions, the norms of Congress are changing.

The Founders' velveteen breeches, frock coats, and white wigs symbolized the drawing room gentility of their circle and helped to mask bitter rivalries. It was Thomas Jefferson, the best known of the gentlemen farmers, who in 1801 wrote the foundational rules for in-chamber conduct for members of the new Congress in an effort to contain the inevitable conflict between Federalist and Anti-Federalist, abolitionist and slave owner. His notes laid the groundwork for Congress's system of informal norms.

Throughout much of the twentieth century, the most important norm was institutional loyalty, the expectation that members would respect their fellow members and Congress itself, especially their own chamber. Personal criticism of one's colleagues was to be avoided, and mutual respect was fostered by such conventions as referring to colleagues by title, such as "the distinguished senator from New York," rather than by name.

In recent years, hostility among members seems as sharp as among those delegates to the First Congress, but scholars differ on the origins of this decline in civility. Some say it dates back decades to the time Democrats had a lock on both chambers, leaving Republicans permanently aggrieved. Some say it began with Watergate—that Nixon's enemies list and Congress's impeachment hearings poisoned the atmosphere. Others tie it to the hearings on the nominations of Robert Bork and Clarence Thomas to the Supreme Court, which were notorious for their overheated exchanges and character bashing. Still others trace the decline to Newt Gingrich's strategy as a minority tactician in the 1980s. He attacked not only the Democratic leaders but Congress as an institution (a severe departure from the institutional loyalty norm) in an attempt to sour the public on Congress so voters would be inclined to turn out incumbent Democrats. Once the Republicans captured control of the House and Gingrich became their leader, he encouraged an aggressive, combative style on the floor of the House.

The growth in partisan voting, illustrated in Figure 4, gives little support to the Democratic majority or Watergate explanations, though there was a small spike in 1974, the year of those investigations, but then partisanship returned to its formerly low levels. The voting data give more support to the Bork, Thomas, and especially the Gingrich explanations, since there was some increase in partisanship in 1987, at the time of the Bork hearing; in 1992 and 1993, after the Thomas hearings; and dramatically in 1995, after Gingrich became majority leader.

It was in this climate that Republicans launched the impeachment hearings against President Clinton, leaving many Democrats wanting revenge for what they felt was an outrageous diversion of time and energy from crucial business. Under Speaker Hastert's leadership, it seemed at first that there would be a trend toward more conciliation and civility in the conduct of House business. But in 2003, the Republican leadership, reinvigorated by gains in the midterm elections and determined to tighten procedural control over the House, called in the Capitol Police to break up a meeting of Democratic members. Several months later, Hastert broke House rules by holding a vote open for three hours while he rounded up the support needed to pass a Bush administration bill.

Although it is still the norm in Great Britain's House of Commons to hear members refer to one another as the "right honorable member" or "my right honorable colleague," never using personal names, today one is apt to hear much more informal and not particularly polite language when members of our Congress talk to and about one another and the institution. And even in the House of Commons, the formal terms of address are a veneer, as Labour and Conservative members sit on opposite sides of a narrow chamber floor hooting and shouting epithets at their fellow Honourables. However, this is a long and well-loved tradition in the House of Commons and not a modern manifestation of increased hostility.

The only reassuring aspect of this intense degree of congressional partisanship is that it is neither new nor destined to last. Congress passes through cycles of greater and lesser civility. Although they may be name-calling now, they are not beating up or shooting at one another as members were in the years leading up to the Civil War. And Jefferson's ears were hardly virgin; a frequent target of gossip and character attacks, he could dish with the best and used paid agents to spread slander about his Federalist opponents.

Specialization

By specializing, a member can become an expert, and possibly influential, in a few policy areas. Given the scope of Congress's legislative authority, members cannot be knowledgeable in all areas, so House members especially specialize in subject areas important to their home districts or related to their committees. The leader of one freshmen class of legislators advised his new colleagues, "If you've got twenty things you want to do, see where everything is. You'll find that maybe ten of those are already being worked on by people and that while you may be supportive in that role, you don't need to carry the ball. . . . If you try to take the lead on everything, you'll be wasting your time and re-creating the work that's already going on."[81]

The Senate's smaller membership cannot support this degree of specialization. In addition, some senators see themselves as potential presidential candidates who need to be well versed on a variety of issues.

Reciprocity

Tied to specialization is the norm of reciprocity. Reciprocity, or "logrolling," is summarized in the statement "You support my bill, and I'll support yours." Reciprocity helps each member get the votes needed to pass legislation favored in his or her district. The traditional way in which reciprocity worked was described by the late Sam Ervin, Democratic senator from tobacco-growing North Carolina: "I got to know Milt Young [then a senator from North Dakota] very well. And I

told Milt, 'Milt, I would just like you to tell me how to vote about wheat and sugar beets and things like that, if you just help me out on tobacco.'"[82] Reciprocity is another informal norm that is disappearing. Open meetings, media scrutiny, stronger party leadership, and more partisan voting have made it more difficult for members to "go along" on bills unpopular in their constituency or with the party leadership.

Making Alliances

Any member who wants to get legislation passed, move into the party leadership, or run for higher office needs to develop a network of allies among colleagues. Crossing ideological lines to find sponsors or votes for a bill is not uncommon. One of the most unusual alliances of recent years was between Sen. Hillary Clinton (D–N.Y.) and the Christian conservative Sen. Sam Brownback (R–Kans.), who joined forces to promote new measures to stop human trafficking, especially the selling of women and children into prostitution.

An increasingly common venue for cooperation among members, especially in the House, is the **special-interest caucus.** Caucuses are organized by members who share partisan, ideological, issue, regional, or iden-

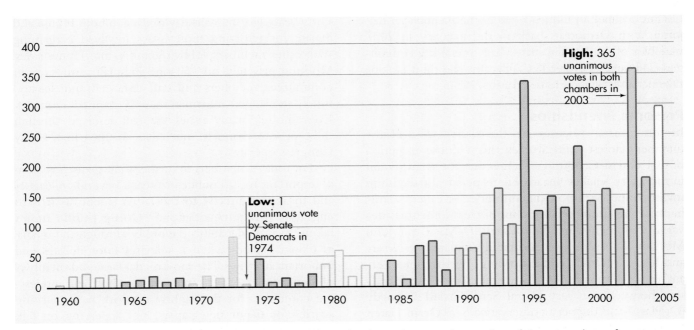

FIGURE 4 • **Partisan Voting Has Increased Significantly** *Shown here are the number of times members of one party unanimously opposed a majority of the other party on a roll-call vote in the House or Senate. These increasing numbers are a sign of hardened lines and heightened partisanship.*
SOURCE: *Congressional Quarterly Weekly Review,* January 3, 2004, 15.

tity interests to pool their strength in promoting shared interests and gaining passage of related legislation. Caucus size ranges from a handful to more than a hundred; almost every member belongs to at least one. The House and Senate have well over one hundred caucuses, many organized cross-chamber. Some caucuses have a narrow focus, such as those promoting bikes, ball bearings, boating, the wine industry, or wireless technology. Some are rooted in personal experience, such as the caucuses of Vietnam veterans and cancer survivors.

Among the most significant of the caucuses are those designed to pool the strength of women and minorities. They develop policy in key issue areas and serve national constituencies. The Caucus for Women's Issues, working across party, racial, and ethnic lines, has managed to recruit almost all women members and many male colleagues as well. With a Republican and a Democrat serving as cochairs, the caucus is regarded as one of the most bipartisan in Congress. Its legislative agenda includes supportive measures for woman-owned businesses, pay equity, and women in the military.

Hispanics, Asians, Native Americans, Asian Indians, and African Americans also have special-interest caucuses. The Black Caucus was organized in 1970 by thirteen House members determined to gain some clout. Today, all forty African Americans in the House are members. The Black Caucus declined in influence under the Republican majority. With Democrats back in the majority in 2007, members of the Black Caucus chair several key committees, and James Clymer (S.C.) became the third-ranking Democrat serving as House Majority Whip.

Personal Friendships

In some cases, caucuses are the source of a House member's closest political allies. But with the exception of its Centrist Coalition, caucuses are not as important in the much smaller Senate. There, personal friendships might count for more than committee or caucus membership, and strong relationships of trust sometimes develop across party lines. John Kerry (D-Mass.) and John McCain (R-Ariz.), two decorated Vietnam War veterans, became friends while working together on veterans' issues. A more unusual example is the close friendship between the very liberal Sen. Edward Kennedy (D-Mass.) and the very conservative Sen. Orrin Hatch (R-Utah). Sometimes the chair of a committee develops both a close working relationship and personal friendship with the ranking minority member, as for example between Senators Richard Lugar (R-Ind.) and

Joseph Biden (D-Del.) of Foreign Relations, or between Arlen Specter (R-Pa.) and Patrick Leahy (D-Vt.) of the Judiciary. In both houses, much of the work gets hammered out in personal conversations and exchanges away from official venues.

Political Action Committees

The most influential members of Congress now have their own PACs for raising campaign funds to disperse to colleagues. Hillary Rodham Clinton (D-N.Y.), a junior senator and former first lady, has been able to use her celebrity and connections to raise millions of dollars for her PAC, Friends of Hillary. By making donations to the reelection campaigns of colleagues, she has built a network of supporters whose chits she can cash in when looking for a committee chair, leadership position, or in a race for the presidency. Nancy Pelosi was able to beat out rivals for the minority leader position in 2001 due in large part to her phenomenal ability to raise and dispense campaign donations for colleagues. By the time she announced that she wanted the position, dozens of fellow House members were in her political debt. **Tom DeLay,** the very powerful former House majority leader, also built his clout by dispensing funds.

Using the Media

Forty years ago, the workday routine in both House and Senate for resolving most issues involved bargaining with other members, lobbyists, and White House aides. Working privately, one-on-one in small groups, or in committees, members and staff discussed and debated issues, exchanged information, and planned strategies. Even though many issues are still resolved through these private channels, much has changed in the way Congress operates.

For today's members to further their goals, it is often as important to "go public," to reach beyond colleagues and to appeal directly to the larger public, as it is to engage in private negotiation.[83] **Going public** means taking an issue debate to the public through the media, as Congress does when it televises floor debates and important hearings. The most media-oriented members of Congress are experts in providing short and interesting comments for the nightly network news, writing articles for major newspapers, and appearing on talk shows and as commentators on news programs.

With every congressional office wired for Internet access, members have not only a faster way to facilitate casework but a means for continual self-promotion.

Every district visit, town meeting, and photo-op is put up on the website immediately. Members with larger political ambitions may maintain their own listservs or blogs, but no one in Congress today has to wait for the press to come to them.

In the early days of television, networks broadcast only important congressional proceedings, such as the McCarthy hearings and testimony on investigations into the Watergate scandal and the Iran-Contra affair. In 1979, after considerable controversy and anxiety, the House began televising its proceedings. Fearful of being overshadowed by the House, in 1986 the Senate followed suit. But today exposure comes daily on C-SPAN (the Cable Satellite Public Affairs Network). Two of the three C-SPAN advertisement-free channels are available with almost all basic cable service and have almost thirty million viewers each week. Although viewership is small compared with commercial networks, the C-SPAN audience is better informed and more interested in both local and national government than the general public; nine out of ten viewers voted in the 2000 election.[84]

Local television listings provide times for daily coverage of House and Senate floor proceedings as well as for committee hearings and other official business. In addition, C-SPAN covers members of Congress on the campaign trail, attending fundraisers, giving stump speeches, and chatting with constituents. Besides its unbroken coverage of events, what sets C-SPAN apart from commercial network coverage of Congress is that there is no intermediary between the viewers and the events and people they are watching. C-SPAN does not use reporters, so televised events are free of commentary and on-the-spot analysis. This may be why C-SPAN is only one of three television new sources to be named as "most trusted" by Republicans, Democrats, and Independents.

The congressional leadership goes public, too. Leaders of both parties regularly call producers of television talk shows to suggest guests. They meet with the press and often have prepared statements. Before important congressional votes on key issues, the leadership plans letters to the editors of important newspapers and floor speeches designed for maximum television coverage.

Balancing the Work

Schedules
Multiple committee assignments, in combination with party caucus work, fundraising, and visits to the district, mean that members have impossible schedules. At times,

committees cannot obtain quorums because members are tied up with other obligations. Members attend meetings with legislative staff in tow to take notes and to consult with during hearings. If they cannot attend or have to leave for floor business or another meeting, a staffer is there to take notes and brief the member later.

Use of Staff
We have already noted the huge staff available to members. Staffers do most of the background work on the complex foreign and domestic issues that cross the members' desks every day, aided when deep expertise is needed by the Congressional Research Service staff. Through their service, staffers gain a great deal of experience and the opportunity to create a network of contacts that can help them should they decide to run for Congress, so it is not surprising that 107 members of the 109th Congress were former congressional staffers.[85]

Congress and the Public

As we have noted, one of the most frustrating things about Congress for the average citizen is the "messiness" of the legislative process. Not only is the process of crafting laws incredibly complex but it provides many places along the way where individual legislators and interest groups, often for seemingly (or truly) selfish motives, can exact concessions from the people who want to pass the bill. Add to that the partisan bickering, with Democrats picking a proposal apart simply because a Republican introduced it or vice versa, and casual observers throw up their hands in exasperation.

It seems that the more media exposure Congress gets, the less supportive the public is of its work. Now as never before, every step—or misstep—that members of Congress take is carried to every part of the nation. Or as one observer commented, "A member's every twitch is blared to the world, thanks to C-SPAN, open meetings laws, financial-disclosure reports, and every misstep is logged in a database for the use of some future office seeker."[86] And that was more than a decade ago; today we must add Blackberries, cell phones, YouTube, and blogs. Members must be aware that every public utterance is almost certainly being monitored by someone and that if it is the least bit newsworthy, it will soon appear in a blog or electronic newsletter.

Media attention is valuable, because we prize open government in a democracy. But too much is not so good, because in a heterogeneous society we rely on compromise to achieve our public goals, and under the harsh glare of media, there are fewer opportunities to compromise and deliberate without fear of losing votes back home.

The public has little patience for extended partisan debates even when they reflect real policy differences among the people. Of the three branches of government, the public has been least supportive of Congress, where the processes of democracy are exposed for all to see. The conflict and gridlock, if not admirable, are not surprising either, given our complex constituencies with competing interests and worldviews. But members contribute to the poor image by belittling colleagues and the institution itself when they seek reelection by running against "Washington."

For some years, the public gave its highest level of support to the Supreme Court, the institution that is most isolated from the public. Unlike legislative debates, little of the disagreement, negotiation, and compromise of the Court has taken place in public view. When the Court meddles in politics, as it did during the 2000 presidential election vote-counting controversy in Florida, its approval ratings decline. Confidence in the presidency and approval ratings for individual presidents can fluctuate wildly, as both Bushes discovered when their approval ratings fell from near 90 percent to the low 30's. A president's support can soar when acting as a national leader (chief of state), especially in wartime, then suffer huge losses as a political leader (head of government) when his policies fail.

The public's attitudes about Congress are also conflicted. In 2004, for example, two-thirds of the public approved of their own representatives, compared with just 41 percent who approved of Congress as a whole.[87] But occasionally the public gets so down on Congress that it affects constituents' attitudes toward their own representatives. Prior to the 2006 midterm elections, Congress's approval ratings stood at 23 percent and some voters expressed doubts about their own members.[88]

A major factor in Congress's low approval ratings is the public's perception that most members care more about power than about the best interests of the nation and more about pleasing lobbyists who can feed their campaign coffers than serving the interests of the district. The public is not mistaken in its impression of a cozy relationship between Congress and special-interest lobbies. Eight members of the 109th Congress worked as lobbyists before running for office, and between 1998 and 2005, 50 percent of the members who left the Senate and 40 percent who left the House became registered lobbyists.[89] Others work as "consultants" and are not required to register as lobbyists, and some members are married to, or have children working as, lobbyists. Ex-House members have had easy access to their former colleagues through their lifetime access to gym and dining facilities and the House floor—although they were prohibited from lobbying on the floor.

The 109th Congress (2005–06) was one of the most scandal-ridden in decades with members of both parties and hundreds of staff members accused of ethics violations for acceptance of gifts, free travel, and questionable campaign contributions from powerful lobbyists. The Republican chair of House Administration, who had close ties to Jack Abramoff, and a Democratic member of the powerful Ways and Means Committee, who was caught with thousands of dollars in his freezer—allegedly a bribe—were forced to give up their committee seats; and the thrice-censured, once-indicted majority leader Tom Delay resigned his leadership position and then his seat in Congress. Two of his top aides were convicted on corruption charges, also in connection with the Abramoff scandal. One of these aides used his time awaiting sentencing to complete a graduate thesis on the House ethics process. The congressional newspaper, The Hill, called it "irony on steroids," and it encapsulates the cynicism much of the public saw in the gap between Congress's rhetoric about ethics and its conduct.[90]

Despite all this, the public values the idea of Congress as a constitutionally mandated "people's house." It is the people in Congress and the way Congress works that the public dislikes. Just over half of all voters turn out for congressional elections (less in years when the president is not being elected), and most of the public is poorly informed about what Congress does. This pattern persists even with C-SPAN coverage and even though many local papers each week print a congressional scorecard with the voting records of local legislators. Constituents are much more likely to know about ethics violations and sexual improprieties of members of Congress than they are about the legislation passed in any session. The public evaluation of Congress as accomplishing "not much" or "nothing at all" stems in part from the public's lack of awareness of what Congress has actually done. However, in the 109th Congress very little actually was done; the House was in session for only 139 days in 2005 and the Senate for little more.

Conclusion: Is Congress Responsive?

Congress is certainly responsive to individual constituents, but is it responsive to the policy demands of the national constituency? The pressures of elections and of constituency service seem to undermine Congress's ability to focus on public policy. Pressure to be in the home district meeting constituents competes with legislators' desires to do a good job at lawmaking and to work more efficiently.

The public wants Congress to be responsive to its individual needs and group interests, but then it looks down on the institution for its pork-barrel politics and big spending. This is the perennial dilemma of representatives and senators: how to meet the demands of the district or state—that is to do the job members are sent to do—in order to get reelected and at the same time serve the national interest.

Pressure to raise money for reelection campaigns incurs obligations to interest groups that may not be consistent with either the members' or the constituents' views. Indeed, congressional leaders from both parties have problems articulating a clear vision in part because so many of them have become dependent on the contributions of PACs for their campaign funding. This puts them in the position of having to support some interests that are not consistent with voters' views or interests.

The procedures and organization of Congress also give individuals and small groups opportunities to block or redirect action. This is particularly true in the Senate, where procedures allow a minority of senators to engage in unlimited debate unless sixty members vote to stop it. The fragmented committee and subcommittee structure in both houses offers many venues in which action can be killed. Political parties have been strengthened in recent years, but neither party discipline nor institutional rules and norms, including ethics guidelines, have kept members from bowing to the pressure of lobbyists or outraged constituents. These factors mean that Congress continues to be more responsive to individual and group interests than to national needs.

The increasing partisanship in Congress has been one of the biggest changes since the mid-1990s. During George W. Bush's administration, the White House intervened heavily to press its policy agenda. Partisan voting hit a record high in 2003 as the legislative process became party dominated. Democrats were shut out of many important stages of the process, including the drafting of final versions of legislation in conference committees. This further heightened the partisan divisions and made the output of Congress less a product of compromise than it had been in earlier years and less responsive to the broader public. Legislation was the product of a single party and the group interests closest to its political base. As Democrats assumed control of Congress in 2007, they promised to restore bipartisanship to the legislative process.

Even in the best of times, Congress best represents those voters who identify with one of the two major parties, even though about a third of the public identify as independents or with a third party. This has complicated what was already a difficult process for the formulation of broadly responsive public policy, namely, the overweening influence of large campaign donors on voting on both sides of the aisle. It is difficult to get consistently good legislation when special interests, partisan concerns, and pork-hungry legislators dominate the lawmaking process. It is especially difficult when only the majority party is making the decisions.

Key Terms

Key Names

1. The Founders intended which branch to be dominant?
   a. The judiciary
   b. Congress
   c. The president
   d. The vice president
   e. The bureaucracy

2. Which is a not restriction on the ability to be elected to Congress?
   a. Must have been a citizen for seven years
   b. Must reside in the state you are elected from
   c. Must reside in the House district you are elected from
   d. Must be 25 to serve in the House
   e. Must be 30 to serve in the Senate

3. Term limits
   a. are less frequent than a decade ago.
   b. have been implemented by several states for their congressional representatives.
   c. are constitutional for congressional seats.
   d. a and b.
   e. a and c.

4. House districts
   a. vary in proportion to the state's population.
   b. are the same number for each state.
   c. are usually redistricted every five years.
   d. are based on population and geographical size.
   e. are drawn to take into account the number of citizens in the district, not illegal residents.

5. A gerrymander
   a. is an attempt to define representation.
   b. means that a district is very competitive.
   c. has not been the subject of judicial decisions.
   d. is an attempt to draw legislative districts to favor a party or group.
   e. is used for congressional districts but not for state legislative seats.

6. "Acting for" representation differs from descriptive representation in that
   a. acting for representation involves policies reflecting public wishes.
   b. acting for representation involves the legislature reflecting the demographic composition of the electorate.
   c. descriptive representation involves policies that describe the characteristics of the electorate.
   d. a and b.
   e. a and c.

7. In congressional elections
   a. challengers to House incumbents fare better than challengers to Senate incumbents.
   b. challengers to Senate incumbents fare better than challengers to House incumbents.
   c. challengers to House incumbents have about a 50 percent chance of winning.
   d. challengers generally spend nearly as much as incumbents.
   e. challengers to Senate incumbents have about a 50 percent change of winning.

8. Which is not a likely explanation for the Democrats' victories in the 2006 midterm elections?
   a. The public thought that the Democrats could do better fighting the war on terror.
   b. Republican congressional scandals took the focus off the Republicans' message in fall 2006.
   c. Public unhappiness with the Iraq War was on the upswing.
   d. Majorities of the public viewed the administration's handling of domestic issues, like the Katrina disaster, as incompetent.
   e. Republican attempts to link Democrats with terrorism no longer worked as well as in 2002 and 2004.

9. Which is true of congressional candidates?
   a. Incumbents in both houses win about 65 percent of the time.
   b. Challengers to Senate incumbents fare better than challengers to House incumbents.
   c. Challengers to House incumbents have about a 50 percent chance of winning.
   d. Challengers generally spend nearly as much as incumbents.
   e. Challengers to Senate incumbents have about a 50 percent chance of winning.

10. As of 2007, Nancy Pelosi was
    a. the Speaker of the House.
    b. the majority leader of the House.
    c. the majority leader of the Senate.
    d. the minority leader of the House.
    e. the minority leader of the Senate.

11. Joseph Cannon, Newt Gingrich, and Thomas Reed were each
    a. majority leaders of the House.
    b. majority leaders of the Senate.
    c. Speakers of the House.
    d. minority leaders of the Senate.
    e. majority leaders of the Senate.

12. In recent years, the most important leader of the Senate has been the
    a. vice president.
    b. president pro-tempore.
    c. majority leader.
    d. minority leader.
    e. chair of the Judiciary committee.

13. Markup sessions
    a. are composed of only the majority party.
    b. are opportunities for the minority party to mark up bills approved by the majority.
    c. are conducted after the bill has been approved in each house.
    d. are conducted by subcommittees considering the bill.
    e. are conducted by full committees considering the bill.

14. Which is **not** true of standing committee membership? Membership
    a. is by random assignment.
    b. differs in prestige from committee to committee.
    c. can help members build power bases for themselves.
    d. is assigned by parties.
    e. sometimes heightens members' conflicts of interests.

15. Congress in the mid-nineteeth century
    a. had U.S. Senators elected by popular vote.
    b. was a collaborative and peaceful group in the pre-Civil War era.
    c. had members serving more terms, in general, than in the late twentieth century.
    d. acted to lead to a peaceful resolution of the slavery issue.
    e. none of the above.

16. Lyndon Johnson, as a member of Congress, was well known for his
    a. leadership in the House of Representatives.
    b. remarkable ability to get agreement for his legislation as leader of the Senate.
    c. chairmanship of the Senate Rules Committee.
    d. ability to persuade fellow members to fund the Vietnam War.
    e. none of the above.

17. Significant differences between the House and Senate include
    a. the stricter rules of procedure in the Senate.
    b. the greater likelihood of House members becoming significant presidential candidates.
    c. the ability of Senators, but not members of the House, to filibuster.
    d. the greater importance of the Rules Committee in the Senate.
    e. the larger size of the Senate.

18. The constitutional provision giving Congress authority to make laws "necessary and proper" to carry out its other charges is
    a. an enumerated power of Congress.
    b. an implied power of Congress.
    c. a minor part of congressional power.
    d. a provision that allows Congress to abolish state powers.
    e. an amendment added after the Civil War.

19. Tools that Congress has to exercise oversight of the executive branch do not include
    a. congressional hearings.
    b. demanding reports from executive agencies.
    c. investigations by the GAO.
    d. investigations by the FBI.
    e. control of the budget.

20. In general, oversight of the executive branch by Congress from 2001 to 2006
    a. was very stringent.
    b. was very lax.
    c. was particularly effective in managing the Iraq War.
    d. was more active than congressional oversight during the Clinton years.
    e. was more effective than in previous administrations.

21. Which is not true of conference committees?
    a. They contain members of both parties.
    b. They have great power in shaping a bill.
    c. They are rare.
    d. They are appointed by the president.
    e. Their chairs are chosen by seniority.

22. A filibuster
    a. is often used by a majority.
    b. is sometimes used by an intense minority.
    c. was used frequently in the early twentieth century by pro-civil rights supporters.
    d. was not used in the debate over the 1964 Civil Rights bill.
    e. can never be stopped.

23. A president's veto
    a. can be overridden by a two-thirds vote.
    b. can be overridden by a simple majority.
    c. can never be overridden.
    d. has been used frequently by George W. Bush.
    e. can be used to veto a single item in a bill.

24. Which is **not** true about budgeting in Congress?
    a. It is an incremental process.
    b. Pay-go provisions are strictly followed.
    c. It is dominated by leaders, important committees, and the executive.
    d. It gives significant power to appropriations committees.
    e. It often results in omnibus bills with many funding provisions.

25. Funding for congressional campaigns
    a. is provided at taxpayers expense.
    b. is effectively regulated so that most funds come from small donors.
    c. while regulated, allows large donors many ways to give.
    d. has never been regulated by federal law.
    e. effectively eliminates non-party groups from spending to help candidates.

Key: 1-b; 2-c; 3-a; 4-a; 5-d; 6-a; 7-b; 8-a; 9-b; 10-a; 11-c; 12-c; 13-d; 14-a; 15-e; 16-b; 17-c; 18-b; 19-d; 20-b; 21-c; 22-e; 23-a; 24-b; 25-c

As commander in chief, George W. Bush took America into war with Iraq. This image is comprised of photos of the first 609 American troops killed there.

President John Kennedy received a call from Senator Everett Dirksen (R-Ill.), who was the minority leader in the Senate, requesting a favor. An aide to former president Dwight Eisenhower was under investigation for income tax evasion and would be indicted (formally charged) the next day. Eisenhower's wife Mamie was a close friend of the aide's wife, and she worried that the aide might commit suicide as a result. The former president didn't know the new president, so he asked his friend and fellow Republican, Dirksen, to request a favor. "I'd like you to ask President Kennedy, as a personal favor to me, to put the . . . indictment in the deep freeze. . . . [A]dvise him he'll have a blank check in my bank if he will grant me this favor."

When Dirksen relayed the request to Kennedy, the president said that he had no knowledge of the matter but would grant the favor. He called his brother Robert, the attorney general, and told him not to sign the indictment. His brother objected: "This will destroy us politically, to grant a special favor to a tax evader." The exchange between the two got hot. Finally, the president told his brother, "I'm president. If you can't comply with my request, then your resignation will be accepted."

Weeks later, the nuclear test ban treaty with the Soviet Union was pending in the Senate. Approval required a two-thirds vote in that chamber, which is always difficult to obtain, and was especially difficult to obtain at the height of the Cold War. Americans didn't trust the Soviets, and conservatives claimed the Soviets would defeat us if the treaty were approved and implemented. A White House aide informed the president that a head count showed the treaty falling short of a two-thirds majority.

Kennedy called Dirksen. "Ev, I must write a check on you and Ike. This atomic treaty is important to me and to the country and, I think, to all mankind. It's imperative that it be approved. Ike said I had coin in his bank, and you say I have coin in yours." Kennedy asked Dirksen to reverse himself and support the treaty. He also asked Dirksen to get Eisenhower to endorse the treaty before the Senate voted. Then, "We'll call it square on that other matter."

With public support from the Republican leader in the Senate and from the former president, who remained popular, enough Republicans joined the Democrats to forge a two-thirds majority. By swapping favors, the president got his treaty.[1]

Pharaohs, consuls, emperors, kings, queens, tsars, prime ministers, and various councils served as executives in other governments before 1789. But no country's government had a president, an elected executive with authority equal to and independent of a national legislature, until **George Washington** became the first president of the United States.

The Founders didn't expect the Presidency to be a very powerful office. Some leaders were reluctant to serve. Washington had to be coaxed out of retirement at his Virginia plantation to lend his esteemed reputation to the fledgling government.

Today, however, the president is universally regarded as the most powerful person in the world. When he enters a room, everyone stands. When he appears at ceremonial functions, the band plays "Hail to the Chief." Wherever he goes, a military aide carries the nuclear "suitcase" containing descriptions of options, protocols, and authentication codes in case he has to launch a nuclear attack. The president is so powerful that some scholars and commentators speak of the **"imperial Presidency."**[2]

Nevertheless, all presidents become frustrated with the limits on their power. At times, they feel that they're saddled with an **"impossible"** or "imperiled" **Presidency**.[3]

Consider the past two presidents. **Bill Clinton** saw his agenda, aside from economic policy and welfare reform, sidetracked by one congressional investigation after another and found himself impeached for lying about a sexual affair. But **George W. Bush,** with a boost from public support after 9/11, started two wars, adopted numerous policies restricting civil liberties, and passed major tax cuts. The Clinton terms suggested an impossible Presidency, whereas the Bush years have sparked renewed talk about an imperial Presidency.

In this chapter, we'll consider the paradox of presidential power and presidential weakness.

George Bush Presidential Library

America does not have a monarchy, but it does have political dynasties. George W. Bush is shown here with his father George H. W. Bush, who served as president and whose father served as a U.S. senator.

Eligibility and Tenure

The Constitution specifies only three conditions to be eligible for the Presidency: one must be a "natural-born citizen," a U.S. resident for at least fourteen years before taking office, and at least thirty-five years old.

Historically, it has helped to be a white male with roots in small-town America; a Protestant with ancestry from England, Germany, or Scandinavia; a resident of a populous state; and a "good family man." In recent decades, this profile has broadened considerably as society

has become more inclusive, the electorate more diverse, and social norms more tolerant of divorce, but sexual, racial, and religious barriers remain. It's not clear whether a woman or a nonwhite could get elected. Although a Catholic (John Kennedy, 1960) has been elected, and a Jew (Joe Lieberman, 2000) has run for vice president, it's clear that a nonbeliever could not get elected today. It's also clear that a gay or lesbian could not get elected yet.

Traditionally, it has helped to be a common man or at least to evoke a common touch. In 1840, William Henry Harrison campaigned as a frontiersman born in a log cabin. Yet he came from an elite family with a Virginia plantation.[4] The "log cabin myth" persisted for years, as candidates who may never have seen a log cabin claimed to have been born in one.[5] Although nine of the ten presidential nominees from the major parties since 1988 have a degree from Harvard or Yale,[6] the public expectations for a common touch continue. George W. Bush, a true blueblood,[7] bought his Texas ranch to convey a cowboy image one year before beginning to campaign for president.[8] In 2004, John Kerrey was derided as an eastern elitist, partly because he spoke French and enjoyed skiing and windsurfing.

Tenure and Succession

Presidents serve four-year terms. The Twenty-second Amendment limits them to serving two terms (or ten years if they complete the term of an incumbent who dies or resigns). Four presidents died from illness (Harrison, Taylor, Harding, and Franklin Roosevelt), and four were assassinated (Garfield, McKinley, Lincoln, and Kennedy).

Presidents can be removed from office by **impeachment** and conviction. The House impeaches—that is, brings the charges against the president—if it finds evidence of "treason, bribery, or other **high crimes and misdemeanors.**" The latter part of this constitutional phrase sows confusion. It doesn't mean all crimes ("high crimes" for our felonies and "misdemeanors" for our misdemeanors). Rather, the language, which was borrowed from English usage, means serious crimes or political abuses, such as violating the Constitution.[9] As a practical matter, however, "high crimes and misdemeanors" means whatever Congress at any time decides it means. As one attorney general declared, "You don't need evidence; all you need is votes."[10] Thus the Republican Congress impeached President Clinton for lying about a sexual affair with intern Monica Lewinsky.[11] After the House brings the charges, the Senate decides whether to remove the president from office. Although the House needs a simple majority to impeach, the Senate needs a two-thirds majority to remove from office.[12]

The Founders intended impeachment as part of the system of checks and balances, a weapon against abuses of power. It wasn't designed for partisan purposes. To guard against this possibility, the Founders divided the power between the House and the Senate. If trying the charges were left to the popularly elected House, Alexander Hamilton wrote in the *Federalist Papers,* "there will always be the greatest danger that the decision will be regulated more by the comparative strength

of parties, than by the real demonstrations of innocence or guilt."[13]

Only three presidents have been targets of extensive impeachment proceedings.[14] Andrew Johnson (1865–1869), who came to office after Abraham Lincoln's assassination, was a southerner and unpopular member of his own party. He was impeached in a dispute over Reconstruction policies in the post–Civil War South. He was spared removal by a single vote. **Richard Nixon** (1969–1974) was investigated for abuse of power and obstruction of justice stemming from the **Watergate scandal.** (The House also had evidence that Nixon cheated on his income taxes, but members decided not to pursue that charge because it wasn't a major crime or a political abuse of power.)[15] He was spared certain impeachment—the House Judiciary Committee had voted to impeach, but the whole House hadn't voted yet—and near-certain removal by resigning. Bill Clinton was impeached by the House but not removed

At few times in American history have five ex-presidents been alive at once. This early 1990s photograph shows, from left, Richard Nixon (1969–1974), Gerald Ford (1974–1977), Jimmy Carter (1977–1981), Ronald Reagan (1981–1989), and George H. W. Bush (1989–1993).

by the Senate. Of these impeachments, Nixon's was the most bipartisan.

Should a president die, resign, be removed, or become incapacitated, the Constitution stipulates that the vice president takes over. But what if the Vice Presidency is vacant, a situation that has occurred eight times?[16] When Lincoln was assassinated and Johnson was elevated to the Presidency, there were no provisions for replacing the vice president. (Had Johnson been removed in the impeachment process, the president pro tempore of the Senate would have become president, according to the rules in effect at the time.)

Not until the death of Franklin Roosevelt had put the unknown Harry Truman (1945–1953) into the White House, did Congress pass the Presidential Succession Act. It established the order of succession should both the president and vice president be unable to serve. The list begins with the Speaker of the House, followed by the president pro tempore of the Senate and the secretaries of the cabinet departments in the order in which the departments were created. The Succession Act has never been used because we have always had a vice president when something has happened to the president.

To ensure that this situation is always the case, the Constitution was amended in 1967. The Twenty-fifth Amendment directs the president to name a vice president acceptable to majorities in the House and Senate if the Vice Presidency becomes vacant. This amendment has been used twice. Nixon chose Gerald Ford to replace Spiro Agnew, who resigned after pleading no contest to charges of taking bribes when he was a public official in Maryland. After Nixon resigned and Ford became president, Ford named Nelson Rockefeller, the former governor of New York, as his vice president.

The Twenty-fifth Amendment also charges the vice president and a majority of the cabinet—or some other body named by Congress—to determine, when there is doubt, whether the president is mentally or physically incapable of carrying out his duties. This provision was meant to cover situations in which it is unclear who is acting as president. When James Garfield was shot in July 1881, he didn't die until mid-September, and he was completely unable to fulfill his duties during this period. Woodrow Wilson had a nervous collapse in the summer and a stroke in the fall of 1919, and he was partially incapacitated for seven months. No one was sure about his condition, however, because his wife restricted access for government officials and kept information from the public.

Under the amendment's provisions, the vice president becomes "acting president" if the president is found mentally or physically unfit to fulfill his duties.[17] Ronald Reagan and George W. Bush followed the spirit of this section. Before they underwent surgery, they sent their vice president a letter authorizing him to act as president while they were unconscious.

The succession issue arose again after the terrorist attacks of 2001 when the Bush administration, just hours after the attacks, activated an emergency plan established during the Eisenhower administration (1953–1961) to provide for continuity of government in case of a nuclear attack. A shadow government of seventy-five to one hundred senior executive branch officials (serving in rotation) operated from a secret fortified location outside the capital where they lived and worked underground twenty-four hours a day.

Now let's turn to the heart of the chapter and examine presidential power.

Growth of the Presidency

The Founders' Expectations

The American colonists chafed under the strong executives—the British king and the royal governors—who exercised authority over them. When the colonists gained their independence and drafted the Articles of Confederation, they made sure that the new government had no strong executive. In fact, it had no separate executive; the legislature wielded executive, as well as legislative, power. But the new government was too weak, incapable of resolving either domestic or foreign crises. So when the Founders drafted the Constitution, they created a separate executive, and they gave this executive, the president, substantial power. Yet their memories of British rule were still fresh. The Founders rejected proposals for a monarchy or anything akin to a monarchy. They wanted a government with a stronger executive than under the Articles but a weaker executive than under the British. Consequently, the Founders intended the legislature, Congress, to be the strongest branch and the executive to be the second strongest. They expected the judiciary, the federal courts, to be the weakest branch.

At its inception, the Presidency was a relatively weak office in an infant country with few international ties and no standing army. John Quincy Adams (1825–1829) reflected the relatively low status of the job when he remarked, "No man who ever held the office would congratulate another on attaining it."

Congressional Government

The Founders' expectations were borne out for many years. Throughout the nineteenth century, except during the Civil War, the real power at the national level resided in Congress, so much so that Woodrow Wilson, who was a political scientist before becoming president, characterized our national government as a "congressional government."[18]

Consequently, between Andrew Jackson in the 1830s and Franklin Roosevelt in the 1930s, most men who sought the Presidency were "ordinary people, with very ordinary reputations"[19]—for example, John Tyler and Zachary Taylor (or was it Zachary Tyler and John Taylor?). There were powerful exceptions, such as Abraham Lincoln, Theodore Roosevelt, and Woodrow Wilson, and a few with exceptional achievements before their presidencies, such as Ulysses Grant (1869–1877) and Herbert Hoover (1929–1233), who fared badly in the White House.

Presidential Expansion

Although Congress was dominant, the Presidency gradually gained power. Critical events, such as wars and depressions, fueled the demands for emergency power. After the crises passed, presidential power rarely returned to "normal" levels. Bold presidents also expanded presidential power.

In the nineteenth century, **Thomas Jefferson** (1801–1809) was offered an opportunity to purchase the Louisiana Territory, but he fretted that doing so would exceed presidential authority. Yet the territory was so desirable that he had the Treasury purchase it anyway.[20] Although ranked as a "near-great" president, Jefferson never considered the office, or his performance in it, very important. His instructions for an epitaph listed what he thought were his three main accomplishments in life—writing the Declaration of Independence and Virginia's religious freedom law and founding the University of Virginia. **Andrew Jackson** (1929–1837) claimed to be "the direct representative of the American people," unlike his predecessors who didn't consider themselves as having a popular constituency. Dubbed "the people's president," he was the first to act to fulfill a popular mandate from a presidential election.[21] He was also the first to veto a bill because he didn't like it. Previous presidents had vetoed a bill only when they thought it was unconstitutional.

Teddy Roosevelt called the Presidency a "bully pulpit" from which he could persuade both legislators and the public to support his programs.

Abraham Lincoln (1861–1865) assumed extraordinary powers during the Civil War, raising and financing an army while Congress was out of session, blockading southern ports, imposing martial law, suspending habeas corpus (which prevents illegal detentions), arresting southern sympathizers, censoring critical newspapers, jailing their editors; and all along interpreting the Constitution to say that the Union was indivisible.

In the twentieth century, **Teddy Roosevelt** (1901–1909) used the Presidency as a "bully pulpit" to challenge corporate power and to advocate labor reform and an improvement in living conditions for average Americans. He also saw an imperial role for the United States in world politics, especially through military expansion, and led the country into "entangling alliances," which George Washington had warned against. Roosevelt constantly pushed back the boundaries of presidential power. When he desired to send the American fleet around the world, as a display of our military might, Congress balked at the cost. So Roosevelt announced that he had enough money in his budget to send the fleet halfway around the world and that if Congress wanted the fleet to return home, it could appropriate the rest of the money. **Woodrow Wilson** (1913–1921) led us into a major war, World War I, and envisioned an international organization that could prevent further world wars. His vision gave birth to the League of Nations, which was the forerunner of the United Nations.[22]

The Depression and Franklin Roosevelt

But it was **Franklin Delano Roosevelt** (1933–1945) who presided over the greatest expansion of presidential power. As Chapter 2 explained, the Great Depression led to a tremendous increase in the size and scope of the federal government. It also led to a significant increase in the power of the Presidency itself.

Roosevelt was elected because Americans hoped he would help them through the crisis. In his first inaugural address, he told people that he would ask Congress for "broad executive power," equivalent to the authority that would be granted if an enemy had invaded the country, to fight the Depression. The flurry of New Deal legislation and programs led to an expansion of the executive branch because new agencies were created and new bureaucrats were hired. The president became more important as a policy maker and a manager. And after the United States entered World War II, Roosevelt assumed additional authority as a hands-on commander in chief.

Roosevelt used radio to extend his power. An integral part of national life by the 1930s, radio gave people a way to follow their presidents and presidents a way to sell their policies. Radio newscasts focused on the president, and his "fireside chats" drew more attention to himself and his policies. Through radio, Roosevelt became a national cheerleader, a one-man band of optimism, persuading the public that solutions were at hand. As his campaign song promised, "Happy Days Are Here Again." Roosevelt's experience showed how the broadcast media—radio, and television when it became popular in the 1950s—would enhance presidential power by making the president the focal point of the government.

Roosevelt was elected for an unprecedented four terms. The country had come a long way from the era of George Washington, who refused to run for a third term because he thought it wouldn't be healthy for democracy if one person accumulated vast power.

After the Depression and the war ended, most Americans gave Roosevelt credit for pulling the country through. Ever since, the public has expected strong presidents.[23]

An Imperial Presidency?

Roosevelt's successors had little opportunity to shrink the Presidency. With the United States emerging from World War II as the preeminent world power and with the Cold War replacing the hot war as the foreign policy challenge, Congress was willing to cede even more authority to presidents to counter the Soviet threat. Responsibilities as the chief diplomat and commander in chief of the world's largest military would make the president a principal actor on the world stage.

The Vietnam War, a small conflict magnified by the Cold War, led to concerns about excessive presidential power. Presidents Kennedy, Johnson, and Nixon all waged war in Vietnam—the use of American troops started during the Kennedy administration, continued through the Johnson and Nixon administrations, and ended during the Ford administration—sometimes in secret and most times without input from Congress.

Theodore Roosevelt Collection, Harvard College Library

Teddy Roosevelt's Presidency marked the emergence of the United States as a world power. Roosevelt built up the navy, as this illustration from the time portrays. He said the United States should wield "a big stick."

While waging the war, President Johnson also marshaled his power for a highly ambitious legislative agenda, and President Nixon claimed vast power under a very expansive constitutional interpretation. Nixon said such power was necessary for "national security," even when there was little threat to national security. He also engaged in the illegal activities that collectively would become known as the Watergate scandal—break-ins; phone taps; unauthorized use of government agencies, from the IRS to the FBI and CIA, to retaliate against administration critics; and then obstruction of justice in covering up the evidence of these acts. The back-to-back presidencies of Johnson and Nixon prompted talk about an imperial Presidency.

Reaction against arrogant presidential power led to the modest presidencies of Gerald Ford (1974–1977) and Jimmy Carter (1977–1981). But Americans' preference for such presidents was short-lived. Ford, who became president when Nixon resigned, couldn't get elected, and Carter couldn't get reelected. Their successors—Ronald Reagan (1981–1989), George H. W. Bush (1989–1993), and Bill Clinton 1993–2001)—all tried to exercise considerable power.

However, under Clinton the Presidency seemed to be imploding. Paula Jones, a former employee of Arkansas' state government, sued Clinton for conduct—allegedly sexual harassment—that occurred when he was governor. Even though the suit wasn't brought until he was president, the Supreme Court ruled that he had no immunity while in office because the conduct occurred before taking office.[24] The justices doubted that a suit would command the attention and time he needed to carry out his duties. This was a colossal misjudgment.[25] The suit not only consumed the attention and time of the president but also diverted the attention of the media and the Washingtonians from his efforts to implement his policies. Critics wondered whether this precedent would encourage aggrieved individuals to sue future presidents for partisan reasons and hamstring the Presidency.[26]

Meanwhile, the Republican majority in Congress, reflecting a combination of moral principles, personal enmity, and partisan rivalry, was opposed to Clinton, even contemptuous of him, demanding special prosecutors and launching ethics investigations, which led to sensational headlines and constant scrutiny of the first family's private lives. The attacks culminated in Clinton's impeachment. The president considered his survival to be his greatest accomplishment, protecting future presidents and the political system itself from partisan-inspired impeachment attempts. Some historians worried that Clinton's impeachment would leave a legacy similar to Andrew Johnson's, which weakened the Presidency for the next half-century.[27] Now, however, it appears that the diminution of the office was temporary and that the Presidency will suffer less than Clinton's reputation.

The Bush Presidency

The Bush Presidency (2001–2009) shows how elastic the institution is. Under Bush, the Presidency has experienced a vast increase in power and sparked renewed talk about an imperial Presidency.[28]

George W. Bush and Vice President Dick Cheney, who long favored a strong Presidency and an opaque rather than open government,[29] came into office believing that the power of the Presidency had eroded since Vietnam and Watergate. They began exploring how they could use the power of the office to bolster the Presidency against congressional oversight, judicial review, and public scrutiny.

Early in Bush's first term, the 9/11 attacks gave the administration the rationale it needed to claim more latitude for unilateral action by a "wartime" president. Following Cheney's lead, Bush demanded the power to take any action he deemed necessary to protect the American people. In search of a legal basis for the sweeping measures they were taking, Bush and Cheney had administration lawyers reinterpret the constitutional limits on presidential power.[30] Calling their reinterpretation the "**New Paradigm**" (*paradigm* means a model or a way of looking at things), the lawyers concluded that a president, using his authority as commander in chief, can take any action he deems necessary for national security without any involvement, oversight, or restriction by Congress or the courts.[31]

At the same time, the lawyers proposed a very broad conception of the president's role as chief executive officer. They argued that the Constitution created a **"unitary executive,"** making the president the sole head of the executive branch with the authority to direct the work of its employees without interference.[32] His directions to federal bureaucrats supersede any directions from congressional laws. His actions are subject to his, rather than the courts', interpretation of the Constitution. Therefore, because the Pentagon and intelligence agencies are in the executive branch, the president has the authority to collect any intelligence— open mail and e-mail, scrutinize bank accounts, seize library records, and wiretap phone calls—as he sees fit, regardless of congressional laws or judicial rulings.

This authority complements the administration's claim, under the "New Paradigm," of unilateral warmaking authority that allows the president to declare any person an enemy combatant, detain the person for an indefinite time without bringing charges or allowing access to lawyers or courts, interrogate the person under rules set by the president independent of international laws and treaties, and try the person by a tribunal outside the military justice system. The president can take all these actions, according to "New Paradigm" reasoning, without congressional oversight or judicial review.

These claims are breathtaking. According to one Republican legal adviser, Bush has "staked out powers that are a universe beyond any other administration."[33] Indeed, they are far beyond the Nixon administration.

Yet, in the political climate following direct attacks on the country, and anticipating more attacks in the future, Congress acquiesced to most of the president's demands. The Republican majority, seeing itself as part of "the Republican team" running a unified government, was loath to challenge the president. Thus Congress was unwilling to exercise its constitutional responsibilities, in our system of separation of powers and checks and balances, to oversee executive branch actions.

The administration's interpretation of the Constitution and the administration's exercise of vast power are especially troubling because of the nature of the "war on terrorism." Such a war has no foreseeable end. As long as people, in one place or another, have grievances, and as long as they resort, in one form or another, to terrorism, the "war on terrorism" can be maintained— and the emergency powers in the hands of the American president can be exercised.

Presidential Power versus Congressional Power

Both presidential power and congressional power have grown as the federal government has grown. However, presidential power has grown relative to congressional power because the Presidency has inherent advantages over Congress.

The president is one person, whereas Congress includes 535 members who are divided into two houses and hundreds of committees and subcommittees. Congressional leaders struggle to develop and articulate policy goals acceptable to their party and their members, and then they struggle to keep the members committed to the goals. While the members of Congress talk and negotiate, the president can decide and act. The president can also attract the attention of the media, which focus on the single president rather than on the multiple members of Congress. Hence the White House gets a bigger megaphone.

In addition, the president has more information, collected by the huge bureaucracy of the executive branch. In foreign affairs, the president has a monopoly, or near monopoly, of information from the intelligence agencies. The president can keep this information secret, revealing as much as necessary to persuade the members of Congress and the public. The president can distort classified information, or falsely claim the existence of classified information, to make his case. In the run-up to the Iraq War, the administration insisted that Iraq had weapons of mass destruction. Secretary of Defense Donald Rumsfeld said the administration even knew where the weapons were. (But no WMDs were found, there or anywhere.) Secretary of State Colin Powell said the administration had evidence that Iraq bought uranium from Niger to use in nuclear weapons. Yet the administration knew this assertion wasn't true.

Despite these advantages, presidential power shouldn't be exaggerated. A prominent presidential scholar reminds us, "The Presidency is not the government. Ours is not a presidential system."[34] Rather, "the most outstanding feature of the American system is the separation of powers."[35] Thus Congress, as a coequal branch of government, has its own power.

So the balance of power swings like a pendulum, depending upon major events at the time, the personality of the president, and the composition of Congress. Sometimes the Presidency is dominant, sometimes Congress is dominant, and other times the two are evenly matched.[36]

Now let's turn to the functions presidents perform and the roles they play, as we further examine presidential power.

Presidential Leadership

Presidents derive their official authority from four sources—explicit powers, which are stated in the Constitution; implicit (or implied) powers, which are implied in the explicit powers; inherent powers, which aren't in

When President Franklin Roosevelt died, most Americans felt a personal loss. Here Chief Petty Officer Graham Jackson plays "Nearer My God to Thee" as the president's body is carried to the train that returned him to Washington for burial.

the Constitution, explicitly or implicitly, but are considered to be a national executive's prerogatives; and delegated powers, which are granted to Congress by the Constitution but given to the president by various statutes. With these powers, presidents play various roles—the head of state, chief executive, fiscal leader, legislative leader, diplomatic and military leader, and party leader.

Head of State

The **head of state** is the official representative of a country and its people. He or she symbolizes the identity and the unity of the nation. In the United States, the president is the head of state. In this capacity, he performs various nonpolitical functions, especially at ceremonial occasions, such as lighting the White House Christmas tree; opening the baseball season; greeting foreign visitors to this country; or attending the swearing in, coronation, or funeral of foreign dignitaries.

The president is also the **head of government.** In this capacity, he is the leader of a political party with a partisan agenda. For these dual roles to be combined in one person is unusual. In most Western democracies, the state and the government are separate entities headed by different officials. The head of state may be a

In 2000, at C-SPAN's request, fifty-seven historians and presidential scholars rated the presidents on ten personal and professional qualities: economic management, moral authority, crisis leadership, public persuasion, relations with Congress, international relations, administrative skills, vision and agenda setting, pursuit of equal justice, and performance in the context of their time. Their overall ranking of the top ten and bottom five was arrived at by averaging those scores. (George W. Bush wasn't rated yet.)

Top Ten (in order)

1. Abraham Lincoln
2. Franklin D. Roosevelt
3. George Washington
4. Theodore Roosevelt
5. Harry S. Truman
6. Woodrow Wilson
7. Thomas Jefferson
8. John F. Kennedy
9. Dwight D. Eisenhower
10. Lyndon B. Johnson

Bottom Five

41. William Henry Harrison
40. Warren G. Harding
39. Franklin Pierce
38. Andrew Johnson
37. James Buchanan

SOURCE: C-SPAN survey, 2000. Full results at www .americanpresidents.org.

king or queen or an elder statesman, and the head of government will be the top political official. (In Great Britain, the head of state is the queen and the head of government is the prime minister.) In the United States, the fusion of these roles gives the president an advantage. Performing the unifying functions as head of state builds up political capital, which the president can use in his divisive role as head of government.

Pardons

The head of state, reflecting the power and the mercy of the nation, is authorized to grant pardons. Through the **pardon power,** the president can erase the guilt and restore the rights of anyone convicted of a federal crime.[37] One of Lincoln's last acts, on the day he would be assassinated, was to pardon a Union Army deserter. Blanket pardons have been issued to Confederate Army veterans and Vietnam draft evaders, but most presidents have used the power to clear the names of offenders who have served their sentences.

Unlike most functions as head of state, granting pardons can be controversial, especially absolving persons convicted of crimes with political overtones. The most controversial was President Ford's pardon of President Nixon for his Watergate crimes. As president, Nixon had immunity from criminal charges, but once he resigned (or was impeached and removed from office), he would no longer have immunity. As a private citizen, he could be indicted. To prevent a trial and possible appeals that could drag on and on, Ford pardoned Nixon in advance. Although Ford's goal was to put Watergate behind the country, his move was highly unpopular— his popularity plummeted from about 70 percent to about 50 percent—and very costly to his election bid two years later. People were so enraged at Nixon that driving him from office wasn't enough for them. In hindsight, however, the pardon looks wiser than many people recognized at the time.

Other pardons have also prompted sharp criticism. George H. W. Bush pardoned Reagan's secretary of defense and five other officials charged with crimes related to the Iran-Contra scandal. The special prosecutor complained that the pardon was a cover-up to prevent investigation of Bush's own role in the scandal.[38] (Once pardoned, the officials couldn't be pressured to reveal what they knew about Bush's role.) In the waning days of his last term, Clinton pardoned a fugitive commodities trader whose ex-wife was a large donor to the Democratic Party.

George W. Bush has granted fewer pardons—just 113 in six years—than any president after World War II.[39] Yet he did cancel Lewis "Scooter" Libby's two-and-one-half-year prison sentence for lying and obstructing justice in the investigation into the leak of the identity of CIA agent Valerie Plame.[40] As chief of staff to the vice president, Libby was an administration stalwart.

Chief Executive

Article II of the Constitution stipulates, "The executive power shall be vested in a president," and it charges him to "take care that the laws be faithfully executed." Thus the president is the **chief executive.** He administers the laws and manages the executive branch.

The Founders expected Congress to make policy and the president to implement it. In this, Congress would be the stronger branch. According to the *Federalist Papers,* the president's responsibilities would be "mere execution" and "executive details."[41] But the president's role as chief executive has proven more potent than the Founders thought.

Appointment and Removal

Although most of the staff in the executive branch are nonpartisan employees hired through the merit system, the president appoints about three thousand people in the departments and agencies. A third—the ones nominated to policy making positions, such as the cabinet secretaries, assistant secretaries, and deputy secretaries—require confirmation by the Senate. The president also appoints White House aides and advisers, who don't require confirmation.

In making these appointments, the president faces some constraints. The president must satisfy the senators in his party. The custom of **senatorial courtesy** gives the senators in his party a virtual veto over appointments to positions, including judgeships, in their states. The president must also satisfy the senators who represent important constituencies by nominating people acceptable to these constituencies. Big businesses expect a well-regarded business executive to be named secretary of commerce, and labor unions expect a person with union ties to be named secretary of labor. Western states, which have the most public land, look for a westerner to be secretary of the interior. When the Senate is controlled by the other party, the president's choices are usually confirmed because of the belief that a president should be able to have the people he wants. But a controversial choice is occasionally rejected due to the heightened partisanship of recent decades.

Although the power to remove political appointees isn't explicit in the Constitution, it's implied from the power to appoint. If presidents can appoint people they want to work with, they must be allowed to remove those they no longer want to work with, even the ones who were confirmed by the Senate. However, presidents can't remove appointees who have fixed terms or who work for regulatory commissions, which are supposed to exercise their authority independent of political pressures.[42] And, of course, presidents can't remove federal judges, who serve for life.

A clear pattern has emerged in George W. Bush's appointments to the bureaucratic agencies. As the president with the closest ties to big business since Herbert Hoover (1929–1933),[43] Bush appointed over 100 executives, lawyers, and lobbyists to positions in which they regulate the corporations they worked for.[44] To head the Environmental Protection Agency's (EPA's) clean air program, he appointed a lawyer for the Chemical Manufacturers Association who had called most environmental problems "myths." To head the Agriculture Department's national forest programs, he appointed a lobbyist for lumber companies that oppose the programs.

Reorganizing Agencies

Presidents can reorganize agencies in the executive branch, merging or abolishing existing offices or creating new ones. But presidents need congressional approval for major reorganizations. With congressional assent, George W. Bush created the new cabinet-level Department of Homeland Security, combining dozens of executive branch agencies and reassigning almost two hundred thousand federal employees.

Inherent Executive Powers

The courts have ruled that presidents have inherent powers, which are neither explicit nor implicit in the Constitution. Rather, they are inherent in the nature of the job. According to the courts, they are necessary for chief executives to perform their duties.

Executive Orders To ensure that "the laws be faithfully executed," presidents can issue orders, including **executive orders.** These directives have the force of law, as long as they don't contradict the Constitution. Thus executive orders are a form of legislative power for the executive branch.

Presidents often use executive orders to address internal procedures or organizational problems. They also use them to implement provisions of treaties and statutes that are ambiguous. They occasionally use them when events require the government to take swift action, because the executive branch has the expertise and ability to act quicker than the legislative branch.[45] In the wake of the 9/11 attacks, George W. Bush issued numerous executive orders.[46]

Executive orders can be controversial when presidents use them to create policy that Congress wouldn't enact. Reagan and both Bushes banned abortion counseling in birth control clinics that received federal

"... to uphold the Constitution and the laws of the United States—as I see them ..."

© Paul Conrad from *The King and Us* (Los Angeles: Clymer Publications, 1974.) Reprinted by permission.

funds and in family planning programs administered by the United Nations that received American money. Clinton restricted road building and oil and gas drilling on environmentally sensitive public land in the West, to the dismay of some westerners who favored more development.

Executive orders can be countermanded by successor presidents, and they can be overridden by Congress. When George W. Bush took office, he countermanded numerous directives by Clinton.

Some orders have had a major impact. Truman issued an order to integrate the military, Kennedy to end racial discrimination in public housing, and Lyndon Johnson to require affirmative action in hiring by firms with federal contracts.

Executive Privilege To ensure that they receive the full and frank advice of their aides and advisers or of any

visitors to the White House, presidents also have **executive privilege,** which is the right to refuse to disclose the contents of private conversations and internal documents to Congress, the courts, or the public.

Presidents since George Washington have asserted executive privilege,[47] usually when Congress has requested certain information. Historically, the disputes have been resolved through give-and-take between the two branches, with presidents retaining the information at times and divulging it at other times.

The Supreme Court has settled several disputes and, in the process, acknowledged the legitimacy of executive privilege in general. At the same time, it has ruled that the privilege is limited and that the courts, rather than presidents themselves, would determine its validity in particular circumstances. In one case, the Court upheld the privilege when national security was involved.[48] In another, it struck down the privilege when the courts needed the evidence of possible wrongdoing for criminal trials.

The latter case was *United States v. Nixon,* which stemmed from the Watergate scandal.[49] A low-level aide revealed that President Nixon had installed a taping device in the Oval Office, which had secretly recorded conversations between the president and everyone he talked to there. The conversations could confirm or refute the charges of White House complicity in the break-in at the national office of the Democratic Party (in the Watergate Hotel), the attempt to place wiretaps on its phones, and then the cover-up of these actions. The special prosecutor demanded the tapes. When the president, citing executive privilege, refused to hand them over, the special prosecutor filed suit and the justices ruled unanimously that the privilege didn't apply in this situation. After twelve days of weighing his options, Nixon decided to comply with the ruling. Although the tapes didn't indicate that he participated in planning the break-in, they did show that he participated in covering it up. (Years later, however, one aide claimed that the president himself had ordered the break-in.)[50] Just seventeen days after the ruling, when it became clear that Congress would impeach and remove him, Nixon resigned.[51]

The George W. Bush administration, which has made the strongest case for presidential power since the Nixon administration, has claimed executive privilege numerous times.[52] Sometimes the administration has asserted the privilege clearly to establish a precedent that it doesn't have to turn over information. For example, it rejected the request of a war scholar for the intelligence briefings given to President Johnson during the Vietnam War. Other times the administration has asserted the privilege when the documents could prove embarrassing. Upon taking office, Vice President Cheney had secret meetings with the executives of energy companies—reportedly the major donors to the Bush campaign—who were invited to determine national energy policy. When a group sought the attendance records and minutes of these meetings to confirm the reports, the Supreme Court accepted the claim of executive privilege because the administration wasn't protecting criminal wrongdoing.[53]

In other cases, the administration claimed the privilege when a reporter tried to confirm officials' statements that the administration had advance warnings of the 9/11 attacks, and when Congress sought information about the CIA's doubts that Iraq had weapons of mass destruction before the war.

The history of executive privilege raises a serious question: Is the privilege used primarily to guarantee effective communication within the White House or to hide embarrassing information from the public?

Fiscal Leader

The president has acquired a role as fiscal leader by attaining the power to manage the budget.

The Founders gave Congress the power of the purse. No money can be spent unless it is appropriated by Congress. This power encompassed the authority to set the government's budget. For many years, Congress created the annual budget. Executive branch agencies sent their budget requests directly to Congress; they bypassed the president. But after World War I, the larger government seemed to require better management. In the Budget and Accounting Act of 1921, Congress delegated key responsibilities for the budget to the president, enabling the administration to dominate the process.

Each year the president, through the Office of Management and Budget (OMB), which lies in the executive branch, recommends the amount of money for each item in the budget. Congress retains the authority to approve or to change the amounts. Nonetheless, this arrangement benefits the president. The budget is huge and complex, and the experts in the OMB work for the president.[54] Thus the administration understands exactly what's in the budget and shapes the debates over the budget.

Legislative Leader

Congress, of course, was expected to dominate the legislative process, but the president has come to play an important role as well. The president is *a* legislative leader, though not necessarily *the* legislative leader. The president sets priorities, proposes solutions, shapes legislation, and vetoes legislation. For some legislation, the president is dominant, for some Congress is dominant, but for most the two branches share responsibility.[55]

As the head of a party with an issue agenda, the president is an advocate of a legislative program, whether packaged as the Square Deal (Teddy Roosevelt), the New Deal (Franklin Roosevelt), the Fair Deal (Truman), the New Frontier (Kennedy), the Great Society (Johnson)—or not packaged with any snappy title.

However, presidents' proposals are rarely new. Most ideas have been around for awhile. A former senator and White House chief of staff exclaimed that "issues are like snakes—they just refuse to die! They keep coming back, time after time."[56] Presidents must fit their agenda into the ongoing issues of their time.

Among these issues, presidents designate their priorities. At any given time, the government's agenda is full to overflowing. Because they can't address everything, members of Congress wait for the president to set the priorities. "As in any organization with too much to do, there is a need for someone in authority to say: 'Let's start here.'"[57] But presidents can't dictate what Congress spends its time on or what the media and the public focus on. In the Clinton years, the press and the people found the Lewinsky affair more fascinating than the president's (legislative) proposals. Now, the catastrophic failure of the Iraq War makes it difficult for Bush to direct public or congressional attention to his legislative program.

Although presidents designate their priorities, members of Congress have their own preferences and initiate their own bills. Even when they deal with a president's proposal, they amend it. Virtually all proposals emerge from Congress in very different form from when they were introduced.

Normally presidents are most effective if they recognize their place in a continuing government that has separation of powers with a strong legislative branch as well. Only occasionally has a president been able to impose his own agenda on the legislative process. Franklin Roosevelt was able to do so because of the public's desperation during the Great Depression and his political skills. **Lyndon Johnson** (1963–1969) was also able to do so because of his experience in Congress—he served in both houses and as majority leader in the Senate—and his inside knowledge of the members and the process, along with his constant drive and ruthlessness. He knew how to put together legislative coalitions, whether in the Capitol or from the White House.

Vetoes

The Constitution gives the president **veto power** over bills passed by Congress. When the president receives a bill passed by Congress, he has three options: he can sign it into law; he can veto it; or he can take no action, in which case the bill becomes a law after ten congressional working days. If he vetoes the bill, Congress can override the veto by mustering two-thirds of both houses. (But if Congress adjourns before ten congressional working days after sending a bill to the White House, the president can pocket the bill—take no action on it—and thus exercise a "pocket veto." The Founders included this option to prevent Congress from passing a bill and adjourning too quickly for the president to veto it.)

The veto, and the ever present threat of a veto, help presidents influence legislation. Mobilizing two-thirds majorities in both houses to override a veto usually is very hard. Presidents call on the loyalty of party members in Congress, and they appeal to the public for support. Thus not only can presidents block a bill but they can force Congress to alter a bill by wagging their veto pen.

Franklin Roosevelt, the longest-serving president, holds the record with 635 vetoes in fourteen years. Congress overrode just nine. Roosevelt understood the political value of the veto power. Once he said to an aide, "Find me something I can veto!" Only eight presidents never vetoed a bill. George W. Bush didn't use the veto until his sixth year, when Congress passed a bill to expand federal funding for embryonic stem cell research. His veto was upheld. He used the veto again in his seventh year, when Congress passed a bill to phase out the deployment of troops in Iraq.

Signing Statements

George W. Bush has tried to establish another presidential power. Applying the "unitary executive" principle, Bush has attached statements to congressional legislation, as he has signed the bills, that indicate his understanding of their content and his intentions for their implementation. Known as **signing statements,** these written comments are deposited with the new laws and recorded in the *Federal Register.*

Previous presidents made limited use of signing statements, primarily to clarify their understanding of vague language in a bill in case it's later contested in the courts. Before the 1980s, just over a dozen had been issued. But a Reagan administration lawyer, Samuel Alito, who has since been appointed to the Supreme Court by George W. Bush, proposed greater use of these statements. In eight years, Reagan issued 71, and Clinton issued 105.[58]

Bush has far exceeded both of them. He attached signing statements to 1 out of 10—more than 750—laws during his first five years in office.[59] More significant than the number, however, is the scope of the statements. In some, he exempted himself from a president's constitutional obligation to provide information to congressional oversight committees. In others, he exempted himself from a president's constitutional obligation to "faithfully execute" the laws passed by Congress. These statements were de facto declarations

of Bush's intention not to enforce, in whole or in part, the laws he was signing, on the grounds that the chief executive has complete authority to instruct executive branch agencies how to implement the laws. For a president to say that he's not obligated to "faithfully execute" the laws is a bizarre interpretation of his constitutional role as the chief executive.

The only power the Constitution gives a president to block congressional legislation is the veto. But vetoes attract publicity and can be overridden. Signing statements escape public notice and provide no opportunity for congressional challenge. They can be used like a line-item veto—a veto of one part of a bill rather than the entire bill—which the Supreme Court declared unconstitutional.[60] And signing statements can mislead the public about the laws the president supports and the ones he opposes. For example, Bush signed into law a bill forbidding the use of torture, but at the same time he attached a statement, which most people wouldn't read or grasp, saying essentially that he had no intention of enforcing the legislation when he thought it interfered with his powers as commander in chief.

Diplomatic and Military Leader

The Constitution includes provisions that make the president the chief diplomat of the country and the commander in chief of the military. Together, these roles enable the president to exercise tremendous power over foreign affairs, greater power than over domestic matters. And most presidents have enjoyed shaping foreign policy more than domestic policy, which Richard Nixon dismissed as having to worry about "outhouses in Peoria."[61]

Chief Diplomat

The Constitution authorizes the president to negotiate treaties, appoint ambassadors, and receive foreign ambassadors. These provisions make the president the chief diplomat.

The president negotiates treaties with foreign countries, although the Senate must approve them by a two-thirds majority before they can take effect. This requirement is a severe limitation on presidential power. Just as it's difficult to obtain two-thirds majorities to override a veto, it's also difficult to obtain a two-thirds majority to approve a treaty. This fact gives the Senate leverage to bargain with the president. After Jimmy Carter (1977–1981) negotiated a treaty to give the Panama Canal and

return the Canal Zone to Panama, the Senate demanded two amendments—that the United States retain the right to intervene militarily against any threats to the canal and get priority passage for U.S. ships during wartime. (Carter renegotiated with Panama and then obtained approval of the amended treaty from the Senate.)

The president evidently can terminate treaties without any involvement by the Senate. The Supreme Court allowed Carter to terminate the 1903 treaty with Panama to make way for the new one.[62] George W. Bush, who entered office with a disdain for international agreements and organizations, unilaterally withdrew the United States from the ABM treaty.[63]

The president also negotiates executive agreements and trade deals with foreign countries. These aren't mentioned in the Constitution, but are considered implicit in the president's diplomatic authority. Both of these are similar to treaties, but they avoid the high hurdle of a two-thirds majority. Some executive agreements and trade deals require congressional approval, though only a simple majority, and others don't require any approval.[64]

The president appoints ambassadors to represent us abroad, although the Senate must confirm them. The president also "receives" ambassadors from other countries. Foreign ambassadors present their credentials upon arriving in the country to begin their posting. What appears to be a ceremonial duty may actually be a significant power. Receiving foreign ambassadors implies recognizing their governments, which means acknowledging the legitimacy of their governments. If a revolution leads to a new government, there may be uncertainty or controversy as to which government is the legitimate government. The authority to "receive" foreign ambassadors thus gives the president the power to decide which government to recognize. The United States didn't recognize the Soviet government until sixteen years after the Bolshevik Revolution or the Communist government of mainland China until twenty-five years after it took power.

From the beginning of the country, officials referred to the president as the "nation's organ for foreign affairs."[65] In 1936, the Supreme Court revised this characterization, calling the president the "sole organ" for foreign affairs.[66] This revision reflected the growth of presidential power by this time. Yet this revision remains controversial, because the Constitution also grants Congress powers over foreign affairs, including treaties and

As commander in chief, the president appoints military officers. During the Civil War, President Lincoln couldn't understand why the Union Army hadn't pressed its advantage over the Confederate army. When he visited the Antietam battlefield, he discovered that his top general, George McClellan, was both pro-Union and pro-slavery. Hoping for a stalemate in the war, McClellan tried to block Confederate advances but refused to rout Confederate troops. Lincoln replaced him.

National Archives

Commander in Chief

The Constitution designates the president as **commander in chief,** which means, according to the *Federalist Papers,* that the president is "first general" and "first admiral."[68] And this means that civilian authority has primacy over military authority; the president can countermand any order of any officer.

Being "first general" and "first admiral" allows the president to determine military strategy. Truman made the decision to drop the atom bomb on Hiroshima during World War II. Later presidents made the decisions to wage limited wars in Korea and Vietnam, concluding that victories over North Korea and North Vietnam weren't worth risking a nuclear holocaust. In the Vietnam War, Johnson and Nixon selected the bombing targets.

In the Persian Gulf War, George H. W. Bush ordered the American commanders not to pursue fleeing Iraqi troops to Baghdad and topple Saddam Hussein's regime. Despite the quick victory in driving the Iraqi army from Kuwait, Bush thought it would be much more difficult to overthrow the regime and occupy the country.[69] In preparation for the Iraq War, George W. Bush's secretary of defense, Donald Rumsfeld, acting under the authority of the president, forced the military leaders to use far fewer troops than they thought necessary.[70]

Being commander in chief also allows the president to appoint and discipline the officers. In the Korean War, Truman, who had been simply an infantry captain in World War I, ordered General Douglas MacArthur, who was the commander of U.S. and United Nations forces in Korea, home for disobeying his order to keep the war contained in Korea. (MacArthur threatened to extend it to China.) Truman effectively ended MacArthur's military career.[71]

However, when Clinton tried to reverse the military's ban on homosexuals, General Colin Powell rallied opposition within the military and behind the scenes in Congress. Powell's conduct verged on insubordination,[72] but his popularity prevented the president from taking disciplinary action. Congressional opposition

ambassadors, as we've seen here, and over war itself, as we'll see in the next section. Nonetheless, the statement accurately conveys the fact that the president dominates foreign policy making.

To underscore the importance of speaking with one voice in foreign affairs, Congress passed the Logan Act in 1799, after a Philadelphia doctor sailed to France to try his hand at diplomacy when it appeared that France and the United States were heading toward war. The act prohibits unauthorized citizens from negotiating with foreign governments. Such negotiations could undermine official attempts to conduct foreign policy. However, there's no record of any prosecutions for violating the act, although prosecutions were threatened during the Vietnam War when peace advocates traveled to North Vietnam and again when Jesse Jackson traveled to Cuba in violation of U.S. policy. But members of Congress and ex-presidents made similar trips to other countries.[67] In 2007, Speaker of the House Nancy Pelosi (D-Cal.) announced a trip to Syria to discuss Middle East policy with the Syrian president. Although President Bush, whose policy was to isolate Syria, asked Pelosi not to go, she nevertheless did go (along with several members of Congress, including one Republican).

forced the president to back down and substitute an ineffectual compromise—the "don't ask, don't tell" policy—instead.[73]

The constitutional designation of commander in chief was not intended to give the president the power to initiate war. The Founders wanted to deny the president the prerogative of war and peace, which the British king had. They feared that the executive would be too eager to wage war. James Madison thought that "the executive is the branch of power most interested in war and most prone to it."[74] The Founders thought that Congress, representing the people who would be fighting and dying, would be more reluctant to embrace war. Therefore, Madison said, the Constitution "vested the question of war in the legislature."[75] Thomas Jefferson thought this arrangement would be an "effectual check to the dog of war."[76]

At the Constitutional Convention, it was proposed that Congress have the power to "make" war, but this was changed to "declare" war so as to allow the president to repel attacks before Congress could convene and act. The Founders also gave Congress the authority to "raise and support"—that is, finance—the military.

With the authority to initiate a war and to finance the military, it's clear that the Founders gave Congress the preponderant power over war making. Yet this intention has become one of the most flagrantly disregarded in the Constitution.

The War Powers Resolution The war-making power exercised by Presidents Johnson and Nixon during the undeclared war in Vietnam inspired the 1970s characterization of the Presidency as "imperial" and led Congress to limit the power of the president to take unilateral military action. Congress passed the **War Powers Resolution** over Nixon's veto in 1973. This law allows the president to use troops abroad without a declaration of war if the military involvement is authorized by Congress (in a resolution rather than an official declaration of war) or if the United States or its military is attacked. If the latter, the president is supposed to consult with Congress beforehand, if possible, and notify it within forty-eight hours afterward. (Nixon had secretly extended the Vietnam War into Cambodia and Laos.) Unless Congress approves the involvement, the president must withdraw the troops within ninety days.[77] At any time, Congress can pass a resolution (not subject to presidential veto) ordering the president to halt the involvement. The goal was to force public debate before it's too late.

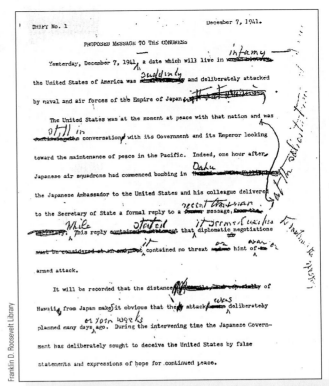

As the nation's foreign policy leader, President Franklin Roosevelt edited his own speech to Congress about the Japanese attack on Pearl Harbor. He added the word infamy that made memorable the phrase "a date which will live in infamy."

Although the law was a serious attempt to retrieve Congress's war powers, it has had little effect. In practice, it has meant that Congress endorses what presidents have already decided. Congress has never used it to prevent presidents from going to war. Even when presidents have violated the letter or spirit of the law, Congress has acquiesced. George H. W. Bush invaded Panama in 1989, although Congress hadn't authorized war and the United States hadn't been attacked. He ordered a half million troops to the Persian Gulf in 1990 and *then* mobilized opinion in the United States and gained support from the United Nations. By the time Congress authorized force against Iraq, the decision to use force had already been made. The same can be said for George W. Bush's decision to invade Iraq in 2003. Way before Congress consented, the decision to attack had been made.

Congress hasn't demanded fealty to the War Powers Resolution for the same reasons it hadn't demanded

Mike Lane and PoliticalCartoons.com

fealty to the constitutional provision about declarations of war. For political reasons, congressional power is limited by patriotic fervor in the public or presidential manipulation of the public. There's almost always a **"rally 'round the flag" effect** when troops are committed to combat.[78] The president asks the public to "support" the troops. The public rarely turns against a war unless it drags on and victory seems unlikely. In such a political climate, Congress is unlikely to mount a real challenge to the president.

In addition to the political climate, the president has gained the upper hand because of the inherent advantages addressed already. Early in the country's history, the president was in office year-round, whereas Congress wasn't. Today, the president has a monopoly or near monopoly of secret information from the intelligence agencies. In 2003, the Bush administration skillfully used this advantage to convince the country that there was no doubt that Iraq had weapons of mass destruction and that there was real evidence that Saddam Hussein was behind the 9/11 attacks.[79] Neither has been borne out, but the public relations campaign was so persuasive that even after Bush renounced his claims millions of Americans still believe them.[80]

In a democracy with a free press, we expect the media to question the administration and demand genuine evidence, where appropriate, so the people can decide whether to begin a war. But we saw in Chapter 4 that the media were more anxious to attract a big audience than to fulfill their journalistic responsibilities during the run-up to the Iraq War. As a result, they were cheerleaders for the war rather than watchdogs with an eye on the government.

Party Leader

The president is the head of his party and the chief advocate for its policy agenda. As party leader, the president uses his reputation and his office to push his party's legislative priorities.

The president is also the party's chief fundraiser, serving as the headliner at fundraising events and hosting or accommodating major donors in various ways. Clinton invited big donors to the White House to have coffee and, in some cases, to stay overnight. He was criticized by members of both parties for making the White House available to "the highest bidder." George W. Bush has exploited his office for partisan fundraising as well. He invited big donors to meet with cabinet officials and to dine with diplomats at an embassy.[81] He offered them a photo op with himself or the first lady.[82] Some big donors were rewarded with jobs in the administration or appointments as ambassadors, and virtually all were ensured access to high-level officials in the White House when they had concerns about government policies.

In addition to raising money, presidents help recruit candidates for House and Senate races. They may dispatch political aides to boost the campaigns of party candidates and may appear themselves to plug the candidates. Seeing presidents in person—seeing a little history in the making—is exciting, so presidents draw big crowds and attract media coverage for the candidates.

Presidential support, however, is no guarantee of electoral success for congressional candidates, especially in off-year elections (see Table 1). Without the party's presidential nominee at the top of the ticket, voters are less likely to support the party's congressional candidates. Since 1934, the president's party has lost an average of twenty-six House seats and three Senate seats in off-year elections.

This pattern is less pronounced in recent decades, due to the high number of safe seats. Most congressional members win reelection even when their presidential candidate loses or is unpopular at midterm.

However, many lost reelection in 1994 and 2006. In 1994, when Clinton was unpopular because of his health care proposal, Republicans gained enough seats to take control of both houses of Congress. In 2006, when Bush was unpopular because of the Iraq War, Democrats regained enough seats to recapture control of both houses.

Presidential Staff

To perform these functions, modern presidents have a large staff. Earlier presidents, however, didn't. Washington paid a nephew out of his own pocket to be his only full-time aide, and Jefferson had only four cabinet officers to advise him. Congress didn't appropriate funds for a presidential clerk until 1857. Even so, Lincoln opened and answered much of the daily mail himself. A decade after a telephone was installed in the White House, Grover Cleveland (1885–1889 and 1893–1897) answered it himself. As late as the 1910s, Wilson typed many of his own speeches.[83]

As the work of the president has expanded, staff size has exploded. Today, as chief executive, the president heads a bureaucracy of fifteen cabinet departments and 2.7 million civil servants.

Executive Office of the President

The bureaucracy that surrounds modern presidents had its origins in the administration of Franklin Roosevelt. Because his small staff was overwhelmed by the administrative demands of New Deal agencies and programs, FDR called in a team of public administration experts to restructure the presidential office. In response, Congress created the **Executive Office of the President** (EOP).[84]

The EOP is the president's personal bureaucracy, sitting atop the executive branch and monitoring the work done in the cabinet departments and agencies to see that the president's policies are carried out. Although many EOP staffers are career civil servants, the president appoints the ones who fill the top positions.

The EOP isn't a single office but a group of offices, councils, and boards. It includes the National Security Council (NSC), which advises the president on foreign policy; the Council of Economic Advisers, which advises the president on economic policy; and the OMB, which prepares the budget. The OMB has its own eight-story building, and it accounts for a large part of the EOP's growth.

Table 1	The President's Tattered Coattails: Congressional Losses for the President's Party in Off–Year Elections		

Seats Gained or Lost by the President's Party

Year	President	House	Senate
1934	Roosevelt (D)	+9	+10
1938	Roosevelt (D)	–71	–6
1942	Roosevelt (D)	–45	–9
1946	Truman (D)	–55	–12
1950	Truman (D)	–29	–6
1954	Eisenhower (R)	–18	–1
1958	Eisenhower (R)	–47	–13
1962	Kennedy (D)	–4	+4
1966	Johnson (D)	–47	–3
1970	Nixon (R)	–12	+2
1974	Ford (R)	–48	–3
1978	Carter (D)	–11	–3
1982	Reagan (R)	–26	0
1986	Reagan (R)	–6	–8
1990	G. H. Bush (R)	–8	–1
1994	Clinton (D)	–52	–9
1998	Clinton (D)	+5	0
2002	G. W. Bush (R)	+6	+2
2006	G. W. Bush (R)	-31	–6
Average, all off-year elections		**–26**	**–3**
Average, all presidential election years		**+20**	**+3**

SOURCES: *Congressional Quarterly Weekly Review,* various issues; Roger H. Davidson and Walter J. Oleszek, *Congress and Its Members,* 9th ed. (Washington, D.C.: CQ Press, 2004), 106.

White House Office

The EOP also includes the White House Office, which houses the president's closest advisers. White House staffers have greater influence than most advisers because the president appointed all of them and works daily with many of them.

Many presidents have counted their wives among their closest advisers, and every first lady has her own office and staff within the White House Office. (See the box "The First Lady: A Twofer.")

President Kennedy's closest adviser was his brother Robert (right), whom he appointed attorney general.

Management of the White House staff varies with the president's personal style. Franklin Roosevelt disdained a hierarchical organizational structure, with rigid lines of responsibility, for a more fluid structure that funneled information to him. He wanted to be made aware of any problems in government programs. He appointed staffers to overlapping, even identical, jobs. This arrangement fostered sharp competition and clashes among the staffers, but it provided more information to the president and pushed policy disputes to the top, so the president could make the decisions.

On the other hand, Nixon valued formal lines of authority with a strong chief of staff. Nixon's chief of staff, H. R. Haldeman, saw his job this way: "Every president needs a son of a bitch, and I'm Nixon's. I'm his buffer and his bastard. I get done what he wants done and I take the heat instead of him."[85]

Reagan prided himself on delegating authority to good people and letting them do their work without interference.[86] Serious problems developed, however, when policy disagreements emerged among his advisers. Reagan was too removed from daily affairs, and given his personality too reluctant to intervene, to resolve the disputes. His detached management style had its costs, most noticeably in the Iran-Contra scandal.[87]

Clinton's appointment of many staffers with little Washington experience and diverse policy positions showed his determination to immerse himself in policy details and to be the final arbiter of many competing views. He directed his first staff chief to channel all paperwork to him. However, this approach prevented him from focusing on his priorities. He got so bogged down in details that his wife complained that he had become the "mechanic-in-chief."[88]

Clinton also rejected a hierarchical organizational structure. In fact, White House meetings resembled college bull sessions. The meetings seemed to occur at all hours of the day or night, with no fixed agenda and no clear list of participants, as aides wandered in and out, many of them casually dressed young people.[89]

George W. Bush has employed the opposite approach to management. As the only president to hold an MBA degree, Bush set out to run the White House like the corporate model. He established crisp lines of authority, kept a tight schedule, and demanded complete team loyalty with no public dissent from the administration's policy.[90] (And after the casual appearance of the Clinton staffers, the White House instituted a strict dress code. A Democratic congressional leader wasn't allowed into a meeting until he buttoned his suit coat.)

Bush has gathered a very small group of advisers[91] and, unlike some presidents, such as Kennedy, Clinton, and his father, hasn't sought information directly from civil servants or outside experts. He has relied on staff reports sent through established channels. This top-down style, with ever-loyal aides, though efficient, has insulated the president, preventing him from receiving essential information. Aides are discouraged from correcting his misconceptions as well as his policies. "The first time I told him he was wrong," a young aide said, "he started yelling at me. Then I showed him where he was wrong, and he said, 'All right. I understand. Good job.' He patted me on the shoulder. I went and had dry heaves in the bathroom."[92] Such an experience doesn't engender the truth telling that's vital to effective decision making. Aides are also discouraged from taking any matters to the president that political appointees further down the ladder can deal with. One consequence was the mismanagement of the crisis spawned by hurricane Katrina. According to a former aide, "His inner circle takes pride in being able to tell him 'everything is under control,' when in this case it was not."[93]

Bush has delegated so much responsibility that his first secretary of the treasury said he seemed disengaged and uninformed on issues during cabinet meetings and one-on-one conversations. He said the president was like "a blind man in a room full of deaf people."[94]

An unusual, perhaps unique, aspect of Bush's organizational structure was the central role played by his political strategist, Karl Rove (until he left in September 2007). Today all presidents have political strategists, of course, but Bush fully integrated Rove (nicknamed "Boy Genius" by the president and "Bush's Brain" by writers) into the policy process in the White House. Rove assessed the political implications of competing policy options and signed off on "every" major decision.[95] Reportedly, it was his idea to persuade the public that Saddam Hussein was involved with Osama bin Laden.[96] Rove's goal was to engineer a permanent Republican majority, so he shaped the administration's domestic and foreign policies toward this end. The result is that partisan calculations influenced government policies to an unprecedented extent.

With the key roles played by Rove and Vice President Cheney, Bush has sometimes appeared to be a secondary figure in his own administration. His press staff has had to work to convince the public that the president is in charge of the White House, and the president himself has reminded the press corps that he is "the decider" and "the commander guy."

Office of the Vice President

The EOP also includes the Office of the Vice President. Today the vice president has his own budget for an office and a staff, housed adjacent to the White House, and an official airplane (*Air Force Two*).

The vice president has few formal duties—to preside over the Senate, which he rarely does (junior senators are assigned to do so); cast tie-breaking votes, which he rarely needs to; and succeed to the Presidency if necessary.[97] Vice presidents have succeeded to the office nine times (following eight deaths and one resignation).

Benjamin Franklin suggested a title for the vice president—"His Superfluous Excellency." For many years, vice presidents had little to do, other than to serve as "standby equipment," in the words of Nelson Rockefeller. Woodrow Wilson's vice president, Thomas Marshall, said

President Johnson worked continuously. When he awoke, he read newspapers, ate breakfast, and met with his staff all before getting out of bed.

that holding the job was like being "a man in a cataleptic fit. He cannot speak, he cannot move. He suffers no pain. He is perfectly conscious of all that goes on. But he has no part in it." Franklin Roosevelt's first vice president, John Nance Garner, less elegantly observed that his job wasn't worth "a pitcher of warm piss."

Until recent times, presidents didn't delegate important responsibilities to them, because vice presidents were usually chosen to balance the ticket geographically or ideologically. They weren't necessarily men who presidents wanted to work with. In 1960, the youthful New Englander, John Kennedy, chose the experienced Texan, Lyndon Johnson. The two had a chilly relationship. Kennedy disdained the less polished Johnson, and the self-made Johnson bristled at the privileged background and Harvard degrees of the Kennedy clan.

Sometimes presidents were reluctant to delegate important responsibilities because they feared that their vice president had an eye on the Presidency and sought to build an independent political base for his own future run. Such ambitions discourage loyal support of the president's agenda.

THE FIRST LADY: A TWOFER

The president's wife has always had to walk a fine line, supporting her husband and presiding over social functions without appearing as though she is exercising more power than she should be.[1]

Concern over the influence and accountability of presidential spouses is as old as the republic. When John Adams's opponents referred to his wife as "Mrs. President," they meant something more than her marital status. Abigail Adams was an accomplished writer with strong political opinions and not afraid to express them (for example, that women would "foment a Rebellion" if made subject to laws without representation). Her views on women's rights and other issues, coupled with the fact that her long and happy marriage to John Adams made her his principal adviser, led both supporters and opponents of the president to believe that she might have "undue" influence on policy decisions.

On the other hand, Louisa Adams, the wife of John Quincy Adams, felt hemmed in by the limits of acceptable behavior, and she titled her autobiography *The Adventures of a Nobody*.[2]

There is no mention of a presidential spouse in the Constitution, and she has no official duties and no government salary. Yet she's expected to serve, in Martha Washington's words, as "the hostess of the nation."[3] (Unmarried presidents have had to borrow a stand-in: the widower Thomas Jefferson often relied on Dolley Madison, the wife of his secretary of state and future president, James Madison.) At the same time, she's expected to demonstrate political savvy. The wealthy Martha Washington arrived in a homespun gown.[4]

In addition to an intense schedule of state social functions, the first lady must oversee the White House domestic staff. And it has become the custom for her to identify causes, usually nonpartisan, on which she focuses attention. Jacqueline Kennedy devoted herself to historic preservation, Lady Bird Johnson to environmental issues, Betty Ford to creative arts and the welfare of the elderly, Nancy Reagan to drug abuse prevention, Barbara and Laura Bush to literacy, and Hillary Rodham Clinton to child welfare.

But it was not until 1978 that Congress made formal budgetary provisions for the Office of the First Lady as an official unit within the EOP's White House office.[5] Still without salary, she does get a $20,000 annual pension upon retirement.

First ladies have been instrumental in their husbands' political campaigns. In Warren Harding's presidential campaign, much of the organizing and financing was done by his wife, Florence, which explains her widely repeated comment: "I got you the Presidency; now what are you going to do with it?" Even first ladies uninterested in electoral politics helped attract votes. Jacqueline Kennedy attained a level of popularity and celebrity that surpassed her husband's. Laura Bush had approval ratings double her husband's during his second term.

In office, first ladies who were so inclined continued their political role. Edith Wilson served what she called a "stewardship" (but what others called "bedside government") during a seven-month period when her husband was disabled by a stroke.[6] She decoded classified diplomatic and military messages, encoded presidential responses, controlled access to her husband, and kept information about his condition from the public.

Although many first ladies have been political advisers to their husbands, no one did it quite so publicly or independently as **Eleanor Roosevelt** (Franklin's wife). She held press conferences for women journalists shut out of the president's briefings, made radio broadcasts, and wrote a syndicated newspaper column read by millions. She discussed policies with her husband, peppered him with memos, and brought supporters of causes she advocated into the White House. She served on countless committees and traveled around the world promoting social justice, racial equality, women's issues, and the war effort. After her husband's death, she served as a delegate to the United Nations, where her efforts in support of human rights and international cooperation earned her the title "First Lady of the World."

So, vice presidents were assigned ceremonial tasks or partisan activities, such as being the president's attack dog—saying what the president wanted to say but couldn't say and still seem presidential. Spiro Agnew fulfilled this role for Richard Nixon. (For a time, Agnew fulfilled another role. "They'll never impeach me as long as I have him here," Nixon said, expressing his view of his Veep.)[98]

Mrs. Roosevelt's stature was attained under the exceptional circumstances of FDR's long tenure during two national crises. Furthermore, after incapacitation from polio years earlier, Franklin had become dependent on Eleanor to keep his political career afloat by serving as his stand-in and surrogate campaigner. In combination with their strained marriage, this meant that Mrs. Roosevelt entered the White House as much her husband's political partner as his wife. Although some thought her too powerful, she always deferred to him in joint appearances, saying it was the job of a wife to "lean back in an open car so voters always see *him*."[7]

Most first ladies haven't been traditional wives who limited themselves to the domestic sphere. Even those who did—Bess Truman, Mamie Eisenhower ("Ike runs the country and I turn the lamb chops"),[8] Pat Nixon, and Barbara Bush—were not without influence on their husbands. Bess Truman was uninterested in Washington politics or social life and spent as much time as possible away from the capital. But Harry Truman still called her "the Boss" and said he frequently consulted her about his speeches and important decisions.

Since the 1960s, strong-willed women have been the norm. Lady Bird Johnson helped finance her husband's congressional campaigns and in his presidential race had her own train to tour the South while her husband worked in Washington. During his Presidency, she initiated the Head Start program for poor children and the highway beautification program that banned junkyards and billboards along federal-funded highways. Betty Ford was an outspoken supporter of the Equal Rights Amendment and abortion rights in defiance of her husband's party's position. Rosalynn Carter attended cabinet meetings, had policy lunches with her husband every week, had policy meetings with foreign heads of state, and chaired the Commission on Mental Health Reform. At times, she was derisively referred to as "copresident." Nancy Reagan, most often seen in public gazing adoringly at her husband, often controlled access to the Oval Office and weighed in on the hiring and firing of key advisers.

The term *copresident* was revived for Hillary Clinton, a lawyer and lobbyist for child welfare causes, who was one of her husband's closest advisers and strategists throughout his career in elective office while also serving as the family's principal wage earner. After her husband's inauguration, she moved the first lady's office into the West Wing amidst the policy makers. She sparked greater opposition than any first lady since Eleanor Roosevelt. But in 2000, she became the first presidential wife to run for and win elective office. It is increasingly likely that professional couples will occupy the White House in this century.

In long and close marriages, it's natural for husbands and wives to become confidants and to rely on one another's judgment. Yet worry persists that the special nature of a marital relationship provides opportunities for influence—of the kind Betty Ford called "pillow talk"—unavailable to others. We frequently refer to lobbyists "getting into bed" with politicians, but wives don't have to pay to get there, and if they change their husband's views, it's likely that money won't have anything to do with it.

[1]Much of the material in this box is drawn from Carol Chandler Waldrop, *Presidents' Wives: The Lives of 44 American Women of Strength* (Jefferson, N.C.: McFarland, 1989); Lewis L. Gould, ed., *American First Ladies* (New York: Garland, 1996); and Kati Marton, *Hidden Power: The Impact of Presidential Marriages on Our Recent History* (New York: Pantheon, 2001).

[2]Edith P. Mayo, ed., *The Smithsonian Book of First Ladies* (Washington, D.C.: Smithsonian Institution, 1996), 11, 43.

[3]Ibid., 11.

[4]Cokie Roberts, *Founding Mothers* (New York: HarperCollins, 2004), 231. The position, according to Barbara Bush's chief of staff, is "filled with banana peels and land mines."

[5]Gil Troy, *Affairs of State: The Rise and Rejection of the First Couple since World War II* (New York: Free Press, 1997), 250. Troy also discusses attempts at reorganizing the first lady's office. See especially 178–188 and 248–258.

[6]Phyllis Lee Levin, *Edith and Woodrow* (New York: Scribner, 2001).

[7]Carl Sferrazza Anthony, "The First Ladies: They've Come a Long Way, Martha," *Smithsonian*, October 1992, 150.

[8]Margaret Sullivan, "The Odd Couple," *Washington Monthly*, January/February, 2004, 54.

Jimmy Carter was the first president to integrate his vice president into the day-to-day operations of the White House.[99] Walter Mondale had the Washington experience that Carter lacked. Carter gave him a White House office and asked him to read the paperwork that crossed Carter's desk. Carter lunched with Mondale weekly and included him in all White House advisory groups and important meetings. Later presidents followed Carter's lead. Now vice presidents have important roles to play.

Prior to the Bush-Cheney administration, the closest working relationship between a president and vice president was that between Bill Clinton and Al Gore. Seasoned political observers thought it was unusual when Clinton chose Gore for his running mate. Although Clinton had domestic policy experience as a governor and Gore had foreign policy experience as a senator, they were of the same age and ideology (moderately liberal) and from the same region (the South, and two states with relatively few electoral votes at that). There was no attempt to balance the ticket. Yet Clinton and Gore hit it off and worked well together. Divisions didn't surface until Gore's campaign for president tried to distance itself from Clinton's escapades.

In anticipation of his presidential nomination, George W. Bush asked **Dick Cheney,** whom he knew from his father's administration, to vet potential running mates. After interviewing the candidates and examining their records, Cheney offered himself for the position instead. Cheney and Bush shared a very conservative ideology, but Cheney, unlike Bush, had extensive Washington experience, having been chief of staff for one president (Ford) and secretary of defense for another (George H. W. Bush) as well as a member of Congress.

Cheney had the goal of "merging" the vice president's office with the president's to create a "single Executive Office" in which the vice president would serve as the president's "executive and implementer."[100] Cheney ran Bush's transition team, which chose the political appointees. Cheney placed his allies in key positions throughout the government, especially in the Defense Department and State Department. These allies would serve as his eyes and ears, informing him about any officials who had contrary views and any proposals that were inconsistent with his preferences. These warnings would give him a real advantage in the bureaucratic maneuvering that would come.

Cheney headed the most important policy making groups in the White House and wrote its energy policy. He created his own national security staff and worked closely on military policy with his old friend Donald Rumsfeld, secretary of defense. Cheney has had unprecedented access to the Oval Office, meeting the president every morning and often more times during the day.

The vice president has also been deeply involved in the administration's legislative strategy, meeting with the Republican caucus at least once a week and, for lobbying purposes, maintaining an office in the Senate and another in the House (the only vice president ever to have an office in that chamber). Bush told members, "When you're talking to Dick Cheney, you're talking to me."[101] As Bush had been a political enforcer in his father's administration, Cheney has played the same role for the younger Bush, using strong arm tactics if necessary to gain passage of bills when Congress was closely split. Pressure to support Bush's tax cut proposal in 2001 was so intense that some Republicans called Cheney's Senate office the "torture chamber."[102]

Cheney has been the most powerful vice president in history.[103] One presidential scholar considers him "almost a deputy president with a shadow operation."[104] Cheney was the driving force behind the administration's efforts to expand presidential power and thwart congressional oversight and its decision to invade Iraq.[105] Before Israel bombed Lebanon in 2006, Israeli officials sought a green light from the U.S. government. They visited Cheney first. After that, they said, "persuading Bush was never a problem."[106] For these and other issues, Cheney has dominated the decision-making process, providing the facts and analyses that have directed the process toward the decisions he favored all along.[107] Cheney's aggressiveness has meshed with Bush's willingness to delegate responsibility to others, although it has meant, according to an insider, that the president has lost control of some policies.[108]

In fact, Cheney believes that it's important for the vice president to keep some information and some decisions from the president, so the president later can deny any knowledge about them in case they prove embarrassing or disastrous. Reagan's aides thought that this practice provided "plausible deniability" for the president. (In the Iran-Contra scandal, Reagan hinted that the administration should find a way to circumvent the congressional ban on supplying aid to the Nicaraguan *contras*. When the administration's actions became known, he claimed that he hadn't "any inkling" what his underlings had done.)[109] George H. W. Bush had demanded all information so he'd be less likely to make bad decisions, but his son evidently has allowed the vice president to shield some information and some decisions from him.

According to a presidential speechwriter, Cheney has played a stealth role in administration policy making. "It was like . . . that experiment where you pass a magnet under the table and you see the iron filings on the top of the table move. You know there's a magnet there because of what you see happening, but you never see the magnet."[110]

Presidential Persuasion

Although presidents have significant constitutional authority, this alone doesn't allow them to exercise great power, because the system of separation of powers gives significant authority to others as well. Members of Congress have their own priorities and views, as do the career bureaucrats in the executive branch. And, of course, so do interest groups, political parties, the media, and the public. Consequently, presidents can't simply order people to adopt and implement controversial policies. Instead, presidents must persuade them.

Persuading Officials

In a discouraged mood, Harry Truman said, "I sit here all day, trying to persuade people to do the things they ought to have sense enough to do, without my persuading them. . . . They talk about the power of the president, how I can just push a button to get things done. Why, I spend most of my time kissing somebody's ass."[111]

Presidents must discuss, cajole, negotiate, bargain, and then, at the right moment, compromise to get as much as they can. *Politics* is a dirty word to many Americans, but the Presidency, after all, is a political job requiring political skills. Dwight Eisenhower (1953–1961), before entering politics, was a general in the army and used to issuing orders down the chain of command and having them obeyed by underlings. This approach didn't work in the government. Along the way, his orders got modified or ignored or disobeyed. Eisenhower needed to be a hands-on president, but he wasn't comfortable even being a politician.[112]

Every president develops a reputation for his persuasiveness among the Washingtonians, who include the members of Congress, professionals in the bureaucracy, leaders and lobbyists of interest groups, and reporters and commentators in the media.[113] A strong reputation contributes to a president's continuing ability to persuade them.

To persuade members of Congress, presidents may simply give them a call. Former Speaker of the House Tip O'Neill (D-Mass.) remarked, "The men and women in Congress love nothing better than to hear from the head guy, so they can go back to their districts and say, 'I was talking to the president the other day.' The constituents love it too."[114] After a call from President Reagan, a Democrat exclaimed, "I was so thrilled, I thought I was talking to the pope."[115]

In phone calls, casual conversations at social events, or formal meetings, presidents can ask for lawmakers' support. Presidents can point out the advantages of their position and, for foreign policy, reveal classified information that bolsters their position.

As the chief executive—the one who provides choice jobs to many people and the one who prepares the budget for the country—and as the party's leader, presidents have various favors and penalties to dispense to enhance their persuasiveness. They can wheel and deal. They might promise to back a bill sponsored by the legislator or appoint an official or judge recommended by the legislator. They might direct government projects to the district or state of the legislator. Or presidents might call in their "chits," reminding the legislator about the time they backed a bill or appointed an official or judge pushed by the legislator or the time they campaigned for the legislator back home. The message? "Now it's your turn to help me."

If the legislator still refuses to heed their request, presidents can threaten retaliation. They might block a bill sponsored by the legislator or refuse to appoint an official or judge recommended by the legislator. They can play hardball, vowing to reduce the party's funding for the legislator in the next election or, as a last resort, even to campaign for the legislator's opponent in the primary election.

In conjunction with overt appeals, presidents offer social attention to make the members more amenable. Invitations to receptions or dinners at the White House are prized. The lavish occasions can be nights to remember. Lyndon Johnson invited Rep. Delbert Latta (Oh.), the ranking Republican on an important committee, and his wife to a fancy dinner. After the dinner, a band played and the couples danced. At one point, Johnson cut in to dance with Mrs. Latta. (This wasn't an affront to the representative, but an honor to think that the president wanted to dance with his wife.) When the couple got home, they were so excited that they awoke their children and Latta announced, "Your mother danced with the president of the United States!" (Their son wasn't impressed. "But, Dad, the president is a Democrat," he reminded them.)[116] Bill Clinton played a round of golf with another representative from Ohio to obtain his vote for a bill.

Presidents also use the trappings of their office. Johnson employed his "taxi" when a member was going to the same event as the president. Johnson offered the member a ride in his limousine, with its motorcycle escort and Secret Service tail and with the lights flashing and sirens wailing. During the exciting ride, Johnson would press his case for a pending bill. Sometimes presidents offer members rides in *Air Force One* when they are traveling to the same part of the country. The lawmakers' awe, and the experience they get from the ride and the story they can tell about it, can make them more pliable.

Thus, presidents have numerous means at their disposal, but they can't use all of them or even many of them on a single issue, because these tactics take considerable time, when multiplied by many members of Congress, and lose their effect if used too often.

No president was more effective in persuading members of Congress than Lyndon Johnson. Having been in both houses of Congress and majority leader in the Senate, he knew how the institution worked and what made its members tick. He knew their views, their favorite programs and least favorite programs, their strengths and weaknesses, their health, their quirks—which ones had "a nagging wife" and which ones liked a 5 o'clock scotch. A congressional leader said LBJ "could talk a bone away from a dog." But his efforts to persuade weren't just sweet talk. One senator remembered, "You needed a bridge built on some highway, and, by God, he got your vote or you didn't get the bridge."[117] When he wanted the vote of Sen. Harry Byrd (D-Va.), who was resisting a civil rights bill, Johnson summoned him to the White House and said, "You know, Harry, [Defense Secretary Robert] McNamara says we got to close that Norfolk naval base down there, and I don't much want to do it," but, Johnson added, he needed Byrd's vote. The Norfolk naval base was the largest in the country, so its closure would have devastated Virginia's economy and undermined Bryd's reputation among his constituents. Byrd rushed back to the Senate and announced his support for the bill.[118]

Johnson also knew where the skeletons were buried. When necessary, he quoted FBI reports about a member having a mistress or IRS reports about a member submitting inaccurate tax returns. His unspoken threat was that he would leak the incriminating information to the media or ask the IRS to conduct an audit.

These efforts were all-consuming. When asked how a president should deal with Congress, Johnson replied: "continuously, incessantly, and without interruption."[119]

As a result of Johnson's tremendous drive and consummate skills working with Congress, he left a legacy of legislative accomplishments. One presidential scholar expressed a common view: "He did more for racial justice than any president since Abraham Lincoln. He built more social protections than anyone since Franklin Roosevelt. He was probably the greatest legislative politician in American history." Unfortunately, he was also "largely responsible for one of the greatest disasters in American history"—the Vietnam War, which he inherited but sharply escalated.[120] The failure of the war, and the divisions in our society it fostered, caused him to not seek reelection. In most people's minds, Johnson would be remembered more for the disastrous war than for his domestic accomplishments.

In contrast, George W. Bush hasn't been effective in persuading members of Congress. Although he had strong support after 9/11, enabling him to get what he wanted from Congress, he has lost much support as the Iraq War has dragged on. He has been unable to get his legislative agenda through Congress, in part because he lacks the skills many predecessors had.

Bush hasn't had close relationships with members of Congress, and by personality doesn't engage in "Washington schmoozing."[121] His early-to-bed, early-to-rise habits keep him from the Capital's social scene, where the politicians become comfortable with and trusting of each other. Presidents chat up the Washingtonians whose support they need. But Bush has shied away from these events. At the same time, he has demonstrated "thinly veiled contempt" for Congress, even when the Republicans controlled both chambers.[122] He treated the Republicans "as if they were his valets," according to one observer, and the Democrats "as if they were infected with tuberculosis."[123] When he met with lawmakers about funding for Iraq, he simply demanded their support. One senator asked a question, and the president interrupted him, saying, "I'm not here to debate you."[124] A presidential and congressional scholar concluded, "If you had to evaluate presidents, 1 to 10, and Johnson is a 10, this president is a 1" in his ability to work with Congress.[125]

Persuading the Public

In addition to persuading officials directly, presidents try to persuade the American public in the hope that citizens will pressure officials to follow the president's lead.

The Founders didn't anticipate that one day the president would be the leader of a national party with a political agenda and accountable to the people. They envisioned a president chosen by the Electoral College and removed from the people.

Our earliest presidents had little contact with the general public. George Washington and Thomas

Jefferson averaged only three speeches a year to the public; John Adams averaged one. Adams spent eight months of his Presidency at home in Massachusetts, avoiding Congress and procrastinating on a decision whether to get involved in a war between England and France.[126] Abraham Lincoln thought it prudent to make few speeches. He told people gathered at Gettysburg the night before his famous address, "I have no speech to make. In my position it is somewhat important that I should not say foolish things. It very often happens that the only way to help it is to say nothing at all."[127]

But now presidents are dependent on a national electorate, and they must have a media strategy. They try to persuade the public directly, and also indirectly by persuading opinion leaders, such as the executives, reporters, columnists, and commentators of the media, and the leaders and lobbyists of interest groups, including the executives of big businesses. These people have the ability to influence the public (and interest groups have the money to provide campaign contributions).

Going Public

The strategy of appealing to the people to gain cooperation from Congress and Washington power brokers is known as **going public.**[128] The strategy entails giving television and radio addresses, holding press conferences, making speeches at various events around the country, and giving interviews, through satellite technology, to local media, big conventions, or other audiences. These techniques have become so important that the president sometimes is referred to as the "salesman in chief." (See box, "If They Can't Get Back from the Moon. . . .")

Franklin Roosevelt pioneered this strategy with his **fireside chats,** which were the first attempt to use the media to speak directly and regularly to the people in their homes. The talks made the president the focal point and public face of the government. In a personalized style and conversational tone, FDR began, "My friends," and even talked about his dog. People gathered around their radios whenever he was on, and many felt as though he was talking directly to them. Whereas predecessor Herbert Hoover (1929–1933) had received an average of forty letters a day, Roosevelt, after initiating his chats, received four thousand a day.[129] He even received some addressed not to himself, by name or position, but simply to "My Friend, Washington, D.C." Whereas Hoover needed one clerk to handle his mail, Roosevelt needed fifty.

IF THEY CAN'T GET BACK FROM THE MOON . . .

When a tragedy strikes, the president is expected to be the "mourner in chief." In the days before American astronauts were sent to the moon in 1969, government officials feared that a malfunction might leave them stranded on the moon, unable to return to Earth. According to documents that surfaced at the National Archives years later, the Nixon administration prepared for this contingency.

A speechwriter penned a speech for President Nixon to give while the astronauts were still alive but had no hope of returning:

> Fate has ordained that the men who went to the moon to explore in peace will stay on the moon to rest in peace.
>
> These brave men . . . know that there is no hope for their recovery. But they also know that there is hope for mankind in their sacrifice.
>
> These . . . men are laying down their lives in mankind's most noble goal: the search for truth and understanding.
>
> In ancient days, men looked at stars and saw their heroes in the constellations. In modern times, we do much the same, but our heroes are epic men of flesh and blood.
>
> Others will follow, and surely find their way home. Man's search will not be denied. But these men were the first, and they will remain the foremost in our hearts.

Before giving the speech, the president would contact the "widows-to-be." After giving the speech, he would instruct NASA to cut off all further communications with the astronauts to cut short the public agony over their deaths. Then a clergyman would follow the protocol used for a burial at sea and conclude with "The Lord's Prayer."

Of course, the president didn't have to implement these plans, as the astronauts, after 21 hours on the moon, returned home safely.

SOURCE: "Nixon Had Words Ready for Moon Disaster," *Lincoln Journal Star,* July 10, 1999.

Roosevelt also pioneered the use of public opinion polls to gauge the public's views. Thus he created a communications loop—to the people and from the people—which helped him sell his policies.

Now when a president is not heard from frequently, the media complain because they count on presidential communications to fill their newscasts and news columns. George W. Bush took heat from the press for giving few press conferences and for spending 535 days at Camp David, his ranch in Texas, and his parents' home in Maine during his first three years in office.[130]

Ronald Reagan, often called the "Great Communicator," spoke in public an average of two hundred times a year. When he spoke, he didn't discuss the details of his proposals. Rather, he dwelled on anecdotes about people he knew earlier in life or people who had written letters to the White House. Like FDR, he personalized his speeches. As Roosevelt was the most effective president on radio, Reagan was the most effective on television. Bill Clinton spoke in public an amazing 550 times a year.[131] Perhaps the most effective extemporaneous speaker, Clinton even revised his formal speeches in the back of the limousine on the way to an event, risking heart attacks among his aides. (These three presidents' use of the media is profiled in Chapter 4.)

Today presidents have a large communications staff, led by a media adviser and a press secretary, to get their message out. Following Reagan's practice, they determine a message for every day and every week, and they direct everyone in the administration to stay "on message"—to repeat the message and to avoid other topics that could deflect attention from the message. Inevitably, other topics will pop up, prompting the administration to regain control of the agenda. When the George W. Bush administration has faced competing news stories that put the president or the administration in an unfavorable light, it has often hyped an alleged terrorist threat to push the unwanted stories off the top of the newscast or front page of the newspaper.[132]

The Bush administration has been the most disciplined in staying on message. On any day, viewers of newscasts or listeners of talk radio hear administration officials delivering the same message in virtually the same words. Running such an operation is a high-pressure job, and press secretaries usually don't last long. When Bush's first press secretary resigned after two years, he said he wanted to do "something more relaxing, like dismantling live nuclear weapons."[133]

Of course, going public, even when staying on message, is no guarantee of success. After winning reelection, Bush identified Social Security privatization as his major domestic goal. For six months, he made one public appearance after another on behalf of this goal, but he couldn't convince the public. In fact, the public was less supportive of privatization after his efforts than it had been before them.[134]

Spectacle Presidency

An important part of going public is being seen as well as heard. And the important reason for being seen is projecting an image that conveys what presidents want their character and style to appear to be. Presidents "make fully realized dramatic characters out of themselves. . . . The character has to bear some relation to the real person . . . but it is still a genuine act of creation."[135] The observation that "politics is theater" is intended as ridicule, but images do matter in presidents' drive for popular support.

Presidents' attempts to shape public perceptions and gain public support by presenting symbolic spectacles—gestures designed to influence the public rather than actions that achieve a goal—led to what some political scientists call the **spectacle Presidency.**[136] Through history, many presidents have tried to shape their image. Teddy Roosevelt cast himself as a manly man—a big-game hunter and a Rough Rider who led a charge in the Spanish-American War. But the television screen was the modern impetus to the spectacle Presidency.

Although television became popular in the 1950s, politicians didn't recognize its potential. Dwight Eisenhower shunned televised speeches because, "I can think of nothing more boring, for the American public, than to have to sit in their living rooms for a whole half hour looking at my face on their television screens."[137] But the young medium became a powerful presence in politics in the 1960s. John Kennedy was the first president to recognize its utility for presidential spectacles. To overcome public concerns about his youth and inexperience, he initiated live television coverage of presidential press conferences. The idea was to court the viewers rather than the reporters asking the questions. He would demonstrate his intelligence and command of the issues and, in the process, leaven it with his wit. In other ways, Kennedy tried to make a virtue of his youth and inexperience by conveying a sense of athleticism, with photo ops of sailing and playing touch football, and by exhorting Americans to take long hikes. And always Kennedy promised "vigor," which became his signature word. (Yet his back was in constant pain, which limited his own activities.)

Another image of his administration, whether created by his wife, his aides, or the press, was that of "Camelot," with the royal couple bringing glamour and sophistication to an uncultured society. The administration left a lasting image of a tuxedoed president and his beautiful wife hosting White House galas for classical musicians and great intellects. Although the first lady may have favored these activities, the president himself preferred listening to Frank Sinatra and reading Ian Fleming's James Bond books.

Ronald Reagan and George W. Bush successfully portrayed themselves as dramatic characters. Both evoked masculine toughness. The characterizations were deliberate. A Reagan aide proposed that the president reflect "America's idealized image of itself."[138] An actor, Reagan had little difficulty projecting an image as a rugged individualist, riding horses and clearing brush at his California ranch, even though he had spent most of his life in Hollywood's studio system.

Bush's persona as a Texas cowboy—he wore cowboy boots to his inaugural and made sure the press photographed him wearing them—was mostly invented. His packaging as a war leader was even more intentional. The staging of the flight-suited commander in chief landing by fighter jet on an aircraft carrier and speaking in front of a *MISSION ACCOMPLISHED* banner was one of the most dramatic image-creating photo opportunities in the history of the Presidency.

The advantage of such bold efforts is that the visual image lingers. But that can also be the disadvantage. Bush announced the end of the war in Iraq far too soon, and the photo op came back to haunt him when critics later castigated him as a reckless rather than resolute war leader.

If a president fails to manage his image, the press or his opponents will do it for him—and in ways he won't like. Bill Clinton intended to convey an image of a knowledgeable leader whose gaze was directed toward the future but who, with his own humble origins, could see the problems of average people buffeted by economic forces beyond their control. Instead, his image for many people became that of a womanizer who palled with Hollywood celebrities and paid for a $200 haircut by a Beverly Hills stylist. Although he was one of the most knowledgeable presidents, many people didn't see that image when they looked at him.

Personal Presidency

As the Presidency has grown since the Depression, and as the media have become pervasive, we have developed what political scientists call a **personal Presidency.**[139]

The public didn't always agree with President Reagan's views or policies, but he remained popular partly because of his image as a rugged individualist.

Ronald Reagan Library

The president is the most powerful and visible figure in the government. The media cover not only presidents' official acts but their private lives as well, so the public learns that Gerald Ford toasted his own English muffins and Bill Clinton wore boxers rather than briefs. Consequently, the people come to feel that they have a personal relationship with their presidents. This relationship prompts the people to entrust them with greater power. In return, however, the people expect them to achieve greater results. "Everybody now expects the man inside the White House to do something about everything."[140] Thus, the people have an unwritten contract with the president.

Presidents themselves fuel the personal Presidency by their willingness to reveal private matters—Clinton didn't have to answer the MTV reporter's question about boxers or briefs—and by their efforts to reach out to the people. One example, among many, is the number of Christmas cards sent by the presidents. Eisenhower, who started the custom, sent eleven hundred; Clinton, in his last year, sent four hundred thousand; and George W. Bush, in 2002, sent one million.[141]

The personal Presidency reached a new level during the Clinton years. The continuous investigations of Clinton by Congress, special prosecutors, the lawyers representing Paula Jones, and conservative groups looking for dirt resulted in media saturation of the most private and intimate details of a president's life ever revealed. At one point, the lawyers representing Paula Jones promised titillating information about the "distinguishing characteristics" of the president's genitals if her suit ever came to trial. "It is entirely possible," one reporter observed, "that the Clinton era will be remembered by historians primarily as the moment when the distance between the President and the public evaporated forever."[142]

The personal Presidency has both advantages and disadvantages for the country. The relationship enables presidents to marshal public support for important goals and thus overcome the inertia of a system with fragmented power. On the other hand, the relationship fosters unrealistic assumptions about what presidents can achieve. Many citizens who don't understand our system assume that presidents are all-powerful. They assign presidents too much blame when things go wrong and give them too much credit when things go right, such as when the economy sags or surges.

Because they hold unrealistic assumptions, citizens encourage, actually pressure, candidates for president to make unrealistic promises. The candidates oblige in order to garner more contributions for their campaign or votes for their election. Jimmy Carter, who was one of our most honest presidents, nonetheless told campaign audiences, "If you ever have any questions or advice for me, please write. . . . I open every letter myself, and read them all."[143] George H. W. Bush promised to send astronauts to Mars, be the "education president," be the

"environmental president," and do many other things while cutting the budget deficit yet promising "no new taxes."

Despite these examples, most presidents deliver, or at least try to deliver, on a majority of their promises.[144] Inevitably, however, they neglect some and Congress blocks others, prompting the presidents to seek more power. They get caught in a cycle in which they grasp more power to honor past promises and then make new promises for which they need even more power. Thus the rise of the personal Presidency has fed the expansion of the office. After 9/11, George W. Bush, boosted by sky-high public support, perceived a mandate from the people to prevent further terrorist attacks. He declared a war on terrorism and presented himself as a wartime president. He used this status to make extraordinary claims of presidential power.

As the people experience one personal president after another, they become disillusioned. Their unrealistic assumptions about presidential power, which prod the presidential candidates to make unrealistic promises, set the presidents up for failure in the eyes of the people. When the presidents can't deliver, the people lose faith. And, all along, the media exposure and scrutiny take a toll. Presidents' novelty wears off and their flaws appear. Few presidents can withstand the media microscope without losing their public esteem. Most presidents suffer a decline in popularity as they continue in office. (See Figure 1.)

Despite presidents' constant concerns about their public support, as measured by their approval ratings, there's no strong correlation between presidents' popularity and their clout in Congress.[145] High approval ratings don't guarantee passage of their legislative proposals, because most constituents never learn whether their representative or senators voted for a president's proposals.

Conclusion: Is the Presidency Responsive?

The Founders invented the concept of a Presidency, and our government remains the only presidential government among the established democratic governments of the world.[146]

The Founders intended Congress—in particular, the House of Representatives—to have close ties to the people, but they intended the president, who would be

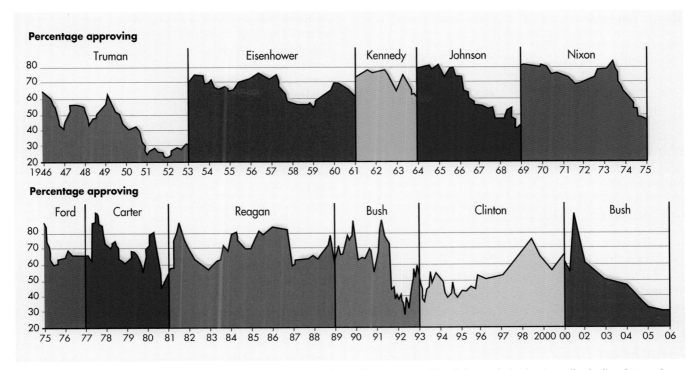

Percentage approving

Truman | Eisenhower | Kennedy | Johnson | Nixon

80, 70, 60, 50, 40, 30, 20

1946 47 48 49 50 51 52 53 54 55 56 57 58 59 60 61 62 63 64 65 66 67 68 69 70 71 72 73 74 75

Percentage approving

Ford | Carter | Reagan | Bush | Clinton | Bush

80, 70, 60, 50, 40, 30, 20

75 76 77 78 79 80 81 82 83 84 85 86 87 88 89 90 91 92 93 94 95 96 97 98 2000 00 02 03 04 05 06

FIGURE 1 • **Presidential Popularity** *Since the end of World War II, presidential popularity has usually declined over time. Only three presidents—Eisenhower, Reagan, and Clinton—left office with ratings at a level comparable to those when they entered.*

SOURCE: Gallup polls, reported in *Public Opinion* and updated at www.gallup.com. The question asked is, "Do you approve or disapprove of the way [name of president] is handling his job as president?" The 2006 approval rating for G. W. Bush is from CBS News/*New York Times* poll data.

chosen by the Electoral College, to be less connected to the people. They didn't foresee that the president would have a popular constituency, so they didn't expect the president to be responsive to the people either.

But as the president became the head of a political party with a political agenda, and as the Electoral College evolved to embrace the voters' participation, the president developed a popular constituency. And as the Presidency grew powerful and the media became pervasive, the president counted on and catered to that constituency. Having a direct and personal relationship with the people, the president is highly responsive to the people, as their views are expressed through the ballot box and public opinion polls. Yet the president uses the media to shape these views.

Although the Presidency has become far stronger than the Founders expected, presidents still must navigate the system of fragmented powers. Therefore, they can't be as responsive as the people may want if Congress has opposing views or priorities. At the same time, there's a danger that presidents may be overresponsive. To remain popular, a president facing national problems may seek symbolic solutions that appeal to many people but don't solve the problems. Or the president may propose short-term solutions that appease many people but neglect long-term needs.

One interesting aspect of this unusual office is its elasticity. Depending upon the demands of the times, and the personality of the president and composition of Congress, the Presidency can be stretched or shrunk from one administration to another or even from the start of one president's tenure to the end. Each occupant makes something quite different of the office than his predecessor. And so we vacillate from thinking that we have either an "imperial Presidency" or an "impossible Presidency."

Key Terms

Key Names

1. The Founders invented the concept of a
   a. Congress.
   b. Presidency.
   c. head of state.
   d. chief executive.
   e. bureaucracy.

2. The "log cabin myth" reflects the fact that
   a. most nineteenth-century presidents were born in a log cabin.
   b. a person needed to be a real frontiersman to be considered for the Presidency in the early 1800s.
   c. all nineteenth-century presidents were from the upper class.
   d. voters prefer a "common man" or at least one with a common touch.
   e. no presidents were born in a log cabin.

3. The constitutional phrase "high crimes and misdemeanors" was intended by the Founders to mean
   a. all crimes.
   b. felonies and misdemeanors.
   c. just serious crimes.
   d. serious crimes and less serious crimes.
   e. serious crimes and abuses of power.

4. In creating the Presidency, the Founders intended it to be
   a. a stronger executive than under the Articles of Confederation.
   b. a weaker executive than the British king.
   c. stronger than the judiciary.
   d. weaker than Congress.
   e. all of the above.

5. Through the nineteenth and early twentieth centuries, our government could be characterized essentially as
   a. an active government.
   b. a presidential government.
   c. a congressional government.
   d. a judicial government.
   e. a balanced government.

6. President _____ presided over the greatest expansion of presidential power.
   a. Franklin Roosevelt
   b. Teddy Roosevelt
   c. Abraham Lincoln
   d. Andrew Jackson
   e. Thomas Jefferson

7. The Presidency of George W. Bush has seen renewed concern about
   a. congressional government.
   b. an imperial president.
   c. an impossible president.
   d. an imperiled president.
   e. judicial supremacy.

8. President George W. Bush's use of the concepts of the "New Paradigm" and a "unitary executive" envisions
   a. an increase in presidential power over foreign affairs.
   b. a vast increase in presidential power over prior presidents.
   c. comparable presidential power to other presidents in recent decades.
   d. a more modest conception of presidential power than that of Clinton.
   e. an increase in presidential power over domestic affairs.

9. Which of the following is not an inherent advantage for the president over Congress?
   a. The president is given more power under the Constitution than Congress is.
   b. The president has access to more information involving foreign affairs than Congress has.
   c. It is easier for one person to develop and articulate goals than 535.
   d. It is easier for the media to focus on one person than on 535.
   e. The president represents the entire nation.

10. In which of these situations is the president acting as head of state?
    a. Raising money for his party
    b. Advocating legislation for Congress to pass
    c. Throwing out the ball for the first Major League baseball game of the season
    d. Performing any of the divisive jobs that presidents are expected to perform
    e. Doing the sorts of things that another country's prime minister might do

11. Due to the merit system, the president has authority to appoint
    a. no one in the executive branch.
    b. only his top aides and advisers.
    c. only the people who work in the White House Office.
    d. about 3000 people in the executive branch.
    e. most employees in the executive branch.

12. With respect to executive privilege, the Supreme Court has ruled all but which of the following?
    a. The privilege exists.
    b. The privilege is limited.
    c. The privilege can be used as presidents see fit.
    d. The validity of the privilege will be determined by the courts.
    e. The privilege is less likely to be considered valid when the courts need the information for criminal trials.

13. The commander-in-chief authority was designed to allow the president to do all but which of the following?
    a. Begin a war
    b. Repel attacks against the United States
    c. Serve as first general
    d. Appoint military officers
    e. Decide military strategy

14. A major change in the responsibilities of modern vice presidents is to
    a. preside over the Senate.
    b. cast tie-breaking votes.
    c. succeed to the Presidency when necessary.
    d. carry out ceremonial functions.
    e. have a policy making role.

15. A president who was especially effective in persuading members of Congress was
    a. Eisenhower.
    b. Kennedy.
    c. Lyndon Johnson.
    d. Nixon.
    e. Carter.

16. The strategy of appealing to the people to gain cooperation from Congress is called
    a. going public.
    b. the personal Presidency.
    c. fireside chats.
    d. the spectacle Presidency.
    e. persuading Washingtonians.

17. Examples of the spectacle Presidency include all but which of the following?
    a. Reagan's image as a rugged individualist
    b. Kennedy's athletic activities
    c. Eisenhower's television speeches
    d. Kennedy's televised press conferences
    e. George W. Bush's persona of a Texas cowboy

18. The term *personal Presidency* refers to an unwritten contract in which the people
    a. entrust the president with vast power.
    b. allow the president to exercise extra power over foreign affairs.
    c. expect the president to deliver results.
    d. permit the president to exercise extra power over domestic affairs.
    e. a. and c.

19. A president's popularity _____ through his tenure in office.
    a. goes up and down about equally
    b. tends to remain constant
    c. tends to increase
    d. tends to decrease
    e. shows no clear pattern

20. Over the years, the Presidency has _____ the Founders expected.
    a. developed much as
    b. become more responsive than
    c. increased in power but remained as responsive as
    d. become less responsive than
    e. tried to avoid the popular constituency that

Key: 1-b; 2-d; 3-e; 4-e; 5-c; 6-a; 7-b; 8-b; 9-a; 10-c; 11-d; 12-c; 13-a; 14-e; 15-c; 16-a; 17-c; 18-e; 19-d; 20-b.

Federal Workders don't all sit at a desk. These workers check for radiation after dismantling equipment at a former nuclear weapons plant in Golden, Colorado.

AP Images/Jack Dempsey

I n 2005, the U.S. Food and Drug Administration issued new guidance to manufacturers concerning labeling of condoms. The FDA directed that the condom container package should specify that condoms can reduce, but not eliminate, possibilities of pregnancy, sexually transmitted disease, and HIV. It further specified that the package should note that the product contained natural latex, which could cause allergic reactions (some people have a serious allergy to rubber latex), and it recommended that manufacturers list on the box the probabilities of pregnancy using various sorts of birth control methods.[1]

Though these facts have been known for some time, and seem like relatively straightforward information, this proposed guidance an-gered some individuals and groups, especially conservatives opposed to contraception. Senator Tom Coburn (R-Ok.) issued a press release[2] criticizing the agency and accusing them of overplaying the usefulness and efficacy of condoms. But on the other hand, a foundation whose mission is to combat HIV AIDs criticized the FDA for moving too slowly to issue the recommendations.[3]

Bureaucrats, then, even when trying to deal with an issue in a factual, scientific way find themselves in the political arena, subject to criticism by groups who don't like the outcome of a report or action. The fact that government (and private) bureaucracies affect our lives from birth to death provides the incentive for groups to try to hold bureaucracies accountable.

When George Wallace ran as a third-party candidate for president in 1968, he campaigned against "pointy-headed bureaucrats" in Washington making decisions that regulated good people's lives. Bureaucrats, according to Wallace, were out of touch with everyday citizens and their concerns. Wallace did not invent bureaucracy bashing, but he helped make it popular among candidates for federal office.

President Reagan never tired of talking about his dissatisfaction with big government and liked to say he preferred flying over Washington to being on the ground because from the air, government looked smaller. And not long after taking office, George W. Bush discounted a report on global warming "put out by the bureaucracy," implying that, given its source, it need not be taken seriously.

When these men refer to "Washington" they mean big government using too much money to do unnecessary things. These critics imply that bureaucrats are not like ordinary citizens. Rather, they are busybodies committed to expanding government's size, spending taxpayers' money, and designing regulations to make life more difficult for individuals and businesses.

Bureaucratic decision making is involved in so much of our lives because government has come to serve many different purposes and interests. The federal government employs butchers, truck drivers, engineers, and three-quarters of all the holders of doctorates in mathematics working in the United States. In all, it employs 2.7 million civilians who work in one hundred agencies at more than eight hundred different occupations. (The armed forces put another 2.3 million on the federal payroll.) Federal bureaucrats do crop research and soil analysis, run hospitals and utilities, fight drug trafficking, check manufacturers' claims about their products, inspect mines, develop high-tech weapons systems, send out Social Security checks, authorize Medicare payments, administer student loan programs, and regulate air traffic, to mention only a few responsibilities.

To some people, the federal bureaucracy has become the symbol of big government and the embodiment of everything they dislike about it. It is seen as equivalent to a fourth branch of government—powerful, uncontrollable, and with a life of its own. In fact, the federal bureaucracy has no independent legislative authority, only that delegated by Congress, and it has no budgetary powers. The bureaucracy's official role is to implement and enforce policies made by elected officials—that is,

by Congress and the president. In doing this, bureaucrats do, in some instances, make new law. But departments and agencies exist at the pleasure of Congress, which can eliminate them or trim their budgets if it does not approve of their behavior. If an agency within the bureaucracy consistently supersedes its authority, it is because Congress is intentionally letting it do so or is failing to fulfill its oversight duties.

As we shall see, government bureaucrats are a lot like everyone else. They are ordinary citizens with attitudes that mirror those of their fellow citizens. Very few of these civil servants, about 16 percent, work in the Washington, D.C., metropolitan area. It may not fit your image of people pushing paper in buildings the size of the Pentagon, but the great majority of federal bureaucrats serve in offices near you; check the U.S. government listing in your telephone book and see how many branch offices of federal agencies are located in or near your hometown. (See the box "Women and Minorities in the Civil Service.")

In this chapter, we look at the evolution of the federal bureaucracy—its growth in size, function, and lawmaking powers. We describe the people who staff the bureaucracy, how they are recruited, what rules govern their work, and how Congress and the president set guidelines for the executive branch and oversee its activities. Finally, we describe ways in which the public can join in the work of monitoring the bureaucracy and have a say in the rules it makes.

The Nature of Bureaucracies

Many people automatically associate the word *bureaucracy* with the federal government. They may visualize rows of cubicles with nameless clerical workers doing monotonous work very inefficiently. Trying to cash in on this stereotype, a Virginia company once sold a "Bureaucrat" doll as "a product of no redeeming social value. Place the Bureaucrat on a stack of papers on your desk, and he will just sit on them."[4] The problem with this joke is that the parodied traits are not necessarily common among government bureaucrats, nor are they unique to bureaucrats. All organizations except the very smallest have bureaucracies: Your college or university has one, as did your local school district; every corporation, most religious denominations, and large philanthropic foundations have them, too, not to mention the Olympics, your favorite sports league, and the unions that represent the players in that league.

All these bureaucracies, public and private, share some common features. For example, all have hierarchies of authority; that is, everyone in a bureaucracy has a place in a pyramidal network of jobs, with fewer near the top and more near the bottom. Almost everyone in a bureaucracy has a boss, and except for those in the bottom tier, most have some subordinates. People advance up the hierarchy on the basis of performance or seniority, so those with more authority tend to be those with more experience and expertise.

Because of the hierarchical structure, bureaucratic behavior is not always consistent with democratic principles. Most bureaucrats are not elected, and as in any hierarchical organization, higher-level authorities can restrict the opportunity of someone lower in the pyramid to express an opinion or share expertise in the decision-making process. In their relative lack of openness, bureaucracies have the potential to restrict consumer and client access to information about their products and services and how they operate and to limit citizens' access to information about their own government. In effect, organizational tendencies, if unrestrained in a government bureaucracy, could transform "citizens" into "subordinates."[5] But our constitutional system provides checks on the power of federal bureaucrats and ways for the public to participate in decision making that few people know about or take advantage of.

Not only are government bureaucracies structurally similar to private ones but they do the same types of work. Employees in both private and public bureaucracies perform a lot of routine tasks. Auditing expense vouchers, managing employee travel, and creating personnel systems, for example, are as routine in business firms as in public agencies. And both also have workers who are productive, honest, and efficient and others who are not. Executives in the Defense Department bought $600 toilet seats and spent more than $75 apiece for metal screws sold elsewhere for 57 cents. During the 1990s, corporations such as Enron, Tyco, and World-Com paid out hundreds of millions of dollars in stock options and bonuses to executives who, in return, ran their businesses into the ground, lied about company earnings, and cost investors billions of dollars.

But there are some distinctions between private and public bureaucracies. Here we look at several.[6]

Goals

Businesses are supposed to make a profit; if they do not, they fail. Public agencies are supposed to promote the "public interest"; if they do not, they fail to serve the people who pay their salaries. Although people disagree over what the public interest is, it is not the same thing as making a profit, just as a government is not a business. This is why we have different words for these two kinds of organizations that exist for completely different reasons.

The goals of a public bureaucracy are defined by elected officials, who collectively determine what is in the public interest. They are sometimes accused of setting goals as if they were in a private bureaucracy—that is, making policies that will help them at the polls rather than policies that best serve the public. But in general, the goals set by these officials are supposed to accomplish tasks and provide services that private bureaucracies cannot. In some cases, such as providing for national security during wartime, they must do so irrespective of cost.

Some part of the public's varying perception of how well the bureaucracy does its job stems from a lack of agreement on the work it is given to do. One person's lazy, red-tape-ridden, uncaring bureaucracy is another's responsive agency. But even when unhappy with its performance, Americans still expect government to provide a vast array of services costing billions of dollars annually, from highways that accommodate high-speed cars to Social Security payments that arrive on time, from clean tap water to safe neighborhoods, from protection from foreign enemies to a cure for cancer.

Performance Standards

It is relatively easy to judge if a private organization is meeting its goals (ignoring for the moment fraudulent accounting) by asking, is it profitable? We might dislike the chocolate-covered raisins that a candy company produces but would still consider the company successful if it made a profit selling them. We would not typically denigrate the company because it makes something we do not approve of. But we rightly use a different standard in judging government. Yet what is the appropriate standard for evaluating the performance of government if making a profit is not the goal?

One obvious method is to determine whether a public agency is efficient and cost-effective. That sounds

AMERICAN DIVERSITY

WOMEN AND MINORITIES IN THE CIVIL SERVICE

Americans expect their public bureaucracies to be open and responsive. Andrew Jackson recognized this when he opened the civil service to people of "common" origins. By putting his frontier supporters in office, he hoped to make the bureaucracy more responsive by making it more representative. In the twentieth century, the expectation that public agencies should be open to all qualified applicants gave some groups, such as Irish, Jewish, and African Americans, more job opportunities than were open to them in the private sector because of segregation and quotas.

In the past two decades, significant progress has been made in making the federal bureaucracy more reflective of American diversity. Thirty-one percent of Americans were identified as minorities in the 2000 census, and they were 32 percent of the civilian federal workforce in 2004. African Americans are particularly well represented, being a substantially larger portion of the fed-

Table 1	Women and Minorities as a Percentage of the Senior Federal Civil Service Workforce		
	1985	1990	2004
Women			26
(Non-Hispanic whites)	8	12	(21)
(Minority women)			(5)
African Americans	4	5	7
Hispanics	1	2	4
Asians and Pacific Islanders	1	1	3
American Indians	—	0.5	0.8

NOTE: Overall, about 1 percent of all federal employees are at this pay grade; minority percentages include men and women.
SOURCE: Office of Personnel Management, "2004 Demographic Profile of the Federal Workforce" (www. opm.gov/feddata/ demograp/table2w); *The Fact Book*, 2005 Edition, 47–48 (www .opm.gov/feddata/factbook/2005). These are the latest data available as of mid-2007.

eral workforce (17 percent) than of the general population. American Indians and Asian Americans have a percentage of federal jobs close to their population share, whereas Hispanics remain significantly underrepresented in the federal workforce, despite an aggressive Hispanic recruitment program (7 percent of federal workers compared with 13 percent of the civilian labor

logical, but any method of assigning dollar values to bureaucratic output must be partly subjective. It is usually easier to place a value on a commodity than on a government service. We can estimate what price to place on a chair or a house by computing the cost of constructing, advertising, and selling it. But placing a dollar value on such public goals as education or consumer safety is much harder. How many children have to die from swallowing pills and medications before government requires pharmaceutical manufacturers to use childproof caps on bottles? How many lives saved makes it worthwhile for government to require auto manufacturers to install air bags? How much was the life of each person killed in the World Trade Center on 9/11 worth

(a calculation made in order to provide reimbursement for their families)? These are questions bureaucrats must answer. They are required to calculate how much a human life is worth and how productive an individual will be during his or her lifetime. Then they have to estimate the costs of putting the policies in place to protect lives, as well as to monitor and enforce the policies.

Private bureaucracies ask the same questions before their leaders decide whether it is profitable to install safer fuel tanks in cars or to remove a low-risk flaw from a child's toy. Although the federal bureaucrat, too, is always weighing costs against benefits, many people believe that the government should not use cost as the primary standard when lives are at risk.

force). However, the Hispanic labor force and census count includes both legal and illegal residents, and the latter would not be eligible for federal jobs. Women are represented almost in exact proportion as in the private sector, filling 44 percent of federal positions compared with 46 percent of private sector jobs, but still not at parity with their 51 percent share of the population.[1]

The relatively good news about the overall profile of the bureaucracy fades at the top of the pay scale. Women and minority men have not yet broken completely through the "glass ceiling" that has kept them out of top management positions. Even after passage of civil rights and equal opportunity legislation, barriers did not disappear because often the individuals who enforced the new regulations were opposed to the policies.

There is progress, however. Women now fill almost 26 percent of senior-grade pay positions (about one-fifth of those are minority women), more than twice the share held fifteen years ago. And, collectively, minorities hold 14 percent of all senior positions.

Federal court rulings and out-of-court settlements in discrimination cases account for some of the improvement in upward mobility. For example, women agents charged the FBI with denying them assignment to SWAT teams, even though experience on such teams was crucial to advancement. Only when they threatened to sue did the FBI change its promotion procedures.[2]

[1]Office of Personnel Management, *The Fact Book*, 2005 Edition, 47 (www.opm.gov/feddata/ factbook/2005).
[2]Katherine C. Naff, "Through the Glass Ceiling: Prospects for the Advancement of Women in the Federal Civil Service," *Public Administration Review* 54 (1994), 513; for an account of discrimination against women in the FBI, see Rosemary Dew and Pat Pap, *No Backup: My Life as a Female FBI Special Agent* (New York: Carroll & Graf, 2003).

© Ted Thai/Time Life Pictures/Getty Images

Federal employment has opened opportunities for African Americans. Shown here are two Bureau of Engraving and Printing employees checking the quality of $20 bills. The woman at right is holding $8000 in printing mistakes.

Another way to evaluate performance is to measure waste that stems from inefficiency and corruption. It is not particularly difficult to calculate how much more an agency paid because it failed to get competitive bids for equipment and supplies, hired more employees than necessary to do a job, contracted consultants to do imaginary work, or erred in calculating welfare payments or farm subsidies. Two spectacular cases of waste in government spending resulted from the Pentagon's awarding five-year, no-bid contracts to Haliburton and its subsidiaries to provide housing, food, laundry, and security services in Iraq that, prior to the 1980s, would have been provided by military personnel, and from the Department of Homeland Security's (DHS's) misman-

agement of rescue and recovery after hurricane Katrina. Millions in housing support was paid out to ineligible applicants and millions more wasted in purchases made on no-bid contracts.

Some kinds of government waste are harder to measure because no matter how well a program may be run, there will always be part of the public opposed to its goals. Perhaps the program is providing services a taxpayer thinks inappropriate for government, or maybe it serves relatively few people at a large cost. These were the criteria many Americans used to evaluate welfare programs. Accusations of waste and fraud were common, but as a percentage of overall expenditures, there was little client fraud in the welfare program. Most criticism stemmed from opposition to the program itself and services provided at great cost to a small clientele without appropriate results. Similar criticism comes from opponents of government health care and social insurance programs; some argue that private health insurance and pension programs are by definition more efficiently run because private businesses exist to make a profit. But in fact the administrative costs of Medicare are well below those of private health care insurers, and many private pension programs have been catastrophically underfunded and either terminated or placed in government receivership.

In a less-publicized example, a government commission called it wasteful to keep open hundreds of very small post offices that served rural communities. The commission was not alleging fraud or mismanagement, but believed that the post offices cost too much for the small number of people served. To the residents of these communities, however, their post offices were a good return on their tax dollars, and paying to keep them open was more efficient than having to drive miles to a distant station.

Citizens have rarely applied this standard of waste to corporate behavior, at least not prior to our more environmentally conscious era. Historically, private corporations have been able to waste more than a government agency of comparable size without the public ever taking notice. If a business or industry makes a profit, most people think it is a job well done, without asking whether the product or service offered is in itself wasteful. Marketing a hundred different kinds of breakfast cereal in packaging twice the size of the contents may not be an efficient use of resources, but if they sell, consumers are inclined to say, "Why not?" We may not like lime green sofas with pink stripes, but we do not consider their manufacturer wasteful for making them as long as the product is profitable. In 2001, when senior managers in the federal bureaucracy got bonuses averaging $11,000, it prompted public scrutiny of their agencies' performances.[7] When CEOs of corporations that lost money got multimillion-dollar bonuses, much of the public simply said, "Whatever the market will allow." (That thinking changed when some CEOs were found to have committed criminal acts.)

We see government expenditures as *our* money, and we feel entitled to complain, especially since payment of that money (taxes) is not voluntary. Only recently has such a large percentage of the public invested in stock that they have begun paying attention to how private bureaucracies manage *investors'* money.

Openness

The openness of public bureaucracy is another feature distinguishing it from a private bureaucracy. Private firms operate with much more secrecy than public agencies do, even when private actions have a significant impact on the public. For example, tobacco companies' lack of openness—long assumed to be their right—cost the lives of many people. The courts ordered tobacco companies to open their files only after much scientific evidence on the dangers of tobacco had accumulated.

In contrast, the greater visibility, or openness, of public agencies helps make them more responsive. Only by having knowledge of both the process and the content of public decisions can interested groups and individuals express their preferences effectively. No one articulated this better than James Madison when he wrote, "A popular Government without popular information or the means of acquiring it, is but a Prologue to a Farce or a Tragedy or perhaps both. Knowledge will forever govern ignorance, and a people who mean to be their own Governors, must arm themselves with the power knowledge gives."[8]

To this end, Congress in 1813 established the federal depository library program, "to guarantee public access to government information by making it available free of charge" in local libraries around the country. Today there are 1250 depository libraries. But as government grew and agencies and paper proliferated, it became harder for the public to keep track of what government was doing. In 1934, Congress passed the Federal Register Act, requiring that all government rules, regulations, and laws be published in the *Federal Register* and that all rules in their final version appear in the *Code of Federal Regulations.* (Today both are available online at www.gpoaccess.gov/fr/index.html.)

Congress went further in 1946 by passing the **Administrative Procedure Act (APA),** which provides for public participation in the rule-making process. All federal agencies must disclose their rule-making procedures and publish all regulations at least thirty days in advance of their effective date to allow time for public comment. Today citizens can often post comments on proposed rules at an agency's website, but it is common for public hearings to be held on controversial rules or those with wide impact. Environmental rules frequently provoke citizen reactions, with comments sometimes numbering in the tens of thousands.

Congress increased public access to the bureaucracy in another way by passing the Freedom of Information

Act in 1966. As amended in 1974, **FOIA** (pronounced "foy-ya") lets any member of the public apply to an agency for access to unclassified documents in its archives. The government also puts out a handbook telling how to take advantage of this right, and every government website is required to have a link to its FOIA office. FOIA cannot be used to gain access to internal records such as personnel files, for example, or sensitive documents on a living person. But it can be used to get your FBI file, should you have one, or the file of a person no longer living. Requests must be made according to a formal procedure, and they must cite specific documents. Agencies are not obligated to give "information," only to provide copies of the documents requested, if they have them and if they are not in an exempt category.

Efforts to make government agencies more open often run up against a desire to limit the distribution of critical or embarrassing information. It is the rare public or private bureaucracy that wants to reveal its failures. Thus an evaluation of FOIA found that agencies used many tactics to discourage people from seeking information, such as delaying responses to requests, charging high fees for copies of records (the State Department once charged $10 a page for copying records), and requiring detailed descriptions of documents requested.[9] The FBI once refused to expedite the release of information to a prisoner on death row who was afraid he would be executed before the information was available. The FBI's judgment that his situation did not show "exceptional need or urgency" was overruled by a federal court.[10]

As the chief executive, a president's views on the openness of agencies are also important. Under Presidents Reagan and George H. W. Bush, federal agencies adopted a narrow reading of the act, making it more difficult to get information.[11] In contrast, President Carter banned classification of documents unless they were clearly related to national security, and President **Clinton** issued an executive order authorizing the declassification of most documents twenty-five-years old or older and other orders that would also make government documents more accessible.[12]

George W. Bush began tightening access to government documents virtually upon taking office, as part of his broader goals of strengthening the Presidency and reducing both congressional and public oversight of the executive branch.[13] Vice President Cheney was a long-standing opponent of FOIA.[14] By executive order, Bush immediately established new rules for access to presi-

dential papers, including his father's, which were due to be opened to the public. (The American Political Science Association was among the plaintiffs who sued to reverse the order.)

One month after 9/11 Bush used national security as grounds for restricting FOIA access to all government papers and reports. His attorney general assured FOIA administrators that when they "decide to withhold records, in whole or in part," the Justice Department "will defend your decisions unless they lack a sound legal basis or present an unwarranted risk of adverse impact on the ability of other agencies to protect important records."[15] Thus under the Bush standard, any FOIA request denied by an agency on any "sound legal basis" could expect Justice Department backing. The administration ordered thousands of scientific and technical documents removed from public release, some from libraries and many from government websites, such as an Environmental Protection Agency (EPA) database on chemicals used at industrial sites.[16] The government also asked scientists' professional associations to restrict what they publish.[17] Some of this censorship just created confusion. For example the Federal Aviation Administration warned pilots they were not to fly in the vicinity of nuclear power plants but at the same time told them it could not say where the plants were located because that was "sensitive security information."[18]

The justification for withdrawal of so much information from public view was a claim in a captured al-Qaeda manual that it "expected" to get most of the information it needed to plan attacks from open sources.[19] Few Americans want to make it easier for terrorists to gain access to detailed site information on nuclear waste dumps, nuclear power plants, or other utilities, or instructions on how to construct nuclear, biological, and chemical weapons. At the same time, most citizens do not want the fear of terrorism to destroy the openness and access to information essential to any democracy. The Bush administration had removed from public view documents on World War II, the Korean War, relations with China, and other foreign policy papers that had been declassified decades ago and have nothing to do with terrorism. Whereas during Clinton's presidency four times as much material had been declassified as in the previous fifteen years, during Bush's first term declassification dwindled to about 10 percent of what it had been at the end of the nineties.[20] By 2004, the Bush administration was classifying an historic high of 125 documents per minute, in large part by creating vague new security classifications.[21]

Bush's narrow definition of public access rights and his penchant for secrecy drew criticism from both conservatives and liberals. The head of the nonpartisan interest group Judicial Watch concluded that the administration's attitude was simply that "the government is not to be questioned."[22] The Cato Institute, a libertarian think tank, accused the administration of being "a law unto itself."[23] Thomas Kean, a Republican appointed by Bush to cochair the commission investigating the 9/11 attack, said that in carrying out their investigation, "three-quarters of the classified material he reviewed . . . should not have been classified in the first place."[24]

Despite the limitations placed on FOIA, it has enabled individuals and groups to gain important and useful information. Citizens have used it to gather injury and fatality information on defective cars, to assess dangerous infant formulas, to reveal a link between aspirin and a disease known as Reye's syndrome, to learn that J. Edgar Hoover authorized the FBI to carry out a four-year investigation of women's rights groups, and to force the Internal Revenue Service (IRS) to release a 40,000-page manual on its auditing procedures.[25] Scholars have used FOIA to retrieve thousands of documents on Cold War diplomacy, to get records of medical experiments on the effect of radioactivity conducted on unwitting subjects, and to retrieve the FBI files of anthropologists kept under surveillance during the Cold War and the McCarthy era.

Public access to records that document experiments on human subjects and surveillance of private citizens is an essential check on abuse of power by federal bureaucrats. Yet some categories of information and types of deliberation among decision makers require privacy, and it is not always easy to balance individual privacy with openness of government. With the movement from paper to electronic files, new controversies arose over what should be classified. FOIA laws were written before the government began storing its records electronically so they did not define what electronic information was in the public domain. The first George Bush took his aides' e-mail tapes with him when he left office and argued that they were not public property. A federal appeals court ruled that these tapes are public records and must be preserved, and it applied the same ruling to Clinton administration requests for exemption. Because of these rulings, the second Bush administration was very cautious about exchanges of views by e-mail, and Bush himself stopped sending personal e-mail.

Another significant law mandating openness in government is the aptly named **Sunshine Act.** Adopted in 1977, it requires that most government meetings be conducted in public and that notice of such meetings must be posted in advance. Regulatory agencies, for example, must give notice of the date, time, place, and agenda of their meetings and follow certain rules to prevent unwarranted secrecy. State governments have adopted their own sunshine laws, and today it is difficult for any public body—city council or planning commission or any of their subgroups—to meet in secret to conduct official business. Results of meetings conducted in closed, unannounced sessions are open to citizen challenge.

Growth of the Federal Bureaucracy

The Founders did not discuss the federal "bureaucracy," but they did recognize the need for an administration to carry out laws and programs. They envisioned administrators with only a little power, charged with "executive details" and "mere execution" of the law. But the growing size and complexity of society and increasing demands that government do more have dramatically changed the nature of the federal bureaucracy.

George Washington's first cabinet included only three departments and the offices of attorney general and postmaster general, and all combined employed just a few hundred people. More people worked at Mount Vernon, Washington's plantation, than in the executive branch in the 1790s.[26] The Department of State had just nine employees. By 1800, the bureaucracy was still small, with only three thousand civil servants. Only the Treasury Department had much to do, collecting import and excise taxes and purchasing military supplies for an army of a few thousand. From then until 1990, the bureaucracy grew continuously, though at an uneven rate.

Why the Bureaucracy Has Grown

As we saw in Chapter 3, government, over time, responded to public wishes by creating federal agencies to assist and promote emerging economic interests of

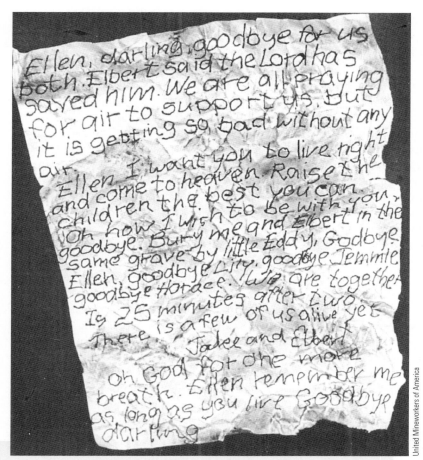

Jacob Vowell wrote this letter shortly before suffocating after a mine collapse in Fraterville, Tennessee, in 1902. Such disasters prompted government regulation of mining, which has since saved many lives. However, mining companies resist some regulations, and occasional disasters, such as the one in West Virginia in 2006, still occur.

business, agriculture, and labor and more recently to provide health and economic protections for workers, consumers, retirees, and other groups.[27] One scholar explained the bureaucracy's growth by pointing to Americans' discovery that "government can protect and assist as well as punish and repress."[28] Thus at the same time we criticize government's growth, we demand education, irrigation projects, roads, airports, job training, effective policing, consumer protection, agricultural subsidies, student loans, and many other services. Each of us might be willing to cut benefits for someone else, but most of us want to keep the benefits *we* have.

When new bureaucracies are created, the intent is to hold them to their original size, but most grow over time because once they are in place, additional responsibilities are assigned to them. After World War II, the Department of Defense did not return to its prewar size or scope because the Cold War gave us a new reason to support a massive military establishment. That era also created additional demands for health care and other services for veterans. The Administrative Procedure Act was passed in 1946 partly because the bureaucracy had grown so much in size and power during the Depression and World War II that Congress believed it needed to increase its oversight.[29]

Bureaucracy usually grows during national crises. After the Cold War, when thoughts turned to downsizing the Defense Department, supporters of military spending found new justifications for expansion in the threat of global terrorism. Forty-five days after 9/11, Congress rushed to pass the USA PATRIOT Act (officially, the Uniting and Strengthening America by Providing Appropriate Tools Required to Intercept and Obstruct Terrorism Act) before members had even read it. That act increased both the power and the size of the federal bureaucracy. Implementation of government's extraordinary new power to wiretap, search e-mail, and gain access to library borrowing records and many business records, both paper and electronic, required more personnel and increased spending. Opponents, however, are more frightened by the loss of privacy and liberty than by the increased size and cost of the bureaucracy.

Bureaucrats cannot produce growth on their own. Every agency and its budget is authorized and approved by Congress and the president and continues to exist because it is valuable to enough people with enough influence to sustain it. Sometimes government grows because the president and Congress want it to be more accountable. This often results in hiring more managers, producing greater inefficiency, and ironically, more difficulty in holding agencies accountable.[30]

The growth of the bureaucracy should be seen in the perspective of the overall growth of our economy and population. For example, the number of federal bureaucrats for every one thousand people in the United States decreased from sixteen in 1953 to nine in 2006. The major growth in public employment in recent decades has been at the state and local levels. Over 37 percent of all government workers were federal employees in 1953; in 2006, fewer than 13 percent were.[31]

Controlling Growth

Once departments are established, their consolidation or elimination is rare. More commonly, departments become so large that they must subdivide (for example, the Department of Commerce and Labor was divided into separate departments of Labor and Commerce) or for offices and agencies to become so big or their work so important they are made into cabinet departments (Veterans Affairs, DHS), where they become even larger.

Yet almost every president since Lyndon Johnson has tried to streamline or downsize the bureaucracy. Most were unsuccessful. For example, for all **Ronald Reagan's** talk against big government, it grew by over two hundred thousand employees during his administration. He even created a new cabinet office, the Department of Veterans Affairs, from what had been an independent agency. The Clinton administration's initiative on "reinventing government" did have limited success; the number of government employees decreased by 1.5 percent during his years in office.

Despite George W. Bush's stated admiration for smaller, more efficient government, the federal bureaucracy grew by 5000 during his first five years in office.[32] Some of the growth was due to the war on terrorism—adding a new cabinet department and increasing defense appointments. But there was also some padding—or thickening—of the bureaucracy through the creation of new positions at the senior level in cabinet departments that have nothing to do with national security.[33] The number of people at the highest pay level more than tripled during Bush's first three years. A 2004 survey showed that the new Department of Homeland Security had jumped from three to twenty-one layers of administration two years after its creation.[34]

Career civil servants are skeptical about the attempt of every administration to take on the bureaucracy and cut it down to size. One explanation of the perception gap is that there is a "natural antipathy" between presidents and career civil servants because the president is elected on his ability to articulate basic human values whereas "civil service is about enforcing rules and procedures and treating all citizens and issues equally."

Bureaucrats are not about values in the sense that politicians use that term.[35] Reform is difficult when presidents fill political leadership positions in agencies with individuals who do not stay around long enough to learn their jobs and have little chance of really reshaping their agencies. Presidents and their appointees find that reality does not always match political slogans. And presidents find that reforming the bureaucracy is much tougher than they anticipated and soon turn to other activities with more immediate payoffs. Thus in the view of a former OMB official, reform is mostly "three yards and a cloud of dust."[36] (See the box "What Do Bureaucrats Want Anyway?")

Agencies within the Federal Bureaucracy

The Constitution says little about the organization of the executive branch other than indicating a need for the president to have a cabinet. As government's role expanded, it became clear that a single type of organization would not be appropriate for every task assigned to the bureaucracy. Cabinet departments, for example, are headed by people who serve at the president's pleasure and who are there to help carry out his policies. But other agencies must implement law without reference to an individual president's preferences. These agencies require protection from political interference, as do those established to carry out highly technical work. In this section, we review the major types of agencies in the executive branch.

Departments

Departments are organizations within the executive branch that form the president's cabinet. Their heads, called secretaries (except for the head of the Justice Department, who is called the Attorney General), are appointed by the president with the consent of the Senate, and they are directly responsible to the president. There are fifteen departments; the newest is DHS (see Figure 1). These departments constitute the lion's share of the federal bureaucracy; the largest employer is the Defense Department, with close to 30 percent of all civil servants.

Cabinet departments exist to carry out the president's policy in specific functional areas: national security, federal law enforcement, fiscal policy, health and welfare, foreign relations, and so forth. They are staffed by career civil servants, but all top policy making posi-

WHAT DO BUREAUCRATS WANT, ANYWAY?

Bureaucrats are not much different from the rest of us. They are no more likely to favor raising taxes or government spending; they have about the same confidence as other citizens in government and other institutions, such as organized religion, business, labor, and the press; and they are about as likely as other Americans to favor or oppose busing and gun control.[1]

When civil servants do differ from other citizens, they seem more open to diversity. For example, they are more likely to say they would vote for an African American or a woman as president and less likely to accept traditional gender roles. They are more likely to vote than are other Americans and are more likely to favor candidates who are supportive of government spending.[2] And they are somewhat *less* likely than other Americans to approve government intrusions into people's private lives. They also are less likely to approve censoring people who hold unpopular views or laws banning pornography or interracial marriage. On only one issue are they more liable to favor "big government": they are somewhat more likely to favor wiretapping.

Federal bureaucrats, like many other Americans, are critical of their own institutions. "Having endured a decade of downsizing, two decades of bureaucratic bashing, three decades of constant reform, four decades of increasing workloads, and five decades of pay and hiring freezes," the attitudes of many federal bureaucrats do not add up to a "healthy public service."[3]

Not surprisingly, federal bureaucrats do not have a particularly high opinion of the political appointees who wander into their agencies for short periods (eighteen to twenty-four months on average) to fill leadership positions and then quickly disappear, often without ever learning very much about what the agency is all about.[4] What most bureaucrats seem to want is for Congress and the president to stop using them as guinea pigs for their management experiments and instead to provide the tools and training they need to do their jobs right. Sixty percent of federal employees said that Congress "generally acts in ways that worsen the management of their organizations," and 41 percent said the same about the president. Overall, the attitude of federal employees is not "Show me the money" but "Let me do my job."[5]

At lower levels of the civil service, employees are especially apt to complain about their lack of access to training, and at most levels there is dissatisfaction over the lack of equipment, especially state-of-the-art computers, necessary to do their work properly and efficiently. Other major concerns are the impact of past reforms that have left many programs without sufficient personnel to carry out their work and the increasing number of positions within the bureaucracy that have been removed from civil service and made appointive. Some people believe that this has made the work of the bureaucracy too politicized. In addition, many of those at lower levels believe that there is too much bureaucracy—too many layers of administration between top and bottom, impeding communication and making their jobs more difficult.

Bureaucrats are very hard on themselves, both their own performance and that of their agencies, citing too many people in positions they are unqualified for, especially senior people and political appointees. They want "to eliminate the 'yes' men (and women) and give responsibility back to the employees."[6]

[1] Gregory B. Lewis, "In Search of the Machiavellian Milquetoasts: Comparing Attitudes of Bureaucrats and Ordinary People," *Public Administration Review* 50 (1990), 220–227.

[2] James Garand, Catherine Parkhurst, and Rousanne Jourdan Seoud, "Bureaucrats, Policy Attitudes, and Political Behavior," *Journal of Public Administration Research and Theory* 1 (1990): 177–212.

[3] Paul C. Light, "What Federal Employees Want from Reform: Reform Watch Brief No. 5," Brookings Institution, March 2002, www.brookings.edu/comm/reformwatch/rw05.htm.

[4] Paul C. Light, "Fact Sheet on the Continued Thickening of Government," Brookings Institution, July 23, 2004, www.brookings.edu/views/papers/light/20040723.htm.

[5] Light, "What Federal Employees Want," 10.

[6] Ibid., 7.

tions in each division of a department are held by presidential appointees. The fifteen cabinet departments have more than 350 such positions. Permanent staff believe that the increase in the number of appointive senior positions makes their work more difficult.

Independent Agencies

Independent agencies differ from departments in that they are usually smaller and their heads do not sit in the cabinet. Agency heads are, however, appointed by and responsible to the president. And occasionally a

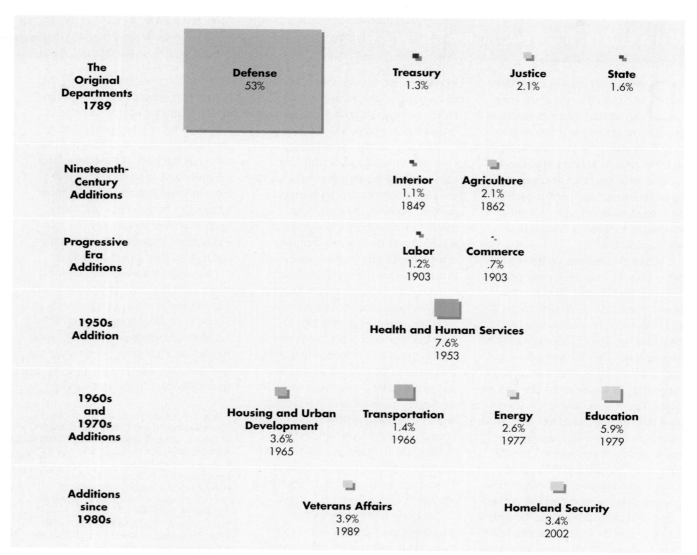

| The Original Departments 1789 | Defense 53% | | Treasury 1.3% | Justice 2.1% | State 1.6% |

FIGURE 1 • **The Development and Relative Size of Cabinet Departments** *Percentages are each department's share of the **discretionary** budget authority for fiscal 2007. The figures add to less than 100% because of noncabinet agencies that are allocated funds (the judicial branch, the independent agencies, etc.). The modern Department of Defense (1949) replaced the Departments of War (1789) and the Navy (1798); the Justice Department (1870) replaced the Department of the Attorney General (1789); the Commerce and Labor Departments were first established in 1903 as a joint enterprise; and the Department of Health, Education and Welfare (1953) was divided in 1979 into the Department of Health and Human Services and the Department of Education.*

SOURCE: *United States Budget for Fiscal Year 2007 Historical Tables* (Washington, D.C.: Government Printing Office, 2006), Tab. 5.5, 117; *Manual of the United States Government, 2003–2004* (Washington, D.C.: Government Printing Office, 2003).

president does extend cabinet status to the head of an independent agency, most notably the director of the EPA. Some agencies, such as the EPA, the CIA, the Social Security Administration, the Peace Corps, and the National Aeronautics and Space Administration (NASA), are well known to the public. Others, such as the Office of Government Ethics, are relatively unknown.

Some independent agencies are responsible for highly specialized areas of policy, such as space exploration (NASA) or law enforcement (FBI). The people appointed to head them usually have an appropriate professional background, not just a political profile acceptable to the president. However, if the agency deals with policy that has widespread impact, as the EPA and CIA do, political credentials are likely to be the president's first consideration in naming a director.

Independent Regulatory Boards and Commissions

Although unfamiliar to most Americans, independent agencies affect almost every aspect of our daily lives—the air we breathe, the water we drink, the interest on a bank loan, the fee at an ATM, the labeling on our food and contaminants allowed in that food, phone and mail service, and the construction of every car, train, plane, or bus we ride on.

Each independent regulatory board and commission regulates a specific area of business or the economy. Examples include the Federal Communications Commission (FCC), which regulates the electronic media; the Securities and Exchange Commission (SEC), which makes and enforces rules regarding stocks, bonds, and securities; and the Federal Reserve System (the Fed), which sets prime interest rates and controls the amount of money in circulation. These and other regulatory agencies are designated "independent" because the work they do is supposed to be removed from politics as much as possible. Congress created the first such commission, the Interstate Commerce Commission, in 1887 to decide such things as interstate freight rates, railroad ticket prices, routes, and conditions of service.

Each of these independent regulatory boards and commissions is directed by five to ten presidential appointees. By law, each board and commission must be balanced with members of both major political parties. Appointees serve staggered terms and cannot be removed by presidents who dislike their decisions. Because of the technical knowledge needed for decision making, appointments are supposed to be based on expertise rather than partisan considerations. Of course, it is almost impossible for politics, in the sense of an individual's values, not to have some impact on decision making. Presidents who want less government regulation appoint commissioners who share that value. Commissioners, in turn, can then make it difficult for the professionals in the agency to carry out their regulatory mission. However, the goal of having these independent commissions is to make politics secondary to professional expertise.

Government Corporations

Government corporations are businesses run by government to provide services the public needs but that no private company will provide because they are not profitable—or were not profitable at the time government began providing the service. The first government corporation, the Tennessee Valley Authority (TVA), was created when no utility company was willing to invest in the infrastructure necessary to bring electricity to what was then a very poor, undeveloped region of the country. The TVA still supplies electricity to its part of the country.

The United States Postal Service, which was originally a cabinet department, was converted to a business operation in 1971. Formerly a government monopoly, it now has competition from UPS and FedEx, for example, for some of the services it provides. In the 1960s, when railroads were no longer willing to provide passenger service, the government created the National Railroad Passenger Corporation (Amtrak). And because no private insurance company would ever bear the risk of insuring private bank deposits, the government established a corporation to protect your savings account (the Federal Deposit Insurance Corporation). Similarly, the government is now the main purveyor of terrorism insurance because after 9/11, private firms were no longer willing to assume the risk, just as after hurricane Katrina, private insurers wanted government to take even greater responsibility for insuring homeowners in coastal areas against flood damage.

Government corporations charge for their services or products but their primary objective is to provide a needed service, not to make a profit. Of course, the government is quite happy if they do or if they at least break even. When a government corporation does become profitable, its assets may be sold to private businesses and the corporation closed. This is what happened with CONRAIL, the government corporation that took over rail freight and turned it back into a profitable enterprise. The U.S. Postal Service also is now showing a profit after decades of needing government subsidies to balance its budget. Opponents of government corporations would like to see both the Postal Service and the unprofitable Amtrak completely privatized. But the services provided are so important to the national economy that without the certainty that private businesses would guarantee their continuation, government would have difficulty justifying the sale of their assets.

What Bureaucracies Do

Having examined forms of bureaucratic organization, we now look in greater detail at the sources of the bureaucracy's authority and the responsibilities assigned to it.

After elected officials make a law, someone must carry it out. That is the primary job of the bureaucracy. Bureaucrats convert laws passed by Congress and signed by the president into rules and actions that have an actual impact on people and things. We call this process **policy implementation.** The general process of policy implementation has two major components: administering policies and making them.

Administering Policy

Public bureaucracy's oldest job is to administer the law. To "administer" is to execute, enforce, and apply the rules that have been made either by Congress or the bureaucracy itself. Thus if policy makers decide to go to war, they must empower agencies to acquire weapons, recruit and train soldiers, and devise a winning strategy. Policy making without administration is tantamount to having no policy at all.

Administration includes thousands of different kinds of activities. It involves writing checks to farmers who receive payments for growing—or not growing—crops, providing direct services to the public, evaluating how well programs are working, prosecuting those who try to defraud the government, and maintaining buildings and offices. For forest rangers, administration involves helping backpackers in the Grand Canyon or putting out a forest fire in northern Minnesota.

Making Policy

Responsibility for administering policy inevitably conferred lawmaking powers on the bureaucracy. This can be illustrated with the example of the Americans with Disabilities Act (ADA). The ADA directs employers to make a "reasonable accommodation" for a competent worker with a disability that "substantially limits" a major life activity such as seeing or walking, except when this causes "undue hardship."[37]

This seemingly straightforward law is in fact extremely complex and its impact far-reaching. Although the act went into effect in 1992, the Equal Employment Opportunity Commission (EEOC), which has respon-

sibility for its implementation, is still clarifying what specific provisions in the act mean. What is the difference between a "reasonable accommodation" and an "undue hardship"? When voters want local governments to spend less, is the $2 million that Des Plaines, Illinois, had to shell out for sidewalks and curb cuts an "undue hardship" or not?[38] Will the EEOC let colleges and universities make only some classrooms and offices accessible to students and staff in wheelchairs, or must every classroom and faculty office be accessible to people with disabilities, at a cost of millions of dollars for large universities?

Answering such questions and formulating rules to implement them is de facto policy making. Implementation requires disseminating the rules and negotiating interpretations with the parties who have to put them in place and enforce them. State and local counterparts of the EEOC and their clients must be informed of the rules, assisted in their attempts to use the rules, and monitored in their progress. Bills must be paid, disputes resolved, and information collected as to how successful the program is. If affected parties reject the EEOC's interpretation or the officials' implementation, the rules can be challenged in federal court. This is where almost all disputed provisions of the ADA are being decided. Bureaucrats very often do not have the last word in determining how a policy is implemented.

The passage of thousands of complex bills like the ADA accounts for the growth in policy making functions of public bureaucracies. Industrialization, population growth, urbanization, and profound changes in science, transportation, and communications have put problems of a more complex nature on government's agenda. The large number and technical nature of these problems, as well as policy differences among its members, have often limited Congress's ability to draft specific policy responses.

Congress often responds to this situation by enacting a general statement of goals and identifying actions that would help achieve them. Congress then delegates the power to an agency with the relevant expertise to draft specific rules that will achieve these goals. This **delegated legislative authority** empowers executive branch agencies to draft, as well as execute, specific policies. Just as the ADA left rule making to the EEOC, any tax reform legislation requires thousands of rules to be written by the IRS and the Treasury Department. Agency-made policy is just as binding as acts of Congress because agencies make it at the direction of Congress. In strictly numerical terms, agencies make much more policy than Congress because agencies issue many new rules and regulations for the implementation of each new law Congress passes.

Many political scientists believe that Congress abdicates its authority and acts in an irresponsible manner by refusing, because of political pressures and its heavy workload, to develop specific guidelines for agencies.[39] This leaves agencies to implement policies without much guidance from Congress beyond the wording of each bill. Sometimes, however, agency complaints about the ambiguities or lack of specificity in legislation are just excuses not to implement disliked policies. Often these lead to partisan conflicts, especially over regulatory policy. Congress can send more detailed directives to agencies. But this does not prevent the political appointees who head executive branch agencies from resisting congressional directives they dislike on the grounds that they are too complex or unrealistic to follow.

In effect, the competition between the White House and Congress was extended to the bureaucracy when Congress delegated legislative authority to agencies. This competition can intensify or subside, depending on whether the president is of the same party as congressional majorities. However, the competition has continued even in those recent years when Republicans controlled both houses of Congress and the White House.

Sometimes agencies are in the difficult position of having to satisfy competing demands. To figure out what Congress, the president, and others want, agency officials read congressional debates and testimony and talk to members of Congress, committee staffers, White House aides, lobbyists, and others. Although agencies also try to determine what the public wants, they are more likely to respond to well-organized and well-funded groups that closely monitor their actions. As a result, agency-made policy is often less responsive to the general public than to particular interests.

Regulation

A special kind of policy making called **regulation** produces rules, standards, or guidelines conferring benefits and imposing restrictions on business conduct and economic activity. Regulations have the force of law and are made by agencies whose directors and board members are appointed by the president and whose operating procedures are generally governed by the Administrative Procedure Act. Regulatory agencies include not only independent regulatory boards and commissions but also some independent agencies, such as the EPA, and some agencies within cabinet departments, such as the Food and Drug Administration (FDA) in Health and Human Services and the Office of Safety and Health Administration (OSHA) in the Labor Department.

Regulatory actions include two steps: making rules and adjudicating their enforcement. Rule making is the establishment of standards that apply to a class of individuals or businesses. Adjudication occurs when agencies try individuals or firms charged with violating standards. To do this, they use procedures that are very similar to those of courts.

Most regulations derive from laws passed by Congress that direct agencies to take actions to accomplish the goals established in the legislation. Environmental legislation, for example, requires regulatory agencies to set standards for clean air, safe disposal of toxic wastes, or safe workplaces that businesses must meet. Businesses are often allowed some flexibility in the methods used to meet the standard, but failure to comply can result in fines or other legal penalties.

Consumer protection legislation directs federal regulators to set quality or safety standards for certain types of products, such as cars, toys, food, and medical equipment. This is why there are seat belts, air bags, and shatterproof windows in cars and why materials used to make children's toys or clothing cannot be flammable or toxic. Regulations may also require businesses to provide information through labeling, such as the cancer warnings on cigarette packages and lists of ingredients noting trans fats, sugar, salt, and vitamin content on packaged food.

Another form of regulation is licensing the right to own or use public properties. For example, the FCC licenses the publicly owned airwaves to people who own and operate radio and television stations.

Data Collection and Analysis

In the course of policy making and administration, the bureaucracy performs other functions. It collects data, as in the decennial census, and it makes information available to the public. Much of what we know about ourselves as a people comes from the government's collection of data on births and deaths, occupations and income, housing and health, crime, and many other things. A cursory glance at the annual *Statistical Abstract of the United States* shows that the government reports on everything from the incidence of abortions to the

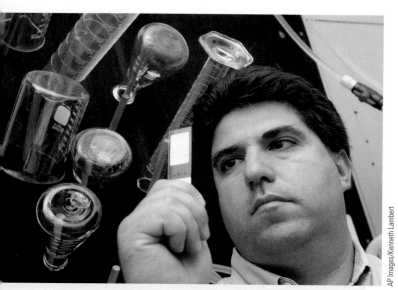

Not all bureaucrats push paper. This scientist with the Food and Drug Administration (FDA) examines breast cancer protein in his lab in Bethesda, Maryland.

AP Images/Kenneth Lambert

export of zinc and in between informs us how much celery we eat and how many DVDs we own.

Bureaucracy also keeps us informed about what government is doing, and the Internet is a valuable tool to assist in this function. Every federal agency has a website with information about its policies and programs and an e-mail link for feedback from the public. If we want to know the rules governing camping in national parks, we can call the National Park Service or go to its website. If we want to know the fate of a bill in Congress or how our representatives voted on it, we can find it posted on the Internet.

The bureaucracy engages in research, too. A prime example is the Department of Agriculture, which for nearly 140 years has conducted research on how to grow bigger and better crops, raise healthier animals, and transport and market products more effectively. Government researchers, such as those at the National Institutes of Health and the Centers for Disease Control and Prevention, do much of the country's medical research, especially that related to mental health and epidemiology. Many vaccines and prescription drugs are also developed in government labs, and the Internet was invented by military bureaucrats. Every cabinet department has career civil servants—geologists, chemists, physicists, engineers, etc.—carrying out research relevant to its area of policy making, be it rocketry, soil

erosion, climate change, space travel, weapons development or high-tech communications and surveillance.

Finally, in addition to its responsibilities in the four major areas just described, the bureaucracy provides continuity in governing. Presidents and members of Congress come and go, and political appointees in the bureaucracy stay an average of two years—many barely learn their jobs by the time they leave. Career civil servants have a much deeper knowledge of their agencies' work, which makes them better at it and more productive than short-term political appointees. They keep government agencies functioning day in and day out so that all essential work continues even as elected and appointed officials come and go from office.

Politics and Professional Standards

As the part of government that implements policies made by elected officials, the bureaucracy cannot escape politics and it is subject to constant lobbying. That does not mean that civil servants have the green light to implement policy in a partisan manner. Today's civil servants are governed by laws that give priority to professional competence over political loyalty. Most Americans want fair, apolitical performance such that the quantity and quality of any government service they receive is not dependent on whether they belong to the same party as the president or their member of Congress. And most of us would prefer to have a civil engineer rather than a political crony in charge of building the dam near our town. The chances that the engineer will get the job over the crony have improved significantly since patronage was outlawed in the federal bureaucracy.

The Merit System

For decades, American public bureaucracies were staffed under the **patronage** system, which allowed elected officials to fill administrative jobs on the basis of political loyalty rather than merit. By providing their supporters with jobs, elected officials could strengthen their political base, and many people regarded this as simply a means for government agencies to provide employment to citizens. Patronage hiring was usually referred to as the spoils system because it operated in rough accordance with the principle "to the victor belong the spoils," as the newly elected filled jobs with their own supporters. At the federal level, **Andrew Jackson**'s presidential election in 1828 was a watershed in using the patronage system. Jackson believed that any white male citizen of average intelligence and goodwill could do a government job well. So he reversed the existing practice of naming mostly well-off people from the East Coast by appointing less-well-off supporters from frontier areas.

The most obvious problem with staffing the bureaucracy with political supporters rather than by competitive recruitment is that jobs will go to people who are not competent to perform their duties. This became a major problem as government work became more technical and specialized. Furthermore, patronage could and frequently did lead to corruption, in particular to deal making between candidates and voters or individuals who controlled blocs of voters. Voters supported candidates who promised them jobs or other favors. Such corruption increasingly sullied city councils, state legislatures, and Congress during the 1800s.

Although patronage was affecting government performance, the influence wielded by the political machines that had grown powerful through its use kept Congress from acting until an unsuccessful job seeker assassinated President James Garfield in 1881. The Pendleton Act of 1883 established the **Civil Service Commission** to fill designated positions within the bureaucracy with people who had proved their competence in competitive examinations. Jobs under the commission's jurisdiction were part of the **merit system.** The new law also protected people holding merit positions from pressure to support or oppose particular candidates and from dismissal for political reasons.

Neutral Competence

The merit system established **neutral competence** as the professional standard for civil service employees. It requires that individuals filling merit positions be chosen for their expertise in executing policy and that they carry out their work in a nonpartisan or neutral manner. This standard assumes that there is no Republican or Democratic way to build a sewer, collect customs duties, enforce laws, or fight a war. In effect, it says that partisan politics have no place in bureaucracy. It also implies that bureaucrats should not profit personally from the decisions they make.

Woodrow Wilson, a strong advocate of neutral competence, believed that bureaucrats could learn to execute policy both expertly and responsively.[40] He saw government jobs as either political or administrative in nature and felt that by knowing which was which, we could create a bureaucracy that elected officials could control. Most current observers are less sanguine about the possibility of completely separating politics from administration.[41]

The Pendleton Act authorized the president to extend merit system coverage to additional federal jobs by executive order. In 1884, the merit system covered about 10 percent of the jobs in the federal bureaucracy, and by the middle of the twentieth century the figure rose to 90 percent. This created a rather rigid system of job classifications, pay, and rank known as the *general schedule.* It limited the president's appointment powers and also made it difficult to remove people for cause. Reforming the system was a central issue in **Jimmy Carter**'s 1976 run for the presidency. The Civil Service Reform Act of 1978 was an attempt to modernize the personnel system and make it more competitive with the private sector. It was also a response to complaints that the commission was concentrating on management at the expense of merit hiring, equal opportunity, and regulation.

The act got rid of the Civil Service Commission and divided its functions among several agencies. The Office of Personnel Management (OPM) today is responsible for managing a merit system for all federal employees nationwide and for working with the president to ensure that appointments to positions in exempt categories also adhere to basic standards of merit and political neutrality. Grievances and discrimination complaints are now handled by separate agencies and a new unit, the Whistleblowers Protection Agency (WBA), designed to defend **whistleblowers** against retaliatory action by their agencies. The act gave managers more opportunity to fire incompetent subordinates, and it established a more flexible classification of civil service positions. It also created the Senior Executive Service (SES) to fill the top management positions in the executive branch in the civil service. Those in the SES may be career civil servants or political appointees; they are not locked into a position but can move from agency to agency, carrying rank with them. They are also paid on the basis of performance and may receive bonuses. A few units have their own personnel systems, such as the State Department's Foreign Service.

At least one-quarter of all positions in the federal bureaucracy are now in categories exempt from the hiring and compensation rules that govern the general schedule of civil service appointments, although all are

SCIENCE, POLITICS, AND THE BUREAUCRACY

The thousands of government scientists, mathematicians, engineers, investigators, and data analyzers who provide the information that informs policy making and implementation were hired specifically for their professional expertise, and it is their mandate as civil servants to provide that information with neutral competence. It is up to elected officials whether they choose to act on the information provided.

All administrations vet scientific reports, and on many issues there is no clear consensus in the findings. A president may cherry-pick reports for the evidence that supports his policy preferences. There are many examples of this, such as whether it is the right or wrong time to raise taxes or cut taxes, to raise the prime interest rate or hold it steady, or approve or ban a new medical procedure. In most cases a president or members of Congress acknowledge disagreements among the experts, but they do not try to change the data. Government researchers whose findings are not followed may not be happy with the policy results,

but if they are not pressured to change their findings, their neutral competence has not been challenged.

For example, President Reagan did not try to alter scientific findings about AIDS, but he did refuse to act on them. However, C. Everett Koop, his surgeon general, against administration wishes but in accordance with his own understanding of his public responsibility, undertook a mass education campaign on AIDS. The mailing of information to every American household helped reduce panic and fear about the disease, change behavior, and undoubtedly contributed to saving many lives. And, even by going against the man who appointed him, Koop managed to keep his job.

The threat to neutral competence comes when a president, or his political appointees in federal agencies, suppress data or actually edit the content of research reports to fit policy. These attempts are most egregious when there is a consensus among experts.[1] For example, George W. Bush did not deny that global warming was occurring, but he did not accept the interna-

tional scientific consensus, nor the findings of government scientists, that human behavior was a major contributing factor. In 2002 and 2003, a White House lawyer who had worked for the oil industry's largest lobby, the American Petroleum Institute, and who had no science training, edited reports on global warming by government scientists to make their conclusions seem far less certain.[2]

In 2006, Jim Hansen, an expert on climate change and the long-time head of NASA's Goddard Institute for Space Studies, complained that the administration had ordered him to stop giving speeches on global warming and not to talk about how his findings differed from administration policy.[3] One of his reports had been edited to bring the conclusions nearer the president's position. The wording changes were made by a twenty-four-year-old political appointee at NASA, previously a public relations aide in Bush's presidential campaign, who had no scientific training and in fact no college degree.

Hanson's case is but one of many attempts by the Bush administration to

supposed to be governed by the basic rules of merit and neutral competence. In fact, there are many more political appointments in the upper levels of bureaucracy today than there were thirty years ago.

Even within the regular civil service, merit is not all that counts. The system favors veterans by adding a five-point bonus to their test scores (disabled veterans get ten points). And positioning counts as well: people already in the system are favored because they know about job openings first and may have skills identical to those in the job listing. As in the private sector, sometimes job descriptions are written to fit particular individuals.

Banning patronage from federal hiring did not end partisan political activity by federal employees, so Congress passed another law expressly defining the limits on such activities. The **Hatch Act** of 1939 prohibited federal employees, and state and local employees supported by federal funds, from active participation in partisan campaigns, even at the state and local levels. Political activities were restricted to voting, attending rallies, and having private conversations. The Hatch Act was controversial from the beginning. Supporters argued that it protected the neutral competence of civil servants from partisan influences. Critics said it made civil servants put policy preferences above neutral competence. The former surgeon general, Richard Carmona, testified in 2007 that high officials in the Bush administration prohibited him from speaking about or reporting on issues ranging from stem cells to contraception and many other health issues. Administration officials "delayed for years and tried to 'water down' a landmark report on secondhand smoke"[4] that when eventually released documented the dangers of even brief exposure to cigarette smoke. He was also asked to mention the president three times on every page of his speeches.[5]

Bush appointees have also ordered changes in scientific papers that are unrelated to policy but illustrate micromanaging of scientific wording to conform to a political sensibility. A discussion of the Big Bang explanation of the origins of the universe, for example, was altered to magnify its uncertainty, presumably to leave room for a biblical interpretation. In another paper a reference by NASA scientists to the death of the sun in the distant future was expunged. A spokeswoman for the

agency said, "NASA is not in the habit of frightening the public with doom and gloom scenarios."[6]

These charges go beyond the surgeon general or NASA. The Union of Concerned Scientists charged Bush with ordering politically motivated changes in the evidence and conclusions of reports prepared by government scientists on climate change, mercury pollution, drug safety, and the effectiveness of sex education in disease prevention.[7]

It is probably easier for political appointees to accept presidential directives than it is for career professionals. A NASA public affairs officer, for example—a political appointee—said his job was "to make the president look good." However, his counterpart at the Goddard Institute said it was not her job nor that of the Institute's. "I'm a career civil servant and Jim Hansen is a scientist."

Falsifying or supressing scientific research in the interest of political goals can obviously work in the short run. In the longer run, however, it undermines the public's faith in government and in

science, too, and can delay making policy choices to deal with the issue that is being surpressed. As a retiring chair of the House Committee on Science remarked, "This is a town where everyone says they are for science-based decision making—until the science leads to a politically inconvenient conclusion."[8]

[1]For an overview of findings on climate change, go to www.realclimate.org.
[2]Andrew Revkin, "Bush Aide Softened Greenhouse Gas Links to Global Warming," New York Times, June 8, 2005, 1.
[3]Andrew C. Revkin, "Climate Expert Says NASA Tried to Silence Him," New York Times, January 29, 2006, 1; Juliet Eilperin, "Censorship Is Alleged at NOAA: Scientists Afraid to Speak Out," Washington Post, February 11, 2006, A7.
[4]Gardiner Harris, "Surgeon General Sees Five Year Term as Compromised," Washington Post, (July 11, 2006). [6]www.nytimes.com/2007/07/11/washington/11surgeon.html?_r=1&oref=slogin.
[5]Ibid.
[6] www.ucsusa.organd also the Federation of American Scientists (www.usfas.org).
[7]"What About Us?" (Editorial), New York Times, July 28, 2006.
[8]Claudia Dreifus, "A Conversation with Sherwood Boehlert: A Science Advocate and 'an Endangered Species,' He Bids Farewell," New York Times, May 9, 2006.

second-class citizens by denying them the First Amendment guarantees of freedom of speech and association. In 1993, Congress changed the law to allow most federal employees to hold office within a political party, to participate in political campaigns, and to raise funds for political action committees when they are not on duty. However, all employees of law enforcement and national security agencies remain under the earlier, more stringent prohibitions.[42]

Sometimes the range within which bureaucrats can exercise neutral competence is severely restricted by their superiors. Agencies and department heads are po-

litical, not merit, appointees, and many are specifically charged with carrying out the programs of the president who appointed them. In addition, some of the policy that bureaucrats are implementing was made by presidential directive or executive order. EPA bureaucrats gearing up to implement Clinton's executive orders on clean water and clean air in December 2000 were required to write very different rules several months later when Bush rescinded Clinton's orders and substituted radically different policies. When an agency appears to be partisan in the way it implements, or fails to implement, congressional acts, it may be because of presidential directives or orders issued by the short-term political appointee temporarily heading the agency. Bureaucrats in the Drug Enforcement Agency were ordered to make campaign appearances in the 2006 election, supporting Republican candidates and making announcements about antidrug grants coming to the candidate's district. Of course, announcing federal largesse to a community right before an election is not new, but it is usually done by elected officials—not bureaucrats.

The politicization of the civil service reached a new high in the Bush administration. A widely publicized example occurred in 2007, when critics charged that the firing of eight U.S. attorneys was done because the attorneys were not willing to follow directives from the attorney general's office to investigate Democratic candidates running for key offices. A congressional investigation led to Attorney General Alberto Gonzales claiming he couldn't remember key details about how it was decided to fire the attorneys, the resignation of the deputy attorney general and two lower-level political operatives in the Justice Department, and a refusal of other administration officials to testify under oath. After congressional committees issued subpoenas requiring testimony under oath to high-level Justice Department officials, Gonzales himself resigned, though the investigation of the events continues. Although U.S. attorneys are political appointments, and often are replaced by new administrations, it is rare to fire them for anything but incompetence during a presidential term. Moreover, the public expects that Justice Department attorneys will act in a neutrally competent way and not use the law to pursue explicitly partisan objectives.

Two other agencies came under heavy fire for not exercising neutral competence. The first was the CIA. The day after the 9/11 attacks, President Bush made clear to the head of his counterterrorism unit and to others in his administration his interest in establishing a connection between Iraq and al-Qaeda.[43] The evidence of a connection was weak, but Bush thought an invasion of Iraq could be justified on the grounds that Saddam Hussein's arsenal of weapons of mass destruction presented an imminent threat. When he asked **George Tenet,** the CIA director, whether there was evidence to support his case to Congress and the public, Tenet told him it was a "slam dunk."[44] (Later, Tenet said he had been misquoted, but he didn't make any correction at the time.) Postwar investigators found no evidence to support the claim that Iraq possessed stockpiles of weapons of mass destruction or even active programs

to develop them.[45] Furthermore, many arms experts within the agency had questioned the validity of the evidence Bush cited in his public statements.

Tenet had been a Clinton appointee whom Bush retained when he became president; his retention and reappointment were dependent on Bush's judgment of his work. Because Bush's policy preferences on Iraq were well known inside and outside the administration, most concluded that Tenet had violated his neutral competence mandate and simply told the president what he wanted to hear. Having lost credibility in Congress and with the public, Tenet was forced to resign. Bush replaced him with Porter Goss, a political ally in Congress—albeit a former CIA employee—with instructions to purge the agency of career agents who would not subordinate their professional views to administration policy. A number of the agency's highest-level, longest-serving agents resigned or were forced out. Many became sources (leaks) for a number of new books on the politicization of intelligence gathering and analysis.[46]

Hurricane Katrina brought to the public eye a politicization of another important federal agency, FEMA, the Federal Emergency Management Agency. During the Clinton administration, the agency had been highly professionalized and performed well during several hurricane emergencies. But President Bush filled top FEMA slots with political supporters or friends of influential Republicans who had no emergency management expertise. Michael Brown, the director of FEMA at the time of hurricane Katrina, was a lawyer whose previous experience was as an administrator in the International Arabian Horse Association. He had been appointed to FEMA by the then director, who had been Bush's campaign manager in 2000. Brown oversaw federal efforts in New Orleans and was told by the president that he was doing "a heckuva job," a comment widely quoted at the time and after as the incompetence of both preparation for the hurricane and the response to it became ever clearer. The director of Homeland Security removed Brown from the New Orleans oversight and Brown later resigned from FEMA.

The neutral competence standard prohibits bureaucrats from gaining materially from their decisions. Civil servants are supposed to make decisions based on their professional judgment and not to advance the cause of something in which they have a financial stake. For example, bureaucrats who are stockholders in chemical companies are not supposed to be making policy about

James Nielsen/AFP/Getty Images

Although the party that wins the presidency no longer controls most government jobs, it still controls the top jobs—several thousands—to which the president usually appoints party members. President Bush appointed political operatives rather than experienced managers to the top jobs at FEMA. When hurricane Katrina hit the Gulf Coast, their incompetence in coordinating evacuation and providing relief was apparent.

chemical waste. Even if it were possible for policy makers to put self-interest aside, holding stakes in firms they regulate automatically takes on the appearance of a conflict of interest. This in turn would allow critics of a decision to challenge the regulation in court. Furthermore, the appearance of a conflict of interest undermines public confidence in government.

To better define what constitutes a conflict of interest, Congress passed the Ethics in Government Act in 1978. The act sought to prevent former public officials with inside information from using it and their contacts to give their new employers an unfair competitive advantage. The act barred former public servants from lobbying their agencies for one year and prohibited for life lobbying on matters in which they "personally and substantially" participated as public officials.

President Clinton issued an executive order requiring many of his political appointees to sign a pledge that they would not lobby the agencies in which they worked for five years after leaving government and would never lobby for foreign political parties and governments. But in 2002, four of Clinton's former cabinet members and other high-level political appointees, including his trade representative and the heads of the FCC and the SEC, each held multiple seats on corporate boards. It is not unthinkable that they were hired for their government contacts, although holding such positions in itself does not violate any ethics rule.

George W. Bush appointed more corporate executives to head government agencies than any other president. Some were responsible for regulating industries whose payrolls they had just left or in which they had held stock. During the corporate accounting scandals of 2001–2002, Bush appointed Harvey Pitt to head the SEC. Pitt was a lawyer whose main work had been to defend the very Wall Street firms he was supposed to regulate as SEC head. Shortly after he took office, Pitt announced that under his direction, the SEC would be "a kinder place for accountants," a statement he undoubtedly wished he had not made after the Enron scandal broke. (Later, public outrage over his unwillingness to enforce regulations led to his resignation.)

Overseeing the Bureaucracy

The principal overseers of the bureaucracy are, of course, the president, who heads it and appoints its top policy makers; the Senate, which holds confirmation powers; Congress as a whole, which has authority to create, monitor, and fund agencies; and the federal courts, which often have to interpret the meaning of regulations or rule on their constitutionality. Congress has also given the public a significant, if vastly under-used, role through legislation that mandates openness in government.

President

The president, constitutionally the chief executive, has primary responsibility for directing executive branch agencies and monitoring their responsiveness. He has several significant means for providing executive leadership, including budgeting, appointment and removal powers, the authority to initiate executive branch reorganizations, and, of course, his power to issue executive orders.

Congress decidedly enhanced the president's administrative powers in 1921 by delegating authority to write the annual budget. In 1937, when Congress approved Franklin Roosevelt's executive branch reorganization, it moved the Bureau of the Budget (BOB) into the new Executive Office of the President (EOP) to help the president manage the bureaucracy. During Nixon's reorganization of the EOP, the newly created Office of Management and Budget (OMB) absorbed BOB and was given specific responsibility for overseeing executive agency performance. (It reports its findings to the public as well as the president by posting them at its website.) This constant monitoring of agencies from within the EOP gives the president more administrative control than does budget writing itself. Presidents can try to cut agency appropriations to limit agencies' range of actions or they can tie conditions to appropriations to make them take specific actions, but Congress does not have to approve White House requests. And because it has power to approve appropriations, Congress has more opportunity than the president to attach strings to funding.

A president's best chance to direct the work of an agency is to put a surrogate in charge of it, that is, to appoint someone who shares his views. It is easiest to do this with cabinet departments because it is accepted that a president is entitled to appoint politically like-minded people to his own cabinet. Thus Reagan and both Bushes filled health care–related positions in the Department of Health and Human Services with people who[47] were against keeping abortion legal, whereas Clinton filled them with people who were pro-choice. George W. Bush's choice to head the Health and Human Services Family Planning programs was a man who felt that contraception was demeaning to women. Appointments to independent and regulatory agencies receive more scrutiny because

neutral competence plays a greater role, but presidents do get most of their choices confirmed. Republican presidents tend to appoint people who favor business, and Democratic presidents appoint those who lean toward the interests of consumers and organized labor. For example, Clinton named a lifelong environmental activist to head the EPA.

Of course, sometimes presidential appointees, despite their being screened for issue positions, may end up—especially if they stay in a position long enough—representing long-standing agency policies and norms rather than the president's interests. Most appointees have less expertise and experience in agency operations than career civil servants, and some come to rely on career officials for information about agency history, procedures, and policy questions. But much depends on the president's leadership, how high a priority change in the agency is for him, and how closely he monitors a particular agency's activities and directions.

Administrative reform is a third means a president can use to increase his control over the bureaucracy. Generally, the more sweeping a president's recommendation for change, the more he must anticipate congressional and interest group resistance. The most audacious attempt at bureaucratic control by a modern president has been George W. Bush's reorganization of the executive branch to create the new cabinet-level Department of Homeland Security. The plan had great scope, affecting twenty-two agencies and 177,000 employees. But what made it bold was Bush's request for exemption from worker protection laws and the authority to transfer funds and personnel from agency to agency without congressional approval. In other words, he asked Congress to cede substantial budgetary and oversight powers to the White House.

The White House can also try to influence independent agencies and commissions by lobbying and mobilizing public opinion. Attempts by presidents of both parties to influence Federal Reserve Board decisions on interest rates, for example, are legion.

Despite these powers, there are many limits on the president's executive leadership. Given the size and complexity of the federal bureaucracy, the president cannot possibly influence every important decision. Moreover, as the civil service expanded, presidents found it increasingly difficult to lead an executive branch with 90 percent of its positions filled by the merit system employees deliberately insulated from presidential control. The creation of the SES and alternative personnel systems allows for short-term and emergency appointments and easier movement within the bureaucracy. In addition, the 1978 law gave managers more opportunity to fire incompetent subordinates and authorized bonuses and a new pay scale for managers to encourage better performance. Despite the changes, presidents often still feel thwarted by the constraints on removing civil servants for poor performance or because they will not do a president's bidding. Although job security is not meant to shield public servants who do poor work, it does make firing incompetent workers difficult and time-consuming. The organization of public employees into unions contributes to this, although unions also protect workers from being dismissed without grounds. The government's rate of discharging people for inefficiency, 0.01 percent a year, did not increase after the 1978 reforms, though no doubt some employees left after being threatened with dismissal or demotion. As one public employee said, "We're all like headless nails down here—once you get us in you can't get us out."[48] This attitude captures what some say is the civil service's built-in bias toward job survival rather than innovation.[49]

Agencies that have strong allies in Congress, in powerful interest groups, or in the public provide another limit on presidential leadership. Presidents have more success controlling agencies that lack strong congressional allies and domestic clientele groups, such as the Treasury and State departments, than agencies that have allies such as the Social Security Administration and the Agriculture and Health and Human Services departments. However, the increasing number of political appointees in senior positions gives the president many more opportunities to exercise his influence over agency operations, even in agencies like the EPA, which has strong bipartisan support in Congress and powerful interest groups monitoring its work.

Not all presidents have the same interest in exercising executive leadership over the bureaucracy. Although all want to appoint people to policy-making positions who are committed to a similar set of goals, the will to pressure these individuals after they have been appointed varies. As discussed in Chapter 11, George W. Bush arguably has interpreted the president's role as chief executive more absolutely than any of his predecessors. He maintained that a president's powers as chief executive are not divided but unitary and that as a **unitary executive** his orders to executive branch agencies trump any directions from Congress or the courts. (See the box "Science, Politics, and the Bureaucracy")

Congress

Although the president has the edge in leadership through his appointment powers, Congress has greater scope for oversight and control. Much of the bureaucracy's power is delegated authority from Congress, and much of its work is implementing laws passed by Congress. Congress has the power to create, reorganize, or eliminate agencies and the ultimate instrument of control—the power of the purse strings. Congress not only has the power to increase or decrease the amount of money the president requests to fund an agency, it can tell an agency how it has to spend the money it allocates. Many special interest projects are funded in this way: Congress, or more often, a congressional committee, tells an agency that it must spend x number of dollars from its budget to pay for a project earmarked by a member of Congress, even though the project does not appear in the budget and the president may oppose the spending or the project itself.

Congress also has dozens of committees (supported by a staff of thousands) to which executive agencies must report. But just as an agency's outside allies can work to thwart presidential control, they can also limit congressional oversight. Agencies frequently work closely with certain congressional committees and interest groups for mutual support and outcomes favorable to all. (These relationships are sometimes called "iron triangles" or "issue networks.") Agencies may adjust their actions to suit the preferences of the congressional committees that authorize their programs and appropriate their funds. For example, decisions by members of independent regulatory commissions are sensitive to the views of members of their congressional oversight committees. When the membership of the committees becomes more liberal or more conservative, so do the decisions regulators make.[50]

Iron triangles make oversight look less like monitoring the bureaucracy and more like collusion. Constituent service, by contrast, provides a motive for members of Congress to try to shape bureaucratic decision making. Members often try to influence agencies to take some action on behalf of constituents or in the interest of their districts. In fact, congressional staff who do casework often have their duties assigned according to the agencies they are responsible for contacting about constituent complaints. This can lead to inefficiencies when bureaucrats are pressured to help members of Congress satisfy constituent demands rather than use neutral competence as a decision standard. It is this kind of pressure that keeps military bases open years beyond their usefulness simply because they are good for the economy of a member's district. This pressure from Congress makes it difficult for bureaucrats to act with neutral competence.

Courts

Federal courts act as another check on the bureaucracy. Judicial decisions shape agency actions by directing agencies to follow legally correct procedures. Of course, the courts cannot intercede in an agency's decision making unless some aggrieved person or corporation files a suit against the agency. Nevertheless, in almost any controversial agency action, there will be aggrieved parties and possibly some with sufficient resources to bring a court action.

The courts interpret lawmakers' intentions by deciding what congressional majorities and the president had in mind when they made a law. This can be difficult. Sometimes, in their haste, lawmakers fail to specify crucial elements of a law, or they may be unable to reach agreement on a provision and leave it ambiguous in order to get the bill passed. Lawmakers may also write a certain amount of vagueness into a law so that agencies will be able to adapt it to unknown future conditions. How the courts read a law may augment or reduce the ability of Congress and the president to influence its implementation. In the current Supreme Court, the conservative majority has increasingly used its authority to interpret the intent of congressional acts in ways that expand the Court's own powers. We discuss these issues in Chapter 13.

Regulators and other agency policy makers appear to be quite sensitive to federal court decisions. For example, when the courts overturn the National Labor Relations Board's decisions in a prolabor direction, the board's decisions soon become more prolabor. Similarly, decisions drift the other way when courts overturn agency decisions in a probusiness direction.[51]

Interest Groups and Individuals

The public has numerous opportunities to oversee and to influence bureaucratic decision making. Most of these rights stem from laws designed to ensure openness in government.

Openness laws also extend to media access and thus provide another important check on bureaucratic abuses. But the media can also make the bureaucracy's work more difficult. Reporters like to cover conflict and bad news and are therefore usually on the lookout for stories about internal policy disputes. Newspapers and other media outlets make frequent use of FOIA to obtain documents from government agencies.

Interest groups and their lobbyists are also part of the public. Lobbyists tend to take much greater advantage of their rights of access than the general public does, and they are the source of much of the public comment on proposed rules received by agencies. Most FOIA requests still come from businesses, interest groups, lawyers, scholars, and the media. In one year, 85 percent of the requests for information submitted to the FDA came from companies that it regulates. That information enabled the companies to evaluate their strategies for influencing agency decisions that affect them. Interest groups want to make sure bureaucracies adopt rules and enforcement practices they favor. An environmental group cannot rest on its laurels just because Congress has passed a law placing new safeguards on toxic waste disposal. The group's job is not over until it makes sure the EPA writes strict rules to enforce the law. Consequently, the group must lobby the regulators as well as Congress.

If an agency seems to be sabotaging the intent of Congress, interest groups can work with friendly congressional committees to put pressure on the agency to mend its ways. And interest groups can also try to rally public opinion to their side to pressure Congress or the president to do something about the agency. Environmental groups are especially skilled at this. Sometimes interest groups pressure an agency so effectively that the agency is said to be "captured."[52] This term is used most frequently for regulatory agencies thought to be controlled by the groups they are supposed to be regulating.

We know that interest groups can influence the bureaucracy, but can individual citizens affect policy too? It is difficult for an individual to influence public agencies when acting alone, but that does not mean there are no opportunities to do so. Perhaps one person posting a comment on a website will not change agency policy, but if all residents opposed to a decision on cleaning up a hazardous waste site in their neighborhood file comments, it can make a difference. Rules have been reversed or amended.

An individual who uses FOIA to retrieve documents that expose agency corruption or abuse can also make a difference by going public with the story. And members of the general public are increasingly taking advantage of openness laws even though the process is not easy for those who try. A lot of paperwork is involved, some costs, and often a long wait, even though government agencies employ over five thousand administrators to process the requests.

Ordinary citizens could have a greater impact if they used all the tools that Congress has given them to oversee and to influence the bureaucracy. They can even be whistleblowers by suing companies with government contracts that defraud the government (and if successful, share in the money recovered).[53] But individual whistleblowers within the bureaucracy often have the best opportunity to monitor agency practices. Some whistleblowing is unsuccessful, but some makes a real difference. One of the most famous whistleblowers was Pentagon employee Daniel Ellsberg, who in 1968 leaked thousands of documents on the conduct of the Vietnam War to the *New York Times*. Henry Kissinger claimed that Ellsberg was the most dangerous man in the world, but Ellsberg's acts helped the public understand that the Johnson and Nixon administrations' private rationale for fighting the war was not the same as the reasons they stated in public.

Bunny Greenhouse, chief contracting officer in the United States Army Corps of Engineers, blew the whistle on a no-bid, five-year, $7-billion offer to Halliburton and its subsidiaries to get Iraqi oilfields running. (Halliburton was the company of which Vice President Cheney was CEO before becoming vice president). After being pressured by superiors to approve that and other contracts that would allow the company essentially to set costs and add a service fee, and without competitive bidding or appropriate controls, she signed the contracts because of the needs of those trying to get Iraq stabilized, but with a note saying she was doing it under pressure and in spite of irregularities. A FOIA request uncovered the documents and her comments. She later testified at a 2005 forum organized by the Democrats looking into charges of overbilling and fraud in Iraq War contracts (the Republican-dominated Congress refused to hold such hearings). She indicated that these agreements were "the worst activity in contracting that I'd ever seen in all my contracting career."[54] Three weeks later, Greenhouse was demoted to a lower civil service grade despite years of exemplary reviews. Although she asked for a full investigation, she is still waiting for her case to be resolved.

Bureaucrats who blow the whistle on mismanagement, sexual or political harassment, or other abuses of

Sometimes federal employees are on the front line of danger. A mail carrier protects herself after other postal workers were infected by anthrax spores sent through the mail in 2001.

power in their agencies are supposed to be protected from arbitrary firing or demotions such as Greenhouse received. But rarely does an agency publicly thank an employee for blowing the whistle, as FBI Director Robert Mueller did when Coleen Rowley went public with that agency's mishandling of a 9/11–related investigation. Rowley, a Minneapolis-based agent involved in the case of Zacarias Moussaoui, an Algerian, under indictment as the so-called twentieth hijacker, had complained to Director Mueller that a midlevel manager had thwarted her attempt to get a search warrant to go through Moussaoui's personal belongings and the contents of his computer.[55] Rowley testified before the Senate Judiciary Committee, but even if her complaints had not become public, they would have been hard for the agency to ignore given her record. Mueller went public to commend her for her actions, but his praise was not so much an indication of changing attitudes toward whistleblowers as a measure of the trouble the agency was in with Congress and also the media attention to Rowley's case. She was one of three whistleblowers (the other two exposed fraud in the private bureaucracies of Enron and WorldCom) named by *Time* magazine when it proclaimed 2002 "The Year of the Whistleblower."

Disclosure of bureaucratic failures increased after 9/11 because many individuals saw that neglected shortcomings could have serious consequences. But retaliation continued. In recent years, airport baggage screeners, border patrol agents, and the chief of the United States Park Police were disciplined or fired for reporting problems in their agencies. The most publicized case was that of Medicare's chief actuary, who was threatened with dismissal by the political appointee who headed his agency if he provided Congress with accurate numbers on the cost of the Bush administration's proposed prescription drug benefit for seniors.

In 2004, Congress responded by writing a new law with stronger protections for whistleblowers, including freedom from reprisal for those, like the Medicare actuary, who provide information to Congress. But the bill was strongly opposed by the Bush administration, which contended that it "unconstitutionally interferes with the president's ability to control and manage the government."[56]

Despite the legal protections, it is the rare person who will set aside cordial relations with colleagues and ambition for promotion in order to challenge the status quo. Most people, whether working in the private or the public sector, find it difficult to expose their employer's dirty laundry. And even if the law does protect their jobs, their careers may be effectively ruined. Rowley, who despite the public commendations probably had little chance for promotion, retired from the FBI and in 2006 ran for Congress. About half of all whistleblowers lose their jobs, half of those lose their homes, and half of those lose their families.[57]

Conclusion: Is the Bureaucracy Responsive?

In 2002, Congress oversaw the biggest reorganization of the federal bureaucracy in a half century when it created the Department of Homeland Security (DHS). The changes were prompted by failures in performance that helped make possible the terrorist attacks of September 11, 2001. Particular targets of the reform were intelligence and law enforcement agencies and customs and immigration services. A reporter noted that the bureaucratic morass in the former Immigration and Naturalization Service was encapsulated in the title of the official put in charge of the reorganization: the "as-sistant deputy executive associate commissioner for immigration services."[58] The failure of the reorganization either to streamline communications, as revealed in DHS's response to hurricane Katrina, or consolidate preparedness for future terrorist attacks was more evidence of the limits of reform. In fact, many observers believe that the reorganization diminished, not enhanced, the functions of agencies (e.g., FEMA and Immigration) incorporated into DHS.

Is the federal bureaucracy an impenetrable forest or an uncontrollable fourth branch of government, as some portray it? The turf wars, miscommunication, and fragmented authority that surfaced after 9/11 certainly indicate that at least part of the federal bureaucracy is an impenetrable forest. It is not surprising that most of the agencies that failed so badly (e.g., the CIA and the FBI) are among the least open to citizens or the media and even to congressional oversight. Those agencies continued to oppose reform even as Congress was implementing the recommendations of the 9/11 Commission to reorganize our fifteen different intelligence agencies under a single directorate to improve communication, gain more central control, and limit interagency rivalries.

But the bureaucracy as a whole is not an errant fourth branch of government. With the exception of supersecret agencies like the National Security Agency, for which Congress has forfeited much of its oversight responsibility in the interests of national security, most of the bureaucracy is subject to presidential and congressional control, providing they are willing to exercise their powers. Indeed, one of the by-products of the Bush administration's attempts to increase presidential control of executive branch agencies at the expense of Congress is that it has reawakened some members of Congress to its oversight lapses.

Our fragmented political system means that our public agencies operate in an environment of uncertainty and competition. Bureaucrats have many bosses: a president, his appointees, Congress and its many committees and subcommittees, and the federal courts. In addition, numerous interest groups try to influence the work of federal agencies. The often contradictory demands for responsiveness and neutral competence contribute to an uncertainty of expectations, too. As a result, agencies try to protect themselves by cultivating the support of congressional committees and interest groups. Even presidents have trouble influencing agencies because of these alliances. Although some presidents, such as Franklin Roosevelt and Jimmy Carter, have occasionally rearranged the status quo, their successes in articulating a vision of national priorities are more the exception than the rule.

There is a vaguely defined but frequently articulated public suspicion that any bureaucracy is destined to be intransigent and inefficient. We have tried to show that some of that attitude stems from lack of consensus on what the work of government should be. If you do not like the work that Congress and the president have assigned to the bureaucracy, there is not much chance you will view the bureaucracy as responsive to your needs. If the dissatisfaction is more over how the bureaucracy does its work, there is hope that at least some areas of performance will meet with your approval. The public does have tools to influence how bureaucrats do their work, but it has many more ways to lobby Congress and the president to change the work they give the bureaucracy to do.

Despite people's negative feelings about the bureaucracy, the mail is delivered, roads built, Social Security paid, anddrivers' licenses issued. Bureaucracy usually does what it is supposed to do. Some agencies, such as Medicare and Social Security, are very efficient and in the case of Medicare, operate with a lower overhead than private insurance companies. But the investigation into the INS, FBI, and CIA actions prior to September 11, 2001, made clear that these agencies had experienced catastrophic failures on 9/11. Part of the problem, as subsequent investigations revealed, was that the bosses in the agencies overrode their own experts, who were not allowed to exercise neutral competence. As a consequence, a number of our most experienced intelligence professionals left the government.

Paradoxically, Americans' opinion of how the government was doing its job and its overall trust in government increased substantially after the 9/11 attacks. But there was also a more serious concern for poorly functioning government agencies. The head of one government watchdog group summarized the feeling this way:"Before September 11 there was a bit of a blasé attitude of 'OK, the government screwed up again.' Now people see the consequences on their lives and see the necessity of government functioning well."[59]

Key Terms

Key Names

1. The federal bureaucracy includes
   a. mathematicians.
   b. butchers.
   c. engineers.
   d. nurses.
   e. all of the above.

2. Which is true of the characteristics of employees in the federal bureaucracy in comparison to employees in the overall civilian labor force?
   a. Women are significantly overrepresented.
   b. African Americans are underrepresented.
   c. Latinos are underrepresented.
   d. Asian Americans are overrepresented.
   e. American Indians are significantly overrepresented.

3. Which is true of bureaucracies?
   a. They are only found in public agencies.
   b. They are only found in private agencies.
   c. They are found in both public and private agencies.
   d. They tend to be run according to democratic principles.
   e. Expertise and experience tend to be ignored.

4. Measuring performance in a public bureaucracy is
   a. a simple matter of assessing profit and loss.
   b. a fairly easy matter to agree on.
   c. very similar to measuring performance in the private sector.
   d. sometimes measured by the amount of waste in government programs.
   e. done regularly and consistently by Congress.

5. Which is **not true** of FOIA and its implementation?
   a. It is intended to make government activities more open.
   b. It is intended to make government more accountable.
   c. Republican presidents have been more likely to open government documents to public scrutiny than have Democratic ones.
   d. It is rarely used by citizens or interest groups.
   e. It probably applies to electronic records.

6. Which is not an explanation why government has grown over time?
   a. Conservatives as well as liberals want their priorities addressed.
   b. Elected officials respond to public demands for action.
   c. National crises produce demands for government to do more.
   d. Liberals have controlled Congress most of the time.
   e. Once established, programs benefitting any group are hard to kill.

7. Which recent president was most successful in decreasing the size of government?
   a. Ronald Reagan
   b. Bill Clinton
   c. George W. Bush
   d. George H.W. Bush
   e. None of the above

8. Which is true about departments, independent agencies, and independent regulatory boards?
   a. Heads of departments form the president's cabinet.
   b. Most heads of independent agencies are part of the president's cabinet.
   c. Regulatory boards and commissions have a minor role in our lives.
   d. Independent regulatory boards are directed by an individual called a "Secretary."
   e. The president appoints, and can remove, members of independent regulatory commissions.

9. In terms of its stance with regard to science policy, the administration of George W. Bush
   a. had no science experts within the administration.
   b. often disagreed with its scientific experts, but always reported accurately what they said.
   c. valued scientific expertise and neutral competence more than most previous administrations.
   d. was careful to keep science and political considerations separate.
   e. sometimes distorted the scientific content of reports and muzzled scientific experts.

10. Policy implementation includes all but
    a. making policy.
    b. regulation.
    c. collecting data.
    d. informing citizens about government action.
    e. doing research.

11. Which is not true of government corporations?
    a. They exist in most countries but not the United States.
    b. They include the TVA.
    c. They include the postal service.
    d. They include Amtrak.
    e. They include the selling of terrorism insurance.

12. Patronage
    a. no longer exists in the public bureaucracy.
    b. is the practice of filling jobs on the basis of political loyalty.
    c. was increased after the Civil Service Commission was established.
    d. makes neutral competence a primary objective.
    e. is the practice by which the Senior Executive Service is staffed.

13. The Ethics in Government Act
    a. was passed at the beginning of the twentieth century.
    b. was opposed by President Clinton.
    c. bars former public bureaucrats from lobbying their agencies for one year.
    d. has been very effective.
    e. prevents bureaucrats from acting unethically in making decisions.

14. Which is true about oversight of the bureaucracy?
    a. The president has little control.
    b. The courts have no oversight powers.
    c. The public has no role.
    d. Whistleblowers can play an important role.
    e. Interest groups are usually uninterested in the bureaucracy.

15. Which is **not** a tool that presidents might use in overseeing the federal bureaucracy?
    a. Reorganization
    b. Power of appointment
    c. Administrative reform
    d. Lobbying
    e. Firing civil service appointees

16. Which is **not** a tool that Congress might use in overseeing the federal bureaucracy?
    a. Eliminating an agency
    b. Controlling agency budgets
    c. Holding hearings on agencies or their policies
    d. Earmarking money
    e. Firing senior bureaucrats

17. Which is **not** a tool that interest groups and the public might use in overseeing the federal bureaucracy?
    a. Lobbying bureaucrats
    b. Holding a referendum on the agency
    c. Making a FOIA request
    d. Working with friendly congressional committees to pressure the agency
    e. Suing companies suspected of wrongdoing in their government contracts

18. Match the whistleblower with his/her act:
    a. Daniel Ellsberg/Halliburton overcharging in Iraqi War
    b. Coleen Rowley/Pentagon documents on the Vietnam war
    c. Bunny Greenhouse/FBI laxity in pre-9/11 investigations
    d. Daniel Ellsberg/Halliburton overcharging in Iraqi War
    e. Coleen Rowley/FBI laxity in pre-9/11 investigations

19. Which is true of the bureaucracy?
    a. It is an independent, fourth branch of government.
    b. It can adopt policies independent of Congress, the Presidency, and the courts.
    c. It is overseen by the Congress, the Presidency, and the courts.
    d. Most of those who work in it are not very similar to the average citizen.
    e. It is immune from reform and reorganization.

20. Which is **not** true of neutral competence?
    a. It assumes there is no Democratic or Republican way to implement policy.
    b. It was an objective of the Pendleton Act.
    c. It is usually linked to the merit system.
    d. It is a professional standard requiring expertise as a criterion for appointment to the civil service.
    e. It is best promoted by the patronage system.

Key: 1-e; 2-c; 3-c; 4-d; 5-c; 6-d; 7-b; 8-a; 9-e; 10-a; 11-a; 12-b; 13-c; 14-d; 15-e; 16-e; 17-b; 18-e; 19-c; 20-e

The newest justices on the Supreme Court, Samuel Alito (left) and John Roberts, are appointees of President George W. Bush.

Samuel Alito, a federal appellate court judge for fifteen years and a Reagan administration lawyer before that, was President George W. Bush's last nominee to the Supreme Court.

Alito appeared to be quite conservative. As a lawyer in the Reagan administration, he wrote that "the Constitution does not protect a right to an abortion."[1] He argued for more presidential power than courts allow and less congressional power than Congress exercises. He maintained, for example, that Congress didn't have power to pass the Truth in Mileage Act, which forbade car dealers from turning back the odometers in used cars and misleading the buyers. As a judge on the appellate court, he usually favored powerful institutions over average individuals when they came in conflict.

When vacancies on the Court occur, the president nominates a replacement and the Senate votes to confirm or reject the nominee. As part of the confirmation process, the **Senate Judiciary Committee** holds hearings in which senators question the nominee about his or her views. Nominees aren't asked how they would decide any particular cases, but they are asked what they think about current legal issues.

The administration's twenty-person confirmation team launched a public relations blitz, orchestrating news conferences, opinion articles, and letters to the editor. Friends, classmates, and former law clerks were contacted for testimonies. Conservative legal scholars were enlisted to answer questions that might arise about the judge's decisions. The goal of these efforts was to persuade the public that Alito was a mainstream conservative rather than an extreme conservative.

The team also prepared Alito. A Republican consultant who had guided numerous judicial nominees through the confirmation process instructed them that "your role in this process is that of a bridegroom at a wedding: stay out of the way, be on time, and keep your mouth shut." Therefore, "the most important rule is the 80–20 rule, which is if the senators are talking 80 percent of the time and you're talking 20 percent of the time, you're winning, and if it's 60–40 you've got a problem, and if it's 50–50, you've lost and you might as well go home."[2]

The team held mock hearings, known as "murder boards," in which administration lawyers, acting as various senators, asked Alito the questions they expected those senators to ask. They devised answers, and Alito rehearsed them. They advised him to be as vague as possible.

Before the hearings, three evangelical ministers were allowed into the Senate Judiciary Committee's room to apply holy oil to the senators' seats.[3]

At the hearings, Alito talked no more than necessary, resisting all attempts to engage in a dialogue. "He was like a chauffeur who speaks only when spoken to, and doesn't presume to converse."[4]

When asked about his past statements, he soft-pedaled them, saying that he was an advocate in the Reagan administration. As a justice, he insisted, he would have no political agenda. Yet, he refused to reveal his actual views.

Even so, Alito was confirmed. Later, the Judiciary Committee chair observed, "The hearings are really. . . a subtle minuet, with the nominee answering as many questions as he thinks necessary in order to be confirmed."[5] With a ten-member advantage in the Senate, the Republican candidate didn't need to answer many questions.

The hearings were so dull that few Americans watched. Their lack of interest and lack of concern that a candidate for a lifetime seat on the highest court in the land wouldn't reveal his views on legal controversies shows that most Americans don't care about judicial appointments, unless the nominees are obviously out of the mainstream.[6]

One disillusioned committee member proposed that the confirmation hearings be abolished because they tell us little about the nominee's views. They tell us little even about the nominee's personality. What we see is a carefully crafted persona fashioned by a public relations team. As a media consultant observed, "Every Court nominee is filtered through a machine that covers them in vanilla topping. . . . It's hard to organize against vanilla."[7]

The public expresses more support for the Supreme Court than for the president or Congress.[8] The public dislikes the disagreements and debates and the negotiations and compromises among governmental officials, and it deplores the efforts of interest groups to influence governmental policies. These messy features of democratic government, which are visible in the executive and legislative branches, aren't visible in the judicial branch. Many people conclude that they don't occur.

Indeed, many people assume that courts are nonpolitical and that judges are objective. People say we have "a government of laws, not of men." But this view is a myth. At any time in our history, "it is individuals who make, enforce, and interpret the law."[9] When judges interpret the law, they are political actors and the courts are political institutions.

Thus public support for the Supreme Court and the lower courts rests partly on false assumptions about the absence of politics in this branch. There is plenty of politics, as will be seen in each of the topics covered in this chapter.

Courts

Due to federalism, the United States has a complete system of national courts side by side with complete systems of state courts, for a total of fifty-one separate systems.[10]

Structure of the Courts

The Constitution mentions only one court—a supreme court—although it allows Congress to set up additional lower courts, which it did in 1789 and again in 1891, completing the basic structure of the federal judiciary.

In the federal system, the **district courts** are trial courts. There are ninety-four, based on population but with at least one in each state. They have multiple judges, although a single judge or a jury decides each case.

The **courts of appeals** are intermediate appellate courts. They hear cases that have been decided by the district courts and then appealed by the losers. There are twelve, based on regions of the country known as "circuits."[11] They have numerous judges, from six to twenty-eight, although a panel of three judges decides each case.[12]

The Supreme Court is the ultimate appellate court. It hears cases that have been decided by the courts of appeals, district courts, or state supreme courts. (Although it can hear some cases—those involving a state or a diplomat—that have not been heard by the lower courts first, in practice it hears nearly all of its cases on appeal.) The group of nine justices decides its cases.

The district courts conduct trials. The courts of appeals and Supreme Court do not; they do not have juries or witnesses to testify and present evidence—just lawyers for the opposing litigants. Rather than determine guilt or innocence, these courts evaluate arguments about legal questions arising in the cases.

The state judiciaries have a structure similar to the federal judiciary. In most states, though, there are two tiers of trial courts. Normally, the lower tier is for criminal cases involving minor crimes, and the upper tier is for criminal cases involving major crimes and for civil cases. In about three-fourths of the states, there are intermediate appellate courts, and in all of the states there is a supreme court (although in a few it is known by another name).

Since 1978, the federal system has also had an unusual secret court, which few Americans are aware of. (See the box "Surveillance Court.")

Jurisdiction of the Courts

As noted, **jurisdiction** is the authority to hear and decide cases. The federal courts can exercise jurisdiction over cases in which the subject involves the U.S. Constitution, statutes, or treaties; maritime law; or cases in which the litigants include the U.S. government, more than one state government, one state government and a citizen of another state, citizens of more than one state,[13] or a foreign government or citizen. The state courts exercise jurisdiction over the remaining cases. These include most criminal cases because the states have authority over most criminal matters and pass most criminal laws. Consequently, the state courts hear far more cases than the federal courts.

Despite this dividing line, some cases begin in the state courts and end in the federal courts. These in-volve state law and federal law, frequently a state statute and a federal constitutional right—for example, a criminal law and a legal question about the search and seizure (Fourth Amendment) or interrogation (Fifth Amendment) conducted by the police. For these cases, there are two paths from the state judiciary to the federal judiciary. One is for the litigant who lost at the state supreme court to appeal to the U.S. Supreme Court.

The other path, available only in a criminal case, is for the defendant who has exhausted all possible appeals in the state courts to appeal to the local federal district court through a writ of **habeas corpus** ("Bring the body!" in Latin). This order demands that the state produce the defendant and justify his or her incarceration. If the district court decides that the state courts violated the defendant's constitutional rights, it will reverse the conviction. After the district court's decision, the losing side can try to appeal to the courts of appeals and the Supreme Court (see Figure 1).

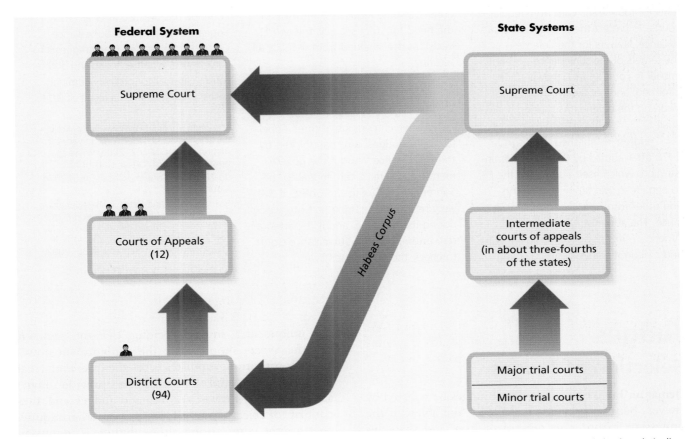

FIGURE 1 • **Federal and State Court Systems** *The arrows indicate the primary avenues of appeal, and the heads indicate the usual number of judges who hear cases in the federal system.*

Behind closed doors in a windowless room in the Justice Department, a highly secretive court meets. The court hears requests from the FBI for electronic surveillance of possible spies and terrorists and sometimes for physical searches of their homes and computers.

The **Foreign Intelligence Surveillance Court (FISC)** operates like no other court in the United States. It consists of eleven district court judges handpicked by the chief justice of the Supreme Court. The members sit in panels of three judges and serve for seven years. Lawyers for the government, acting on behalf of the FBI, seek approval for electronic surveillance, much as law enforcement officers seek search warrants for routine searches from regular courts. To protect the secrecy of the surveillance, lawyers for the defense—the targets of the surveillance—do not appear in court. In fact, they are not informed, and not aware, that a case involving the defendants is being heard at all.

Congress established the court in 1978 after abuses by the Nixon administration, which itself authorized the FBI to engage in wiretapping, bugging, and other forms of electronic surveillance. The administration spied on American citizens active in the antiwar and civil rights movements, claiming that these protesters were threats to "national security," and then tried to disrupt their organizations and harass their leaders. Yet Congress recognized that the government might need to use electronic surveillance when national security actually was at stake—from foreign agents or American citizens spying for foreign countries. Congress established the court to approve the surveillance when it was justified and to check the government when it was overzealous.

However, the court has been little more than a rubber stamp for the government. Since its inception, the court has approved almost 19,000 requests and denied just 4.[1] (In recent years, the court has made "substantive modifications" to some requests.)[2] Because of the need for strict secrecy, the court's decisions are shielded from virtually all scrutiny.

If the government loses, it can appeal the court's decision to the Foreign Intelligence Surveillance Court of Review, which consists of three appellate court judges, also handpicked by the chief justice. (And if the government loses here, it can appeal to the Supreme Court.) But the Court of Review has heard just one pair of cases during its existence, and it thwarted a rare attempt by the Surveillance Court to check the government.

The Surveillance Court had turned down the government's request in one pair of cases when the judges realized that the FBI had been misleading the court. When the FBI had lacked sufficient evidence to obtain approval for surveillance in ordinary criminal cases—not spying or terrorism cases—from regular courts, it had tried to circumvent the law by going to the Surveillance Court, which requires less evidence to grant surveillance because of the seriousness of spying and terrorism.[3] The furious judges admonished the FBI to discontinue this practice. But the Bush administration appealed, and the Court of Review overturned the decision, concluding that the USA PATRIOT Act had broadened the law to allow the FBI to continue this practice after all. Thus it appears that the secret Surveillance Court will be hearing many requests for surveillance, whether for spying and terrorism cases or for ordinary criminal cases, in the future as a result of 9/11.

[1] "Foreign Intelligence Surveillance Act Orders, 1979–2005," Electronic Privacy Information Center, May 2, 2006, www.epic.org/privacy/wiretap/stats/fisa_stats.html.
[2] In 2005, sixty-one modifications in 2074 requests. Ibid.
[3] John Podesta and Peter Swire, "Speaking Out about Wiretaps," *Washington Post National Weekly Edition*, September 9, 2002, 27; Seymour M. Hersh, "The Twentieth Man," *New Yorker*, September 30, 2002, 56–76.

Judges

Selection of Judges

Benjamin Franklin proposed that judges be selected by lawyers because lawyers would pick "the ablest of the profession in order to get rid of him, and share his practice among themselves."[14] The Founders rejected this unique idea, instead deciding that the president and the Senate should share the appointment power. The Constitution stipulates that the president shall nominate judges and the Senate shall provide "advice and consent"—that is, recommend judges and then confirm or reject them.[15] There are no other requirements in the Constitution, although there is an unwritten requirement that judges be trained as lawyers.

The Founders expected these appointments to be based on merit rather than on politics. However, as soon as political parties developed, presidents and senators used politics as well as merit in making these appointments.

Mechanics of Selection

For the lower courts, lawyers who want to become judges get politically active in their party and make financial contributions to it. When vacancies arise, they lobby political officials, bar association leaders, or interest group leaders in the hope that these elites will recommend them to the administration.

They especially focus on their senators, who play a key role through the practice of **senatorial courtesy.** This tradition allows senators in the president's party to recommend, or veto, candidates for judgeships in their state. This practice applies not only to district courts, which lie within individual states, but also to courts of appeals, which span several states. For courts of appeals, senators informally divide the seats among the states within the circuit. (This practice doesn't apply to the Supreme Court because it has too few seats to divide among the states.)

Senatorial courtesy can limit the president's choices. During President Kennedy's term, the practice was ironclad. In deference to southern senators, the president, who advocated civil rights, was forced to appoint southern judges who favored segregation. One of them characterized the Supreme Court's desegregation ruling as "one of the truly regrettable decisions of all time," and another even called black litigants "niggers" and "chimpanzees" from the bench.[16] However, senatorial courtesy is not as ironclad now as it was then. Since the 1970s, most administrations have sought certain candidates for their ideology or diversity, so they have pressured senators to cooperate. Consequently, there is more give-and-take between the senators and the president than there used to be. Nevertheless, in 1999 Senator Orin Hatch (R–Utah), chair of the Judiciary Committee, blocked all of President Clinton's nominees for six months until the president agreed to nominate one of Hatch's allies for a judgeship in Utah.

For the Supreme Court, lawyers who want to become justices also try to become prominent in the legal profession. They write articles or give speeches designed to attract officials' attention. When vacancies arise, political officials, bar association leaders, and interest group leaders urge consideration of certain candidates. The administration also conducts a search for acceptable candidates. Sometimes even sitting justices make a recommendation. Chief Justice Warren Burger, who dis-

couraged President Nixon from choosing a woman, claiming that not one was qualified, recommended Harry Blackmun, a childhood pal and the best man at his wedding. Justice William Rehnquist recommended Sandra Day O'Connor, a law school classmate whom he had dated occasionally.

Once the president has chosen a candidate, he submits the nomination to the Senate, where it goes to the Judiciary Committee for hearings. Senators question the nominee about his or her judicial philosophy, and interest groups voice their concerns. If a majority of the committee consents, the nomination goes to the whole Senate. If a majority of the Senate consents, the nomination is confirmed.

The Judiciary Committee is the battleground for controversial nominations. The committee is controlled by the party that has a majority in the Senate, so the committee reflects the views of that party. If the committee confirms the nominee, usually the whole Senate will confirm the nominee. If the committee rejects the nominee, usually the president will have to submit another one.

The mechanics of selection for all federal courts are similar, but the process of selection for the Supreme Court is more politicized at every stage because the Court is more powerful and visible, so its seats are fought over more intensely.

Criteria Used by Presidents

Although presidents want judges who demonstrate merit, they choose judges who meet various political criteria. Presidents normally nominate members of their party. In fact, they normally nominate active members who have served in public office or contributed to party candidates. In the twentieth century, presidents selected members of their party from 82 percent of the time (William Howard Taft) to 99 percent of the time (Woodrow Wilson).[17] This practice has become so established that senators of the opposition party usually confirm the president's nominees.

Some presidents want judges who hold certain ideological views. President Theodore Roosevelt sought judges who opposed business monopolies and supported labor unions, and President Franklin Roosevelt sought judges who favored his New Deal policies. President Nixon sought conservatives who would reverse the direction of the Supreme Court and prompt southern whites to join the Republican Party.[18]

The Reagan administration was the first to establish systematic procedures for choosing lower court judges as well as Supreme Court justices according to ideology.

The George H. W. Bush administration did the same. These two administrations sought conservatives who would roll back the rulings of previous courts. They had candidates fill out lengthy questionnaires and then submit to daylong interviews probing their positions. They expected candidates, for example, to oppose the right to abortion, the Supreme Court's ruling establishing the right, and the Supreme Court's reasoning in the case.[19]

The George W. Bush administration has followed a similar process. The unusual feature, however, has been the role of Vice President Dick Cheney, who has taken the lead. He has sought conservative judges, especially those who have a broad interpretation of presidential power and a narrow interpretation of congressional authority, so they will be likely to uphold the administration's sweeping claims of presidential power in the war on terror. After rigorous screening and interviewing of the candidates, Cheney submitted a list of five names for Bush to choose from. In this way, Cheney steered Bush toward his conservative nominees for the Supreme Court—John Roberts and Samuel Alito.[20]

These three Republican administrations—Reagan's, George H. W. Bush's, and George W. Bush's—have made the most concerted efforts to select judges according to ideology.

Some presidents want judges who provide more diversity on the courts. In the past, presidents chose westerners to balance the easterners who dominated the bench and Catholics and Jews to balance the Protestants who dominated the bench. In 1967, President Johnson chose the first black justice, **Thurgood Marshall;** in 1981, President Reagan chose the first woman justice, **Sandra Day O'Connor.** Presidents bowed to the pressure from various groups to solidify their support from these groups. Reagan, who wasn't an advocate of women's rights, pledged to appoint a woman to the Court to shore up his support among female voters. (After fulfilling this pledge, he felt no need to appoint many women to the lower courts.)

Now Hispanics want a seat on the Supreme Court. Both parties, who see support from this growing group as crucial to future electoral success, would welcome the opportunity to appoint the first Hispanic justice.

Presidents Carter and Clinton appointed numerous women and minorities to the lower courts. Before Carter took office, only eight women had ever served on the federal bench.[21] Sixteen percent of Carter's appointees were women, and 21 percent were racial minorities.[22] Twenty-nine percent of Clinton's appointees were women, and 25 percent were racial minorities.[23]

These two Democratic administrations, which were not as driven by ideology, made the most concerted efforts to select judges for diversity.

President George W. Bush has also made an effort, greater than previous Republican administrations, to appoint women and minorities to the lower federal courts.[24] However, he has passed over most female and all minority candidates for Supreme Court vacancies because those under consideration either were not conservative enough for the interest groups that wield power within the Republican Party or too conservative for the moderate senators and voters to accept.

Demands for diversity can reduce presidents' choices, but presidents can acquiesce to these demands and still find candidates with the desired party affiliation and ideological views. When Thurgood Marshall retired in 1991, President George H. W. Bush felt obligated to nominate another African American for this seat, but he wanted to nominate a conservative. He chose **Clarence Thomas,** a court of appeals judge. Whereas Marshall had been an ardent champion of civil rights, Thomas opposes affirmative action and other policies favored by many black leaders. Whereas Marshall had been one of the most liberal justices on the Warren Court, Thomas is the most conservative justice in many years, espousing a return to some positions abandoned by the Court in the 1930s.[25] Occasionally, groups have to satisfy themselves with the symbolic benefits from having "one of their own" on the Court. Thus many blacks get the psychological lift from having an African American on the bench but not the additional satisfaction from having one who reflects their policy views. (Also, see the box "Do Women Judges Make a Difference?")

Criteria Used by Senators

Although the Senate played a vigorous role in the appointment process in the nineteenth century, rejecting twenty-two of eighty-one presidential nominations to the Supreme Court between 1789 and 1894, it routinely accepted the president's nominations in the first half of the twentieth century, rejecting only one nomination until 1968.[26] Then it rejected two by President Johnson, two by President Nixon, and two by President Reagan.[27]

Of these six nominees, most were qualified in an objective sense.[28] Although some were accused of ethical lapses, most were rejected for ideological reasons.[29] Johnson's were deemed too liberal, while Nixon's and Reagan's were deemed too conservative.

Nominations to the Supreme Court have been contentious since the 1960s partly because of the Court's activism—both liberals and conservatives have seen what the Court can do—and partly because of the divided government that has characterized our government for most years since the late 1960s. Often Republicans dominated the presidency while Democrats dominated Congress (although in the 1990s, the situation was the reverse), so both have fought over the judiciary to tip the balance. Nominations have also become contentious because of the culture wars between reformers and traditionalists, of which the abortion debate is the most obvious manifestation, and the corresponding rise of interest groups on the left and the right that scrutinize the appointments, pressuring presidents and senators on their side to nominate and vote their way.

Even nominations to the lower courts, especially to the courts of appeals, which serve as "farm teams" for future justices, have become contentious in recent decades.[30] This reflects the polarization of American politics and the role of interest groups today. "You go out on the streets of Raleigh," Sen. Jesse Helms of North Carolina said, "and ask one hundred people: 'Do you give a damn who is on the Fourth Circuit Court of Appeals?' They'll say: 'What's that?'"[31] But political activists representing interest groups on the left and the right do know and do care, deeply, because they see the connection between the lower court judges and the interest groups' goals. In elections, these political activists mobilize their party's base of voters. Thus they have influence on their party, which needs their help. They can persuade, sometimes demand, that their party's senators fight a nomination by the other party's president.[32]

Results of Selection

Judges are drawn from large law firms or the federal government, and higher court judges are often drawn from the lower courts. These established legal circles are dominated by white men, so most judges have been white men. Although recent presidents have appointed more minorities and women, the bench's composition changes slowly because of judges' life tenure.

Despite the efforts to provide racial and sexual diversity, no effort has been made to reflect socioeconomic diversity. Throughout history, judges have come from a narrow, elite slice of society. Most have come from upper-middle-class or upper-class families with prestige and connections as well as expectations for achievement.[33] No Supreme Court justice since Warren Burger in 1969 has attended a public university or graduate school. Every justice since then has had a degree from one of four prestigious, private schools—Chicago, Harvard, Stanford, or Yale.[34] Many justices—at least six on the current Court—have been millionaires.[35] Many lower court judges have been millionaires, too. Forty percent of Clinton's appointees were and 58 percent of Bush's appointees are.[36] With the power to nominate judges, presidents have a tremendous opportunity to shape the courts and their decisions (see Figure 2).

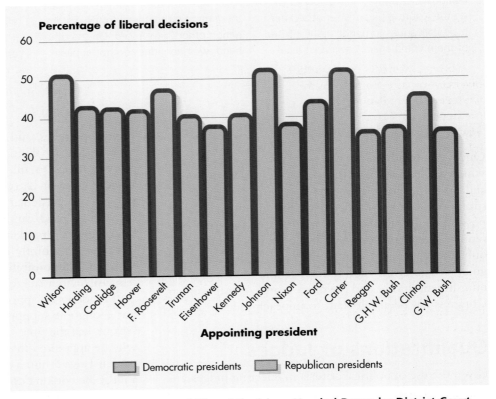

Percentage of liberal decisions

Appointing president

Democratic presidents ☐ Republican presidents ☐

FIGURE 2 • **Percentage of Liberal Decisions Handed Down by District Court Appointees of Presidents Woodrow Wilson through George W. Bush** *Appointees of Democratic and Republic presidents tend to decide cases somewhat differently.*
SOURCE: Robert A. Carp, Ronald Stidham, and Kenneth L. Manning, *Judicial Process in America*, 6th ed. (Washington, D.C.: CQ Press, 2004), fig. 7-1.

DO WOMEN JUDGES MAKE A DIFFERENCE?

Some people believe that there should be more women judges because women are entitled to their "fair share" of all governmental offices, including judgeships. Others believe that there should be more so women will feel that the courts represent them too. Still others believe that there should be more because women hold different views than men and therefore would make different decisions.

A study of Justice Sandra Day O'Connor, the first woman on the Supreme Court, shows that although she generally voted as a conservative, she usually voted as a liberal in sex discrimination cases. Moreover, her presence on the Court apparently sensitized her male colleagues to gender issues. Most of them voted against sex discrimination more frequently after she joined the Court.[1]

Some studies find similar results for women justices on state supreme courts. Even women justices from opposite political parties support a broad array of women's rights in cases ranging from sex discrimination to child support and property settlement.[2]

But studies that compare voting patterns on issues less directly related to gender have less clear findings. Women judges appear more liberal than men in cases involving employment discrimination and racial discrimination. Perhaps the treatment they have experienced as women has made them more sympathetic to the discrimination others have faced. On the other hand, women judges do not appear more liberal or conservative than men in cases involving obscenity or criminal rights.[3]

Studies that compare the sentencing of criminal defendants in state courts find scant differences between men and women judges.[4] However, women judges do tend to sentence convicted defendants somewhat more harshly.[5]

Women judges in Harris County, Texas, which includes Houston, have applied the death penalty with "greater ferocity" than their male predecessors. This *county,* a majority of whose judges are female, has given the death penalty to more defendants than all other *states* but one.[6]

But the studies comparing men and women judges find more similari-

Tenure of Judges

Once appointed, judges can serve for "good behavior," which means for life, unless they commit "high crimes and misdemeanors." These are not defined in the Constitution but are considered to be serious crimes or, possibly, political abuses. Congress can impeach and remove judges as it can presidents, but it has impeached only thirteen and removed only six. The standard of guilt—"high crimes and misdemeanors"—is vague, the punishment drastic, and the process time-consuming, so Congress has been reluctant to impeach judges.[37]

Qualifications of Judges

Given the use of political criteria in selecting judges, are judges well qualified?

Political scientists who study the judiciary consider federal judges generally well qualified. This is especially true of Supreme Court justices, apparently because most presidents realize they will be held responsible for their appointees, and the presidents don't want to be embarrassed by them. Also, because presidents have so few vacancies to fill, they can confine themselves to persons of their party and political views and even to persons of a particular region, religion, race, and sex and still locate good candidates. This is less true of lower court judges. Presidents and senators (through senatorial courtesy) jointly appoint them, so both can avoid taking full responsibility for them. These judges are also less visible, so a lack of merit is not as noticeable.

Presidents do appoint some losers. President Truman put a longtime supporter on a court of appeals who was "drunk half the time" and "no damn good." When asked why he appointed the man, Truman candidly replied, "I . . . felt I owed him a favor; that's why, and I thought as a judge he couldn't do too much harm, and he didn't."[38] Sometimes presidents appoint qualified persons who later become incompetent. After serving for many years, they incur the illnesses and infirmities of old age, and perhaps one-tenth become unable to perform their job well.[39] Yet they hang on because they are allowed to

ties than differences. This should not be surprising, because the two sexes were subject to the same training in law school and the same socialization in the legal profession, and they became judges in the same ways as others in their jurisdiction.

Perhaps the greatest difference women judges have made is to protect the credibility of women lawyers and witnesses. In court, some men judges and lawyers made disparaging remarks about women lawyers, suggesting that they should not be in the profession—for example, calling them "lawyerettes." Many male judges and lawyers made paternalistic or personal remarks to female lawyers and witnesses, referring to them by their first name or by such terms as "young lady,"

"sweetie," or "honey." Or the men, in the midst of the proceedings, commented about their perfume, clothing, or appearance. "How does an attorney establish her authority when the judge has just described her to the entire courtroom as 'a pretty little thing'?"[7] Even if the men considered their remarks harmless compliments rather than intentional tactics, their effect was to undermine the credibility of women lawyers and witnesses in the eyes of jurors. Women judges have squelched such remarks.

[1]Karen O'Connor and Jeffrey A. Segal, "Justice Sandra Day O'Connor and the Supreme Court's Reaction to Its First Female Member," in *Women, Politics, and the Constitution*, ed. Naomi B. Lynn (New York: Haworth Press, 1990), 95–104.

[2]David W. Allen and Diane E. Wall, "Role Orientations and Women State Supreme Court Justices," *Judicature* 77 (1993), 156–165.

[3]Sue Davis, Susan Haire, and Donald R. Songer, "Voting Behavior and Gender on the U.S. Courts of Appeals," *Judicature* 77 (1993), 129–133; Thomas G. Walker and Deborah J. Barrow, "The Diversification of the Federal Bench," *Journal of Politics* 47 (1985), 596–617.

[4]John Gruhl, Cassia Spohn, and Susan Welch, "Women as Policymakers: The Case of Trial Judges," *American Journal of Political Science* 25 (1981), 308–322.

[5]Darrell Steffensmeier and Chris Hebert, "Women and Men Policymakers: Does the Judge's Gender Affect the Sentencing of Criminal Defendants?" *Social Forces* 77 (1999), 1163–1196.

[6]Jeffrey Toobin, "Women in Black," *New Yorker*, October 30, 2000, 48.

[7] William Eich, "Gender Bias in the Courtroom: Some Participants Are More Equal than Others," *Judicature* 69 (1986), 339–343.

serve for "good behavior," and they prevent other lawyers from filling their seats on the bench.

This problem has prompted proposals for a constitutional amendment setting a term limit of eighteen years[40] or a mandatory retirement age of seventy. Either of these changes would have a substantial impact because over one-third of all Supreme Court justices have served longer than twenty years and past age seventy-five. But constitutional amendments are difficult to pass, and mandatory retirement ages are out of favor now. Furthermore, some of the best judges have done some of their finest work late in their career.

Independence of Judges

Given the use of political criteria in selecting judges, can judges be independent on the bench? Can they decide cases as they think the law requires? Or do they feel pressure to decide cases as presidents or senators want them to?

Because judges are not dependent on presidents for renomination or senators for reconfirmation, they can be independent to a great extent. When President Nixon claimed executive privilege to keep the Watergate tapes secret, three of his appointees joined the other justices in ruling against him.[41] When President Clinton asserted presidential immunity from Paula Jones's lawsuit charging sexual harassment, both of his appointees joined the Republican justices in deciding against him.[42] After surveying the Warren and Burger Court decisions involving desegregation, obscenity, abortion, and criminal defendants' rights, one scholar observed, "Few American politicians even today would care to run on a platform of desegregation, pornography, abortion, and the 'coddling' of criminals."[43]

Presidents have scoffed at the notion that their appointees become their pawns. A study concluded that one-fourth of the justices deviated from their president's expectations.[44] Theodore Roosevelt placed Oliver Wendell Holmes on the Court, believing that Holmes shared his views on trusts. But in an early antitrust case, Holmes

Ruth Bader Ginsburg, appointed by President Clinton, was the second female justice and is the only one now. Although she tied for first place in her graduating class from Columbia Law School in 1959, she was turned down for a clerkship by Justice Felix Frankfurter and for law jobs with New York City firms. As a Jew, a woman, and a mother with young children, she had three liabilities at that time. Instead, she taught law and served as an attorney with the ACLU. In the 1970s, she argued six sex discrimination cases before the Supreme Court, winning five.

voted against Roosevelt's position, prompting Roosevelt to declare, "I could carve out of a banana a judge with more backbone than that!"[45] Holmes had ample backbone; he just didn't agree with Roosevelt's position in this case. Likewise, President Eisenhower placed Earl Warren on the Court, assuming that Warren was a moderate. But Warren turned out to be a liberal. Later Eisenhower said his appointment of Warren was "the biggest damn fool thing I ever did"[46] (although many legal scholars rank Warren as a great justice). President Truman concluded that "packing the Supreme Court simply can't be done. . . . I've tried it and it won't work. . . . Whenever you put a man on the Supreme Court he ceases to be your friend."[47] Truman exaggerated, although some presidents have had trouble "packing" the courts. They have not been able to foresee the issues

their appointees would face or the ways their appointees would change on the bench. (During Harry Blackmun's confirmation hearings, no senators asked about his views on abortion law, yet within six months *Roe* v. *Wade* would reach the Court, and Blackmun would author the controversial opinion.)[48] Nevertheless, presidents who have made a serious effort to find candidates with similar views usually have been able to.[49]

Access to the Courts

In our litigation-prone society, many individuals and groups want courts to resolve their disputes. Whether these individuals and groups get their "day in court" depends on their case, their wealth, and the court involved.

Courts hear two kinds of cases. **Criminal cases** are those in which governments prosecute persons for violating laws. **Civil cases** are those in which persons sue others for denying their rights and causing them harm. Criminal defendants, of course, must appear in court. Potential civil litigants, however, often cannot get access to court.

Wealth Discrimination in Access

Although the courts are supposed to be open to all, most individuals don't have enough money to hire an attorney and pay the costs necessary to pursue a case. Only corporations, wealthy individuals, or seriously injured victims suing corporations or wealthy individuals do. (Seriously injured victims with a strong case can obtain an attorney by agreeing to pay the attorney a sizable portion of what they win in their suit.) In addition, a small number of poor people supported by legal aid programs can pursue a case.

The primary expense is paying an attorney. New lawyers in law firms charge approximately $100 an hour; established partners may charge several times that.[50] Other expenses include various fees for filing the case, summoning jurors, paying witnesses, and also lost income from missed work due to numerous meetings with the attorney and hearings in court.

Even if individuals have enough money to initiate a suit, the disparity continues in court. Those with more money can develop a full case, whereas others must proceed with a skeletal case that is far less likely to persuade judges or jurors. Our legal system, according to one judge, "is divided into two separate and unequal systems of justice: one for the rich, in which the courts take limitless time to examine, ponder, consider, and deliberate over hundreds of thousands of bits of evidence and days of testimony, and hear elaborate, endless appeals and write countless learned opinions" and one for the nonrich, in which the courts provide "turnstile justice."[51] (During the week that one judge spent conducting the preliminary hearing to determine whether there was sufficient evidence to require O. J. Simpson to stand trial for murdering his ex-wife and her friend, other judges in Los Angeles disposed of 474 preliminary hearings for less wealthy defendants.) Consequently, many individuals are discouraged from pursuing a case in the first place.

Interest Group Help in Access

Interest groups, with more resources than most individuals, help some individuals gain access to the courts. The groups sponsor and finance these individuals' cases. Of course, the groups don't act out of altruism. They choose the cases that will advance their goals. An attorney for the **American Civil Liberties Union (ACLU),** which takes criminal cases to prod judges to protect constitutional rights, admitted that the defendants the ACLU represents "sometimes are pretty scurvy little creatures, but what they are doesn't matter a whole hell of a lot. It's the principle that we're going to be able to use these people for that's important."[52]

Some liberal groups—especially civil liberties organizations such as the ACLU, civil rights organizations such as the National Association for the Advancement of Colored People (NAACP), environmental groups such as the Sierra Club, and consumer and safety groups such as Ralph Nader's organizations—use litigation as a primary tactic. Other groups use it as an occasional tactic. In the 1980s and 1990s, some conservative groups began to use litigation as aggressively as these liberal groups. The Rutherford Institute arose to help persons who claimed that their religious rights were infringed, representing children who were forbidden from reading the Bible on the school bus or praying in the school cafeteria. The institute also funded Paula Jones's suit against President Clinton. Today the Alliance Defense Fund, which sponsors eighty to one hundred cases at a time, prods the courts to reflect conservative Christian values in disputes involving education, homosexuality, and embryonic stem cell research.[53] Interest groups have become ubiquitous in the judicial process. About half of all Supreme Court cases involve a liberal or con-

servative interest group,[54] and many lower court cases do as well. Even so, interest groups can help only a handful of the individuals who lack the resources to finance their cases.

Proceeding through the Courts

Cases normally start in a district court. Individuals who lose have a right to have their case decided by one higher court to determine whether there was a miscarriage of justice. They normally appeal to a court of appeals. Individuals who lose at this level have no further right to have their case decided by another court, but they can appeal to the Supreme Court. However, the Court can exercise almost unlimited discretion in choosing cases to review. No matter how important or urgent an issue seems, the Court doesn't have to hear it.

When the husband of Terri Schiavo, who was brain dead but physically alive in a persistent vegetative state, sought to have her feeding tube removed, her parents, with the help of pro-life groups, sued to take custody from her husband, then to maintain the feeding tube, and, once taken out, to reinsert it. They appealed to the Supreme Court six times. Although congressional leaders, thundering about federal judges, made her situation a political cause, the Supreme Court refused to hear the case each time it was appealed. Sen. Tom Coburn (R-Okla.) responded, "I don't want to impeach judges; I want to impale them."[55]

Litigants who appeal to the Supreme Court normally file a petition for a **writ of *certiorari*** ("made more certain" in Latin). The Court grants the writ—agrees to hear the case—if four of the nine justices vote to do so. The rationale for this "rule of four" is that a substantial number, though not necessarily a majority, of the justices should deem the case important enough to review. Generally, the Court agrees to review a case when the justices think an issue hasn't been resolved satisfactorily or consistently by the lower courts.

From over eight thousand petitions each year, the Court selects about eighty to hear, thus exercising considerable discretion.[56] The oft-spoken threat "We're going to appeal all the way to the Supreme Court" is usually just bluster. Likewise, the notion that the Court is "the court of last resort" is misleading. Most cases never get beyond the district courts or courts of appeals.

That the Supreme Court grants so few writs means that the Court has tremendous power to control its docket and determine which policies to review. It also means that the lower courts have considerable power because they serve as the court of last resort for most cases.

Deciding Cases

In deciding cases, judges need to interpret statutes and the Constitution and determine whether to follow precedents. In the process, they exercise discretion and make law.

Interpreting Statutes

In deciding cases, judges start with **statutes**—laws passed by legislatures. Often statutes are ambiguous. Then judges need to interpret them in order to apply them to their cases.

For example, Congress passed the **Americans with Disabilities Act** to protect people from discrimination in employment and public accommodations (businesses open to the public, such as stores, restaurants, hotels, and health care facilities). The act applies to people who have a "physical impairment" that "substantially limits" any of their "major life activities." The statute does not define these terms. Thus the courts have to do so, and in the process they determine the scope of the act.

When a dentist refused to fill a cavity for a woman with HIV, she sued, claiming discrimination under this act. The Supreme Court agreed by a 5–4 vote.[57] The majority concluded that HIV was a "physical impairment," although the woman was in the early stages and the disease didn't prevent her from performing any activity yet. The majority acknowledged that HIV would limit the "major life activity" of reproduction, because the disease could infect her fetus if she got pregnant. (Of course, HIV would also affect other important life activities as well.) The dissenters interpreted the statute to mean repetitive activities that are essential for daily existence rather than important activities that rarely occur in a person's life. Therefore, they denied that reproduction is a "major life activity."

When a woman developed carpal tunnel syndrome on the assembly line at a manufacturing plant, she sued, claiming that the company didn't make the reasonable accommodation—give her a different job that didn't require repetitive manual labor—that was required under the act. She said her condition limited her "major life activities" of performing manual tasks at work and at home, including lifting, sweeping, and gardening; playing with her children; and driving long distances.

The Court ruled that these aren't "major life activities,"[58] because they aren't of central importance to daily life, as seeing, hearing, and walking are.

Thus the Court had discretion. It interpreted the act broadly when it covered persons with HIV but narrowly when it refused to cover workers with less serious ailments.

Interpreting the Constitution

After interpreting statutes, judges determine whether the statutes are constitutional. Or if the cases involve actions of government officials rather than statutes, judges determine whether the actions are constitutional. For either, they need to interpret the Constitution.

Compared to constitutions of other countries, our Constitution is short and therefore ambiguous. It speaks in broad principles rather than in narrow details. The Fifth Amendment states that persons shall not be "deprived of life, liberty, or property without due process of law." The Fourteenth Amendment states that persons shall not be denied "the equal protection of the laws." What is "due process of law"? "Equal protection of the laws"? Generally, the former means that people should be treated fairly and the latter means that they should be treated equally. But what is fairly? Equally? These are broad principles that need to be interpreted in specific cases.

Sometimes the Constitution uses relative terms. The Fourth Amendment provides that persons shall be "secure . . . against unreasonable searches and seizures." What are "unreasonable" searches and seizures? Other times the Constitution uses absolute terms, which appear more clear-cut but aren't. The First Amendment provides that there shall be "no law . . . abridging the freedom of speech." Does "no law" mean literally no law? Then what about a law that punishes someone for falsely shouting "Fire!" in a crowded theater and causing a stampede that injures some patrons? Whether relative or absolute, the language needs to be interpreted in specific cases.

Occasionally, politicians, following the lead of Richard Nixon, assert that judges ought to be "strict constructionists," that they ought to interpret the Constitution "strictly." This is nonsense. Judges can't interpret ambiguous language strictly. When politicians or commentators use this phrase, they're trying to persuade voters that judges from the other party are deciding cases incorrectly, as though they are departing from some clear and fixed standard.

When judges interpret the Constitution, they exercise discretion. As former Chief Justice Charles Evans Hughes candidly acknowledged, "We are under a constitution, but the Constitution is what the Supreme Court says it is."[59]

Restraint and Activism

All judges exercise discretion, but not all engage in policy making to the same extent. Some, classified as restrained, are less willing to declare laws or actions of government officials unconstitutional, whereas others, classified as activist, are more willing to do so.

Restrained judges believe that the judiciary is the least democratic branch because (federal) judges are appointed for life rather than elected and reelected. Consequently, they should defer to the other branches, whose officials are elected. That is, they should accept the laws or actions of the other branches rather than substitute their own views. They should be wary of "government by judiciary." They should recognize, Justice Harlan Stone said, that "courts are not the only agency of government that must be presumed to have the capacity to govern. For the removal of unwise laws from the statute books, appeal lies not to the courts, but to the ballot and the processes of democratic government."[60]

Restrained judges also maintain that the power to declare laws unconstitutional is more effective if it is used sparingly. Justice Louis Brandeis concluded that "the most important thing we do is not doing."[61] That is, the most important thing judges do is declare laws constitutional and thereby build up political capital for the occasional times that they declare laws unconstitutional.

Ultimately, restrained judges contend that showing appropriate deference and following proper procedures are more important than reaching desired results. When a friend taking leave of Justice Oliver Wendell Holmes one morning said, "Well, Mr. Justice, I hope you do justice today," Holmes replied, "My job is not to do justice but to follow the law."

Justice Harry Blackmun, appointed by President Nixon, reflected this view in a capital punishment case:

I yield to no one in the depth of my distaste, antipathy, and, indeed, abhorrence for the death penalty, with all its aspects of physical distress and fear and of moral judgment exercised by finite minds. That distaste is buttressed by a belief that capital punishment serves no useful purpose that can be demonstrated. For me, it violates childhood's training and

Although many children worked long days in unhealthy conditions, the Supreme Court declared initial laws prohibiting child labor unconstitutional. This girl working in a spinning mill in the early 1900s.

Library of Congress, #LC-DIG-nclc-01830

life's experiences, and is not compatible with the philosophical convictions I have been able to develop. It is antagonistic to any sense of "reverence for life." Were I a legislator, I would vote against the death penalty.

But as a judge, he voted for it.[62]

Activist judges are less concerned with showing appropriate deference and following proper procedures. Some are more concerned with the results; others are more outraged at injustice. Chief Justice Earl Warren said that the courts' responsibility was "to see if justice truly has been done." He asked lawyers who emphasized technical procedures during oral arguments, "Yes, yes, yes, but is it right? Is it good?"[63]

Activist judges don't believe that the judiciary is the least democratic branch. Warren, who had served as governor of California, saw that the legislators, though elected, were often the captives of special interests. As a result of these attitudes, activist judges have a flexible view of separation of powers. District court judge Frank Johnson, who issued sweeping orders for Alabama's prisons and mental hospitals, replied to critics, "I didn't

A study of all cases in which congressional statutes were at stake (sixty-four) in the last eleven terms of the Supreme Court under Chief Justice Rehnquist (1994–2005) reveals that the most conservative justice—Clarence Thomas—was the most activist. He voted to strike down the law in 65.6 percent of these cases. The next most conservative justices—Antonin Scalia and William Rehnquist—were among the most activist. The most liberal justices—John Paul Stevens, Ruther Bader Ginsburg, Steven Breyer, and David Souter—were the most restrained. (All but Rehnquist and O'Connor are on the current Supreme Court.)

Justice	% Votes to Strike Down Congressional Statute
Thomas	65.6
Kennedy	64.1
Scalia	56.3
Rehnquist	46.9
O'Connor	46.8
Souter	42.2
Stevens	39.3
Ginsburg	39.1
Breyer	28.1

SOURCE: Paul Gewirtz and Chad Golder, "So Who Are the Activists?" *New York Times*, July 6, 2005, www.nytimes.com/2005/07/06/opinion/06gewirtz.html?ei=5070&en=5b5cf694fb8.

tend to be restrained, whereas others tend to be activist; most fall somewhere in between.

Both conservatives and liberals have practiced both restraint and activism depending on the political climate at the time. In the late nineteenth and early twentieth centuries, the Court was conservative and activist, striking down regulations on business. After the switch in the 1930s, the Court was liberal and restrained, upholding regulations on business. Then in the 1950s and 1960s, the Court was liberal and activist, striking down restrictions on individual rights. (See the box "Who Are the Activists?")

Although restraint and activism are useful concepts, we should not make too much of them. It usually is more important to know whether a judge is conservative or liberal than whether the judge purports to be restrained or activist. Political science research shows that justices' votes reflect their ideology: conservative justices vote for the conservative position, and liberal justices vote for the liberal position in most cases. When justices claim to be restrained, their decision, allowing a particular law or policy to continue, produces the conservative or liberal outcome they prefer.[65] Thus some political scientists conclude that "judicial restraint" is little more than "a cloak for the justices' policy preferences."[66] It enables them to proclaim their "restraint" while actually voting on the basis of their ideology—without ever admitting this to the public.

We should be skeptical when we hear judges or politicians using these terms, whether touting their "restraint" to pacify the public or deriding opponents' "activism" to inflame the public.

Following Precedents

In interpreting statutes and the Constitution, judges are expected to follow precedents established by their court or higher courts in previous cases. This is the rule of *stare decisis* ("stand by what has been decided" in Latin).

Stare decisis provides stability in the law. If different judges decided similar cases in different ways, the law would be unpredictable, even chaotic. "*Stare decisis*," Justice Brandeis said, "is usually the wise policy; because in most matters it is more important that the applicable rule of law be settled than that it be settled right."[67] *Stare decisis* also promotes equality in the law. If different judges decided similar cases in different ways, the courts would appear discriminatory toward some litigants.

When in 1962 the Supreme Court held unconstitutional a New York law requiring public school students

ask for any of these cases. In an ideal society, all of these . . . decisions should be made by those to whom we have entrusted these responsibilities. But when governmental institutions fail to make these . . . decisions in a manner which comports with the Constitution, the federal courts have a duty to remedy the violation."[64] Activist judges don't believe that the power to declare laws unconstitutional is more effective if it is used sparingly. Rather, they claim that the power is enhanced if it is used frequently—essentially, they urge their colleagues to "use it or lose it"—because the public gets accustomed to it.

Thus judicial restraint and judicial activism are belief systems and role concepts that people think judges should follow when they decide cases. Some judges

to recite a nondenominational prayer every day, the ruling became a precedent.[68] The following year, the Court held unconstitutional a Baltimore school policy requiring students to recite Bible verses.[69] The Court followed the precedent it had set the year before. In 1980, the Court held unconstitutional a Tennessee law forcing public schools to post the Ten Commandments in all classrooms.[70] Although this law differed from the previous ones in that it did not require recitation, the majority concluded that it reflected the same goal—to use the public schools to promote the Christian religion—so it violated the same principle—separation of church and state. In 1992, the Court ruled that clergy cannot offer prayers at graduation ceremonies for public schools.[71] Although this situation, too, differed from the previous ones in that it did not occur every day at school, the majority reasoned that it, too, reflected the same goal and violated the same principle. Finally, in 2000, the Court ruled that schools cannot use, or allow clergy or students to use, the public address system to offer prayers before high school football games.[72] For almost four decades, the Court followed the precedent it originally set when it initially addressed this issue.

However, sometimes it's not clear which precedent to follow. There might not be any precedents that are controlling but several that are relevant, and these might point in contrary directions. Then the justices have discretion. In 1996, the justices weighed government regulation of indecent programming on cable television. They had precedents that governed broadcast television, telephones, and bookstores. But as Justice Stephen Breyer observed, none of these really paralleled cable television, which looks like broadcast television but which uses telephone lines rather than airwaves to transmit its signals. He was uncertain which precedent to use. Apparently the others were uncertain also, as the nine justices split three ways and wrote six opinions.[73]

Making Law

Many judges deny that they make law. They say that it is already there, that they merely "find" it or, with their education and experience, "interpret" it. They imply that they use a mechanical process. Justice Owen Roberts wrote for the majority that struck down a New Deal act in 1936:

> It is sometimes said that the Court assumes a power to overrule . . . the people's representatives. This is a misconception. The Constitution is the supreme law of the land. . . . All

legislation must conform to the principles it lays down. When an act of Congress is appropriately challenged in the courts as not conforming to the constitutional mandate, the judicial branch of government has only one duty—to lay . . . the Constitution . . . beside the statute . . . and to decide whether the latter squares with the former.[74]

In other words, the Constitution itself dictates the decision.

However, by now it should be apparent that judges do not use a mechanical process. They *do* exercise discretion, and they *do* make law—when they interpret statutes, when they interpret the Constitution, and when they determine which precedents to follow or disregard.[21] In doing so, they reflect their own political preferences. As Justice Benjamin Cardozo said, "We may try to see things as objectively as we please. Nonetheless, we can never see them with any eyes except our own."[76] They do not shed their attitudes, even their prejudices, when they don their robes.

But to say that judges make law is not to say that they make law as legislators do. Judges make law less directly. They make it in the process of resolving disputes brought to them. They usually make it by telling governments what they cannot do, rather than what they must do and how they must do it. And judges make law less freely. They start not with clean slates, but with established principles embodied in statutes, the Constitution, and precedents. They are expected to follow these principles. If they deviate from them, they are expected to explain their reasons, and they are subjected to scrutiny by the legal profession.

Deciding Cases at the Supreme Court

The Supreme Court's term runs from October through June. Early in the term, the justices decide which cases to hear, and by the end of the term, they decide how to resolve those cases.

After the Court agrees to hear a case, litigants submit written arguments. These "briefs" identify the issues and marshal the evidence—statutes, constitutional provisions, and precedents—for their side. (The word *briefs* is a misnomer, as some run to more than one hundred pages.)

Often interest groups and governments, whether federal, state, or local, submit briefs to support one side. These **friend of the court briefs** present additional evidence or perspectives not included in the litigants' briefs. Major cases can prompt many briefs. A pair of affirmative action cases from the University of Michigan in 2003 had a record 102 briefs.[77]

Several weeks after receiving the briefs, the Court holds oral arguments. The justices gather in the robing room, put on their black robes, and file into the courtroom, taking their places at the half-hexagon bench. The chief justice sits in the center, with the associate justices extending out in order of seniority. The crier gavels the courtroom to attention and announces:

The Honorable, the Chief Justice and Associate Justices of the Supreme Court of the United States! Oyez, oyez, oyez! [Give ear, give ear, give ear!] All persons having business before the Honorable, the Supreme Court of the United States are admonished to draw near and give attention, for the Court is now sitting. God save the United States and this Honorable Court.

The chief justice calls the case. The lawyers present their arguments, although the justices interrupt with questions whenever they want. When Thurgood Marshall, as the counsel for the NAACP before becoming a justice, argued one school desegregation case, he was interrupted 127 times. The justices ask about the facts of the case: "What happened when the defendant . . . ?" They ask about relevant precedents that appear to support or rebut the lawyers' arguments: "Can you distinguish this case from . . . ?" They ask about hypothetical scenarios: "What if the police officer . . . ?" These questions help the justices determine what is at stake, how a ruling would relate to existing doctrine, and how a ruling might govern future situations. They are experienced at pinning lawyers down. Chief Justice Rehnquist, who was affable toward his colleagues, was tough on the lawyers appearing before him. When asked whether the lawyers were nervous, he replied, "I assume they're all nervous—they should be."[78] Occasionally, one faints on the spot.

The chief justice allots a half hour per side. When time expires, a red light flashes on the lectern, and the chief justice halts any lawyer who continues. Rehnquist, who valued efficiency and punctuality, cut lawyers off in mid-sentence when their time was up.

The oral arguments identify and clarify the major points of the case for any justices who did not read the briefs, and they assess the potential impact of the possible rulings. The oral arguments also serve as a symbol: they give the litigants a chance to be heard in open court, which encourages the litigants to feel that the eventual ruling is legitimate. However, the oral arguments rarely sway the justices, except occasionally when a lawyer for one side is especially effective or ineffective.

The Court holds Friday conferences to make a tentative decision and assign the opinion. The decision affirms or reverses the lower court's decision; it indicates who wins and who loses. The opinion explains why. It expresses principles of law and establishes precedents for the future. It tells lower courts how to resolve similar cases.

A portrait of Chief Justice John Marshall presides over the conference. To ensure secrecy, no one is present but the justices. They begin with handshakes. (During his tenure, Chief Justice Marshall suggested that they begin with a drink whenever it was rainy. But even when it was sunny, Marshall sometimes announced, "Our jurisdiction extends over so large a territory that the doctrine of chances makes it certain that it must be raining somewhere."[79] Perhaps this accounts for his extraordinary success in persuading his colleagues to adopt his views.) Then the justices get down to business. The chief justice initiates the discussion of the case. He indicates what the issues are and how they ought to be decided, and he casts a vote. The associate justices follow in order of seniority. Although the conference traditionally featured give-and-take among the justices, discussion was perfunctory under Rehnquist, and the conference became a series of quick votes.[80] The Court reaches a tentative decision based on these votes. If the chief justice is in the majority, he assigns the writing of the opinion to himself or another justice. If he is not in the majority, the most senior associate justice in the majority assigns it. This custom reveals the chief justice's power. Although his vote counts the same as each associate justice's vote, his authority to assign the opinion can determine what the opinion says. He knows that certain colleagues will use strong language and lay down broad principles, whereas others will use guarded language and hew closely to specific facts in the case.

Before Marshall became chief justice, each justice wrote his own opinion. But Marshall realized that one opinion from the Court would carry more weight. He often convinced the other justices to forsake their opinions for his. As a result, he wrote almost half of the more than eleven hundred opinions the Court handed down during his thirty-four years. Recent chief justices have assigned most opinions—82 to 86 percent—but have written just slightly more than their share—12 to 14 percent.[81] Some Court watchers believe that Rehnquist downplayed his conservative views after he became chief justice to stay in the majority and retain control of the opinion.[82]

After the conference, the Court produces the opinion. This is the most time-consuming stage in the process. After Justice Brandeis died, researchers found in his files the thirty-seventh draft of an opinion he had written but still had not been satisfied with.

Because the justices are free to change their vote anytime until the decision is announced, the justice assigned the opinion tries to write it to command support of the justices in the original majority and possibly even some in the original minority. The writer circulates the draft among the others, who suggest revisions. The writer circulates more drafts. These go back and forth as the justices attempt to persuade or cajole, nudge or push their colleagues toward their position.

Unlike legislators, however, the justices don't engage in horse-trading—if you join me on this, I'll join you on that. According to one justice, there's "[n]one of that, zero. The coalitions float. Each . . . case is a new day."[83] Sometimes the outcome changes between the tentative vote in the conference and the final vote in the decision. According to Justice Blackmun's notes, eleven times during his last three years on the Rehnquist Court, one or more justices switched sides to fashion a new majority from the original minority. In the case involving graduation prayers, Justice Anthony Kennedy was writing the **majority opinion** to allow such prayers, but he was unable to persuade himself. He abandoned the majority and joined the minority, thus making it the eventual majority.[84]

These inner workings underscore the politicking among the justices. **Justice William Brennan,** a liberal activist on the Warren and Burger Courts, was a gregarious and charming Irish American who was well liked by his colleagues. After drafting an opinion, he sent his clerks to other justices' clerks to learn whether their justices had any objections. Then he tried to redraft it to satisfy them. If they still had qualms, he went to their offices and tried to persuade them. If necessary, he compromised. He didn't want "to be 100 percent principled and lose by one vote," a law professor observed.[85] Brennan was so adept at persuasion that some scholars consider him "the best coalition builder ever to

Justice Clarence Thomas shares a laugh with his clerks in his chambers.

sit on the Supreme Court."[86] In fact, some say the Warren and Burger Courts should have been called the Brennan Court.

Justice Antonin Scalia, a conservative activist on the Rehnquist Court, is a brilliant and gregarious Italian American who, when appointed by President Reagan, was expected to dominate his colleagues and become the leader of the Court. Yet he has not fulfilled this expectation. He has been brash and imprudent, appearing to take more pleasure in insulting his colleagues than in persuading them.[87] In a case in which Justice O'Connor, also conservative but more cautious, did not want to go as far in limiting abortion rights as he did, Scalia wrote that her arguments "cannot be taken seriously."[88] In another case in which Chief Justice Rehnquist, who usually voted with Scalia, voted opposite him, Scalia wrote that his arguments were "implausible" and suggested that any lawyer who advised his client as Rehnquist urged should be "disbarred."[89] As a result, Scalia has not been as effective in forging a consensus among conservatives as Brennan was among liberals.

Leadership, by someone, is necessary with nine strong-willed individuals, each of whom has risen to the top of the legal profession and each of whom is essentially operating a one-person law firm. Sometimes the chief justice becomes the informal leader. Marshall set the standard; Warren and Rehnquist were also effective leaders. Burger, however, possessed neither the interpersonal skills nor the intellectual firepower to earn the respect of his colleagues. From all indications, new Chief Justice Roberts has the potential to become an effective leader.

If the opinion does not command the support of some justices in the original majority, they write a **concurring opinion.** This indicates that they agree with the decision but not the reasons for it. Meanwhile, the justices in the minority write a **dissenting opinion.** This indicates that they do not agree even with the decision. Both concurring and dissenting opinions weaken the force of the majority opinion. They question its validity, and they suggest that at a different time with different justices, there might be a different ruling. Chief Justice Hughes used to say that a dissenting opinion is "an appeal to the brooding spirit of the law, to the intelligence of a future day."[90] Unlike the high courts of many other countries, which don't report any dissents, the Supreme Court of the United States routinely does, and the American people usually accept the existence of such doctrinal disagreements.[91] In recent terms, about 60 percent of the Court's cases have had dissents.[92] But too many dissents indicate a fractious Court. One-third of the Rehnquist Court's cases were decided by a 5–4 vote in 2001, possibly the highest proportion ever.[93]

Finally, the print shop in the Court's basement prints the opinions, thus preventing the leaks that might occur if the opinions were printed elsewhere, and the Court announces its decisions and distributes the opinions in public session.

Exercising Power

The use of judicial review by the courts and the exercise of political checks against the courts reveal the extent of their power.

Use of Judicial Review

The Founders expected the judiciary to be the weakest branch of government. In the *Federalist Papers,* Alexander Hamilton wrote that Congress would have power to pass the laws and appropriate the money; the president would have power to execute the laws; but the courts would have "merely judgment"—that is, only power to resolve disputes in cases brought to them. In doing so, they would exercise "neither force nor will." They would not have any means to enforce decisions, and they would not use their own values to decide cases. They would simply apply the Constitution and laws as written. Consequently, the judiciary would be the "least dangerous" branch.[94]

This prediction was accurate for the early years of the Republic. The federal courts seemed inconsequential. The Supreme Court was held in such low esteem that some distinguished men refused to accept appointment to it; others accepted appointment but refused to attend sessions. The first chief justice thought the Court was "inauspicious,"[95] without enough "weight and dignity" to play an important role.[96] So he resigned to be governor of New York. The second chief justice resigned to be envoy to France.

When the nation's capital was moved to Washington, D.C., in 1801, new homes were built for Congress and the president but not for the Supreme Court. Planners considered the Court too insignificant for more than a small room in the Capitol. But the Court couldn't even keep this room. For decades, it would be shunted from one location to another, from the marshal's office to the clerk's office, from the clerk's home to the Capitol's cellar—a dark and damp chamber in which visitors joked that Lady Justice wouldn't need to wear a blindfold because she couldn't see anyway—and from one committee room to another.[97] It wouldn't get its own building until 1935.

However, the status of the Court began to change after the appointment of the fourth chief justice, **John Marshall.** Under his leadership, the Court began to develop "weight and dignity" and to play an important role in government.

The Founding Era
In the Founding era, the Supreme Court established judicial review and national supremacy.

Establishing judicial review Judicial review is the authority to declare laws or actions of government officials unconstitutional. The Constitution doesn't mention judicial review. Although the idea was proposed at the Constitutional Convention, it was strongly opposed by some delegates who feared that it would strengthen the federal courts too much and, ultimately, weaken the state governments. The delegates who favored judicial review did not press for its inclusion because they worried that doing so might jeopardize the Constitution's ratification.[98]

Nevertheless, the Supreme Court claimed the authority of judicial review in the case of ***Marbury v. Madison*** in 1803.[99] The dispute originated in 1800, when the Federalist president, John Adams, was defeated in his bid for reelection by Thomas Jefferson and many Federalist members of Congress were defeated by

Jeffersonians. With both the Presidency and Congress lost, the Federalists tried to maintain control of the judiciary. The lame-duck president and lame-duck Congress added more judgeships, most of which were unnecessary. (Forty-two were for justices of the peace for the District of Columbia, which was sparsely populated.) They hoped to fill these positions with loyal Federalists before the new president and new Congress took over.

In addition, Adams named his secretary of state, John Marshall, to be chief justice. At the time, though, Marshall was still secretary of state and responsible for delivering the commissions to the new appointees. But he ran out of time, failing to deliver four commissions for District of Columbia justices of the peace. He assumed that his successor would deliver them. But Jefferson, angry at the Federalists' efforts to pack the judiciary, told his secretary of state, James Madison, not to deliver the commissions.[100] Without the signed commissions, the appointees could not prove that they had in fact been appointed.[101]

William Marbury and the three other appointees petitioned the Supreme Court for a writ of *mandamus* ("we command" in Latin), an order that forces government officials to do something they have a duty to do. In this case, it would force Madison to deliver the commissions.

As chief justice, Marshall was in a position to rule on his administration's efforts to appoint these judges. Today this would be considered a conflict of interest, and he would be expected to disqualify himself. But at the time, people were not as troubled by such conflicts.

Marshall could issue the writ, but Jefferson would tell Madison to disobey it, and the Court would be powerless to enforce it. Or Marshall could decline to issue the writ, and the Court would appear powerless to issue it. Either way, the Court would reflect weakness rather than project strength.

Marshall shrewdly found a way out of the dilemma. He interpreted a provision of a congressional statute in a questionable way and then a provision of the Constitution in a questionable way as well.[102] As a result, he could claim that the statute violated the Constitution. Therefore, the statute was unconstitutional, and the Court couldn't order the administration to give the commissions. Thus Marshall exercised judicial review. He wrote, in a statement that would be repeated by courts for years to come, "It is emphatically the province and duty of the judicial department to say what the law is."

Marshall sacrificed the commissions—he couldn't have gotten them anyway—and established the power of judicial review instead. In doing so, with one hand he gave the Jeffersonians what they wanted— permission not to deliver the commissions—while with the other he gave the Federalists something much greater—judicial review. And all along he claimed he did what the Constitution required him to do.

Jefferson saw through this. He said the Constitution, in Marshall's hands, was "a thing of putty,"[103] adding that Marshall's arguments were "twistifications." But the decision didn't require Jefferson to do anything, so he couldn't do anything but protest. Most of Jefferson's followers were satisfied with the result. They weren't upset that the Court had invalidated a Federalist law, even though it had established judicial review to do so.

Of course, they were shortsighted because this decision laid the cornerstone for a strong judiciary. A case that began as a "trivial squabble over a few petty political plums"[104] became perhaps the most important case the Court has ever decided.

Establishing national supremacy After *Marbury*, the Marshall Court declared numerous state laws unconstitutional.[105] These decisions solidified the authority of judicial review, and they symbolized the supremacy of the national government over the state governments.

The Court also advanced the supremacy of the national government by broadly construing congressional power. In **McCulloch v. Maryland**, discussed in Chapter 2, the Court interpreted the **"necessary and proper clause"** to allow Congress to legislate in many matters not mentioned in the Constitution and not anticipated by the Founders.[106]

Now let's leap forward to the modern era, where we'll see how the Court has used judicial review and national supremacy.

The Modern Era

The modern era for the Supreme Court began when President Dwight Eisenhower, fulfilling a campaign pledge to a presidential rival, **Earl Warren,** appointed him chief justice. In the 1950s and 1960s, the **Warren Court** decided many cases involving civil liberties and civil rights. These cases pitted individuals against the government. Often they pitted minority individuals—whether a political minority, a racial minority, or a religious minority—against the majority of the public, whose views were reflected in government policy.

Chief Justice Earl Warren

he appointed **Warren Burger** to be chief justice. Then Nixon and his former vice president, President Gerald Ford, appointed four more justices as vacancies occurred. They sought to slow, halt, or even reverse the Court's liberal doctrine. They expected the **Burger Court** to bring about a "constitutional counterrevolution."

But the Burger Court in the 1970s and 1980s did not. Although it eroded some liberal doctrine,[108] it left most intact. And it initiated new liberal doctrine in two areas where the Warren Court had been silent—sexual discrimination and abortion. Although it was not as committed to civil liberties and civil rights as the Warren Court, the Burger Court was more committed to them than any earlier Court.

President Ronald Reagan and his former vice president, George H. W. Bush, also sought to reverse the Court's liberal doctrine. When Burger retired, Reagan elevated **William Rehnquist,** the most conservative associate justice, to be chief justice. Then Reagan and Bush appointed five more conservatives as vacancies occurred. By this time, Republican presidents had named ten justices in a row.

President Bill Clinton's election led to the first Democratic justices since 1967. Although these two moderate liberals slowed any further swing to the right, the conservative justices controlled the **Rehnquist Court** in the 1980s, 1990s, and early 2000s. But conflicts among the conservatives splintered their bloc. Some were bold, eager to sweep away liberal precedents and substitute conservative principles. Others were cautious, willing to uphold liberal precedents they would not have agreed to set in the first place and inclined to decide cases on narrow bases rather than on broad principles. In some terms, the former group dominated, but in other terms, the latter group dominated.[109] Overall, the Rehnquist Court, though markedly more conservative than the Burger Court,[110] did not bring about a "constitutional counterrevolution" either.

The Rehnquist Court also practiced judicial activism, though from the right rather than from the left. For example, it struck down laws implementing gun registration, affirmative action, legislative districts that help racial minorities elect their candidates, and governmental policies that help religious minorities practice their religion. It also invalidated a series of congressional laws regulating the states. In eight of the last years of the Rehnquist Court, the justices invalidated thirty-three federal laws, the highest annual average ever.[111]

In ***Bush v. Gore,*** which arose from the disputed presidential election of 2000, the conservative major-

Historically, the courts had paid little attention to civil liberties and civil rights, allowing the government to ignore these constitutional rights. But the Warren Court reversed this lax attitude. It replaced traditional legal doctrine involving racial segregation, legislative reapportionment, criminal defendants' rights, libel, obscenity, and religion. It also modified traditional legal doctrine involving political speech. In the process, it held many laws, especially state laws, unconstitutional. The Warren Court was more activist in civil liberties and civil rights cases than any Supreme Court had ever been (see Figure 3).

The Warren Court sympathized with powerless groups and unpopular individuals when they challenged government policies. Thus the most elite institution in our government used its power to benefit many non-elites in our society. In its sympathies, the Warren Court differed sharply from previous Courts, which typically favored the haves over the have-nots and the efforts to preserve the status quo over the struggles to change it.

The Warren Court's decisions brought about a conservative backlash.[107] President Richard Nixon vowed to change the Court's direction, and after Earl Warren retired

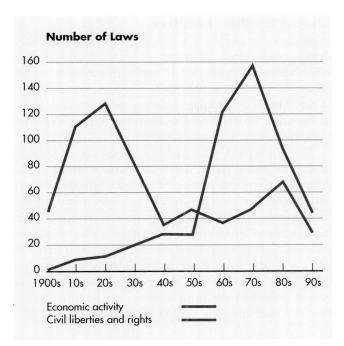

Number of Laws

FIGURE 3 • Laws Regulating Economic Activity and Restricting Civil Liberties and Rights Declared Unconstitutional by the Supreme Court since 1900 *The Supreme Court was nearly as activist in striking down laws in the 1910s, 1920s, and 1930s, as it was in the 1950s, 1960s, and 1970s. But in the former years, it was activist in economic cases (usually those involving government regulation of business), whereas in the latter years, it was activist in civil liberties and rights cases.*

SOURCE: Congressional Research Service, *The Constitution of the United States: Analysis and Interpretation* and its 1998 supplement (Washington, D.C.: U.S. Government Printing Office, 1996 and 1999); Kenneth Jose, *The Supreme Court Yearbook, 1998–1999* (Washington, D.C.: CQ Press, 2000); Lawrence Baum, *The Supreme Court,* 8th ed. (Washington, D.C.: CQ Press, 2004), 181.

ity deliberately intervened—essentially, picked the president—although the Constitution lays out the procedures to resolve electoral deadlocks.[112] These procedures give Congress, not the courts, primary authority to choose the president.

President George W. Bush, like recent Republican presidents, has tried to fashion a more conservative Court. When William Rehnquist died in 2005, he appointed **John Roberts** to be chief justice. He then appointed another conservative, Samuel Alito. The **Roberts Court** is developing as a more conservative court than the Rehnquist Court.

In the modern era, the Court has used judicial review to be a policy maker. In general, the Warren Court was a liberal policy maker, the Burger Court a moderate policy maker, and the Rehnquist Court a conservative policy maker. All three courts were activist rather than restrained.

The Role of Judicial Review

Judicial review is the most powerful tool courts use to wield power. When the courts declare a law or action unconstitutional, they not only void that law or action but also might put the issue on the public agenda, and they might speed up or slow down the pace of change in the government's policy.

When the Supreme Court declared Texas's abortion law unconstitutional in *Roe* v. *Wade* in 1973, the Court put the abortion issue on the public agenda.[113] It hadn't been a raging controversy before the decision.

The Court used judicial review as a catalyst to speed up change in the desegregation cases in the 1950s. At the time, President Eisenhower wasn't inclined to act, and Congress wasn't able to act because both houses were dominated by senior southerners who, as committee chairs, blocked civil rights legislation. The Court broke the logjam.

The Court used judicial review as a brake to slow down change in the business cases in the first third of the twentieth century. After the Industrial Revolution swept the United States, powerful corporations abused their employees, their customers, and their competitors. Although Congress and state legislatures passed laws to regulate these abuses, the Court, dominated by justices who had been lawyers for corporations, often struck down the laws. The Court delayed some policies for several decades.

Judicial review, an American contribution to government, was for years unique to this country. It is now used in numerous other countries, but not as extensively or as effectively as in the United States.

The Supreme Court alone has struck down over 150 provisions of federal laws and over 1200 provisions of state and local laws.[114] The number of laws struck down, however, isn't a true measure of the importance of judicial review. Instead, the ever-present threat of review has prevented the legislatures from enacting many laws they feared would be struck down.

By using judicial review to play a strong role in government, the Court has contradicted the Founders' expectation that the judiciary would always be the weakest branch. Usually it has been the weakest branch, but occasionally it has been stronger. Arguably, these times include some years during the early nineteenth

Chief Justice William Rehnquist

Lynn Johnson/Aurora Photos

century, when the Court established national supremacy; the late nineteenth century and early twentieth century, when the Court thwarted efforts to regulate business; and the 1950s and 1960s, when the Court extended civil liberties and civil rights.

Nevertheless, the extent to which the Court has played a strong role in government shouldn't be exaggerated. At any given time, the Court has focused on one broad area of the law—in the modern era, civil liberties and civil rights—and has paid little attention to other areas. Moreover, this area has always involved domestic policy. Traditionally, the Court has been reluctant to intervene in foreign policy.[115]

Use of Political Checks against the Courts

The courts have exercised judicial review cautiously because they're subject to various political checks by the other branches.

Checks by the Executive

Presidents can impose the most effective check. If they dislike courts' rulings, they can appoint new judges when vacancies occur. Many appointees remain on the bench two decades after their president has left the White House.[116] President Nixon resigned in disgrace in 1974, but his appointee William Rehnquist stayed on the Court until he died in 2005.

Presidents and state and local executives, such as governors and mayors and even school officials and police officers, can refuse to enforce courts' rulings. School officials have disobeyed decisions requiring desegregation and invalidating class prayers. Police officers have ignored decisions invalidating some kinds of searches and interrogations. Yet executives who refuse to enforce courts' rulings risk losing public support, unless the public also opposes the rulings. Even President Nixon complied when the Court ordered him to turn over the incriminating Watergate tapes.

Checks by the Legislature

Congress and state legislatures can overturn courts' rulings by adopting constitutional amendments. They have done so four times (with the Eleventh, Fourteenth, Sixteenth, and Twenty-sixth Amendments).[117]

They can also overturn courts' rulings by passing new statutes. When courts base decisions on their interpretations of statutes, or when they make decisions in the absence of statutes, legislatures can pass new statutes, with clear language, that negate the decisions. From 1967 through 1990, Congress passed statutes to negate 121 Supreme Court rulings.[118] In 1986, the Court ruled that the Air Force didn't have to allow an ordained rabbi to wear his yarmulke with his uniform.[119] The next year, Congress passed a statute permitting military personnel to wear some religious apparel while in uniform.

Legislatures can refuse to implement courts' rulings, especially when money is necessary to implement them. The legislators simply don't appropriate the money.

Although these checks are the most common, Congress has invoked others, though only rarely. It can alter the structure of the lower federal courts, it can limit the appellate jurisdiction of the Supreme Court, and it can impeach and remove judges. It can also limit the use of *habeas corpus*. In 2005, it prohibited federal courts from hearing any cases brought by alien detainees at Guantanamo Bay, Cuba.[120]

As a result of occasional checks or threatened checks, the courts have developed a strong sense of self-restraint to ensure self-preservation. This, more than the checks themselves, limits their use of judicial review.

Table 1	Modern Supreme Courts
Warren Court	1953–1969
Burger Court	1969–1986
Rehnquist Court	1986–2005
Roberts Court	2005–present

Conclusion: Are the Courts Responsive?

The courts tend to reflect the views of the public. Studies comparing 185 Supreme Court rulings from the mid-1930s through the mid-1990s with public opinion polls on the same issues found that the rulings mirrored the polls in approximately 60 percent of the cases.[121] The justices reflected the views of the public about as often as elected officials did. Thus the justices either responded to the public or, having been appointed by political officials chosen by the public, simply reflected the views of the public as political officials did.

Research shows that citizens know almost nothing about the judges; more adults can identify the character names of the Three Stooges than a single justice on the Supreme Court.[122] They also know little about the cases, but they do remember controversial decisions and they do recognize broad trends.[123] If they dislike these decisions or trends, their opinions pressure presidents and members of Congress to appoint justices with different views.

Although the courts are directly or indirectly responsive to the public, the Founders did not intend for them to be very responsive. The Founders gave judges life tenure so the courts would be relatively independent of both officials and the public. Indeed, the courts are more independent of political pressures than the other branches are. This enables them, in the words of appellate court judge Learned Hand, to stand as a bulwark against the "pressure of public panic." They can provide a "sober second thought."[124]

The courts can even protect the rights of various minorities—racial minorities, religious minorities, political dissidents, and criminal defendants—against the demands and the wrath of the majority. Chapters 12 and 13 will show how courts extended civil liberties and civil rights to unpopular groups and individuals who lacked clout with the other branches and support from the public. Yet protecting the rights of these groups and individuals has historically been the exception rather than the rule. It was typical of the Warren Court and to some extent the Burger Court, but it was not typical of Supreme Courts before and has not been typical of the Courts since.

The courts are part of the political process and are sensitive to others in the process, especially to the president, Congress, and the public. Although they enjoy relative independence, they aren't immune to political pressure. They have therefore "learned to be a political institution and to behave accordingly" and have "seldom lagged far behind or forged far ahead" of public opinion.[125]

Key Terms

Key Names

TEST YOURSELF

1. The battleground over judicial appointments usually is the
   a. Senate Judiciary Committee.
   b. House Judiciary Committee.
   c. whole Senate.
   d. whole House.
   e. Congress.

2. Federal courts have jurisdiction over
   a. cases that involve the Constitution.
   b. cases that involve congressional statutes.
   c. cases in which the U.S. government is a party.
   d. most criminal cases.
   e. all but d.

3. Due to senatorial courtesy,
   a. presidents are courteous when they submit nominations to the Senate.
   b. senators in the president's party recommend or veto candidates for judgeships in their state.
   c. presidents play virtually no role in nominations to the lower courts.
   d. senators in the opposite party of the president have a say in judicial nominations.
   e. lawyers who want to become judges feel no need to get to know their senators.

4. Of the criteria that presidents consider when nominating judges, which is the most common?
   a. nominating persons who demonstrate merit
   b. nominating members of their party
   c. nominating persons who share their ideology
   d. nominating persons who reflect racial and sexual diversity
   e. nominating persons who are uncontroversial

5. Presidents have made an effort to appoint judges who reflect diversity except _____ diversity.
   a. racial
   b. religious
   c. sexual
   d. socioeconomic
   e. geographic

6. When the Senate has refused to confirm presidential nominees to federal courts in recent decades, it's usually been because of the nominees'
   a. merit.
   b. party affiliation.
   c. ideology.
   d. race.
   e. religion.

7. Federal judges serve for
   a. two years.
   b. four years.
   c. six years.
   d. eight years.
   e. "good behavior."

8. When litigants appeal to the Supreme Court, they normally file a petition for a
   a. writ of *certiorari*.
   b. "forma pauperis."
   c. writ of *habeas corpus*.
   d. "friend of the court."
   e. writ of *mandamus*.

9. The Supreme Court hears _____ of the cases appealed to it.
   a. a tiny fraction
   b. a relatively small number
   c. a fairly large number
   d. a very large number
   e. the vast majority

10. The FISA Court
    a. approves warrants for searches of drug dealers.
    b. serves as a vigilant check on overzealous investigations.
    c. was used by the Nixon administration to spy on protestors.
    d. hears prosecutors for the government and defense attorneys for defendants.
    e. approves FBI requests for electronic surveillance of possible spies and terrorists.

11. Judges have to interpret the Constitution
    a. only if statutes are ambiguous.
    b. only if they're not strict constructionists.
    c. because the Constitution is short and general.
    d. only if they want to make law.
    e. only if precedents aren't clear.

12. Activist judges tend to be
    a. liberal.
    b. conservative.
    c. moderate.
    d. cautious.
    e. none of the above; there's no clear pattern.

13. Supreme Court cases involving the Americans with Disabilities Act show
    a. how ambiguous the statute is.
    b. how much discretion courts have.
    c. a. and b.
    d. how precise most statutes are.
    e. how judges "find" the law rather than make it.

14. The chief justice of the Supreme Court has more power than the associate justices because
    a. he can prevent another justice from sitting on a case.
    b. he decides which cases will be heard.
    c. his vote counts more than another justice's vote.
    d. he assigns the opinion if he's in the majority.
    e. he can prevent another justice from writing his or her own opinion.

15. The Founders expected the judiciary to be
    a. the weakest branch.
    b. stronger than Congress but weaker than the presidency.
    c. stronger than the presidency but weaker than Congress.
    d. equal in power with the other branches.
    e. the most dangerous branch.

16. The case of *Marbury* v. *Madison* is important because the Supreme Court
    a. broadly interpreted the necessary and proper clause.
    b. claimed the authority of judicial review.
    c. demonstrated how it could be nonpolitical.
    d. showed that judges don't have much discretion when they interpret statutes and constitutional provisions.
    e. showed that judges don't have much discretion when they interpret statues but do when they interpret constitutional provisions.

17. The case of *McCulloch* v. *Maryland* is important because the Supreme Court
    a. advanced the supremacy of the federal government.
    b. broadly interpreted the "necessary and proper" clause.
    c. limited the power of states to interfere with federal programs.
    d. broadly construed congressional power.
    e. all of the above.

18. Which Supreme Court is known for expanding individual rights?
    a. Warren Court
    b. Burger Court
    c. Rehnquist Court
    d. Roberts Court
    e. No particular court; they've all decided individual rights cases similarly.

19. In the modern era, the Supreme Court's docket of cases has focused especially on
    a. disputes between the nation and states.
    b. business regulation.
    c. legal issues involving television and computers.
    d. civil liberties and rights.
    e. disputes between the president and Congress.

20. If presidents don't approve of Supreme Court decisions, their most effective check is to
    a. reduce the Court's jurisdiction.
    b. appoint new justices when vacancies arise.
    c. urge Congress to impeach justices.
    d. adopt a new statute to negate the decisions.
    e. reduce the justices' salary.

Key: 1-a; 2-e; 3-b; 4-b; 5-d; 6-c; 7-e; 8-a; 9-a; 10-e; 11-c; 12-e; 13-c; 14-d; 15-a; 16-b; 17-e; 18-a; 19-d; 20-b.

A cell block in the prison at Guantanmo Bay, Cuba

When the Olympic Torch Relay passed through Juneau, Alaska, on its way to Salt Lake City, Utah, for the 2002 Winter Games, high school students were dismissed early to watch. They lined the street. The school's cheerleaders and marching band waited to greet the relay.

Joseph Frederick, a senior, and his friends had planned a prank. They had created a banner that said, "BONG HITS 4 JESUS." They waited across the street from the school. As the relay passed and television cameras filmed the scene, they unfurled their banner. The principal was not amused. She crossed the street and ordered the students to take down the banner. Frederick refused, and she suspended him for ten days.

Frederick's family sued the school and the principal, claiming that the punishment violated his First Amendment right to free speech, because the incident didn't disrupt the students' education or even occur on the school's property. Frederick said the phrase was "meaningless and funny, in order to get on television."

In 2007, the Supreme Court agreed to hear the case—its first student speech case since 1988.[1] By a 5–4 vote, the Roberts Court upheld the punishment. The five most conservative justices ruled that public schools can prohibit student speech, in the schools or at school events, that might be interpreted as celebrating or encouraging drug use. And this was a school event because it occurred during school hours, was sanctioned by school administrators, and was supervised by school teachers.

The ruling raised the possibility that school administrators could censor student speech that addressed matters other than drugs, such as political or social issues. But two justices in the majority said the ruling wouldn't apply to such speech.[2] One said it wouldn't apply even to student criticism of the war on drugs. Nevertheless, the ruling underscores the fact that students below the college level have narrower speech rights than adults.

Civil Rights → Equal rights for person regardless ethnics & background obligate. Gov @ some level. Take action. Positive action to protect citizens. from other citizens or protect from Gov. Agencies.

14th Amend.
↑
Guarantee equal protection of law.

Americans value their "rights." Eighteenth-century Americans believed that people had **"natural rights"** by virtue of being human. Given by God, not by government, the rights could not be taken away by government. Contemporary Americans do not normally use this term, but they do think about their rights much as their forebears did.

Yet Americans have a split personality when assessing their rights. Most people tell pollsters they believe in constitutional rights in the abstract, but many do not accept these rights in concrete situations. During the Cold War, most people said they believe in free speech, but many said communists, socialists, or atheists should not be allowed to speak in public or teach in schools.

Surveys show that Americans remain divided over their support for civil liberties. Many would ban expression that might upset others.[3] One-third said they wouldn't allow a rally that might offend community members. Two-thirds said they wouldn't allow people to say things in public that might offend racial groups, and over one-half said they wouldn't allow people to say things in public that might offend religious groups. One-fifth said they wouldn't allow newspapers to publish without government approval of the articles.[4]

Conflicts over civil liberties and rights have dominated the courts since the Great Depression. This chapter, covering civil liberties, and the next, covering civil rights, describe how the courts have interpreted these rights and tried to resolve these conflicts. We'll explain the most important rights and recount the struggles by individuals and groups to achieve them. We'll see how judges act as referees between litigants, brokers among competing groups, and policy makers in the process of deciding these cases.

The Constitution and the Bill of Rights

Individual Rights in the Constitution

stopping Govern. actions against citizens!

Although the term *civil liberties* usually refers to the rights in the Bill of Rights, a few rights are granted in the body of the Constitution. The Constitution bans religious qualifications for federal office and guarantees jury trials in federal criminal cases. It bans bills of attainder, which are legislative acts rather than judicial trials pronouncing specific persons guilty of crimes, and *ex post facto* ("after the fact") laws, which are legislative

acts making some behavior illegal that wasn't illegal when it was done. The Constitution also prohibits suspension of the writ of *habeas corpus,* except during rebellion or invasion of the country.

The Bill of Rights

Origin and Meaning

The Constitution originally didn't include a bill of rights; the Founders didn't think traditional liberties needed specific protections because federalism, separation of powers, and checks and balances would prevent the national government from becoming too powerful. But to win support for ratification, the Founders promised to adopt constitutional amendments to provide such rights. James Madison proposed twelve, Congress passed them, and in 1791 the states ratified ten of them, which came to be known as the **Bill of Rights.**[5]

The first eight grant specific rights. (See the box "Civil Liberties in the Bill of Rights.") The Ninth Amendment says that the listing of these rights does not mean they are the only ones the people have, and the Tenth says that any powers not granted to the federal government are reserved for the state governments.

The Bill of Rights provides rights against the government. According to Justice Hugo Black, it is a list of "Thou shalt nots" directed at the government.[6] In practice, it provides rights for political, religious, or racial minorities against the majority, because government policy toward civil liberties tends to reflect the views of the majority.

As explained in Chapter 2, the Founders set up a government to protect property rights for the well-to-do minority against the presumably jealous majority. The Constitution's fragmentation of power and some specific provisions (see box "Constitutional Provisions Protecting Property" in that chapter) were designed to prevent the masses from curtailing the rights of the elites. However, as Americans became more egalitarian and as the masses gained more opportunity to participate in politics in the nineteenth and twentieth centuries, the relative importance of property rights declined while the relative importance of other rights increased. Thus the Bill of Rights became the means to protect the fundamental rights of political, religious, and racial minorities—people who are out of the mainstream and often unpopular and powerless—when they come in conflict with the majority.

Responsibility for interpreting the Bill of Rights lies with the federal courts. Because federal judges are appointed for life, they are more independent of majority pressure than elected officials are.

✗ Exam → Civil Liberties & Civil Rights ✗

[handwritten at top: Liberties → limit government substantively or procedurally.]
[handwritten: ↑ are contains in the Bill of Rights]

Application

For many years, the Supreme Court applied the Bill of Rights only to the federal government, not to the state governments (or to the local governments, which are under the authority of the state governments). That is, the Bill of Rights restricted the actions only of the federal government.[7]

In ruling this way, the Court followed the intentions of the Founders, who assumed that the states, with their capitals closer to their people, would be less likely to violate their peoples' liberties.[8] The Founders didn't realize that the states would in fact be more likely to violate their peoples' liberties. Because the state governments represent smaller, more homogeneous populations, they tend to reflect majority sentiment more closely than the federal government, so they often ignored—and sometimes obliterated—the rights of political, religious, or racial minorities or of criminal defendants.

However, in the twentieth century there was a growing sense that individual rights are important and that the state governments, as well as the federal government, should accord them. Starting in 1925[9] and continuing through 1972,[10] the Supreme Court gradually applied most provisions of the Bill of Rights to the states.[11] In addition, the Court established some rights not in the Bill of Rights, and it applied these to the states, too—presumption of innocence in criminal cases, right to travel within the country, and right to privacy. Thus most provisions in the Bill of Rights, and even some not in it, now restrict the actions of both the federal and the state governments.

To see how the Court has interpreted these provisions, we'll look at four major areas—freedom of expression, freedom of religion, rights of criminal defendants, and right to privacy—and also look at implications for civil liberties from the war on terrorism. We'll put the major rulings of the Supreme Court in italics because the Court's doctrine is complex.

[handwritten: Liberties are Not Absolute.]

Freedom of Expression

The **First Amendment** guarantees freedom of expression, which includes freedom of speech, assembly, and association, and freedom of the press.[12] The amendment also guarantees freedom of religion, which will be addressed in the next section. (Take note, in case you're asked. In 2006, Americans could name more members of *The Simpsons* cartoon family and more judges on *American Idol* than they could rights in the First Amendment.)[13]

CIVIL LIBERTIES IN THE BILL OF RIGHTS

[handwritten: ★ Review ★]

- First Amendment grants
  freedom of religion
  freedom of speech, assembly, and association
  freedom of the press

- Second Amendment grants
  right to keep and bear arms

- Third Amendment forbids
  quartering soldiers in houses during peacetime

- Fourth Amendment forbids
  unreasonable searches and seizures

- Fifth Amendment grants
  right to a grand jury in criminal cases
  right to due process

  [handwritten: No cruel & unusual punishment.]

- Fifth Amendment forbids
  double jeopardy (more than one trial for the same offense)
  compulsory self-incrimination
  taking private property without just compensation

- Sixth Amendment grants
  right to speedy trial
  right to public trial
  right to jury trial in criminal cases
  right to cross-examine adverse witnesses
  right to present favorable witnesses
  right to counsel

- Seventh Amendment grants
  right to jury trial in civil cases

- Eighth Amendment forbids
  excessive bail and fines
  cruel and unusual punishment

[handwritten: 14th Amend → Due process of law. States should be bound to Bill of Rights]

The amendment states that "Congress shall make no law" abridging these liberties. The language is absolute, but no justices interpret it literally.[14] They cite the example of the person who falsely shouts "Fire!" in a crowded theater and causes a stampede that injures someone. Surely, they say, the amendment doesn't protect this expression. So the Court needs to draw a line between expression the amendment protects and that which it doesn't.

Freedom of Speech

Freedom of speech, Justice Black asserted, "is the heart of our government."[15] There are important theoretical justifications for freedom of speech. By creating an open atmosphere, it promotes individual autonomy and self-fulfillment. By encouraging a wide variety of opinions, it furthers the advancement of knowledge and the discovery of truth. The English philosopher **John Stuart Mill,** who championed freedom of speech, observed that individuals decide what is correct by comparing different views. Unpopular opinions might be true or partly true. Even if completely false, they might prompt a reevaluation of accepted opinions. By permitting citizens to form opinions and express them to others, freedom of speech helps them participate in government. It especially helps them check inefficient or corrupt government. Thus the American philosopher John Dewey remarked that "democracy begins in conversation."[16] Finally, by channeling conflict toward persuasion, freedom of speech promotes a stable society. Governments that deny freedom of speech become inflexible. Unintentionally, they force conflict toward violence and foster rebellion.[17]

Because of our tradition and constitutional guarantee, almost all speech is allowed. However, there are some restrictions on the content of speech—what is said—and other restrictions on the manner of speech—how it is said. We'll first examine the restrictions on the content of speech, focusing on seditious speech, offensive speech, hate speech, and sexual speech. We'll then examine the restrictions on the manner of speech.

Seditious Speech

Seditious speech is speech that encourages opposition to or rebellion against the government.[18] The public becomes most hostile to seditious speech, and the government becomes most likely to prosecute people for such speech, during or shortly after war, when society is most sensitive about patriotism and loyalty. Criminal prosecution for seditious speech strikes at the heart of our principle of freedom of speech, which is supposed to protect individuals and groups who criticize the government and its officials.

World War I era Numerous prosecutions came with World War I and the Russian Revolution, which brought the Communists to power in the Soviet Union in 1917. The Russian Revolution prompted the **Red Scare,** in which people feared conspiracies to overthrow the U.S. government. Congress passed laws that prohibited "disloyal, profane, scurrilous, or abusive language about the form of government, Constitution, soldiers and sailors, flag or uniform of the armed forces."[19] State legislatures passed similar laws.

The federal government prosecuted almost two thousand and convicted almost nine hundred persons under these acts, and the state governments prosecuted and convicted many others. They prosecuted individuals for saying that war is contrary to the teachings of Jesus, that World War I should not have been declared until after a referendum was held, and that the draft was unconstitutional. Officials even prosecuted an individual for remarking to women knitting clothes for the troops, "No soldier ever sees those socks."[20]

These cases gave the Supreme Court numerous opportunities to rule on seditious speech. In six major cases, the Court upheld the governments' laws and affirmed the defendants' convictions.[21] The Court concluded that *these defendants' speech constituted a "clear and present danger"* to the government. Justice Edward Sanford wrote, "A single revolutionary spark may kindle a fire that, smoldering for a time, may burst into a sweeping and destructive conflagration."[22] In reality, there was nothing clear or present about the danger; the defendants' speech had little effect. The Court, reflecting our society at the time, was simply intolerant of dissent.

Cold War era More prosecutions came after World War II, as the uneasy alliance between the United States and the Soviet Union during the war gave way to the Cold War between the two countries in the 1950s. Politicians, especially Sen. **Joseph McCarthy** (R–Wisc.), exploited the tensions. McCarthy claimed that many government officials were Communists. He said he had a list of 205 "known Communists" in the State Department alone. He had little evidence—and provided no list.[23] Other Republicans also accused the Democratic Truman administration of covering for Communists in government. They goaded it into prosecuting Communists outside government so it would not appear "soft on communism."

Congress passed an act that prohibited advocating overthrow of the government by force and organizing or joining individuals who advocated overthrow.[24] The government used the act against the Communists. The Court upheld the act and affirmed the convictions of eleven upper-echelon leaders of the American Communist Party.[25] These leaders organized the party, and the party advocated overthrowing the government by force, but the leaders had not attempted to overthrow the government. (If they had, they clearly would have

At congressional hearings, Sen. Joseph McCarthy identified the supposed locations of alleged Communists and "fellow travelers."

and continued after McCarthy's tenure in the 1950s, as other politicians and the Senate's Internal Security Committee and House's Un-American Activities Committee used similar tactics.)[26]

Although McCarthy and others were bullies who hurt many innocent or harmless people, there actually were Communist spies in the federal government, from the atomic labs at Los Alamos, New Mexico, to the State Department and the White House, according to records revealed after the collapse of the Soviet Union. Apparently most spies were discovered before the 1950s, but some were never uncovered.[27]

In the meantime, two new members, including Chief Justice **Earl Warren,** joined the Supreme Court. In a series of cases in the mid- to late 1950s and early 1960s, the **Warren Court** made it more difficult to convict Communists.[28] It incurred the wrath of the public, Congress, and President Dwight Eisenhower. In a private conversation at the White House, Eisenhower criticized the rulings. Warren asked Eisenhower what he thought the Court should have done with the Communists. Eisenhower replied, "I would kill the S.O.B.s."[29]

Ultimately, the Warren Court created new doctrine for seditious speech.[30] The justices drew a distinction between advocacy and incitement. *People can advocate, enthusiastically, even heatedly, as long as they don't incite illegal action—that is, urge immediate action to violate any laws.* This doctrine protects most criticism of the government, whether at a rally, from a pulpit, or through the media, and it remains in effect today.

Thus after many years and many cases, the Court concluded that the First Amendment protects seditious speech as much as other speech. Justice William Douglas noted that "the threats were often loud but always puny."[31] Even the attorney general who prosecuted the major Communist cases later admitted that the cases were "squeezed oranges. I didn't think there was much to them."[32] Nevertheless, the Court had permitted public fear to overwhelm the First Amendment for a long time.

The Vietnam War didn't prompt the same concerns as did the Red Scare during World War I or the Cold War following World War II. Congress didn't pass any comparable laws. Nonetheless, the federal government took some actions against individuals and groups. Antiwar groups were harassed by federal grand juries, and their leaders were spied on by the U.S. Army. Some prominent opponents were prosecuted for conspiring against the draft.[33] However, opposition to this war was so widespread that the government's actions didn't silence the protesters' speech.

been guilty of crimes.) Even so, the Court concluded that *they were a clear and present danger.* After the Court's decision, the government prosecuted and convicted almost one hundred lower-level Communists as well.

The public's fear was so consuming that the government's actions extended beyond criminal prosecutions to other measures, and beyond active Communists to former Communists—some Americans had dabbled with communism during the Great Depression in the 1930s—and even to individuals who had never been Communists but who were lumped together as "Commie dupes" or "comsymps" (Communist sympathizers).

The federal government and some state governments required government employees to take "loyalty oaths" and then fired those who refused, even on principle, and those who (purportedly) lied. Some state governments banned Communists, former Communists, and alleged subversives from public jobs such as teaching or private jobs such as practicing law or serving as union officers. Federal and state legislative committees held hearings to expose and humiliate them. These actions cost an estimated ten thousand Americans their jobs.

Eventually, the Cold War thawed somewhat, and the Senate condemned McCarthy after he tried to bully the Army. His method was likened to witch hunts, and the tactic of making political accusations or name-calling based on little or no evidence came to be known as **McCarthyism.** (However, McCarthyism began before

Something disallowed:
(1) libel → written statement made w/ reckless of truth.
Difficult to win

The First Amendment prevents governments—not businesses—from restricting your speech. When Lorrie Heasley boarded a Southwest Airlines plane, she wore a T-shirt featuring President Bush, Vice President Cheney, Secretary of State Rice, and the title of the movie Meet the Fockers except an expletive was substituted. The flight crew removed her from the plane. Although the government could not restrict this expression, the airline could.

© Melanie Conner/The New York Times/Redux

The collapse of the Soviet Union and the demise of the Cold War made communism less threatening, but this doctrine remains important. After the Oklahoma City bombing in 1995, government surveillance of right-wing militia groups increased, but prosecution of the members, under terrorism laws, was limited because most of the evidence was fiery rhetoric, which is protected speech (unless it urges immediate action to violate any laws).

After the terrorist attacks in 2001, pressure to conform—to temper criticism and to support the government's policies—mounted. An organization identified forty college professors with "un-American" agendas, in an effort to prod the schools to discipline and restrain their professors. (Negative reaction prompted the organization to remove the names from its website.)[34] A tenured professor at the University of New Mexico who cracked, "Anyone who can blow up the Pentagon gets my vote," was reprimanded, and a lawsuit demanding his termination was filed.[35] During the Iraq War, pressure to conform was linked to support for our troops. Critics were branded as "unpatriotic" and "disloyal" by conservative commentators who stoked their listeners' anger.[36] Pressure to conform was muted only when the initial victory unraveled in the invasion's aftermath and the public's criticism increased.

Although the government didn't adopt laws during the war on terrorism or the war in Iraq comparable to those adopted during the twentieth century, it did take other actions that have important implications for civil liberties. These measures will be covered later in this chapter.

The state and federal governments have also limited offensive speech, hate speech, and sexual speech, which will be covered now.

Offensive Speech

Arrests for swearing, especially at police officers or in the presence of police officers, were common. In the District of Columbia, for example, about ten thousand people per year were arrested for swearing (and charged with "disorderly conduct").[37] As swearing became more common in the 1960s and 1970s, and as it became a clear manifestation of the poor relations between inner-city residents and the officers who patrolled their neighborhoods, the justices decided that *swearing in many situations is protected speech* (though not on radio or television, as we'll see). They expect police, who are trained to face emotionally charged situations, to tolerate swearing.[38]

During the Vietnam War, a man on his way to observe a trial walked through the corridors of the Los Angeles County courthouse wearing a jacket with the words "Fuck the Draft" emblazoned on the back. A cop arrested him, and a judge convicted him. The Supreme Court reversed the young man's conviction, as seventy-two-year-old Justice John Harlan remarked that "one man's vulgarity is another's lyric."[39] Harlan recognized that "much linguistic expression serves a dual communicative function: it conveys not only ideas capable of relatively precise, detached explication, but otherwise inexpressible emotions as well. In fact, words are often chosen as much for their emotive as their cognitive force. . . . [The former] may often be the more important element of the overall message."

Hate Speech

Hate speech is derogatory speech—racial, ethnic, sexual, or religious slurs—usually aimed at a group rather than at an individual. When aimed at an individual, the words impugn characteristics the individual shares with the group. Hate speech demeans people for characteristics that are innate, such as race, ethnicity, or sexuality, or characteristics that are deeply held, such as religious faith. Such speech can cause emotional or psychological harm.

Even so, it can be difficult to distinguish hate speech from other speech. What one person considers hate speech another may consider a simple observation or a valid criticism. And because of the First Amendment, *hate speech normally can't be prohibited by governments.*[40]

Lower federal courts required the Chicago suburb of Skokie to permit the American Nazi Party to demonstrate in 1978.[41] The Nazis intentionally chose Skokie as the site for their demonstration because many Jews lived there—forty thousand of the seventy thousand residents. Hundreds were survivors of German concentration camps during World War II, and thousands were relatives of people who had died in the camps. The city, in anticipation of the demonstration, passed ordinances that prohibited wearing "military-style" uniforms and distributing material that "promotes and incites hatred against persons by reason of their race, national origin, or religion." These ordinances were an attempt to bar the demonstration, and the courts threw them out. One court quoted Justice Oliver Wendell Holmes's statement that "if there is any principle of the Constitution that more imperatively calls for attachment than any other it is the principle of free thought—not free thought for those who agree with us but freedom for the thought we hate."[42]

Cross burning by the Ku Klux Klan presents a more difficult question. In the Klan's heyday, a cross-burning was a clear threat to the black families it was directed toward. Today a cross-burning *might* be nothing more than a rallying symbol to the Klan's members. The Supreme Court ruled that persons who burn a cross to intimidate or to threaten—for example, to frighten their black neighbors—can be prosecuted, but those who burn a cross at a KKK rally in a private field hidden from other people and passing cars cannot be prosecuted.[43]

Despite the First Amendment, many colleges and universities adopted hate speech codes in the 1980s and 1990s. They worried that such speech created a hostile and intimidating environment for the victims.[44] A student who was jeered nightly by taunts of "Faggot!" said, "When you are told you are not worth anything, it is difficult to function."[45] Some students were disciplined under the codes. But colleges and universities, more than other institutions in our society, have traditionally fostered free expression and debate. And the codes, which were inherently difficult to write, were often too broad or too vague. Some were struck down by lower courts, and others were abandoned by the schools. Some were rewritten to focus on harassment and threats, which can be prohibited, and to apply to computers. George Mason University forbade students from using computers "to harass, threaten, or abuse others." Virginia Tech disciplined a student for posting a message on the home page of a gay men's group calling for gays to be castrated and to "die a slow death."[46]

Some conservative Christians, funded by evangelical ministries and interest groups, have launched an attack on tolerance policies toward gays and lesbians. They demand that schools and workplaces revoke their policies, including speech codes and, in lower grades, dress codes prohibiting antigay T-shirts. A Georgia Tech student who was reprimanded for sending a letter that berated students who came out as gay filed suit, claiming that her faith compelled her to speak out against homosexuality.[47]

These disputes highlight the fine line between harassment and free speech. So far, the Supreme Court hasn't addressed college and university speech codes.

Sexual Speech

In some contexts, sexual speech—that is, language or situations that fall short of obscenity—has been prohibited. (Obscenity, whether in print or film or on radio or television, is never allowed. But its legal definition and judicial doctrine are complex and beyond the scope of this text.)

Governments can forbid nude dancing,[48] although it is expression. Through zoning, *they can restrict pornographic theaters or sex shops* from most (though not all) parts of their cities.[49]

The Federal Communications Commission (FCC) can forbid radio and television stations from broadcasting some sexual language and situations. A California radio station broadcast a monologue by comedian George Carlin. Titled "Filthy Words," it lampooned society's sensitivity to seven words that "you couldn't say on the public airwaves . . . the ones you definitely wouldn't say, ever." The seven words, according to the FCC report, included "a four-letter word for excrement" repeated seventy times in twelve minutes. A majority of the Court ruled that although the monologue was part of a serious program on contemporary attitudes toward language, it was not protected under the First Amendment because people, including children, tuning the radio could be subjected to the language in their homes.[50] Now the FCC forbids indecent material, except "fleeting" profanities, on radio and noncable television between 6 A.M. and 10 P.M. and fines any media that violate the ban.[51] (Large fines were levied on the *Howard Stern Show,* before it moved to satellite radio, and on a New York City radio station that broadcast a tape of a couple having sex in Saint Patrick's Cathedral.)[52] Yet the Court struck down a Utah law restricting indecent material on cable television. By subscribing to and paying for cable television, its customers are accepting exposure to its programming.[53]

In each of these areas—seditious speech, offensive speech, hate speech, and sexual speech—courts allow more freedom for individuals today because the Supreme Court broadened its interpretation of the First Amendment during the second half of the twentieth century.

We'll now examine the restrictions on the manner of speech, focusing on demonstrations and symbolic speech.

Demonstrations

Protesters want people to see or hear their demonstrations, so they seek locations where people congregate and provide an audience. Although some people won't like their message or their use of public places to disseminate it, protesters have a right to demonstrate.

Individuals are allowed to use public places, such as streets, sidewalks, parks, theaters,[54] and the grounds around public buildings,[55] *to express their views on public issues.* These places constitute the **public forum** and serve as "the poor person's printing press."

Private property is not part of the public forum, so *individuals have no right to demonstrate on private property* without the owner's permission.[56] Shopping malls usually forbid demonstrations. During the run-up to the Iraq War, a sixty-year-old man wore a T-shirt with the slogan "Give Peace a Chance" at a mall in Albany, New York. Security guards ordered him to take off the shirt or leave the mall. When he refused, he was arrested.[57]

Although his shirt was not what we think of as a demonstration, it did express his views, and the mall could forbid such expression.

Even in the public forum, individuals can't demonstrate whenever or however they want. The streets, sidewalks, parks, and theaters in the public forum are used for purposes other than demonstrations—especially for transportation and recreation—so individuals can't disrupt these activities. They can't, Justice Arthur Goldberg remarked, hold "a street meeting in the middle of Times Square at the rush hour."[58]

Therefore, abortion protesters can demonstrate on public streets and public sidewalks near abortion clinics, and they can approach staffers and patients who come and go. But *protesters cannot block access* (and to ensure this, judges can order them not to come within a certain distance—for example, fifteen feet—of driveways and doorways).[59] Moreover, they cannot demonstrate at the doctor's house even if they stand on a public sidewalk. After protesters repeatedly picketed at a doctor's residence in a Milwaukee suburb, the town passed an ordinance forbidding such picketing. The Court ruled that protesters can march through residential neighborhoods but *cannot focus on particular houses,* because such picketing interferes with the privacy of the home.[60]

To ensure that potential demonstrations don't disrupt the normal activities of the places in the public forum, *governments can require groups to obtain a permit, which can specify the place, time, and manner of the demonstration. Officials can establish restrictions to avoid disruptions. However, officials cannot use these restrictions to censor speech.* They cannot allow one group to demonstrate but forbid another, no matter how much they dislike the group or its message. They cannot forbid the group even if they say they fear violence (unless the group actually threatens violence).

Symbolic Speech

Some demonstrations feature **symbolic speech,** which is the use of symbols rather than words to convey ideas. Sometimes symbolic speech has been prohibited when actual speech, with the same message, would have been permitted.

During the Vietnam War, some young men burned their draft cards to protest the war and the draft. Their action was powerful expression—symbolic speech was a novelty in the 1960s—and Congress tried to stifle it by passing a law prohibiting the destruction of draft cards. The justices upheld the law and expressed their discomfort with the concept of symbolic speech.[61]

But the Court came to accept symbolic speech in the late 1960s and early 1970s.[62] To protest the war, a Massachusetts man wore a flag patch on the seat of his pants and was arrested and sentenced to six months in jail. A Washington student taped a peace symbol on a flag and then hung the flag upside down outside his apartment. The Court reversed both convictions.[63]

When a member of the Revolutionary Communist Youth Brigade burned an American flag outside the Republican convention in 1984, the justices faced the issue of *flag desecration*—the ultimate symbolic speech. A bare majority of the **Rehnquist Court** *permitted* this symbolic speech.[64] Justice William Brennan wrote that the First Amendment can't be limited just because this expression offends most people. "We do not consecrate the flag by punishing its desecration, for in doing so we dilute the freedom that this cherished emblem represents." The ruling invalidated the laws of forty-eight states and the federal government.

In a dissent, Chief Justice **William Rehnquist** emotionally criticized the decision. He said the First Amendment shouldn't apply because the flag is a unique national symbol. He recounted the history of "The Star-Spangled Banner" and the music of John Philip Sousa's "Stars and Stripes Forever," he quoted poems by Ralph Waldo Emerson and John Greenleaf Whittier that refer to the flag, and he discussed the role of the Pledge of Allegiance.

Civil liberties advocates praised the decision, but veterans' groups were outraged and many Americans were upset. President George H. W. Bush proposed a constitutional amendment to override the decision. Members of Congress, always eager to appear patriotic, lined up in support. But others, mostly Democrats, criticized the proposal for creating an unprecedented exception to the First Amendment. Eventually, instead of an amendment, Congress passed a statute prohibiting flag desecration. Apparently, a majority felt that a statute, not as permanent and not a part of the Constitution, would be an acceptable compromise between the Court's doctrine and the public's anger. Yet the justices, dividing the same way, declared the new statute unconstitutional for the same reasons they reversed the prior convic-

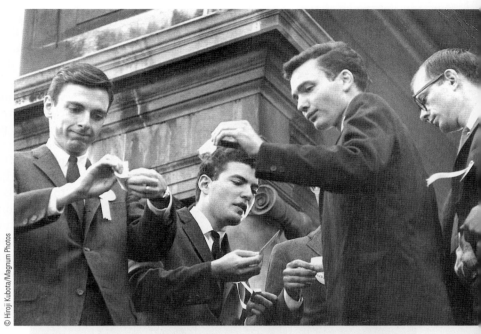

When young men illegally burned their draft cards to protest the Vietnam War, the Supreme Court refused to protect their action as symbolic speech.

© Hiroji Kubota/Magnum Photos

tion.[65] By now, the public's anger had ebbed.[66] Even so, congressional Republican leaders periodically propose an amendment to overturn the ruling as a way to rally their conservative base. In 2006, they fell just one vote short in the Senate. With one vote more, the amendment would have been sent to the states for ratification.

In this chapter so far, we've focused on adult speech. Now we'll turn to student speech. Students below the college level are considered children rather than adults, so they aren't afforded full First Amendment rights yet.

Student Speech

During the Vietnam War, junior and senior high school students in Des Moines, Iowa, wore black armbands to protest the war. When they were suspended, their families sued school officials. The Warren Court ruled that the schools must allow the students freedom of speech, as long as the students don't disrupt the schools.[67] Public schools, Justice Abe Fortas said, "may not be enclaves of totalitarianism."

However, this case, which involved political speech, has proven to be the exception to the rule. According to the **Burger Court** and the Rehnquist Court, *administrators in public or private schools can restrict student speech*

an article about the class valedictorian who succeeded despite the death of her mother, the desertion of her father, and her own pregnancy. North Carolina administrators shut down a high school newspaper and fired its adviser because of three articles, including a satirical story about the "death" of the writer after eating a cheeseburger from the school cafeteria.

Some principals have tried to restrict their students from using the Internet to criticize school officials or policies. But like the underground newspapers of the 1960s and 1970s, web pages created off campus (rather than in class) can't be censored and their creators can't be disciplined by administrators, unless the pages urge illegal action or make terrorist threats. A Georgia student was arrested for suggesting that the principal be shot, his daughter kidnapped, his car keyed, and its locks clogged with Superglue.

Freedom of Association

Although the First Amendment does not mention *association,* the Supreme Court has interpreted the right to speak, assemble, and petition the government for a redress of grievances, all of which the amendment does list, to encompass a **freedom of association** for individuals to join with others to do these things.

This freedom implicitly entails a right not to associate as well. Therefore, groups can exclude individuals.

The right is strongest when the organization forms for "expressive association"—that is, when it speaks, assembles, and petitions the government for a redress of grievances. The right is also strong when the organization forms for "intimate association"—that is, when it is relatively personal, selective, and small, such as a social club or a country club.

Organizations formed for expressive or intimate association can exclude others. The Supreme Court allowed organizers of Boston's Saint Patrick's Day parade to exclude a group of gays, lesbians, and bisexuals.[70] Because the organizers were private individuals—the parade wasn't sponsored by the city—and because a parade is an expressive activity, the organizers didn't have to allow any views contrary to their views. The Supreme Court also allowed the Boy Scouts of America to expel an assistant scoutmaster who was openly gay.[71] The Court concluded that the Boy Scouts is an expressive organization, which espouses various values, including an opposition to homosexuality.

The right is weakest when the organization forms for "commercial association"—that is, when it is de-

Toni Kay Scott was sent home from her middle school in Napa, California, for wearing Tigger socks. To combat gangs, the school's dress code required solid colors—no patterns. Her parents sued, claiming that the students in public schools have a right to express themselves through their attire.

for educational purposes. They can restrict speech or clothing that is lewd or vulgar[68] or that promotes sex, drugs, or violence. They can restrict hate speech as well. Conflicts over hate speech arise in public schools because many administrators and teachers believe they should encourage tolerance. Disputes over antigay speech have been especially controversial.

Administrators can also censor student publications, even serious articles that don't promote sex, drugs, or violence or contain hate speech. The Rehnquist Court allowed censorship of student newspaper articles about the impact of pregnancy and of parents' divorce on teenagers.[69]

After the ruling, a Colorado principal blocked an editorial criticizing his study hall policy while allowing another editorial praising it. A Texas principal banned

signed to enhance business interests of its members and is relatively large, unselective, and impersonal. *Organizations formed for commercial association, such as civic clubs, can't exclude others* (in states or cities that adopt nondiscrimination laws). Their right to associate can be overridden by individuals' right to be free from discrimination.[72] Therefore, the Jaycees (the Junior Chamber of Commerce), which was a business organization of young men, and the Rotary Club, which was a civic organization of men, can't discriminate against women in states that have laws forbidding sex discrimination.[73]

Freedom of the Press

Freedom of the press may be as important as freedom of speech in a democracy. Indeed, it may be more important in a mass society where most people hear opposing views through the media rather than from person to person.

Prior Restraint

The core of **freedom of the press** is freedom from prior restraint—censorship. If the press violates laws prohibiting, for example, libelous or obscene material, it can be punished after publishing such materials. But freedom from prior restraint means the press can disseminate the information it considers appropriate and the public can see this information.

Yet freedom from prior restraint isn't absolute. During the Vietnam War, the secretary of defense in the Johnson administration, Robert McNamara, ordered a thorough study of our engagement. The study, known as the **Pentagon Papers,** laid bare the reasons the country was embroiled—reasons not as honorable as ones the officials had fed the public—and it questioned the effectiveness of military policy. The study was so revealing that McNamara confided to a friend, "They could hang people for what's in there."[74] He classified the papers "top secret" so few persons could see them. One of the authors, Daniel Ellsberg, who was a planner in the war, originally supported the war but later turned against it. Haunted by his involvement, he photocopied the papers and passed them to the *New York Times* and *Washington Post* in the hope that their publication would sway public opinion and force the government to halt the war. (He also passed them to the television networks—ABC, CBS, and NBC—but they were afraid to use them.)[75]

The newspapers began to publish excerpts of the papers. Although the information implicated the Kennedy and Johnson administrations, President Richard Nixon was still fighting the war, and their publication infuriated him. Summoning his chief of staff and national security adviser, he demanded:

I have a project I want somebody to take. . . . This takes eighteen hours a day. It takes devotion and loyalty and diligence such as you've never seen. . . . I really need a son of a bitch . . . who will work his butt off and do it dishonorably. . . . And I'll direct him myself. I know how to play this game and we're going to start playing it. . . . I want somebody just as tough as I am for a change. . . . We're up against an enemy, a conspiracy. They're using any means. We're going to use any means.[76]

This tirade set in motion the developments that would culminate in the Watergate scandal.

Nixon sought injunctions to restrain the newspapers from publishing more excerpts. In the *Pentagon Papers Case,* the Supreme Court refused to grant them.[77] Most justices said they would grant the injunctions if publishing the papers clearly jeopardized national security. But the information in the papers was historical; its disclosure didn't hinder the current war effort.[78] Thus *the rule—no prior restraint—remained, but some exceptions could be made.*

One exception occurred in 1979 when *The Progressive,* a monthly political magazine, planned to publish technical material about the design of hydrogen bombs. The article, "The H-Bomb Secret: How We Got It, Why We're Telling It," argued against secret classification of this material. Although the article wasn't a "do-it-yourself guide," it might have helped a medium-size nation develop a bomb sooner than the nation could otherwise. At the government's request, a federal judge granted an injunction prohibiting the magazine from publishing the article.[79]

The press in the United States is freer than that in Great Britain, where freedom from prior restraint began. Britain has no First Amendment and tolerates more secrecy. The government banned radio and television interviews with all members of the outlawed Irish Republican Army and its political party, including its sole representative in Parliament.[80] The French government banned the sale of a song critical of the West during the Persian Gulf War, and it blocked the broadcasting of anti-Semitic programming by an Arab channel in 2005. The German government, which has prohibited the display of the Nazi swastika since World War II, banned the sale of music by skinhead groups after neo-Nazi violence in recent years. The Austrian government im-

The press chief of the Washington Post hails the Court's decision allowing publication of the Pentagon Papers.

prisoned a British historian for publicizing his book denying the Holocaust. (Austria is the birthplace of Hitler.)

Restrictions on Gathering News

Although prior restraint is an obvious limitation on freedom of the press, restrictions on gathering news are less obvious but no less serious. They also keep the news from the public.

The Burger Court *denied reporters the right to keep the names of their sources confidential.* In investigative reporting, reporters frequently rely on sources who demand anonymity in exchange for information. The sources might have sensitive positions in government or relations with criminals that would place them in jeopardy if their names were publicized. A Louisville reporter was allowed to watch persons make hashish from marijuana if he kept their names confidential. But after publication of his story, a grand jury demanded their names. When the reporter refused to reveal them, he was cited for contempt of court, and his conviction was upheld by the Supreme Court.[81] The majority said reporters' need for confidentiality isn't as great as courts' need for information about crimes. So reporters face a difficult choice: Either do not guarantee anonymity to a potential source, which means they might not obtain infor-

mation for an important story; or do guarantee anonymity, which means, if the courts demand their source, they might be cited for contempt and jailed for months. Grand juries have demanded reporters' sources increasingly in recent years.[82]

Invasion of Privacy

The right to a free press can conflict with an individual's desire for privacy when the press publishes personal information. The Supreme Court has *permitted the press to publish factual information.* For example, although Georgia law prohibited the press from releasing the names of crime victims, to spare them embarrassment, an Atlanta television station announced the name of a high school girl who was raped by six classmates and left unconscious on the lawn to die. When her father sued the station, the Court said the press needs freedom to publish factual information from the public record so that citizens can scrutinize the workings of the judicial system.[83]

When a man in a crowd watching President Gerald Ford noticed a woman, close by, pull out a gun, he grabbed the gun and prevented an assassination. Reporters wrote stories about this hero, including the fact that he was a homosexual. This coverage caused him considerable embarrassment and practical problems as well, so he sued. The courts sided with the press again. The man's good deed made him newsworthy, whether he wanted to be or not.[84] Persons who become newsworthy are granted little privacy. Justice Brennan said this is a necessary evil "in a society which places a primary value on freedom of speech and of press."[85]

However, the Court has prohibited the press from sending reporters and photographers with law enforcement officers when they conduct a search or make an arrest at someone's home.[86] The Court decided that the police department's desire for good publicity and the local media's desire for interesting stories didn't justify the invasion of a defendant's or a resident's privacy.

Libel

Libel consists of printed or broadcast statements that are false and that tarnish someone's reputation. Victims are entitled to sue for money to compensate them for the harm done.

Historically, the justices considered libelous material irrelevant to the exposition of ideas and search for truth envisioned by the framers of the First Amendment. The minimal benefit such material might have had was outweighed by the greater need to protect persons' reputations. For many years, the Court allowed the states to adopt libel laws as they saw fit.

However, the Warren Court recognized that state libel laws could be used to stifle legitimate political criticism; they could be used to thwart freedom of the press. The justices forced radical changes in these laws in the landmark case *New York Times* v. *Sullivan* in 1964.[87]

The *Times* ran an ad by black clergymen criticizing Montgomery, Alabama, officials for their response to racial protests. The ad contained trivial inaccuracies. Although the ad didn't name any officials, the commissioner of police claimed that it implicitly referred to him, and he sued. A local jury ordered the *Times* to pay him a half million dollars. Meanwhile, another local jury ordered the *Times* to pay another commissioner another half million dollars for the same ad. It was apparent that traditional libel laws could be used to wreak vengeance on a critical press—in this case, on a detested northern newspaper for its coverage of controversial civil rights protests.

The Court, ruling against the commissioner, made it more difficult for public officials to win libel suits. It held that *officials must show not only that the statements made about them were false, but also that the statements were made with "reckless disregard for the truth."* This standard gives the press some leeway to make mistakes—to print inaccurate statements—as long as the press is not careless to the point of recklessness.

This protection for the press is necessary, according to Justice Brennan, because the "central meaning of the First Amendment" is that citizens should have the right to criticize officials. This statement prompted one legal scholar to herald the decision "an occasion for dancing in the streets."[88]

In later cases, the Court *extended this ruling to public figures*—other persons who have public prominence or who thrust themselves into public controversies. These included candidates for public office[89] and activists for various causes.[90] The Court reasoned that it should be more difficult for public figures, as for public officials, to win libel suits because they also influence public policy and also are newsworthy enough to get media attention to rebut any accusations against them.[91]

In sum, the Warren Court's doctrine shifted the emphasis from protection of personal reputation to protection of press freedom.

This shift in emphasis has helped the press report the news—and helped the public learn about the government—during a time when media coverage of controversial events has angered many people. Since the 1960s, individuals and groups have sued the press not primarily to gain compensation for damage to their reputation, but to punish the press for its coverage. For example, a lawyer for a conservative organization that sued CBS for its depiction of the army general who commanded the U.S. military in Vietnam admitted that the organization sought the "dismantling" of the network through libel suits.[92]

Freedom of Religion

Some people came to America for religious liberty, but once they arrived, many didn't want to grant this liberty to others. Some communities became as intolerant as those in the Old World from which the people had fled.[93] But the colonists came with so many religious views that the diversity gradually led to grudging tolerance. By the time the Constitution and the Bill of Rights were adopted, support for religious liberty was fairly widespread.

Both the diversity and the tolerance are reflected in the two documents. Unlike the Declaration of Independence, the Constitution is a secular document. It doesn't mention "God," "Creator," "Providence," or "divine."[94] It doesn't claim to be a compact between the people and God (or, like some monarchies, between the rulers and God); rather, it's a compact among the people, as the Preamble underscores—"We the people . . . ."

The Bill of Rights grants freedom of religion in the First Amendment, which states, "Congress shall make no law respecting an establishment of religion, or prohibiting the free exercise thereof." These two clauses—the establishment clause and the free exercise clause—were intended to work in tandem to provide freedom for people's religions and, by implication, freedom from others' religions.

The Founders recoiled from Europeans' experience of continuous conflict and long wars fought over religious schisms. Consequently, **Thomas Jefferson** explained, the clauses were designed to build "a wall of separation between church and state."[95] Each would stay on its own side of the wall and not interfere or even interact with the other. **Separation of church and state** was a novel idea; according to one historian, although the phrase isn't in the Constitution, it's the "most revolutionary" aspect of the document.[96]

When the District of Columbia was designed, a triangular configuration popular at the time was adopted. In one corner was the Capitol building for Congress, and in another was the White House for the president. In the third corner in many other nations, a large church representing the state religion reflected the spiritual power. Due to separation of church and state, the Founders didn't want a church in that corner. (They could have put the Supreme Court there, but the Court wasn't considered important then and wouldn't get its own building until 1935.) Instead, they located the Patent Office in that corner to represent the spirit of innovation. They anticipated many inventions.[97] (Now the building houses the National Portrait Gallery and the Museum of American Art.)

Today some deeply religious people scorn the idea of separation of church and state. They think it devalues the importance of religion. But the Founders saw it as a means to preserve the peace that had eluded European states. In addition, they saw it as a way to protect religion itself. Without interference by government officials, whether to hinder or to help, churches would be free to determine their dogma and establish their practices as they saw fit. They would be free to flourish. Indeed, religion is stronger in the United States than in Europe, where churches endorsed and supported by the government sit mostly empty.

Despite the Founders' intention, as society became more complex and government became more pervasive, church and state came to interact, sometimes to interfere, with each other. Inevitably, the wall began to crumble, and the courts had to devise new doctrine to keep church and state as separate as possible while still accommodating the needs of each.

Free Exercise of Religion

The **free exercise clause** allows individuals to practice their religion without government coercion.

Direct Restrictions

Government has occasionally restricted free exercise of religion directly. Early in the country's history, some states prohibited Catholics or Jews from voting or holding office, and as late as 1961, Maryland prohibited nonbelievers from holding office.[98] In the 1920s, Oregon prohibited students from attending parochial schools.[99] More recently, prisons in Illinois and Texas prohibited Black Muslims and Buddhists from receiving religious publications and using prison chapels.[100] The Supreme Court *invalidated each of these restrictions.*

A suburb of Miami tried to ban the Santeria religion in 1987. Santeria blends ancient African rites and Roman Catholic rituals, but its distinguishing feature is animal sacrifice. Adherents believe that animal sacrifice is necessary to win the favor of the gods, and they practice it at initiations of new members and at births, marriages, and deaths. They kill chickens, ducks, doves, pigeons, sheep, goats, and turtles. When adherents, who had practiced their religion underground since refugees from Cuba brought it to Florida in the 1950s and 1960s, announced plans to construct a church building, cultural center, museum, and school, the city passed ordinances against ritualistic animal sacrifice, essentially forbidding adherents from practicing their religion. The Court struck down the ordinances.[101] "Although the practice of animal sacrifice may seem abhorrent to some," Justice Anthony Kennedy wrote, "religious beliefs need not be acceptable, logical, consistent, or comprehensible to others in order to merit First Amendment protection."

Indirect Restrictions

Government has also restricted free exercise of religion indirectly. As society has become more complex, some laws have interfered with religion, even when not designed to do so. The laws have usually interfered with minority religions, which don't have many members as legislators looking out for their interests.

At first the Court distinguished between belief and action: individuals could believe what they wanted, but they could not act accordingly if such action was against the law. In 1878, male Mormons who believed their religion required polygamy could not marry more than one woman.[102] The Court rhetorically asked, "Suppose one believed that human sacrifices were a necessary part of religious worship?" Of course, belief without action gave little protection and scant satisfaction to the individuals involved.

In the 1960s, the Warren Court recognized this problem and broadened the protection by *granting exemptions to laws.* A Seventh-Day Adventist who worked in a textile mill in South Carolina quit when the mill shifted from a five-day to a six-day workweek that included Saturday—her Sabbath. Unable to find another job, she applied for unemployment benefits, but the state refused to provide them. To receive them, she had to be "available" for work, but the state said she wasn't available because she wouldn't accept any jobs that re-

The country's religious diversity has led to demands for some exotic exemptions. Inspired by the Bible's statement that Jesus's followers "shall take up serpents" and "if they drink any deadly thing, it shall not hurt them," members of the Holiness Church of God in Jesus's Name handle snakes and drink strychnine. Some become enraptured and entranced to the point of hysteria, and occasionally some die. The Tennessee Supreme Court forbade such practices, saying that the state has "the right to guard against the unnecessary creation of widows and orphans." However, these practices continue in some places.

quired Saturday work. The Court ordered the state to grant an exemption to its law.[103] The Burger Court, which followed the Warren Court's doctrine, ruled that employers need to make a reasonable effort to accommodate employees' requests to fit work schedules around their Sabbath.[104]

Congress, too, has granted some exemptions. It excused the Amish from participating in the Social Security program because the Amish support their own elderly. And in every draft law, it excused conscientious objectors from participating in war.

The Court has been most reluctant to exempt individuals from paying taxes. It didn't excuse either the Amish[105] or the Quakers, who as pacifists tried to withhold the portion of their income taxes that funded the military.[106] The Court worried that many other persons would try to avoid paying taxes, too.

The Rehnquist Court, which was less sensitive to minority rights, *refused to grant such exemptions.*[107] The Native American church uses peyote, a hallucinogen derived from a cactus, in worship ceremonies. Church members believe that the plant embodies their deity and that ingesting the plant is an act of communion. Although peyote is a controlled substance, Congress has authorized its use on Indian reservations, and many states have authorized its use off the reservations by church members. But when two members in Oregon, a state that didn't allow its use off the reservations, were fired from their jobs and denied unemployment benefits for using the drug, the Court refused to grant an exemption.[108] A five-justice majority rejected the doctrine and precedents of the Warren and Burger Courts. Justice Antonin Scalia, a Catholic, admitted that denying such exemptions will put minority religions at a disadvantage but insisted that this is an "unavoidable consequence of democratic government." That is, denying minority rights is an inevitable and acceptable result of majority rule. This rationale, of course, could emasculate not only the free exercise clause but other provisions of the Bill of Rights as well.

As a result of the decision, some adherents of minority religions weren't allowed to practice the tenets of their religions. Families of deceased Jews and Laotians, whose religions reject autopsies, were overruled. Muslim prisoners, whose religion forbids them to eat pork, were denied other meat as a substitute. Sikh construction workers, whose religion requires them to wear turbans, had been exempted from the law mandating hard hats at construction sites; after the decision, this exemption was rescinded.[109]

Even mainstream churches worried about the ruling's implications, and a coalition of religious groups lobbied Congress to overturn it. Congress passed an act reversing the ruling and substituting the previous doctrine from the Warren and Burger Courts. But the Rehnquist Court invalidated the act because it challenged the justices' authority and altered their interpretation of the First Amendment without going through the process required to amend the Constitution.[110]

Establishment of Religion

Two competing traditions reflecting the role of government toward religion have led to intense conflict over the **establishment clause.** Many settlers were Christians who wanted the governments to reinforce their religion, yet the framers of the Constitution were products of the Enlightenment, which emphasized the importance of reason and deemphasized the role of religion. Many Founders, including the six considered most important—John Adams, Benjamin Franklin, Alexander Hamilton, Thomas Jefferson, James Madison, and George Washington—were Deists rather than Christians. They believed in a Supreme Being but rejected much religious dogma.[111]

The two considered most responsible for the religious guarantees in the First Amendment, Thomas Jefferson and **James Madison,** especially feared the divisiveness of religion. They wanted separation of church and state, advocating not only freedom *of* religion for believers but freedom *from* religion for others.[112]

Even some religious groups wanted separation of church and state. The Baptists and the evangelicals had been harassed and persecuted by the Anglicans (Episcopalians) and Congregationalists, and they feared that these larger groups would use the power of the state to promote their views and practices.[113]

The Supreme Court initially reflected the first of these traditions. In 1892, Justice David Brewer proclaimed that "this is a Christian nation."[114] But as the country became more pluralistic, the Court moved toward the second of these traditions. Since the 1960s, the Court has *generally interpreted the establishment clause to forbid government not only from designating an official church,* like the Church of England, which receives tax money and special privileges, *but also from aiding one religion over another or even from aiding religion over nonreligion.*

School Prayers

Courts have used the clause to resolve disputes about prayer in public schools. In 1962 and 1963, the Warren Court initiated its prayer rulings. At the start of each day, New York had students recite a nondenominational prayer, and Pennsylvania and Baltimore had students recite the Lord's Prayer or Bible verses. The Court, with only one justice dissenting, ruled that *these practices violated the establishment clause.*[115] Although the prayers officially were voluntary—students could leave the room—the Court doubted that the prayers really were voluntary. The justices noted that nonconforming students would face tremendous pressure from teachers and peers. The Court therefore concluded that the prayers fostered religion. According to Justice Black, "Government in this country should stay out of the business of writing and sanctioning official prayers and leave that purely religious function to the people themselves and to those the people . . . look to for religious

guidance." Although schools could teach religion as a subject, they could not promote religion. For similar reasons, the Court ruled that Kentucky *could not require public schools to post the Ten Commandments* in classrooms.[116]

Many people sharply criticized the rulings. A representative from Alabama lamented, "They put the Negroes in the schools, and now they've driven God out."[117] Students, of course, can still pray on their own at any time.

Empirical studies in the years after the rulings found that prayers and Bible readings decreased but by no means disappeared, especially in the South.[118] A Tennessee school official asserted, "I am of the opinion that 99 percent of the people in the United States feel as I do about the Supreme Court's decision—that it was an outrage. . . . The remaining 1 percent do not belong in this free world."[119]

News reports in recent years indicate that some schools, especially in the rural South, still use prayers or Bible readings in violation of the Court's rulings. These practices are reinforced by social pressure. A woman whose family had moved to Pontotoc, Mississippi, discovered that Christian prayers were being broadcast on the intercom and the Bible was being taught in a class. When she objected, rumors circulated that she was an outside agitator paid by the ACLU to force the town to change. One of her children had a teacher who told the class that he didn't believe in God, while another of her children kept "getting jumped" in the bathroom. Then the woman lost her job in a convenience store after customers threatened to boycott the store.[120] News reports also indicate that officials in Kentucky and Ohio allowed volunteers to put the Ten Commandments inside or outside public schools in violation of the Court's ruling.[121]

Although many people wanted a constitutional amendment to allow official prayers in public schools, Congress never passed one. Some people supported the rulings. Other people, who supported the Court, didn't want to challenge its authority and set a precedent for other groups on other matters. Some religious leaders doubted that the religious groups would ever agree on specific prayers. America's religious diversity means that any prayers would offend some students or parents. Prayers that suit Christians might offend Jews; those that suit Jews might offend adherents of other faiths. Recent immigrants from Asia and the Middle East, practicing Buddhism, Shintoism, Taoism, and Islam, have made the country even more pluralistic. Now, ac-

Muslim students in Dearborn, Michigan, reflect our religious pluralism. The Detroit area has the second-largest concentration of Arabs outside the Middle East.

cording to one researcher, America's religious diversity is greater than that of any country in recorded history.[122] Asking the students in this country to say a prayer would be like "asking the members of the United Nations to stand and sing the national anthem of one country."[123]

However, many small communities don't reflect this nationwide diversity, and their residents often assume that everyone, or at least "normal" people, share their views toward religion.

In lieu of an amendment, about half of the states have passed laws providing for a "moment of silence" to begin each school day. Although the laws are ostensibly for meditation, some legislators admit they are really for prayer. Yet a majority of justices indicated that they *would approve a moment of silence if students were not urged to pray.*[124]

The Rehnquist Court reaffirmed and extended the prayer rulings of the Warren Court. It held that *clergy can't offer prayers at graduation ceremonies* for public elementary, middle, and high schools.[125] The prayers in question were brief and nonsectarian, but the majority reasoned, "What to most believers may seem nothing more than a reasonable request that the nonbeliever respect their religious practices, in a school context may appear to the nonbeliever or dissenter to be an attempt to employ the machinery of the state to enforce a religious orthodoxy." Although attendance at the ceremony was voluntary, like participation in school prayers, the majority didn't consider it truly voluntary. Justice Kennedy wrote, "Everyone knows that in our society and in our culture high school graduation is one of life's most significant occasions. . . . Graduation is a time for family and those closest to the student to celebrate success and express mutual wishes of gratitude and respect."

Although the Court's language here was emphatic, its stance on student-led prayers has been ambiguous. In 1992, the Court refused to review a federal court of appeals ruling that allowed student-led prayers at graduation ceremonies.[126] A Texas school board permitted the senior class to decide whether to have a prayer and, if so, which student to give it. The appellate court held that this policy wasn't precluded by the Supreme Court's ruling because the decision wasn't made by officials and the prayer wasn't offered by a clergy member, so official coercion wasn't present. But in 1996, the Court also refused to review a federal court of appeals ruling from a different circuit that prohibited student-led prayers.[127] The Court's reluctance to resolve this controversy means that the ruling of each court of appeals remains but applies only to the schools in its circuit.

The first appellate court's holding encouraged opponents of the Supreme Court's rulings to use the same approach to circumvent these rulings as well. Several southern states passed laws allowing student-led prayers to start each school day. Some school officials, who selected the students, let them give the prayers over the intercom. Federal courts in Alabama and Mississippi invalidated these laws because school officials were involved and because all students were required or at least pressured to listen to the prayers.

The Rehnquist Court did invalidate the use of schools' public address systems by clergy or students to give prayers at high school football games.[128] Although student attendance is voluntary, the games are official school events.

The public desire for official school prayers is fueled by nostalgia for the less troubling times before the 1960s. As one writer perceived, the desire "doesn't have much to do with prayer anyway, but with a time, a place, an ethos that praying and pledging allegiance at the beginning of school each day represent."[129] For some people, buffeted by the upheavals and dislocations of our times, the reinstitutionalization of school prayers would symbolize that our society still stands for appropriate values.

The public desire for official school prayers is also fueled by occasional reports of school officials who mistakenly believe that court rulings require them to forbid all forms of religious expression. Some confused administrators have prohibited a few students from wearing religious jewelry, reading the Bible while riding the bus, and praying before eating their lunch.[130]

In another case, the Supreme Court held that the University of Missouri at Kansas City had to make its meeting rooms available to students' religious organizations on an equal basis with other organizations, even if the religious organizations used the rooms for prayer or worship.[131] Otherwise, the university would be discriminating against religion.

After this decision, Congress passed a law that *requires public high schools as well as colleges and universities to allow meetings of students' religious, philosophical, or political groups outside class hours.* The Court accepted this law in 1990.[132] Justice Sandra Day O'Connor said that high school students "are likely to understand that a school does not endorse or support student speech that it merely permits on a nondiscriminatory basis." Students have established Bible clubs in one-quarter of public high schools, according to one estimate.[133] (As a result of this act, students have also established gay-straight clubs—organizations of gay and straight students who support the rights of gays, lesbians, and bisexuals—in more than seven hundred high schools.)[134] The Rehnquist Court also held that the University of Virginia had to provide funding, from students' fees, to students' religious organizations on an equal basis with other campus organizations, even if a religious organization sought the money to print a religious newspa-

per.[135] Following this precedent, a federal court of appeals ruled that the University of South Alabama had to provide funding to a gay organization.

Religious Symbols

Despite its prayer rulings, the Court has been *reluctant to invalidate traditional religious symbols.* It has not questioned the motto "In God We Trust," on our coins since 1865 and paper money since 1955, or the phrase "one nation under God," in the Pledge of Allegiance since 1954.[136]

In 2002, a federal court of appeals held the phrase "under God" in the Pledge unconstitutional when recited in the public schools. The court said it promotes religion as much as if it professed that we are a nation "under Jesus" or "under Vishnu" or "under Zeus" or "under no god." It promotes Christianity and leaves out not only atheists and agnostics but believers of other deities, such as Buddhists and many Native Americans. Although the ruling was a logical extension of the prayer rulings, it was a lightning rod for the public's anger, and the Supreme Court sidestepped the issue (deciding that the student's father, an atheist, lacked authority to bring suit on the student's behalf because the student's mother, a born-again Christian, had custody of the child after their divorce).[137]

The Burger Court upheld the display of a nativity scene on government property, at least when it is part of a broader display for the holiday season.[138] Pawtucket, Rhode Island, had a crèche, Christmas tree, Santa Claus, sleigh with reindeer, and talking wishing well. The Court said that Christmas had become a secular as well as a religious holiday and that the secular decorations diluted any religious impact the nativity scene would have. A crèche by itself, however, would be impermissible.[139]

The chief justice of Alabama's supreme court had a granite marker bearing the Ten Commandments installed in Alabama's Judicial Building in the middle of the night. Lower federal courts ruled this display, which stood by itself, a violation of the establishment clause. When the chief justice defied a federal court order to remove the 5300-pound marker, he was suspended by his own court.

The Rehnquist Court addressed Ten Commandments displays and ruled much like the Burger Court did for Christmas nativity scenes. A Ten Commandments monument on the Texas capitol grounds could remain because it was just one of sixteen other monuments and twenty-one historical markers, which were secular, and because it had been there for forty years.[140] But copies of the Ten Commandments in two Kentucky courthouses could not remain because they were not part of historical displays[141] and they were posted recently for religious purposes.[142]

Evolution

Courts have also used the establishment clause to resolve disputes about teaching evolution in schools. In 1968, the Supreme Court invalidated Arkansas' forty-year-old law forbidding schools from teaching evolution.[143] Arkansas and Louisiana then passed laws requiring schools that teach evolution to also teach "creationism"—the biblical version of creation.[144] In 1987, the Court *invalidated these laws because their purpose was to advance the fundamentalist Christian view.*[145]

Evolution remains controversial. In 2005, at least twenty states considered antievolution proposals. A suburban Atlanta school district pasted disclaimers onto ninth-grade biology textbooks stating "Evolution is a theory, not a fact" and it should be "critically considered." A federal court ordered the disclaimers removed because their denigration of evolution reflected a religious view.

Critics of evolution also promoted "intelligent design"—the notion that some life is so complex that it must have been designed by an intelligent creator rather than have evolved through natural selection and random chance, as the theory of evolution posits.[146] In 2005, the Dover, Pennsylvania, school district required teachers to discuss intelligent design. A federal court invalidated the policy because intelligent design isn't a science. Its proponents invoke a supernatural designer—that is, God[147]—whereas science deals with natural phenomena. Although intelligent design proponents make scientific critiques of evolution, intelligent design itself isn't based on empirical evidence and doesn't offer testable hypotheses.

Other Policies

Conservative Christians have pushed Republican officials to adopt policies and programs reflecting their beliefs. Despite the establishment clause, the Bush administration has limited scientific research with stem cells, withheld federal money from family planning

A megachurch with 12,000 members in Memphis, Tennessee, unveiled its "Statue of Liberation Through Christ" in 2006. In contrast to the Statue of Liberty, this monument holds a cross rather than a torch and, with the other arm, the Ten Commandments. She also has a tear running down her cheek because of modern secularism, legal abortions, and the absence of school prayers. According to the pastor, the purpose of the monument is to let people know that "God is in the foundation of our nation." Hence the merger of church and state.

organizations and programs in the United States and abroad, given federal money to abstinence education programs, and given federal money to hundreds of church-run marriage, child care, and drug treatment programs. As a result, for example, the government gave federal money to Louisiana, which funneled it to Protestant groups to teach abstinence through Bible lessons and to Catholic groups to hold prayer sessions at abortion clinics.[148] So far, the courts haven't ruled that these policies and programs violate the establishment clause.

Despite ever-present tensions and frequent conflicts, the effort to separate church and state has enabled the United States to manage, even nourish, its religious pluralism. The effort has kept potential religious fights out of the political arena. But today this practical arrangement is opposed by those religious conservatives who most fear the changes in modern society. They consider their religion a shield protecting their family against these changes, and they want the authority of the government to reinforce their religion.

Rights of Criminal Defendants

The Fourth, Fifth, Sixth, and Eighth Amendments provide numerous **due process** rights for criminal defendants. When the government prosecutes defendants, it must give them the process—that is, the procedures—they are due; it must be fair and "respect certain decencies of civilized conduct,"[149] even toward uncivilized people.

One defense attorney said that many of his clients "had been monsters—nothing less—who had done monstrous things. Although occasionally not guilty of the crime charged, nearly all my clients have been guilty of something."[150] Then why do we give them rights? We give criminal defendants rights because we give all individuals rights in court. As Justice Douglas observed, "respecting the dignity even of the least worthy . . . citizen raises the stature of all of us."[151]

But why do we give all individuals rights in court? We do so because we have established the **presumption of innocence.** This presumption is "not . . . a naive belief that most or even many defendants are innocent, or a cavalier attitude toward crime." It reflects a mistrust of the state, as it recognizes the possibility of an overzealous prosecutor or an unfair judge. It requires the state to prove the defendant's guilt, essentially saying, "We won't take your word for it."[152] Of course, when the crime rate is high or a particular crime is heinous, many people fear the state less than the criminals. Then they want to give officials more authority and defendants fewer rights. But this is the way all people eventually lose their rights.

Search and Seizure

England fostered the notion that a family's home is its castle, but Parliament made exceptions for the American colonies. It authorized writs of assistance, which allowed customs officials to conduct general searches for goods imported by the colonists without paying taxes to the crown. The English tradition of home privacy combined with the colonists' resentment of these writs led to adoption of the Fourth Amendment, which forbids **unreasonable searches and seizures.**

In these cases, the Supreme Court has tried to walk a fine line between acknowledging officials' need for evidence and individuals' desire for privacy. This judicial doctrine is so complex that we will note just its basic principles here.

One type of seizure is the arrest of a person. *Police must have evidence to believe that a person committed a crime.*

Another type of seizure is the confiscation of illegal contraband. *The general requirement is that police must get a search warrant from a judge by showing evidence that a particular thing is in a particular place.*

However, *the Court has made numerous exceptions to this requirement* that complicate the law. These exceptions account for most searches. If persons consent to a search, police can conduct a search without a warrant. If police see contraband in plain view, they can seize it; they don't have to close their eyes to it. If police have evidence to arrest someone, they can search the person and the area within the person's control. If police have reason to suspect that someone is committing a crime but lack evidence to arrest the person, they can "stop and frisk" the person—conduct a pat-down search. If police have reason to believe that a person's life is in jeopardy, they can search for weapons. In some situations, if police want to search a motor vehicle, they can do so because vehicles are mobile and could be gone by the time police get a warrant.

Customs and border patrol officials can search persons and things coming into the country to enforce customs and immigration laws. Airport guards can search passengers and luggage to prevent hijackings and terrorism. And prison guards can search prisoners to ensure security. (See the box "When a Court Reverses a Conviction. . . .")

Exclusionary Rule

To enforce search and seizure law, the Supreme Court has *established the* **exclusionary rule**, *which bars from the courts any evidence obtained in violation of the Fourth Amendment.* The purpose is to deter illegal conduct by police officers.

Although the Court created this rule for federal courts in 1914,[153] it didn't impose the rule on state courts until 1961 in *Mapp* v. *Ohio.*[154] Until this time, police in many states had ignored search and seizure law. *Mapp* was one of the Warren Court's most controversial rulings. Many people didn't think that evidence of guilt should be barred, even if search and seizure law had been violated by police.

The decision still hasn't been widely accepted. The Burger Court created an exception to it. In a pair of cases, the justices allowed evidence obtained illegally to be used in court because the police had acted "in good faith."[155] The Roberts Court has also created an exception to it.[156]

Electronic Surveillance

The Fourth Amendment traditionally applied to searches involving a physical trespass and seizures producing a tangible object. Electronic surveillance, however, does not require a physical trespass or result in a tangible object.

This posed a problem for the Supreme Court when it heard its first wiretapping case in 1928. Federal prohibition agents tapped a bootlegger's telephone by installing equipment on wires in the basement of the bootlegger's apartment building. The Court's majority rigidly adhered to its traditional doctrine, saying that this was not a search and seizure, so the agents did not need a warrant.[157]

In a classic example of keeping the Constitution up-to-date with the times, the Warren Court overruled this precedent in 1967.[158] Because electronic eavesdropping might threaten privacy as much as traditional searching, *officials must get judicial authorization,* similar to a warrant, *to engage in such eavesdropping.*

Self-Incrimination

The Fifth Amendment stipulates that persons shall not be compelled to be witnesses against themselves—that is, to incriminate themselves. Because defendants are presumed innocent, the government must prove their guilt.

This right means that *defendants on trial don't have to take the witness stand and answer the prosecutor's questions,* and neither the prosecutor nor the judge can call attention to their decision to exercise this right. Neither can suggest or imply that the defendants must have something to hide and must therefore be guilty. (But if the defendants do take the stand, they thereby waive their right, so the prosecutor can cross-examine them and they must answer.)

This right also means that *prosecutors can't introduce into evidence statements or confessions from defendants that weren't voluntary.* However, the meaning of *voluntary* has changed over time.

For years, police used physical brutality—"the third degree"—to get confessions. After 1936, when the Supreme Court ruled that confessions obtained in this manner were invalid,[159] police used psychological techniques. They held suspects incommunicado, preventing them from contacting relatives or lawyers and delaying them from going to court, to pressure them to confess.[160] They interrogated suspects for long periods of time without food or rest, in one case with alternating teams of interrogators for thirty-six hours straight,[161] to wear them down and break their will. The Court ruled

WHEN A COURT REVERSES A CONVICTION . . .

. . . the defendant does not necessarily go free. An appellate court only evaluates the legality of the procedures used by officials; it does not determine guilt or innocence. Therefore, when it reverses a conviction, it only indicates that officials used some illegal procedure in convicting the defendant—for example, evidence from an improper search and seizure. Then the prosecutor can retry the defendant, without this evidence, if the prosecutor thinks there is enough other evidence. Often prosecutors do retry the defendants, and frequently judges or juries reconvict them.

that confessions obtained by these techniques were also invalid.

The Warren Court still worried that many confessions weren't truly voluntary, so it issued a landmark decision in 1966. Arizona police arrested a poor, mentally disturbed man, Ernesto Miranda, for kidnapping and raping a woman. After the woman identified him in a lineup, police interrogated him, prompting him to confess. He hadn't been told that he could remain silent or be represented by an attorney. In *Miranda v. Arizona,* the Court concluded that his confession wasn't truly voluntary.[162] Chief Justice Warren, as a former district attorney, knew the advantage that police officers have in interrogation and thought the suspects needed more protection. The Court ruled that *officials must advise suspects of their rights before interrogation.* These came to be known as the **Miranda rights:**

> You have the right to remain silent.
>
> If you talk, anything you say can be used against you.
>
> You have the right to be represented by an attorney.
>
> If you can't afford an attorney, one will be appointed for you.

The Burger and Rehnquist Courts did not require police and prosecutors to follow *Miranda* as strictly as the Warren Court did but, contrary to expectations, did not abandon it. In 2000, the Rehnquist Court reaffirmed *Miranda* by a 7–2 vote.[163]

Even with the warnings, most suspects talk anyway. Some don't understand the warnings. Others think the police, who may rattle off the warnings fast or in a monotone, give them as a formality but wouldn't follow them. Also, suspects being interrogated face a coercive atmosphere and law enforcement tactics designed to exploit their weaknesses. Detectives are trained to persuade suspects to talk despite the warnings. One said, —"Before you ever get in there, the first thing an investigator usually thinks about is . . . how can I breeze through this *Miranda* thing so I don't set the guy off and tell him not to talk to me, song and dance it, sugarcoat it, whatever."[164] So detectives frequently lie and trick suspects.

Counsel

The Sixth Amendment provides the **right to counsel** in criminal cases. Initially, it meant that defendants could hire an attorney to help them prepare a defense, and later it meant that defendants could also have the attorney represent them at the trial. But it was no help to most defendants because they were too poor to hire an attorney for either. Consequently, the Supreme Court required federal trial courts to furnish an attorney to all indigent defendants in 1938.[165] But most criminal cases are state cases, and the Court was reluctant to require state trial courts also to furnish an attorney.[166]

However, the Warren Court was willing to do so in 1963. It heard the case of Clarence Earl Gideon, who was charged with breaking into a pool hall and stealing beer, wine, and change from a vending machine. At trial, Gideon asked the judge for a lawyer. The judge wouldn't appoint one, leaving Gideon to defend himself. The prosecutor didn't have a strong case, but Gideon wasn't able to point out its weaknesses. He was convicted and sentenced to five years. On appeal, the Warren Court unanimously declared that Gideon was entitled to be represented by counsel.[167] Justice Black explained that "lawyers in criminal courts are necessities, not luxuries." The Court finally established a broad rule: state courts must provide an attorney to indigent defendants in felony cases.

When he was tried again, Gideon was given a lawyer, who proved the Court's point. The lawyer did an effective job defending him, which Gideon hadn't been able to do himself. Gideon wasn't convicted this time.

The Burger and Rehnquist Courts expanded the rule: state courts must provide an attorney to indigent defendants in misdemeanor cases, too, except those that result in no incarceration (or probation),[168] because misdemeanor cases as well as felony cases are too complex for the defendants to defend themselves. Thus *all*

Courtesy of the National Archives

Clarence Earl Gideon, convinced that he was denied a fair trial because he was not given an attorney, read law books in prison so he could petition the Supreme Court for a writ of certiorari. Although he had spent much of his life in prison, he was optimistic. "I believe that each era finds an improvement in law [and] each year brings something new for the benefit of mankind. Maybe this will be one of those small steps forward."

courts must offer an attorney to indigent defendants in all cases except the most minor ones, such as traffic violations. The Supreme Court also decided that in addition to an attorney for the trial, *the courts must provide an attorney for one appeal.*[169]

Receiving counsel doesn't necessarily mean receiving effective counsel, however. Some assigned attorneys are inexperienced, some are incompetent, and most are overworked and have little time to prepare the best possible defense.

Some jurisdictions make little effort to provide effective counsel, even in murder cases where capital punishment looms. In Illinois, at least thirty-three convicts on death row had been represented at trial by attorneys who were later disbarred or suspended.[170] In

Louisiana, a defendant was represented by an attorney who was living with the prosecutor in the case. In Florida, a defendant was represented by an attorney who was a deputy sheriff at the time. In Georgia, a black defendant was represented by a white attorney who had been the Imperial Wizard of the local Ku Klux Klan for fifty years.[171] Also in Georgia, an attorney was so unversed in criminal law that when he was asked to name criminal rulings he was familiar with, he could think of only one (*Miranda*).[172] In three murder cases in one recent year in Texas, defense attorneys slept through the trials. When one of these defendants appealed his conviction on the ground that he didn't receive his constitutional right to counsel, the appellate court announced that "the Constitution doesn't say the lawyer has to be awake."[173] (Stung by criticism, the appellate court sat *en banc*—that is, the entire court, rather than a three-judge panel, reheard the case—and overruled itself.) At least these attorneys were present. In Alabama, a defendant was represented by an attorney who failed to appear when his case was argued before the state supreme court. The defendant lost and was executed.[174]

In recent years, the issue of legal counsel for the defendants subject to capital punishment has received more scrutiny because new investigations and technologies have demonstrated that dozens of people on death row didn't commit the murder they were convicted of and sentenced for. Nonetheless, there is little effort to provide effective counsel for criminal defendants because few groups, other than lawyers' associations, urge adequate representation. Criminal defendants have no political power in our system, and the public has limited sympathy for their rights.[175]

Jury Trial

The Sixth Amendment also provides the **right to a jury trial** in "serious" criminal cases. The Supreme Court has defined "serious" cases as those that could result in more than six months' incarceration.[176]

The right was adopted to prevent oppression by a "corrupt or overzealous prosecutor" or a "biased . . . or eccentric judge."[177] It has also served to limit governmental use of unpopular laws or enforcement practices. Regardless of the evidence against a defendant, a jury can refuse to convict if it feels that the government overstepped its bounds.

The jury is supposed to be impartial, so persons who have made up their minds before trial should be dismissed. It is also supposed to be "a fair cross section" of the community, so no group should be systematically excluded.[178] But the jury need not be a perfect cross section and in fact need not have a single member of a particular group.[179] Most courts use voter registration lists to obtain the names of potential jurors. These lists are not closely representative because poor people do not register at the same rate as others, but the courts have decided that the lists are sufficiently representative. And the "motor voter law," which requires drivers' license and welfare offices to offer voter registration forms, has prompted more people to register to vote and thus to make themselves available to serve on juries.

Cruel and Unusual Punishment

The Eighth Amendment forbids **cruel and unusual punishment** but doesn't define it. The Supreme Court had defined it as torture or any punishment grossly disproportionate to the offense, but the Court had seldom used the provision until applying it to capital punishment in the 1970s.

Because the death penalty was used at the time the amendment was adopted and had been used ever since, it was assumed to be constitutional.[180] But the Burger Court (albeit with Chief Justice Burger and the other three Nixon appointees in dissent) held that *capital punishment as it was then being administered was cruel and unusual.*[181] The laws and procedures allowed too much discretion by those who administered the punishment and resulted in too much arbitrariness and discrimination for those who received it. The death penalty was imposed so seldom, according to Justice Potter Stewart, that it was "cruel and unusual in the same way that being struck by lightning is cruel and unusual." Yet when it was imposed, it was imposed on black defendants convicted of murder more often than on other defendants.

The decision invalidated the laws of forty states and commuted the death sentences of 629 inmates. But because the Court didn't hold capital punishment cruel and unusual in principle, about three-fourths of the states adopted new laws that permitted less discretion in an attempt to be less arbitrary and discriminatory.

These changes satisfied a majority of the Court, which ruled that *capital punishment is not cruel and unusual for murder if administered fairly.*[182] But it can't be imposed automatically for everyone convicted of murder, because the judge or jury must consider any mitigating factors that would justify a lesser punishment.[183] Also, it can't be imposed for rape, as some states legislated, because it's disproportionate to that offense.[184]

The new laws have reduced but not eliminated discrimination. Although past studies showed discrimination against black defendants, recent studies show discrimination against black or white defendants who murder white victims. People who affect the decision to impose the death penalty—prosecutors, defense attorneys, judges, and jurors—appear to value white lives more. Despite evidence that in Georgia those who killed whites were more than four times as likely to be given the death penalty as those who killed blacks, the Rehnquist Court, by a 5–4 vote, upheld capital punishment in the state.[185]

The new laws have not addressed an equally serious problem—inadequate representation given to poor defendants who face the death penalty—which we discussed in conjunction with the right to counsel.

For years, most people dismissed any suggestions that innocent defendants might be put to death. They assumed that the criminal justice system used careful procedures and made no mistakes in these cases at least. However, since capital punishment was reinstated and stricter procedures were mandated in the 1970s, at least 117 inmates awaiting execution have been released because new evidence, including DNA tests, revealed their innocence.[186] This number represents one exoneration for every seven or eight executions—a disturbing frequency for the ultimate punishment.[187] Some were the victims of sloppy or biased police or overzealous prosecutors; some were the victims of mistaken witnesses; others were the victims of emotional or prejudiced jurors. Many were the victims of inadequate representation.

Due to the patterns of racial discrimination and inadequate representation, the American Bar Association and some state governors have called for a moratorium on the use of capital punishment. Although a majority of the public still supports capital punishment, that support is declining as more inmates are being found innocent.[188] Juries are becoming more reluctant to impose it, instead opting for life in prison.[189]

Even the Rehnquist Court, long a staunch supporter of the death penalty, reflected the public's mood. In 2002, it ruled that states can't execute the mentally retarded.[190] Previously, it had allowed execution of the retarded, including a man who had the mental capacity of a seven-year-old and still believed in Santa Claus.[191] But now, the six-justice majority observed, there was a new "national consensus" against such executions. In 2005, it ruled that states can't execute juveniles who were younger than eighteen when they killed.[192] Previously, it had allowed execution of juveniles as young as sixteen. But Justice Kennedy noted the "evolving standards of decency" in society. Nonetheless, most states retain the death penalty for adults even though nearly all other developed countries (except Japan) have abolished it.[193]

Rights in Theory and in Practice

Overall, the Supreme Court has interpreted the Bill of Rights to provide an impressive list of rights for criminal defendants (although a significant change from the Warren Court to the Burger and Rehnquist Courts was a narrowing of the rights for criminal defendants). Yet not all rights are available for all defendants in all places. Some police, prosecutors, and judges don't comply with Supreme Court rulings.

When the rights are available, most defendants don't take advantage of them. About 90 percent of criminal defendants plead guilty, and many of them do so through a **plea bargain.** This is an agreement among the prosecutor, the defense attorney, and the defendant, with the explicit or implicit approval of the judge, to reduce the charge or the sentence in exchange for a guilty plea. A plea bargain is a compromise. For officials, it saves the time, trouble, and uncertainty of a trial. For defendants, it eliminates the fear of a harsher sentence. However, it also reduces due process rights. A guilty plea waives the defendants' right to a jury trial, at which the defendants can present their own witnesses and cross-examine the government's witnesses and at which they can't be forced to incriminate themselves. A guilty plea also reduces the defendants' right to counsel because it reduces their lawyers' need to prepare a defense. Consequently, most attorneys pressure their clients to forgo a trial so that the attorneys don't have to spend the time to investigate and try the case. Despite these drawbacks for due process rights, the Supreme Court allows plea bargaining, and the trial courts encourage the practice because it enables judges and attorneys to dispose of their cases quickly.[194]

Right to Privacy

Neither the Constitution nor the Bill of Rights mentions privacy. Nevertheless, the right to privacy, Justice Douglas noted, is "older than the Bill of Rights,"[195] and the framers undoubtedly assumed that the people would have such a right. In fact, the framers did include several amendments that reflect a genuine concern for privacy: The First Amendment protects privacy of association; the Third, privacy of homes from quartering soldiers; the Fourth, privacy of persons and places where they live from searches and seizures; and the Fifth, privacy of knowledge and thoughts from compulsory self-incrimination. The Supreme Court would use these to establish an explicit **right to privacy.**

So far, the Court's right-to-privacy doctrine reflects a right to autonomy—what Justice Louis Brandeis called "the right to be left alone"—more than a right to keep things confidential. As noted earlier in the chapter, the Court has been reluctant to punish the press for invading people's privacy.[196]

Birth Control

The Warren Court explicitly *established a right to privacy* in *Griswold* v. *Connecticut* in 1965. In violation of an 1879 law, which prohibited distributing or using contraceptives or even disseminating information about them, Planned Parenthood and a professor at Yale University Medical School established a birth control clinic in New Haven. After authorities shut it down, the founders challenged the law, and the Court struck it down.[197] To enforce the law, the state would have had to police people's bedrooms, and the Court said the very idea of policing married couples' bedrooms was absurd. Then the Court struck down Massachusetts and New York laws that prohibited distributing contraceptives to unmarried persons.[198] "If the right of privacy means anything," Justice Brennan said, "it is the right of the individual, married or single, to be free from unwarranted governmental intrusion into matters so fundamentally affecting a person as the decision whether to bear or beget a child."[199]

Abortion

When twenty-two-year-old Norma McCorvey became pregnant in 1969, she was distraught. She had one young daughter, she had relinquished custody of two previous children, and she was divorced. She sought an abortion, but Texas prohibited abortions unless the mother's life was in danger. "No legitimate doctor in Dallas would touch me," she discovered. "I found one doctor who offered to abort me for $500. Only he didn't have a license, and I was scared to turn my body over to him. So there I was—pregnant, unmarried, unemployed, alone, and stuck."[200]

Unaware of states that permitted abortions, McCorvey put her baby up for adoption. But the state law rankled her. When she met two women attorneys who recently graduated from law school and also disliked the law, they offered to take her case to challenge the law. She adopted the name Jane Roe to conceal her identity.

In *Roe* v. *Wade* in 1973, the Burger Court *extended the right to privacy from birth control to abortion.*[201] Justice Harry Blackmun surveyed the writings of doctors, theologians, and philosophers over the years and found that these thinkers didn't agree when life begins. Therefore, the majority on the Court concluded that judges shouldn't assert that life begins at any particular time, whether at conception, which would make a fetus a person and abortion murder, or at birth. Without this factor in the equation, a woman's privacy, or control, of her body became paramount.

The Court ruled that *women have a **right to abortion** during the first six months of pregnancy.* States can prohibit an abortion during the last three months because the fetus becomes viable—it can live outside the womb—at this point. (However, states must allow an abortion for a woman whose life is endangered by continuing her pregnancy.) Thus the right is broad but not absolute. The justices, as revealed in memos discovered years later, acknowledged that their division of the nine-month term was "legislative," but they saw this as a way to balance the rights of the mother in the early stages of pregnancy with the rights of the fetus in the later stage.[202]

The case has had an enormous impact on American politics. The Court's ruling invalidated the abortion laws of forty-nine states[203] and increased the number of abortions performed in the country (see Figure 1). It put abortion on the public agenda, and it galvanized conservative groups who saw the ruling as a symbol of loosening social restraints at a time of rampaging social problems. Disparate groups, such as Roman Catholics and evangelical Protestants (and some Orthodox Jews), rural residents and urban ethnics, who rarely saw eye to eye, coalesced around this issue and exercised leverage within the Republican Party.

In hindsight, some observers believe that the Court's ruling may have been imprudent or at least premature. Before the ruling, some states began liberalizing their laws, but there wasn't time for others to follow or for the citizens to ponder the issue. There was little public debate, let alone the extended debate necessary to de-

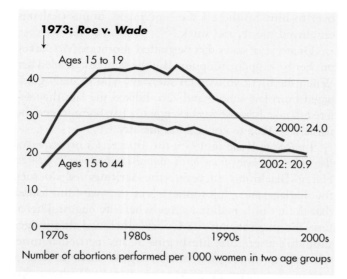

FIGURE 1 • **Abortion Rate since *Roe***
The abortion rate climbed after Roe and peaked in the 1980s. Since then it has declined steadily.
SOURCE: *New York Times,* November 6, 2005.

velop a broad consensus. The Court's ruling short-circuited the normal political process and prompted opponents to mobilize and supporters to countermobilize. Both sides scorned the compromises that typify political solutions to most issues.[204]

The right-to-life movement pressured presidents and senators to appoint justices and lower court judges who opposed the ruling. The movement also lobbied members of Congress and state legislatures to overturn or circumvent the ruling. Although Congress refused to pass constitutional amendments banning abortions or allowing states to regulate them, Congress and state legislatures did pass statutes limiting abortions in various ways.

The Burger Court invalidated most of these statutes,[205] but it upheld a major limitation. The Medicaid program, financed jointly by the federal and state governments, had paid for abortions for poor women. As a result, the program had paid for a third of the abortions in the country each year.[206] But Congress eliminated federal funding (except when pregnancy threatens the life of the mother or is the result of rape or incest), and thirty-three state legislatures eliminated state funding. In these states, poor women need to pay the entire cost. The Court upheld these laws, ruling that *governments have no obligation to finance abortions,* even if this means that some women cannot take advantage of their right to have them.[207]

For some women, these laws delay abortions while the women search for the money. For an estimated 20 percent of the women, these laws deny abortions because the women can't obtain the money.[208]

Many people, including pro-choice advocates, support these bans because they dislike welfare spending. Yet according to an analysis of the states that do provide abortion funding for poor women, the states save money. For every $1 they spend on abortions, they save $4 in welfare and medical expenses in what would have been the first two years of the child's life.[209] They save much more over a longer period. Ironically, public distaste for welfare spending actually leads to more welfare spending here.

Presidents Reagan and George H. W. Bush sought justices who opposed *Roe,* and after they filled their fifth vacancy on the Court, pro-life advocates expected the Court to overturn it. Yet the Rehnquist Court didn't overturn it.[210] In 1992, a bare majority reaffirmed the right to abortion.[211] At the same time, the majority *allowed more restrictions on the right—as long as the restrictions don't place an "undue burden" on the women seeking abortions.* In other words, states must permit abortions but can discourage them.[212]

Therefore, the majority upheld Pennsylvania's twenty-four-hour waiting period between the time a woman indicates her desire to have an abortion and the time a doctor can perform one. Although a twenty-four-hour waiting period is not a burden for many women, it can be for poor women who live in rural areas and must travel to cities for abortions. One Mississippi woman hitchhiked to the city and planned to sleep on outdoor furniture in the Kmart parking lot until the clinic offered to pay for her motel room.[213]

A waiting period can also affect teenagers. Some pro-life groups note the license numbers of cars driven to clinics by teenagers. After looking up the name and address of the family, they inform the parents in the hope that the parents will persuade or pressure their daughter to change her mind during the waiting period.

The majority struck down Pennsylvania's requirement that a married woman notify her husband before having an abortion.[214] This was an undue burden because a woman who fears physical abuse from her husband would be deterred from seeking an abortion. Justice O'Connor wrote that a state "may not give to a man the kind of dominion over his wife that parents exercise over their children."

The Court upheld thirteen states' requirement that unmarried minors notify their parents and twenty-one states' requirement that unmarried minors obtain their parents' consent before having an abortion.[215] For either requirement, if a daughter doesn't want to tell her parents, she can seek permission from a judge. She must convince the judge that an abortion would be in her best interest or that she is mature enough to make the decision herself. If she isn't mature enough, she must become a mother. These laws, Justice Thurgood Marshall wrote in dissent, force "a young woman in an already dire situation to choose between two fundamentally unacceptable alternatives: notifying a possibly dictatorial or even abusive parent or justifying her profoundly personal decision in an intimidating judicial proceeding to a black-robed stranger."[216]

Pro-life groups advocated these laws with the expectation that they would result in fewer abortions. They believed that many teenagers would go to their parents rather than face the forbidding atmosphere of a court hearing and that their parents would persuade or pressure them not to have the abortion. Some evidence indicates that the laws have had this effect.[217]

When teenagers do go to court, they routinely get waivers in some states but not in others.

After the Rehnquist Court reaffirmed the right to abortion, pro-life groups tried to prohibit one abortion procedure known as "intact dilation and extraction" in medicine but referred to as "partial-birth abortion" in politics—a rhetorical success of antiabortion supporters. In this procedure, a doctor delivers the fetus except for the head, punctures the skull and drains the contents, and then removes the fetus from the woman. Because the procedure seems gruesome, pro-life groups used it to sway undecided people in the abortion debate. Numerous states passed laws banning the procedure. A bare majority of the Rehnquist Court struck down the laws in 2000.[218] But Justice Sandra Day O'Connor, who supported abortion rights, retired, and Justice Samuel Alito, who opposes abortion rights, replaced her. Congress passed a similar law for the whole country. A bare majority of the **Roberts Court** upheld the law in 2007.[219] For the majority, Justice Kennedy said the law protects women from themselves. "While we find no reliable data to measure the phenomenon," he concluded that some women "regret their choice to abort," so the law prevents other women from making that choice.

For the time being, a five-justice majority, including Kennedy, supports the basic right to abortion. But the ruling will encourage state legislatures to pass more restrictions on abortion.

The pro-life movement is divided over its current tactics. Some factions prefer an incremental strategy, passing numerous restrictions that might go unnoticed by most people, rather than a frontal attack that might prompt a backlash by the majority. When South Dakota, which had no doctors who performed abortions—Minnesota doctors flew in to the state's sole facility—banned all abortions in 2005, abortion supporters petitioned to put the issue on the ballot in 2006. Voters repealed the law.

In some states, pro-life groups have quietly pressed the legislatures to enact extra-stringent building codes for abortion clinics. These codes specify such things as the heights of ceilings, widths of hallways and doorways, dimensions of counseling rooms and recovery rooms, rates of air circulation, and the types and angles of jets in drinking fountains. (Although all states have construction codes for their buildings, these new laws apply only to abortion clinics.) Some codes require equipment or levels of staffing, such as a registered nurse rather than a licensed practical nurse, beyond what is normal in these clinics. Although the stated goal is health and safety, the real purpose is to drive up the clinics' expenses so they have to increase their patients' fees to the point where many women can no longer afford to have an abortion.[220] When South Carolina's law, which mandates twenty-seven pages of requirements just for abortion clinics, was challenged, a lower court upheld the law and the Supreme Court refused to hear the case, thus allowing the law to stand.

Despite dissatisfaction by activists on both sides of this controversy—pro-life groups are disappointed that the conservative Supreme Court has upheld the right to abortion, whereas pro-choice groups are critical that it has upheld some restrictions on abortion—it is worth noting that the nonelected, nonmajoritarian Supreme Court has come closer to forging a policy reflective of public opinion than most politicians have. Polls show that the public is ambivalent. A majority believes that abortion is murder, but a two-thirds majority opposes banning it. This two-thirds majority favors letting women choose. Over half of those who believe that abortion is murder nonetheless favor letting women choose.[221] (See Figure 2.) Thus many people support the right to abortion but are uncomfortable with it and willing to allow restrictions on it. The Court's doctrine articulates this position.[222]

But the Court's rulings aren't necessarily the final word in this controversy, as they haven't been the final word in some other controversies. Frustrated by the

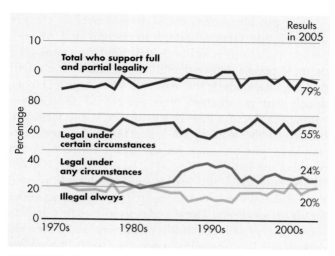

FIGURE 2 • Opinion on the Legality of Abortions
People were asked, "Do you think abortions should be legal under any circumstances, legal only under certain circumstances, or illegal in all circumstances?"
SOURCE: *New York Times,* November 6, 2005.

Court's refusal to overturn *Roe,* activists in the pro-life movement (not most of the pro-life supporters) adopted more militant tactics. First they targeted abortion clinics. Organizations such as Operation Rescue engaged in civil disobedience, blockading clinics and harassing workers and patients as they came and went. Some activists sprayed chemicals inside clinics, ruining carpets and fabrics and leaving a stench that made the clinics unusable. Such incidents occurred fifty times in one year alone.[223]

Then activists targeted doctors, nurses, and other workers of the clinics. Operation Rescue ran a training camp in Florida that instructed members how to use public records to locate personal information about clinic employees, how to tail them to their homes, and how to organize demonstrations at their homes. Activists put up "Wanted" posters, with a doctor's picture, name, address, and phone number and then encouraged people to harass the doctor, the doctor's spouse, and even their children. (One thirteen-year-old was confronted in a restaurant and told that he was going to burn in hell.)[224] Letters containing powder and threatening death by anthrax were sent to over one hundred doctors and clinics.[225] Some extremists even advocated killing the doctors. One minister wrote a book—*A Time to Kill*—and marketed a bumper sticker reading "execute abortionists–murderers."[226]

In this climate, three doctors, two clinic receptionists, and one clinic volunteer were killed, and seven other doctors, employees, and volunteers were wounded.[227] Numerous clinics were firebombed.

The tactics have had their intended effect on doctors.[228] They have made the practice of providing abortions seem dangerous and undesirable. Fewer medical schools offer abortion classes, fewer hospitals provide abortion training, fewer doctors study abortion procedures, and fewer gynecologists and obstetricians, despite most being pro-choice, perform abortion operations.[229] As a result, the number of abortion providers has dropped significantly.[230]

One pro-life leader proclaimed, "We've found the weak link is the doctor."[231] Another observed, "When you get the doctors out, you can have all the laws on the books you want and it doesn't mean a thing."[232]

Abortions remain available in most metropolitan centers but not in most rural areas. Eighty-six percent of U.S. counties, containing 32 percent of the American women aged fifteen to forty-four, have no doctor who performs abortions. Some states have only one and others have only two cities where women can obtain abortions.[233] Nevertheless, an abortion is still one of the most common surgical procedures for American women.

Birth Control, Revisited

Although the pro-life movement has been frustrated by its inability to overturn *Roe,* it has been stimulated by the conservatism of the Bush administration and the appointment of new justices to the Supreme Court. Now the movement has trained its sights on contraception in addition to abortion.[234] Initially the pro-life movement was dominated by Catholics, whose church opposes contraceptives. The movement's leaders muted their views to avoid scaring off potential supporters. (Ninety-three percent of all Americans, and 90 percent of Catholics, supported contraceptives in 2005.)[235] The pro-life movement was joined by conservative Protestants who didn't oppose birth control. Recently, however, more movement leaders, Protestants as well as Catholics, have voiced opposition to contraception. The president of the American Life League declared, "We oppose all forms of contraception."[236] Now religious interest groups, such as the Christian Coalition and Focus on the Family, address birth control. Increasing numbers of evangelical theologians oppose it and evangelical churches discuss it. A cluster of representatives and senators spearheads congressional efforts against some forms of birth control. Members have spoken out against condoms, charging that they don't prevent pregnancy or disease to the extent people believe.

The Bush administration has shifted federal family planning policy from contraception to abstinence—from sex education, including information about birth control, to abstinence education—at least for individuals who aren't married. For 2007, the administration budgeted more than $200 million for abstinence education. The administration has also shifted federal aid to foreign countries for AIDS prevention from contraception to abstinence.[237]

President Bush, when asked whether he supports *the right* to use contraceptives, has refused to answer.[238] (His father, as a member of Congress, was so insistent that foreign aid include contraceptives that he was nicknamed "Rubbers" by other members of the committee.)[239]

Current opposition to contraception makes it difficult for the two sides in the abortion controversy to find common ground. Some on each side had called for greater availability of contraceptives so there would be less need for abortions. But this common ground is giving way as more who oppose abortion also oppose contraception.

What this indicates is that for some in the pro-life movement it's not so much about abortion as it is about sex. One leader said, "We see a direct connection between the practice of contraception and the practice of abortion." They both reflect "an anti-child mindset."[240] Both serve "the selfish demands of the individual."[241] The president of the Southern Baptist Theological Seminary stated, "The effective separation of sex from procreation may be one of the most important defining marks of our age—and one of the most ominous."[242] Their goal is to reverse the sexual revolution of the 1960s, when "the pill" became commonplace, and instead to confine sex to marriage.

This debate reflects sharp cultural differences between European countries and the United States. In those countries, contraceptives are readily available, and unintended pregnancies and abortions are less frequent. There, "these things are in the open, and the only issue is to be careful. Here in the U.S., people are still arguing about whether it's O.K. to have sex."[243]

Homosexuality

For years, states prohibited adultery, fornication, and sodomy. Reflecting Christian doctrine, the statutes targeted various forms of nonmarital sex and nonprocreative sex (including masturbation and withdrawal prior

to ejaculation).[244] After the "sexual revolution" of the 1960s, many states repealed these statutes. However, most states retained their sodomy statutes, which prohibited oral or anal sex (performed by heterosexuals or homosexuals) because of the legislators' disgust at homosexual practices and opposition to the emerging gay rights movement.[245] Although these statutes were primarily symbolic, they were occasionally enforced against homosexuals.

The Supreme Court refused to extend the right to privacy to protect homosexual practices in 1986,[246] but the Rehnquist Court reversed itself in 2003. When a neighbor phoned a false report of an armed intruder, police responded and discovered two men violating Texas's law. The men were arrested, jailed, and fined. The Texas courts affirmed their conviction, but in *Lawrence* v. *Texas,* the Supreme Court overturned it and *invalidated the sodomy laws* of the thirteen states that still had them.[247] In a broad opinion, Justice Kennedy wrote, "Liberty presumes an autonomy of self that includes freedom of thought, belief, expression, and certain intimate conduct." Therefore, homosexuals are entitled to "dignity" and "respect for their private lives."

A sizable shift in public opinion had occurred in the seventeen years between the two rulings.[248] As more homosexuals "came out," they gained greater acceptance from straights. Most Americans say they know someone who is gay or lesbian, and a majority say they are sympathetic to the gay and lesbian communities. Numerous states repealed their sodomy statutes after the 1986 ruling (even though the ruling allowed the states to keep the statutes). Thus in the *Lawrence* case, according to one law professor, "The Court legitimized and endorsed a cultural consensus."[249] (See Table 1.)

Although the majority in *Lawrence* said the ruling would not necessarily extend to same-sex marriages, the dissenters feared that establishing a right to privacy for homosexual practices would indeed lead to a right to marry for homosexual couples. Congress adopted the Defense of Marriage Act, which allows states to disregard same-sex marriages performed in other states. (About forty states have passed laws to do so.) The act also forbids federal recognition of same-sex marriages and thus denies federal benefits, such as Social Security, to same-sex couples.[250]

Although marriage was a fantasy for most homosexuals, their lack of legal rights was both a cause for concern and a source of anger. In the 1980s and 1990s, the AIDS epidemic swept gay communities across the United States. "Lovers, friends, and AIDS 'buddies' were

Table 1	Coming Out

The largest percentage increases in same-sex couples willing to identify themselves as homosexual in government surveys between 2000 and 2005.

New Hampshire	106%
Wisconsin	81
Minnesota	76
Nebraska	71
Kansas	68
Ohio	62
Colorado	58
Iowa	58
Missouri	56
Indiana	54

SOURCE: Gary J. Gates, "Same-Sex Couples and the Gay, Lesbian, Bisexual Population: New Estimates from the American Community Survey," (Williams Institute on Sexual Orientation Law and Public Policy, n.d.), as reported in "Leaving the Closet," *Atlantic Monthly,* January-February, 2007, 44.

spooning food, emptying bedpans, holding wracked bodies through the night. They were assuming the burdens of marriage at its hardest."[251] Yet gay partners had no legal rights. They encountered problems involving health insurance, hospital visitation, disability benefits, funeral planning, and estate settling. Gays were often unable to participate fully in these life-and-death matters due to legal impediments that didn't exist for married couples. In the same decades, lesbians gave birth using donated sperm, and gays got children through adoption and surrogate mothers, yet homosexual couples realized that they didn't have legal protections for their families. These developments increased the calls for legal rights commensurate with the rights of heterosexual couples.[252]

In 1999, the Vermont supreme court ruled that the state must either legalize same-sex marriages or equalize the rights and benefits received by same-sex couples and traditional married couples. The legislature decided to equalize the rights and benefits. To implement this policy, the legislature established "civil unions," with procedures for couples to become official partners (similar to marriage) and procedures for them to dissolve their relationship (similar to divorce).

Although these civil unions provide most of what regular marriages provide, the unions don't apply when couples move from Vermont to other states. And they don't apply to federal benefits. By one count, 1138 federal laws apply to married couples that don't apply to unmarried couples. Some impose responsibilities; most provide rights and benefits, such as tax breaks.[253] Also, of course, the unions don't provide the symbolism that regular marriages do.

So the pressure for same-sex marriages continued. In 2004, the Massachusetts Supreme Judicial Court, hearing a suit brought by seven couples, ruled that same-sex marriages were allowed under the state's constitution. Otherwise, same-sex couples are relegated to "a different status. . . . The history of our nation has demonstrated that separate is seldom, if ever, equal."[254]

In quick succession, officials in San Francisco; Portland, Oregon; and smaller cities in New York, New Jersey, and New Mexico were inspired to issue marriage licenses to same-sex couples. State courts halted the licenses but not until thousands of beaming couples had married and posed for news photos. Although the marriages were pronounced invalid, the head of the Lambda Legal Defense and Education Fund observed, "You can't put the toothpaste back in the tube."[255]

There was an immediate backlash. Polls showed that a majority of the public opposed same-sex marriages. President Bush proposed a constitutional amendment. One congressional sponsor claimed, "There is a master plan out there from those who want to destroy the institution of marriage." (However, Massachusetts, where same-sex marriage is lawful, has the nation's lowest divorce rate.)[256] Another senator, comparing the threat of gay marriage to that of terrorism, called the amendment "the ultimate homeland security." An evangelist predicted that "the family as it has been known for five millennia will crumble, presaging the fall of Western civilization itself."[257] Yet there was more fire from the pulpits than there was in the pews. Evangelical leaders expressed puzzlement and frustration that there was no loud outcry from their faithful.[258] But many people who oppose gay marriage don't feel threatened by it. Consequently, the amendment failed to pass. Nevertheless, voters in over half of the states adopted such amendments to their state constitution, most by a wide margin.

Despite many people's objections, gay rights leaders predict that once homosexuals begin to marry and straights see that "the sky doesn't fall," people will stop opposing their marriages.[259] Indeed, the initial backlash against Massachusetts' same-sex marriages dissipated. Other northeastern states—Maine, New Hampshire, and New Jersey—and California passed domestic-partnership laws that formally recognize same-sex partnerships and provide them some or all rights associated with marriage.

Meanwhile, homosexuals have gained equal benefits at some workplaces. Large corporations especially have been willing to grant health care packages to same-sex couples as a way to attract and retain good workers. Some cities and states also offer these benefits.

Yet homosexuals remain vulnerable at other workplaces. In most states, employees can be fired merely for being homosexual. Although some states and cities have passed laws barring discrimination in employment, housing, credit, insurance, and public accommodations, Congress rejected a bill barring discrimination in employment at the same time it passed the Defense of Marriage Act.[260]

Thirteen states have also passed laws barring discrimination against transgendered persons—those who are born as one gender but live as the opposite gender.[261]

Holding their twin daughters, this couple exchanges marriage vows in San Francisco before same-sex marriages were invalidated there.

Right to Die

The Court has broadened the right to privacy to provide a limited right to die. When Nancy Cruzan's car skidded off an icy road and flipped into a ditch in 1983, doctors were able to save her life but not her brain. She never regained consciousness. She lived in a vegetative state, similar to a coma, and was fed through a tube. Twenty-five at the time of the accident, she was expected to live another thirty years. When her parents asked the doctors to remove the tube, the hospital objected, and the state of Missouri, despite paying $130,000 a year to maintain her, also objected. This issue became entangled in other issues. Pro-life groups contended that denying life support was analogous to abortion; disability groups, claiming that her condition was merely a disability, argued that withholding food and water from her would lead to withholding treatment from others with disabilities.[262]

When Cruzan's parents filed suit, the Rehnquist Court established a limited **right to die.**[263] The justices ruled that *individuals can refuse medical treatment, including food and water, even if this means they will die.* But individuals must make their decision while competent and alert. They can also act in advance, preparing a "living will" or designating another person as a proxy to make the decision if they're unable to.

Cruzan's parents presented evidence to a Missouri court that their daughter would prefer death to being kept alive by machines. Three of Cruzan's coworkers testified that they recalled conversations in which she said she'd never want to live "like a vegetable." The Missouri court granted her parents' request to remove the feeding tube. She died twelve days later.

Although the legal doctrine is clear, various practical problems and emotional issues limit its use. Many people do not make their desires known in advance. Approximately ten thousand people in irreversible comas now did not indicate their decision beforehand.[264] Some people who do indicate their decision beforehand waver when they face death. Some doctors, who are in the habit of prolonging life even when their patients have no chance of enjoying life, resist their patients' decision.[265]

The Rehnquist Court *refused* patients' pleas *to expand the limited right into a broader right to obtain assistance in committing suicide.*[266] The Court drew a distinction between stopping treatment and assisting suicide; individuals have a right to demand the former but not the latter. The justices seemed tentative, as is typical with an issue new to the courts. Chief Justice Rehnquist emphasized, "Our holding permits this debate to continue, as it should in a democratic society."

Oregon decided to allow assisted suicide. The law provides some safeguards. The patient must submit written requests in the presence of two witnesses, get two doctors to concur that he or she has less than six months to live, and wait fifteen days. The pro-life Bush administration challenged Oregon's law, claiming that individual states can't allow assisted suicide. But the Supreme Court rebuffed the Bush administration and *allowed the state law to stand*.[267] So far, a modest number of terminally ill patients—about thirty a year—have taken advantage of the law.[268]

A majority of the public favors a right to assisted suicide,[269] but conservative religious groups oppose one. They insist that people, even when facing extreme pain and no hope of recovery, shouldn't take their life. In addition, ethicists worry that patients will be pressured to give up their life because of the costs, to their family or health care provider, of continuing it. The ethicists fear that a right will become a duty.

Meanwhile, the practice, even where officially illegal, is widely condoned, much as abortion was before *Roe*. Almost a fifth of the doctors who treat cancer patients in Michigan admitted in a survey that they have assisted suicide, and over half of two thousand doctors who treat AIDS patients in San Francisco also admitted that they have done so.[270]

Implications for Civil Liberties from the War on Terrorism

Although the **George W. Bush administration** was lax about the terrorist threat before September 11, 2001, since then it has been aggressive in investigating and pursuing possible terrorists around the world. The administration's policies were devised mostly by Vice President **Dick Cheney** and the legal team working under him.[271] These policies have serious implications for civil liberties.

This section will address detention of suspects, interrogation of detainees, surveillance of Americans and foreigners, and provisions of the USA PATRIOT Act. These issues all pose the question, Can we wage an effective war against the radical Islamists and still maintain our civil liberties?

Detentions

Since the attacks, almost 800 men from forty-four countries have been rounded up and flown to the United States Naval Base at Guantanamo Bay, Cuba, where they have been detained as terrorist suspects. Most were captured in Afghanistan or Pakistan. Vice President Cheney called them "the worst of a very bad lot." Secretary of Defense Donald Rumsfeld called them "among the most dangerous, best-trained, vicious killers on the face of the earth."[272] Officials said they would be detained indefinitely.

"Gitmo" consists of forty-five square miles of land and water along the southeastern coast of Cuba. The United States acquired the base after the Spanish-American War in 1898.[273] It has complete control of the territory.

The families of some captives filed suit, petitioning courts for a writ of **habeas corpus,** which criminal defendants use to challenge the legality of their confinement. As explained in Chapter 11, *habeas corpus* is a traditional and integral component of English and American law, mandating that the government's prosecutors must justify a defendant's incarceration. The Constitution stipulates that *habeas corpus* can't be suspended unless there is a rebellion or foreign invasion. A congressional statute grants federal courts jurisdiction to hear petitions for *habeas corpus* from anyone claiming to be held in violation of the Constitution, laws, or treaties of the United States. The statute doesn't distinguish between American citizens and aliens, and it doesn't distinguish between peacetime and wartime.[274]

The administration claimed that these provisions shouldn't apply to the prisoners at Guantanamo Bay because the naval base isn't part of the United States. The administration also claimed that international law shouldn't apply because the naval base is our military base. In other words, the administration, reflecting Cheney's views, maintained that no laws applied to the base and no rights protected the prisoners (not even the minimal rights of prisoners of war).[275] Essentially, the detainees were in a legal black hole.[276] This may be the first time that the United States officially held anyone outside of all legal processes.[277]

The Bush administration made another sweeping claim. It insisted that the president, as commander in chief, has expanded power during wartime that the courts can't review or question.[278]

The Supreme Court, however, rejected these contentions and rebuffed the president, telling him that he,

too, must follow the law. The justices decided that federal courts do have the authority to review the detentions and that the detainees had the right to challenge their designation as "enemy combatants."[279]

The Court's ruling was a tentative step. Its opinion didn't specify what procedures should be used or what rights, such as a right to an attorney, should be accorded the detainees.[280]

The administration interpreted the ruling as narrowly as possible. The Pentagon began military hearings before military officers, rather than before federal judges, and denied the detainees an actual lawyer (although it allowed them a "personal representative" chosen by the military). Even so, numerous detainees were released.

Other detainees, who weren't released, sought a review by federal courts. Their appeals prompted Congress to pass a law stripping the Guantanamo detainees of *habeas corpus* rights (at least until a military tribunal issues a final ruling in their case).[281] The Supreme Court agreed to hear a challenge to this law in its 2007–2008 term.[282]

The files of many detainees, including those who were released and others who were not released, were opened to the media. The files show that the most dangerous terrorists had been taken to the CIA's secret prisons around the world. Although some al-Qaeda members had been housed at Gitmo, many innocent or at least harmless people had also been housed at Gitmo.

The president and vice president said the prisoners were "picked up off the battlefield," but according to the files only 5 percent were. Eighty-six percent were apprehended by Afghani or Pakistani warlords or tribes-

men and turned over to the United States. Some were captured because they were rivals or enemies of the warlords or tribesmen; others were captured because, as purported "terrorists," they would bring a bounty from the United States (reportedly $1000 a head).[283] Others were foreigners who worked for Muslim organizations operating charities, clinics, and schools.[284] At least ten wore the wrong watch—a Casio model used by al-Qaeda bombers because of its timer, but also worn by many Arabs because it is cheap and has a compass, which enables them to point toward Mecca when they pray.[285] A thorough review of the government's files concluded, "Most, when captured, were innocent of any terrorist activity, were Taliban foot soldiers at worst, and were often far less than that. And some, perhaps many, were guilty only of being foreigners in Afghanistan or Pakistan at the wrong time."[286] The former head of the CIA's bin Laden unit concluded that many were "absolutely . . . the wrong people."[287] The U.S. military was under so much pressure to find al-Qaeda members that it accepted the persons who were delivered by the warlords and tribesmen. With too few experienced interpreters and interrogators, it couldn't separate the terrorists from the others.

The problems continued at Gitmo. During interrogation, one Yemeni who was asked whether he knew bin Laden said, "I saw bin Laden five times: three times on al Jazeera [TV] and twice on Yemeni news." In his file, the interrogator noted, "Detainee admitted to knowing Osama bin Laden."[288] Interrogators were under tremendous pressure from Washington to identify terrorists and, knowing that al-Qaeda trained its agents to lie, were reluctant to conclude that prisoners were innocent.

The indefinite detentions put the detainees under great stress. Many tried to hang themselves and three succeeded.[289] The human rights group Amnesty International, referring to the notorious Soviet prison for dissidents, called Guantanamo the "gulag of our times."[290] European leaders and a United Nations committee, in addition to American politicians, urged the administration to shut down the prison. President Bush has expressed a desire "to close Guantanamo," but Vice President Cheney has resisted.[291]

In 2006, the Court issued another rebuke to the president. A slim majority ruled that the administration's plan to try terrorism suspects by military commissions violated both U.S. law and international law because the commissions weren't established courts and wouldn't afford adequate rights to the suspects.[292]

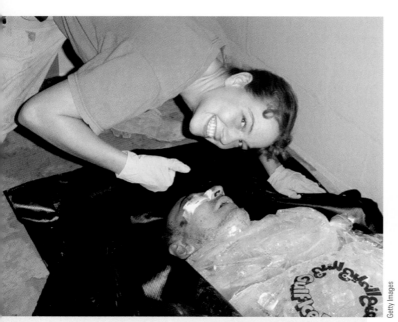

An American soldier poses with the body of an Iraqi prisoner who died during his interrogation at Abu Ghraib prison.

Taken together, the Court's rulings on detentions and military commissions challenge the president's assertion that he alone can determine how to fight terrorism. And the rulings reflect the justices' belief that at least some constitutional standards must be followed even during wartime.

Interrogations

The restrictions on police interrogations of criminal suspects, explained earlier in the chapter, don't apply outside the United States or to enemy combatants captured in a war. Nevertheless, these restrictions create norms of behavior, reflecting standards of civility and decency that we have come to expect. Do no-holds-barred methods of interrogation of suspected terrorists violate these norms and standards? Might they undermine our methods of interrogation of criminal defendants?

Methods

For suspected terrorists, the Bush administration, again reflecting the vice president's views, authorized procedures it calls **"stress and duress"** and which others call "torture lite"[293] (but which many in the public and for-

eign countries call simply "torture"). Prisoners may be locked, naked and wet, in a cold cubicle in which they cannot stand, sit, or lie. They have to kneel or squat in "stress positions." They may be bound and have a hood put over their head or dark goggles put over their eyes to keep them disoriented. Or they may be subjected to bright lights, perhaps strobe lights, and loud noise—cacophonous sounds such as babies' cries, cats' meows, and heavy metal music—to keep them awake. (Interrogators also experimented with children's songs, such as "Barney's" song, to drive them crazy. We haven't heard whether interrogators tried Barry Manilow's albums.) If prisoners doze, they may be awakened. (One suspect was sleep-deprived for twenty hours a day for seven weeks.[294]) They may be beaten. They may be fed irregularly. Through their food, they may be drugged. This "stress and duress" process, according to one government official, is "not pulling out fingernails, but it's pretty brutal."[295]

At Guantanamo Bay, some prisoners were shackled for twenty-four hours and left in their own excrement. Other prisoners were subjected to sexual humiliation. Female interrogators rubbed their breasts against detainees and squeezed the genitals of detainees.[296] One wiped red ink, which she said was her menstrual blood, on a detainee. By violating sexual taboos, the interrogators tried to make the men feel unclean and unable to pray to their god for strength.[297]

For key suspects, interrogators have used waterboarding, which simulates drowning. The suspect is bound to a board, which is inclined so his head is lower than his feet. Then water is poured up his nose.[298] Although the United States had prosecuted military personnel for using this tactic since 1901, Vice President Cheney approved it. (The only tactic that the CIA requested approval for that was denied was threatening to bury a prisoner alive.)[299]

International law forbids torture, which is generally defined as acts that intentionally inflict "severe pain or suffering, whether physical or mental."[300] International law also forbids "outrages upon personal dignity, in particular humiliating and degrading treatment."[301] Domestic law prohibits torture as well, and the Uniform Code of Military Justice commands military personnel not to engage in "cruelty" or "maltreatment" toward prisoners or to threaten or assault them.

The Bush administration claims that its tactics don't amount to torture.[302] After 9/11, however, it secretly redefined *torture* to encompass only such pain which produces the impairment of a function, the failure of an organ, or death. Under this definition, the "stress and duress" procedures, including most beatings, wouldn't constitute torture. Of course, the administration can't unilaterally alter the definition of torture. But by redefining the term, the administration can insist that the government doesn't engage in torture.

Many people would countenance torture, and certainly "torture lite," against terrorists if there is a "ticking time bomb" and lives could be saved. But such scenarios, though common on television, are rare in reality. (Military officers and veteran interrogators have urged television producers of shows such as "24" to offer more realistic scenarios.)[303] And once rough treatment is used, there is a tendency for it to be extended to other enemies and other situations that are less urgent.

When the insurgency in Iraq proved difficult to control, American officials became frustrated. A general who had overseen the interrogations at Guantanamo Bay was sent to Baghdad to introduce similar tactics there.[304] But many arrestees in Iraq were neither terrorists nor insurgents. When attacks occurred, the American military, adopting a tactic used by the Israeli military for suicide bombings, conducted a sweep of the area, rounding up all men, roughly interrogating them, and weeding out the ones who seemed innocent.[305] Intelligence officers have estimated that 70 to 90 percent of the men who have been arrested and interrogated in Iraq have been innocent.[306] Yet they have been subjected to harsh treatment.

Another problem is that it becomes difficult for interrogators using rough methods to restrain themselves when their approach isn't producing any results.[307] We know that severe beatings have been administered to detainees (and burning cigarettes have been put in their ears).[308] As many as thirty-four prisoners may have been killed during interrogations in Afghanistan and Iraq.[309]

In response to the photos of the horrors at Abu Ghraib, Congress adopted a law that prohibits cruel treatment of our prisoners.[310] The law was proposed by Sen. John McCain (R-Ariz.), who was tortured during the Vietnam War. The administration opposed the proposal, but the president was forced to sign it into law by strong congressional support for it. Yet the president issued a signing statement indicating that he wouldn't feel bound by the law.[311]

Renditions

For some important prisoners, the government has arranged with countries to interrogate the prisoners for us. In a procedure called **rendition,** the CIA seizes suspects in foreign countries and whisks them away to other countries whose intelligence services have ties with the CIA. Islamic extremists have been seized not only from the Middle East but also from countries in Africa, Asia, and Europe and taken to Egypt, Jordan, Morocco, Saudi Arabia, Syria, and Uzbekistan, all of which are known to use torture.[312] "We don't kick the [expletive] out of them," an American official said. "We send them to other countries so *they* can kick the [expletive] out of them."[313]

The transfers are made in secret, using unmarked airplanes in remote corners of airports at night. The transfers ignore legal formalities, such as extradition procedures, and have defied national laws. Six suspects were taken from Bosnia even though the Bosnian supreme court had ordered them released. The secrecy reduces court battles and minimizes the publicity that could tip off suspects' comrades or inflame public opinion, especially where the government feels threatened by rebellious groups with numerous sympathizers. An official in Indonesia, which has the world's largest Muslim population, said, "We can't be seen cooperating too closely with the United States."[314]

People in Germany, Italy, and Sweden expressed outrage when they learned that the CIA had snatched suspects from their countries. Prosecutors in Germany and Italy have issued arrest warrants for the CIA agents involved. Renditions do appear to violate international agreements signed by the United States.[315]

Secret Prisons

For its most important prisoners, the government established a covert prison system run by the CIA. These "black sites," as they were known, were located in at least six countries in Eastern Europe and Asia. Until the *Washington Post* broke this story, these prisons were unknown to all but a handful of government officials.[316] And, of course, they were unknown to the International Red Cross, which monitors prisoners' treatment. (In 2006, the administration announced that these prisons would be shut down, but we don't know whether they have been.)[317]

Surveillance

Soon after 9/11, the government began to intercept international calls and domestic calls of American citizens without judicial approval.[318] The **National Security Agency,** which is our largest intelligence agency, conducts this program. The NSA was established in secret in 1952 to obtain intelligence of our adversaries' communications. Located at Fort Meade in Maryland, the agency was so secretive that for years the government refused to acknowledge its existence. (Washingtonians joked that "NSA" stood for No Such Agency.) Today its existence is acknowledged, and the huge agency has its own off-ramp from the Baltimore-Washington Parkway, marked "NSA Employees Only."

The agency operates two programs relevant here, one monitoring international calls and emails and another monitoring domestic calls.

Monitoring International Calls and Emails

The NSA eavesdrops on phone calls and e-mails between people in the United States and people in foreign countries. It uses computer searches to look for telltale words and phrases that might be used by terrorists.

When the revelations about this program broke, President Bush said, "[I]f you're talking to a member of al-Qaeda, we want to know why."[319] Vice President Cheney downplayed the revelations. "If you're calling Aunt Sadie in Paris, we're probably not really interested." A White House representative emphasized that the NSA was recording calls "from very bad people to very bad people."[320] Apparently, however, the program has been more extensive than the administration has admitted until recently. Thousands of ordinary Americans have had their conversations recorded.[321]

The snooping occurs without judicial authorization. The Foreign Intelligence Surveillance Act required the government to obtain authorization from the Surveillance (FISA) Court, as explained in Chapter 11.[322] Although it was easy to get authorization from this court, the government had to have some evidence to do so. The administration had no evidence—it was conducting "a fishing expedition"—so it was unable to get authorization.

This program, according to legal experts, was a clear violation of the FISA law. At the administration's request, Congress amended the FISA law to allow this program in 2007.[323]

Monitoring Domestic Calls

The NSA also monitors calls between people within the United States. (It's not clear whether the agency monitors long-distance calls only or local calls as well.) The agency has direct access to the data from the major communications companies. The data include the callers' and receivers' numbers; the date, time, and duration of the calls; and possibly the content of the calls as well.

The goal is to uncover hidden terrorists through social network analysis. Al-Qaeda is so amorphous and diffuse that it's difficult for outsiders to identify its members. By correlating calls, computers map patterns of interactions among people. If the government knows that one person is a member of al-Qaeda, social network analysis might identify other members as well.

Initial reports indicated that this domestic monitoring program, unlike the international monitoring program, did not access the content of the calls. However, later reports indicate that the monitoring program does in fact access the content of the calls. As a result, the government has examined the calls of "tens of thousands" of Americans without seeking judicial authorization.[324]

It's unclear whether either program has identified any terrorists.

Most legal experts believe that the international monitoring program violates the Fourth Amendment (and violated the FISA law until Congress amended the law in 2007). If the domestic monitoring program accesses the content of the calls, it probably violates the Fourth Amendment and the FISA law also.[325] However, our conclusions must be tentative because at the time of this edition the administration was revealing as little information as possible.

USA PATRIOT Act

The **USA PATRIOT Act** also extends surveillance of people within the United States. (The title is an acronym for Uniting and Strengthening America by Providing Appropriate Tools Required to Intercept and Obstruct Terrorism.) This act, which was passed in a rush after 9/11, with limited congressional consideration and little public debate,[326] also has important implications for civil liberties.

The Patriot Act expands domestic intelligence gathering. It shifts the FBI's primary function from solving crimes to gathering intelligence within the country. (The CIA and other agencies gather intelligence outside the country.) The act allows the FBI and CIA to share intelligence, which had been prohibited after abuses by both agencies in the 1960s and 1970s. The goal is to coordinate their information and their efforts.

The act loosens some restrictions on searches and seizures and on wiretaps. The act enables the FBI to obtain various papers and records, including the records of books bought from bookstores or checked out from libraries and the records of websites visited on library computers. For other computers, including personal computers, the act allows surveillance of the websites visited and key words used in search engines, and header information (to, from, and subject lines) of e-mail messages. (A later act encourages Internet service providers to turn over the *contents* of their customers' e-mail messages.)[327] The act extends surveillance to financial data—where people make and spend money, including what they buy online and what they borrow and invest.

Because some 9/11 terrorists entered the country on student visas, the act establishes a database to monitor foreign students in American colleges. When foreign students apply for a visa, their data is logged into the database. Each semester the schools are required to forward information about the students' classes and activities on campus. When government officials investigate particular students, the schools are forbidden from telling the students that their records were checked.

Because most 9/11 terrorists lived in the United States for some time before the attacks, the act authorizes the government to monitor foreign visitors in the country. The U.S. Citizenship and Immigration Services (USCIS) requires nonresident aliens who are male and over sixteen and who come from an Arab or Muslim country to report to its offices to be fingerprinted, photographed, and interrogated. The men must notify the agency of any new address within ten days, and they must reappear annually.

The Patriot Act puts in place a surveillance state more extensive than Americans have ever experienced.[328] Yet the act is difficult to evaluate—how it is implemented and what impact it has had—because the Bush administration is unusually secretive, shielding its policies and their effects from congressional oversight, judicial review, and public scrutiny.

For government policies involving detention, interrogation, and surveillance, a pattern has appeared. When President Bush and Vice President Cheney don't like particular constitutional limitations or congressional laws, the administration unilaterally reinterprets—essentially, overrides—the limitations or laws. The officials, asserting an expansive interpretation of presidential war power, claim that their policies are necessary to protect the country against the terrorists and will remain necessary as long as the threat from the terrorists continues. And, for six years, Congress failed to check the executive branch because its Republican majority

considered itself part of the same "team" as the White House rather than part of an independent branch of government.

During other crises in our history, well-meaning political leaders, responding to peoples' fears, took bold action that affected civil liberties. During the Civil War, President Lincoln suspended the writ of *habeas corpus*. During World War II, President Roosevelt ordered the internment of Japanese Americans. In response to the Russian Revolution, the executive and legislative branches launched the Red Scare. In response to the Cold War, history repeated itself, as Congress pursued efforts that led to McCarthyism. In hindsight, all of these actions have been condemned as overreactions. All of them have been considered unnecessary infringements of civil liberties and rights.[329] Might some of our current efforts to ferret out terrorists be categorized in this way by later generations?

Conclusion: Are the Courts Responsive in Interpreting Civil Liberties?

The Supreme Court has interpreted the Constitution to provide valuable civil liberties. The Warren Court in the 1950s and 1960s, which included four of the most committed and forceful advocates of the Bill of Rights ever to sit on the High Court—Chief Justice Warren and Justices Black, Brennan, and Douglas—expanded civil liberties more than any other Court in history. It applied many provisions of the Bill of Rights to the states. It greatly broadened First Amendment rights and criminal defendants' rights. It also established a right to privacy.

Observers predicted that the Burger Court would lead a constitutional counterrevolution. However, it didn't. The Burger Court in the 1970s and 1980s narrowed some rights, especially for criminal defendants. But the Court accepted the core of the Warren Court's doctrine and even extended the right to privacy to encompass abortions.

Nor did the Rehnquist Court in the 1980s, 1990s, and 2000s produce a constitutional counterrevolution. It, too, narrowed some rights, but it also accepted most of the Warren Court's doctrine and even extended the right to privacy to encompass homosexual practices.

The decisions by these Courts show the extent to which the Supreme Court is responsive to the people in civil liberties cases. The majority of the people support civil liberties in general but not necessarily in specific situations. The majority support civil liberties less than the elites. As the Court has expanded civil liberties, it has been more responsive to various minorities—political and religious minorities and unpopular groups such as criminal defendants—and to the elites rather than to the majority.

When the Supreme Court has upheld civil liberties, it has fulfilled what many legal scholars consider the quintessential role of the highest court in a democracy—"to vindicate the constitutional rights of minorities, of dissidents, of the unrepresented, of the disenfranchised, of the unpopular." The other branches of government, whose officials are elected every two, four, or six years, are sensitive to the needs of "the majority, the politically powerful, the economically influential, and the socially popular."[330] According to this view, the judicial branch should be sensitive to the needs of the others.

Because the Founders didn't intend the Court to be very responsive to the majority, they gave it substantial independence. Therefore, it doesn't have to mirror public opinion, although it can't ignore this opinion either. The Warren Court went too far too fast for too many people. It produced a backlash that led to the Burger and Rehnquist Courts, which were somewhat more responsive to majority opinion—and somewhat less vigilant in protecting civil liberties.

Key Terms

Key Names

1. Americans tend to
   a. strongly support civil liberties.
   b. support civil liberties in the abstract.
   c. be neutral toward civil liberties.
   d. oppose civil liberties in practice.
   e. b and d.

2. In practice, the Bill of Rights provides rights
   a. against the government.
   b. for various minorities.
   c. for the majority.
   d. for unpopular groups.
   e. for all but c.

3. Under judicial doctrine, the Bill of Rights now limits what _____ can do to individuals.
   a. all governments
   b. the federal government
   c. state governments
   d. private businesses
   e. all of the above

4. Freedom of speech promotes
   a. individual self-fulfillment.
   b. the discovery of truth.
   c. participation in government.
   d. the advancement of knowledge.
   e. all of the above.

5. McCarthyism refers to
   a. the rise of Irish Americans in U.S. government.
   b. the process of exposing Communist spies during the Cold War.
   c. political accusations based on little evidence.
   d. the attempt to promote loyalty among Americans during the Cold War.
   e. the role of communists and socialists in U.S. government.

6. Today hate speech can be prosecuted if it
   a. is aimed at individuals rather than at entire groups of people.
   b. demeans people for innate characteristics.
   c. is used intentionally to upset people.
   d. constitutes a clear threat to the people it's directed at.
   e. all of the above.

7. Students below the college level have
   a. no right to freedom of speech.
   b. less right to freedom of speech than adults.
   c. a right to freedom of speech but no right to freedom of the press for student publications.
   d. a right to freedom of speech if they're responsible.
   e. a right to freedom of speech if they don't engage in antigay speech.

8. The core of freedom of the press is freedom
   a. to gather news.
   b. from punishment after publishing.
   c. from prior restraint.
   d. from punishment for libelous articles.
   e. to invade individuals' privacy.

9. The Warren Court overhauled libel doctrine by
   a. allowing states to establish libel laws as they see fit.
   b. making it difficult for public officials and figures to win libel suits.
   c. making it difficult for victims to sue if the statements were true.
   d. making it impossible for public officials and figures to win libel suits.
   e. allowing victims to sue more easily for coverage that tarnishes their reputation.

10. The concept of "separation of church and state"
    a. isn't explicit in the Constitution.
    b. was a novel idea when the Constitution was drafted.
    c. was promoted by Jefferson to provide harmony between church and state.
    d. contrasted with European policies toward church and state.
    e. all of the above.

11. Controversy over the scope of the establishment clause today is due to
    a. activist judges.
    b. early Christian settlers, who wanted government to reinforce their religion.
    c. the Founders, who wanted freedom from religion as well as freedom of religion.
    d. b and c.
    e. politicians who don't follow the will of the people concerning religion.

12. Of the following practices by public schools, which one hasn't been forbidden by the Supreme Court?
    a. having students recite Bible verses at the start of each school day
    b. having students recite a nondenominational prayer at the start of each school day
    c. allowing students to give a prayer at graduation
    d. allowing clergy to give a prayer through the PA system at football games
    e. having schools post the Ten Commandments

13. Due process rights include
    a. a prohibition against unreasonable searches and seizures.
    b. a prohibition against compulsory self-incrimination.
    c. a right to counsel.
    d. a prohibition against cruel and unusual punishment.
    e. all of the above.

14. The *Miranda* warnings were designed to
    a. make sure confessions are voluntary.
    b. prompt police to look harder for other evidence than confessions.
    c. keep suspects from talking to police.
    d. limit police in their efforts to obtain evidence.
    e. give suspects the advantage during interrogations.

15. The Supreme Court has used the right to privacy in cases involving
    a. birth control.
    b. abortions.
    c. homosexual sex.
    d. the withholding of water, food, or treatment for terminally ill patients.
    e. all of the above.

16. According to the Supreme Court, there's a right to abortion
    a. for three months of pregnancy.
    b. for six months of pregnancy.
    c. for the entire pregnancy.
    d. only if the father approves.
    e. only if the woman lives in a state that allows it.

17. The legal concept central to deciding the legal status of the Guantanamo detainees is
    a. bills of attainder.
    b. a writ of *mandamus.*
    c. *habeas corpus.*
    d. a writ of *certiorari.*
    e. *ex post facto* laws.

18. The government agency that seeks intelligence of our adversaries' communications is the
    a. Department of Defense.
    b. FBI.
    c. CIA.
    d. NSA.
    e. Department of Communications.

19. The primary goal of the USA PATRIOT Act is to
    a. expand domestic intelligence gathering.
    b. settle turf battles between the FBI and CIA.
    c. increase foreign intelligence gathering.
    d. authorize wiretaps of Americans' phone calls.
    e. broaden interrogation methods that can be used on terrorist suspects.

20. The Court most associated with expanding individual rights was
    a. the Warren Court.
    b. the Burger Court.
    c. the Rehnquist Court.
    d. the Roberts Court.
    e. each of these courts about equally.

Key: 1–e; 2–e; 3–a; 4–e; 5–c; 6–d; 7–b; 8–c; 9–b; 10–e; 11–d; 12–c; 13–e; 14–a; 15–e; 16–b; 17–c; 18–d; 19–a; 20–a.

The civil rights movement helped propel many African Americans into the middle class.

The Rev. Al Sharpton, a civil rights activist in New York, recently learned that his ancestors were owned by the ancestors of former Senator Strom Thurmond of South Carolina. An avowed segregationist, Thurmond split from the Democratic Party to run for president on the Dixiecrat ticket in 1948. During the campaign, he told screaming crowds, "There's not enough troops in the army to force the southern people to break down segregation and admit the nigra race into our theaters, into our swimming pools, into our schools, and into our homes." When the Democratic Party continued to push for civil rights, Thurmond joined the Republican Party.

Through DNA testing, Sharpton learned that his family was enslaved by Thurmond's family. It was "the shock of my life." His family was owned by a man named Alexander Sharpton, whose son was married to Julia Ann Thurmond. When Alexander Sharpton's son died in debt, Al Sharpton's great-grandfather, with his wife and two children, was sent from South Carolina to Liberty, Florida, to work off the Sharpton-Thurmond family's debts.

"You're always kind of thinking that your ancestors were slaves," Sharpton said, but "this hit home." He added, "Words cannot fully describe the feelings I had when I learned the awful truth. Not only am I the descendant of slaves, but my family had to endure the particular agony of being slaves to the Thurmonds, the symbol of everything about America that I have fought to change."

Nevertheless, he vowed, "My family and the Thurmond family must rise above the ugly, shameful past that binds us, just as America must . . . seek to repair the damage that slavery has done and to eliminate the bigotry that still lingers."[1]

The term **civil rights** means equal rights for persons regardless of their race, sex, or ethnic background.

The **Declaration of Independence** proclaimed that "all men are created equal." The author, **Thomas Jefferson,** knew that all men were not created equal in many respects, but he meant that they should be considered equal in their rights and equal before the law. This notion represented a break with Great Britain, where rigid classes with unequal rights existed; nobles enjoyed more rights than commoners.

The Declaration's promise didn't include nonwhites or women, however. So although colonial Americans advocated equality, they envisioned it only for white men. Other groups eventually gained more equality, but the Declaration's promise remains unfulfilled for some.

Race Discrimination

African Americans, Hispanics, and American Indians all have endured and continue to experience discrimination. This chapter recounts the struggle for equal rights by these groups.

Discrimination against African Americans

Slavery

The first Africans came to America in 1619, just twelve years after the first whites. Like many whites, the Africans initially came as indentured servants. In exchange for their passage across the ocean, they were bound to an employer, usually for four to seven years, and then freed. Later in the century, however, the colonies passed laws making the Africans and their children slaves for life.

Once slavery was established, the slave trade flourished. In the South, slavery provided the foundation for an agricultural economy with huge and prosperous plantations. In the North, slavery also was common. Large plantations in Connecticut, Massachusetts, and Rhode Island shipped agricultural products to the West Indies in exchange for molasses used to make rum. Tradesmen and households in the cities also used slaves. In the mid-1700s, New York City had more slaves than any city in the colonies except Charleston. About 40 percent of its households owned slaves (though, unlike southern plantations, an average of only two slaves per household).[2] In the North, however, slavery lost favor,

and most slaves were freed by the time of the Revolutionary War.

During the war, the British, attempting to disrupt American society, promised freedom for the slaves. (The promise was a tactical maneuver rather than an ethical stand, as British generals themselves had slaves.) Perhaps as many as eighty thousand escaped and fought alongside the Redcoats.[3] After the war, some fled to Canada with the Loyalists; some sailed to Caribbean islands, where they would be enslaved again; and others shipped to Sierra Leone. Most remained in America.

By the time of the Constitutional Convention, there were sharp differences between northern and southern attitudes toward slavery. In most parts of the North, slavery was condemned,[4] but in the South it was accepted and ingrained.

As a result of the compromises between northern and southern states, the Constitution protected slavery. It allowed the importation of slaves until 1808, when Congress could bar further importation, and it required the return of escaped slaves to their owners.

In 1808, Congress barred the importation of slaves but not the practice of slavery. Yet Thomas Jefferson, a Virginia slave owner, foresaw its demise, "whether brought on by the generous energy of our own minds" or by a "bloody process."[5]

Abolitionists called for an end to slavery. In response, southerners began to question the Declaration of Independence and to repudiate its notion of natural rights, attributing this idea to Jefferson's "radicalism."[6]

The Supreme Court tried to quell the antislavery sentiment in the **Dred Scott case** in 1857.[7] Dred Scott, a slave who lived in Missouri, was taken by his owner to the free state of Illinois and the free territory of Wisconsin and, after five years, was returned to Missouri. The owner died and passed title to his wife, who moved and left Scott in the care of people who opposed slavery. They arranged for Scott to sue his owner for his freedom. They argued that Scott's time in a free state and a free territory made him a free man even though he was returned to a slave state. The owner also opposed slavery, so she could have simply freed Scott, but they all sought a major court decision to keep slavery out of the territories.

In this infamous case, Chief Justice Roger Taney, from Tennessee, stated that blacks, whether slave or free, were not citizens and were, in fact, "so far inferior that they had no rights which the white man was bound to respect." Taney could have stopped here—if Scott wasn't a citizen, he couldn't sue in federal court at the time—but Taney continued. He declared that Congress had no power to control slavery in the territories. This meant that slavery could extend into the territories that Congress had declared free. It also raised the possibility that slavery might extend into the states that had prohibited it.

By this time, slavery had become the hottest controversy in American politics, and this decision fanned the flames. It provoked vehement opposition in the North and produced bitter polarization in the country, leading to the Civil War. Today it is cited among the worst decisions ever made by the Supreme Court. (Yet Taney had freed his slaves, whom he had inherited from his parents, three decades earlier, and he remained with the Union when the war broke out.)[8]

Although Scott received his freedom from his owner, most other slaves weren't so lucky (see the box "Black Masters"). When the Civil War began, one of every nine black people in America was free; the other eight were slaves. The slaves were so integral to the southern economy that the paper money of some Confederate states depicted slaves harvesting cotton.[9]

The North's victory in the Civil War gave force to President Lincoln's Emancipation Proclamation ending slavery.[10] But blacks would find short-lived solace.

Reconstruction

After the war, Congress passed and the states ratified three constitutional amendments. The Thirteenth Amendment prohibited slavery. (In 1995, Mississippi became the last state to ratify the amendment, but of course the state's ratification was merely a symbolic action by then.) The Fourteenth Amendment granted citizenship to blacks, thus overruling the Dred Scott decision, and also granted "equal protection of the laws" and "due process of law." The **equal protection clause** would eventually become the primary guarantee that government would treat people equally. The Fifteenth Amendment gave black men the right to vote.

These amendments not only granted specific rights for African Americans but also transformed the relationship between the federal and state governments. Each amendment included the stipulation that "Congress shall have power to enforce" the provisions of the amendment. (In the wake of the war, Congress didn't trust the southern states to enforce the constitutional provisions.) This stipulation granted the federal government new power—whatever power was necessary to guarantee these rights. This power was in marked contrast to the Founders' original understanding that the federal government would have limited power. The Civil War and

AMERICAN DIVERSITY

BLACK MASTERS

Although most slave owners were white, some were black. William Ellison of South Carolina was one. Born a slave, he bought his freedom and then his family's by building and repairing cotton gins. Over time, he earned enough money to buy slaves himself and operate a plantation. With sixty slaves, Ellison ranked in the top 1 percent of all slaveholders, black or white.

Ellison was unusual, but he was not unique. In Charleston, South Carolina, alone, more than one hundred African Americans owned slaves in 1860. Most, however, owned fewer than four.[1]

Although part of the slave-owning class, the black owners weren't accepted as equals by whites. Ellison's family was granted a pew on the main floor of the Episcopal church, but they had to act deferentially toward whites. Failure to maintain the norms of black-white relations could mean instant punishment.

And as the Civil War approached, whites increasingly viewed free blacks, even slaveholders, as a threat to the established order. State legislatures passed harsh legislation to regulate free blacks. For example, they had to have a white "guardian" to vouch for

their moral character, and they had to carry special papers to prove their free status. Without these papers, they could be sold back into slavery.

Some black slaveholders showed little sign that they shared the concerns of black slaves. Indeed, Ellison freed none of his slaves.[1]

SOURCE: Michael Johnson and James L. Roark, *Black Masters* (New York: Norton, 1984).

[1]For an acclaimed novel exploring the moral intricacies for black slave owners, read Edward P. Jones, *The Known World* (New York: Amistad, 2003).

these amendments together thus constituted a constitutional revolution, as explained in Chapter 2.[11]

Congress also passed a series of Civil Rights Acts, which allowed blacks to buy, own, and sell property; to make contracts; to sue; to serve as witnesses and jurors in court. The acts also allowed blacks to use public transportation, such as railroads and steamboats, and to patronize hotels and theaters.[12]

Even so, freed blacks faced bleak conditions. Congress rejected proposals to break up the plantations and give former slaves "forty acres and a mule" or to provide aid to establish schools. Without land or education, the former slaves had to work for their former masters as hired hands—as **sharecroppers.** They weren't much better off than they had been.

Landowners designed a system to make them dependent. A landowner allowed his sharecroppers to sell half of their crop and keep the proceeds, but he paid so little, regardless of how hard the farmers worked, that the families had to borrow to tide themselves over the winter. The next year, they had to work for the same landowner again to pay off their debts. The cycle continued, year after year. And lacking education, most sharecroppers didn't keep any records, so they didn't know how much they owed, and many were cheated.

During Reconstruction, the Union Army, which occupied the South, enforced the new amendments and acts. Military commanders established procedures to register voters and hold elections. The commanders also started schools for the children of former slaves. But the army didn't have enough troops in the region to maintain Reconstruction policies (just as our military didn't have enough troops in Iraq to maintain order). And in state after state, the South resisted.

Eventually, the North capitulated. The 1876 presidential election between Republican Rutherford Hayes and Democrat Samuel Tilden was disputed in some states. To resolve the dispute, Republicans, most of whom were northerners, and Democrats, many of whom were southerners, agreed to a compromise: Hayes would be named president, and the remaining Union troops would be removed from the South. Without the Union troops, there was no way to enforce the Reconstruction policies.

The collapse of Reconstruction limited the impact of the Civil War. In effect, the South was allowed to nullify one result of the war—granting legal and political rights to blacks—in exchange for accepting two other results—preserving the Union and abolishing slavery.

In hindsight, it isn't surprising that Reconstruction didn't accomplish more. It was difficult, if not impossible, to integrate four million former slaves into a society that was bitter in its defeat and weak in its economy. Northerners who expected progress to come smoothly were naive. When it didn't come quickly, they grew weary. At the same time, there was a desire for healing between the regions and lingering feelings for continuity with the past.

Public attitudes during Reconstruction thus began a recurring cycle that continues to this day: periodically the public gets upset about the treatment of African Americans and determined to improve the conditions. But the public is naive and impatient, and when the efforts don't produce the results they expect as soon as they expect, the public becomes disillusioned with the efforts and dissatisfied with their costs. Then the public forces the government to put the race problem on the back burner until some future generation picks it up again.[13]

Segregation

In both the South and the North, blacks came to be segregated from whites.

Segregation in the South The reconciliation between Republicans and Democrats—northerners and southerners—was effected at the expense of blacks.

A rest stop for Greyhound bus passengers between Louisville, Kentucky, and Nashville, Tennessee, in 1943 depicts the segregation at the time.

Library of Congress # LC-USW3-037919

Removing the troops enabled the South to govern itself again, and this enabled the South to reduce blacks to near-slave status.

Before the Civil War, there was no segregation in rural areas, where slaves' shacks sat near plantation mansions, or in urban areas, where few blocks were solidly black. Segregation would have been inconvenient, with blacks and whites working in proximity, and it would have been unnecessary—slavery itself kept blacks at the bottom of society. But after slavery was abolished, southerners established segregation as a new way to keep blacks "in their place."

The southern states established a pervasive pattern of **Jim Crow laws** by the turn of the century.[14] These laws segregated residential areas—city blocks or whole neighborhoods. Some small towns excluded blacks altogether, either by passing explicit laws or by adopting **sundown laws,** which required blacks to be off the streets by dark or 10 P.M.

Other Jim Crow laws segregated schools, which blacks had been allowed to attend during Reconstruction, and even textbooks (black schools' texts had to be stored separately from white schools' books).

Many laws segregated public accommodations, such as hotels, restaurants, bars, theaters, and streetcars. Other laws segregated sporting events, circuses, and parks. They separated black and white checkers players in Birmingham and districts for black and white prostitutes in New Orleans.

The laws were pervasive, segregating entrances, exits, ticket windows, waiting rooms, restrooms, and drinking fountains. They segregated the races in prisons, hospitals, and homes for the blind. They even segregated the races in death—in morgues, funeral homes, and cemeteries.

Although blacks were denied access to better locations or facilities, the greatest damage from segregation is that they were degraded. The system of Jim Crow laws was "an officially organized degradation ceremony, repeated day after day." Segregation told blacks that they were inferior and did not belong in the communities in which they lived.[15]

In addition to the laws, blacks were forced to defer to whites in informal settings as well—for instance, to move off the sidewalk when a white pedestrian approached. Failure to defer could bring punishment for being "uppity." Blacks were "humiliated by a thousand daily reminders of their subordination."[16]

Meanwhile, northern leaders, who had championed the cause of the slaves before and during the Civil War, abandoned African Americans a decade after the war.

Congress declined to pass new laws, presidents refused to enforce existing laws, and the Supreme Court gutted the constitutional amendments and Civil Rights Acts.[17]

Then the Court upheld segregation itself. Louisiana passed "an Act to promote the comfort of passengers," which mandated separate accommodations in trains. New Orleans black leaders sponsored a test case challenging the act's constitutionality. Homer Adolph Plessy sat in the white car. When the conductor ordered him to move to the black car, Plessy refused. He maintained that the act was unconstitutional under the Fourteenth Amendment. In **Plessy v. Ferguson** in 1896, the Court disagreed, claiming that the act was not a denial of equal protection because it provided equal accommodations.[18] The Court established the **separate-but-equal doctrine,** which allowed separate facilities if they were "equal." Of course, government required separate facilities only because people thought the races were not equal, but the Court brazenly commented that the act did not stamp "the colored race with a badge of inferiority" unless "the colored race chooses to put that construction on it." Only Justice John Harlan, a former Kentucky slaveholder, dissented: "Our Constitution is

Lynching occurred not only in the South but also in northern cities such as Marion, Indiana, in 1930. The girls on the left hold pieces of the victims' clothing, torn off as "souvenirs."

color-blind, and neither knows nor tolerates classes among citizens."

Three years later, the Court accepted segregation in schools.[19] A Georgia school board turned a black high school into a black elementary school without establishing a new high school for blacks or allowing them to attend the existing high schools for whites. Nevertheless, the Court said this action was not a denial of equal protection. Its ruling set a pattern in which separate but equal meant separation but not equality.

Segregation in the North Although Jim Crow laws were not as pervasive in the North as in the South, they were quite common. In fact, sundown laws were more prevalent in the North, especially in the Midwest. In the 1930s, Hawthorne, California, posted a sign at its city limits: "Nigger, Don't Let The Sun Set On YOU In Hawthorne."[20] Jim Crow laws in the northern states prompted one writer to proclaim, "The North has surrendered!"[21]

Yet job opportunities were better in the North. While southern blacks were sharecropping—by 1930, 80 percent of those who farmed were still working somebody else's land[22]—northern factories were offering jobs. Between 1915 and 1940, more than a million southern blacks headed north in the **Great Migration.** Although they got decent jobs, they were forced to live in black ghettos because they couldn't afford better housing and weren't allowed to live in some areas anyway.

Denial of the Right to Vote

With the adoption of the Fifteenth Amendment, many African Americans voted and elected fellow African Americans to office during Reconstruction, but southern states began to disfranchise them in the 1890s (as explained in Chapter 7).

Violence

To solidify their control, whites engaged in violence against blacks. In the 1880s and 1890s, whites lynched about one hundred blacks a year. In the 1900s, vigilante "justice" continued (see Table 1). For example, a mob in Livermore, Kentucky, dragged a black man accused of murdering a white man into a theater. The ringleaders charged admission and hanged the man. Then they allowed the audience to shoot at the swinging body—those in the balcony could fire once; those in the better seats could empty their revolvers.[23]

Lynchings often began with a false report of a white woman being sexually assaulted by a black man. An irate mob would gather and, after locating the man, would subject him to an excruciating ordeal. Usually they castrated him before they killed him. Frequently, they hacked off his fingers and ears as well.[24]

Lynchings were not the result of a few troublemakers; rather, they were a social institution in the South. The ritualized spectacles were a desperate attempt to cling to the antebellum order upset by the Civil War. At the same time, lynchings were an outgrowth of the increase in white women who worked outside the home at the turn of the century. As these women experienced greater independence, insecure men feared that the women would become too independent, perhaps even leave them for black men. Hence the ritual of castration.[25] Through lynchings, then, white men could remain in charge—at home as well as in society—while appearing to defend women's honor.

Lynchings were considered entertaining as well as essential to maintain order. They would be photo-

Table 1	Why Whites Lynched Blacks in 1907

Whites gave the following reasons for lynching blacks, who may or may not have committed the acts cited.

Reason	Number of Lynchings
Murder	5
Attempted murder	5
Manslaughter	10
Rape	9
Attempted rape	11
Burglary	3
Harboring a fugitive	1
Theft of 75 cents	1
Having a debt of $3	2
Winning a fight with a white man	1
Insulting a white man	1
Talking to white girls on the telephone	1
Being the wife or son of a rapist	2
Being the father of a boy who "jostled" white women	1
Expressing sympathy for the victim of mob violence	3

SOURCE: Adapted from Ray Stannard Baker, *Following the Color Line* (New York: Harper & Row, 1964), 176–177.

graphed and, later, postcards would be sold (though after 1907 they could no longer be mailed, according to a postal regulation).

In 1919, twenty-five race riots erupted in six months. White mobs took over cities in the North and South, burning black neighborhoods and terrorizing black residents for days on end.[26] In 1921, ten thousand whites burned down thirty-five blocks of Tulsa's black neighborhood. The incident that precipitated the riot was typical—a report of an assault by a black man on a white woman. The report was false, fabricated by the woman (and later retracted), but residents were inflamed by a racist newspaper and encouraged by the city's officials. Almost three hundred people were shot, burned alive, or tied to cars and dragged to death. Survivors reported corpses stacked like firewood on street corners and piled high in dump trucks.[27]

The white supremacist **Ku Klux Klan,** which began during Reconstruction and started up again in 1915, played a major role in inflaming prejudice and terrorizing blacks. It was strong enough to dominate many southern towns and even the state governments of Oklahoma and Texas. It also made inroads into some northern states such as Indiana.

In addition, bands of white farmers known as "Whitecaps" nailed notes, with a drawing of a coffin and a warning to leave or die, on the doors of black farmers. Their goal was to drive black farmers off the land. Then the local governments put the land up for auction or simply gave it to the white families who owned the adjacent land.[28] The impact of this intimidation continued for many generations and, in fact, continues to this day. The black families lost wealth, for themselves and their descendants, and the white families gained wealth that is appreciating in value for their descendants today, many of whom may be unaware of how "their" land changed hands.

Federal officials contended that racial violence was a state problem—presidents refused to speak out, and Congress refused to pass legislation making lynching a federal offense—yet state officials did nothing.

For at least the first third of the twentieth century, white supremacy reigned—in the southern states, the border states, and many northern states. It also pervaded the nation's capital, where President Woodrow Wilson instituted segregation in the federal government.[29]

Overcoming Discrimination against African Americans

African Americans fought white supremacy primarily in three arenas: the courts, the streets, and Congress. In general, they fought in the courts first and Congress last, although as they gained momentum they increasingly fought in all three arenas at once.

The Movement in the Courts

The first goal was to convince the Supreme Court to overturn the separate-but-equal doctrine of *Plessy* v. *Ferguson.*

The NAACP In response to racial violence, a group of blacks and whites founded the National Association for

Tulsa's black neighborhood after whites burned it down in 1921.

Tulsa Historical Society

the Advancement of Colored People, or **NAACP,** in 1909. In its first two decades, it was led by **W. E. B. Du Bois,** a black sociologist. In time, it became the major organization fighting for blacks' civil rights.

Frustrated by presidential and congressional inaction, the NAACP decided to appeal to the courts, which are less subject to political pressure from the majority. The association assembled a cadre of lawyers, mainly from Howard University Law School, a historically black school in Washington, D.C., to bring lawsuits attacking segregation and the denial of the right to vote. In 1915, they persuaded the Supreme Court to strike down the grandfather clause (which exempted persons whose ancestors could vote from the literacy test);[30] two years later, they convinced the Court to invalidate residential segregation laws.[31] But the Court continued to allow most devices to disfranchise blacks and most efforts to segregate.

In 1938, the NAACP chose a thirty-year-old attorney, **Thurgood Marshall,** to head its litigation arm.[32] Marshall—whose mother had to pawn her engagement and wedding rings so he could go to an out-of-state law school because his in-state school, the University of Maryland, didn't admit blacks—would become a tireless and courageous advocate for equal rights. (In 1946, after defending four blacks charged with attempted murder during a riot in rural Tennessee, he would narrowly escape a lynch mob.)[33]

Desegregation of schools Seventeen states and the District of Columbia segregated their schools (and four other states allowed cities to segregate their schools). The states gave white students better facilities and white teachers larger salaries. Overall, they spent from two to ten times more on white schools than on black ones.[34] Few of these states had graduate schools for blacks: as late as 1950, they had fifteen engineering schools, fourteen medical schools, and five dental schools for whites and none for blacks; they had sixteen law schools for whites and five for blacks.

The NAACP's tactics were first to show that "separate but equal" actually resulted in unequal schools and then, attacking the concept head-on, to argue that "separate but equal" led to unequal status in general.

The NAACP challenged segregation in graduate schools. Missouri provided no black law school but offered to reimburse blacks who went to out-of-state law schools. In 1938, the Supreme Court said the state had to provide black students a law school or admit them to the white school.[35] Texas established a black law school,

but it was clearly inferior to the white law school at the University of Texas. In 1950, the Court said the black school had to be substantially equal to the white school.[36] Oklahoma allowed a black student to attend the white graduate school at the University of Oklahoma but designated a separate section of the classroom, library, and cafeteria for the student. The Court said this, too, was inadequate because it deprived the student of the exchange of views with fellow students necessary for education.[37] The Court didn't invalidate the separate-but-equal doctrine in these decisions, but it made segregation almost impossible to implement in graduate schools.

The NAACP turned its attention to the lower levels of the school system. Marshall filed suits in two southern states, one border state, one northern state, and the District of Columbia. The suit in the northern state was brought against Topeka, Kansas, where Linda Brown could not attend the school just four blocks from her home because it was a white school. Instead, she had to go to a school twenty-one blocks away.[38]

When the cases reached the Supreme Court, the justices were split. Although Chief Justice Fred Vinson might have had a majority to uphold the separate-but-equal doctrine, the Court put off a decision and rescheduled oral arguments for its next term. Between the Court's terms, Vinson suffered a heart attack, and President **Dwight Eisenhower** appointed **Earl Warren** to take his place. When the Court reheard the case, the president pressured his appointee to rule in favor of segregation. Eisenhower invited Warren and the attorney for the states to the White House for dinner. When the conversation turned to the segregationists, Eisenhower said, "These are not bad people. All they are concerned about is to see that their sweet little girls are not required to sit in schools alongside some big overgrown Negroes."[39] However, Warren not only voted against segregation but used his considerable determination and charm to persuade the other justices, some of whom had supported segregation, to vote against it too. Justice Felix Frankfurter later said Vinson's heart attack was "the first indication I have ever had that there is a God."[40]

In the landmark case of ***Brown v. Board of Education*** in 1954, the **Warren Court** ruled unanimously that school segregation violated the Fourteenth Amendment's equal protection clause.[41] In the opinion, Warren asserted that separate but equal not only resulted in unequal schools but was inherently unequal because it made black children feel inferior.

In overruling the *Plessy* doctrine, the Court showed how revolutionary the equal protection clause was—or could be interpreted to be. The Court required the segregated states to change their way of life to a degree unprecedented in American history.

After overturning laws requiring segregation in schools, the Court overruled laws mandating segregation in other places, such as public parks, golf courses, swimming pools, auditoriums, courtrooms, and jails.[42]

In *Brown,* the Court had ordered the schools to desegregate "with all deliberate speed."[43] This standard was a compromise between justices who thought schools should do so immediately and those who thought communities would need to do so gradually.[44] The ambiguity of the phrase, however, allowed the communities to do so slowly, even imperceptibly. The ruling prompted much deliberation but little speed.

The South engaged in massive resistance. The Court needed help from the other branches, but Congress was controlled by southerners and President Eisenhower was reluctant to tell the states to change. In fact, the president criticized the decision. With his power and immense popularity, he could have speeded implementation by speaking out in support of the ruling, yet he offered no help for three years. When nine black students tried to attend a white high school under a desegregation plan in Little Rock, Arkansas, the governor's and state legislature's inflammatory rhetoric against desegregation encouraged local citizens to take the law into their own hands. Finally, Eisenhower acted, sending federal troops and federalizing the state's national guard to quell the riot.

President Kennedy also used federal marshals and paratroopers to stop the violence after the governor of Mississippi blocked the door to keep James Meredith from registering at the University of Mississippi. Kennedy again sent troops when the governor of Alabama, **George Wallace,** proclaiming "segregation now, segregation to-

Dorothy Counts, the first black student to attend one white high school in Charlotte, North Carolina, is escorted by her father in 1957.

AP/WideWorld Photos

morrow, segregation forever," blocked the door to keep blacks from enrolling at the University of Alabama.

After outright defiance, some states attempted to circumvent the ruling by shutting down their public schools and providing tuition grants, textbooks, and recreation facilities for students to use at new private schools, which at the time could segregate.

The states also tried less blatant schemes, such as "freedom of choice" plans that allowed the students to choose the school they wanted to attend. Of course, virtually no whites chose a black school, and due to social pressure very few blacks chose a white school. The idea was to achieve desegregation on paper, or token desegregation in practice, in order to avoid actual desegregation. But the Court rebuffed these schemes and even forbade private schools from discriminating.[45]

To black southerners, the Court's persistence raised hopes. Chief Justice Warren, according to Thurgood Marshall, "allowed the poor Negro sharecropper to say, 'Kick me around Mr. Sheriff, kick me around Mr. County Judge, kick me around Supreme Court of my state, but there's one person I can rely on.'"[46]

To white southerners, however, the Court's rulings reflected a federal government, a distant authority, that was exercising too much control over their traditional practices. The rulings engendered much bitterness. Justice Hugo Black, who was from Alabama, was shunned by former friends from the state, and his son was driven from his legal practice in the state. The justice wasn't even sent an invitation to his fiftieth reunion at his alma mater, the University of Alabama.[47]

Despite the Court's rulings, progress was excruciatingly slow. If a school district was segregated, a group like the NAACP had to run the risks and spend the money to bring a suit in a federal district court. Judges in these courts reflected the views of the state or local political establishment, so the suit might not be successful. If it was, the school board would prepare a desegregation plan. Members of the school board reflected the views of the community and the pressures from the segregationists, so the plan might not be adequate. If it was, the segregationists would challenge it in a federal district court. If the plan was upheld, the segregationists would appeal to a federal court of appeals. Judges in these courts, based in Richmond and New Orleans, came from the South, but they were not as tied to the state or local political establishment, and they usually ruled against the segregationists. But then the segregationists could appeal to the Supreme Court. The segregationists knew they would lose sooner or later, but the process took several years, so they could delay the inevitable.

Thus the segregationists tried to resist, then to evade, and finally to delay. In this they succeeded. In 1964, a decade after *Brown,* 98 percent of all black children in the South still attended all-black schools.[48]

By this time, the mood in Congress had changed. Congress passed the Civil Rights Act of 1964, which, among other things, cut off federal aid to school districts that continued to segregate. The following year, it passed the first major program providing federal aid to education. This was the carrot at the end of the stick; school districts complied to get the money.

Finally, by 1970, only 14 percent of all black children in the South still attended all-black schools. Of course, some went to mostly black schools. Even so, the change was dramatic.

Busing

Brown and related rulings addressed **de jure segregation**—segregation enforced by law. This segregation can be attacked by striking down the law. *Brown* didn't address **de facto segregation**—segregation based on

residential patterns—typical of northern cities and large southern cities, where most blacks live in black neighborhoods and most whites live in white neighborhoods. Students attend their neighborhood schools, which are mostly black or mostly white. This segregation is more intractable because it doesn't stem primarily from a law, so it can't be eliminated by striking down a law.

Civil rights groups proposed busing some black children to schools in white neighborhoods and some white children to schools in black neighborhoods. They hoped to improve black children's education, their self-confidence, and eventually, their college and career opportunities. They also hoped to improve black and white children's ability to get along together.

The **Burger Court** authorized busing within school districts—ordinarily cities. These included southern cities where there was a history of *de jure* segregation, and northern cities where there was a pattern of *de facto* segregation and evidence that school officials had located schools or assigned students in ways that perpetuated this segregation.[49]

However, busing for desegregation was never extensive. In one typical year, only 4 percent of students were bused for desegregation. Far more students were bused, at public expense, to segregated public and private schools.[50]

Even so, court orders for mandatory busing ran into a wall of hostile public opinion. White parents criticized the courts sharply. Their reaction stemmed from a mixture of prejudice against black people, bias against poor persons, fear of the crime in inner-city schools, worry about the quality of inner-city schools, and desire for the convenience of neighborhood schools.[51]

Due to the opposition of white parents, busing—and publicity about it—prompted an increase in "white flight" as white families moved from public schools to private schools and from the cities to the suburbs to avoid the busing in the cities.[52] This trend overlapped other trends, especially a reduction in the white birthrate and an increase in the nonwhite immigration rate, which altered the racial and economic composition of our big cities. As a result, there were fewer white students to balance enrollments and fewer middle-class students to provide stability in the cities' schools.

Therefore, even extensive busing couldn't desegregate the school systems of most big cities, where blacks and other minorities together were more numerous than whites. Consequently, civil rights groups proposed busing some white children from the suburbs to the cities and some black children from the cities to the suburbs. This approach would provide enough of both races to achieve balance in both places.

The Burger Court rejected this proposal by a 5–4 vote in 1974.[53] It ruled that busing isn't appropriate between school districts unless there is evidence of intentional segregation in both the city and its suburbs. Otherwise, such extensive busing would require too long a ride for students and too much coordination by administrators.

Although there was intentional segregation by many cities and their suburbs,[54] the evidence is not as clear-cut as that of the *de jure* segregation by the southern states, so it was difficult to satisfy the requirements laid down by the Court. The ruling made busing between the cities and their suburbs very rare.

Thurgood Marshall, by then a Supreme Court justice, dissented and predicted that the ruling would allow "our great metropolitan areas to be divided up each into two cities—one white, the other black." Indeed, the ruling was the beginning of the end of the push to desegregate public schools in urban areas.

In 1991, the **Rehnquist Court** ruled that school districts have no obligation to reduce *de facto* segregation, and the Court also diminished their obligation to reduce the vestiges of *de jure* segregation.[55] This ruling relieved the pressure on school districts, and most stopped busing.[56] The result was increasing resegregation.

Some districts tried other ways to balance enrollments. The county that includes Louisville, Kentucky, voluntarily adopted a "managed choice" program in which parents indicated their preference for the schools their children would attend, but the school district kept the black enrollment in each school between 15 and 50 percent. To do this, the district used extensive busing. Yet the plan was popular with most parents, including white parents, almost all of whom got their first or second choice of schools.[57] Louisville became one of the most desegregated cities in the nation.

In 2007, however, the **Roberts Court** invalidated the Louisville program and a limited program in Seat-

Busing led to riots in cities such as Boston. In 1976, protesters assault Ted Landsmark, a lawyer who came around the corner at the wrong time.

© Stanley J. Forman, Pulitzer Prize, 1977

tle.[58] The five-justice majority ruled that school districts can't use race as a basis for assigning students. The ruling may jeopardize the programs in a thousand school districts across the country.[59]

The Court's decisions in the 1990s and 2000s reflect none of "the moral urgency of *Brown*."[60] Instead, they reflect hostility toward government efforts, even school districts' voluntary efforts, to achieve desegregation. For most justices, desegregation is relatively unimportant, certainly less important than allowing white parents unfettered choice where they send their children. In this way, the Court's majority mirrors the views of the Republican presidents who appointed them.

The Movement in the Streets

After the NAACP's early successes in the courts, other blacks, and some whites, took the fight to the streets. Their bold efforts gave birth to the modern civil rights movement.

The movement came to public attention in Montgomery, Alabama, in 1955, when Rosa Parks refused to move to the back of the bus. Her courage, and her arrest, roused others to boycott city buses. For their leader they chose a young Baptist minister, Dr. **Martin Luther King Jr.** The boycott catapulted the movement and King to national attention (as explained in Chapter 5).

King was the first charismatic leader of the movement. He formed the Southern Christian Leadership Conference (SCLC) of black clergy and adopted the tactics of Mahatma Gandhi, who had led the movement to free India from the British. The tactics included direct action, such as demonstrations and marches, and civil disobedience—intentional and public disobedience of unjust laws. The tactics were based on nonviolence, even when confronted with violence. This strategy was designed to draw support from whites by contrasting the morality of the movement's position with the immorality of the opponents' discrimination and violence toward blacks.

For a long time, some southern whites, focusing on movement leaders and college students from other states, and fearing even infiltration by foreign communists, deluded themselves into thinking that "outside agitators" were responsible for the turmoil in their communities.[61] But the movement grew from the grass roots, and it eventually shattered this delusion.

The movement spread among black students. In 1960, four students of North Carolina A&T College sat at the lunch counter in Woolworth's, a chain of dime stores, and asked for a cup of coffee. The waitress refused to serve them, but they remained until they were arrested. On successive days, as whites waved the Confederate flag and jeered, more students sat at the lunch counter.[62] Within a year, such sit-ins occurred in more than one hundred cities.

When blacks asserted their rights, whites often reacted with violence. In 1963, King led demonstrators in Birmingham, Alabama, seeking desegregation of public facilities. Police unleashed dogs to attack the marchers. In 1964, King led demonstrators in Selma, Alabama, for voting rights. State troopers clubbed some marchers, and vigilantes beat and shot others.

In the summer of 1964, black and white college students mounted a voter registration drive in Mississippi. By the end of the summer, one thousand had been arrested, eighty beaten, thirty-five shot, and six killed.[63] When a black cotton farmer, who had tried to register to vote, was shot in the head in broad daylight by a white state legislator, the act wasn't even treated as a crime.[64]

Indeed, perpetrators of the violence usually were not apprehended or prosecuted. When they were, they usually were not convicted. Law enforcement was fre-

quently in the hands of bigots, and juries were normally all white.[65]

During these years, whites told pollsters they disliked the civil rights movement's speed and tactics: "They're pushing too fast and too hard." At the same time, most said they favored integration more than ever. And they seemed repelled by the violence. The brutality against black demonstrators generated more support for black Americans and their cause.

The media, especially national organizations based in northern cities such as the *New York Times,* the Associated Press, and the major television networks, played a role simply by covering the conflict. The leaders of the civil rights movement staged events that captured attention, and violent racists played into their hands. As northern reporters and photographers relayed the events and violence to the nation, the movement gained public sympathy in the North. Yet the national press became as vilified as the federal government in the South. (This anger would fuel southerners' distrust of the media for many years.)[66]

Although the movement's tactics worked well against southern *de jure* segregation, they did not work as well against northern *de facto* segregation or against job discrimination in either region. By the mid-1960s, prog-

President Lyndon Johnson and Martin Luther King Jr., compatriots with a tense relationship.

ress had stalled and dissatisfaction had grown. Young blacks from the inner city, who hadn't been involved in the movement, questioned two of its principles: interracialism and nonviolence. As James Farmer, head of the Congress of Racial Equality (CORE), explained, they asked, "What is this we-shall-overcome, black-and-white-together stuff? I don't know of any white folks except the guy who runs that store on 125th Street in Harlem and garnishes wages and repossesses things you buy. I'd like to go upside his head. [Or] the rent collector, who bangs on the door demanding rent that we ain't got. I'd like to go upside his head."[67] These blacks criticized King and his tactics. In place of the integration advocated by King, some leaders began to call for "black power." This phrase, which implied black pride and self-reliance, meant different things to different people. To some it meant political power through the ballot box, and to others it meant economic power through business ownership. To a few it meant violence in retaliation for violence by whites. The movement splintered further.

The Movement in Congress

As the civil rights movement expanded, it pressured presidents and members of Congress to act. President **John Kennedy,** who was most concerned about the Cold War, considered civil rights a distraction. President **Lyndon Johnson,** who was a champion of "the poor and the downtrodden and the oppressed"—a biographer calls him our second most compassionate president, after Abraham Lincoln[68]—supported civil rights but felt hamstrung by the southerners in Congress who, through the seniority system, chaired key committees and dominated both houses. As a result, the presidents considered the civil rights leaders unreasonable, because their movement alienated the southerners on whom the presidents had to rely for other legislation.

But once the movement demonstrated real strength, it convinced the officials to act. After two hundred thousand blacks and whites marched in Washington in 1963, President Kennedy introduced civil rights legislation. His successor, President Johnson, with consummate legislative skill, forged a coalition of northern Democrats and northern Republicans to overcome southern Democrats and pass the Civil Rights Act of 1964. After one thousand blacks and whites had been attacked and arrested in Selma, Johnson introduced and Congress passed the Voting Rights Act of 1965. Three years later, Johnson introduced and Congress passed the Civil Rights Act of 1968. Within a span of four years,

Congress passed legislation prohibiting discrimination in public accommodations, employment, housing, and voting. These would become the most significant civil rights acts in history.

It is impossible to exaggerate how controversial these laws were. In 1964, the Republican nominee for president, Sen. Barry Goldwater of Arizona, opposed the Civil Rights Act. He had been assured by two advisers—Phoenix attorney William Rehnquist and Yale professor Robert Bork—that it was unconstitutional.[69] The conservative Republican Ronald Reagan, preparing to run for California governor, also strongly opposed the act.[70] (Years later, as president, Reagan would appoint Rehnquist as chief justice and nominate Bork to serve as an associate justice on the Supreme Court.)

Although President Johnson believed he was doing the right thing, he realized the political ramifications. He said he was handing the South to the Republican Party "for the next fifty years."[71] And that's exactly what happened. In less than a decade, the South went from the most Democratic region to one of the most Republican regions in the country.[72]

After the 1966 congressional elections, when it was evident that the party was losing southern voters, Democratic governors in southern and border states demanded a meeting with Johnson. They criticized administration efforts to desegregate the schools and even suggested that the president was a traitor to his heritage. The next day Johnson was still fuming. To an aide he vented, "'Niggah! Niggah! Niggah!' That's all they said to me all day. Hell, there's one thing they'd better know. If I don't achieve anything else while I'm president, I intend to wipe that word out of the English language and make it impossible for people to come here and shout 'Niggah! Niggah! Niggah!' to me and the American people."[73]

Desegregation of public accommodations The **Civil Rights Act of 1964** prohibits discrimination on the basis of race, color, religion, or national origin in public accommodations.[74] The act doesn't cover private clubs, such as country clubs, social clubs, or fraternities and sororities, on the principle that the government shouldn't tell people with whom they may or may not associate in private. (The Court has made private schools an exception to this principle to help enforce *Brown,* so they can't discriminate.)

Desegregation of employment The Civil Rights Act of 1964 also prohibits employment discrimination on the basis of race, color, religion, national origin, or sex and (as amended) physical disability, age, or Vietnam-era veteran status. The act covers employers with fifteen or more employees and unions.[75]

In addition to practicing blatant discrimination, some employers practiced more subtle discrimination. They required applicants to meet standards unnecessary for the jobs, a practice that hindered blacks more than whites. A high school diploma for a manual job was a common example. The Court held that the standards must relate to the jobs.[76]

Desegregation of housing Although the Supreme Court had struck down laws that prescribed segregation in residential areas, whites maintained segregation by making **restrictive covenants**—agreements among neighbors not to sell their houses to blacks. In 1948, the Court ruled that courts could not enforce these covenants because doing so would involve the government in discrimination.[77]

Real estate agents also played a role in segregation by practicing **steering**—showing blacks houses in black neighborhoods and whites houses in white neighborhoods. Unscrupulous real estate agents practiced **blockbusting.** After a black family bought a house in a white neighborhood, the agents would warn white families that more blacks would move in. Because of prejudice and fear that their houses' values would decline, whites would panic and sell to the agents at low prices. Then the agents would resell to blacks at higher prices. In this way, neighborhoods that might have been desegregated were instead resegregated—from all white to all black.

Banks and savings and loans also played a role. They were reluctant to lend money to blacks who wanted to buy a house in a white neighborhood. Some engaged in **redlining**—refusing to lend money to people who wanted to buy a house in a racially changing neighborhood. The lenders worried that if the buyer could not keep up with the payments, the lender would be left with a house whose value had declined.

The government also played an important role. The Veterans Administration and the Federal Housing Authority, which guaranteed loans to some buyers, were reluctant to authorize loans to blacks who tried to buy houses in white neighborhoods (but they did provide loans to whites who fled from the cities to buy houses in all-white suburbs). And the federal government, which funded low-income housing, allowed local governments to locate such housing in ghettos. In these

ways, the governments fostered and extended residential segregation (which is at the heart of the segregation of the schools and other activities such as neighborhood sports and commerce).[78]

The **Civil Rights Act of 1968** bans discrimination in the sale or rental of housing on the basis of race, color, religion, or national origin and (as amended) on the basis of sex, having children, or having a disability. The act covers 80 percent of the housing and prohibits steering, blockbusting, and redlining.

Restoration of the right to vote The Voting Rights Act of 1965, which implemented the Fifteenth Amendment, includes measures that enable blacks to vote (as explained in Chapter 7).

Continuing Discrimination against African Americans

African Americans have overcome much discrimination but still face lingering prejudice. Overt laws and blatant practices have been struck down, but subtle manifestations of old attitudes persist—and in ways far more numerous and with effects far more serious than this one chapter can convey.[79] Moreover, African Americans must cope with the legacy of generations of slavery, segregation, discrimination, and for many, the effects of poverty.

They also must cope with the attitudes of whites. Although few people say they want to return to the days of legal segregation, about half reject the dream of an integrated society.[80] (See the box "How Much Is White Skin Worth?" on page 402 for a hypothetical but telling response to discrimination.)

Discrimination in Education

Segregated schools Some black children, mostly those who have affluent parents who pay for private schools or live in well-off neighborhoods with good public schools, go to integrated schools. However, most black children, especially those who live in big cities or areas where private schools predominate, go to segregated schools.

Although *de jure* segregation of schools has been eliminated, *de facto* segregation remains. In fact, this segregation is getting worse. After progress in the 1960s, 1970s, and 1980s, the trend toward desegregation reversed itself in the 1990s. "For the first time since the *Brown* v. *Board* decision," one study concluded, "we are going backwards"[81] (see Figure 1). A smaller proportion of black and Latino students attend schools that have a majority of white students than at any time since 1968.[82] One-third of black students attend schools that are 90 to 100 percent minority.[83]

The segregation is worse in the North, where it has been *de facto,* than in the South, where it had been *de jure.*[84] In the Northeast and Midwest, more than one-fourth of black and Latino students attend schools that are 99 to 100 percent nonwhite.[85]

The resegregation is due to white flight to private schools and to the suburbs, leaving fewer white children, and due to higher nonwhite birthrates and immigration rates, bringing more nonwhite children to the public schools.

These changes affect the decisions of white parents who look for schools with low numbers of racial minorities.[86] Although many say they move for "better schools," few ever visit the schools or check the schools' test scores before moving. They use racial composition as a proxy for school quality. The more racial minorities, the poorer the quality, they assume.[87]

To an extent, the resegregation is also due to a shift in government policies and court decisions, which sent the message to school districts that desegregation is no longer an important national goal.[88]

The persistence of *de facto* segregation and the waning of society's commitment to integration have led national, state, and local officials to adopt a resigned attitude: "We still agree with the goal of school desegregation, but it's too hard, and we're tired of it, and we give up."[89]

Reforms proposed for urban schools rarely include desegregation. Officials speak of a ghetto school that is more "efficient" or one that gets more "input" from ghetto parents or offers more "choices" for ghetto children. But they seem to accept segregated education as "a permanent American reality."[90]

A writer who visited many central-city classrooms and talked with students, teachers, and administrators observed that Martin Luther King was treated as "an icon, but his vision of a nation in which black and white kids went to school together seemed to be effaced almost entirely. Dutiful references to 'The Dream' were often seen in school brochures and on wall posters in February, when 'Black History' was celebrated in the public schools, but the content of the dream was treated as a closed box that could not be opened without ruining the celebration."[91]

Indeed, many cities have a school named after King—a segregated school in a segregated neighborhood—"like a terrible joke on history," a fourteen-year-old, wise beyond her years, remarked.[92] In fact, if you want to find a school that's really segregated, look for the schools named after champions of integration— Jackie Robinson, Rosa Parks, and Thurgood Marshall.[93]

Some minorities have gotten so frustrated that they themselves have questioned the goal of school desegregation. Instead, they have voiced greater concern about improving the quality and safety of their schools and neighborhoods.[94] However, one education analyst observes, "For African Americans to have equal opportunity, higher test scores will not suffice. It is foolhardy to think black children can be taught, no matter how well, in isolation and then have the skills and confidence as adults to succeed in a white world where they have no experience."[95]

Unequal schools In areas where the schools are segregated, their quality varies enormously—from "the golden to the godawful," in the words of a Missouri judge.[96] And of course, blacks and Latinos are more likely to be in the "godawful" ones.

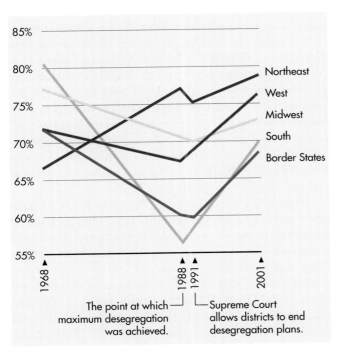

FIGURE 1 • **Resegregation of Schools** *Percentage of black students attending predominantly minority schools (schools in which 50%–100% of students are nonwhite)* SOURCE: The Civil Rights Project, Harvard University. Chart by L. Eckstein.

HOW MUCH IS WHITE SKIN WORTH?

*Y*ou will be visited tonight by an official you have never met. He begins by telling you he is extremely embarrassed. The organization he represents has made a mistake, something that hardly ever happens.

According to the group's records, he goes on, you were to have been born black—to another set of parents, far from where you were raised.

However, the rules being what they are, this error must be rectified, and as soon as possible. So at midnight tonight, you will become black. And this will mean not simply a darker skin but the bodily and facial features associated with African ancestry. However, inside you will be the person you always were. Your knowledge and ideas will remain intact. But outwardly you will not be recognizable to anyone you now know.

Your visitor emphasizes that being born to the wrong parents was in no way your fault.

Consequently, his organization is prepared to offer you some reasonable recompense. Would you, he asks, care to name a sum of money you might consider appropriate? He adds that his group is by no means poor. It can be quite generous when the circumstances warrant, as they seem to in your case. He finishes by saying that the records show you are scheduled to live another fifty years— as a black man or woman in America.

How much financial recompense would you request?

A professor who puts this parable to white college students finds that most feel $1 million per year—$50 million total—would be appropriate. This much would protect them from, and reimburse them for, the danger and discrimination they would face if they were perceived as black. In acknowledging that white skin is worth this much, the students also are admitting that treatment of the races is not nearly equal.

SOURCE: Andrew Hacker, *Two Nations: Black and White, Separate, Hostile, Unequal* (New York: Scribner, 1992), 31–32.

By virtually every measure of school quality—school funding, class size, teacher credentials, teacher salaries, breadth of curriculum, number of computers, opportunities for gifted students—these black and Latino children attend worse schools.[97]

Public schools are financed largely by property taxes paid by homeowners and businesses. Wealthy cities, where property costs more to buy and is assessed more in taxes, collect more in taxes than poor ones. In modern America, this means that suburban school districts have more to spend per pupil than central-city school districts.[98]

In about three-fourths of the states, school districts with the highest percentage of black and Latino children receive less funding than the districts with the fewest.[99] Nationwide, the difference amounts to $25,000 less per *classroom* per year for school districts with the most black and Latino children. In Illinois, the difference totals $47,000 less per classroom, and in New York, it totals $50,000 less.[100] And these official figures don't count the extra money that affluent parents, on their own or through PTAs, contribute to hire additional teachers to reduce class sizes or to provide art and music instruction, or to buy books for the library or equipment for the gym and playground.

Spending-per-pupil figures don't take into account the fact that the needs of poor children, after years of neglect and with scores of problems in their homes and neighborhoods, are greater than the needs of other children. Schools for poor children would require *more* funding to provide their students an *equal* education.

So many inner-city schools are bleak institutions, filthy and in disrepair. A 30-year veteran of seven District of Columbia schools said all should be condemned. Of her current school, she said, "I have to cover books, computers, and student work stations with plastic to catch the falling plaster and water from the leaking roof. In the school cafeteria, 55-gallon garbage cans are strategically placed to catch the water from gaping holes in the ceiling."[101] Teachers in some Los Angeles schools said the children count the rats.[102]

Most inner-city schools are overcrowded. They lack up-to-date texts and paper and pencils. They lack books for literature classes, chemicals for chemistry classes, and computers for computer classes. (Teachers *talk* about using computers.)[103]

Most inner-city schools can't attract enough good teachers. A New York City principal said he is forced to take the "tenth-best" teachers. "I thank God they're still breathing."[104] Even then, the schools can't fill all of their positions, so they must employ armies of substitute teachers to get through the year.

Despite the pattern of unequal funding, cash alone would not solve the problems of inner-city schools. Cultural and economic factors in these communities also restrict the quality of education available in these schools. But cash would help.

Some states have equalized funding for public schools, but the attempts to do so in other states have encountered fierce opposition. Some states have considered supplementary funding for inner-city schools, as an alternative to equalized funding, but people's priorities run in other directions. In 1999, the Pennsylvania legislature approved $160 million of public financing for new stadiums for the Eagles and Phillies and another $160 million of public financing for new stadiums for the Steelers and Pirates, while the schools in Philadelphia and Pittsburgh languished.[105]

Discrimination in Employment

Although the Civil Rights Act of 1964 and affirmative action (discussed later in the chapter) have prompted more employers to hire and promote African Americans, discrimination remains.

Researchers sent out fictional résumés for fictional applicants in response to help-wanted ads in Boston and Chicago newspapers. The fictional applicants with white-sounding names, such as Emily or Greg, received significantly more responses than the fictional applicants with black-sounding names, such as Lakisha or Jamal, even though all applicants had similar credentials.[106]

Other researchers used pairs of white and black high school graduates, matched according to their job histories and demeanors, to apply for low-skilled positions in Milwaukee. The white male applicants had a fictional record that included eighteen months in prison for possession of cocaine with intent to sell, while the black male applicants had no criminal record. Nonetheless, the whites received slightly more callbacks than the blacks.[107]

Many blacks who are hired encounter negative stereotypes that question their competence on the job. These workers are passed over when they could be promoted.[108] Other blacks who are hired face racial slurs in comments, notes, and graffiti from coworkers. They endure an unfriendly or hostile environment.[109] Although most upper-level executives realize that it is economically advantageous to have a diverse workforce, some middle-level white managers and lower-level white workers interact poorly with the black employees.

Discrimination in Housing

The Civil Rights Act of 1968, which prohibits discrimination in housing, has fostered some desegregation of housing, but extensive segregation persists.

One reason is economic. Many blacks don't have enough money to buy homes in white neighborhoods. But another reason is discrimination. Social pressure and occasional violence discourage blacks who try to move into white neighborhoods. Continuing discrimination by homeowners, real estate agents, lenders, and insurers also stymies them. A study of twenty metropolitan areas, using white and minority testers responding to house and apartment ads, found that blacks who try to buy a house face discrimination 17 percent of the time, and those who try to rent an apartment do so 22 percent of the time.[110] If callers sound black, landlords may claim that the apartment has already been rented.[111]

Although residential segregation remains pervasive in metropolitan areas, it is declining. The 2000 census shows that the fast-growing suburban areas in the West and South are much more likely to have integrated neighborhoods than a decade earlier, though the stagnant "rust belt" cities in the East and Midwest are integrating too, but more slowly.[112] Middle-class blacks who escape the ghetto often end up in black neighborhoods in the suburbs of these cities.[113]

Segregation doesn't continue because black people "want to live among their own kind," as some whites insist. Surveys show that only about 15 percent want to live in segregated neighborhoods, and most of them cite their fear of white hostility as the reason. Eighty-five percent would prefer mixed neighborhoods. Many say the optimal level would be half black and half white. But whites tend to move out when the concentration of blacks reaches 8 to 10 percent.[114] These contrasting attitudes make integration an elusive goal. Blacks constitute 13 percent of the population in the country but a much larger percentage in some cities.

These patterns and attitudes are all the more troublesome because residential segregation, of course, is at the heart of school segregation.

Discrimination in Other Ways

Law enforcement African Americans face discrimination from police officers. The practice of **racial profiling,** which is based on the assumption that minorities, especially males, are more likely to commit crimes, especially those involving drugs, targets minorities for stops and searches. Without evidence, officers stop minority drivers and search them and their vehicles.[115] Sometimes officers stop minority pedestrians as well. Although police departments deny profiling, statistics show clear evidence of the practice.

Nationwide, black, Latino, and white drivers are equally likely to be stopped, though black and Latino drivers are twice as likely to be searched. And white drivers are more likely to receive a written or verbal warning.[116] In some places, profiling is more pronounced. In Los Angeles, blacks are two times as likely to be stopped and four times as likely to be searched as other drivers. However, they are less likely to be found with illegal substances.[117] Interstate 95 from Florida to New York also has a notorious reputation.

African Americans speak of the moving violation "DWB"—*driving while black*. A Chicago journalist who was stopped at least every other time he traveled through the Midwest learned not to rent flashy Mustangs or wear his beret. Others avoid tinted windshields or expensive sunglasses—any flamboyance—to avoid the cops.[118] Former Rep. J. C. Watts (R-Okla.) was pulled over by police six times in one day in his home state.[119]

Profiling might be justified if it led to the apprehension of dangerous criminals, but apparently it does not. Although African American young men evidently do commit a larger percentage of certain crimes,[120] profiling does not lead the police to many criminals. When police stop motorists, they find no greater evidence of crimes by blacks and Hispanics than by whites.[121] Meanwhile, the encounters often humiliate those who are stopped and spark animosity toward the police in these communities (as the movie *Crash* so clearly depicted).

Some states and many counties and cities have taken steps to reduce profiling, such as recording data on every stop to see whether the police, or individual officers, are prone to profile. Yet the cops on the beat, who feel that profiling is useful, are reluctant to change their habits.

Other discrimination from police officers is less common but more serious. Sometimes officers arrest black citizens without legal cause, and occasionally they use excessive force against them. Numerous examples attest to improper beatings.[122] Sometimes officers lie while testifying against black suspects in court. As a result, even prominent African Americans say their "worst fear" is to go before the criminal justice system.[123] It is little wonder that black jurors hearing the O. J. Simpson trial and black citizens following it put less faith in the police testimony than white observers did.

Cautious parents teach their children how to avoid sending the wrong signals to police. Some parents urge their children not to wear street fashions and not to use cell phones, which from a distance might be mistaken as weapons. Some schools offer survival workshops for police encounters. Minority officers instruct the students what to do when they get stopped: Don't reach for an ID unless the officer asks for one; don't mumble or talk loudly; don't antagonize by asking for a badge number or threatening to file a complaint.[124]

Insults Most blacks, even professionals, face insults because of their race. Black women tell of being mistaken for hotel chambermaids by white guests at the hotels.[125] They tell of being mistaken for prostitutes, while waiting in hotel lobbies, by white men and police officers. A distinguished black political scientist was mistaken for a butler in his own home. Black doctors tell of dressing up to go shopping to avoid being regarded as shoplifters. But dressing up is no guarantee. A black lawyer, a senior partner in a large law firm, arrived at work early one morning, before the doors were unlocked. As he reached for his key, a young white lawyer, a junior associate in the firm, arrived at the same time, blocked his entrance, and asked, repeatedly and demandingly, "May I help you?" The white associate had taken the black partner for an intruder.[126] Although in these encounters the insults were unintentional, the stings hurt just the same. The accumulation of such incidents, which more than eight in ten blacks say they occasionally experience, has created a "black middle-class rage" among many.[127]

Overall, discrimination against African Americans continues. Whites speak of "past discrimination"—sometimes referring to slavery, sometimes to official segregation—but this phrase is misleading. Of course, there is a lot less discrimination now due to the civil rights movement, Supreme Court decisions, and congressional acts. However, there is nothing "past" about much "past discrimination."[128] The effects linger, and the discrimination itself persists.

Even when blacks point out the discrimination, some whites insist that little discrimination is left. These whites apparently assume that they know more than blacks do about what it is like to be black. Indeed, the perceptual gap between blacks and whites about the existence of discrimination is a real barrier to improved race relations. Whites who believe nothing is wrong don't favor actions to fix what they see as a nonexistent problem.

Improving Conditions for African Americans?

Despite continuing discrimination, African Americans have taken long strides toward achieving equal rights. These strides have led to much better living conditions for them and to a healthier racial climate in society. But serious problems remain.

Progress

Since the 1960s, blacks' lives have improved in most ways that can be measured.[129] Blacks have a lower poverty rate and a longer life expectancy than before. They have completed more years of education, with larger numbers attending college and graduate school. They have attained higher occupational levels—for example, tripling their proportion of the country's professionals[130]—and higher income levels. Many—well over half—have reached the middle class.[131] Almost half own their own homes,[132] and a third have moved to the suburbs.[133]

During the years that blacks' lives have improved, whites' racial attitudes have also improved. Although answers to pollsters' questions cannot be accepted as perfect reflections of people's views, especially on sensitive matters such as racial attitudes, the answers can be considered general indicators of these views. The polls show that whites' views have changed significantly (even assuming that some whites gave socially acceptable answers rather than express their real feelings).[134]

Whites and blacks both report more social contact with members of the other race since the 1960s, and both report more approval of interracial dating and marriage. The acceptance of interracial dating and marriage is especially significant because these practices were the ultimate taboos when official segregation ruled. Interracial couples represented the clearest breach, and their potential offspring the greatest threat, to continued segregation.

According to one survey, four of every ten Americans said they had dated someone of another race, and almost three of every ten said it had been a "serious" relationship.[135] According to the 2000 census, 6.7 percent of all marriages—up from 4.4 percent in the 1990 census—are interracial. (And many cohabitations, which aren't included in the census, are interracial as well.) Thirteen percent of marriages involving blacks are interracial; a third of those involving Hispanics and Asians are also.[136]

Some whites, of course, remain blatant racists. Due to socioeconomic reasons, these whites are more likely

AP Images/Rick Bowmer

African American communities often have tense relationships with local police departments. After hurricane Katrina, Leonard Thomas's family was living in its flooded home when a SWAT team burst in, believing that the family was squatting in another family's house.

to have contacts with blacks—to live and work in proximity to them—than are tolerant whites, who are more educated and more prosperous. Even so, blatant racist behavior occurs less frequently and is condemned more quickly than before.

Problems

Although the push for civil rights has opened many doors, some blacks are not in a position to pass through. About a quarter of the black population lives in poverty—two and one-half times the rate among the white population—and about a tenth, the poorest of the poor, exists in a state of economic and social "disintegration."[137] This "underclass" is trapped in a cycle of self-perpetuating problems from which it is extremely difficult to escape.

The problems of the lower class and the underclass were exacerbated by economic changes that intensified in the 1970s and have continued since then. These changes hit the poor the hardest. Good-paying manufacturing jobs in the cities—the traditional path out of poverty for immigrant groups—disappeared. Chicago lost over three hundred thousand jobs, New York over five hundred thousand.[138] Many jobs were eliminated by automation, while many others were moved to foreign countries or to the suburbs. Although service jobs increased, most were outside the cities and required more education or paid lower wages than the manufacturing jobs had.

As black men lost their jobs, they lost their ability to support a family. This led to a decrease in the number of "marriageable" black men and an increase in the number of households headed by black women.[139] The percentage of such households rose from 20 percent of all black families in 1960 to 45 percent in 2000.[140] And 60 percent of black children live in such households. These families are among the poorest in the country.

Meanwhile, much of the black middle class fled the inner cities to the suburbs. Their migration left the ghettos with fewer healthy businesses and strong schools to provide stability and fewer role models to portray mainstream behavior.[141] By 1996, one Chicago ghetto with sixty-six thousand people had just one supermarket and one bank but forty-eight state-licensed lottery agents and ninety-nine state-licensed liquor stores and bars.[142]

The combination of chronic unemployment in the inner cities and middle-class migration from the inner cities created an environment that offers ample opportunity and some incentive to use drugs, commit crimes, and engage in other types of antisocial behavior. The development of crack, a cheap form of cocaine, in the mid-1980s aggravated these conditions. It led to more drug use and drug trafficking and, because of steady demand by users and huge profits for dealers, much more violence. As a result, crack overwhelmed whole neighborhoods.[143] The spread of AIDS, rampant among intravenous drug users, further aggravated these conditions.

Now, about 44 percent of federal and state prisoners are black, though only 13 percent of the U.S. population is black.[144] Almost 10 percent of black men between 25 and 29 are in prison.[145] According to one study in Washington, D.C., one-fourth of black males born in the 1960s were charged with drug dealing between the ages of eighteen and twenty-four.[146] (This is partly due to greater enforcement of drug laws against black offenders than against white offenders.)

It is commonly recognized that the plight of young black men is worse than that of any other group in society. More black men receive their GED (high school equivalence degree) in prison than graduate from college.[147] About half as many black men as black women attend college. A black man in Harlem has less chance of living past forty than a man in Bangladesh.[148]

These problems affect even middle-class blacks who escaped to the suburbs. While returning from the city to see their relatives or old friends or to get a haircut, they may be in the wrong place at the wrong time. They may wear the wrong color shirt, wrong logo hat, or wrong brand of shoes and get caught up in gang violence. A father asks, "How many cultures can you say that when a guy turns twenty-five, he actually celebrates because he didn't think he would make it?"[149]

After widespread riots in the 1960s, the Kerner Commission, appointed by President Johnson to examine the cause of the riots, concluded, "What white Americans have never fully understood—but what the Negro can never forget—is that white society is deeply implicated in the ghetto. White institutions created it, white institutions maintain it, and white society condones it." After the riots, however, governments did little to improve the conditions that precipitated the riots.

After the riots in Los Angeles following the trial of police officers who beat Rodney King in 1992, there was more talk about improving the conditions in the ghetto. But a columnist who had heard such talk before commented, "My guess is that when all is said and done, a great deal more will be said than done. The truth is we don't know any quick fixes for our urban ills and we lack the patience and resources for slow fixes."[150]

These problems are all the more difficult to resolve because the cities have lost political power as they have lost population due to white flight and black migration. Since 1992, more voters (including many blacks) have lived in the suburbs than in the cities. Suburban voters don't urge action on urban problems. Sometimes they resist action if it means an increase in their taxes or a decrease in their services.

For the black lower class, and especially for the black underclass, it is apparent that civil rights aren't enough. As one black leader said, "What good is a seat in the front of the bus if you don't have the money for the fare?"[151]

But most blacks don't fall in the lower class or underclass, and most don't dwell in the inner cities. It would be a serious mistake to hold the stereotypical view that the majority reside in the inner cities and that a majority of them live in dysfunctional families filled with crackheads and prone to violence. Although black men lag behind, black women especially have vastly improved lives—academically, professionally, and financially—over the span of one generation.[152]

© Ethan Hill

Black women are making great progress. They are more likely than black men to graduate from college and professional schools. At Tuskegee University, they dominate the veterinary school.

Discrimination against Hispanics

Hispanics, also called Latinos, never endured slavery,[153] but they have faced discrimination. Although some Hispanics are Caucasian, many Puerto Ricans and Cubans have African ancestry, and many Mexicans have Indian ancestry, so they have darker skin than non-Hispanic whites. Like blacks, Hispanics have faced discrimination in education, employment, housing, and voting.[154]

Latinos also encounter discrimination due to immigration. The flood of illegal immigrants pouring in from Latin America, especially from Mexico, has produced a wave of anti-immigration sentiment throughout the United States, even in the areas with few immigrants.[155] This sentiment affects not only illegal immigrants but the Latinos who are legal residents and U.S. citizens; it even affects those who are native-born Americans, because the average person or law enforcement officer can't tell, simply by watching or listening to them, which people who look like Latinos are legal and which are illegal.

Border patrol agents and local police officers often stop Latinos for questioning. Because illegal immigrants can't get driver's licenses and most don't get driver's insurance, the officers expect to identify illegal immigrants by asking for these documents. Border patrol agents stopped the mayor of Pomona, California, a hundred miles from the Mexican border and ordered him to produce papers proving that he is a legal resident.

Even when the officials are well intentioned, their conduct seems like harassment to law-abiding residents. The officers also assume that many Latinos are involved in drug trafficking, so they practice profiling, as they do toward blacks.[156]

Latino immigrants who are farmworkers face additional problems. Agriculture has long avoided regulations imposed on other businesses. For decades, the minimum wage law didn't apply to farmworkers. Even today, the laws providing overtime pay and the right to organize don't apply. In many states, the laws establishing workers' compensation and unemployment benefits programs don't apply. Farmworkers' lack of governmental protection, coupled with their economic desperation, makes them vulnerable to unscrupulous employers. The Department of Justice has investigated more than one hundred cases of involuntary servitude—slavery—and has prosecuted a half dozen from South Florida in recent years.[157]

Discrimination in Education

In some places, Hispanic children were not allowed to attend any schools. In other places, they were segregated into "Mexican" schools that were inferior to Anglo schools.[158] When the Supreme Court declared segregation illegal, many school districts achieved "integration" by combining Hispanics with blacks, leaving non-Hispanic whites in their own schools.[159]

Although *de jure* segregation has been struck down,[160] *de facto* segregation exists in cities where Latinos are concentrated. Many Latinos attend schools with

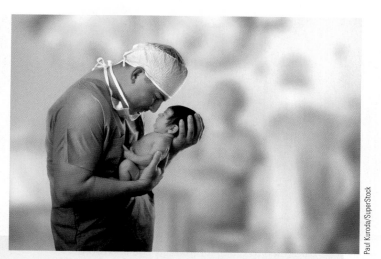

Latinos are gradually improving their status as more go to college and graduate school and become professionals, such as this doctor.

Paul Kuroda/SuperStock

more than 90 percent minorities, and most attend schools with more than 50 percent minorities.[161]

Predominantly Latino schools, like predominantly black schools, aren't as well funded as other schools because they're located in poor communities that don't get as much revenue from property taxes. In San Antonio, wealthy families, who were concentrated in one section of the city, got their section incorporated as a separate school district, though it was surrounded by the rest of the city. As a separate district, its property taxes financed its schools only. When Mexican American parents sued, the Burger Court ruled that the Fourteenth Amendment's equal protection clause doesn't require states to equalize funding among school districts, even where artificial districts have been carved out of a city.[162]

Despite the Court's ruling, this case highlighted the problem of unequal funding, prompting some states to equalize funding, though allowing other states to maintain the status quo.

Latinos' primary problem in education, however, is the language barrier. Many are unable to speak English, causing them to fail in school and drop out of school at higher rates than other students, even African Americans. One-third of Latinos drop out before graduating from high school.[163]

Bilingual education was created to help such students. Bilingual classes use the students' native language to teach the students English and their other subjects. The goal is to transition them from their native language to English rather than to immerse them in a foreign language—English—that they don't understand.

In 1968, Congress encouraged bilingual education by providing funding, and in 1974 the Supreme Court, in a case brought by Chinese parents in San Francisco, held that schools must teach students in a language they can understand.[164] This can be their native language, or it can be English if they have been taught English. These federal actions prompted states to establish bilingual education programs. More than 150 languages, from Chinese to Yapese, have been offered. Because three-fourths of the students who don't speak English are Hispanic, Spanish has been the most common.[165]

Bilingual programs have faced numerous problems. They are expensive because they require more teachers and smaller classes. They are impractical because schools can't find enough teachers in various languages. Schools in California, where half of all students in bilingual programs lived, fell twenty-one thousand teachers short in one year.[166] They couldn't offer bilingual education to two-thirds of the students who were eligible.[167]

Bilingual programs have been controversial as well. Although Latino groups have advocated these programs as a way to preserve Latino culture, Latino parents want their children to learn English and to learn it well. They worry that bilingual programs will delay their mastery of English. Seventy-five percent of recent immigrants, including 56 percent of Mexican immigrants, oppose these programs.[168] Many Anglos also oppose these programs. Bilingualism prompts concerns, even fears, about the continuing dominance of Anglo culture in American society. For all of these reasons, California citizens voted to abolish bilingual programs in 1998.

Despite the decline in bilingual programs and widespread perceptions of many Americans, current immigrants are learning English just as previous waves of European immigrants learned it. Among Spanish speakers in the United States, 90 percent speak English (though 18 percent say they don't speak it well).[169] Although about half of those who arrived as teenagers or adults don't speak English proficiently, almost all of those who arrived as young children or who are in the second generation speak it proficiently.[170] Cuban Americans are learning it as fast or faster than any group in history.[171] Mexican Americans are learning it as they reside longer in the United States. Although many of those who come for work and plan to return to Mexico don't speak English, most of those who plan to remain in the United States learn to speak some English, and almost all of their children learn to speak fluent English.[172]

The drive to learn English is so strong that only a third of Latinos born in the United States are bilingual. Most can't speak Spanish.[173]

It is true that some immigrant communities, especially Cubans in South Florida and Mexicans in parts of the Southwest, are so large that people can survive without learning English. But most feel pressure to learn English to function in the broader society and for their children to succeed in school. Indeed, 89 percent believe that those who immigrate must learn English to succeed in the United States.[174] (For further evidence of their inclination to assimilate, see the box "Latinos Choose Anglo Names.")

Combating Discrimination against Hispanics

In the 1960s, Hispanic advocacy groups tried to imitate African American groups by using protests and other forms of direct action. The Chicano movement attempted to forge a powerful bloc from the diverse population of Hispanics. **César Chávez** successfully led a coalition of labor, civil rights, and religious groups to obtain better working conditions for migrant farmworkers in California. But few other visible national leaders or organizations emerged.

Latinos remain more diverse and less cohesive than blacks. Most don't even consider themselves part of a common group.[175] They identify strongly with their national origin and have little contact with Latinos of other national origins. And they lack a shared, defining experience in their background, such as slavery for blacks, to unite them.

Where Latinos are highly concentrated, they are increasingly powerful at the local and state levels of government. Yet Latino politicians haven't shaped a common agenda, perhaps because Latino people don't share a common agenda.[176]

They are potentially powerful at the national level as well. When Congress considered harsh measures toward illegal immigrants in 2006, hundreds of thousands of Latinos rallied against the measures. Many families include legal and illegal residents—children who were born here living with parents who are illegal, or nuclear families who are legal residents living with grandparents or aunts and uncles who are illegal—so congressional

threats of deportation sparked real fears in these families. Politicians' comments that immigrants are taking jobs from citizens and not contributing anything to society ignited their anger. In their passion, some observers saw the stirrings of political activism among young Latinos especially.

With their huge numbers, Latinos are a coveted bloc of voters. Yet many are not citizens, and many of those who are citizens do not register and vote. Although the Latino population is slightly larger than the African American population, six million fewer Latinos are registered to vote.[177]

Meanwhile, Latino individuals are moving up society's ladder. More attend college and become managers and professionals. At least those who speak educated English appear to be following the pattern of earlier generations of immigrants from Southern and Eastern Europe—arriving poor, facing discrimination, but eventually working their way up. Along the way, they are also assimilating through high rates of marriage to non-Latinos.

LATINOS CHOOSE ANGLO NAMES

Despite Anglos' concern that Latinos are not assimilating, Latinos are favoring Anglo names for their children. For Hispanic children born in Texas in a recent year, the most popular names for boys were:

And for girls were:

Jose	Ashley
Daniel	Jennifer
Jonathan	Emily
David	Samantha
Christopher	Maria

In New York City, the most popular names for Hispanic boys were:

And for Hispanic girls were:

Justin	Ashley
Christopher	Jennifer
Kevin	Emily
Anthony	Brianna
Brandon	Samantha

SOURCE: Sam Roberts, "In a Changing Nation, Smith Is Still King," *New York Times*, July 11, 2004.

Discrimination against American Indians

More than two million American Indians live in the United States. Most live in the West, and half live on reservations. Although some native Americans are Eskimos and Aleuts from Alaska, most are Indians, representing more than 550 tribes with different histories, customs, and languages. Proud of their tribal heritage, they prefer to be known by their tribal name, such as Cheyenne or Sioux, than by the collective terms *Indians* or *Native Americans*.[178] (Of the collective terms, they prefer to be called *Indians,* so our text will follow their preference.)

American Indians have endured treatment quite different from what African Americans or Hispanics have experienced.

Government Policy toward American Indians

Government policy toward Indians has ranged from forced separation at one extreme to forced assimilation at the other.

Separation Initially, the policy was separation. People believed that the North American continent was so vast that most of its interior would remain wilderness populated by Indians who would have ample room to live and hunt. The Constitution reflects this belief. It grants Congress authority to "regulate commerce with foreign nations, and among the several states, and with the Indian tribes." In early cases, Chief Justice John Marshall described the tribes as "dependent domestic nations."[179] They were within U.S. borders but outside its political process.

Early treaties reinforced separation by establishing boundaries between Indians and non-Indians. The boundaries were intended to minimize conflict. White hunters or settlers who ventured across the boundaries could be punished by the Indians. But as the country grew, it became increasingly difficult to contain the settlers within the boundaries. Mounting pressure to push the Indians farther west led to the Indian Removal Act of 1830, which mandated removal of tribes east of the Mississippi River and relocation on reservations west of the river. At the time, people considered the Great Plains as a great desert, unfit for habitation by whites but suitable for Indians.

Assimilation As more settlers moved west, the vision of a separate Indian country far beyond white civilization faded. In the 1880s, the government switched its policy to assimilation. Prompted by Christian churches, government officials sought to "civilize" the Indians—to integrate them into American society, whether they wanted to be integrated or not. In place of their traditional means of subsistence, rendered useless once the tribes were removed from their historical homelands, the government subdivided reservation land into small tracts and allotted these tracts to tribe members in the hope that they would turn to farming as white and black settlers had.

Bureau of Indian Affairs (BIA) agents, who supervised the reservations, tried to root out Indian ways and replace them with white dress and hairstyles, the English language, and the Christian religion. Government boarding schools separated Indian children from their families to instill these new practices.

Since the adoption of the Constitution, Native Americans were not considered citizens but members of separate nations.[180] In 1890, after government policy had switched to assimilation, Congress permitted Indians who remained on reservations to become citizens. In a formal ceremony marking his new citizenship, the Indian shot his last arrow and then took hold of the handles of a plow to demonstrate his assimilation.[181] After World War I, Congress granted citizenship to those who served in the military during the war, and

"I love the way you make those yams. You'll have to give me the recipe before your culture is obliterated from the face of the earth."

finally, in 1924, Congress extended it to all who were born in the United States.

Citizenship enabled Indians to vote and hold office, though some states effectively barred them from the polls for decades. Arizona denied them the right to vote until 1948, Utah until 1956.[182]

Tribal restoration By the 1930s, the government recognized the consequences of coerced assimilation. Most Indians, though able to speak English, were poorly educated. And with their traditional means of earning a living gone, most were poverty-stricken. The policy had led to the destruction of native culture without much assimilation into white society. Consequently, in 1934 Congress implemented a new policy of tribal restoration that recognized Indians as distinct persons and tribes as autonomous entities encouraged to govern themselves once again. Traditional cultural and religious practices were accepted, and Indian children, no longer forced to attend boarding schools, were taught some Indian languages.

Reflecting the policy of tribal restoration and the efforts of other minorities in the 1960s and 1970s, Indian interest groups became active. Indian law firms filed lawsuits, seeking to protect not only tribal independence and traditional ways but also land, mineral, and water resources.

The diversity and the dispersion of the tribes—they are divided by culture and by geography, often located in the remotest and poorest parts of the country—make it difficult for them to present a united front. Nevertheless, they have been able to wrest some autonomy from the government. In particular, they have gained more authority over the educational and social programs administered by the BIA for the tribes.[183]

In recent years, Indians have fought for the return of some tribal land and for an accounting of the money owed them for the use of their individual land held in trust by the government. In the early nineteenth century, the government took tribal land and put it in trust for the Indians. But then the government divided the land, classified large tracts as "surplus," and offered the tracts to white settlers. In return, it paid individual In-

Dilos Lonewolf became Tom Torlino during his transformation at a boarding school in Carlisle, Pennsylvania. Indians were shorn of their hair and clothes and trained to adopt white ways.

dians a pittance. In this way, the Indians lost two-thirds of their territory. The government held the remaining land in trust for the Indians, leasing it to ranchers, loggers, and miners. The government collected the rents and royalties for the Indians. But the BIA didn't bother to keep accurate records or even to preserve its records. A class-action lawsuit, dubbed "the Indian Enron case," seeks a reckoning of the accounts and a payment to the Indians who are owed money.[184]

After a Supreme Court ruling and a congressional law in the 1980s underscored tribal sovereignty on tribal land, tribes could establish gambling casinos on reservations, even if their state didn't allow casinos.[185] Almost three hundred tribes have done so, although less than a dozen have found a bonanza—mostly small tribes in populous states where the casinos attract numerous customers.[186] And many of the casinos are bankrolled by unknown investors who keep most of the profits. A Malaysian businessman owns one, a South African developer another. From these casinos, little money trickles down to tribal members.[187]

With their casino businesses, some tribes have begun to buy into the political process, as other groups have done. Threatened by gambling interests in Las Vegas and Atlantic City, which fear that tribal casinos will lure away their customers, the tribes have formed a lobby, the National Indian Gaming Association, and made political contributions. These contributions reportedly total more than the contributions by individual corporations such as AT&T, Boeing, or General Motors.[188]

Now more Indians share the views of one activist who says, "You have a federal government, state governments, and tribal governments—three sovereigns in one country. This is the civil rights movement of Native Americans."[189] Indeed, Indians enjoy renewed pride, which has led tribes to establish programs to preserve their language and culture.[190]

Nevertheless, Indians remain at the bottom of America's racial and ethnic ladder. They are the least educated and most unemployed group, the poorest and sickest group, with the highest alcoholism rates and lowest life expectancy, of any people in the country.

Sex Discrimination

Most sex discrimination has been directed at women, though some has been directed at men.

Discrimination against Women

The Traditional View

People used to believe that natural differences between the sexes required men and women to occupy separate spheres of life. Men would dominate the public domain of work and government, and women would dominate the private domain of the home. Both domains were important, and men were considered superior in one and women were considered superior in the other.

Thomas Jefferson, the most egalitarian of the male Founders, reflected this view when he said, "Were our state a pure democracy there would still be excluded from our deliberations women, who, to prevent deprivation of morals and ambiguity of issues, should not mix promiscuously in gatherings of men."[191] That is, women are more moral than men, so they would be corrupted by politics, and they are more irrational, so they would confuse the issues. For both reasons, they should not participate in politics.

So, women were denied the right to vote, and married women were denied other rights—to manage property they acquired before marriage, to manage income they received from jobs, to enter into contracts, and to sue. Some states eventually granted these rights, but when disputes arose within families, male judges hesitated to tell other men how to treat their wives.

Even women's citizenship was tied to their husbands' citizenship. If a foreign woman married an American man, she automatically became a United States citizen. But if an American woman married a foreign man, she automatically lost her United States citizenship. (Women's citizenship wouldn't become independent of their husbands' citizenship until 1922.)

Women were barred from schools and jobs. Before the Civil War, they were not admitted to public high schools. Because they were being prepared for motherhood, education was considered unnecessary, even dangerous. According to the *Encyclopaedia Britannica* in 1800, women had smaller brains than men.[192] Education would fatigue them and might ruin their reproductive organs. For the same reasons, women were not encouraged to hold jobs. Those who did were shunted into jobs that were seen as extensions of the domestic domain, such as producing textiles, clothes, and shoes in sex-segregated factories.[193]

This traditional conception of gender roles created problems for women who didn't fit the standard mold. After the Civil War, Myra Bradwell ran a private school, founded a weekly newspaper, and worked for various civic organizations. She was active in the women's suffrage movement and instrumental in persuading the Illinois legislature to expand women's legal rights. After learning the law, however, she was denied a license to practice it solely because she was a woman. The Supreme Court upheld the Illinois policy in 1873.[194] Justice Joseph Bradley declared:

> *Law, as well as nature itself, has always recognized a wide difference in the respective spheres and destinies of man and woman. Man is, or should be, the woman's protector and defender. The natural and proper timidity and delicacy which belongs to the female sex evidently unfits it for many of the occupations of civil life. . . . The constitution of the family organization . . . indicates the domestic sphere as that which properly belongs to the domain and functions of womanhood. The harmony . . . of interests and views which belong, or should belong, to the family institution is repugnant to the idea of a woman adopting a distinct and independent career from that of her husband. . . . The paramount destiny and mission of woman are to fulfill the noble and benign offices of wife and mother. This is the law of the Creator. And the rules of civil society must be adapted to the general constitution of things, and cannot be based upon exceptional cases.*

It was difficult to distinguish between this separate-but-equal view and clear discriminatory treatment. In the 1860s and 1870s, the doctors who practiced scientific medicine formed the American Medical Association (AMA) to drive out other people who offered medical services. These people included not only hucksters and quacks but also women who served as midwives or abortionists. Although abortions had been widely available, the AMA, drawing on popular fears about the women's suffrage movement, convinced state legislatures that abortions were "a threat to social order and to male authority." The woman who seeks an abortion, the AMA explained, is "unmindful of the course marked out for her by Providence, she overlooks the duties imposed on her by the marriage contract. She yields to the pleasure—but shrinks from the pains and responsibilities of maternity. . . . Let not the husband of such a wife flatter himself that he possesses her affection."[195]

Sometimes the discriminatory treatment was even more blatant. The Mississippi Supreme Court acknowledged a husband's right to beat his wife.[196] Using the "rule of thumb," the court held that a husband could not beat his wife with a weapon thicker than his thumb.

The Women's Movement

Early feminists were determined to remedy these inequities. Many had gained political and organizational experience in the abolitionist movement. It wasn't considered "unladylike" for women to campaign for abolition of slavery because that movement was associated with religious groups. Yet the women weren't allowed to participate fully in the major antislavery society. They formed their own antislavery society, but when they attended a convention of abolitionist groups, they weren't allowed to sit with the male delegates.

Angry at such treatment, the women held a meeting to discuss the "social, civil, and religious rights of women." In 1848, this Women's Rights Convention adopted a declaration of rights based on the Declaration of Independence, proclaiming, "We hold these truths to be self-evident: that all men and women are created equal." The convention also passed a resolution calling for women's suffrage.

After the Civil War, the women who had worked in the abolitionist movement expected that women, as well as blacks, would get legal rights and voting rights. When the Fourteenth and Fifteenth Amendments did not include women, they felt betrayed, and they disassociated themselves from the black movement. They formed their own organizations to campaign for women's suffrage. This movement, led by **Susan B. Anthony** and **Elizabeth Cady Stanton,** succeeded in 1920, when the Nineteenth Amendment gave women the right to vote.

Then dissension developed within the movement. Many groups felt that the Nineteenth Amendment was just the first step in the struggle for equal rights. They proposed the Equal Rights Amendment to remedy remaining inequities. Other groups felt that the battle had been won. They opposed the Equal Rights Amendment, arguing that it would overturn labor laws recently enacted to protect women. Due to this dissension and the conservatism in the country at the time, the movement became dormant.[197]

The movement reemerged in the 1960s. As a result of the civil rights movement, many women recognized their own inferior status. Female writers sensitized other women. **Betty Friedan** published *The Feminine Mystique,* which grew out of a questionnaire she circulated at her fifteenth college reunion. The book addressed the malaise that afflicted college-educated women who were socialized into the feminine role but found it unsatisfying.[198] Friedan observed that women reared the children, shopped for groceries, cooked the meals, and cleaned the house, while secretly wondering, "Is this all?" Friedan's manifesto became the best-selling nonfiction paperback in 1964. Its popularity spurred Friedan and other upper-middle-class, professional women to form the **National Organization for Women (NOW)** in 1966. They resolved "to bring women into full participation in the mainstream of American society *now.*"

Other women, also middle class but veterans of the civil rights and antiwar movements, had developed a taste for political action. They formed other organizations. Where NOW fought primarily for women's political and economic rights, the other organizations fought broadly for women's liberation in all spheres of life. Together these organizations pushed the issue of women's rights back onto the public agenda.

Nevertheless, they weren't taken seriously for years. In 1970, *Time* magazine reported, "No one knows how many shirts lay wrinkling in laundry baskets last week as thousands of women across the country turned out for the first big demonstration of the women's liberation movement. They took over [New York City's Fifth Avenue], providing not only protest but some of the best sidewalk ogling in years."[199]

Although the movement tried to broaden its base beyond upper-middle-class and college-educated women, it was unable to do so. The movement fostered an image of privileged women who looked on other women with disdain. *Housewife* became a derisive term. Traditional women viewed the movement as antimotherhood and antifamily and, when it became more radical in the 1970s, prolesbian. This image gave "women's liberation" a bad name, even though most women agreed with most goals of the movement.[200] This image persists. More Americans believe that extraterrestrials have visited the earth than think that the word *feminist* is a compliment.[201] (It is unclear, however, whether this says more about Americans' attitudes toward gender equality or their penchant for paranoid conspiracy theories.)

The Movement in Congress and the Courts

Congress initially didn't take the women's movement seriously either. When the House debated a bill forbidding racial discrimination in employment, eighty-one-year-old Rep. Howard Smith (D-Va.) proposed an amendment to add sex discrimination to the bill. A staunch foe of equal rights for blacks, Smith thought his proposal so ludicrous and so radical that it would help defeat the entire bill. Indeed, during their debate on the amendment, members of Congress laughed so hard that they could barely hear each other speak.[202] But the joke was on these members, because the amendment, and then the bill—the Civil Rights Act of 1964—passed.

Equal Rights Amendment Congress also passed the **Equal Rights Amendment (ERA).** The amendment simply declared, "Equality of rights under the law shall not be denied or abridged by the United States or by any state on account of sex." Introduced in 1923 and every year thereafter, Congress passed the amendment in 1972.

It looked like the amendment would zip through the states. Both parties endorsed it, and a majority of the public supported it. But the amendment stalled. Observers speculated that it could make women subject to the draft for the military (if there was another draft). Opponents charged, falsely, that it would result in unisex restrooms and homosexual rights.

The main problem, however, was the amendment's symbolism. For many women, the ERA represented an attack on the traditional values of motherhood, the family, and the home. Early feminists had emphasized equal employment so much that they gave some women the impression that they opposed these values. Traditional women sensed implicit criticism for becoming housewives.[203] To underscore the symbolism, the women in anti-ERA groups baked bread for state legislators scheduled to vote on ratification.

Consequently, numerous women, even some who favored equality, opposed the amendment. Although many young women supported it, fewer middle-age and elderly women did; and although many working women supported it, fewer housewives did. Women's organizations hadn't created an effective grassroots campaign to sway traditional women. Their disaffection allowed male legislators to vote according to their male attitudes. They didn't need to worry about a backlash from their female constituents.[204]

In 1980, the Republican Party became the first party not to endorse the ERA since 1940, and President Reagan became the first president not to support the amendment since Truman.

When the deadline for ratification set by Congress expired in 1982, the ERA fell three states short of the

The more WOMEN at work the sooner we WIN!

WOMEN ARE NEEDED ALSO AS:

FARM WORKERS   WAITRESSES   TIMEKEEPERS   LAUNDRESSES
TYPISTS   BUS DRIVERS   ELEVATOR OPERATORS   TEACHERS
SALESPEOPLE   TAXI DRIVERS   MESSENGERS   CONDUCTORS
— and in hundreds of other war jobs!

SEE YOUR LOCAL U.S. EMPLOYMENT SERVICE

A World War II poster thanks women for performing the jobs of the men called to the war. After the war, however, the women were urged to give up their factory jobs to the returning veterans.

three-fourths necessary. As with the Nineteenth Amendment, it was opposed primarily by the Southern states.

Supreme Court rulings But women would assert their rights in court.

Historically courts upheld laws that limited women's participation in the public domain and occasionally even laws that diminished their standing in the private domain. As late as 1970, the Ohio supreme court ruled that a wife is a husband's servant with "no legally recognized feelings or rights."[205]

The Burger Court finally reversed this pattern. In 1971, for the first time, the Court struck down a law that discriminated against women,[206] heralding a long series of rulings that invalidated a variety of such laws. The Court used the congressional statutes and broadened the Fourteenth Amendment's equal protection clause to apply to women as well as to racial minorities.

The change was especially apparent in a pair of cases involving the selection of jurors. For the pool of potential jurors, some states drew the names of men, but not women, from voter registration or other lists. These states allowed women to serve only if they voluntarily signed up at the courthouse. Consequently, few women served. In 1961, the Court let Florida use these procedures because the "woman is still regarded as the center of home and family life."[207] In 1975, however, the Court forbade Louisiana from using similar procedures,[208] thus overturning a precedent only fourteen years old.

The Court's rulings rejected the traditional stereotypes that men are the breadwinners and women the child rearers in society. The Court invalidated Utah's law that required divorced fathers to support their daughters until eighteen but their sons until twenty-one.[209] The state assumed that the daughters would get married and be supported by their husbands, whereas the sons would need to get educated for their careers. But the Court noted, "No longer is the female destined solely for the home."

Congressional laws Congress adopted legislation to forbid sex discrimination in employment and education.

The Civil Rights Act of 1964 forbids discrimination on the basis of both sex and race in hiring, promoting, and firing. It prohibits discrimination on the basis of sex, except where sex is a "bona fide occupational qualification" for the job. Sex is considered a legitimate qualification for very few jobs, such as restroom attendants, lingerie salesclerks, models, or actors. It is not considered a legitimate qualification for jobs men traditionally held, such as those that entail heavy physical labor, unpleasant working conditions, late-night hours, overtime, or travel. Employers can no longer reserve these jobs for male applicants.

However, discrimination in hiring, promoting, and firing persists, even forty years after the act. A major study examined the records in lawsuits alleging sex discrimination in one recent year. A surprising and staggering number, they required employers to pay $263 million to the female plaintiffs in that year alone.[210] Testimony by midlevel managers revealed that higher executives instructed them, "We do not employ women," or, "The day I hire a woman will be a cold day in hell." In dozens of cases, the managers were told to throw women's applications into the trash.[211]

The same result occurs when male managers decide according to their "gut instinct" that a man is more qualified. Their "gut instinct" may be biased without them realizing it.

The discrimination occurs up and down the ladder. Huge lawsuits have been brought against both Merrill Lynch and Wal-Mart in recent years. But the discrimination appears most prevalent for traditional male, blue-collar jobs. Some men don't want to work with women; they don't want to break up the "good-ol'-boys' clubhouse."[212] Mysteriously, a woman's application disappears; or the letter telling her when to come for the interview gets lost in the mail; or her examination is invalidated for some reason.[213]

Some companies that fill their positions through hiring agencies instruct the agencies to send them only men for traditional male jobs and only women for traditional female jobs.[214]

Discrimination in firing, especially for pregnancy, continues as well, despite the **Pregnancy Discrimination Act** of 1978, which forbids firing or demoting women when they become pregnant or after they return from maternity leave.[215] Some women have been fired as soon as they mentioned being pregnant, others as soon as their body showed it. Many have seen their performance evaluations drop as their bellies swelled, even though their actual performance did not decline.[216] Others have been demoted after giving birth. "When I returned from maternity leave," a lawyer recounted, "I was given the work of a paralegal and I wanted to say, 'Look, I had a baby, not a lobotomy.'"[217]

The cases examined in these studies probably represent the tip of the iceberg. To sue an employer for sex discrimination is to embark on an expensive and exhausting legal battle that will take several years of one's life. It requires a strong-willed woman who has experienced discriminatory behavior egregious enough for her to persuade a lawyer to take the case and then a company to settle or a judge or jury to find for her. Although there are some frivolous lawsuits in our legal system, there is more discriminatory behavior in our workplaces than is ever brought to court.

The **Equal Pay Act** of 1963 requires that women and men receive equal pay for equal work. The act makes exceptions for merit, productivity, and seniority.

As a result of the act, the gap between what women and men earn has slowly shrunk. In the 1960s, working women earned just 59 cents for every dollar men earned.[218] Today, working women earn 80 cents for every dollar men earn—an improvement but far short of real equality.[219]

One reason for the gap is old-fashioned sex discrimination. Despite the Equal Pay Act, some male employers with ingrained attitudes are reluctant to pay women equally. The act allows exceptions for merit and productivity, which usually are determined subjectively. The employer may insist, whether sincerely or not, that the man is more meritorious or productive. Legions of women believe that they need to perform better to be paid equally.[220]

Now the Roberts Court has made it more difficult for women to bring lawsuits for pay discrimination.[221] To bring a suit, the law requires victims to file a complaint within 180 days of the discrimination. The Equal Employment Opportunity Commission (EEOC), which administers the law, had interpreted the law to require victims to file a complaint within 180 days of their *last* paycheck reflecting the discriminatory salary or wages. Thus the 180-day clock reset after each paycheck. In 2007, a five-justice majority of the Roberts Court, however, interpreted the provision to require victims to file a complaint within 180 days of their *first* paycheck. At this time, few employees would be aware of any pay differential and new employees would be leery of filing a formal complaint anyway. The Court's decision means that fewer suits will be brought, even when clear discrimination exists. (The Court's decision reflects its change in membership. Justice Samuel Alito, who replaced Justice Sandra Day O'Connor, cast the tie-breaking vote.)

Another reason for the gap between what women and men earn is because women and men have different jobs, whether due to discrimination or to choice. Despite the Civil Rights Act of 1964 and the societal changes—the blurring lines between genders—many women have traditional women's jobs and most men have traditional men's jobs. And traditional women's jobs pay less.

Historically, women were shunted into a small number of jobs. Even by 2000, two-thirds of working women were crowded into just twenty-one of the occupations identified by the Department of Labor.[222] These "pink-collar" jobs include secretaries (98 percent are women), household workers (97 percent), child care workers (97 percent), nurses (93 percent), bank tellers (90 percent), librarians (83 percent), elementary school teachers (83 percent), and health technicians (81 percent). In contrast, few women are carpenters (1 percent), firefighters (2 percent), mechanics (4 percent), or truck drivers (5 percent).[223] Although the Equal Pay Act mandates equal pay for equal work, it does not require equal pay for comparable work—usually called **comparable worth.** According to a study in Washington state, maintenance carpenters and secretaries performed comparable jobs in terms of the education, the skill, or other qualifications required, but the carpenters, mostly men, made about $600 a month more than the secretaries, mostly women. In general, "men's jobs" paid about 20 percent more than comparable "women's jobs." Yet courts rejected demands by public employees that government employers boost the pay for "women's jobs." Nonetheless, some state and city governments implemented comparable worth for their employees after prodding by labor unions and women's groups. Private companies, however, did not, because doing so would require them to pay many female employees more.

Although the push for comparable worth has stalled, in recent years grassroots campaigns organized by labor unions and church groups have called for laws mandating a **living wage.**[224] These laws would require employers to pay more than the federal minimum wage, to pay whatever is necessary so a full-time worker doesn't fall below the poverty line. Underlying a living wage is the ethical principle that no one who works full time should have to live in poverty (as full-time workers paid the minimum wage now do).

Some proposals would apply only to government employees and to the employees of the companies that do business with the government. Other proposals would apply to all employees within a city or state. Still other proposals would apply just to the employees of "big-box stores," such as Wal-Mart and Home Depot, because these companies drive down the wages for workers throughout society. Most proposals would exempt small businesses with fewer than twenty-five workers.

So far, some cities (Baltimore, San Francisco, and Santa Fe) and one state (Nevada) have adopted such laws.[225] If many cities and states did, living wage laws would have a significant impact on women and minorities, because women and minorities hold a disproportionate number of the lowest-paying jobs. In addition, living wage laws would have a ripple effect, prompting employers to raise the wages of the workers just above the lowest level.

Another reason for the gap between what women and men earn is because women have children. The gap is mostly between married women and married men. Single women and single men between the ages of twenty-one and thirty-five receive nearly equal pay. But when the women get married and have children, their pay lags. Some interrupt their career until their children start school. Others continue to work but shift from the fast track to the so-called "mommy track," working fewer hours due to child care and household responsibilities.[226] Still others fall victim to stereotypes—that mothers aren't serious about their careers, that mothers aren't dependable because they won't show up when their children get sick, or that mothers will quit sooner or later anyway.[227] Through such stereotypes, managers move mothers to the "mommy track" in their own minds, whether the mothers want that track or not.

Mothers with young children confront more obstacles than unequal pay. Male employers do little to accommodate the demands of child rearing. Most companies don't provide paid maternity leave, paid sick days, on-site day care, or flexible schedules. The United States lags far behind most other countries, including all wealthy countries, in creating family-friendly policies. Of 173 countries, all but the United States, Papua New Guinea, and three African countries guarantee paid maternity leaves. Sixty-five countries even provide paid paternity leaves. (In the United States, only California provides partly paid family leaves.) One hundred forty-five countries provide paid sick days.[228]

Congress passed and President Clinton signed a bill requiring employers to grant unpaid maternity and paternity leaves. Companies must allow unpaid leaves for up to three months for workers with newborn or recently adopted children or with seriously ill family members. The act applies to companies that have fifty employees and to workers who work twenty-five hours a week for a year.[229] This covers about half of American workers.

But relatively few workers take advantage of these leaves. Most workers can't afford to take unpaid leaves. Moreover, many managers don't support such measures, and some coworkers resent the additional burdens, so employees are reluctant to ask for leaves. When companies are laying off workers to cut costs, "If you look like you are not career oriented, you can lose your job."[230]

Due to the influx of women workers, "the workforce has changed enormously in the last thirty years, but the workplace has not kept pace."[231] The workplace is "stuck in a time warp, modeled for [*Leave it to Beaver's*] Ward and June Cleaver when the reality feels more like . . . 'Survivor.'"[232]

Workers in the United States put in longer hours than those in other industrialized countries, and these hours, for both sexes, have increased since the 1970s.[233] The result is that mothers and fathers with young children often face unreasonable demands on their time. Neither spouse has the time to do what the housewife once did. In many families, the woman tries to do these tasks at night and on weekends, but both spouses frequently feel stretched thin and stressed out. Two-thirds of parents say they don't have enough time with their children, and nearly two-thirds of married workers say they don't have enough time with their spouse.[234]

Consequently, among men with children, those who have a housewife rise up the career ladder faster than those who have a wife with a job outside the home. The latter men apparently put in less "face time" at the office. Executives who reach the higher rungs are "almost always" men who have a housewife.[235] An executive of a Fortune 500 company admitted that his company still prefers to hire men who are married to a housewife.[236]

So even though women have gained greater acceptance in the workplace, they—and their spouses—have not overcome the expectations that developed long before they were ever allowed in the workplace. And these expectations are exacerbated by Americans' glorification of work and, with new communications technology, a perverse celebration of a "24/7 workweek." "We glorify an all-work, all-the-time lifestyle," notes one commentator, "and then weep crocodile tears for kids whose parents are never home."[237]

In addition to their difficulties in getting hired, promoted, and paid equally, some women also face sexual harassment (see the box "Sexual Harassment at Work").

The Education Amendments of 1972 (to the Civil Rights Act of 1964) forbid discrimination on the basis

The Supreme Court has ruled that sexual harassment is a form of job discrimination prohibited by the Civil Rights Act of 1964,[1] and Congress has passed a law allowing victims to sue employers and collect money for distress, illness, or loss of their job due to such behavior. Although sexual harassment can be directed toward either sex,[2] it is usually directed toward women.

Courts recognize two types of **sexual harassment.** The most obvious is *quid pro quo,* in which a supervisor makes unwanted sexual advances and either promises good consequences (for example, a promotion or pay raise) if the employee goes along or threatens bad consequences (for example, an undesirable reassignment) if the employee refuses. The less obvious type is creating a hostile environment that interferes with the employee's ability to perform the job. To prove that a hostile environment existed, the employee must demonstrate that the offensive conduct was severe or persistent.

Paula Jones's suit against President Clinton, who as Arkansas' governor allegedly asked her for oral sex, was dismissed because the sexual advance was considered neither severe enough nor, as a single incident, persistent enough to constitute a hostile environment. If it happened, the judge said, it was "boorish and offensive" but not technically harassment.

Despite many men's fears, occasional innocuous comments, jokes, or requests for dates would not be classified as harassment. Justice Antonin Scalia emphasized that the law did not create "a general civility code."[3]

Yet confusion persists because several outlandish examples have received widespread publicity. A library employee filed a complaint against a co-worker who had posted a *New Yorker* cartoon in his cubicle.[4] A graduate teaching assistant filed a complaint against another who had placed a photograph of his wife, wearing a bikini, on his desk in their office at the University of Nebraska. If sexual harassment were defined this broadly, it would interfere with freedom of speech. (Anyone can file a complaint, as anyone can bring a lawsuit, but of course this doesn't mean that a bureaucratic agency or court agrees with the person filing the complaint or bringing the lawsuit. Yet the publicity gives many people this impression.)

Confusion also persists because some employers, who can be held responsible for sexual harassment by their employees,[5] have adopted "zero-tolerance" policies to insulate them from potential lawsuits. These policies are stricter than the law, and they have led to the firing of a few men who would not have been convicted under the law. For example, a male executive told a female coworker about the plot of the *Seinfeld* show the night before. Seinfeld

of sex in schools and colleges that receive federal aid. The amendments were prompted by discrimination against women by undergraduate and graduate colleges, especially in admissions and financial aid.

The language of the amendments, often referred to as **Title IX,** is very broad, and the Department of Education, which administers the provisions, has established extensive rules that cover more aspects of education than Congress expected.[238] The department has used Title IX to prod institutions into employing and promoting more female teachers and administrators, opening vocational training classes to girls and home economics classes to boys, and offering equal athletic programs to girls and women. If institutions don't comply, the government can cut off their federal aid. (See Table 2.)

Title IX has affected athletic programs especially. Before, schools provided far fewer sports for females than for males, and they spent far fewer dollars—for scholarships, coaches, and facilities—on women's sports. Now the department interprets Title IX to require a school either to have approximately the same percentage of female athletes as female undergraduates, to continually expand opportunities for female athletes, or to fully accommodate the interests and abilities of female students. (The latter would occur if female students at a school were satisfied that there were sufficient opportunities for them, given their interests and abilities, even if the opportunities were unequal to those for men.)

Very few colleges meet the first requirement. To comply, most are trying to meet the second requirement by expanding the number of women's sports. But they worry that they will have to fulfill the first requirement eventually. And they fear that they will have to cap the squad size of their football team, which has the most

had told his friends about a woman he met but whose name he could not remember except that it rhymed with a female body part. The coworker complained of sexual harassment, and Miller Brewing Company fired the executive, despite his nineteen years with the company. (When the executive sued the company, however, a mostly female jury awarded him millions of dollars for being wrongfully dismissed.)

Women in traditional female jobs, such as secretaries, are more likely to be subjected to *quid pro quo* harassment from supervisors, whereas women in traditional male jobs, especially blue-collar jobs, are more likely to be subjected to hostile-environment harassment from coworkers. Examples abound of male laborers posting sexual pictures or writing sexual messages in women's lockers or restrooms or leaving plastic penises in their toolboxes; taunting the women with sexual questions and comments or addressing

them as "Bitch," "Slut," or "Whore" instead of by name; and grabbing their breasts, buttocks, or genitals. Worse for new workers, however, is having supervisors or coworkers who will not train them or help them, or coworkers who will sabotage their work, making them appear slow and shoddy, to drive them off the job. Some coworkers have even sabotaged the women's machinery or equipment—for example, male firefighters have disabled their female colleagues' life-saving equipment—and thus endangered the women's lives.

The dynamics of sexual harassment don't revolve around sex as much as they reflect abuse of power. A supervisor or coworker makes a woman feel vulnerable and thus exercises psychological dominance over her. He wants her to leave the workplace or, at least, to suffer inferior status if she remains there.

Consultants have found that a very small percentage of men harass

women, but these men do it a lot. Perhaps three to five men out of one hundred create problems, but these men might affect fifty women. They typically feel bitter toward women or threatened by them. Some also have been bullies toward men as well.[6]

Surveys and stories from women indicate that many more have been sexually harassed than have sued. Relatively few have filed formal complaints, let alone brought lawsuits, because they need their jobs.

[1]*Mentor Savings Bank* v. *Vinson,* 91 L.Ed.2d 49 (1986).
[2]*Oncale* v. *Sundowner Offshore Services,* 140 L.Ed.2d 201 (1998).
[3]*Oncale* v. *Sundowner Offshore Services.*
[4]Henry Louis Gates Jr., "Men Behaving Badly," *New Yorker,* August 18, 1997, 5.
[5]*Faragher* v. *Boca Raton,* 141 L.Ed.2d 662 (1998); *Burlington Industries* v. *Ellerth,* 141 L.Ed.2d 633 (1998).
[6]Kirsten Downey Grimsley, "Confronting Hard-Core Harassers," *Washington Post National Weekly Edition,* January 27, 1997, 6.

players and costs the most money, to do so. This would lessen the imbalance in the numbers of male and female athletes, and it would free more money for women's teams.

Some colleges have resisted the enforcement of Title IX, partly because athletic departments are struggling to balance their budget and partly because the act threatens deeply ingrained cultural values reflected in men's athletics. Administrators and boosters fear that women's sports will take money from men's sports and thereby weaken the primacy of men's athletics.

When Brown University tried to eliminate women's volleyball and gymnastics (at the same time it dropped men's golf and water polo), members of the women's teams sued. More than sixty schools filed briefs supporting Brown's decisions and criticizing the department's interpretations of Title IX. Lower courts ruled against Brown, and in 1997, the Supreme Court refused

to hear the case, leaving the lower courts' rulings intact. Thus the department's interpretations remain.

Already Title IX has had a major impact. Colleges have increased their women's teams—more than three times as many as in the early 1970s—and their female athletes—more than ten times as many as before.[239] Women now make up 42 percent of all college athletes and receive 42 percent of the scholarship money (though their teams have lower coaches' salaries and operating expenses than men's teams, and their teams have a smaller proportion of women coaches than they used to).[240]

Colleges with successful football or basketball programs have increased their women's teams the most because these sports generate revenue that funds women's sports. Colleges with no football program have also increased their women's teams. Colleges with football programs that don't generate a profit (and most don't)

Table 2	Taking Strides

Since 1970, women have made dramatic gains in higher education.

Women are graduating from college at a higher rate than men.

percentage of bachelor's degrees earned by women:

1970: 40%

1980: 47

1990: 54

2004: 57

Women are graduating from law and medical school at nearly the rate of men.

percentage of law degrees earned by women::

1970: 5%

1980: 28

1990: 42

2000: 46

2004: 49

percentage of medical degrees earned by women:

1970: 8%

1980: 23

1990: 34

2000: 43

2004: 46

SOURCES: National Center for Education Statistics; *Statistical Abstract of the U.S. 1999*, tab. 333 and 329; 2007, tab. 293.

lag behind. They pour money into football but lack revenue from television or bowl contracts to fund women's sports.[241]

To reduce the gender imbalance, many colleges have eliminated low-profile men's teams, especially wrestling, gymnastics, tennis, and track. Marquette University eliminated men's wrestling even though the team was financed mostly by private donations.[242]

Title IX has also had a major impact on high schools, which have increased their girls' teams. Before Title IX, 1 of every 27 girls played on a high school team; now 1 of every 2.5 girls does.[243]

But supporters have a broader goal in mind as well. "If girls are socialized the way boys are to take part in sports," the editor of a women's sports magazine says, and "if boys and girls grow up with the idea that girls are strong and capable, it will change the way girls and women are viewed—by themselves and by society."[244]

Overall, Congress and the courts have moved steadily toward legal equality for the sexes. Women have accomplished through congressional and judicial action much of what they would have accomplished with the ERA. It is an indication of the success of the movement that young women today take their equality for granted and focus on their personal lives rather than on the need for further progress.

However, challenges remain. Besides the noncompliance with congressional laws, as noted above, the demands on working parents are overwhelming. The workplace needs reform. "The failure of the workplace to make accommodations for working parents is one of the biggest unmet demands of American voters."[245] The family also needs reform. After work, most wives come home to face their "second shift." According to one survey, 40 percent feel that their husbands create more work around the house than they perform.[246]

Discrimination against Men

The traditional conception of gender roles has also created problems for men who don't fit the standard mold.

When the Burger Court rejected stereotypes that led to discrimination against women, it also rejected some that led to discrimination against men. It invalidated Mississippi's law barring men from a state university's nursing school.[247] It also invalidated Alabama's law allowing only women to seek alimony upon divorce.[248] Thus the Court rejected stereotypes that only women become nurses and only women are dependent on their spouses.

On the other hand, the Burger Court upheld some laws that were designed to protect women but that discriminate against men. It affirmed laws prohibiting statutory rape—intercourse with a minor, with consent—by males but not by females.[249] It also affirmed a law mandating draft registration for males but not for females.[250] It rationalized that registration eventually could lead to the draft and the draft eventually could lead to combat, and it insisted that most women aren't capable of combat. Thus the Court accepted the stereotypes that only men initiate sex with under-age partners and only men can fight in war.

In the absence of a draft, the most significant discrimination against men may occur in divorce cases, where the norm is to grant custody of children to

Men resisted the expansion of women's athletics. The Boston Marathon was traditionally for men only. When the first woman tried to participate in 1967, a marathon official assaulted her.

mothers and require payment of support by fathers. Although courts give fathers visitation rights, they permit mothers to move miles away, making visitation difficult and sporadic. And although governments have taken steps to enforce support payments, they have done little to enforce visitation rights. This practice reflects the stereotype that fathers are capable of funding their children but not of raising them. The Supreme Court has ignored this problem.

Other discrimination against men may occur in cases of unintended pregnancy. Women may choose abortion, adoption, or raising the child. Men have no choice. The Supreme Court invalidated laws requiring a husband's consent before his wife's abortion, because the woman carries the fetus so she is most affected by the decision.[251] But consider a different situation. A twenty-five-year-old man repeatedly told his girlfriend that he didn't want to have a child, but she assured him—falsely—that she couldn't get pregnant because of a physical condition. After unprotected sex, however, she got pregnant. She did want to have the child, and a Michigan court ordered the man, now her ex-boyfriend, to pay $500 a month in child support. With help from the National Center for Men, he filed a lawsuit, nicknamed *Roe* v. *Wade for Men*.[252]

According to traditional notions of morality, fashioned before the right to abortion, if you engage in intercourse, you risk becoming a parent and shoulder-

ing financial responsibilities. But the right to abortion changes the calculus. It frees women from the unintended consequences of pregnancy. Should a comparable right free men from the unintended consequences of pregnancy? Assuming men have no say over the decision to give birth, should a comparable right allow men to opt out of financial obligations at least? Should this man, who evidently was deceived, be saddled with eighteen years of child support? Or is the unfairness to him overridden by the child's need for financial support from two parents?

Affirmative Action

Assume that a black runner and a white runner compete at a track meet. But the officials force the black runner to carry heavy weights, and he falls behind. Eventually, the officials realize that this is unfair, and they take the weights off. Of course, the black runner is still behind. Would this be fair? Assume instead that the officials not only take the weights off but also allow him to catch up. Would this be fairer?[253]

This scenario captures the dilemma of civil rights policy today. Although most discrimination has been repudiated by the courts and legislatures, the effects of past discrimination survive. Now the question is whether civil rights policy should ignore race and sex or take race and sex into account to compensate for the effects of past discrimination. That is, should the policy require nondiscrimination only or **affirmative action** as well?

Affirmative action applies to employers for hiring and promoting minorities and women, colleges and universities for admitting minorities and women, and governments for reserving a portion of their contracts for businesses owned by minorities and women. We'll examine the first two of these.

In Employment

The Civil Rights Act of 1964, which bars discrimination in employment, does not mention affirmative action, but it does authorize the bureaucracy to make rules to end discrimination. In 1969, the Department of Labor called for affirmative action by companies doing business with the federal government. Later, the Equal Employment Opportunities Commission called for affirmative action by governments, and the Office of Education called for affirmative action by colleges as

Although most single parents are women, an increasing number are men, such as this father of an eleven-year-old in Dallas.

well. Presidents from Nixon through Carter supported it with executive orders, and the Supreme Court sanctioned it in a series of cases.[254] Many state and local governments also adopted it.

Affirmative action requires positive steps to ensure that qualified minorities and women receive a fair share of the jobs at each level. Just what the positive steps and the fair share should be are the subject of considerable controversy.

If the number of minorities or women who work in a company that has government contracts is less than the number in the local labor force, the company must agree to recruit more minorities or women or, in serious cases, draw up an affirmative action plan. The plan must include goals to hire or promote more minorities or women and a timetable to reach these goals. If the company does not reach them, it must show that it made an effort to do so. If the company cannot satisfy the government, it can be denied future contracts (though in reality these companies are seldom penalized). Similar requirements apply if the number of minorities or women who work in a government agency is less than the number in the local labor force.

Although the requirements for affirmative action plans speak of "goals," critics charge that they mandate quotas and that quotas amount to "reverse discrimination" and result in lower standards.[255] The terms do blur; if employers are pressured to meet goals, they might interpret *goals* to mean *quotas*. But only after a finding of deliberate and systematic discrimination does affirmative action entail actual quotas.[256]

Furthermore, the courts scrutinize the plans to make sure that they do not prevent all white men from being hired and promoted and that they are temporary (usually until the percentage of minority or female employees reaches the percentage of minority or female workers in the community).

Affirmative action applies to hiring and promoting but not to laying off workers. Because of a belief that affirmative action shouldn't impose much burden on innocent individuals, the Court has struck down the use of affirmative action—any protection for minorities and women—when employers pare their workforce for economic reasons. Instead, the Court has accepted the traditional practice, based on seniority, that the last hired can be the first fired, even if the last hired were minorities and women.[257]

In addition to these limits on affirmative action, the Rehnquist Court made it more difficult for governments to adopt affirmative action for themselves or to require it for companies.[258] Governments must show clear evidence of some particular past discrimination by the government or company or industry, rather than simply point to the pervasive historical discrimination in society, as their justification for adopting or requiring affirmative action.

Affirmative action has definitely helped minorities and women. White men dominate public and private institutions, and as the personnel director of a Fortune 500 company observed, "People tend to hire people like themselves."[259] Thus affirmative action has prodded employers to hire more minorities and women.[260] It has also prodded managers to promote more minorities and women who previously had been stuck in low-level positions.[261]

Although affirmative action is controversial among the public, it is routinely used and even championed, under the name of "diversity," by big businesses. It enables them to locate untapped talent in overlooked groups and to gain new insights for selling their products to minority and female consumers.[262]

Whether affirmative action is mandated by governments or practiced by businesses, it has helped some blacks move up a rung—from the lower middle class to the middle class or from the middle class to the upper middle class.[263] But affirmative action has not pulled blacks out of the underclass. Many of them, in families mired in poverty, lack the education and skills necessary to compete for available jobs.[264] And affirmative action cannot create new jobs or better jobs, so it is not as helpful to minorities or women as a flourishing economy is.

In short, affirmative action should not be given more credit or more blame than it deserves. It has boosted some minorities and women, but it cannot help many others. It has displaced some white men, but it has not affected most others.

Yet 13 percent of white men think they lost a job or promotion because of their race, and 10 percent think they did because of their sex.[265] Many others claim they "heard about" another white man who did. Yet affirmative action is not as pervasive as most people assume.[266] Many people view affirmative action as they do handicapped parking. When looking for a parking space in a crowded lot, numerous drivers see an empty handicapped space and think, "If it weren't for that, I could park here." Of course, if the space wasn't reserved for handicapped drivers, only one other driver could park there.[267] So it is with affirmative action. Many white men think they would get a particular job if it weren't for affirmative action, but only one would. Meanwhile, the rest feel victimized by the policy.

For both sides in the controversy, affirmative action has become a symbol. For civil rights leaders, it represents fairness and a step toward equality and progress. For critics, it represents unfairness and an attack on individuality and merit. It's important to debate these values, but it's also important to recognize that affirmative action is neither the key public policy for racial and sexual equality, as some supporters portray it, nor a big stumbling block for individual achievement, as some detractors characterize it. In fact, some supporters argue that affirmative action reaches so few individuals that it is an attempt to achieve "racial justice on the cheap," without facing up to the greater problem of the underclass.[268]

In College Admissions

Affirmative action also applies to college and university admissions. Colleges and universities began to use affirmative action in the 1970s. Some schools used limited programs that gave a boost to minority applicants, while other schools used extensive programs that reserved seats—essentially, set quotas—for minority applicants. The medical school of the University of California at Davis reserved sixteen seats in its class of one hundred students for minorities. In *University of California v. Bakke*, the Burger Court upheld the use of race as a factor in admissions, emphasizing the value of diversity, but struck down the use of quotas (unless the school had a history of intentional discrimination).

The Supreme Court would not rule on this issue again until 2003. In the meantime, voters in California and Washington and the governor of Florida mandated an end to the use of race in admissions to public universities in those states.

The moves against affirmative action prompted concerns that minority enrollments would plunge. Some state legislatures and universities decided not to let this happen. The Texas legislature passed a law guaranteeing admission to its state universities for all high school graduates in the top 10 percent of their class. The University of California Board of Regents guaranteed admission to at least one of the UC campuses for those in the top 4 percent.

These programs use geography instead of race; in particular, they use residential segregation, which has stymied the efforts to desegregate the schools from grade schools through high schools, as a way to diversify the universities. Minority students who perform well in their schools can get admitted to the universities, even if their segregated schools provide a lower-quality education than the white schools offer.

Although the programs in both states have increased the numbers of minorities above the levels they would have had without the programs, the numbers are lower than they had been with affirmative action.[269] Asians—not whites—have been the prime beneficiaries of the demise of affirmative action in these states, as they would be with the end of affirmative action throughout the country.[270]

The Rehnquist Court revisited the *Bakke* ruling in 2003. In a pair of cases from the University of Michigan, one directed at undergraduate admissions and one directed at law school admissions, five justices upheld affirmative action but only as part of a "holistic review" that gives "individualized consideration" to each application. Schools can't use formulas that add points for minority status; they must use a more labor-intensive review.[271] The decision to uphold affirmative action came as a surprise, because the Rehnquist Court had narrowed the practice in employment cases.

FROM THE DETROIT FREE PRESS

MIKE THOMPSON, COPLEY NEWS SERVICE

Reprinted with permission by Copley News Service

Some justices may have been influenced by friend of the court briefs. A record number of these—102—were prepared, most supporting affirmative action. They were filed not only by universities but also by dozens of Fortune 500 companies. One was filed by twenty-one retired generals and admirals, including three former superintendents of the military academies. This brief recalled the Vietnam War, when there were few minority officers and there was much tension between black troops and white officers. Since then, affirmative action has produced an integrated officer corps and consequently a more effective military, according to the retired brass. Justice Sandra Day O'Connor, who provided the crucial fifth vote, acknowledged that selective universities—the ones that use affirmative action—train the leaders of our society and that an integrated leadership helps govern a diverse people.

The future of affirmative action is in doubt, however, because Justice O'Connor was replaced by the more conservative Justice Alito, and at least four, if not five, justices on the new Roberts Court are hostile to any use of race to ameliorate past discrimination.[272]

Just as some white men believe that affirmative action cost them a job or promotion, some white students believe that it cost them, or will cost them, a seat in the college or university of their choice. But 60 percent of colleges admit nearly all students who apply; only 20 percent are selective enough to use affirmative action.[273] Students who apply to elite schools are more likely to lose a seat because parents of other applicants are alumni of these schools, and these schools give preferential treatment to their "legacies." (This practice encourages the alumni to donate to their school.) Typically, a fifth of Harvard's students receive preferential treatment because their parents attended the school. Harvard's "legacies" are more than twice as likely to be admitted as blacks or Latinos. A similar advantage exists at other selective schools, including public schools such as the Universities of California and Virginia.[274]

Affirmative action may be more widespread in graduate and professional schools.[275] For some beneficiaries of affirmative action in law schools, recent social science research has found a mismatch between these students' abilities and the schools' demands. These students attended law schools that were too difficult for them, making it harder for them to graduate, pass the bar exam, and join the legal profession.[276] These findings are controversial, but, if confirmed, suggest that some schools may need to adjust the scope of their affirmative action programs.

Conclusion: Is Government Responsive in Granting Civil Rights?

When summarizing civil rights progress for minorities and women, an apt analogy is a glass that is half full but also half empty. The same idea is expressed in a website's title—the Half Changed World.

Blacks and women have taken long strides toward equality since the time when people would say, "A Negro's place is in the cotton field" or "A woman's place is in the home."

The civil rights movement and the women's movement initiated the changes. They protested inequality, and they put that issue on the public agenda. As the movements grew and garnered support, they pressured the government. Eventually, a century after the movements began, the government responded.

Within the government, the Supreme Court exercised decisive leadership. In the 1950s and 1960s, the Warren Court was activist in striking down racial segregation, and in the 1970s and 1980s, the Burger Court was activist in striking down sexual discrimination. The Courts' efforts may go down in history as their major achievements. But the Courts' rulings themselves weren't sufficient. Because the Court lacks the means to enforce its decisions, the president and Congress had to help overcome public resistance.

Thus the areas of racial and sexual discrimination show the power, and the limits of the power, of the courts. The Supreme Court exercised power because it articulated society's emerging views that racial segregation and sexual discrimination by law are wrong and because it forced the government to address this discrimination. But the Court could not bring about the changes by itself. And the Court could not bring about further changes to overcome residential segregation, which leads to school segregation and school inequality, or to ameliorate the poverty that renders many blacks unable to take advantage of their rights. These intractable conditions will require concerted action by the other branches and the other levels of government as well.

The changes in racial and sexual policies over the years illustrate the responsiveness of the government. In its subjugation of blacks until the 1950s and its treatment of women until the 1970s, the government was responding to majority opinion. When blacks and women organized to protest their status, the government began responding to them and to the shifts in majority opinion that their protests prompted.

In pressuring the government to respond, African Americans have benefited from being numerous, visible, and—with their common legacy of slavery, segregation, and discrimination—cohesive. Their concentration in large northern cities and some southern states has helped them exercise political power. Their legacy, though, has fostered the ghetto, with its debilitating conditions, and denied them the resources to make faster progress.

Thus there are two black Americas—a middle class that has benefited tremendously from the civil rights movement and the changes in our society and a lower class, especially the underclass, that has been left behind to fend for itself.[277]

Latinos, whose movement is younger, have also taken strides toward equality. With increased immigration, they have become more numerous, and in coming years they will become even more numerous, giving them a large voting bloc. Their concentration in some western and southwestern states has enabled them to influence state and local governments. Their diversity and lack of cohesiveness, however, have hindered their ability to influence the national government.

American Indians are the smallest, most isolated, and least organized minority, so they have had the poorest success in pressuring the government.

As minority groups grow—together they are expected to make up half of the U.S. population by 2050—they will be able to exert pressure on government more effectively. But they will increasingly come into conflict with each other, especially when economic conditions are stagnant and government jobs and services are scarce. Already there are tensions. Some blacks resent the faster progress of Latinos and Asians. These blacks say African Americans were here before most Hispanics and all Asians, they suffered more and struggled longer, and so they should reap the rewards sooner. On the other hand, Latino leaders resent the reluctance of black groups to help them with their issues.[278] There have been conflicts, even riots. Blacks have rioted in Miami from frustration with the Cuban-dominated leadership. Latinos have rioted in Washington, D.C., out of anger with the black power structure. Continuing illegal immigration could exacerbate the tensions by pitting new immigrants against poor blacks in competition for jobs.

Nonminority women were never subjugated as much as minority men and women, so they have had less to overcome. Moreover, women are a majority, they vote as frequently as men, and they have well-organized and well-funded interest groups. Consequently, they have made the greatest strides toward equality.

Key Terms

Key Names

1. According to the Founders, the phrase "all men are created equal" in the Declaration of Independence meant
   a. people are born with equal virtue.
   b. people are born with equal intelligence and ability.
   c. people should have equal rights.
   d. white men should have equal rights.
   e. very little—the phrase was simply intended to rally Americans for the revolution.

2. The *Dred Scott* decision was significant for all but which of the following?
   a. It proclaimed slavery unconstitutional.
   b. It polarized Americans further.
   c. It held that even free blacks weren't citizens.
   d. It contributed to the climate that fostered the Civil War.
   e. It held that Congress couldn't control slavery in the territories.

3. Which constitutional provision is usually cited and debated when litigants complain of discrimination?
   a. Thirteenth Amendment
   b. equal protection clause
   c. Fifteenth Amendment
   d. due process clause
   e. exclusionary rule

4. Jim Crow laws in the South
   a. broke up the plantations after the Civil War.
   b. maintained order during Reconstruction.
   c. implemented the Thirteenth, Fourteenth, and Fifteenth Amendments.
   d. established official segregation.
   e. made blacks sharecroppers.

5. The *Plessy* v. *Ferguson* ruling was important because it
   a. led to the Civil War.
   b. led to *de jure* segregation.
   c. articulated the separate-but-equal doctrine to justify segregation.
   d. invalidated segregation in the North.
   e. finally allowed black children in the South to get an education.

6. The Supreme Court's ruling in *Brown v. Board of Education*
   a. maintained the precedent set in the *Dred Scott* case.
   b. maintained the precedent set in the *Plessy* v. *Ferguson* case.
   c. fostered *de jure* segregation.
   d. applied the Fifteenth Amendment to the states.
   e. used the Fourteenth Amendment's equal protection clause against segregation.

7. *De facto* segregation is
   a. due to Jim Crow laws.
   b. due to sundown laws.
   c. based on residential patterns.
   d. typical in small towns.
   e. typical in the South.

8. Which of the following statements about busing for desegregation isn't true?
   a. It was used extensively throughout the United States.
   b. It prompted an increase in white flight to the suburbs.
   c. It was mostly used within school districts.
   d. There was far less busing for desegregation than there was busing to segregated schools.
   e. It was rarely used to bus inner-city kids to suburban schools or suburban kids to inner-city schools.

9. Martin Luther King's tactics of direct action and nonviolence worked
   a. well against job discrimination in the North.
   b. poorly against *de facto* segregation.
   c. ineffectively in the television age.
   d. poorly against *de jure* segregation.
   e. well against job discrimination in the South.

10. Which of the following statements about school desegregation in recent decades isn't true?
    a. We made significant progress in the 1960s, 1970s, and 1980s.
    b. School segregation has gotten worse in the past decade.
    c. Most minority children go to mostly minority schools.
    d. *De facto* segregation remains.
    e. *De jure* segregation continues.

11. Compared with schools attended by white children, those attended by black and Latino children tend to be
    a. better.
    b. just as good.
    c. almost as good.
    d. worse.
    e. none of the above. There's no clear pattern.

12. The lives of _____ blacks have improved greatly since the 1950s, but the lives of _____ blacks have not.
    a. middle-class; underclass
    b. middle-class; upper-class
    c. upper-class; middle-class
    d. underclass; middle-class
    e. lower-class; upper-class

13. Which generalization about current immigrants tends to be true?
    a. Only Asians are learning English.
    b. Among Hispanics, only Cubans are learning English.
    c. Most Hispanics don't feel pressure to learn English.
    d. Even Mexicans who live here a long time don't learn English.
    e. Immigrants' children almost all learn fluent English.

14. Latinos have had trouble making political gains because of all but which of the following?
    a. They come from diverse cultures.
    b. They're not as cohesive as African Americans.
    c. They're not as numerous as African Americans.
    e. They don't register to vote at the same rates as African Americans.
    e. They identify with the country they come from.

15. The women's movement in the 1970s and 1980s especially attracted
    a. lower-class women who were most affected by job discrimination.
    b. traditional women.
    c. lower-middle-class women who wanted to move further up in the middle class.
    d. housewives.
    e. upper-middle-class women who were college educated.

16. The Equal Rights Amendment wasn't ratified by the states primarily because
    a. of opposition from working women.
    b. it would provide equal rights for homosexuals.
    c. it symbolized an attack on traditional values of motherhood and family.
    d. it wouldn't provide equal rights for men.
    e. of opposition from younger women.

17. Women often receive less pay than men because
    a. they have children.
    b. they have different jobs than men.
    c. they face discrimination.
    d. Congress refused to pass a law mandating equal pay for equal work.
    e. all but d.

18. Evidence shows that affirmative action has
    a. had little effect in the public sector.
    b. helped many blacks move up to the middle or upper-middle class.
    c. led to the creation of new jobs.
    d. helped many blacks escape from the underclass.
    e. had little effect in the private sector.

19. Which statement about affirmative action in college admissions today isn't correct?
    a. Affirmative action isn't allowed anymore.
    b. Quotas for minorities or women aren't allowed.
    c. Automatic points for being minority aren't allowed.
    d. Race can be taken into account, as a plus, if each applicant receives individual consideration.
    e. The use of race is justified by the need for diversity.

20. The _____ Court was the one primarily responsible for rulings restricting race discrimination, while the _____ Court was the one primarily responsible for rulings restricting sex discrimination.
    a. Warren; Burger
    b. Warren; Rehnquist
    c. Burger; Warren
    d. Burger; Rehnquist
    e. Burger; Roberts

Key: 1-d; 2-a; 3-b; 4-d; 5-c; 6-e; 7-c; 8-a; 9-b; 10-e; 11-d; 12-a; 13-e; 14-c; 15-e; 16-c; 17-e; 18-b; 19-a; 20-a.

AP Images/Haraz Ghanbari

Sister Roseanne Cook, a medical doctor, checks the heartbeat of her patient in Pine Apple, Alabama. Forty-six million Americans are uninsured, and federal health care programs are limited.

ecently, former basketball star Scottie Pippen was featured not on the sports pages, but on pages reporting farm news. Why? Pippen, like billionaire Ted Turner, founder of CNN and TNT, and David Rockefeller, one of the heirs to the Rockefeller fortune, and at least twenty Fortune 500 companies received agricultural support checks. Several members of Congress also received the checks, the former Speaker of the House, the ranking Democrat on the House Agriculture Committee, and the former chair of the Senate Finance Committee, Charles Grassley. Grassley, who claims to be primarily a farmer and not to live in Washington, D.C., "except Monday through Fridays," has received payments as large as $110,936—mailed to his Washington residence.

The reason for the program in the beginning was to support the family farmer and to keep farmers on the land. But small family farmers get little of the subsidy. Most of the funds go to the largest farms, many owned by corporations. As one writer, publishing in the newsletter of the conservative Cato Foundation, pointed out, "The biggest 10 percent of farm businesses have received 72 percent of farm subsidies."[1] In fact, farm families, on averge, earn more than the average household.

Even though most conservatives and liberals oppose farm subsidies in theory, most on both sides of the partisan divide continue to support them for fear of alienating corporate donations, being perceived as not sympathetic to the hypothetical "family farmer," and hence losing the next election. Agriculture and the "family farm" hold a special place in the American identity— they represent the country's breadbasket, its Corn and Bible Belts, conjuring up images of waving fields of grain, pioneers, and an "authentic" America that politicians love to be associated with, even if that is not where the farm subsidy funds are going.

Most Americans believe that government should be fairly small. And yet, few Americans eschew benefits targeted to their own groups, whether those groups be age specific, occupational, racial, or something else. Farmers wants support for their crops and for not growing crops; veterans want government help to compensate them for their service to their country and perhaps for the injuries sustained during that service, businesses want tax breaks so they can create new jobs or pay a higher dividend to their shareholders, senior citizens want government to ensure they can live their old age in dignity, and so on. Moreover, Americans want government to protect them, too. We want protection not just from foreign enemies or domestic criminals, but also from unsafe food and drugs, hazardous working conditions, fraudulent businesses, and dangerous air or auto travel, among other things.

To meet the needs of its citizens and to protect the country from potential enemies, governments raise money through taxes and spend it in many different ways to achieve national goals. In the course of this, governmental taxing and spending differentially benefits various groups in society. Most of the political discussion in the United States (and other countries too) is about how to raise and spend money and how much each group should contribute to the revenue and benefit from the spending. Though much of that discussion is cloaked in rhetoric about the national interests, in fact, groups see the national interest in large part through the lenses of their own interests. Americans tend to view their own benefits—scholarships and guaranteed loans for students; price supports and credit assistance to farmers; preferred mortgage rates to veterans; retirement benefits and medical care for seniors; billions in annual tax deductions for savings plans, home ownership, education, private health care, and charitable giving—as entitlements reflecting a good use of their tax dollars.

Although a discussion of all government policies is far beyond the scope of this chapter, we will focus on how government raises money through taxation and how funds are allocated through a variety of social welfare spending policies adopted to serve the needs of specific groups of Americans. We will put these discussions in the context of income inequality. Although federal social welfare programs aid almost all groups—rich, poor, and almost everyone in between—more social welfare spending is targeted at the well-off than at the poor. Thus government taxing and spending policies exacerbate the differences between the rich and poor.

Income Distribution

We will start by considering the question of how income is distributed. Should government help those at the lower end of the income spectrum through progressive taxation (placing a lower tax burden on middle- and lower-income families than on the wealthy) and government spending to help lower-income Americans? Or should government help those at the upper end of the income distribution through tax breaks and subsidized services for them in the expectation that they will create jobs and benefits for poor people? Those who believe private property is the preeminent right in a capitalist society tend to oppose the use of tax and spending policy to diminish income inequality. Those who believe that a society of haves and have-nots, with relatively few in the middle, is inherently unstable and a threat to democracy are more supportive of taxing and spending to prevent extreme maldistribution of income.

Since the passage of civil rights and affirmative action laws, our society has become progressively more democratic in terms of equality before the law and equal opportunity in the marketplace. However, the distribution of wealth is more unequal than at any time since the 1930s.[2] See Table 1.

What has caused income distribution to become so unbalanced? First, wages for blue-collar jobs have not kept pace with overall wage increases. In the immediate post–World War II era, family income grew more than 3 percent a year,[3] so workers could see continuing income growth. But since the 1970s, blue-collar workers started falling behind.[4] In fact, in the 1980s, in real terms,

Table 1	Distribution of Household Income in the United States Is Becoming More Lopsided		

Percentage of Income Earned			
Percentage of Households	**1980**	**1990**	**2001**
Lowest 20%	4.3	3.9	3.5
Next lowest 20%	10.3	9.6	8.7
Middle 20%	16.9	15.9	14.6
Next highest 20%	24.9	24.0	23.0
Highest 20%	43.7	46.6	50.1
Top 5%	15.8	18.6	22.4

SOURCE: U.S. Census Bureau, Income Inequality Table, IE-3, 1980–2001, www.census.gov/hhes/www/income/histinc/ie3.html/.

The American postwar economy lifted millions of families into middle-class status. At left is thirty-two-year-old Florence Thompson and her three daughters in 1936 after drought and the Depression drove them from Oklahoma to look for a better future in California. The family was living in a migrant labor camp and surviving on vegetables dug up from fields and birds killed by the children. Publication of the photo prompted the government to send twenty thousand pounds of food to the camp. At right is the same family forty-three years later in Modesto, California, where Mrs. Thompson's children eventually were able to buy her a home. But before her death in 1983, they had to solicit contributions to pay for her medical care.

blue-collar workers were earning less than their parents did at a comparable age, and growth in living standards nearly stopped. There were fewer well-paying jobs for them than there had been twenty years earlier because heavy industries that traditionally paid high wages to unionized workers fell on hard times. Wage concessions were made by workers worried about job security. The proportion of workers in unions dropped from 47 percent in the immediate postwar years, to 13 percent today.[5] With less powerful unions, workers lost both economic power and political clout since unions were an important part of the political coalition supporting civil rights, health and education reform, and other progressive policies closely tied to equality and well-being.

Except for the most highly educated, the *lifetime* earnings of men have been declining since the 1980s,

even though earnings for the high-skill workers have increased.[6] Virtually all wage growth since 1973 has gone to the top 20 or 30 percent of earners. In fact, in 1973 the median wage for male workers was $15.24; in 2004, adjusted for inflation, it was only 2 cents more.[7]

Even during the 1990s, when the United States experienced a remarkable nine years of low unemployment, economic growth, and low inflation, income inequalities increased. Jobs were plentiful, but the rich got richer faster than the middle class and poor improved their status.

This leads to the second reason for growing income inequality. The earnings of those at the top of the income scale have skyrocketed. As real wages stagnated and the average income of the poorest fifth fell, by 2005 the average corporate executive was earning more in one day than the average American worker earned in a year (Figure 1).[8] In many cases, CEO compensation was set by a board of directors appointed by the CEO, and amounts were unrelated to the economic performance of the company.

Recent tax changes favoring upper-income Americans are the third reason for growing inequalities. Tax policies have reduced taxes on the very wealthy much more than on lower- and middle-income Americans. A series of tax cuts during the past decade have favored the wealthiest Americans. For example, the 2006 tax cuts provided an average of $20 for each family in the bottom 20 percent of income and $44,600 for those in the top 1 percent of income. Millionaires got tax breaks of over more than $100,000.[9]

Politicians of all stripes quote data in a way that adds greatest support to their positions, so the income increases that went lopsidedly to a single demographic group are also used as evidence of a strengthening economy. But it is always necessary to look beyond average and median income to see how aggregate wealth in real dollars is distributed across all income groups, both before and after taxes, to understand the health of the economy. Here is a common illustration: nine men—firefighters, factory workers and police officers—with an average income of $50,000 are sitting in a neighborhood bar talking when Bill Gates walks through the door. The average income of the ten men in the room is now $45 billion. When an example is that extreme, it is easy to see the problem of income averaging.

The wealth gap is far greater than income alone suggests, because those in the highest brackets have money to save, invest in the stock market, and buy homes. This made it possible for those already well off to take advantage of the real estate and stock booms of the 1990s in ways unavailable to those with little capital. The concentration of wealth and privilege (especially access to higher education in elite institu-

tions) has become so pronounced that one observer refers to the formation of an "overclass."[10] (See Figure 2.)

Government and the Economy

Human nature does not change in 30 years, so these changes in income distribution must be due to government or the economy or both. Our Constitution specifies only a little about the nature of our economic system. It emphasizes private property rights and gives government monetary, taxation, and regulatory powers. By contrast, the governments of most countries, whether democracies or dictatorships, have constitutions that link their political system to a form of economic organization and give government major responsibilities for achieving economic goals.

Types of Economic Systems

The role of government in the economy largely determines the kind of economic system a country has. An economy in which individuals and corporations own its capital goods or productive capacity—businesses, facto-

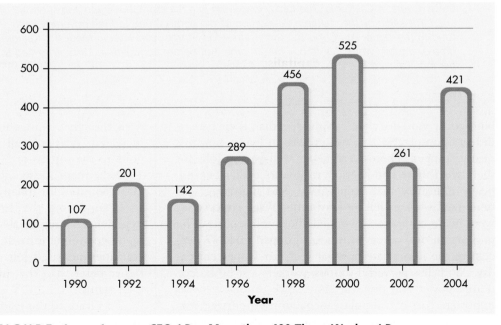

FIGURE 1 • Average CEOs' Pay More than 400 Times Workers' Pay

The pay of the average corporate CEO is now almost 400 times that of the average worker.

SOURCE: Institute for Policy Studies and United for a Fair Economy. CEO compensation based on *Business Week* annual compensation surveys; pay of average worker based on Bureau of Labor statistics data.

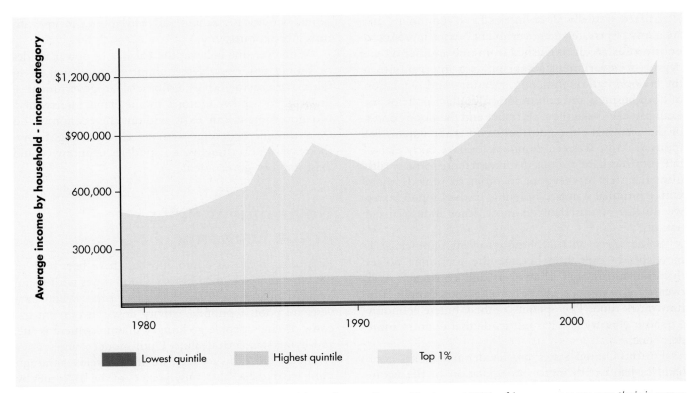

FIGURE 2 • **The Income Gap between the Rich and Poor Grows** *The lowest 20% of income earners saw their incomes increase by $800, in real terms, between 1979 and 2004. The highest 1% of income earners saw their real income increase by more than $500,000 in that period.*
SOURCE: Reported in *The New York Times Sunday Magazine,* June 10, 2007, 60. Data from the Congressional Budget Office, Historical Effective Tax Rates: 1979–2004, December, 2006. Chart by MGMT.Design. These data are pretax income.

ries, and farms—is called a **capitalist economy,** or sometimes a free market, free enterprise economy. In a pure capitalist economy, prices, profits, working conditions, and wages would be totally determined by private sector decisions rather than by the government. Manufacturers would sell goods at what the market could bear, pay workers as little as possible, and manufacture products as cheaply as possible, concerned with health and safety only to the extent dictated by individual morality and the necessity to maintain consumer loyalty.

The idea that a capitalist economy would promote prosperity was popularized in 1776 by the British economist **Adam Smith** in *The Wealth of Nations.*[11] In his view, as each person seeks to maximize his or her own economic well-being, the collective well-being is enhanced. Businesses become more efficient, sell more at lower costs, hire more workers, and hence promote the economic well-being of the workers as well as the owners. Smith spoke of the "invisible hand" of the marketplace bringing about these positive outcomes.

In practice, there are no pure capitalist systems, and there never have been. Nor have there been pure socialist systems, where government owns all means of production. Instead, all economies have a mix of private and government-owned. Even Adam Smith believed there was some role for government intervention in a capitalist system, such as to ensure conditions for fair competition in the marketplace. Our own system is a mixture of private enterprise and government ownership combined with considerable government intervention through taxation and regulation. The U.S. government owns power-generating dams, some railroads, and 27 percent of all land, and it acts as an insurer of individual and corporate assets. It has loaned money to corporations to save them from bankruptcy, and it has bailed out large banks in danger of failing. In other modern societies, such as Great Britain, France, Sweden, Germany, and the former communist nations of Eastern Europe, it is not unusual for government to own airlines, television networks, and telephone systems.

In fact, virtually all countries have economies that are a mix of private and government ownership. **Mixed economies** are distinguished from one another by the degree of government ownership and intervention in the economy through taxing, spending, and regulation of both business and consumption. Budget policies, for example, can make the rich richer and the poor poorer, or they can make the poor better off at the expense of the rich. Most Western democracies have fairly elaborate social welfare systems that redistribute some wealth from the rich to the poor in order to provide them with a minimal standard of living. In the United States, we do less of this than do most other industrialized nations.

Some argue that evolution toward democracy is inevitable in capitalism because the economic power that individuals gain as workers and consumers will, over time, lead to their political empowerment. But how much time? The opening of the Chinese economy a quarter century ago has not made that country more democratic.

For the United States, greater democracy has gone hand-in-hand with increased regulation of the economy. In nineteenth-century America, government involvement in the economy was much less than it is today. Public anger over unsafe working conditions, unsafe foods and drugs, and child labor led to increased government regulation of wages, working conditions, the content of food and drugs, and more. And government responded because, as suffrage expanded, elected officials had to answer to an increasingly broader segment of the public.

There is an undeniable tension between capitalism and democracy. The capitalist marketplace rewards and encourages inequities that, if unchecked, threaten democratic beliefs about individual equality. For example, capitalist systems place no upper limits on the accumulation of wealth, even though wealth can be used to buy greater access to decision makers and hence dilutes democratic practices and norms, such as one person, one vote.

In systems where most power is concentrated in the government and in those where it is concentrated primarily in the hands of the corporate elite, democracy will suffer. Gravitation of political power to an unaccountable government will undermine democracy. Extreme maldistribution of wealth will also produce inequality of access and the loss of any meaningful practice of political equality. This is why in democratic capitalist systems, some government regulation of economic activity is essential and why most end up with mixed economies.

Wherever one believes the balance of power resides or should reside—with economic decision makers in the private sector or elected officials in government—governments and economies are inevitably intertwined. No government can exist without an economy, and even though economic systems existed long before there were governments, no modern economy could exist without government.

Government Roles in the Economy

Economic cycles of boom and bust have been one of the constants of human history. Good times with rising living standards are followed by bad times when harvests are poor, economic activity slows, investment income declines, people go hungry, unemployment is rife, and living standards decline. Until modern times, governments did little to regulate these cycles, although some tried to ease the consequences of the bad times by distributing grain to people who were starving or by providing temporary shelters for the homeless. In the United States, it was not until the 1930s that government tried, through economic policies, to prevent these cycles from occurring.

The idea that government intervention could ease the boom-and-bust cycle of the economy was revolutionary. Classical economists had argued that the market would adjust itself without government action. But as governments became larger and more powerful, people expected government at least to try to alleviate economic problems. Since the Great Depression, government has almost always been linked in the public mind to poor performance by the economy, whether or not government's policies contributed much to the failures. And whether or not the public is willing to credit public policies for a robust economy, the president and Congress will certainly try to take credit for it.

Government can have an impact on some of the economic problems of greatest concern to the average citizen—unemployment, interest rates and inflation, the high cost of food and gasoline, low income, fair employment practices, minimum wage, and barriers to trade. But it cannot do as much as many people have come to expect because much of the decision-making power lies in the private sector and outside our borders.

However, government can and does do many things. Imagine for a minute that you are a farmer in a chronically drought-stricken African country. If your cattle die or your crops fail, the chances of malnutrition and even starvation are fairly high. There is no crop insurance, no agricultural extension service, no income support or food vouchers, no public health service, and perhaps no schools to teach your children skills other than farming. Governments often do not have the reach, the resources, or sometimes even the will to provide a safety net.

This is what capitalism without a social welfare program would be like. It is closer to what our system was like in the early 1930s when American farmers fled the Dust Bowl states trying to find work to allow them to feed their children. Religious and other private charities and state and local governments provided some services, but all their resources combined could not cope with the dislocation and needs created by the Great Depression. The federal government's response to the Depression was the beginning of large-scale federal welfare and social insurance programs.

Dorothea Lange snapped this historic photo of a homeless Oklahoma family during the Great Depression. Most major federal welfare programs were adopted in the 1930s.

Fiscal Policy

Government has three primary tools to help achieve its economic goals: the fiscal, monetary, and regulatory powers granted by the Constitution. Here we will focus on fiscal policy.

Government decisions on how much money it will spend and how much tax it will levy determine **fiscal policy.** Increased spending stimulates the economy and increases employment; lower government spending helps slow the economy and decreases inflation. How great an impact government has depends on how much it spends in relation to the size of the economy. The United States spends a smaller percentage of its GDP on government than other Western industrial countries. For the past forty years, federal government spending has hovered near 20 percent of GDP and state and local government spending accounts for another 10 percent. Thus 70 percent of the GDP is accounted for by private spending.

The size of the annual budget tells us the federal government's share of the domestic economy and indicates the potential for fiscal policy to affect the nation's economy. The federal budget also reflects the country's political goals and values, because who is taxed, at what rates, and what government spends the money on reflect national priorities. Government spending is often discussed within the larger debate over fundamental political values, and disagreements on taxation have always been linked to the debate over the proper size and role of government in both a democracy and a free market economy.

Taxes are generally pegged to spending, so that government takes in enough revenue each year to cover its outlays. But tax policy is also used to help regulate economic cycles. Tax cuts leave more money in the hands of the consumer, thus stimulating private spending and reducing unemployment. Increased taxes take more money out of the hands of the consumer, slow the economy, and thus reduce inflation. Taxes also affect the income shares of different segments of society.

Government's ability to regulate economic activity through spending and taxation is limited, in part because it accounts for less than one-third of all economic activity. Moreover, our economy is linked to the global market and thus is affected by conditions over which we have little control, such as energy prices or demands for products or labor.

Who makes fiscal policy? In the United States, laws regarding taxation and spending require approval by

Congress and the president. In making his recommendations to Congress about taxes, spending, and other economic matters, the president has the assistance, among others, of three key people: the secretary of the treasury; the head of the Office of Management and Budget (OMB), who is responsible for preparing the annual budget message; and the chair of the Council of Economic Advisers, a group of economists within the White House Office who are specialists in fiscal policy matters. Sometimes, of course, these three advisers to the president are at odds with each other or with the president's political aides or are uncertain their advice is sound. Indeed, President Harry Truman once said he was in search of a one-armed economist so that the person could never make a recommendation and then say "on the other hand."[12] Economics, like political science, is an inexact science!

Congress has its own fiscal specialists on committees such as Appropriations and Budget, and members also rely heavily on the director of the nonpartisan Congressional Budget Office (CBO).

Keynesian Economics

That government can have a substantial impact on the economy through its fiscal policy has been accepted wisdom since the British economist **John Maynard Keynes** published *A General Theory of Employment, Interest and Money*.[13] In 1935, Keynes argued that government could stimulate the economy by increasing spending in a time of high unemployment. This would put more money into the economy, thus stimulating the demand for goods and services and, in turn, causing factories to produce more and hire more workers. Therefore, even if government had to borrow to increase spending, the deficit could be justified because eventually higher employment rates would increase tax revenue.

Keynesian economics ran counter to the conventional wisdom of the time. At the outset of the Great Depression in 1929, President Hoover believed that if the government went into debt, it would make the Depression worse, not better. His opponent in the 1932 election, **Franklin D. Roosevelt,** also ran on a pledge of a balanced federal budget. It was only after Roosevelt was elected that he adopted the Keynesian idea that the government could stimulate the economy by spending money, borrowing it if it had to, and in this way help the nation get out of the Depression.

Keynesian thinking dominated fiscal policy for several decades. Well into the 1960s, economists were optimistic that government could successfully regulate the economy to maintain high levels of employment and reasonable inflation. But by the 1970s, this confidence disappeared because of simultaneous high unemployment and high inflation. These conditions led to increasing dissatisfaction with existing fiscal policy.

Supply-Side Economics

In 1981, the **Reagan** administration came to the White House with a new policy, **supply-side economics,** that promised to reduce inflation, lower taxes, and balance the budget simultaneously. The basic premise of this theory is that as government lowers taxes, more money is freed for private investment. Therefore, when the economy is sluggish, supply-siders advocate tax cuts to stimulate growth. They believe people will save some of the money they would have paid in taxes, thus making more money available to lend to businesses for expansion and modernization. Taxpayers would also be left with more money to spend on consumption, and to satisfy the increased demand, businesses would hire more workers. With increased employment, there would be more people paying taxes and fewer collecting unemployment compensation. So, according to supply-side economics, it is possible both to promote economic growth and to balance the budget by lowering the tax rate.

These ideas appeal to conservatives because they offer an economic rationale for smaller budgets and thus smaller government. They also have broad appeal to Republicans, who, since the Great Depression, have drawn substantial electoral support from the wealthiest Americans. Whereas Keynesian economics has been used to endorse across-the-board tax cuts to stimulate consumer spending, the supply-side approach puts more emphasis on tax cuts for the highest income groups as a means of encouraging private investment.

Keynesians and supply-siders have fundamentally different views on government regulation of the economy. Keynesians believe that government intervention can be effective both in steering the economy and in cushioning the blow to consumers of a sluggish or overheated economy. Supply-siders believe that taxing and spending for these purposes are inappropriate and inefficient uses of government powers. They believe it is better to leave as many decisions on spending and investing, and as much money as possible, in the hands of consumers.

Supply-side economics, as implemented by Reagan's economic team and continued by George H. W. Bush's

By G.B. Trudeau

administration (despite Bush having labeled it "voodoo economics"), created record-smashing budget deficits and led to disillusionment with the policy. Savings rates among the wealthy did not increase, and, although the economy did grow at a faster rate for a few years, revenues as a percentage of GDP were lower than at any time since World War II, leading to even higher record deficits.

Tax Reform

During the **Clinton** years, deficits were reduced and, at the end of his term, eliminated, thanks to both tax increases and a prosperous economy. Major deficits recurred under George W. Bush because of a slowing economy and a series of tax cuts for the wealthiest Americans. The Bush tax policies have again brought the issue of tax policy to the fore.

Tax policy is always on the agenda. Though debates over income tax may seem arcane, and sometimes are, tax policy says a lot about who the winners and losers in society are. There are many reasons for trying to revise or reform the tax code: to simplify it, to achieve greater fairness, to increase revenue to pay for new spending or to balance the budget, or to decrease revenue as a way of downsizing government or of stimulating the economy in periods of sluggish growth. Reagan's tax cuts of the early 1980s were intended to stimulate the economy and to decrease government spending in favor of private investment. Clinton's tax legislation targeted fairness and deficit reduction. **George W. Bush** focused on cutting taxes for the rich to encourage investment and to remove the lowest income groups (who pay a tiny proportion of overall taxes) from the tax rolls. None of these tax policies—Reagan's, Clinton's, or Bush's—made the system simpler.

Americans think they are highly taxed, but compared with citizens in other developed countries, they are not. Twenty-seven percent of all tax filers pay no federal income tax, and as a share of household income, income tax for most has been falling since the 1990s.[14] In 2001, a household with a median income of $64,600 paid about 7 percent of it in *income* taxes, the lowest amount since 1957.[15] Overall, in 2001, federal personal income, payroll, and other taxes (such as taxes on alcohol, gasoline, and cigarettes) took an average of 16.3 percent of the income of the middle fifth of American taxpayers.[16] This is the lowest percentage since the CBO began publishing such data.[17] Of course, most households also pay some combination of state income tax, sales, excise, and local taxes in addition to federal income and payroll taxes. The average taxpayer must work from January 1 until about mid–April each year to cover all these tax obligations.[18]

Americans' collective tax burden is equal to about 28 percent of GDP; the only other industrialized nation that has as low a tax burden is Japan. The average for European nations is 37 percent; Swedes have the highest taxes, with combined tax payments equal to 51 percent of GDP.[19]

Tax Fairness

In tax language, "fairness" means spreading the tax burden among households according to their ability to pay. A tax structure based on the principle of wealthy and middle-income households paying higher percentages of their income in taxes than poorer households is called a **progressive tax.** A tax that requires the poor to pay proportionately more than those in middle- and upper-income brackets is a **regressive tax**.

Experts do not agree on the degree of progressivity of current income tax law. If the Bush tax cuts are looked at in dollar savings or share of tax benefits, current rates look more regressive than in the 1990s. We have already reported that recent tax cuts have provided little relief for the poor and large windfalls for the rich. Supporters of the Bush tax cuts point out that the wealthiest Americans pay the largest share of income tax revenue because they have the largest share of the country's wealth (Figure 2). The top 1 percent of earners accounted for 34 percent of all income taxes paid in 2002; the bottom half paid about 3 percent.[20] Seventy-five percent of those earning less than $10,000 paid no income tax at all.[21]

Payroll taxes, however, are regressive. The reason that payroll taxes disproportionately hit lower- and middle-income taxpayers is that each year a ceiling is set on how much income is subject to Social Security tax (in 2007, the tax was assessed on the first $97,500 of earnings). Interest and dividend income is not subject to Social Security taxes either, and this is primarily earned by wealthier Americans.

A second kind of fairness is economic or tax neutrality—tax policy that does not single out for favor certain kinds of economic activity over others. Our current tax code is definitely not economically neutral, as evidenced in our complex scheme of tax breaks and deductions (discussed below). It favors home ownership over renting, raising children over having none, oil exploration over the development of solar energy and wind power, and—in what some economists think is the most worrisome preference of all—it favors consumption over saving. Supporters of greater tax neutrality want to structure a tax system so that it does not favor one form of economic activity over another.[22]

Tax Simplification

President Franklin D. Roosevelt once said that our tax code "might as well have been written in a foreign language," and the laws are dozens of times more complex now. Since 1986 there have been 15,000 amendments to the tax code.[23] It offers 17,500 pages of explanation for filling out more than 650 different forms. According to the IRS, in 2003 it took the average taxpayer thirteen hours and thirty-five minutes to complete Form 1040; it is thus not surprising that more than half of all filers hire professionals to do their returns.[24] The rules are so Byzantine that a 2003 Treasury Department survey of

IRS walk-in services found 43 percent of the questions received no answer or were answered incorrectly.[25]

Why is the tax code so complex when most policy makers claim to want to simplify it? The complexity occurs because tax policy is used to achieve a variety of social goals and to reward various constituencies with what some call tax "candy." These are more commonly known as exemptions and deductions. A deduction is the amount taxpayers have spent for some item, such as mortgage interest or business equipment, that they are allowed by law to subtract from their income before figuring their tax liability. Congress values families, so it provides tax credits for child care; Congress wants to encourage business growth, so it gives credits and deductions for investment. It thinks that charitable giving is a good thing, so there are deductions for gifts to charity. Congress wants to encourage Americans to become home owners, so it provides a deduction for home mortgage interest, and so on and on with thousands of deductions for activities or objects that the majority of Congress values. (See Figure 3.)

Though each of these is wanted and lobbied heavily for by interest groups, together they create a tax code that is difficult to understand and one that favors wealthier Americans who are able to take advantage of the greatest number of deductions. To get a good idea

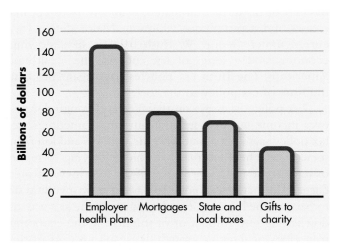

FIGURE 3 • **Tax Deductions Mostly Benefit Middle- and Higher-Income Families** *Billions of tax revenue dollars are lost through deductions, largely benefiting middle- and upper-class families. The figure shows total cost, in billions, of 2007 deductions for each category.*
SOURCE: "Estimates of Total Income Tax Expenditures," *Budget of the United States 2007: Analytic Perspectives* (Washington, D.C.: Government Printing Office, 2006), tab. 19-1, 288–289.

of just how complex these breaks make our tax system, go to the IRS website (www.irs.gov), click on "Forms and Publications," and scroll through the vast array of forms that must be filed when claiming deductions.

Both Reagan and Clinton tried tax reform that altered rates but did not change the basic code, and because they did not significantly reduce deductions and loopholes, their changes offered no simplification of the system. George W. Bush's tax cuts were more radical in their size, but by targeting upper-income groups with a vast array of new deductions and credits, they made the code even more complex. And because Bush's estate, personal, and corporate tax cuts were passed as phase-in programs, they require taxpayers to deal with different numbers and rules each year until 2010. Furthermore, Congress regularly approves "extenders" or special, limited-time tax breaks for business groups or other special categories of taxpayers. Each year Congress has to either suspend or renew them. All of this piecemeal legislating adds thousands of pages to the tax code.

Then, too, sometimes influential members of Congress add special deductions for favored corporations or interests. Every budget bill contains hundreds of these special exemptions. Tax legislation is so voluminous other members may not even realize that they are voting for a special deal for an individual corporation or a small class of them. These giveaways are seldom debated, and each of them makes the tax code more complicated and less equitable.

There are four nominal personal income tax rates (not counting zero) ranging from 10 to 35 percent. The corporate tax rate is 34 percent. Sometimes people talk about these rates as if they do, in fact, reflect the share of income paid to the government. However, because of credits, exemptions, and deductions, individuals and corporations pay the nominal rate only on their net, not their gross incomes. According to the 2006 tax returns released by President Bush and Vice President Cheney, George and Laura Bush had $765,801 in taxable income and an effective tax rate of 24.4 percent; Dick and Lynn Cheney had taxable income of $1.8 million and an effective tax rate of 23.4 percent.[26] (Both benefited considerably from the Bush tax cuts). Others whose gross income puts them in the highest tax bracket have even lower effective rates than Bush and Cheney because of the skill of their accountants and lawyers in sheltering their income.

The same generalization applies to corporations. Many pay no tax at all, and others pay effective rates from 5 percent to 33 percent, depending on how they are able to use tax law to shelter or exempt profits.[27] The overall amount of taxes corporations are paying, however, is on the rise because of record profits and because the Bush administration raised some types of corporate taxes to offset the cuts for individuals.

How taxable income is computed and what write-offs are available to which people is the most complex part of the tax code. No reform that deals only with rates and ignores deductions can simplify the code or make it fairer. Sixty percent of Americans favor a progressive tax system, but the public also appears to favor a simpler, more straightforward system. This is the attraction of single-rate or form-free reform proposals.

Flat Tax

One of the most frequently proposed tax reforms would abolish our present tax code and replace it with a **flat tax**—that is, a single rate for all income groups. One version of the flat tax proposed by a former member of the congressional leadership calls for a single rate of 17 percent for all Americans and the elimination of all deductions except for one large standard deduction of about $35,000 for a family of four. Its supporters argue that it would simplify the tax code, cut millions from the federal budget for IRS administration, and reduce the present U.S. 1040 form to a single-page or a postcard-sized form.

Flat-tax advocates believe that a progressive tax policy punishes people for earning more and creating wealth. They argue that fairness can be better achieved by requiring all Americans to pay the same proportion of their income to the government.

Though the proposed tax rate is flat in theory, in practice it could be modestly progressive. There would be a *de facto* zero tax rate for an estimated ten million of the poorest Americans. For example, using a flat rate of 17 percent with a $35,000 exemption for a family of four, those families making less than $35,000 would pay nothing; those making $135,000 would pay $17,000 (17 percent on $135,000 minus the $35,000 deduction), an effective rate of about 12.5 percent, and those making $1,035,000 would pay $170,000, or 17 percent of $1 million, an effective rate of 16.4 percent. Megamillionaires would pay close to the 17 percent rate. Middle-income taxpayers, those making $50,000 to $75,000, would pay effective rates of 5 percent to 9 percent.

The flat tax would disadvantage some low-income families, however. Most of the lowest-income households are not subject to income tax now. Some would be worse off with a flat rate because they would lose the earned income tax credit (EITC) they can claim under our current system (a reverse tax payment made to the working poor, discussed below).

Moreover, many wealthy households would likely pay even less than their current effective tax rate and, depending on where the flat rate is set, the middle class could end up paying more. Under the existing system, every taxpayer receives a standard deduction and a personal exemption amounting to more than $22,000 for a family of four, *without* itemizing any deductions. For those middle-class families able to deduct their home mortgage interest, health insurance and medical expenses, and IRA contributions, and claim education and child care credits, deductions under the current system might be greater than the single large deduction allowed under some flat-rate plans. And everyone would still have to pay Social Security and Medicare taxes, as well as state and local taxes.

Even if a flat tax were adopted, it is nearly impossible to imagine that Congress or the president would refrain from adding exemptions and deductions to the basic rate. All the special interests that now have a place in a tax code that is nominally progressive will also want a place in a code that is nominally flat. And exemptions and deductions would soon make a flat tax more regressive, that is, lower-income people would pay more than those with higher incomes.

National Sales Tax

Another proposal is to replace the personal income tax with a national sales, or consumption, tax. Under this tax regime, our current tax code would be abolished and taxes would be levied on what we buy, not on what we earn. All but five states currently levy sales taxes, usually ranging from 4 to 7 percent, but often more for luxury items. A national sales tax would work the same way, with consumers paying as they spend, ending the need to file a tax return.

Sales taxes can be very regressive because poor people spend a higher proportion of their income than the well-off, who can afford to invest a significant portion of their incomes. Purchases such as clothing, appliances, and cars take a much higher proportion of the incomes of poor and middle class than of wealthy families. Thus, a national sales tax could compound the regressivity of state and local taxes.[28] To reduce the regressivity of the tax, basic necessities, such as food, on which the lowest-income groups spend a high proportion of their earnings, would have to be exempt, as they are now in many states. But to replace the revenue gen-

erated by other taxes, the sales tax would have to be extremely high, perhaps more than 50 percent of the purchase price or cost of service to recover all of the revenue if all other taxes were eliminated.[29]

Reducing Tax Subsidies

Tax breaks are a hidden subsidy for various groups. A tax subsidy permits some people and corporations to pay much less in taxes than they would if the nominal rate for their income bracket were applied. Tax reformers seek to close these various tax break loopholes.

The biggest winners in the tax subsidies are corporations. The usual reason cited for extending so many tax incentives to business is to encourage economic and job growth that will benefit the population at large. Although some tax breaks do lead to the creation of jobs, many do not, or at least not domestically.

The vast array of current tax breaks for business are seen by their critics as a form of welfare. **Corporate welfare** has been defined as "any action by local, state, or federal government that gives a corporation or an entire industry a benefit not offered to others." The benefit can be in the form of services, low-interest loans, grants, concessions of land, or tax exemptions, deferrals, or lowered rates.[30] Mining and logging companies, for example, lease federal land at bargain-basement prices. Tax write-offs for capital gains cost taxpayers more than income support to the elderly poor and disabled, and deductions for charitable contributions cost the Treasury more than it spends on food stamps.

It would be easy to go on at length listing costs of various business tax breaks, but they only count as welfare if taxpayers get nothing in return for the subsidies. In many instances, this seems to be the case. During the 1990s, when AT&T, Bechtel Corp., Boeing, General Electric, and McDonnell Douglas Corp. were awarded 40 percent of all loans and grants made by the Export-Import Bank, employment by those firms dropped by 38 percent. During a period in the late 1980s and early 1990s, when General Electric was buying up other companies, including RCA, it received several billion dollars in tax breaks while reducing its workforce by 165,000.[31] And while Enron was receiving government subsidies for developing oil fields, it was bilking shareholders and California's utility customers out of billions of dollars.

Tax breaks to encourage job creation are among the most controversial. State, local, and federal tax breaks offered to attract businesses to relocate are estimated to cost taxpayers from $44,000 to $29 million per job created.[32] Policy makers continue to subscribe to the argument that tax breaks for corporations will produce new jobs despite the fact that most job growth in the United States has long come from small businesses. (They have their own government support agency—the Small Business Administration, which writes or sells off millions in loans each year.)

Corporations may be the biggest winners of tax subsidies, but the government has not neglected mainstream America. It is "working families" that Congress most likes to cite as the beneficiaries of tax breaks and tax cuts, and indeed, some are not trivial. In 2007, the tax deduction for mortgage interest, for example, will cost the U.S. Treasury five times as much as welfare payments to the poor. Families also receive tax credits for child care, adoption costs, school and college tuition, out-of-pocket health care costs, and tax deferrals for private savings plans.

Direct aid for the poor often produces outrage; even health care and income support (Medicare and Social Security) for the middle class have their critics. But subsidized services (mortgage underwriting, college scholarships, and grazing rights, for example) and tax breaks for the middle class and the well-off are subjected to much less scrutiny, perhaps because these benefits are more hidden and different in kind than benefits for senior citizens and the poor. It may also be because the most well-off, through their campaign contributions, have a greater say in the content of public debates.

One particular tax subsidy does benefit poor Americans. The **earned income tax credit (EITC)** has been in place since 1975 and was expanded during the Clinton administration. A tax break for the working poor, EITC is a negative income tax, which gives both single and married individuals, with and without dependent children, credits against their tax liability. The credit can be used to reduce taxes owed, but for families whose income is so low that they have no income tax liability, the credit is returned as a direct payment from the government. Claims for the credit are filed on a form attached to one's annual income tax report. In 2003, more than nineteen million families and individuals—about one of every seven tax returns filed—claimed the credit. An estimated five million families were lifted above the official poverty threshold by an EITC payment.[33]

This approach to poverty rewards work and allows poor families to receive government aid without becoming a client of the welfare bureaucracy. President Reagan called the EITC the "best antipoverty, best pro-family, best job creation measure to come out of Congress." That both the Clinton and Bush administrations were able to expand EITC is a measure of its bipartisan support. But it is still a frequent target of budget cutters.

Politics of Tax Reform

Many politicians talk about tax reform but few propose any significant changes because identifying oneself with any specific scheme is considered a "career killer."[34] At the outset of his second term, Bush said he was committed to reforming the tax code and was open to consideration of both flat and national sales tax proposals. But he also said that certain deductions, such as for home mortgage and charitable contributions, were untouchable and that he hoped to eliminate tax on capital gains and dividend income. But as his second term wore on and his popularity diminished, he stopped discussing sweeping tax reform and concentrated on making his tax cuts permanent.

Like Bush, many Democrats would like to see the tax code simplified, but their primary objective is to keep the tax structure progressive. Therefore, Democrats have not been the principal advocates for the flat tax or a national sales tax; instead, they recommend undoing Bush's tax cuts and making incremental changes in the rate structure or number of deductions.

Radical tax reform has not been a winning issue for any recent politician, and in this time, when spending far outpaces revenue, it is even more chancy to kill the bird in hand. Americans have to want a simpler, fairer tax code enough to give up their tax candy.

Social Welfare Policies

Fiscal policy includes not only taxation but also spending. Spending directed toward individuals is often labeled social welfare spending, that is, direct or indirect government subsidies for individuals and families who are often grouped by category such as "the poor," "the disabled," "farmers," and "the elderly," for example. Direct subsidies are payments government makes to individuals by checks, vouchers, or credits. Social Security payments, price support payments to farmers, cash assistance to the poor, and food vouchers are direct subsidies. Indirect subsidies are goods or services provided by the government to the public or to a specified group at below market value—for example, public education, health care, water and grazing rights to western farmers and ranchers, and public hous-

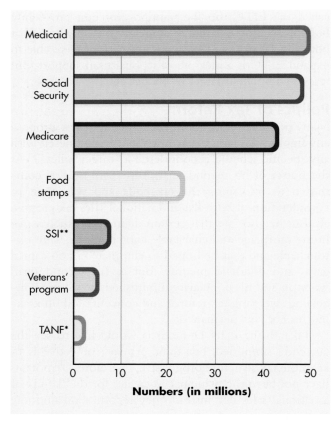

FIGURE 4 • **Direct Federal Aid** *More than 80 million Americans receive direct federal aid. This figure does not include indirect subsidies or tax subsidies. (The numbers in this figure add up to more than 80 million because millions of people benefit from more than one federal program.)*

*Temporary Assistance for Needy Families, the program that replaced Aid to Families with Dependent Children. This program is what most people think of when they think of "welfare."

**Supplemental Security Income, the aid program for the needy elderly and disabled.

SOURCE: *Budget of the United States, Fiscal Year 2007,* 238, 289; Appendix, 173, 452, 1102.

ing. If you are enrolled at a public college or university, for example, chances are that your tuition and fees cover no more than half of the real costs, possibly less—taxpayers pick up the difference.

Why Social Welfare Policies?

Why does government do it? And should it be doing it? Whether it should be providing so many benefits is a philosophical question about which there will never be agreement. But there are many motivations for adopting such a wide variety of support programs. As we

noted above, a political system like ours is predicated on equality of opportunity, and various social welfare policies help individuals take advantage of opportunities. This support in turn helps foster economic growth because every country's development is dependent on a healthy, educated population.

As government has grown and become involved in all segments of society, we have come to rely on its help to cushion life's blows for the least well-off. At the same time, we give even more support to the middle class and the rich because policy makers could not get elected if they were not responsive to the expectations of their most powerful supporters and constituents.

Few people in any industrialized country today think they should be left completely at the mercy of natural or market forces. They look to social welfare policies to take the worst risks out of living in a capitalist system, offering protection for the ill, disabled, elderly poor, and unemployed. At the same time our government also provides a sturdy safety net for businesses.

Where does the authority come from to do all this? According to the Preamble to the Constitution, promotion of the "general Welfare" was one purpose for creation of the Union. Article I assigns the responsibility of providing for the general welfare to Congress, but the scope of the formal powers granted to Congress is a topic of continuing debate. Congress's authority to enact social welfare programs stems from powers implied by the "general welfare" phrase and from its formal power to tax. Government's taxing authority allows it to accumulate the resources needed to provide social services as well as a means for taking income from some people and redistributing it to others. Sometimes redistribution is from the rich to the poor and sometimes from the less well-off to the wealthy.

The Evolution of Social Welfare Policies

At the time the Constitution was written, no level of government was involved in providing aid to families and individuals. Local governments were responsible for the poor but gave little aid. Orphaned or destitute children were apprenticed to better-off families, where they worked as servants. Local authorities established workhouses for the able-bodied poor and in some places gave minimal assistance to the old or sick.[35] Churches and other private charities helped the "deserving" poor and unfortunate. Those thought to be undeserving were treated harshly.

These attitudes reflected the belief that individuals bore the primary responsibility for their own fate.

While government took little responsibility for the well-being of individuals, it *was* involved in the economic development of the country and the creation of jobs. In at least one case (the Homestead Act, passed during the Civil War), this resulted in direct benefits to families and individuals: to encourage settlement of the western states, the government gave away 246 million acres of land, in 160-acre allotments, to 1.5 million homesteaders. If settlers stayed on the land for five years and developed it, they received title free and clear.

Government also encouraged development through its immigration policies, although it did little to help new residents after their arrival. The great waves of immigration at the end of the nineteenth century and the beginning of the twentieth generated a desperate need for health care, housing, and education in the big cities, but that demand was met primarily with services from private charities or settlement houses, such as Chicago's Hull House, or from local political party organizations. Settlement houses taught literacy and work skills and provided lessons in hygiene and rudimentary health care for infants and children. The big cities' political machines, such as New York's Tammany Hall, helped new arrivals find housing and jobs and traded those favors for votes.

The idea that government should provide extensive public services such as education, hospitals, and asylums developed in the nineteenth century. But the concept of paying individuals benefits is a twentieth-century idea. Gradually, the belief grew that government has a responsibility to help at least some of those at the bottom of the ladder. These changed attitudes led to the enactment of state laws, beginning in 1911, to establish aid programs for poor children and their mothers. Fifteen years later, most states had such laws, freeing many children from apprenticeships and poorhouses.

Most of our major federal social welfare programs were developed in the 1930s as part of the New Deal's response to the Great Depression. These programs provided support to farmers, poor families, and the elderly poor. After World War II, the GI bill provided many entitlements to veterans and helped millions become part of the middle class (see box, "The GI Bill of Rights"). During the 1960s' War on Poverty, old programs were expanded and major new ones to assist with health care—Medicare and Medicaid—were added.

Over the decades, the United States has amassed a large number of social welfare programs (see Figure 4),

but that does not make us a "welfare state." Welfare states have a coordinated set of income support programs to ensure access to basic necessities in a uniform way, not just for those in need, but for the population as a whole. These are governments that accept the premise that jobs, health care, education, and the basic material necessities of life are entitlements or human rights, and some may even have that principle incorporated into their constitutions. In contrast, our social welfare programs are largely uncoordinated efforts designed to solve the particular problems of specific groups (for example, college students, the poor, farmers, the elderly) on a piecemeal basis. We shall look at two categories of programs: income support programs and health care.

Income Support Programs

Today the federal government has programs providing income support to retirees and their dependents, the disabled and their dependents, farmers, poor families, and the unemployed, in addition to pension plans for its civilian and military personnel.

Retirees and Their Dependents

The earliest and the most comprehensive of income support programs is the Old Age Survivors Disability and Health Insurance Program, adopted in 1935 to ensure that the elderly would not live in poverty after retirement. President Roosevelt and the other New Dealers who initiated the program would be astounded at its current magnitude. **Social Security** has evolved into a government-managed retirement fund for American workers from all income groups, a life insurance program for surviving dependents and spouses, and an income support program for people with disabilities. Participation is not voluntary, and over the decades, the program has grown to cover 96 percent of all workers. Social Security covers so many Americans that each of us is issued a Social Security identification number at birth.

Social Security is financed through a payroll tax on employees and employers. The employee's contribution, slightly over 6.2 percent (7.65 percent, including Medicare) of the first $97,500 of earnings (periodically adjusted upward), is withheld from wages; employers

More than 400,000 American soldiers were killed in World War II. By 1945, public attention turned to the fate of the more than 12 million soldiers who survived and were returning home after the war was won.

World War I "doughboys" had received a tiny cash payment on mustering out but were promised a small annuity to be paid near retirement age. But those who fell on hard times in the early years of the Great Depression couldn't wait for retirement. In 1932, when they marched on Washington to demand early payment of their "bonuses," U.S. Army units under the command of General Douglas MacArthur violently suppressed their demonstration. The spectacle of our military assaulting its veterans was a black mark on the national conscience.

Nevertheless, the following year when Franklin Roosevelt took office he rejected the idea that citizen soldiers were entitled to benefits not available to all.[1] But during the course of World War II, opinions changed. The overwhelming majority of the American public favored some kind of bonus for vets. When the GI Bill—officially titled the Serviceman's Readjustment Act—was signed into law in 1944, neither President Roosevelt nor Congress thought they were passing a transformative piece of legislation. They just wanted to help millions of veterans reintegrate into civilian life and the labor force. But today the bill is often called the "greatest piece of legislation Congress ever passed," a "Marshall Plan for America," and "a magic carpet to the middle class." No one foresaw the consequences of the bill's three major benefits: a living stipend and tuition vouchers for college, low-interest mortgages for purchase of a first home, and loans for starting new businesses. These measures set off a chain reaction that helped shape modern America.

That was true because the typical World War II GI had completed only one year of high school and came from a family for whom college was financially out of reach.[2] Had these young men and women not served in the war and received the GI benefit, most could never have gone back to school.

Many educators and college presidents opposed the voucher program, arguing that they would have to lower their standards and admit students with poor educational backgrounds. But veterans returned to school in record numbers, more than a million in 1946 alone, when they accounted for almost half of all college enrollments in the United States. Even as late as 1950, almost a quarter of all college students were veterans.[3] The GI Bill thus stimulated a tremendous growth in public and private higher education, creating the need to hire more faculty and build new facilities, eventually giving rise to a new system of state colleges in many states.

With college educations, many working-class families moved into the middle class, making it possible for them to afford to send their children to college and continue the families' upward mobility. With federally guaranteed mortgages, many vets were also able to leave rental housing in the cities for homes in the outlying areas. So many new homeowners entered the market that it prompted the building of housing developments such as Levittown, stimulating the suburbanization of America. This in turn fostered the building of highways and schools and the whole infrastructure necessary to support new towns.

The bill did not work equally well for everyone, in part because African Americans did not have the same choices as whites in using their benefits. Because housing was segregated in most new suburban areas, including

contribute an equal amount. Self-employed workers must pay both the workers' and employers' share and send payments to the IRS with their income tax returns. Social Security taxes are credited to a special off-budget trust fund and invested in government securities until they are needed to cover benefit payments. In other words, Social Security benefits are not paid out of the general revenue funds that come from personal and corporate income or excise taxes. They are paid entirely from contributions made to the trust fund by employers, their employees, and the self-employed, plus the accrued interest.

Social Security taxes will produce more than 36 percent of federal revenues in 2007, and payments to beneficiaries will account for just over 21 percent of federal spending. It is the single largest expenditure in

Levittown, the route out of the city to affordable housing was less possible for blacks than for whites. Although black vets got the same educational benefits, they did not have the range of choices in schools, given segregation in some universities and the use of a quota system in others. But thousands did get to college, among them many of those who would become leaders of the modern civil rights movement.

The GI Bill's significance stemmed from providing benefits that made it possible for young veterans to become more productive citizens for the remainder of their lives. It gave education vouchers to eight million veterans. It doubled home ownership, from one in three before the war to two in three afterward. It returned $5 to $12 in tax revenues for each dollar spent.[4] And it expanded higher education dramatically, preparing the way for the information-based society. For these reasons, its passage may in the future be seen "as one of the most important events of the twentieth century."[5]

Courtesy: Indiana University Archives

With support from the GI Bill, returning veterans flooded America's universities by the millions, changing the face of higher education. The facilities at Indiana University, like those of so many other schools, were soon overtaxed, forcing relocation of student registration to its field house.

[1]Suzanne Mettler, *Soldiers to Citizens: The G.I. Bill and the Making of the Greatest Generation* (New York: Oxford University Press, 2005), 19.

[2]Doris Kearns Goodwin, on "Remembering the GI Bill," *NewsHour with Jim Lehrer,* PBS, July 4, 2000.

[3]Michael J. Bennett, *When Dreams Come True: The GI Bill and the Making of Modern America* (Washington, D.C.: Brassey's, 1996), 18.

[4]Spencer Michaels, on "Remembering the GI Bill," *NewsHour with Jim Lehrer,* PBS, July 4, 2000.

[5]Peter Drucker, *Post-Capitalist Society* (New York: HarperBusiness, 1993), 3.

the federal budget, although spending on national security is now close behind.

Lower-income workers are hardest hit by these taxes because all their earnings are subject to the tax. Americans who earn more than the $97,500 subject to the tax pay a smaller proportion of their income into Social Security. Lower-income retirees receive more benefits relative to their earnings than do wealthier participants, but 60 percent of Social Security payments do go to individuals living above the poverty line.[36] For this reason, and also to shore up the trust fund, middle- and upper-income beneficiaries are required to pay taxes on 85 percent of their Social Security income at the same rate at which the rest of their income is taxed.

The size of the monthly stipend received by beneficiaries is determined by how many years they worked,

Social Security helps senior citizens endure the bumps of old age.

of increased life spans, a sixty-five-year-old can expect to collect Social Security for more than seventeen.

Social Security has grown from about 220,000 recipients in 1940 to 49 million in 2006. Ninety percent of Americans sixty-five years of age or older currently receive Social Security benefits; most of the rest will receive payments in their later sixties. Older people and their dependents receive the largest share of benefits paid; the disabled and their dependents account for most of the rest. The average monthly benefit to a retired worker has risen from a mere $13 in 1940, when many fewer people were covered and withholding was much less, to $1,007 in 2006.[37] Due to annual cost-of-living adjustments, the monthly stipend increases by a small amount each year.

Gradually over the years, Social Security payments have become a principal part of retirement income. In 1950, they accounted for only 3 percent of retirees' income, but by 2006, 41 percent. For 43 percent of unmarried or widowed retirees, Social Security accounts for 90 percent of income. It forms a larger part of elderly women's income because women earn less over the life course and have fewer private pensions, savings, or other investments.[38] Without Social Security, almost half of our senior citizens would be poor, but for those sixty-five and older the poverty rate fell to a historic low of 9.8 percent in 2004 (see Figure 2).[39] (In contrast, the poverty rate has been rising for children.) To the extent that continued payments from the fund keep people above the poverty line, they are doing what Social Security was intended to do.

Social Security has stayed afloat because of ever-increasing numbers of people paying in at steadily rising rates. The taxes withheld from the paychecks of today's workers provide the payouts to current retirees just as they supported the generation before them. The aging of the population and the declining ratio of workers to retirees does present a threat to the long-term solvency of the system.

how much they earned, and whether they are alone or have dependents. The age of eligibility for full benefits rises in small increments with one's birth year. Beginning in 2008, a retiree will have to be 66 years old to collect full Social Security benefits, though reduced benefits can be taken at age 62. For each year up to age seventy that retirement is postponed, the monthly stipend increases.

Social Security is categorized as social insurance rather than a welfare program because it covers people in all income groups and because only those who have paid into the program, or their survivors, can collect benefits. Since people do not have to show financial need to participate, everyone can accept it without the public stigma of being on welfare. This aspect of the program increases its political popularity. Yet it is a mistake to think that all beneficiaries get back only what they and their employers paid into the program through payroll deductions, plus accumulated interest. This is true for some short-lived people. But given our longer life span, Social Security pays most of its recipients more than they paid in (private insurance plans pay many people more than they paid in, but many others less). In 1935, a sixty-five-year-old was expected to collect benefits for a little more than twelve years; by 2006, because

Issues with the Program

As a retirement program for everyone, Social Security continues to be politically popular among all groups, save the very young, because it alleviates some of the economic risks of growing old. It is a great public policy success story, but the program does have problems. The aging of the population in combination with the heavy borrowing from the trust fund to pay current expenses has left the program in need of reform. Its popularity, however, makes a frank discussion of basic changes in the fundamental nature of the program politically risky, as Bush discovered when he tried to sell his partial privatization program in 2005. There is also serious disagreement over how much trouble the system is in and whether it needs another modest rules adjustment, such as it received in the 1970s and 1980s, or a radical overhaul.

Two major problems confront the Social Security system. One is that the ratio of active workers to retirees is decreasing. Even though immigration keeps us from zero growth, there will be only 2.2 active workers for each Social Security beneficiary in 2031, compared with 3.3 in 2006. This reduction in the ratio of active to retired workers is because the number of people over age sixty-five is growing and is expected to almost double from thirty-seven million in 2006 to seventy-one million in 2031.[40]

The second problem is the fact that presidents and Congress continue to use Social Security trust fund surpluses to offset budget deficits. In 2007, the fund will collect over $300 billion more than it needs to make payments to current retirees. The years of overcollection were by design, in anticipation of the drain on the trust fund that will occur as the baby boom generation (those born between 1946 and 1964) reaches retirement age. Reforms passed in the 1980s increased payroll tax rates and the amount of income taxed and forced virtually all U.S. workers into the program. The intention was to lock down this surplus so that as the population aged and the number of younger workers paying into the program declined, the surplus would be there to cover payouts to the growing number of retirees. But during years when general revenue funds are insufficient to cover government spending, budget makers in the White House and Congress borrow from the Social Security trust fund to reduce deficits.

When the years of overpayments end and the money in the trust fund is needed to pay benefits, the government will have to repay what it has borrowed from the fund. Although the government will surely find a way to make good on its commitment to retirees, millions of Americans are skeptical; one poll showed that young people were more likely to believe in flying saucers than in the viability of the Social Security system.[41] Some advocates of privatizing the system want to spread doubt and even panic about its stability and repeatedly predict that the Social Security trust fund will go broke "in the next few years" unless changes are made. However, the program's trustees say that Social Security will be financially able to make full payments to all beneficiaries until 2018 and payments of about three-fourths of the current benefit level from then until 2042 even if no changes are made in the program.

Those who are opposed to the idea of a government-managed retirement system tend to favor restructuring Social Security. The most significant and persistent of these proposals involve some degree of privatization of the payroll withholding tax. The Bush administration favored this approach, although it refused to call it *privatization* because that word is not popular with the public. The Bush proposal would have allowed people who want to invest some of the money now withheld from their paychecks for Social Security in stocks, bonds, or funds of their choosing to set up their own retirement accounts.

But reductions in contributions in even small percentages would put the fund in an even more tenuous financial position as the number of beneficiaries explodes over the next few decades. However, supporters of the privatization approach believe that those who invest on their own will be able to get a much higher rate of return than the government does on its investment of money in the trust fund, which invests solely in low-risk, low-interest government securities.

There are two formidable obstacles to the partial privatization plan. If the stock market falters or if bad investment decisions are made, millions of seniors may end up having insufficient retirement income. Most people have no special expertise in investment strategies, and whereas putting the money in stocks and bonds or mutual funds will provide a windfall in commissions for investment firms, there is no guarantee that the money will earn a higher rate of return for the investor or even that it will not be lost. The stock market and mutual funds were rocked by fraud and corruption from 2001 to 2004, and private pension plans have been failing at an alarming rate, leaving taxpayers to pay part of the bill for bankrupt companies. When retirement arrives for individuals who have lost the money invested or earned a lower return than Social Security could have provided, would they have the right to turn to the government to supplement their lower Social Security benefits, and if so, where would government get the money?

A more immediate problem in the privatization idea is where the trust fund will get the money to pay benefits to retirees if younger workers are allowed to take up to a third of their contributions into the private market. The government would need to find enough lenders to fund Social Security and to cover the rest of the shortfall in government spending. Even many Republicans argue that that much borrowing is unrealistic and that partial privatization cannot happen without raising taxes, reducing benefits, or both.

Reducing benefits would present another set of problems because 52 percent of the workforce has no private pension coverage to supplement Social Security benefits and 31 percent of Americans have no retirement savings other than what they have paid into Social Security.[42]

For more than two million of these retirees, Social Security payments are already insufficient to meet the cost of living, so a further reduction could cause an even greater number to look to supplemental payments from other government programs, such as SSI (discussed later).

In lieu of big structural changes in the system, small changes similar to those made in the 1980s are being phased in; one is a gradual and modest increase in the age when one can collect full benefits (soon to be 66)—something that makes sense given how much longer people are living and working (though this is a hardship for those working at demanding physical labor). There are also periodic increases in the share of earnings subject to payroll tax. Many argue that an individual's whole salary should be taxed, a change that would significantly increase the trust fund. Other tweaking that has been tried is reducing the automatic annual cost-of-living increases recipients receive. Another possibility, not yet considered, is to reverse the income tax cut for the highest income earners instead of making it permanent as the Bush administration wants. The extra revenue would go a long way toward ending budget deficits and the need to borrow from the Social Security trust fund.

The Poor

Federal income support programs for the poor began as part of the original Social Security legislation, which established a national program of unemployment insurance, along with the Social Security program. Unemployment insurance was introduced in order to combat the effects of the Great Depression, when nearly a quarter of the workforce was unemployed and state and local programs did not have the resources to meet demand. Except for Social Security itself, which is funded and managed entirely at the federal level, income support programs for the poor have been run jointly by federal, state, and local governments, and sometimes state programs predated federal ones.

Eligibility

A major difference between beneficiaries of an inclusive program such as Social Security and one that exclusively targets the poor is that qualification for participation requires a **means test.** Participants must periodically demonstrate eligibility by showing that they are poor—they must have both limited income and few assets.

The definition of who is poor is revised each year by the Census Bureau, which makes adjustments to account for changes in inflation and the cost of living. It does not set a single income level but many, depending on age and household composition. In 2006, for example, a single person under sixty-five years of age was considered poor if his or her income was below $9800; the comparable figure for a family of four was $20,000. Not everyone agrees with the Census Bureau's poverty estimates because they do not take into account many "in-kind" benefits poor people receive, such as food and housing subsidies and medical care. If these were added to income, critics of the threshold say, the poverty rate would be reduced by about 4 percent. Others argue that the Census Bureau *understates* the amount of poverty by using 1960s standards that focused on the price of food and underestimated the cost of housing, fuel, education, and health care. A common alternative estimate of living costs for a family of four is $30,000 to $34,000.[43]

The Elderly and the Disabled

One of the first grant-in-aid programs established under Social Security authority, **Supplemental Security Income (SSI),** provides income support for the blind and people with disabilities and for the elderly not covered by Social Security or whose Social Security benefits are not large enough to lift them out of poverty. For 20 percent of seniors, Social Security is their only income, which may be insufficient to meet their basic living costs. Other SSI recipients are workers or survivors of workers who were not covered by the Social Security program (something unlikely to happen much in the future given the expansion of Social Security to virtually all jobs). Although created by Social Security legislation and run by the same agency, SSI is funded from general tax revenues, not Social Security payroll taxes, and many recipients receive a supplement from the state government as well.

In 2006, just over seven million Americans received SSI; about one-third were Social Security recipients whose benefits were too low to meet basic needs, and most of the remainder were people under age sixty-five with disabilities.[44] SSI payments are generally quite small, ranging from $603 per month for an individual to $904 for a couple.[45] SSI recipients are automatically eligible under federal standards for food stamps and health insurance (discussed later), but states have considerable leeway to change eligibility standards.

Poor Families

Aid to Families with Dependent Children (AFDC) was another grant-in-aid program that grew out of Social Security legislation. The purpose was to strengthen maternal and child welfare services being provided by the states. Coverage was soon extended to mothers as well as their dependent children and later to both fathers and mothers with dependent children. Because AFDC was a joint federal-state program administered at the state level, eligibility and benefits varied from state to state.

Despite the success that AFDC had in providing food and shelter to dependent children, critics argued that it fostered dependency instead of encouraging independence and hard work. The largest growth in number of recipients came when economic times were hard. This suggests that the economy, not work ethic or responsibility, drove the numbers. However, when the economy improved, the rolls did not always fall back to their previous level, suggesting something else was also driving the numbers. Part of that "something else" is that even in years when the economy was growing, many of the new jobs being created did not pay enough to meet basic living costs. But welfare rolls also grew because of the increase in the number of births to unmarried women without job skills who were often still children themselves; about 80 percent of these unwed mothers went on welfare at some point.

In contrast to the common stereotype, however, the increase in welfare recipients was not tied to the size of welfare stipends, which in real terms (adjusted for inflation) began a steady decline in the 1970s.

The number of births to single women continues to be high: 68 percent of all African American, 43 percent of all Hispanic, and 28 percent of all white births are to unmarried women, but the number of unmarried teenage women giving birth has been declining since 1990.[46]

Our society made it very difficult for women to choose low-paid work over welfare. Workers were often worse off because of child care costs and the loss of medical benefits that came with AFDC but not with most low-paying jobs. Nevertheless, the majority of AFDC recipients collected benefits for a relatively short time.[47] They found a job or married someone who earned more than poverty wages (or both). But nearly one-quarter of the women who went on AFDC stayed for ten years or more, and another 20 percent stayed for six to nine years. Though most AFDC recipients were white, long-term recipients were more likely to be black or Hispanic unmarried teenage mothers with no high school diploma.

AFDC became the main target for critics of cash assistance to the poor. Its cost was much lower than other income support programs, but to its critics it appeared to be rewarding the wrong kind of behavior and getting no results. They saw AFDC as discouraging work, encouraging out-of-wedlock births, and allowing fathers to take no responsibility for their children.

In response to criticisms of the program, in 1993, President Clinton took office promising to end welfare "as we know it." In the 1994 elections, the Republican's "Contract with America" promised even more dramatic reform. After heated debate, in 1996 Congress passed, and President Clinton signed, a welfare reform bill that abolished AFDC and with it the concept of welfare as an entitlement to all those who met federal guidelines. Instead, in the **Temporary Aid to Needy Families (TANF)** program, states were mandated to set up their own welfare systems under loose federal guidelines to be funded by block grants from the federal government.

TANF is a results-oriented program that sets time limits on eligibility and requires participants to move "from welfare to work," the signature slogan of the reform bill. States receiving TANF funds were to have, at minimum, 30 percent of the people on their welfare rolls working at least thirty hours a week during the program's initial five years. "Work" included job training, community service, and continuing education. TANF recipients are required to hold jobs within two years of entering the program, and working families can receive assistance for a lifetime maximum of five years. States were allowed to exempt up to 20 percent of the people receiving assistance from this requirement (for example, people who are physically or mentally unable to hold a job or parents with young children and no child care).

Later modifications were made to allow recipients to receive child care, transportation, and other noncash assistance beyond the two-year cutoff. These modifications were designed to help those who took low-paying jobs and who needed such additional assistance to keep their families intact.[48] However, states have the authority to enact more stringent limits.

The impact of reform Most analysts agree that the TANF program was a success from the standpoint of getting people off welfare and into the labor force. The new time limits and work requirements forced many states to reorient their efforts toward helping clients develop job and life skills instead of passive assistance to see that they had food and shelter. By 2005, the number of people on welfare rolls had dropped by 60 percent and the percentage of never-married mothers in the labor force had jumped from 49 to 63 percent.[49]

It is likely that some of the decrease in the welfare rolls occurred because of the rapidly growing economy in the late 1990s that led employers to hire people who would not be hired if there were more workers available. Evidence for the latter explanation is that in most states the decline in welfare enrollments began three years before TANF went into effect. By some estimates, the strong economy accounted for 35 to 45 percent of the decline in caseloads and the reforms themselves for 25 to 35 percent. A third factor, which may have reduced the number of households on welfare by another 20 or 30 percent, was the expanded EITC program.[50] Some of the decline may also be attributed to the complexity of the rules and pressure from caseworkers trying to meet their welfare-to-work quotas.

There have been blips in the pattern of declining caseloads. Welfare enrollments increased in the early 2000s after several years of net job losses in the private sector and a rising poverty rate. But the rolls fell again as the economy improved.

TANF has shown that, at least in good economic times, welfare rolls can be reduced and more people employed. For people healthy and skilled enough to hold down jobs and lucky enough to find them, "welfare to work" has been successful in reducing dependency on cash assistance. However, perhaps fewer than half of all mothers who left welfare found full-time jobs; others found only part-time work. Based on state reports, average earnings are about $8 an hour, or $16,000 a year, and that is for those lucky enough to find full-time work.[51] Lack of suitable skills for today's economy is a significant impediment to getting a job that pays a living wage, as are the mental or physical disabilities, learning disabilities, and substance abuse problems

plaguing a sizable proportion of those on welfare. Any one of these conditions makes finding and keeping a job difficult, and many unemployed have more than one of these problems.[52] It remains to be seen whether the welfare rolls will rise when the economy turns down.[53]

TANF has undergone changes since 2000 under the Republican administration. The work requirement was increased, though not all states have been able to find enough jobs for recipients.[54] Bush's initiative to support "healthy marriage and family formation" was funded.[55] The purpose of the program is to encourage welfare recipients to marry on the assumption that children do better in two-parent households and that child care would be more workable and less costly.[56] Poverty rates in two-parent households are significantly lower than in single-parent households (see Table 2), and poverty rates in households headed by women are poorest of all, partly because women earn on average 75 cents for every dollar earned by a man. Finally, broader authority was given to states to waive poverty program standards and requirements, an action desired by Bush because it reduces federal responsibility for welfare programs.[57]

Why Welfare Reform?

There will never be agreement among welfare reformers on what kinds of reforms are necessary because there is no basic agreement on why people are poor. Those who think that poverty is the fault of the poor because they are deficient in character or effort are far less likely to support government help for the poor than are those who believe that poverty is a product of the economic system, bad luck, and parentage (the wealth of your parents determines a lot about your own opportunities to get ahead).

Although the cost to taxpayers is a frequently stated goal of reform and was one of the forces driving the 1996 welfare reform, it was probably not the primary objective. Income support for the poor pales in comparison to income support and indirect subsidies to millions of far better-off Americans. In 2006 we were spending more on interest payments to service the national debt than we were spending on welfare for the poor. It is likely that the distaste for "welfare" and the idea that some recipients are getting something for nothing were at least as important a motivation for reform as saving money.

Improving program performance and getting results for the individual are far more compelling reasons than cost reduction for trying to reform welfare. This would

Table 2	Poverty Is Much More Common in Female-Headed and Minority Families	
		Percentage in Poverty
All families		11
White, non-Hispanic		7
Black		24
Hispanic*		21
Asian		8
Married-couple families		5
White, non-Hispanic		5
Black		8
Hispanic*		16
Asian		8
Female-headed families, no husband present		31
White, non-Hispanic		22
Black		40
Hispanic*		39
Asian		13

*Hispanics can be of any race.

SOURCE: U.S. Census Bureau, "Historical Poverty Tables," tab. 2 (www.census.gov); 2006 *Statistical Abstract of the United States*, tab. 699.

be better for the individual clients and also for the economy and society as a whole. In America, we like to think that everyone can have a chance to achieve to the best of his or her ability and that parents can have a reasonable hope that their children's lives will be better than their own. Moreover, democracies function better when there are no permanent classes of haves and have-nots (see Table 1). People who must worry about how to feed and house their families are not going to be full participants in the political process. By helping sustain an underclass, we undermine the political system itself.

Farmers

Farmers, especially corporate farmers, are another group receiving government welfare. Direct federal aid has accounted for almost half of total farm income since the 1980s, and it has been as high as 70 percent in some farm states. **Farm subsidies** are a means by which government underwrites part of the cost of agriculture;

they include direct payments to farmers or agribusinesses to reduce the economic risks of growing food and other crops. More than 90 percent of subsidies are paid out in price supports; the government guarantees set prices—usually more than the market commands—for crops such as corn, wheat, rice, cotton, and soybeans, to name the most heavily subsidized. If the market price falls below the guaranteed level, the government pays the difference while also purchasing and storing tons of surplus crops each year. Some of that surplus goes to federal programs such as food stamps and subsidized school lunches.

The government also pays farmers to withhold land from production, either to promote conservation or to reduce the production of crops or farm products (cheese, butter, dried milk) that the government holds in surplus. Collectively, these farm support programs have made agriculture the most subsidized industry in the United States.

Like Social Security, income support for farmers was originally motivated by the urgent needs and dire living conditions of one segment of the American population. Because food self-sufficiency is regarded by many as essential to national security and because many farmers were being forced off the land, providing federal aid took on a special urgency. All of the rhetorical justification for continuing the program still focuses on family farms, but in fact small farmers have been going out of business by the tens of thousands since the 1970s. By 1997, there were only two million farms left in the United States, and about half of these were hobby farms, having less than $10,000 in gross sales.[58] Thus farm aid has evolved into an income support program primarily for the largest and most profitable farming enterprises, not for poor or marginal family farms.

Unlike Social Security, where even the top payments are modest and all participants get some minimum payments, farm aid provides staggeringly large sums to the wealthiest farmers, whereas 60 percent of farmers receive no subsidies at all.[59] In 2000, of 1.6 million individuals receiving farm aid, about 57,500 got more than $100,000; at least 154 got more than $1 million. $17 million went to farms operated by government agencies, and millions more to university farms.[60]

Of course, the operating costs of large farms are staggering, and a good share of government aid is used to defray these expenses.[61] The question is whether taxpayers' money should make the difference between agribusinesses' and corporate farms' staying in or going out of business.

Our society is rich, but still many people do not have enough to eat. The federal government provides several kinds of food subsidies, including targeted food subsidies for pregnant women and preschool children.[1] But the largest food subsidy program is the Department of Agriculture's **food stamp** program.

Until 2004, food stamps were paper coupons that served as vouchers redeemable in grocery stores for food. Now this food subsidy is issued in the form of an electronic credit accessed by a debit card. The credit may be used only to purchase unprepared food and cannot be used for dining out or for liquor or tobacco.[2] The average food stamp allotment per poor household ranges from about $160 to $350 a month, depending on the state.

The food stamp program began as a temporary measure of support during the last years of the Great Depression but was revived and made permanent as part of Lyndon Johnson's War on Poverty. Its coverage expanded during the early 1970s in response to an investigation that revealed that tens of thousands of Americans suffered from malnourishment, resulting in retarded growth, anemia, protein deficiencies, high rates of infant mortality, scurvy and rickets (from insufficient vitamin C,

vitamin D, and milk), and an impaired ability to learn. In the first years of the program, malnutrition among the poor decreased, as did the incidence of diseases caused by poor nutrition.

Even though the food stamp program was pared back during the 1980s, one of every ten Americans was receiving the coupons in the years just before the 1996 welfare reforms.

Farmers and the Department of Agriculture (DoA) are other beneficiaries of the food stamp program. Food stamps have always been seen as a constructive means for reducing food surpluses (which are warehoused by

the DoA), as well as for fighting hunger. Government's purchase of surplus food from farmers is, in part, justified by the food stamp program.

The rising poverty rate in the past decade has led to a steady increase in food stamp recipients, who numbered twenty-three million in 2004. This is still only 60 percent of those eligible to participate.[3]

[1] Jay Mathews, "Study Shows Early Head Start Gains," *State College* (Pa.) *Centre Daily Times,* June 5, 2002, 1.

[2] Robert Pear, "Electronic Cards Replace Coupons for Food Stamps," *New York Times,* June 23, 2004, 1.

[3] Food and Nutrition Service, "Food Stamp Participation Rates: 2004" (www.usda.gov).

AP Images/Grand Junction Free Press, Jim Noelker

A homeless family rides the bus during the day to stay warm in Grand Junction, Colorado. At night the family stays in a homeless shelter.

As one farm state senator (Richard Lugar (R–Ind.)) asserted, "subsidies distort markets by encouraging overproduction to drive prices lower in a self-perpetuating cycle."[62] And a House colleague warned that with the current level of subsidies "we are in danger of systematically turning farmers into dependent serfs of the federal government."[63]

Farm subsidies are constant targets of budget cutters and free marketers, but political support for their retention is formidable. After anti–big government Republi-

cans took control of Congress, some of them made a halfhearted attempt to phase out income supports for certain crops over a seven-year period. Instead, the conservative Congress and administration quadrupled payments. And Congress has continued to increase subsidies right through recession, tax cuts, budget deficits, and rising farm income. Between 2002 and 2004, farm income doubled, yet farm subsidies still rose 40 percent.[64] They rose again in 2007, with the Democrats in control of Congress.

President Bush, who has advocated cutting subsidies on rice and cotton, nevertheless signed into law the largest-ever farm subsidy bill in 2002, describing farm and ranch families as embodying "some of the best values of our nation: hard work and risk taking."[65] Of course, this statement, like many others that officials make about the farm program, ignores the reality of who gets the subsidies. Not surprisingly, current programs are not well regarded by the small family farmers whom politicians like to claim they are saving. By 2001, fully 73 percent of rural Nebraskans polled believed that caps should be set on the amount of subsidies any individual can receive.[66]

Farm subsidies are a good example of why government continues to grow. Both liberals and conservatives want to be seen supporting income subsidies for "family farmers," and both, including the conservatives who decry big government, vote for what they believe is beneficial to their constituents and campaign donors. In that sense they are also an example of how government welfare policies often end up responding to the lobbying influence of the well-off.

If farm subsidies are to be reformed, the pressure will probably come from abroad. Continued spending on price supports for agricultural commodities conflicts with the U.S. commitment to free trade and its obligations as a member of the World Trade Organization (see Chapter 15). The United States is a party to international trade agreements that, to ensure fair competition among the world's farm exporters, limit how much a government can pay in price supports. Unless we are found in violation of the agreements, farm subsidies will continue to reduce, if not eliminate, risk taking primarily for the wealthiest farm industries, not for the average family farmer. This is why some in rural America call it "farming the government, not farming the land."[69]

The Impact of Income Support Programs

Income support programs for the elderly, disabled, and dependent children played a major role in reducing poverty rates in the United States from their highs in the 1930s. Due in part to the Great Society programs of the 1960s, the proportion of families in poverty dropped from 21 percent in 1959 to 10 percent in 1973, the lowest point ever achieved in the United States.[70] It then increased steadily, reaching a high of 14 percent in 1993, before the booming economy of the 1990s sent it

© Brad Doherty, Brownsville, TX

This 55,000-ton pile of raw sugar is part of the surplus that costs taxpayers $1.4 million a month to store. Sugar subsidy programs cost American consumers $2 billion annually.

downward. On the rise again, it stood at 13 percent in 2005 (thirty-seven million people). One of every three poor persons is a child, and fifteen million people live in extreme poverty (below one-half of the poverty line).[71]

Income support payments for farmers do not have the same effect. They are less public (though well publicized among those who follow national politics). They do not help poor or marginal farmers, but rather make corporate farmers richer. In fact, they probably make it harder for small farmers to remain on the land by contributing to increasing land prices and providing incentives to sell land to big corporations. The crop subsidies keep marginal land in production, resulting in overproduction and lower prices. Corn is one of many examples. From 2000 to 2004, the average farmer lost up to $128 an acre raising corn, but farmers continue to plant more corn because during those same four years taxpayers covered their losses with $25 billion in subsidies.[72] Industrial farms producing these single, heavily subsidized commodities average 14,000 acres, about the size of Manhattan. Despite all the rhetoric, government does little specifically for family farmers struggling to make it.[73]

Health Care Programs

About 16 percent of the nation's economy is spent on health care: $6280 a person, a figure that grows ever higher.[74] About half is paid for by various government programs. After the Medicare drug benefit for seniors went into full effect in 2006, the government also was paying for half of all prescription drugs sold in the country.

The irony is that though we spend twice as much per capita than the country that ranks second to us in health spending, we have less to show for it. We rank below all other countries in the industrial world in infant mortality and life expectancy. And, according to a study by the *Journal of the American Medical Association,* the richest one-third of Americans are sicker than the poorest one-third in England, even though Britain spends only about 40 percent as much per person on health care as the United States.[75] The movie *Sicko* (see viewing list at end of chapter) exaggerated the perfection of other systems but was accurate in portraying inadequacies in ours.

Big spending has not made us careful or efficient either: the Institute of Medicine of the National Academy of Sciences has estimated that up to 98,000 Americans die needlessly each year because of medical errors in the nation's hospitals and that medication errors harm 1.5 million people and kill several thousand each year.[76] Nor has spending given us comprehensive coverage; forty-seven million Americans remain uninsured. About eighteen thousand adults between the ages of twenty-five and sixty-four die every year for lack of health coverage, and the economy loses $65 to $130 billion in productivity and other costs.[77]

The Government's Role in Health Care

In the United States, government aid for health care is a social benefit for some people in all income groups but not for all people. It is a patchwork of public and private programs, which mesh together very poorly and create tremendous inefficiencies and inequities. Health care is by far the most costly indirect government subsidy. Half of all federal, state, and local spending on means-tested programs is for medical care.[78] Through Medicare, Medicaid, and Veterans Affairs, the government is the largest health care provider in the country.

The federal government has been involved in some aspects of health care for decades, but before 1965, there was no general federal support for individual health care. In 1965, after years of debate over government's responsibility, concern about the problems of millions of Americans who could not afford adequate health care prompted President Johnson to propose and Congress to pass two programs, Medicare (for the elderly) and Medicaid (for low-income people).

Health Care for Seniors

Medicare is a public health insurance program that funds many medical expenses for the elderly and disabled. It includes hospital insurance, and additional voluntary coverage helps pay for physicians' services, outpatient hospital services, and some other costs.

Hospital insurance is paid for by the Medicare payroll tax, and the elective portion is financed through general revenues and monthly premiums paid by participants. Everyone eligible for Social Security benefits is eligible for Medicare, and over 90 percent of Social Security recipients buy the optional insurance. In 2007, the program will cover more than forty million people at a cost of $390 billion.

There are many factors that explain the improved health profile of the elderly over the past forty years, including scientific breakthroughs in the treatment of some diseases, but Medicare is responsible for many of the gains. Compared with the period before 1965, more seniors are able to see doctors now, and the elderly have more but shorter hospital stays. There have been declines in death rates from diseases affecting the elderly, such as heart attacks and strokes, and a decrease in the number of days of restricted activity that older people experience.[79]

Despite these substantial accomplishments, Medicare has not been a complete success. It is expensive, and many of those who need it have trouble paying their portion of the costs. There has been extensive fraud in the program, especially overbilling by doctors and HMOs.

The maximum fees the government has set for services are lower than some doctors have been willing to accept, and as a consequence, they refuse to treat Medicare patients. Patients themselves have been criticized for driving up costs by making unnecessary doctor or hospital visits and having unrealistic expectations about what medical care can do to resolve their health problems. Experts of all political persuasions continue to predict that the Medicare program will go broke within the next few decades unless changes are made or a national health care system is put in place, but it is hard to imagine that the government would let such a popular and essential program fail. A similar cost problem afflicts the other major federal health care program, Medicaid.

Health Care for the Poor and Disabled

Medicaid is a federal-state program that pays for medical care for disabled and unemployed people as well as some of the working poor who do not have coverage and cannot afford to buy it. States set their own Medicaid eligibility standards, within federal guidelines. Nationwide, 11 percent of Americans receive health coverage through Medicaid, with some variation among states.[80] Medicaid pays for one-third of all births, two-thirds of nursing home stays, and provides nearly half of the public funds for AIDS patients.[81]

Medicaid, which will cover about fifty million people in 2007, has now surpassed Medicare as the second most expensive entitlement program (after Social Security). The federal government continues to shift more of the responsibility for funding and setting program standards to state governments. On average, states spend 22 percent of their budgets on Medicaid, and its rapid growth is crowding out spending for education and other needs.[82] Even with Medicare, Medicaid, and private health insurance provided through the workplace, more than forty-seven million Americans remain without health insurance, two-thirds from wage-earning families whose income is above the poverty line.

To ensure greater coverage of children, in 1997 the government created the State Children's Health Insurance Program (SCHIP). Working through existing state programs, it set a goal of insuring all children whose parents do not qualify for Medicaid and who cannot afford private insurance. About six million children have received coverage under this program. However, the states determine eligibility, and eligibility standards vary widely. With medical costs soaring, at least eleven states have begun making it harder for children to qualify and other states have established their own comprehensive programs. In 2007, the president and Congress could not agree on funding for SCHIP, and as of this writing, the issue is not resolved.

Health Care for Veterans

In addition to Medicare, Medicaid, and SCHIP, the government also funds a national system of hospitals, outpatient clinics, nursing homes, and psychiatric clinics, run by the Department of Defense and Veterans Affairs (VA), that provide health care to five million veterans. (The VA also maintains a national system of cemeteries for veterans and their families.) The wars in Afghanistan and Iraq are creating a new generation of combat veterans and an increased need for health care and rehabilitation. Fewer soldiers than in past wars are dying on the battlefield in Iraq; modern medicine can save many who would have died even as recently as the Vietnam War. But those saved often have severe brain injuries and mental illnesses from traumatic experience and have lost one or more limbs. The veterans' hospital and medical system has proved inadequate to meeting veteran's needs in an effective and timely way.

Problems with the Existing System

For years, policy makers have heaped scorn on nations with national health care systems, arguing that care in those countries was poorer and rationed. But now we see that the outcomes in our health care system are inferior to those in many other nations.

Rationing by Income, Race, and Age

It is clear that, though we pretend otherwise, in reality we, too, have a rationing system for medical care; it is rationed by ability to pay. If you can afford it or if you have the right insurance, you can have the most expensive treatment, even if it will prolong your life only a few days or make you only marginally better off or not better off at all. If you do not have the money or insurance coverage, you may die at an early age even though you have a treatable condition. Even if you have money, you may wait a long time for appropriate treatment.

Medical care is also not equally accessible to all racial and ethnic groups. Analysts have concluded that neither income nor educational differences explain the poorer health of African Americans compared with the United States population overall; they conclude that racial discrimination plays a large part in explaining why blacks receive less and poorer-quality health care than others.[83]

Medical care is also not well rationed over the life cycle; we spend a very large proportion of health care resources on people in the last year of their lives. Thirty percent of all Medicare costs are incurred for last-year care, much of it for the last month of treatment!

Other nations also ration medical care, but they do it in a different way. In Canada, which has a government-funded national health care system, more is spent on preventive medicine. Expensive tests are reserved for those with a high probability of benefiting from them. People sometimes have to wait for elective surgery, imposing an inconvenience but ensuring that facilities will be used more efficiently. In several European countries, rationing is done by a kind of triage process that determines who should have first priority for expensive procedures. For example, except in life-threatening circumstances, priority for an elective hip replacement would be given to a middle-aged working person over an elderly person.

Costs

Health premiums are rising faster than inflation; the average cost of private health insurance for a family of four in 2006 was more than $11,000. Although families are spending proportionately less on food and clothing than they did thirty years ago, they are spending much more on housing and health care.[84] For families who cannot afford health insurance, a major illness can lead to bankruptcy or worse, death. The millions who cannot afford

"Kids, your mother and I have spent so much money on health insurance this year that instead of vacation we're all going to go in for elective surgery."

health insurance often go untreated. President Bush's casual comment in 2007 that those without insurance can get their treatment in emergency rooms illustrated both the lack of understanding of the lives of many poor and working-class people but also the limitations of a health system where, for some people, emergency care is the best alternative possible. Emergency care deals not at all with prevention nor with follow-up of problems identified in the emergency treatment.

By comparison, a patient in Sweden never has to spend more than $118 a year out-of-pocket for visits to the doctor, and the state pays all medical costs above $236 a year. In Belgium, where the "right to health" is an article in the constitution, a three-day treatment for a cancer patient costs only $2000, and the patient pays only $36.[85]

Why are our costs so high? There are several reasons. First, our system is a costly mixture of private and public. Because it is such a complicated mix, administration consumes 25 percent of health care costs, largely because we have so many different providers. Each has its own rules, forms, and systems for managing paperwork.[86] Waste and inefficiency, partly from negotiating amongst all these systems, account for another 10 to 20 percent of health care costs.[87]

New drugs and new medical technology that make it possible to do more for more people are a second major contribution to escalating costs.[88] Not only are better, more complicated drugs being developed to treat diseases that we couldn't treat before (AIDS for example) but people are taking more of them. The growing reliance on high technology such as CT scanners, MRI, dialysis, and laser equipment, intensive care units, and other sophisticated medical tools costs billions of dollars. High technology has made possible organ transplants and other procedures unheard of a few years ago available today, but at a huge cost. There is often a technology arms race among hospitals in a community, driving up costs for everyone.

When better procedures become available, more people want them, so even if the new procedures are cheaper than the old, the total cost can be higher. Surgery for cataracts, an eye disease affecting many elderly, is an example. Until two decades ago, surgery was painful and often ineffective. Now new techniques and materials allow plastic lenses to be inserted into the eye surgically, greatly improving vision. As a consequence, many more people receive the surgery, at a greatly increased overall cost, even though the individual procedures cost less.[89] And sometimes new, more costly procedures are not more effective than older ones, but are more in demand anyway.[90]

The aging population is a third reason for higher costs. One out of six people can now expect to live to the age of one hundred. The elderly have more and more serious health problems than younger people, so as their numbers increase, the demand for medical services rises.

The financial and even legal pressure to perform many unnecessary procedures is a fourth factor driving up costs. One-quarter to one-third of all medical procedures are unneeded or are actually harmful.[91] It is telling that patients' likelihood of surgery for common problems may vary more with where they live than with their conditions. Moreover, costs from region to region and city to city vary widely for a particular procedure, and those spending levels are unrelated to quality of care.[92]

Damage to American industry Health care costs are a burden on corporations as well as families. Our system penalizes corporations which provide health insurance coverage and rewards corporations which do not. After corporate income taxes, employee benefits are the largest structural cost to business. In 2002, General Motors spent $4.5 billion on health care for its employees.[93] By one estimate, if we had a government-funded national health insurance plan similar to those in Canada and Europe, U.S. automakers could save at least $1300 per vehicle.[94] High health costs drive employers to relocate abroad where the cost of labor is low, as in developing countries, or where the government picks up the costs of health care, as in Canada, Europe, and Japan.

On the other hand, some corporations fail to provide health insurance and, essentially, pass on the costs to taxpayers. Wal-Mart has become the most egregious and visible example. With over $312 billion in sales in 2005, it offered health insurance to fewer than half its employees, many of whom ended up on Medicaid. State policy makers are not amused, and more than a dozen states have passed laws trying to force Wal-Mart and other large corporations to spend a set fraction of their earnings on employee benefits.

Possible Reforms of the Health Care System

Though the fear of "socialized" medicine has been an obstacle to thorough health care reform for decades, the irrationality and cost of the existing system is changing the opinions of some powerful interests, including cor-

porations saddled with the high costs of health insurance benefits.

In 2004, almost eight thousand U.S. doctors (about 1 percent of all practicing physicians) published a letter in the *Journal of the American Medical Association* arguing that private sector solutions have failed and calling for the elimination of for-profit hospitals and HMOs. The physicians who signed the letter advocate a government-financed health insurance system covering every American. They said it would save billions.[95] This idea has picked up some support as we approach the 2008 election. Several of the leading Democratic presidential candidates have offered some variation of a plan to finance health insurance for every American.

A single-payer system, with individuals choosing their own doctors, would likely save significant administrative costs. Currently, the administrative costs of private health maintenance organizations are higher than those for Medicare because, in the attempt to be as profitable as possible, the private organizations are highly selective. They spend a great deal of money sorting policy applicants to find those at least risk for health problems. Medicare covers everyone sixty-five and older who has paid into the program. Moreover, a single-payer system would reduce the administrative costs endemic in the multiplicity of systems and their inefficient duplication and interaction.

An inclusive program would also allow more attention to prevention, preventing or delaying the onset of diseases that impose untold costs in productivity and treatment further down the road. The incidence of those health problems predicted to be the greatest burden on the health care system in coming years—obesity, diabetes, AIDS, for example—could all be reduced through preventive health care.

The Bush administration reforms have focused on privatization, encouraging people on Medicare and Medicaid to enroll in HMOs and private drug insurance programs. Bush has increased tax credits for the purchase of private health insurance and created new deductions for medical savings accounts. Relying more on private solutions is an idea also advanced by several of the Republican presidential candidates.

But tax credits will not do anything to address rising costs, nor will they improve access and decrease costs for low-income families who do not have the money to buy insurance or open medical savings accounts. Moreover, our mixed private-public system has proven to be a failure for millions of people, and seems unlikely to be significantly improved with tinkering.

for corn, which allows agribusiness to churn out the cheap fructose-laden foods and sodas that are available in every vending machine.

Conclusion: Are Domestic Policies Responsive?

The past thirty years of increasing maldistribution of wealth has been paralleled by the rising influence of money in politics and an increase in legislation that benefits the well-off. Our taxing and spending policies have certainly been responsive to the needs of wealthier Americans.

However, looking at our vast array of social welfare benefits, it would be easy to conclude that government is not only responsive to the American public but hyperresponsive. Through income support programs, subsidized services, and tax breaks, social welfare provides something for everyone while reflecting government's greater responsiveness to individuals and groups who wield political influence. The poor, although comprising more than 12 percent of the population, do not have the influence, organization, or access to win public support for programs benefiting them. In hard times, when support is most needed, programs for the poor often take the brunt of budget cuts. But not all Americans view politics solely in terms of what they get, and some have learned that the growth of an underclass harms everyone.

Most taxpayers define themselves as middle income, and they support services for themselves and others like them. Benefits to the upper classes are tolerated to a large extent because they often take the form of technical or specially tailored tax breaks that most of the public has never heard of. When they do catch the public's attention, often because of abuse—such as offshore tax shelters or business deductions for stock options given to CEOs—they can trigger resentment and reform.

The making of social welfare policy also illustrates our government's lack of an overarching policy or philosophy about its responsibilities for ensuring basic human services. Instead, it responds in piecemeal fashion to crises or to pressure from the most influential interest groups and lobbyists and gives far too little attention to long-term planning. Though Americans worry about the viability of the country's health care system, Con-

The fact that government insurance programs cover many of the people most likely to be sick—the elderly and the poor—and private health insurers cover those at least risk—the young, the well, and the well-off—means that it is very hard to hold down costs of publicly funded programs in the current system. To compensate, state governments, which bear a large share of the costs, are tightening access to Medicaid and increasing premiums, and the federal government is limiting the amount it will reimburse doctors and hospitals for services provided to patients enrolled in Medicare and Medicaid.[96] These moves exacerbate the problems of access.

With runaway budget deficits and public spending on health now rising faster than private spending, government has to take some action to contain costs. But Congress has shown little interest in major reform. It continues to approach health care much like all other social welfare issues: with changes and benefits targeted at specific groups. There is no commitment to an overall policy on health care and no consensus on who is responsible for providing it.

Moreover, Congress unintentionally but surely with knowledge is an enabler of poor health practices, encouraging unhealthful foods and drugs by providing subsidies for tobacco, which ends up in cigarettes and

gress is too often preoccupied with responding to short-term demands, such as holding down drug costs or capping jury awards in malpractice suits.

Finally, it is clear that Congress has established a massive tangle of support programs to protect individuals and businesses from the risks of the same market-place whose self-regulating properties it loves to praise. Two of the central questions about domestic policies today have to be whether government assumes too much risk for individuals and for business and whether it assumes more risk for the powerful than for the weak.

Key Terms

capitalist economy   435
mixed economies   436
fiscal policy   437
Keynesian economics   438
supply-side economics   438
progressive tax   439
regressive tax   440
flat tax   441

corporate welfare   442
earned income tax credit (EITC)   443
Social Security   445
means test   450
Supplemental Security Income (SSI)   450
Temporary Aid to Needy Families (TANF)   451
farm subsidies   453
food stamps   454
Medicare   456
Medicaid   457

Key Names

Adam Smith   435
John Maynard Keynes   438

Franklin D. Roosevelt   438
Ronald Reagan   438
Bill Clinton   439
George W. Bush   439

For Viewing

Dark Days (2000). An award-winning documentary at the Sundance Film Festival, this film looks at the lives of homeless people who live in the train tunnels beneath Manhattan.

The Farmer's Wife (1998). This PBS documentary watched by millions explores what one farm couple had to do to survive economically and the impact on family life. The first hour can be viewed online at www.pbs.org/frontline. Compare this documentary treatment of a real farm family to two commercial films released in 1984 inspired by the despair in farming communities during the wave of farm foreclosures in the 1970s and 1980s: *The River,* with Sissy Spacek and Mel Gibson, and *Country,* with Jessica Lange and Sam Shepard.

Harvest of Shame (1960). This CBS documentary, narrated by Edward R. Murrow, at the time one of the country's most respected newscasters, generated public awareness of malnutrition and poverty among migrant workers in the United States and helped build support for the war on poverty.

The Hospital (1971). Chaos in a hospital—or as it was once billed, "Madness, Murder, and Malpractice"—was never so entertaining as in this Oscar-winning black comedy.

The Hudsucker Proxy (1994). This comedy by the Coen brothers is about a company that installed a moron as president in order to drive the company into the ground and carry out a stock scam.

Roger and Me (1989). Documentary filmmaker Michael Moore shadowed General Motors' CEO, Roger Smith, hoping to get him to visit his hometown, Flint, Michigan, so he could see firsthand how GM's factory closings led to the city's economic decline. This film made many of the ten-best lists for 1989.

Sicko (2007). Filmaker Michael Moore sets out to see how the American health care system works, especially in the access that individuals have to good care. He compares our system with publicly funded systems elsewhere, including Cuba. Though criticized for idealizing other systems, few dispute his portrayal of America's broken health care system.

Wall Street (1987). This film captured public disenchantment with the "Me Decade" obsession with personal enrichment at all costs.

1. Agricultural subsidies
   a. go mostly to low income farmers.
   b. go mostly to middle-income farmers.
   c. go mostly to high-income farmers.
   d. were designed to get farmers off the land.
   e. were discontinued in 2000.

2. The idea that capitalism would promote prosperity was first associated with
   a. Adam Smith
   b. Karl Marx
   c. John Maynard Keynes
   d. Ronald Reagan
   e. Bill Clinton

3. Which is true of economic systems?
   a. Capitalist systems are always democratic.
   b. There are many examples of pure capitalist countries.
   c. Most countries have economies that are a mixture of public and private ownership.
   d. In most countries, government owns most of the economic enterprises and regulates prices and labor.
   e. Modern economies can exist without government.

4. Which is **not** true of fiscal policy?
   a. Tax levels and types of taxes are part of it.
   b. Spending levels are part of it.
   c. It cannot completely regulate economic activity.
   d. In the United States, it is made by the president and Congress.
   e. It has always been recognized that government can affect the economy.

5. Which is **not** true of supply-side economics?
   a. It was called "voodoo economics" by George H.W. Bush.
   b. It assumes that lower taxes will stimulate growth without harming government revenue.
   c. It offers an economic rationale for smaller governments.
   d. It was used by President Clinton to justify tax increases at the beginning of his term.
   e. It contributed to record budget deficits.

6. Reasons for growing income inequality in the past thirty years include
   a. stagnation of wages for blue collar workers.
   b. tax policies that favored the wealthy.
   c. a sharp rise in the salaries of CEOs.
   d. the rising cost of education.
   e. all of the above.

7. Levels of taxation in America are
   a. higher than in most other industrialized countries.
   b. lower than in most other industrialized countries.
   c. about the same as in most other industrialized countries.
   d. rising rapidly.
   e. higher than they have been for many years.

8. A progressive tax
   a. taxes the rich at a higher rate than the middle income or poor.
   b. taxes the poor at a higher rate than the rich or middle income.
   c. is exemplified by the Social Security tax.
   d. is exemplified by the sales tax.
   e. is exemplified by the proposed flat tax.

9. EITC is an example of a tax break for
   a. the rich.
   b. farmers.
   c. the working poor.
   d. homeowners.
   e. corporations.

10. Spending for social welfare needs
    a. was an important part of government activity in the early nineteenth century.
    b. increased dramatically in the Hoover administration.
    c. is authorized in Article I of the Constitution.
    d. was rolled back during the New Deal.
    e. has led to a completely publically funded health insurance system.

11. Which is **not** true of Social Security?
    a. It was introduced as part of Great Society legislation under Lyndon Johnson.
    b. It was part of Roosevelt's New Deal.
    c. It taxes workers' salaries up to a maximum of close to $100,000.
    d. Taxes to support it produce more than one-third of government revenues.
    e. It has lifted millions of older people out of poverty.

12. Which of the following programs does not have a means test?
    a. TANF
    b. SSI
    c. Social Security
    d. Food stamps
    e. Medicaid

13. The Census Bureau considers a family of four "poor," if its income is less than
    a. $50,000.
    b. $40,000.
    c. $30,000.
    d. $20,000.
    e. $10,000 .

14. TANF
    a. was introduced as part of the New Deal.
    b. was introduced in the Reagan administration.
    c. requires participants to work or enroll in education or training.
    d. is run exactly the same in every state.
    e. was replaced by AFDC.

15. Since the introduction of TANF,
    a. welfare rolls have decreased.
    b. welfare rolls have increased.
    c. welfare rolls have not changed.
    d. the economy has shrunk.
    e. support for the program has eroded.

16. The food stamp program
    a. covers only those receiving TANF benefits.
    b. is no longer in place, since few Americans go hungry.
    c. was made permanent as part of the War on Poverty.
    d. is generally supported by agricultural interests.
    e. only serves rural areas.

17. Which is true of the American health care system?
    a. It costs more than health care in other developed countries.
    b. It is the reason why Americans live longer than people in other countries.
    c. It is almost entirely private.
    d. It is a uniform national system.
    e. It provides for significant preventive heath care.

18. The GI Bill of Rights
    a. provided educational benefits for returning World War II veterans.
    b. helped World War II veterans buy houses.
    c. led to the expansion of higher education.
    d. moved millions of families into the middle class.
    e. all of the above.

19. Our health care system
    a. rations health care by ability to pay.
    b. has failed to contain costs.
    c. is a burden on corporate America.
    d. provides more spending on the last year of life than for children.
    e. all of the above.

20. Which is **not** a factor in driving up health care costs?
    a. growth of high technology in medicine
    b. an aging population
    c. complex administration necessary to manage our multiple providers and insurers
    d. legal pressures to perform more procedures
    e. universal health insurance

I n 2005, the Department of Homeland Security named Weeki Wachee Springs near St. Petersburg, Florida, one of the nation's top terrorist targets. Weeki Wachee is a tiny town featuring a natural spring and shows by "live mermaids." It had its peak in the 1960s when as many as a half million tourists visited annually, and even now is a thriving roadside tourist attraction.

Upon hearing of the designation as a terrorism target, the Weeki Wachee park manager first reflected that it was hard to see why Osama bin Laden would focus on blowing up his mermaids. But, he continued, with terrorists, who knows what they are thinking?[1]

And, as a next step? The manager is working with the county sheriff's office to get some of the federal government's counterterrorism funds. Plans were afoot to "harden the target" by securing the mermaid pond and other park features.[2] However, the manager lamented, "Walt Disney World is a bigger attraction and likely to receive more counterterrorism funds."

Weeki Wachee was fingered in a list of 80,000 potential targets compiled by the Department. The list was kept largely secret so that terrorists would not be able to read about the nation's vulnerabilities. Based on Weeki Wachee and a few other examples leaked to the press, the list soon became fodder for comedians more than a roadmap for terrorists or a useful aid for those trying to protect the U.S. against terrorism.

The foreign policy of the United States has a substantial impact on the world, yet we are not all-powerful. We are one of many nations; decisions about war and peace and about trade and diplomacy are made by people in all nations. In this sense, public expectations about what we can achieve have often been unrealistically high.

Yet we are the world's most powerful nation in terms of both military and economic strength. Thus our power, and how we use it, has a tremendous impact on people throughout the world.

In the 1990s, many of the resources that had been devoted to competition with the former Soviet Union were redirected toward other goals. We suffered from a sense of uncertainty because the Cold War with Soviet bloc countries, which had defined much of our foreign policy since the late 1940s, was over. The nature of international cooperation and competition changed, and we were forced to rethink the means we use to pursue our foreign policy objectives. During the unprecedented period of peace and prosperity at the end of the century, we were more inward looking and less willing to devote as much of our energies and resources to foreign policy as we had in the past. As we shifted from a world divided between East and West to one increasingly linked by the forces of globalization, much of the world left behind the great power struggles of the Cold War and immersed itself in trade rivalries and economic competition.

At the outset of the twenty-first century, as the sole remaining superpower, we settled into a kind of triumphalism grounded in a belief that the Western ideals of democracy, capitalism, and free trade had become the world's agenda. One pundit even called it "The End of History."[3] In this atmosphere of unrivaled military power, the United States experienced the first attack on its territory since the Japanese bombed Pearl Harbor in 1941 and the first attack on the continental United States since the War of 1812.

In this chapter, we examine past and present foreign policy goals, how foreign policy decisions are made, and how foreign policy concerns have changed over time. Then we discuss why the challenges policy makers face in an era of globalization and new security threats require adjustments in how we pursue our foreign policy goals.

Foreign Policy Goals

The goals any nation has and the means it uses to pursue them are influenced by its traditions, core values, ideology, and geopolitical situation (that is, the advantages and limitations imposed by geographical location, size, and wealth relative to other nations). Foreign policies are the strategies adopted and actions taken by a government to achieve its goals in its relationships with other nations. These actions range from informal negotiations to waging war, from writing position papers to initiating trade boycotts. They may require economic, political, cultural, or military resources.

The art of foreign policy making includes choosing means suitable to the objective sought. Due to our size and great wealth, huge diplomatic corps, military forces, and intelligence establishment, we have the fullest possible range of foreign policy instruments at our disposal. Sometimes the possession of so many means of pursuing foreign policy objectives affects the setting of goals; that is, the more a country is able to do, the more it may try to do.

Our primary foreign policy goal, like that of every other nation, is to protect our physical security. Until the era of long-range bombers and ballistic missiles, achieving this goal meant preventing land invasions, and in this we have been successful. Our success was due largely to our separation from the other major powers by two oceans and being bounded on the north and south by two friendly countries. In the nuclear era, when we could be attacked by air by long-range bombers and intercontinental ballistic missiles launched by land or sea, we had to develop an air as well as a ground defense.

In today's era of terrorist attacks—with conventional weaponry or biological, chemical, or nuclear weapons of mass destruction—physical security must be defended against both external and internal attacks. Since September 11, 2001, greater emphasis has been placed on how to prevent terrorist attacks from within and how to stop the proliferation of weapons of mass destruction (WMD). As we will discuss later, how we provide for our physical security in an age of high technology and globalization is undergoing serious rethinking.

A second goal is to help protect the physical security of our neighbors and major democratic allies. Since World War II, we have committed ourselves, through the North Atlantic Treaty Organization (NATO), to join in the defense of Canada and Western, Southern, and now even some Eastern European nations. We also have treaty commitments to Japan, South Korea, and the nations of South and Central America and a bilateral agreement on defense with Taiwan.

A third goal is to protect our economic security. Although the United States is blessed with many natural resources, we must purchase such essential resources as oil, manganese, and tin elsewhere. Safeguarding access to these resources may include stabilizing the governments of producing nations or protecting the sea lanes in which goods are shipped.

Our economic well-being is equally dependent on selling our goods abroad, which in turn depends on how cheaply we can manufacture or grow products desired in other parts of the world and how willing our trading partners are to buy them.

Economic self-interest is almost always a factor in foreign policy, even in dealings with our closest allies, because they do not always want to import U.S. goods that compete with their own. Thus trade missions and participation in the international organizations that govern trade relations are crucial to achieving our foreign policy goals, even though most of the public paid scant attention to them before the 1990s. Today the electronic flow of capital into and out of the country is also essential to our economic viability, so ensuring the privacy of information transfers, including financial transactions, and securing computer systems against hackers are becoming as important to national security as protecting sea lanes.

A fourth overlapping goal is to extend our sphere of influence. Historically, this has meant keeping foreign powers out of the Caribbean and Latin America.

In the 1780s, Thomas Jefferson said he hoped Spain would hold on to its territory in South America until "our population can be sufficiently advanced to gain it from them piece by piece."[4] Since the beginning of the nineteenth century, we have warned off foreign powers from meddling in the affairs of any country in the Americas, and there is still a tendency to see Latin America as "our turf." Since World War II, our sphere of interest has extended around the world. We have sought to influence security arrangements on all continents. Even after the post–Cold War base closures, we still have more military bases and more troops outside our borders than any other country.

We also try to spread our influence by promoting democracy, capitalism, and Western cultural values. Our State Department maintains a system of public libraries around the world to disseminate information on our government, economy, and popular culture and also funds thousands of cultural and academic exchanges between American and foreign artists and scholars each year. More proactively, we fund (to the tune of almost $2 billion in 2006) a good deal of both open and covert democracy promotion through political parties and

AP/Wide World Photos

Some Americans think humanitarian aid should be a goal of U.S. foreign policy, but others, especially policy makers, prefer to focus on U.S. self-interest, despite dire needs around the globe. Here malnourished Sudanese children wait for aid from international relief agencies.

front organizations in other countries. The Orange Revolution that brought down Ukraine's authoritarian government after it tampered with election results was achieved with financial support from the United States. Optimally, we offer our political and economic systems as models of development and at a minimum we try to foster a favorable attitude toward the United States that will make it easier for us to achieve our foreign policy goals. But these efforts can be undercut by foreign policy actions that seem to conflict with the values and ideals we promote; the Iraq War, for example, has made it very difficult to promote or sustain favorable attitudes toward the United States, even among our allies.

Our specific foreign policy objectives, such as protecting access to oil in the Middle East, drying up funding sources for terrorist operations, removing trade barriers, and increasing U.S. exports, are almost always

IDEALS AND NATIONAL INTEREST IN MIDDLE EAST FOREIGN POLICY

overnment's first obligation is to protect the physical and economic security of the country. Many Americans also want our relations with other nations to be consistent with our fundamental values and political ideals. But people do not agree on what makes us secure or which foreign policies best reflect our values.

George W. Bush brought a new wrinkle to the debate over finding the proper balance among the national interest, democratic values, and human rights in foreign policy. After the 9/11 attacks, Bush divided the world into good and evil forces, between those who shared our civilization's values, or supported our efforts to preserve them, and those who were enemies of "civilization." This led Bush to conclude that the only way we could be secure is if other people in the world shared our political values—democracy and freedom, he said, were divine gifts to which all people were entitled.[1]

Bush's basic premise implies that our ideals and national self-interest go hand in hand. In positing democracy as a divine gift he was also saying that all people want to live in democratic systems and therefore if we "bring" it to them, even by force, we will be acting in both their interests and our own. He made the Middle East his test case and in doing so set himself apart from predecessors he saw as too willing to tolerate dictatorships in the name of national interest. So now it is fair to ask, in comparison to his predecessors, how responsive has his foreign policy been to American ideals and political values?

The United States has been actively trying to influence politics and shape governments in the Middle East for almost sixty years. After World War II broke up the empires of the colonial powers—Britain, France, and Germany—that dominated the area, the United States moved in. The main objectives of successive administrations were to keep the area stable, out of Soviet control, and the oil supply lines open. For the most part, this meant staying on good terms with monarchs and dictators, training their armies, and sending billions of dollars in military aid.

When the rare regime change was attempted it was not in support of democracy. A 1953 CIA-backed coup overthrew the elected government of Iran (which was considering nationalization of oil resources) and restored the monarchy, putting on the throne a family handpicked decades earlier by the British. The Shah of Iran's rule, which featured secular, pro-Western polices and a brutal secret police we trained and equipped, created such dissent in Iran that it fomented the Islamic revolution of 1979, which replaced the Shah with an even more oppressive Shia Muslim theocracy. We have not had normal diplomatic relations with Iran since.

To counter the unfriendly Shia regime in Iran, the Reagan administration established close ties with neighboring Iraq's dictator, Saddam Hussein, a secular Sunni Muslim, trained and equipped his army, and supported him through a war with Iran that we hoped would bring down the virulently anti-American Iranian theocracy. The war produced nothing but hundreds of thousands of deaths, some of them caused by Saddam's use of chemical weapons (obtained with the help of the United States) against Iraqi dissidents as well as Iranians.

In 1991, when Saddam invaded neighboring Kuwait, threatening oil exports from that country, the first Bush administration put together an international force under UN auspices to drive Saddam's army back into Iraq. After achieving our goals of reinstating a friendly Kuwaiti monarchy and ensuring access to its oil fields, we withdrew rather than moving on to Baghdad and removing Saddam (whom George H. W. Bush had equated with Hitler) from power. U.S. decision makers, aware that Saddam's dictatorship was what held together Iraq's conflictive Kurds, Shia, and Sunni Muslims under one government, preferred the status quo and political stability over regime change. Even when the majority Shia Muslims rebelled against Saddam, we left them to die at Saddam's hand.

In Saudi Arabia, Jordan, Pakistan, and Egypt, national interest rather than ideals has also led us to support monarchies and military dictatorships that suppress opposition and resist elections. Our closest Arab ally, Saudi Arabia, has funded a worldwide system of schools that train students in *Wahhabism,* a branch of Muslim teaching subscribed to by many Islamist fundamentalists, that preaches virulent anti-Semitism and a severe restriction of women's freedoms.

Even with Israel, our most stalwart ally in the Middle East and the one with whom we share by far the closest political and cultural ties, our alliance was driven primarily by national interest. Israel was created in 1948, but it was not until its display of military prowess in the 1967 Six Day War against neighboring Arab countries that we began to see it as a valuable ally against Soviet intrusion into the Middle East.

Despite our commonality of interests with Israel, we have been unable, in thirty years of trying, to negotiate a settlement of the land dispute between the Israelis and Palestinians. The significant achievement of **Jimmy Carter** in negotiating a peace agreement between Israel and Egypt ended in the assassination of Anwar Sadat, the Egyptian president who signed the accords. And Israeli Prime Minister Yitzhak Rabin was assassinated by an Israeli religious zealot after he signed a later peace settlement brokered by Bill Clinton.

However much we have in common with the Israelis, our national interests differ: ours is regional stability and access to oil and theirs is survival. Many Israelis felt withdrawal from occupied territories or sharing control of Jerusalem would endanger their security (and some religious fundamentalists felt it morally wrong to give away land that, in their view, was theirs by Biblical right). We cannot define their national interest for Israelis.

George W. Bush sought to change business as usual in the Middle East with his program of "Democracy and Economic Freedom in the Muslim World."[2] With this policy, he tried to align foreign policy goals with American values. He refused to deal with the Palestinian leader Yasir Arafat and made known his support for Israel and his willingness to use force if Israel was attacked (the first American president to make that pledge). And when he invaded Iraq to overthrow Saddam, he expected it to be the tipping point for the emergence of a "new Middle East" of friendly democratic governments.

However, what Bush labeled the equal pursuit of ideals and national interest compromised our national security, diminished our moral authority, and increased regional instability. Bush's refusal to deal with Yasir Arafat stalled the peace process for several years. There were new rounds of suicide bombings by Palestinians, followed by Israeli incursions into Palestinian-controlled territory and the building of a wall separating those territories from Israel. The elections Bush called for to replace the obstinate Arafat brought to power Hamas, a militant Islamic faction that refuses to recognize Israel's right to exist. The democratic process did not produce leaders who shared democratic values or believed in the peaceful resolution of differences with Israel.

The overthrow of Saddam Hussein in 2003 unleashed the kind of religious and ethnic conflict that George H. W. Bush had feared when he decided to end the Gulf War short of regime change. The nation fell into sectarian warfare, attracted outside jihadists, and spawned a new generation of terrorists in a nation where before the invasion there had been few outside of Saddam's government.

Moreover, in fighting a war to promote democracy, the Bush administration endorsed actions never before sanctioned by our government: torturing those suspected of being enemy combatants and holding them for years without charges being filed or the right to see evidence against them. When Bill Clinton, through NATO and the UN, involved the United States in nation building in the Balkans, Haiti, and Somalia, Bush called it "misplaced idealism."[3] Bush's own approach to foreign policy has been a combination of brutal realism (pursuing national interest at the expense of international law) and very poorly executed idealism (the promotion of democracy through regime change). Unwilling to commit enough troops to stop the violence in Iraq, the Bush policy made the United States look feckless in the eyes of the world. The wars in Iraq and Afghanistan left the armed forces with virtually no battle-ready troops other than those already deployed. American credibility sank to an all-time low and anti-Americanism rose to an all-time high.

American policy in the Middle East illustrates once again that foreign policy cannot be based on simple ideas of good and evil; good motives often fall prey to real limitations on our ability to change things and our misunderstandings about what can be changed.

[1]U.S. State Department, "Fiscal Yr 2004–2009 Department of State and USAID Strategic Plan" (www.state.gov).
[2]Ibid., 3.
[3]Steven R. Weisman, "Democracy Push by Bush Attracts Doubters in Party," *New York Times,* March 17, 2006.

The United States is offering millions of dollars for information leading to the capture of Osama bin Laden. The reward is printed on matchbooks and posters. However, many villagers are sympathetic to him, and they are aware that anyone who turns him in will not be safe.

tions and individuals who in some way influence the process of making and implementing foreign policy: the president, members of Congress, heads of relevant cabinet departments and independent agencies, foreign service officers, chiefs of the armed services, White House staff and other political advisers, interest groups, lobbyists, the media, the public, and even leaders of other countries. (For example, when he made the decision to invade Iraq, President Bush told the Saudi Arabian ambassador, whose country he would need to use as a staging area, before he informed his own secretary of state.)

Historically, inconsistencies in our foreign policy were rarely caused by differences among policy makers over fundamental goals but rather over specific actions that should be taken. Recently, though the direct attack on U.S. soil on 9/11 crystallized our foreign policy focus and Americans united behind the goal of destroying al-Qaeda's terrorist network, disagreement has emerged on how much intervention in the internal affairs of another country is justifiable, what form that intervention should take, and to what extent fundamental principles of government should be compromised in the name of national security.

Here we look at some of the groups and individuals who influence the foreign policy-making process and how division and conflict among them can affect U.S. policy.

related to achieving one or more of these four general goals.

Making Foreign Policy in a Democracy

Alexis de Tocqueville was one of the first to remark that it is difficult to have a coherent foreign policy in a democracy. His sentiments have been echoed thousands of times since and certainly apply to the United States. Why has the United States had such difficulty articulating a coherent and consistent set of objectives?

Some of the confusion in foreign policy making arises because we elect new leaders every four or eight years. As leaders change, so do their policy priorities. Inconsistencies within a single administration can also be partly explained by the sheer number of organiza-

The President and His Inner Circle

As head of state and commander in chief of the armed forces, the president is in control of the nation's diplomatic and military establishments. In addition, he has the most complete and privileged access to the nation's diplomatic and military communications and intelligence networks. In times of crisis, without immediately available alternative sources of reliable information, members of Congress and the public have historically almost always relied on the president's sources. The Clinton years of divided government were a partial exception to this rule; with no overt foreign policy crises, presidential decisions, even those made in response to attacks on U.S. facilities and forces abroad, were constantly challenged by an especially contentious Congress.

Given the central role of the president in foreign policy making and the fact that most presidents enter

This Iranian mother and daughter reflect the split between the traditionalists and the modernists in Iranian society. U.S. policymakers hope that younger, westernized Iranians will help transform their religious government

Members of the Joint Chiefs of Staff are military professionals who give advice to the president on both the readiness of their service arms and the appropriateness of their use in specific situations. Members of Congress may be consulted because they are political allies of the president, because they are in leadership positions crucial for mobilizing support on an issue, or because they have developed expertise in military or foreign policy issues through their committee assignments.

The president may also consult his wife or friends and advisers outside government, not because of their policy expertise, but because he trusts in their good judgment and wants the perspective of people close to him who have no organizational interests or policy agenda to advance.

Who the president draws into his inner circle of advisers depends in large part on his experience and decision-making style. President Kennedy, who had almost no foreign policy experience, assembled a committee of cabinet heads and close advisers to help him construct his response to the Soviets during the Cuban Missile crisis. But during the Persian Gulf crisis, the first President Bush reportedly made the decision to send troops to Saudi Arabia relying almost exclusively on his own judgment and that of a few close advisers.

If a president comes to office with a foreign policy agenda and expects to make his political reputation and leave his mark on history in this policy area, as Richard Nixon and the first George Bush did, he will surround himself with like-minded people and replace those who disagree with him or ignore their advice. George H. W. Bush appointed both members of the foreign policy establishment who had held high positions in previous administrations and several associates from his tenure as the Central Intelligence Agency (CIA) director, an organizational tie that made many in Congress uncomfortable.

Ex-governors such as Carter, Reagan, Clinton, and George W. Bush can compensate for their lack of foreign policy experience when they become president by surrounding themselves with experts. Nevertheless, Carter and Reagan chose foreign policy advisers with limited experience and had difficulty maintaining unity among them. In contrast, Clinton appointed an experienced team of advisers, including a number from the Carter administration, but was himself more focused on domestic policy and less decided on foreign policy goals early in his presidency.

George W. Bush came to office with even less international experience than Clinton and a pronounced

office with very little foreign policy expertise, it is important to know who advises him. Though he doesn't have to, usually the president gives at least a perfunctory hearing to people who head departments and agencies involved with making or implementing policy. The government officials best positioned to advise the president on foreign policy include the secretaries of defense and state, the national security adviser, and the head of the National Intelligence Agency (NIA). The president also frequently consults others, including the Joint Chiefs of Staff and influential members of Congress.

These individuals represent a wide range of experience and bring different perspectives to the analysis of foreign policy issues. The secretary of state is usually concerned with the nation's diplomatic relations and the use of diplomatic channels to implement the president's policies. The secretary of defense (a civilian) is primarily concerned with military and security issues and the use of the military to pursue foreign policy goals. The national security advisor heads the National Security Council, a team of security specialists working within the Executive Office of the President. They are essentially political advisors whose job is to vet all security-related information coming into the White House and make recommendations to the president.

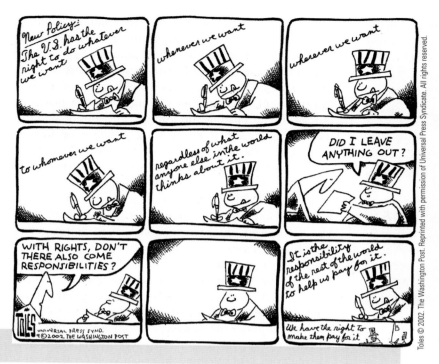

and almost all members of the Foreign Service. Although they must implement the president's policy as directed, when giving advice their job is to exercise neutral competence, not to serve a political agenda. However, their briefings may simply be ignored if they do not support policy choices preferred by their superiors. Turf battles between advisers and their agencies can result in incomplete or inaccurate information reaching the highest levels. Agency separation, competition, and even antagonism led to many of the failures and misuses of intelligence prior to and after the September 11 attacks.

The principal office for carrying out the president's foreign policy, the State Department, has eleven thousand Foreign Service officers who are experts on every policy area and region of the globe. Ambassadors, the president's personally appointed emissaries to other countries, are often career professionals, but in some of the largest and most important embassies and in some of the smaller but very desirable posts, the ambassador may be a political appointee chosen from among the president's friends or campaign contributors.

We should not assume that even the career professional experts present neutral information that is somehow mechanically cranked out as public policy. Even if the experts do their best to provide the most accurate information and most comprehensive policy alternatives possible, top policy makers see the information through their own perceptual and ideological lenses. Our Vietnam policies failed in part because many of our best Asia experts had been purged from the State Department during the McCarthy era. The second Bush administration ignored both intelligence reports and advice from experts in the State Department in its rush to war in Iraq. High turnover in specialist positions has at times put us at a disadvantage relative to our adversaries and allies.

Another group of specialists that is important in formulating foreign and military policy is intelligence experts who collect and collate economic, military, and diplomatic information gathered in the government's fifteen intelligence agencies. The best known of these is the CIA, but several cabinet departments (Treasury, State, Defense, and Energy) also have intelligence-gathering offices, and Justice has the FBI. The National

disinterest in international politics. He chose his entire first-tier foreign policy advisers, and part of the second tier, from those who had served in his father's and earlier Republican administrations. Arguably they were, collectively, the most experienced group of foreign policy advisers assembled by any president since the end of World War II. But some came with predetermined worldviews and their own policy agendas. Donald Rumsfeld wanted to transform the military and brought with him neoconservatives associated with his longtime colleague Vice President Dick Cheney. This subset of advisers had a list of objectives, including the overthrow of **Saddam Hussein,** that it had publicized in the 1990s.[5] Their influence, exercised through the Department of Defense and the vice president's office, dwarfed advice received from the State Department and the president's own National Security Council. Bush's administration is the only one in American history in which foreign policy is as closely—perhaps more closely associated—with the vice president than the president.

Specialists

Much further removed from the president are the career specialists in the federal bureaucracy who are not political appointees: the staff of intelligence agencies, area specialists in the State and Defense departments,

Security Agency is so secret its employees cannot be photographed; its funding is part of the "black budget," unknown to the public and to much of Congress (hence its nickname, No Such Agency).

Though novels written about intelligence work focus on undercover agents, and our agencies have many of those, in fact most of the work done by intelligence agencies involves routine fact collecting, research, and report writing rather than covert operations. Intelligence agencies also use electronic and satellite surveillance.[6]

In 2005 all fifteen intelligence operations were put under the supervision of a sixteenth, the National Intelligence Agency, whose head briefs the president daily. How successful the NIA will be in diminishing turf wars, improving data sharing, and discouraging "analysis shopping," (choosing whichever agency's data best supports policy preferences),[7] remains to be seen.[8]

Congress

The leading members of congressional committees on foreign affairs and armed services and of the oversight committees for intelligence agencies play a larger role in foreign policy than the average member plays. But Congress as a whole has specific constitutional authority to act as a check on the president's policies through its power to declare and fund wars and the requirement for Senate ratification of treaties and confirmation of ambassadorial and high-level State and Defense department and intelligence agency officials. Because Congress appropriates all money for carrying out foreign policy, the president is limited in the scope of the actions he can take without congressional approval.

Sometimes there is rivalry between the White House and Congress in foreign policy making. Nowhere is conflict greater than over the use of the military to achieve foreign policy goals. Politicians and scholars have been arguing for more than two hundred years about how Congress's constitutional authority to "declare war" limits the president's authority as commander in chief. The Founders, believing it too dangerous to give war powers to the president alone, were also unwilling to accept wording that would have given Congress the power to "make war." Instead, they gave Congress the power to "declare war," leaving the president, according to James Madison's notes on the debate, "the power to repel sudden attacks."[9] This left Congress and the president to struggle over what constitutes an attack on the United States and when a military intervention is a war.

There have been more than two hundred occasions when the president has sent troops into combat situations without congressional approval. In fact, Congress has exercised its power to declare war only five times, and on only one of those occasions, the War of 1812, did it conduct a debate before issuing the declaration. Yet the two undeclared wars in Korea and Vietnam alone produced almost one hundred thousand American deaths, more than the combined losses of all of our declared wars, except World War II and the Civil War.[10]

The 1973 War Powers Resolution, which was intended to curb what Congress believes is presidential usurpation of its authority, limits the president's ability to commit troops to combat to three conditions: (1) when Congress has declared war; (2) when Congress has given the president specific authority to send troops into combat; or (3) when an attack on the United States or its military creates a national crisis. The War Powers Resolution has been opposed by every president since Nixon, whose veto of the resolution was overridden by Congress. Some presidents have ignored the resolution. Both Presidents Bush sought it for their actions in Iraq only under pressure. During the Clinton administration, Democrats tried to strengthen the act and Republicans to repeal it; neither effort was successful. As one supporter of the act commented, "Every president finds Congress inconvenient, but we're a democracy, not a monarchy."[11]

In his dealings with Congress over use of the military, George W. Bush paid little attention to the War Powers Resolution, concentrating instead on establishing a new interpretation of the president's powers as commander in chief. As part of their attempt to argue that the presidency is a unitary executive with complete authority to direct the work of all executive branch agencies, Justice Department attorneys claimed virtually unchecked powers for the commander in chief in committing and directing the armed forces in combat and in all domestic actions a president judges necessary to achieving military goals. (This issue is discussed in greater detail in Chapter 9.)

Whatever their differences with Congress, presidents in the postwar era have usually proclaimed their desire to have a "bipartisan" foreign policy; that is, they want support from both parties in order to present a united front to the world. Presidents will often try to frame policies in a national security context as a way to pressure Congress into accepting their position, but Congress's role is not simply to rubber-stamp executive

Most presidents have resented Congressional oversight during wars. And members of Congress are equally resentful when a president sends American soldiers into combat without asking Congress for authorization. And when wars are unpopular, this tension becomes a focal point of controversy. Members of Congress become frustrated at their inability to significantly affect the course of the war. The Vietnam War illustrated this dynamic well. And the current war in Iraq provides a striking current example.

The decision to invade Afghanistan, where there was clear evidence that the Afghan government was harboring and supporting al-Qaeda, won bipartisan support from members of Congress. But Congress and the president have been at odds over the Iraq War from the beginning. In October 2002, several months before we invaded, a strong majority of both houses of Congress voted to give Bush the power to go to war against Iraq. Even so, there were significant dissenters. In both the House and Senate, overwhelming majorities of Republicans favored the resolution. But only a minority of House Democrats did, and Senate Democrats were split, though a majority supported the resolution.

Many members of Congress, especially Democrats, questioned the president's rationale for the war and raised questions about whether the administra-

tion really had evidence that Saddam Hussein's government had weapons of mass destruction or that he was involved in the 9/11 attacks, both of which the president claimed. Some members were also concerned that the war would be easy to get into and tough to get out of. And others also argued that the war was a diversion from the war against al-Qaeda in Afghanistan.[2]

The administration did not have the evidence that it claimed to have, and as the war itself began to go badly, Congressional criticism increased. Moreover, as troops died, members of Congress began to discover that the troops were undermanned and poorly equipped for the war they were fighting. The president had sent fewer troops than military leaders thought were necessary, those troops lacked the body armor to protect them from gunfire, and their vehicles lacked proper protection from roadside bombs, the deadly improvised explosive devices (IEDs).

Individual soldiers were rotated through Iraq, and then sent back for additional tours of duty.[3] Forces were overstretched and the readiness of the military declined to its lowest point since World War II. In 2003, Secretary of Defense Donald Rumsfeld infuriated many members of Congress when he remarked that, "As you know, you go to war with the Army you have. They're not the Army you might want

or wish to have at a later time," as if the administration had not chosen the time and place for this preemptive war.

Over time, as the war became more and more unpopular, more Republicans joined their Democratic colleagues in criticism. Yet Republicans, wanting to protect "their" president, continued to support him in congressional votes. Then, too, though no president can fight a war without funding, most members of Congress, including Democrats, would not consider cutting appropriations, a move that could put troops at risk.

Despite growing unpopularity because of the war, President Bush was reelected in 2004. The majority of the public gave the president higher marks on national security issues than they did his challenger, John Kerry. But, having reelected the president, the public continued to oppose the war, and by larger proportions.

Finally, a year after that election, the Democratic House Caucus decided to back Rep. John Murtha (D-Pa.), a former medal-winning Marine officer and one of the congressional experts on the military, when he introduced a resolution criticizing the war and urging the president to change direction.[4] At a press conference on November 17, 2005, Murtha said, "The war in Iraq is not going as advertised. It is a flawed policy wrapped in illusion." He continued, "It is time to bring [the troops]

---

branch policies. Presidents especially need bipartisan support when treaties are to be ratified because it is rare for one party to have the necessary two-thirds majority in the Senate or for members of each party to be united in their ranks.

Presidents like to say that in facing the rest of the world, Americans are all on the same side. But this view

is too simplistic. Americans come from all over the world and, once here, look out on the rest of the world from very different vantage points. Party positions, too, differ on these as on most other issues, as shown in roll-call votes.[12] Democrats tend to favor lower levels of military spending and higher levels of foreign aid than Republicans and to support interest group demands for

home."[5] The resolution he prepared for a House vote proposed three actions: no new troops would be deployed to Iraq and those already there would be withdrawn "at the earliest practicable date"; a quick strike force would be deployed in a neighboring country; and the stabilization of Iraq would be pursued by diplomatic means.

The next day, as Murtha walked onto the House floor to debate his resolution, Democrats cheered and Republicans went on the attack. A junior Republican member was sent to the podium to call Murtha a coward and to remind the decorated veteran that Marines "never cut and run." Democrats stormed into the aisles with raised fists demanding an apology and removal of the insult from the daily record. They screamed, "You're pathetic, you're pathetic" at the Republican name-callers; one of their number crossed to the Republican side to mix it up with those attacking Murtha but the Majority Leader arrived and restored order.[6]

Murtha's resolution was never allowed to come to a vote because the Republican majority controlled how bills and resolutions worked their way through the House. They substituted Murtha's page-long proposal for withdrawal of troops at "the earliest practicable date" with a twenty-one-word, one-sentence resolution calling for "immediate termination" of the U.S.

presence in Iraq.[7] Of course, this was not what Murtha was proposing, and, as Republicans knew, virtually no one would vote for a measure that said U.S. troops should just get on a plane and go home. The resolution went down on a 403–3 vote with Murtha voting in the majority.

But the fight was only beginning. The administration brought out its big guns to attack Murtha.[8] And, predictably, Murtha was swift-boated; within a few days of his press conference, conservative blogs were questioning whether he really earned the two Purple Hearts he was awarded for service in Vietnam.

But public opposition to the war continued to increase and by 2006, public discontent contributed significantly to the Republicans' defeat in the off-year elections. The party lost its majority in both houses of Congress. But even with the Democrats nearly united against the war, they found it difficult to do anything about it. Indeed, ignoring advice of a distinguished task force he had appointed, the president actually escalated the war in early 2007 with a "surge" of troops.

But by mid-2007, even influential Republicans like Richard Lugar (R-Ind.) and John Warner (R-Va.) began to speak out against the war and urged the administration to find a way out. Yet, they refused to join Democrats in passing a resolution setting timetables

for withdrawal. Like the president, they insisted on waiting for a fall 2007 report on the progress of the war.

These events illustrate the upper hand a president has in wartime. Until 2006, the White House could get away with accusing opponents of the war, including a thrice-decorated veteran and military hawk, of being unpatriotic cowards simply because they had the temerity to criticize war policy. The president also retained his ability to harness his party to his ends; even with his record-low approval ratings, he was able to get Republican members to vote against resolutions to withdraw troops. This is especially noteworthy because by 2006, a significant majority of the public was opposed to the war, including majorities in several Republican districts.

[1] Howard Fineman, "Politics," *Newsweek*, November 28, 2005, 28.

[2] Letter from John P. Murtha to the Democratic Caucus, December 14, 2005. (www.murtha.house.gov).

[3] "Murtha Responds to Rumsfeld," August 30, 2006. This press release from Murtha's office lists claims made by Rumsfeld about the war in Iraq and counters with a list of "facts" to refute them. (www.murtha.house.gov).

[4] Ibid.

[5] "War in Iraq," press release from Murtha's office, November 17, 2005 (www.murtha.house.gov).

[6] Fineman, "Politics," 29.

[7] H. Res. 571, *Congressional Record*, November 18, 2005, HR1005.

[8] "War-Backer Dem Wants Out," *New York Post*, November 18, 2005, 26.

worker and environmental protection restrictions on trade agreements, the funding of international agencies, and working multilaterally to achieve goals. Republicans are more likely to support unrestricted trade and military intervention to protect U.S. economic interests and to oppose family planning aid to poor countries and working through the United Nations.[13]

It often seems that the opposition party has no coherent alternative to the president's policy. This is probably because under normal circumstances, most members of Congress spend their time on the domestic issues that are so important to their constituents (especially at election time). Then too, in times of crisis, as when U.S. troops are committed to combat, the opposition party usually rallies in support of administration policy so that the country can present a united front to the world.

Once these troops are actually engaged in battle, those who continue to oppose the president's actions can find themselves in the position of appearing to give higher priority to their policy preferences than to the safety of U.S. troops. At this point, it is very difficult for the opposition party to oppose the president's policy effectively. There are notable exceptions, such as bipartisan criticism of Johnson's and Nixon's Vietnam policies, but this dissent came late in the course of the fighting, when public opinion was turning against the war and administration policies did not seem to be working. Even then, Congress approved virtually all expenditures requested to wage the war.

A similar scenario is playing out in Iraq. Even as criticism of George W. Bush's handling of the Iraq war mounted, and the majority of Americans have turned against the war, very few Republicans or Democrats voted against supplemental funding to pay the costs. Most members are fearful that their vote will be seen not as opposition to policy, but as a refusal to support U.S. troops, and the president's party loyalists are eager to paint a dissenting vote that way.

Interest Groups

A multiplicity of interest groups are concerned with foreign policy issues: international businesses; public interest groups, such as those that lobby on environmental and human rights issues; veterans' organizations; farmers who grow crops for export; labor unions; and ethnic groups interested in their ancestral lands, such as African, Jewish, Muslim, Arab, Irish, Cuban, Mexican, and Polish Americans.

In general, it is harder for interest groups to affect foreign policy than to influence domestic policy. Part of the reason for this is that the president and the executive branch have greater weight than Congress in day-to-day foreign policy decision making. But interest group activity has always been effective in some policy areas, especially those related to containing communism and regulating trade and foreign investment. For example, electronics industries lobby against national security restrictions that keep them from exporting computer equipment and software that have military applications. Farm and business organizations lobby on behalf of import quotas and tariffs to protect their domestically produced goods and against trade restrictions and embargoes that prevent them from selling their products abroad.

Americans have a long history of trying to win favorable U.S. policy for their countries of birth or ancestry. Some have even undertaken private action in support of home countries: Irish Americans have sold guns to the Irish Republican Army and Jewish Americans to Jews in Palestine trying to establish an independent state (in the territory that became Israel). Cuban Americans have trained a military force on U.S. soil to overthrow the Castro government in Cuba (even though it is illegal to do so under U.S. law). Mexican Americans have mobilized millions for street demonstrations supporting legal residency for Mexican nationals who entered the country without permission. Arab and Muslim Americans,

Cubans in Miami celebrate upon hearing that Cuban leader Fidel Castro was ill and had ceded power to his brother. Cuban Americans' bitterness toward Castro has influenced American policy toward Cuba.

© Richard Patterson/Getty Images

seeing the effectiveness of these lobbies, are only now seriously organizing to try to influence foreign policy toward Middle Eastern countries.

Perhaps no other nationality group has had as much success in setting the foreign policy agenda for their homeland as Cuban Americans. The strength of their lobby is due in part to a predisposition in Congress for their policy preference and in part to the concentration of their population in one state with a large number of electoral votes (Florida). The Cuban American lobby has been the driving force behind preferential treatment for Cuban immigrants (special terms of entry and financial help from the government) and the maintenance of an economic embargo against the Castro government. In recent years, however, the Cuba lobby has seen its influence decline. Farm and business lobbies in the United States, afraid of losing export and investment opportunities on the island to Canada and Europe, succeeded in getting Congress to lift the sanctions on food exports and lighten travel restrictions. As an indication of how important an electoral force Cuban Americans are in Florida, Bush toughened sanctions on travel and humanitarian aid before the 2004 election. He did not, however, interfere with agricultural trade deals.

During the past quarter century, three factors have opened up the foreign policy decision-making process to greater influence by interest groups. The first is the growing importance of campaign spending and the rise of political action committees (PACs). Both the president and members of Congress depend on large campaign contributions from interest groups and are thus more vulnerable to their demands.

Second, the personal Presidency, in combination with the rise of identity politics, has increased the need of presidents to serve a multitude of constituencies and interests. Under pressure from African American interest groups, Clinton gave U.S. policy toward Africa a prominence it had never had previously. His twelve-day trip to six African nations in 1998 was the first by a U.S. president in twenty years and the most extensive ever. Women's and religious interest groups have also become important lobbies, affecting policies on foreign aid, family planning, abortion, immigration, and women's rights. Women's groups found an advocate in Madeleine Albright, the first woman to serve as secretary of state; she identified the promotion of women's rights and ending the trafficking of women and children as among the Clinton administration's priority issues.

Third, the globalization of economic activity has intensified interest groups' efforts to influence trade policy because of their concern about its impact on wages, job opportunities, child labor, worker safety, and the environment. This has led to new and very vocal alliances among trade unions and environmental and human rights groups who oppose some aspects of current trade policy. During a conference of the world's top trade officials in Seattle in 1999, thousands of protesters took to the streets and managed to shut down parts of the city and interrupt the proceedings at this and at each succeeding summit meeting. They have launched similarly high-profile attacks on international monetary policy, driving economic summit organizers to move the meetings to ever-more-remote locations.

Public Opinion

Overall, the views of the public on foreign policy are not that different from those of elected policy makers. When they do vary, public opinion has little direct effect except on high-profile issues that could make a difference at the polls. One reason is that much of our foreign policy is made incrementally over a long period of time and out of public view. Public opinion also has little short-term impact on decisions made in "crisis" situations or in secrecy for national security reasons.

Another factor limiting the public's ability to influence foreign policy decisions is that only a minority of Americans know much about even the most publicly discussed issues, and many have no opinion about them. The public has always been more interested in domestic issues that impinge directly on daily life, such as the availability of jobs and the cost of consumer goods. Although there is growing awareness of the impact of foreign policy, especially trade issues, on daily life, it is difficult for the public to be well informed on the technical problems involved in trade and tariff negotiations.

People who rely on television as their main news source, as a majority of Americans do, see only a few minutes of foreign coverage each day. Responding to their viewers' primary interest in domestic issues, network television news programs cut back international coverage substantially during the 1990s. After 9/11, when viewers began expressing more interest in foreign policy and information about other countries, especially those with Muslim populations, television news increased coverage of international affairs. But in polls taken one month after the attacks, Americans were saying again that their primary concerns were jobs and the economy.

An Iraqi prisoner of war comforts his four-year-old son.

In general, the public is more likely to concede its ignorance on a wider range of issues in foreign policy than in domestic policy and to accept the judgments of decision makers. Therefore, on most issues, it is easier for the president to influence public opinion on foreign affairs through use of the media than it is for public opinion to change the president's foreign policy. President Bush's consistent linking of al-Qaeda and Iraq was hugely successful in convincing the public that Iraq had had a role in the 9/11 attacks. Three years later, well after the president and secretary of defense conceded publicly that there was no evidence for such a link, 40 percent of Americans continued to believe that Saddam Hussein had been "personally involved" in the attacks.[14] That belief appeared to be an important factor in Bush's reelection in 2004, a campaign in which national security was the main issue. Only after public opinion turned against the war in Iraq did the public show signs of separating it from the 9/11 attacks; by late 2006, 41 percent of those surveyed said Iraq was not a part of the war on terrorism.[15]

Sometimes public opinion resists attempts to change it. Even as the Bush administration discounted our ties to our traditional allies when they refused to support the invasion of Iraq—countries Rumsfeld referred to as "old Europe"—66 percent of the public continued to believe our partnership with Western Europe on security and diplomatic matters should remain as close as it has always been.[16] Deeply held opinions like these are more resistant to administration pressure.

Trade policy provides a good illustration of the limits on the ability of public opinion to change the president's position on a foreign policy issue. Interest group opposition to the North American Free Trade Agreement (NAFTA), which eliminated trade barriers among Mexico, Canada, and the United States, was so strong that it led most Democrats, who were then the majority in Congress, to openly oppose their own party's president on this issue. One member said, "All of the traditional groups we count on to reelect us [Democrats] are against NAFTA."[17] Despite this opposition from his own party's leadership and from traditional Democratic constituencies, Clinton never wavered in his support for NAFTA because increasing trade was the cornerstone of both his domestic and his foreign policies.

Ultimately, without some public support, foreign policy objectives that require substantial commitments of time and resources will prove unsuccessful. So the government attempts to manipulate public access to information. This is most common during wartime, when the government can justify press censorship on national security grounds. Withholding negative information (for example, high casualty rates, slow progress, civilian losses) can help keep public support high.

In the Iraq War, in an attempt to generate sympathetic press coverage, the Defense Department embedded reporters with the troops, partly on the assumption that living with the troops in combat zones and being under fire with them would be a bonding experience. The Defense Department also prohibited the photographing of soldiers' coffins as they were returned to the United States for burial. The department said it was to protect family privacy, but it was also a way to divert public attention from the rising body count. In addition, official casualty counts issued by the Department of Defense included only troops wounded in combat, not those who were wounded in the line of duty but outside of combat, and no tally at all was kept of Iraqi civilian deaths. This policy understated the actual casualty count by thousands.

A few years into the war, the Defense Department was forced to change its policy on reporting both American and Iraqi casualties because interest groups and international agencies were posting their counts on websites for all the world to see. Similarly, the public learned about prisoner abuse in the Abu Ghraib prison camp—which the International Red Cross and government officials had known about months earlier—because digital photos taken by troops at the site were e-mailed to friends and relatives and were circulating on the Internet.

In general, because of the revolution in information technology, it is becoming harder for the president, or the president and Congress together, to appeal for public support based on a claim of privileged information. The press, interest groups, and the general public now have many more sources of information on foreign policy issues than they had a decade ago. More Americans are in e-mail contact with people in other countries and have access to the websites of foreign newspapers, governments, and think tanks, as well as to declassified documents in electronic archives. In fact, private firms here and abroad, including some run by former Soviet intelligence operatives, will even sell satellite reconnaissance photography to order and Internet sites such as Earth Google regularly show high-altitude shots of secret locales such as North Korea's suspected nuclear test sites.[18]

Changing Approaches to U.S. Foreign Policy

Isolationism

Historically, noninvolvement with other nations outside the Americas was a principal goal of our foreign policy. This policy is called **isolationism.** In the nineteenth and early twentieth centuries, Americans generally stayed aloof from European conflicts and turned inward, busy with domestic expansion and development.

One important exception was our continuing military and political involvement in Latin America, which was justified by the **Monroe Doctrine** of 1823. In articulating this doctrine, President James Monroe warned European powers that were not already in Latin America to stay out. This was a brazen move because we were a minor power challenging the major powers of the time.

As European powers withdrew from the region in the late nineteenth and early twentieth centuries, the United States began to play an increasingly active and at times interventionist role. With little regard for national sovereignty, we sent troops to protect U.S. citizens or business interests and to replace existing governments with those more sympathetic to our wishes. Paradoxically, the Monroe Doctrine derived primarily from isolationist, not interventionist, sentiment. By keeping foreign powers on their side of the ocean and out of our hemisphere, we believed we would be less likely to be drawn into conflicts abroad.

During this time, Americans did not think it appropriate to intervene in the problems of Europe or to keep a large standing army at home. This attitude was an offshoot of the predominant mood in domestic affairs: preoccupation with economic growth and fear of a strong central government. Isolationism was also a realistic position in the sense that the United States was not yet a world power. Another source of isolationist sentiment was the belief that the United States was unique and that the more entangling alliances it entered into with foreign countries, the more likely it would "be corrupted and its unique nature . . . subverted."[19] This isolationist sentiment lapsed briefly in 1917–1919, when America entered World War I on the side of the British and French against Germany, but rapidly revived at its close. Despite the wishes of President Woodrow Wilson, the U.S. Senate refused to join the League of Nations, the ill-fated precursor to the United Nations. Although we have no public opinion polls from these early years, 70 percent of Americans polled in 1937 thought, in hindsight, it had been a mistake to enter World War I.

Yet the United States was never truly isolationist in its actions. Throughout the whole early isolationist era, we frequently intervened diplomatically and militarily in the Caribbean and Central America and consistently sought to expand U.S. commercial and cultural influence throughout the world. Even President McKinley, who was labeled an "imperialist" by Democrats for his military adventures in the Caribbean and the Philippines, was easily reelected. And his successor, Theodore Roosevelt, is better characterized as an interventionist than an isolationist. Polls from the post–World War I era show that Americans overwhelmingly favored joining an international peacekeeping body like the League of Nations. And historians have pointed out that there were enough votes in the Senate to ratify participation in the League had President Wilson been willing to accept amendments to the treaty agreement.[20]

Americans have almost always been willing to participate in world affairs to defend our national interests. But we are often slow to recognize just what is at stake. In 1939, we refused to join Britain in its war to stop Nazi Germany's attempted conquest of Europe. It was not until the December 1941 Japanese attack on Pearl Harbor, Hawaii, that the public was willing to support entry into World War II. When Germany and Italy then declared war on the United States, we fought in Europe alongside Britain, the Soviet Union, and remnant armies from the occupied nations of Europe.

Containment

The Allied victory in 1945 brought a split between the Soviet Union and its Western allies. The Soviet Union lost at least twenty million people in the war (the United States lost four hundred thousand). Given these losses in a German invasion that was only one of many invasions of Russian territory over the centuries, the Soviet government was determined, especially as a protection against Germany, to have friendly neighbors in Europe, just as we wanted them in Latin America. To ensure this, the Soviet Union was willing to use any means, including intervention, to secure communist governments in the ring of nations surrounding it—Poland, Czechoslovakia, Romania, Hungary, and Bulgaria. Our wish for free elections in these nations was seen by the Soviet Union as an attempt to isolate it. The Russians believed we wanted to surround them with anti-Soviet governments, thus making their sacrifices in World War II futile. Many of our policy makers saw the subversion of Eastern European governments as the beginning of a Soviet effort to conquer all of Europe.

As the only major power not decimated by the war, the United States was unable to return to its isolationist prewar stance. In 1947, the **Harry S. Truman** administration formulated a policy to limit the spread of communism by meeting any action taken by the Soviet Union to spread its influence with counterforce or a countermove by the United States. Known as **containment** (also called the Truman Doctrine), this policy led U.S. decision makers to see most of the world's conflicts in terms of rivalry between the Soviet Union and the United States. The Soviet coup d'état in Czechoslovakia in 1948 and the 1949 rise to power of a communist government in China fueled U.S. fears that the Communists would try to expand the area under their control as far as possible. Consequently, when communist North Korea attacked South Korea in 1950, we intervened as the nucleus of a United Nations force, believing we had to stop the spread of communism in Korea before the Soviets undertook further expansion.

Containment was aimed at limiting the Russians to their post–World War II reach and out of our sphere of influence. Instead of trying to roll back Soviet power, containment was designed to keep it from expanding to a point that changed the global power balance or dragged the United States into unwanted conflicts.

Containment philosophy was at work in the Marshall Plan, which provided economic relief to the nations of Western Europe in 1947 (aid was offered to some Eastern European governments, but they refused it). In addition, the United States entered into military alliances with friendly nations in Europe and Asia to stop the spread of Soviet influence or even to roll it back. The most important of these was the **North Atlantic Treaty Organization,** which in 1949 joined the United States, Canada, and their Western European allies in a mutual defense pact against Soviet aggression in Europe. Building these military alliances to compete with the Soviet Union and its Eastern European allies was a response to the **Cold War** era that we had now entered. We were not in a military battle (or hot war) with the Russians, but the deep hostility between the two nations threatened to turn any conflict into a major armed confrontation.

Nuclear Deterrence

The nuclear era began in 1945, when the United States dropped atomic bombs on the Japanese cities of Hiroshima and Nagasaki. Although the debate on the necessity and ethics of dropping these bombs still continues, Japan surrendered, bringing the war in the Pacific to an end and making an invasion of the island by the Allies unnecessary.

At the close of the war, the United States was the only nuclear power. The Soviet Union exploded its first bomb in 1949, but it did not have an operational warhead until the mid-1950s and for a while thereafter had no intercontinental bombers or missiles to deliver the bombs. Despite our nuclear superiority, we found our power limited. Nuclear weapons were of little use in the pursuit of most foreign policy objectives because the threat of inflicting mass destruction to achieve a nonvital objective was not credible to opponents. Hence during the period of nuclear superiority, the United States saw its Chinese Nationalist allies lose to Communists in China, its French allies lose to Ho Chi Minh in Indochina (Vietnam), and an anti-communist uprising in Hungary in 1956 crushed by Soviet tanks.

In 1955, the Soviet Union and its Eastern European satellites formed the Warsaw Pact, a military alliance to counter NATO. People began to see all international relations as part of the bipolar competition between a

During the Cold War, communism generated real fear among Americans, as this poster for a 1962 Hollywood documentary shows. Soviet Premier Nikita Khrushchev had proclaimed, "We'll bury you!"

Reprinted from *Better Dead Than Red* by Michael Barson (Hyperion).

Western bloc of countries united under the U.S. nuclear umbrella and an Eastern bloc of nations operating under the protection of the Soviet nuclear umbrella.

American nuclear dominance began to erode in the late 1950s. *Sputnik,* the Soviet satellite that was the first to orbit Earth, showed that the Soviet Union had successfully built large rockets capable of firing missiles that could reach the United States. The fear of Soviet rocketry advances led to a program to build and deploy nuclear-tipped intercontinental ballistic missiles (ICBMs) to supplement our bomber force.

Even with Soviet advances, American nuclear superiority was maintained for another decade. Yet everyone agreed that neither side could attack the other without the certain knowledge that both the attacker and the attacked would suffer enormous damage. No sane leader would risk so much damage by striking first.[21] This capability is called **mutual assured destruction,** referred to by the fitting acronym **MAD.**

Despite public frustration with the Cold War—being neither totally at war nor at peace—successive administrations found that "rolling back" communism in the nuclear age was not possible without the kind of risk and commitment of resources most Americans were unwilling to assume. Although the Kennedy administration did risk nuclear war over Soviet placement of nuclear weapons in Cuba, ninety miles from our shores, we stood by and avoided such risks when the Soviet Union invaded Hungary in 1956, Czechoslovakia in 1968, and Afghanistan in 1979. And the Soviet Union stood down when we tried to overthrow Castro in 1961 and when we forced the removal of Russian missiles from the island in 1962 and avoided confrontation when we sent military forces to oppose a Russian-backed nationalist movement in Vietnam.

One of the basic premises of containment was that all communist nations were controlled by the Soviet Union. But as the 1950s progressed, it became clear that this was not true. Both Albania and Yugoslavia spurned Moscow's control. The Chinese became increasingly independent and in the early 1960s broke with the Soviet Union, declaring that "there are many paths to socialism." Despite this, we continued to define most international events in terms of Communists versus anti-Communists, no matter how poorly the characterization fit. This conviction formed the basis of the **domino theory,** the proposition that if one country fell to communist rule, it would set off a chain reaction in neighboring countries, just as a long line of dominoes standing on end will fall in sequence when the first one is toppled. If U.S. intervention could prevent the first country to come under attack from falling, others would stand firm. This rationale led us into Vietnam, our longest war to date.

Vietnam Early period

If one were ranking the landmark events of the twentieth century, surely World War II would rank at the top. We live in a completely different world than would have existed had Hitler not been defeated. Fighting alongside Britain and the Soviet Union, the United States achieved its greatest military victory and forged the alliance with Western Europe that led to our most important treaty relationship. Yet the Vietnam War has had a far greater impact on U.S. military policy since its end in 1975. We will try to explain why.

When we became involved in Vietnam, it was still part of the French colonial territory of Indochina. After the defeat of the Japanese occupying forces in World War II, the Indochinese Communist Party, led by **Ho Chi Minh**, engaged the returning French forces in a war for independence. Ho appealed several times to the United States—a critic of both British and French colonial policies—for support in this effort but was rebuffed. As the war in Indochina dragged on, the Cold War settled in, and containment became the organizing concept in American foreign policy. By 1954, when Ho's troops defeated the French in a major battle, the United States was underwriting 80 percent of the cost of the French effort in Vietnam. But after considerable deliberation, the Eisenhower administration refused to provide troops or air support to save the French because Eisenhower believed this could bog us down in a long war requiring many troops, certainly a prescient view.

At a conference in Geneva in 1954, a temporary boundary was established separating the territory of Ho's government in the North from that of the French- and U.S.-backed government in the South until elections could be held to choose leaders for all of Vietnam. The new prime minister in the South, Ngo Dinh Diem, was a staunch anti-communist Catholic with influential friends in the U.S. Catholic community and Congress. Diem's government refused to participate in the elections scheduled for 1956, and the United States backed him because it feared that Ho's communist government would win the election. The temporary partition between the North and South continued. After the assassination of Diem in 1963, it soon became clear that the South Vietnamese government would collapse without more U.S. intervention.

Armed intervention

In 1964, President **Lyndon Johnson** won congressional approval for massive intervention in Vietnam. In an August television address to the American public, Johnson claimed that two U.S. destroyers had been attacked by North Vietnamese torpedo boats while on routine patrol in international waters near the Gulf of Tonkin. He announced his intention to retaliate by bombing sites in North Vietnam. The next day, after presenting misleading information about the role of the U.S. destroyers in initiating the attack, he asked Congress to endorse the Gulf of Tonkin Resolution authorizing him

Jack Kightlinger/Lyndon Baines Johnson Library

President Johnson listens in anguish to a tape sent by his son-in-law (Charles Robb, then an officer in Vietnam and later a U.S. senator from Virginia) talking about the men lost in battle in Vietnam.

"to take all necessary measures to repel any armed attack against the forces of the U.S. and to prevent further aggression." Johnson said the resolution was like "grandma's nightshirt. It covers everything."[22] He and President Nixon used the Tonkin Resolution to justify each act of escalation in the war. This deception laid the groundwork for the gradual erosion of congressional support for the war effort.

In early 1965, Johnson sent in U.S. troops in the belief that the war would be over "in a matter of months." After all, the United States had sophisticated equipment and training and complete air superiority. But three years later, after a half million U.S. troops had been committed to combat, the Vietcong—North Vietnam's southern allies—were able to launch a major offensive that demonstrated that all our military efforts had not made one square foot of Vietnam truly secure. When the Joint Chiefs of Staff requested more than two hundred thousand additional troops, a stunned President Johnson decided to undertake a review of Vietnam policy. Even the Joint Chiefs were not sure how many years and troops it might take to win. As public opposition to the war grew, Johnson called for peace talks and announced that he would not run for reelection in 1968. The talks began in May 1968 and dragged on through the administration of Johnson's successor, Richard Nixon.

President Nixon wanted to leave Vietnam without appearing to have lost the war. To accomplish this, he tried "Vietnamizing" the war by forcing the South Vietnamese government to give more responsibility to its own army. He authorized the massive bombing of Hanoi and began withdrawing U.S. troops.

Nixon's most controversial war policy was his decision to expand the war into neighboring Cambodia, supposedly to destroy a huge underground headquarters of the North Vietnamese army near the Vietnamese border. In addition to igniting the largest public protests of the war, the invasion finally led to significant congressional opposition. The Gulf of Tonkin Resolution was repealed, and a resolution was passed prohibiting the president from using budgeted funds to wage a ground war in Cambodia. Nixon had planned to withdraw the troops from Cambodia anyway and did so quickly. But bombing in Cambodia continued until 1973, when Congress forbade the use of funds for this purpose. This was the only time Congress actually blocked presidential policies in the war.

In 1973, the United States and North Vietnam signed a peace agreement. We might have reached the same agreement in 1969, but President Nixon had believed this would jeopardize his reelection chances in 1972 and perhaps other foreign policy goals, too.[23] The victory of the Vietcong and North Vietnamese finally occurred in 1975 as the South Vietnamese army disintegrated in the face of a communist attack.

Lessons from Vietnam

Much of our thinking about the use of the military today is still informed by the lessons of policy failures in Vietnam.[24] Even though at its peak in 1968–1969 our military force in Vietnam exceeded half a million, had sophisticated equipment and training, and had complete air superiority, we were eventually defeated. Why did we fail?

We did not have clear goals Policy makers never agreed on whether we were fighting China, the Soviet Union, North Vietnam, or rebels in the South (the Vietcong). It was not clear what or whom we were trying to defend or what Vietnam was supposed to look like after the North was defeated.

We did not understand the political aspects of the war Supporting a series of unpopular South Vietnamese governments, we were at first oblivious to the vast indigenous opposition to the South Vietnamese government from Communists, other nationalists, and Buddhists. Our inability to construct an effective policy for "winning the hearts and minds" of the domestic opposition to the South Vietnamese government appears to have been a fatal weakness of policy makers from Eisenhower through Nixon.

In 1995, on the twentieth anniversary of the war's end, Robert McNamara, secretary of defense in the Kennedy and Johnson administrations and a principal architect of early Vietnam policy, wrote a book publicly stating for the first time that by 1967 he had come to the conclusion that the war was a mistake and could not be won. Principal among his eleven reasons for the loss were the incompetence of the South Vietnamese government and armed forces and American underestimation of the North Vietnamese.[25] President Johnson's refusal to accept this conclusion led McNamara to leave—or be made to leave—the cabinet in 1968. But as revealed by the release of the tapes of Johnson's phone calls, at the very time he was making large troop commitments, Johnson was saying, "I don't see any way of winning."[26]

We did not understand the nature of guerrilla warfare For much of the war, we did not fight against a standing army dressed in the uniform of an enemy force. It was often impossible for our troops to tell soldier from civilian or enemy from ally. Although we inflicted heavy casualties on the Vietcong and North Vietnamese forces, we killed thousands of civilians in the process. Our opponents were able to demonstrate to the people of the South that their government and its ally, the United States, could not protect them or their villages. In fact, the Vietcong were able to dominate much of the rural South. Our policies—to "destroy villages in order to save them" and to take people from their own villages to "strategic hamlets," where presumably they were safe from the Vietcong—were bitterly resented by many South Vietnamese.

We were impatient with the war and were unwilling to devote unending resources to winning We knew from the British experience in defeating communist guerrillas in Malaysia that we would need at least ten soldiers to the guerrillas' one and that we might need ten years to win the war, but no leader

This photo of a naked South Vietnamese girl screaming after a napalm attack by "friendly" forces became one of the most famous photographs of the war and a major incitement to antiwar protest. The girl, Kim Phue, survived, despite enduring pain and long-term treatment for her wounds. Now living in Canada, she is pictured at right with her son, Huan (his name means "prospects"). She notes, "I know my picture did something to help stop the war. I have to show [my son] what happened to his mom, to her country, and that there should never be war again."

dared tell the public that we must commit ourselves for that long. We were unwilling to invest the resources or time needed to defeat a guerrilla enemy. Since the goals were unclear, few wanted to risk use of the ultimate weaponry that could have destroyed the North. Although this stance was rational, it did not seem to lead to the obvious question of whether our objectives were worth the effort we were making.

We did not have public support Although public opinion was generally supportive during the first years of the war, support eroded as it became clear that we were bogged down in an interminable and indecisive conflict. Only about 20 percent of the public favored an immediate withdrawal in 1965, but by mid-1969, support for withdrawal began to increase and reached 50 percent within the next year. By 1971, public support for withdrawal grew to overwhelming proportions.[27]

The United States persisted in Vietnam for nearly eleven years because most policy makers believed in standing firm against what they saw as communist aggression and because no president wanted to be responsible for losing a war. But Vietnam shattered the belief in containment and U.S. illusions that it could serve as the world's police force. Many Americans believed that both our aims and tactics in Vietnam were immoral. Others believed that our aims were just but unachievable. Still others thought that we should have stayed

until we won. All these sentiments led to a good deal of public self-examination.

The failure of our Vietnam policy produced the **Vietnam syndrome,** an attitude among the public and officials of uncertainty about our foreign policy goals and our ability to achieve them through military means. Decision makers became more reluctant to commit troops to combat situations or to threaten military action to pursue containment goals. Some people regarded this new caution as a positive development that would keep us from becoming involved in new military entanglements we could not win. But many others believed that this national self-doubt tied the hands of decision makers and prevented them from using the full range of our capabilities to pursue national interests abroad.

These differences persist among policy makers today. Colin Powell, former chairman of the Joint Chiefs of Staff and George W. Bush's first secretary of state, did two tours of duty in Vietnam. His experience there was the basis of what is now called the *Powell doctrine:* never commit U.S. forces to combat abroad without clear goals and an exit plan. It led to Powell's initial opposition both to committing troops to the Persian Gulf War in 1991 and to unilateral military action against Iraq in 2003.

During the first years of the Iraq War, President Bush disavowed any comparisons with the Vietnam quagmire, but then in 2007 stated that we should have stayed in Vietnam longer to prevent the negative outcomes when we left.

Détente

Richard Nixon came to office after public opinion had begun to turn against the war, and he immediately began looking for ways to shape international relations in the post–Vietnam War era. As a man whose career was built on making political hay out of his staunch anticommunism, President Nixon was well placed to make diplomatic overtures to the Soviet Union without fear of being attacked by any but the most die-hard Cold Warriors. Thus Nixon and his national security adviser and later secretary of state, **Henry Kissinger,** developed a policy called **détente,** which was designed to deescalate Cold War rhetoric and to promote the notion that relations with the Soviet Union could be conducted in ways other than confrontation.

With a policy of détente, we could reward the Soviet Union for "good behavior" on the international scene and at the same time reduce our own military expenditures, slow the arms race, and perhaps step back from the brink of war. The détente doctrine recognized that although the Soviet Union would remain our adversary, it, too, had legitimate interests in the world. Détente also recognized the growing military strength of the Soviet Union and the fact that it was in our interests to pursue bilateral agreements, such as on arms control, that would try to limit this strength. Among the most notable achievements of the détente policy were the treaty agreements limiting the number of defensive antiballistic missile (ABM) launchers that each side could possess and freezing the number of offensive missiles in each side's stockpile.

During this era of new diplomacy with the Soviet Union, President Nixon also sent out feelers to see whether China was interested in reestablishing diplomatic ties. Even though it was home to one-fifth of the world's population, China had been shut out of the mainstream diplomatic community, largely due to U.S. pressure, since the communist victory in 1949. After two years of negotiations through third parties, the first cultural exchange (a visit by the U.S. Ping-Pong team) was arranged in 1971. By the time of President Nixon's visit in 1972, many nations had resumed diplomatic relations with China, and it had regained its seat in the United Nations Security Council. Full diplomatic recognition by the United States, however, did not come until the Carter administration.

The resumption of diplomatic relations between China and the United States was one of the most remarkable achievements of Nixon's and Kissinger's attempts to break the Cold War stalemate. Nonetheless, it was consistent with their balance-of-power approach to foreign policy. By making this effort during a period of hostility in relations between the Soviet Union and China, Nixon was probably hoping to gain leverage in dealings with the Soviet Union (what some referred to as "playing the China card").

The Nixon-Kissinger visits to China were all the more remarkable because they occurred while U.S. troops were still fighting in Vietnam. It had been the specter of a Sino–Soviet-led communist bloc and a near paranoid fear of "yellow hordes" (in the racist parlance of the time) advancing throughout Asia that led us to fight in Korea and Vietnam. Within a few short years, China's image was recast from dreaded enemy to friendly ally, and Cold War fears of world communist domination were greatly diminished.

The doctrine of détente complemented the mood of isolationism and weariness that grew in the wake of the Vietnam War. Public and elite opinion after the war was divided. Isolationist, go-it-alone sentiment peaked immediately after the war but then declined.

A new spirit of cooperative internationalism characterized the early Carter administration.[28] Carter and his advisers saw the world as far more complex than Cold War rhetoric suggested. They believed that problems of global poverty, inequitable distribution of wealth, abuse of human rights, and regional competitiveness were substantial threats to world order and that the United States should work with other nations to solve these problems.

In 1979, Carter signed a new agreement with the Soviet Union placing limits on offensive missiles. But the Soviets' stunning invasion of Afghanistan that same year ended the chance of gaining Senate approval for the treaty. Public and elite opinion shifted, and Cold War views, never completely abandoned, became much more respectable again.

Cold War Revival and Death

The Reagan administration took office in 1981 determined to challenge the Soviet Union in every way possible. During his first term, **Ronald Reagan** totally renounced the Nixon-Kissinger principle of détente

One of the first major achievements of the Nixon-Kissinger policy of détente was to reestablish normal relations with the People's Republic of China, governed by the Communist Party since 1949. Here Nixon attends a state banquet in Beijing with then premier Zhou Enlai.

Courtesy of the National Archives

and labeled the Soviet Union an "evil empire." He and his advisers continued to view the world largely in light of a U.S.-Soviet competition. They painted a simple picture of an aggressive, reckless, and brutal Soviet Union and a peace-loving and virtuous United States. Despite the rhetoric, however, the administration did not risk direct confrontation.

Reagan's approach differed from containment because it was more ideologically than strategically driven; he sought not just to contain the Soviets but to undo the status quo. One method Reagan endorsed was stepping up the arms race and, by forcing them to keep pace, drive the Soviets into economic ruin. The centerpiece of this policy was his plan to build an antimissile defense system, the Strategic Defense Initiative (SDI), derisively known as Star Wars. The plan was based on a laser technology that did not yet exist but that was supposed to intercept and destroy nuclear-tipped ballistic missiles before they reached their targets in the United States. Its projected cost was tens of billions of dollars. Reagan's SDI and military build-up programs increased military spending to record peacetime levels.

Though the election of Reagan put a Cold Warrior in the White House, the public was not willing to buy Cold War arguments wholeheartedly. By Reagan's second term, a dramatic drop in public support for in-

creased military spending and growing public pressure for progress on arms control helped push the administration toward a less belligerent stance. Violent rhetoric was toned down, and conciliatory gestures multiplied.[29] Common wisdom was that President Reagan wanted to reach some agreement with the Soviets in order to be remembered as a peacemaking president.

The moderation in Reagan's rhetoric was also a response to changes in the Soviet Union. In 1985, **Mikhail Gorbachev,** the new general secretary of the Communist Party of the Soviet Union, called for "new thinking" and began to shake up Soviet society as it had not been shaken since the Russian Revolution in 1917.[30] Faced with a stagnating economy and an antireform Soviet leadership, Gorbachev encouraged competition in the economy, criticism of corruption and inefficiencies by government agencies, and free elections of some government legislative bodies.

In addition to his domestic reforms, Gorbachev challenged the status quo in the international community with his policy of *glasnost,* or opening to the outside world. He encouraged foreign investment and requested foreign aid to help rebuild the Soviet economy; he made it easier for Soviet citizens to emigrate, pulled Soviet troops out of Afghanistan, and reduced aid to Soviet-backed governments in Nicaragua and Cuba.

Gorbachev also took the initiative in resuming arms control negotiations with President Ronald Reagan. In 1987, the two men reached an agreement on intermediate-range nuclear forces. To ensure compliance, the United States sent inspectors or monitors to the Soviet Union and the Soviets sent them to Western Europe and the United States to observe production facilities and the dismantling and removal of the missiles.

During the first two years of **George H. W. Bush's** administration, the Soviet empire in Eastern Europe disintegrated with such rapidity that all policy makers (and intelligence agencies too) were caught off-guard. The Soviet-dominated governments were dismantled, communist parties changed their names, opposition parties formed, and free multiparty elections were held.

In late 1989, demonstrators assaulted the most visible symbol of the Cold War, the Berlin Wall (built by the Soviets in 1961 to divide Soviet-occupied East Berlin from NATO-occupied West Berlin), and began tearing it down. A year later, the reunification of Germany marked the end of the post–World War II power alliance in Europe.

Then, in 1991, after a brief, unsuccessful coup against him, Gorbachev resigned as head of the Communist Party and stripped the party of its role in government. Facing massive restructuring problems, he made major foreign policy concessions to Western governments in order to obtain economic aid. Among them was an agreement to remove Soviet military forces from Cuba, the last vestige of Cold War competition in the Western Hemisphere.

With no strong center left in Moscow, the non-Russian states of the Soviet Union declared their independence. Gorbachev was left with no country to lead, his power supplanted by the presidents of the fifteen newly independent republics. As the Soviet Union passed from the scene, all nations had to adjust to a realignment of the world order.

Early in the 1990s, the first President Bush spoke of a "new world order," although no one was quite certain what it meant in terms of concrete foreign policies, other than the absence of U.S.-Soviet military competition. In the new order, foreign policies would presumably be less dependent on military capabilities. Still, some Americans feared that as the world's sole remaining military superpower, the United States would feel freer to use its military advantage in pursuit of its foreign policy goals. However, without the Soviet threat to justify expenditures, the United States began to shrink its military.

There was also strong public pressure to avoid new foreign entanglements. With the Cold War over, Americans seemed weary of trying to understand and change the world. They were more impressed by the failures of foreign aid, military intervention, and diplomacy than by foreign policy successes, more weighed down by problems at home than by those in other countries. George H. W. Bush found that he could justify intervention in the Persian Gulf, and later in the civil war in Somalia, only through cost sharing and participation in an international force under UN auspices.

Merchant Diplomacy and Multilateralism

Bill Clinton took office as the first president born after World War II. He was a self-described child of the Cold War, an opponent of the Vietnam War, one of twelve presidents never to have served in the military, and more shaped by the skepticism of the Vietnam era than by memories of the Allied victory in World War II. In his campaign, he reminded voters that we had not defeated the Soviet Union in battle but that it had collapsed from within due to "economic, political, and spiritual failure." He believed that the best foreign policy was to have a strong economy.[31]

With this as his theme, Clinton signaled a change in approach to foreign policy. Befitting the end of the Cold War, greater emphasis would be given to economic rather than to military instruments of foreign policy, and more attention would be paid to using our economic strength to achieve political goals, such as promotion of democracy and human rights, which Clinton said we had neglected in our pursuit of strategic interests.

Clinton was an exception among modern Democratic presidents in that he was openly committed to free trade. **Free trade** is a policy of minimum intervention by governments in trade relations. Its advocates, or free traders, believe that government regulation of trade, for economic or political reasons, reduces the efficiency of the world economy, thus preventing countries from maximizing their income.[32] Free trade, like capitalism, is relative; all countries place some restrictions on trade to protect domestic labor and business interests. In fact, forms of protection historically, and today, apply to as much as 40 percent of all trade.

Protectionism is government intervention to protect domestic producers and their employees against competition from foreign producers of manufactured and agricultural goods. Protectionist policies can take the form of a ban on goods from abroad, quotas on imports, or taxes (tariffs) on imports to make them more expensive and therefore less competitive in the United States. We have used protectionist policies to help American farmers and the manufacturers of automobiles, textiles, steel, clothing, computer chips, and other goods.

When Clinton came to office many Americans, especially those who worked in manufacturing and agriculture, still expected the president, especially a Democrat, to take action to protect their jobs. But believing globalization was not reversible and that the shift at home to a high-tech, service economy was unstoppable, Clinton believed jobs and capital should gravitate wherever market forces took them as long as all countries played by a common set of rules.[33] In other words, increasing trade with China, India, and African countries would create jobs in the United States and raise living standards in poorer countries while costing the American taxpayer virtually nothing in aid. At the same time, eradicating trade barriers for those countries would create a huge new pool of customers for American goods and services.

The war on terror is one of the key features of the Bush presidency. Based on the notion of a globally linked network of terrorists waging war on the United States, Bush launched this war shortly after the attacks of 9/11. While it is possible that in the beginning, the president had a more specific target in mind, the war on terror soon took on the meaning of fighting terrorism wherever it was found. In pursuit of that war, we invaded two nations, undermined the civil liberties of Americans with a massive wiretapping program, legitimized violations of international law against torture and holding people without trial, and, of course, saw the deaths of more than 4000 U.S. soldiers, the wounding of another 30,000, and the deaths of tens of thousands of Iraqis and Afghanis (all as of mid-2007).

Is the war on terror a war? Does it make sense as a coherent strategy to accomplish our foreign policy objectives? These questions were not widely asked in the months following 9/11 but are now being asked with increasing frequency and urgency.

Terrorists have existed for millennia. That creates a problem with thinking about the war on terror as a foreign policy or even as a strategy. Terrorism is a tactic rather than an enemy. In antiquity (first century C.E.), for example, the Zealots of Judea terrorized the Roman occupiers of their lands. During the French Revolution (1789–1799), a "Reign of Terror" was instigated by the Revolutionary Government, and opponents fought back with their own campaign of assassination and intimidation. During the twentieth century, terrorist organizations on most continents, and including the Middle East, used tactics of assassinations and threats of violence to pursue their aims, often demands for national sovereignty.

In the 1960s, America had its own terrorists, as radical elements of the Weatherman organization blew up buildings in protest against the Vietnamese War and big government. (They sought to avoid human casualties by calling to announce the bombings beforehand, however). Again, in 1995, domestic terrorists blew up the federal building in Oklahoma City, killing 168 people. Thus terrorism is a tactic that has been used throughout the ages, and almost by definition, a war on terror will last forever.

Moreover, it is realistic to ask what real danger terrorists pose here in the United States. Some now argue that the terrorist threat has been greatly exaggerated. Of course, there are real, on-the-ground wars that terrorists are involved in, as in Afghanistan. But aside from wars and insurgencies, as one observer pointed out, "international terrorism generally kills a few hundred people a year worldwide—not much more, usually, than the number who drown each year in bathtubs in the

---

Of course, Clinton was no pure free trader; no American president has been, in large part because pressure from interest groups to retain certain protections, such as agricultural subsidies, is too great. But he moved his party away from advocacy of protectionism and made free trade a cornerstone of American foreign policy.

Clinton's foreign policy was so rooted in the pursuit of national economic interests that almost all issues were discussed in terms of their value to U.S. trade relations. (Clinton's second-term national security adviser was an international trade lawyer.) This led some observers to label his foreign policy "merchant diplomacy."[34] Deemphasizing military in favor of economic diplomacy suited the public mood, which, although not one of withdrawal from world affairs, was leery of new political entanglements.

Despite the deemphasis on military force, there were many occasions during Clinton's administration when its use was deemed necessary. But unlike previous presidents, Clinton was reluctant to rely on the unilateral use of force. When he ordered troops to Haiti in 1994 to oust a military dictatorship and restore the elected president, it was only after gaining UN backing. It marked the first time an American president had sought prior international approval for a military intervention in the Caribbean. To some, it was a radical departure from, or even an end to, the Monroe Doctrine.[35] But it was compatible with Clinton's view of the post–Cold War world as a community of nations becoming increasingly linked through the forces of globalization and in which every country should assume part of the burden for maintaining international peace and security. Avoiding costly military entanglements also helped end the huge budget deficits run up by the military spending and tax cuts of the Reagan era.

The difficulty with a multilateral approach to achieving foreign policy goals is that the national interests

United States."[1] Your lifetime chances of being killed by a terrorist are about the same as being hit by an asteroid or comet.[2] All Americans killed by terrorists since the late 1960s (when we began counting) "is about the same as the number killed over the same period by lightning, or by accident-causing deer, or by severe allergic reaction to peanuts."[3] Americans are much more insecure about terrorism than any real assessment of risk would warrant.

In fact, by lumping together many different organizations under the rubric of "terrorists" and declaring war on them, we may inadvertently strengthen and legitimize them. Certainly invading Iraq ostensibly as part of a war on terror undermined the president's credibility with the public and the rest of the world when the facts became known. Though few mourned the loss of Saddam Hussein, a brutal dictator, the war in Iraq, it is generally agreed, has fostered terrorism in that country.

Terrorism can no more be squelched completely than, say, drunk driving (which kills thousands of Americans every year). Moreover, antiterrorist measures taken in the United States have resulted in not one conviction for terrorism despite the fact that we've imprisoned more than 5000 foreign nationals, registered more than 80,000 foreign Muslims and Arabs, and tapped hundreds of thousands of phone conversations.

Obviously, there are individuals and groups around the world that would like to harm or destroy the United States. We do read occasionally of groups within the United States picked up by the police for alleged terrorist activity. But in all cases so far, the plots were just ideas hatched by disgruntled individuals who were far from carrying them out. In fact, protecting every vulnerable target is impossible—we couldn't afford it nor would we want to live with the consequences of that much security in our daily lives.

Of course, the past is not a perfect predictor of the future, and somewhere a sophisticated terrorist cell may be lurking in the United States. It's in the perceived interests of some in government to lead the public to believe that this is highly likely, partly to sustain our defense establishment but also to make it possible for elected officials and bureaucrats to say "we told you so," if a terrorist incident really does occur. Moreover, a fearful public is likely to give government more authority to protect them, a mindset that complemented the Bush administration's vision of a strong executive with virtually unlimited powers. But as a strategic foundation for sound foreign policy, the war on terror seems based on an unsustainable illusion.

[1] John Mueller, *Overblown* (New York: The Free Press, 2006), 2.
[2] Ibid.
[3] Ibid., 13.

(and therefore the motivation for intervening) that each country has at stake in any international dispute vary. This can paralyze the policy process and make military cooperation to resolve a conflict impossible to achieve. Reluctance to act alone kept the United States on the sidelines when its intervention might have saved hundreds of thousands of lives. Clinton did not intervene to stop ethnic cleansing in the breakaway republics of Yugoslavia until thousands had died. When we did get involved, it was as part of a NATO force, with shared costs and troop commitments.

The most glaring failure of multilateralism during Clinton's administration was the decision to follow the UN's lead in not intervening to stop the genocide in Rwanda, a conflict that cost an estimated eight hundred thousand lives. Both Clinton and the intervention-shy UN leadership later admitted this was a drastic failure of preventive diplomacy and international peacekeeping.

Regime Change and Preemptive War

When he campaigned for the presidency, George W. Bush advocated a foreign policy that was even less interventionist than Clinton's had been. He opposed any long-term or open-ended commitment of U.S. troops to international combat units or peacekeeping missions. He said that we had to be "humble" about our role in the world and that we should not be engaged in nation building in countries where our troops were committed. Bush's selection as his secretary of state, Colin Powell, the former chair of the Joint Chiefs of Staff and a man famously reluctant to commit U.S. troops to combat, was considered further evidence of his cautious approach to military involvement around the world.

Bush's early actions also indicated a shrinking back from diplomatic engagement, and he soon established himself as someone who preferred going it alone. The United States did not withdraw from international organizations, but Bush's rhetoric suggested that he would only *consult* with other countries, not deal with them as equals. He announced his opposition to a number of treaty arrangements. He withdrew U.S. involvement in the Kyoto agreements on global warming, which Clinton had signed, because he thought it placed unreasonable burdens on American businesses and too few on those in poorer countries. He refused to renew the ABM treaty because it would keep him from pursuing the development of the space-based antimissile defense system Reagan had begun, and he refused to agree to U.S. participation in an international court to try war crimes and human rights abuses because he thought it would make American peacekeeping troops subject to false accusations.

These early actions contributed to the view that Bush's foreign policy approach would shift the U.S. stance from multilateralism to unilateralism. The terrorist attacks of September 11, 2001, reinforced certain aspects of this approach but changed others. Bush did organize a multinational force before taking military action in Afghanistan, suggesting an accommodation with multilateralism. But laying claim to Reagan's "evil empire" terminology, he labeled three nations—Iraq, Iran, and North Korea—an "axis of evil" and agents of state-sponsored terrorism.

The conviction that an international ring of state-sponsored terrorists was lying in wait to launch other attacks led to a major redefinition of U.S. defense policy. Whereas historically the United States had maintained a posture of defensive response, striking only after being attacked, the Bush national security team endorsed a strategy of **preemption,** or striking first.[36] In a much-quoted speech delivered at West Point after 9/11, Bush said, "The war on terrorism will not be won on the defensive. . . . We must take the battle to the enemy, disrupt its plans, and confront the worst threats before they emerge. For that reason, this struggle will [only] end . . . with complete and utter destruction" of terrorist networks.[37]

Preemption is not a new idea in U.S. foreign policy; it has always been there as an option in defense policy.[38] It is unlikely that any president would fail to strike first in a situation where it was certain it would prevent a lethal attack on the United States. The distinctive aspect of the Bush position is his use of preemption, not as one option, but as a guiding principle in military policy.

Bush put his policy into effect shortly after announcing it by calling for a preemptive strike against Iraq. If the administration had argued that it had proof that an attack on the United States was imminent, probably few analysts would have seen preemption as a policy shift. But Bush's Iraq policy was based not on known capabilities or actual plans but on assumed *intent.* And it was unclear whether it was to be a unique operation or just the first in a series of strikes against the "axis of evil." Many members of Congress argued that invoking the policy to send thousands of combat troops to invade a sovereign nation encroached on Congress's constitutional prerogative to declare war.

After less than two years in office, Bush, certainly with the prodding of Vice President Cheney, drastically revised his approach to foreign policy from a passive unilateralism to an interventionist unilateralism. Opponents of preemptive war believe that attacking a country to prevent the possibility that it *might* one day attack us sets a frightening precedent for international rules of engagement, legitimizing preemptive military or nuclear strikes by other countries against their enemies (or against us).

Bush did put together a "coalition of the willing" to participate in the invasion of Iraq, but of the more than thirty countries signing on, only Great Britain contributed any serious contingent of combat troops. Troops and civilian personnel from other countries served mainly in support and humanitarian roles and sometimes numbered only a handful. And Great Britain's contribution of nearly thirty thousand troops for the invasion was immediately reduced to eight thousand after U.S. troops reached Baghdad and therefore were gone when the major fighting began. And whereas the coalition partners George H. W. Bush put together to fight the first Gulf War paid for virtually all of the war's cost, we paid most of George W. Bush's coalition partners (other than Great Britain and Australia) to participate.

Although Clinton's multilateralism slowed U.S. response to crises where lives could have been saved had we acted more quickly, it was an approach that rationed the use of U.S. military force and spending, maintaining the bulk of strength for response to vital national security threats. It was also an approach that tried to augment our worldview by factoring our allies' assessments of foreign policy crises into our own analyses. Multilateralism slows response time, but it can prevent precipitous entry into situations we do not fully understand. Bush's preemptive unilateralism, a token multilateralism, pushed U.S. military strength to its limits, leaving no ready reserve for responding to other substantial threats.

In its execution, unilateralism led the Bush administration back to multilateralism because alone we did not have the economic and military resources to stabilize and reconstruct Iraq and carry on the war in Afghanistan. By 2005, NATO troops were the bulk of the military presence in Afghanistan.

Spreading democracy was a corollary of preemptive war because waging a war not just to disarm a country but to overthrow its government inevitably led to nation building. Bush justified the imposition of a new government on Iraq by saying that in establishing a model for democratic government there he was laying the groundwork for regime change across the Middle East. By fostering the creation of governments more in our own image, he argued, we would be helping to ensure our physical and economic security. Bush suggested he would follow a similar policy toward other countries in the "axis of evil," and subsequent mission statements of his State Department listed democracy promotion as a fundamental goal of U.S. foreign policy.

Bush's policies unleashed a wave of anti-Americanism throughout Europe and parts of Asia as well as the Middle East. After 9/11, world opinion was almost entirely sympathetic, but the U.S. decision to launch a preemptive war and to overthrow the government of a sovereign country triggered fear and hatred in many parts of the world. Even among our closest allies, including Britain, Canada, Germany, and Australia, public opinion was against the war. International criticism increased after revelations about rendition (sending prisoners to other countries where laws do not prevent use of torture), secret CIA prisons for holding suspected terrorists, and the use of torture in American-run prisons in Iraq and Afghanistan. Animosity deepened when Bush claimed he did not have to abide by all the terms of the Geneva Convention on prisoners of war. By 2006, anti-Americanism was at an historic peak. (See Table 1.)

Of course, American presidents do not have to be directly responsive to worldwide opinion, but negative world opinion can have serious consequences if other governments refuse to help the United States achieve its objectives. When Bush had to go to NATO to ask that more troops be sent to Afghanistan and to ask allies to share the burden for reconstructing Iraq, he found himself working against public sentiment in those countries. In an intensely interdependent world, the leaders of activist governments must court world, as well as domestic, opinion.

Table 1	Global Attitudes toward the U.S. Have Become Less Favorable in the Iraqi War Era	
	1999–2000	2006
Great Britain	83	56
France	62	39
Germany	78	37
Spain	50	23
Russia	37	43
Indonesia	75	30
Turkey	52	12
Jordan	25*	15
Pakistan	23	27

*The figure is from 2002.

SOURCE: Pew Global Attitudes Project, June 13, 2006, "America's Image Slips, But Allies Share U.S. Concerns on Iran and Hamas," pewglobal.org/reports. In March and April, 2006, 17,000 people were surveyed in fifteen nations. The margin of error in each nation is 3–4 percent.

Security Issues in the Global Age

The international environment is always in a state of flux. Sometimes shifts in the international power structure force profound changes in how a country pursues its foreign policy goals. We saw this after World War I and the Russian Revolution, again after World War II, and with the breakup of the Soviet empire and the end of a bipolar balance of power. We began as a nation that feared standing armies and foreign involvements but have developed the largest conventional armed forces in the world. We moved on to acquire a nuclear arsenal capable of destroying the earth many times over. Each policy outlived its effectiveness as new threats emerged.

For more than forty years after World War II we thought our military strength was our most important asset in our effort to keep the world "free." Relying on the strategy of MAD, we built up an arsenal of nuclear-tipped missiles and bombers capable of delivering nuclear warheads. But we neglected other aspects of our military capability, including the capacity to fight limited wars with conventional weaponry. These conventional capabilities take on new importance in today's world.

At the beginning of the twenty-first century, the emergence of nonstate actors as global security threats and the rise of new economic giants to challenge the dominance of the old Western industrial powers brought about other shifts. International exchanges of people and goods are ubiquitous and pose new challenges. There are many new points of vulnerability, including the computer systems on which international business and finance and national security systems are now completely dependent. Globalization means that foreign problems left unattended find their way to our door, not only armed conflicts but also financial and environmental crises and epidemic diseases that can spread rapidly from one country to another. In this section we look at some of the security issues in the modern world.

Defense Policy

The end of the Cold War removed the need to prepare for a major nuclear confrontation with the Soviet Union. The arsenal of warheads, ICBMs, and nuclear bombers was drastically cut, and many domestic and foreign bases closed. After the Persian Gulf War, the size of the military was cut by a third, and base closings continued. We also reached tentative agreement with Russia to reduce our stockpile of 10,400 operable nuclear weapons to 2000. By the turn of the century, military spending was at its lowest level—3 percent of gross domestic product (GDP)—since before World War II.

By the beginning of the Clinton administration it was clear that the old defense strategies did not address the major security threats—terrorism, nuclear proliferation, environmental degradation, and political instability caused by poverty and disease.[39]

Today, the primary objective of military reform is to make our armed forces more mobile, capable of a quick response, and armed with lighter, more flexible, high-tech weaponry. A major showdown over this change came at the outset of Secretary of Defense **Donald Rumsfeld's** tenure. Rumsfeld wanted to kill new heavy-weapons programs and use the funds to outfit a mobile light infantry more suitable to counterterrorism. He won despite opposition by some of the Army's top leadership.

In 2001, in response to the 9/11 attacks, the Pentagon began to prepare the armed forces for **asymmetrical warfare**—conflict between combatants of very unequal strength. In this type of warfare, the weaker antagonist, knowing that direct military confrontation would lead to certain defeat, identifies and attacks a weak spot in the armor of the stronger opponent. Al-Qaeda found a security vulnerability in one of our strengths—the openness and easy access of American society—and used it to its advantage in organizing the attack, training the operatives, and eventually gaining control of commercial airliners to use as weapons against American citizens.

Transforming the military to fight this new kind of warfare requires a break with old strategies, weaponry, training, traditions, and career paths established in the armed forces over a period of decades. It has not been easy for civilian leaders to win acceptance from military professionals who have prepared for everything from guerrilla and limited warfare to all-out nuclear confrontation and some of whom believe we have not seen the last of traditional ground warfare. Rumsfeld forced out those who resisted, including the Army's chief of staff and others who opposed an Iraq invasion plan that was based on the new thinking—fewer troops, with lighter-weight, more mobile equipment. The top leaders argued that Rumsfeld was asking for fewer troops than needed to carry out the mission, especially for stabilizing Iraq after Saddam Hussein's overthrow. In addition, many of the lightweight, unarmored vehicles that troops had to use to patrol postinvasion Iraq and to transport supplies became death traps. Three years into the war, despite all evidence to the contrary, Rumsfeld insisted that the war plan had succeeded.

Rumsfeld also built on the policy of outsourcing military functions that dates back to the 1980s. The armed services bolster service personnel with military contractors—private citizens—to help train recruits and do other combat-related work. In Bosnia in 1996, one of every ten Americans in the peacekeeping force was a civilian under contract to the Pentagon.[40] The numbers are at least as high in Iraq, where low-paid infantry officers can be assigned to protect civilian employees earning three to four times as much and who are not subject to the same rules, discipline, or chain of command as regular military personnel.

There are two reasons for outsourcing—one is the assumption that private companies can provide logistical and support services more cheaply than the military. But many, if not all, privatized services have proven to be more, not less, costly, and the contracting process has been riddled with fraud. The second reason is that both civilian and military leaders have opted to stay with an all-volunteer force rather than reinstating the draft, which Nixon abolished in 1971 to quell anti–Vietnam War protests. By outsourcing much of the work troops would have done, the military can get by with far fewer personnel.

The conversion to all-volunteer armed services more than thirty years ago produced enough enlistees to meet the military's combat needs until the wars in Afghanistan and Iraq required a large-scale commitment of troops for a prolonged period. Now with National Guard and army reserves accounting for more than 40 percent of all troops in Iraq, and Congress and the administration unwilling to support the draft, the Defense Department is more dependent than ever on privatization.

Nuclear Proliferation

A few years ago, it was hard to imagine that we might look back at the Cold War as a simpler and even safer time, yet today's world is more complex than it was in the days of MAD. Nuclear proliferation makes defense against a nuclear strike exceedingly difficult because it is no longer sufficient just to monitor national defense establishments. It is less certain from where or from whom an attack might come. The CIA's failure to predict India's nuclear tests, despite years of surveillance of its arms program, is not reassuring regarding our ability to determine when other countries, let alone nonstate actors, have gained access to nuclear, chemical, and biological weapons or missile technology.

Both the Clinton and the Bush administrations declared that unsecured nuclear material and its possible acquisition by terrorist groups constituted the primary threat to world peace and the country's most difficult security challenge: how to stop terrorist groups, acting alone or in concert with a state hostile to the United States, from gaining access to missile technology and to the materials needed to make biological, chemical, or nuclear weapons. During the Cold War, only five nations (the United States, the Soviet Union, Britain, France, and China) produced and stockpiled nuclear weapons. The MAD strategy was rooted in, and dependent on, the conviction that the fairly small number of people who were in a position to make decisions about the use of nuclear weapons were sane and rational and had something to lose if their countries were destroyed and that the threat of mutual destruction would keep any leader from launching a first strike.

But now, many states are trying to gain a nuclear capability, and the materials and technology to make nuclear weapons have proliferated across the globe. When India and Pakistan conducted tests in 1998, the number of nuclear-ready countries increased to seven. Now there are at least nine nations—and perhaps as many as forty more nations—that have the capacity to produce warheads. The head of Pakistan's nuclear program has admitted selling materials and parts to China and Iran and perhaps other countries as well (perhaps with tacit official consent, since he received only token punishment).

And large reservoirs of enriched uranium and plutonium needed to make nuclear weapons lie unsecured and undocumented at sites in Russia and other parts of the former Soviet Union. Substantial black market trafficking in these materials is well documented.[41] Once the material is acquired, the technology necessary to build a simple uranium bomb like the one dropped on Hiroshima in 1945 is available to "anyone with a personal computer."[42] Although it is not as simple to assemble an operational bomb as that quote suggests, the likelihood that nuclear weapons will fall into the hands of terrorist groups continues to grow.

Defense Spending

Although Rumsfeld tried to shift planning and training away from preparing for large conventional ground warfare, he had virtually no impact on how defense dollars are spent. Despite administration claims that the greatest threats to national security come from terrorists planning to attack our chemical plants, public utilities, transportation facilities, and nuclear storage sites or to smuggle in WMD through our ports or by air cargo, we still spend ten times as much (more than a half trillion dollars in 2007) preparing for conventional warfare abroad than on homeland security.

Before spending on defense can be redirected to homeland security, the grip that arms manufacturers, military leaders, and their congressional allies have on the defense budget will have to be loosened. This iron triangle is the military-industrial-political complex President Eisenhower spoke of as he left office in 1961. Recognizing the potential for profit-hungry defense industries and pork-hungry congressional allies to drive military spending, determine the kind of weaponry purchased, and encourage the use of military force to achieve objectives, Eisenhower warned: "The conjunction of an immense military establishment and a large arms industry is new in the American experience," and "we must not fail to comprehend its grave implications. . . . The potential for the disastrous rise of misplaced power exists and will persist. We must never let the weight of this combination endanger our liberties or democratic processes." Sen. John McCain (R–Ariz.) is one of many who thinks Eisenhower's "fear became a reality long ago. He was worried that priorities are set by what benefits corporations as opposed to what benefits the country."[43]

Trying to change military spending priorities is like trying to turn around an ocean liner on a dime. This is perhaps the largest challenge we face in formulating effective national security policy. But if protecting our physical security depends on stopping terrorist attacks on our own soil, a drastic reordering of military spending must happen soon.

Trade Policy

Although some still see the world as unipolar in terms of military power, in the economic sphere the competition is intense. Although the public eye is focused on Iraq and terrorism, much of our foreign policy establishment is involved with economic affairs. We are always looking for new markets for exports to close the trade gap and create more jobs at home and to limit our vulnerability to foreign creditors.[44]

Trade problems loom large. At the end of World War II, the United States was the world's greatest trading power; half of all world trade passed through our ports. Today that figure has fallen to 14 percent, and we have lost much of the power we once had to regulate the flow of trade.[45] This is especially significant because trade now accounts for about a quarter of our GDP and one-third of our economic growth.[46]

We import far more goods from other countries than they import from us, creating a trade deficit. For years, this deficit has been climbing, reaching a new high with virtually each successive quarter of financial reporting. We have not had a trade surplus since 1975 and have become the world's largest debtor nation because of our trade shortfall and the deficit created by our government's spending hundreds of billions more than it receives in revenues. We need to borrow a great deal of money; by one estimate we need an inflow of at least $3 billion per day to keep our economy afloat. In 2005, foreign investors spent more than $1 trillion on Treasury bonds, equities in American companies, and other securities. Much of that money came from China and the Middle East.[47]

Our huge trade deficit has greatly weakened the dollar. Although that should improve our trade imbalance (because it makes American goods cheaper to buy abroad), it has not. Americans continue to buy massive

Carol Guzy/The Washington Post. Reprinted with permission.

A demonstrator refuses to give way to a police horse during protests against economic policies toward developing nations.

quantities of imported goods because they are so much cheaper than American-produced goods, and American investors continue to take their money abroad looking for cheaper labor and less government regulation. Despite the demand for cheap, foreign goods, American workers and producers still make it difficult for our trade negotiators and financiers by lobbying for restrictions (import quotas, tariffs, and surcharges) to protect domestic goods from foreign competition.

The ability of our, or any, government to adopt protectionist measures and have them stick is limited by membership in the **World Trade Organization (WTO).** The WTO, headquartered in Geneva, Switzerland, was founded in 1995 to remove barriers to free trade and to mediate trade disputes between member countries. WTO policies are set primarily by consensus of its member countries, represented by their trade ministers. Countries can be sanctioned for not abiding by WTO decisions.[48]

The near-universal membership of the WTO includes many smaller and poorer countries that do not have the legal infrastructure or the political freedoms that exist in the United States. This has created concern among U.S. interest groups that membership in the WTO will cause a rollback in regulatory standards to the lowest level existing in any member country. Unions worry they will lose good-paying jobs with benefits to nonunionized workers in poorer countries who will work for low wages, no benefits, and few safety protections and who in some cases lack the freedom to unionize. And environmental activists fear that none of the regulations applied to food production and distribution in the United States will be enforced for foodstuffs imported from countries without a commitment to environmental protection or even food safety. They claim that globalization and free trade are hastening the relocation of industry to countries where there are no limitations on toxic emissions into the air and water or regulation of the dumping and storing of hazardous waste. Human rights groups claim that free trade is adding to the already widespread abuse of child labor, unequal pay for women, and the exploitation of prison labor. They do not want to trade with, or invest in, countries controlled by dictatorships, fearing that by helping build up these economies, we will strengthen their governments and contribute to even greater human rights abuses.

Protecting American workers and industries sounds patriotic. Supporters of protectionism argue that these policies protect new industries until they can get established and support old industries essential to our defense and basic self-sufficiency. But protectionist policies usually result in higher consumer prices because of the elimination of competition from foreign labor and the products they produce.

Free traders, who include all presidents since Ronald Reagan, argue that it is cheaper to compensate displaced domestic workers and retrain them for other jobs than it is to pay the higher cost for protected goods and labor. They also claim that in addition to increasing prices, protectionism also discourages industry efficiency, just as the lack of domestic competition does. Finally, critics of protectionism say that imposing quotas or tariffs on other nations' goods just leads them to respond in kind, limiting our export markets and creating a trade war. Presidents Clinton and Bush advocated for and signed into law agreements (NAFTA and CAFTA)

that established the United States, Mexico and the states of Central America as a free trade area.

But demand for protectionist measures continues because job retention and creation are major issues in all industrialized countries. George W. Bush elevated free trade to a "moral principle," but this did not keep him from imposing quotas or tariffs on steel, textiles, beef, and other goods to satisfy the demands of a number of interest groups.[49] Such actions may temporarily relieve domestic political pressure, but most of Bush's measures ended up in international arbitration.

The strongest free trade area is the **European Union (EU).** Formerly called the European Economic Community or European Common Market, the EU was formed in 1957 to foster political and economic integration in Europe. In 1992, the EU removed all internal economic barriers and customs posts for member nations, and in 2002, it began phasing in a common currency (the euro). The membership of the EU has expanded to twenty-five from its original six members, with four more awaiting entry. The EU, with a single trade policy, a single agricultural policy, and a single market of 440 million people, is the world's biggest trading bloc.

Despite the near complete focus on the war on terrorism, trade will continue to be a—if not *the*—central foreign policy issue for most Americans because of what it means for job security and the cost of goods.

Conclusion: Is Our Foreign Policy Responsive?

As the head of the world's largest military and economic power and a partner in major military and trade alliances, the president has a constituency larger than the American public. He is often called on to be responsive to the needs of other people or countries— victims of famines, civil wars, natural disasters, and human rights abuses or countries in need of military and economic assistance.

But is the direction of our foreign policy responsive to public opinion, and should it be, given how poorly informed most Americans are on specific issues? Public attitudes can constrain the general policy directions of the president and Congress, but presidents can do a lot to shape these attitudes. Over the long term, as in Vietnam, the administration must be somewhat responsive to public sentiment that intensely opposes administration policy. But it is far harder for the public to have a short-term impact on military policy. Because everyone agrees on the general goal of protecting the nation from external attack, the public is far less inclined to be critical of military policy than it is of other areas of foreign policy. But this free rein has led to excessive secrecy, inefficiencies, and extravagant spending that are surely not in the public interest.

After 9/11, there was no need to convince the public that a threat existed, and the public gave the president unprecedented support for military action against al-Qaeda. As long as the public believed in a connection between Iraq and the 9/11 attacks, there was substantial backing for President Bush's preemptive war policy. But when evidence for such a connection failed to materialize and the war turned into an occupation characterized by urban warfare and sectarian conflict, public support waned. Nevertheless, it is difficult for a government to respond to public opinion shifts once troops are engaged in combat. The commitment has been made, and responsiveness to public mood has to wait.

In other areas of foreign policy, the public has more opportunity for influence than in the past, even on more technical issues such as trade, immigration, and human rights. The rise of powerful lobbies and the voting blocs of "hyphenated" Americans, for example, can have a significant impact on policy decisions. The information revolution also has given the public a much greater opportunity to be informed on the whole range of foreign policy issues, even, on occasion, on classified war policy. Without the dissemination of photographs showing prisoner abuse at the Abu Ghraib prison in Iraq, public pressure might never have been brought to bear to end the practices.

Because of our greater connectedness to all parts of the world through the Internet and because of globalization in general, Americans are far more aware than before of the relationships between foreign policy and their everyday lives and standard of living. In the day-to-day world of diplomacy, Foreign Service officers work tirelessly to promote American agricultural and other exports and American business interests in general. The State Department's own description of its work cites creating jobs and opening markets as central to its mission. Representing American policy as a vehicle for the promotion of individual economic interests is in itself an indication of how necessary policy makers feel it is to at least have the appearance of being responsive to the public.

Key Terms

Key Names

1. It is generally agreed that the most important goal of a country's foreign policy is to
   a. protect its physical security.
   b. protect its neighbor's security.
   c. protect its economic security.
   d. extend its sphere of influence.
   e. bring peace to all nations.

2. All but which one are explanations why it is difficult to have a coherent foreign policy in a democracy?
   a. We elect new leaders every few years.
   b. Many people participate in the foreign policy process.
   c. Usually, policy makers disagree on fundamental goals.
   d. Congress and the president do not always agree on specific actions.
   e. Interest groups and the media sometimes influence the process.

3. Which is **not** true of the president and foreign policy?
   a. Those without foreign policy experience often appoint very experienced foreign policy advisors.
   b. A president typically consults the secretaries of defense and state and the national security advisor on important foreign policy questions.
   c. In times of immediate crisis, Congress usually defers to the president and his sources on foreign policy.
   d. George W. Bush choose an inexperienced group of foreign policy advisors.
   e. Bill Clinton and George W. Bush came to office with little international experience.

4. Foreign policy specialists
   a. always play a major role in foreign policy decisions.
   b. are in short supply in the U.S. government.
   c. always work together across agencies, recognizing that the overall success of American foreign policy is more important than turf issues.
   d. advised George W. Bush to invade Iraq.
   e. are sometimes not given important roles, such as Asian experts in the Vietnam War.

5. Which is true of the War Powers Resolution? It
   a. was intended to curb congressional usurpation of presidential power to declare war.
   b. urged President Johnson to send troops to Vietnam.
   c. authorizes the president to send troops into combat only under specific situations.
   d. has been popular with modern presidents.
   e. was passed during the War of 1812.

6. Which is **not** true about partisan differences on foreign policy?
   a. They are usually apparent in the parties' national platforms.
   b. The opposition party usually rallies around the president in times of national crises.
   c. When troops are fighting on foreign soil, it is hard for Congress to vote against supporting them.
   d. The party that does not control the White House often has a difficult time speaking with one voice on foreign policy.
   e. Americans usually see foreign policy in much the same way, regardless of party.

7. Interest group influence in foreign policy
   a. is nonexistent.
   b. is generally greater than in domestic policy.
   c. is generally less than in domestic policy.
   d. has decreased in the past 25 years.
   e. does not include groups organized around their common ethnic or national heritage.

8. The fact that a substantial minority of the public still believes that Sadaam Hussein had something to do with 9/11 is an example of
   a. the sophistication of the American public on foreign policy issues.
   b. the president's ability to shape attitudes about foreign policy.
   c. the influence of Iraqi American immigrants.
   d. the results of the press being embedded with the troops.
   e. the impact of public opinion on presidential decisions.

9. The Reagan administration supported the regime of Sadaam Hussein because
   a. they saw Iraq as a counterbalance to a hostile Iran.
   b. they saw Iraq as a counterbalance to a hostile Saudi Arabia.
   c. they saw Iraq as a possible ally of Israel.
   d. they wanted help overthrowing the Shah of Iran.
   e. they opposed Kurdish rights.

10. George H. W. Bush did not try to topple Saddam Hussein because
    a. we lacked military power to do so.
    b. the Hussein regime promised to change some of its policies.
    c. he wanted to let his son do it.
    d. the Shia Muslims would oppose regime change.
    e. he feared ethnic conflict and instability.

11. In which era was isolationism most prominent?
   a. 1942–1952
   b. 1962–1972
   c. 1902–1912
   d. 2000–2007
   e. 1992–2000

12. Containment was a foreign policy that was
   a. designed to win World War II by containing the Nazis.
   b. designed to limit the spread of Communism after World War II.
   c. designed to maintain the peace in the Middle East.
   d. very relevant after the end of the communist empire.
   e. originated in the Presidency of John F. Kennedy.

13. "We will bury you" is a phrase most associated with
   a. Adolph Hitler.
   b. Ho Chi Minh.
   c. Mikhail Gorbechev.
   d. Saddam Hussein.
   e. Nikita Khrushchev.

14. The domino theory assumed that
   a. communist countries were independent of one another.
   b. cultural exchanges could improve international relations.
   c. if Vietnam was taken over by the communists, other nations would fall too.
   d. if one Muslim nation in the Middle East were a democracy, others would follow.
   e. if the president allowed one interest group to influence policy, others would demand a voice.

15. Which is true of the Vietnam War?
   a. Congress, early and often, denied funding for the war.
   b. The war began with the North Vietnamese army attacking Saigon.
   c. The United States had planned for a long-drawn-out war.
   d. Republicans generally did not support the war.
   e. Our massive intervention began with the Gulf of Tonkin resolution.

16. In which way is the Iraqi War **not** similar to the Vietnam War?
   a. Public support started high and eroded over the course of the war.
   b. The administration expected a quick war.
   c. The president won congressional approval for sending troops on the basis of "facts" that later proved to be false.
   d. To facilitate possible withdrawal of American troops, training and then turning over the fighting to indigenous troops (Vietnamese or Iraqi) was stated as an important goal by American decision makers.
   e. The president authorized torture and holding of combatants outside the restraints of international law.

17. Détente as a foreign policy is most associated with
   a. Richard Nixon.
   b. Bill Clinton.
   c. Ronald Reagan.
   d. George W. Bush.
   e. John F. Kennedy.

18. The doctrine of preemption was used to justify
   a. America's involvement in World War II.
   b. America's intervention in the Vietnam War.
   c. our invasion of Afghanistan.
   d. our invasion of Iraq.
   e. America's involvement in World War I.

19. The war on terror
   a. has limited objectives.
   b. seems to be drawing to a successful conclusion.
   c. was launched by President Eisenhower.
   d. is hard to implement.
   e. is fought only overseas.

20. Trade as a foreign policy area
   a. displays internation competition.
   b. is regulated by the World Trade Organization (WTO).
   c. has significant interest group involvement.
   d. reflects a division between free traders and protectionists.
   e. All are true.

In Congress, July 4, 1776.

A Declaration by the Representatives of the United States of America, in General Congress assembled.

When in the Course of human Events, it becomes necessary for one People to dissolve the Political Bonds which have connected them with another, and to assume among the Powers of the Earth, the separate and equal Station to which the Laws of Nature and of Nature's God entitle them, a decent Respect to the Opinions of Mankind requires that they should declare the causes which impel them to the Separation.

We hold these Truths to be self-evident, that all Men are created equal, that they are endowed by their Creator with certain unalienable Rights, that among these are Life, Liberty, and the Pursuit of Happiness—That to secure these Rights, Governments are instituted among Men, deriving their just Powers from the Consent of the Governed, that whenever any Form of Government becomes destructive of these Ends, it is the Right of the People to alter or to abolish it, and to institute new Government, laying its Foundation on such Principles, and organizing its Powers in such Forms, as to them shall seem most likely to effect their Safety and Happiness. Prudence, indeed, will dictate that Governments long established should not be changed for light and transient Causes; and accordingly all Experience hath shewn, that Mankind are more disposed to suffer, while Evils are sufferable, than to right themselves by abolishing the Forms to which they are accustomed. But when a long Train of Abuses and Usurpations, pursuing invariably the same Object, evinces a Design to reduce them under absolute Despotism, it is their Right, it is their Duty, to throw off such Government, and to provide new Guards for their future Security. Such has been the patient Sufferance of these Colonies; and such is now the Necessity which constrains them to alter their former Systems of Government. The History of the present King of Great Britain is a History of repeated Injuries and Usurpations, all having in direct Object the Establishment of an absolute Tyranny over these States. To prove this, let facts be submitted to a candid World.

He has refused his Assent to Laws, the most wholesome and necessary for the public Good.

He has forbidden his Governors to pass Laws of immediate and pressing Importance, unless suspended in their Operation till his Assent should be obtained; and when so suspended, he has utterly neglected to attend to them.

He has refused to pass other Laws for the Accommodation of large Districts of People, unless those People would relinquish the Right of Representation in the Legislature, a Right inestimable to them, and formidable to Tyrants only.

He has called together Legislative Bodies at Places unusual, uncomfortable, and distant from the Depository of their Public Records, for the sole Purpose of fatiguing them into Compliance with his Measures.

He has dissolved Representative Houses repeatedly, for opposing with manly Firmness his Invasions on the Rights of the People.

He has refused for a long Time, after such Dissolutions, to cause others to be elected; whereby the Legislative Powers, incapable of Annihilation, have returned to the People at large for their exercise; the State remaining in the mean time exposed to all the Dangers of Invasion from without, and Convulsions within.

He has endeavoured to prevent the Population of these States; for that Purpose obstructing the Laws for Naturalization of Foreigners; refusing to pass others to encourage their Migration hither, and raising the Conditions of new Appropriations of Lands.

He has obstructed the Administration of Justice, by refusing his Assent to Laws for establishing Judiciary Powers.

He has made Judges dependent on his Will alone, for the Tenure of their offices, and the Amount and payments of their Salaries.

*The spelling, capitalization, and punctuation of the original have been retained here.

He has erected a Multitude of new Offices, and sent hither Swarms of Officers to harass our People, and eat out their Substance.

He has kept among us, in times of Peace, Standing Armies, without the consent of our Legislatures.

He has affected to render the Military independent of, and superior to the Civil Power.

He has combined with others to subject us to a Jurisdiction foreign to our Constitution, and unacknowledged by our Laws; giving his Assent to their Acts of pretended Legislation:

For quartering large Bodies of Armed Troops among us:

For protecting them, by a mock Trial, from Punishment for any Murders which they should commit on the Inhabitants of these States:

For cutting off our Trade with all Parts of the World: For imposing Taxes on us without our Consent: For depriving us, in many cases, of the Benefits of Trial by Jury:

For transporting us beyond Seas to be tried for pretended Offences:

For abolishing the free System of English Laws in a neighbouring Province, establishing therein an arbitrary Government, and enlarging its Boundaries, so as to render it at once an Example and fit Instrument for introducing the same absolute Rule into these Colonies:

For taking away our Charters, abolishing our most valuable Laws, and altering fundamentally the Forms of our Governments:

For suspending our own Legislatures, and declaring themselves invested with Power to legislate for us in all Cases whatsoever.

He has abdicated Government here, by declaring us out of his Protection and waging War against us.

He has plundered our Seas, ravaged our Coasts, burnt our towns, and destroyed the Lives of our People.

He is, at this Time, transporting large Armies of foreign Mercenaries to compleat the works of Death, Desolation, and Tyranny, already begun with circumstances of Cruelty and Perfidy, scarcely parallelled in the most barbarous Ages, and totally unworthy the Head of a civilized Nation.

He has constrained our fellow Citizens taken Captive on the high Seas to bear Arms against their Country, to become the Executioners of their Friends and Brethren, or to fall themselves by their Hands.

He has excited domestic Insurrections amongst us, and has endeavoured to bring on the Inhabitants of our Frontiers, the merciless Indian Savages, whose known Rule of Warfare is an undistinguished Destruction, of all Ages, Sexes and Conditions.

In every state of these Oppressions we have Petitioned for Redress in the most humble Terms: Our repeated Petitions have been answered only by repeated Injury. A Prince, whose Character is thus marked by every act which may define a Tyrant, is unfit to be the Ruler of a free People.

Nor have we been wanting in Attentions to our British Brethren. We have warned them from Time to Time of Attempts by their Legislature to extend an unwarrantable Jurisdiction over us. We have reminded them of the Circumstances of our Emigration and Settlement here. We have appealed to their native Justice and Magnanimity, and we have conjured them by the Ties of our common Kindred to disavow these Usurpations, which would inevitably interrupt our Connections and Correspondence. They too have been deaf to the Voice of Justice and of Consanguinity. We must, therefore, acquiesce in the Necessity, which denounces our Separation, and hold them, as we hold the rest of Mankind, Enemies in War, in Peace Friends.

We, therefore, the Representatives of the UNITED STATES OF AMERICA, in General Congress Assembled, appealing to the Supreme Judge of the World for the Rectitude of our Intentions, do, in the Name, and by Authority of the good People of these Colonies, solemnly Publish and Declare, That these United Colonies are, and of Right ought to be, Free and Independent States; that they are absolved from all Allegiance to the British Crown, and that all political Connection between them and the State of Great Britain, is and ought to be totally dissolved; and that as Free and Independent States, they have full Power to levy War, conclude Peace, contract Alliances, establish Commerce, and to do all other Acts and Things which Independent States may of right do. And for the support of this declaration, with a firm Reliance on the Protection of divine Providence, we mutually pledge to each other our Lives, our Fortunes, and our sacred Honor.

CONSTITUTION OF THE UNITED STATES OF AMERICA*

We the people of the United States, in Order to form a more perfect Union, establish Justice, insure domestic Tranquility, provide for the common defence, promote the general Welfare, and secure the Blessings of Liberty to ourselves and our posterity, do ordain and establish this Constitution for the United States of America.

Article I

Section 1. All legislative Powers herein granted shall be vested in a Congress of the United States, which shall consist of a Senate and House of Representatives.

Section 2. The House of Representatives shall be composed of Members chosen every second Year by the People of the several States, and the Electors in each State shall have the Qualifications requisite for Electors of the most numerous Branch of the State Legislature.

No person shall be a Representative who shall not have attained to the Age of twenty-five Years, and been seven Years a Citizen of the United States, and who shall not, when elected, be an Inhabitant of that State in which he shall be chosen.

Representatives and direct [Taxes][1] shall be apportioned among the several States which may be included within this Union, according to their respective Numbers [which shall be determined by adding to the whole Number of free Persons, including those bound to Service for a Term of Years, and excluding Indians not taxed, three fifths of all other Persons].[2] The actual Enumeration shall be made within three Years after the first Meeting of the Congress of the United States, and within every subsequent Term of ten Years, in such Manner as they shall by Law direct. The Number of Representatives shall not exceed one for every thirty Thousand, but each State shall have at Least one Representative; and until such enumeration shall be made, the State of New Hampshire shall be entitled to chuse three, Massachusetts eight, Rhode Island and Providence Plantations one, Connecticut five, New-York six, New Jersey four, Pennsylvania eight, Delaware one, Maryland six, Virginia ten, North Carolina five, South Carolina five, and Georgia three.

When vacancies happen in the Representation from any State, the Executive Authority thereof shall issue Writs of Election to fill such Vacancies.

The House of Representatives shall chuse their Speaker and other Officers; and shall have the sole Power of Impeachment.

Section 3. The Senate of the United States shall be composed of two Senators from each State [chosen by the Legislature thereof],[3] for six Years; and each Senator shall have one Vote.

Immediately after they shall be assembled in Consequence of the first Election, they shall be divided as equally as may be into three Classes. The Seats of the Senators of the first Class shall be vacated at the Expiration of the second year, of the second Class at the Expiration of the fourth Year, and of the third Class at the Expiration of the sixth Year, so that one third may be chosen every second Year [and if Vacancies happen by Resignation, or otherwise, during the Recess of the Legislature of any State, the Executive thereof may make temporary Appointments until the next Meeting of the Legislature, which shall then fill such Vacancies.][4]

No Person shall be a Senator who shall not have attained to the Age of thirty Years, and been nine Years a Citizen of the United States, and who shall not, when elected, be an Inhabitant of that State for which he shall be chosen.

The Vice President of the United States shall be President of the Senate, but shall have no Vote, unless they be equally divided.

---

*The spelling, capitalization, and punctuation of the original have been retained here. Brackets indicate passages that have been altered by amendments to the Constitution.

1. Modified by the Sixteenth Amendment.
2. Modified by the Fourteenth Amendment.

3. Repealed by the Seventeenth Amendment.
4. Modified by the Seventeenth Amendment.

The Senate shall chuse their other Officers, and also a President pro tempore, in the Absence of the Vice President, or when he shall exercise the Office of President of the United States.

The Senate shall have the sole Power to try all Impeachments. When sitting for that Purpose, they shall be on Oath or Affirmation. When the President of the United States is tried, the Chief Justice shall preside: And no Person shall be convicted without the Concurrence of two thirds of the Members present.

Judgment in Cases of Impeachment shall not extend further than to removal from Office, and disqualification to hold and enjoy any Office of honor, Trust or Profit under the United States; but the Party convicted shall nevertheless be liable and subject to Indictment, Trial, Judgment and Punishment, according to Law.

Section 4. The Times, Places and Manner of holding Elections for Senators and Representatives, shall be prescribed in each State by the Legislature thereof; but the Congress may at any time by Law make or alter such Regulations, except as to the Places of chusing Senators.

[The Congress shall assemble at least once in every Year, and such Meeting shall be on the first Monday in December, unless they shall by Law appoint a different Day.][5]

Section 5. Each House shall be the Judge of the Elections, Returns and Qualifications of its own Members, and a Majority of each shall constitute a Quorum to do Business; but a smaller Number may adjourn from day to day, and may be authorized to compel the Attendance of absent Members, in such Manner, and under such Penalties as each House may provide.

Each House may determine the Rules of its Proceedings, punish its Members for disorderly Behaviour, and, with the Concurrence of two thirds, expel a Member.

Each House shall keep a Journal of its Proceedings, and from time to time publish the same, excepting such Parts as may in their Judgment require Secrecy; and the Yeas and Nays of the Members of either House on any question shall, at the Desire of one fifth of those present, be entered on the Journal.

Neither House, during the Session of Congress, shall, without the Consent of the other, adjourn for more than three days, nor to any other Place than that in which the two Houses shall be sitting.

Section 6. The Senators and Representatives shall receive a Compensation for their Services, to be ascertained by Law, and paid out of the Treasury of the United States. They shall in all Cases, except Treason, Felony and Breach of the Peace, be privileged from Arrest during their Attendance at the Session of their respective Houses, and in going to and returning from the same; and for any Speech or Debate in either House, they shall not be questioned in any other Place.

No Senator or Representative shall, during the Time for which he was elected, be appointed to any civil Office under the Authority of the United States, which shall have been created, or the Emoluments whereof shall have been encreased during such time; and no Person holding any Office under the United States, shall be a Member of either House during his Continuance in Office.

Section 7. All Bills for raising Revenue shall originate in the House of Representatives; but the Senate may propose or concur with Amendments as on other Bills.

Every Bill which shall have passed the House of Representatives and the Senate, shall, before it become a Law, be presented to the President of the United States; If he approves he shall sign it, but if not he shall return it, with his objections to that House in which it shall have originated, who shall enter the Objections at large on their Journal, and proceed to reconsider it. If after such Reconsideration two thirds of that House shall agree to pass the Bill, it shall be sent, together with the Objections, to the other House, by which it shall likewise be reconsidered, and if approved by two thirds of that House, it shall become a Law. But in all such Cases the Votes of both Houses shall be determined by yeas and Nays, and the Names of the Persons voting for and against the Bill shall be entered on the Journal of each House respectively. If any Bill shall not be returned by the President within ten Days (Sun- days excepted) after it shall have been presented to him, the Same shall be a Law, in like Manner as if he had signed it, unless the Congress by their Adjournment prevent its Return, in which Case it shall not be a Law.

Every Order, Resolution, or Vote to which the Concurrence of the Senate and House of Representatives may be necessary (except on a question of Adjournment) shall be presented to the President of the United States; and before the Same shall take Effect, shall be approved by him, or being disapproved by him, shall be repassed by two thirds of the Senate and House of Representatives, according to the Rules and Limitations prescribed in the Case of a Bill.

Section 8. The Congress shall have Power To lay and collect Taxes, Duties, Imposts and Excises, to pay the Debts and provide for the common Defence and general Welfare of the United States; but all Duties, Imposts and Excises shall be uniform throughout the United States;

To borrow Money on the credit of the United States; To regulate Commerce with foreign Nations, and among the several States, and with the Indian Tribes;

To establish a uniform Rule of Naturalization, and uniform Laws on the subject of Bankruptcies throughout the United States;

To coin Money, regulate the Value thereof, and of foreign Coin, and fix the Standard of Weights and Measures;

---

5. Changed by the Twentieth Amendment.

To provide for the Punishment of counterfeiting the Securities and current Coin of the United States.

To establish Post Offices and post Roads; To promote the Progress of Science and useful Arts, by securing for limited Times to Authors and Inventors the exclusive Right to their respective Writings and Discoveries;

To constitute Tribunals inferior to the supreme Court; To define and punish Piracies and Felonies committed on the high Seas, and Offences against the Law of Nations;

To declare War, grant Letters of Marque and Reprisal, and make Rules concerning Captures on Land and Water;

To raise and support Armies, but no Appropriation of Money to that Use shall be for a longer Term than two Years;

To provide and maintain a Navy; To make Rules for the Government and Regulation of the land and naval Forces;

To provide for calling forth the Militia to execute the Laws of the Union, suppress Insurrections and repel Invasions;

To provide for organizing, arming, and disciplining the Militia, and for governing such Part of them as may be employed in the Service of the United States, reserving to the States respectively, the Appointment of the Officers, and the Authority of training the Militia according to the discipline prescribed by Congress;

To exercise exclusive Legislation in all Cases whatsoever, over such District (not exceeding ten Miles square) as may, by Cession of particular States, and the Acceptance of Congress, become the Seat of the Government of the United States, and to exercise like Authority over all Places purchased by the Consent of the Legislature of the State in which the Same shall be, for the Erection of forts, Magazines, Arsenals, dock-Yards, and other needful Buildings;—And

To make all Laws which shall be necessary and proper for carrying into Execution the foregoing Powers, and all other Powers vested by this Constitution in the Government of the United States, or in any Department or Officer thereof.

Section 9. The Migration or Importation of such Persons as any of the States now existing shall think proper to admit, shall not be prohibited by the Congress prior to the Year one thousand eight hundred and eight, but a Tax or duty may be imposed on such Importation, not exceeding ten dollars for each Person.

The Privilege of the Writ of Habeas Corpus shall not be suspended, unless when in Cases of Rebellion or Invasion the public Safety may require it.

No Bill of Attainder or ex post facto Law shall be passed. [No Capitation, or other direct, Tax shall be laid, unless in Proportion to the Census or Enumeration herein before directed to be taken.][6]

No Tax or Duty shall be laid on Articles exported from any State.

No Preference shall be given by any Regulation of Commerce or Revenue to the Ports of one State over those of another; nor shall Vessels bound to, or from, one State, be obliged to enter, clear, or pay Duties in another.

No Money shall be drawn from the Treasury, but in Consequence of Appropriations made by Law; and a regular Statement and Account of the Receipts and Expenditures of all public Money shall be published from time to time.

No Title of Nobility shall be granted by the United States; and no Person holding any Office or Profit or Trust under them, shall, without the Consent of the Congress, accept of any present, Emolument, Office, or Title, of any kind whatever, from any King, Prince, or foreign State.

Section 10. No state shall enter into any Treaty, Alliance, or Confederation; grant Letters of Marque and Reprisal; coin Money; emit Bills of Credit; make any Thing but gold and silver Coin a Tender in Payment of Debts; pass any Bill of Attainder, ex post facto Law, or Law impairing the Obligation of Contracts, or grant any Title of Nobility.

No State shall, without the Consent of the Congress, lay any Imposts or Duties on Imports or Exports, except what may be absolutely necessary for executing its inspection Laws; and the net Produce of all Duties and Imposts, laid by any State on Imports or Exports, shall be for the Use of the Treasury of the United States; and all such Laws shall be subject to the Revision and Controul of the Congress.

No State shall, without the Consent of Congress, lay any duty of Tonnage, keep Troops, or Ships of War in time of Peace, enter into any Agreement or Compact with another State, or with a foreign Power or engage in War, unless actually invaded, or in such imminent Danger as will not admit of delay.

Article II

Section 1. The executive Power shall be vested in a President of the United States of America. He shall hold his Office during the Term of four Years, and, together with the Vice President, chosen for the Same Term, be elected, as follows.

Each State shall appoint, in such Manner as the Legislature thereof may direct, a Number of Electors, equal to the whole Number of Senators and Representatives to which the State may be entitled in the Congress; but no Senator or Representative, or Person holding an Office of Trust or Profit under the United States, shall be appointed an Elector.

[The Electors shall meet in their respective States, and vote by Ballot for two Persons of whom one at least shall not be an Inhabitant of the same State with themselves. And they shall make a List of all the Persons voted for, and of the Number of Votes for each; which List they shall sign and certify, and transmit sealed to the Seat of the Government of

---

6. Modified by the Sixteenth Amendment.

the United States, directed to the President of the Senate. The President of the Senate shall, in the Presence of the Senate and House of Representatives, open all the Certificates, and the Votes shall then be counted. The Person having the greatest Number of Votes shall be the President, if such Number be a Majority of the whole Number of Electors appointed; and if there be more than one who have such Majority, and have an equal Number of Votes, then the House of Representatives shall immediately chuse by Ballot one of them for President; and if no Person have a Majority, then from the five highest on the List the said House shall in like Manner chuse the President. But in chusing the President, the Votes shall be taken by States, the Representation from each State having one Vote; A quorum for this Purpose shall consist of a Member or Members from two thirds of the States, and a Majority of all the states shall be necessary to a Choice. In every Case, after the Choice of the President, the Person having the greatest Number of Votes of the Electors shall be the Vice President. But if there should remain two or more who have equal Votes, the Senate shall chuse from them by Ballot the Vice President.][7]

The Congress may determine the Time of chusing the Electors, and the Day on which they shall give their Votes; which Day shall be the same throughout the United States.

No person except a natural born Citizen, or a Citizen of the United States, at the time of the Adoption of this Constitution, shall be eligible to the Office of President; neither shall any Person be eligible to that Office who shall not have attained to the Age of thirty five Years, and been fourteen Years a Resident within the United States.

[In Case of the Removal of the President from Office, or of his Death, Resignation, or Inability to discharge the Powers and Duties of the said Office, the same shall devolve on the Vice President, and the Congress may by Law provide for the Case of Removal, Death, Resignation or Inability, both of the President and Vice President, declaring what Officer shall then act as President, and such Officer shall act accordingly, until the Disability be removed, or a President shall be elected.][8]

The President shall, at stated Times, receive for his Services, a Compensation, which shall neither be increased nor diminished during the Period for which he shall have been elected, and he shall not receive within that Period any other Emolument from the United States, or any of them.

Before he enter on the Execution of his Office, he shall take the following Oath or Affirmation:—"I do solemnly swear (or affirm) that I will faithfully execute the Office of President of the United States, and will to the best of my Ability, preserve, protect and defend the constitution of the United States."

Section 2. The President shall be Commander in Chief of the Army and Navy of the United States, and of the Militia of the several States, when called into the actual Service of the United States; he may require the Opinion, in writing, of the principal Officer in each of the executive Departments, upon any Subject relating to the Duties of their respective Offices, and he shall have Power to grant Reprieves and Pardons for Offences against the United States, except in Cases of Impeachment.

He shall have Power, by and with the Advice and Consent of the Senate, to make Treaties, provided two thirds of the Senators present concur; and he shall nominate, and by and with the Advice and Consent of the Senate, shall appoint Ambassadors, other public Ministers and Consuls, Judges of the supreme Court, and all other Officers of the United States, whose Appointments are not herein otherwise provided for, and which shall be established by Law; but the Congress may by Law vest the Appointment of such inferior Officers, as they think proper, in the President alone, in the Courts of Law, or in the Heads of Departments.

The President shall have Power to fill up all Vacancies that may happen during the Recess of the Senate, by granting Commissions which shall expire at the end of their next Session.

Section 3. He shall from time to time give to the Congress Information of the State of the Union, and recommend to their Consideration such Measures as he shall judge necessary and expedient; he may, on extraordinary Occasions, convene both Houses, or either of them, and in Case of Disagreement between them, with Respect to the Time of Adjournment, he may adjourn them to such Time as he shall think proper; he shall receive Ambassadors and other public Ministers; he shall take Care that the Laws be faithfully executed, and shall Commission all the Officers of the United States.

Section 4. The President, Vice President and all civil Officers of the United States, shall be removed from Office on Impeachment for, and Conviction of, Treason, Bribery, or other high Crimes and Misdemeanors.

Article III

Section 1. The judicial Power of the United States shall be vested in one supreme Court, and in such inferior Courts as the Congress may from time to time ordain and establish. The Judges, both of the supreme and inferior Courts, shall hold their Offices during good Behaviour, and shall, at stated Times, receive for their Services a Compensation, which shall not be diminished during their Continuance in Office.

Section 2. The judicial Power shall extend to all Cases, in Law and Equity, arising under this Constitution, the Laws of the United States, and Treaties made, or which shall be

---

7. Changed by the Twelfth Amendment.
8. Modified by the Twenty-fifth Amendment.

made, under their Authority;—to all Cases affecting Ambassadors, other public Ministers and Consuls;—to all Cases of admiralty and maritime Jurisdiction;—to Controversies to which the United States shall be a Party;—to Controversies between two or more States;—[between a State and Citizens of another State;][9]—between Citizens of different States,—between Citizens of the same State claiming Lands under Grants of different States, [and between a state, or the Citizens thereof, and foreign States, Citizens or Subjects.][10]

In all cases affecting Ambassadors, other public Ministers and Consuls, and those in which a State shall be Party, the supreme Court shall have original Jurisdiction. In all the other Cases before mentioned, the supreme Court shall have appellate Jurisdiction, both as to Law and Fact, with such Exceptions, and under such Regulations as the Congress shall make.

The Trial of all Crimes, except in Cases of Impeachment, shall be by Jury; and such Trial shall be held in the State where the said Crimes shall have been committed; but when not committed within any State, the Trial shall be at such Place or Places as the Congress may by Law have directed.

Section 3. Treason against the United States, shall consist only in levying War against them, or in adhering to their Enemies, giving them Aid and Comfort. No Person shall be convicted of Treason unless on the Testimony of two Witnesses to the same overt Act, or on Confession in open Court.

The Congress shall have Power to declare the Punishment of Treason, but no Attainder of Treason shall work Corruption of Blood, or Forfeiture except during the Life of the Person attainted.

Article IV

Section 1. Full Faith and Credit shall be given in each State to the public Acts, Records, and judicial Proceedings of every other State. And the Congress may by general Laws prescribe the Manner in which such Acts, Records and Proceedings shall be proved, and the Effect thereof.

Section 2. The Citizens of each State shall be entitled to all Privileges and Immunities of Citizens in the several States.

A Person charged in any State with Treason, Felony, or other Crime, who shall flee from Justice, and be found in another State, shall on Demand of the executive Authority of the State from which he fled, be delivered up, to be removed to the State having Jurisdiction of the Crime.

[No Person held to Service or Labour in one State under the Laws thereof, escaping into another, shall, in Consequence of any Law or Regulation therein, be discharged from such Service or Labour, but shall be delivered up on Claim of the Party to whom such Service or Labour may be due.][11]

Section 3. New States may be admitted by the Congress into this Union; but no new State shall be formed or erected within the Jurisdiction of any other State; nor any State be formed by the Junction of two or more States, or Parts of States, without the Consent of the Legislatures of the States concerned as well as of the Congress.

The Congress shall have Power to dispose of and make all needful Rules and Regulations respecting the Territory or other Property belonging to the United States; and nothing in this Constitution shall be so construed as to Prejudice any Claims of the United States, or of any particular State.

Section 4. The United States shall guarantee to every State in this Union a Republican Form of Government, and shall protect each of them against Invasion, and on Application of the Legislature, or of the Executive (when the Legislature cannot be convened) against domestic Violence.

Article V

The Congress, whenever two thirds of both Houses shall deem it necessary, shall propose Amendments to this Constitution, or on the Application of the Legislatures of two thirds of the several States, shall call a Convention for proposing Amendments, which, in either Case, shall be valid to all Intents and Purposes, as Part of this Constitution, when ratified by the Legislatures of three fourths of the several States, or by Conventions in three fourths thereof, as the one or the other Mode of Ratification may be proposed by the Congress; Provided that no Amendment which may be made prior to the Year One thousand eight hundred and eight shall in any Manner affect the first and fourth Clauses in the Ninth Section of the first Article; and that no State, without its Consent, shall be deprived of its equal Suffrage in the Senate.

Article VI

All Debts contracted and Engagements entered into, before the Adoption of this Constitution, shall be as valid against the United States under this Constitution, as under the Confederation.

This Constitution, and the laws of the United States which shall be made in Pursuance thereof; and all Treaties made, or which shall be made, under the Authority of the United States, shall be the supreme Law of the Land; and the Judges in every State shall be bound thereby, any Thing in the Constitution or Laws of any State to the Contrary notwithstanding.

The Senators and Representatives before mentioned, and the Members of the several State Legislatures, and all executive and judicial Officers, both of the United States and of

---

9. Modified by the Eleventh Amendment.
10. Modified by the Eleventh Amendment.

11. Repealed by the Thirteenth Amendment.

the several States, shall be bound by Oath or Affirmation, to support this Constitution; but no religious Test shall ever be required as a Qualification to any Office or public Trust under the United States.

Article VII

The Ratification of the Conventions of nine States, shall be sufficient for the Establishment of this constitution between the States so ratifying the Same.

Done in Convention by the Unanimous Consent of the States present the Seventeenth Day of September in the Year of our Lord one thousand seven hundred and Eighty seven and of the Independence of the United States of America the Twelfth. IN WITNESS whereof we have hereunto subscribed our Names.

Go. WASHINGTON *Presid't. and deputy from Virginia*
Attest William Jackson *Secretary*
Delaware
Geo. Read
Gunning Bedford jun
John Dickinson
Richard Basset
Jaco. Broon
Massachusetts
Nathaniel Gorham
Rufus King
Connecticut
Wm. Saml. Johnson
Roger Sherman
New York
Alexander Hamilton
New Jersey
Wh. Livingston
David Brearley
Wm. Paterson
Jona. Dayton
Pennsylvania
B. Franklin
Thomas Mifflin
Robt. Morris
Geo. Clymer
Thos. FitzSimons
Jared Ingersol
James Wilson
Gouv Morris
Virginia
John Blair
James Madison Jr.
North Carolina
Wm. Blount
Richd. Dobbs Spaight
Hu Williamson

South Carolina
J. Rutledge
Charles Cotesworth Pinckney
Charles Pinckney
Pierce Butler
Georgia
William Few
Abr. Baldwin
New Hampshire
John Langdon
Nicholas Gilman
Maryland
James McHenry
Dan of St Thos. Jenifer
Danl. Carroll

Amendment I[12]

Congress shall make no law respecting an establishment of religion, or prohibiting the free exercise thereof; or abridging the freedom of speech, or of the press; or the right of the people peaceably to assemble, and to petition the Government for a redress of grievances.

Amendment II

A well regulated militia, being necessary to the security of a free State, the right of the people to keep and bear arms, shall not be infringed.

Amendment III

No Soldier shall, in time of peace be quartered in any house, without the consent of the owner, nor in time of war, but in a manner to be prescribed by law.

Amendment IV

The right of the people to be secure in their persons, houses, papers, and effects, against unreasonable searches and seizures, shall not be violated, and no warrants shall issue, but upon probable cause, supported by oath or affirmation, and particularly describing the place to be searched, and the persons or things to be seized.

Amendment V

No person shall be held to answer for a capital, or otherwise infamous crime, unless on a presentment or indictment of a Grand Jury, except in cases arising in the land or naval forces, or in the militia, when in actual service in time of war or public danger; nor shall any person be subject for the same offence to be twice put in jeopardy of life or limb; nor shall be compelled in any criminal case to be a witness against him-

---

12. The first ten amendments were passed by Congress on September 25, 1789, and were ratified on December 15, 1791.

self, nor be deprived of life, liberty, or property, without due process of law; nor shall private property be taken for public use, without just compensation.

Amendment VI

In all criminal prosecutions, the accused shall enjoy the right to a speedy and public trial, by an impartial jury of the State and district wherein the crime shall have been committed, which district shall have been previously ascertained by law, and to be informed of the nature and cause of the accusation; to be confronted with the witnesses against him; to have compulsory process for obtaining witnesses in his favor, and to have the assistance of counsel for his defence.

Amendment VII

In Suits at common law, where the value in controversy shall exceed twenty dollars, the right of trial by jury shall be preserved, and no fact tried by a jury, shall be otherwise re-examined in any Court of the United States, than according to the rules of the common law.

Amendment VIII

Excessive bail shall not be required, nor excessive fines imposed, nor cruel and unusual punishments inflicted.

Amendment IX

The enumeration in the Constitution, of certain rights, shall not be construed to deny or disparage others retained by the people.

Amendment X

The powers not delegated to the United States by the Constitution, nor prohibited by it to the States, are reserved to the States respectively, or to the people.

Amendment XI (Ratified February 7, 1795)

The Judicial power of the United States shall not be construed to extend to any suit in law or equity, commenced or prosecuted against one of the United States by Citizens of another State, or by Citizens or Subjects of any Foreign State.

Amendment XII (Ratified June 15, 1804)

The Electors shall meet in their respective states, and vote by ballot for President and Vice-President, one of whom, at least, shall not be an inhabitant of the same state with themselves; they shall name in their ballots the person voted for as President, and in distinct ballots the person voted for as Vice President, and they shall make distinct lists of all persons voted for as President, and of all persons voted for as Vice-President, and of the number of votes for each, which lists they shall sign and certify, and transmit sealed to the seat of the government of the United States, directed to the President of the Senate;—The President of the Senate shall, in the presence of the Senate and House of Representatives, open all the certificates and the votes shall then be counted;—The person having the greatest number of votes for President, shall be the President, if such number be a majority of the whole number of Electors appointed; and if no person have such majority, then from the persons having the highest numbers not exceeding three on the list of those voted for as President, the House of Representatives shall choose immediately, by ballot, the President. But in choosing the President, the votes shall be taken by states, the representation from each state having one vote; a quorum for this purpose shall consist of a member or members from two-thirds of the states, and a majority of all the states shall be necessary to a choice. [And if the House of Representatives shall not choose a President whenever the right of choice shall devolve upon them, before the fourth day of March next following, then the Vice-President shall act as President, as in the case of the death or other constitutional disability of the President.][13]—The person having the greatest number of votes as Vice-President, shall be the Vice-President, if such number be a majority of the whole number of Electors appointed, and if no person have a majority, then from the two highest numbers on the list, the Senate shall choose the Vice-President; a quorum for the purpose shall consist of two-thirds of the whole number of Senators, and a majority of the whole number shall be necessary to a choice. But no person constitutionally ineligible to the office of President shall be eligible to that of Vice-President of the United States.

Amendment XIII (Ratified on December 6, 1865)

Section 1. Neither slavery nor involuntary servitude, except as a punishment for crime whereof the party shall have been duly convicted, shall exist within the United States, or any place subject to their jurisdiction.

Section 2. Congress shall have power to enforce this article by appropriate legislation.

Amendment XIV (Ratified on July 9, 1868)

Section 1. All persons born or naturalized in the United States, and subject to the jurisdiction thereof, are citizens of the United States and of the State wherein they reside. No State shall make or enforce any law which shall abridge the privileges or immunities of citizens of the United States; nor shall any State deprive any person of life, liberty, or property, without due process of law; nor deny to any person within its jurisdiction the equal protection of the laws.

---

13. Changed by the Twentieth Amendment.

Section 2. Representatives shall be apportioned among the several States according to their respective numbers, counting the whole number of persons in each State, excluding Indians not taxed. But when the right to vote at any election for the choice of electors for President and Vice President of the United States, Representatives in Congress, the Executive and Judicial officers of a State, or the members of the Legislature thereof, is denied to any of the male inhabitants of such State, being [twenty-one][14] years of age, and citizens of the United States, or in any way abridged, except for participation in rebellion, or other crime, the basis of representation therein shall be reduced in the proportion which the number of such male citizens shall bear to the whole number of male citizens twenty-one years of age in such State.

Section 3. No person shall be a Senator or Representative in Congress, or elector of President and Vice President, or hold any office, civil or military, under the United States, or under any State, who having previously taken an oath, as a member of Congress, or as an officer of the United States, or as a member of any State legislature, or as an executive or judicial officer of any State, to support the Constitution of the United States, shall have engaged in insurrection or rebellion against the same, or given aid or comfort to the enemies thereof. But Congress may by a vote of two-thirds of each House, remove such disability.

Section 4. The validity of the public debt of the United States, authorized by law, including debts incurred for payment of pensions and bounties for services in suppressing insurrection or rebellion, shall not be questioned. But neither the United States nor any State shall assume or pay any debt or obligation incurred in aid of insurrection or rebellion against the United States, or any claim for the loss or emancipation of any slave, but all such debts, obligations and claims shall be held illegal and void.

Section 5. The Congress shall have power to enforce, by appropriate legislation, the provisions of this article.

Amendment XV
(Ratified on February 3, 1870)

Section 1. The right of citizens of the United States to vote shall not be denied or abridged by the United States or by any State on account of race, color, or previous condition of servitude.

Section 2. The Congress shall have power to enforce this article by appropriate legislation.

Amendment XVI
(Ratified on February 3, 1913)

The Congress shall have power to lay and collect taxes on incomes, from whatever source derived, without apportionment among the several States, and without regard to any census or enumeration.

Amendment XVII
(Ratified on April 8, 1913)

The Senate of the United States shall be composed of two Senators from each State, elected by the people thereof, for six years; and each Senator shall have one vote. The electors in each State shall have the qualifications requisite for electors of the most numerous branch of the State legislatures.

When vacancies happen in the representation of any State in the Senate, the executive authority of such State shall issue writs of election to fill such vacancies: Provided, That the legislature of any State may empower the executive thereof to make temporary appointments until the people fill the vacancies by election as the legislature may direct.

This amendment shall not be so construed as to affect the election or term of any Senator chosen before it becomes valid as part of the Constitution.

Amendment XVIII
(Ratified on January 16, 1919)

Section 1. After one year from the ratification of this article the manufacture, sale, or transportation of intoxicating liquors within, the importation thereof into, or the exportation thereof from the United States and all territory subject to the jurisdiction thereof for beverage purposes is hereby prohibited.

Section 2. The Congress and the several States shall have concurrent power to enforce this article by appropriate legislation.

Section 3. This article shall be inoperative unless it shall have been ratified as an amendment to the Constitution by the legislatures of the several States, as provided in the Constitution, within seven years from the date of the submission hereof to the States by the Congress.[15]

Amendment XIX
(Ratified on August 18, 1920)

The right of citizens of the United States to vote shall not be denied or abridged by the United States or by any State on account of sex.

Congress shall have power to enforce this article by appropriate legislation.

Amendment XX
(Ratified on January 23, 1933)

Section 1. The terms of the President and Vice President shall end at noon on the 20th day of January, and the terms of Senators and Representatives at noon on the 3rd day of January, of the years in which such terms would have ended

---

14. Changed by the Twenty-sixth Amendment.

15. The Eighteenth Amendment was repealed by the Twenty-first Amendment.

if this article had not been ratified, and the terms of their successors shall then begin.

Section 2. The Congress shall assemble at least once in every year, and such meeting shall begin at noon on the 3rd day of January, unless they shall by law appoint a different day.

Section 3. If, at the time fixed for the beginning of the term of the President, the President elect shall have died, the Vice President elect shall become President. If a President shall not have been chosen before the time fixed for the beginning of his term, or if the President elect shall have failed to qualify, then the Vice President elect shall act as President until a President shall have qualified; and the Congress may by law provide for the case wherein neither a President elect nor a Vice President elect shall have qualified, declaring who shall then act as President, or the manner in which one who is to act shall be selected, and such person shall act accordingly until a President or Vice President shall have qualified.

Section 4. The Congress may by law provide for the case of the death of any of the persons from whom the House of Representatives may choose a President whenever the rights of choice shall have devolved upon them, and for the case of the death of any of the persons from whom the Senate may choose a Vice President whenever the right of choice shall have devolved upon them.

Section 5. Sections 1 and 2 shall take effect on the 15th day of October following the ratification of this article.

Section 6. This article shall be inoperative unless it shall have been ratified as an amendment to the Constitution by the legislatures of three-fourths of the several States within seven years from the date of its submission.

Amendment XXI
(Ratified on December 5, 1933)

Section 1. The eighteenth article of amendment to the Constitution of the United States is hereby repealed.

Section 2. The transportation or importation into any State, Territory, or possession of the United States for delivery or use therein of intoxicating liquors, in violation of the laws thereof, is hereby prohibited.

Section 3. This article shall be inoperative unless it shall have been ratified as an amendment to the Constitution by conventions in the several States, as provided in the Constitution, within seven years from the date of the submission hereof to the States by the Congress.

Amendment XXII
(Ratified on February 27, 1951)

No person shall be elected to the office of the President more than twice, and no person who has held the office of President, or acted as President, for more than two years of a term to which some other person was elected President shall be elected to the office of the President more than once. But

this Article shall not apply to any person holding the office of President when this Article was proposed by the Congress, and shall not prevent any person who may be holding the office of President, or acting as President, during the term within which this Article becomes operative from holding the office of President or acting as President during the remainder of such term.

Amendment XXIII
(Ratified on March 29, 1961)

Section 1. The District constituting the seat of Government of the United States shall appoint in such manner as the Congress may direct:

A number of electors of President and Vice President equal to the whole number of Senators and Representatives in Congress to which the District would be entitled if it were a State, but in no event more than the least populous State; they shall be in addition to those appointed by the States, but they shall be considered, for the purposes of the election of President and Vice President, to be electors appointed by a State; and they shall meet in the District and perform such duties as provided by the twelfth article of amendment.

Section 2. The Congress shall have power to enforce this article by appropriate legislation.

Amendment XXIV
(Ratified on January 23, 1964)

Section 1. The right of citizens of the United States to vote in any primary or other election for President or Vice President, for electors for President or Vice President, or for Senator or Representative in Congress, shall not be denied or abridged by the United States or any State by reason of failure to pay any poll tax or other tax.

Section 2. The Congress shall have power to enforce this article by appropriate legislation.

Amendment XXV
(Ratified on February 10, 1967)

Section 1. In case of the removal of the President from office or of his death or resignation, the Vice President shall become President.

Section 2. Whenever there is a vacancy in the office of the Vice President, the President shall nominate a Vice President who shall take office upon confirmation by a majority vote of both Houses of Congress.

Section 3. Whenever the President transmits to the President pro tempore of the Senate and the Speaker of the House of Representatives his written declaration that he is unable to discharge the powers and duties of his office, and until he transmits to them a written declaration to the contrary, such powers and duties shall be discharged by the Vice President as Acting President.

Section 4. Whenever the Vice President and a majority of either the principal officers of the executive departments or of such other body as Congress may by law provide, transmit to the President pro tempore of the Senate and the Speaker of the House of Representatives their written declaration that the President is unable to discharge the powers and duties of his office, the Vice President shall immediately assume the powers and duties of the offices as Acting President.

Thereafter, when the President transmits to the President pro tempore of the Senate and the Speaker of the House of Representatives his written declaration that no inability exists, he shall resume the powers and duties of his office unless the Vice President and a majority of either the principal officers of the executive department or of such other body as Congress may by law provide, transmit within four days to the President pro tempore of the Senate and the Speaker of the House of Representatives their written declaration that the President is unable to discharge the powers and duties of his office. Thereupon Congress shall decide the issue, assembling within forty-eight hours for that purpose if not in session. If the Congress, within twenty-one days after receipt of the latter written declaration, or, if Congress is not in session, within twenty-one days after Congress is required to assemble, determines by two-thirds vote of both Houses that the President is unable to discharge the powers and duties of his office, the Vice President shall continue to discharge the same as Acting President; otherwise; the President shall resume the powers and duties of his office.

Amendment XXVI
(Ratified on July 1, 1971)

Section 1. The right of citizens of the United States, who are eighteen years of age or older, to vote shall not be denied or abridged by the United States or by any State on account of age.

Section 2. The Congress shall have the power to enforce this article by appropriate legislation.

Amendment XXVII
(Ratified on May 7, 1992)

No law, varying the compensation for the services of the Senators and Representatives, shall take effect, until an election of Representatives shall have intervened.

→ Read for Chapter 2

Faction Definition ↓

Must preserve individuals liberty).

Among the numerous advantages promised by a well-constructed Union, none deserves to be more accurately developed than its tendency to break and control the violence of faction. The friend of popular governments never finds himself so much alarmed for their character and fate as when he contemplates their propensity to this dangerous vice. He will not fail, therefore, to set a due value on any plan which, without violating the principles to which he is attached, provides a proper cure for it. The instability, injustice, and confusion introduced into the public councils have, in truth, been the mortal diseases under which popular governments have everywhere perished, as they continue to be the favorite and fruitful topics from which the adversaries to liberty derive their most specious declamations. The valuable improvements made by the American constitutions on the popular models, both ancient and modern, cannot certainly be too much admired; but it would be an unwarrantable partiality to contend that they have as effectually obviated the danger on this side, as was wished and expected. Complaints are everywhere heard from our most considerate and virtuous citizens, equally the friends of public and private faith and of public and personal liberty, that our governments are too unstable, that the public good is disregarded in the conflicts of rival parties, and that measures are too often decided, not according to the rules of justice and the rights of the minor party, but by the superior force of an interested and overbearing majority. However anxiously we may wish that these complaints had no foundation, the evidence of known facts will not permit us to deny that they are in some degree true. It will be found, indeed, on a candid review of our situation, that some of the distresses under which we labor have been erroneously charged on the operation of our governments; but it will be found, at the same time, that other causes will not alone account for many of our heaviest misfortunes; and, particularly, for that prevailing and increasing distrust of public engagements and alarm for private rights which are echoed from one end of the continent to the other. These must be chiefly, if not wholly, effects of the unsteadiness and injustice with which a factious spirit has tainted our public administration.

By a faction I understand a number of citizens, whether amounting to a majority or minority of the whole, who are united and actuated by some common impulse of passion, or of interest, adverse to the rights of other citizens, or the permanent and aggregate interests of the community.

There are two methods of curing the mischiefs of faction: the one, by removing its causes; the other, by controlling its effects.

There are again two methods of removing the causes of faction: the one, by destroying the liberty which is essential to its existence; the other, by giving to every citizen the same opinions, the same passions, and the same interests.

It could never be more truly said than of the first remedy that it was worse than the disease. Liberty is to faction what air is to fire, an aliment without which it instantly expires. But it could not be a less folly to abolish liberty, which is essential to political life, because it nourishes faction than it would be to wish the annihilation of air, which is essential to animal life, because it imparts to fire its destructive agency.

The second expedient is as impracticable as the first would be unwise. As long as the reason of man continues fallible, and his is at liberty to exercise it, different opinions will be formed. As long as the connection subsists between his reason and his self-love, his opinions and his passions will have a reciprocal influence on each other; and the former will be objects to which the latter will attach themselves. The diversity in the faculties of men, from which the rights of property originate, is not less an insuperable obstacle to a uniformity of interests. The protection of these faculties is the first object of government. From the protection of different and unequal faculties of acquiring property, the possession of different degrees and kinds of property immediately results; and from the influence of these on the sentiments and views of the respective proprietors ensues a division of the society into different interests and parties.

Faculties → Differ in intelligence

The latent causes of faction are thus sown in the nature of man; and we see them everywhere brought into different degrees of activity, according to the different circumstances of civil society. A zeal for different opinions concerning religion, concerning government, and many other points, as well of speculation as of practice; an attachment to different leaders ambitiously contending for preeminence and power; or to persons of other descriptions whose fortunes have been interesting to the human passions, have, in turn, divided mankind into parties, inflamed them with mutual animosity, and rendered them much more disposed to vex and oppress each other than to cooperate for their common good. So strong is this propensity of mankind to fall into mutual animosities that where no substantial occasion presents itself the most frivolous and fanciful distinctions have been sufficient to kindle their unfriendly passions and excite their most violent conflicts. But the most common and durable source of factions has been the various and unequal distribution of property. Those who hold and those who are without property have ever formed distinct interests in society. Those who are creditors, and those who are debtors, fall under a like discrimination. A landed interest, a manufacturing interest, a mercantile interest, a moneyed interest, with many lesser interests, grow up of necessity in civilized nations, and divide them into different classes, actuated by different sentiments and views. The regulation of these various and interfering interests forms the principal task of modern legislation and involves the spirit of party and faction in the necessary and ordinary operations of government.

No man is allowed to be a judge in his own cause, because his interest would certainly bias his judgment, and, not improbably, corrupt his integrity. With equal, nay with greater reason, a body of men are unfit to be both judges and parties at the same time; yet what are many of the most important acts of legislation but so many judicial determinations, not indeed concerning the rights of single persons, but concerning the rights of large bodies of citizens? And what are the different classes of legislators but advocates and parties to the causes which they determine? Is a law proposed concerning private debts? It is a question to which the creditors are parties on one side and the debtors on the other. Justice ought to hold the balance between them. Yet the parties are, and must be, themselves the judges; and the most numerous party, or in other words, the most powerful faction must be expected to prevail. Shall domestic manufacturers be encouraged, and in what degree, by restrictions on foreign manufacturers? are questions which would be differently decided by the landed and the manufacturing classes, and probably by neither with a sole regard to justice and the public good. The apportionment of taxes on the various descriptions of property is an act which seems to require the most exact impartiality; yet there is, perhaps, no legislative act in which greater opportunity

and temptation are given to a predominant party to trample on the rules of justice. Every shilling with which they overburden the inferior number is a shilling saved to their own pockets. It is in vain to say that enlightened statesmen will be able to adjust these clashing interests and render them all subservient to the public good. Enlightened statesmen will not always be at the helm. Nor, in many cases, can such an adjustment be made at all without taking into view indirect and remote considerations, which will rarely prevail over the immediate interest which one party may find in disregarding the rights of another or the good of the whole.

The inference to which we are brought is that the *causes* of faction cannot be removed and that relief is only to be sought in the means of controlling its *effects*.

If a faction consists of less than a majority, relief is supplied by the republican principle, which enables the majority to defeat its sinister views by regular vote. It may clog the administration, it may convulse the society; but it will be unable to execute and mask its violence under the forms of the Constitution. When a majority is included in a faction, the form of popular government, on the other hand, enables it to sacrifice to its ruling passion or interest both the public good and the rights of other citizens. To secure the public good and private rights against the danger of such a faction, and at the same time to preserve the spirit and the form of popular government, is then the great object to which our inquiries are directed. Let me add that it is the great desideratum by which alone this form of government can be rescued from the opprobrium under which it has so long labored and be recommended to the esteem and adoption of mankind.

By what means is this object attainable? Evidently by one of two only. Either the existence of the same passion or interest in a majority at the same time must be prevented, or the majority, having such coexistent passion or interest, must be rendered, by their number and local situation, unable to concert and carry into effect schemes of oppression. If the impulse and the opportunity be suffered to coincide, we well know that neither moral nor religious motives can be relied on as an adequate control. They are not found to be such on the injustice and violence of individuals, and lose their efficacy in proportion to the number combined together, that is, in proportion as their efficacy becomes needful.

From this view of the subject it may be concluded that a pure democracy, by which I mean a society consisting of a small number of citizens, who assemble and administer the government in person, can admit of no cure for the mischiefs of faction. A common passion or interest will, in almost every case, be felt by a majority of the whole; a communication and concert results from the form of government itself; and there is nothing to check the inducements to sacrifice the weaker party or an obnoxious individual. Hence it is that such democracies have ever been spectacles of turbulence and contention; have ever been found incompatible with personal security or the rights of property; and have in general been as short in their lives as they have been violent in their deaths. Theoretic politicians, who have patronized this species of government, have erroneously supposed that by reducing mankind to a perfect equality in their political rights, they would at the same time be perfectly equalized and assimilated in their possessions, their opinions, and their passions.

A republic, by which I mean a government in which the scheme of representation takes place, opens a different prospect and promises the cure for which we are seeking. Let us examine the points in which it varies from pure democracy, and we shall comprehend both the nature of the cure and the efficacy which it must derive from the Union.

The two great points of difference between a democracy and a republic are: first, the delegation of the government, in the latter, to a small number of citizens elected by the rest; secondly, the greater number of citizens and greater sphere of country over which the latter may be extended.

The effect of the first difference is, on the one hand, to refine and enlarge the public views by passing them through the medium of a chosen body of citizens, whose wisdom may best discern the true interest of their country and whose patriotism and love of justice will be least likely to sacrifice it to temporary or partial considerations. Under such a regulation it may well happen that the public voice, pronounced by the representatives of the people, will be more consonant to the public good than if pronounced by the people themselves, convened for the purpose. On the other hand, the effect may be inverted. Men of factious tempers, of local prejudices, or of sinister designs, may, by intrigue, by corruption, or by other means, first obtain the suffrages, and then betray the interests of the people. The question resulting is, whether small or extensive republics are most favorable to the election of proper guardians of the public weal; and it is clearly decided in favor of the latter by two obvious considerations.

In the first place it is to be remarked that however small the republic may be the representatives must be raised to a certain number in order to guard against the cabals of a few; and that however large it may be they must be limited to a certain number in order to guard against the confusion of a multitude. Hence, the number of representatives in the two cases not being in proportion to that of the constituents, and being proportionally greatest in the small republic, it follows that if the proportion of fit characters be not less in the large than in the small republic, the former will present a greater option, and consequently a greater probability of a fit choice.

In the next place, as each representative will be chosen by a greater number of citizens in the large than in the small republic, it will be more difficult for unworthy candidates to practice with success the vicious arts by which elections are too often carried; and the suffrages of the people being more free, will be more likely to center on men who possess the most attractive merit and the most diffusive and established characters.

It must be confessed that in this, as in most other cases, there is a mean, on both sides of which inconveniencies will be found to lie. By enlarging too much the number of electors, you render the representative too little acquainted with all their local circumstances and lesser interests; as by reducing it too much, you render him unduly attached to these, and too little fit to comprehend and pursue great and national objects. The federal Constitution forms a happy combination in this respect; the great and aggregate interests being referred to the national, the local and particular to the State legislatures.

The other point of difference is the greater number of citizens and extent of territory which may be brought within the compass of republican than of democratic government; and it is this circumstance principally which renders factious combinations less to be dreaded in the former than in the latter. The smaller the society, the fewer probably will be the distinct parties and interests composing it; the fewer the distinct parties and interests, the more frequently will a majority be found of the same party; and the smaller the number of individuals composing a majority, and the smaller the compass within which they are placed, the more easily will they concert and execute their plans of oppression. Extend the sphere and you take in a greater variety of parties and interests; you make it less probable that a majority of the whole will have a common motive to invade the rights of other citizens; or if such a common motive exists, it will be more difficult for all who feel it to discover their own strength and to act in unison with each other. Besides other impediments, it may be remarked that, where there is a consciousness of unjust or dishonorable purposes, communication is always checked by distrust in proportion to the number whose concurrence is necessary.

Hence, it clearly appears that the same advantage which a republic has over a democracy in controlling the effects of faction is enjoyed by a large over a small republic—is enjoyed by the Union over the States composing it. Does this advantage consist in the substitution of representatives whose enlightened views and virtuous sentiments render them superior to local prejudices and to schemes of injustice? It will not be denied that the representation of the Union will be most likely to possess these requisite endowments. Does it consist in the greater security afforded by a greater variety of parties, against the event of any one party being able to outnumber and oppress the rest? In an equal degree does the increased variety of parties comprised within the Union increase this security. Does it, in fine, consist in the greater obstacles opposed to the concert and accomplishment of the secret wishes of an unjust and interested majority? Here again the extent of the Union gives it the most palpable advantage.

The influence of factious leaders may kindle a flame within their particular States but will be unable to spread a general conflagration through the other States. A religious sect may degenerate into a political faction in a part of the Confederacy; but the variety of sects dispersed over the entire face of it must secure the national councils against any danger from that source. A rage for paper money, for an abolition of debts, for an equal division of property, or for any other improper or wicked project, will be less apt to pervade the whole body of the Union than a particular member of it, in the same proportion as such a malady is more likely to taint a particular county or district than an entire State.

In the extent and proper structure of the Union, therefore, we behold a republican remedy for the diseases most incident to republican government. And according to the degree of pleasure and pride we feel in being republicans ought to be our zeal in cherishing the spirit and supporting the character of federalists.

To what expedient, then, shall we finally resort, for maintaining in practice the necessary partition of power among the several departments as laid down in the Constitution? The only answer that can be given is that as all these exterior provisions are found to be inadequate the defect must be supplied, by so contriving the interior structure of the government as that its several constituent parts may, by their mutual relations, be the means of keeping each other in their proper places. Without presuming to undertake a full development of this important idea I will hazard a few general observations which may perhaps place it in a clearer light, and enable us to form a more correct judgment of the principles and structure of the government planned by the convention.

In order to lay a due foundation for that separate and distinct exercise of the different powers of government, which to a certain extent is admitted on all hands to be essential to the preservation of liberty, it is evident that each department should have a will of its own; and consequently should be so constituted that the members of each should have as little agency as possible in the appointment of the members of the others. Were this principle rigorously adhered to, it would require that all the appointments for the supreme executive, legislative, and judiciary magistracies should be drawn from the same fountain of authority, the people, through channels having no communication whatever with one another. Perhaps such a plan of constructing the several departments would be less difficult in practice than it may in contemplation appear. Some difficulties, however, and some additional expense would attend the execution of it. Some deviations, therefore, from the principle must be admitted. In the constitution of the judiciary department in particular, it might be inexpedient to insist rigorously on the principle: first, because peculiar qualifications being essential in the members, the primary consideration ought to be to select that mode of choice which best secures these qualifications; second, because the permanent tenure by which the appointments are held in that department must soon destroy all sense of dependence on the authority conferring them.

It is equally evident that the members of each department should be as little dependent as possible on those of the others for the emoluments annexed to their offices. Were the executive magistrate, or the judges, not independent of the legislature in this particular, their independence in every other would be merely nominal.

But the great security against a gradual concentration of the several powers in the same department consists in giving to those who administer each department the necessary constitutional means and personal motives to resist encroachments of the others. The provision for defense must in this, as in all other cases, be made commensurate to the danger of attack. Ambition must be made to counteract ambition. The interest of the man must be connected with the constitutional rights of the place. It may be a reflection on human nature that such devices should be necessary to control the abuses of government. But what is government itself but the greatest of all reflections on human nature? If men were angels, no government would be necessary. If angels were to govern men, neither external nor internal controls on government would be necessary. In framing a government which is to be administered by men over men, the great difficulty lies in this: you must first enable the government to control the governed; and in the next place oblige it to control itself. A dependence on the people is, no doubt, the primary control on the government; but experience has taught mankind the necessity of auxiliary precautions.

This policy of supplying, by opposite and rival interests, the defect of better motives, might be traced through the whole system of human affairs, private as well as public. We see it particularly displayed in all the subordinate distributions of power, where the constant aim is to divide and arrange the several offices in such a manner as that each may be a check on the other—that the private interest of every individual may be a sentinel over the public rights. These inventions of prudence cannot be less requisite in the distribution of the supreme powers of the State.

But it is not possible to give to each department an equal power of self-defense. In republican government, the legislative authority necessarily predominates. The remedy for this inconveniency is to divide the legislature into different branches; and to render them, by different modes of election and different principles of action, as little connected with each other as the nature of their common functions and their common dependence on the society will admit. It may even be necessary to guard against dangerous encroachments by still further precautions. As the weight of the legislative authority requires that it should be thus divided, the weakness of the executive may require, on the other hand, that it should be fortified. An absolute negative on the legislature appears, at first view, to be the natural defense with which the executive magistrate should be armed. But perhaps it would be neither altogether safe nor alone sufficient. On ordinary occasions it might not be exerted with the requisite firmness, and on extraordinary occasions it might be perfidiously abused. May not this defect of an absolute negative be supplied by some qualified connection between this weaker department and the weaker branch of the stronger department, by which the latter may be led to support the constitutional rights of the former, without being too much detached from the rights of its own department?

If the principles on which these observations are found be just, as I persuade myself they are, and they be applied as a criterion to the several State constitutions, and the federal Constitution, it will be found that if the latter does not perfectly correspond with them, the former are infinitely less able to bear such a test.

There are, moreover, two considerations particularly applicable to the federal system of America, which place that system in a very interesting point of view.

First. In a single republic, all the power surrendered by the people is submitted to the administration of a single government; and the usurpations are guarded against by a division of the government into distinct and separate departments. In the compound republic of America, the power surrendered by the people is first divided between two distinct governments, and then the portion allotted to each subdivided among distinct and separate departments. Hence a double security arises to the rights of the people. The different governments will control each other, at the same time that each will be controlled by itself.

Second. It is of great importance in a republic not only to guard the society against the oppression of its rulers, but to guard one part of the society against the injustice of the other part. Different interests necessarily exist in different classes of citizens. If a majority be united by a common interest, the rights of the minority will be insecure. There are but two methods of providing against this evil: the one by creating a will in the community independent of the majority—that is, of the society itself; the other, by comprehending in the society so many separate descriptions of citizens as will render an unjust combination of a majority of the whole very improbable, if not impracticable. The first method prevails in all governments possessing an hereditary or self-appointed authority. This, at best, is but a precarious security; because a power independent of the society may as well espouse the unjust views of the major as the rightful interests of the minor party, and may possibly be turned against both parties. The second method will be exemplified in the federal republic of the United States. Whilst all authority in it will be derived from and dependent on the society, the society itself will be broken into so many parts, interests and classes of citizens, that the rights of individuals, or of the minority, will be in little danger from interested combinations of the majority. In a free government the security for civil rights must be the same as that for religious rights. It consists in the one case in the multiplicity of interests, and in the other in the multiplicity of sects. The degree of security in both cases will depend on the number of interests and sects; and this may be presumed to depend on the extent of country and number of people comprehended under the same government. This view of the subject must particularly recommend a proper federal system to all the sincere and considerate friends of republican government, since it shows that in exact proportion as the territory of the Union may be formed into more circumscribed Confederacies, or States, oppressive combinations of a majority will be facilitated; the best security, under the republican forms, for the rights of every class of citizen, will be diminished; and consequently the stability and independence of some member of the government, the only other security, must be proportionally increased. Justice is the end of government. It is the end of civil society. It ever has been and ever will be pursued until it be obtained, or until liberty be lost in the pursuit. In a society under the forms of which the stronger faction can readily unite and oppress the weaker, anarchy may as truly be said to reign as in a state of nature, where the weaker individual is not secured against the violence of the stronger; and as, in the latter state, even the stronger individuals are prompted, by the uncertainty of their condition, to submit to a government which may protect the weak as well as themselves; so, in the former state, will the more powerful factions or parties be gradually induced, by a like motive, to wish for a government which will protect all parties, the weaker as well as the more powerful. It can be little doubted that if the State of Rhode Island was separated from the Confederacy and left to itself, the insecurity of rights under the popular form of government within such narrow limits would be displayed by such reiterated oppressions of factious majorities that some power altogether independent of the people would soon be called for by the voice of the very factions whose misrule had proved the necessity of it. In the extended republic of the United States, and among the great variety of interests, parties, and sects which it embraces, a coalition of a majority of the whole society could seldom take place on any other principles than those of justice and the general good; whilst there being thus less danger to a minor from the will of a major party, there must be less pretext, also, to provide for the security of the former, by introducing into the government a will not dependent on the latter, or, in other words, a will independent of the society itself. It is no less certain than it is important, notwithstanding the contrary opinions which have been entertained, that the larger the society, provided it lie within a practicable sphere, the more duly capable it will be of self-government. And happily for the republican cause, the practicable sphere may be carried to a very great extent by a judicious modification and mixture of the federal principle.

ABRAHAM LINCOLN'S GETTYSBURG ADDRESS

Four score and seven years ago our fathers brought forth on this continent a new nation, conceived in liberty and dedicated to the proposition that all men are created equal. Now we are engaged in a great Civil War, testing whether that nation or any nation so conceived and so dedicated can long endure. We are met on a great battlefield of that war. We have come to dedicate a portion of that field as a final resting place for those who here gave their lives that that nation might live. It is altogether fitting and proper that we should do this. But in a larger sense, we cannot dedicate—we cannot consecrate—we cannot hallow this ground. The brave men, living and dead, who struggled here have consecrated it far above our poor power to add or detract. The world will little note nor long remember what we say here, but it can never forget what they did here. It is for us the living, rather, to be dedicated here to the unfinished work which they who fought here have thus far so nobly advanced. It is rather for us to be here dedicated to the great task remaining before us—that from these honored dead we take increased devotion to that cause for which they gave the last full measure of devotion—that we here highly resolve that these dead shall not have died in vain, that this nation, under God, shall have a new birth of freedom, and that government of the people, by the people, for the people shall not perish from the earth.

NOTES

Chapter 1

[1]Claudia Kolb, "In Our Blood," *Newsweek,* February 6, 2006, 55; "Man as 'Black' for 50 Years Finds Out He's Probably Not," http://www.chinadaily.com.cn/en/doc/2003-12/29/content_294229.htm.

[2]See John Hibbing and Beth Theiss-Morse, *Congress as Public Enemy: Public Attitudes toward American Political Institutions* (Cambridge, England: Cambridge University Press, 1995); John Hibbing and Beth Theiss-Morse, "Civics Is Not Enough: Teaching Barbarics in K–12," *PS,* March 1996, 57–62.

[3]Hibbing and Theiss-Morse, *Congress.*

[4]Michael Kinsley, "In Defense of Partisan Bickering," *Time,* February 5, 2007, 41.

[5]Ibid.

[6]In the view of many political scientists, the term *politics* encompasses a wider spectrum than actions directed toward government policy; it applies to all power relationships and to all attempts to influence the distribution of resources in the private sphere as well.

[7]Gore Vidal, "Coached by Camelot," *New Yorker,* December 1, 1997, 88.

[8]Walt Whitman, Preface to *Leaves of Grass* (1855), in *Leaves of Grass and Selected Prose,* ed. Lawrence Buell (New York: Random House, 1981), 449.

[9]Edward Countryman, *Americans: A Collision of Histories* (New York: Hill & Wang, 1996).

[10]As noted by historian Carl Wittke. John Elson, "The Great Migration," *Time,* Fall, 1983, 28.

[11]John Sugden, *Tecumseh: A Life* (New York: Holt, 1998).

[12]This system has undergone considerable tinkering, including an amnesty that gave permanent residency to 2.6 million illegal residents between 1989 and 1992.

[13]Jessica Mintz, "Limited Time Offer," *Lincoln Journal Star,* April 8, 2007, F1.

[14]*2004 Yearbook of Immigration Statistics* (Washington, D.C.: Department of Homeland Security, 2004), tab. 3 (uscis.gov).

[15]Rachel L. Swarns, "Republican Split on Immigration Reflects Nation's Struggle," *New York Times,* March 29, 2006, 1; U.S. Census Bureau, "The Foreign-Born Population in the United States: 2003" (report issued August 2004) (www.census.gov).

[16]For many years, the flag was not flown in battle or over government buildings or public schools.

[17]The Spanish-American War and World War I also gave a boost to efforts to use the flag as a symbol.

[18]James Q. Wilson, "The History and Future of Democracy," lecture delivered at the Ronald Reagan Presidential Library, November 15, 1999.

[19]"Religion and the Founding of the American Republic. Part I: America as a Religious Refuge: The Seventeenth Century," Library of Congress exhibit (lcweb.loc.gov/exhibits/religion).

[20]Michael J. Sandel, *Democracy's Discontent: America in Search of a Public Philosophy* (Cambridge, Mass.: Belknap Press, 1997), 56–57.

[21]Sarah Mondale and Sarah B. Patton, eds., *School: The Story of American Public Education* (Boston: Beacon Press, 2001), 36.

[22]Elizabeth Becker, "All White, All Christian, and Divided by Diversity," *New York Times,* June 10, 2001, sec. 4, 7. Becker was writing about her hometown.

[23]Census Bureau, *U.S. Statistical Abstract, 2006,* tab. 69, 58. These numbers are derived from self-reports because the Census Bureau does not collect data on religious affiliation. The number of Muslims in the United States is variously stated as from 1 to 8 million. The higher estimates are from Muslim clergy.

[24]Alan Cowell, "After a Century," an American Writer's Library Will Go to America," *New York Times,* December 15, 2005.

[25]On identity politics, see Walter Benn Michaels, *Our America: Nativism, Modernism, and Pluralism* (Durham, N.C.: Duke University Press, 1997).

[26]Felicity Barringer, "Ethnic Pride Confounds the Census," *New York Times,* May 9, 1993, E3.

[27]Jack Hitt, "The Newest Indians," *New York Times Magazine,* August 21, 2005, 38.

[28]ABC Evening News with Peter Jennings, February 21, 2005.

[29][no author] "Survey: Hispanics Reject Cohesive Group Identity," *Lincoln Journal,* December 15, 1992.

[30]Darryl Fears, "The Power of a Label," *Washington Post National Weekly Edition,* September 1, 2003, 29.

[31]Lynne Duke, "English Spoken Here," *Washington Post National Weekly Edition,* December 21, 1992, 37.

[32]U.S. Census Bureau, *General Social and Economic Characteristics: U.S. Summary* (Washington, D.C.: Government Printing Office, 1990), pt. 1, tab. 12.

[33]Census Bureau, *Statistical Abstract, 2005,* tab. 54.

[34]Gregory Rodriguez, "Mongrel America," *Atlantic Monthly,* January-February, 2003, 96.

[35]Michael Lind, "The Beige and the Black," *New York Times Magazine,* August 16, 1998, 38; Randall Kennedy, Interracial Intimacies (New York: Pantheon, 2003).

[36]According to sociologists Zhenchao Qian and Daniel Lichter. Jeff Gammage, "Immigration Changes the Mating Game," *Lincoln Journal Star,* April 3, 2007, 8A.

[37]The origins of governmental systems are discussed by John Jay in *Federalist Paper 2.*

[38]Garry Wills, *Lincoln at Gettysburg: The Words That Remade America* (New York: Simon & Schuster, 1992), 145.

[39]Carl F. Kaestle, "Introduction," in *School,* ed. Mondale and Patton, 13.

[40]Ibid., 16.

[41]"The Educated Citizen," in *School,* ed. Mondale and Patton, 22.

[42]Ibid.

[43]Adam Cohen, "According to Webster: One Man's Attempt to Define 'America,'" *New York Times,* February 12, 2006, Sec. 4, 13.

[44]Noah Webster quoted in Jack Lynch, "Dr. Johnson's Revolution," *New York Times,* July 2, 2005.

[45]Michael Thompson, Richard Ellis, and Aaron Wildavsky, *Cultural Theory* (Boulder, Colo.: Westview, 1990), 216.

[46]Seymour Martin Lipset, "Why No Socialism in the United States?" in Seweryn Bialer and Sophis Sluzar, eds., *Sources of Contemporary Radicalism* (Boulder, Colo: Westview, 1977), 86.

[47]For an examination of the theory of path dependence and a persuasive argument that the views of early immigrants affect the views of today's Americans, see John W. Kingdon, *America, the Unusual* (Boston: Bedford/St. Martin's, 1999).

[48]The writings of Thomas Hobbes also shaped this belief. Hobbes wrote that individuals give some rights they would have in "a state of nature" to government in exchange for government protection of their remaining rights.

[49]Survey conducted by Peter D. Hart and Robert Teeter for the Council for Excellence in Government in 1999 and cited in David S. Broder, "Where Did Our Government Go?" *Washington Post National Weekly Edition,* July 19–26, 1999, 37.

[50]For the parallels between a country's emphasis on individual liberty and its deemphasis upon government help for less fortunate or successful citizens, see Kingdon, *America, the Unusual.*

[51]Wilfred M. McClay, "Communitarianism and the Federal Idea," in *Community and Political Thought Today,* Peter Augustine Lawler and Dale McConkey, eds. (Westport, Conn.: Praeger, 1998), 102.

[52]President Johnson quoted in Tim Funk, "Civil Rights Act of 1964 Paved Way for Prosperity," *Champaign-Urbana News Gazette,* July 11, 2004, B1.

[53]Alexis de Tocqueville, *Democracy in America* (New York: Knopf, 1945; originally published 1835).

[54]See Michael Parenti, *Democracy for the Few,* 7th ed. (Belmont, Calif.: Wadsworth, 2001), on "permanent losers."

[55]For elaboration, see Thomas G. West, *Vindicating the Founders: Race, Sex, Class, and Justice in the Origins of America.* (Lanham, Md.: Rowman & Littlefield, 1997), 43-54.

[56]This discussion draws from Sidney Verba and Norman Nie, *Participation in America* (New York: Harper & Row, 1972); Stephen Earl Bennett and Linda L.M. Bennett, "Political Participation," in *Annual Review of Political Science,* Samuel Long, ed. (Norwood, N.J.: Ablex, 1986).

[57]Alan Wolfe, "Couch Potato Politics," *New York Times,* March 15, 1998, Sec. 4, 17.

[58] League of Conservative Voters poll, March 2002.

Chapter 2

[1]The clause would not necessarily lead to these results. The courts could interpret the clause, which usually applies to "adversarial proceedings" such as lawsuits, including divorces, not to marriages.

[2]The Indians, of course, had their own governments, and the Spanish may have established Saint Augustine, Florida, and Santa Fe, New Mexico, before the English established Jamestown. The Spanish settlements were extensions of Spanish colonization of Mexico and were governed by Spanish officials in Mexico City.

[3]This is not to suggest that the Pilgrims believed in democracy. Apparently, they were motivated to draft the compact by threats from some on the *Mayflower* that when the ship landed they would "use their owne libertie; for none had power to command them." Thus the compact was designed to bind them to the laws of the colony. Richard Shenkman, "*I Love Paul Revere, Whether He Rode or Not*" (New York: HarperCollins, 1991), 141-142.

[4]David Hawke, *A Transaction of Free Men* (New York: Scribner, 1964), 209.

[5]For an account of the foreign affairs problems under the Articles of Confederation, see Frederick W. Marks III, *Independence on Trial: Foreign Affairs and the Making of the Constitu-tion* (Baton Rouge: Louisiana State University Press, 1973).

[6]Louis Fisher, *President and Congress* (New York: Free Press, 1972), 14.

[7]The government under the Articles, however, could boast one major accomplishment: the Northwest Ordinance, adopted in 1787, provided for the government and future statehood of the land west of Pennsylvania (land that would become most of the Great Lakes states). The law also banned slavery in this territory.

[8]Gordon S. Wood, "The Origins of the Constitution," *This Constitution: A Bicentennial Chronicle,* Summer 1987, 10–11.

[9]Eric Black, *Our Constitution* (Boulder, Colo.: Westview Press, 1988), 6.

[10]For development of this idea, see Kenneth M. Dolbeare and Linda J. Medcalf, "The Political Economy of the Constitution," *This Constitution: A Bicentennial Chronicle,* Spring 1987, 4–10.

[11]Black, *Our Constitution,* 59.

[12]The Constitution would, however, retain numerous positive aspects of the Articles. See Donald S. Lutz, "The Articles of Confederation as the Background to the Federal Republic," *Publius* 20 (Winter 1990), 55–70.

[13]Robert McCloskey, *The American Supreme Court* (Chicago: University of Chicago Press, 1960), 29.

[14]Fred Barbash, "James Madison: A Man for the '80s," *Washington Post National Weekly Edition,* March 30, 1987, 23.

[15]Robert A. Dahl, *A Preface to Democratic Theory* (Chicago: University of Chicago Press, 1956), 5.

[16]Yet according to a poll in 1987, the bicentennial of the Constitution, only 1 percent of the public identified Madison as the one who played the biggest role in creating the Constitution. Most—31 percent—said Thomas Jefferson, who was a diplomat in France during the convention. Black, *Our Constitution,* 15.

Some argue that Hamilton, rather than Madison, was the driving force behind the Constitution, especially if his efforts after ratification—as an influential member of Washington's cabinet and later—are taken into account. Kenneth M. Dolbeare and Linda Medcalf, "The Dark Side of the Constitution," in *The Case Against the Constitution: From the Antifederalists to the Present,* eds. Kenneth M. Dolbeare and John F. Manley (Armonk, N.Y.: Sharpe, 1987), 120–141.

[17]Only Hamilton suggested a monarchy, and only one delegate—Gouverneur Morris of Pennsylvania—suggested an aristocracy.

[18]Dahl, *How Democratic,* 11–12.

[19]Ibid., 14.

[20]The large states did extract a concession that all taxing and spending bills must originate in the house in which representation is based on population. This provision would allow the large states to take the initiative on these important measures.

[21]Paul Finkelman, "Slavery at the Philadelphia Convention," *This Constitution: A Bicentennial Chronicle* (1987), 25–30.

[22]Ibid., 29.

[23]Ibid., 18.

[24]Quoted in Thomas G. West, *Vindicating the Founders: Race, Sex, Class, and Justice in the Origins of America* (Lanham, Md.: Rowman & Littlefield, 1997), 15.

[25]Theodore J. Lowi, *American Government* (Hinsdale, Ill.: Dryden, 1976), 97.

[26]William Gladstone, quoted in C. Herman Pritchett, *Constitutional Law of the Federal System* (Englewood Cliffs, N.J.: Prentice Hall, 1984), xi.

[27]Quoted in Richard Hofstadter, *The American Political Tradition* (New York: Vintage, 1948), 6–7.

[28]Under some state constitutions.

[29]*Federalist Paper* 51.

[30]Although we use this term today, neither it nor the word *federal* appears in the Constitution.

[31]In the United States, each state government is unitary with respect to its local governments. The state government can alter or eliminate cities, counties, townships, or school districts.

[32]James Madison, *Federalist Paper* 10.

[33]Madison also saw our vast territory as a way to limit factions, because it would be difficult for a group to extend its influence throughout the entire country.

[34]Creating a separate executive branch and making the selection of president independent of Congress also strengthened the national government, because it gave the president a political base from which to exercise national leadership.

[35]However, the amendment's checkered history indicates that the amendment hasn't always played a significant role in limiting the national government.

[36]Max Farrand, *The Framing of the Constitution of the United States* (New Haven, Conn.: Yale University Press, 1913).

[37]Charles O. Jones, *The Presidency in a Separated System* (Washington, D.C.: Brookings Institution, 1994), 14.

[38]Charles O. Jones, *Separate but Equal Branches* (Chatham, N.J.: Chatham House, 1995), 12.

[39]*Federalist Paper* 51.

[40]Jones, *Presidency in a Separated System,* 16, thus modifying Neustadt's classic definition of "a government of separated institutions sharing powers." Richard E. Neustadt, *Presidential Power and the Modern Presidents* (New York: Macmillan, 1990), 29.

[41]Locke called for majority rule but never resolved the conflict between majority rule and natural rights—in particular, the rights of the minority.

[42]Donald S. Lutz, "The Relative Influence of European Writers on Later Eighteenth-Century American Political Thought," *American Political Science Review* 78 (1984), 139–197.

[43]Alpheus T. Mason and Richard H. Leach, *In Quest of Freedom: American Political Thought and*

Practice, 2nd ed. (Englewood Cliffs, N.J.: Prentice Hall, 1973), 51.

[44]John P. Roche, "The Founding Fathers: A Reform Caucus in Action," *American Political Science Review* 56 (1962), 799–816.

[45]Benjamin F. Wright Jr., "The Origins of the Separation of Powers in America," in *Origins of American Political Thought,* ed. John P. Roche (New York: Harper & Row, 1967), 139–162.

[46]John R. Roche, "The Founding Fathers: A Reform Caucus in Action," *American Political Science Review* 55 (December, 1961), 805.

[47]James MacGregor Burns, *The Vineyard of Liberty* (New York: Knopf, 1982), 33.

[48]Bernard Bailyn, *Voyagers to the West* (New York: Knopf, 1982), 20.

[49]The Boston Tea Party, contrary to myth, was not prompted by higher taxes on British tea. Parliament lowered the taxes to give the British East India Company, facing bankruptcy, an advantage in the colonial market. This threatened American shippers who smuggled tea from Holland and controlled about three-fourths of the market. The shippers resented Parliament's attempt to manipulate the economy from thousands of miles away. Shenkman, "*I Love Paul Revere,*" 155.

[50]*Federalist Paper* 10.

[51]Of the fifty-five delegates, forty were owners of government bonds that had depreciated under the Articles, and twenty-four were moneylenders. Black, *Our Constitution,* 21.

[52]For elaboration, see Dolbeare and Medcalf, "Dark Side of the Constitution."

[53]Calvin C. Jillson and Cecil L. Eubanks, "The Political Structure of Constitution Making," *American Journal of Political Science* 29 (1984), 435–458.

[54]Jonathan Elliot, *The Debates in the Several State Conventions on the Adoption of the Federal Constitution as Recommended by the General Convention at Philadelphia, in 1787,* 2nd ed., 5 vols. (Philadelphia, 1896), 2: 102.

[55]On Anti-Federalist thinking, see William B. Allen and Gordon Lloyd, eds., *The Essential Antifederalist,* 2nd ed. (Lanham, Md.: University Press of America, 2002); John F. Manley and Kenneth M. Dolbeare, *The Case against the Constitution* (Armonk, N.Y.: Sharpe, 1987).

[56]Richard S. Randall, *American Constitutional Development,* vol. 1, *The Powers of Government* (New York: Longman, 2002), 54.

[57]"A Fundamental Contentment," *This Constitution: A Bicentennial Chronicle* (Fall 1984), 44.

[58]Quoted in Charles Warren, *The Making of the Constitution* (Boston: Little, Brown, 1928), xiv. Jefferson made this observation from afar, as he was serving as ambassador to France at the time of the Constitutional Convention.

[59]Keith Perine, "Congress Shows Little Enthusiasm for Bush's Marriage Amendment," *CQ Weekly* (February 28, 2004), 533.

[60]Alan P. Grimes, *Democracy and the Amendments to the Constitution* (Lexington, Mass.: Lexington Books, 1978). Grimes also shows how the adoption of new amendments reflects the rise of new power blocs in society.

[61]4 Wheaton 316 (1819).

[62]Historian James McPherson, quoted in George P. Fletcher, *Our Secret Constitution: How Lincoln Redefined American Democracy* (New York: Oxford University Press, 2001), 57. For a similar view, see Bruce Ackerman, *We the People,* vol. 2, *Transformations* (Cambridge, Mass.: Belknap Press, 1998), 10. This discussion borrows heavily from Fletcher and Ackerman and also from Garry Wills, *Lincoln at Gettysburg* (New York: Simon & Schuster, 1992). For a complementary view, see Charles Black, *A New Birth of Freedom: Human Rights, Named and Unnamed* (New York: Grosset/Putnam, 1997).

[63]Many of Lincoln's prejudicial comments came in response to more blatant racist remarks by his opponents. Lincoln abandoned his support for black emigration before he was elected to a second term as president. For a critical perspective on Lincoln's racial views, see Lerone Bennett Jr., *Forced into Glory: Abraham Lincoln's White Dream* (Chicago: Johnson, 2000). For a positive perspective, see William Lee Miller, *Lincoln's Virtues: An Ethical Biography* (New York: Knopf, 2002).

[64]Fletcher, *Our Secret Constitution,* 24.

[65]These paragraphs rely on the interpretations of Wills, *Lincoln at Gettysburg,* and Fletcher, *Our Secret Constitution.*

[66]Fletcher, *Our Secret Constitution,* 53.

[67]A precursor of this view was the era of Jacksonian democracy in the 1830s.

[68]A contemporaneous celebration of the nation as an entity can be seen in the poetry of Walt Whitman.

[69]Wills, *Lincoln at Gettysburg,* 38. Wills insists that this was not a coincidence, and he debunks the notion that Lincoln hastily dashed off his remarks while on his way to the town or to the speech itself (27–31).

[70]Fletcher, *Our Secret Constitution,* 35, 4. Others might nominate Lincoln's second inaugural address, in which he offered reconciliation to the South, or Martin Luther King Jr.'s "I Have a Dream" speech.

[71]The *Dred Scott* case is explained in Chapter 13.

[72]The equal protection clause is covered fully in Chapter 13, and the due process clause is covered fully in Chapter 12.

[73]Fletcher, *Our Secret Constitution,* 25.

[74]In this vein, Congress first experimented with an income tax during the war. It would return to this tax in the decades after the war.

[75]For example, the abolitionist movement and the Fifteenth Amendment would fuel the drive for women's suffrage, as explained in Chapter 15.

[76]This section borrows heavily from Ackerman, *We the People,* and Theodore J. Lowi, *The Personal President* (Ithaca, N.Y.: Cornell University Press, 1985). For a different view about the impact of the New Deal, see G. Edward White, *The Constitution and the New Deal* (Cambridge, Mass.: Harvard University Press, 2001).

[77]We never had a pure laissez-faire approach—there always was some governmental regulation—but this is the term most associated with the attitudes of the time.

[78]At least one legal scholar dismisses the notion that the Court's "old men" were reactionaries or fools. Although today people consider them mistaken, at the time they were following established doctrine. Ackerman, *We the People.*

[79]Lowi, *Personal President,* 49. Writers during the Depression and in the decades after it also recognized this as a revolution. Ernest K. Lindley, *The Roosevelt Revolution, First Phase* (New York: Viking, 1933); Mario Einaudi, *The Roosevelt Revolution* (New York: Harcourt, Brace & World, 1959).

[80]Karl Vick, "A President Who Woke Up Washington," *Washington Post National Weekly Edition,* April 28, 1997, 8.

[81]Ibid., 9.

[82]Lowi, *Personal President,* 44.

[83]Ibid., xi.

[84]This era also saw a shift to a more presidency-centered government that persists to a significant degree today. Lowi, *Personal President.*

[85]President Ronald Reagan in the 1980s and congressional Republicans in the early 1990s mounted major challenges to the changes initiated by the Depression and the New Deal. President George W. Bush has also mounted significant challenges. These will be addressed in later chapters. In addition, some conservative judges and legal scholars support the "Constitution in exile" movement, which claims that the changes in legal doctrine during and after the 1930s have been illegitimate.

[86]Of course, the process was evolutionary; the changes did not spring solely from these two crises. Moreover, some might maintain that the Supreme Court under the leadership of Chief Justice Earl Warren in the 1950s and 1960s also remade the Constitution because of its rulings expanding the Bill of Rights. Yet the changes brought about by the Warren Court probably had less impact overall than those wrought by Reconstruction or the New Deal.

[87]For a discussion of the role played by the philosophy of pragmatism in resolving these conflicts, see Fletcher, *Our Secret Constitution,* ch. 11.

[88]Henry Steele Commager, *Living Ideas in America* (New York: Harper & Row, 1951), 109.

[89]West, *Vindicating the Founders,* xi.

[90]Parts of the Constitution have been copied by some Latin America countries, Liberia (founded by Americans), and the Philippines (formerly an American territory).

[91]"South Africa Looks at U.S. Constitution," *Lincoln Journal Star,* October 7, 1990; David Remnick, "'We, the People,' from the Russian," *Washington Post National Weekly Edition,* September 10, 1990, 11.

[92]European countries, Australia, Canada, Costa Rica, Israel, Japan, and New Zealand.

[93]Dahl, *How Democratic . . . ?* tabs. 1 and 2, 164–165. Dahl counts only countries that have "strong" federalism, bicameralism, and judicial review.

[94]Rep. Barney Frank (D-Mass.), quoted in Michael Grunwald, "Everybody Talks about States' Rights," *Washington Post National Weekly Edition,* November 1, 1999, 29. Frank was referring to Republicans, but his comments apply to Democrats as well.

[95]Jones, *Presidency in a Separated System,* xiii

[96]Dahl, *How Democratic . . . ?* 115.

[97]Jones, *Presidency in a Separated System,* 3.

[98]Kingdon, *America the Unusual,* 7–22. Exceptions include education and regulation of civil rights and the environment. They also include a massive national defense establishment and an extensive criminal justice system. In these aspects, our government is bigger than in many other advanced industrialized countries.

[99]Richard Morin, "Happy Days Are Here Again," *Washington Post National Weekly Edition,* August 25, 1997, 35.

[100]About 25 percent split their ticket between candidates for president and representative. In addition, others split their vote between candidates for president and senator or between candidates for representative and senator. For an examination of the research about divided government, see Morris Fiorina, *Divided Government,* 2nd ed. (Boston: Allyn & Bacon, 1996), 153.

[101]Lewis Lapham, "Get Me Rewrite!" *New York Times Book Review,* February 4, 1996, 11.

Chapter 3

[1]Sheila Dewan and John Broder (with others), "Massacre in Virginia: Rampage Gunman Was Student; Warning Lag Tied to Bad Lead," *New York Times* (April 18, 2007), http://select.nytimes.com/search/restricted/article?res=F00A1FFA355B0C7B8DDDAD0894DF404482; N. R. Kleinfield (and others), "Massacre in Virginia: The Gunman," *New York Times* (May 2, 2007), http://select.ny-times.com/search/restricted/article?res=F70E1EFE3C5A0C718EDDAD0894DF404482.

[2]Gallup Poll, "Gallup's Pulse of Democracy," www.galluppoll.com/content/default.aspx?ci=1645.

[3]Timothy E. Cook, "The Bear Market in Political Socialization and the Costs of Misunderstood Psychological Theories," *American Political Science Review* 79 (1985), 1079–1093.

[4]S. W. Moore et al., "The Civic Awareness of Five- and Six-Year-Olds," *Western Political Quarterly* 29 (1976), 418.

[5]R. W. Connell, *The Child's Construction of Politics* (Carlton, Australia: Melbourne University Press, 1971).

[6]Fred I. Greenstein, *Children and Politics* (New Haven, Conn.: Yale University Press, 1965), 122; see also Fred I. Greenstein, "The Benev-

olent Leader Re-visited: Children's Images of Political Leaders in Three Democracies," *American Political Science Review* 69 (1975), 1317–1398; Robert D. Hess and Judith V. Torney, *The Development of Political Attitudes in Children* (Chicago: Aldine, 1967).

[7]Amy Carter and Ryan Teten, "Assessing Changing Views of the President: Ravishing Greenstein's Children and Politics," *Presidential Studies Quarterly* 32 (2002), 453–462.

[8]Greenstein, *Children and Politics.*

[9]Hess and Torney, *The Development of Political Attitudes in Children;* Connell, *The Child's Construction of Politics.*

[10]Greenstein, *Children and Politics;* Greenstein, "The Benevolent Leader Revisited: Children's Images of Political Leaders in Three Democracies"; and Hess and Torney, *The Development of Political Attitudes in Children.*

[11]Connell, *The Child's Construction of Politics.*

[12]Carter and Teten, "Assessing Changing Views."

[13]F. Christopher Arterton, "The Impact of Watergate on Children's Attitudes toward the President," *Political Science Quarterly* 89 (1974), 269–288; see also P. Frederick Hartwig and Charles Tidmarch, "Children and Political Reality: Changing Images of the President," paper presented at the 1974 Annual Meeting of the Southern Political Science Association; J. Dennis and C. Webster, "Children's Images of the President and Government in 1962 and 1974," *American Politics Quarterly* 4 (1975), 386–405; Robert Hawkins, Suzanne Pingree, and D. Roberts, "Watergate and Political Socialization," *American Politics Quarterly* 4 (1975), 406–436.

[14]Gallup Organization, "Public Trust in Federal Government Remains High," January 8, 1999.

[15]Michael Delli Carpini, *Stability and Change in American Politics: The Coming of Age of the Generation of the 1960s* (New York: New York University Press, 1986), 86–89.

[16]Richard M. Merelman, *Political Socialization and Educational Climates* (New York: Holt, Rinehart and Winston, 1971), 54; more recently, the percentage of liberals among college freshmen and the public is about the same.

[17]Roberta Sigel and Marilyn Hoskin, *The Political Involvement of Adolescents* (New Brunswick, N.J.: Rutgers University Press, 1981).

[18]John R. Hibbing and Elizabeth Theiss-Morse, *Congress as Public Enemy: Public Attitudes toward American Political Institutions* (Cambridge, England: Cambridge University Press, 1995). It is plausible to assume that the content of early political socialization influences what is learned later, but the assumption has not been adequately tested. Thus we might expect the positive opinions toward government and politics developed early in childhood to condition the impact of traumatic events later in life; David Easton and Jack Dennis, *Children in the Political System: Origins of Regime Legitimacy* (New York: Mc-

Graw-Hill, 1969); Robert Weissberg, *Political Learning, Political Choice, and Democratic Citizenship* (Englewood Cliffs, N.J.: Prentice Hall, 1974). See also Donald Searing, Joel Schwartz, and Alden Line, "The Structuring Principle: Political Socialization and Belief System," *American Political Science Review* 67 (1973), 414–432.

[19]Jack Citrin, "Comment: The Political Relevance of Trust in Government," *Washington Post National Weekly Edition* 68, September 1974, 973–1001; Jack Citrin and Donald Green, "Presidential Leadership and the Resurgence of Trust in Government," *British Journal of Political Science* 16 (1986), 431–453.

[20]John Alford, Carolyn Funk, and John Hibbing, "Are Political Orientations Genetically Transmitted," *American Political Science Review* 99 (May, 2005), 153–168. How do scientists determine hereditary traits from those environmentally determined? Much of this research looks at identical twins, who share the exact same genetic traits, and compares them with nonidentical twins, who do not.

[21]Christopher Achen, "Parental Socialization and Rational Party Identification," *Political Behavior* 24 (June, 2002), 151–170.

[22]Dean Jaros, Herbert Hirsch, and Frederic J. Fleron Jr., "The Malevolent Leader: Political Socialization in an American Subculture," *American Political Science Review* 62 (1968), 564–575.

[23]Kent Tedin, "The Influence of Parents on the Political Attitudes of Adolescents," *American Political Science Review* 68 (1974), 1579–1592.

[24]M. Kent Jennings, *Generations and Politics* (Princeton, N.J.: Princeton University Press, 1981).

[25]Kathleen Dolan, "Attitudes, Behaviors, and the Influence of the Family: A Re-examination of the Role of Family Structure," *Political Behavior* 17 (1995), 251–264.

[26]On the impact of the public schools and teachers on political socialization, particularly with respect to loyalty and patriotism, see Hess and Torney, *The Development of Political Attitudes in Children.*

[27]Gabriel A. Almond and Sidney Verba, *The Civic Culture: Political Attitudes and Democracy in Five Nations, an Analytic Study* (Boston: Little, Brown, 1965); John R. Hibbing and Elizabeth Theiss-Morse, "Civics Is Not Enough: Teaching Barbarics in K–12," *PS: Political Science and Politics* (1996), 12; Norman H. Nie, Jane Junn, and Kenneth Stehlik-Barry, *Education and Democratic Citizenship in America* (Chicago: University of Chicago Press, 1996).

[28]Nie et al., *Education and Democratic Citizenship in America.*

[29]Hibbing and Theiss-Morse, *Congress as Public Enemy: Public Attitudes toward American Political Institutions.*

[30]Richard G. Niemi and Jane Junn, *Civic Education: What Makes Students Learn* (New Haven, Conn.: Yale University Press, 1998). See also Richard G. Niemi and Julia Smith, "En-

rollments in High School Government Classes: Are We Shortchanging Both Citizenship and Political Science Training?" *PS: Political Science and Politics* 34 (2001), 281–288. Honors and advanced placement (AP) programs, along with active learning, can improve student understanding and achievement in American history.

[31]Stephen Bennett, Staci Rhine, and Richard Flickinger, "Reading's Impact on Democratic Citizenship in America," *Political Behavior* 22 (2000), 167–195.

[32]Nie et al., *Education and Democratic Citizenship in America.*

[33]Alfonso Damico, M. Margaret Conway, and Sandra Bowman Damico, "Patterns of Political Trust and Mistrust: Three Moments in the Lives of Democratic Citizens," *Polity* 32 (2000), 377–400.

[34]Joel Westheimer and Joseph Kahne, "Educating the 'Good' Citizen: Political Choices and Pedagogical Goals," *PS: Political Science and Politics* 2 (2004), 241–247.

[35]Richard M. Merelman, "Democratic Politics and the Culture of American Education," *American Political Science Review* 74 (1980), 319–332; Hibbing and Theiss-Morse, "Civics Is Not Enough: Teaching Barbarics in K–12"; Nie et al., *Education and Democratic Citizenship in America.*

[36]Material for this section is drawn from Everett C. Ladd and Seymour M. Lipset, *The Divided Academy: Professors and Politics* (New York: McGraw-Hill, 1975); Charles Kesler, "The Movement of Student Opinion," *National Review,* November 23, 1979, 29; Ernest L. Boyer, *College: The Undergraduate Experience in America* (New York: Harper & Row, 1987); "Fact File: Attitudes and Characteristics of This Year's Freshman," *Chronicle of Higher Education,* January 11, 1989, A33–A34; General Social Survey, *National Opinion Research Center,* 1984, 87. During the early 1970s, more college freshmen identified themselves as liberal compared with the public at large.

[37]David Horowitz, *The Professors: The 101 Most Dangerous Academics in America* (Regency Publishing 2006)

[38]Rebecca Trounson, "Poll Says College Freshmen Lean Left," www.commondreams.org/headlines02/0128-01.htm.

[39]Alexander W. Astin, William S. Korn, and Linda Sax, *The American Freshman: Thirty Year Trends* (Los Angeles: Higher Education Research Institute, Graduate School of Education and Information, 1997).

[40]Thomas Bartlett, "Evaluating Student Attitudes Is More Difficult This Year," *Chronicle of Higher Education,* February 1, 2002, A35–A38. See also Linda Sax, Alexander W. Astin, and William S. Korn, *The American Freshman: National Norms for Fall 1998* (Los Angeles: Higher Education Research Institute, Graduate School of Education and Information Studies, 1998).

[41]"College Freshman More Politically Liberal Than in the Past, UCLA Survey Reveals,"

2001 CIRP Press Release: CIRP Freshman Survey, January 28, 2001.

[42]Linda Sax, Alexander W. Korn, and Kathryn M. Mahoney, *The American Freshman: National Norms for Fall 1999* (Los Angeles: Higher Education Research Institute, Graduate School of Education and Information Studies, 1999).

[43]"Attitudes and Characteristics of Freshmen," *Chronicle of Higher Education,* August 27, 2004, 19.

[44]Maxwell McCombs and Donald Shaw, "The Agenda Setting Function of the Media," *Public Opinion Quarterly* 36 (1972), 176–187.

[45]Benjamin I. Page, Robert Y. Shapiro, and Glenn R. Dempsey, "What Moves Public Opinion?" *American Political Science Review* 81 (1987), 23–44.

[46]Herbert F. Weisberg, "Marital Differences in American Voting," *Public Opinion Quarterly* 51 (1987), 335–343.

[47]Michael A. Fletcher, "On Campus, a Patriotic Surge," *Washington Post National Weekly Edition,* December 10, 2001, 31.

[48]Philip E. Converse, Aage R. Clausen, and Warren E. Miller, "Electoral Myth and Reality: The 1964 Election," *American Political Science Review* 59 (1965), 321–326.

[49]John P. Robinson, "The Press as Kingmaker: What Surveys Show from the Last Five Campaigns," *Journalism Quarterly* 49 (1974), 592.

[50]See jacob@jacbian.org; also Nick Anderson, "Kerry Wins the Paper Endorsement Derby, for What It's Worth," *Los Angeles Times,* October 29, 2004, A5. Two hundred twelve newspapers endorsed Kerry; 199 recommended Bush. Newspapers endorsing Kerry had a circulation of twenty-two million; Bush, sixteen million.

[51]For a review of the history of polling, see Bernard Hennessy, *Public Opinion,* 4th ed. (Monterey, Calif.: Brooks/Cole, 1983), 42–44, 46–50. See also Charles W. Roll and Albert H. Cantril, *Polls: Their Use and Misuse in Politics* (New York: Basic Books, 1972), 3–6.

[52]Peverill Squire, "Why the 1936 Literary Digest Poll Failed," *Public Opinion Quarterly* 52 (1988), 125–133; see also Don Cahalan, "The Digest Poll Rides Again," *Public Opinion Quarterly* 53 (1989), 107–113.

[53]Hennessy, *Public Opinion,* 4th ed., 46.

[54]"Consulting the Oracle," *U.S. News and World Report,* December 4, 1995, 52–55; Joshua Green, "The Other War Room," *Washington Monthly,* April 2002, 11–16.

[55]Green, "The Other War Room."

[56]Joe Klien, *The Natural* (New York: Doubleday, 2002), 7.

[57]Green, "The Other War Room."

[58]Harris, "Presidency by Poll."

[59]Steven Mufson and John E. Harris, "Clinton's Global Growth," *Washington Post National Weekly Edition,* January 22, 2001, 8–9.

[60]Ibid., 11.

[61]Lawrence R. Jacobs and Robert Y. Shapiro, *Politicians Don't Pander: Political Manipulation and the Loss of Democratic Responsiveness* (Chicago: University of Chicago Press, 2000).

[62]Ibid., 12.

[63]Richard Morin, "Surveying the Surveyors," *Washington Post National Weekly Edition,* March 2, 1992, 37.

[64]David Broder, "Push Polls Plunge Politics to a New Low," *Lincoln Journal Star,* October 9, 1994, 5E.

[65]Bill Kovack and Tom Rosensteil, "Campaign Lite," *Washington Monthly,* January–February 2001, 31–38.

[66]"All Things Considered," National Public Radio, October 30, 1992.

[67]Richard Morin, "Voters Are Hung Up on Polling," *Washington Post National Weekly Edition,* November 1–7, 2004, 12.

[68]Ibid.

[69]Ibid.

[70]Claudia Deane, "And Why Haven't You Been Polled?" *Washington Post National Weekly Edition,* January 18, 1999, 34; Richard Morin, "The Election Post Mortem," *Washington Post National Weekly Edition,* September 30, 1996, 37.

[71]Real Clear Politics, www.realclearpolitics.com/polls.html; see also "Pre-Election Polls Largely Accurate," *The Pew Research Center for the People and the Press,* November 23, 2004, www.peoplepress.org/commentary/display.php3?AnalysisID5 102.

[72]Richard Morin and Claudia Deane, "Why the Florida Exit Polls Were Wrong," *Washington Post,* November 8, 2000.

[73]Diana Owen, "Media Mayhem: Performance of the Press in Election 2000," in *Overtime! The Election 2000 Thriller,* ed. Larry J. Sabato (New York: Longman, 2002), 144.

[74]Steve Freeman, *Polling Bias or Corrupted Count* (Philadelphia: American Statistical Association, Philadelphia Chapter, October 14, 2005). (Freeman is a faculty member at the University of Pennsylvania).

[75]*The New Yorker,* March 20, 1999, 18.

[76]Richard Morin, "Tuned Out, Tuned Off," *Washington Post National Weekly Edition,* February 5, 1996, 6–8.

[77]Ibid., 8.

[78]Ibid., 8.

[79]Richard Morin, "They Know Only What They Don't Like," *Washington Post National Weekly Edition,* October 3, 1994, 37.

[80]National Election Study, 2004.

[81]Ibid.

[82]Morin, "They Know Only What They Don't Like," 35.

[83]Center for Political Studies, 1986 National Election Study, University of Michigan, "Wapner Top Judge in Recognition Poll," *Lincoln Journal Star,* June 23, 1989, 1.

[84]Michael Delli Carpini and Scott Keeter, "Stability and Change in the U.S. Public's Knowledge of Politics," *Public Opinion Quarterly* (1991), 583–612.

[85]Richard Morin, "We Love It—What We Know of It," *Washington Post National Weekly Edition,* September 22, 1997, 35.

[86]Ibid.

[87]Richard Morin, "Foreign Aid: Mired in Misunderstanding," *Washington Post National Weekly Edition,* March 20, 1995, 37.

[88]Richard Morin, "What Informed Public Opinion?" *Washington Post National Weekly Edition,* April 10, 1995, 36.

[89]Vladimer Orlando Key, *The Responsible Electorate* (Cambridge, Mass.: Harvard University Press, 1966); Norman H. Nie, Sidney Verba, and John R. Petrocik, *The Changing American Voter* (Cambridge, Mass.: Harvard University Press, 1976), ch. 18; Samuel L. Popkin, *The Reasoning Voter: Communication and Persuasion in Presidential Campaigns* (Chicago: University of Chicago Press, 1994).

[90]Gallup Organization, poll conducted April 6, 2004.

[91]Popkin, *The Reasoning Voter: Communication and Persuasion in Presidential Campaigns.*

[92]Morin, "Tuned Out, Turned Off," 8.

[93]Gallup Organization, poll conducted June 16, 2003.

[94]*Newsweek,* poll conducted September 2–3, 2004.

[95]Harold Meyerson, "Fact-Free News," *Washington Post National Weekly,* October 10–26, 2003, 26.

[96]Andrew Sullivan, article found on www.andrewsullivan.com/main_article.php?artnum520040126.

[97]General Social Survey, 2002.

[98]Jonathan Rauch, "Bipolar Disorder," *Atlantic Monthly* (January-February 2005), 102.

[99]John Sperling, *The Great Divide: Retro and Metro America* (USA: PoliPoint Press, 2004), 212.

[100]Ibid., 165, 178, 192.

[101]E. J. Dionne Jr., "One Nation Deeply Divided," *Washington Post,* November 7, 2004, A31, quoted in Morris P. Fiorina with Samuel J. Abrams and Jeremy C. Pope, *Culture War? The Myth of the Polarized America* (New York: Pearson Longman, 2005), 6.

[102]Matthew Dowd, quoted in Fiorina, ibid., 6.

[103]Conducted by the Gallup Organization for the online dating service Match.com during July 2004. Cited in Jonathan Rauch, "Bipolar Disorder," *Atlantic Monthly,* January-February, 2005, 105.

[104]Various studies are summarized in Rauch, "Bipolar Disorder," 102–110.

[105]Editorial, "A Polarized Nation?" *Washington Post,* November 14, 2004, 6. Several of these ideas were summarized nicely in this article.

[106]This section draws heavily on Howard Schuman, Charlotte Steeh, and Lawrence Bobo, *Racial Attitudes in America* (Cambridge, Mass.: Harvard University Press, 1985); Howard Schuman, Charlotte Steeh, Lawrence Bobo, and Maria Krysan, *Racial Attitudes in America,* rev. ed. (1997); data summaries are drawn from the General Social Surveys of the National Opinion Research Center, University of Chicago, and National Elections Studies of CPS, University of Michigan; see also Lee Sigelman and Susan Welch, *Black Americans' Views of Racial Inequality* (Cambridge, Mass.: Cambridge University Press, 1991).

[107]General Social Survey, 1996; Richard Morin, "Polling in Black and White: Sometimes the Answers Depend on Who's Asking the Questions," *Washington Post National Weekly Edition,* October 30, 1989, 37.

[108]General Social Survey, 1996;"Whites Retain Negative Views of Minorities, a Survey Finds," *New York Times,* January 10, 1991, C19; Mary R. Jackman, "General and Applied Tolerance: Does Education Increase Commitment to Racial Inequality?" *American Journal of Political Science* 25 (1981), 256–269; Donald Kinder and David Sears, "Prejudice and Politics: Symbolic Racism versus Racial Threats to the Good Life," *Journal of Personality and Social Psychology* 40 (1981), 414–431.

[109]Richard Morin, "We've Moved Forward, but We Haven't," *Washington Post National Weekly Edition,* October 5, 1998, 34.

[110]"Whites Retain Negative Views of Minorities, a Survey Finds," C19.

[111]General Social Survey, 1998; see also Donald Kinder and Lynn Saunders, *Divided by Color: Racial Politics and Democratic Ideals* (Chicago: University of Chicago Press, 1996); Howard Schuman and Lawrence Bobo, "Survey-Based Experiments on White Attitudes toward Residential Integration," *American Journal of Sociology* 94 (1988), 519–526; see also Schuman et al., *Racial Attitudes in America,* rev. ed.

[112]General Social Survey, 1998.

[113]Richard Morin, "It's Not as It Seems," *Washington Post National Weekly Edition,* July 16, 2001, 34.

[114]Ibid.

[115]Morin, "It's Not as It Seems"; ABC/ *Washington Post* poll, 1981 and 1986.

[116]General Social Survey, 1998.

[117]Benjamin I. Page and Robert Y. Shapiro, "Effects of Public Opinion on Policy," *American Political Science Review* 77 (1983), 175–190.

[118]Morin, "Voters Are Hung Up on Polling."

[119]Lawrence Jacobs and Robert Y. Shapiro, *Politicians Don't Pander* (Chicago: University of Chicago Press, 2000).

[120]Ibid.

Chapter 4

[1]Frank Rich, *The Greatest Story Ever Sold* (New York: Penguin, 2006), 109.

[2]The correction of the record has been covered heavily, including in Dana Priest, William Booth, and Susan Schmidt, "Saving Private Lynch," *Washington Post National Weekly Edition,* June 23–29, 2003, 8–10; Nancy Gibbs, "The Private Jessica Lynch," *Time,* November 17, 2003, 24–46; and Frank Rich, "Saving Private England," *New York Times,* May 16, 2004, AR1.

[3]"All Things Considered," NPR, March 23, 2004.

[4]Rich, *The Greatest Story Ever Sold,* 81.

[5]James David Barber, *The Pulse of Politics* (New York: Norton, 1980), 9.

[6]Kevin Phillips, "A Matter of Privilege," *Harper's,* January 1977, 95.

[7]Media time overlaps with work time per day, because many people listen to music, watch TV, or surf the Web while working. Richard Harwood, "So Many Media, So Little Time," *Washington Post National Weekly Edition,* September 7, 1992, 28.

[8]Edwin Diamond, *The Tin Kazoo* (Cambridge, Mass.: MIT Press, 1975), 13.

[9]Study by Kaiser Family Foundation, cited in Lauran Neergaard, "Parents Encouraging TV Use among Young Kids, Study Says," *Lincoln Journal Star,* May 25, 2006, 4A, and in Ruth Marcus, "Is Decency Going Down the Tubes?" *Washington Post National Weekly Edition,* June 26–July 9, 2006, 26.

[10]Lindsey Tanner, "Studies Suggest Watching TV Harms Children Academically," *Lincoln Journal Star,* July 5, 2005, 6A.

[11]Doris A. Graber, *Mass Media and American Politics* (Washington, D.C.: Congressional Quarterly Press, 1980), 2.

[12]William Lutz, *Doublespeak* (New York: Harper & Row, 1989), 73–74.

[13]Robert W. McChesney and John Nichols, "It's the Media, Stupid," in *Voices of Dissent,* 5th ed., eds. William F. Grover and Joseph G. Peschek (New York: Longman, 2004), 116–120.

[14]According to the Kaiser Family Foundation. Claudia Wallis, "The Multitasking Generation," *Time,* March 27, 2006, 50–51.

[15]Rob McGann, "Internet Edges Out Family Time More than TV Time," ClickZ, January 5, 2005, www.clickz.com/stats/sectors/demographics/article.php/3455061.

[16]Shanto Iyengar, *Is Anyone Responsible? How Television Frames Political Issues* (Chicago: University of Chicago Press, 1991), 1.

[17]James Rainey, "More News Outlets, Fewer Stories: New Media 'Paradox,'" *Los Angeles Times,* March 13, 2006, www.latimes.com/news/nationworld/nation/la-nanews13mar13,0,2018145. story?

[18]Elizabeth Gleick, "Read All about It," *Time,* October 21, 1998, 66; Dana Millbank, "A Bias for Mainstream News," *Washington Post National Weekly Edition,* March 28–April 3, 2005, 23. See also Tom Rosenstiel, *The State of the News Media, 2004* (Washington, D.C.: Project for Excellence in Journalism, 2004).

[19]"Ticker," 128.

[20]Scott Althaus, "American News Consumption during Times of National Crisis," *PS,* September 2002, 517–521.

[21]Millbank, "A Bias for Mainstream News."

[22]Michael J. Wolf and Geoffrey Sands, "Fearless Predictions," *Brill's Content,* July-August 1999, 110. For a discussion of the future impact of the Internet on media concentration and diversity, see Robert W. McChesney, *The Problem of the Media* (New York: Monthly Review Press, 2004), 211–217.

[23]Eve Gerber, "Divided We Watch," *Brill's Content,* February 2001, 110–111.

[24]Donald Kaul, "Effects of Merger between AOL, Time Warner Will Be Inescapable," *Lincoln Journal Star,* January 18, 2000; Ken Auletta, "Leviathan," *New Yorker,* October 29, 2001, 50.

[25]McChesney, *Problem of the Media,* 182–183.

[26]For examination of this development, see Lawrence Lessing, *The Future of Ideas* (New York: Random House, 2001). For an alternative view, see McChesney, *Problem of the Media,* 205–209.

[27]Benjamin M. Compaine, *Who Owns the Media?* (White Plains, N.Y.: Knowledge Industry Publications, 1979), 11, 76–77; Michael Parenti, *Inventing Reality* (New York: St. Martin's Press, 1986), 27; Paul Farhi, "You Can't Tell a Book by Its Cover," *Washington Post National Weekly Edition,* December 5, 1988, 21; Andrews, "A New Tune for Radio."

[28]Robert McChesney, "AOL–Time Warner Merger Is Dangerous and Undemocratic," *Lincoln Journal Star,* January 17, 2000.

[29]Rosenstiel, *State of the News Media,* 9.

[30]Daren Fonda, "National Prosperous Radio," *Time,* March 24, 2003, 50; Marc Fisher, "Sounds All Too Familiar," *Washington Post National Weekly Edition,* May 26, 2003, 23.

[31]McChesney, *Problem of the Media,* 178.

[32]Ibid., 188.

[33]Mary Lynn F. Jones, "No News Is Good News," *American Prospect,* May 2003, 39.

[34]"Clear Channel Growth the Result of 1996 Deregulation," *Lincoln Journal Star,* October 5, 2003.

[35]"Weekend Edition," NPR, October 28, 2006.

[36]David Gram, "Opponents of War Have Trouble Getting Message Out," *Lincoln Journal Star,* February 25, 2003.

[37]"Broadcaster: *Nightline* Won't Air on Its Stations," *Lincoln Journal Star,* April 30, 2004.

[38]money.cnn.com/2004/10/11/news/newsmakers/sinclair_kerry/index.htm?cnn5yes

[39]Elizabeth Lesly Stevens, "Mouse.Ke.Fear," *Brill's Content,* December 1998–January 1999, 95. For other examples, see Jane Mayer, "Bad News," *New Yorker,* August 14, 2000, 30–36.

[40]Jim Hightower, *There's Nothing in the Middle of the Road but Yellow Stripes and Dead Armadillos* (New York: HarperCollins, 1997), 121.

[41]The Project for Excellence in Journalism, affiliated with Columbia University's Graduate School of Journalism, concluded after a five-year study that newscasts by stations owned by smaller companies were significantly higher in quality than newscasts by stations owned by larger companies. "Does Ownership Matter in Local Television News?" February 17, 2003 (www.journalism.org).

[42]Neil Hickey, "Money Lust," *Columbia Journalism Review,* July-August 1998, 28.

[43]*Now, with Bill Moyers,* PBS, April 11, 2003.

[44]Ted Turner, "Break Up This Band!" *Washington Monthly,* July-August, 2004, 35.

[45]In response, ABC made all of its prime-time programming available in Spanish in 2005.

[46]Howard Kurtz, "Welcome to Spin City," *Washington Post National Weekly Edition,* March 16, 1998, 6. See also Roger Parloff, "If This Ain't Libel . . . ," *Brill's Content,* Fall 2001, 95–113.

[47]Times Mirror Center for the People and the Press, *The Vocal Minority in American Politics* (Washington, D.C.: Times Mirror Center for the People and the Press, 1993).

[48]In addition, she received $50,000 for a book elaborating on her story, $250,000 for posing nude for *Penthouse* magazine, and about $20,000 for appearing on German and Spanish television shows. "Flowers Says She Made Half Million from Story," *Lincoln Journal Star,* March 21, 1998.

[49]Ernest Tollerson, "Politicians Try to Balance Risk against Rewards of Reaching Talk-Radio Audiences," *New York Times,* March 31, 1996, 12.

[50]McChesney, *Problem of the Media,* 96; Paul Taylor, "The New Political Theater," *Mother Jones,* November-December 2000, 30–33.

[51]David Halberstam, "Preface," in Bill Kovach and Tom Rosenstiel, *Warp Speed: America in the Age of Mixed Media* (New York: Century Foundation Press, 1999), x.

[52]None of the "Swift Boat Veterans for Truth" served with Kerry on his boat. The charges were disputed by Kerry's crewmates and contradicted by Navy records. Evidently, the "Swift Boat Veterans for Truth" were motivated by their anger toward Kerry's antiwar stance after he returned from Vietnam, which became the subject of the group's second commercial. Todd Gitlin, "Swifter Than Truth," *American Prospect,* November, 2004, 29–30.

[53]Quoted in Richard Corliss, "Look Who's Talking," *Time,* January 23, 1995, 25.

[54]Lev Grossman, "Meet Joe Blog," *Time,* June 21, 2004, 66.

[55]Scott Shane, "For Liberal Bloggers, Libby Trial is Fun and Fodder," *New York Times,* February 15, 2007, www.nytimes.com/2007/02/15/washington/15bloggers.html?hp&ex=1171602000&en=5afe9e7498071C7f&ei=50948partner=homepage.

[56]Matt Bai, "Can Bloggers Get Real?" *New York Times Magazine,* May 28, 2006, 13.

[57]Elizabeth LeBel, "Life in This Girl's Army," www.sgtlizzie.blogspot.com, cited in Jonathan Finer, "The New Ernie Pyles: Sgtlizzie and 67cshdocs," www.washingtonpost.com/wp-dyn/content/article/2005/08/11/AR2005081102168.

[58]Ibid.

[59]Richard A. Posner, "Bad News," *New York Times Book Review,* July 31, 2005, 10–11. Posner, however, argues that the number of bloggers provides a fact-correcting mechanism in the blogosphere.

[60]Garance Franke-Ruta, "Blog Rolled," *American Prospect,* April, 2005, 40.

[61]Dom Bonafede, "Press Paying More Heed to Substance in Covering 1984 Presidential Election," *National Journal,* October 13, 1984, 1923.

[62]Seth Mnookin, "Advice to Ari," *Brill's Content,* March 2001, 97.

[63]Ken Auletta, "Fortress Bush," *New Yorker,* January 19, 2004, 53.

[64]Charles Peters, *How Washington Really Works* (Reading, Mass.: Addison-Wesley, 1980), 18.

[65]Auletta, "Fortress Bush," 54.

[66]Matthew Brzezinski, *Fortress America: On the Front Lines of Homeland Security—an Inside Look at the Coming Surveillance State* (New York: Bantam, 2004).

[67]William Greider, "Reporters and Their Sources," *Washington Monthly,* October 1982, 13–15.

[68]See, for example, Jeffrey Toobin, *A Vast Conspiracy: The Real Story of the Sex Scandal That Nearly Brought Down a President* (New York: Simon & Schuster, 1999), 310.

[69]Murray Waas, "Why Novak Called Rove," *National Journal,* December 17, 2005, 3874–3878.

[70]There is some uncertainty whether the initial leak, by State Department official Richard Armitage, was intended as retaliation, but at least the subsequent leaks, by White House officials, were. For examination of this incident and the practice of leaking, see Max Frankel, "The Washington Back Channel," *New York Times Magazine,* March 25, 2007, 40.

[71]When a spy's identity becomes public, foreign governments try to retrace the spy's movements and determine his or her contacts to see how the CIA operated in their country.

[72]Howard Kurtz, "Lying Down on This Job Was Just Fine," *Washington Post National Weekly Edition,* April 19, 1999, 13.

[73]Ann Devroy, "The Republicans, It Turns Out, Are a Veritable Fount of Leaks," *Washington Post National Weekly Edition,* November 18, 1991, 23.

[74]Daniel Schorr, "A Fact of Political Life," *Washington Post National Weekly Edition,* October 28, 1991, 32.

[75]Howard Kurtz, "How Sources and Reporters Play the Game of Leaks," *Washington Post National Weekly Edition,* March 15, 1993, 25.

[76]Dan Eggen, "Bush's Plumbers," *Washington Post National Weekly Edition,* March 13–19, 2006, 11.

[77]Nancy Franklin, "Rather Knot," *New Yorker,* October 4, 2004, 108–109.

[78]Samuel Kernell, *Going Public: New Strategies of Presidential Leadership* (Washington, D.C.: Congressional Quarterly Press, 1986), 59. Woodrow Wilson also tried to cultivate correspondents and host frequent sessions, but he did not have the knack for this activity and so scaled back the sessions. Kernell, *Going Public,* 60–61. He did perceive that "some men of brilliant ability were in the group, but I soon discovered that the interest of the majority was in the personal and the trivial rather than in principles and policies." James Bennet, "The Flack Pack," *Washington Monthly,* November 1991, 27.

[79]Dwight Eisenhower was actually the first president to let the networks televise his press conferences, but he did not do so to reach the public. When he wanted to reach the public, he made a formal speech. The networks found his conferences so untelegenic that they stopped covering the entire session each time. Kernell, *Going Public,* 68.

[80]Bennet, "The Flack Pack," 19.

[81]Frank Rich, "The Armstrong Williams NewsHour," *New York Times,* June 26, 2005, WK13.

[82]Dom Bonafede, " 'Mr. President,' " *National Journal,* October 29, 1988, 2756.

[83]Charles Hagen, "The Photo Op: Making Icons or Playing Politics?" *New York Times,* February 9, 1992, H28.

[84]Frank Rich, "Operation Iraqi Infoganda," *New York Times,* March 28, 2004, AR21.

[85]"The Man behind the Curtain Award," *Mother Jones,* September-October 2002, 67.

[86]Molly Ivins, "It's Up to Us to Stop This War, and Now," *Lincoln Journal Star,* January 7, 2007, 8C. This incident is also shown and discussed in the documentary *Control Room.*

[87]Kiku Adatto, cited in Howard Kurtz, "Networks Adapt to Changed Campaign Role," *Washington Post,* June 21, 1992, A-19. See also Diana Owen, "Media Mayhem: Performance of the Press in Election 2000," in *Overtime! The Election 2000 Thriller,* ed. Larry J. Sabato (New York: Longman, 2002), 123–156.

[88]Lance Morrow, "The Decline and Fall of Oratory," *Time,* August 18, 1980, 78.

[89]David Halberstam, "How Television Failed the American Voter," *Parade,* January 11, 1981, 8.

[90]George E. Reedy, *The Twilight of the Presidency* (New York: New American Library, 1970), 112.

[91]Sam Donaldson, quoted in Thomas Griffith, "Winging It on Television," *Time,* March 14, 1983, 71.

[92]Auletta, "Fortress Bush," 61–62.

[93]W. Lance Bennett, *News: The Politics of Illusion,* 2nd ed. (White Plains, N.Y.: Longman, 1988).

[94]Larry J. Sabato, *Feeding Frenzy: How Attack Journalism Has Transformed American Politics* (New York: Free Press, 1991).

[95]Deborah Tannen, *The Argument Culture* (New York: Ballantine, 1998), 81.

[96]Ibid., 55.

[97]Orville Schell, "Preface" to Michael Massing, *Now They Tell Us: the American Press and Iraq* (New York: New York Review of Books, 2004), xiv.

[98]Fallows, *Breaking the News,* 62–63.

[99]Joan Konner, "Diane 'Got' Gore. But What Did We Get?" *Brill's Content,* September 1999, 59–60.

[100]See Sabato, *Feeding Frenzy,* for additional reasons for this increase.

[101]"Ticker," *Brill's Content,* July-August 1998, 152, citing the Project for Excellence in Journalism, "Changing Definitions of News: A Look at the Mainstream Press over 20 Years," March 6, 1998.

[102]Fallows, *Breaking the News,* 196.

[103]An examination of 224 incidents of criminal or unethical behavior by Reagan administration appointees found that only 13 percent were uncovered by reporters. Most were discovered through investigations by executive agencies or congressional committees, which then released the information to the press. Only incidents reflecting personal peccadilloes of government officials, such as sexual offenses, were exposed first by reporters. John David Rausch Jr., "The Pathology of Politics: Government, Press, and Scandal," *Extensions* (University of Oklahoma), Fall 1990, 11–12. For the Whitewater scandal, reporters got most of their tips from a Republican Party operation run by officials from Republican presidential campaigns. Regarding sexual matters, reporters got most of their tips from prosecutors for the independent counsel, lawyers for Paula Jones, or a book agent for Linda Tripp. See Brill, "Pressgate," 134.

[104]Except for a reporter at a small paper in North Carolina. Charles Peters, "Tilting at Windmills," *Washington Monthly,* October/November, 2005, 15.

[105]Charles Peters, "Tilting at Windmills," *Washington Monthly,* March, 2006, 8. Only a reporter for a Charleston, West Virginia, newspaper sounded an alarm.

[106]William Rivers, "The Correspondents after 25 Years," *Columbia Journalism Review* 1 (Spring 1962): 5.

[107]Coolidge, in his reelection campaign, was actually the first president to use radio as a means of addressing the public directly.

[108]James David Barber, *Presidential Character* (Englewood Cliffs, N.J.: Prentice Hall, 1992), 238.

[109]Reagan got his start in show business as a radio sportscaster in Des Moines, Iowa, announcing major league baseball games "live." Of course, he was not actually at the games: he got the barest details—who was at bat, whether the pitch was a strike or a ball or a hit—from the wireless and made up the rest to create a commentary that convinced listeners that he was watching in person.

[110]Timothy J. Russert, "For '92, the Networks Have to Do Better," *New York Times,* March 4, 1990, E23.

[111]Smith, *Power Game,* 420.

[112]Steven K. Weisman, "The President and the Press," *New York Times Magazine,* October 14, 1984, 71–72; Dick Kirschten, "Communications Reshuffling Intended to Help Reagan Do What He Does Best," *National Journal,* January 28, 1984, 154.

[113]Sidney Blumenthal, "The Syndicated Presidency," *New Yorker,* April 5, 1993, 45.

[114]Brit Hume, of NBC News.

[115]For an extensive examination of this phenomenon, see Toobin, *Vast Conspiracy.*

[116]John F. Harris, "Bush's Lucky Break," *Washington Post National Weekly Edition,* May 14, 2001, 23.

[117]For examination of coverage during Clinton's early days in office, see William Glaber-son, "The Capitol Press vs. the President: Fair Coverage or Unreined Adversity?" *New York Times,* June 17, 1993, A11; Christopher Georges, "Bad News Bearers," *Washington Monthly,* July-August 1993, 28–34; and Toobin, *Vast Conspiracy,* 247–248.

[118]Howard Kurtz, "Assessing—and Controlling—the Damage to the Presidency," *Washington Post National Weekly Edition,* February 2, 1998, 21.

[119]Auletta, "Fortress Bush," 60.

[120]Ibid., 54, 57, 64.

[121]*All Things Considered,* NPR, March 21, 2006.

[122]Ibid., 55.

[123]David Barstow and Robin Stein, "Is it News or Public Relations? Under Bush, Lines Are Blurry," *New York Times,* March 13, 2005, YT1. The Clinton administration also used these, though less extensively.

[124]According to a report by the Government Accountability Office (GAO). Christopher Lee, "Report: White House Spent $1.6 Billion on PR," *Lincoln Journal Star,* February 19, 2006, 3A.

[125]John F. Harris, "On the World Stage, Bush Shuns the Spotlight," *Washington Post National Weekly Edition,* April 23, 2001, 11; Ronald Brownstein, "Bush Forced into Role He May Not Want: Communicator," *Lincoln Journal Star,* September 15, 2001.

[126]John F. Harris and Dan Balz, "A Well-Oiled Machine," *Washington Post National Weekly Edition,* May 14, 2001, 6.

[127]James Carville, quoted in John F. Harris, "Bush's Lucky Break," *Washington Post National Weekly Edition,* May 14, 2001, 23.

[128]Aides claimed that *Air Force One* was a target, but it was revealed that this claim was an exaggeration to parry the criticism that Bush received. Eric Pooley and Karen Tumulty, "Bush in the Crucible," *Time,* September 24, 2001, 49.

[129]Calvin Woodward, "Warrior Bush: It Doesn't Come Naturally," *Lincoln Journal Star,* October 6, 2002.

[130]Michael Duffy, "Marching Alone," *Time,* September 9, 2002, 42.

[131]Presidential historian Henry Graff, cited in Ron Fourier, "President Stumbles with Mideast Rhetoric," *Lincoln Journal Star,* April 20, 2002.

[132]Joe Klein, "Why the 'War President' Is Under Fire," *Time,* February 23, 2004, 17.

[133]For an empirical examination, see David Domke, *God Willing? Political Fundamentalism in the White House, the War on Terror, and the Echoing Press* (Ann Arbor, Mich.: Pluto, 2004). Domke also examines the intolerance of dissent reflected in speeches and remarks issued by the administration.

[134]David Greenberg, "Fathers and Sons," *New Yorker,* July 12 and 19, 2004, 97.

[135]David L. Greene, "Bush Often Great Miscommunicator," *Lincoln Journal Star,* October 6, 2002.

[136]Philip Gourevitch, "Bushspeak," *New Yorker,* September 13, 2004, 38.

[137]Stephen Hess, *Live from Capitol Hill!* (Washington, D.C.: Brookings Institution, 1991), 62; Timothy E. Cook, *Making Laws and Making News: Media Strategies in the U.S. House of Representatives* (Washington, D.C.: Brookings Institution, 1989), 2.

[138]Hess, *Live from Capitol Hill!* 102.

[139]Joe Klein, *The Natural* (New York: Doubleday, 2002), 109.

[140]Robert Schmidt, "May It Please the Court," *Brill's Content,* October 1999, 74.

[141]For analysis, see Rorie L. Spill and Zoe M. Oxley, "Philosopher Kings or Political Actors? How the Media Portray the Supreme Court," *Judicature,* July-August 2003, 22–29.

[142]Ibid.

[143]Edward Jay Epstein, *News from Nowhere* (New York: Random House, 1973), 13.

[144]Graber, *Mass Media and American Politics,* 62.

[145]Milton Coleman, "When the Candidate Is Black Like Me," *Washington Post National Weekly Edition,* April 23, 1984, 9.

[146]Roper Organization, "A Big Concern about the Media: Intruding on Grieving Families," *Washington Post National Weekly Edition,* June 6, 1984. See also Cappella and Jamieson, *Spiral of Cynicism,* 210.

[147]In 1987 Reagan appointees to the Federal Communications Commission (FCC) abandoned the Fairness Doctrine, which had required broadcasters to maintain editorial balance. When Congress reinstated the doctrine, President Reagan vetoed the bill, thus allowing broadcasters to cater to any audience.

[148]McChesney, *Problem of the Media,* 116.

[149]Karen Tumulty, "I Want My Al TV," *Time,* June 30, 2003, 59. A new liberal network, Air America Radio, which reaches some of these cities, began in 2004. Even the Sunday talk shows of the major television networks lean right. Significantly more guests are conservative or Republican than liberal or Democrat, and the journalists who question them are more conservative than liberal, according to a study of the shows from 1997 through 2005. Paul Waldman, "John Fund Again? It's Not Your Imagination— the Sunday Shows Really Do Lean Right," *Washington Monthly,* March, 2006, 9–13.

[150]Liddy, who was convicted in the Watergate scandal, instructed listeners where to aim when shooting agents of the Bureau of Alcohol, Tobacco, and Firearms to kill them.

[151]McChesney, *Problem of the Media,* 117.

[152]According to the Center for American Progress. Rob Hotakainen, "Congress Braces for Battle on the Fairness Doctrine," *Champaign-Urbana News-Gazette,* July 15, 2007, B1.

[153]For a history of the origins of Fox News, see David Carr, *Crazy Like a Fox* (New York: Portfolio, 2004).

[154]For analysis, see Ken Auletta, "Vox Fox," *New Yorker,* May 26, 2003, 58.

[155]Geneva Overholser, "It's Time for News Networks to Take Sides," *Lincoln Journal Star,* August 26, 2001.

[156]Robert S. Boynton, "How to Make a Guerrilla Documentary," *New York Times Magazine,* July 11, 2004, 22. See also the documentary *Outfoxed* (2004).

[157]According to the Project for Excellence in Journalism. David Bauder, "Study: Fox Spends Less Time on Iraq War than MSNBC, CNN," *Lincoln Journal Star,* June 14, 2007. In the first three months of 2007, Fox devoted half as much airtime to the war as MSNBC did and considerably less than CNN did.

[158]Nicholas D. Kristof, "A Challenge for Bill O'Reilly," *New York Times,* December 18, 2005, WK13. The crusade coincided with publication of a book on this subject by a Fox broadcaster.

[159]Auletta, "Vox Fox," 63–64.

[160]Overholser, "It's Time"; David Plotz, "Fox News Channel," *Slate,* November 22, 2000 (slate.msn.com).

[161]Jeff Cohen and Jonah Goldberg, "Face-Off: Beyond Belief," *Brill's Content,* December 1999-January 2000, 54.

[162]For examination, see Tommy Nguyen, "The Reel Liberal Majority," *Washington Post National Weekly Edition,* August 2–8, 2004, 14.

[163]Edith Efron, *The News Twisters* (Los Angeles: Nash, 1971); L. B. Bozell and B. H. Baker, "And That's the Way It Isn't," *Journalism Quarterly* 67 (1990), 1139; Bernard Goldberg, *Bias* (New York: Regnery, 2002); Alterman, *What Liberal Media?*

[164]S. Robert Lichter, Stanley Rothman, and Linda S. Lichter, *The Media Elite* (Bethesda, Md.: Adler & Adler, 1986), 21–25. See also Hess, *Live from Capitol Hill!* app. A, 110–130.

[165]John Johnstone, Edward Slawski, and William Bowman, *The Newspeople* (Urbana: University of Illinois Press, 1976), 225–226.

[166]Stanley Rothman and S. Robert Lichter, "Media and Business Elites: Two Classes in Conflict?" *Public Interest* 69 (1982), 111–125; S. Robert Lichter and Stanley Rothman, "Media and Business Elites," *Public Opinion,* October-November 1981, 44.

[167]Stephen Hess, *The Washington Reporters* (Washington, D.C.: Brookings Institution, 1981), 89; see also Lichter et al., *Media Elite,* 127–128.

[168]James Fallows, "The Stoning of Donald Regan," *Washington Monthly,* June 1984, 57.

[169]Sometimes media executives or editors pressure reporters because they have contrary views. Kimberly Conniff, "All the Views Fit to Print," *Brill's Content,* March 2001, 105.

[170]Howard Kurtz, *Media Circus* (New York: Random House, 1994), 48.

[171]Russell J. Dalton, Paul A. Beck, and Robert Huckfeldt, "Partisan Cues and the Media Information Flows in the 1992 Presidential Election," *American Political Science Review* 92 (March 1998), 118.

[172]C. Richard Hofstetter, *Bias in the News* (Columbus: Ohio State University Press, 1976); Graber, *Mass Media and Politics,* 167–168; Michael J. Robinson, "Just How Liberal Is the News?" *Public Opinion,* February-March 1983, 55–60; Maura Clancy and Michael J. Robinson, "General Election Coverage: Part I," *Public Opinion,* December 1984-January 1985, 49–54, 59; Michael J. Robinson, "The Media Campaign, '84: Part II," *Public Opinion,* February-March 1985, 43–48.

[173]Dave D'Alessio and Mike Allen, "Media Bias in Presidential Elections: A Meta-Analysis," *Journal of Communication* 50 (2000), 133–156. Some studies did find some bias against incumbents, front-runners, and emerging challengers. For these candidates, the media apparently took their watchdog role seriously. Clancy and Robinson, "General Election Coverage"; Robinson, "Media Campaign, '84"; Michael J. Robinson, "Where's the Beef? Media and Media Elites in 1984," in *The American Elections of 1984,* ed. Austin Ranney (Durham, N.C.: Duke University Press, 1985), 184; Michael J. Robinson, "News Media Myths and Realities: What Network News Did and Didn't Do in the 1984 General Campaign," in *Elections in America,* ed. Kay Lehman Schlozman (Boston: Allen & Unwin, 1987), 143–170; Kim Fridkin Kahn and Patrick J. Kenney, *The Spectacle of U.S. Senate Campaigns* (Princeton, N.J.: Princeton University, 1999), 126–129.

[174]Robert Shogan, *Bad News: Where the Press Goes Wrong in the Making of the President* (Chicago: Dee, 2001), 231.

[175]It helped the Democrat Carter in 1976 but hurt him in 1980. It helped the Republican Bush in 1988 but hurt him in 1992. Thomas E. Patterson, *Out of Order* (New York: Vintage, 1994), 131. It helped the Democrat Clinton in 1996, and at different stages of the campaign, it helped the Republican Bush or the Democrat Gore in 2000.

[176]Shogan, *Bad News,* 204–245; Clymer, "Better Campaign Reporting."

[177]Fewer than one in ten stories on the 2000 debates focused on policy differences; seven in ten focused on candidates' performance or strategy. Bill Kovach and Tom Rosenstiel, "Campaign Lite," *Washington Monthly,* January-February 2001, 31–32. For a perceptive analysis, see Clymer, "Better Campaign Reporting."

[178]The media, however, did pay a lot of attention to Ross Perot's presidential bid in 1992 because he said he would spend $100 million on his campaign and because polls showed he could compete with Bush and Clinton.

[179]For a recounting of his 2000 campaign, see Ralph Nader, "My Untold Story," *Brill's Content,* February 2001, 100.

[180]"Clinton Gains More Support from Big Papers," *Lincoln Journal Star,* October 25, 1992. Newspapers insist that there is little relationship between their editorial endorsements and their news coverage or even their political columns. An endorsement for one candidate does not mean more positive coverage or columns for that candidate because American media have established a tradition of autonomy in the newsroom. Dalton et al., "Partisan Cues," 118. However, some research shows that when papers endorse candidates,

the papers show a small bias toward the candidates in their news stories (if the candidates are incumbents). Kim Fridkin Kahn and Patrick J. Kenney, "The Slant of the News: How Editorial Endorsements Influence Campaign Coverage and Citizen's Views of Candidates," *American Political Science Review* 96 (June 2002), 381–394.

[181]Hofstetter, *Bias in the News;* Hess, *Live from Capitol Hill!* 12–13.

[182]Robinson, "Just How Liberal . . . ?" 58; Arthur H. Miller, Edie N. Goldenberg, and Lutz Erbring, "Type-Set Politics," *American Political Science Review* 73 (January 1979), 69; Patterson, *Out of Order,* 6; Charles M. Tidmarch and John J. Pitney Jr., "Covering Congress," *Polity* 17 (Spring 1985), 463–483.

[183]Richard Morin, "The Big Picture Is out of Focus," *Washington Post National Weekly Edition,* March 6, 2000, 21.

[184]Steven Brill, "Quality Control," *Brill's Content,* July-August 1998, 19–20.

[185]Patterson, *Out of Order,* 25, 245.

[186]Stanley Rothman and S. Robert Lichter, "The Nuclear Energy Debate," *Public Opinion,* August-September 1982, 47–48; Stanley Rothman and S. Robert Lichter, "Elite Ideology and Risk Perception in Nuclear Energy Policy," *American Political Science Review* 81 (June 1987), 383–404; Lichter et al., *Media Elite,* ch. 7; Sabato, *Feeding Frenzy,* 87, and sources cited therein. But a study examining twenty years' coverage of governors and their states' unemployment and murder rates shows no bias toward Democratic or Republican governors. David Niven, "Partisan Bias in the Media?" *Social Science Quarterly* 80 (December 1999), 847–857.

[187]Goldberg, *Bias,* ch. 5; Alterman, *What Liberal Media?* ch. 7.

[188]Alterman, *What Liberal Media?* 104–117.

[189]For examination of "24," see Jane Mayer, "Whatever It Takes," *New Yorker,* February 19 and 26, 2007, 66.

[190]Mireya Navarro, "On Abortion, Hollywood Is No Choice," *New York Times,* June 10, 2007, ST1.

[191]Ibid., 118–138. For an analysis of the coverage of the economy in the booming 1990s, see John Cassidy, "Striking It Rich: The Rise and Fall of Popular Capitalism," *New Yorker,* January 14, 2002, 63–73.

[192]Bruce Nussbaum, "The Myth of the Liberal Media," *Business Week,* November 11, 1996; Fallows, *Breaking the News,* 49.

[193]Further, the media give scant attention to labor matters, except when strikes inconvenience commuters. Mark Crispin Miller, "The Media and the Bush Dyslexicon," in Grover and Peschek, *Voices of Dissent,* 137–146. In 2001, the three main television networks used representatives of corporations as sources thirty times more often than representatives of unions. McChesney, *Problem of the Media,* 70–71.

[194]McChesney, *Problem of the Media,* 106.

[195]Robinson, "Just How Liberal . . . ?" 59.

[196]Parenti, *Inventing Reality,* ch. 7–11; Charles E. Lindblom, *Politics and Markets* (New York: Basic Books, 1977); J. Fred MacDonald, *One Nation under Television: The Rise and Decline of Network TV* (New York: Pantheon Books, 1990); Dan Nimmo and James E. Combs, *Mediated Political Realities* (White Plains, N.Y.: Longman, 1983), 135; Benjamin I. Page and R.Y. Shapiro, *The Rational Public* (Chicago: University of Chicago Press, 1992); John R. Zaller and Dennis Chiu, "Government's Little Helper: U.S. Press Coverage of Foreign Policy Crises, 1945–1991," *Political Communication* 13 (1996), 385–405.

[197]John R. MacArthur, *Second Front: Censorship and Propaganda in the Gulf War* (New York: Hill & Wang, 1992); James Bennet, "How They Missed That Story," *Washington Monthly,* December 1990, 8–16; Christopher Dickey, "Not Their Finest Hour," *Newsweek,* June 8, 1992, 66.

[198]In the 1950s and early 1960s, newspapers, magazines, and television networks sent few correspondents to Vietnam, so most accepted the government's account of the conflict. Susan Welch, "The American Press and Indochina, 1950–1956," in *Communication in International Politics,* ed. Richard L. Merritt (Urbana: University of Illinois Press, 1972), 207–231; Edward J. Epstein, "The Selection of Reality," in *What's News?,* ed. Elie Abel (San Francisco: Institute for Contemporary Studies, 1981), 124. When they did dispatch correspondents, many filed pessimistic reports, but their editors believed the government rather than the correspondents and refused to print these reports. Instead, they ran articles quoting optimistic statements by government officials. See David Halberstam, *The Powers That Be* (New York: Dell, 1980), 642–647. In 1968, the media did turn against the war, but rather than sharply criticize it, they conveyed the impression that it was futile. Daniel C. Hallin, *The "Uncensored War": The Media and Vietnam* (New York: Oxford University Press, 1986).

[199]David Domke, *God Willing? Political Fundamentalism in the White House, the "War on Terror," and the Echoing Press* (London: Pluto, 2004).

[200]"Return of Talk Show Is Healthy Sign," *Lincoln Journal Star,* October 6, 2001.

[201]Alterman, *What Liberal Media?* 202.

[202]Anthony Collings, "The BBC: How to Be Impartial in Wartime," *Chronicle of Higher Education,* December 21, 2001, B14.

[203]*Weapons of Mass Deception,* a documentary film by Danny Schechter (Cinema Libre Distribution, 2005).

[204]Alterman, *What Liberal Media?* 29; Todd Gitlin, "Showtime Iraq," *American Prospect,* November 4, 2002, 34–35.

[205]*Weapons of Mass Deception*

[206]Bill Moyers, "Our Democracy Is in Danger of Being Paralyzed," Keynote address to the National Conference on Media Reform, November 8, 2003, www.truthout.org/docs_03/printer_111403E.shtml.

[207]James Poniewozik, "What You See vs. What They See," *Time,* April 7, 2003, 68–69. For example, that U.S. searches caused considerable damage to Iraqi homes and that these raids swept up many innocent family members, *Morning Edition,* National Public Radio, May 4, 2004. Also, that in the run-up to the war, U.S. agents had bugged the homes and offices of United Nations Security Council members who had not proclaimed support for the war, Camille T. Taiara, "Spoon-Feeding the Press," *San Francisco Bay Guardian,* March 12, 2003 (www.sfbg.com/37/24/x_media-beat.html).

[208]Frank Rich, "The Spoils of War," *New York Times,* April 13, 2003, AR1; Paul Janensch, "Whether to Show Images of War Dead Is Media Dilemma," *Lincoln Journal Star,* March 31, 2003.

[209]Terry McCarthy, "Whatever Happened to the Republican Guard?" *Time,* May 12, 2003, 38.

[210]Frank Rich, *The Greatest Story Ever Told* (New York: Penguin Press, 2006), 155.

[211]Todd Gitlin, "Embed or in Bed?" *American Prospect,* June 2003, 43.

[212]Schell, "Preface," vi.

[213]Massing, *Now They Tell Us,* 7.

[214]For an examination, see Massing, *Now They Tell Us.*

[215]"Buying the War," PBS, April 25, 2007.

[216]Howard Kurtz, quoted in Todd Gitlin, "The Great Media Breakdown," *Mother Jones,* November-December, 2004, 58.

[217]Rich, *The Greatest Story Ever Sold,* 87.

[218]"The Times and Iraq," *New York Times,* May 26, 2004, A10; Daniel Okrent, "Weapons of Mass Destruction? Or Mass Distraction?" *New York Times,* May 30, 2004, WK1.

[219]Jim Thompson, "Letters to the Public Editor," *New York Times,* June 6, 2004, WK2.

[220]Reporters turn to officials because it is easy and because, ironically, they want to avoid charges of bias. They believe that their superiors and the public consider officials to be reliable, so ignoring or downplaying them might be construed as showing bias against them. Cook, *Making Laws and Making News,* 8. See also Leon V. Sigal, *Reporters and Officials* (Lexington, Mass.: Heath, 1973), 120–121; Lucy Howard, "Slanted 'Line'?" *Newsweek,* February 13, 1989, 6; Hess, *Live from Capitol Hill!* 50. Trivia buffs might wonder who has been the subject of the most cover articles in *Time* magazine—the answer is Richard Nixon (fifty-five). "Numbers," *Time,* March 9, 1998, 189.

[221]W. Lance Bennett, "Toward a Theory of Press-State Relations in the United States," *Journal of Communication* 40 (1990), 103–125.

[222]Three times as many people believe the media are "too liberal" than believe they are "too conservative" (45 percent to 15 percent). McChesney, *Problem of the Media,* 114.

[223]M. D. Watts, D. Domke, D.V. Shah, and D. P. Fan, "Elite Cues and Media Bias in Presidential Campaigns: Explaining Public Perceptions

of a Liberal Press," *Communication Research* 26 (1999), 144–175.

[224]William Kristol, quoted in Alterman, *What Liberal Media?* 2–3.

[225]Elizabeth Wilner, "On the Road Again," *Washington Post National Weekly Edition,* June 6–12, 2005, 22.

[226]Robert Vallone, Lee Ross, and Mark R. Lepper, "The Hostile Media Phenomenon," *Journal of Personality and Social Psychology* 49 (1985), 577–585; Roger Giner-Sorolla and Shelly Chaiken, "The Causes of Hostile Media Judgments," *Journal of Experimental Social Psychology* 30 (1994), 165–180.

[227]Dalton et al., "Partisan Cues and the Media."

[228]W. Phillips Davison, "The Third-Person Effect in Communication," *Public Opinion Quarterly* 47 (1983), 1–15.

[229]Dave D'Alessio, "An Experimental Examination of Readers' Perceptions of Media Bias," unpublished manuscript, University of Connecticut, n.d.; Mark Peffley, James M. Avery, and Jason E. Glass, "Public Perceptions of Bias in the News Media," paper presented at the annual meeting of the Midwest Political Science Association, Chicago, April 19–22, 2001.

[230]According to a statement by a CNN producer in the documentary *Outfoxed.*

[231]And HBO postponed a documentary film, *Last Letters Home,* based on excerpts of letters from soldiers later killed in Iraq, because this powerful film might have turned viewers against the war. *All Things Considered,* NPR, November 11, 2004.

[232]Ted Koppel, "And Now, a Word for Our Demographic," *New York Times,* January 29, 2006, WK16.

[233]Goldberg, *Bias,* 92

[234]Theodore H. White, *America in Search of Itself* (New York: Harper & Row, 1982), 186.

[235]Goldberg, *Bias,* 92

[236]"Anchorwoman Verdict Raises Mixed Opinions," *Lincoln Journal Star,* August 9, 1983.

[237]Kovach and Rosenstiel, *Warp Speed,* 64

[238]Hess, *Live from Capitol Hill!* 34; Rosenstiel, *State of the News Media,* 21.

[239]Molly Ivins, "Media Conglomerates Profit at Expense of News, Public," *Lincoln Journal Star,* October 26, 2001.

[240]James Fallows, "On That Chart," *Nation,* June 3, 1996, 15

[241]Maureen Dowd, "Flintstone Futurama," *New York Times,* August 19, 2001, WK 13

[242]A poll of reporters and executives found that a third admitted to avoiding stories that would embarrass an advertiser or harm the financial interests of their own organization. "Poll: Reporters Avoid, Soften Stories," *Lincoln Journal Star,* May 1, 2000; David Owen, "The Cigarette Companies: How They Get Away with Murder, Part II," *Washington Monthly,* March 1985, 48–54. See also Daniel Hellinger and Dennis R. Judd, *The Democratic Facade,* 2nd ed. (Belmont, Calif.: Wadsworth,

1994), 59. Through the 1920s, newspapers refrained from pointing out that popular "patent medicines" were usually useless and occasionally dangerous because the purveyors bought more advertising than any other business. Mark Crispin Miller, "Free the Media," *Nation,* June 3, 1996, 10.

[243]Roger Mudd, quoted in *Television and the Presidential Elections,* ed. Martin A. Linsky (Lexington, Mass.: Heath, 1983), 48.

[244]"Q&A: Dan Rather on Fear, Money, and the News," *Brill's Content,* October 1998, 117.

[245]Barry Sussman, "News on TV: Mixed Reviews," *Washington Post National Weekly Edition,* September 3, 1984, 37.

[246]Bill Carter, "Networks Fight Public's Shrinking Attention Span," *Lincoln Journal Star,* September 30, 1990.

[247]Epstein, *News from Nowhere,* 4.

[248]William A. Henry III, "Requiem for TV's Gender Gap," *Time,* August 22, 1983, 57.

[249]Richard Morin, "The Nation's Mood? Calm," *Washington Post National Weekly Edition,* November 5, 2001, 35.

[250]According to the Tyndall Report, cited in Nicholas Kristof, "Please, Readers, Help Bill O'Reilly!" *New York Times,* February 7, 2006, A21.

[251]Charles Peters, "Tilting at Windmills," *Washington Monthly,* September, 2006, 7.

[252]For an examination of how the media exaggerated the Whitewater scandal, see Gene Lyons, *Fools for Scandal* (New York: Franklin Square Press, 1996).

[253]The third and final special prosecutor concluded that there might be some evidence of wrongdoing in the law firm rec-ords of Hillary Clinton but that there was not enough evidence to justify prosecution.

[254]The pope was making a historic visit to Cuba. The networks had considered this so important that they had sent their anchors to Havana. At the same time, renewed violence in Northern Ireland threatened to scuttle the peace talks between Catholics and Protestants, and continued refusal from Iraq to cooperate with United Nations biological and chemical weapons inspectors threatened to escalate to military conflict.

[255]Eric Pooley, "Monica's World," *Time,* March 2, 1998, 40.

[256]Quoted in Fallows, *Breaking the News,* 201.

[257]Samuel G. Freedman, "Fighting to Balance Honor and Profit on the Local News," *New York Times,* September 30, 2001, sec. 2, 26.

[258]Lawrie Mifflin, "Crime Falls, but Not on TV," *New York Times,* July 6, 1997, E3. According to one researcher, crime coverage is also "the easiest, cheapest, laziest news to cover" because stations just listen to the police radio and then send a camera crew to shoot the story.

[259]Heather Maher, "Eleven O'Clock Blues," *Brill's Content,* February 2001, 99.

[260]Molly Ivins, "Don't Moan about the Media, Do Something," *Lincoln Journal Star,* November 1999.

[261]David S. Broder, "Can We Govern?" *Washington Post National Weekly Edition,* January 31, 1994, 23.

[262]Newspaper ads were placed in college papers by Holocaust deniers, claiming that there is no proof that gas chambers actually existed. The editor of one paper justified accepting the ad by saying, "There are two sides to every issue and both have a place on the pages of any open-minded paper's editorial page." Tannen, *Argument Culture,* 38. For examination of this phenomenon, see Deborah E. Lipstadt, *Denying the Holocaust: The Growing Assault on Truth and Memory* (New York: Plume, 1993).

[263]Howard Kurtz, quoted in Tannen, *Argument Culture,* 29.

[264]Patterson, *Out of Order,* 53–59.

[265]Lee Sigelman and David Bullock, "Candidates, Issues, Horse Races, and Hoopla: Presidential Campaign Coverage, 1888–1988," *American Politics Quarterly* 19 (January 1991), 5–32. So was emphasis on human interest. In 1846, the *New York Tribune* described the culinary habits of Representative William "Sausage" Sawyer (D-Ohio), who ate a sausage on the floor of the House every afternoon: "What little grease is left on his hands he wipes on his almost bald head which saves any outlay for Pomatum. His mouth sometimes serves as a finger glass, his shirtsleeves and pantaloons being called into requisition as a napkin. He uses a jackknife for a toothpick, and then he goes on the floor again to abuse the Whigs as the British party." Cook, *Making Laws and Making News,* 18–19.

[266]Patterson, *Out of Order,* 74; Marion R. Just, Ann N. Crigler, Dean E. Alger, Timothy E. Cook, Montague Kern, and Darrell M. West, *Crosstalk: Citizens, Candidates, and the Media in a Presidential Campaign* (Chicago: University of Chicago Press, 1996); Mathew Robert Kerbel, *Remote and Controlled* (Boulder, Colo.: Westview Press, 1995); Bruce Buchanan, *Electing a President* (Austin: University of Texas Press, 1991).

[267]Owen, "Media Mayhem," 127.

[268]Richard Morin, "Toward the Millennium, by the Numbers," *Washington Post National Weekly Edition,* July 7, 1997, 35.

[269]Patterson, *Out of Order,* 81–82.

[270]Fallows, *Breaking the News,* 162, 27.

[271]Epstein, *News from Nowhere,* 179, 195.

[272]Rosenstiel, *State of the News Media,* 18.

[273]John Horn, "Campaign Coverage Avoids Issues," *Lincoln Journal Star,* September 25, 1988. Another survey found that 28 percent of women and 40 percent of men change channels every time during commercial breaks. "Ticker," *Brill's Content,* September 1999, 128.

[274]John Eisendrath, "An Eyewitness Account of Local TV News," *Washington Monthly,* September 1986, 21.

[275]Michael Deaver, "Sound-Bite Campaigning: TV Made Us Do It," *Washington Post National Weekly Edition,* November 7, 1988, 34.

276Fred Friendly, quoted on *All Things Considered,* National Public Radio, March 4, 1998.
277Thomas E. Patterson, *The Vanishing Voter* (New York: Knopf, 2002), 92.
278Graber, *Mass Media,* 244; Doris Graber, *Processing News: How People Tame the Information Tide* (White Plains, N.Y.: Longman, 1984). A 1993 survey concluded that almost half of Americans over sixteen have such limited reading and math skills that they are unfit for most jobs. One task the survey included was to paraphrase a newspaper story. Many people could scan the story but not paraphrase it when they finished it. Paul Gray, "Adding Up the Under-Skilled," *Time,* September 20, 1993, 75. For a critique, claiming that the oligopolistic structure of the media makes it impossible to know if people are getting what they actually want, see McChesney, *Problem of the Media,* 198–202.
279Reuven Frank, quoted in Neil Hickey, "Money Lust," *Columbia Journalism Review,* July-August 1998, 35.
280Patrick D. Healy, "Believe It: The Media's Credibility Headache Gets Worse," *New York Times,* May 22, 2005, WK4. At least this is an improvement. In the late 1990s, reporters ranked lower than lawyers. Joe Klein, "Dizzy Days," *New Yorker,* October 5, 1998, 45.
281Marta W. Aldrich, "Support for Media Freedoms Waning," *Lincoln Journal Star,* July 4, 1999.
282James Poniewozik, "Don't Blame It on Jayson Blair," *Time,* June 9, 2003, 90.
283Kathleen Hall Jamieson, quoted in Howard Kurtz, "Tuning Out the News," *Washington Post National Weekly Edition,* May 29, 1995, 6; William Raspberry, "Blow-by-Blow Coverage," *Washington Post National Weekly Edition,* November 6, 1995, 29.
284Michael J. Robinson, "Public Affairs Television and the Growth of Political Malaise," *American Political Science Review* 70 (1976), 409–432; Miller et al., "Type-Set Politics."
285"Study: Public More Cynical than Media," *Champaign-Urbana News-Gazette,* May 22, 1995.
286Fallows, *Breaking the News,* 202–203.
287See Cappella and Jamieson, *Spiral of Cynicism.*
288Fallows, *Breaking the News,* 247.
289Stephen Earl Bennett, "Trends in Americans' Political Information," *American Politics Quarterly* 17 (October 1989), 422–435; Richard Zoglin, "The Tuned-Out Generation," *Time,* July 9, 1990, 64.
290Robert N. Entman, *Democracy without Citizens: Media and the Decay of American Politics* (New York: Oxford University Press, 1989), 17.
291See McChesney, *Problem of the Media,* 96–97.
292Peters, *How Washington Really Works,* 32.

Chapter 5

1This vignette is drawn from Warren Brown, "From Victim to Advocate," *Washington Post National Weekly Edition,* June 28, 1999, 30.

2Jeffrey H. Birnbaum, *The Lobbyists: How Influence Peddlers Get Their Way in Washington* (New York: Times Books, 1993), 32.
3Mark A. Peterson and Jack L. Walker, Jr., "Interest Group Responses to Partisan Change: The Impact of the Reagan Administration upon the National Interest Group System," in *Interest Group Politics,* 2nd ed., ed. Allan J. Cigler and Burdett A. Loomis (Washington, D.C.: CQ Press, 1987), 162.
4Alexis de Tocqueville, *Democracy in America* (New York: Knopf, 1945), 191. (Originally published 1835.)
5Gabriel Almond and Sidney Verba, *Civil Culture* (Boston: Little, Brown, 1965), 266–306.
6David Truman, *The Governmental Process* (New York: Knopf, 1964), 25–26.
7Ibid., 59.
8James Q. Wilson, *Political Organizations* (New York: Basic Books, 1973), 198.
9Graham K. Wilson, *Interest Groups in America* (Oxford: Oxford University Press, 1981), ch. 5; see also Graham K. Wilson, "American Business and Politics," in *Interest Group Politics,* 2nd ed., ed. Cigler and Loomis, 221–235.
10Kay Lehman Schlozman and John T. Tierney, "More of the State: Washington Pressure Group Activity in a Decade of Change," *Journal of Politics* 45 (1983), 335–356.
11Christopher H. Foreman Jr., "Grassroots Victim Organizations: Mobilizing for Personal and Public Health," in *Interest Group Politics,* 4th ed., ed. Allan J. Cigler and Burdett A. Loomis (Washington, D.C.: CQ Press, 1994), 33–53.
12William Brown, "Exchange Theory and the Institutional Impetus for Interest Group Formation," in *Interest Group Politics,* 6th ed., ed. Allan J. Cigler and Burdett A. Loomis (Washington, D.C.: CQ Press, 2002), 313–329; William Brown, "Benefits and Membership: A Reappraisal of Interest Group Activity," *Western Political Quarterly* 29 (1976), 258–273; Terry M. Moe, *The Organization of Interests: Incentives and the Internal Dynamics of Political Interest Groups* (Chicago: University of Chicago Press, 1980).
13This applies to public, or collective, goods, rather than to private goods available only to the members.
14Mancur Olson, *The Logic of Collective Action* (Cambridge, Mass.: Harvard University, 1971).
15Nicholas Babchuk and Ralph V. Thompson, "The Voluntary Associations of Negroes," *American Sociological Review* 27 (1962), 662–665; see also Patricia Klobus-Edwards, John N. Edwards, and David L. Klemmack, "Differences in Social Participation of Blacks and Whites," *Social Forces* 56 (1978), 1035–1052.
16Robert D. Putnam, *Bowling Alone* (New York: Simon & Schuster, 2000).
17Theda Skocpol, "The Narrowing of Civic Life," *American Prospect,* June 2004, A5–A7
18Richard Stengel, "Bowling Together," *Time,* July 22, 1996, 35.
19Theda Skocpol, "Associations without Members," *American Prospect,* July-August 1999, 66–73.

20Mark T. Hayes, "The New Group Universe," in *Interest Group Politics,* 2nd ed., ed. Cigler and Loomis, 133–145.
21Walker, "Origins and Maintenance of Interest Groups"; E. E. Schattschneider, *Semi-Sovereign People* (New York: Holt, Rinehart and Winston, 1960), 118.
22David S. Broder and Michael Weisskopf, "Finding New Friends on the Hill," *Washington Post National Weekly Edition,* October 3, 1994, 11.
23Charles E. Lindblom, "The Market as Prison," *Journal of Politics* 44 (1982), 324–336; Michael Genovese, *The Presidential Dilemma: Leadership in the American System* (New York: HarperCollins, 1995).
24M. Asif Ismail, "Drug Lobby Second to None," The Center for Public Integrity, www.publicintegrity.org/rx/report.aspx?aid=723.
25Ibid.
26*Democracy on Drugs: The Medicare Prescription Drug Bill: A Study in How Government Shouldn't Work.* Common Cause, May 18, 2004, www.commoncause.org/atf/cf/%7BFB3C17E2 CDD1-4DF6-92BE-BD4429893665%7D/democracy_on_drugs.pdf.
27"Pharmaceutical Industry Ranks as Most Profitable Industry—Again," *Public Citizen,* April 18, 2002, www.citizen.org/pressroom/release.cfm?ID51088.
28Unions contributed to their decline by becoming complacent toward the recruitment of new members. Instead, they focused on achieving greater gains for existing members. Harold Myerson, "Organize or Die," *American Prospect,* September 2003, 39–42.
29Steven Greenhouse, "Union Membership Rose in '98, but Unions' Percentage of Workforce Fell," *New York Times,* January 20, 1999, A22; Paul E. Johnson, "Organized Labor in an Era of Blue-Collar Decline," in *Interest Group Politics,* 3rd ed., ed. Allan J. Cigler and Burdett A. Loomis (Washington, D.C.: CQ Press, 1991), 33–62.
30Thomas B. Edsall, "Working With the Union You Have," *Washington Post National Weekly Edition,* March 14–20, 2005, 15.
31Steven Greenhouse, "Report Faults Laws for Slowing Growth of Unions," *New York Times,* October 24, 2000, A14.
32Jeffrey Goldberg, "Selling Wal-Mart," *New Yorker,* April 2, 2007, 33.
33Harold Meyerson, "Wal-Mart Comes North," *American Prospect,* April, 2007, 28–29.
34Joshua Green, "The New War Over Wal-Mart," *Atlantic Monthly,* June, 2006, 38–44.
35Steven Greenhouse, "The Most Innovative Figure in Silicon Valley? Maybe This Labor Organizer," *New York Times,* November 14, 1999, 26.
36Steven Greenhouse, "Graduate Students Push for Union Membership," *New York Times,* May 15, 2001, A18.
37Information on annual expenditures is found in U.S. Census Bureau, *Statistical Abstract of the United States, 2003* (Washington,

D.C.: Government Printing Office, 2003), tab. 812.

[38]Andrew S. McFarland, *Common Cause: Lobbying in the Public Interest* (Chatham, N.J.: Chatham House, 1984); see also Andrew S. McFarland, *Public Interest Lobbies: Decision Making on Energy* (Washington, D.C.: American Enterprise Institute, 1976).

[39]Ronald G. Shaiko, "More Bang for the Buck: The New Era of Full-Service Public Interest Groups," in *Interest Group Politics*, 3rd ed., ed. Cigler and Loomis, 109.

[40]For a discussion of the evolution of NOW and its success in lobbying Congress, see Anne N. Costain and W. Douglas Costain, "The Women's Lobby: Impact of a Movement on Congress," in *Interest Group Politics*, ed. Cigler and Loomis.

[41]Richard Morin and Claudia Deane, "The Administration's Right-Hand Women," *Washington Post National Weekly Edition,* May 7, 2001, 12.

[42]Eric M. Uslaner, "A Tower of Babel on Foreign Policy," in *Interest Group Politics*, 3rd ed., ed. Cigler and Loomis, 309.

[43]Kenneth D. Wald, *Religion and Politics* (New York: St. Martin's Press, 1985), 182–212.

[44]Sidney Blumenthal, "Christian Soldiers," *New Yorker,* July 18, 1994, 36.

[45]James L. Guth, John C. Green, Lyman A. Jellstedt, and Corwin E. Struck, "Onward Christian Soldiers: Religious Activist Groups in American Politics," in *Interest Group Politics*, 3rd ed., ed. Cigler and Loomis, 57; Charles Levendosky, "Alternative Religious Voice Finally Being Raised," *Lincoln Journal Star,* March 3, 1996, 7B.

[46]Michael Lind, "The Right Still Has Religion," *New York Times,* December 9, 2001, sec. 4, 13; Blumenthal, "Christian Soldiers."

[47]Frank Rich, "The Reverend Falwell's Heavenly Timing," *New York Times,* May 20, 2007, WK13.

[48]Sam Tanenhaus, "Down, But Maybe Not Out," *New York Times,* May 20, 2007, WK14.

[49]"Citing 'Moral Crisis,' a Call to Oust Clinton," *New York Times,* October 23, 1998, Al, A8.

[50]Richard Parker, "On God and Democrats," *American Prospect,* March 2004, 40.

[51]Harold Meyerson, "Target of Opportunism," *Washington Post National Weekly Edition,* March 28–April 3, 2005, 26.

[52]David Kuo, *Tempting Faith: An Inside Story of Political Seduction* (New York: Free Press, 2006).

[53]Levendosky, "Alternative Religious Voice."

[54]Lynette Clemetson, "Clergy Group to Counter Conservatives," *New York Times,* November 17, 2003, A15.

[55]Christopher J. Bosso, "Adaptation and Change in the Environmental Movement," in *Interest Group Politics*, 3rd ed., ed. Cigler and Loomis, 155–156.

[56]Ibid., 162.

[57]Katharine Q. Seelye, "Bush Team Still Reversing Environmental Policies," *New York Times,* November 18, 2001, A20.

[58]Brent Kendall, "License to Kill," *Washington Monthly,* January/February, 2003, 11–14.

[59]John Mintz, "Would Bush Be the NRA's Point Man in the White House?" *Washington Post National Weekly Edition,* May 8, 2000, 14; Mike Doming, "NRA Promises an All-Out Assault on Al Gore's Presidential Campaign," *Lincoln Journal Star,* May 21, 2000, 2A; Thomas B. Edsall, "Targeting Al Gore with $10 Million," *Washington Post National Weekly Edition,* May 29, 2000, 11.

[60]Linda Greenhouse, "U.S., in a Shift, Tells Justices Citizens Have a Right to Guns," *New York Times,* May 8, 2002, A1.

[61]Blaine Harden, "The NRA Moves Away from Bush," *Washington Post National Weekly Edition,* January 15-21, 2007, 12.

[62]Robin Toner, "Abortion's Opponents Claim the Middle Ground," *New York Times,* April 25, 2004, sec. 4, 1.

[63]David S. Broder, "Let 100 Single-Issue Groups Bloom," *Washington Post,* January 7, 1979, C1–C2; see also David S. Broder, *The Party's Over: The Failure of Politics in America* (New York: Harper & Row, 1972).

[64]Wilson, *Interest Groups in America,* ch. 4.

[65]Robert Pear, "Lobbyists Seek Special Spin on Federal Bioterrorism Bill," *New York Times,* December 11, 2001, A1, A18

[66]Lowell Bergman and Jeff Gerth, "Power Trader Tied to Bush Finds Washington All Ears," *New York Times,* May 25, 2001, A1.

[67]Charles Peters, "Tilting at Windmills," *Washington Monthly,* July/August, 2004, 4.

[68]Sheryl Gay Stolberg, "Bush in Political Hot Spot in Picking an FDA Chief," *New York Times,* February 8, 2002, A17; Sheryl Gay Stolberg, "Deputy Is Appointed to Direct Food and Drug Agency as Impasse Continues," *New York Times,* February 26, 2002, A22.

[69]"Some Funny Facts About D.C.," *Parade Magazine,* March 19, 2006, 25.

[70]And this was in 1986! This admission was reported only because it surfaced during a divorce. Charles Peters, "Tilting at Windmills," *Washington Monthly,* May, 1986, 6, quoting *Washingtonian* magazine, April, 1986.

[71]As revealed in the documentary *Sicko.*

[72]Purdum, op. cit.

[73]David Segal, "Bob Dole Leads the Cast of Rainmakers," *Washington Post National Weekly Edition,* September 27, 1997, 20.

[74]For an examination of Enron's influence in this process, see Lowell Bergman and Jeff Gerth, "Power Trader Tied to Bush Finds Washington All Ears," *New York Times,* May 25, 2001, A1.

[75]Quote attributed to Lord Acton, a nineteenth-century historian.

[76]Jeffrey H. Birnbaum, "Seeking Influence," *Washington Citizens National Weekly Edition,* April 30–May 6, 2007, 17.

[77]Diana M. Evans, "Lobbying the Committee: Interest Groups and the House Public Works and Transportation Committee in the Post-Webster Era," in *Interest Group Politics*, 3rd ed., ed. Cigler and Loomis, 257–276.

[78]Birnbaum, *Lobbyists,* 40.

[79]Todd S. Purdum, "Go Ahead, Try to Stop K Street," *New York Times,* January 8, 2006, WK 4.

[80]Elizabeth Drew, *Politics and Money: The New Road to Corruption* (New York: Macmillan, 1983), 78.

[81]Ibid.

[82]Tina Daunt, "Hollywood Leans Right, Too," *Los Angeles Times,* November 3, 2006, www.calendarlive.com/printedition/calendar/cl-et-cause3nov03,0,498316,print .story. However, individual contributions, rather than company contributions, went mostly to Democratic candidates.

[83]Samuel Kernell, *Going Public: New Strategies of Presidential Leadership* (Washington, D.C.: CQ Press, 1986), 34.

[84]William P. Browne, *Groups, Interests, and U.S. Public Policy* (Washington, D.C.: Georgetown University Press, 1998) 23.

[85]Richard Harris, "If You Love Your Grass," *New Yorker,* April 20, 1968, 57.

[86]Ibid.

[87]"MoveOn's Big Moment," *Time,* November 24, 2003, 32.

[88]Kate Aurthur, "Lifetime's Place Is in the House (and Senate)," *New York Times,* October 16, 2005, sec. 2, 30.

[89]Stephanie Mencimer, *Blocking the Courthouse Door* (New York: Free Press, 2007)

[90]Birnbaum, *Lobbyists,* 40.

[91]The Union of Concerned Scientists. Britain's leading scientific academy drew similar conclusions. "Scientists: ExxonMobil Misleads the Public," *Lincoln Journal Star,* January 4, 2007, 3A.

[92]There have also been charges that Exxon-Mobil funded scientists who aren't experts in climatology and whose research wasn't reviewed by scholars in the field. Greenpeace, *Denial and Deception: A Chronicle of ExxonMobil's Efforts to Corrupt the Debate on Global Warming* (Washington, D.C.: Greenpeace, 2002).

[93]"Lobbyist Blitzkrieg Criticized," *Lincoln Journal Star,* September 23, 1994.

[94]For many examples, see David Cay Johnston, *Perfectly Legal* (New York: Portfolio/Penguin, 2003).

[95]Dan Clawson, Alan Neustadt, and Denise Scott, *Money Talks* (New York: Basic Books, 1992), 91.

[96]John Christensen (R–Neb.), from Omaha. [no author] "It Takes Only One Cook to Spoil the Batter," *Time,* July 7, 1997, 18.

[97]E. E. Schattshneider, *Semi-Sovereign People* (New York: Holt, Rinehart and Winston, 1960), 35.

[98]David S. Broder, "Can We Govern?" *Washington Post National Weekly Edition,* January 31, 1994, 23.

[99]Robert Wright, "Hyper Democracy," *Time,* January 23, 1995, 18.

[100]Comment "Reckless Driver," *New Yorker Magazine,* March 8, 2004, 25. Nader may also be the person most responsible for the election of George W. Bush to the presidency, but that's another story.

Chapter 6

[1]*National Journal*'s daily newsletter *Hotline* posed questions to presidential campaign personnel, congressional staffers, and state party chairs of both major parties. The operatives weren't randomly chosen, so the conclusions are tentative. The authors analyzed the responses to 306 interviews from September 21, 2003, through June 1, 2005. Jonathan Bernstein, Rebecca E. Bromley, and Krystle T. Meyer, "Republicans and Golf, Democrats and Outkast: Or, Party Political Culture from the Top," *The Forum*, vol. 4, no. 3, www.bepress.com/forum/vo14/iss3/art8.

[2]The preference for the *New Yorker* may reflect the magazine's political content as much or more than its literary content. But the Democrats cited other literary magazines as well.

[3]E. E. Schattschneider, *Party Government* (New York: Holt, Rinehart and Winston, 1960), 1.

[4]Frank J. Sorauf, *Political Parties in the American System*, 4th ed. (Boston: Little, Brown, 1980).

[5]Maurice Duverger, *Political Parties* (New York: Wiley, 1963). See also Edward R. Tufte, "The Relationship between Seats and Votes in Two-Party Systems," *American Political Science Review* 67 (1973), 540–554.

[6]In a few PR systems, citizens vote for multiple candidates rather than for a party slate.

[7]Robert G. Kaiser, "Hindsight Is 20/20," *Washington Post National Weekly Edition*, February 19, 2001, 11. Similar dynamics cost Gore a victory in New Hampshire.

[8]"Republicans Helping Nader," NewsMax.com, July 12, 2004 (www.newsmax.com/archives/ articles/2004/7/11/160540.shtml). This amounted to about $50,000 of the $1 million Nader had raised at the time.

[9]Ralph Nader, "My Untold Story," *Brill's Content*, February 2001.

[10]*CQ Weekly*, January 12, 2002, 136; *CQ Weekly*, January 2, 2004, 53.

[11]Frank J. Sorauf, *Money in American Elections* (Glenview, Ill.: Scott, Foresman, 1988), 121–153; Paul Herrnson, *Party Campaigning in the 1980s* (Cambridge, Mass.: Harvard University Press, 1988).

[12]Janet Hook, "Meet the Powers Behind the Democrats' Strategy," *Los Angeles Times*, July 5, 2006, www.latimes.com/news/nationworld/nation/la-na-dems5jul05,0,1314589,print.story?c.

[13]Richard Hofstadter, *The Idea of the Party System: The Rise of Legitimate Opposition in the United States, 1780–1840* (Berkeley: University of California Press, 1969).

[14]Theodore Lowi, *The Personal President* (Ithaca, N.Y.: Cornell University Press, 1985), 35.

[15]James MacGregor Burns, *The Vineyard of Liberty* (New York: Knopf, 1982).

[16]Instead of the party's members in Congress.

[17]In 1820, there had been around 1.2 million free white men over twenty-five years of age; by 1840, there were 3.2 million white men of over the age of twenty.

[18]When Harvard students established a charity for poor people in the city, they got few takers because the machine was already providing welfare for these people, so they shut down the charity.

[19]William L. Riordon, *Plunkitt of Tammany Hall* (New York: E.P. Dutton, 1963), 28.

[20]They also were allowed to dispense jobs with private companies, such as streetcar, gas, electric, and phone companies, that wanted to curry favor with local officials.

[21]Milton L. Rakove, *Don't Make No Waves, Don't Back No Losers* (Bloomington: Indiana University Press, 1975), 112.

[22]Benjamin Ginsberg and Martin Shefter, *Politics by Other Means* (New York: Viking, 1999), 19.

[23]Ibid.

[24]When independent newspapers emerged as profit-making businesses, the party papers declined. But the independent papers tended to favor one side or the other for many years as a way to attract and retain readers used to the advocacy of party papers.

[25]Walter Dean Burnham, *Critical Elections and the Mainstream of American Politics* (New York: Norton, 1970); Helmut Norpoth and Jerrold Rusk, "Partisan Dealignment in the American Electorate," *American Political Science Review* 76 (1982), 522–537; David W. Rhode, "The Fall Elections: Realignment and Dealignment," *Chronicle of Higher Education*, December 14, 1994, 131–132.

[26]National Election Studies, Center for Political Studies, University of Michigan, 1952–2000 (www.umich.edu/nes). Although many people who claim to be independent regularly vote for candidates of the same party, their unwillingness to identify themselves as party members indicates some detachment from the party.

[27]Everett Carill Ladd, *Where Have All the Voters Gone?* (New York: Norton, 1982).

[28]Martin P. Wallenberg, *The Rise of Candidate-Centered Politics* (Cambridge, Mass.: Harvard University Press, 1991).

[29]Thomas E. Patterson, *The Vanishing Voter* (New York: Knopf, 2002).

[30]For a discussion of party influence on voting in Congress, see William R. Shaffer, *Party and Ideology in the United States Congress* (Lanham, Md.: University Press of America, 1980).

[31]Bruce I. Oppenheimer, "The Importance of Elections in a Strong Congressional Era," in *Do Elections Matter?* eds. Benjamin Ginsberg and Alan Stone (Armonk, N.Y.: Sharpe, 1996), 120–138.

[32]Mary Lunn F. Jones, "Rock and a Hard Place," *American Prospect*, June 2003, 18–19.

[33]Dan Carney, "As Hostilities Rage on the Hill, Partisan-Vote Rate Soars," *Congressional Quarterly Weekly Report*, January 27, 1996, 199–200.

[34]In this realignment, the Republicans went from a bare majority to an overwhelming majority, so they remained the dominant party.

[35]James L. Sundquist, *Dynamics of the Party System: Alignment and Realignment of Political Parties in the United States* (Washington, D.C.: Brookings Institution, 1973).

[36]Kevin Phillips, *The Emerging Republican Majority* (New York: Doubleday, 1969).

[37]Patrick Reddy, "Why It's Got to Be All or Nothing," *Washington Post National Weekly Edition*, October 18, 1999, 23.

[38]Tali Mendelberg, *The Race Card* (Princeton, N.J.: Princeton University Press, 2001).

[39]Ibid., 97.

[40]Ibid., 3.

[41]Thomas F. Shaller, "Forget the South," *Washington Post National Weekly Edition*, November 24, 2003, 21.

[42]Thomas B. Edsall, "The Fissure Running through the Democratic Party," *Washington Post National Weekly Edition*, June 6, 1994, 11.

[43]John R. Petrocik and Frederick T. Steeper, "The Political Landscape in 1988," *Public Opinion*, September–October 1987, 41–44; Helmut Norpoth, "Party Realignment in the 1980s," *Public Opinion Quarterly* 51 (1987), 376–390.

[44]Edsall, "Fissure," 11.

[45]Thomas B. Edsall, "The Shifting Sands of America's Political Parties," *Washington Post National Weekly Edition*, April 9, 2001, 11.

[46]Ibid.

[47]According to Pew Research Center surveys. Ross Douthat, "Crises of Faith," *The Atlantic*, July/August, 2007, 38.

[48]Quoted in Robert B. Reich, "Deepening the Religious Divide," *American Prospect*, May 2005, 40.

[49]Frank Newport and Joseph Carroll, "GOP Identification, Party Image, Bush Approval Down as Rove Leaves," *Gallup News Service*, www.galluppoll.com/content/default.aspx?ci=28429.

[50]Kevin Phillips, "All Eyes on Dixie," *American Prospect*, February 2004, 24.

[51]Gallup Poll, May 12, 2006.

[52]Gebe Martinez and Mary Agnes Carey, "Erasing the Gender Gap Tops Republican Playbook," *CQ Weekly*, March 6, 2004, 565.

[53]Mary Agnes Carey, "Democrats Want Women: Party Targets Single Female Voters," *CQ Weekly*, March 6, 2004, 567.

[54]Robert A. Dahl, *How Democratic Is the American Constitution?* (New Haven, Conn.: Yale University Press, 2003), 30.

Chapter 7

[1]Kevin Phillips, *American Theocracy: The Peril and Politics of Radical Religion, Oil, and Borrowed Money in the 21st Century*. New York: Viking, 2006.

[2]William H. Flanigan, *Political Behavior of the American Electorate*, 2nd ed. (Boston: Allyn and Bacon, 1972), 13. See also Chilton Williamson, *American Suffrage from Property to Democracy 1760–1860* (Princeton, N.J.: Princeton University Press, 1960).

[3]James MacGregor Burns, *Vineyard of Liberty* (New York: Knopf, 1982), 363.

[4]August Meier and Elliot M. Rudwick, *From Plantation to Ghetto: An Interpretive History of American Negroes* (New York: Hill & Wang, 1966), 69.

[5]Robert Darcy, Susan Welch, and Janet Clark, *Women, Elections, and Representation* (Lincoln: University of Nebraska Press, 1994).

[6]Ralph G. Neas, "The Long Shadow of Jim Crow: Voter Intimidation and Suppression in America Today," *People for the American Way Foundation,* August 2004, or online at www .naacp.org/inc/pdf/jimcrow.pdf.

[7]Grandfather clause: *Guinn v. United States,* 238 U.S. 347 (1915); white primary: *Smith v. Allwright,* 321 U.S. 649 (1944).

[8]Data on black and white voter registration in the southern states are from the *Statistical Abstract of the United States* (Washington, D.C.: U.S. Bureau of the Census, various years).

[9]California, Florida, Michigan, New Hampshire, New York, and South Dakota.

[10]Richard J. Timpone, "Mass Mobilization or Government Intervention? The Growth of Black Registration in the South," *Journal of Politics* 57 (1995), 425–442.

[11]*City of Mobile v. Bolden,* 446 U.S. 55 (1980).

[12]*Thornburg v. Gingles,* 478 U.S. 301 (1986).

[13]Bob Benenson, "Arduous Ritual of Redistricting Ensures More Racial Diversity," *Congressional Quarterly Weekly Report,* October 24, 1992, 3385. For a very thorough review of the legal and behavioral impact of the Voting Rights Act, see Joseph Viteritti, "Unapportioned Justice: Local Elections, Social Science, and the Evolution of the Voting Rights Act," *Cornell Journal of Law and Public Policy* (1994), 210–270.

[14]*Shaw v. Reno,* 125 L.Ed.2d 511, 113 S.Ct. 2816 (1993); *Miller v. Johnson,* 132 L.Ed.2d 762, 115 S.Ct. 2475 (1995); *Bush v. Vera,* 135 L.Ed.2d 248, 116 S.Ct. 1941 (1996).

[15]Darcy et al., *Women, Elections, and Representation.*

[16]Speech in 1867 by George Williams cited in Peter Pappas's "Re-defining the Role of Women in Industrial America" at www .peterpappas.com/ journals/industry/ women3.pdf.

[17]The discussion in this paragraph is drawn largely from Lois W. Banner, *Women in Modern America: A Brief History* (New York: Harcourt Brace Jovanovich, 1974), 88–90; Glenn Firebaugh and Kevin Chen, "Vote Turnout of Nineteenth Amendment Women," *American Journal of Sociology* 100 (1995), 972–996.

[18]Alabama, Florida, Virginia, and Kentucky.

[19]Thompson, ibid., 18.

[20]"Groups Report Progress against Laws Banning Felons from Voting," *Lincoln Journal Star* (June 22, 2005), 4a.

[21]Thompson, ibid., 20.

[22]Tom Fiedler, "The Perfect Storm," in *Overtime!: The Election 2000 Thriller,* ed. Larry J. Sabato (New York: Longman, 2002), 11.

[23]Liz Krueger, "Budgeting for Another Florida," *New York Times,* February 8, 2004, 14.

[24]Dale Keiger, "E-lective Alarm," *Johns Hopkins Magazine,* February 2004, 50.

[25]See report of Electionline.org on voting law changes at www.electionline.org/site/docs/ pdf/2004.Election.Preview.Final.Report.pdf.

[26]Sasha Abramsky, *Conned: How Millions Went to Prison, Lost the Vote, and Helped Send George W. Bush to the White House* (New York: The New Press: 2006). This book is partly anecdotal but does point out the huge numbers of people disenfranchised by both laws and intimidation.

[27]See www.Tallahassee.com/mld/tallahassee/ news/9202503.htm.

[28]Richard Jensen, "American Election Campaigns: A Theoretical and Historical Typology," paper delivered at the 1968 Midwest Political Science Association Meeting, quoted in Walter Dean Burnham, *Critical Elections and the Main-springs of American Politics* (New York: Norton, 1970), 73.

[29]Frances Fox Piven and Richard A. Cloward, *Why Americans Don't Vote* (New York: Pantheon Books, 1988), 30.

[30]These examples are from editorial, "Barriers to Student Voting," *New York Times,* September 28, 2004, 26.

[31]Part of the explanation for declining voting rates is that the number of citizens who are ineligible to vote has increased, which depresses voter-turnout statistics. Immigrants, other noncitizens, and, in some states, convicted felons are not eligible to vote. When those individuals are removed from the calculation of proportion voting, the proportion voting is increased by about five points; and most of the turnout decline occurred in the 1960s. See Michael P. McDonald and Samuel Popkin, "The Myth of the Vanishing Voter," *American Political Science Review* 95 (2001), 963–974.

[32]*Statistical Abstract of the United States 2006,* tab. 405. This self-report is probably an overestimate.

[33]*Statistical Abstract of the United States 2006,* tab. 406.

[34]Daniel J. Elazar, *American Federalism: A View from the States* (New York: Crowell, 1972); *Statistical Abstract of the United States 2006,* tab. 406.

[35]Norman H. Nie, Sidney Verba, Henry Brady, Kay Lehman Schlozman, and Jane Junn, "Participation in America: Continuity and Change," presented at the Midwest Political Science Association, April 1988. The standard work, though now dated, on American political participation is Sidney Verba and Norman H. Nie, *Participation in America: Political Democracy and Social Equality* (New York: Harper & Row, 1972).

[36]Piven and Cloward, *Why Americans Don't Vote,* 162; *Statistical Abstract of the United States 2001,* tab. 401; Piven and Cloward, *Why Americans Still Don't Vote: And Why Politicians Want It That Way* (Boston: Beacon Press, 2001).

[37]G. Bingham Powell, "American Voter Turnout in Comparative Perspective," *American Political Science Review* 80 (1986), 30; Piven and Cloward, *Why Americans Don't Vote,* 119; Arend Lijphart, "Unequal Participation: Democracy's Unresolved Dilemma," *American Political Science Review* 91 (1997), 1–14.

[38]Brady et al., "Beyond SES: A Resource Model of Political Participation."

[39]Nie et al., "Participation in America: Continuity and Change"; Verba and Nie, *Participation in America: Political Democracy and Social Equality.*

[40]Steven Hill and Rashad Robinson, "Demography vs. Democracy: Young People Feel Left Out of the Political Process," *Los Angeles Times,* November 5, 2002, 2. Posted by the Youth Vote Coalition (www.youthvote.org/ news/newsdetail. cfm?newsid56). The survey cited was conducted by Harvard University.

[41]Eric Plutzer, "Becoming a Habitual Voter: Inertia, Resources, and Growth in Young Adulthood," *American Political Science Review* 96 (2002), 41–56.

[42]Anna Greenberg, "New Generation, New Politics," *American Prospect,* October 1, 2003, A3.

[43]Paul Allen Beck and M. Kent Jennings, "Political Periods and Political Participation," *American Political Science Review* 73 (1979), 737–750; Nie et al., "Participation in America: Continuity and Change."

[44]George F. Will, "In Defense of Nonvoting," *Newsweek,* October 10, 1983, 96.

[45]Richard Morin, "The Dog Ate My Forms, and, Well, I Couldn't Find a Pen," *Washington Post National Weekly Edition,* November 5, 1990, 38.

[46]Lawrence R. Jacobs and Robert Y. Shapiro, *Politicians Don't Pander: Political Manipulation and the Loss of Democratic Responsiveness* (Chicago: University of Chicago Press, 2000).

[47]Richard Lau, Lee Sigelman, Caroline Heldman, and Paul Babbitt, "The Effects of Negative Political Advertisements," *American Political Science Review* 93 (1999), 851–875; Steven E. Finkel and John Geer, "A Spot Check: Casting Doubt on the Demobilizing Effect of Attack Advertising," *American Journal of Political Science* 42 (1998), 573–595. Research on turnout is found in Stephen Ansolabehere and Shanto Iyengar, *Going Negative* (New York: Free Press, 1996). In her book *Packaging the Presidency: A History and Criticism of Presidential Campaign Advertising* (New York: Oxford University Press, 1984), Kathleen Jamieson also argues that there are checks on misleading advertising, but later ("Is the Truth Now Irrelevant in Presidential Campaigns?"), she notes that these checks do not always work well. See Jamieson, *Dirty Politics: Deception, Distraction, and Democracy* (New York: Oxford University Press, 1992).

[48]Thomas E. Patterson, *The Vanishing Voter* (New York: Knopf, 2002); Curtis B. Gans, "The Empty Ballot Box," *Public Opinion* 1 (September–October 1978), 54–57; Curtis Gans, quoted in Jack Germond and Jules Witcover, "Listen to the Voters—and Nonvoters," *Minneapolis Star Tribune,* November 26, 1988. This effect was foreshadowed by Michael J. Robinson, "American Political Legitimacy in

an Era of Electronic Journalism," in *Television as a Social Force: New Approaches to TV Criticism,* eds. Douglass Cater and Richard Adler (New York: Praeger, 1975). See also Austin Ranney, *Channels of Power: The Impact of Television on American Politics* (New York: Basic Books, 1983); and Richard Boyd, "The Effect of Election Calendars on Voter Turnout," paper presented at the Annual Meeting of the Midwest Political Science Association, April 1987, Chicago.

[49]Boyd, "The Effect of Election Calendars on Voter Turnout," 43. See Piven and Cloward, *Why Americans Don't Vote,* 196–197, for illustrations of these kinds of informal barriers, and Piven and Cloward, *Why Americans Still Don't Vote: And Why Politicians Want It That Way,* for further examples.

[50]Ibid.

[51]Ruy Texeira, *Why Americans Don't Vote: Turnout Decline in the United States 1960–1984* (Boulder, Colo.: Greenwood, 1987); Texeira, *The Disappearing American Voter* (Washington, D.C.: Brookings Institute, 1992); and Peverill Squire, Raymond Wolfinger, and David Glass, "Residential Mobility and Voter Turnout," *American Political Science Review* 81 (1987), 45–66.

[52]Jennifer Joan Lee, "Pentagon Blocks Site for Voters Outside U.S.," *International Herald Tribune,* September 20, 2004. The site was run by the Pentagon for both military and civilian overseas citizens.

[53]Piven and Cloward, *Why Americans Don't Vote,* 17.

[54]Ibid.

[55]Raymond E. Wolfinger and Steven J. Rosenstone, *Who Votes?* (New Haven, Conn.: Yale University Press, 1980), tab. 6-1.

[56]Steven J. Rosenstone and Raymond E. Wolfinger, "The Effect of Registration Laws on Voter Turnout," *American Political Science Review* 72 (1978), 22–45; Glenn Mitchell and Christopher Wlezien, "Voter Registration Laws and Turnout, 1972–1982," paper presented at the Annual Meeting of the Midwest Political Science Association, April 1989, Chicago; Mark J. Fenster, "The Impact of Allowing Day of Registration Voting on Turnout in U.S. Elections from 1960 to 1992," *American Politics Quarterly* 22 (1994), 74–87.

[57]Kim Quaile Hill and Jan E. Leighley, "Racial Diversity, Voter Turnout, and Mobilizing Institutions in the United States," *American Politics Quarterly* 27 (1999), 275–295.

[58]"Block the Vote," *New York Times,* (May 30, 2006), editorial.

[59]Piven and Cloward, *Why Americans Don't Vote,* 230–231.

[60]Stephen Knack, "Does 'Motor Voter' Work?" *Journal of Politics* 57 (1995), 796–811.

[61]Michael Martinez and David Hill, "Did Motor Voter Work?" *American Politics Quarterly* 27 (1999), 296–315; Piven and Cloward, *Why Americans Still Don't Vote: And Why Politicians Want It That Way.*

[62]More recent studies of turnout include Richard J. Timpone, "Structure, Behavior and Voter Turnout in the United States," *American Political Science Review* 92 (1998), 145–158; Henry Brady, Sidney Verba, and Kay Lehman Schlozman, "Beyond SES: A Resource Model of Political Participation," *American Political Science Review* 89 (1995), 271–294.

[63]Bill Winder, "The Roller Coaster of Class Conflict: Class Segments, Mass Mobilization, and Voter Turnout in the United States, 1840–1996." For a review of this literature, see John Petrocik, "Voter Turnout and Electoral Preference," in *Elections in America,* ed. Kay Lehman Schlozman (Boston: Allen & Unwin, 1987). See also Bernard Grofman, Guillermo Owen, and Christian Collet, "Rethinking the Partisan Effects of Higher Turnout," *Public Choice* 99 (1999), 357–376.

[64]Tom Hamburger and Peter Wallsten, "Parties Are Tracking Your Habits," *Los Angeles Times,* July 24, 2005: www.latimes.com/news/nationworld/nation/lanarncdnc24jul24,0,535024, full.story

[65]Kim Quaile Hill, Jan Leighley, and Angela Hinton-Anderson, "Lower-Class Mobilization and Policy Linkage in the U.S. States," *American Journal of Political Science* 39 (1995), 75–86.

[66]Jo Becker, "Voters May Have Their Say before Election Day," *Washington Post,* August 26, 2004, A01.

[67]Texas, Minnesota, Louisiana, and Missouri are the only states west of the Mississippi not allowing unrestricted absentee voting; Florida, North Carolina, Vermont, and Maine are the only states east of the Mississippi who do. See Michael Moss, "Parties See New Promise When Ballot Is in the Mail," *New York Times,* August 22, 2004, 12; R. W. Apple, Jr., "Kerry Pins Hopes in Iowa on Big Vote from Absentees," *New York Times,* September 28, 2004, 18.

[68]These examples are drawn from Raymond Wolfinger, Benjamin Highton, and Megan Mullin, "How Postregistration Laws Affect the Turnout of Blacks and Latinos," paper presented at the 2003 Annual Meeting of the American Political Science Association, Philadelphia, Pennsylvania, August 28–31.

[69]Diane Feldman and Cornell Belcher, "Democracy at Risk, the 2004 Election in Ohio," report for the Democratic National Committee found online at a9.g.akamai.net/7/9/8082/v001 www.democrats.org/pdfs/ohvrireport/ fullreport.pdf.

[70]Miles Rapoport, "The Democracy We Deserve," *Prospect* (January, 2005): A7.

[71]"Numbers," *Time* (May 15, 2006), 17.

[72]Anthony Downs, *An Economic Theory of Democracy* (New York: Harper, 1957).

[73]Morin, "The Dog Ate My Forms, and, Well, I Couldn't Find a Pen."

[74]Kay Lehman Schlozman, Sidney Verba, and Henry Brady, "Participation's Not a Paradox: The View from American Activists," *British Journal of Political Science* 25 (1995), 1–36.

[75]The following discussion draws heavily upon John H. Aldrich, *Before the Convention: Strategies and Choices in Presidential Nomination Campaigns* (Chicago: University of Chicago Press, 1980).

[76]Ibid. See also David W. Rohde, "Risk Bearing and Progressive Ambition: The Case of Members of the United States House of Representatives," *American Journal of Political Science* 23 (1979), 1–26.

[77]Quoted in Audrey A. Haynes, Paul-Henri Gurian, and Stephen M. Nichols, "The Role of Candidate Spending in Presidential Nomination Campaigns," *Journal of Politics* 59 (February 1997), 213–225.

[78]"The Fall Campaign," *Newsweek Election Extra,* November-December 1984, 88.

[79]Hendrick Hertzberg, "This Must Be the Place," *New Yorker,* January 31, 2000, 36–39.

[80]B. Drummond Ayres Jr., "It's Taking Care of Political Business," *New York Times,* July 18, 1999, 22.

[81]Katharine Q. Seelye and Marjorie Connelly, "Republican Delegates Leaning to Right of G.O.P. and the Nation," *New York Times,* August 29, 2004, 13.

[82]Gerald M. Pomper and Susan S. Lederman, *Elections in America: Control and Influence in Democratic Politics* (New York: Longman, 1980), ch. 7.

[83]Quote from Gerald M. Pomper in Adam Nagourney, "What Boston Can Do for Kerry," *New York Times,* July 18, 2004, 5.

[84]David Carr, "Whose Convention Is It? Reporters Outnumber Delegates 6 to 1," *New York Times,* July 27, 2004, E1.

[85]Lee Sigelman and Paul Wahlbeck, "The 'Veep-stakes': Strategic Choice in Presidential Running Mate Selection," *American Political Science Review* 94 (1997), 855–864.

[86]Ibid.

[87]Ibid.

[88]Robert L. Dudley and Ronald B. Rapaport, "Vice-Presidential Candidates and the Home State Advantage: Playing Second Banana at Home and on the Road," *American Journal of Political Science* 33 (1989), 537–540.

[89]*New York Times,* July 11, 2004, 16.

[90]Daron Shaw, "A Study of Presidential Campaign Event Effects from 1952 to 1992," *Journal of Politics* 61 (1999), 387–422.

[91]See *Congressional Quarterly,* July 23, 1988, 2015; Thomas M. Holbrook, "Campaigns, National Conditions and U.S. Presidential Elections," *American Journal of Political Science* 38 (1994), 973–998.

[92]Benjamin I. Page and Richard A. Brody, "Policy Voting and the Electoral Process: The Vietnam War Issue," *American Political Science Review* 66 (1972), 979–995.

[93]The discussion of the functions of the media relies heavily on the excellent summary found in Stephen Ansolabehere, Roy Behr, and Shanto Iyengar, "Mass Media and Elections," *American Politics Quarterly* 19 (1991), 109–139.

[94]Kathleen Hall Jamieson, "Ad Wars," *Washington Post National Weekly Edition,* October 4, 2004, 22.

[95]L. Marvin Overby and Jay Barth," Radio Advertising in American Political Campaigns," *American Politics Research* 34 (July, 2006): 451–478.

[96]Robert MacNeil, *People Machine: The Influence of Television on American Politics* (New York: Harper & Row, 1968), 182.

[97]Elisabeth Bumiller, "Selling Soup, Wine and Reagan," *Washington Post National Weekly Edition,* November 5, 1984, 6–8.

[98]Jim Rutenberg, "Seeking Voters through Habits in TV Viewing," *New York Times,* July 18, 2004, 1.

[99]Data are drawn from Rutenberg, ibid. See Thomas E. Mann, "Elections and Change in Congress," in *The New Congress,* eds. Thomas E. Mann and Norman J. Ornstein (Washington, D.C.: American Enterprise Institute for Public Policy Research, 1981), 32–54; David Mayhew, *Congress: The Electoral Connection* (New Haven, Conn.: Yale University Press, 1974); Glenn R. Parker and Roger H. Davidson, "Why Do Americans Love Their Congressmen So Much More Than Their Congress?" *Legislative Studies Quarterly* 4 (1979), 53–62.

[100]Daron Shaw, "The Methods behind the Madness: Presidential Electoral College Strategies, 1988–1996," *Journal of Politics* 61 (1999), 893–913, shows the evolution of advertising focus during these three elections.

[101]Through early summer, about three-fourths of Bush's were negative, whereas only one-fourth of Kerry's were. As election day drew nearer, the proportion of negative ads increased. Dana Milbank and Jim VandeHei, "The Mean Season Is in Full Bloom," *Washington Post National Weekly Edition,* June 7, 2004, 13. Both campaigns agreed the figures were accurate.

[102]John Theilmann and Allen Wilhite, "Campaign Tactics and the Decision to Attack," *Journal of Politics* 60 (1998), 1050–1062.

[103]The study of negative advertising research was done by Richard Lau, Lee Sigelman, Caroline Heldman, and Paul Babbitt, "The Effects of Negative Political Advertisements," *American Political Science Review* 93 (1999), 851–875.

[104]Democratic consultants are more likely to find negative advertising distasteful than Republican consultants. However, this does not necessarily translate into partisan differences in use.

[105]Paul Taylor, "Pigsty Politics," *Washington Post National Weekly Edition,* February 13, 1989, 6.

[106]Howard Kurtz, "The Ad-Slingers in the TV Corral," *Washington Post,* October 10, 2004, A06.

[107]Ansolabehere and Iyengar, *Going Negative.*

[108]Jamieson, *Packaging the Presidency: A History and Criticism of Presidential Campaign Advertising.*

[109]Eileen Shields West, "Give 'Em Hell These Days Is a Figure of Speech," *Smithsonian* (October 1988), 149–151. The editorial was from the *Connecticut Courant.*

[110]Charles Paul Freund, "But Then, Truth Has Never Been Important," *Washington Post National Weekly Edition,* November 7, 1988, 29.

[111]Quoted in Freund, "But Then, Truth Has Never Been Important," 29.

[112]Thomas E. Patterson, *The Mass Media Election: How Americans Choose Their President* (New York: Praeger, 1980), 3.

[113]Martin Schram, *The Great American Video Game: Presidential Politics in the Television Age* (New York: Morrow, 1987).

[114]Mike Allen, "Bush's Isolation from Reporters Could Be a Hindrance," *Washington Post,* October 8, 2004, A09.

[115]Daron Shaw, "A Study of Presidential Campaign Event Effects from 1952 to 1992," *Journal of Politics* 61 (May, 1999), 387–422, reports on a systematic study of campaign events and their impact on the elections.

[116]Adam Nagourney, "Internet Injects Sweeping Change into U.S. Politics," *New York Times,* April 2, 2006, 1ff.

[117]David Perlmutter, "Political Blogs: The New Iowa?" *Chronicle of Higher Education* (May 26, 2006), B6.

[118]Jimmy Breslin, *How the Good Guys Finally Won: Notes from an Impeachment Summer* (New York: Ballantine, 1974), 14.

[119]Elizabeth Drew, *Politics and Money* (New York: Collier, 1983), 9.

[120]Glen Justice, "Irrelevance Stalks a Post-Watergate Invention," *New York Times,* November 16, 2003, 3.

[121]David Kirkpatrick, "Death Knell May be Near for Public Election Funds," *New York Times,* January 23, 2007. www.nytimes .com/2007/01/23/us/politics/23donate.html ?ex=1182139200&en=6462e8ba43abb196& ei=5070.

[122]Ibid.

[123]Glen Justice, "Kerry's Campaign Finances Soar," *International Herald Tribune,* June 28, 2004, 7.

[124]*Buckley* v. *Valeo,* 424 U.S. 1 (1976); the Vermont case is *Randall* v. *Sorrell* 548 U.S. (2006).

[125]*Federal Election Commission* v. *National Conservative PAC,* 470 U.S. 480 (1985).

[126]To judge whether an ad is a campaign ad, rather than an issue ad, the Court's rule is whether the ad uses language such as "vote for" or "vote against." However, this is a meaningless criterion because only 4 percent of the ads sponsored by the candidates themselves use these phrases. David S. Broder, "Both Major Parties Abuse Soft Money Loophole," *State College* (Pa.) *Centre Daily Times,* May 30, 2000, 6A.

[127]Pauol Farhi, "A Team Effort," *Washington Post National Weekly Edition,* March 29, 2004, 12.

[128]See Larry J. Sabato and Glenn Simpson, *Dirty Little Secrets: The Persistence of Corruption in American Politics* (New York: Times Books, 1996); Marick Masters and Gerald Keim, "Determinants of PAC Participation among Large Corporations," *Journal of Politics* 47 (1985), 1158–1173; and J. David Gopoian, "What Makes PACs Tick?" *American Journal of Political Science* 28 (1984), 259–281.

[129]See Kevin Grier and Michael Mangy, "Comparing Interest Group PAC Contributions to House and Senate Incumbents," *Journal of Politics* 55 (1993), 615–643.

[130]J. David Gopoian, "Change and Continuity in Defense PAC Behavior," *American Politics Quarterly* 13 (1985), 297–322; Richard Morin and Charles Babcock, "Off Year, Schmoff Year," *Washington Post National Weekly Edition,* May 14, 1990, 15.

[131]Recent legislation has attempted to close part of the soft money loophole by banning soft money contributions to national political parties. However, it left a huge loophole allowing soft money contributions to various independent groups and, to a lesser extent, to state and local parties.

[132]Walter Lippmann, "A Theory about Corruption," in *Political Corruption,* ed. Arnold J. Heidenheimer (New York: Holt, Rinehart and Winston, 1970), 294–297.

[133]Robert Dahl, *How Democratic Is the American Constitution?* (New Haven, Conn.: Yale University Press, 2001).

[134]Akhil Reed Amar, *America's Constitution: A Biography* (New York: Random House, 2005).

[135]Ibid.

[136]Paul Abramson, John H. Aldrich, and David Rohde, *Change and Continuity in the 2000 Elections* (Washington, D.C.: CQ Press, 2003).

[137]Ibid.

[138]In recent elections, the percentages able to identify correctly general differences between the major party candidates varied between 26 and 55 percent.

[139]Abramson, Aldrich, and Rohde, *Change and Continuity, 2000.*

[140]Ibid.

[141]Paul Abramson, John H. Aldrich, and David Rohde, *Change and Continuity in the 1996 Elections* (Washington, D.C.: CQ Press, 1998).

[142]Morris Fiorina, *Retrospective Voting in American National Elections* (New Haven, Conn.: Yale University Press, 1981).

[143]Edward R. Tufte, *Political Control of the Economy* (Princeton, N.J.: Princeton University Press, 1978); Douglas Hibbs, "The Mass Public and Macroeconomic Performance," *American Journal of Political Science* 23 (1979), 705–731; John Hibbing and John Alford, "The Electoral Impact of Economic Conditions: Who Is Held Responsible," *American Journal of Political Science* 25 (1981), 423–439.

[144]Quoted in Alan M. Dershowitz, *Supreme Injustice: How the High Court Hijacked Election 2000* (New York: Oxford University Press, 2001), 25.

[145]Hendrik Hertzberg, "Up for the Count," *New Yorker,* December 18, 2000, 41.

[146]Kosuke Imai and Gary King, "Did Illegally Counted Overseas Absentee Ballots Decide the 2000 U.S. Presidential Election?" available at gking.Harvard.edu.

[147]Ibid.

[148]David Barstow and Don Van Natta Jr., "How Bush Took Florida: Mining the Overseas Absentee Vote," *New York Times,* July 15, 2001, available at www.nytimes. com/2001/07/15/ www. national/15ball.

149Ibid.

150Jonathan Wand, Kenneth Shotts, Jasjeet Sekhon, Walter R. Mebane Jr., Michael Herron, and Henry Brady, "The Butterfly Did It: The Aberrant Vote for Buchanan in Palm Beach," *American Political Science Review* 95 (2001), 793–809. They examined the Palm Beach Buchanan vote in relation to all other counties in the United States to the absentee ballots (which did not use the butterfly format) in Palm Beach County, precinct-level data, and individual ballots.

151Tom Fiedler, "The Perfect Storm," in *Overtime! The Election 2000 Thriller,* ed. Larry J. Sabato (New York: Longman, 2002), 8.

152Imal and King, 3.

153Jimmy Carter, quoted from *NPR* in Kéllia Ramares's special report "House Strikes Truth from the Record," *Online Journal,* July 23, 2004. You can find the full Ramares article at www.onlinejournal.com/Special_Reports/072304Ramares/072304ramares.html.

154Andrew Gelman, Boris Shor, Joseph Bafumi, David Park, "Rich State, Poor State, Red State, Blue State: What's the Matter with Connecticut?" abstract and slides can be found at home.uchicago.edu/~bshor/papers. A summary can be found at harrisschool.uchicago.edu/about/publications/HarrisView/ spring06/shor.asp.

155Alan Abramowitz, "Terrorism, Gay Marriage, and Incumbency: Explaining the Republican Victory in the 2004 Presidential Election," *The Forum* 2 (Issue 4); 2004. Found online at the Berkeley Electronic Press: www.bepress.com/forum.

156For example, see *The Permanent Campaign and Its Future,* eds. Norman J. Ornstein and Thomas E. Mann (Washington, D.C.: American Enterprise Institute and the Brookings Institution, 2000).

157Data on voters' issue preferences on Election Day can be found in the article "41% Said National Security Issues Most Important," *Rasmussen Reports,* November 2, 2004 at www.rasmussenre ports.com/Issue%20Clusters_Election%20Night.htm.

158Editorial, "A Polarized Nation?" *Washington Post,* November 14, 2004, 6. Several of these ideas were summarized nicely in this article.

159Benjamin I. Page and Robert Y. Shapiro, "Effects of Public Opinion on Policy," *American Political Science Review* 77 (1983), 175–190.

160Arthur Schlesinger Jr., *Wall Street Journal,* December 5, 1986. But see also Jacobs and Shapiro, *Politicians Don't Pander: Political Manipulation and the Loss of Democratic Responsiveness.*

Chapter 8

1Josephine Hearn, "Civility Caucus? No Way," The Politico, dyn.politico.com/dyn.politico.com/printstory.cfm?uuid=03079B81-3048-5C12-00BD283871F5093F; Matt Stearns, "In Congress, Civility Struggles to Appear," *Lincoln Journal Star* (March 26, 2007): 9A. McClathy Newspaper story.

2Ibid.

3Eric Schmitt, "Uproar in House as Parties Clash on Iraq Pullout," *New York Times* (November 19, 2005).

4Hearn.

5Ibid.

6James R. Chiles, "Congress Couldn't Have Been This Bad, or Could It?" *Smithsonian,* November 1995, 70–80.

7Susan Webb Hammond, "Life and Work on the Hill: Careers, Norms, Staff, and Informal Caucuses," in *Congress Responds to the Twentieth Century,* eds. Sunil Ahuja and Robert Dewhirst (Columbus: Ohio State University Press, 2003), 74.

8Quoted in Kenneth J. Cooper and Helen Dewar, "No Limits on the Term Limits Crusade," *Washington Post National Weekly Edition,* May 29, 1995, 14.

9By the late 1990s, enthusiasm for term limits in the *state legislatures* had waned. By 2007 only fifteen states still had them.

10*Baker v. Carr,* 369 U.S. 186 (1962).

11*Wesberry v. Sanders,* 376 U.S. 1 (1964).

12See the report on *Miller v. Johnson,* 515 U.S. 900 (1995); see *New York Times,* July 2, 1995, E1, E4.

13"Congress of Relative Newcomers Poses Challenge to Bush, Leadership," *Congressional Quarterly Weekly Review,* January 20, 2001, 179–181.

14"Datafile," *Congressional Quarterly Weekly Review,* February 21, 2004, 456. "For the Record," *CQ Monthly Report,* November 13, 2006, 3068–3075.

15Hanna F. Pitkin, *The Concept of Representation* (Berkeley: University of California, 1967), 60.

16Ibid., 60–61.

17Leslie Laurence, "Congress Makes Up for Neglect," *Lincoln Journal Star,* December 5, 1994, 8.

18Roger H. Davidson and Walter J. Oleszek, *Congress and Its Members,* 9th ed. (Washington, D.C.: CQ Press, 2004), 132–134; Richard Fenno, *Home Style: House Members in Their Districts,* 2nd ed. (New York: Longman, 2003), 232–247.

19Carl M. Cannon, "State of Our Disunion," *National Journal,* January 21, 2006, 23; Norman Ornstein and Barry McMillion, "One Nation, Divisible," *New York Times,* June 23, 2005.

20See Thomas E. Mann, "Elections and Change in Congress," in *The New Congress;* Mayhew, *Congress: The Electoral Connection;* Parker and Davidson, "Why Do Americans Love Their Congressmen So Much More Than Their Congress?"

21Edie N. Goldenberg and Michael W. Traugott, *Campaigning for Congress* (Washington, D.C.: CQ Press, 1984); Gary C. Jacobson and Samuel Kernell, *Strategy and Choice in Congressional Elections* (New Haven, Conn.: Yale University Press, 1981).

22Edward Walsh, "Wanted: Candidates for Congress," *Washington Post National Weekly Edition,* November 25, 1985, 9.

23Larry Makinson and Joshua Goldstein, *Open Secrets: The Cash Constituents of Congress,* 2nd ed. (Washington, D.C.: CQ Press, 1994), 23.

24Amy Dockser, "Nice PAC You've Got There . . . A Pity If Anything Should Happen to It," *Washington Monthly,* January 1984, 21.

25See Paul Feldman and James Jondrow, "Congressional Elections and Local Federal Spending," *American Journal of Political Science* 28 (1984), 152; Glenn R. Parker and Suzanne Parker, "The Correlates and Effects of Attention to District by U.S. House Members," *Legislative Studies Quarterly* 10 (1985), 239.

26Christopher Buckley, "Hangin' with the Houseboyz," *Washington Monthly* (June 1992), 44.

27Linda L. Fowler and Robert D. McClure, *Political Ambition: Who Decides to Run for Congress?* (New Haven, Conn.: Yale University Press, 1989), 47; John Hibbing and Sara Brandes, "State Population and the Electoral Success of U.S. Senators," *American Journal of Political Science* 27 (1983), 808–819. See also Glenn R. Parker, "Stylistic Change in the U.S. Senate, 1959–1980," *Journal of Politics* 47 (1985), 1190–1202.

28Thomas E. Mann, *Unsafe at Any Margin: Interpreting Congressional Elections* (Washington, D.C.: American Enterprise Institute for Public Policy Research, 1978).

29"Women, Minorities Join Senate," *CQ Almanac* (1992), 8A–14A; "Wave of Diversity Spared Many Incumbents," *CQ Almanac* (1992), 15A–21A, 24A; "The Elections," *Congressional Quarterly,* November 12, 1994, 3237.

30See Gary C. Jacobson, *The Politics of Congressional Elections,* 2nd ed. (Boston: Little, Brown, 1987), 51 for a discussion of financial needs in the 1980s.

31Ibid.

32Barbara Hinckley, "The American Voter in Congressional Elections," *American Political Science Review* 74 (1980), 641–650; Barbara Hinckley, "House Reelections and Senate Defeats: The Role of the Challenger," *British Journal of Political Science* 10 (1980), 441–460.

33John Alford and John R. Hibbing, "The Disparate Electoral Security of House and Senate Incumbents," paper presented at the Annual Meeting of the American Political Science Association, September 1989, Atlanta, Georgia, 107.

34A good review of these arguments is found in John R. Hibbing and Sara L. Brandes, "State Population and the Electoral Success of U.S. Senators," *American Journal of Political Science* 27 (1983), 808–819. See also Eric Uslaner, "The Case of the Vanishing Liberal Senators: The House Did It," *British Journal of Political Science* 11 (1981), 105–113; Abramowitz, "A Comparison."

35Hibbing and Brandes, "State Population and the Electoral Success of U.S. Senators." See also Glenn R. Parker, "Stylistic Change in the U.S. Senate, 1959–1980," ibid.

36See Gerald C. Wright Jr. and Michael B. Berkman, "Candidates and Policy in United

States Senate Elections," *American Political Science Review* 80 (1986), 567–588; Robert S. Erikson and Gerald C. Wright, "Voters, Candidates, and Issues in Congressional Elections," in *Congress Reconsidered,* eds. Lawrence C. Dodd and Bruce I. Oppenheimer, 7th ed. (Washington, D.C.: CQ Press, 2001), 67–95.

[37]See James Campbell, "Explaining Presidential Losses in Midterm Elections," *Journal of Politics* 47 (1985), 1140–1157. See also Barbara Hinckley, "Interpreting House Midterm Elections," *American Political Science Review* 61 (1967), 694–700; Samuel Kernell, "Presidential Popularity and Negative Voting," *American Political Science Review* 71 (1977), 44–66; Edward Tufte, "Determinants of the Outcomes of Midterm Congressional Elections," *American Political Science Review* 69 (1975), 812–826; Alan Abramowitz, "Economic Conditions, Presidential Popularity and Voting Behavior in Midterm Elections," *Journal of Politics* 47 (1985), 31–43.

[38]Davidson and Oleszek, 114.

[39]John Alford and John Hibbing, "The Disparate Electoral Security of House and Senate Incumbents," paper presented at the annual meeting of the American Political Science Association, Atlanta, Georgia, September 1989.

[40]Fenno, *Home Style.*

[41]John Cochran, "A New Medium for the Message," *Congressional Quarterly Weekly Review,* March 13, 2006, 657.

[42]Ibid., 145.

[43]*Budget of the United States, Fiscal 2007: Appendix* (Washington, D.C.: Government Printing Office, 2006), 15–18.

[44]Quoted in Kenneth Shepsle, "The Failures of Congressional Budgeting," *Social Science and Modern Society* 20 (1983), 4–10. See also Howard Kurtz, "Pork Barrel Politics," *Washington Post,* January 25, 1982.

[45]Congressional Quarterly, *The Origins and Development of Congress* (Washington, D.C.: CQ Press, 1976).

[46]Neil McNeil, *Forge of Democracy* (New York: McKay, 1963), 306–309.

[47]Historian David S. Reynolds quoting a newspaper reporter of the time in Sheryl Gay Stolberg, "What Happened to Compromise," *New York Times,* May 29, 2005, sec. 4, 4.

[48] The House also approved the amendment in 1912.

[49]Mark Hankerson, "Participation Hits Record," *Congressional Quarterly Weekly Review,* December 11, 1999, 2979.

[50]David Nather, "Hastert Keeps His Cool, and His Post," *Congressional Quarterly Weekly Review,* February 6, 2006, 313.

[51]Rep. Barney Frank (D-Mass.), quoted in David D. Kirkpatrick, "As Dust Settles, The Speaker of the House Emerges, Still Standing," *New York Times,* February 5, 2006, 24.

[52]Ibid.

[53]Michael Barone, Richard E. Cohen, and Charles E. Cook Jr., *Almanac of American Politics, 2002* (Washington, D.C.: National Journal, 2002), 46.

[54] Ibid.

[55]For a review of all congressional committees and subcommittees, see the special report, "CQ Guide to the Committees," *Congressional Quarterly Weekly Review,* March 13, 2006, 659–693. Every January CQ publishes a special report on committees, their memberships and agendas.

[56]Davidson and Oleszek, *Congress and Its Members,* 198.

[57]See Roger Davidson, "Subcommittee Government," in *The New Congress,* eds. Thomas E. Mann and Norman J. Ornstein (Washington, D.C.: American Enterprise Institute for Public Policy Research, 1981), 110–111. Some of this occurs because members of Congress tend to be wealthy, and the wealthy make investments in corporations. It also occurs because members' financial interests are often similar to the interests in their districts (for example, representatives from farm districts are likely to be involved in farming or agribusiness).

[58]Jonathan Weisman and Charles S. Babcock, "The Currency of Corruption," *Washington Post National Weekly Edition,* February 6, 2006, 15.

[59]Sara Brandes Crook and John Hibbing, "Congressional Reform and Party Discipline: The Effects of Changes in the Seniority System on Party Loyalty in the U.S. House of Representatives," *British Journal of Political Science* 15 (1985), 207–226.

[60]Davidson and Oleszek, *Congress and Its Members,* 204.

[61]For a review of how the task force has been used, see Walter J. Oleszek, "The Use of Task Forces in the House," Congressional Research Service Report No. 96-8, 3-GOV, 1996, www .house.gov/rules/96-843.htm.

[62]*Budget of the United States, Fiscal 2007: Appendix* (Washington, D.C.: Government Printing Office, 2006), 15–38.

[63]Harlan Coben, "Rock and a Hard Place," *New York Times,* November 25, 2005. http:// www.nytimes.com/ 2005/11/25/opinion/25coben.html

[64]Ronald Moe and Steven Teel, "Congress as a Policy-Maker: A Necessary Reappraisal," *Political Science Quarterly* 85 (1970), 443–470.

[65] "The State of Congress," *National Journal* (Special Issue), January 10, 2004, 92.

[66] Thomas Geoghegan, "Bust the Filibuster," *Washington Post National Weekly Edition,* July 12, 1994, 25.

[67] Michael Malbin, "Leading a Filibustered Senate," in *Extensions* (Carl A. Albert Center, University of Oklahoma), Spring 1985, 3.

[68]Clinton aide Chuck Brain, quoted in Richard E. Cohen, "The Third House Rises," *National Journal,* July 28, 2001, 2395.

[69]Paul C. Light, "Filibusters Are Only Half the Problem," *New York Times,* June 3, 2005.

[70]David J. Vogler, *The Third House: Conference Committees in the United States Congress* (Evanston, Ill.: Northwestern University Press, 1971); see also Lawrence D. Longley and Walter J. Oleszek, *Bicameral Politics* (New Haven, Conn.: Yale University Press, 1989).

[71]Morris Ogul, "Congressional Oversight: Structures and Incentives," in *Congress Reconsidered,* eds. Dodd and Oppenheimer; see also Loch Johnson, "The U.S. Congress and the CIA: Monitoring the Dark Side of Government," *Legislative Studies Quarterly* 5 (1980), 477–501.

[72]Joseph Califano, "Imperial Congress," *New York Times Magazine,* January 23, 1994, 41.

[73][64]Richard E. Cohen, Kirk Victor, and David Bauman, "The State of Congress," *National Journal,* January 10, 2004, 104–105.

[74]Quoted in ibid., 105.

[75]Henry A. Waxman, "Free Pass from Congress," *Washington Post,* July 6, 2004, A19.

[76]"Investi-Gate," *Washington Monthly,* May 29, 2006, 3.

[77]Norman J. Ornstein, "Relationship between President, Congress Is Still Dysfunctional," *Roll Call,* April 26, 2006 (online version at www.aei.org, along with other Ornstein articles on the same subject). Another leading congressional expert whose work is frequently critical of Congress's poor performance on oversight is Thomas Mann, whose articles can be found at www.brookings.edu.

[78]Testimony from former CIA officers involved in writing the National Intelligence Estimate and providing other intelligence for the Bush administration prior to the Iraq invasion can be heard in the investigative report "The Dark Side," aired on *Frontline* in 2006. In it, former chair of the Senate Select Committee on Intelligence Bob Graham (D-Fla.) describes conditions under which senators were allowed access to intelligence reports. (The program can be viewed online at www. pbs.org/frontline.) Also see Ron Suskind, *The One Percent Doctrine* (New York: Simon and Schuster, 2006), 177–179.

[79]Cohen, Victor, and Bauman, "State of Congress," 96.

[80]Herbert Asher, "Learning of Legislative Norms," *American Political Science Review* 67 (1973), 499–513. Michael Berkman points out that freshmen who have had state legislative experience—who now account for more than half of all House members—adapt to the job faster than other members. See "Former State Legislators in the U.S. House of Representatives: Institutional and Policy Mastery," *Legislative Studies Quarterly* 18 (1993), 77–104.

[81]Rep. Jim DeMint (R-S.C.), quoted in Davidson and Oleszek, *Congress and Its Members,* 264.

[82]*Minot* (N.D.) *Daily News,* June 17, 1976.

[83]Samuel Kernell, *Going Public* (Washington, D.C.: CQ Press, 1986).

[84]Viewer statistics are available at C-SPAN's website (www.c-span.org). These are from July 2002 but are the most recent posted.

[85]Profile of the 109th Congress (www.cspan .org).

[86]Michael Wines, "Washington Really Is in Touch. We're the Problem," *New York Times,* October 16, 1994, 4: 2.

[87]Gallup poll, June 2004, www.gallup.com.

[88]*New York Times*/CBS poll, May, 2006.

[89]Editorial, "A Richer Life Beckons Congress," *New York Times,* August 8, 2005.

[90]Editorial, "Ethical Notes on the Reforming Class," *New York Times,* May 6, 2006.

Chapter 9

[1]This vignette is drawn from Bobby Baker (with Larry L. King), *Wheeling and Dealing: Confessions of a Capitol Hill Operator* (New York: W.W. Norton, 1978), 97–99.

[2]Arthur M. Schlesinger Jr., *The Imperial Presidency* (Boston: Houghton Mifflin, 1973). Schlesinger has published an updated version based on the Presidency of George W. Bush: *War and the American Presidency* (New York: Norton, 2004).

[3]Harold M. Barger, *The Impossible Presidency* (Glenview, Ill.: Scott, Foresman, 1984).

[4]Carl M. Cannon, "Untruth and Consequences," *The Atlantic,* January-February, 2007, 59.

[5]Evidently coined by historian Edward Pessen. Richard Brookhiser, "The People's Choice," *Time,* March 12, 2007, 25.

[6]Bob Dole, a Republican who ran in 1996, was the exception. David Leonhardt, "Who's in the Corner Office?" *New York Times,* November 27, 2005, BU 1.

[7]Since World War II, the only presidents with blueblood origins were Kennedy and the Bushes. Charles O. Jones, *The Presidency in a Separated System* (Washington, D.C.: Brookings, 1994), 43.

[8]Warren Vieth, "Burnishing an Image at the USA Corral," *Los Angeles Times,* August 29, 2005, www.latimes.com/news/nationworld/nation/la-na-ranch29aug,0,216556,print.story.

[9]"High misdemeanors" were political abuses.

[10]Richard Kleindienst, who served in the Nixon administration.

[11]Although members of Congress called it "perjury," it wouldn't have been considered perjury in court, because the lie was deemed irrelevant to the matter under investigation by a federal court. To be perjury, a lie must be relevant and important in a case.

[12]Two-thirds of those present.

[13]#65.

[14] Information on all three impeachment proceedings can be found at www.historyplace.com

[15] Jeffrey Toobin, *A Vast Conspiracy* (New York: Touchstone, 1999), 333–334.

[16]During the presidencies of John Tyler, Millard Fillmore, Andrew Johnson, Chester Arthur, Theodore Roosevelt, Calvin Coolidge, Harry Truman, and Lyndon Johnson.

[17]As the title suggests, the conferral of power is temporary; the president can resume office by giving Congress written notice of his recovery. If the vice president and other officials who determined the president unfit do not concur in his judgment that he has recovered, they can challenge his return to office by notifying Congress in writing. Then it falls to Congress to decide whether the president is capable of resuming his duties.

[18]Woodrow Wilson, *Congressional Government: A Study in American Politics* (New Brunswick, N.J.: Transaction, 2002). Originally published in 1885.

[19]Theodore Lowi, *The Personal President: Power Invested, Promise Unfulfilled* (Ithaca, N.Y.: Cornell University Press, 1985).

[20]Jefferson's management of the Presidency is described in Joseph J. Ellis, *American Sphinx: The Character of Thomas Jefferson* (New York: Knopf, 1997), 186–228.

[21]Michael Lind, "The Out-of-Control Presidency," in Robert E. DiClerico and Allan S. Hammock, *Points of View,* 9th ed. (Boston: McGraw Hill, 2004), 188.

[22]However, he couldn't persuade the Senate to ratify the treaty that would have authorized U.S. membership.

[23]With the possible exception of the 1950s, when the people, who had lived through the Depression, World War II, and the Korean War, were tired of government activity and ready to focus on their private lives. For veterans, this meant a college education or a new job. For many, it meant a new house, perhaps a move to the growing suburbs or to the beckoning states of California or Florida. Even so, President Dwight Eisenhower (1953–1961) was expected to protect the country during the Cold War.

[24]*Clinton v. Jones,* 137 L.Ed.2d 945 (1997).

[25]There was an alternative. A legal record could be established then, and the suit itself could be tried after he left office, thus preserving Jones' opportunity to sue.

[26]When the suit went to trial, the federal court ruled that Clinton's conduct was "boorish" but not illegal. When Jones appealed, the two parties settled out of court.

[27]See, for example, the comments of Arthur M. Schlesinger Jr. in Cannon, "Judging Clinton," 22; Steven A. Holmes, "Losers in Clinton-Starr Bouts May Be Future U.S. Presidents," *New York Times,* August 23, 1998, 18; and Adam Clymer, "The Presidency Is Still There, Not Quite the Same," *New York Times,* February 14, 1999, 4: 1.

[28] This has become a common assessment of the Bush Presidency. For a libertarian view, see George Healey and Timothy Lynch, "Power Surge: the Constitutional Record of George W. Bush" (Washington, D.C.: Cato Institute, 2006); for a classical conservative view, see the *National Review,* especially essays by its founder, William S. Buckley; for a liberal view within Congress, see Henry Waxman's report to the Committee on Government Reform, "Secrecy in the Bush Administration," at the website of the committee's Democrats (www.democrats.reform.house.gov); for an academic treatment, see Andrew Rudalevige, *The New Imperial Presidency* (Ann Arbor: University of Michigan, 2005), 211–285.

[29]See, for example, his paper, "Congressional Overreaching in Foreign Policy," American Enterprise Institute, 1989, cited in Paul Starobin, "Long Live the King!" *National Journal,* February 18, 2006, 25.

[30] The two principals were long-time Cheney aide, David Addington, and Deputy Assistant Attorney General John Yoo, who elaborated on his ideas in *The Powers of War and Peace: The Constitution and Foreign Affairs After 9/11* (Chicago: University of Chicago Press, 2005). For others involved, see Keith Perine, "Imbalance of Power," *CQ Weekly,* February 27, 2006, 545.

[31]Jane Mayer, "The Hidden Power," *New Yorker,* July 3, 2006, 44.

[32]Charlie Savage, "Bush Challenges Hundreds of Laws: President Cites Powers of His Office," *Boston Globe,* April 30, 2006, A1.

[33]Bruce Fein, Associate Deputy Attorney General in the Reagan administration, quoted in Mayer, "Hidden Power," 46.

[34]Charles O. Jones, *The Presidency in a Separated System* (Washington, D.C.: Brookings, 1994), 1.

[35]Charles O. Jones, *Separate But Equal Branches* (Chatham, N. J.: Chatham House, 1995), 107.

[36]Jones found that evenly matched was more common in his study. Jones, *Presidency in a Separated System,* 293.

[37]A president can't pardon a president who has been impeached, because impeachment isn't a criminal charge and removal isn't a criminal conviction.

[38]Michael J. Sniffen, "Pardons Can Cause Relief, Grief," *Lincoln Journal Star,* March 12, 2007, 5A.

[39]Ibid.

[40] Bush didn't *pardon* Libby; he left Libby's conviction, fine, and probation intact (as of fall, 2007).

[41]#69, by Alexander Hamilton.

[42]These appointees have quasi-legislative and quasi-judicial responsibilities, unlike typical executive agencies. For discussion of the president's removal powers in light of a 1988 Supreme Court decision regarding independent counsels, see John A. Rohr, "Public Administration, Executive Power, and Constitutional Confusion," and Rosemary O'Leary, "Response to John Rohr," *Public Administrative Review* 49 (1989), 108–115.

[43]According to presidential historians Alan Brinkley and Robert Dallek, quoted in Thomas B. Edsall, "Always the Winner," *Washington Post National Weekly Edition,* February 16–22, 2004, 19.

[44]Todd Gitlin, "From the Left," *New York Times,* October 17, 2004, WK2.

[45]Michael Nelson, ed., *Presidency A to Z* (Washington, D.C., CQ Press, 1998), 169.

[46]The Bush White House provides a link to all executive orders issued by the president at the White House home page (www.whitehouse.gov).

[47]Although the phrase itself doesn't go back that far. For historical examination, see Schlesinger, *Imperial Presidency.*

48 *United States v. Reynolds*, 345 U.S. 1 (1953). Years later, however, it was found that national security wasn't at stake after all. The Eisenhower administration had claimed executive privilege to spare the Air Force embarrassment over a plane crash that was due to poor maintenance and pilot error. "Morning Edition," National Public Radio, September 9, 2005.

49 418 U.S. 683 (1974).

50 Jeb Stuart Magruder, "Ex-aide: Nixon Ordered Watergate Break-in," *Lincoln Journal Star*, July 27, 2003.

51 The courts also rejected a claim of executive privilege by Clinton to prevent a White House aide from testifying about possible criminal wrongdoing.

52 Peter Baker, "Reasserting Authority," *Washington Post National Weekly Edition*, August 8–14, 2005, 11.

53 *Cheney v. United States District Court*, 542 U.S. 367 (2004).

54 Congress's nonpartisan budget office, the Congressional Budget Office (CBO), prepares budget reports that are regarded as more reliable than those of the OMB, but the administration has the initiative because it prepares the initial budget proposal.

55 Jones, *The Presidency in a Separated System*, 209.

56 Howard Baker, quoted in Ibid., 202.

57 Ibid., 181.

58 Andrew Sullivan, "We Don't Need a New King George," *Time*, January 23, 2006, 74.

59 Charlie Savage, "Bush Challenges Hundreds of Laws: President Cites Powers of His Office," *Boston Globe*, April 30, 2006, A1.

60 *Clinton v. New York City*, 524 U.S. 417 (1998).

61 Richard J. Barnet, "Reflections: The Disorders of Peace," *New Yorker*, January 20, 1992, 64.

62 Rather than expressly authorizing the president to abrogate a treaty by himself, the majority ruled that the dispute was a "political question," which avoided a ruling on the merits of Carter's claim. Thus the Court allows, but doesn't authorize, the president to take this action. *Goldwater v. Carter*, 444 U.S. 996 (1979).

63 He also "unsigned" the treaty creating the International Criminal Court, which Clinton had signed but never submitted for Senate approval. Thus the United States wasn't a party to the treaty, but because Clinton had signed it, the United States was a participant in discussions of rules for the court. Bush's "unsigning," for symbolic reasons, pulled the United States out of these discussions.

64 For some trade deals, Congress delegates power to the president in advance.

65 John Marshall, as a member of the House of Representatives. Later, Marshall would become chief justice of the Supreme Court.

66 *United States v. Curtiss-Wright Export Corporation*, 299 U.S. 304 (1936).

67 As ex-presidents, Nixon and Carter made foreign trips in apparent violation of this law.

68 Alexander Hamilton, #69. Hamilton indicates that this authority is "nothing more" than being "first general" and "first admiral."

69 John Barry, "What Schwarzkopf's Book Leaves Out," *Newsweek*, September 28, 1992, 68.

70 A good overview of Rumsfeld's attempts to transform the military and his role in planning and directing the war in Iraq can be found in the transcript of the PBS program *"Rumsfeld's War,"* broadcast October 26, 2004, available at www.pbs.org/wgbh/pages/frontline/shows/pentagon.

71 During the Depression, MacArthur commanded federal troops at a demonstration. He refused to obey President Hoover's orders, which were given twice, not to use force on demonstrators. Hoover himself took the blame for the incident, rather than explaining his orders and disciplining MacArthur. "The Great Depression," PBS, October 25, 1993. Hoover's behavior may have fueled MacArthur's boldness.

72 Michael Steinberger, "Misoverestimated," *American Prospect*, April, 2004, 23. As a candidate for president, Clinton had promised to end the military's ban. Nine days before Clinton took office, Powell urged midshipmen at the Naval Academy to resign in protest if they couldn't accept the change. At this time, Clinton wasn't commander in chief, but Powell's actions continued after the president was sworn in.

73 The "don't ask, don't tell" policy retains the ban but forbids the military from asking the personnel about their sexual orientation. However, if any personnel admit homosexual orientation or engage in certain practices, such as holding hands or dancing with a person of the same sex, they can be booted from the military.

74 Quoted in "Notes and Comment," *New Yorker*, June 1, 1987, 23.

75 Ibid.

76 Ibid.

77 The law specifies sixty days but gives the president an additional thirty days if necessary to protect the troops.

78 For analysis, see Marc J. Hetherington and Michael Nelson, "Anatomy of a Rally Effect: George W. Bush and the War on Terrorism," *PS*, January, 2003, 37–42.

79 British spy novelist John Le Carre observed, "How Bush and his junta succeeded in deflecting America's anger from bin Laden to Saddam Hussein is one of the great public relations conjuring tricks in history." "Verbatim," *Time*, January 27, 2003, 15.

80 For analysis of the public relations campaign, see Frank Rich, *The Greatest Story Ever Sold* (New York: Penguin, 2006).

81 Mike Allen, "Does an Embassy Trump the Lincoln Bedroom?" *Washington Post National Weekly Edition*, May 7, 2001, 14.

82 Mike Allen, "The Mother of All Fundraisers," *Washington Post National Weekly Edition*, May 20, 2002, 13.

83 Thomas F. Cronin, *The State of the Presidency* (Boston: Little, Brown, 1975), 118.

84 Congress's anger at Roosevelt's court-packing scheme held up the reorganization for two years.

85 Quoted in Richard Pious, *The American Presidency* (New York: Basic Books, 1979), 244.

86 Ann Reilly Dowd, "What Managers Can Learn from Manager Reagan," *Fortune*, September 15, 1986, 32–41.

87 See John H. Kessel, "The Structures of the Reagan White House," *American Journal of Political Science* 28 (1984), 231–258.

88 Hillary Rodham Clinton, quoted in Carol Gelderman, *All the Presidents' Words: The Bully Pulpit and the Creation of the Virtual Presidency* (New York: Walker, 1997), 160.

89 A good description of Clinton's relationship to his White House staff can be found in Joe Klein, *The Natural: The Misunderstood Presidency of Bill Clinton* (New York: Doubleday, 2002).

90 For more on Bush's management style, see the several articles in the special section "C.E.O. U.S.A.," *New York Times Magazine*, January 14, 2001, 24–58.

91 Ron Suskind, *The Price of Loyalty: George W. Bush, the White House, and the Education of Paul O'Neill* (New York: Simon & Schuster, 2004), 224–227; 293; Lawrence B. Wilkerson, "The White House Cabal," *Los Angeles Times*, October 25, 2005, www.latimes.com/news/opinion/la-oe-wilkerson25oct25,0,1845763,print.story. Wilkerson served as chief of staff to Secretary of State Colin Powell from 2002 to 2005.

92 Mike Allen, "Living Too Much in the Bubble?" *Time*, September 19, 2005, 44.

93 Ibid. It didn't help that political strategist Karl Rove was in the hospital, recovering from kidney stones, and Vice President Cheney and Chief of Staff Andrew Card were on vacation, and close adviser Condoleeza Rice was shopping in New York City when Katrina hit.

94 Suskind, *The Price of Loyalty*, 149.

95 James C. Moore, "Karl Rove: Counting Votes While Bombs Drop," *Lincoln Journal Star*, May 11, 2003, 5E. Moore co-authored the biography of Rove. James Moore and Wayne Slater, *Bush's Brain: How Karl Rove Made George W. Bush Presidential* (Hoboken, N.J.: John Wiley and Sons, 2003).

96 Ibid.

97 For a review of the backgrounds of men who have served in the Vice Presidency and the roles they have played, see L. Edward Purcell, *Vice Presidents* (New York: Facts on File, 2001); Michael Nelson, *A Heartbeat Away* (New York: Priority, 1988); Paul C. Light, *Vice-Presidential Power: Advice and Influence in the White House* (Baltimore: Johns Hopkins University Press, 1984); and George Sirgiovanni, "The 'Van Buren Jinx': Vice Presidents Need Not Beware," *Presidential Studies Quarterly* 18 (1988), 61–76.

[98]Seymour M. Hersh, "Nixon's Last Cover-up: The Tapes He Wants the Archives to Suppress," *New Yorker*, December 14, 1992, 94.

[99]Purcell, *Vice Presidents*, 380.

[100]Jane Mayer, "The Hidden Power," *The New Yorker*, July 3, 2006, 50.

[101]Nicholas Lemann, "The Quiet Man," *New Yorker*, May 7, 2001, 68.

[102]Janet Hook, "Bush Gets Personal on Social Security," *Los Angeles Times*, April 25, 2005, www.latimes.com/news/nationworld/nation/la-na-bushlobby25apr25.story.

[103]According to several presidential scholars. "What Will History Rate Cheney?" *Time*, February 27, 2006, 28–29.

[104]Paul Light, quoted in Tom Raum, "Trial Shines Revealing Light on White House," *Lincoln Journal Star*, February 12, 2007, 7A.

[105]According to presidential scholars Robert Dallek and Stephen Hess, quoted in "What Will History Rate Cheney?" and according to officials in the administration, quoted in Michael Duffy, "Cheney in Twilight," *Time*, March 19, 2007, 25; and Glenn Kessler, "Iraq, Enemy No. 1," *Washington Post National Weekly Edition*, January 20–26, 2003, 16. See also Bob Woodward, *Plan of Attack* (New York: Simon & Schuster, 2004).

[106]According to a government consultant, quoted in Seymour M. Hersh, "Watching Lebanon," *New Yorker*, August 21, 2006, 30.

[107]As described by one Washington insider. Duffy, "Cheney in Twilight," 25.

[108]The insider chose to remain anonymous. Kessler, "Iraq, Enemy No. 1."

[109]Suskind, *One Percent Doctrine*, 173–174.

[110]David Frum, quoted in Jo Becker and Barton Gellman, "A Strong Push from Backstage," *Washington Post National Weekly Edition*, July 16–22, 2007, 8.

[111]Barger, *Impossible Presidency*, 145.

[112]Fortunately, in the 1950s, the public, worn out from government activity during the Great Depression and World War II, didn't expect the president to accomplish much. People focused on their private lives. Eisenhower does receive high marks for a steady hand during the Cold War. For an examination of presidential persuasion, particularly the Truman and Eisenhower presidencies, see Richard E. Neustadt, *Presidential Power: The Politics of Leadership from FDR to Carter* (New York: Wiley, 1980).

[113]These ideas come especially from Neustadt, *Presidential Power*.

[114]Thomas P. O'Neill Jr., with William Novak, *Man of the House* (New York: Random House, 1987), 341–342.

[115]The representative wasn't identified. "Contra Proposal Heads for Showdown in House," *Lincoln Journal*, June 25, 1986, A1.

[116]David Pomerantz, "Political Booknotes," *Washington Monthly*, March, 1990, 57.

[117]Sen. Barry Goldwater (R-Ariz.), who was referring to Johnson's tenure as majority leader, although the same could have been said about his tenure as president. Burton

Bernstein, "Profiles—AuH₂O," *New Yorker*, April 28, 1988, 64.

[118]According to Sen. Dale Bumpers (D-Ark.), quoted in Lloyd Grove, "Replacing the Carrot with a Stick," *Washington Post National Weekly Edition*, April 12–18, 1993, 12.

[119]Doris Kearns Goodwin, *Lyndon Johnson and the American Dream* (New York: Harper & Row, 1976), 226.

[120]Presidential historian Alan Brinkley in "The Making of a War President," *New York Times Book Review*, August 20, 2006, 10.

[121]Sheryl Gay Stolberg, "As Agenda Falters, Bush Tries a More Personal Approach in Dealing with Congress," *New York Times*, June 11, 2006, YT26.

[122]According to congressional scholar Thomas Mann, quoted in Hook, "Bush Gets Personal on Social Security."

[123]E.J. Dionne Jr., "The System at Work," *Washington Post National Weekly Edition*, June 18–24, 2007, 31.

[124]Hook, "Bush Gets Personal on Social Security." However, when the president pushed his proposal for Social Security in 2006, he did make an effort to meet with and listen to lawmakers, once he realized that his proposal was in trouble.

[125]James A. Thurber, quoted in Stolberg, "As Agenda Falters, Bush Tries a More Personal Approach in Dealing with Congress."

[126]Jeffrey K. Tulis, *The Rhetorical Presidency* (Princeton, N.J.: Princeton University Press, 1987).

[127]Quoted in Garry Wills, *Lincoln at Gettysburg* (New York: Simon & Schuster, 1992), 31.

[128]Samuel Kernell, *Going Public: New Strategies of Presidential Leadership* (Washington, D.C.: CQ Press, 1986), 15.

[129]David Halberstam, *The Powers That Be* (New York: Dell, 1980), 30.

[130]"Travels of the President," *New York Times*, August 8, 2004, 18.

[131]Michael Waldman, Clinton's former chief speechwriter, interviewed on *Morning Edition*, National Public Radio, January 1, 2002.

[132]Frank Rich, "One Step Closer to the Big Enchilada," *New York Times*, October 30, 2005, WK12.

[133]Ari Fleischer, quoted in *Congressional Quarterly Today News*, May 19, 2004, www.cq.com.

[134]Janet Hook, "Social Security Plan Hits Shoals," *Los Angeles Times*, June 27, 2005, www.latimes.com/news/nationworld/nation/la-na-social27jun27,0,7154171,full.story.

[135]Nicholas Lemann, "Remember the Alamo," *New Yorker*, October 18, 2004, 153.

[136]Bruce Miroff, "The Presidency and the Public: Leadership and Spectacle," in *The Presidency and the Political System*, 5th ed., ed. Michael Nelson (Washington: CQ Press, 1998), 320. This section draws heavily from Miroff's observations.

[137]James David Barber, *The Presidential Character*, 2nd ed. (Englewood Cliffs, N.J.: Prentice Hall, 1977), 157.

[138]Ibid.

[139]Theodore Lowi coined this term and our discussion will draw from Lowi, *The Personal President*.

[140]Richard E. Neustadt, *Presidential Power* (New York: Wiley, 1960), 5–6.

[141]Malcolm Gladwell, "Comment: The Politics of Politesse," *New Yorker*, December 23 and 30, 2002, 57.

[142]Klein, *The Natural*, 208.

[143]Benjamin C. Bradlee, "When They Made George Washington, They Broke the Mold," *Washington Post National Weekly Edition*, November 25–December 1, 1991, 23.

[144]Thomas E. Patterson, *The Vanishing Voter* (New York: Knopf, 2002), 54.

[145]Jones, *The Presidency in a Separated System*, chap. 4.

[146]Some countries have a "president," but that office doesn't resemble our president's. Robert A. Dahl, *How Democratic is the American Constitution?* (New Haven, Conn.: Yale University Press, 2003), 111.

Chapter 10

[1]www.fda.gov/cdrh/comp/guidance/1548.html.

[2]coburn.senate.gov/public/index.cfm?FuseAction=LatestNews.PressReleases&ContentRecord_id=7602b477-6536-4c3c-a715-bb40fb9752ec.

[3]http://www.medicalnewstoday.com/articles/33503.php

[4]Bruce Adams, "The Frustrations of Government Service," *Public Administration Review* 44 (1984), 5. For more discussion of public attitudes about the civil service, see Herbert Kaufman, "Fear of Bureaucracy: A Raging Pandemic," *Public Administration Review* 41 (1981), 1.

[5]The classic early work on Western bureaucracy is Max Weber's. See H. H. Gerth and C. Wright Mills, trans., from Max Weber: *Essays on Sociology* (New York: Oxford University Press, 1946), 196–239.

[6]On distinctions between public and private bureaucracies see Barry Bozeman, *All Organizations Are Public: Bridging Public and Private Organizational Theories* (San Francisco: Jossey-Bass, 1987).

[7]"Federal Executives' Bonuses Scrutinized," *Champaign-Urbana News-Gazette*, January 23, 2002, A4.

[8]From a letter to W. T. Barry, quoted in "A Citizen's Guide on Using the Freedom of Information Act and the Privacy Act of 1974 to Request Government Records," report to the U.S. House of Representatives 50 (1999), 2.

[9]Reported in Sam Archibald, "The Early Years of the Freedom of Information Act, 1955–1974," *PS: Political Science and Politics*, December 1993, 730.

[10]Debra Gersh Hernandez, "Many Promises, Little Action," *Editor and Publisher*, March 26, 1994, 15.

[11]Government Accounting Office, *Freedom of Information Act: State Department Request Processing* (Washington, D.C.: Government Printing Office, 1989).

[12]Clinton administration policy on compliance with FOIA can be found in Federation of American Scientists, Project on Govern-

ment Secrecy, "Clinton Administration Documents on Classification Policy," 2003, www .fas.org/sgp/clinton/index.html.

[13]Linda Greenhouse, "A Penchant for Secrecy," *New York Times,* May 5, 2002, WK1.

[14]As a presidential aide in the Ford administration, Cheney encouraged President Ford to veto the 1974 bill that strengthened FOIA rights. Congress ultimately passed the bill over Ford's veto.

[15]Memo from Attorney General John Ashcroft, October 12, 2001. The text of this memo and all major Bush administration statements and documents regarding its FOIA and openness in government policies are posted at the Federation of American Scientists website, www.fas.org. Also see openthe-government.org.

[16]Useful websites for tracking data removed from government websites include: www .ombwatch.org, openthegovernment.org, and www.fas.org.

[17]William S. Broad, "U.S. Is Tightening Rules on Keeping Scientific Secrets," *New York Times,* February 17, 2002, 1, 13.

[18]David Nather, "Pilots Need-to-Know Conundrum," *CQ Weekly,* July 18, 2005, 1966.

[19]Christopher Drew, "Efforts to Hide Sensitive Data Pit 9/11 Concerns against Safety," *New York Times,* March 5, 2005.

[20]Ellen Nakashima, "Frustration on the Left—and the Right," *Washington Post National Weekly Edition,* March 11, 2002, 29; Scott Shane, "Increase in the Number of Documents Classified by the Government," *New York Times,* July 3, 2005, 12.

[21]Shane, "Increase in the Number of Documents Classified by the Government," 12; David Nather, "Classified: A Rise in State Secrets," *CQ Weekly,* July 18, 2005, 1960.

[22]Nakashima, "Frustration."

[23]Greenhouse, "Penchant for Secrecy."

[24](Senators) Trent Lott and Ron Wyden, "Hiding the Truth in a Cloud of Black Ink," *New York Times,* August 26, 2004, A27.

[25]Evan Hendricks, *Former Secrets: Government Records Made Public through the Freedom of Information Act* (Washington, D.C.: Campaign for Political Rights, 1982); "Behind the Freedom of Information Act," *Now with Bill Moyers,* PBS, April 5, 2002.

[26]Joyce Appleby, "That's General Washington to You," *New York Times Book Review,* February 14, 1993, 11, a review of Richard Norton Smith, *Patriarch* (Boston: Houghton Mifflin, 1993). See also James Q. Wilson, "The Rise of the Bureaucratic State," *Public Interest* 41 (1975), 77–103.

[27]Wilson, "Rise of the Bureaucratic State."

[28]Leonard D. White, *Introduction to the Study of Public Administration,* 4th ed. (New York: Macmillan, 1955), 4.

[29]David H. Rosenbloom, "'Whose Bureaucracy Is This Anyway?' Congress's 1946 Answer," *PS: Political Science and Politics* (December 2001), 773.

[30]Paul C. Light, *Thickening Government: Federal Hierarchy and the Diffusion of Accountability*
(Washington, D.C.: Brookings Institution, 1995).

[31]U.S. Census Bureau, *Statistical Abstract of the United States,* 2006 (Washington, D.C.: Government Printing Office, 2005), tab. 451.

[32]*Statistical Abstract of the U.S. 2007,* tab. 480.

[33]Paul C. Light, "Fact Sheet on the Continued Thickening of Government," Brookings Institution, July 23, 2004, www.brookings. edu/views/papers/light/20040723.htm.

[34]Ibid. Light does an "inventory" of senior positions in cabinet departments every six years.

[35]Jim Hoagland, "Dissing Government," *Washington Post National Weekly Edition,* December 8, 2003, 5.

[36]Paul C. Light, "What Federal Employees Want from Reform: Reform Watch Brief No. 5," Brookings Institution, March 2002, www .brookings. edu/comm/reformwatch/rw05 .htm.

[37]For a discussion of these issues, see Peter T. Kilborn, "Big Change Likely as Law Bans Bias toward Disabled," *New York Times,* July 19, 1992, 1, 16.

[38]Jill Smolows, "Noble Aims, Mixed Results," *Time,* July 31, 1995, 54.

[39]Theodore Lowi, *The End of Liberalism* (New York: Norton, 1969).

[40]Woodrow Wilson, "The Study of Administration," *Political Science Quarterly* 56 (1941), 481–506. Originally published in 1887.

[41]See David H. Rosenbloom, "Have an Administrative Rx? Don't Forget the Politics!" *Public Administration Review* 53 (1993), 503–507.

[42]The changes in allowable political activities made possible by the Hatch Act Reform Amendments are outlined by Office of Personnel Management in its online history, "Biography of an Ideal." See the section "Hatch Act Revisited and Transformed" (www.opm.gov).

[43]This was revealed by the head of the Clinton and Bush counterterrorism unit, Richard A. Clarke, who spoke with Bush on September 12, 2001, in the war room and recounted the event in *Against All Enemies* (New York: Free Press, 2004) and in public testimony before the televised 9/11 Commission hearings in 2004.

[44]Public testimony before the televised 9/11 Commission hearings, 2004.

[45]Report issued by the chief U.S. arms inspector, Charles A. Duelfer, October 2004.

[46]See, for example, James Risen, *State of War: The Secret History of the CIA and the Bush Administration* (New York: The Free Press, 2006), and Ron Suskind, *The One Percent Doctrine* (New York: Simon and Schuster, 2006). George Tenet himself was a major source for Suskind's book. In 2007, Tenet wrote his own book, *At the Center of the Storm: My Years with the CIA,* in which he told a different version of his "slam dunk" comment.

[47]Christopher Lee, "Bush's Family Planning Appointee Worked for Anti-Contraception Group," *Washington Post,* November 17, 2006.

[48]Charles Peters, *How Washington Really Works* (Reading, Mass.: Addison-Wesley, 1980), 46–47.
[49]Nicolas Thompson, "Finding the Civil Service's Hidden Sex Appeal," *Washington Monthly,* November 2000, 31.

[50]Terry More, "Regulators' Performance and Presidential Administrations," *American Journal of Political Science* 26 (1982), 197–224; Terry More, "Control and Feedback in Economic Regulation," *American Political Science Review* 79 (1985), 1094–1116.

[51]More, "Control and Feedback."

[52]Use of the term *capture* by political scientists studying regulation seems to have originated with Samuel Huntington, "The Marasmus of the ICC," *Yale Law Journal* 61 (1952), 467–509; it was later popularized by Marver Bernstein, *Regulating Business by Independent Commission* (Princeton, N.J.: Princeton University Press, 1955).

[53]W. John Moore, "Citizen Prosecutors," *National Journal,* August 18, 1990, 2006–2010.

[54]Interview with David Brancaccio, *NOW* (PBS), October 14, 2005.

[55]Steve Fainaru and Dan Eggen, "Chief among the Charges," *Washington Post National Weekly Edition,* June 10, 2002, 30.

[56]Robert Pear, "Congress Moves to Protect Federal Whistleblowers," *New York Times,* October 3, 2004, 21.

[57]Fred Alford, quoted in Barbara Ehrenreich, "All Together Now," *New York Times,* July 15, 2004, A23.

[58]Eric Schmitt, "The Rube Goldberg Agency," *New York Times,* March 24, 2002, WK5.

[59]Schmitt, "Is This Any Way to Run a Nation?"

Chapter 11

[1]"Judging Samuel Alito," *New York Times,* January 8, 2006, WK13.

[2]Tom Korologos, "Roberts Rx: Speak Up, but Shut Up," *New York Times,* September 4, 2005, WK12.

[3]Harold Meyerson, "Up Front," *American Prospect,* February, 2006, 6.

[4]Janet Malcolm, "The Art of Testifying," *New Yorker,* March 13, 2006, 74.

[5]Arlen Specter (R-Pa.), quoted in Jeffrey Toobin, "Comment: Unanswered Questions," *New Yorker,* January 23 and 30, 2006, 30.

[6]As Robert Bork was. Or unless the hearings are sensational, as Clarence Thomas's were.

[7]David Axelrod, quoted in James A. Barnes, "Confirming Their Frustration," *National Journal,* January 21, 2006, 54.

[8]John Hibbing and Elizabeth Theiss-Morse, *Congress as Public Enemy: Public Attitudes toward American Political Institutions* (New York: Cambridge University Press, 1995), chs. 2 and 3.

[9]John R. Schmidhauser, *Justices and Judges* (Boston: Little, Brown, 1979), 11.

[10]However, federalism doesn't require this exact arrangement. Most federal countries have one national court over a system of regional courts.

[11]In addition, there is the Court of Appeals for the Federal Circuit, which handles customs and patents cases.

[12]Occasionally, for important cases, the entire group of judges in one circuit will sit together, "en banc." (In the large Ninth Circuit, eleven judges will sit.)

[13]If at least $75,000 is at stake, according to congressional law.

[14]Quoted in Henry J. Abraham, "A Bench Happily Filled," *Judicature* 66 (1983), 284.

[15]For elaboration on the Senate's role, see Stephen B. Burbank, "Politics, Privilege, and Power: The Senate's Role in the Appointment of Federal Judges," *Judicature* 86 (2002), 24.

[16]Victor Navasky, *Kennedy Justice* (New York: Atheneum, 1971), 245–246.

[17]Harry P. Stumpf, *American Judicial Politics,* 2nd ed. (Upper Saddle River, N.J.: Prentice Hall, 1998), 175. After Taft nominated a Catholic to be chief justice, the Speaker of the House cracked, "If Taft were Pope, he'd want to appoint some Protestants to the College of Cardinals." Henry J. Abraham, *Justices and Presidents: A Political History of Appointments to the Supreme Court,* 2nd ed. (New York: Oxford University Press, 1985), 168.

[18]The Nixon administration was the first to recognize that it could accomplish some policy goals by selecting lower court judges on the basis of ideology. Elliot E. Slotnick, "A Historical Perspective on Federal Judicial Selection," *Judicature* 86 (2002), 13.

[19]For an analysis of internal documents that established this process in the Reagan administration, see Dawn Johnsen, "Tipping the Scale," *Washington Monthly,* July–August 2002, 1–18.

[20]Jo Becker and Barton Gellman, "The Veep Steered While Vetting Conservatives for the Court," *Washington Post National Weekly Edition,* July 16–22, 2007, 9. For Bush's second nomination to the Court, the president departed from Cheney's list, selecting White House Counsel Harriet Miers. The vice president was miffed, commenting, "Didn't have the nerve to tell me himself," and conservative groups were concerned that Miers wasn't reliably conservative. After these groups torpedoed her nomination, Bush selected a name—Alito's—from Cheney's list.

[21]Marilyn Nejelski, *Women in the Judiciary: A Status Report* (Washington, D.C.: National Women's Political Caucus, 1984).

[22]Sheldon Goldman, "Reagan's Second-Term Judicial Appointments," *Judicature* 70 (1987), 324–339.

[23]Sheldon Goldman, Elliott E. Slotnick, Gerard Gryski, Gary Zuk, and Sara Schiavoni, "W. Bush Remaking the Judiciary: Like Father Like Son?" *Judicature* 86 (2003), 304, 308. For further examination, see Rorie L. Spill and Kathleen A. Bratton, "Clinton and Diversification of the Federal Judiciary," *Judicature,* March–April, 2001, 256.

[24]Ibid.

[25]Especially congressional power under the commerce clause.

[26]David Greenberg, "Actually, It Is Political," *Washington Post National Weekly Edition,* July 26-August 1, 2004, 23.

[27]One of President Reagan's nominees, Douglas Ginsburg, withdrew his nomination due to widespread opposition in the Senate, so officially his nomination was not denied.

[28]Nixon's nomination of G. Harold Carswell was a notable exception. At his confirmation hearing, a parade of legal scholars called him undistinguished. Even his supporters acknowledged that he was mediocre. Nixon's floor manager for the nomination, Senator Roman Hruska (R-Neb.), blurted out in exasperation, "Even if he is mediocre, there are a lot of mediocre judges and people and lawyers. They are entitled to a little representation, aren't they, and a little chance? We can't have all Brandeises, Cardozos, and Frankfurters, and stuff like that there." Abraham, *Justices and Presidents,* 6–7.

[29]For an examination of the relationship between ethical lapses and ideological reasons, see Charles M. Cameron, Albert D. Cover, and Jeffrey A. Segal, "Senate Voting on Supreme Court Nominees: A Neoinstitutional Model," *American Political Science Review* 84 (1990), 525–534.

[30]For some time, the Senate confirmed fewer nominees to the lower courts in the fourth year of a president's term when the Senate's majority was from the other party. The senators hoped their candidate would capture the White House in the next election. They delayed confirmation so there would be numerous vacancies for their president and, through senatorial courtesy, for themselves to fill as well. Jeffrey A. Segal and Harold Spaeth, "If a Supreme Court Vacancy Occurs, Will the Senate Confirm a Reagan Nominee?" *Judicature* 69 (1986), 188–189.

[31]Quoted in Savage, "Clinton Losing Fight for Black Judge," *Los Angeles Times,* July 7, 2000, A1.

[32]Scherer, "Judicial Confirmation Process," 240–250.

[33]Schmidhauser, *Justice and Judges,* 55–57.

[34]David Leonhardt, "Who Has a Corner Office?" *New York Times,* November 27, 2005, BU4.

[35]All except Kennedy, Thomas, and possibly Alito.

[36]Goldman et al., "W. Bush Remaking the Judiciary," 304, 308.

[37]As an alternative, Congress in 1980 established other procedures to discipline lower court judges. Councils made up of district and appellate court judges can ask their fellow judges to resign or can prevent them from hearing cases, but they cannot actually remove them. The procedures have been used infrequently, although their existence has prompted some judges to resign before being disciplined.

[38]Merle Miller, *Plain Speaking* (New York: Berkeley Putnam, 1974), 121.

[39]Harold W. Chase, *Federal Judges* (Minneapolis: University of Minnesota Press, 1972), 189.

[40]John Gruhl, "The Impact of Term Limits for Supreme Court Justices," *Judicature* 81 (1997), 66–72.

[41]The fourth, Rehnquist, disqualified himself because he had worked on the administration's policy toward executive privilege.

[42]*Jones v. Clinton,* 137 L.Ed.2d 945, 117 S. Ct. 1636 (1997).

[43]Martin Shapiro, "The Supreme Court: From Warren to Burger," in *The New American Political System,* ed. Anthony King (Washington, D.C.: American Enterprise Institute, 1978), 180–181.

[44]Robert Scigliano, *The Supreme Court and the Presidency* (New York: Free Press, 1971), 147–148.

[45]Quoted in Abraham, *Justices and Presidents,* 62.

[46]Earl Warren, *The Memoirs of Earl Warren* (Garden City, N.Y.: Doubleday, 1977), 5.

[47]Quoted in Abraham, *Justices and Presidents,* 63.

[48]Linda Greenhouse, "In the Confirmation Dance, the Past but Rarely the Prologue," *New York Times,* July 24, 2005, WK5.

[49]For elaboration, see Lee Epstein and Jeffrey A. Segal, *Advice and Consent* (New York: Oxford University Press, 2005), ch. 5.

[50]"How Much Do Lawyers Charge?" *Parade,* March 23, 1997, 14.

[51]Lois G. Forer, *Money and Justice* (New York: Norton, 1984), 9, 15, 102.

[52]Jonathan Casper, "Lawyers Before the Supreme Court: Civil Liberties and Civil Rights, 1957–1966," *Stanford Law Review,* February, 1970, 509.

[53]Peter Slevin, "Courting Christianity," *Washington Post National Weekly Edition,* July 17–23, 2006, 29.

[54]Karen O'Connor and Lee Epstein, "The Rise of Conservative Interest Group Litigation," *Journal of Politics* 45 (1983), 481. See also Richard C. Cortner, *The Supreme Court and the Second Bill of Rights* (Madison: University of Wisconsin Press, 1981), 282.

[55]Rick Perlstein, "Christian Empire," *New York Times Book Review,* January 7, 2007, 15.

[56]Epstein and Segal, *Advice and Consent,* 12. The Court also takes about this many to decide summarily—without oral arguments and full written opinions.

[57]The dentist agreed to fill the cavity only in a hospital, where the procedure would be far more expensive. *Bragdon* v. *Abbott,* 141 L. Ed.2d 540 (1998).

[58]*Toyota Motor Manufacturing* v. *Williams,* 151 L.Ed.2d 615 (2001).

[59]Abraham, *Judicial Process,* 324.

[60]*United States* v. *Butler,* 297 U.S. 1, at 94.

[61]Murphy and Pritchett, *Courts, Judges, and Politics,* 586.

[62]*Furman* v. *Georgia,* 408 U.S. 238 (1972). Blackmun did vote against the death penalty later in his career.

[63]Quoted in Alexander Bickel, *The Morality of Consent* (New Haven, Conn.: Yale University Press, 1975), 120.

[64]"Judicial Authority Moves Growing Issue," *Lincoln Journal,* April 24, 1977.

[65]Jeffrey A. Segal and Albert D. Cover, "Ideological Values and the Votes of U.S. Supreme Court Justices," *American Political Science Review* 83 (1989), 557–564. For different findings for state supreme court justices, see John M. Scheb II, Terry Bowen, and Gary Anderson, "Ideology, Role Orientations, and Behavior in the State Courts of Last Resort," *American Politics Quarterly* 19 (1991), 324–335.

[66]Harold Spaeth and Stuart Teger, "Activism and Restraint: A Cloak for the Justices' Policy Preferences," in *Supreme Court Activism and Restraint,* eds. Stephen P. Halpern and Clark M. Lamb (Lexington, Mass.: Lexington Books, 1982), 277.

[67]*Burnet* v. *Coronado Oil and Gas,* 285 U.S. 293 (1932), at 406.

[68]*Engel* v. *Vitale,* 370 U.S. 421 (1962).

[69]*Abington School District* v. *Schempp,* 374 U.S. 203 (1963).

[70]*Stone* v. *Graham,* 449 U.S. 39 (1980).

[71]*Lee* v. *Weisman,* 120 L.Ed.2d 467 (1992).

[72]*Santa Fe Independent School District* v. *Doe,* 147 L.Ed.2d 295 (2000).

[73]*Denver Area Educational Telecommunications Consortium* v. *Federal Communications Commission,* 116 S. Ct. 2374 (1996).

[74]*United States* v. *Butler,* 297 U. S. 1 (1936), at 79.

[75]Some might say that judges, rather than make law, mediate among various ideas that rise to the surface, killing off some and allowing others to survive. Robert Cover, "Nomos and Narrative," *Harvard Law Review* 97 (1983), 4.

[76]Quoted in Murphy and Pritchett, *Courts, Judges, and Politics,* 25.

[77]*Gratz* v. *Bollinger,* 156 L.Ed.2d 257 (2003); *Grutter* v. *Bollinger,* 156 L.Ed.2d 304 (2003).

[78]Quoted in David J. Garrow, "The Rehnquist Reins," *New York Times Magazine,* October 6, 1996, 70.

[79]Quoted in Robert Wernick, "Chief Justice Marshall Takes the Law in Hand," *Smithsonian,* November 1998, 162.

[80]Joan Biskupic, "Here Comes the Judge? Maybe Not," *Washington Post National Weekly Edition,* February 14, 2000, 30.

[81]Jeffrey A. Segal and Harold J. Spaeth, *The Supreme Court and the Attitudinal Model* (New York: Cambridge University Press, 1993), 262–264.

[82]Jeffrey Rosen, "Rehnquist's Choice," *New Yorker,* January 11, 1999, 31.

[83]Justice Breyer, quoted by Jeffrey Toobin, "Breyer's Big Idea," *New Yorker,* October 31, 2005, 43.

[84]*Morning Edition,* National Public Radio, March 5, 2004.

[85]Michael S. Serrill, "The Power of William Brennan," *Time,* July 22, 1985, 62.

[86]Ibid.

[87]David J. Garrow, "One Angry Man," *New York Times Magazine,* October 6, 1996, 68–69.

[88]*Webster* v. *Reproductive Health Services,* 492 U. S. 490 (1989).

[89]*United States* v. *Virginia,* 135 L.Ed.2d 735, 787–789 (1996).

[90]Charles Evans Hughes, *The Supreme Court of the United States* (New York: Columbia University Press, 1928), 68.

[91]Interview with Justice Ruth Bader Ginsburg, *Morning Edition,* National Public Radio, May 2, 2002. Ginsburg said that foreign jurists admit they disagree with each other but do not make it public.

[92]Craig R. Ducat, *2005 Supplement for Constitutional Interpretation,* 8th ed. (Belmont, Calif.: Wadsworth, 2006), 3.

[93]Linda Greenhouse, "The High Court and the Triumph of Discord," *New York Times,* July 15, 2001, sec. 4, 1. Perhaps this calls into question Rehnquist's reputation as an effective leader.

[94]*Federalist Paper* 78.

[95]Henry J. Abraham, *Justices and Presidents* (New York: Oxford University Press, 1974), 74.

[96]Henry J. Abraham, *The Judicial Process,* 3rd ed. (New York: Oxford University Press, 1975), 309.

[97]Drew Pearson and Robert S. Allen, *The Nine Old Men* (New York: Doubleday/Doren, 1937), 7; Barbara A. Perry, *The Priestly Tribe: The Supreme Court's Image in the American Mind* (Westport, Conn.: Praeger, 1999), 8–9.

[98]There's evidence that many Founders expected the federal courts to use judicial review eventually. Some state courts already used judicial review, and in *Federalist Paper* 78 Hamilton said that the federal courts would have authority to void laws contrary to the Constitution.

[99]5 U.S. 137 (1803). Technically, *Marbury* was not the first use of judicial review, but it was the first clear articulation of judicial review by the Court.

[100]Jefferson was also angry at the nature of the appointees. One had led troops loyal to England during the Revolutionary War. Eric Black, *Our Constitution: The Myth That Binds Us* (Boulder, Colo.: Westview Press, 1988), 66.

[101]Debate arose over whether the four should be considered appointed. Their commissions had been signed by the president, and the seal of the United States had been affixed by Marshall, as secretary of state. Yet it was customary to require commissions to be delivered, perhaps because of less reliable record keeping by government or less reliable communications at the time.

[102]Marbury had petitioned the Court for a writ of *mandamus* under the authority of a provision of the Judiciary Act of 1789 that permitted the Court to issue such a writ. Marshall maintained that this provision broadened the Court's original jurisdiction and thus violated the Constitution. (The Constitution allows the Court to hear cases that have not been heard by any other court before—if they involve a state or a foreign ambassador. Marbury's involved neither.) Yet it was quite clear that the provision did not broaden the Court's original jurisdiction—so

clear, in fact, that Marshall did not even quote the language he was declaring unconstitutional. Furthermore, even if the provision did broaden the Court's original jurisdiction, it is not certain that the provision would violate the Constitution. (The Constitution does not say that the Court shall have original jurisdiction only in cases involving a state or a foreign ambassador.) Many members of Congress who had drafted and voted for the Judiciary Act had been delegates to the Constitutional Convention, and it is unlikely that they would have initiated a law that contradicted the Constitution. And Oliver Ellsworth, who had been a coauthor of the bill, then served as chief justice of the Supreme Court before Marshall. But these interpretations allowed Marshall a way out of the dilemma.

[103]Quoted in Walter F. Murphy and C. Herman Pritchett, *Courts, Judges, and Politics,* 3rd ed. (New York: Random House, 1979), 4.

[104]John A. Garraty, "The Case of the Missing Commissions," in *Quarrels That Have Shaped the Constitution,* ed. John A. Garraty (New York: Harper & Row, 1962), 13.

[105]*Fletcher* v. *Peck,* 10 U.S. 87 (1810); *Martin* v. *Hunter's Lessee,* 14 U.S. 304 (1816); *Cohens* v. *Virginia,* 19 U.S. 264 (1821).

[106]In other cases, the Court narrowly construed state power, especially to regulate commerce. *Gibbons* v. *Ogden,* 22 U.S. 1 (1824).

[107]However, the Warren Court may not have been as out of step with the political branches as is often believed. See Lucas A. Powe, *The Warren Court and American Politics* (Cambridge, Mass.: Harvard University Press, 2000), 160–178.

[108]Particularly regarding criminal defendants' rights.

[109]One legal scholar says the most striking feature about Supreme Court decision making in the 1990s was the effort by five justices to resolve most issues as narrowly as possible, shunning sweeping pronouncements for case-by-case examination. Cass R. Sunstein, *One Case at a Time: Judicial Minimalism on the Supreme Court* (Cambridge, Mass.: Harvard University Press, 2001).

[110]The Rehnquist Court reduced the scope of criminal defendants' rights, racial minorities' rights, and affirmative action. It also tightened access to the courts for individuals and groups trying to challenge government policies, and it limited efforts by Congress to impose new regulations on the states. However, the Court did take the first step toward homosexuals' legal rights.

[111]Thomas M. Keck, *The Most Activist Supreme Court in History* (Chicago: University of Chicago Press, 2004).

[112]531 U.S. 98 (2000).

[113]*Roe* v. *Wade,* 410 U.S. 113 (1973).

[114]Baum, *Supreme Court,* 170, 173.

[115]Craig R. Ducat and Robert L. Dudley, "Federal Appellate Judges and Presidential Power," paper presented at the Midwest Political Science Association meeting, April 1987.

[116]Sheldon Goldman, "How Long the Legacy?" *Judicature* 76 (1993), 295.

[117]The Eleventh Amendment overturned *Chisholm v. Georgia* (1793), which had permitted the federal courts to hear suits against a state by citizens of another state. The Fourteenth overturned the Dred Scott case, *Scott v. Sandford* (1857), which had held that blacks were not citizens. The Sixteenth overturned *Pollock v. Farmers' Loan and Trust* (1895), which had negated a congressional law authorizing a federal income tax. The Twenty-Sixth overturned *Oregon v. Mitchell* (1970), which had negated a congressional law allowing eighteen-year-olds to vote in state elections.

[118]William N. Eskridge Jr., "Overriding Supreme Court Statutory Interpretation Decisions," *Yale Law Journal* 101 (1991), 338.

[119]*Goldman v. Weinberger,* 475 U.S. 503 (1986).

[120]Detainee Treatment Act of 2005.

[121]Thomas R. Marshall, "Public Opinion and the Rehnquist Court," in *Readings in American Government and Politics,* 3rd ed. (Boston, Mass.: Allyn & Bacon, 1999), 115–121.

[122]Richard Morin, "A Nation of Stooges," *Washington Post,* October 8, 1995, C5.

[123]Gregory A. Caldeira, "Neither the Purse nor the Sword," paper presented at the American Political Science Association meeting, August 1987.

[124]Quoted in Abraham, *Justices and Presidents,* 342–343.

[125]Robert G. McCloskey, *The American Supreme Court* (Chicago: University of Chicago Press, 1960), 225.

Chapter 12

[1]*Frederick v. Morse,* 168 L.Ed.2d 290 (2007).

[2]Chief Justice Roberts and Justice Alito.

[3]Richard Morin, "The High Price of Free Speech," *Washington Post National Weekly Edition,* January 8, 2001, 34.

[4]After 9/11, support for civil liberties dropped, reflecting people's fears. By 2005, however, support returned to pre-9/11 levels. First Amendment Center, in cooperation with the *American Journalism Review.* Survey conducted May 13–23, 2005. (*N* = 1003; sampling error = 3%).

[5]The states didn't ratify a proposed amendment that would have required at least one representative in Congress for every fifty thousand people. That amendment would have put about five thousand members in today's Congress. The states also didn't ratify, until 1992, another proposed amendment that would have prohibited a salary raise for members of Congress from taking effect until after the next election to Congress.

[6]*Reid v. Covert,* 354 U.S. 1 (1957).

[7]*Barron v. Baltimore,* 32 U.S. 243 (1833).

[8]Also, many states had their own bill of rights at the time, and other states were expected to follow.

[9]*Gitlow v. New York,* 268 U.S. 652 (1925). *Gitlow* is usually cited as the first because it initiated the twentieth-century trend. However,

Chicago, Burlington and Quincy R. Co. v. Chicago, 166 U.S. 266 (1897), was actually the first. It applied the Fifth Amendment's just compensation clause, requiring government to pay owners "just compensation" for taking their property.

[10]*Argersinger v. Hamlin,* 407 U.S. 25 (1972).

[11]It hasn't applied the Fifth Amendment's guarantee of a grand jury in criminal cases or the Seventh Amendment's guarantee of a jury trial in civil cases. The grand jury no longer serves as a protective shield for potential criminal defendants; rather, it's become a prosecutorial tool. The Seventh Amendment guarantees a jury trial in civil cases when $20 or more is at stake, so that would require a commitment of scarce resources even for trivial cases.

[12]The amendment also includes a right "to petition the government for a redress of grievances," which is incorporated in freedom of speech and assembly. The language doesn't explicitly include freedom of association, but the Court has interpreted the amendment to encompass this right.

[13]Anna Johnson, "Know Your First Amendment Rights? Poll Shows Many Don't," *Lincoln Journal Star,* March 1, 2006, 10A.

[14]Even Justice Black, who claimed that he interpreted it literally. To do so, he had to define some speech as "action" so that it wouldn't be protected.

[15]*Milk Wagon Drivers Union v. Meadowmoor Dairies,* 312 U.S. 287 (1941).

[16]Quoted in Deborah Tannen, *The Argument Culture* (New York: Ballantine, 1998), 25.

[17]Thomas I. Emerson, *The System of Freedom of Expression* (New York: Random House/Vintage, 1971), 6–8.

[18]For a history of speech cases between the Civil War and World War I, see David M. Rabban, *Free Speech in Its Forgotten Years* (New York: Cambridge University Press, 1997).

[19]The Sedition Act of 1918. In addition, the Espionage Act of 1917 prohibited interfering with military recruitment, inciting insubordination in military forces, and mailing material advocating rebellion.

[20]Zechariah Chafee Jr., *Free Speech in the United States* (Cambridge, Mass.: Harvard University Press, 1941), 51–52.

[21]*Schenk v. United States,* 249 U.S. 47 (1919); *Frohwerk v. United States,* 249 U.S. 204 (1919); *Debs v. United States,* 249 U.S. 211 (1919); *Abrams v. United States,* 250 U.S. 616 (1919); *Gitlow v. New York,* 268 U.S. 652 (1925); *Whitney v. California,* 274 U.S. 357 (1927).

[22]*Gitlow v. New York.*

[23]Novelist Philip Roth observes, "McCarthy understood better than any American politician before him that people whose job was to legislate could do far better for themselves by performing; McCarthy understood the entertainment value of disgrace and how to feed the pleasures of paranoia. He took us back to our origins, back to the seventeenth century and the stocks. That's how the country began: moral disgrace as public entertainment."

I Married a Communist (New York: Vintage, 1999), 284.

[24]The Smith Act (1940). This act wasn't as broad as the World War I acts because it didn't forbid criticizing the government.

[25]*Dennis v. United States,* 341 U.S. 494 (1951).

[26]For the role of the Senate's Internal Security Committee, see Michael J. Ybarra, *Washington Gone Crazy: Senator Pat McCarran and the Great American Communist Hunt* (Hanover, N. H.: Steerforth, 2004).

[27]The records included some code names that haven't been linked to real people. Charles Peters, "Tilting at Windmills," *Washington Monthly,* May, 2006, 8. See also Ted Morgan, *Reds: McCarthyism in Twentieth-Century America* (New York: Random House, 2003).

[28]In the cases of *Yates v. United States,* 354 U.S. 298 (1957), and *Scales v. United States,* 367 U.S. 203 (1961), among others.

[29]Earl Warren, *The Memoirs of Earl Warren* (Garden City, N.Y.: Doubleday, 1977), 6.

[30]The doctrine was created in a case in which a Ku Klux Klan leader said at a rally that the Klan might take "revengeance" against the president, Congress, and the Supreme Court if they continued "to suppress the white, Caucasian race." *Brandenburg v. Ohio,* 395 U.S. 444 (1969).

[31]*Brandenburg v. Ohio.*

[32]Attorney General Tom Clark, quoted in *Esquire,* November 1974.

[33]Cole, "Course of Least Resistance," 1.

[34]Jean E. Jackson, "ACTA Report Criticizes Professors," *Anthropology News,* March 2002, 7.

[35]Gia Fenoglio, "Is It 'Blacklisting' or Mere Criticism?" *National Journal,* January 19, 2002, 188.

[36]For some examples, see Michael Tomasky, "Dissent in America," *American Prospect,* April 2003, 22. See also Ann Coulter, *Treason: Liberal Treachery from the Cold War to the War on Terrorism* (New York: Crown Forum, 2003), and Sean Hannity, *Deliver Us from Evil* (New York: Regan Books/HarperCollins, 2004).

[37]C. Herman Pritchett, *The American Constitution,* 2nd ed. (New York: McGraw-Hill, 1968), 476, n. 2. However, police in some places continue to arrest for swearing. Judy Lin, "ACLU Fights Police on Profanity Arrests in Pittsburgh Area," *Lincoln Journal Star,* July 11, 2002.

[38]*Gooding v. Wilson,* 405 U.S. 518 (1972); *Lewis v. New Orleans,* 408 U.S. 913 (1972).

[39]*Cohen v. California,* 403 U.S. 15 (1971).

[40]However, businesses can restrict the speech of their employees at work because they're private entities.

[41]*Collin v. Smith,* 447 F.Supp. 676 (N.D. Ill., 1978); *Collin v. Smith,* 578 F.2d 1197 (7th Cir, 1978).

[42]*United States v. Schwimmer,* 279 U.S. 644 (1929).

[43]*Virginia v. Black,* 155 L.Ed.2d 535 (2003). Previously, the Court invalidated a St. Paul, Minnesota, ordinance prohibiting the display of a Nazi swastika or a cross-burning on pub-

lic or private land. *R.A.V. v. St. Paul,* 120 L.Ed.2d 305 (1992).

44For a legal analysis supporting these codes, see Richard Delgado and David H. Yun, "Pressure Valves and Bloodied Chickens: An Analysis of Paternalistic Objections to Hate Speech Regulation," *University of California Law Review,* 82 (1994), 716.

45Mary Jordan, "Free Speech Starts to Have Its Say," *Washington Post National Weekly Edition,* September 21–27, 1992, 31.

46Michael D. Shear, "A Tangled World Wide Web," *Washington Post National Weekly Edition,* October 30–November 5, 1995, 36.

47Stephanie Simon, "Christians Sue for Right Not to Tolerate Policies," *Los Angeles Times,* April 10, 2006, www.latimes.com/news/nationworld/nation/la-nachristians10apr10,0,6204444.story?

48*Barnes v. Glenn Theater,* 501 U.S. 560 (1991).

49*Young v. American Mini Theatres,* 427 U.S. 50 (1976); *Renton v. Playtime Theatres,* 475 U.S. 41 (1986).

50*FCC v. Pacifica Foundation,* 438 U.S. 726 (1968).

51By "fleeting" profanities, the FCC evidently means brief and spontaneous profanities that the networks couldn't foresee and bleep.

52Jonathan D. Salant, "FCC Wants to Up Fine for Cursing," *Lincoln Journal Star,* January 15, 2004.

53*Wilkinson v. Jones,* 480 U.S. 926 (1987).

54*Southeastern Promotions v. Conrad,* 420 U.S. 546 (1975).

55*Jeannette Rankin Brigade v. Chief of Capital Police,* 409 U.S. 972 (1972); *Edwards v. South Carolina,* 372 U.S. 229 (1963); *United States v. Grace,* 75 L.Ed.2d 736 (1983). The grounds around jails and military bases are off-limits due to the need for security. *Adderley v. Florida,* 385 U.S. 39 (1966); *Greer v. Spock,* 424 U.S. 828 (1976).

56According to the Burger Court, which emphasized property rights over First Amendment rights. *Lloyd v. Tanner,* 407 U.S. 551 (1972); *Hudgens v. NLRB,* 424 U.S. 507 (1976).

57Leonard Pitts Jr., "Intolerance Meets Its Nemesis at an Albany Mall," *Lincoln Journal Star,* March 10, 2003.

58*Cox v. Louisiana,* 379 U.S. 536 (1965).

59*Schenk v. Pro-Choice Network,* 137 L.Ed.2d 1 (1997).

60*Frisby v. Schultz,* 101 L.Ed.2d 420 (1988).

61*United States v. O'Brien,* 391 U.S. 367 (1968).

62*Tinker v. Des Moines School District* (1969).

63*Smith v. Goguen,* 415 U.S. 566 (1974); *Spence v. Washington,* 418 U.S. 405 (1974).

64*Texas v. Johnson,* 105 L.Ed.2d 342 (1989).

65*United States v. Eichman,* 110 L.Ed.2d 287 (1990).

66However, in 1995, after Republicans became the majority in Congress, they renewed efforts to adopt a constitutional amendment but fell just three votes short in one house.

67*Tinker v. Des Moines School District,* 393 U.S. 503 (1969).

68*Bethel School District v. Fraser,* 478 U.S. 675 (1986).

69*Hazelwood School District v. Kuhlmeier,* 98 L.Ed.2d 592 (1988).

70*Hurley v. Irish-American Gay, Lesbian and Bisexual Group of Boston,* 515 U.S. 557 (1995).

71*Boy Scouts of America v. Dale,* 147 L.Ed.2d 554 (2000).

72The Court invalidated racial discrimination in labor unions and private schools and sexual discrimination in law firms, despite claims of freedom of association. *Railway Mail Association v. Corsi,* 326 U.S. 88 (1945); *Runyon v. McCrary,* 427 U.S. 160 (1976); *Hison v. King & Spalding,* 467 U.S. 69 (1984) 6957.

73*Roberts v. U.S. Jaycees,* 468 U.S. 609 (1984); *Board of Directors of Rotary International v. Rotary Club of Duarte,* 481 U.S. 537 (1987).

74Quoted in David Halberstam, *The Best and the Brightest* (Greenwich, Conn.: Fawcett, 1969), 769.

75Bill Moyers, "Our Democracy Is in Danger of Being Paralyzed," Keynote Address to the National Conference on Media Reform, November 8, 2003, www.truthout.org/docs_03/printer_ 111403E.shtml.

76Ibid.

77*New York Times v. United States,* 403 U.S. 713 (1971). In addition to seeking injunctions, the Nixon administration sent a telegram to the *New York Times* demanding that it cease publication of the excerpts, but the FBI had the wrong telex number for the newspaper, so the telegram went first to a fish company in Brooklyn. R. W. Apple, "Lessons from the Pentagon Papers," *New York Times,* June 23, 1996, E5.

78Actually, the Pentagon Papers did include some current information regarding ongoing negotiations and the names of CIA agents in Vietnam, but Ellsberg had not passed this information to the newspapers. However, the government and the Court were unaware of this, so the government argued that publication could affect national security, and the Court decided the case with this prospect in mind. Thus the Court's ruling was stronger than legal analysts realized at the time. Erwin N. Griswold, "No Harm Was Done," *New York Times,* June 30, 1991, E15.

79*United States v. Progressive,* 467 F.Supp. 990 (W.D., Wisc., 1979).

80Then radio and television stations used actors with Irish accents to dub the comments made by IRA members. In 1994, the government lifted the ban.

81*Branzburg v. Hayes,* 408 U.S. 665 (1972).

82Jeffrey Toobin, "Name That Source," *New Yorker,* January 16, 2006, 30.

83*Cox Broadcasting v. Cohn,* 420 U.S. 469 (1975).

84This was not a Supreme Court case.

85*Time v. Hill,* 385 U.S. 374 (1967).

86*Wilson v. Layne,* 143 L.Ed.2d 818 (1999); *Hanlon v. Berger,* 143 L.Ed.2d 978 (1999).

87*New York Times v. Sullivan,* 376 U.S. 254.

88Harry Kalven, "*The New York Times* Case: A Note on 'the Central Meaning of the First Amendment,'" *Supreme Court Review* (1964): 221.

89*Monitor Patriot v. Roy,* 401 U.S. 265 (1971).

90*Associated Press v. Walker,* 388 U.S. 130 (1967); *Greenbelt Cooperative v. Bresler,* 398 U.S. 6 (1970). This set of rulings began with *Curtis Publishing v. Butts,* 388 U.S. 130 (1967).

91*Gertz v. Robert Welch,* 418 U.S. 323 (1974), and *Time v. Firestone,* 424 U.S. 448 (1976).

92Eric Press, "Westmoreland Takes on CBS," *Newsweek,* October 22, 1984, 62.

93The Pilgrims, who had experienced religious toleration in Holland (after persecution in England), left because they wanted a place of their own, not because they could not worship as they pleased. The Dutch were so tolerant that the Pilgrims' children had begun to adopt Dutch manners and ideas. Richard Shenkman, *I Love Paul Revere, Whether He Rode or Not* (New York: HarperCollins, 1991), 20–21.

94The only religious reference in the Constitution occurs in the date when the document was written: "Year of our Lord one thousand seven hundred and eighty-seven." And that may have been mere convention; "year of our Lord" is the English equivalent of A.D.

95Apparently Roger Williams, a clergyman and the founder of Rhode Island, was the first to use this metaphor. Lloyd Burton, "The Church in America," *New Yorker,* September 29, 2003, 10. James Madison was another of the Founders who pioneered our religious freedom. For an analysis of his views, see Vincent Phillip Munoz, "James Madison's Principle of Religious Liberty," *American Political Science Review,* 97 (2003), 17–32.

96Gary Wills, quoted on *Thomas Jefferson,* PBS, February 18, 1997.

97According to Mark Pachter, Curator of the National Portrait Gallery, *Morning Edition,* NPR, June 25, 2006.

98*Torcaso v. Watkins,* 367 U.S. 488 (1961).

99*Pierce v. Society of Sisters,* 268 U.S. 510 (1925).

100*Cooper v. Pate,* 378 U.S. 546 (1963); *Cruz v. Beto,* 405 U.S. 319 (1972).

101*Church of the Lukumi Babalu Aye v. Hialeah,* 124 L.Ed.2d 472 (1993).

102*Reynolds v. United States,* 98 U.S. 145 (1879). Most Mormons, however, didn't approve of polygamy. Even when polygamy was most popular, perhaps only 10 percent of Mormons practiced it. Shenkman, *I Love Paul Revere,* 31. Yet today reports indicate that polygamy is still flourishing among Mormons, perhaps more than ever. Lawrence Wright, "Lives of the Saints," *New Yorker,* January 21, 2002, 43.

103*Sherbert v. Verner,* 374 U.S. 398 (1963).

104Although a congressional statute mandates "reasonable accommodation," the Court interpreted it so narrowly that it essentially requires only minimal accommodation. *Trans World Airlines v. Hardison,* 432 U.S. 63 (1977). For analysis, see Gloria T. Beckley and Paul Burstein, "Religious Pluralism, Equal Opportunity, and the State," *Western Political Quarterly* 44 (1991), 185–208. For a related case, see *Thornton v. Caldor*, 86 L.Ed.2d 557 (1985).

[105]*United States v. Lee*, 455 U.S. 252 (1982).

[106]*United States v. American Friends Service Committee*, 419 U.S. 7 (1974).

[107]*Goldman v. Weinberger*, 475 U.S. 503 (1986); *O'Lone v. Shabazz*, 482 U.S. 342 (1986).

[108]*Employment Division v. Smith*, 108 L.Ed.2d 876 (1990).

[109]Congress did pass the American Indian Religious Freedom Act of 1994 to allow Indians to use peyote, but this law did not address the broader implications of the ruling. Ruth Marcus, "One Nation, under Court Rulings," *Washington Post National Weekly Edition*, March 18, 1991, 33.

[110]*Boerne v. Flores*, 138 L.Ed.2d 624 (1997). Congress then passed another law that addressed just two kinds of government action—zoning and the rights of inmates at public correctional and mental institutions. The law required state and local governments to consider exceptions for religious practices. Although this was another attempt to override the Court's ruling, the Court upheld the law. *Cutter v. Wilkinson*, 125 S.Ct. 2113 (2005).

[111]Brooke Allen, *Moral Minority: Our Skeptical Founding Fathers* (Chicago: Ivan R. Dee, 2006).

[112]William Lee Miller, "The Ghost of Freedoms Past," *Washington Post National Weekly Edition*, October 13, 1986, 23–24.

[113]Steven Waldman, "The Framers and the Faithful," *Washington Monthly*, April, 2006, 33–38.

[114]*Church of Holy Trinity v. United States*, 143 U.S. 457 (1892).

[115]*Engel v. Vitale*, 370 U.S. 421 (1962); *Abington School District v. Schempp*, 374 U.S. 203 (1963).

[116]*Stone v. Graham*, 449 U.S. 39 (1980). The Ten Commandments themselves have been divisive. In 1844, six people were killed in a riot in Philadelphia over which version of the Ten Commandments to post in the public schools. E. J. Dionne Jr., "Bridging the Church-State Divide," *Washington Post National Weekly Edition*, October 11, 1999, 21.

[117]George W. Andrews (D-Ala.), quoted in C. Herman Pritchett, *The American Constitution*, 3rd ed. (New York: McGraw-Hill, 1977), 406.

[118]Kenneth M. Dolbeare and Phillip E. Hammond, *The School Prayer Decisions* (Chicago: University of Chicago Press, 1971).

[119]Robert H. Birkby, "The Supreme Court and the Bible Belt," *Midwest Journal of Political Science* 10 (1966), 304–315.

[120]Julia Lieblich and Richard N. Ostling, "Despite Rulings, Prayer in School Still Sparks Debate, Still Practiced," *Lincoln Journal Star*, January 16, 2000.

[121]"Five Schools Get Ten Commandments," *Lincoln Journal Star*, August 12, 1999.

[122]J. Gordon Melton, quoted in Jon D. Hull, "The State of the Union," *Time*, January 30, 1995, 55.

[123]Peter Cushnie, "Letters," *Time*, October 15, 1984, 21.

[124]The Supreme Court invalidated Alabama's law that authorized a moment of silence "for meditation or voluntary prayer" because the wording of the law endorsed and promoted prayer. But most justices signaled approval of a moment of silence without such wording. *Wallace v. Jaffree*, 86 L.Ed.2d 29 (1985).

[125]*Lee v. Weisman*, 120 L.Ed.2d 467 (1992).

[126]*Jones v. Clear Creek*, 977 F.2d 965 (5th Cir., 1992).

[127]*Moore v. Ingebretsen*, 88 F.3d 274 (1996).

[128]*Santa Fe Independent School District v. Doe*, 530 U.S. 290 (2000).

[129]Anna Quindlen, "School Prayer: Substitutes for Substance," *Lincoln Journal Star*, December 8, 1994.

[130]A current guide for public school teachers, addressing practices that are permissible and those that are advisable in various situations, is Charles C. Haynes and Oliver Thomas, *Finding Common Ground* (Nashville, Tenn.: First Amendment Center, 2002).

[131]*Widmar v. Vincent*, 454 U.S. 263 (1981). The law requires high schools that receive federal funds to allow meetings of students' religious, philosophical, or political groups if the schools permit meetings of any "noncurriculum" groups. Schools could prohibit meetings of all noncurriculum groups. A Salt Lake City high school banned all nonacademic clubs rather than let students form an organization for homosexuals in 1996. Interviews with teachers and students two years later indicated that as a result of the ban on clubs, school spirit declined and class and racial rifts expanded. Clubs no longer brought students together, and clubs such as Polynesian Pride and the Aztec Club, for Latinos, no longer provided a link between these students and their school. "Club Ban Aimed at Gays Backfires," *Lincoln Journal Star*, December 6, 1998.

[132]*Board of Education of the Westside Community Schools v. Mergens*, 496 U.S. 226 (1990).

[133]David Van Biema, "Spiriting Prayer into School," *Time*, April 27, 1998, 28–31.

[134]Harriet Barovick, "Fear of a Gay School," *Time*, February 21, 2000, 52.

[135]*Rosenberger v. University of Virginia*, 132 L. Ed.2d 700 (1995). Yet the Rehnquist Court later ruled that states that provide scholarships for students at colleges and universities don't have to provide them for students preparing for the ministry. *Locke v. Davey*, 158 L.Ed.2d 21 (2004).

[136]For the nation's first celebration of Columbus Day in 1892, Francis Bellamy wrote, "I pledge allegiance to my flag and the republic for which it stands, one nation indivisible, with liberty and justice for all." For Bellamy, the key words were *indivisible*, which referred to the Civil War and emphasized the Union over the states, and *liberty and justice for all*, which emphasized a balance between freedom for individuals and equality between them. During the Cold War in the 1950s, Americans feared "godless communism." Some objected to communism as much because of the Soviet Union's official policy of atheism as because of its totalitarianism. A religious revival swept the United States as preachers such as Billy Graham warned that Americans would perish in a nuclear holocaust unless they opened their arms to Jesus Christ. Congress replaced the traditional national motto—"E Pluribus Unum" ("Out of Many, One")—with "In God We Trust," and it added this new motto to our paper money. Fraternal organizations, especially the Catholic Knights of Columbus, and religious leaders campaigned to add "under God" to the Pledge of Allegiance. The Presbyterian pastor of President Eisenhower's church in Washington urged the addition in a sermon as the president sat in a pew. With little dissent, Congress passed and the president signed a bill to do so in 1954. The legislative history of the act stated that the intent was to "acknowledge the dependence of our people and our government upon . . . the Creator . . . [and] deny the atheistic and materialistic concept of communism." The president stated that "millions of our school children will daily proclaim in every city and town . . . the dedication of our nation and our people to the Almighty." Thus the phrase was adopted expressly to endorse religion. David Greenberg, "The Pledge of Allegiance: Why We're Not One Nation 'under God,'" *Slate*, June 28, 2002, slate.msn.com/?id_2067499 S.

[137]*Elk Grove Unified School District v. Newdow*, 159 L.Ed.2d 98 (2004).

[138]*Lynch v. Donnelly*, 79 L.Ed.2d 604 (1984).

[139]*Allegheny County v. ACLU*, 106 L.Ed.2d 472 (1989).

[140]*Van Orden v. Perry*, 162 L.Ed. 2d 607 (2005).

[141]Initially they stood alone. As the cases proceeded through the lower courts, officials added other historical documents but never made a sincere effort to integrate them.

[142]*McCreary County v. ACLU*, 162 L.Ed.2d 729 (2005).

[143]*Epperson v. Arkansas*, 393 U.S. 97 (1968).

[144]Some groups use the more sophisticated-sounding term *creation science*. Although these groups do address the science of evolution, courts consider creationism and creation science as interchangeable.

[145]*Edwards v. Aguillard*, 482 U.S. 578 (1987).

[146]They do acknowledge that some limited evolution has occurred.

[147]However, to avoid court rulings similar to those against creationism—that it reflects a religious view—they try to avoid mention of God.

[148]Wendy Kaminer, "The God Bullies," *American Prospect*, November 18, 2002, 9.

[149]*Rochin v. California*, 342 U.S. 165 (1952).

150Seymour Wishman, *Confessions of a Criminal Lawyer* (New York: Penguin, 1981), 16.

151*Stein* v. *New York,* 346 U.S. 156 (1953).

152Wendy Kaminer, *It's All the Rage* (Reading, Mass.: Addison-Wesley, 1995), 78.

153*Weeks* v. *United States,* 232 U.S. 383 (1914).

154*Mapp* v. *Ohio,* 367 U.S. 643 (1961).

155This exception applies when police use a search warrant that they did not know was invalid. *United States* v. *Leon,* 82 L.Ed.2d 677 (1984); *Massachusetts* v. *Sheppard,* 82 L.Ed.2d 737 (1984). The Roberts Court has also created an exception to the exclusionary rule. When police have a search warrant but fail to knock and announce their presence before entering, as they have traditionally been required to do, any evidence seized may be used against the suspect despite the violation of the Fourth Amendment. *Hudson* v. *Michigan,* 165 L.Ed.2d 56 (2006).

156In situations in which police are required by law to knock and identify themselves before entering a residence, they can still use any evidence they find inside, even though the search is illegal because of their failure to knock and identify themselves. *Hudson* v. *Michigan,* 165 L.Ed.2d 56 (2006).

157*Olmstead* v. *United States,* 277 U.S. 438 (1928).

158*Katz* v. *United States,* 389 U.S. 347 (1967).

159*Brown* v. *Mississippi,* 297 U.S. 278 (1936).

160*McNabb* v. *United States,* 318 U.S. 332 (1943); *Mallory* v. *United States,* 354 U.S. 449 (1957); *Spano* v. *New York,* 360 U.S. 315 (1959).

161*Ashcraft* v. *Tennessee,* 322 U.S. 143 (1944).

162*Miranda* v. *Arizona,* 384 U.S. 436 (1966).

163*Dickerson* v. *United States,* 530 U.S. 428 (2000).

164Jan Hoffman, "Police Tactics Chipping Away at Suspects' Rights," *New York Times,* March 29, 1998, 35.

165*Johnson* v. *Zerbst,* 304 U.S. 458 (1938).

166The Court did require state courts to furnish an attorney when there were "special circumstances" involved. *Powell* v. *Alabama,* 287 U.S. 45 (1932).

167*Gideon* v. *Wainwright,* 372 U.S. 335 (1963).

168*Argersinger* v. *Hamlin,* 407 U.S. 25 (1972); *Scott* v. *Illinois,* 440 U.S. 367 (1974); *Alabama* v. *Shelton,* 152 L.Ed.2d 888(2002).

169*Douglas* v. *California,* 372 U.S. 353 (1953).

170Wendy Cole, "Death Takes a Holiday," *Time,* February 14, 2000, 68.

171Jill Smolowe, "Race and the Death Penalty," *Time,* April 29, 1991, 69.

172Peter Applebome, "Indigent Defendants, Overworked Lawyers," *New York Times,* May 17, 1992, E18.

173Alan Berlow, "Texas, Take Heed," *Washington Post National Weekly Edition,* February 21, 2000, 22.

174Richard Carelli, "Death Rows Grow, Legal Help Shrinks," *Lincoln Journal Star,* October 7, 1995.

175The Burger Court did rule that the right to counsel entails the right to "effective"

counsel, but the Court set such stringent standards for establishing the existence of ineffective counsel that few defendants can take advantage of this right. See *Strickland* v. *Washington,* 466 U.S. 668 (1984), and *United States* v. *Cronic,* 466 U.S. 640 (1984).

176*Baldwin* v. *New York,* 339 U.S. 66 (1970); *Blanton* v. *North Las Vegas,* 489 U.S. 538 (1989).

177*Duncan* v. *Louisiana,* 391 U.S. 145 (1968).

178*Taylor* v. *Louisiana,* 419 U.S. 522 (1975).

179 *Swain* v. *Alabama,* 380 U.S. 202 (1965).

180The Court implicitly upheld the death penalty in *Wilkerson* v. *Utah,* 99 U.S. 130 (1878), and *In re Kemmler,* 136 U.S. 436 (1890).

181*Furman* v. *Georgia,* 408 U.S. 238 (1972).

182*Gregg* v. *Georgia,* 428 U.S. 153 (1976).

183*Woodson* v. *North Carolina,* 428 U.S. 289 (1976).

184*Coker* v. *Georgia,* 433 U.S. 584 (1977).

185*McCleskey* v. *Kemp,* 95 L.Ed.2d 262 (1987). Studies of Florida, Illinois, Mississippi, and North Carolina have found similar results. Fox Butterfield, "Blacks More Likely to Get Death Penalty, Study Says," *New York Times,* June 7, 1998, 16.

186Jeffrey Toobin, "Killer Instincts," *New Yorker,* January 17, 2005, 54.

187Leonard Pitts Jr., "Fate of 100 Innocent Men Casts Doubt on Capital Punishment," *Lincoln Journal Star,* April 13, 2002.

188Frank R. Baumgartner, Suzanna De Boef, Amber E. Boydstun, *The Decline of the Death Penalty and the Discovery of Innocence* (Cambridge, England: Cambridge University Press, 2008).

189Adam Liptak, "Juries Reject Death Penalty in Nearly All Federal Trials," *New York Times,* June 15, 2003, 12; Alex Kotlowitz, "In the Face of Death," *New York Times Magazine,* June 6, 2003, 34.

190*Atkins* v. *Virginia,* 153 L.Ed. 2d 335 (2002).

191*Penry* v. *Lynaugh,* 106 L.Ed.2d 256 (1989).

192*Roper* v. *Simmons,* 161 L.Ed.2d 1 (2005).

193Some Asian countries (notably China) and many Middle Eastern countries also retain it.

194*Brady* v. *United States,* 397 U.S. 742 (1970).

195*Griswold* v. *Connecticut,* 38 U.S. 479 (1965).

196For a rare exception, see *Time* v. *Hill,* 385 U.S. 374 (1967).

197*Griswold* v. *Connecticut.*

198*Eisenstadt* v. *Baird,* 405 U.S. 438 (1972); *Carey* v. *Population Services International,* 431 U.S. 678 (1977).

199*Eisenstadt* v. *Baird.*

200Lloyd Shearer, "This Woman and This Man Made History," *Parade,* 1983.

201*Roe* v. *Wade,* 410 U.S. 113 (1973).

202Bob Woodward, "The Abortion Papers," *Washington Post National Weekly Edition,* January 30, 1989, 24–25.

203All but New York's. Three other states allowed abortion on demand, though not quite as extensively as *Roe,* so the ruling also invalidated their laws. Jeffrey A. Segal and Harold J. Spaeth, *The Supreme Court and the Attitudinal*

Model (New York: Cambridge University Press, 1993), 333.

204For example, Alan Dershowitz, *Supreme Injustice* (New York: Oxford University, 2001), 191–196. For a contrast with same-sex marriage, see Jonathan Rauch, "A Separate Peace," *Atlantic Monthly,* April, 2007, 21.

205*Akron* v. *Akron Center for Reproductive Health,* 76 L.Ed.2d 687 (1983).

206"The Supreme Court Ignites a Fiery Abortion Debate," *Time,* July 4, 1977, 6–8.

207*Beal* v. *Doe,* 432 U.S. 438 (1977); *Maher* v. *Roe,* 432 U.S. 464 (1977); *Poelker* v. *Doe,* 432 U.S. 519 (1977); *Harris* v. *McRae* 448 U.S. 297 (1980).

208"The Abortion Dilemma Come to Life," *Washington Post National Weekly Edition,* December 25, 1989, 10–11.

209Alan Guttmacher Institute, *Facts in Brief: Abortion in the United States* (New York: Alan Guttmacher Institute, 1992); Stephanie Mencimer, "Ending Illegitimacy as We Know It," *Washington Post National Weekly Edition,* January 17, 1994, 24.

210*Webster* v. *Reproductive Health Services,* 106 L.Ed.2d 410 (1989).

211*Planned Parenthood of Southeastern Pennsylvania* v. *Casey,* 120 L.Ed.2d 674 (1992). Justice Anthony Kennedy changed his mind after the justices' conference, from essentially overturning *Roe* to reaffirming it. His was the fifth vote to reaffirm, as it would have been to overturn.

212Kathleen Sullivan, cited in Robin Toner and Adam Liptak, "In New Court, *Roe* May Stand, So Foes Look to Limit Its Scope," *New York Times,* July 10, 2005, YT16.

213William Booth, "The Difference a Day Makes," *Washington Post National Weekly Edition,* November 23, 1992, 31.

214*Planned Parenthood of Southeastern Pennsylvania* v. *Casey,* 120 L.Ed.2d 674 (1992).

215*Hodgson* v. *Minnesota,* 111 L.Ed.2d 344 (1990); *Ohio* v. *Akron Center for Reproductive Health,* 111 L.Ed.2d 405 (1990); *Planned Parenthood Association of Kansas City* v. *Ashcroft,* 462 U.S. 476 (1983). Number of states from Holly Ramer, "Never-Enforced Abortion Law to Go before Supreme Court," *Lincoln Journal Star,* November 27, 2005, 4A.

216*Hodgson* v. *Minnesota,* 111 L.Ed.2d 344 (1990).

217Margaret Carlson, "Abortion's Hardest Cases," *Time,* July 9, 1990, 24.

218*Stenberg* v. *Carhart,* 530 U.S. 914 (2000).

219*Gonzales* v. *Carhart,* 167 L.Ed.2d 480 (2007). The Court didn't overrule the 2000 decision, because that Nebraska law, unlike this congressional law, was too broad.

220Barry Yeoman, "The Quiet War on Abortion," *Mother Jones,* September-October 2001, 46–51.

221"Survey Reveals U.S. Views on Abortion to Be Contradictory," *Lincoln Journal Star,* June 19, 2000.

222For an analysis of the political dynamics that produced this moderate result, see William Saleton, *Bearing Right: How Conservatives Won the Abortion War* (Berkeley: University of California Press, 2003). The title is an exaggeration.

[223]Alissa Rubin, "The Abortion Wars Are Far from Over," *Washington Post National Weekly Edition,* December 21, 1992, 25.

[224]Richard Lacayo, "One Doctor Down, How Many More?" *Time,* March 22, 1993, 47.

[225]Rebecca Mead, "Return to Sender the Usual Hate Mail," *New Yorker,* October 29, 2001, 34.

[226]Douglas Frantz, "The Rhetoric of Terror," *Time,* March 27, 1995, 48–51.

[227]Dan Sewell, "Abortion War Requires Guns, Bulletproof Vests," *Lincoln Journal Star,* January 8, 1995.

[228]"Blasts Reawaken Fear of Domestic Terrorism," *Lincoln Journal Star,* January 17, 1997.

[229]Richard Lacayo, "Abortion: The Future Is Already Here," *Time,* May 4, 1992, 29; Jack Hitt, "Who Will Do Abortions Here?" *New York Times Magazine,* January 18, 1998, 20.

[230]Jodi Enda, "The Women's View," *American Prospect,* April, 2005, 26.

[231]Randall Terry, quoted in Anthony Lewis, "Pro-Life Zealots 'Outside the Bargain,'" *Lincoln Journal Star,* March 14, 1993.

[232]Joseph Scheidler, quoted in Sandra G. Boodman, "Bringing Abortion Home," *Washington Post National Weekly Edition,* April 15, 1993, 6.

[233]Stanley K. Henshaw, "Abortion Incidence and Services in the United States, 1995–1996," *Family Planning Perspectives,* November–December 1998.

[234]Much of this section is taken from Russell Shorto, "Contra-Contraception," *New York Times Magazine,* May 7, 2006, 48–55, 68..

[235]Ibid., Harris Poll, 54.

[236]Judie Brown, quoted in Ibid., 50.

[237]Ibid., 50, 68.

[238]Ibid., 51, 53.

[239]Nicholas D. Kristof, "Abortion, Condoms and Bush," *New York Times,* November 5, 2006, WK13.

[240]Judie Brown, quoted in Ibid., 50.

[241]As the author concludes from the leaders' statements. Ibid., 54.

[242]R. Albert Mohler, Jr., quoted in Ibid., 50.

[243]Sarah Brown of the National Campaign to Prevent Teen Pregnancy, quoted in Ibid., 83.

[244]For an elaboration of this history, see "In Changing the Law of the Land, Six Justices Turned to Its History," *New York Times,* July 20, 2003, WK7.

[245]Four states at this time revised their statutes to bar sodomy only between homosexuals: Kansas, Missouri, Oklahoma, and Texas.

[246]*Bowers v. Hardwick,* 92 L.Ed.2d 140 (1986); see also *Doe v. Commonwealth's Attorney,* 425 U.S. 901 (1976).

[247]*Lawrence and Garner v. Texas,* 539 U.S. 558 (2003).

[248]"Gays Getting More Acceptance as They're More Open, Poll Says," *Lincoln Journal Star,* April 11, 2004.

[249]Paul Gewirtz, quoted in Joe Klein, "How the Supremes Redeemed Bush," *Time,* July 7, 2003, 27.

[250]The House sponsor of the act, Robert Barr (R-Ga.), said the act was necessary because "the flames of hedonism, the flames of narcissism, the flames of self-centered morality are licking at the very foundation of our society, the family unit." At the time he was protecting the family unit, he was in his third marriage. Margaret Carlson, "The Marrying Kind," *Time,* September 16, 1996, 26.

[251]Jonathan Rauch, "Families Forged by Illness," *New York Times,* June 11, 2006, WK15

[252]For elaboration, see David Von Drehle, "Same-Sex Unions Take Center Stage," *Washington Post National Weekly Edition,* December 1, 2003, 29.

[253]John Cloud, "1,138 Reasons Marriage Is Cool," *Time,* March 8, 2004, 32. A few go in the opposite direction, such as eligibility for Medicaid, which takes into account a spouse's income.

[254]Advisory Opinion on Senate No. 2175, Supreme Judicial Court of Massachusetts, February 3, 2004.

[255]David J. Garrow, "Toward a More Perfect Union," *New York Times Magazine,* May 9, 2004, 54.

[256]Hendrik Hertzberg, "Comment: Distraction," *New Yorker,* June 19, 2006, 30.

[257]Senator Wayne Allard (R-Colo.); Senator Rick Santorum (R-Pa.); James Dobson. Andrew Sullivan, "If at First You Don't Succeed . . .," *Time,* July 26, 2004, 78.

[258]Alan Cooperman, "Anger without Action," *Washington Post National Weekly Edition,* June 28, 2004, 30.

[259]Garrow, "Toward a More Perfect Union," 57.

[260]The Supreme Court did invalidate a Colorado constitutional amendment prohibiting laws barring discrimination against homosexuals, saying that the amendment singled out homosexuals and denied them the opportunity enjoyed by others to seek protection from discrimination. This put the brakes on a drive to adopt similar provisions in other states. *Roemer v. Evans,* 134 L.Ed.2d 855 (1996).

[261]Geoff Mulvihill, "Transgender Protection Law Begins in New Jersey," *Lincoln Journal Star,* June 13, 2007, 7A.

[262]Al Kamen, "When Exactly Does Life End?" *Washington Post National Weekly Edition,* September 18, 1989, 31; Alain L. Sanders, "Whose Right to Die?" *Time,* December 11, 1989, 80.

[263]*Cruzan v. Missouri Health Department,* 111 L.Ed.2d 224 (1990).

[264]Otto Friedrich, "A Limited Right to Die," *Time,* July 9, 1990, 59.

[265]Tamar Lewin, "Ignoring 'Right to Die' Directives, Medical Community Is Being Sued," *New York Times,* June 2, 1996, 1.

[266]*Washington v. Glucksberg,* 138 L.Ed.2d 772 (1997); *Vacco v. Quill,* 138 L.Ed.2d 834 (1997).

[267]*Gonzales v. Oregon,* 163 L.Ed.2d 748 (2006).

[268]Kathy Barks Hoffman, "On Eve of Kevorkian Release from Prison, Little Has Changed," *Lincoln Journal Star,* May 29, 2007, 6A.

[269]David E. Rosenbaum, "Americans Want a Right to Die—or So They Think," *New York Times,* June 8, 1997, E3.

[270]Ibid.

[271]Barton Gellman and Jo Becker, "A 'Surrogate Chief of Staff,'" *Washington Post National Weekly Edition,* July 9–15, 2007, 6–12.

[272]Ian James, "Importance of Gitmo Questioned," *Lincoln Journal Star,* June 26, 2004.

[273]When the United States granted Cuba independence four years later, it retained the right to lease the base as a refueling station. In 1934, it renegotiated the treaty to remain in effect as long as the United States wants it to. The terms specify that the United States has complete control and jurisdiction.

[274]The Supreme Court did rule that *habeas corpus* does not apply to aliens who are outside of U.S. territory. *Johnson v. Eisentrager,* 339 U.S. 763 (1950).

[275]The administration also claims that international law doesn't apply because the detainees, as (alleged) members of al-Qaeda, don't represent an official army of an actual country, so they are "unlawful combatants."

[276]This wasn't a coincidence. Administration officials talked among themselves of finding the legal equivalent of outer space. Michael Isikoff and Stuart Taylor Jr., "The Gitmo Fallout," *Newsweek,* July 17, 2006, 23.

[277]Joseph Margulies, "At Guantanamo Bay, a Year in Limbo," *Washington Post National Weekly Edition,* January 6, 2003, 22.

[278]A related argument is that the military has discretion on the battlefield, and in the war on terrorism, all American territory, including foreign bases, is part of the battlefield.

[279]*Rasul v. Bush,* 159 L.Ed.2d 548 (2004). On the same day, the Court decided a similar case involving an American citizen who had been raised in Afghanistan and captured during the war against the Taliban. The Court ruled similarly, although the fact that he was an American citizen prompted eight justices (all but Thomas) to declare that he was entitled to contest his detention and four justices to conclude that his detention was unlawful. *Hamdi v. Rumsfeld,* 159 L.Ed.2d 578 (2004).

[280]The Court gave the government a distinct advantage in this process, stipulating that the government merely has to pre-sent credible evidence against the detainees. Then they have to prove that they aren't enemy combatants; that is, they have to prove their innocence. If they are determined to be enemy combatants, they can be held for the duration of the conflict.

[281]The Detainee Treatment Act of 2005. Petitions for a writ of *habeas corpus* were filed for all detainees before this law was passed, so the courts might conclude that the law doesn't apply to these cases already in progress.

282In April 2007, the Court refused to hear this case, but in June 2007, it changed its mind. In the intervening months, military officers and lawyers asserted that the panels were biased and the procedures made it impossible for detainees to defend themselves.

283*This American Life*, NPR, March 12, 2006.

284Corine Hegland, "Guantanamo's Grip," *National Journal*, February 1, 2006, 20–34.

285Ibid., 29.

286Ibid., 28.

287Michael Scheuer, quoted in Ibid., 31.

288Ibid., 30–31.

289"Military: Detainees Attempted Mass Hanging Protest in 2003," *Lincoln Journal Star*, January 25, 2005, 6A. By this date, the guards had logged 120 instances in which prisoners had tried to hang themselves, although the military says the majority were done in protest rather than in an attempt to commit suicide.

290Hegland, "Guantanamo's Grip," 23.

291Gellman and Becker, "A 'Surrogate Chief of Staff,'" 12.

292*Hamdan v. Rumsfeld*, 165 L.Ed.2d 723 (2006).

293For the vice president's role, see Gellman and Becker, "A 'Surrogate Chief of Staff.'" For a very useful article on the concept of torture, see Mark Bowden, "The Dark Art of Interrogation," *Atlantic Monthly*, October, 2003, 51–76.

294Adam Zagorin, "One Life Inside Gitmo," *Time*, March 13, 2006, 22.

295Anonymous official, quoted in Jodie Morse, "How Do We Make Him Talk?" *Time*, April 15, 2002, 92.

296Neil A. Lewis and Eric Schmitt, "Inquiry Finds Abuses at Guantanamo Bay," *New York Times*, May 1, 2005, YT23.

297Paisley Dodds, "Guantanamo Translator Tells of Sexual Tactics Used on Detainees," *Lincoln Journal Star*, January 28, 2005, 5A.

298For more information, including the role of medical personnel in devising the tactics, see Jane Mayer, "The Experiment," *New Yorker*, July 11 and 18, 2005, 60–71.

299Gellman and Becker, "A 'Surrogate Chief of Staff,'" 10.

300According to the Geneva Conventions and the United Nations Convention Against Torture and also under treaty law, to which the United States is a party, and customary law, which is binding on all nations.

301From the Geneva Conventions.

302The administration also claims that al-Qaeda members aren't entitled to the protection of international law because as stateless fighters they are "unlawful enemy combatants" and because neither al-Qaeda nor the Taliban regime of Afghanistan were a party to the Geneva Conventions.

303Martin Miller, "'24' Gets a Lesson in Torture from the Experts," *Los Angeles Times*, February 13, 2007, www.calendarlive.com/printedition/calendar/cl-et-torture13feb13,0,2384998; Jane Mayer, "What-

ever It Takes," *New Yorker*, February 19 and 26, 2007, 66.

304Mayer, "The Experiment," 70.

305*Marketplace*, NPR, May 5, 2004.

306Rajiv Chandrasekaran and Scott Wilson, "Many in Prison in Error," *Lincoln Journal Star*, May 11, 2004. These conclusions have been confirmed by General Antonio Taguba, who prepared the army's official report on Abu Ghraib. Seymour M. Hersh, "The General's Report," *New Yorker*, June 25, 2007, 64.

307The phenomenon is known as "force drift." Mayer, "The Experiment," 70.

308According to the government's own documents. For more incidents and documents, see Mark Danner, *Torture and Truth* (New York: New York Review of Books, 2004).

309Ninety-eight have died, and thirty-four of these have been suspected or confirmed homicides, according to Human Rights First, a human rights group. Drew Brown, "Report: 98 Died in U.S. Custody," *Lincoln Journal Star*, February 23, 2006, 3A.

310The law is essentially a statement of our policy. It doesn't authorize prisoners to bring lawsuits to stop such treatment or to penalize the interrogators.

311In a signing statement, he said that he would interpret the law "in a manner consistent with the constitutional authority of the President to supervise the unitary executive branch and as Commander in Chief and consistent with the constitutional limitations on the judicial power."

312Don Van Natta Jr., "How Ally with Abuse Record Became a Surrogate U.S. Jailer," *New York Times*, May 1, 2005, YT1.

313Dana Priest and Barton Gellman, "U.S. Decries Abuse but Defends Interroga-tions; 'Stress and Duress' Tactics Used on Terrorism Suspects Held in Secret Overseas Facilities," *Washington Post*, December 26, 2002, A1.

314Rajiv Chandrasekaran and Peter Finn, "Interrogating Terrorist Suspects 'in a Way We Can't Do on U.S. Soil,'" *Washington Post*, March 12, 2002, A1.

315U.N. Convention against Torture and Other Cruel, Inhuman, or Degrading Treatment or Punishment of 1984, signed in 1994.

316Dana Priest, "The CIA's Secret Prisons," *Washington Post National Weekly Edition*, November 7–13, 2005, 10–11.

317Warren P. Strobel, "Report: U.S. Has 39 Secret Detainees," *Lincoln Journal Star*, June 7, 2007, 3A.

318There are assertions that the administration notified two judges on the FISA court, but it did not seek official approval.

319Barton Gellman, Dafna Linzer, and Carol D. Leonnig, "Spying That Yields Little," *Washington Post National Weekly Edition*, February 13–19, 2006, 6.

320Zev Borow, "Very Bad People," *New Yorker*, February 6, 2006, 44.

321Ibid.

322The law allows warrantless wiretapping for just three days. The administration sought

congressional authority for warrantless wiretapping for long periods, but Congress refused to grant this authority.

323The Protect America Act allows the government to monitor these phone calls and e-mails, usually without obtaining any warrants and without going through any courts, including the FISA Court. Warrants are required only if the administration believes that the conversations involve persons who are the prime targets of the administration's investigations. The act was slated to expire in six months after it took effect.

324Seymour M. Hersh, "National Security Dept.: Listening In," *New Yorker*, May 29, 2006, 25.

325If it doesn't access the content of the calls, it probably doesn't violate the Fourth Amendment, although it might violate federal laws protecting the privacy of phone records.

326In just forty-five days after the 9/11 attacks. There were few hearings, and there was no committee report, and during this time senators were evacuated from their offices because of the anthrax attacks. In 2005, the act, with minor revisions, was made permanent.

327The Homeland Security Act.

328Although the act focuses on intelligence gathering, it contains other important provisions that enhance the government's ability to detain and prosecute aliens. Those suspected of committing a crime related to terrorism can be detained, without trial, longer than before. And those accused of providing "material support" to organizations involved in terrorism can be prosecuted more easily than before.

329Joseph J. Ellis, "Finding a Place for 9/11 in American History," *New York Times*, January 28, 2006. Available online at www.select.nytimes.com/search/restricted/article?res=FB0A13F93A5B0C 7B8EDDA8089.

330Alan M. Dershowitz, *Supreme Injustice: How the High Court Hijacked Election 2000* (New York: Oxford University Press, 2001), 189.

Chapter 13

1Vignette is drawn from Al Sharpton Jr., "My Link to Strom Thurmond," *Los Angeles Times*, March 1, 2007, www.latimes.com/news/opinion/la-oe-sharpton1mar01,05069644,print.story?coll=la-. . . ; Bob Herbert, "Slavery is Not Dead. It's Not Even Past," *New York Times*, March 1, 2007.

2Exhibition "Slavery in New York," New York Historical Society, November, 2005. For more details, see Ira Berlin and Leslie M. Harris, ed., *Slavery in New York* (New York: New York Historical Society/New Press, 2006).

3Gary B. Nash, *The Forgotten Fifth* (Cambridge, Mass.: Harvard University Press, 2006). See also Simon Schama, *Rough Crossings: Britain, the Slaves, and the American Revolution* (New York: Ecco, 2006).

4In most of the North, slavery was officially abolished shortly after ratification of the

Constitution, although New York didn't abolish it until 1827 and New Jersey didn't until 1865.

[5]Adam Goodheart, "Setting Them Free," *New York Times Book Review,* August 7, 2005, 1.

[6]Russell Nye, *Fettered Freedom* (Lansing: Michigan State University Press, 1963), 187, 227–229.

[7]*Scott v. Sandford,* 60 U.S. 393 (1857).

[8]Taney considered slavery "a blot on our national character." Richard Shenkman, *I Love Paul Revere, Whether He Rode or Not* (New York: HarperCollins, 1991), 168.

[9]*Fresh Air Weekend,* NPR, August 18, 2002.

[10]The Emancipation Proclamation, issued during the Civil War in 1863, was apparently a tactical move to discourage European countries from aiding the Confederacy. It gave the Civil War a moral purpose, making foreign intervention less likely. The proclamation could not free southern slaves at the time because the Union did not control the southern states, which had seceded.

[11]Bruce Ackerman, *We the People: Transformations* (Cambridge, Mass.: Harvard University Press, 1998); George Fletcher, "Unsound Constitution: Oklahoma City and the Founding Fathers," *New Republic,* June 23, 1997, 14–18. These conclusions make dubious the arguments that judges should be guided only by the intentions of the original Founders as they resolve contemporary cases. Ignoring the transformation that occurred as a result of the Civil War and these amendments amounts to using a highly selective and self-serving version of history.

[12]Civil Rights Act of 1866; Civil Rights Act of 1871; Civil Rights Act of 1875. These acts reversed the "Black Codes" that southern states passed to deny rights to former slaves.

[13]See Eric Foner, *Reconstruction: America's Unfinished Revolution* (New York: Harper & Row, 1988).

[14]The name Jim Crow came from a white performer in the 1820s who had a vaudeville routine in which he blackened his face with burnt cork and mimicked black men. He sang "Wheel About and Turn About and Jump, Jim Crow." This routine led to minstrel shows in high schools and colleges, with students portraying and satirizing blacks. The shows were popular into the 1960s.

[15]Kenneth Karst, "Equality, Law, and Belonging: An Introduction," in *Before the Law,* 5th ed., ed. John J. Bonsignore et al. (Boston: Houghton Mifflin, 1994), 429.

[16]C. Vann Woodward, *The Strange Career of Jim Crow,* 2nd ed. (London: Oxford University Press, 1966), 44.

[17]*Civil Rights Cases,* 109 U.S. 3 (1883).

[18]*Plessy v. Ferguson,* 163 U.S. 537 (1896). The Court's ruling prompted states to expand their Jim Crow laws. Before *Plessy,* states segregated just trains and schools.

[19]*Cumming v. Richmond County Board of Education,* 175 U.S. 528 (1899). Then the Court enforced segregation in colleges. It upheld a criminal conviction against a private college for teaching blacks together with whites. *Berea College v. Kentucky,* 211 U.S. 45 (1908).

[20]See, generally, James W. Loewen, *Sundown Towns: A Hidden Dimension of American Racism* (New York: New Press, 2005).

[21]Woodward, *The Strange Career of Jim Crow,* 113. Before the Civil War, northern states had passed some Jim Crow laws, which foreshadowed the more pervasive laws in southern states after the war. Leon F. Litwack, *Trouble in Mind: Black Southerners in the Age of Jim Crow* (New York: Knopf, 1998).

[22]Jacqueline Jones, *The Dispossessed: America's Underclasses from the Civil War to the Present* (New York: Basic Books, 1992), 83. And they were still being cheated. One sharecropper went to the landowner at the end of the season to settle up but was told he would not receive any money that year because the landowner needed it to send his son to college. The sharecropper moved to the North. Interview with the sharecropper's son on *The Best of Discovery,* Discovery television channel, June 11, 1995.

[23]Richard Kluger, *Simple Justice* (New York: Knopf, 1976), 89–90.

[24]Philip Dray, *At the Hands of Persons Unknown* (New York: Random House, 2002).

[25]Ibid.

[26]Woodward, *The Strange Career of Jim Crow,* 114.

[27]Yet talk of the riot was banished from newspapers, textbooks, and everyday conversations. After some years, most Oklahomans were unaware of it, except those who lived through it. In the 1990s, newspaper articles prompted the state to establish a commission to investigate the riot, leading to more awareness. Jonathan Z. Larsen, "Tulsa Burning," *Civilization,* February-March 1997, 46–55; Brent Staples, "Unearthing a Riot," *New York Times Magazine,* December 19, 1999, 64–69. For an examination, see James S. Hirsch, *Riot and Remembrance: The Tulsa Race War and Its Legacy* (New York: Houghton Mifflin, 2002).

[28]"Torn from the Land," Associated Press, wire.ap.org. The website offers an investigative report with numerous stories. For an illuminating look at the lives and status of black people in the Deep South in the 1920s, see Nan Woodruff, *American Congo: The African American Freedom Struggle in the Delta* (Cambridge, Mass.: Harvard University Press, 2003).

[29]Wilson apparently opposed segregation in government but still allowed it to appease southerners who were a major portion of his Democratic Party and whose support was essential for his economic reforms.

[30]*Guinn v. United States,* 238 U.S. 347 (1915). This clause had been written into election laws to make it more difficult for freed blacks and their children to qualify to vote (their grandfathers having been illiterate slaves) while effectively exempting whites from having to submit to literacy testing.

[31]*Buchanan v. Warley,* 245 U.S. 60 (1917).

[32]In 1939, the NAACP established the NAACP Legal Defense and Educational Fund as its litigation arm. In 1957, the Internal Revenue Service, pressured by southern members of Congress, ordered the two branches of the NAACP to break their connection or lose their tax-exempt status. Since then, they have been separate organizations, and further references in this chapter to the NAACP are in fact to the NAACP Legal Defense and Educational Fund.

[33]Juan Williams, "The Case for Thurgood Marshall," *Washington Post,* February 14, 1999, W16.

[34]Kluger, *Simple Justice,* 134.

[35]*Missouri ex rel. Gaines v. Canada,* 305 U.S. 337 (1938).

[36]*Sweatt v. Painter,* 339 U.S. 629 (1950).

[37]*McLaurin v. Oklahoma State Regents,* 339 U.S. 637 (1950).

[38]Esther Brown, a white woman from a Kansas City suburb, had a black maid who lived in nearby South Park. In 1948, when Brown saw the decrepit school for black students in South Park, she complained to the board of education in the town. At a meeting, she said, "Look, I don't represent these people. One of them works for me, and I've seen the conditions of their school. I know none of you would want your children educated under such circumstances. They're not asking for integration, just a fair shake." From the audience, Brown received catcalls and demands to go back where she came from. A woman behind her tried to hit her. The school board responded by gerrymandering the black neighborhood out of the South Park school district. Kluger, *Simple Justice,* 388–389.

[39]Earl Warren, *The Memoirs of Earl Warren* (Garden City, N.Y.: Doubleday, 1977), 291.

[40]Kluger, *Simple Justice,* 656.

[41]*Brown v. Board of Education of Topeka,* 347 U.S. 483 (1954).

[42]*Holmes v. Atlanta,* 350 U.S. 879 (1955); *Baltimore v. Dawson,* 350 U.S. 877 (1955); *Schiro v. Bynum,* 375 U.S. 395 (1964); *Johnson v. Virginia,* 373 U.S. 61 (1963); *Lee v. Washington,* 390 U.S. 333 (1968).

[43]*Brown v. Board of Education II,* 349 U.S. 294 (1955).

[44]Justice Tom Clark later told a political science conference that one justice had proposed desegregating one grade a year, beginning with kindergarten or first grade, but this concrete standard was rejected because the other justices felt it would take too long. In retrospect, it might have been quicker, and easier, than the vague standard used.

[45]*Griffin v. Prince Edward County School Board,* 377 U.S. 218 (1964); *Norwood v. Harrison,* 413 U.S. 455 (1973); *Gilmore v. Montgomery,* 417 U.S. 556 (1974); *Green v. New Kent County School Board,* 391 U.S. 430 (1968).

[46]Quoted in James F. Simon, *In His Own Image* (New York: McKay, 1974), 70.

[47]*All Things Considered,* NPR, December 10, 2003.

[48]William Cohen and John Kaplan, *Bill of Rights* (Mineola, N.Y.: Foundation Press, 1976), 622.

[49]*Swann v. Charlotte-Mecklenburg Board of Education*, 402 U.S. 1 (1971); *Columbus Board of Education v. Penick*, 443 U.S. 449 (1979); *Dayton Board of Education v. Brinkman*, 443 U.S. 526 (1979); *Keyes v. School District 1, Denver*, 413 U.S. 921 (1973).

[50]Lee A. Daniels, "In Defense of Busing," *New York Times Magazine*, April 17, 1983, 36–37.

[51]Some black parents opposed busing because it disrupted their children's lives and because it implied that their children could learn only by sitting beside white children. But other black parents favored busing because it offered their children an opportunity to go to better schools.

[52]White flight began after World War II as affluent families moved to the suburbs. Although white flight continued for economic reasons, it increased because of busing as well.

[53]*Milliken v. Bradley*, 418 U.S. 717 (1974).

[54]For example, some suburbs of Kansas City, Missouri, didn't allow black students to attend high schools. Some black families, then, moved back to the city, aggravating both school segregation and residential segregation. James S. Kunen, "The End of Integration," *Time*, April 29, 1996, 41.

[55]*Board of Education of Oklahoma City v. Dowell*, 112 L.Ed.2d 715 (1991). The Court said that school districts could stop busing when "the vestiges of past discrimination had been eliminated to the extent practicable." See also *Freeman v. Pitts*, 118 L.Ed.2d 108 (1992).

[56]*Missouri v. Jenkins*, 132 L.Ed.2d 63 (1995).

[57]Julie Rawe, "When Public Schools Aren't Color-blind," *Time*, December 4, 2006, 54–56.

[58]*Parents Involved in Community Schools v. Seattle School District* 168 L.Ed.2d 508 (2007).

[59]These districts use race in some way, although most don't use it as extensively as Louisville did. David G. Savage, "Justices Reject School Integration Efforts," *Los Angeles Times*, June 29, 2007, www.latimes.com/news/la-na-scotus29jun29,0,2236400,print.story?coll=la-tot-topst. Unlike most justices in the majority, Anthony Kennedy indicated that he may be willing to allow some efforts to promote desegregation.

[60]Anjetta McQueen, "Desegregation Waning," *Lincoln Journal Star*, May 16, 1999.

[61]FBI director J. Edgar Hoover ordered wiretaps that he hoped would link King with communists. When the taps failed to reveal any connection, Hoover had agents bug a hotel room, where they heard King having extramarital sex. Taylor Branch, *Pillar of Fire: America in the King Years, 1963–65* (New York: Simon & Schuster, 1998).

[62]Although this sit-in usually is cited as the first, a sit-in at a lunch counter in a drugstore in Wichita, Kansas, actually was the first—in 1958. But the Greensboro sit-in prompted the wave of sit-ins through the South.

[63]Woodward, *The Strange Career of Jim Crow*, 186.

[64]This incident occurred in 1961. Nicholas Lemann, "The Long March," *New Yorker*, February 10, 2003, 88.

[65]The Supreme Court had struck down discrimination in choosing juries, but discrimination continued through informal means. *Norris v. Alabama*, 294 U.S. 587 (1935); *Smith v. Texas*, 311 U.S. 128 (1940); *Avery v. Georgia*, 345 U.S. 559 (1952).

[66]An excellent collection of articles is presented in *Reporting Civil Rights: American Journalism, 1941–1973* (New York: Library of America, 2003).

[67]Henry Louis Gates Jr., "After the Revolution," *New Yorker*, April 29 and May 6, 1996.

[68]Robert A. Caro, "The Compassion of Lyndon Johnson," *New Yorker*, April 1, 2002, 56.

[69]Louis Menand, "He Knew He Was Right," *New Yorker*, March 26, 2001, 95.

[70]Lemann, "Long March," 86.

[71]Patrick Reddy, "Why It's Got to Be All or Nothing," *Washington Post National Weekly Edition*, October 18, 1999, 23.

[72]This was true for national elections. The transformation took longer for state and local elections.

[73]Joseph A. Califano, Jr., *The Triumph and Tragedy of Lyndon Johnson* (New York: Simon & Schuster, 1991), 177–178.

[74]The Supreme Court unanimously upheld the law. *Heart of Atlanta Motel v. United States*, 379 U.S. 421 (1964).

[75]For discussion of organized labor's ambivalence toward enactment and enforcement of the employment provisions of the act, see Herbert Hill, "Black Workers, Organized Labor, and Title VII of the 1964 Civil Rights Act: Legislative History and Litigation Record," in *Race in America*, eds. Herbert Hill and James E. Jones (Madison: University of Wisconsin Press, 1993), 263–341.

[76]*Griggs v. Duke Power*, 401 U.S. 424 (1971). However, standards that hinder blacks more than whites aren't necessarily unlawful. Washington, D.C., required police applicants to pass an exam. Although a higher percentage of blacks failed to pass, the Court said the exam related to the job. *Washington v. Davis*, 426 U.S. 229 (1976).

[77]*Shelley v. Kraemer*, 334 U.S. 1 (1948).

[78]Less directly, the numerous national and state policies that encouraged urban sprawl—e.g., road building—provided the opportunity for middle-class whites to flock to the suburbs, leaving the cities disproportionately black.

[79]For more extensive examination, see Andrew Hacker, *Two Nations: Black and White, Separate, Hostile, Unequal* (New York: Scribner, 1992).

[80]Richard Morin, "Southern Discomfort," *Washington Post National Weekly Edition*, July 15, 1996, 35.

[81]Gary Orfield, quoted in Mary Jordan, "Separating the Country from the *Brown* Decision," *Washington Post National Weekly Edition*, December 20, 1993, 33. See also Maia Davis, "Harvard Study Finds New Segregation," *Lincoln Journal Star*, January 20, 2003.

[82]Jonathan Kozol, *The Shame of the Nation: The Restoration of Apartheid Schooling in America* (New York: Crown, 2005), 19.

[83]Adam Cohen, "The Supreme Struggle," *New York Times*, January 18, 2004, E22.

[84]Kozol, *The Shame of the Nation*, 226–227.

[85]Ibid., 19.

[86]Consequently, magnet schools in minority neighborhoods often don't attract many white students. Sandy Banks, "Mixed Results for L.A.'s Magnet Schools," *Los Angeles Times*, January 20, 2006, www.latimes.com/news/local/la-me-magnet20jan20,0,6132919,fullstory?coll= la-home-headlines.

[87]Thomas M. Shapiro, *The Hidden Cost of Being African American* (New York: Oxford University, 2004), 170–179.

[88]Jordan, "Separating the Country from the *Brown* Decision."

[89]Kunen, "End of Integration," 39.

[90]Jonathan Kozol, *Savage Inequalities: Children in America's Schools* (New York: HarperPerennial, 1992), 4.

[91]Ibid., 3.

[92]Ibid., 35. However, only three public schools in Alabama are named after King, a native of the state. "Numbers," *Time*, January 24, 2000, 23.

[93]Kozol, *The Shame of the Nation*, 24–25.

[94]Rob Gurwitt, "Getting off the Bus," *Governing*, May 1992, 30–36; Jervis Anderson, "Black and Blue," *New Yorker*, April 29 and May 6, 1996.

[95]Richard Rothstein, quoted in Kozol, *The Shame of the Nation*, 230.

[96]"That's Quite a Range," *Lincoln Journal*, January 21, 1993.

[97]Shapiro, *Hidden Cost*, 144–145.

[98]In addition, cities have numerous nonprofit institutions—colleges, museums, hospitals—that benefit the entire urban area but don't pay property taxes. According to one estimate, 30 percent of the cities' potential tax base is tax-exempt, compared with 3 percent of the suburbs'. There are a few exceptions.

[99]Kozol, *The Shame of the Nation*, 245.

[100]Ibid., 60.

[101]Charles Peters, "Tilting at Windmills," *Washington Monthly*, March, 2006, 6.

[102]Kozol, *The Shame of the Nation*, 172

[103]Ibid., 171.

[104]Ibid., 53, 84.

[105]Steve Lopez, "Money for Stadiums but Not for Schools," *Time*, June 14, 1999, 54.

[106]"Employers' Replies to Racial Names," *NBER Digest*, September 2003, 1.

[107]David Wessel, "Studies Suggest Potent Race Bias in Hiring," *Wall Street Journal*, September 4, 2003, A2.

[108]Earl G. Graves, *How to Succeed in Business without Being White* (New York: Harper Business, 1997).

[109]Reed Abelson, "Anti-Bias Agency Is Short of Will and Cash," *New York Times,* July 1, 2001, BU1.

[110]These figures from 2002 are about 25 percent lower than the results from 1989, which was the last time the government had conducted this research. "Hispanics Face More Bias in Housing," *Lincoln Journal Star,* November 8, 2002. Another study found similar discrimination in fairly progressive northern cities. "Professional Should Address Discrimination," *Lincoln Journal Star,* April 24, 2002.

[111]Most Americans can identify a telephone caller as white or black. *All Things Considered,* NPR, August 5, 2001.

[112]John Iceland and Daniel Weinberg with Erika Steinmetz, *Racial and Ethnic Residential Segregation in the United States, 1980–2000* (Washington, D.C.: United States Census, 2002), ch. 5. Available on the web at www.census.gov/hhes/www/ housing/housing_patterns/pdf/censr-3.pdf.

[113]James Traub, "The Year in Ideas," *New York Times Magazine,* December 9, 2001, 94.

[114]Hacker, *Two Nations,* 35–38. For information on why blacks do not want to live in white neighborhoods, see Maria Krysan and Reynolds Farley, "The Residential Preferences of Blacks: Do They Explain Persistent Segregation?" *Social Forces* 80 (2002), 937–980.

[115]According to the Supreme Court's interpretation of Fourth Amendment search and seizure law, police can stop and frisk individuals who officers have a "reasonable suspicion" to believe are committing a crime. But officers must have more than a hunch to meet the standard of "reasonable suspicion" (though less than the "probable cause" required to obtain a search warrant). A person's race is not a valid criterion, except when the person's race and physical description match those of a particular suspect being sought.

[116]Eugene Robinson, "Pulling Over for Prejudice," *Washington Post National Weekly Edition,* May 5-13, 2007, 31.

[117]Sandy Banks, "Growing Up on a Tightrope," *Los Angeles Times,* March 3, 2006, www.latimes.com/ news/local/la-me boys3mar03,0,2282338.full.story.

[118]Michael A. Fletcher, "May the Driver Beware," *Washington Post National Weekly Edition,* April 8, 1996, 29.

[119]Jake Tapper, "And Then There Were None," *Washington Post National Weekly Edition,* January 13, 2003, 9.

[120]Jeffrey Goldberg, "The Color of Suspicion," *New York Times Magazine,* June 20, 1999, 53.

[121]David Cole and John Lamberth, "The Fallacy of Racial Profiling," *New York Times,* May 13, 2001, sec. 4, 13.

[122]Pierre Thomas, "Bias and the Badge," *Washington Post National Weekly Edition,* December 18, 1995, 6–9.

[123]Henry Louis Gates Jr., "Thirteen Ways of Looking at a Black Man," *New Yorker,* October 23, 1995, 59; Anderson, "Black and Blue," 64.

[124]Tammerlin Drummond, "Coping with Cops," *Time,* April 3, 2000, 72–73.

[125]Laura M. Markowitz, "Walking the Walk," *Networker,* July-August 1993, 22.

[126]William Raspberry, "The Little Things That Hurt," *Washington Post National Weekly Edition,* April 18, 1994, 29. See also Ellis Cose, *The Rage of a Privileged Class* (New York: HarperCollins, 1993).

[127]Richard Morin and Michael H. Cottman, "The Invisible Slap," *Washington Post National Weekly Edition,* July 2, 2001, 6.

[128]Kozol, *Savage Inequalities,* 179–180.

[129]Stephan Thernstrom and Abigail Thernstrom, *America in Black and White: One Nation, Indivisible* (New York: Simon & Schuster, 1997), especially part 3. Some improvement began before the civil rights movement, when southern blacks migrated to northern cities in the 1940s.

[130]Andrew Tobias, "Now the Good News about Your Money," *Parade,* April 4, 1993, 5.

[131]James Smith and Finis Welch, "Race and Poverty: A 40-Year Record," *American Economic Review* 77 (1987), 152–158.

[132]However, their rate of home ownership—48 percent—is the same as the national rate was in the 1940s. Whites' rate is 74 percent now. Deborah Kong, "Strides Made, but Still Much Disparity between Blacks, Whites," *Lincoln Journal Star,* July 22, 2002.

[133]Joel Garreau, "Candidates Take Note: It's a Mall World after All," *Washington Post National Weekly Edition,* August 10, 1992, 25.

[134]Thernstrom and Thernstrom, *America in Black and White,* 500.

[135]Francine Russo, "When Love Is Mixing It Up," *Time,* November, 2001, Bonus Section, F5.

[136]Benedict Carey, "In-laws In the Age of the Outsider," *New York Times,* December 18, 2005, WK1.

[137]Orlando Patterson, quoted in Anderson, "Black and Blue," 62.

[138]From 1967 to 1987, according to calculations by William Julius Wilson. David Remnick, "Dr. Wilson's Neighborhood," *New Yorker,* April 29 and May 6, 1996.

[139]Sociologist William Julius Wilson develops this idea extensively in *The Truly Disadvantaged* (Chicago: University of Chicago Press, 1987).

[140]U.S. Census Bureau, *Statistical Abstract of the United States, 2001* (Washington, D.C.: Government Printing Office, 2001), tab. 38.

[141]Wilson, *The Truly Disadvantaged.*

[142]Remnick, "Dr. Wilson's Neighborhood," 98.

[143]Samuel Walker, *Sense and Nonsense about Crime and Drugs,* 3rd ed. (Belmont, Calif.: Wadsworth, 1994), xviii, 3.

[144]According to the U.S. Bureau of Justice Statistics, cited in Fox Butterfield, "Despite Drop in Crime, an Increase in Inmates," *New York Times,* November 8, 2004.

[145]Ibid.

[146]Peter Reuter, "Why Can't We Make Prohibition Work Better? Some Consequences of Ignoring the Unattractive," in *Perspectives on Crime and Justice, 1996–1997 Lecture Series* (Washington, D.C.: National Institute of Justice, 1997), 30–31.

[147]Rosa A. Smith, "Saving Black Boys," *American Prospect,* February 2004, 49.

[148]"Doctor: Harlem's Death Rate Worse than Bangladesh's," *Lincoln Journal,* January 18, 1990.

[149]Banks, "Growing Up on a Tightrope."

[150]Donald Kaul, "Only Surprise Is That Riots Didn't Happen Sooner," *Lincoln Journal,* May 19, 1992.

[151]Drummond Ayres Jr., "Decade of Black Struggle: Gains and Unmet Goals," *New York Times,* April 2, 1978, sec. 1, 1.

[152]See Veronica Chambers, *Having It All?* (New York: Doubleday, 2003).

[153]Except for some immigrant farmworkers, who will be discussed.

[154]According to the most recent research, in 2002, Hispanics might face somewhat more discrimination in housing than blacks. Hispanics who tried to buy a house faced discrimination 20 percent of the time, and those who tried to rent an apartment did so 25 percent of the time. "Hispanics Face More Bias in Housing."

[155]Fifty-nine percent of voters in counties in which immigrants are less than 5 percent of the population say that all illegals should be deported. Joe Klein, "Bush Is Smart on the Border—and the G.O.P. Isn't," *Time,* May 29, 2006, 25.

[156]Tammerlin Drummond, "It's Not Just in New Jersey," *Time,* June 14, 1999, 61.

[157]John Bowe, "Nobodies," *New Yorker,* April 21, 2003, 106.

[158]Guadalupe San Miguel, "Mexican American Organizations and the Changing Politics of School Desegregation in Texas, 1945–1980," *Social Science Quarterly* 63 (1982), 701–715.

[159]Ibid., 710.

[160]Even children of illegal aliens have been given the right to attend public schools by the Supreme Court. The majority assumed that most of these children, although subject to deportation, would remain in the United States, given the large number of illegal aliens who do remain here. Denying them an education would deprive them of the opportunity to fulfill their potential and would deprive society of the benefit of their contribution. *Plyler v. Doe,* 457 U.S. 202 (1982).

[161]Luis Ricardo Fraga, Kenneth J. Meier, and Robert E. England, "Hispanic Americans and Educational Policy: Structural Limits to Equal Access and Opportunities for Upward Mobility," unpublished paper, University of Oklahoma, 1985, 6.

[162]*San Antonio Independent School District v. Rodriguez,* 411 U.S. 1 (1973).

[163]Anjetta McQueen, "Dual-Language Schools Sought," *Lincoln Journal Star,* March 16, 2000.

[164]*Lau v. Nichols,* 414 U.S. 563 (1974).

[165]McQueen, "Dual-Language Schools Sought."

[166]"Bilingualism's End Means a Different Kind of Change," *Champaign-Urbana News-Gazette,* June 7, 1998.

[167]Margot Hornblower, "No Habla Español," *Time,* January 26, 1998, 63.

[168]James Traub, "The Bilingual Barrier," *New York Times Magazine,* January 31, 1999, 34–35.

[169]U.S. Census Bureau, "Social and Economic Characteristics," *2000 Census of the Population* (factfinder.census.gov/servlet/QTTable?_bm5y&-geo_id5D&-qr_name5DEC_2000). Four percent of Asian language speakers do not speak English.

[170]Nancy Landale and R. S. Oropesa, "Schooling, Work, and Idleness among Mexican and Non-Latino White Adolescents," working paper, Pennsylvania State University, Population Research Institute, 1997.

[171]Thomas Boswell and James Curtis, *The Cuban American Experience* (Totowa, N.J.: Rowman & Allanheld, 1983), 191.

[172]Kevin F. McCarthy and R. Burciaga Valdez, *Current and Future Effects of Mexican Immigration in California—Executive Summary* (Santa Monica, Calif.: RAND Corp., 1985), 27.

[173]Ruben Navarrette Jr., "Hispanics See Themselves as Part of United States," *Lincoln Journal Star,* December 23, 2002.

[174]Ibid.

[175]"Survey: Hispanics Reject Cohesive Group Identity," *Lincoln Journal,* December 15, 1992.

[176]Gregory Rodriguez, "Finding a Political Voice," *Washington Post National Weekly Edition,* February 1, 1999, 22–23.

[177]Karen Tumulty, "Courting a Sleeping Giant," *Time,* June 11, 2001, 74.

[178]A 1995 Census Bureau Survey indicated that 49% of Native people preferred being called *American Indian,* 37% preferred *Native American,* 3.6% preferred "some other term," and 5% had no preference. Bureau of Labor Statistics, U.S. Census Bureau Survey, May 1995. www.census.gov/prod/2/gen/96arc/ivatuck.pdf.

[179]*Cherokee Nation v. Georgia,* 30 U.S. 1 (1831); *Worcester v. Georgia,* 31 U.S. 515 (1832).

[180]Treaties made exceptions for those who married whites and those who left their tribes and abandoned tribal customs.

[181]Vine Deloria Jr. and Clifford M. Lytle, *American Indians, American Justice* (Austin: University of Texas Press, 1983), 221.

[182]Ibid., 222–225.

[183]Indian Self-Determination Act (1975).

[184]Ellen Nakashima and Neely Tucker, "A Fight over Lost Lands, Money Owed," *Washington Post National Weekly Edition,* April 29, 2002, 30.

[185]According to the Indian Gaming Regulatory Act (1988), tribes can establish casinos if their reservation lies in a state that allows virtually any gambling, including charitable "Las Vegas nights."

[186]Kathleen Schmidt, "Gambling a Bonanza for Indians," *Lincoln Journal Star,* March 23, 1998.

[187]Donald L. Bartlett and James B. Steele, "Wheel of Misfortune," *Time,* December 16, 2002, 44–48.

[188]Ibid., 47.

[189]W. John Moore, "Tribal Imperatives," *National Journal,* June 9, 1990, 1396.

[190]Jack Hitt, "The Newest Indian," *New York Times Magazine,* August 21, 2005, 40–41.

[191]Quoted in Ruth B. Ginsburg, *Constitutional Aspects of Sex-Based Discrimination* (Saint Paul, Minn.: West, 1974), 2.

[192]Karen De Crow, *Sexist Justice* (New York: Vintage, 1975), 72.

[193]Nadine Taub and Elizabeth M. Schneider, "Women's Subordination and the Role of Law," in *The Politics of Law: A Progressive Critique,* rev. ed., ed. David Kairys (New York: Pantheon, 1990), 160–162.

[194]*Bradwell v. Illinois,* 83 U.S. 130 (1873).

[195]From an *amicus curiae* ("friend of the court") brief by 281 historians filed in the Supreme Court case, *Webster v. Reproductive Health Services,* 106 L.Ed.2d 410 (1989).

[196]Donna M. Moore, "Editor's Introduction" in *Battered Women,* ed. Donna M. Moore (Beverly Hills, Calif.: Sage, 1979), 8.

[197]Barbara Sinclair Deckard, *The Women's Movement,* 2nd ed. (New York: Harper & Row, 1979), 303.

[198]In the early 1960s, a board game for girls—What Shall I Be?—offered these options: teacher, nurse, stewardess, actress, ballerina, and beauty queen. David Owen, "The Sultan of Stuff," *New Yorker,* July 19, 1999, 60.

[199]Reprinted in "Regrets, We Have a Few," *Time Special Issue: 75 Years of Time,* 1998, 192.

[200]For an examination of Betty Friedan's role in the movement and the political dynamics among the various factions in the movement, see Judith Hennessee, *Betty Friedan: Her Life* (New York: Random House, 1999). For an examination of women's views toward feminism, see Elinor Burkett, *The Right Women* (New York: Scribner, 1998).

[201]Robert Alan Goldberg, *Enemies Within* (New Haven, Conn.: Yale University Press, 2002).

[202]De Crow, *Sexist Justice,* 119.

[203]This is why Betty Friedan later felt compelled to write a book espousing the concept of motherhood: *The Second Stage* (New York: Summit, 1981).

[204]For a discussion of these points, see Jane Mansbridge, *Why We Lost the ERA* (Chicago: University of Chicago Press, 1986); Mary Frances Berry, *Why ERA Failed* (Bloomington: Indiana University Press, 1986); Janet Boles, "Building Support for the ERA: A Case of 'Too Much, Too Late,'" *PS: Political Science and Politics* 15 (1982), 575–592.

[205]Shenkman, *I Love Paul Revere,* 136–137.

[206]*Reed v. Reed,* 404 U.S. 71 (1971).

[207]*Hoyt v. Florida,* 368 U.S. 57 (1961).

[208]*Taylor v. Louisiana,* 419 U.S. 522 (1975).

[209]*Stanton v. Stanton,* 421 U.S. 7 (1975).

[210]Cases were from 2002. They were compiled by The WAGE Project (www.wageproject.org) and examined and reported in Evelyn F. Murphy, with E. J. Graff, *Getting Even: Why Women Don't Get Paid Like Men—and What to Do about It* (New York: Simon & Schuster, 2005), 40–48. This total also includes sexual harassment suits, which, of course, reflect a type of sexual discrimination.

[211]Ibid., 56.

[212]Ibid., 157.

[213]Ibid., 153

[214]Ibid., 60–61.

[215]Ibid., 84–85.

[216]Ibid., 200.

[217]Ibid., 199.

[218]Ibid., 4.

[219]David Leonhardt, "Gender Pay Gap, Once Narrowing, Is Stuck in Place," *New York Times,* December 24, 2006, YT18.

[220]Murphy, *Getting Even,* 185.

[221]*Ledbetter v. Goodyear Tire and Rubber,* 167 L. Ed.2d 982 (2007).

[222]Ibid., 146.

[223]U.S. Census Bureau, *Statistical Abstract of the United States, 1997* (Washington, D.C.: Government Printing Office, 1997), tab. 645.

[224]The phrase itself is not new. It was used by workers in the nineteenth century and as the title of a book by a Catholic priest in 1906. Jon Gertner, "What Is a Living Wage?" *New York Times Magazine,* January 15, 2006, 42.

[225]For discussion, see ibid., 38.

[226]Lisa McLaughlin, "In Brief," *Time,* October 9, 2000, G12.

[227]For discussion, see Murphy, *Getting Even,* 194–213.

[228]David Crary, "U.S. Among Worst in Family vs. Work Policies," *Lincoln Journal Star,* February 1, 2007, 5A. There's no federal law requiring employers to provide paid sick days. Most do provide them for salaried employees but not for hourly employees.

[229]The Family and Medical Leave Act. The act also requires employers to continue health insurance coverage during the leave and to give the employee the same job or a comparable one upon her or his return.

[230]Lisa Genasci, "Many Workers Resist Family Benefit Offers," *Lincoln Journal Star,* June 28, 1995.

[231]Ellen Bravo, "The Architecture of Work and Family," *American Prospect,* March, 2007, A5.

[232]Jodie Levin-Epstein, "Responsive Workplaces," *American Prospect,* March, 2007, A16.

[233]Joan C. Williams, "The Opt-Out Revolution Revisited," *American Prospect,* March, 2007, A14.

[234]Heather Boushey, "Values Begin at Home, but Who's Home?" *American Prospect,* March, 2007, A2.

[235]Nancy R. Gibbs, "Bringing Up Father," *Time,* June 28, 1993, 55–56.

[236]In a conversation with business professors at a southwestern university not long ago. One of the participants conveyed his remark to the author of this chapter.

[237]Ann Crittenden, "Parents Fighting Back," *American Prospect,* June 2003, 22.

[238]Joyce Gelb and Marian Lief Palley, *Women and Public Policies* (Princeton, N.J.: Princeton University Press, 1982), 102. The author of Title IX, Rep. Patsy Mink (D.-Hawaii), had applied to medical schools but was not considered because she was a woman. Mink intended Title IX to open the doors. She said it was "never intended to mean equal numbers or equal money" in athletics. Susan Reimer, "Title IX Has Unintended Consequences," *Lincoln Journal Star,* April 9, 2000.

[239]R. Vivian Acosta and Linda Jean Carpenter, *Women in Intercollegiate Sport: A Longitudinal, National Study. Twenty-nine Year Update,* 2006, www.womenssportsfoundation.org/cgi-bin/iowa/issues/part/article.html?record=1107.

[240]Welch Suggs, "Uneven Progress for Women's Sports," *Chronicle of Higher Education,* April 7, 2000, A52–A56; Bill Pennington, "More Men's Teams Benched as Colleges Level the Field," *New York Times,* May 9, 2002, A1; Susan Welch and Lee Sigelman, "Who Calls the Shots: Women Coaches in Division I Women's Sports," forthcoming *Social Science Quarterlly,* 2008.

[241]Suggs, "Uneven Progress for Women's Sports," A52.

[242]Michele Orecklin, "Now She's Got Game," *Time,* March 3, 2003, 57.

[243]"Title IX Facts Everyone Should Know," www.womensportsfoundation.org/cgibin/iowa/issues/geena/record,html?record=862.

[244]Mary Duffy, quoted in E. J. Dionne Jr., "Nothing Wacky about Title IX," *Washington Post National Weekly Edition,* May 19, 1997, 26.

[245]Karen Kornbluh, "The Joy of Flex," *Washington Monthly,* December 2005, 30.

[246]Linda R. Hirshman, "Homeward Bound," *American Prospect,* December, 2005, 25.

[247]*Mississippi University for Women* v. *Hogan,* 458 U.S. 718 (1982).

[248]*Orr* v. *Orr,* 440 U.S. 268 (1979).

[249]*Michael M.* v. *Sonoma County,* 450 U.S. 464 (1981).

[250]*Rostker* v. *Goldberg,* 453 U.S. 57 (1981).

[251]*Planned Parenthood of Southeastern Pennsylvania* v. *Casey,* 120 L.Ed.2d 674 (1992).

[252]David Crary, "Man Sues for Right to Decline Fatherhood," *Lincoln Journal Star,* March 9, 2006, 7A. But a federal court of appeals rejected his suit in 2007.

[253]This scenario was used by President Johnson in support of affirmative action.

[254]Early decisions include *University of California Regents* v. *Bakke,* 438 U.S. 265 (1978); *United Steelworkers* v. *Weber,* 443 U.S. 193 (1979); and *Fullilove* v. *Klutznick,* 448 U.S. 448 (1980).

[255]Two critics include Thomas Sowell, *Preferential Policies: An International Perspective* (New York: Morrow, 1990), and Dinesh D'Souza, *Illiberal Education* (New York: Free Press, 1991).

[256]*United Steelworkers* v. *Weber; Sheet Metal Workers* v. *EEOC,* 92 L.Ed.2d 344 (1986); *Firefighters* v. *Cleveland,* 92 L.Ed.2d 405 (1986); *United States* v. *Paradise Local Union,* 94 L.Ed.2d 203 (1987).

[257]*Firefighters* v. *Stotts,* 467 U.S. 561 (1985); *Wygant* v. *Jackson Board of Education,* 90 L.Ed.2d 260 (1986).

[258]*Richmond* v. *Croson,* 102 L.Ed.2d 854 (1989); *Adarand Constructors* v. *Pena,* 132 L. Ed.2d 158 (1995). The perception that minorities are taking over is also reflected in a peculiar poll finding: The average American estimated that 32 percent of the U.S. population was black and 21 percent was Hispanic at a time when they were just 12 percent and 9 percent. Richard Nadeau, Richard G. Niemi, and Jeffrey Levine, "Innumeracy about Minority Populations," *Public Opinion Quarterly* 57 (1993), 332–347.

[259]Quoted in Robert J. Samuelson, "End Affirmative Action," *Washington Post National Weekly Edition,* March 6, 1995, 5.

[260]Private companies that have government contracts, and therefore are subject to affirmative action, have shown more improvement in hiring minorities and women than other companies have. State and local governments, also subject to affirmative action, have shown more improvement in hiring than private companies have.

[261]James E. Jones, "The Genesis and Present Status of Affirmative Action in Employment," paper presented at the annual meeting of the American Political Science Association, Washington, D.C., September, 1984; Nelson C. Dometrius and Lee Sigelman, "Assessing Progress toward Affirmative Action Goals in State and Local Government," *Public Administration Review* 44 (1984), 241–247; Peter Eisinger, *Black Employment in City Government* (Washington, D.C.: Joint Center for Political Studies, 1983); Milton Coleman, "Uncle Sam Has Stopped Running Interference for Blacks," *Washington Post National Weekly Edition,* December 19, 1983.

[262]This "is one of the better kept secrets of the debate." Alan Wolfe, "Affirmative Action, Inc.," *New Yorker,* November 25, 1996, 107. See also the numerous sources cited there.

[263]Gertrude Ezorsky, *Racism and Justice: The Case for Affirmative Action* (Ithaca, N.Y.: Cornell University Press, 1991), 48–49, 63–65.

[264]Wilson, *The Truly Disadvantaged.*

[265]Donald Kaul, "Privilege in Workplace Invisible to White Men Who Enjoy It," *Lincoln Journal-Star,* April 9, 1995; Richard Morin and Lynne Duke, "A Look at the Bigger Picture," *Washington Post National Weekly Edition,* March 16, 1992, 9.

[266]Eisinger, *Black Employment in City Government.*

[267]Thomas J. Kane, "Racial and Ethnic Preference in College Admissions," paper presented at the Ohio State University College of Law Conference, "Twenty Years after *Bakke,*" Columbus, April 1998.

[268]Stephen Carter, quoted in David Owen, "From Race to Chase," *New Yorker,* June 3, 2002, 54.

[269]Jeffrey Rosen, "How I Learned to Love Quotas," *New York Times Magazine,* June 1, 2003, 54; Lee Hockstader, "The Texas 10 Percent Solution," *Washington Post National Weekly Edition,* November 11, 2002, 30. A major effect on the University of California system has been "cascading," with minority enrollments dropping at the most competitive UC campuses but increasing at the less competitive ones. Minorities have been cascading from the top tier to the next tiers, where their academic records more closely match those of the other students. James Traub, "The Class of Prop. 209," *New York Times Magazine,* May 2, 1999, 51.

[270]Jacques Steinberg, "The New Calculus of Diversity on Campus," *New York Times,* February 2, 2003, WK3; Timothy Egan, "Little Asia on the Hill," *New York Times,* January 7, 2007, Education Life, 26.

[271]*Gratz* v. *Bollinger,* 156 L.Ed.2d 257; *Grutter* v. *Bollinger,* 156 L.Ed.2d 304.

[272]Chief Justice Roberts and Justices Alito, Scalia, and Thomas. The question mark is Justice Kennedy.

[273]Traub, "Class of Prop. 209."

[274]John Larew, "Why Are Droves of Unqualified, Unprepared Kids Getting into Our Top Colleges?" *Washington Monthly,* June 1991, 10–14; Theodore Cross, "Suppose There Was No Affirmative Action at the Most Prestigious Colleges and Graduate Schools," *Journal of Blacks in Higher Education,* March 31, 1994, 47, 50; Joe Klein, "There's More Than One Way to Diversify," *Time,* December 18, 2006, 29.

[275]For an examination of the *Bakke* ruling and its impact on graduate schools, see Susan Welch and John Gruhl, *Affirmative Action and Minority Enrollments in Medical and Law Schools* (Ann Arbor: University of Michigan Press, 1998).

[276]Richard H. Sander, "House of Cards for Black Law Students," *Los Angeles Times,* December 20, 2004, www.latimes.com/news/opinion/la-oe-sander20dec20,0,436015,print. story; Adam Liptak, "For Blacks in Law School, Can Less Be More?" *New York Times,* February 13, 2005, WK3.

[277]For further discussion, see David T. Canon, *Race, Redistricting, and Representation* (Chicago: University of Chicago Press, 1999), 23–25. Of course, there's also a small upper class of wealthy business people, entertainers, and athletes.

[278]Dick Kirschten, "Not Black-and-White," *National Journal,* March 2, 1991, 496–500.

Chapter 14

[1]Chris Edwards, "Ten Reasons to Cut Farm Subsidies," Center for Trade Policy Studies, Cato Institute, June 28, 2007, freetrade.org/node/697.

[2]Arloc Sherman and Aviva Aron-Dine, "New CBO Data Shows Income Inequality Continues to Widen," Center on Budget and Policy Priorities, January 23, 2007, cbpp.org/1-23-07inc.htm#_ftn1. Data from the Congressional Budget Office.

[3]John Berry, "The Legacy of Reaganomics," *Washington Post National Weekly Edition,* December 19, 1988; Spencer Rich, "Are You Really Better Off Than You Were Thirteen Years Ago?" *Washington Post National Weekly Edition,* September 8, 1986, 20; Levy, "We're Running Out of Gimmicks to Sustain Our Prosperity," *Washington Post National Weekly Edition,* December 29, 1986, 18–19.

[4]Editorial, "Two Trillion Dollars Is Missing," *New York Times,* January 8, 1989, E28.

[5]Louis Uchitelle, "For Employee Benefits, It Pays to Wear the Union Label," *New York Times,* July 16, 1995, F10.

[6]Stephanie Aronson, "The Rise in Lifetime Earnings Inequality among Men," Federal Reserve Board Staff Report, Finance and Economics Discussion Series, March 2002, 4 (www. federalreserve.gov).

[7]Bruce Stokes, "The Lost-Wages of Immigration," *National Journal,* January 7, 2006, 58.

[8]Economic Policy Institute.

[9]Sherman and Aron-Dine, "New CBO Data Shows Income Inequality Continues to Widen."

[10]Michael Lind, *The Next American Nation: The New Nationalism and the Fourth American Revolution* (New York: Free Press, 1995), 139–216.

[11]Adam Smith, *Inquiry into the Nature and Causes of the Wealth of Nations* (1776; reprinted in several editions, including Indianapolis: Bobbs-Merrill, 1961).

[12]Quoted in John Greenwald, "Knitting New Notions," *Time,* January 30, 1989, 46.

[13]John Maynard Keynes, *The General Theory of Employment, Interest and Money* (New York: Harcourt, Brace, 1935).

[14]Jill Barshay, "The Uneven Field," *CQ Weekly,* February 7, 2005, 292. Data cited is from Congress's Joint Economic Committee.

[15]The government raises small amounts of revenue by taxing consumption through the levies it places on the sale or manufacture of some luxury and nonessential items such as liquor and cigarettes, as well as on a few essential products such as gasoline. These excise taxes are designed not only to raise revenue but also to limit or discourage use of scarce or dangerous products, which is why they are sometimes called "sin taxes."

[16]Isaac Shapiro, "Overall Federal Tax Burden on Most Families—Including Middle-Income Families—at Lowest Levels in More Than Two Decades," Center on Budget and Policy Priorities Report, April 10, 2002, 2.

[17]Data are from the Center on Budget and Policy Priorities Report (www.cbpp .org), quoted in "Middle-Class Tax Blow Hits Lowest Level Since 1957," *Champaign-Urbana News-Gazette,* April 15, 2002, A8.

[18]John Cranford, "Code Words: Tax Neutrality," *CQ Weekly,* February 7, 2005, 288–290.

[19]Joseph J. Schatz, "National Sales Tax: The Pros and Cons," *CQ Weekly,* June 13, 2005, 1558.

[20]U.S. Congress, Joint Economic Committee.

[21]Barshay, "The Uneven Field."

[22]Cranford, "Code Words: Tax Neutrality," 289. The economist quoted is Alice Rivlin, former director of the CBO and the OMB, and former vice-chair of the Fed.

[23]Roger Lowenstein, "Tax Break: Who Needs the Mortgage-Interest Deduction?" *New York Times Magazine,* March 5, 2006, 78.

[24]"Rich vs. Poor," *CQ Weekly,* February 7, 2007, 297.

[25]"Problems Cited at IRS Help Centers," *Champaign-Urbana News-Gazette,* September 4, 2003, 1.

[26]David Cay Johnston, "A Taxation Policy to Make John Stuart Mill Weep," *New York Times,* April 18, 2004, WK14.

[27]Jill Barshay, "Business Lobby Storms Senate to Shape Corporate Tax Bill," *CQ Weekly,* May 8, 2004, 1073.

[28]Citizens for Tax Justice, "State and Local Taxes Hit Poor and Middle Class Far Harder than the Wealthy." Report issued June 26, 1996. See the report online at www.ctj.org/ html/whopays.htm.

[29]Institute on Taxation and Economic Policy, "The Effects of Replacing Most Federal Taxes with a National Sales Tax: A State-by-State Distributional Analysis." Paper issued September 2004, 2.

[30]Barlett and Steele, "Corporate Welfare," 38.

[31]Ibid., 87.

[32]See Donald L. Barlett and James B. Steele, "Paying a Price for Polluters," November 23, 1998, 77, and "Corporate Welfare," 39.

[33]Nicholas Johnson, Joseph Llobrera, and Bob Zahradnik, "A Hand Up: How State Earned Income Tax Credits Help Working Families Escape Poverty in 2003," Center on Budget and Policy Priorities, March 3, 2003 (www .cbpp.org/3-3-03sfp.htm). Seventeen states also offer the EITC against state income taxes.

[34]Joseph L. Schatz, "The Power of the Status Quo," *CQ Weekly,* February 6, 2006, 322.

[35]Patricia Dunn, "The Reagan Solution for Aiding Families with Dependent Children: Reflections of an Earlier Era," in *The Attack on the Welfare State,* eds. Anthony Champagne and Edward Harpham (Prospect Heights, Ill.: Waveland, 1984), 87–110.

[36]Melinda Upp, "Relative Importance of Various Income Sources of the Aged, 1980," *Social Security Bulletin,* January 1983, 5.

[37]All of the statistics on Social Security recipients are from Social Security Administration, "Social Security Basic Facts" (www.socialsecurity.gov/pressoffice/basicfact.htm).

[38]Social Security Administration, "Social Security Information for Women" (www.ssa .gov/women).

[39]U.S. Census Bureau, "Poverty: 2004 Highlights" (www.census.gov/hhes/poverty/poverty04/pov0 4hi.html).

[40]Social Security Administration, "Social Security Basic Facts 2006," 2 (www.socialsecurity.gov/pressoffice/basicfactalt.htm).

[41]Robert Pear, "AARP Opposes Bush Plan to Replace Social Security with Private Accounts," *New York Times,* November 12, 2004, A19.

[42]Social Security Administration, "Social Security Basic Facts, 2006," 2.

[43]Barbara Ehrenreich, who writes on working-class life, is one who believes that the poverty level is set too low. Swanee Hunt, "Number of Poor May Be Far Higher Than Government Statistics Indicate," *Champaign-Urbana News-Gazette,* December 7, 2003, B1.

[44]Social Security Administration, "Social Security Basic Facts 2006", 1 (www.socialsecurity.gov/pressoffice/basicfact.htm).

[45]Social Security Administration, "Social Security Highlights 2005–2006," 2 (www .socialsecurity. gov/policy/docs/quickfacts/proghighlights. index.html).

[46]U.S. Census Bureau, *Statistical Abstract of the United States, 2006* (Washington, D.C.: Government Printing Office, 2005), tabs. 80 and 81.

[47]Greg J. Duncan, *Years of Poverty, Years of Plenty: The Changing Economic Fortunes of American Workers and Families* (Ann Arbor: Survey Research Center, Institute for Social Research, University of Michigan, 1984); Spencer Rich, "Who Gets Help and How," *Washington Post National Weekly Edition,* May 15, 1989, 37.

[48]Department of Health and Human Services, Temporary Assistance for Needy Families (TANF) Program, Administration for Children and Families, final rule summary (www. acf.dhhs. gov/programs/ofa/exsumcl.htm); Liz Schott, Ed Lazere, Heidi Goldberg, and Eileen Sweeney, "Highlights of the Final TANF Regulations," Center on Budget and Policy Priorities, April 29, 1999 (www.cbpp .org/4-29-99wel.htm).

[49]Department of Health and Human Services, "Reauthorization of the Temporary Assistance for Needy Families Program," 4 (www.aphsa. org). Program renewal was part of the Deficit Reduction Act of 2005.

[50]Douglas J. Besharov, "End Welfare Lite as We Know It," *New York Times,* August 15, 2006.

[51]Ibid.

[52]Eileen P. Sweeney, "Recent Studies Indicate That Many Parents Who Are Current or Former Welfare Recipients Have Disabilities," Center on Budget and Policy Priorities, February 29, 2000 (www.cbpp.org/2-29-00wel. pdf); Erica Goode, "Childhood Abuse and Adult Stress," *New York Times,* August 2, 2000, A22.

[53]Gordon Berlin, vice president of MDRC, a nonpartisan research group, quoted in Hegland, "What Works for Welfare?" 108.

[54]Kevin Freking, "Many States Facing Welfare Dilemma," *Champaign-Urbana News-Gazette,* September 10, 2006, C-3.

[55]*Budget of the United States 2007,* 116.

56On Bush's marriage initiative and work requirements, see Bill Swindell, "Welfare Reauthorization Becomes Another Casualty in Congress's Partisan Crossfire," *Congressional Quarterly Weekly,* April 3, 2004, 805–806.

57Ibid., 3–6.

58U.S. Census Bureau, *Statistical Abstract of the United States, 2001* (Washington, D.C.: Government Printing Office, 2001), tab. 801.

59Nicholas Kristof, "Farm Subsidies That Kill," *New York Times,* July 5, 2002, A21.

60John Kelly, "Lion's Share of Farm Subsidies Going to a Select Few," *State College* (Pa.) *Centre Daily Times,* September 10, 2001, 1.

61John Lancaster, "Our Farm-Friendly Lawmakers," *Washington Post National Weekly Edition,* September 10, 2001, 11.

62Quoted in ibid.

63Gebe Martinez, "Free-Spending Farm Bill a Triumph of Politics," *Congressional Quarterly Weekly Review,* May 4, 2002, 114. The first quote is from John Boehner (R-Ohio) and Cal Dooley (D-Calif.), the second from Patrick Toomey (R-Pa.).

64Timothy Egan, "Big Farms Reap Two Harvests with Aid as Bumper Crop," *New York Times,* December 26, 2004, sec. 1, 36.

65Press release from the office of Senator Tim Hutchinson, May 13, 2002.

66Elizabeth Becker, "As House Prepares Farm Bill, Questions of Who Needs Help and How Much," *New York Times,* September 9, 2001, 22.

67Kristof, "Farm Subsidies That Kill."

68Richard B. Freeman, "Labor Market Institutions and Earnings Inequality," *New England Economic Review,* May-June 1996, 158; U.S. Census Bureau, "Current Population Survey," March 1960 to 2001 (www.census.gov).

69U.S. Census Bureau, "2003 Poverty Tables." For an analysis of the data in these tables, see "Census Data Show Poverty Increased, Income Stagnated, and the Number of Uninsured Rose to a Record Level in 2003," Center on Budget and Policy Priorities, August 27, 2004 (www
.cbpp.org/8-26-04pov.htm).

70Nicholas D. Kristof, "A Gift to the World, and Ourselves," *New York Times,* December 25, 2005, WK9.

71Dan Barber, "Stuck in the Middle," *New York Times,* November 23, 2005.

72Robert Pear, "Growth of National Health Spending Slows Along With Drug Sales," *New York Times,* January 10, 2006.

73Paul Krugman, "Our Sick Society," *New York Times,* May 5, 2006.

74"Hospital-Caused Deaths" (Editorial), *New York Times,* July 5, 2006; Gardiner Harris, "Report Finds a Heavy Toll From Medication Errors," *New York Times* July 21, 2006.

75Institute of Medicine study, cited in Hillary Rodham Clinton, "Now Can We Talk About Health Care?" *New York Times Magazine,* April 18, 2004, 20.

76Mark Murray, Marilyn Werber Serafini, and Megan Twohey, "Untested Safety Net," *National Journal,* March 10, 2001, 691.

77Clarke E. Cochran et al., *American Public Policy,* 6th ed. (New York: St. Martin's/Worth, 1999), 282.

78Rebecca Adams, "America's Unraveling Safety Net," *Congressional Quarterly Weekly Review,* May 22, 2004, 1225.

79Ibid., 1226; Robert Pear, "Nursing Home Inspections Miss Violations, Report Says," *New York Times,* January 16, 2006.

80Erin Heath, "Medicaid: The Pendulum Swings," *National Journal,* August 9, 2003, 2546.

81The findings of a study on this subject can be found in "Racial Differences in Health Care," *New England Journal of Medicine* (Aug 2005).

82Elizabeth Warren and Amelia Warren Tyagi, *The Two-Income Trap: Why Middle-Class Mothers and Fathers Are Going Broke* (New York: Basic Books, 2003).

83"Europe Mulls Private Medical Care," *Champaign-Urbana News-Gazette,* November 29, 2003, A3.

84Clinton, "Now Can We Talk?" 30

85Steve Lohr, "Health Care Costs Are a Killer but Maybe That's a Plus," *New York Times,* September 26, 2004, WK5.

86Lohr, "Health Care Costs Are a Killer"; Malcolm Caldwell, "High Prices," *New Yorker,* October 25, 2004, 88.

87Ibid.

88Gina Kolata, "More May Not Mean Better in Health Care, Studies Find," *New York Times,* July 21, 2002, sec. 1, 20.

89Erik Eckholm, "Those Who Pay Health Costs Think of Drawing Lines," *New York Times,* March 28, 1993, 1.

90Gina Kolata, "Research Suggests More Health Care May Not Be Better," 20.

91Daniel Gross, "Whose Problem Is Health Care?" *New York Times,* February 8, 2004, BU6.

92Robert Fitch, "Big Labor's Big Secret," *New York Times,* December 28, 2005.

93Mark Sherman, "Doctors Call for National Coverage," *Lincoln Journal Star,* August 13, 2003, 1.

94Robert Pear, "House and Senate Still Far Apart on Medicaid Changes," *New York Times,* December 12, 2005.

Chapter 15

1Mary Spicuzza, "Weeki Wachee Mermaids in Terrorist Cross Hairs?" *St. Petersburg Times,* April 22, 2005. This incident was featured in John Mueller, *Overblown. Free Press,* 2006, 1.

2Ibid.

3Francis Fukuyama, *The End of History and the Last Man* (New York: Free Press, 1992).

4Walter LaFeber, "Marking Revolution, Opposing Revolution," *New York Times,* July 3, 1983, sec. 4, 13.

5The group was known as the Project for the New Century (PNAC); it circulated its call for the overthrow of Saddam Hussein in 1995.

6Philip Bobbitt, "Why We Listen," *New York Times,* January 30, 2006.

7For a discussion of how the Bush administration cherry-picked intelligence data to support the invasion of Iraq in 2003, see James Risen, *State of War: the Secret History of the CIA and the Bush Administration* (New York: Free Press, 2006).

8The findings of the congressional investigation into intelligence failures prior to and after 9/11 can be read at the website for the Senate Select Intelligence Committee (www
.intelligence.senate.gov). See transcripts of the testimony of Eleanor Hill, director of the Joint Inquiry staff.

9Madison's notes from *Documents Illustrative of the Formation of the Union of the American States,* quoted in Joan Biskupic, "Constitution's Conflicting Clauses Underscored by Iraqi Crisis," *Congressional Quarterly Weekly Report,* January 5, 1991, 34.

10Ronald D. Elving, "America's Most Frequent Fight Has Been the Undeclared War," *Congressional Quarterly Weekly Report,* January 5, 1991, 37.

11Rep. Toby Roth (R-Wis.), quoted in Katharine Q. Seelye, "House Defeats Bid to Repeal 'War Powers,'" *New York Times,* June 11, 1995, A7.

12Barry B. Hughes, *The Domestic Context of American Foreign Policy* (San Francisco: Freeman, 1978), ch. 5.

13Robert Weissberg, *Public Opinion and Popular Government* (Englewood Cliffs, N.J.: Prentice Hall, 1976).

14Tom Zeller, "The Iraq-Qaeda Link: A Short History," *New York Times,* June 20, 2004, WK4.

15*New York Times*/CBS News poll, August, 2006.

16Andrew Kohut, "Speak Softly and Carry a Smaller Stick," *New York Times,* March 24, 2006. Kohut is a pollster for the Pew Foundation.

17Carl M. Cannon, "Judging Clinton," *National Journal,* January 1, 2000, 21.

18Robert Wright, "Private Eyes," *New York Times Magazine,* September 5, 1999, 50–54; William J. Broad, "North Korea's Nuclear Intentions, Out There for All to See," *New York Times,* October 8, 2006, WK5; and www.
earth.google.com.

19Historian Michael Hogan, quoted in John M. Broder, "Gentler Look at the U.S. World Role," *New York Times,* October 31, 1999, 14.

20Paul Johnson, "The Myth of American Isolationism," *Foreign Affairs,* May-June 1995, 162.

21Bruce Russett, *The Prisoners of Insecurity* (San Francisco: Freeman, 1983).

22Quoted in Robert Dallek, *Lyndon B. Johnson, Portrait of a President* (New York: Oxford University Press, 2004), 179.

23See James Nathan and James Oliver, *United States Foreign Policy and World Order,* 2nd ed. (Boston: Little, Brown, 1981), 359–361.

24For one view of the impact of Vietnam on the thinking of today's high-ranking officers, see H. R. McMaster, *Dereliction of Duty* (New York: HarperCollins, 1997).

[25]Robert S. McNamara, *In Retrospect: The Tragedy and Lessons of Vietnam* (New York: Times Books, 1995).

[26]Michael Beschloss, *Reaching for Glory: Lyndon Johnson's Secret White House Tapes, 1964–1965* (New York: Simon & Schuster, 2001), 166.

[27]Weissberg, *Public Opinion and Popular Government,* 144–148.

[28]Ole Holsti, "The Three-Headed Eagle," *International Studies Quarterly* 23 (1979), 339–359; Michael Mandelbaum and William Schneider, "The New Internationalisms," in *The Eagle Entangled: U.S. Foreign Policy in a Complex World,* eds. Kenneth Oye, Donald Rothchild, and Robert J. Lieber (New York: Longman, 1979), 34–88.

[29]For an analysis of U.S.-Soviet relations in the Reagan era, see Alexander Dallin and Gail Lapidus, "Reagan and the Russians," and Kenneth Oye, "Constrained Confidence and the Evolution of Reagan Foreign Policy," in *Eagle Resurgent?* eds. Kenneth Oye, Robert Lieber, and Donald Rothchild (Boston: Little, Brown, 1987); and John Newhouse, "The Abolitionist" (pts. 1 and 2), *New Yorker,* January 2 and 9, 1989.

[30]See George F. Kennan, "After the Cold War," *New York Times Magazine,* February 5, 1989, 32ff.

[31]Bill Clinton, "A Democrat Lays Out His Plan," *Harvard International Review,* Summer 1992, 26.

[32]For a concise summary of the advantages and disadvantages of protectionism and free trade, see Paul Krugman, *The Age of Diminished Expectations* (Cambridge, Mass.: MIT Press, 1992), 101–113.

[33]Bill Clinton, quoted in Jane Perlez, "At Conference on Trade, Clinton Makes Pitch for Poor," *New York Times,* January 30, 2000, 6.

[34]Thomas Friedman, "What Big Stick? Just Sell," *New York Times,* October 2, 1995, E3.

[35]Elaine Sciolino, "Monroe's Doctrine Takes Another Knock," *New York Times,* August 7, 1994, E6. For a discussion of the U.S. turn to multilateralism, see Stanley Hoffmann, "The Crisis of Liberal Internationalism," *Foreign Policy* 98 (1995, 159–177).

[36]"National Security Strategy of the United States," September 2002. The president's annual report to Congress is posted at www.whitehouse.gov.

[37]"Bush Plans 'Strike First' Military Policy," *Champaign-Urbana News-Gazette,* June 10, 2002, A-3.

[38]Fred Kaplan, "JFK's First-Strike Plan," *Atlantic Monthly,* October 2001, 81–86.

[39]U.S. Department of Defense, *Quadrennial Defense Review Report* (Washington, D.C.: Government Printing Office, 2001), 17. The full report is at the Pentagon's website (www.dod.gov/pubs/qdr2001.pdf).

[40]Leslie Wayne, "America's For-Profit Secret Army," *New York Times,* October 13, 2002, sec. 3, 10.

[41]Material in this section is drawn from Michael R. Gordon, "A Whole New World of Arms Races to Contain," *New York Times,* May 3, 1998, sec. 4, 1; John Kifner and Jo Thomas, "Singular Difficulty in Stopping Terrorism," *New York Times,* January 18, 1998, 16; Keith Easthouse, "The Stewardship Debate," *Champaign- Urbana News-Gazette,* June 14, 1998, B1, B4–B5; and Michael R. Gordon, "Russian Thwarting U.S. Bid to Secure a Nuclear Cache," *New York Times,* January 5, 1997, 1, 4.

[42]"What Does It Take to Make a Bomb?" *Frontline,* PBS, 1998 (www.pbs.org/wgbh/pages/ frontline/shows/nukes/stuff /faqs.html).

[43]Interview for the documentary *Why We Fight,* 2005. (See the For Viewing section.)

[44]Joan Spero, an undersecretary of state, quoted in David E. Sanger, "How Washington Inc. Makes a Sale," *New York Times,* February 19, 1995, sec. 3, 1.

[45]"Diplomacy's New Hit Man: The Free-Market Dollar," *New York Times,* May 24, 1998, sec. 4, 5.

[46]Julie Kosterlitz, "Trade Crusade," *National Journal,* May 9, 1998, 1054–1055.

[47]Estimate by Clyde Prestowitz, former Reagan official and president of the Economic Strategy Institute, cited in Eduardo Porter, "Dubai Deal's Collapse Prompts Fears Abroad on Trade With U.S.," *New York Times,* March 10, 2006.

[48]For a description of WTO structure, membership, and activities, see "WTO: Special Report," *Congressional Quarterly Weekly Report,* November 27, 1999, 2826–2838.

[49]"National Security Strategy of the United States," 18.

527 groups Tax-exempt groups, named after the provision in the tax code, that are organized to provide politically relevant advertising, usually with the aim of helping particular candidates or parties. Technically they are supposed to be independent but in reality are often closely linked to the candidates.

Activist judges Judges who are not reluctant to overrule the other branches of government by declaring laws or actions of government officials unconstitutional.

Administrative Procedure Act (APA) Legislation passed in 1946 that provides for public participation in the rule-making process. All federal agencies must disclose their rule-making procedures and publish all regulations at least thirty days in advance of their effective date to allow time for public comment.

Adversarial relationship A relationship in which the parties are constantly in conflict with each other.

Affirmative action A policy in job hiring or university admissions that gives special consideration to members of historically disadvantaged groups.

Agents of political socialization Sources of information about politics; include parents, peers, schools, the media, political leaders, and the community.

Aid to Families with Dependent Children (AFDC) A program that provides income support for the poor. Replaced by TANF.

American Civil Liberties Union (ACLU) A nonpartisan organization that seeks to protect the civil liberties of all Americans.

Americans with Disabilities Act Passed to protect those with disabilities from discrimination in employment and public accommodations, such as stores, restaurants, hotels, and health care facilities.

Antifederalists Those who opposed the ratification of the U.S. Constitution.

Antitrust law Laws that prohibit **monopolies.**

Appropriations Budget legislation that specifies the amount of authorized funds that will actually be allocated for agencies and departments to spend.

Articles of Confederation The first constitution of the United States; in effect from 1781 to 1789.

Asymmetrical warfare Conflict between combatants of very unequal military strength.

Authorizations Budget legislation that provides agencies and departments with the legal authority to operate; may specify funding levels but do not actually provide the funding (the funding is provided by **appropriations**).

Baker v. *Carr* A 1962 Supreme Court decision giving voters the right to use the courts to rectify the malapportionment of legislative districts.

Battleground states Also known as "swing states." During a presidential election, these are states whose Electoral College votes are not safely in one candidate's pocket; candidates will spend time and more money there to try to win the state.

Bible Belt A term used to describe portions of the South and Midwest that were strongly influenced by Protestant fundamentalists.

Bilingual education Programs where students whose native language is not English receive instruction in substantive subjects such as math in their native language.

Bill of Rights The first 10 amendments to the U.S. Constitution.

Bills of attainder Legislative acts that pronounce specific persons guilty of crimes.

Black Codes Laws passed by Southern states following the **Civil War** that denied most legal rights to the newly freed slaves.

Blockbusting The practice in which realtors would frighten whites in a neighborhood where a black family had moved by telling the whites that their houses would decline in value. The whites in panic would then sell their houses to the realtors at low prices, and the realtors would resell the houses to blacks, thereby resegregating the area from white to black.

Block grants A system of giving federal funds to states and localities under which the federal government designates the purpose for which the funds are to be used but allows the states some discretion in spending.

Blog Common term for independent web log, which is an independent website created by an individual or group to disseminate opinions or information.

Blue states These are the states that voted Democratic in 2000 and 2004 and in general more liberal in outlook. They include New England, Middle Atlantic, Upper Midwest, and Pacific Coast states.

Broadcasting An attempt by a network to appeal to most of the television or radio audience.

Brown v. *Board of Education* The 1954 case in which the U.S. Supreme Court overturned the **separate-but-equal doctrine** and ruled unanimously that segregated schools violated the Fourteenth Amendment.

Budget and Accounting Act of 1921 This act gives the president the power to propose a budget and led to presidential dominance in the budget process. It also created the **Bureau of the Budget,** changed to the **Office of Management and Budget** in 1970.

Budget deficit Occurs when federal spending exceeds federal revenues.

Bureau of the Budget Established in 1921 and later changed to the **Office of Management and Budget,** the BOB was designed as the president's primary means of developing federal budget policy.

Burger Court The U.S. Supreme Court under Chief Justice Warren Burger (1969–1986). Though not as activist as the **Warren Court,** the Burger Court maintained most of the rights expanded by its predecessor and issued important rulings on abortion and sexual discrimination.

Bush v. *Gore* U.S. Supreme Court case in 2000 where the Supreme Court set aside the Florida Supreme Court's order for a manual recount of the presidential votes cast in the state. The Court's decision meant that Bush got Florida's electoral votes, giving him a majority of all electoral votes and, thus, the election.

Cannonism The attributes of a strong Speaker of the House of Representatives, based on the tenure of Joseph Cannon (R—Ill.), speaker from 1903-1911, who controlled the House with the force of his personality and his use of the rules at the time. He blocked legislation he did not like, controlled debate, and punished those who opposed him.

Capitalist economy An economic system in which the means of production are privately owned and prices, wages, working conditions, and profits are determined solely by the market.

Captured agencies Refers to the theory that regulatory agencies often end up working on behalf of the interests they are supposed to regulate.

Casework The assistance members of Congress provide to their constituents; includes answering questions and doing personal favors for those who ask for help. Also called **constituency service.**

Caucus Today, a meeting of local residents who select delegates to attend county, state, and national conventions where the delegates nominate candidates for public office. Originally, caucuses were limited to party leaders and officeholders who selected the candidates.

Central Intelligence Agency (CIA) Created after World War II, the CIA is a federal agency charged with coordinating overseas intelligence activities gathering and analysis.

Checkbook members People who "join" an interest group only in the sense that they donate money to the group.

Checks and balances The principle of government that holds that the powers of the various branches should overlap to avoid power becoming overly concentrated in one branch.

Chief executive Another title of the president of the United States. This phrase also refers specifically to the president's responsibilities in running the executive branch.

Christian right A collective term referring to the conservative Christian organizations and churches active in American politics.

Civil case A case in which individuals sue others for denying their rights and causing them harm.

Civil disobedience Peaceful but illegal protest activity in which those involved allow themselves to be arrested and charged.

Civil liberties The individual rights in the Constitution, most of which are in the Bill of Rights.

Civil rights The principle of equal rights for persons regardless of their race, sex, or ethnic background.

Civil Rights Act of 1964 Major civil rights legislation that prohibits discrimination on the basis of race, color, religion, or national origin in public accommodations.

Civil Rights Act of 1968 Civil rights legislation that prohibits discrimination in the sale or rental of housing on the basis of race, color, religion, or national origin; also prohibits **blockbusting, steering,** and **redlining.**

Civil Service Commission An agency established by the **Pendleton Act of 1883** to curb **patronage** in the federal bureaucracy and replace it with a merit system.

Civil War The war between the Union and the Confederacy (1861–1865), fought mainly over the question of whether the national or state governments were to exercise ultimate political power. Secession and slavery were the issues that precipitated this great conflict.

Classical democracy A system of government that emphasizes citizen participation through debating, voting, and holding office.

Closed primary A primary election where participation is limited to those who are registered with a party or declare a preference for a party.

Cloture A method of stopping a **filibuster** by limiting debate to only 20 more hours; requires a vote of three-fifths of the members of the Senate.

Coalition A network of **interest groups** with similar concerns that combine forces to pursue a common goal; may be short-lived or permanent.

Coalition building The union of **pressure groups** that share similar concerns.

Cold War The era of hostility between the United States and the Soviet Union that existed between the end of World War II and the collapse of the Soviet Union.

Commander in Chief The president's constitutional role as head of the armed forces with power to direct their use

Commercial bias A slant in news coverage to please or avoid offending advertisers.

Committee of the Whole Refers to the informal entity the House of Representatives makes itself into to debate a bill.

Commodity interest groups Associations that represent producers of specific products, such as cattle, tobacco, or milk producers.

Comparable worth The principle that comparable jobs should pay comparable wages.

Concurring opinion The opinion by one or more judges in a court case who agree with the decision but not with the reasons given by the majority for it. The concurring opinion offers an alternate legal argument for the ruling.

Confederal governments A system in which the central government has only the powers given to it by the subnational governments.

Conference committee A committee composed of members of both houses of Congress that is formed to try to resolve the differences when the two houses pass different versions of the same bill.

Conflict of interest The situation when government officials make decisions that directly affect their own personal livelihoods or interests.

Conscientious objectors Persons who oppose all wars and refuse military service on the basis of religious or moral principles.

Conservative A person who believes that the domestic role of government should be minimized and that individuals are responsible for their own well-being.

Constituency Both the geographic area and the people a member of Congress represents. For a senator, the state and all its residents; for a member of the House, a congressional district and all its residents.

Constituency service The assistance members of Congress provide to residents in their districts (states, if senators); includes answering questions and doing personal favors for those who ask for help. Also called **casework.**

Constitution The body of basic rules and principles that establish the functions, limits, and nature of a government.

Constitutional Convention The gathering in Philadelphia in 1787 that wrote the U.S. Constitution; met initially to revise the **Articles of Confederation** but produced a new national **constitution** instead.

Containment A policy formulated by the Truman administration to limit the spread of communism by meeting any action taken by the Soviet Union with a countermove; led U.S. decision makers to see most conflicts in terms of U.S.- Soviet rivalry.

Contribution limits Ceilings set on the overall amount of money that individuals and groups give to candidates.

Cooperative federalism The day-to-day cooperation among federal, state, and local officials in carrying out the business of government.

Cooperative internationalism The belief that problems of global poverty, inequitable distribution of wealth, abuse of human rights, and regional competitiveness are substantial threats to world order, and that the United States should work with other nations to solve these problems.

Corporate welfare Tax breaks or financial subsidies given by government to corporations.

Court-packing plan President Franklin D. Roosevelt's attempt to expand the size of the U.S. Supreme Court in an effort to obtain a Court more likely to uphold his New Deal legislation.

Courts of appeals Intermediate courts between trial courts (**district courts** in the federal system) and the supreme court (the U.S. Supreme Court in the federal system).

Cracking, stacking, and packing Methods of drawing district boundaries that minimize black representation. With cracking, a large concentrated black population is divided among two or more districts so that blacks will not have a majority anywhere; with stacking, a large black population is combined with an even larger white population; with packing, a large black population is put into one district rather than two so that blacks will have a majority in only one district.

Crafted talk Politicians use the words and phrases that public opinion research has found to be the most effective in persuading people to support particular policies.

Criminal case A case in which a government (national or state) prosecutes a person for violating its laws.

Cruel and unusual punishment Torture or any punishment that is grossly disproportionate to the offense; prohibited by the Eighth Amendment.

Dealignment Term used to refer to the diminished relevance of political parties.

Declaration of Independence The document proclaiming the American colonies' determination to break with England and become a separate country.

De facto segregation Segregation that is based on residential patterns and is not imposed by law; because it cannot be eliminated by striking down a law, it is more intractable than **de jure segregation.**

Deficit A budgetary condition in which government expenditures exceed revenues.

De jure segregation Segregation imposed by law; outlawed by **Brown v. Board of Education** and subsequent court cases.

Delegated legislative authority The power to draft, as well as execute, specific policies; granted by Congress to executive branch agencies when a problem requires technical expertise.

Democratic Party One of two major American political parties, founded in the 1820s and 1830s to emphasize the "common man."

Democracy A system of government in which sovereignty resides in the people.

Depression A period of prolonged high unemployment.

Deregulation Ending **regulation** in a particular area.

Detente A policy designed to deescalate **Cold War** rhetoric and promote the notion that relations with the Soviet Union could be conducted in ways other than confrontation; developed by President Richard M. Nixon and Secretary of State Henry Kissinger.

Direct democracy A system of government in which citizens govern themselves directly and vote on most issues; e.g., a New England town meeting.

Direct lobbying Direct personal encounters between lobbyists and the public officials they are attempting to influence.

Direct primary An election in which voters select a party's candidates for office.

Discretionary spending Spending levels set by the federal government in annual **appropriations** bills passed by Congress; includes government operating expenses and salaries of many federal employees.

Dissenting opinion The opinion by one or more judges in a court case who do not agree with the decision of the majority. The dissenting opinion urges a different outcome.

District courts The trial courts (lower-level courts) in the federal system.

Divided government The situation when one political party controls the presidency and the other party controls one or both houses of Congress.

Dixiecrat A member of a group of southern segregationist Democrats who formed the States' Rights Party in 1948.

DNA testing Testing that can determine a person's genetic make-up. By analyzing evidence left on a crime victim, it is also used to identify the criminal or rule out a suspect.

Domino theory The idea that if one country fell under communist rule, its neighbors would also fall to communism; contributed to the U.S. decision to intervene in Vietnam.

Dred Scott case An 1857 case in which the U.S. Supreme Court held that blacks, whether slave or free, were not citizens and that Congress had no power to restrict slavery in the territories; contributed to the polarization between North and South and ultimately to the **Civil War.**

Due process The 14th Amendment guarantee that the government will follow fair and just procedures when prosecuting a criminal defendant.

Earmark A specific amount of money designated—or set aside—at the request of a member of Congress, for a favored project, usually in his or her district. The dollar amount may be included in one of the budget authorization bills, but more commonly is in the committee report attached to the bill that instructs the relevant executive branch agency how to spend the money authorized for its operations.

Earned income tax credit (EITC) A negative income tax. On filing income tax reports, persons with low incomes receive a payment from the government or a credit toward their taxes owed.

Electoral College A group of electors selected by the voters in each state and the District of Columbia; the electors officially elect the president and vice president.

Emancipation Proclamation Abraham Lincoln's 1863 proclamation that the slaves "shall be . . . forever free." At the time, applied only in the Confederate states, so had little practical impact, because the Union did not control them. However, it had an immense political impact, making clear that the Civil War was not just to preserve the Union but to abolish slavery.

Enumerated powers Explicit grants of authority to Congress in the Constitution.

Environmental Protection Agency (EPA) The regulatory agency with responsibility for pollution control; created in 1970 by President Richard M. Nixon.

Equal Employment Opportunity Commission (EEOC) The EEOC enforces the **Civil Rights Act of 1964,** which forbids discrimination on the basis of sex or race in hiring, promotion, and firing.

Equal Pay Act A statute enacted by Congress in 1963 that mandates that women and men should receive equal pay for equal work.

Equal protection clause The Fourteenth Amendment clause that is the Constitution's primary guarantee that everyone is equal before the law.

Equal Rights Amendment (ERA) A proposed amendment to the Constitution that would prohibit government from denying equal rights on the basis of sex; passed by Congress in 1972 but failed to be ratified by a sufficient number of states.

Establishment clause The First Amendment clause that prohibits the establishment of a state religion.

European Union (EU) A union of European nations formed in 1957 to foster political and economic integration in Europe; formerly called the European Economic Community or Common Market.

Exclusionary rule A rule that prevents evidence obtained in violation of the Fourth Amendment from being used in court against the defendant.

Executive leadership The president's control over the bureaucracy in his capacity as chief executive; achieved through budgeting, appointments, administrative reform, lobbying, and mobilizing public opinion.

Executive Office of the President The president's personal bureaucracy, which monitors the cabinet departments. The EOP includes the White House staff and the Office of Management and the Budget.

Executive orders Rules or regulations issued by the president that have the force of law; issued to implement constitutional provisions or statutes.

Executive privilege The authority of the president to withhold specific types of information from the courts and Congress.

Exit polls Election-day poll of voters leaving the polling places, conducted mainly by television networks and major newspapers.

Experimental laboratories Because of federalism, each state in the United States retains enough authority to adopt many public policies on its own. If these policies succeed, they may be copied by other states or by the federal government. Thus, the states serve as experimental laboratories for these policies.

Ex post facto **law** A statute that makes some behavior illegal that was not illegal when it was done.

Externality A cost or benefit of production that is not reflected in the product's market price. **Regulation** attempts to eliminate negative externalities.

Faithless elector A member of the **Electoral College** who votes on the basis of personal preference rather than the way the majority of voters in his or her state voted.

Farm subsidies Government payments to farmers for withholding land from production or to guarantee set prices for certain crops.

Federal Communication Commission (FCC) A regulatory agency that controls interstate and foreign communication via radio, television, telegraph, telephone, and cable. The FCC licenses radio and television stations.

Federal Election Campaign Act A 1974 statute that regulates campaign finance; provided for public financing of presidential campaigns, limited contributions to campaigns for federal offices, and established the **Federal Election Commission,** among other things.

Federal Election Commission Created in 1975, the commission enforces federal laws on campaign financing.

Federalism A system in which power is constitutionally divided between a central government and subnational or local governments.

Federalist Papers A series of essays in support of ratification of the U.S. Constitution; written for New York newspapers by Alexander Hamilton, James Madison, and John Jay during the debate over ratification.

Federalists Originally, those who supported the U.S. Constitution and favored its ratification; in the early years of the Republic, those who advocated a strong national government.

Federal Register A government publication that provides official notification of executive orders, agency rulings and federal statutes.

Federal Reserve Board Created by Congress in 1913, the board regulates the lending practices of banks and plays a major role in determining **monetary policy.**

Felonies Crimes considered more serious than **misdemeanors** and carrying more stringent punishment.

Fifteenth Amendment An amendment to the Constitution, ratified in 1870, that prohibits denying voting rights on the basis of race, color, or previous condition of servitude.

Filibuster A mechanism for delay in the Senate in which one or more members engage in a continuous speech to prevent the Senate from voting on a bill.

Fireside chats Short radio addresses given by President Franklin D. Roosevelt to win support for his policies and reassure the public during the Great Depression.

First Amendment The first amendment to the United States Constitution, guaranteeing freedom of expression, which includes freedom of speech, religion, assembly, association, and freedom of the press.

Fiscal policy Government's actions to regulate the economy through taxing and spending policies.

Flat tax A tax structured so that all income groups pay the same rate.

Focus groups A group of a dozen or so average men and women brought together by political consultants and pollsters to share their feelings and reactions to different things in an effort to develop a campaign strategy that will attract voters to or away from a particular candidate.

FOIA The Freedom of Information Act, passed in 1966 and amended in 1974, lets any member of the public apply to an agency for access to unclassified documents in its archives.

Food stamp program A poverty program that gives poor people electronic credits redeemable in grocery stores for food.

Foreign Intelligence Surveillance Court Created by the Foreign Intelligence Surveillance Act of 1978, this secretive court hears requests from the U.S. government to conduct electronic surveillance, or physical searches of the home and computer, of suspected spies or terrorists.

Freedom of association Guarantees the right of an individual to join with others to speak, assemble, and petition the government for a redress of grievances. This right allows a minority to pursue interests without being prevented from doing so by the majority.

Freedom of speech The First Amendment guarantee of a right of free expression.

Freedom of the press Freedom from censorship, so the press can disseminate the news, information, and opinion that it deems appropriate.

Free exercise clause The First Amendment clause that guarantees individuals the right to practice their religion without government intervention.

Free rider problem Interest groups realize that many people may benefit if the groups achieve their goals but most of these people—the "free riders"—won't join the groups or otherwise help the groups accomplish the goals. Interest groups try various means to lure these people into their groups.

Free trade A policy of minimum intervention by government in trade relations.

Friend of the court briefs Legal arguments filed in court cases by individuals or groups who aren't litigants in the cases. These briefs often provide new information to the court and usually urge the judges to rule one way.

Full faith and credit A clause in the U.S. Constitution that requires the states to recognize contracts that are valid in other states.

Gaining access Getting the opportunity to talk to the government officials who determine the policy that a group or organization wants to shape or benefit from.

Game orientation The assumption in political reporting that politics is a game and that politicians are the players; leads to an emphasis on strategy at the expense of substance in news stories.

Gender gap An observable pattern of modest but consistent differences in opinion between men and women on various public policy issues.

Gerrymander A congressional district whose boundaries are drawn so as to maximize the political advantage of a party or racial group; often such a district has a bizarre shape.

Gettysburg Address Famous 1863 speech by President Lincoln to dedicate the battlefield where many had fallen during the Civil War. Lincoln used the occasion to advance his ideal of equality and to promote the Union.

Globalization The international dispersion of economic activity through the networking of companies across national borders.

Going public The process in which Congress or its members carry an issue debate to the public via the media; e.g., televising floor debates or media appearances by individual members.

GOP Grand Old Party or **Republican Party**, which formed in 1856 after the Whig Party split. The GOP was abolitionist and a supporter of the Union.

Government contracts Agreements in which the government pays private businesses to supply products or services to the government.

Grandfather clause A device used in the South to prevent blacks from voting; such clauses exempted those whose grandfathers had the right to vote before 1867 from having to fulfill various requirements that some people could not meet. Since no blacks could vote before 1867, they could not qualify for the exemption.

Grand jury A jury of citizens who meet in private session to evaluate accusations in a given **criminal case** and to determine if there is enough evidence to warrant a trial.

Grants-in-aid Federal money provided to state and, occasionally, local governments for community development and to establish programs to help people such as the aged poor or the unemployed; began during the New Deal.

Grassroots lobbying The mass mobilization of members of an **interest group** to apply pressure to public officials, usually in the form of a mass mailing.

Great Compromise The decision of the **Constitutional Convention** to have a bicameral legislature in which representation in one house would be by population and in the other house, by states; also called the Connecticut Compromise.

Great migration The movement of southern blacks to the North in the search of better jobs between 1915 and 1940.

Habeas corpus Latin for "have ye the body." A writ of *habeas corpus* is a means for criminal defendants who have exhausted appeals in state courts to appeal to a federal **district court.**

Hatch Act A statute enacted in 1939 that limits the political activities of federal employees in partisan campaigns.

Hate speech Racial, ethnic, sexual, or religious slurs which demean people for characteristics that are innate or beliefs that are deeply held.

Head of government The president's partisan, policy-making role as head of the executive branch and as head of his party in government, in contrast to his nonpartisan duties as head of state and representative of the country.

Head of state The president's role as a symbolic leader of the nation and representative of all the people.

High crimes and misdemeanors The standard for impeachment of presidents, federal judges, and other officials stipulated in the Constitution. Borrowed from England, this phrase means serious crimes or the abuse of political power. It does not mean misdemeanors as this word is used in modern criminal law.

Horse race coverage The way in which the media reports on the candidates' polling status and strategies, rather than covering their positions on relevant issues.

House of Representatives The chamber of Congress in which people are represented on the basis of population, with voters electing representatives from districts of equal size.

Hyperpluralism The idea that it is difficult for government to arrive at a solution to problems because **interest groups** have become so numerous and so many groups have a "veto" on issues affecting them.

Identity politics The practice of organizing on the basis of sex, ethnic or racial identity, or sexual orientation to compete for public resources and influence public policy.

Ideology A highly organized and coherent set of opinions.

Impeachment The process provided for in the Constitution by which the House of Representatives can indict (impeach) a president for "Treason, Bribery, or other High Crimes and Misdemeanors." If the House votes to lodge formal charges against the president he is impeached. But a president cannot be removed from office unless two-thirds of the Senate finds him guilty of the charges.

Imperial presidency A term that came into use at the end of the 1960s to describe the growing power of the presidency.

Implied powers clause The clause in the U.S. Constitution that gives Congress the power to make all laws "**necessary and proper"** for carrying out its specific powers.

Impossible presidency A phrase that captures the frustration that presidents, or observers of presidents, feel when presidential efforts are stymied by others in the political process. The phrase is used especially during periods when presidential power seems at a low ebb.

Independent A voter who is not aligned with any political party.

Independent agencies Government bureaus that are not parts of **departments.** Their heads are appointed by and responsible to the president.

Independent spending Spending on political campaigns by groups not under the control of the candidates.

Indirect democracy A system of government in which citizens elect representatives to make decisions for them.

Indirect lobbying Attempts to influence legislators by persuading citizens who then persuade legislators.

Individualistic political culture One in which politics is seen as a way of getting ahead, of obtaining benefits for oneself or one's group, and in which corruption is tolerated. See also **moralistic** and **traditionalistic political cultures.**

Individual liberty A synonym for freedom. In our system, individuals are free to do what they want within broad limits set by the government.

Inflation The situation in which prices increase but wages and salaries fail to keep pace with the prices of goods.

Informal norms Unwritten rules designed to help keep Congress running smoothly by attempting to diminish friction and competition among the members.

Infotainment A word for television newscasts that attempt to entertain as they provide information.

Initiative A process in which citizens or interest groups circulate petitions calling for a new state law. If they gather enough signatures, the proposal will be put on the ballot for citizens to vote for or against in the next election.

Institutional loyalty An **informal norm** of Congress that calls for members to avoid criticizing their colleagues and to treat each other with mutual respect; this norm has eroded in recent decades.

Interest groups Organizations that try to achieve at least some of their goals with government assistance.

Isolationism A policy of noninvolvement with other nations outside the Americas; generally followed by the United States during the nineteenth and early twentieth centuries.

Issue voting Refers to citizens who vote for candidates whose stands on specific issues are consistent with their own.

Jacksonian democracy An era during the 1820s and 1830s emphasizing the "common man" rather than the elites and extending the right to vote to more people, including those who did not own property, and for more officials.

Jeffersonian Republicans (Jeffersonians) Opponents of a strong national government. They challenged the **Federalists** in the early years of the Republic.

Jim Crow laws Laws enacted in southern states that segregated schools, public accommodations, and almost all other aspects of life.

Joint resolutions Measures approved by both houses of Congress and signed by the president that have the force of law.

Judicial review The authority of the courts to declare laws or actions of government officials unconstitutional.

Jurisdiction The authority of a court to hear and decide cases.

Justices of the peace Magistrates at the lowest level of some state court systems, responsible mainly for acting on minor offenses and committing cases to higher courts for trial.

Keynesian economics The argument by John Maynard Keynes that government should stimulate the economy during periods of high unemployment by increasing spending even if it must run **deficits** to do so.

Ku Klux Klan A white supremacist organization, which originally began during **Reconstruction** and then started up again in 1915. The KKK inflamed prejudice and instigated violence against African Americans, and it became a force in some state governments during the first half of the twentieth century.

Labor unions Workers' organizations that represent the workers in negotiations with their employers.

Leaks Disclosures of information that some government officials want kept secret.

Legislative calendar An agenda or calendar containing the names of all bills or resolutions of a particular type to be considered by committees or either legislative chamber.

Libel Printed or broadcast statements that are false and that tarnish someone's reputation.

Liberal A person who believes in government activism to help individuals and communities in such areas as health, education, and welfare.

Limited government A government that is strong enough to protect the people's rights but not so strong as to threaten those rights; in the view of John Locke, such a government was established through a **social contract.**

Literacy tests Examinations ostensibly carried out to ensure that voters could read and write but actually a device used in the South to disqualify blacks from voting.

Living wage A wage that is high enough to allow full-time workers' to meet the basic cost of living, something the minimum wage does not do.

Lobbyist A representative of a group or organization who tries to persuade government officials to do what the group or organization wants them to do.

Lobbying The efforts of **interest groups** to influence government.

Majority leader The title of both the leader of the Senate, who is chosen by the majority party and the head of the majority party in the House of Representatives who is second in command to the **Speaker.**

Majority-minority district A congressional district whose boundaries are drawn to give a minority group a majority in the district.

Majority opinion The joint opinion by a majority of the judges in a federal court case which explains why the judges ruled as they did.

Majority rule A decision rule in which the preference of the majority takes precedence over the wishes of the minority.

Mandate A term used in the media to refer to a president having clear directions from the voters to take a certain course of action; in practice, it is not always clear that a president, even one elected by a large majority, has a mandate or, if so, for what.

Marble cake federalism The idea that different levels of government work together in carrying out policies; governments are intermixed, as in a marble cake.

Marbury v. Madison The 1803 case in which the U.S. Supreme Court enunciated the doctrine of **judicial review.**

Markup The process in which a congressional subcommittee rewrites a bill after holding hearings on it.

McCarthyism Methods of combating communism characterized by irresponsible accusations made on the basis of little or no evidence; named after Senator Joseph McCarthy of Wisconsin who used such tactics in the 1950s.

McCulloch v. Maryland An 1819 U.S. Supreme Court decision that broadly interpreted Congress's powers under the **implied powers clause.**

Means test An eligibility requirement for poverty programs under which participants must demonstrate that they have low income and few assets.

Media event An event, usually consisting of a speech and a photo opportunity, that is staged for television and is intended to convey a particular impression of a politician's position on an issue.

Media malaise A feeling of cynicism and distrust toward government and officials that is fostered by media coverage of politics.

Medicaid A federal-state medical assistance program for the poor.

Medicare A public health insurance program that pays many medical expenses of the elderly and the disabled; funded through **Social Security** taxes, general revenues, and premiums paid by recipients.

Merit system A system of filling bureaucratic jobs on the basis of competence instead of **patronage.**

Minority leader The leader of the minority party in either the House of Representatives or the Senate.

Minority rights Rights that a minority, whether a racial, religious, or political minority, has despite the predominance of majority rule.

Miranda rights A means of protecting a criminal suspect's **rights against self-incrimination** during police interrogation. Before interrogation, suspects must be told that they have a right to remain silent; that anything they say can be used against them; that they have a right to an attorney; and that if they cannot afford an attorney, one will be provided for them. The rights are named after the case *Miranda v. Arizona.*

"Mischiefs of faction" A phrase used by James Madison in the *Federalist Papers* to refer to the threat to the nation's stability that self-interested groups could pose.

Misdemeanors Crimes of less seriousness than **felonies,** ordinarily punishable by fine or imprisonment in a local rather than a state institution.

Mixed economies Countries that incorporate elements of both capitalist and socialist practices in the workings of their economies.

Moderates Also referred to as "middle of the roaders," these are persons with centrist positions on issues that distinguish them from **liberals** and **conservatives.**

Monetary policy Actions taken by the **Federal Reserve Board** to regulate the economy through changes in short-term interest rates and the money supply.

Monopoly One or a few firms that control a large share of the market for certain goods and can therefore fix prices.

Monroe Doctrine A doctrine articulated by President James Monroe in 1823 that warned European powers not already involved in Latin America to stay out of that region.

Moralistic political culture One in which people feel obligated to take part in politics to bring about change for the better, and in which corruption is not tolerated. See also **individualistic** and **traditionalistic political cultures.**

Motor voter law A statute that allows people to register to vote at public offices such as welfare offices and drivers' license bureaus.

Multiparty system A type of political party system where more than two groups have a chance at winning an election.

Mutual assured destruction (MAD) The capability to absorb a nuclear attack and retaliate against the attacker with such force that it would also suffer enormous damage; believed to deter nuclear war during the **Cold War** because both sides would be so devastated that neither would risk striking first.

NAACP (National Association for the Advancement of Colored People) An organization founded in 1909 to fight for black rights; its attorneys challenged segregation in the courts and won many important court cases, most notably, *Brown v. Board of Education.*

Nader's Raiders The name given to people who work in any of the "public interest" organizations founded by consumer advocate and regulatory watchdog Ralph Nader.

Narrowcasting An attempt by a network to appeal to a small segment of the television or radio audience rather than to most of the audience.

Nation-centered federalism The view that the Constitution was written by representatives of the people and and ratified by the people. Nation-centered federalists believe that the national government is the supreme power in the federal relationship. (Hamilton articulated this view in the *Federalist Papers*.) Nation-centered federalism was the view used by northerners to justify a war to prevent the southern states from seceding in 1861. The alternative view, state-centered federalism, holds that the Constitution is a creation of the states.

National party chair The head of a political **party organization,** appointed by the **national committee** of that party, usually at the direction of the party's presidential nominee.

National committee The highest level of **party organization;** chooses the site of the national convention and the formula for determining the number of delegates from each state.

National debt The total amount of money owed by the federal government; the sum of all budget **deficits** over the years.

National Organization for Women (NOW) A group formed in 1966 to fight primarily for political and economic rights for women.

National Security Agency (NSA) The U.S. government's largest intelligence service, which uses electronic surveillance to obtain the communications of possible adversaries.

NATO (North Atlantic Treaty Organization) A mutual defense pact established by the United States, Canada, and their western European allies in 1949 to protect against Soviet aggression in Europe; later expanded to include other European nations.

Natural rights Inalienable and inherent rights such as the right to own property (in the view of John Locke).

"Necessary and proper" A phrase in the **implied powers clause** of the U.S. Constitution that gives Congress the power to make all laws needed to carry out its specific powers.

Neutral competence The concept that bureaucrats should make decisions in a politically neutral manner in policymaking and should be chosen only for their expertise—not their political affiliation.

New Deal A program of President Franklin D. Roosevelt's administration in the 1930s aimed at stimulating economic recovery and aiding victims of the Great Depression; led to expansion of the national government's role.

New Deal coalition The broadly based coalition of southern conservatives, northern liberals, and ethnic and religious minorities that sustained the Democratic Party for some 40 years.

New Paradigm The reinterpretation of the president's constitutional powers by the George W. Bush administration based on the president's authority as commander-in-chief. According to this reinterpretation, the president can take any action he deems necessary for national security without any involvement, oversight, or restriction by Congress or the courts.

News release A printed handout given by public relations workers to members of the media, offering ideas or information for new stories.

Nineteenth Amendment An amendment to the Constitution, ratified in 1920, guaranteeing women the vote.

Obscenity Sexual material that is patently offensive to the average person in the community and that lacks any serious literary, artistic, or scientific value.

Obstruction of justice A deliberate attempt to impede the progress of a criminal investigation or trial.

Occupational Safety and Health Administration (OSHA) An agency formed in 1970 and charged with ensuring safe and healthful working conditions for all American workers.

Office of Management and Budget (OMB) A White House agency with primary responsibility for preparing the federal budget.

Open primary A primary election that is not limited to members of a particular party; a voter may vote in either party's primary.

Outsourcing (offshoring) Companies' transfer of jobs abroad in order to increase their profit (because they pay foreign workers less).

Oversight Congress's responsibility to make sure the bureaucracy is administering federal programs in accordance with congressional intent.

Pardon power The president's authority to erase the guilt or commute the sentence of persons convicted in federal court. The power can also be used before prosecution and conviction, as President Ford pardoned former President Nixon.

Parliamentary government A system in which voters elect only their representatives in parliament; the chief executive is chosen by parliament, as in Britain.

Partisan Pertaining to a particular political party. For example, a "partisan attack" or an official who acts as a "partisan."

Party boss The head of a **political "machine,"** a highly disciplined state or local **party organization** that controls power in its area.

Party caucus Meetings of members of political parties, often designed to select party nominees for office, or of all members of a party in the House or Senate to set policy and select their leaders.

Party convention A gathering of party delegates, on the local, state, or national level, to set policy and strategy and to select candidates for elective office.

Party identification A psychological link between individuals and a political party that leads those persons to regard themselves as members of that party.

Party in government Those who are appointed or elected to office as members of a political party.

Party in the electorate Those who identify with a political party.

Party organization The "professionals" who run a political party at the national, state, and local levels.

Party system The configuration of parties in a political system. Usually noted in conjunction with the number of parties in the system—one party system, two party system, or multiparty system.

Patronage A system in which elected officials appoint their supporters to administrative jobs; used by **political machines** to maintain themselves in power.

Paygo ("pay-as-you-go") Budgetary rules adopted by Congress that set caps on spending and bars legislation to increase spending without offsetting cuts in spending or increases in revenue.

Pendleton Act of 1883 This act created the **Civil Service Commission,** designed to protect civil servants from arbitrary dismissal for political reasons and to staff bureaucracies with people who have proven their competence by taking competitive examinations.

Pentagon Papers A top-secret study, eventually made public, of how and why the United States became embroiled in the Vietnam War; the study was commissioned by Secretary of Defense Robert McNamara during the Johnson administration.

Permanent campaign The situation in which elected officials are constantly engaged in a campaign; fund-raising for the next election begins as soon as one election is concluded.

Personal presidency A concept proposed by Theodore Lowi that holds that presidents since the 1930s have amassed tremendous personal power directly from the people and, in return, are expected to make sure the people get what they want from government.

Photo op A "photo opportunity" that frames the politician against a backdrop that symbolizes the points the politician is trying to make.

Platform committee The group that drafts the policy statement of a political party's convention.

Plea bargain An agreement between the prosecutor, defense attorney, and defendant in which the prosecutor agrees to reduce the charge or sentence in exchange for the defendant's guilty plea.

Plessy v. *Ferguson* The 1896 case in which the U.S. Supreme Court upheld segregation by enunciating the **separate-but-equal doctrine.**

Pluralism The theory that American government is responsive to groups of citizens working together to promote their common interests and that enough people belong to **interest groups** to ensure that government ultimately hears everyone, even though most people do not participate actively in politics.

Pocket veto A legislative bill dies by pocket veto if a president refuses to sign it and Congress adjourns within 10 working days.

Policy implementation The process by which bureaucrats convert laws into rules and activities that have an actual impact on people and things.

Political action committee (PAC) A committee established by corporation, labor union, or **interest group** that raises money and contributes it to a political campaign.

Political bias A preference for candidates of particular parties or for certain stands on issues that affects a journalist's reporting.

Political culture A shared body of values and beliefs that shapes perceptions and attitudes toward politics and government and, in turn, influences political behavior.

Political efficacy A person's feeling that he or she can make a difference in politics.

Political equality The principle that every citizen of a democracy has an equal opportunity to try to influence government.

Political machines Political organizations based on **patronage** that flourished in big cities in the late nineteenth and early twentieth centuries. The machine relied on the votes of the lower classes and, in exchange, provided jobs and other services.

Political patronage Party leaders who, once in office, openly award government jobs and other benefits to their supporters.

Political socialization The process of learning about politics by being exposed to information from parents, peers, schools, the media, political leaders, and the community.

Political trust The extent to which citizens place trust in their government, its institutions, and its officials.

Politics A means by which individuals and **interest groups** compete, via political parties and other extragovernmental organizations, to shape government's impact on society's problems and goals.

Poll tax A tax that must be paid before a person can vote; used in the South to prevent blacks from voting. The Twenty-fourth Amendment prohibits poll taxes in federal elections.

Popular sovereignty Rule by the people.

Pork barrel Funding for special projects, buildings, and other public works in the district or state of a member of Congress. Members support such projects because they provide jobs for constituents and enhance the members' reelection chances, rather than because the projects are necessarily wise.

Power to persuade The president's informal power to gain support by dispensing favors and penalties and by using the prestige of the office.

Practice of objectivity The attempt by mainstream media to be as neutral as possible in their news stories. They quote each side in a controversy and refrain from evaluating the accuracy of either side's statements.

Precedents In law, judicial decisions that may be used subsequently as standards in similar cases.

Precinct The basic unit of the American electoral process—in a large city perhaps only a few blocks— designed for the administration of elections. Citizens vote in precinct polling places.

Preemption Military strategy of "striking first." Endorsed by the Bush national security team after the September 11, 2001, terrorist attacks.

Pregnancy Discrimination Act A congressional act from 1978 that forbids firing or demoting employees for becoming pregnant.

Presidential preference primary A **direct primary** where voters select delegates to presidential nominating conventions; voters indicate a preference for a presidential candidate, delegates committed to a candidate, or both.

Presidential press conference A meeting at which the president answers questions from reporters.

Pressure group An organization representing specific interests that seeks some sort of government assistance or attempts to influence public policy. Also known as an **interest group.**

Presumption of innocence A fundamental principle of the U.S. criminal justice system in which the government is required to prove the defendant's guilt. The defendant is not required to establish his innocence.

Pretrial hearings Preliminary examinations of the cases of persons accused of a crime.

Primary elections Before the general election, each party holds primary elections in which the party chooses its nominees for the general election.

Prior restraint Censorship by restraining an action before it has actually occurred; e.g., forbidding publication rather than punishing the publisher after publication has occurred.

Private interest groups Interest groups that chiefly pursue economic interests that benefit their members; e.g., business organizations and labor unions.

Probable cause In law, reasonable grounds for belief that a particular person has committed a particular crime.

Productivity The ratio of total hours worked by the labor force to total goods and services produced.

Professional association A **pressure group** that promotes the interests of a professional occupation, such as medicine, law, or teaching.

Progressive Movement Reform movement designed to wrest control from political machines and the lower-class immigrants they served. These reforms reduced corruption in politics, but they also seriously weakened the power of political parties.

Progressive reforms Election reforms introduced in the early twentieth century as part of the Progressive movement; included the **secret ballot**, **primary elections**, and **voter registration laws**.

Progressive tax A tax structured so that those with higher incomes pay a higher percentage of their income in taxes than do those with lower incomes.

Prohibition Party A political party founded in 1869 that sought to ban the sale of liquor in the United States.

Pro-life groups Organizations that oppose abortions and abortion rights.

Proportional representation An election system based on election from multimember districts. The number of seats awarded to each party in each district is equal to the percentage of the total the party receives in the district. Proportional representation favors the **multiparty system**.

Protectionism Government intervention to protect domestic producers from foreign competition; can take the form of **tariffs**, quotas on imports, or a ban on certain imports altogether.

Public disclosure The requirement that names of campaign donors be made public.

Public forum A public place such as a street, sidewalk, or park where people have a **First Amendment** right to express their views on public issues.

Public interest A term generally denoting a policy goal, designed to serve the interests of society as a whole, or the largest number of people. Defining the public interest is the subject of intense debate on most issues.

Public interest groups Interest groups that chiefly pursue benefits that cannot be limited or restricted to their members.

Public opinion The collection of individual opinions toward issues or objects of general interest.

Push poll A public opinion poll presenting the respondent with biased information favoring or opposing a particular candidate. The idea is to see whether certain "information" can "push" voters away from a candidate or a neutral opinion toward the candidate favored by those doing the poll. Push polls seek to manipulate opinion.

Quorum calls A roll call of members of a legislative body to determine if enough members are present to conduct business; often used as a delaying tactic.

Racial profiling Practice that targets a particular group for attention from law enforcement based on racial stereotypes, A common occurrence is black drivers being stopped by police disproportionately.

Rally 'round the flag effect When the president takes dramatic action involving foreign policy, the president's standing in the polls increases, usually significantly, as Americans express support for the president as the leader of the nation.

Realignment The transition from one stable party system to another, as occurred when the **New Deal coalition** was formed.

Reapportionment The process of redistributing the 435 seats in the House of Representatives among the states based on population changes; occurs every 10 years based on the most recent census.

Recall elections States allow people, by gathering enough signatures on petitions, to request an election in which they vote whether to replace or retain a state or local official.

Recession Two or more consecutive three-month quarters of falling production.

Reciprocity An **informal norm** of Congress in which members agree to support each other's bills; also called logrolling.

Reconstruction The period after the **Civil War** when black rights were ensured by a northern military presence in the South and by close monitoring of southern politics; ended in 1877.

Reconstruction Amendments Three amendments (13th, 14th, and 15th), adopted after the Civil War from 1865 through 1870, that eliminated slavery (13), gave blacks the right to vote (15), and guaranteed due process rights for all (14).

Redistricting The process of redrawing the boundaries of congressional districts within a state after a census to take account of population shifts.

Redlining The practice in which bankers and other lenders refused to lend money to persons who wanted to buy a house in a racially changing neighborhood.

"Red Scare" Prompted by the Russian Revolution in 1917, this was a large-scale crackdown on so-called seditious activities in the United States.

Red states These are the states that voted for George Bush in 2000 and 2004 and in general more conservative in outlook. They include the states of the South, Great Plains, and Rocky Mountain West.

Reelection constituency Those individuals a member of Congress believes will vote for him or her. Differs from a geographical, loyalist, or personal constituency.

Referendum A state legislature puts a proposal on the ballot for citizens to vote for or against.

Regressive tax A tax structured so that those with lower incomes pay a larger percentage of their income in tax than do those with higher incomes.

Regulation The actions of regulatory agencies in establishing standards or guidelines conferring benefits or imposing restrictions on business conduct.

Rehnquist Court The U.S. Supreme Court under Chief Justice William Rehnquist (1986–2005); a conservative Court, but one that did not overturn most previous rulings.

Religious tests Tests once used in some states to limit the right to vote or hold office to members of the "established church."

Rendition The process in which the CIA seizes terrorist suspects in foreign countries and takes them to other countries for interrogation. The purpose is to have other countries use methods of

interrogation, often torture, that the U.S. would not use.

Republic A system of government in which citizens elect representatives to make decisions for them; an **indirect democracy.**

Republican Party One of two major American political parties, founded in 1860 to oppose slavery.

Responsible party government A governing system in which political parties have real issue differences, voters align according to those issue differences, and elected officials are expected to vote with their party leadership or lose their chance to run for office.

Responsiveness The extent to which government conforms to the wishes of individuals, groups, or institutions.

Restrained judges Judges who are reluctant to overrule the other branches of government by declaring laws or actions of government officials unconstitutional.

Restrictive covenants Agreements among neighbors in white residential areas not to sell their houses to blacks.

Retrospective voting Voting for or against incumbents on the basis of their past performance.

Right against self-incrimination A right granted by the Fifth Amendment, providing that persons accused of a crime shall not be compelled to be witnesses against themselves.

Right to abortion U.S. Supreme Court ruling in *Roe* v. *Wade* (1973) established that women have a right to terminate a pregnancy during the first six months. States can prohibit an abortion during the last three months because at that time the fetus becomes viable—it can live outside the womb.

Right to a jury trial The Sixth Amendment's guarantee of a trial by jury in any **criminal case** that could result in more than six months' incarceration.

Right to counsel The Sixth Amendment's guarantee of the right of a criminal defendant to have an attorney in any **felony or misdemeanor** case that might result in incarceration; if defendants are indigent, the court must appoint an attorney for them.

Right to die Rehnquist court ruling that individuals can refuse medical treatment, including food and water, even if this means they will die. Individuals must make their decision while competent and alert. They can also act in advance, preparing a "living will" or designating another person as a proxy to make the decision if they are unable to.

Right to own property A right for individuals to buy, use, and sell private property.

Right to privacy A right to autonomy—to be left alone—that is not specifically mentioned in the U.S. Constitution, but has been found by the U.S. Supreme Court to be implied through several amendments.

Roberts Court The current Supreme Court under the leadership of Chief Justice John Roberts (2005–).

Rules Committee The committee in the House of Representatives that sets the terms of debate on a bill.

Sample A subset of a larger population that researchers use to draw conclusions about the larger population.

Scientific polls Systematic, probability-based sampling techniques that attempt to gauge public sentiment based on the responses of a small, selected group of individuals.

Scoop To obtain information before another reporter; also the information so obtained.

Second Amendment "The right of the people to keep and bear arms." Some interpret this as an individual right to own and use guns, others as only an indication that guns can be owned if one is part of a state militia.

Secret ballot A vote that is cast in such a way that election officials or other voters cannot see which candidates a particular person voted for.

Seditious speech Speech that encourages rebellion against the government.

Senate The chamber of Congress in which people are represented as members of states, with voters electing two representatives from each state.

Senate Judiciary Committee The committee that plays the greatest role in Senate confirmation of presidential nominations to the federal courts. The committee holds hearings on the nominees.

Senatorial courtesy The custom of giving senators of the president's party a virtual veto over appointments to jobs, including judicial appointments, in their states.

Senior Executive Service The SES was created in 1978 to attract high-ranking civil servants by offering them challenging jobs and monetary rewards for exceptional achievement.

Seniority rule The custom that the member of the majority party with the longest service on a particular congressional committee becomes its chair; applies most of the time but is occasionally violated.

Separate-but-equal doctrine The principle, enunciated by the U.S. Supreme Court in **Plessy v. Ferguson** in 1896, that allowed separate facilities for blacks and whites as long as the facilities were equal.

Separation of church and state Constitutional principle that is supposed to keep church and state from interfering with each other. In practice it restricts government from major efforts either to inhibit or advance religion.

Separation of powers The principle of government under which the power to make, administer, and judge the laws is split among three branches—legislative, executive, and judicial.

Setting the agenda Influencing the process by which problems are deemed important and alternative policies are proposed.

Sexual harassment A form of job discrimination prohibited by the **Civil Rights Act of 1964**. Sexual harassment can consist of either 1) a supervisor's demands for sexual favors in exchange for a raise or promotion or in exchange for not imposing negative consequences; or 2) the creation of a hostile environment which prevents workers from doing their job.

Sharecroppers Tenant farmers who lease land and equipment from landowners, turning over a share of their crops in lieu of rent.

Shays's Rebellion A revolt of farmers in western Massachusetts in 1786 and 1787 to protest the state legislature's refusal to grant them relief from debt; helped lead to calls for a new national **constitution**.

Signing Statements Written comments a president may attach to a law after signing it and sending it to the Federal Register for publication. Historically they have been used to indicate provisions in a law the president believes the federal courts may find unconstitutional. George W. Bush

used them frequently to indicate sections of laws he would refuse to implement, thus setting up a conflict between the executive and legislative branches.

Single-issue groups Interest groups that pursue a single public interest goal and are characteristically reluctant to compromise.

Single-member districts Where only one individual is elected from a particular electoral district.

Social contract An implied agreement between the people and their government in which the people give up part of their liberty to the government in exchange for the government protecting the remainder of their liberty.

Social insurance A social welfare program such as **Social Security** that provides benefits only to those who have contributed to the program and their survivors.

Socialism An economic system in which the government owns the country's productive capacity—industrial plants and farms—and controls wages and the supply of and demand for goods; in theory, the people, rather than the government, collectively own the country's productive capacity.

Social issue An important, noneconomic issue affecting significant numbers of the populace, such as crime, racial conflict, or changing values.

Social Security A **social insurance** program for the elderly and the disabled.

Soft money Contributions to national party committees that do not have to be reported to the federal government (and sometimes not to the states) because they are used for **voter registration** drives, educating voters on the issues, and the like, rather than for a particular candidate; the national committees send the funds to the state parties, which operate under less stringent reporting regulations than the federal laws provide.

Sound bite A few key words or phrase included in a speech with the intent that television editors will use the phrase in a brief clip on the news.

Southern strategy Based primarily on exploiting the race issue, the Southern strategy was the successful attempt by the **Republican Party** to wrest control of the heretofore Democratic South. Presidential candidate Barry Goldwater planted the seeds, Richard Nixon cultivated them, and later Republicans continued the effort. This strategy has also relied on mobilization of conservative evangelical Christians. By controlling the electoral votes of the South, the Republicans have significantly increased their chances of winning the presidency.

Speaker of the House The leader and presiding officer of the House of Representatives; chosen by the majority party.

Special interest caucuses Groups of members of the House of Representatives and Senate who are united by some personal interest or characteristic; e.g., the Black Caucus.

Specialization An **informal norm** of Congress that holds that since members cannot be experts in every area, some deference should be given to those who are most knowledgeable about a given subject related to their committee work.

Special prosecutor A prosecutor charged with investigating and prosecuting alleged violations of federal criminal laws by the president, vice president, senior government officials, members of Congress, or the judiciary.

Spectacle presidency Term used to describe presidents who are mostly seen by the public as actors

in public spectacles, stage-managed photo ops, featuring the president in a dramatically staged event or setting.

Spin What politicians do to portray themselves and their programs in the most favorable light, regardless of the facts, often shading the truth.

Split-ticket voting Voting a for a member of one party for one office and another party for a different office, such as for a Republican presidential candidate but a Democratic House candidate.

Spoils system The practice of giving political supporters government jobs or other benefits.

Stagflation The combination of high inflation and economic stagnation with high unemployment that troubled the United States in the 1970s.

Standing committees Permanent congressional committees.

Stare decisis Latin for "stand by what has been decided." The rule that judges should follow **precedents** established in previous cases by their court or higher courts.

"Star Wars" The popular name for former President Reagan's proposed space-based nuclear defense system, known officially as the Strategic Defense Initiative.

State-centered federalism The view that our constitutional system should give precedence to state sovereignty over that of the national government. State centered federalists argue that that the states created the national government and the states are superior to the federal government.

States' rights The belief that the power of the federal government should not be increased at the expense of the states' power.

Statutes Laws passed by the legislative body of a representative government.

Steering The practice in which realtors promoted segregation by showing blacks houses in black neighborhoods and whites houses in white neighborhoods.

Straw polls Unscientific polls.

Stress and duress Also called "torture lite," this term refers to a wide variety of measures that constitute rough interrogation just short of serious physical injury.

Subcommittee bill of rights Measures introduced by Democrats in the House of Representatives in 1973 and 1974 that allowed members of a committee to choose subcommittee chairs and established a fixed jurisdiction and adequate budget and staff for each subcommittee.

Subpoena A court order requiring someone to appear in court to give testimony under penalty of punishment.

Suffrage The right to vote.

Sundown laws Laws that required blacks to leave a town by sundown or by a particular time, so they couldn't remain overnight and therefore couldn't live in the town.

Sunshine Act Adopted in 1977, this act requires that most government meetings be conducted in public and that notice of such meetings must be posted in advance.

Super Tuesday The day when most southern states hold **presidential preference primaries** simultaneously.

Supplemental Security Income (SSI) A program that provides supplemental income for those who are blind, elderly, or disabled and living in poverty.

Supply-side economics The argument that tax revenues will increase if tax rates are reduced, on the assumption that more money will be available for business expansion and modernization. This in turn would stimulate employment and economic growth and result in higher tax revenues.

Supremacy clause A clause in the U.S. Constitution stating that treaties and laws made by the national government take precedence over state laws in cases of conflict.

Symbiotic relationship A relationship in which the parties use each other for mutual advantage.

Symbolic speech The use of symbols, rather than words, to convey ideas; e.g., wearing black armbands or burning the U.S. flag to protest government policy.

Tariff A special tax or "duty" imposed on imported or exported goods.

Tax deductions Certain expenses or payments that may be deducted from one's taxable income.

Tax exemptions Certain amounts deductible from one's annual income in calculating income tax.

Teapot Dome scandal A 1921 scandal in which President Warren Harding's secretary of the interior received large contributions from corporations that were then allowed to lease oil reserves (called the Teapot Dome); led to the Federal Corrupt Practices Act of 1925, which required reporting of campaign contributions and expenditures.

Temporary Aid to Needy Families (TANF) A program that provides income support for the poor; successor to **Aid to Families with Dependent Children (AFDC)**.

Tenth Amendment Constitutional amendment stating that powers not delegated to the federal government nor prohibited to the states are reserved to the states and to the people. This amendment has generally not had much impact, though a few recent Supreme Court cases have referred to it.

Third party A political party established in opposition to two dominant parties, often advocating radical change or pushing single issues.

Three-fifths Compromise The decision of the **Constitutional Convention** that each slave would count as three-fifths of a person in apportioning seats in the House of Representatives.

Ticket splitting Voting for a member of one party for a high-level office and a member of another party for a different high-level office.

Title IX Equal Opportunity in Education Act that forbids discrimination on the basis of sex in schools and colleges that receive federal aid. The amendment was prompted by discrimination against women by colleges, especially in admissions, sports programs, and financial aid.

Tracking polls Continuous polling throughout an election campaign to determine the candidates' standing.

Trade association An **interest** or **pressure group** that represents a single industry, such as builders.

Traditionalistic political culture One in which politics is left to a small elite and is viewed as a way to maintain the status quo. See **individualistic** and **moralistic political cultures**.

Treason The betrayal of one's country by knowingly aiding its enemies.

Turnout The proportion of eligible citizens who vote in an election.

Two-party system A political system like that in the U.S. in which only two parties have a realistic chance of winning most government offices. This system is rare among the world's other democracies.

Unanimous consent agreements Procedures by which the Senate may dispense with standard rules and limit debate and amendments.

Underdogs Candidates for public office who are thought to have little chance of being elected.

Unfunded mandates Federal laws that require the states to do something without providing full funding for the required activity.

Unitary executive A minority interpretation of Article II of the Constitution made by lawyers in the Bush administration that claims the president has sole power to direct the work of executive branch agencies, without interference from Congress or the federal courts. This interpretation is considered at odds with the conventional understanding of the **checks and balances** built into our system of three branches of government.

Unitary governments A system in which the national government is supreme; subnational governments are created by the national government and have only the power it allocates to them.

Unreasonable searches and seizures Searches and arrests that are conducted without a warrant or that do not fall into one of the exceptions to the warrant requirement; prohibited by the Fourth Amendment.

Unscientific polls Unsystematic samplings of popular sentiments; also known as **straw polls**.

USA PATRIOT Act Passed shortly after 9/11, this act expands the government's authority to conduct surveillance in an attempt to prevent future terrorist attacks.

U.S. Census Every ten years the federal government sends census takers around the country to count the American people and record demographic and social data about them. The Census is used to apportion the seats in the House of Representatives and, for government researchers and social scientists, to identify trends in society.

U.S. v. Nixon Case in which the Supreme Court ruled that President Nixon must turn over the Watergate tapes to the special prosecutor because he did not have executive privilege to keep them.

Veto power The president's constitutional authority to refuse to sign a law passed by Congress. Vetoes may be overridden by a two-thirds vote in each house of Congress.

Vietnam syndrome An attitude of uncertainty about U.S. foreign policy goals and our ability to achieve them by military means; engendered among the public and officials as a result of the U.S. failure in Vietnam.

Voter registration The requirement that eligible voters record their name and address with county officials, usually ten days or more before election day. If properly registered, then persons are allowed to vote in the election.

Voting Rights Act (VRA) A law passed by Congress in 1965 that made it illegal to interfere with anyone's right to vote. The act and its subsequent amendments have been the main vehicles for expanding and protecting minority voting rights.

War Powers Resolution A 1973 statute enacted by Congress to limit the president's ability to commit troops to combat without congressional approval.

Warren Court The U.S. Supreme Court under Chief Justice Earl Warren (1953–1969); an activist Court that expanded the rights of criminal defendants and racial and religious minorities.

Watergate scandal The attempt to break into Democratic National Committee headquarters in 1972 that ultimately led to President Richard M. Nixon's resignation for his role in attempting to cover up the break-in and other criminal and unethical actions.

Weber, Max German social scientist, author of pioneering studies on the nature of bureaucracies.

Whigs Members of the Whig Party, founded in 1834 by National Republicans and several other factions who opposed Jacksonian Democrats.

Whips Members of the House of Representatives who work to maintain party unity by keeping in contact with party members trying to ensure they vote for party-backed bills. Both the majority and the minority party have a whip and several assistant whips.

Whistleblower An individual employee who exposes mismanagement and abuse of office by government officials.

White primary A device for preventing blacks from voting in the South. Under the pretense that political parties were private clubs, blacks were barred from voting in Democratic primaries, which were the real elections because Democrats always won the general elections.

Whitewater investigation An investigation conducted by a **special prosecutor** into the activities of President Bill Clinton and Hillary Rodham Clinton in connection with an Arkansas land deal and other alleged wrongdoings.

Winner-take-all The outcome of an election where only one individual is elected from a district or state, the individual who receives the most votes. It is contrasted with multi-member systems where more than one person wins seats in an election.

Wire services News-gathering organizations such as the Associated Press and United Press International that provide news stories and other editorial features to the media organizations that are their members.

World Trade Organization (WTO) Founded in 1995 to remove barriers to free trade and to mediate trade disputes between member countries. WTO policies are set primarily by consensus of its member countries, represented by their trade ministers. Its general council, to which all members belong, is empowered to resolve trade disputes.

Writ of *certiorari* An order issued by a higher court to a lower court to send up the record of a case for review; granting the writ is the usual means by which the U.S. Supreme Court agrees to hear a case.

PHOTO CREDITS

Front Matter TOC

iv Chapter 1, Copyright 2006 Mark Alan Stamarty. Reprinted with permission; Chapter 2, Chuck Nacke/Woodfin Camp & Associates. **v** Chapter 3, © Gianni Muratore/Alamy; Chapter 4, REUTERS/Blake Sell/Landov; Chapter 5, © David McNew/Getty Images; Chapter 6, AP Images/Andrew Rush. **vi** Chapter 7, Callie Shell/Aurora Photos. **vii** Chapter 8, © Mannie Garcia/AFP/Getty Images; Chapter 9, Courtesy Joe Wezorek; Chapter 10, AP Images/Jack Dempsey. **viii** Chapter 11, Stephen Voss/WPN; Chapter 12, © Mark Wilson/Getty Images. **ix** Chapter 13, © Stewart Cohen/Taxi/Getty Images; Chapter 14, AP Images/Haraz Ghanbari: Chapter 15, © Michael Kamber/Polaris.

Chapter 1

xx Copyright 2006 Mark Alan Stamarty. Reprinted with permission; **3** © Bettmann/Corbis; **7** © AP Images/Pablo Martinez Monsivais; **9** Courtesy of Wayne Joseph; **10** © Jason Tanaka Blaney Photography; **14** AP Images/St. Petersburg Times, Danile Wallace.

Chapter 2

18 Chuck Nacke/Woodfin Camp & Associates; **23** The Metropolitan Museum of Art, Bequest of Charles Alan Munn, 1924 (24-90-35); **32** © Tom Myers, San Francisco Chronicle; **34** Library of Congress; **36** Library of Congress; **38** The David J. and Janice L. Frent Collection; **39** AP Images.

Chapter 3

46 © Gianni Muratore/Alamy; **51** Robin Nelson/Black Star; **53** © Sungsu Cho/Polaris Images **56** © Bettmann/Corbis; **58** Todd Yates/The Facts, Clute, TX.

Chapter 4

74 REUTERS/Blake Sell/Landov; **78** Copyright © 2003. Reprinted by permission of Cagle Cartoons; **81** © The New Yorker Collection 2006 Peter C. Vey from cartoonbank.com. All rights reserved; **82** Henry Groskinsky, New York City; **84** © Carol Joynt/Getty Images; **85** © Bettmann/Corbis; **86** © Brooks Kraft/Corbis; **90** © Bettmann/Corbis; **97** © Todd Heisler, Rocky Mountain News/Polaris; **102** © Time Life Pictures/Getty Images; **104** Copyright © The Granger Collection, New York.

Chapter 5

110 © David McNew/Getty Images; **112** Getty Images; **114** Library of Congress, Image # LC-USZ62-83799; **119** AP Images; **121** © The New Yorker Collection 2002 Dana Fradon from cartoonbank.com. All rights reserved; **124** © The New Yorker Collection 2002 Alex Gregory from cartoonbank.com. All rights reserved; **126** Jim West/Alamy; **130** © Fred Blackwell/Jackson Daily News. Used by permission of the Clarion Ledger; **133** AP/Wide World Photos.

Chapter 6

138 AP Images/Andrew Rush; **143** above, AP Images/Darron Cummings; below, AP Images/Reed Saxon; **148** right, Courtesy of the Smithsonian Institute, neg. # 98-4290; **149** The David J. and Janice L. Frent Collection; **154** The David J. and Janice L. Frent Collection; **155** © AFP/Stephen Jaffe/Getty Images; **156** Andy Levin/Photo Researchers, Inc.; **157** © David Scull.

Chapter 7

166 Callie Shell/Aurora Photos; **169** Library of Congress; **171** © Bettmann/Corbis; **172** AP Images/Christopher Morris/VII; **176** Courtesy of the Smithsonian Institutution; **184** Courtesy of the Smithsonian Institution; **187** Courtesy of the Smithsonian Institution; **188** © Cynthia Johnson/Liaison/Getty Images; **190** © Brooks Kraft/Corbis; **191** AP Images/Charlie Neibergall; **193** © Bettmann/Corbis; **201** © The New Yorker Collection 19709 Whitney Darrow, Jr. from cartoonbank.com. All rights reserved.

Chapter 8

210 © Mannie Garcia/AFP/Getty Images; **213** National Archives; **214** Paul Szep, Reprinted with permission; **217** © David McNew/Getty Images; **220** AP Images; **225** AP Images/Al Grillo; **228** Library of Congress; **230** © George Tames/Redux.

Chapter 9

252 Courtesy Joe Wezorek; **254** George Bush Presidential Library; **256** AP/Wide World Photos; **258** Brown Brothers; **259** Theodore Roosevelt Collection, Harvard College Library; **261** © Time Life Pictures/Getty Images; **264** © Tribune Media Services, Inc. All rights reserved. Reprinted with permission; **266** TOLES © 2006 The Washington Post. Reprinted with permission of UNIVERSAL PRESS SYNDICATE. All rights reserved; **268** National Archives; **269** Franklin D. Roosevelt Library; **270** © Mike Lane and PoliticalCartoons.com; **272** © Hank Walker/Time Life Pictures/Getty Images; **273** Lyndon B. Johnson Library; **281** Ronald Reagan Library.

Chapter 10

288 AP Images/Jack Dempsey; **293** © Ted Thai/Time Life Pictures/Getty Images; **297** United Mineworkers of America; **304** AP Images/Kenneth Lambert; **309** © James Nielsen/AFP/Getty Images; **313** © Stefano Paltera/Gamma Presse, Inc.

Chapter 11

318 Stephen Voss/WPN; **328** © AP Images/Nati Harnik; **331** Library of Congress, #LC-DIG-ncic-01830; **335** © David Hume Kennerly/Getty Images; **338** AP Images/Henry Burroughs; **340** © Lynn Johnson/Aurora.

Chapter 12

344 © Mark Wilson/Getty Images; **349** © Bettmann/Corbis; **350** © Melanie Coner/Redux; **353** © Hiroji Kubota/Magnum Photos; **354** © Markham Johnson-2007; **356** AP/Wide World Photos; **359** Courtesy of National Archives; **361** © Sylvia Plachy, photographed for the New Yorker; **363** © Aisling Maki/AFP/Getty Images; **366** Courtesy of National Archives; **375** Kim Kullish/Corbis; **377** © Margulies 2004. Reprinted with permission; **378** © Getty Images.

INDEX

Note: Page references in **boldface** refer to photographs and tables.

on regime changes and
preemptive war, 489–491
retrospective voting for, 202–203
signing statements of, 266–267,
379
Social Security reform, 449
speeches leading up to Iraq War,
83
strength in primaries, 181
tax cuts of, 86, 434, 438, 439–
441, **440**
taxes paid by, 441
on torture, 378–379, **378**, 469,
478, 491
as unitary executive, 260, 311
use of bureaucrats during
elections, 308
on use of polling, 57
vetoes by, 266
War on Terror, 488–489 (*See also*
War on Terror)
on War Powers Resolution, 473
Bush, Laura, 274
Bush v. *Gore,* 338–339. *See also*
Election of 2000
Business
corporate tax subsidies, 442–443
corporation tax rates, 441
government corporations, 301
interest groups, 115–116, **116,**
125
unionization of, 117, **117** (*See also*
Unions and unionization)
Busing for racial balance, 396–397,
397
Butterfly ballots, 59, 202
Byrd, Harry, 278
Byrd, Robert C., 96

Cabinet, 298–299, **300**
Cable television, 78, 79, 104, 245
Cady Stanton, Elizabeth, 172, 173,
413
CAGW (Citizens Against
Government Waste), 226
Calendars, congressional, 235
Calhoun, John, 225
California
abolition of bilingual education
in, 408
minority access to public
universities in, 423
paper backups for voting
machines in, 175
proposed Electoral College
division in, 200
racist tactics of Republican party
in, 182
Cambodia, bombing of, 483
Campaigns, 188–200. *See also*
Campaign finance
congressional, 219–225, **220, 221**
e-campaigning, 194
Electoral College strategy, 189, 199
image creation in, 189–190, **190**
issues in, 201–202
media and, 190–192, **191**
national conventions, 185–188,
186, 187

organization of, 189
permanent, 204–205
responsiveness of government
and, 205–206
role of parties in, 149
strategies, 189–190, **190,** 199
voters "turned off" by, 178
Campaign finance, 194–198. *See
also* Campaign finance
business interest groups, 115
conflicts of interest and, 195, 198
in congressional campaigns, 219,
220–221, 244
contribution limits, 196
disclosure laws, 196
527 groups, 115, 198
impact of system, 198
importance of money in winning,
194–195
incumbents and, 224
from lobbyists, 128
McCain-Feingold Act, 195
political action committees, 115,
196–197, **197,** 219, 224
by presidents, 270
public funds for, 196
reforms of the 1970s, 194–195
soft money, 195, 198
spending limits, 196–198, **197**
Canada, health care system in, 458,
459
Candidates. *See* Nominations,
presidential
Cannon, Joseph, 227
Cannonism, 227
Capitalist economy, 435–436
Capital punishment, **66,** 326,
366–368
Capito, Shelly Moore, 211
Cardozo, Benjamin, 333
Carlin, George, 351–352
Carmona, Richard, 307
Carpal tunnel syndrome, 330
Carter, Jimmy
civil service reform by, 305
in debates, 193
election of, 155, 204
on election standards in Florida in
2000, 204
foreign policy of, 267, 469, 471,
485
Israeli-Palestinian negotiations
of, 469
judicial appointments by, 324
Mondale and, 275
nomination of, **149,** 183
on openness in government, 295
Panama Canal treaty, 267
personal presidency of, 282
photograph of, **256**
public opinion of, 200, **283**
swamp rabbit incident, 88
Carter, Rosalynn, 275
Casework, 223–224
Casey, Bob, 219
Catholic Church and Catholics
on abortion, 156
on birth control, 372
church-run schools, 6

Know-Nothing Party and, 4, 6
party identification of, 156, 159
restrictions on, 358
against women's suffrage, 174
CATO Institute, 296
Catt, Carrie Chapman, 174
Caucuses, presidential, 184
Caucus for Women's Issues, 244
CBO (Congressional Budget
Office), 234, 240–241, 438
CBS, 78, 84, 87, 92, 100–102
Censorship, 87, 478. *See also*
Freedom of speech
Census Bureau, 9, 303–304, 450
Centers for Disease Control and
Prevention (CDC), 304
Central Intelligence Agency (CIA)
Iraq prewar intelligence, 308
political appointments to, 301
purge of career agents under
Bush, 308
secret prisons and renditions,
377, 379
Centrist Coalition, 236
CEO compensation, 434, **434**
Chávez, César, 409
Checkbook members, 115
Checks and balances, 30, **31,** 312
Cheney, Dick
civil liberties and, 376
cursing by, 211
energy policy task force of, 265
on FOIA, 295
on Guantanamo detainees, 376,
377
Halliburton connections, 313
hunting accident of, 88
on interrogation techniques, 378
on judicial appointments, 324
leaking information to influence
events, 83
role as vice president, 229, 276
taxes paid by, 441
on unilateralism, 490
on wiretapping, 380
Chicano movement, 409. *See also*
Hispanics
Chief executive, president as,
262–265
Children
born to single women, 451
child labor laws, **331,** 495
political socialization of, 50–51
of same-sex parents, 374
social welfare programs for,
451–452
China, diplomatic relations with,
485, **486**
Cho Seung-Hui, 47
Christian Coalition, 121
Christian right
on abortion, 156
on assisted suicide, 376
attack on tolerance policies
toward gays and lesbians,
351
on birth control, 372–373
court access and, 329
freedom of religion and, 363

on homosexual rights, 129, 351
public interest groups, 120–123,
329
on same-sex marriages, 374
on Terri Schiavo, 123
CIA. *See* Central Intelligence
Agency
Citizens Against Government Waste
(CAGW), 226–227
Citizenship
of African Americans, 37
of American Indians, 410–411,
411
of women, 412
Civics courses, 52
Civil cases, 328
Civil disobedience, 130–131, **130,**
132–133, **133**
Civility Hour, 211
Civil liberties. *See also* Civil rights
affirmative action policies, 264,
421–424
employment discrimination,
399–400, 403
freedom of association, 354–355
freedom of religion, 357–363, **363**
freedom of speech, 345–346
freedom of the press, 105,
335–336
of Guantanamo Bay detainees,
340, 376–377
housing discrimination, 400, 403
Internet use and, 381
interrogations, 378–379
libel, 356–357
listed in the Bill of Rights, 347
racial profiling, 403–404
renditions, 377, 379
responsiveness of government in,
381–382
rights of criminal defendants,
364–368
right to privacy, 356, 364–365,
368–376
school desegregation, 334, 394–
396, **395,** 400–403, **401**
secret prisons, 377, 379
sex discrimination, 412–421
USA PATRIOT Act and, 322,
380–381
Warren Court on, 338
Civil rights. *See also* Civil Rights
Act of 1964; Civil rights
movement
of American Indians, 412
"black power," 399
busing of students, 396–397, **397**
civil disobedience, 130–131, **130,**
132–133, **133**
Civil Rights Act of 1968, 399,
400, 403
Civil Rights Acts during
Reconstruction, 37–38, 390
definition of, 388
under Eisenhower, 41–42
filibusters against, 236
immigration restrictions and, 4
Japanese-American internment,
381

southern whites and, 152–155,
155
strict father model and, 160
Responsible party government, 151
Responsiveness of government
bureaucracy and, 314–315
in civil liberties, 381–382
in civil rights, 424–425
Congress and, 247
Constitution and, 40–42
in domestic policies, 460–461
elections and, 205–206
in foreign policy, 495–496
interest groups and, 133–134
judiciary and, 341
media and, 105–106
political parties and, 160–161
presidency and, 282–283
public opinion and, 68–69
public participation, 13–15
Restrained judges, 331–332, **332**
Restrictive covenants, 400
Retrospective voting, 201–202
Revolutionary War, slavery and,
388
"Revolving door" phenomenon,
127
Rhode Island, religious freedom
in, 5
Rights. *See also* Bill of Rights
in the body of the Constitution,
346
to counsel, 366–367
of criminal defendants, 364–368,
376–378
to die, 123
economic, 13
homosexual (*See* Homosexual
rights)
natural, 11, 346
to own property, 13
to privacy (*See* Privacy, right to)
voting (*See* Voting rights)
Right to counsel, 366–367
Right to die, 123, 329, 375–376
Right to own property, 13
Right to privacy. *See* Privacy, right
to
RINOs (Republicans in name
only), 151
Roberts, John, **318,** 324, 335, 339
Roberts, Owen, 333
Roberts Court
on abortion, 371
on busing of students, 397
dates of, **341**
on exclusionary rule, 364
future of affirmative action and,
424
as more conservative, 339
on sex discrimination in
employment, 416
on student speech, 345
Robertson, Pat, 121
Robinson, Jo Ann, 132
Rockefeller, David, 431
Rockefeller, Nelson, 256, 273
Roe v. *Wade,* 328, 339, 369. *See also*
Abortion

Roe v. *Wade for Men,* 421
Roman Catholic Church. *See*
Catholic Church and Catholics
Roosevelt, Eleanor, 274–275
Roosevelt, Franklin. *See also* New
Deal
death of, 256, **261**
faulty polling during election of,
55, 56
fireside chats, 89, 279
growth of presidency under, 258
Japanese American internment, 381
judicial appointments by, 323
Keynesian economics of, 438
liberalism and, 62
management style of, 272
political party realignment and, 152
press conferences of, 84–85, **85**
on tax complexity, 440
use of polls, 280
on veterans' benefits, 446
vetoes by, 266
World War II, **269,** 480
Roosevelt, Theodore
growth of presidency under, 258,
258, 259
interventionist foreign policy
of, 479
judicial appointments by, 323,
327–328
spectacle presidency of, 280
Square Deal of, 265
Rove, Karl, 100, 156, 273
Rowley, Coleen, 313, 314
Rule of thumb, 413
Rules Committee, House, 226,
229, 232, 235
Rumsfeld, Donald
Cheney and, 276
Congress and, 474
on Guantanamo Bay detainees, 376
on military reform, 268, 472, 492
on "old Europe," 478
preexisting agenda of, 472
on troop numbers in Iraq, 268
on weapons of mass destruction
in Iraq, 261
Rutherford Institute, 329
Rwanda, lack of intervention in
genocide in, 489

Sadat, Anwar, 469
Saddam Hussein. *See also* Iraq War
early U.S. support for, 468
efforts to link to 9/11 terrorist
attacks, 61, 270, 273, 474,
478
Iran-Iraq War, 468
Persian Gulf War, 268, 269, 468,
471
U.S. objective to overthrow, 472
Salazar, Ken, 215
Sales tax, national, 442
Salon, 79
Same-sex marriages
full faith and credit clause and, 19
legalization in individual states,
373, 374–375
public opinion on, 48, 374

Sample, random, 56
Sanchez, Linda, **217**
Sanchez, Loretta, **217**
Sanders, Bernie, 141
Sanford, Edward, 348
Santeria religion, 358
Santorum, Rick, 219, 239
Saudi Arabia, 468
Scalia, Antonin, **332,** 335, 359, 418
Scandals
Abramoff, 246
Clinton, 50, 79, 102–103, 121,
282
congressional, 222–223, 246
election outcomes and, 223
involving congressional pages,
222–223, 229
Iran-Contra, 206, 262, 276
Teapot Dome, 206
Watergate, 152, 198, 255, 259,
262
Schattschneider, E. E., 140
Schiavo, Terri, 123, 329
SCHIP (State Children's Health
Insurance Program), 457
Schmidt, Jean, 211
School desegregation, 334,
394–396, **395,** 400–403, **401**
School prayers, 332–333, 335,
360–362
Schools. *See* Education; Public
schools
Schumer, Charles, **143**
Science, politics and, 306–307
SCLC (Southern Christian
Leadership Conference), 398
Scoops, 84
Search and seizure, 347, 364–365
SEC (Securities and Exchange
Commission), 127, 238, 301,
309
Second Amendment, 123, 347, 506
Secondhand smoke, 307
Secretary of defense, 471
Secretary of state, 471
Secret ballots, 147, **148**
Secret prisons, run by the CIA,
377, 379
Securities and Exchange
Commission (SEC), 127, 238,
301, 309
Sedition Act of 1798, 87
Sedition Act of 1918, 348
Seditious speech, 348–350
Segregation. *See also* Desegregation
de jure and *de facto,* 396–403, **401**
Jim Crow laws, 391, 392
Montgomery bus boycott,
132–133, **133,** 397–398
in the North, 392, 398–399, 401
presently, in schools, 400–403, **401**
school desegregation, 334, 394–
396, **395,** 400–403, **401**
separate-but-equal doctrine,
391–392, 394
in the South, 390–392, 397–398
sundown laws, 391, 392
Supreme Court rulings on,
391–392

Select committees, 233
Self-incrimination, 365–366
Senate. *See also* Congress
in budget-making process,
240–241
calendars in, 235
evolution of organization of, 25,
225–226, 227–228
incumbent elections in, 219–225,
221
judicial nomination approval by,
319–320, 323, 324–325
lawmaking process in, 234–238
(*See also* Bills)
leadership positions in, 229–231,
230
pay and perks of, 218, 222, 224
presidential appointment approval
by, 263
qualifications for, 212
role of vice president in, 229, 273
unequal representation of citizens
in, 26–27, **27**
Senate Judiciary Committee, 319,
323
Senatorial courtesy, 263, 323
Senior Executive Service (SES),
305, 310
Seniority rule, 232–233
Seniors
Medicare, 116, 232, 294, 314,
456–457, 459
Social Security, 445–450
Supplemental Security Income,
450–451
voting rates of, 6
Separate-but-equal doctrine,
391–392, 394
Separation of church and state,
357–358, 360
Separation of powers, 29–30
September 11, 2001 attacks. *See*
9/11/2001 terrorist attacks
SES (Senior Executive Service),
305, 310
Settlement houses, 445
Seventeenth Amendment, 508
Seventh Amendment, 507
Seventh-Day Adventists, 358–359
Sex discrimination, 412–421
Burger Court on, 338, 415
Civil Rights Act of 1964, 414,
415, 417–418
in employment, 415–417
Equal Rights Amendment, 413,
414
harassment, 417, 418–419
against men, 420–421
Title IX, 418–420
traditional view of, 412–413
women judges on, 326
women's movement, 23,
413–420
Sexual harassment, 417, 418–419
Sexual relations, government and,
62–63, 373
Sexual scandals
of Clinton, 50, 79, 102–103,
121, 282

Presidents, Elections, and Congresses, 1789–2007 (cont.)

Year	President	Vice President	Party of President	Election Year	Election Opponent with Most Votes*
1889–1893	Benjamin Harrison	Levi P. Morton	Rep	(1888)	Grover Cleveland
1893–1897	Grover Cleveland	Adlai E. Stevenson	Dem	(1892)	Benjamin Harrison
1897–1901	William McKinley	Garret A. Hobart (to 1901)	Rep	(1896)	William Jennings Bryan
		Theodore Roosevelt (1901)		(1900)	William Jennings Bryan
1901–1909	Theodore Roosevelt	(No VP, 1901–1905)	Rep		Took office upon death of McKinley
		Charles W. Fairbanks (1905–1909)		(1904)	Alton B. Parker
1909–1913	William Howard Taft	James S. Sherman	Rep	(1908)	William Jennings Bryan
1913–1921	Woodrow Wilson	Thomas R. Marshall	Dem	(1912)	Theodore Roosevelt
				(1916)	Charles Evans Hughes
1921–1923	Warren G. Harding	Calvin Coolidge	Rep	(1920)	James Cox
1923–1929	Calvin Coolidge	(No VP, 1923–1925) Charles G. Dawes (1925–1929)	Rep	(1924)	Took office upon death of Harding John Davis
1929–1933	Herbert Hoover	Charles Curtis	Rep	(1928)	Alfred E. Smith
1933–1945	Franklin D. Roosevelt	John N. Garner (1933–1941)	Dem	(1932)	Herbert Hoover
		Henry A. Wallace (1941–1945)		(1936)	Alfred Landon
		Harry S. Truman (1945)		(1940)	Wendell Willkie
				(1944)	Thomas Dewey
1945–1953	Harry S. Truman	(No VP, 1945–1949) Alban W. Barkley	Dem		Took office upon death of Roosevelt
				(1948)	Thomas Dewey
1953–1961	Dwight D. Eisenhower	Richard M. Nixon	Rep	(1952)	Adlai Stevenson
				(1956)	Adlai Stevenson
1961–1963	John F. Kennedy	Lyndon B. Johnson	Dem	(1960)	Richard M. Nixon
1963–1969	Lyndon B. Johnson	(No VP, 1963–1965) Hubert H. Humphrey (1965–1969)	Dem	(1964)	Took office upon death of Kennedy Barry Goldwater
1969–1974	Richard M. Nixon	Spiro T. Agnew	Rep	(1968)	Hubert H. Humphrey
		Gerald R. Ford (appointed)		(1972)	George McGovern
1974–1977	Gerald R. Ford	Nelson A. Rockefeller (appointed)	Rep		Took office upon Nixon's resignation
1977–1981	Jimmy Carter	Walter Mondale	Dem	(1976)	Gerald R. Ford
1981–1989	Ronald Reagan	George Bush	Rep	(1980)	Jimmy Carter
				(1984)	Walter F. Mondale
1989–1993	George Bush	J. Danforth Quayle	Rep	(1988)	Michael Dukakis
1993–2001	William J. Clinton	Albert Gore	Dem	(1992)	George Bush
				(1996)	Robert Dole
2001–2006	George W. Bush	Dick Cheney	Rep	(2000)	Albert Gore
				(2004)	John Kerry